DATE DUE

~~JN 26 '98~~			
~~DE 18 '03~~			

DEMCO 38-296

The Geological Society of America
Memoir 174

The Nature and Origin of Cordilleran Magmatism

Edited by

J. Lawford Anderson
Department of Geological Sciences
University of Southern California
Los Angeles, California 90089-0740

1990

Published by The Geological Society of America, Inc.
3300 Penrose Place, P.O. Box 9140, Boulder, Colorado 80301

GSA Books Science Editor Campbell Craddock

Printed in U.S.A.

Library of Congress Cataloging-in-Publication Data

The Nature and origin of Cordilleran magmatism / edited by J. Lawford
   Anderson.
        p.   cm. — (Memoir / Geological Society of America ; 174)
      Includes bibliographical references.
      ISBN 0-8137-1174-6
      1. Magmatism—West (U.S.)   2. Geology, Stratigraphic—Mesozoic.
   3. Geology, Stratigraphic—Tertiary.   I. Anderson, J. Lawford.
   II. Series: Memoir (Geological Society of America); 174.
   QE461.N366   1990
   552'.1'0978—dc20   90-2825
                                                 CIP

10 9 8 7 6 5 4 3 2

Contents

Contents

Preface

The North American Cordillera records the tectonic, metamorphic, and magmatic history of a continental margin that has been active since the middle Paleozoic. Although special volumes have been directed at regional tectonics (Ernst, 1981; Smith and Eaton, 1978), metamorphism (Ernst, 1988), core complexes (Crittenden and others, 1977), and paleogeography (Howell and McDougall, 1978), no comparable volume has dealt with the magmatic origin of the remarkable compositional span of igneous activity that characterizes the orogen. This memoir was produced with this goal in mind and grew from a special GSA symposium on the subject held at the 83rd Cordilleran Section meeting at Hilo, Hawaii. The objective was to bring together not review papers, but rather, contributions from individuals doing research in specific areas. Much of the emphasis is on magma genesis, including the role of multiple source control and changes of magmatic trends caused by fractional crystallization, assimilative fractional crystallization, and mixing. For a recent summary of Mesozoic age patterns and a review of regional compositional trends, the reader is also referred to Armstrong and Ward (1990). The 23 chapters in this volume contain an abundance of new data and exciting interpretations on the Mesozoic and Tertiary igneous suites of the Cordillera from Baja California to Alaska (Fig. 1) and build on a previous, broader collection of work on circum-Pacific plutonic terranes (Roddick, 1983).

PENINSULAR RANGES BATHOLITH

The Peninsular Ranges batholith of southern California and Baja California has long been known for an east-west zonation in age and composition (Gastil, 1975; Silver and others, 1979; Todd and Shaw, 1979; Gromet and Silver, 1987; Taylor, 1988). The first article of the memoir is a report by Walawender and others on internally zoned Cretaceous plutons (La Posta–type) in the eastern portions of the batholith, which they show to be composed of outer margins of metaluminous, ocean-crust–derived tonalites and interior peraluminous, continental-crust–derived granites. A separate paper by Gastil and others describes an important mineralogical aspect regarding the zonation of the batho-

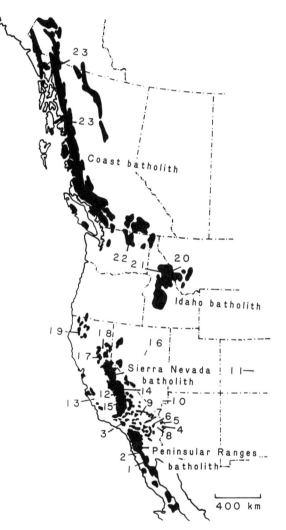

Figure 1. Location of the major batholiths of the North American Cordillera. Areas of study (numbered) reported in this volume are as follows: (1) Walawender and others, (2) Gastil and others, (3) Barth, (4) Anderson and Cullers, (5) John and Wooden, (6) Miller and others, (7) Fox and Miller, (8) Hazlett, (9) Glazner, (10) Smith and others, (11) Stein and Crock, (12) Liggett, (13) Mattinson, (14) Saleeby and others, (15) Kistler, (16) Barton, (17) Beard, (18) Christe and Hannah, (19) Barnes and others, (20) Foster and Hyndman, (21) Fleck, (22) Carlson and Moye, and (23) Barker and Arth.

lith, one that specifically relates the change from magnetite-series (western portion of the batholith) to ilmenite-series (eastern portion) granitoids to conditions of melt generation and crystallization.

TRANSVERSE RANGES AND MOJAVE DESERT REGION OF SOUTHERN CALIFORNIA

Triassic- to Cretaceous-age plutons are widespread in southern California and are compositionally distinct, reflecting source control on magma generation and the variable role of crustal involvement. Triassic plutons are least abundant and are characteristically low in silica, alkalic, and high in Sr; Jurassic plutons are also high in K and usually low in silica, but are less Sr enriched and part calc-alkalic; Cretaceous suites are more siliceous, all calc-alkalic, and range from metaluminous granodiorite to peraluminous granite.

The complexes are quite diverse, in part reflecting the striking range of crustal depth now exposed at the surface. While most igneous terranes represent upper crustal levels, several represent middle crustal exposures of the magmatic arc (Anderson and others, 1988; Anderson and others, 1990). An example of the latter are plutons of the "suspect" San Gabriel or Tujunga terrane of the San Gabriel Mountains and other portions of the eastern Transverse Range. In his chapter, Barth has documented that Triassic and Cretaceous plutons have the four mineralogic attributes of deep-seated crystallization—magmatic epidote, aluminous hornblende, calcic garnet, and silica-rich muscovite (see also Zen, 1989)—requiring portions of the San Gabriel terrane to have resided at middle crustal levels (19 to 28 km) throughout the Mesozoic, if not since the Proterozoic. Likewise, Anderson and Cullers report on plutonism in the Whipple Mountains core complex and discuss the origin of (1) Cretaceous two-mica granites and hornblende quartz diorites emplaced when the crystalline section resided at middle crustal levels (>27 km) and (2) younger igneous suites emplaced during transport of the complex to an upper crustal setting (<7 km) during middle Tertiary extension. The chapter by John and Wooden follows with a detailed investigation of another core complex, that of Chemehuevi Mountains, where melting of granulitic Proterozoic crust and subsequent assimilation and fractionation are envisioned to yield another deep-level (15 to 22 km) composite batholith of Late Cretaceous age. Many of the plutonic suites are composed of near-coeval metaluminous and peraluminous members. In the chapter by Miller and others, Sr, Nd, Pb, and O isotopic data are interpreted to indicate a crustal, non-sedimentary melt origin for metaluminous and two-mica Cretaceous granites of the Old Woman–Piute Range.

In contrast to the widespread nature of Cretaceous plutons, those of Jurassic age form a narrow transect across the Mojave Desert (John, 1981). They are also much different in composition and origin. The chapter by Fox and Miller reports on upper crustal plutons in the Bristol and Providence Mountains and the Colton Hills. High-K diorite to quartz syenite and syenogranite are inferred to have formed from melting of an eclogitic to amphibolitic upper mantle/lower crustal source followed by hornblende-dominated fractionation and late albitization, the latter being a common attribute of the Jurassic arc in this region.

TERTIARY PLUTONISM AND VOLCANISM—CALIFORNIA TO COLORADO

Tertiary igneous activity of the Cordillera is marked by dramatic age progressions. While magmatism in the western Cordillera subsided in the late Cretaceous, the focus of igneous activity shifted 1,000 km eastward to as far as Colorado. Stein and Crock report on the REE and Nd isotopic composition of Tertiary plutons of the Colorado mineral belt and differentiate two suites: Laramide-age (45 to 75 Ma) monzonites inferred to have formed from mafic granulitic crust, and younger (10 to 45 Ma) granodiorite to granite from melting of intermediate to felsic crust.

The Miocene brought a return of igneous activity to the western Cordillera marked by explosive rhyolitic ignimbrites and basaltic to intermediate lavas. It was also a time of widespread extension. The chapter by Hazlett describes 14- to 22-Ma volcanics of the Mopah Range of the eastern Mojave Desert, California, which were erupted contemporaneously with crustal extension and detachment faulting. Chapters by Glazner and Smith and others discuss the origin of similar-aged volcanic sequences in the central Mojave and Lake Mead regions (Nevada and Arizona), respectively; both argue for the importance of mixing of basalt and rhyolite to form intermediate magmas and deviatory trends due to coupled mixing and fractionation. Late potassium metasomatism has affected some of the Lake Mead volcanics, a common attribute of Miocene volcanics in extended terranes.

SIERRA NEVADA BATHOLITH AND SALINIAN MAGMATIC ARC

Moving northward, a set of six chapters treats the magmatic construction of the Sierra Nevada and Salinia. Lingren (1915) was the first to recognize the west-to-east changes across the Sierra Nevada batholith, further documented in terms of rock type (Moore, 1959), elemental and isotopic compositions (Bateman and Dodge, 1970; Kistler and Peterman, 1973; Taylor, 1988; DePaolo, 1981), and age trends that include an eastward younging of Cretaceous plutons (Evernden and Kistler, 1970; Stern and others, 1981).

While most western Sierran plutons are metaluminous and non-felsic, a distinct peraluminous belt of plutons occurs in the southwest portion of the batholith. The chapter by Liggett investigates the origin and condition of emplacement of the calcic, garnet- and two-mica–bearing Tharps Peak granodiorite, concluding that hornblende-plagioclase fractionation plus assimilation of metasedimentary country rock is required to account for major-element, REE, and oxygen-isotope variations.

Paleozoic and early to middle Mesozoic accretion added

considerable volumes of crust to the western portions of the orogen, which was variably imaged by post-accretionary plutons, such as the Tharps Peak. The prebatholithic units are exposed as highly deformed pendants within, and as screens between, plutons of the batholith. Saleeby and others have investigated the stratigraphy, structure, and age of pendants in the central Sierra Nevada, showing that (1) deformation in middle Cretaceous volcanic sequences is coeval with batholithic emplacement, and (2) two different early Mesozoic substrates underlie the Cretaceous sequences; they are separated by a tectonic break. Kistler extends this line of work and, using Sr, Nd, and O isotopic data for plutons and wall rocks of the Sierra Nevada, concludes that a dual east-west zonation exists within the batholith. Two different lithospheres are thought to have contributed to the magmatism: (1) an eastern North American lithosphere that has yielded primitive mantle-derived magmas with an $Sr_i < 0.706$, and Proterozoic crust-enriched magmas, largely granitic, with $Sr_i > 0.706$; and (2) a western "Panthalassan" lithosphere that has yielded magmas with $Sr_i < 0.706$ from a depleted mantle source, and peraluminous granitic magmas with $Sr_i > 0.706$ having a significant sedimentary component in their source.

Origin of the displaced Salinian magmatic arc has been the subject of considerable recent debate. Whereas paleomagnetic data indicate a pre-Cretaceous northward movement on the order of 2,100 to 5,600 km (Kanter and Debiche, 1985), geological and isotopic data show that with removal of 305 km of Neogene slip, Salinia has isotopic patterns consistent with those of the southern Sierras and the western Mojave Desert (Ross, 1984; Silver and Mattinson, 1986). In his chapter, Mattinson shows that plutons of the Salinian magmatic arc have typical Cordilleran isotopic trends such as found in the Sierra Nevada and Peninsular Ranges batholiths. Ages range from 76 to 110 Ma, younging to the east. West to east trends for Sr, Pb, and Nd initial isotopic ratios require an increased easterly contribution of Proterozoic crust, implying that the arc "straddled the margin of the craton" during Cretaceous construction.

In the northern Sierra Nevada batholith, papers by Christe and Hannah and Beard further characterize wall-rock assemblages. Christe and Hannah report on an 11-km-thick, early Mesozoic sequence of high-potassium andesite to latite. In the Smartville complex, Beard investigates mingling and mixing of gabbro and melt produced during contact metamorphism of mafic to intermediate volcanic host rocks.

GREAT BASIN, NEVADA

Cretaceous plutonism in the Great Basin of Nevada shows striking temporal variations. Barton and others have summarized age, major-element, and isotopic data for Cretaceous plutons and associated mineral deposits, which they conclude to be the result of an increased crustal component in the younger magmatic suites. Systematic changes for early to late Cretaceous intrusions include (1) a shift from metaluminous diorite and monzonite to peraluminous granondiorite and granite; (2) isotopic change of

Sr_i from 0.706 to 0.719, ϵNd from -4.1 to -14.0, and $\delta^{18}O$ from 8.7 to 11.2 ‰; and (3) a change in mineralization style from porphyry Cu, Mo-Cu, and base metal to F-rich, lithophile element skarns and greisen deposits.

KLAMATH MOUNTAINS, CALIFORNIA AND OREGON

The Klamath Mountains represent a collage of Paleozoic and Mesozoic oceanic and island-arc terranes perforated by numerous pre- to post-accretion Jurassic plutons. Traditionally, Klamath plutons are regarded as mantle derived (Farmer and DePaolo, 1983), but a recent study by Barnes and others indicates a more complex magmatic history. Two plutons are shown to be tilted, representing 9 km of structural depth into an upwardly zoned magma system ranging from gabbro and tonalite (lower) to granite. Striking elemental and oxygen isotopic ($\delta^{18}O$ from 8.1 to 11.2 ‰) changes and minimal variations in initial Sr (0.7043 to 0.7046) are accounted for by combined magma mixing, fractional crystallization, and assimilation.

IDAHO BATHOLITH, IDAHO AND MONTANA

Two independent chapters on the Idaho batholith reach the same conclusion, that mixing of mafic magma and granitic melt is an important process in the production of intermediate rock types. Foster and Hyndman provide vivid descriptions of three types of magma interaction: mingling, mixing, and combined mingling and mixing of gabbro and granite, yielding near-linear arrays of major- and trace-element data. The chapter by Fleck incorporates Nd and Sr isotopic data and an expanded trace-element data set to distinguish three hybrid suites involving a high-Sr, arc-type magma and melts derived from Proterozoic lower and upper crust and Proterozoic metasedimentary rocks.

COLVILLE IGNEOUS COMPLEX, WASHINGTON

While the early Cenozoic was a time of magmatic quiescence throughout much of the Cordillera (Armstrong and Ward, 1990), Paleocene to Eocene igneous activity yielded batholith-sized granitic intrusions in the Okanagan, Kettle, and Lincoln complexes of northeastern Washington and adjacent British Columbia. Carlson and Moye describe three episodes of magmatism composing the Colville batholith: (1) 65-Ma mylonitic orthogneisses, (2) 54- to 61-Ma peraluminous leucogranites, and (3) 47- to 53-Ma silicic volcanics and shallow plutons.

COAST BATHOLITH, SOUTHEASTERN ALASKA AND BRITISH COLUMBIA

The Coast batholith (or Coast plutonic complex) is the largest Cordilleran batholith of North America, stretching more than 1,700 km from northern Washington to the Yukon (Fig. 1). Barker and Arth report on results from two detailed traverses across the batholith. Emplaced entirely into accreted terranes of oceanic origin, the plutons of the batholith range in timing from syn- to post-acretionary and range in age from Early Cretaceous to Eocene. Calc-alkaline, moderate in K, and high in Sr (to 900–1,070 ppm), the batholithic rocks are principally of tonalite with lesser amounts of quartz diorite, granodiorite, granite; pillow-form mafic inclusions are interpreted as mingled high-Al ba-

salt. Barker and Arth model the magma trends as the result of melting of accreted oceanic to continental slope material modified by hornblende-plagioclase fractionation and mixing with minor, crust-derived melt.

J. Lawford Anderson

REFERENCES CITED

Anderson, J. L., Barth, A. P., and Young, E. D., 1988, Mid-crustal Cretaceous roots of Cordilleran metamorphic core complexes: Geology, v. 16, p. 366–369.

Anderson, J. L., and 7 others, 1990, Plutonism across the Tujunga–North American terrane boundary; A middle to upper crustal view of two juxtaposed magmatic arcs, *in* Bartholomew, M. J., Hyndman, D. W., Mogk, D. V., and Mason, R., eds., Characterization and composition of ancient (Precambrian to Mesozoic) continental margins; Proceedings of the 8th International Conference on Basement Tectonics: Holland, D. Reidel Company (in press).

Armstrong, R. L., and Ward P., 1990, Late Triassic to earliest Eocene magmatism in the North American Cordillera; Implications for the western interior basin: Geological Society of Canada Special Paper (in press).

Bateman, P. C., and Dodge, F.C.W., 1970, Variations in major chemical constituents across the central Sierra Nevada batholith: Geological Society of America Bulletin, v. 81, p. 409–420.

Crittenden, M. D., Coney, P. J., and Davis, G. H., 1980, Cordilleran metamorphic core complexes: Geological Society of America Memoir 153, 490 p.

DePaolo, D. J., 1981, A neodymium and strontium isotopic study of Mesozoic calc-alkaline granitic batholiths of the Sierra Nevada and Peninsular Ranges, California: Journal of Geophysical Research, v. 86, p. 10470–10488.

Ernst, W. G., 1981, The geotectonic development of California; Rubey Volume 1: Englewood Cliffs, New Jersey, Prentice-Hall, 706 p.

——, 1988, Metamorphism and crustal evolution of the western United States; Rubey Volume 7: Englewood Cliffs, New Jersey, Prentice-Hall, 1153 p.

Everden, J. F., and Kistler, R. W., 1970, Chronology of emplacement of Mesozoic batholithic complexes in California and western Nevada: U.S. Geological Survey Professional Paper 623, 42 p.

Farmer, G. L., and DePaolo, D. J., 1983, Origin of Mesozoic and Tertiary granite in the western United States and implications for pre-Mesozoic crustal structure; 1, Nd and Sr isotopic studies in the geocline of the northern Great Basin: Journal of Geophysical Research, v. 88, p. 3379–3401.

Gastil, G., 1985, Terranes of Peninsular California and adjacent Sonora, *in* Howell, D. G., ed., Tectonostratigraphic terranes: Houston, Texas, Circum-Pacific Council for Energy and Mineral Resources, p. 273–284.

Gromet, L. P., and Silver, L. T., 1987, REE variations across the Peninsular Ranges batholith; Implications for batholithic petrogenesis and crustal growth in magmatic arcs: Journal of Petrology, v. 28, p. 75–125.

Howell, D. G., and McDougal, K. A., 1978, Mesozoic paleogeography of the western United States; Pacific Coast Paleogeography Symposium 2: Los Angeles, California, Pacific Section, Society of Economic Paleontologists and Mineralogists, 573 p.

John, B. E., 1981, Reconnaissance study of Mesozoic plutonic rocks in the Mojave Desert region, *in* Howard, K. A., Carr, M. D., and Miller, D. M., eds., Tectonic framework of the Mojave and Sonoran Deserts, California

and Arizona: U.S. Geological Survey Open-File Report 81–503, p. 49–51.

Kanter, L. R., and Debiche, M., 1985, Modeling the motion histories of the Point Arena and central Salinia Terranes, *in* Howell, D. G., ed., Tectonostratigraphic terranes of the circum-Pacific region: Houston, Texas, Circum-Pacific Council for Energy and Mineral Resources Earth Science Series 1, p. 227–238.

Kistler, R. W., and Peterman, Z. E., 1973, Variations in Sr, Rb, K, Na, and initial $^{87}Sr/^{86}Sr$ in Mesozoic granitic rocks and intruded wall rocks in central California: Geological Society of America Bulletin, v. 84, p. 3489–3512.

Lindgren, W., 1915, The igneous geology of the Cordillera and its problems, *in* Problems of American geology: New Haven, Connecticut, Yale University Silliman Foundation, p. 234–286.

Moore, J. G., 1959, The quartz diorite boundary line in the western United States: Journal of Geology, v. 67, p. 197–210.

Roddick, J. A., 1983, Circum-Pacific plutonic terranes: Geological Society of America Memoir 159, 316 p.

Ross, D. C., 1984, Possible correlations of basement rocks across the San Andreas, San Gregorio–Hosgri, and Rinconada–Reliz–King City faults, California: U.S. Geological Survey Professional Paper 1317, 37 p.

Silver, L. T., and Mattinson, J. M., 1986, "Orphan Salinia" has a home: EOS Transactions of the American Geophysical Union, v. 67, p. 1215.

Silver, L. T., Taylor, H. P., and Chappell, B. W., 1979, Some petrological, geochemical, and geochronological observations of the Peninsular Ranges batholith near the international border of the U.S.A. and Mexico, *in* Abbott, P. L., and Todd, V. R., eds., Mesozoic crystalline rocks; Geological Society of America annual meeting guidebook: San Diego, California, San Diego State University, p. 83–110.

Smith, R. B., and Eaton, G. P., 1978, Cenozoic tectonics and regional geophysics of the western Cordillera: Geological Society of America Memoir 152, 388 p.

Stern, T. W., Bateman, P. C., Morgan, B. A., Newell, M. F., and Peck, D. L., 1981, Isotopic U-Pb ages of zircon from granitoids from the central Sierra Nevada, California: U.S. Geological Survey Professional Paper 1185, 17 p.

Taylor, H. P., 1988, Oxygen, hydrogen, and strontium isotope constraints on the origin of granites: Transactions of the Royal Society of London, v. 79, p. 317–338.

Todd, V. R., and S. E., 1979, Metamorphic, intrusive, and structural framework of Peninsular Ranges batholith in southern San Diego County, California, *in* Abbott, P. L., and Todd, V. R., eds., Mesozoic crystalline rocks; Geological Society of America annual meeting guidebook: San Diego, California, San Diego State University, p. 177–232.

Zen, E-An, 1989, Plumbing the depths of batholiths: American Journal of Science, v. 289, p. 1137–1157.

Acknowledgments

This memoir has benefitted greatly from thoughtful and careful reviews by the following individuals:

Bob Anderson
Ernie Anderson
Jim Anderson
Dick Armstrong
Vicki Bennett
Pat Bickford
Ken Cameron
Eric Christiansen
Maria Crawford
Bob Cullers
Gerald Czamanske
Warren Day
Dave Dellinger
Frank Dodge
Mary Donato
Mike Dungan
George Dunne
Perry Ehlig
Richard Fiske

Virgil Frizzell
Tom Frost
Peter Gromet
Gary Girty
Bill Hackett
Alex Halliday
Jane Hammarstrom
William Hart
Dave Harwood
Gordon Haxel
Bill Hirt
Keith Howard
Jeff Keith
Bill Leeman
Nancy McMillan
Elizabeth Miller
Eldridge Moores
Jean Morrison
Jonathan Patchett

Zell Peterman
Jane Pike
John Reid
Steve Reynolds
Brady Rhodes
Dean Rinehart
Peter Schiffman
Bob Scott
Warren Sharp
Sorena Sorensen
Frank Spera
Robert Stull
Vicki Todd
Tom Vogel
Peter Weigan
Howard Wilshire
Joe Wooden
Ed Young

The Geology of North America
Memoir 174
1990

Chapter 1

Origin and evolution of the zoned La Posta-type plutons, eastern Peninsular Ranges batholith, southern and Baja California

M. J. Walawender, R. G. Gastil, J. P. Clinkenbeard, W. V. McCormick, B. G. Eastman, R. S. Wernicke, M. S. Wardlaw, and S. H. Gunn*
Department of Geological Sciences, San Diego State University, San Diego, California 92182
B. M. Smith*
Unocal Science and Technology, P.O. Box 76, Brea, California 92621

ABSTRACT

The Peninsular Ranges batholith has been subdivided into two zones based on geochemical, geophysical, and lithologic parameters. Plutons in the eastern zone (La Posta-type) are typically larger and inwardly zoned from hornblende-bearing tonalite margins to muscovite-bearing monzogranite cores. U-Pb ages on zircon are generally in the 100 to 90 Ma range. They tend to be more discordant in the cores of the plutons and have upper concordia intercepts near 1300 Ma. Rb-Sr systematics on mineral separates yield an Sr_i range from 0.7030 to 0.7044, although one pluton is reported to have a rim-to-core variation from 0.7043 to 0.7074. Whole-rock $\delta^{18}O$ is lowest in the hornblende-bearing facies (8.3 to 10.9 per mil) and highest in the muscovite-bearing facies (10.2 to 11.8 per mil); the level of variation is pluton dependent. $\delta^{18}O$ for quartz separates indicate an eastward-directed asymmetry toward heavier oxygen rather than the facies control observed in the whole-rock data. REE patterns from two plutons have nearly identical LREE enrichment and lack any Eu anomaly.

Associated with the La Posta-type plutons are a series of small, compositionally restricted, garnet-bearing monzogranites. They are 1 to 5 m.y. younger than the surrounding La Posta-type plutons and contain zircons inherited from a 1200- to 1300-Ma source. Whole-rock $\delta^{18}O$ values between 12.5 and 13.2 per mil and $Sr_i = 0.706$ reflect a continental contribution to these magmas.

La Posta-type melts were generated by subduction-related anatexis of amphibolite- or eclogite-grade oceanic crust. The relatively short emplacement interval and large size of the plutons suggest rapid separation of large volumes of melt from the source region under elevated P_{H2O}. Rise toward the present erosional level occurred along the juncture between oceanic lithosphere and the older (ca. 1300 Ma) continental margin. Interaction with the continental crust produced the present-day eastward bias toward higher $\delta^{18}O$ and zircon discordance.

*Present addresses: Gunn, Branch of Isotope Geology, U.S. Geological Survey, 345 Middlefield Road, Menlo Park, California 94025; Smith, Berkeley Center for Isotope Geochemistry, Earth Sciences Division, Lawrence Berkeley Laboratory, 1 Cyclotron Road, Berkeley, California 94720.

Walawender, M. J., Gastil, R. G., Clinkenbeard, J. P., McCormick, W. V., Eastman, B. G., Wernicke, R. S., Wardlaw, M. S., Gunn, S. H., and Smith, B. M., 1990, Origin and evolution of the zoned La Posta-type plutons, eastern Peninsular Ranges batholith, southern and Baja California, *in* Anderson, J. L., ed., The nature and origin of Cordilleran magmatism: Boulder, Colorado, Geological Society of America Memoir 174.

INTRODUCTION

Gastil (1975) first recognized that a major discontinuity separates the Peninsular Ranges batholith (PRB) into western and eastern zones. West of this discontinuity, the batholith is characterized by smaller diameter plutons (less than 10 km), moderate grades of metamorphism, and the presence of gabbro. This contrasts with the larger (up to 40 km) plutons, sillimanite-bearing and migmatitic prebatholithic rocks, and the absence of gabbroic plutons to the east. Silver and others (1979) described regional isotopic variations in the batholith and established that the plutonic rocks in the eastern zone were younger and had higher Sr_i and $\delta^{18}O$ relative to the western zone. The boundaries established by these parameters generally coincide with the discontinuity of Gastil (1975). Todd and Shaw (1979) recognized that the plutons to the west are part of a syntectonic assemblage characterized by locally intense deformation, whereas the eastern plutons are essentially undeformed and form a late- to post-tectonic sequence.

Todd and Shaw (1985) suggested an I-S line that separates a western I-type succession from an eastern series consisting of both I- and S-type granitoids. This sinuous line, limited to San Diego County, is crudely coincident with the previously established boundaries in that area. On a more regional scale, Diamond and others (1985) and Gastil and others (1986) delineated a magnetite-ilmenite line that extends from Riverside County southward through the state of Baja California (Fig. 1). Plutons west of this line contain both ilmenite and magnetite as primary oxide phases, whereas those to the east contain only ilmenite.

The near coincidence of all of these boundaries indicates that fundamental differences exist between the plutonic rocks on either side of the axis of the batholith. These differences cannot be constrained by local variations within the prebatholithic assemblage and must therefore reflect different patterns of plate interaction and magma generation. This paper describes four eastern-zone plutons in terms of their structural, geochemical, isotopic, and geochronologic framework and compares this to the regional characteristics of the western-zone plutons as established from published sources.

STRUCTURE AND PETROGRAPHY

The large, undeformed plutons of the eastern zone of the PRB have distinct structural and petrographic characteristics that set them apart from plutons with similar compositions in the western zone of the batholith. Although the data presented here are limited to the four plutons shown in Figure 1, reconnaissance mapping indicates that these plutons retain their defining characteristics southward to the 28th parallel.

The largest of these bodies, the La Posta pluton (Miller, 1935), straddles the international border and has an estimated exposure area of 1400 km². Although the extreme northern part of this pluton and the part south of the international border have been mapped only in reconnaissance fashion, approximately 750

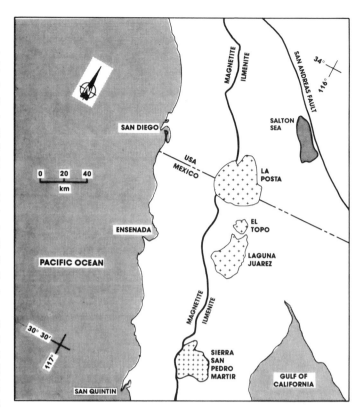

Figure 1. Location map showing the four plutons described in this report.

km² in San Diego and Imperial counties (Fig. 2) have been studied in detail (Kimzey, 1982; Sinfield, 1983; Clinkenbeard, 1987). These and other studies cited later in this report were used to establish the structural and textural features listed below, which define the La Posta–type plutons of the eastern Peninsular Ranges.

1. Concentric zones ranging from tonalite margins inward to granodiorite/monzogranite cores;

2. Internal contacts that are gradational over distances of several tens of meters;

3. Sharply euhedral, inclusion-free crystals of hornblende and biotite;

4. Large (to 0.5 cm) honey- to amber-colored prismatic sphene crystals;

5. Primary muscovite coexisting with biotite in the innermost zone;

6. Local development of megacrystic quartz and oikocrystic alkali feldspar in the inner parts of the pluton;

7. Absence of foliation.

Although individual La Posta–type plutons have the above characteristics, each also has additional structural and textural features that reflect differences in their cooling and emplacement histories.

La Posta pluton

Field mapping by Kimzey (1982), Sinfield (1983), and Walawender and others (1983) established that this pluton (Fig.

2) varies inward from a sphene-hornblende-biotite tonalite rim to a muscovite-biotite granodiorite core (Table 1). A banded border facies (Kofron, 1981), consisting of alternating bands rich in hornblende (± biotite) and plagioclase (± quartz), is locally developed along contacts with older igneous rocks of the batholith's western zone but is not included in Figure 2. Structurally, the pluton is massive; it is foliated only near its margins or near metasedimentary roof pendants where the foliation is steep and parallel to the contact. The sphene-hornblende-biotite tonalite found in the outer zone (hornblende-biotite facies) consists of large (up to 1 cm), inclusion-free hornblende euhedra, pseudohexagonal books of biotite, and smaller (up to 0.5 cm) sphene prisms. Plagioclase is the most abundant phase and displays mild oscillatory zoning. Cores commonly consist of several smaller crystals joined in a synneusis relationship and mantled by later growth as a single crystal. Quartz occurs as discrete anhedral grains with weakly developed undulatory extinction. The hornblende-biotite facies grades inward to the large-biotite facies, a sphene-biotite granodiorite, by gradual loss of the large hornblende euhedra and increase in oikocrystic feldspar. This facies is characterized by its abundance of large (up to 1 cm) pseudohexagonal books of biotite which impart a distinct "salt and pepper" appearance to the outcrops.

The transition into the small-biotite facies is observed as a gradual loss of the large biotite books and an increase in the amount of smaller (1 to 4 mm) but still euhedral biotite grains. There also appears to be a general decrease in grain size in this unit, although the alkali feldspar oikocrysts locally reach 5-cm widths. The muscovite-biotite facies is defined on the basis of visible muscovite in hand specimen, which ranges up to 1 percent and meets the textural criteria of Miller and others (1981) for primary origin. Ilmenite appears to be the sole opaque phase in all of the facies.

Scattered within the western half of the pluton are series of small, isolated blocks of hornblende diorite. These blocks rarely exceed 100 m in maximum dimension and contain up to 60 percent euhedral hornblende. Plagioclase with minor quartz and biotite are the remaining phases and are interstitial to the hornblende. Kimzey (1982) suggested that these blocks represent remnants of a zone of hornblende accumulation and that hornblende fractionation is responsible for the lithologic variations observed within the pluton. Mineral chemistries for the above units are reported by Clinkenbeard and Walawender (1989). Typical modes are reported in Table 1.

Sierra San Pedro Martir pluton

This pluton (Eastman, 1986; McCormick, 1986) is located approximately 150 km south-southeast of Ensenada (Fig. 1) and affords some of the most spectacular scenery in Baja California, with elevations in excess of 3,000 m. At its widest point, this kidney-shaped body is 30 km long and 20 km wide and is exposed over about 400 km^2. Compositional zones are crescent shaped and are successively displaced to the east (Fig. 3). Foliation is strongest near the rim, but decreases rapidly inward into a large undeformed central region. Where present, the foliation dips steeply inward toward the core.

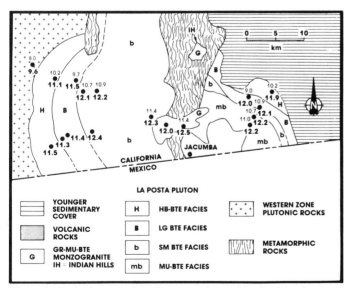

Figure 2. Geologic map of the La Posta pluton. Distribution of oxygen isotope data is shown for both whole rocks (small characters) and quartz separates (large characters).

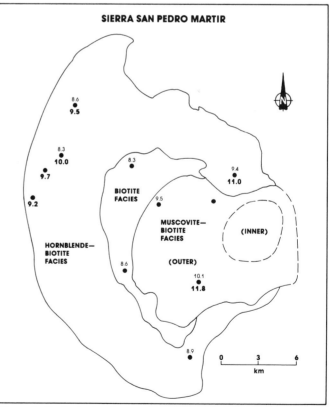

Figure 3. Geologic sketch map of the Sierra San Pedro Martir pluton (Eastman, 1986). Oxygen isotope data for whole rock and quartz separates given in small and large characters, respectively.

TABLE 1. AVERAGE VALUES FOR MODAL ABUNDANCES AND FOR MAJOR- AND TRACE-ELEMENT ANALYSES
OF THE MAIN FACIES OF THE FOUR PLUTONS IN THIS STUDY*

	La Posta				Laguna Juarez			
	Hnb-Bte	Lrg Bte	Sm Bte	Musc-Bte	Hnb-Bte	Bte	Musc-Bte	F Musc-Bte
n	9	10	12	9	17	6	14	4
SiO_2	67.28 (1.86)	68.59 (1.44)	69.15 (0.63)	73.35 (0.69)	64.27 (2.85)	70.80 (1.85)	73.28 (1.20)	73.59 (0.53)
Al_2O_3	16.14 (0.67)	15.97 (0.79)	16.15 (0.53)	15.00 (0.45)	17.02 (0.79)	15.78 (0.65)	15.03 (0.44)	15.13 (0.52)
Total Fe	3.85 (0.62)	3.24 (0.61)	2.75 (0.23)	2.33 (0.37)	4.52 (0.)	2.23 (0.)	1.72 (0.)	1.24 (0.)
Na_2O	0.61 (0.16)	3.64 (0.20)	3.88 (0.24)	3.68 (0.18)	3.61 (0.36)	3.67 (0.15)	3.68 (0.20)	3.91 (0.24)
K_2O	1.84 (0.42)	1.95 (0.35)	2.00 (0.39)	1.87 (0.58)	2.14 (0.41)	2.78 (0.43)	3.09 (0.72)	3.37 (0.13)
CaO	4.29 (0.49)	3.84 (0.40)	3.43 (0.18)	2.67 (0.31)	4.81 (0.84)	2.89 (0.63)	2.17 (0.51)	1.80 (0.11)
TiO_2	0.69 (0.14)	0.65 (0.15)	0.46 (0.05)	0.28 (0.05)	0.73 (0.14)	0.39 (0.15)	0.25 (0.07)	0.19 (0.06)
MgO	1.69 (0.36)	1.45 (0.28)	1.04 (0.12)	0.64 (0.14)	2.35 (0.77)	0.88 (0.36)	0.59 (0.20)	0.59 (0.12)
MnO	0.06 (0.01)	0.05 (0.01)	0.05 (0.01)	0.03 (0.01)	0.08 (0.01)	0.04 (0.01)	0.04 (0.01)	0.03 (0.01)
P_2O_5	0.18 (0.05)	0.14 (0.04)	0.13 (0.02)	0.08 (0.02)	0.16 (0.03)	0.19 (0.22)	0.08 (0.01)	0.07 (0.01)
n	9	10	12	9				
Ba	942 (132)	921 (257)	943 (142)	1421 (370)				
Sr	546 (72)	509 (49)	487 (31)	433 (19)	Sr:	200 - 600 ppm (Gunn, 1984)		
Rb	69 (7)	71 (11)	79 (13)	65 (8)				
Zr	165 (31)	166 (40)	163 (33)	212 (12)				
Sr_i	——	——	0.7044	——	0.7043	0.7051	0.7067	0.7074
n	6	5	11	6	16	9	13	9
Quartz	27.5 (3.8)	28.5 (4.3)	28.6 (2.4)	34.3 (4.9)	24.8 (6.6)	35.3 (3.7)	32.5 (401)	32.5 (4.6)
Plag	50.3 (7.9)	46.5 (4.3)	45.4 (2.7)	45.3 (4.9)	46.8 (6.1)	40.5 (4.0)	42.0 (4.3)	42.0 (5.2)
K-felds	3.4 (1.4)	11.0 (0.9)	14.0 (4.9)	11.0 (3.6)	7.0 (5.8)	15.5 (3.8)	16.4 (3.9)	14.8 (4.8)
Hrnblnd	3.2 (1.6)	1.0 (1.0)	tr	0	7.2 (4.)	0	0	0
Biotite	15.2 (5.6)	12.3 (3.2)	11.9 (2.3)	9.0 (1.6)	11.8 (4.8)	7.7 (1.6)	6.2 (2.2)	6.4 (3.6)
Muscovite	0	0	0	0.5 (0.4)	0	tr	2.2 (1.3)	4.2 (1.4)
Garnet	0	0	0	0	0	0	0	0
Sphene	0.6 (0.6)	0.7 (0.5)	0.1 (0.1)	0	tr	tr	0	0

Three principal units with internal gradational contacts have been defined within the pluton (Eastman, 1986). Although these units are virtually indistinguishable from those in the La Posta pluton, several important differences exist.

1. Magnetite coexists with ilmenite in well-defined zones.

2. Although a large-biotite facies has not been identified, a zone of biotite pseudomorphs after hornblende occurs between the biotite and hornblende-biotite facies.

3. Sparse, fist-sized inclusions of milky-white quartz occur in the muscovite facies.

4. The muscovite-biotite facies can be subdivided into an outer portion with muscovite visible in hand specimen and an inner zone with muscovite visible only in thin section.

5. Hornblende-rich diorites with cumulate textures are absent.

Modal vaariations within the Sierra San Pedro Martir are listed in Table 1. As in the La Posta pluton, hornblende and sphene decrease in abundance inward and are absent from the muscovite-bearing facies. In addition, average grain size in the muscovite-biotite facies is smaller than in the outer facies, despite the fact that the size of the quartz megacrysts increases inward to well over 1 cm.

Laguna Juarez pluton

This oval pluton (Gunn, 1984, 1986) is located approximately 800 km east of Ensenada (Fig. 1) and is exposed over an area of 700 km^2 (Fig. 4). It is zoned inward from a sphene-hornblende-biotite tonalite (hornblende-biotite facies) through a biotite granodiorite (biotite facies) into a core zone of muscovite-biotite monzogranite (muscovite-biotite facies). This latter unit has been further subdivided into a coarser grained outer and a finer grained inner subfacies. All internal contacts are gradational over distances of several tens of meters. Foliation is present only in the marginal facies where it is vertical and parallel to the outer contact. Foliation intensity is strongest at the margins but diminishes rapidly inward to unfoliated rocks in the biotite facies.

The Laguna Juarez pluton differs mineralogically from both

TABLE 1. AVERAGE VALUES FOR MODAL ABUNDANCES AND FOR MAJOR- AND TRACE-ELEMENT ANALYSES OF THE MAIN FACIES OF THE FOUR PLUTONS IN THIS STUDY (continued)*

| | Sierra San Pedro Martir | | | El Topo | | |
| | Hnb-Bte | Bte | Musc-Bte | Hnb-Bte | Bte | |
n	25	5	7	9	8	
SiO_2	65.30 (2.49)	67.81 (1.45)	70.80 (1.45)	67.88 (1.76)	73.32 (1.43)	
Al_2O_3	15.91 (0.92)	15.80 (0.56)	15.07 (0.64)	15.24 (0.78)	14.33 (0.65)	
Total Fe	3.77 (1.09)	2.97 (0.56)	2.31 (0.40)	4.49 (0.66)	1.56 (0.79)	
Na_2O	3.75 (0.52)	3.89 (0.53)	3.77 (0.30)	3.30 (0.26)	3.57 (0.50)	
K_2O	1.62 (0.49)	1.73 (0.12)	1.68 (0.13)	2.18 (0.66)	4.28 (1.18)	
CaO	4.41 (0.56)	3.63 (0.08)	3.10 (0.28)	3.28 (0.58)	1.27 (0.59)	*Number in parentheses is one standard
TiO_2	0.60 (0.07)	0.51 (0.13)	0.30 (0.07)	0.44 (0.07)	0.13 (0.08)	deviation, n = number of analyses.
MgO	1.63 (0.70)	1.24 (0.41)	0.60 (0.13)	1.60 (0.23)	0.32 (0.22)	Sr_i data are single analyses on each
MnO	0.06 (0.01)	0.05 (0.01)	0.04 (0.01)	0.09 (0.01)	0.04 (0.01)	facies, except for SSPM (Biotite Fa-
P_2O_5	0.14 (0.03)	0.13 (0.02)	0.09 (0.02)	0.16 (0.02)	0.08 (0.01)	cies) where the average of two analyses
						is listed. Sr_i for the Biotite Facies
n	10	5	7	9	8	of the Laguna Juarez pluton courtesy of
						J. Calhoun (unpublished data, 1987).
Ba	670 (173)	817 (118)	762 (188)	1077 (185)	759 (321)	
Sr	498 (140)	507 (67)	493 (15)	86 (19)	113 (53)	
Rb	81 (23)	99 (37)	79 (9)	268 (37)	129 (23)	
Zr	175 (54)	182 (25)	166 (15)	117 (15)	59 (36)	
Sr_i	0.7039	0.7041	0.7040	0.7029		
n	7	4	5	6	6	
Quartz	26.4 (3.2)	30.5 (6.3)	38.6 (3.9)	31.2 (5.6)	33.8 (4.1)	
Plag	53.6 (3.5)	44.9 (4.6)	40.3 (2.4)	47.6 (7.2)	41.2 (5.8)	
K-felds	3.1 (1.2)	8.3 (2.8)	10.9 (2.7)	6.1 (4.4)	17.0 (8.4)	
Hrnblnd	3.6 (2.5)	0	0	2.0 (2.0)	0	
Biotite	12.2 (3.8)	15.9 (5.4)	7.8 (1.6)	11.2 (3.1)	5.3 (2.8)	
Muscovite	0	0	2.5 (1.1)	0	0.3 (0.8)	
Garnet	0	0	0	0	tr	
Sphene	0.8 (0.7)	0.4 (0.4)	0	tr	0	

the Sierra San Pedro Martir and the La Posta plutons in that scarce remnant pyroxene cores are found in some hornblende euhedra (Gunn, 1984), and from the Sierra San Pedro Martir pluton in that megacrystic quartz is not reported and the opaque mineral is ilmenite alone. As in the other two plutons, muscovite has the textural criteria for primary origin, synneusis relations in plagioclase and oikocrystic alkali feldspar are common, sphene and hornblende do not coexist with muscovite, and the innermost zone is finer grained than the remainder of the pluton.

El Topo pluton

Located approximately 40 km northeast of Ensenada (Fig. 1), the El Topo pluton (Wernicke, 1987) is exposed over an area of approximately 100 km² (Fig. 5). In addition to being the smallest of the La Posta–type plutons studied to date, it is a maverick in terms of several others features. Concentric lithologic zones with gradational internal contacts occur, but in a reverse pattern so that the core zone is composed of hornblende-biotite

tonalite/granodiorite (hornblende-biotite facies), which grades outward into a biotite granodiorite/monzogranite (biotite facies).

Both facies of the El Topo pluton contain oikocrystic alkali feldspar. The biotite facies does not contain sphene euhedra, has sparse biotite pseudomorphs after hornblende irregularly distributed throughout, and is garnet- (± muscovite) bearing up to 100 m from its contact with the metasedimentary wall rocks. Foliated rocks are present only in the hornblende facies immediately adjacent to the gradational contact with the biotite facies. The foliation is parallel to the contact and dips steeply inward. The two facies have very different geomorphic expressions in that the outer biotite facies forms a topographic high that towers more than 200 m above the inner hornblende facies.

GEOCHRONOLOGY

Krummenacher and others (1975) reported K-Ar cooling ages on hornblende (and biotite) for the La Posta pluton that

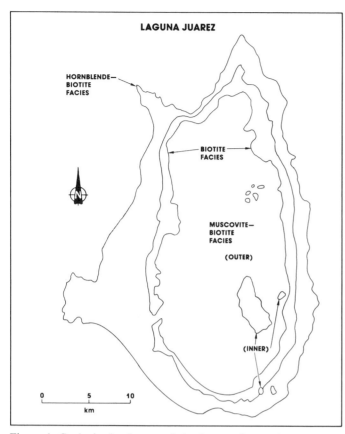

Figure 4. Geologic sketch map of the Laguna Juarez pluton (Gunn, 1984).

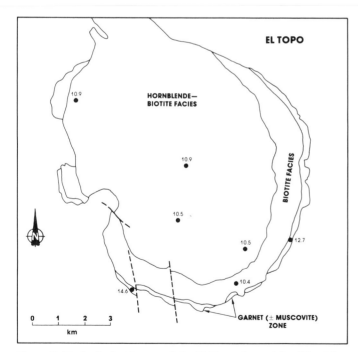

Figure 5. Geologic sketch map of the El Topo pluton (after Wernicke, 1987) and distribution of whole-rock oxygen isotope data.

decreased from approximately 100 (90) Ma on the west to 85 (75) Ma in the east. These values, however, do not decrease smoothly but fall into a western and an eastern group on either side of the central metamorphic screen (Fig. 2). Biotite cooling ages are, for example, 91 to 83 Ma and 78 to 73 Ma for the two groups. Silver and others (1979) reported zircon U-Pb ages of 98 and 97 Ma for two samples presumably taken from the western side of the La Posta pluton. Additional sample locations are shown in their Figure 1 within either what they show as or what we now recognize as the La Posta pluton. However, these are not specifically tied to that pluton in the text.

Multiple zircon fractions (Table 2) were analyzed from three sample localities within the La Posta pluton (Clinkenbeard, 1987). Five fractions from the sample of the eastern hornblende facies, including one air-abraded fraction, yield consistent data that indicate a crystallization age of 93 ± 1 Ma. Data from four zircon fractions from a sample of the western hornblende facies are also consistent and indicate an age of 95 ± 1 Ma. However, an air-abraded fraction gave a slightly higher $^{206}Pb/^{238}U$ age, possibly suggesting a small inherited lead component. The third sample, taken from the western small biotite facies, gave slightly discordant $^{206}Pb/^{238}U$ and $^{207}Pb/^{235}U$ ages. Weighting in favor of the $^{206}Pb/^{238}U$ age gave a value, consistent with the other samples, that represents a maximum age for this sample. These, and all other U-Pb zircon data presented in this paper, were determined at the Baylor Brooks Institute of Isotope Geology at San Diego State University.

A Rb-Sr isochron was also obtained for the sample from the western small-biotite facies; the data are reported in Table 3. Although four points were generated for the isochron, three have comparable Rb/Sr (apatite, whole rock, and hornblende) and reduce the system to an effective two-point isochron. This, however, yielded a calculated age of 92 ± 2.8 Ma that is consistent with the average zircon U-Pb age of 94 ± 2 Ma.

Krummenacher and others (1975) noted the differences in K-Ar cooling ages on either side of the large metasedimentary screen in the La Posta pluton and suggested that the eastern side represented a downthrown block. The U-Pb zircon ages on either side of the pluton are consistent within the given error limits but do not preclude the existence of such a medial fault. However, the general symmetry of the map units around the screen and the consistency of their petrographic characteristics argue that, if such a structure exists, movement was dominantly vertical and juxtaposed different levels of the same pluton.

K-Ar cooling ages on biotite from the three major facies in the Sierra San Pedro Martir pluton progressively decrease inward, from 87 ± 3 Ma in the hornblende-biotite facies to 83 ± 3 Ma in the biotite facies to 72 ± 2 Ma in the innermost muscovite-biotite facies. Zircon fractions were also analyzed from four separate samples (Table 4) within the pluton (McCormick, 1986). These yield discordant points that plot on a chord (Fig. 6) with a lower-intercept age of 93.6 ± 2.8 Ma and an upper-intercept age of 1305 ± 430 Ma. The lower intercept age is interpreted as the zircon closure age for the pluton and is comparable to the re-

TABLE 2. U-Pb ZIRCON DATA FOR THE LA POSTA PLUTON*

Fraction	Concentration (ppm) U	Concentration (ppm) Pb	Measured Ratios $\frac{^{204}Pb}{^{206}Pb}$	Measured Ratios $\frac{^{207}Pb}{^{206}Pb}$	Measured Ratios $\frac{^{208}Pb}{^{206}Pb}$	Radiogenic Ratios (Age [Ma]) $\frac{^{206}Pb}{^{238}U}$	Radiogenic Ratios (Age [Ma]) $\frac{^{207}Pb}{^{235}U}$	Radiogenic Ratios (Age [Ma]) $\frac{^{207}Pb}{^{206}Pb}$
*Unit: Western Hornblende-Biotite Facies*
nm(-3) -200	780	11	0.000420	0.05469	0.09440	0.01468 (94)	0.0981 (95)	0.04850 (124)
nm(-3)	680	10	0.000510	0.05597	0.09941	0.01466 (94)	0.0979 (95)	0.04850 (120)
M(-3)	732	11	0.000180	0.05131	0.08780	0.01477 (95)	0.0991 (96)	0.04863 (131)
m(-2)	687	11	0.001080	0.06371	0.13024	0.01497 (96)	0.0986 (95)	0.04777 (88)
m(-3) aa	590	9	0.000909	0.06203	0.13263	0.01507 (96)	0.1010 (98)	0.04863 (130)
*Unit: Eastern Hornblende-Biotite Facies*
nm(-3)	400	8	0.004770	0.11905	0.27368	0.01441 (92)	0.0969 (94)	0.04878 (137)
nm(-3)	418	6	0.000315	0.05342	0.10678	0.01435 (92)	0.0965 (94)	0.04878 (113)
m(-3)	422	6	0.000496	0.05548	0.11317	0.01455 (93)	0.0966 (94)	0.04817 (108)
m(-2)	424	6	0.000339	0.05307	0.10845	0.01449 (93)	0.0961 (93)	0.04807 (103)
m(-3)	450	7	0.000215	0.05118	0.10422	0.01461 (94)	0.0967 (94)	0.04802 (100)
*Unit: Western Small-Biotite Facies*
nm(-2)	634	9	0.000710	0.06052	0.09332	0.01471 (94)	0.1015 (98)	0.05007 (198)
nm(-2)	672	10	0.000540	0.05816	0.08769	0.01447 (93)	0.1002 (97)	0.05022 (205)
-200 (bulk)	647	10	0.001208	0.06718	0.11320	0.01470 (94)	0.1001 (97)	0.04942 (168)

*Radiogenic lead corrected for blank $^{206}Pb/^{204}Pb$ = 18.85; $^{207}Pb/^{204}Pb$ = 15.64; $^{208}Pb/^{204}Pb$ = 38.29) and common lead derived from feldspar analysis (J. Wooden, personal communication, 1968: $^{206}Pb/^{204}Pb$ = 18.88; $^{207}Pb/^{204}Pb$ = 15.66; $^{208}Pb/^{204}Pb$ = 38.71). nm = nonmagnetic; m = magnetic at given side tilt on a Franz Isodynamic Separator. Front tilt was 20°. Samples were spiked with a $^{208}Pb/^{235}U$ mixed spike. Dissolution and chemical separations were modified after Krogh (1973). Blank lead averaged 0.5 ng during the course of this study. Data were reduced according to the methods of Ludwig (1984). Uncertainties in the $^{206}Pb/^{238}U$ and $^{207}Pb/^{235}U$ ratios are 1 percent and 2 percent, respectively, at the 95-percent confidence level and result in an errror of approximately ±2 Ma. Analytical uncertainty has produced an error in the $^{207}Pb/^{206}Pb$ age as larrge as 25 Ma, based on repeated analyses of individual zircon fractions. Lead ratios were normalized for mass fractionation of 0.1 ± 0.03 percent per mass unit, based on replicate analyses of NBS lead standards 982 and 983. The uranium ratio was normalized for mass fractionation of 0.12 ± 0.06 percent per mass unit, based on replicate analyses of NBS uranium standard U-050. Decay constants used: Lambda U^{238} = 0.000155125 and Lambda U^{235} = 0.00098485 decays per m.y. (Jaffey and others, 1971). Melissa Wardlaw, analyst.

TABLE 3. Rb-Sr DATA FOR THE LA POSTA AND INDIAN HILL PLUTONS*

Sample	$^{87}Sr/^{86}Sr$	Sr (ppm)	Rb (ppm)	$^{87}Rb/^{86}Sr$
Unit: Western Small-Biotite Facies				
Whole rock	0.70555	419	57	0.39
Biotite	0.81490	13	387	84.30
Apatite	0.70483	384	1.1	0.01
Hornblende	0.70410	37.6	7.4	0.65
Age = 91.9 ± 2.8 Ma	Sr_i = 0.70437 ± 0.00057			
Unit: Gar-musc-bte monzogranite, Indian Hill Pluton				
Whole rock	0.70743	261	88	0.95
Biotite	0.74126	58.7	598	28.80
Apatite	0.70614	233	1.6	0.02
Muscovite	0.72040	79.5	292	10.38
Age = 89.6 ± 2.6 Ma	Sr_i = 0.70628 ± 0.00025			

*Age and Sr_i determined using a York II regression. Analyst: Terry Davis, California State University, Los Angeles.

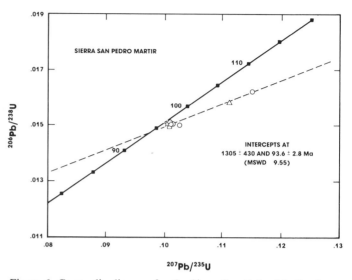

Figure 6. Concordia diagram for the Sierra San Pedro Martir pluton. Star and square symbols represent the outer hornblende-bearing facies, circles represent the biotite facies, and the triangle represents the muscovite-bearing facies. The most discordant sample from the biotite facies was air abraded.

ported ages of the La Posta pluton. The upper intercept reflects a zircon component inherited from a 1300-Ma source.

Multiple zircon fractions from two samples of the El Topo pluton (Wernicke, 1987) yielded concordant ages of 109 ± 1 Ma for the inner hornblende-biotite facies and 106 ± 1 Ma for the outer biotite facies (Table 5) and represent the oldest reported emplacement ages for the La Posta–type plutons. These ages are consistent with models involving stoping of the roof (hornblende-biotite facies) into a more fractionated lower portion of the pluton (biotite facies) or resurgence of the fractionated melt into ring faults (caldera related?) around a partly crystalline carapace; i.e., relative movement of the roof and still-molten interior of the pluton. A similar origin has been suggested for the zoning within the nearby El Pinal pluton (Duffield, 1968).

Gunn (1986, personal communication to RGG) has determined a zircon U-Pb emplacement age of 90 Ma for the inner zone of the Laguna Juarez pluton. A K-Ar age on hornblende (Gunn, 1986) of 89 Ma is generally consistent with those reported for the La Posta and Sierra San Pedro Martir plutons.

Intrusive into many La Posta–type plutons or their surrounding sillimanite-grade metasedimentary envelopes are a series of small garnet (±muscovite ±biotite) monzogranite plutons and/or dikes (Walawender and others, 1983; Clinkenbeard and others, 1986; Parrish and others, 1986). The Indian Hill pluton (Parrish and others, 1986) is entirely surrounded by high-grade metamorphic rocks which, in turn, are within the larger envelope of the La Posta pluton (Fig. 2). Five zircon fractions, including two air-abraded ones from a single sample of the Indian Hill

pluton, yielded discordant $^{206}Pb/^{238}U$ and $^{208}Pb/^{235}U$ ages that plot on a chord with a lower intercept of 84 ± 6 Ma and an upper intercept age of 1162 ± 430 Ma (Table 6, Fig. 7). A Rb-Sr four-point isochron (Table 3) for the same sample gave a regression age of 90 + 2.6 Ma. Given the error limits on the latter, an emplacement age of about 89 Ma is preferred. The U-Pb upper intercept age of 1162 Ma probably represents the average age of continental rocks involved in the formation of the Indian Hill pluton. A similar body of garnet-muscovite-biotite monzogranite cuts both the La Posta pluton and the central metasedimentary screen near Jacumba, California (Fig. 2). U-Pb zircon ages on three fractions from this unit (Table 6) yielded an emplacement age of 93 ± 1 Ma that is consistent with the observed field relations.

A large dike of garnet-muscovite-biotite monzogranite cuts the outer biotite facies of the El Topo pluton. U-Pb data on three zircon fractions from this dike plot on a chord (Fig. 8) whose lower-intercept (emplacement) age of 101 Ma is compatible with a host-rock age of 105 Ma. The upper intercept age of 1278 Ma again signals the involvement of a source with an average age near 1300 Ma and its proximity to the locus of emplacement of the La Posta–type plutons.

INITIAL STRONTIUM RATIOS (Sr_i)

Silver and others (1979) described an eastward increase in Sr_i from approximately 0.703 to 0.707, with Sr_i isopleths parallel to the north-northeast structural grain of the batholith. The La

TABLE 4. U-Pb ZIRCON DATA FOR THE SAN PEDRO MARTIR PLUTON*

| Fraction | Concentration (ppm) | | Measured Ratios | | | Radiogenic Ratios (Age [Ma]) | | |
	U	Pb	$\frac{^{204}Pb}{^{206}Pb}$	$\frac{^{207}Pb}{^{206}Pb}$	$\frac{^{208}Pb}{^{206}Pb}$	$\frac{^{206}Pb}{^{238}U}$	$\frac{^{207}Pb}{^{235}U}$	$\frac{^{207}Pb}{^{206}Pb}$
Unit: Hornblende-Biotite Facies								
nm(-2)	290	5	02.001838	0.07518	0.19403	0.01499 (96)	0.0996 (96)	0.04820 (109)
m(-2) +200	280	4	0.000462	0.05583	0.13860	0.01492 (95)	0.1009 (98)	0.04905 (150)
Unit: Biotite Facies								
M(-2) -200	640	10	0.00162	0.05066	0.11911	0.01507 (96)	0.1003 (97)	0.4828 (113)
m(-2)	593	9	0.000182	0.05165	0.10941	0.01509 (97)	0.1019 (99)	0.04898 (147)
Unit: Biotite Facies								
nm(-2) -200	675	11	0.000233	0.05202	0.13968	0.01507 (96.4)	0.1010 (97.7)	0.04860 (128.7)
nm(-2)	630	10	0.000365	0.05546	0.13593	0.01501 (96)	0.1037 (100)	0.050100 (200)
nm(-2)	640	10	0.000522	0.05667	0.13294	0.01501 (96)	0.1015 (98)	0.049021 (149)
m(-2)	645	10	0.000540	0.05795	0.14323	0.01510 (97)	0.10421 (101)	0.050034 (197)
m(-2)	672	11	0.000715	0.06019	0.14440	0.01497 (96)	0.1026 (99)	0.049701 (181)
nm(-2) aa	578	10	0.000485	0.05856	0.14172	0.01622 (104)	0.1152 (111)	0.051533 (265)
Unit: Muscovite-Biotite Facies								
bulk	994	15	0.000762	0.06222	0.09857	0.01583 (101)	0.115 (107)	0.051088 (245)

*Abbreviations and corrections as in Table 2. Analyst: Melissa Wardlaw.

Posta–type plutons of the eastern Peninsular Ranges batholith appear to lie east of the 0.705 isopleth (see also Hill, 1984). Initial strontium ratios of 0.7044 and 0.7063 have been determined for the La Posta and Indian Hill plutons, respectively, by using four-point isochrons (Table 3). Note that in both cases, the low Rb apatite separates gave a present-day $^{87}Sr/^{86}Sr$ very close to the zero-Rb regression intercept.

Apatite separates from four samples in a rim-to-core traverse of the Sierra San Pedro Martir pluton (Table 1) have average present-day Sr ratios of 0.7040 + 0.0001. Rb content of these apatites was less than 0.6 ppm, so the present-day ratios must closely approximate their Sr_i. The data show neither a geographic nor lithologic control on Sr_i in this pluton. Apatite separates from the hornblende facies of the El Topo pluton yielded a present-day $^{87}Sr/^{86}Sr$ of 0.7030. Samples from the biotite facies did not yield sufficient apatite concentrates for isotopic analysis.

TABLE 5. U-Pb ZIRCON DATA FOR THE EL TOPO PLUTON AND ASSOCIATED DIKE ROCKS*

| | Concentration (ppm) | | Measured Ratios | | | Radiogenic Ratios (Age [Ma]) | | |
| | U | Pb | $\frac{^{204}Pb}{^{206}Pb}$ | $\frac{^{207}Pb}{^{206}Pb}$ | $\frac{^{208}Pb}{^{206}Pb}$ | $\frac{^{206}Pb}{^{238}U}$ | $\frac{^{207}Pb}{^{235}U}$ | $\frac{^{207}Pb}{^{206}Pb}$ |
Fraction								
Unit: Hornblende-Biotite Facies								
nm(-1) -200	840	14.22	0.000344	0.05371	0.09262	0.1711	0.1148	0.04865
m(-1) -200	1020	16.82	0.000171	0.05321	0.08787	0.01682 (108)	0.1132 (109)	0.04881 (139)
Unit: Biotite Facies								
nm (-2) -200	918	15.0	0.000647	0.05816	0.07715	0.01660 (106)	0.1113 (107)	0.04864 (131)
m(-2) -200	1396	23.8	0.001351	0.06854	0.10155	0.01652 (106)	0.1108 (107)	0.04866 (131)
m(-1) -200	1776	31.0	0.001839	0.07592	0.11740	0.01643 (105)	0.1107 (107)	0.04888 (142)
m0 -200	2035	36.94	0.002576	0.08618	0.14319	0.01633 (104)	0.1086 (105)	0.4825 (112)
Unit: Gar-musc-bte monzogranite dike								
nm(-1)	864	17.3	0.001965	0.08225	0.13383	0.01848 (118)	0.1363 (120)	0.05350 (350)
m(-1)	1387	29.4	0.003782	0.10734	0.19935	0.01749 (112)	0.1252 (130)	0.05192 (282)
m1	2314	46.6	0.003799	0.10515	0.20673	0.01659 (106)	0.1139 (110)	0.04981 (186)

*Abbreviations and corrections as in Table 1. Analyst: Melissa Wardlaw.

Gunn (1986 and 1987 personal communication to RGG) determined whole-rock, present-day $^{87}Sr/^{86}Sr$ for three of four lithologic zones in the Laguna Juarez pluton and calculated Sr_i based on a 90-Ma emplacement age. A crude west to east progression from 0.7043 at the margin to 0.7074 in the core (Table 1) suggests a lithologic and/or geographic control on Sr_i.

OXYGEN ISOTOPIC SYSTEMATICS

Previous work on the oxygen isotopic systematics of the plutonic rocks in the PRB include studies of individual plutons by Turi and Taylor (1971) and Hill (1984). Taylor and Silver (1978), Silver and others (1979), and Taylor (1986) recognized a regional pattern of increasing $\delta^{18}O$ from west to east, with whole-rock values ranging from approximately 6 per mil in the

west to as high as 12.8 per mil in the east. In addition, a $\delta^{18}O$ "step" was defined by closely spaced contours of 8.5 and 9.0 per mil. This "step" closely corresponds to the western margin of the La Posta pluton in San Diego County and to the western limit of the La Posta–type plutons in northern Baja California.

Oxygen isotope determinations reported here were carried out at Unocal Science and Technology using BrF_5 as the fluorinating agent (Clayton and Mayeda, 1963). After liberated oxygen was converted to CO_2, isotope ratio measurements were performed on a Finnigan-MAT 251 mass spectrometer with a typical uncertainty of ± 0.2 percent. Our value for NBS-28 quartz was 9.67 ± 0.14 per mil during the course of the study.

Whole-rock $\delta^{18}O$ values for the La Posta pluton range from 9.0 to 11.4 per mil (Fig. 1). The value of 8.0 per mil from tonalitic rocks outside the pluton is distinctly lower than the 10.2

TABLE 6. U-Pb ZIRCON DATA FOR GARNET-BEARING MONZOGRANITES*

| Fraction | Concentration (ppm) | | Measured Ratios | | | Radiogenic Ratios (Age [Ma]) | | |
	U	Pb	$\frac{^{204}Pb}{^{206}Pb}$	$\frac{^{207}Pb}{^{206}Pb}$	$\frac{^{208}Pb}{^{206}Pb}$	$\frac{^{206}Pb}{^{238}U}$	$\frac{^{207}Pb}{^{235}U}$	$\frac{^{207}Pb}{^{206}Pb}$
Unit: Garnet-bearing Granodiorite/Monzogranite								
nm(-2)	522	8	0.000790	0.06003	0.10760	0.01467 (94)	0.0978 (95)	0.04836 (117)
m(-2)	652	10	0.001586	0.07205	0.13149	0.014737 (92)	0.0964 (93)	0.04868 (132)
m(-1)	692	11	0.002240	0.08160	0.14684	0.01433 (92)	0.0959 (93)	0.04856 (126)
Unit: Gar-musc-bte monzogranite, Indian Hill pluton								
nm(-2)	637	9	0.000845	0.06286	0.11084	0.01423 (91)	0.09896 (96)	0.050450 (216)
m(-2)	785	12	0.001270	0.06898	0.12957	0.01416 (91)	0.09824 (95)	0.050306 (209)
m(-1)	867	14	0.002443	0.08567	0.16748	0.01425 (91)	0.09774 (95)	0.049762 (184)
m(-2)aa	566	9	0.000702	0.06153	0.11341	0.01499 (96)	0.10593 (102)	0.051239 (252)
m(-1)aa	699	11	0.000702	0.06323	0.11086	0.01554 (99)	0.11346 (109)	0.052960 (323)

*Abbreviations and corrrections as in Table 2. Analyst: Melissa Wardlaw.

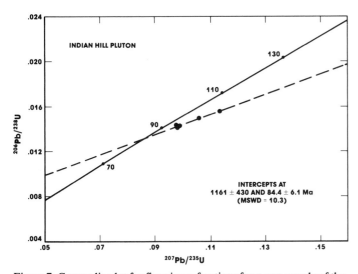

Figure 7. Concordia plot for five zircon fractions from one sample of the Indian Hill pluton (Parrish and others, 1986).

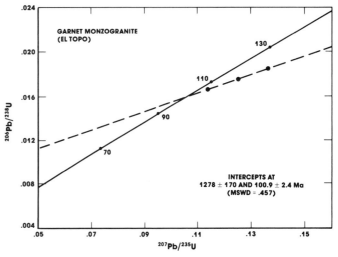

Figure 8. Concordia plot for three zircon fractions from a garnet-bearing monzogranite dike cutting the El Topo pluton (Wernicke, 1987).

per mil found in the western hornblende facies and is consistent with the presence of a $\delta^{18}O$ "step" near the western boundary of the pluton. Whole-rock $\delta^{18}O$ values for the La Posta pluton are generally highest (up to 11.4 per mil) in the interior of the pluton, but some of the scatter in this parameter reflects facies-dependent differences in modal mineralogy. For example, the low values of 9.0 and 9.7 per mil (Fig. 5) for two of the large-biotite facies samples reflect higher concentrations of vermicultic and chloritic biotite (Smith and Walawender, 1987). Hill (1984) accounted for similar variations in whole-rock $\delta^{18}O$ of the Poppet Creek granodiorite in the San Jacinto Mountains by a change in color index. The pattern of increasing $\delta^{18}O$ seen in the whole-rock data is more apparent in the slightly broader data base for quartz separates (Fig. 9). The depression seen in the large-biotite facies, however, is absent, supporting a modal variation as the cause for the whole-rock data of 10 per mil or less in this pluton. The rim to core increase in $\delta^{18}O$ (quartz) for the eastern side of the La Posta pluton is more subdued than on the western side and indicates that the bulk of the pluton, especially the eastern side, has a consistent $\delta^{18}O$ (quartz) of about 12 per mil.

A similar $\delta^{18}O$ pattern exists for the Sierra San Pedro Martir pluton (Fig. 3), but at substantially reduced levels for both whole rock and quartz. Whole-rock $\delta^{18}O$ ranges from 8.3 to 10.1 per mil, whereas quartz ranges from 9.5 to 11.8 per mil. The highest values are found in the inner muscovite-biotite facies, but the pattern may also be geographically controlled in that the easternmost prongs of the hornblende-biotite facies exhibit higher $\delta^{18}O$. Gunn (1986) reported a whole-rock $\delta^{18}O$ range at the Laguna Juarez pluton from 7.4 per mil (hornblende-biotite facies) to 12.1 per mil (muscovite-biotite facies), a pattern consistent with either a lithologic or a geographic control on the oxygen systematics.

Whole-rock $\delta^{18}O$ for both facies of the El Topo pluton are consistently near 10.5 per mil. However, two samples taken from the marginal (garnet + muscovite) zone adjacent to the contact with metasedimentary host rocks yield values of up to 14.7 per mil (Fig. 5).

Three samples from the Indian Hill pluton (Fig. 2) yield whole-rock $\delta^{18}O$ between 11.7 and 12.1 per mil. Quartz separates range between 12.6 and 13.2 per mil, and indicate that this pluton is richer in ^{18}O than the La Posta–type plutons.

GEOCHEMISTRY

Silver and others (1979) described the Peninsular Ranges batholith as the most calcic segment of the circum-Pacific batholiths with an alkali-lime index of 63 to 65. The La Posta pluton has a projected alkali-lime index of 64 (Kimzey, 1982; Clinkenbeard, 1987), making it the most calcic of the four eastern (La Posta–type) plutons studied to date. Alkali-lime indices for the Sierra San Pedro Martir (McCormick, 1986), Laguna Juarez (Gunn, 1984), and El Topo (Wernicke, 1987) plutons are 61, 62, and 60, respectively, and straddle the boundary between calc-alkalic and calcic compositions (Peacock, 1935).

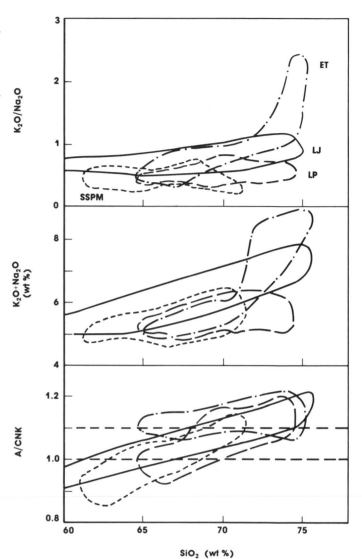

Figure 9. Harker diagrams for the four La Posta–type plutons described in this study. LP = La Posta, LJ = Laguna Juarez, SSPM = Sierra San Pedro Martir, ET = El Topo.

Average major and trace element analyses for each map unit in each pluton are listed in Table 1. A rim to core increase in SiO_2 is observed in all plutons except El Topo, where the interior facies have the lowest SiO_2 values. In all plutons, CaO, MgO, total Fe, TiO_2, MnO, and P_2O_5 decrease smoothly with increasing SiO_2. The alkalis, however, tend to have flat or slightly positive slopes with respect to SiO_2. Total alkalis are plotted against SiO_2 in Figure 10 and indicate that all four plutons have a positive correlation of that parameter with SiO_2. However, the Laguna Juarez pluton has consistently elevated $K_2O + Na_2O$ with respect to the Sierra San Pedro Martir and La Posta plutons. El Topo shows an abrupt increase in total alkalis at high SiO_2 values, but is virtually indistinguishable from the Sierra San Pedro Martir and La Posta plutons at lower SiO_2. Alkali ratios (Fig. 10) show

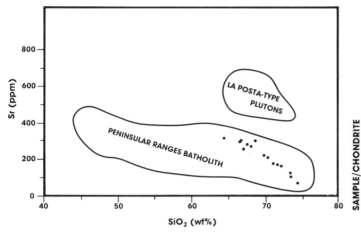

Figure 10. Sr-SiO$_2$ variation diagram. Field for PRB from Todd and Shaw (1979) modified with data from the garnet-bearing monzogranites described in this study. La Posta field defined from 13 points (Todd and Shaw, 1979), 54 points (this study), and 6 points (Lampe, 1987). Data for the El Topo pluton are shown as solid circles.

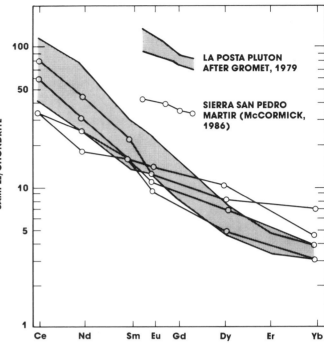

Figure 11. REE patterns for the La Posta pluton (shaded) after Gromet (1979) and the Sierra San Pedro Martir pluton (points) after McCormick (1986). The two patterns with the highest LREE concentrations are from the interior facies of the pluton.

a similar pattern in that the Laguna Juarez pluton has higher K$_2$O/Na$_2$O than the Sierra San Pedro Martir and La Posta plutons, and in that the El Topo pluton shows an abrupt increase in the alkali ratio at high SiO$_2$. For both the El Topo and Laguna Juarez plutons, the increase in total alkalis and alkali ratios are geographic in the sense that the highest values are found at or near the margin of the El Topo pluton and in the innermost facies of the Laguna Juarez pluton.

Figure 10 also shows the relation between A/CNK (molecular proportions of Al$_2$O$_3$ divided by the sum of CaO + Na$_2$O + K$_2$O) and SiO$_2$. The increase in A/CNK against SiO$_2$ also corresponds to a general rim to core increase in that ratio for all plutons except El Topo. Outer zones (hornblende-biotite facies) are weakly metaluminous and change smoothly inward to a peraluminous character in the muscovite-bearing facies. At El Topo, although the pluton margins (garnet-bearing biotite facies) are peraluminous and in contrast to the weakly metaluminous core (hornblende-biotite facies), the relation of A/CNK to facies lithology is the same as in the other plutons.

The most distinctive single geochemical characteristic of La Posta–type plutons is their high Sr content (see also Todd and Shaw, 1979; Hill, 1984), with values typically between 400 and 600 ppm (Table 1). This contrasts with Sr abundances found elsewhere in the plutonic rocks of the batholith (Fig. 11) and suggests a fundamental difference in source-region characteristics. Sr abundances decrease with increasing SiO$_2$ in the La Posta pluton but are essentially constant in all zones of the Sierra San Pedro Martir pluton (Table 1). Gunn (1984) reported Sr ranging from 200 to 600 ppm in the Laguna Juarez pluton, with highest values in the outer hornblende facies. El Topo is once again the maverick pluton in that Sr abundances vary only between 100

and 300 ppm. The lowest values are found in the marginal biotite facies, and its Sr-SiO$_2$ relation matches that of the western-zone plutons (Fig. 11).

Gromet and Silver (1979) presented rare earth element (REE) patterns for three samples from the La Posta pluton and one sample from a separate, unnamed La Posta–type pluton to the north. All four samples were moderately to strongly enriched in LREE, with steep slopes and negligible Eu anomalies (Fig. 12). The two easternmost samples have the most highly fractionated patterns and led to a subdivision of the La Posta terrane into a central zone with moderate LREE enrichment and an eastern zone with strong LREE enrichment. McCormick (1986) presented four REE patterns for rocks from the three main zones of the Sierra San Pedro Martir pluton (Fig. 12). These patterns overlap the two REE-based batholith subdivisions proposed by Gromet and Silver (1979) and indicate that these subdivisions may be due to variable REE abundances within individual facies. Gromet and Silver (1983) pointed out that most of the REE reside within trace minerals such as sphene and allanite. Both minerals appear to be slightly more abundant in the eastern side of the La Posta pluton (Clinkenbeard, 1987), possibly accounting for the higher REE abundances in that area. In addition, allanite ($\pm$ monazite) is more abundant in the interior (biotite and muscovite-biotite) facies of the Sierra San Pedro Martir pluton and could account for the higher REE abundances in those facies (Fig. 11).

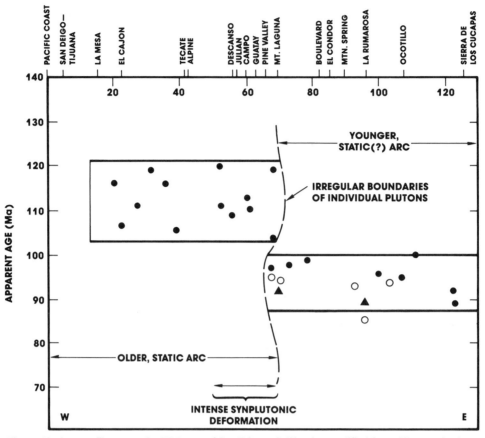

Figure 12. Age profile across the PRB east of San Diego, California (modified from Silver and others, 1979). Our diagram reflects a repositioning of the age step such that a point from the quartz norite of Las Bancas (104 Ma at the position of Mt Laguna; L. T. Silver, 1980, personal communication) falls into the western terrane. Todd and Shaw (1979) also argued that this unit is part of the older synkinematic series. The base line of 89 Ma for the younger static (?) arc is drawn through the preferred age of the Indian Hill pluton rather than its U-Pb zircon age (see text).

DISCUSSION

The U-Pb zircon ages for the La Posta pluton as reported here are 2 to 5 m.y. younger than those reported by Silver and others (1979) but still within the 100 to 89 Ma range of their eastern arc. Figure 13 shows the distribution of available data in a traverse across the batholith east of San Diego. At that latitude, the age step is well established, even to the point that both the Laguna Juarez and Sierra San Pedro Martir plutons well to the south have emplacement ages that fall into the established eastern zone. What is less apparent, however, is the eastward decrease in emplacement ages that gave rise to the "migrating" arc concept of Silver and others (1979). In addition, the El Topo pluton, which is located just south of the traverse, gave ages of 109 and 106 Ma, and a garnet-bearing monzogranite dike within that pluton yielded an emplacement age of 101 Ma. These are the oldest ages reported in the eastern zone of the batholith and suggest that the simplicity of the age step shown in Figure 13 may be a local feature.

Zircon fractions from four samples of the Sierra San Pedro Martir pluton plot on a chord with an upper concordia intercept of 1305 Ma (Fig. 6). Most points cluster near the lower concordia intercept; only one air-abraded fraction and one zircon fraction from the innermost facies fall farther out along the chord. The upper intercept age is considered to represent the average age of zircons in the source region with which the rising diapir interacted. Zircon U-Pb ages for the marginal facies of the La Posta pluton and for both facies of the El Topo pluton (Tables 2 and 5) plot very close to concordia. Three zircon fractions from an interior facies of the La Posta pluton (Table 2, sample LP16), however, show greater discordance and suggest that interior portions of the La Posta–type plutons contain greater proportions of older zircons.

Two garnet-bearing monzogranites, the Indian Hill pluton and a dike within the El Topo pluton (Figs. 6 and 5), have upper intercept ages of 1161 and 1278 Ma. These bodies are spatially associated with La Posta–type plutons and their source rocks contain a zircon component of similar age (1,200 to 1,300 Ma). This suggests that both magmatic systems had access to a common zircon source.

Early and Silver (1973) and Silver and others (1979) pointed out that Sr_i isopleths tend to be evenly spaced across and

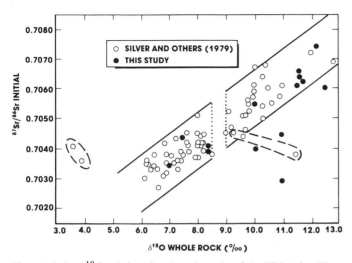

Figure 13. Sr_i-$\delta^{18}O$ relations for plutonic rocks of the PRB (after Silver and others, 1979). Solid points reflect data from this study and include La Posta–type units as well as five spatially and temporally related garnet-bearing monzogranites (Indian Hill, Parrish and others, 1986; the garnet-muscovite monzogranite dike at El Topo pluton, Wernicke, 1987; three garnetiferous monzogranite bodies spatially associated with the Laguna Juarez pluton, J. Calhoun, 1987, unpublished data). One point is from the Valle Pedregoso pluton (B. Chadwick, 1987, unpublished data).

parallel to the structural grain of the batholith. Their $\delta^{18}O$ "step" (Silver and others, 1979; Fig. 8), as noted earlier, appears to divide the batholith into a western zone with Sr_i less than 0.7045 and an eastern zone with Sr_i greater than 0.7045. Western zone plutons located within a limited geographic area (few square kilometers) tend to have very similar Sr_i.

The La Posta–type plutons of the eastern zone described here display a range in Sr_i that matches the range reported by Silver and others (1979) for the batholith as a whole. The Sierra San Pedro Martir pluton is quite consistent in Sr_i over its range of lithologies (Table 1), with an average value of 0.7040 ± 0.0001. The one value from the La Posta pluton (Table 3) is comparable to the Sierra San Pedro Martir pluton; both are somewhat lower than the values reported by Silver and others (1979) for eastern zone plutons. The Laguna Juarez pluton, however, has a remarkable lithologic and/or geographic control on Sr_i such that a rim-to-core traverse would essentially match the range of values reported by Silver and others for the eastern zone plutons. The two innermost samples have sufficiently high Sr_i to necessitate a contribution to these facies from a source region enriched in radiogenic Sr.

The hornblende-biotite facies of the El Topo pluton yielded the lowest Sr_i (0.7030) reported for a granitic rock within the PRB (Fig. 12, Table 1). This value is more consistent with the western zone plutons and with derivation from a source region with low abundances of radiogenic Sr.

The oxygen isotope data for the four plutons indicate that they are more enriched in ^{18}O than their counterparts in the western zone of the batholith and that the level of enrichment is pluton-dependent. Using the hornblende-biotite facies in each pluton as a control, $\delta^{18}O$ ranges from a low of 7.4 per mil at Laguna Juarez to a high of 10.7 per mil at El Topo, with Sierra San Pedro Martir and La Posta at 8.8 and 10.4 per mil, respectively. Such variations and the level at which they occur suggest that the magmas from which these plutons were derived included variable amounts from a high ^{18}O reservoir. Silver and others (1979) argued convincingly that the regional isotopic patterns are not consistent with processes involving assimilation of high-level crustal rocks. On a pluton scale, however, Turi and Taylor (1971) found evidence of isotopic exchange in the Domenigoni Valley granodiorite up to 600 m inward from its contact with metasedimentary wall rocks. A similar pattern exists at the El Topo pluton in that the two high whole-rock values occur less than 100 m from the wall-rock contact and in the sporadically developed garnet (±muscovite) zone. These, and similarly positioned samples, have anomalously high K_2O+Na_2O and K_2O/Na_2O (Fig. 10), a characteristic consistent with high-level exchange. We do not, however, consider this process to be the cause of the range in $\delta^{18}O$ found in the La Posta–type plutons, because such a mechanism would require severe restrictions in terms of the geometry of each magma chamber.

Limited variation in whole-rock $\delta^{18}O$ of the La Posta–type plutons can be modeled on the basis of modal mineralogy (see also Hill, 1984). However, the inward increase in whole-rock $\delta^{18}O$ observed in the three larger La Posta–type plutons is not consistent with modal variations alone. Quartz separates, which have limited abilities to exchange oxygen isotopes even at high temperatures (Taylor 1979), will thus largely retain $\delta^{18}O$ values 1 to 2 per mil higher than the melt from which they crystallized. Hence, the high $\delta^{18}O$ values for quartz and their inward and/or eastward increase must be a reflection of the isotopic character of the melt at its emplacement level.

Geological reasonable reservoirs of heavy oxygen can be limited to rocks that have been subjected to a weathering cycle. These include crustal sedimentary/metasedimentary packages and the upper few kilometers of hydrothermally altered oceanic crust. Taylor (1986) calculated that more than enough oceanic material with high $\delta^{18}O$ and Sr_i had been subducted beneath the strike length of the PRB to produce the estimated volume of eastern-zone (La Posta–type) plutons. He pointed out, however, that derivation of these plutons from altered oceanic crust alone is inconsistent with the isotopic evidence from circum-Pacific island-arc systems and the Nd-Sr studies in the batholith (DePaolo, 1981). In addition, we submit that the presence of 1200- to 1300-Ma zircons in some of the La Posta–type plutons and in younger, spatially associated garnet monzogranite bodies argues for the involvement of continentally derived materials. The eastward bias toward heavier oxygen and increasing zircon discordance in the La Posta–type plutons implies that this terrane must have existed just eastward from the locus of emplacement of these plutons.

Gromet (1979) and Gromet and Silver (1987) stated that

the REE patterns for the eastern zone (La Posta–type) plutons are best met by subduction-related anatexis of eclogite-facies basaltic materials. This source material was richer and more fractionated in the REE than the source for the western-zone tonalites, and is consistent with a "garnet-bearing but plagioclase-poor" residual assemblage (Gromet, 1979). In addition, Gromet (1979) argued that this source material was "broadly equivalent" to the source rocks of the western-zone tonalites in which he modeled hornblende as a residual phase. The Sr "spike" of the La Posta–type plutons (excluding El Topo) can be interpreted as signalling the presence of plagioclase in the source region for these plutons. Combined with Gromet's (1979) residual assemblage of garnet and hornblende, a source region of amphibolitic oceanic crust would also appear to satisfy the trace element constraints, providing that all plagioclase was removed during the melting event.

Taylor (1986), expanding upon the arguments of Silver and others (1979), prefers either mantle or oceanic lithosphere as the source region for the western zone granitic plutons based on their combined ^{18}O-Sr_i characteristics. The near linear correlation of δ^{18}O with Sr_i in the eastern zone (La Posta–type) plutons was interpreted to have formed by a mixing of low Sr-^{18}O western melt with a single, higher Sr-^{18}O source, most likely a Franciscan-type eugeosynclinal assemblage. When our more limited data are added to the base provided by Silver and others (1979), it leads to two critical refinements. First, some of the La Posta–type (eastern zone) plutons have isotopic characteristics of the western plutons such that the δ^{18}O "step" and Sr_i isopleths may show considerable local deviation from the regional patterns established by Silver and others (1979). Second, of the two end members necessary to form to La Posta–type plutons, the low Sr_i-δ^{18}O component would appear to be different from that in the western zone ($Sr_i = 0.704$, δ^{18}O $= 8.0$ versus $Sr_i = 0.703$, δ^{18}O $= 6.0$), and the high δ^{18}O component appears to have a more variable Sr_i (0.704 to 0.707).

CONCLUSIONS

We offer the following model for the generation of the PRB based on the compiled geochronologic, isotopic, and geochemical constraints to stimulate further discussion on the origin and evolution of batholithic terranes.

The subduction of partially altered oceanic crust caused the development of greenschist-facies assemblages, followed in turn, by a conversion to amphibolite-facies mineralogy. Volatiles released during the latter process fluxed the overlying mantle wedge and led to the generation of hydrous basaltic melts. The released volatiles were partitioned into the melt and thus removed from the oceanic crust. Subsequent rise and solidification of these melts at depths of 10 km or less produced the early hornblende-rich gabbroic rocks so prominent in the western zone of the batholith (Walawender and Smith, 1980). The contribution of the older oceanic crust, other than its volatile content, to these magmas is unknown but was, most likely, minimal. The rising diapirs were emplaced into oceanic lithosphere and an overlying sedimentary

apron outboard of the leading edge of the continent (Gastil, 1975). Generation of the granitic components of the western zone, however, is more problematic and may have been due to either single- or multiple-stage melting within the overlying mantle wedge (Silver and others, 1979; Gromet, 1979; Taylor, 1986) during the interval from about 130 to 105 Ma. However, the spatial and temporal association of the granitic plutons with, and their isotopic affinities for, the early gabbroic units argue for an origin by remelting of a gabbroic underplate.

At approximately 105 Ma, magmatism of the style and character of the western zone effectively ceased but overlapped in time with the onset of La Posta–type magmatism. The El Topo pluton has characteristics of both the western zone (size, Sr, Sr_i) and La Posta–type (texture, mineralogy, δ^{18}O) plutons. This suggests that it was derived, to some extent, from two source regions, and that at about 105 Ma, critical changes took place in plate dynamics.

An increase in the spreading rate may have caused the subduction plane to become shallow, buckle, and eventually shear away from the older plate remnant (Luyendyk, 1970). It is during such a tectonic transition that we envision the generation of modest amounts of composite magmas such as those responsible for the El Topo pluton. The shallower oceanic-crust portion of the subduction plane continued to dewater, but the overlying mantle wedge was now below its water-saturated solidus. The released volatiles must diffuse from the crust-mantle interface rather than partitioning into and rising with mantle-derived melts. Hence, the downgoing slab could retain much of its released structural water and undergo greater degrees of partial melting once the volatile-controlled solidus for basaltic rocks (amphibolite?) is intersected. This would produce larger volumes of intermediate composition (La Posta–type) magmas, with slightly higher Sr_i reflecting the increased radiogenic Sr in altered oceanic crust. The δ^{18}O would also be higher, but unless only the upper kilometer or less of oceanic crust was involved in the melting event, that source region alone could not account for La Posta–type plutons with whole-rock δ^{18}O of up to 11.8 per mil. The presence of zircon with an average age of 1200 to 1300 Ma in the interior of some of the La Posta–type plutons and in spatially related but compositionally distinct garnet monzogranites indicates an additional source region above the subduction plane.

The eastward-directed isotopic asymmetry observed in the large La Posta–type plutons most likely formed during emplacement. Rising from the subduction plane, the La Posta–type melts must have encountered and interacted with a terrane/source region somewhat enriched in ^{18}O and radiogenic Sr, and containing 1200- to 1300-Ma zircon. A geometrically attractive but isotopically unknown source region for this interaction is granulite-facies(?) lower continental crust. If the La Posta–type diapirs rose through the juncture of older sialic crust and oceanic lithosphere, as suggested by Gastil (1975), the proposed isotopic interaction would have been limited to the eastern part of the diapirs. Some effects of this interaction may have been partially distributed through the diapir via convective mixing and/or diffusion processes, but the overall asymmetry was retained. The final asymmetry was produced when the head of the diapir rose to its emplacement level within the overlying sedimentary apron and spread laterally. The isotopically enriched zone adjacent to the sialic crust rose as the tail of the diapir and entered the ballooned chamber eastward from the locus of emplacement to produce the core of the magma chamber. Inward crystallization of this zoned magma chamber produced the lithologic and isotopic patterns observed within the La Posta–type plutons. Scenarios involving variable amounts of deep crustal interaction and different erosional levels can be used to account for the differences between individual plutons.

ACKNOWLEDGMENTS

This study was supported by NSF Grant EAR-8306663 to Walawender and Gastil. The authors thank Unocal Science and Technology for general support to B. M. Smith, David Maas for performing many of the oxygen extractions, and L. Peter Gromet for his comprehensive and insightful review. Our interpretations of the U-Pb systematics reported in this study were greatly enhanced by numerous discussions with G. H. Girty.

REFERENCES CITED

Clayton, R. N., and Mayeda, T. K., 1963, The use of bromide pentafluoride in the extraction of oxygen from oxides and silicates for isotopic analysis: Geochemica et Cosmochimica Acta, v. 27, p. 43–53.

Clinkenbeard, J. P., 1987, The mineralogy, geochemistry, and geochronology of the La Posta pluton, San Diego and Imperial counties, California [M.S. thesis]: San Diego, California, San Diego State University, 215 p.

Clinkenbeard, J. P., and Walawender, M. J., 1989, Mineralogy of the La Posta pluton: Implications for the origin of zoned plutons in the eastern Peninsular Ranges batholith, southern and Baja California: American Mineralogist (in review).

Clinkenbeard, J. P., Walawender, M. J., Parrish, K. E., Wardlaw, M. S., and Smith, B., 1986, The geochemical and isotopic composition of the La Posta granodiorite, San Diego County, California: Geological Society of America Abstracts with Programs, v. 18, p. 95.

DePaolo, D. J., 1981, A neodymium and strontium isotopic study of the Mesozoic calc-alkaline granitic batholiths of the Sierra Nevada and Peninsular Ranges, California: Journal of Geophysical Research, v. 86, p. 10470–10488.

Diamond, J. L., Knaack, C. M., Gastil, R. G., Erskine, B., Walawender, M. J., Marshall, M., and Cameron, G. J., 1985, The magnetite-ilmenite line in the Peninsular Ranges batholith, southern and Baja California, USA and Mexico: Geological Society of America Abstracts with Programs, v. 17, p. 351.

Duffield, W. A., 1968, The petrology and structure of the El Pinal tonalite, Baja California, Mexico: Geological Society of America Bulletin, v. 79, p. 1351–1374.

Early, T. O., and Silver, L. T., 1973, Rb-Sr isotopic systematics in the Peninsular Ranges batholith of southern and Baja California [abs.]: EOS (America Geophysical Union, Transactions), v. 54, p. 494.

Eastman, B. G., 1986, The geology, petrography, and geochemistry of the Sierra San Pedro Martir pluton, Baja California, Mexico [M.S. thesis]: San Diego, California, San Diego State University, 154 p.

Gastil, R. G., 1975, Plutonic zones in the Peninsular Ranges of southern California and northern Baja California: Geology, v. 3, p. 361–363.

Gastil, R. G., Diamond, J., and Knaack, C., 1986, The magnetite-ilmenite line in

peninsular California: Geological Society of America Abstracts with Programs, v. 18, p. 109.

Gromet, L. P., 1979, Rare earths abundances and fractionations and their implications for batholithic petrogenesis in the Peninsular ranges batholith, California, U.S.A., and Baja California, Mexico [Ph.D. thesis]: Pasadena, California Institute of Technology, 337 p.

Gromet, L. P., and Silver, L. T., 1979, Profile of rare earth element characteristics across the Peninsular Ranges batholith near the international border, southern California, U.S.A., and Baja California, Mexico, *in* Abbott, P. L., and Todd, V. R., eds., Mesozoic crystalline rocks: San Diego, California, San Diego State University, Department of Geological Sciences, p. 133–142.

—— , 1983, Rare earth element distributions among minerals in a granodiorite and their petrogenetic implication: Geochimica et Cosmochimica Acta, v. 47, p. 925–939.

—— , 1987, REE variations across the Peninsular Ranges batholith; Implications for batholithic petrogenesis and crustal growth in magmatic arcs: Journal of Petrology, v. 28, part 1, p. 75–125.

Gunn, S. H., 1984, The geology, petrography, and geochemistry of the Laguna Juarez pluton, Baja California, Mexico [M.S. thesis]: San Diego, California, San Diego State University, 166 p.

—— , 1986, Isotopic constraints on the origin of the Laguna Juarez pluton, Baja California, Mexico: Society of America Abstracts with Programs, v. 18, p. 111.

Hill, R. I., 1984, Petrology and petrogenesis of batholithic rocks, San Jacinto Mountains, southern California [Ph.D. thesis]: Pasadena, California Institute of Technology, 660 p.

Jaffey, A. H., Flynn, K. F., Glendenin, L. E., Bentley, W. C., and Essling, A. M., 1971, Precision measurement of half-lives and specific activities of ^{235}U and ^{238}U: Physics Review, v. C4, p. 1889–1906.

Kimzey, J. A., 1982, Petrology and geochemistry of the La Posta granodiorite [M.S. thesis]: San Diego, California, San Diego State University, 81 p.

Kofron, R. J., 1981, The geochemistry of the west contact of the La Posta pluton [Undergraduate research report]: San Diego, California, San Diego State University, 22 p.

Krogh, T. E., A low-contamination method for hydrothermal decomposition of zircon and extraction of U and Pb for isotopic age determination: Geochimica et Cosmochimica Acta, v. 37, p. 485–494.

Krummenacher, D., Gastil, R. G., Bushee, J., and Doupont, J., 1975, K-Ar apparent ages, Peninsular Ranges batholith, southern California and Baja California: Geological Society of America Bulletin, v. 86, p. 760–768.

Lampe, C., 1987, Geology of the Granite Mountain area: Implications of the extent and style of deformation along the southeast portion of the Elsinore fault [M.S. thesis]: San Diego, California, San Diego State University, 150 p.

Ludwig, K. L., 1984, PBDAT; A program for reduction of Pb-U-Th isotope data for use with HP-86/87 microcomputers; U.S. Geological Survey Open-File Report 84–113, 54 p.

Luyendyk, B. P., 1970, Dips of downgoing lithospheric plates beneath island arcs: Geological Society of America Bulletin, v. 81, p. 3411–3416.

McCormick, W. V., 1986, The geology, mineralogy, and geochronology of the Sierra San Pedro Martir pluton, Baja California, Mexico [M.S. thesis]: San Diego, California, San Diego State University, 123 p.

Miller, C. F., Stoddard, E. F., Bradfish, L. J., and Dollase, W. A., 1981, Composition of plutonic muscovite; Genetic implications: Canadian Mineralogist, v. 19, p. 25–34.

Miller, W. J., 1935, A geologic section across the southern Peninsular Range of California: California Journal of Mines and Geology, v. 31, p. 115–142.

Parrish, K. E., Walawender, M. J., Clinkenbeard, J. P., Wardlaw, M. S., and Smith, B., 1986, The Indian Hill granodiorite, a peraluminous, garnet-bearing granitoid, eastern Peninsular Ranges: Geological Society of America Abstracts with Programs, v. 18, p. 169.

Peacock, M. A., 1931, Classification of igneous rock series: Journal of Geology, v. 39, p. 54–67.

Silver, L. T., Taylor, H. P., Jr., and Chappell, B., 1979, Some petrological, geochemical, and geochronological observations of the Peninsular Ranges batholith near the international border of the U.S.A. and Mexico, *in* Abbott,

P. L., and Todd, V. R., eds., Mesozoic crystalline rocks: San Diego, California, San Diego State University, Department of Geological Sciences, p. 83–110.

Sinfield, L., 1983, The geology of the eastern facies of the La Posta pluton [Undergraduate research report]: San Diego, California, San Diego State University, 44 p.

Smith, B. M., and Walawender, M. J., 1987, Stable isotope relations among rocks and minerals of the La Posta pluton, eastern Peninsular Ranges batholith, southern California: Geological Society of America Abstracts with Programs, v. 19, p. 848.

Taylor, H. P., Jr., 1979, Oxygen and hydrogen isotope relationships in hydrothermal mineral deposits, *in* Barnes, H. L., ed., Geochemistry of hydrothermal ore deposits (second edition): New York, John Wiley and Sons, Inc., p. 236–277.

—— , 1986, Igneous rocks; 2, Isotopic case studies of circum Pacific magmatism, *in* Valley, J. W., Taylor, H. P., Jr., and O'Neil, J. R., eds., Stable isotopes in high-temperature geological processes: Mineralogical Society of America, p. 273–317.

Taylor, H. P., Jr., and Silver, L. T., 1978, Oxygen isotope relationship in plutonic igneous rocks of the Peninsular Ranges batholith, southern and Baja California, *in* Zartman, R. E., ed., Short papers of the fourth international conference, geochronology, cosmochronology, isotopic geology: U.S. Geological Survey Open-File Report 78–701, p. 423–426.

Todd, V. R., and Shaw, S. E., 1979, Structural, metamorphic, and intrusive framework of the Peninsular Ranges batholith in southern San Diego County, California, *in* Abbott, P. L., and Todd, V. R., eds., Mesozoic crystalline rocks: San Diego, California, San Diego State University, Department of Geological Sciences, p. 177–232.

—— , 1985, S-type granitoids and an I-S line in the Peninsular Ranges batholith, southern California: Geology, v. 13, p. 231–233.

Turi, B., and Taylor, H. P., Jr., 1971, An oxygen and hydrogen isotope study of a granodiorite pluton from the southern California batholith: Geochimica et Cosmochimica Acta, v. 35, p. 383–406.

Walawender, M. J., and Smith, T. E., 1980, Geochemical and petrologic evolution of the basic plutons of the Peninsular Ranges batholith, southern California: Journal of Geology, v. 88, p. 233–242.

Walawender, M.J., Gunn, S. H., and Calhoun, J. M., 1983, Peraluminous granitoid rocks of the eastern Peninsular Ranges: Geological Society of America Abstracts with Programs, v. 15, p. 41.

Wernicke, R. S., 1987, Origin and emplacement of the El Topo pluton, northern Baja California [M.S. thesis]: San Diego, California, San Diego State University, 205 p.

MANUSCRIPT SUBMITTED JUNE 7, 1987
REVISED MANUSCRIPT SUBMITTED JANUARY 28, 1988
MANUSCRIPT ACCEPTED BY THE SOCIETY FEBRUARY 7, 1989

Chapter 2

The problem of the magnetite/ilmenite boundary in southern and Baja California California

Gordon Gastil, Judith Diamond*, Charles Knaack*, Michael Walawender, Monte Marshall, Carolyn Boyles,*
and Burton Chadwick*
Department of Geological Sciences, San Diego State University, San Diego, California 92182
Bradley Erskine*
University of California at Berkeley, Berkeley, California 94720

ABSTRACT

The Peninsular Ranges of southern and Baja California are divided into a western, predominantly magnetite-bearing plutonic subprovince and an eastern, predominantly magnetite-free plutonic subprovince. The boundary that separates the two subprovinces corresponds roughly to the southwestern margin of the La Posta superunit, but in some places extends into the La Posta granitic province. Neither the pre–La Posta foliated granitic rocks nor the garnet- or muscovite-bearing rocks of the eastern Peninsular Ranges contain magnetite.

The magnetite/ilmenite distinction occurs on three scales: regional variations that appear to be independent of host rock or individual plutons, variations paralleling modal facies within zoned plutons, and contact loss of magnetite in the outer margin of a pluton (from meters to more than a kilometer in width).

Observations to date indicate that the regional distribution of magnetite- and ilmenite-series granitic rocks may result from generation of parental magma within the dehydration zone of a subduction plane. The gradation within zoned plutons probably results from a lowering of oxygen fugacity in the magma during progressive crystallization. The contact effect appears to be a consequence of reactions between the cooling pluton, the host rocks, and water-rich fluids from a variety of sources.

INTRODUCTION

The recognition of regional provinces of granitic rocks that are magnetite-bearing as opposed to others that are ilmenite-bearing and magnetite-free is largely the contribution of Ishihara

(1977, 1979, 1984), Ishihara and Ulriksen (1980), and Ishihara and Terashima (1985), who established the classification of "magnetite-series" and "ilmenite-series" granitic rocks based on the identity of opaque oxides and the magnetic susceptibility of the rocks. The observation that ilmenite-series rocks compose the eastern portion of the Peninsular Ranges batholith, southern California, was made by Erskine and Marshall (1980) during a paleomagnetic survey. Since then, this preliminary study has been augmented by a U.S. Department of Energy (1980) aeromagnetic survey, a ground survey of magnetic susceptibility that includes approximately 2,500 outcrop localities in southern and Baja California (Erskine, 1982; Diamond and others, 1985), detailed mapping and magnetic susceptibility contouring of individual

*Present addresses: Diamond, Department of Geology and Geophysics, University of Wyoming, Laramie, Wyoming 82071; Knaack, Department of Geological Sciences, Washington State University, Pullman, Washington 99164; Erskine, National Asbestos Laboratories Inc., 2235 Polverosa Ave., Suite 220, San Leandro, California 94577; Boyles, E.A. Engineering and Technology Inc., 41 Lafayette Circle, Lafayette, California 94549; Chadwick, Harding-Lawson Associates, 15621 Red Hill Blvd., Suite 100, Tustin, California 92680.

Gastil, G., Diamond, J., Knaack, C., Walawender, M., Marshall, M., Boyles-Reaber, C., Chadwick, B., and Erskine, B., 1990, The problem of the magnetite/ilmenite boundary in southern and Baja California, *in* Anderson, J. L., ed., The nature and origin of Cordilleran magmatism: Boulder, Colorado, Geological Society of America Memoir 174.

plutons (Eastman, 1986; McCormick, 1986; Reabor, 1989), and detailed examinations of portions of the magnetite/ilmenite boundary (Chadwick, 1987; Boyles-Reaber, 1987). Figure 1 shows the boundary resulting from these studies.

Following the criteria of Ishihara (1977), we report magnetic susceptibilities measured on a Geoinstruments JH-8 susceptibility meter. Magnetic susceptibility describes the acquired magnetization of a substance in the presence of an external magnetic field (Sharma, 1976). It is defined as $\vec{J} = k\vec{H}$, where $\vec{J}$ is the intensity of magnetization, $\vec{H}$ is the applied magnetic field, and k is the magnetic susceptibility. The magnitude of k is measured in dimensionless susceptibility index (SI) units, which can be converted to the c.g.s. system by the relation: $k(SI)/4\pi = k(emu/g)$. Magnetite accounts for most of the susceptibility measured in rocks, and has a susceptibility roughly three orders of magnitude higher than ilmenite. The volume percent magnetite in granitic rocks can be approximated from susceptibility readings. Our experiments show that pure magnetite in grains 0.1 to 0.5 mm will read approximately 1650×10^{-5} SI units at 0.5 percent volume, 590 at 0.25 percent, and 300 at 0.125 percent. This is in essential agreement with Lindsley and others (1966, Fig. 25-3).

Ishihara (1977, 1979) determined that magnetite-series granitic rocks have a high magnetite content (greater than 0.1 volume percent), high magnetic susceptibility (greater than 130×10^{-5} SI), and high bulk Fe_2O_3/FeO. The ilmenite-series granite rocks contain minor ilmenite and almost no magnetite (both are less than 0.1 volume percent), low magnetic susceptibility (less than 130×10^{-5} SI), and low bulk Fe_2O_3/FeO. We agree with this division because it falls between the typical bimodal distribution of values in the Peninsular Ranges batholith. The majority of the samples we measured (Fig. 2) fall above 200×10^{-5} SI (magnetite series), or below 25×10^{-5} SI (ilmenite series). The variation of magnetic susceptibility with grain size is not significant for grains larger than 40 μm (Shandley and Bacon, 1966).

Within a single outcrop of the Peninsular Ranges batholith, the distribution of magnetite, determined by magnetic susceptibility, can vary appreciably. Fine-grained igneous rocks typically yield consistent magnetic susceptibilities over large areas, but coarse-grained rocks commonly vary by 10 percent and rarely by as much as 100 percent. Susceptibility measurements on a few slightly magnetic or extremely magnetic rocks are even more variable.

Petrographic examination of the opaque oxides shows that in many ilmenite-series rocks of the batholith, ilmenite is com-

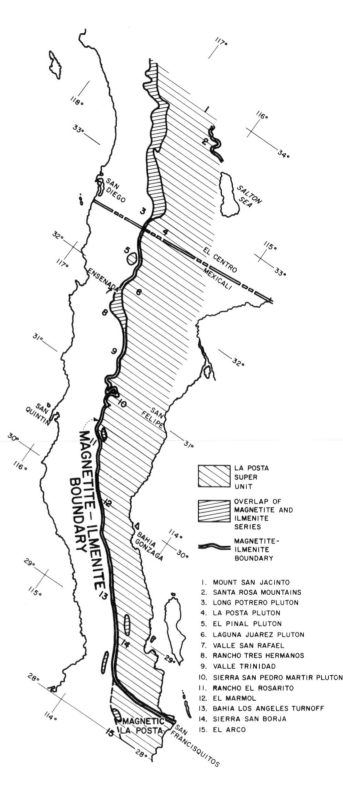

Figure 1. Positions of text localities and the boundary between the magnetite- series (to the west) and ilmenite-series (to the east) granitic rocks in the Peninsular Ranges batholith, southern and Baja California. (1) Mount San Jacinto; (2) Santa Rosa Mountains; (3) Long Potrero pluton; (4) La Posta pluton; (5) El Pinal pluton; (6) Laguna Juarez pluton; (7) Valle San Rafael; (8) Rancho Tres Hermanos; (9) Valle Trinidad; (10) Sierra San Pedro Martir pluton; (11) Rancho El Rosarito; (12) El Marmol; (13) Bahia de Los Angeles turnoff; (14) Sierra San Borja; (15) El Arco.

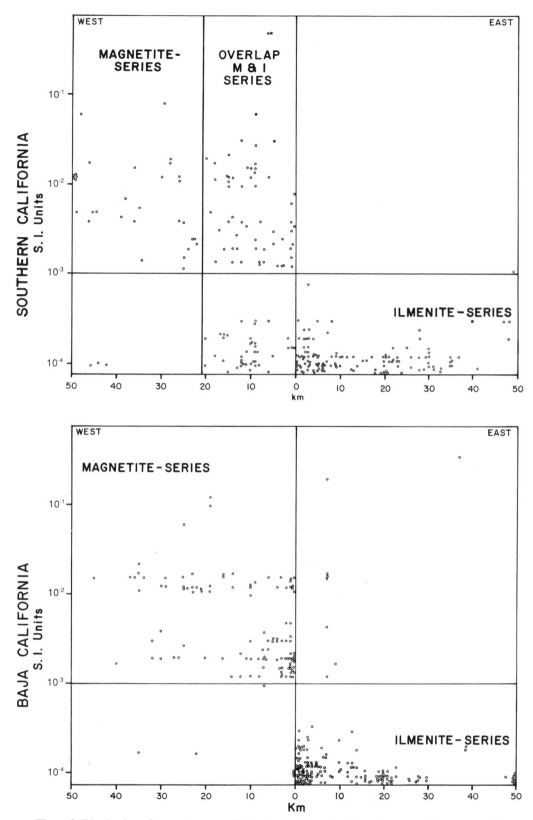

Figure 2. Distribution of magnetic susceptibility for granitic rocks in the Peninsular Ranges batholith, southern and Baja California. Sample localities are plotted in kilometers east and west of the magnetite/ilmenite boundary (after Knaack, 1985; Diamond, 1985). The horizontal line at 10^{-3} illustrates the abrupt lower limit of magnetite-series rocks.

monly the only opaque oxide phase (Hill, 1984; Walawender and others, this volume). However, within some of the magnetite-series granitic rocks we find a significant amount of ilmenite and hematite in addition to magnetite.

REGIONAL DISTRIBUTION OF THE MAGNETITE/ILMENITE BOUNDARY

The majority of granitic rock terranes surrounding the Peninsular Ranges batholith belong to the magnetite series. To the north, this includes the San Gabriel and San Bernardino Mountains; to the northeast, the Little San Bernardino Mountains and other ranges east of the San Andreas fault; and from fragmentary data across the Gulf of California, the rocks of coastal Sonora and Sinaloa, Nyarit, Jalisco, Michoacan, Guerrero, and Oaxaca, Mexico.

Many previous studies have described lithologic, geochemical, geophysical, and geochronological variations across the axis of the Peninsular Ranges batholith (Larsen, 1948; Gastil and others, 1978, 1971; Krummenacher and others, 1975; Silver and others, 1979; Todd and Shaw, 1979, 1985; Diamond and others, 1985). These variations divide the Peninsular Ranges batholith into two distinct subprovinces separated by the magnetite/ilmenite boundary. The western, predominantly magnetite-bearing (magnetite series) subprovince is generally composed of metaluminous rocks older than 105 Ma (Silver and others, 1979). The eastern, predominantly magnetite-free (ilmenite series) subprovince contains two families of granitic rocks. One family consists of mostly peraluminous, highly foliated rocks older than 100 Ma with high $\delta^{18}O$ and high initial strontium ratios. The second family consists of rocks that are generally peraluminous and younger than 97 Ma, with initial strontium and lead ratios characteristic of I-type rocks (Chappell and White, 1974) and showing no regional foliation. This ilmenite-series plutonic subprovince has been informally referred to as the La Posta province (Walawender and others, 1987, and this volume), or La Posta superunit in the terminology of Cobbing and Pitcher (1983), because many of its plutons are lithologically and geochemically similar to the large La Posta pluton (Fig. 1, locality 4).

The magnetite/ilmenite boundary begins east of the Elsinore fault in Riverside County, southern California, and extends southward through the communities of Perris, Pala, Rincon, Ramona, Descanso, and Campo to the U.S.-Mexico border (Fig. 3). South of the border, the magnetite/ilmenite boundary follows the western edge of the Sierra Juarez (Fig. 1, localities 5 and 6), swings to the western side of Valle San Rafael (locality 7), and continues south to Rancho Tres Hermanos (locality 8), and then southeast to Valle Trinidad (locality 9). The boundary follows an irregular path along the western edge of the Sierra San Pedro Martir (locality 10). It crosses the 30th parallel west of El Marmol (locality 12) and closely follows Highway 1 south to the Bahia de Los Angeles turnoff (locality 13). There it swings southeastward, roughly following the western edge of the Sierra San Borja (locality 14) to approximately 28°30', where it swings nearly due east, passing into the Gulf of California at Bahia de San Francisquitos.

The magnetite/ilmenite boundary roughly corresponds to the western limit of the La Posta superunit. The eastern boundary of the ilmenite-series subprovince appears to be in the eastern foothills of the San Jacinto and Santa Rosa Mountains (Fig. 1, locality 2), about 15 km west of the San Andreas fault (Fig. 3). The magnetic granitic rocks in this area are in the upper plates of east-over-west thrusts (Erskine and Wenk, 1985). The positions of both the western and eastern boundaries of the ilmenite-series subprovince agree with the DOE magnetic profiles (Fig. 3).

Some variations between magnetite-series and ilmenite-series rocks become apparent only when the boundary is examined in detail. In many localities, the boundary occurs between outcrops that are only meters apart, whereas in other areas, the boundary is in valleys that are several kilometers wide between adjacent plutons. Some magnetite-ilmenite distinctions may occur at the contact between igneous intrusions over a distance of centimeters. Boyles-Reaber (1987) mapped an area of 25,000 m^2 along the magnetite/ilmenite boundary 4 km south of Interstate 8 in San Diego County (Fig. 1, between 3 and 4) for magnetic susceptibility. The host rock is a magnetite-bearing, leucocratic granodiorite that has been intruded by a nonmagnetic hornblende-biotite tonalite of the ilmenite series. The contact is discontinuously exposed and complicated by patches of enigmatic "selvage" material. Despite these problems, the magnetic contrasts are so sharp that both maximum and minimum values occur within a few centimeters along the contact. Locally, there are visible patches of magnetite crystals just on the magnetic side of the contact.

Within the magnetite-series subprovince, some of the more highly differentiated rocks have magnetic susceptibilities equal to or slightly less than 130×10^{-5} SI. Similar low susceptibility readings in highly differentiated magnetite-series rocks are reported in Japan by Ishihara (1977), and have been observed by Gastil in the Separation Point suite of South Island, New Zealand. In contrast, some low-iron pegmatites and other leucocratic granitic rocks in the Peninsular Ranges batholith have magnetic susceptibilities well above 130×10^{-5} SI.

More significant to our study are strongly magnetic rocks within the ilmenite-series subprovince. Most of the gabbros in the ilmenite-series subprovince are nonmagnetic, although some are petrographically similar to strongly magnetic gabbros in the magnetite-series subprovince. However, in several localities in the ilmenite-series subprovince we find gabbros with magnetic susceptibilities that vary irregularly from 25×10^{-5} SI to values that are several orders of magnitude higher. The zones of overlap where these magnetic gabbros occur within the areas of nonmagnetic rocks are not obvious from the aeromagnetic profiles (Figs. 1 and 3). This is because on the aeromagnetic map, the magnetite/ilmenite boundary is located between the jagged profiles, produced by magnetic gabbro intruded into nonmagnetic plutons, and the flat profiles of the ilmenite-series rocks. The occurrence of these highly magnetic younger intrusions within the ilmenite-series subprovince suggests a time-related eastward shift of the magnetite/ilmenite boundary.

MAGNETITE-ILMENITE VARIATIONS WITHIN INDIVIDUAL PLUTONS

There are a number of ilmenite-series plutons that grade inward from metaluminous hornblende-bearing outer zones to peraluminous muscovite-bearing inner zones, although at least one pluton varies in the opposite sense (Walawender and others, this volume). Most of these plutons contain no detectable magnetite, but a few, such as the Sierra San Pedro Martir pluton (Fig. 1, locality 10) and the Long Potrero pluton (Fig. 1, locality 3),

contain magnetite in their outer zones and grade inward to magnetite-free cores.

Over 1,000 magnetic susceptibility measurements in the 400 km^2 Sierra San Pedro Martir pluton have been contoured (Fig. 4A). Magnetic susceptibility and magnetite content vary in three ways. First, the outer, highly foliated margin, which is part of the hornblende-biotite tonalite facies, is essentially nonmagnetic, despite a realtively high total opaque oxide content. Second, thin-section petrography and calculations of volume percent from magnetic susceptibility show that the magnetite content in the hornblende-biotite tonalite facies decreases gradually from west to east. Third, there is a progressive decrease in magnetite content inward from the hornblende-biotite tonalite facies, through the

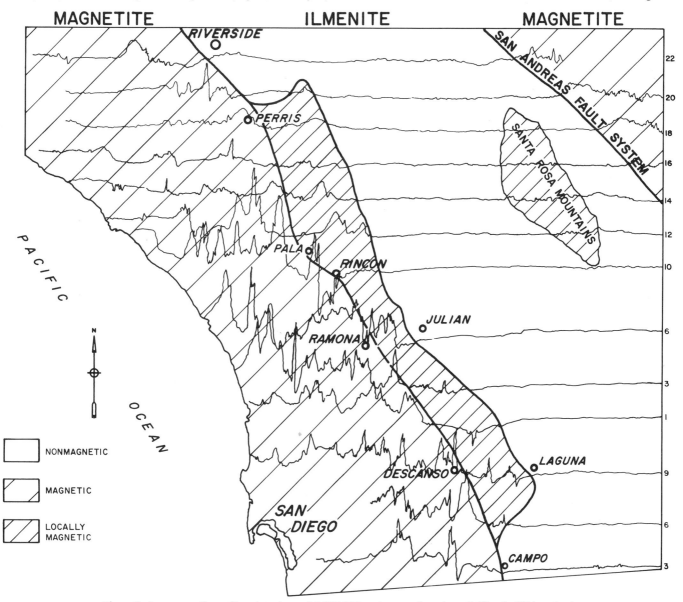

Figure 3. Aeromagnetic profiles plotted on a 1:1,000,000-scale map of southern California. Wide striped pattern represents magnetite-series rocks, unpatterned represents ilmenite-series rocks, and narrow striped pattern represents a zone of overlap along the magnetite/ilmenite boundary. Numbers along the right margin refer to DOE flight lines.

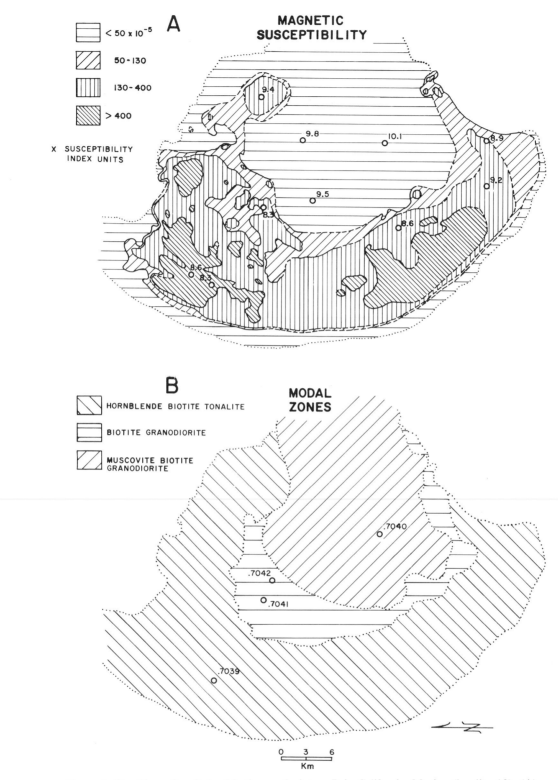

Figure 4. The Sierra San Pedro Martir zoned pluton, Baja California, Mexico (locality 10), (A) contoured for magnetic susceptibility (units are 10^{-5}SI) with values of whole rock δ^{18}O, (B) and modal zones with values of strontium initial ratios in apatite (after Eastman, 1986; McCormick, 1986).

biotite granodiorite facies, to the muscovite-biotite granodiorite facies in the core. The smaller Long Potrero pluton (Fig. 1, locality 3) is similarly zoned (Rector, 1989).

CONTACT LOSS OF MAGNETITE ALONG THE MAGNETITE/ILMENITE BOUNDARY

At several localities within the Peninsular Ranges batholith, plutons that are totally magnetite-bearing or have an outer magnetite-bearing facies display a zone of very low magnetic susceptibilities at the contact with a nonmagnetic host rock. Within the Peninsular Ranges, this contact loss of magnetite appears to be a general feature where magnetite-bearing or partially magnetite-bearing granitic rocks are emplaced within nonmagnetic plutonic or metasedimentary rocks.

The Tres Hermanos area (Fig. 1, locality 8) contains a striking example of magnetite depletion. Here dikes cut both older foliated nonmagnetic plutons northeast of the magnetite/ilmenite boundary and, in a few localities, cut younger magnetic plutons southwest of the magnetite/ilmenite boundary. The dikes include fine-grained mafic and gabbroic rocks, as well as pegmatitic, aplitic, and hypabyssal felsic rocks. Although the dikes display sharp crosscutting contact relations, they appear to have been emplaced when the host rocks were still at metamorphic temperatures, because they have metamorphic fabrics and mineralogies. Where dikes cut a nonmagnetic host rock, they are nonmagnetic; where they cut a magnetic rock, they have magnetic susceptibilities as high as those of the host.

The Valle Pedregoso pluton, in the same area (locality 8), consists of a magnetite-bearing, hornblende-biotite tonalite which is largely surrounded by nonmagnetic, thinly bedded metasandstone and phyllite of greenschist metamorphic grade. At the contact and extending into the pluton for less than 170 m is a zone of progressive magnetite depletion. For the first 40 m in from the contact, ilmenite is the only opaque oxide. Between 40 and 170 m, discrete crystals of both magnetite and ilmenite are present. From 170 m inward to the core of the pluton, magnetite is the primary opaque oxide. Magnetic susceptibility along this transect ranges from 20×10^{-5} SI at the contact to more than $2,000 \times 10^{-5}$ SI at a locality 170 m inward from the contact.

On the western edge of the Sierra San Pedro Martir pluton (Fig. 1, locality 10), the demagnetized margin extends more than a kilometer inward from the contact with the host rocks. Microprobe analyses and polished section studies (Diamond, 1989) show magnetite and ilmenite in the outer hornblende-biotite tonalite facies. Magnetite contains fine ilmenite lamellae and inclusions of ilmenite. The ilmenite intergrowths represent "oxyexsolution" (Buddington and Lindsley, 1964; Haggerty, 1976) of primary titanomagnetite (Usp-Mt) and are present in small amounts (less than 10 percent) in magnetite grains throughout the outer facies of the pluton. However, in the outermost kilometer, ilmenite intergrowths increase to almost 100 percent of the oxide grain.

Ilmenite grains contain blebs of hematite, indicating exsolu-

tion of an ilmenite-hematite solid solution. The ratio of exsolved hematite to primary ilmenite in these grains also increases in the outer kilometer of the pluton. Grains at the contact with the nonmagnetic host rock are almost entirely composed of hematite. Magnetic susceptibilities in the demagnetized zone of the Sierra San Pedro Martir pluton are consistent with the compositions and observed textures of Fe-Ti oxide minerals.

Locally, swarms of mafic inclusions register the same magnetic susceptibilities as the enclosing granitic rocks. In other areas, the inclusions register values that vary from twice to half the susceptibility of the enclosing rock, and the boundary between the contrasting values may be as sharp as the edge of the inclusion. We have found magnetic inclusions within nonmagnetic granitic rocks, and nonmagnetic inclusions within magnetic granitic rocks.

Synplutonic dikes of intermediate composition that cut the hornblende-biotite tonalite and biotite granodiorite facies of La Posta–type plutons (Hill, 1984; Stensrude and Gastil, 1978) commonly contain mafic-free spots, 1 to 2 cm in diameter, that are centered by sphene. Less common, but locally associated with the sphene-bearing spots, are mafic-free spots that contain a single euhedral magnetite crystal up to 0.5 cm across. These spotted dikes cut both magnetic and nonmagnetic host rocks, and with the exception of the rare magnetite-bearing spots, are all nonmagnetic. Ishihara (1977) reported similar anomalous relations in Japan.

OXIDATION STATE, TRACE ELEMENTS, AND ISOTOPES

Ishihara and Terashima (1985) found a close correlation between total rock Fe_2O_3/FeO and the presence or absence of magnetite. However, the Fe_2O_3/FeO ratio that distinguishes between magnetite- and ilmenite-series granitic rocks is not the same in all the Japanese provinces. Investigations of elemental carbon in contaminated ilmenite-series granitic rocks and their host rocks (Ishihara and Terashima, 1985; Ishihara and others, 1986) show that reactions between the intruding magma and graphite in the host rock can significantly affect the oxygen fugacity of the magma. Host-rock assimilation should be reflected in trace element concentrations and strontium, oxygen, and sulfur isotopic compositions, but data for ilmenite-series rocks in Japan and Asia do not everywhere confirm the contamination model (Ishihara, 1984; Ishihara and others, 1986).

As yet, very little Fe_2O_3/FeO, and no carbon or sulfur data, are available for the granitic rocks of the Peninsular Ranges. Strontium and lead isotopic data and trace-element concentrations for the ilmenite-series Sierra San Pedro Martir pluton (Fig. 1, locality 10) (Eastman, 1986; McCormick, 1986) suggest an origin by differentiation from a single magma pulse with little contamination by sedimentary host rocks. FeO and Fe_2O_3 discrimination in iron-bearing minerals in this pluton show a gradual increase in reduced iron paralleling the change in bulk composition from a metaluminous outer facies to a peraluminous core. In the Valle Pedregoso pluton (locality 8), iron oxidation states in Fe-Ti oxides indicate the relatively reduced nature of the demagnetized rim.

Unpublished whole-rock and mineral $\delta^{18}O$ patterns in the Valle Pedregoso pluton show slightly but significantly higher $\delta^{18}O$ values in the demagnetized rim. This is consistent with patterns reported by Turi and Taylor (1971) for the Domenigoni Valley pluton in the northern part of the Peninsular Ranges batholith, and suggests an oxygen isotopic exchange between the host rock and the margin of the pluton.

THE RELATION OF THE MAGNETITE/ILMENITE BOUNDARY TO OTHER GEOCHEMICAL, GEOPHYSICAL, AND GEOCHRONOLOGICAL BOUNDARIES

Silver and others (1975) reported an age step at 105 Ma between the western and eastern granitic rocks of the Peninsular Ranges batholith. A similarly placed drop in K-Ar cooling ages was reported by Krummenacher and others (1975). Silver and others (1979) reported that $\delta^{18}O$ contours for the plutonic rocks in the northern part of the batholith formed a marked "step" (Fig. 5). Baird and Meisch (1984) noted a sharp west-to-east discontinuity in major-element compositions for the southern California portion of the batholith. Gromet and Silver (1979) found marked differences in trace-element chemistry between the western and eastern batholithic rocks. Also in southern California, Oliver (1980) reported Bouguer gravity anomalies that show a gravity "bench" on the western side of the batholith. Similar gravity measurements in Baja California (Gastil and others, 1975) can be used to extrapolate the edge of the gravity "bench" down the length of the batholith (Fig. 6). Bird and Baumgardener (1984) placed the axis of a negative heat-flow anomaly in approximately the same position as these other boundaries. Todd and Shaw (1985) drew an I-S line to distinguish the westernmost occurrence of syntectonic granitic rocks with S-type affinities. Figure 7 shows how several of these geophysical, geochronologic, and geochemical boundaries relate to a hypothetical crustal profile. If indeed they do indicate some fundamental terrane boundary, or "suture," there are rationales as to why they do not occur at exactly the same place on the surface (Todd and Shaw, 1985; Weslow, 1985).

Detailed sampling of individual plutons shows that many of these boundaries are far more complex than indicated in Figure 7. Unpublished zircon U-Pb studies from the older foliated granitic rocks in the eastern ilmenite-series subprovince yield ages older than 105 Ma. These rocks may be as old as or older than any of the western magnetite-series rocks (M. S. Wardlaw, Baylor Brooks Institute of Isotope Geology, 1986, written communication). Similarly, the range in $\delta^{18}O$ and Sr initial ratios within some of the ilmenite-series plutons is contrary to the concept of a simple regional gradient (Gunn, 1985; Clinkenbeard, 1986; McCormick, 1986; Walawender and others, this volume).

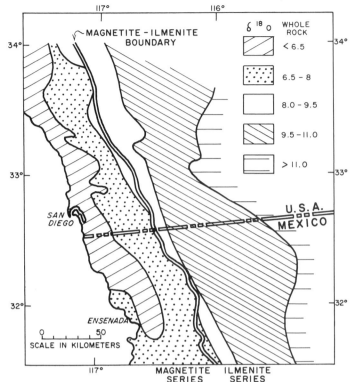

Figure 5. Position of the magnetite/ilmenite boundary relative to the $\delta^{18}O$ contours of Silver and others (1979) in the northern Peninsular Ranges.

The magnetite/ilmenite boundary does not correspond precisely with any docking suture such as the adhesion of a fringing arc to the craton (Gastil and others, 1978; Rangin, 1978). At Rancho Tres Hermanos (Fig. 1, locality 8) Mesozoic phyllites are continuously exposed across the magnetite/ilmenite boundary and are intruded by a large hypabyssal dike swarm that not only crosses the boundary, but intrudes plutonic rocks on either side of the boundary. If such a suture exists it would have to be older than any of the rocks exposed at the surface.

DISCUSSION

On a regional scale, the association of magnetite-series rocks with a specific type of tectonic province is not clear. Ishihara (1979, 1981) related the ilmenite-series granitic rocks to peraluminous, metasedimentary Sn-W–bearing provinces, as opposed to metaluminous volcanic-arc provinces with porphyry copper–type mineralization. In southern Honshu, Japan, the magnetite-series plutons occur close to the Sea of Japan, and the ilmenite-series plutons occur on the Pacific side. Almost the reverse relation occurs in the northern part of Honshu. The eastern edge of Asia is largely fringed by magnetite-series granitic rocks, the ilmenite-series rocks appear toward the continent, and additional magnetite-series volcano-plutonic belts are present farther inland.

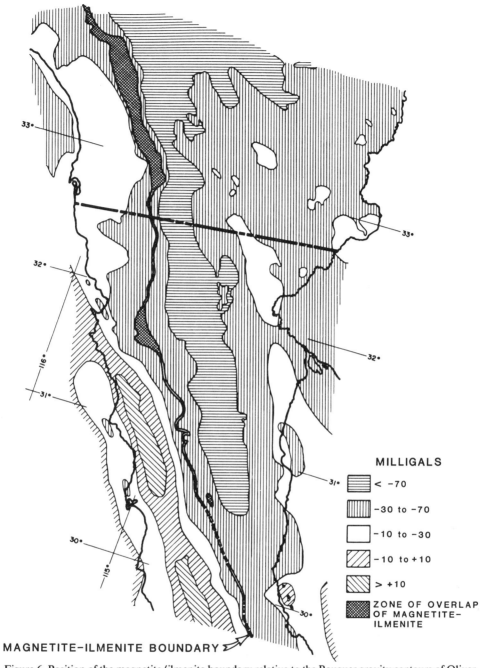

Figure 6. Position of the magnetite/ilmenite boundary relative to the Bouguer gravity contours of Oliver (1980) and Gastil and others (1975) in southern and Baja California.

The majority of the Japanese ilmenite-series granitic rocks occur in a complex of accretionary wedge and associated rocks, an environment associated with deposition off the edge of a continent, onlapping oceanic crust. This is hardly an S-type environment. In North America, the western foothills of both the Peninsular Ranges batholith and the Sierra Nevada batholith contain prebatholithic rocks with island-arc affinities, whereas the eastern part of the ranges contain craton-derived metasedimentary rocks. Yet in the Peninsular Ranges, the magnetite-series granitic rocks are clearly in the west; in the Sierras, the more strongly magnetic rocks are to the east (Dodge, 1972; Ishihara, 1984). In Chile, Paleozoic ilmenite-series granitic rocks occur in the west, close to the trench, whereas Mesozoic-Cenozoic magnetite-series granitic rocks occur in the east, farther from the trench (Ishihara and Ulriksen, 1980).

Shimizu (1986) reported that several plutons in Japan contain areas in which magnetite is present and areas that are magnetite-free. His detailed study of the 600-km^2 Tokuwa pluton shows that magnetic granitic rocks occur adjacent to metavolcanic host rocks, and nonmagnetic granitic rocks occur adjacent to metasedimentary host rocks. In parts of the Tokuwa pluton, the effect of the host rock appears to be limited to a very narrow margin at the rim of the pluton. This contact effect may be similar to the demagnetized margins of the Valle Pedregoso (locality 8) and Sierra San Pedro Martir (locality 10) plutons in Baja California. It is not clear if the magnetic and nonmagnetic phases in the Tokuwa pluton are entirely or only partly due to the contact magnetic depletion reactions.

One surprising aspect of our study in the Peninsular Ranges batholith is that we see no regional correlation between plutonic "kinship" and the magnetite/ilmenite distinction. La Posta–type plutons occur the length of the Peninsular Ranges, from the San Jacinto Mountains (Fig. 1, locality 1) to 28° north latitude in Baja California. The 1400-km^2 La Posta pluton (locality 4) and the 900-km^2 Laguna Juarez pluton (locality 6) are nonmagnetic in all facies and are east of the magnetite/ilmenite boundary. The 300-km^2 El Pinal pluton (locality 5) is a La Posta–type pluton, but is magnetic and lies west of the magnetite/ilmenite boundary. The 400-km^2 Sierra San Pedro Martir pluton (locality 10; Eastman, 1986; McCormick, 1986), and the 30-km^2 Long Potrero pluton (locality 3; Rector, 1989) have outer hornblende-bearing facies that are, at least in part, magnetite-bearing. The hornblende-bearing rocks of the Sierra San Pedro Martir pluton are almost identical to the outer facies of the La Posta pluton

(Kimzey, 1982; Clinkenbeard, 1986), and the Sierra Juarez pluton (Gunn, 1985). In the southernmost part of the batholith, between El Arco (locality 15) and Bahia de San Francisquitos, many kilometers of rock are megascopically identical to Kimzey's (1982) hornblende-biotite and large biotite facies of the nonmagnetic La Posta pluton, but all are magnetic, with susceptibilities up to 3,000 × 10^{-5} SI. The plutonic superunit (Cobbing and Pitcher, 1983) of La Posta–type rocks is not constrained by the magnetite/ilmenite boundary.

The development of either magnetite- or ilmenite-series granitic rocks appears to depend on the depth at which the parental magma formed, and what, if any, subsequent crustal processes or interactions have changed the initial composition. Magnetite-series granitic rocks may crystallize from magmas generated at shallower depths than ilmenite-series rocks, and subsequently undergo oxidation (H$_2$O saturation) prior to cooling (Czamanske and others, 1981). Rare earth element variations across the Peninsular Ranges batholith (Gromet and Silver, 1979, 1987) suggest that the eastern ilmenite-series subprovince was generated at a deeper level than the western magnetite-series subprovince.

Various workers (Ishihara and others, 1986; Shimizu, 1986) attributed the apparent magmatic reduction of iron in ilmenite-series granitic rocks to interaction with sedimentary rocks containing crustal graphite. Presumably, this interaction would occur through stoping and assimilation of sedimentary rocks. Ishihara and others (1986) calculated that the composition of the Miyako pluton in northeastern Japan required approximately 9 percent contamination from sedimentary rocks. The estimated amount of contamination by host rocks in the Tokuwa pluton is as much as 20 percent of the total composition (Shimizu, 1986).

Unfortunately, there are no analyses of Peninsular Ranges rocks for graphite content. However, the proportion of inherited zircons, initial strontium ratios, and the isotopic compositions of strontium and lead in both the magnetite-bearing and magnetite-free facies of the Sierra San Pedro Martir pluton suggest only minor contamination by continental crust (McCormick, 1986).

Portions of the contacts of both the Sierra San Pedro Martir and Valle Pedregoso plutons are against older ilmenite-series plutonic rocks. Similarly, the hypabyssal dikes in the Rancho Tres Hermanos area cut ilmenite-series plutonic rocks as well as metasedimentary rocks. In all these examples, the effect of older ilmenite-series granitic rocks appears to be the same as the effect of the metasedimentary host on the intruding magma. Therefore, it seems that contamination by metasedimentary graphite is an insufficient explanation.

Within the Sierra San Pedro Martir pluton (Figs. 4, 8), opaque oxides decrease in quantity and grain size both inward and eastward within the pluton. This decrease tends to parallel the progressive change in bulk composition toward a more siliceous, more peraluminous, less mafic rock. These variations could be explained by assuming that the muscovite-bearing core zone originated as a diapiric tail that was contaminated in its deeper position by the assimilation of graphite-bearing metasedimentary rocks. However, the strontium initial ratios of all three

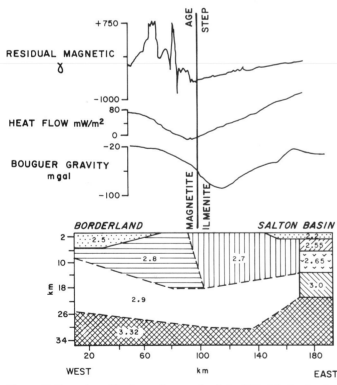

Figure 7. Crustal profile drawn just north of the U.S.–Mexico border relating the position of the magnetite/ilmenite boundary to geophysical variations (after Weslow, 1985). Patterns reflect proposed differences in rock density.

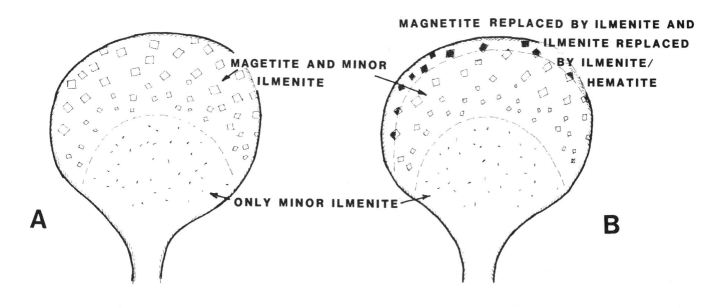

INITIAL CRYSTALLIZATION

**OUTER MARGIN LOSS
OF MAGNETITE**

MAGNETITE REPLACED BY ILMENITE AND
ILMENITE REPLACED
BY ILMENITE/
HEMATITE

MAGETITE AND MINOR
ILMENITE

ONLY MINOR ILMENITE

A

B

SIERRA SAN PEDRO MARTIR PLUTON

Figure 8. Interpretive profiles showing the Sierra San Pedro Martir zoned pluton as a simple diapir: (A) after initial crystallization, and (B) after subsequent loss of magnetite in the outer margin. The outer margin initially contained magnetite plus minor ilmenite (squares) as the primary opaque oxides. The proportion of magnetite to ilmenite decreased inward, with only ilmenite (short dashes) occurring in the core. The filled squares represent crystals in which magnetite (Usp-Mt) is "oxyexsolved" to ilmenite, and late-stage ilmentite is exsolved to ilmenite-hematite.

mineralogically defined facies are essentially 0.7040 (Fig. 4B), and both the lead isotope ratios and rare earth element patterns (McCormick, 1986) suggest a common parental magma with little contamination by crustal rocks for all three modal zones. The modal and chemical variations in the Sierra San Pedro Martir pluton therefore appear to be largely the result of crystal fractionation and inward cooling, not the result of progressive contamination.

The oxidation state of iron in stable iron-bearing minerals of a pluton will reflect the oxygen fugacity of the magma. Distribution and composition of opaque oxides depend on the initial abundance of titanium and iron and on f_{O_2} (Haggerty, 1976). Magnetite (Usp-Mt) can be expected to form in magmas having high f_{O_2} and low f_{H_2O}, and a range of ilmenite and hematite solid solutions in magmas with lower f_{O_2} and higher f_{H_2O}. With continuing differentiation, silica activity and Fe/(Fe + Mg) will increase, and f_{O_2} may decrease. Work in progress in the Sierra San Pedro Martir pluton suggests two populations of magmatic Fe-Ti oxides. Magnetite is the primary opaque oxide phase in the hornblende-biotite and biotite facies, and ilmenite is the primary opaque oxide in the muscovite-bearing core.

The mineralogy in the outer kilometer of the western margin

indicates that the phase relations here are much more complex. In addition to early-stage magnetite, late-stage ilmenite is present, and both oxide phases are highly exsolved. Away from this marginal zone, the opaque oxides are only slightly, if at all, exsolved.

GENERAL OBSERVATIONS CONCERNING THE MAGNETITE-ILMENITE DISTINCTION IN GRANITIC ROCKS

1. The magnetite/ilmenite distinction in granitic rocks is not clearly related to a particular tectonic environment.

2. Pyroxene-bearing, intermediate to siliceous granitic rocks are rarely nonmagnetic. All muscovite- and/or garnet-bearing granitic rocks are nonmagnetic in the Peninsular Ranges batholith.

3. Magnetite-series granitic rocks emplaced at mid-crustal depths against nonmagnetic rocks, either igneous or sedimentary, undergo contact demagnetization at their margins by "oxyexsolution" or direct oxidation of magnetite-ulvospinel solid solutions to less magnetic Fe-Ti opaque oxide phases.

4. In the paired magnetite/ilmenite provinces of the Sierra Nevada batholith, the Peninsular Ranges batholith, and the batho-

liths of Chile and Japan, the ilmenite-series subprovince is more deeply eroded than the magnetite-series subprovince.

5. The magnetite-free peraluminous facies of the zoned La Posta–type plutons in the Peninsular Ranges batholith cannot all be explained by the assimilation of different proportions of sedimentary rock.

6. There is no compelling evidence in the Peninsular Ranges batholith that crustal graphite is responsible for the reduction of iron in otherwise magnetic granitic rocks, and there are several localities where some other mechanism or agent must be responsible.

7. The regional inconsistencies between host-rock terrane and magnetic susceptibility require that some more fundamental variant accounts for the existence of regional magnetite/ilmenite boundaries.

8. In the northern portion of the Peninsular Ranges batholith, it appears that the magnetite/ilmenite boundary has stepped eastward with time.

9. Plutonic superunits, such as the La Posta–type plutons, may cross magnetite/ilmenite boundaries.

CONCLUSIONS

The regional magnetite-ilmenite boundary

The apparently confusing observation that La Posta–type rocks occur on both sides of the magnetite/ilmenite boundary may be explained by differential uplift. A greater amount of uplift in the east and less to the west agrees with the gravity "bench" (Fig. 6) observed in southern California by Oliver (1980). Although depth of erosion may explain in part magnetic variations within individual plutons, we believe that regional magnetite/ilmenite province boundaries are governed by differences in water and oxygen concentrations of the parental magmas. The nature of melt generation is related to the depth to the subduction plane, and the depth at which the subducting slab will no longer support the retention of structural water in hydrous mineral phases. In dehydration reactions, such as

$$K(Mg,Fe)_3(AlSi_3O_{10})(OH)_2 + 3SiO_2 = 2KAlSi_3O_8) + 3(Mg,Fe)SiO_3 + 2H_2O$$
biotite   quartz potassium feldspar hypersthene   water

hydroxyl groups are removed from metamorphosed rock, and half the oxygen from the (OH) is retained to form new anhydrous minerals (Fig. 9). The partial melt generated along the subduction plane will migrate upward containing this liberated OH$^-$ and H$^+$ in the form of a volatile component. Melts generated in this manner will have high initial f_{H_2O} and very low f_{O_2}. We suggest that the large ilmenite-series plutons in the eastern subprovince of the Peninsular Ranges batholith formed in this manner, and conclude that the regional magnetite/ilmenite boundary on the surface identifies the location on the underlying subduction plane where metamorphic dehydration took place.

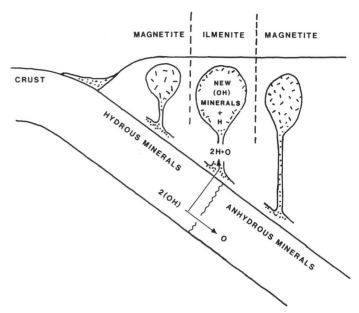

Figure 9. A depth-dependent model for the generation of magma along (or above) a subduction plane. Volatile content of the parental magma will determine whether magnetite-series or ilmenite-series granitoids crystallize. A parental magma that forms at depths where the subducted slab dehydrates will have a higher f_{H_2O} and lower f_{O_2} than magmas generated at either shallower or deeper levels.

Magnetite-ilmenite distinctions within individual plutons

We begin with the premise that the parental magma is generated at some depth, and subsequently emplaced within the crust. During its ascent through the crust, the magma composition changes as a function of fractional crystallization, assimilation of crustal material, and exchange of fluids or volatiles during emplacement, decompression, and early stages of cooling. If the f_{O_2} is sufficiently high, or f_{H_2O} is low, the pluton can crystallize as magnetite series. If the reverse is true, the pluton will be ilmenite series. This implies that an ilmenite-series pluton with magnetite at its margin must have crystallized magnetite until differentiation in the magma lowered the oxygen fugacity below the level necessary for magnetite crystallization. For example, the Sierra San Pedro Martir pluton first crystallized hornblende, biotite, plagioclase, quartz, sphene, and magnetite in its outer and upper reaches (Fig. 8A). This crystallization removed Fe, Mg, Ti, Ca, and lowered the f_{O_2} of the convecting magma. The inward and eastward decrease in magnetite within the hornblende-biotite tonalite facies may be due to the inward and eastward migration of the solidus of the cooling pluton (Eastman, 1986; McCormick, 1986). This migration retarded complete crystallization along the eastern margin until f_{O_2} conditions were such that magnetite could no longer form.

Ilmenite-series plutons without magnetite, such as the La Posta pluton, may have contained upper magnetite-bearing zones prior to uplift and erosion. The presence or absence of a magnetite-bearing outer zone may in part be a function of erosion, or perhaps magnetite never crystallized in these plutons because f_{O_2} in the parental magma was initially too low.

Contact loss of magnetite

The fact that metamorphic minerals such as andalusite are commonly recrystallized to white mica in the contact aureoles of granitic intrusions suggests the increased activity of H_2O in this zone during plutonic cooling. On the western margin of the Sierra San Pedro Martir pluton, the outer hornblende-biotite tonalite zone, which elsewhere is magnetite bearing, is largely nonmagnetic within one kilometer of the contact with the host rock (Fig. 8B). In this pluton, the loss of magnetite is due to "oxyexsolution" of early-stage titanomagnetite (Usp-Mt) to single crystal intergrowth of hematite and ilmenite or pseudobrookite. Exsolution and recrystallization patterns in Fe-Ti oxides suggest an interaction with low-f_{O_2} fluids. In the 170-m-wide rim of the Valle Pedregoso pluton, the contact effect is produced by the direct formation of ilmenite. However, oxygen isotopes suggest an exchange of fluids in this narrow rim.

We believe that the contact loss of magnetite occurred late in the cooling history of the plutons through an interaction with water-rich, low-f_{O_2} fluids. We have not yet determined whether these fluids were escaping from progressively cooling plutons, if the fluids were drawn into the plutons from the adjacent host rocks, or if late-stage magma was involved.

Many small-scale features, including the dikes described in an earlier section, and the exact nature of the reacting fluids still defy explanation by any of the hypotheses offered here. We assume that there are other phenomena involved in addition to those we have discussed. We propose these solutions only to provoke the reader's imagination.

ACKNOWLEDGMENTS

Our research has been assisted by the National Science Foundation and San Diego State University. Much of the work was done by students, not all of whom are acknowledged individually. We thank the Department of Geology, Pomona College, for making available more than 400 specimens of Peninsular Ranges granitic rocks that had been chemically and modally analyzed by the late Alex Baird and associates. In particular, we are indebted to Melissa Wardlaw of the Baylor Brooks Institute of Isotope Geology for U-Pb analyses; Terry Davis of California State University, Los Angeles, for feldspar, lead, and Rb/Sr analyses; and Brian Smith, then of UNOCAL Research, for oxygen isotope analyses. We also thank Sunsho Ishihara, Masaaki Shimizu, and Yoshiaki Tainosho for discussions on their work in Japan and other regions, and Victoria Todd, Gerald Czamanske, and J. Lawford Anderson for their careful and constructive review of our paper.

REFERENCES CITED

Baird, A. K., and Meisch, A. T., 1984, Batholithic rocks of southern California; A model for the petrochemical nature of their source materials: U.S. Geological Survey Professional Paper 1284, 42 p.

Bird, P., and Baumgardener, J., 1984, Fault friction, regional stress, and crust-mantle coupling in southern California from finite element models: Journal of Geophysical Research, v. 89, p. 1932–1944.

Boyles-Reaber, C. B., 1987, A study of the magnetite-series/ilmenite-series rocks, 3 km south of Interstate 8, San Diego County, California [B.S. thesis]: San Diego, California, San Diego State University, Department of Geological Sciences, 20 p.

Buddington, A. F., and Lindsley, D. H., 1964, Iron-titanium oxide minerals and synthetic equivalents: Journal of Petrology, v. 5, p. 310–357.

Chadwick, B., 1987, Petrology, geochemistry, and geochronology of the Tres Hermanos–Santa Clara region, Baja California, Mexico [M.S. thesis]: San Diego, California, San Diego State University, Department of Geological Sciences, 207 p.

Chappell, B. W., and White, A.J.R., 1974, Two contrasting granite types: Pacific Geology, v. 8, p. 173–174.

Clinkenbeard, J., 1986, Mineralogy, chemistry, and geochronology of the La Posta pluton, San Diego County, California [M.S. thesis]: San Diego, California, San Diego State University, Department of Geological Sciences, 215 p.

Cobbing, E. J., and Pitcher, W. S., 1983, Andean plutonism in Peru and its relationship to volcanism and metallogenesis at a segmented plate edge, *in* Roddick, J. A., ed., Circum-Pacific plutonic terranes: Geological Society of America Memoir 159, p. 277–291.

Czamanske, G. K., Ishihara, S., and Atkin, S. A., 1981, Chemistry of rock-forming minerals of the Cretaceous–Paleocene batholith in southwestern Japan and implications for magma genesis: Journal of Geophysical Research, v. 86, p. 10431–10469.

Diamond, J. L., 1985, The magnetite/ilmenite line in the Peninsular Ranges batholith, Baja California, Mexico [B.S. thesis]: San Diego, California, San Diego State University, Department of Geological Sciences, 54 p.

—— , 1989, Mineralogical controls on rock magnetism in the Sierra San Pedro Martir pluton, Baja California [M.S. thesis]: University of Wyoming, Department of Geology and Geophysics, 77 p.

Diamond, J. L., Knaack, C. M., Gastil, R. G., Erskine, B. G., Walawender, M. J., Marshall, M., and Cameron, G. J., 1985, The magnetite/ilmenite line in the Peninsular Ranges batholith, southern and Baja California, U.S.A. and Mexico: Geological Society of America Abstracts with Programs, v. 17, p. 351.

Dodge, F.C.W., 1972, Variation of ferrous-ferric ratios in the central Sierra Nevada batholith: U.S. Geological Survey Bulletin 1314–F, p. F1–13.

Eastman, B. G., 1986, The geology, petrography, and geochemistry of the Sierra San Pedro Martir pluton, Baja California, Mexico [M.S. thesis]: San Diego, California, San Diego State University, Department of Geological Sciences, 154 p.

Eastman, B. G., McCormick, W. V., Gastil, R. G., Walawender, M. J., and Wardlaw, M. S., 1986, Petrogenesis of the Sierra San Pedro Martir zoned pluton, Baja California, Mexico: Geological Society of America Abstracts with Programs, v. 18, p. 591.

Erskine, B. G., 1982, A paleomagnetic, rock magnetic, and magnetic mineralogic investigation of the northern Peninsular Ranges batholith, southern California [M.S. thesis]: San Diego, California, San Diego State University, Department of Geological Sciences, 146 p.

Erskine, B. G., and Marshall, M., 1980, Magnetite- and ilmenite-series sub-belts in the northern Peninsular Ranges batholith, southern California; Their association with magnetic stability and implications on source regions: EOS Transactions of the American Geophysical Union, v. 62, p. 849.

Erskine, B. G., and Wenk, H. R., 1985, Evidence for Late Cretaceous crustal thinning in the Santa Rosa mylonite zone, southern California: Geology, v. 13, p. 274–277.

Gastil, R. G., Morgan, G., and Krummenacher, D., 1978, Mesozoic history of peninsular California and related areas east of the Gulf of California, *in* Howell, D. G., and McDougall, K. A., eds., Mesozoic paleogeography of the western United States: Society of Economic Paleontologists and Mineralogists, Pacific Coast Paleogeography Symposium 2, p. 107–115.

—— , 1981, The tectonic history of peninsular California and adjacent Mexico, *in* Ernst, W. G., ed., The geotectonic development of California; Rubey Volume 1: Englewood Cliffs, New Jersey, Prentice-Hall, p. 284–305.

Gastil, R. G., Phillips, R. P., and Allison, E. C., 1975, Reconnaissance geology of the State of Baja California: Geological Society of America Memoir 140, 170 p.

Gromet, L. P., and Silver, L. T., 1979, Profile of rare earth elements characteristics across the Peninsular Ranges batholith near the international border, southern California, U.S.A., and Baja California, Mexico, *in* Abbott, P. L., and Todd, V. R., eds., Mesozoic crystalline rocks: San Diego, California, San Diego State University, Department of Geological Sciences, p. 133–141.

—— , 1987, REE variations across the Peninsular Ranges batholith; Implications for batholithic petrogenesis and crustal growth in magmatic arcs: Journal of Petrology, v. 28, part 1, p. 75–125.

Gunn, S. H., 1985, Geology, petrography, and geochemistry of the Laguna Juarez pluton, Baja California, Mexico [M.S. thesis]: San Diego, California, San Diego State University, Department of Geological Sciences, 166 p.

Haggerty, S. E., 1976, Opaque mineral oxides in terrestrial igneous rocks, *in* Rumble, D., III, ed., Oxide minerals: Mineralogical Society of America Short Course Notes, v. 3, p. Hg-1-300.

Hill, R. I., 1984, Petrology and petrogenesis of batholithic rocks, San Jacinto Mountains, southern California [Ph.D. thesis]: Pasadena, California Institute of Technology, 700 p.

Ishihara, S., 1977, The magnetite-series and ilmenite-series granitic rocks: Mining Geology, v. 27, p. 293–305.

—— , 1979, Lateral variation of magnetic susceptibility of the Japanese granitoids: Geological Society of Japan Journal, v. 85, no. 8, p. 509–523.

—— , 1981, The granitoid series and mineralization, *in* Skinner, B. S., ed., Economic Geology, 75th Anniversary Volume: Economic Geology Publishing Co., p. 458–484.

—— , 1984, Granitoid series and Mo/W-Sn mineralization in east Asia: Geological Society of Japan Report 263, p. 173–208.

Ishihara, S., and Terashima, S., 1985, Cenozoic granitoids of central Hokkaido, Japan; An example of plutonism along collisional belt: Geological Society of Japan Bulletin, v. 36, no. 12, p. 653–680.

Ishihara, S., and Ulriksen, C. E., 1980, The magnetite-series and ilmenite-series granitoids in Chile: Mining Geology, v. 30, no. 3, p. 183–190.

Ishihara, S., Matsuhisa, Y., Sasaki, A., and Terashima, S., 1986, Wallrock assimilation by magnetite-series granitoid at the Miyako pluton, Kitakami, northeastern Japan: Geological Society of Japan Bulletin, v. 91, no. 10, p. 679–690.

Kimzey, J. A., 1982, Petrography and geochemistry of the La Posta granodiorite [M.S. thesis]: San Diego, California, San Diego State University, Department of Geological Sciences, 64 p.

Knaack, C. M., 1985, Magnetite/ilmenite division within Peninsular Ranges, southern California [B.S. thesis]: San Diego, California, San Diego State University, Department of Geological Sciences, 54 p.

Krummenacher, D., Gastil, R. G., Bushee, J., and Doupont, J., 1975, Potassium-argon apparent ages in the Peninsular Ranges batholith, southern California and northeastern Mexico: Geological Society of America Bulletin, v. 86, no. 6, p. 760–768.

Larsen, E. S., Jr., 1948, Batholithic and associated rocks, Corona, Elsinore, and San Luis Rey quadrangles, southern California: Geological Society of Amer-

ica Memoir 29, 182 p.

Lindsley, D. H., Andeason, G. E., Balsley, J. R., 1966, Magnetic properties of rocks and minerals, *in* Clark, S. P., ed., Handbook of physical constants (Revised edition): Geological Society of America Memoir 97, p. 543–552.

McCormick, W. V., 1986, Geology, mineralogy, and geochronology of the Sierra San Pedro Martir pluton, Baja California, Mexico [M.S. thesis]: San Diego, California, San Diego State University, Department of Geological Sciences, 123 p.

Oliver, H. W., 1980, Interpretation of the gravity map of California and its continental region: California Division of Mines and Geology Bulletin 205, 52 p.

Rangin, C., 1978, Speculative model of Mesozoic geodynamics, central Baja California to northwestern Sonora (Mexico), *in* Howell, D. G., and McDougall, K. A., eds., Mesozoic paleogeography of the western United States: Society of Economic Paleontologists and Mineralogists, Pacific Coast Paleogeography Symposium 2, p. 85–106.

Rector, R., 1989, The Long Potrero pluton: San Diego County, California [thesis]: San Diego, California, San Diego State University, Department of Geological Sciences, 54 p.

Shandley, P. D., and Bacon, L. D., 1966, Analysis for magnetite utilizing magnetic susceptibility: Geophysics, v. 31, no. 2, p. 398–409.

Sharma, P. V., 1976, Geophysical methods in geology, *in* Methods in geochemistry and geophysics, v. 12: New York, Elsevier, 428 p.

Shimizu, M., 1986, The Tokuwa batholith, central Japan: University Museum, University of Tokyo Bulletin 28, 143 p.

Silver, L. T., Early, T. O., and Anderson, T. H., 1975, Petrological, geochemical, and geochronological symmetries of the Peninsular Ranges batholith: Geological Society of America Abstracts with Programs, v. 7, p. 375–376.

Silver, L. T., Taylor, H. P., Jr., and Chappell, B., 1979, Some petrological, geochemical, and geochronological observations of the Peninsular Ranges batholith near the international border of the U.S.A. and Mexico, *in* Abbott, P. L., and Todd, V. R., eds., Mesozoic crystalline rocks: San Diego, California, San Diego State University, Department of Geological Sciences, p. 83–110.

Stensrude, H. L., and Gastil, R. G., 1978, Spotted tonalite dikes from the eastern margin of the southern California batholith: Geological Society of America Abstracts with Programs, v. 10, p. 148.

Todd, V. R., and Shaw, S. E., 1979, Structural, metamorphic, and intrusive framework of the Peninsular Ranges batholith in southern San Diego County, California, *in* Abbott, P. L., and Todd, V. R., eds., Mesozoic crystalline rocks: San Diego, California, San Diego State University, Department of Geological Sciences, p. 177–231.

—— , 1985, S-type granitoids and an I-S line in the Peninsular Ranges batholith, southern California: Geology, v. 13, p. 231–233.

Turi, B., and Taylor, H. P., Jr., 1971, An oxygen and hydrogen isotope study of a granodiorite pluton from the southern California batholith: Geochimica et Cosmochimica Acta, v. 35, p. 383–406.

U.S. Department of Energy, 1980, Airborne gamma-ray spectrometer and magnetometer survey, San Diego and Santa Ana quadrangles, California: Subcontract, High Life Helicopters, Inc./QEB, Inc., Final report, v. 2, 51 p.

Walawender, M. J., Gastil, R. G., Wardlaw, M., Calhoun, J. M., and Smith, B. M., 1987, Geochemical, geochronologic, and isotopic constraints on the origin and evolution of the eastern zone of the Peninsular Ranges batholith: Geological Society of America Abstracts with Programs, v. 19, p. 460.

Weslow, V., 1985, Magnetotelluric profiling of the Peninsular Ranges in northern Baja California, Mexico [M.S. thesis]: San Diego, California, San Diego State University, Department of Geological Sciences, 174 p.

Manuscript Submitted June 1, 1987
Revised Manuscript Submitted January 28, 1988
Manuscript Accepted by the Society February 7, 1989

The Geology of North America
Memoir 174
1990

Chapter 3

Mid-crustal emplacement of Mesozoic plutons, San Gabriel Mountains, California, and implications for the geologic history of the San Gabriel terrane

Andrew P. Barth*
Department of Geological Sciences, University of Southern California, Los Angeles, California 90089-0740

ABSTRACT

Mesozoic plutonism in the San Gabriel Mountains has temporal and geochemical similarities to plutonism in the eastern, inboard part of the Sierran–Mojave Desert Mesozoic arc, including the presence of Late Triassic quartz-poor, alkali-enriched plutons, Middle Jurassic(?) melanodiorites and porphyritic monzodiorites, a pre–Late Cretaceous bimodal dike swarm, and a Late Cretaceous calc-alkalic suite ranging from metaluminous quartz diorite to peraluminous garnet two-mica granite. Mineralogical evidence demonstrates that these plutonic rocks were emplaced at significantly deeper, mid-crustal levels in comparison to their counterparts on the North American craton. Hornblende barometry in metaluminous rocks yields emplacement depths of 19 to 28 km (5 to 7.5 kbar). The presence of late magmatic epidote in hornblende biotite granodiorite and quartz diorite is consistent with these estimates. Epidote is richer in pistacite component, and thus is indicative of slightly lower pressures of crystallization at higher f_{O_2}, in comparison to recent studies of magmatic epidote-bearing plutons. In Late Cretaceous peraluminous rocks, celadonitic muscovite yields estimated emplacement depths of 22 to 33 km (6 to 9 kbar). Calculations indicate that the presence of calcic magmatic garnet in the Late Triassic Mount Lowe intrusion is in accord with these pressure estimates.

Mesozoic plutonic rocks in the San Gabriel Mountains are part of an extensive basement terrane (San Gabriel terrane) in southern California, adjacent Arizona, and northern Sonora. The presence of mid-crustal plutonic rocks in the San Gabriel Mountains is geometrically consistent with juxtaposition on the Vincent thrust fault above Pelona Schist, which was metamorphosed at high pressure in a Late Cretaceous–Paleocene subduction event. However, this mid-crustal Mesozoic history appears to characterize only the southern part of the San Gabriel terrane. A northern subterrane of the San Gabriel terrane, containing Proterozoic and Triassic basement rocks correlative with those in the San Gabriel Mountains, had an upper crustal post–Early Jurassic history in close proximity to the North American craton. The mode and timing of juxtaposition of the San Gabriel terrane with autochthonous North America is unclear, but the similarity in histories of Mesozoic arc construction suggests close ties with Mesozoic North America. Much of the distinctive character of the San Gabriel terrane may be a consequence of exposure of rocks formed in the middle crust of an evolving continental margin magmatic arc.

*Present address: Department of Geology, Indiana University–Purdue University, Indianapolis, Indiana 46202.

Barth, A. P., 1990, Mid-crustal emplacement of Mesozoic plutons, San Gabriel Mountains, California, and implications for the geologic history of the San Gabriel terrane, *in* Anderson, J. L., ed., The nature and origin of Cordilleran magmatism: Boulder, Colorado, Geological Society of America Memoir 174.

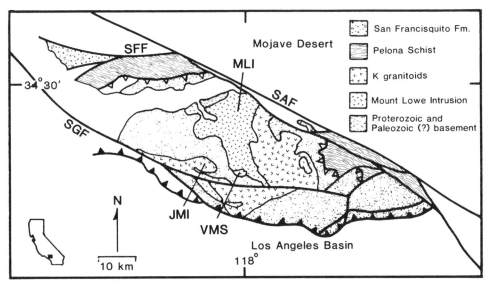

Figure 1. Simplified geologic map of the San Gabriel Mountains (modified from Ehlig, 1981). SAF = San Andreas fault, SGF = San Gabriel fault, SFF = San Francisquito fault, JMI = Josephine Mountain intrusion, VMS = Vetter Mountain stock, MLI = Mount Lowe intrusion.

INTRODUCTION

The San Gabriel Mountains are composed primarily of a tectonic slice of continental crust trapped between the San Andreas and San Gabriel fault zones. The pioneering studies of Crowell (1962, 1975), Silver (1968, 1971), and Ehlig (1981; Ehlig and others, 1975) documented the displacement histories of these faults and led to recognition of a regionally extensive terrane of continental crust (San Gabriel terrane of Silver, 1982) in southeastern California and western Arizona. The San Gabriel terrane lies above Mesozoic regional thrust faults that separate it from terranes of uncertain affinity, including the Joshua Tree (Powell, 1982) and Baldy terranes (Pelona-Orocopia schists; Ehlig, 1981; Jacobson, 1983). The sense of displacement on these thrusts, and thus the roots of the San Gabriel terrane, are uncertain.

In the San Gabriel terrane exposed in the San Gabriel Mountains, a Proterozoic gneiss and anorthosite complex is intruded by Mesozoic plutonic rocks (Fig. 1). These plutonic rocks have temporal and geochemical affinities to the eastern Cordilleran magmatic arc of the Sierra Nevada and Mojave Desert regions. These similarities include the presence of Late Triassic, quartz-poor, alkali-enriched plutons; Jurassic(?) melanodiorites and porphyritic monzodiorites; a pre–Late Cretaceous dike swarm; and a Late Cretaceous calc-alkalic suite, ranging from metaluminous quartz diorite to peraluminous garnet two-mica leucogranite. This chapter summarizes preliminary observations of an ongoing study which suggest a significantly deeper level of exposure of Mesozoic plutonic rocks in the San Gabriel Mountains in comparison to the Cordilleran arc of the craton to the northeast. This observation has important implications for the place of origin and mechanism of emplacement of the San Ga-

briel terrane, as well as for the nature of the middle crust in an evolving continental margin magmatic arc.

GEOLOGIC SETTING

The oldest dated Mesozoic plutonic rocks in the San Gabriel Mountains are plutons of the Mount Lowe intrusion of Late Triassic age (Silver, 1971; Joseph and others, 1978), a chemically and mineralogically zoned composite intrusion made up of at least two distinct plutons. The marginal-zone pluton is zoned inward from metaluminous hornblende quartz monzodiorite to peraluminous garnet biotite quartz monzodiorite and granodiorite. The central zone is composed of more homogeneous biotite monzodiorite. The intrusion is alkali-enriched and quartz-poor (Table 1), similar to Late Triassic and Early Jurassic plutonic rocks of the eastern part of the cratonal Mesozoic arc described by Miller (1977, 1978). The magma(s) that formed the intrusion were derived almost exclusively from subcrustal, probably eclogitic, sources, as inferred from low silica, Rb, and initial $^{87}Sr/^{86}Sr$; high Sr, Ba, and K/Rb; HREE depletion; and lack of a Eu anomaly.

An undated pluton of probable Middle Jurassic age in the north-central San Gabriel Mountains is composed of melanodiorite and monzodiorite, locally containing conspicuous orthoclase phenocrysts (Cox and others, 1983). These rocks are texturally and compositionally similar to rocks of the Middle Jurassic arc extending from Arizona and northern Sonora into southeastern California (Tosdal and others, 1989; R. M. Tosdal and R. E. Powell, 1987, personal communication). East of the San Andreas fault, numerous Middle Jurassic plutons intrude and suture the San Gabriel and underlying Joshua Tree terranes (Powell, 1982). This compositionally and texturally distinctive suite comprises the 160 to 165 Ma Cargo Muchacho Mountains and Kitt Peak–Trigo Peaks superunits of Tosdal and others (1989).

Triassic and Jurassic(?) plutons in the San Gabriel Mountains are cut by a bimodal dike swarm (Table 1). The dikes range from tens of centimeters up to 15 m in thickness, but most are 2 to 3 m thick. Mafic dikes range from olivine tholeiitic to alkalic hornblende microdiorites and lamprophyres. Most have been partly recrystallized in the greenschist to lower amphibolite facies, but some original textures are preserved. Felsic dikes are porphyritic microgranites and aplites containing quartz and, less commonly, alkali feldspar phenocrysts. The groundmass of these dikes commonly contains muscovite, accessory garnet, and intergrown quartz and feldspar. Tosdal and others (1989) report U-Pb zircon ages of 158 and 148 Ma on lithologically similar dikes in the San Gabriel terrane east of the San Andreas fault. This swarm is thus compositionally and temporally (at least in part) akin to the Independence swarm of the eastern Sierra Nevada and northern Mojave Desert regions to the north (Moore and Hopson, 1961; Chen and Moore, 1979).

A compositionally expanded Late Cretaceous calc-alkalic suite is well exposed in the San Gabriel Mountains part of the San Gabriel terrane. In the Josephine Mountain intrusion, early hornblende biotite quartz diorite and tonalite are intruded by isolated sheets and plutons of garnet two-mica leucogranite (Table 1). A granite from this intrusive complex yielded a U-Pb zircon age of 80 ± 10 Ma (Carter and Silver, 1971; L. T. Silver, 1986, personal communication), and a hornblende K-Ar age of 74.8 ± 2.2 Ma was obtained nearby from the host quartz diorite (Miller and Morton, 1980). The Vetter Mountain stock, of inferred Late Cretaceous age, is a relatively poorly exposed heterogeneous stock ranging from hornblende biotite granite to two-mica leucogranite and garnet two-mica aplite. Similar lithologies are present in the Mount Wilson–Waterman Mountain areas to the east (Ehlig, 1981). This suite has some similarity to the inner Cordilleran peraluminous belt described by Miller and Bradfish (1980), characterized by the abundance of muscovite-bearing plutons, in contrast to their scarcity in the main frontal Cordilleran arc.

MINERALOGIC EVIDENCE OF EMPLACEMENT DEPTH

Epidote

Epidote of inferred late magmatic origin occurs in all diorite to granodiorite plutons examined in the San Gabriel Mountains. Subhedral epidote with euhedral terminations in contact with biotite and irregular intergrowths with plagioclase and quartz are common (Fig. 2a). Less commonly, coarse subhedral epidote encloses early-formed hornblende (Fig. 2b), the hornblende locally showing evidence of resorption, a common texture noted by Zen and Hammarstrom (1984) in their discussion of magmatic epidote textural relations. The Late Triassic Mount Lowe intrusion contains abundant epidote of uncertain paragenesis, but two textural variations are here inferred to be of magmatic origin;

TABLE 1. REPRESENTATIVE WHOLE-ROCK ANALYSES OF MESOZOIC PLUTONIC ROCKS, SAN GABRIEL MOUNTAINS

Specimen*	A2	E1	C2b	C13	J54	J28
SiO_2	61.93	63.35	48.10	74.30	57.2	73.6
Al_2O_3	18.91	20.90	16.75	14.54	18.0	14.5
Fe_2O_3[†]	4.00	1.42	8.83	0.47	6.74	0.81
MgO	0.72	0.39	6.20	0.10	2.7	0.15
CaO	5.00	2.60	11.92	0.51	6.42	1.11
Na_2O	4.75	8.40	3.28	4.81	3.9	4.1
K_2O	2.95	1.36	0.22	4.13	1.89	4.69
TiO_2	0.45	0.25	1.46	0.05	0.78	0.13
MnO	0.18	0.03	0.19	0.14	0.12	0.08
P_2O_5	0.18	——	——	——	0.43	0.06
LOI	0.97	0.41	2.11	0.33	0.50	0.25
Sum	100.04	99.11	99.07	99.28	98.68	99.48
qz	10.15	2.51	——	29.02	10.17	29.19
or	17.55	7.84	1.30	24.41	11.17	27.72
ab	42.96	73.64	27.64	40.70	33.00	34.69
an	21.60	12.59	30.33	2.53	26.03	5.11
di	——	——	23.09	——	2.42	——
hy	4.47	1.68	——	0.81	8.19	0.77
mt	1.40	0.46	4.22	0.23	4.35	0.51
il	0.63	0.34	2.77	0.09	1.48	0.25
ap	0.38	——	——	——	1.00	0.14
co	——	0.94	——	1.23	——	0.80
wo	0.87	——	——	——	——	——
ol	——	——	6.87	——	——	——

*Specimen A2, quartz monzodiorite of marginal zone of Mount Lowe Intrusion; E1, monzodiorite of central zone of Mount Lowe Intrusion; C2b and C13, Jurassic(?) dikes; J54 and J28, quartz diorite and garnet two-mica granite of Josephine Mountain Intrusion. Analyses J54 and J28 by Branch of Geochemistry, USGS, Menlo Park.

†Total Fe as Fe_2O_3.

epidote occurs as subhedral prismatic phenocrysts up to 5 cm in long dimension, many with allanite cores, and as euhedral prismatic inclusions paralleling growth zones in unaltered, Carlsbad-twinned orthoclase phenocrysts.

The region of *P-T* overlap between the maximum thermal stability of epidote + quartz (Liou, 1973) and the solidus curve for water-saturated tonalite indicates the potential barometric significance of magmatic epidote (Zen and Hammarstrom, 1984; Fig. 3). Although the data appear to suggest minimum pressures as low as 4 kbar for magmatic epidote-bearing granitoids, this minimum is probably unlikely to be realized in natural systems. Most intermediate to felsic igneous rocks crystallize at oxygen fugacities significantly below the Fe_2O_3–Fe_3O_4 (HM) buffer and activities of water well below unity, the effect of which is to raise the actual pressure of intersection of the solidus and epidote + quartz curves. In addition, epidote in a calc-alkalic magma is unlikely to have its

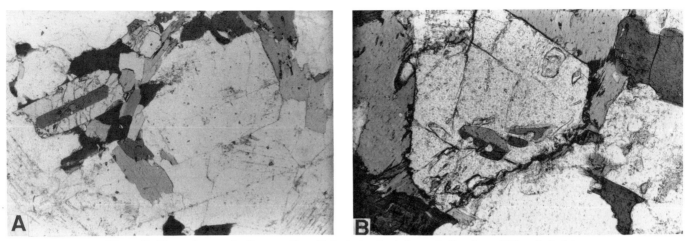

Figure 2. Photomicrograph of magmatic epidote textural relations. A: Specimen J21, euhedral to subhedral epidote with magmatic biotite. Note cores of allanite euhedra and associated unaltered plagioclase. Width of field of view approximately 2 mm. B: Specimen J19, subhedral to anhedral, embayed hornblende enclosed in euhedral epidote and associated biotite. Width of field of view approximately 1 mm.

stability enhanced (thus lowering the minimum pressure of intersection) by solution of additional components. Available compositional data for magmatic epidotes (Naney, 1983; Zen and Hammarstrom, 1984; Barth, unpublished data) suggest no significant solid solution beyond the epidote-clinozoisite binary. However, solid solution in phases of the high-temperature–low-pressure breakdown assemblage in a silicate magma will result in significantly reduced thermal stability for epidote + quartz relative to experimental curves determined in simplified chemical systems. On the basis of these considerations, Zen (1985, 1986) concluded that the stability of epidote in calc-alkalic magmas of intermediate oxygen fugacity is restricted to pressures not less than 6 kbar. Because the experimental studies of Naney (1983) indicate that epidote is a near-solidus phase, its presence should be indicative of conditions near those of final emplacement.

Plutons in the San Gabriel Mountains appear to have crystallized under more oxidizing conditions than those studied by Zen and Hammarstrom (1984), and thus, magmatic epidote may have been stable at pressures slightly lower than those inferred in their study. Magmatic epidote in rocks studied thus far ranges from Ps_{26} to Ps_{32} (percent pistacite = $Fe^{3+}/[Fe^{3+} + Al^{vi}]$). These compositions are similar to epidote crystallized in synthetic granodiorite by Naney (1983) between the Ni-NiO (NNO) and HM buffers, but are less aluminous than those described by Zen and Hammarstrom (1984), inferred to have crystallized at oxygen fugacity near the NNO buffer. Given broadly similar bulk compositions, these data suggest higher oxygen fugacity for the San Gabriel Mountains plustons relative to those studied by Zen and Hammarstrom (1984). The epidote-bearing tonalites of the Josephine Mountain intrusion also contain coexisting subhedral to euhedral magnetite and ilmeno-hematite ($Hm_{62}Il_{36}Py_2$). Compositions lie in an uncalibrated region of T-f_{O_2} space, but are con-

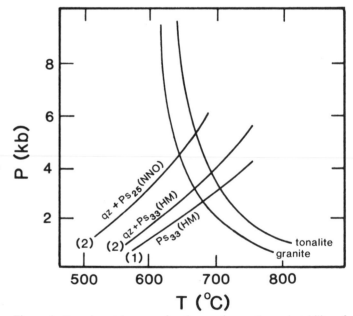

Figure 3. Experimental curves for the maximum thermal stability of epidote (curve 1; Holdaway, 1972) and epidote + quartz (curves 2; Liou, 1973) compared to water-saturated solidii for granite and tonalite (Stern and others, 1975). Ps = pistacite ($Fe^{3+}/[Fe^{3+} + Al^{vi}]$) content of epidote on the experimental curve. Oxygen fugacity conditions relevant to experiment: HM = hematite-magnetite buffer, NNO = nickel-nickel oxide buffer.

sistent with the experimental data of Lindsley (1973) for the ilmenite-hematite join at magmatic temperatures, and may record unusually high f_{O_2}, approaching HM. The presence of andraditic magmatic garnet in the Mount Lowe intrusion (Barth, 1984) is also suggestive of relatively oxidizing conditions.

Hornblende

Hornblende occurs as an early crystallizing phase in dioritic rocks of the Mount Lowe and Josephine Mountain intrusions and the Vetter Mountain stock. Hornblende typically shows irregular optical and compositional zoning; rims of individual grains are enriched in Al^t, Fe, Na, and K and depleted in Mg and Ti relative to cores. An inverse correlation of Al^t and Ti is characteristic of these hornblendes (Fig. 4). Depletion of Ti in rocks having a Ti-saturating phase (sphene, ilmenite) is generally attributed to decreasing temperature accompanying crystallization (Anderson, 1980; Czamanske and others, 1981). The positive correlation of Al^t with Fe/(Fe+Mg) and the negative correlation of Al^t with Ti (Figs. 4 and 5) suggests the operation of a Mg-tschermak substitution, $Al^{iv} + Al^{vi} = Si + Mg$, with Al^{vi} enrichment enhanced by a Ti substitution, e.g., $2Al^{vi} = Ti^{vi} + Mg^{vi}$. A Mg-tschermak substitution can result from Fe being favored over Mg in the M2 octahedral site with increasing Al^{vi}, and increase in Fe/Mg with increasing Al^{iv} to enhance the fit of tetrahedral and octahedral chains (Hawthorne, 1981). Hollister and others (1987) suggested that tschermakite substitution in amphibole in a crystallizing calc-alkalic magma is controlled by the reaction

2 quartz + 2 anorthite + biotite = tschermakite + orthoclase.

This reaction provides a possible explanation for the observed compositional variation in hornblende, which could be a function of rising a_{SiO_2} at constant pressure; quartz is texturally late in all the samples studied, and is rare as inclusions in hornblende (cf. Hammarstrom and Zen, 1986).

The striking compositional feature of hornblende in this study is high Al_2O_3 content, ranging from 8.5 to 12.5 weight percent (Table 2). In comparison, hornblendes in rocks of similar bulk composition from the Sierra Nevada and Mojave Desert regions typically contain 5.5 to 9.5 weight percent Al_2O_3 (Dodge and others, 1968; Miller, 1977; Beckerman and others, 1982; Noyes and others, 1983). Brand (1985) reported hornblende with 8.0 to 9.1 weight percent Al_2O_3 in early Mesozoic(?) granitoids intruding the Joshua Tree terrane in the Pinto Mountains.

Hammarstrom and Zen (1986) and Hollister and others (1987) have empirically calibrated a barometer based on the aluminum content of hornblende in calc-alkalic plutons by comparison with presure estimates from petrologically well-characterized wall-rock assemblages. Both studies have emphasized the importance of reducing the variance of the metaluminous system by choosing samples with the assemblage plagioclase + alkali feldspar + quartz + amphibole + biotite + magnetite + sphene. The more recent calibration of Hollister and others (1987) is important in that it largely confirms that of Hammarstrom and Zen (1986), and significantly reduces the initial uncertainty in the barometer (from ± 3 to ± 1 kbar). Hollister and others (1987) further restricted uncertainty due to the effect of (1) variable temperature (e.g., Nabelek and Lindsley, 1985) by utilizing only rim compositions in plutons crystallized at greater than 2

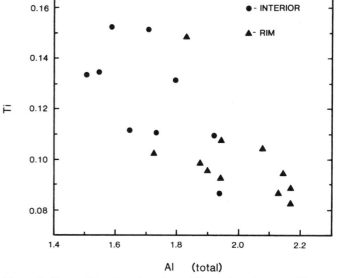

Figure 4. Compositional zoning of amphiboles, in cations per 23 oxygens, for the Josephine Mountain intrusion. Specimen J60, hornblende biotite epidote quartz diorite.

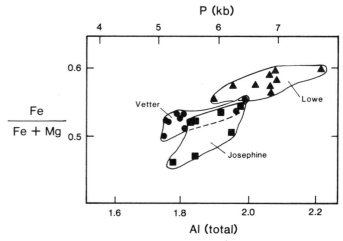

Figure 5. Hornblende barometric results for Mesozoic plutons. All plotted analyses are rim compositions in contact with interstitial quartz. Isobars are based on the calibration of Hollister and others (1987); those based on Hammarstrom and Zen (1986) are displaced a few hundred bars to the right, yielding lower calculated pressures.

kbar, and (2) variable composition by utilizing only rocks with plagioclase rim compositions of An_{25-35}. The data in Table 2 and Figure 5 are for hornblende from samples that satisfy all these limiting criteria, with the sole exception that plagioclase rims in the Josephine Mountain intrusion are somewhat more calcic (An_{31-39}) in the samples studied. Calculated pressures (Fig. 5) are based on low-Ti rim compositions in equilibrium with late interstitial quartz, thus providing the closest approach to solidus

TABLE 2. REPRESENTATIVE MICROPROBE ANALYSES OF AMPHIBOLES

Specimen*	J60		J95		L-85-6-3	
Spot†	3-1c	3-1r	1-1c	1-1r	3-4c	3-4r
SiO₂	44.85	42.40	43.85	42.08	40.58	40.17
Al₂O₃	8.69	10.72	9.64	10.88	11.33	11.19
FeO‡	16.90	17.89	15.66	19.73	20.81	20.16
MgO	11.32	9.83	11.87	9.51	8.21	8.65
CaO	11.59	11.51	11.30	11.46	11.20	11.05
Na₂O	1.11	1.29	1.69	1.51	1.58	1.49
K₂O	0.70	0.93	1.13	1.32	1.77	1.51
TiO₂	1.19	0.93	2.23	0.66	1.14	0.68
MnO	0.48	0.48	0.60	0.61	1.58	1.54
Sum	96.83	95.98	97.97	97.76	98.20	96.44

[cations per 23 oxygen formula unit]

Si	6.777	6.530	6.555	6.445	6.283	6.309
Al^{IV}	1.223	1.470	1.445	1.555	1.717	1.691
Al^{VI}	0.325	0.476	0.253	0.409	0.351	0.380
Fe	2.136	2.304	1.958	2.527	2.695	2.648
Mg	2.550	2.257	2.645	2.171	1.895	2.025
Mn	0.061	0.063	0.076	0.079	0.207	0.205
Ti	0.135	0.108	0.251	0.076	0.133	0.080
Ca	1.876	1.899	1.810	1.881	1.858	1.859
Na	0.325	0.385	0.490	0.448	0.474	0.454
K	0.135	0.183	0.215	0.258	0.350	0.303

*Specimen J60, quartz diorite of Josephine Mountain Intrusion; J95, granodiorite of Vetter Mountain Stock; L-85-6-3, quartz monzodiorite of marginal zone of Mount Lowe Intrusion.

†c = core, r = rim, all rim analyses are from grains in contact with interstitial quartz.

‡Total Fe as FeO.

conditions and the best estimate of emplacement depth. Results are 5.6 ± 0.5 and 5.9 ± 0.7 kbar for the Late Cretaceous Josephine Mountain intrusion and Vetter Mountain stock, respectively, and 6.7 ± 0.6 for the Late Triassic Mount Lowe intrusion. Data are not yet sufficient to evaluate whether the pressure difference between early and late Mesozoic plutons has spatial or temporal significance, although increasing pressure toward the northeast is not unexpected, based on the antiformal nature of exposures of structurally underlying rocks (Pelona Schist) in the eastern San Gabriel Mountains (Ehlig, 1981; Fig. 1).

Muscovite

In peraluminous leucogranites and aplites of the Josephine Mountain intrusion and Vetter Mountain stock, two generations of white mica are observed. Subhedral grains with sharp boundaries, locally interpenetrating with biotite, are inferred to be primary magmatic phases, whereas secondary grains generally are more ragged in form and partially or wholly enclosed in feldspars. Inferred primary magmatic muscovite is typically characterized by higher TiO₂ content in comparison to secondary muscovite and sericite (Anderson and others, 1980; Anderson and Rowley, 1981; Miller and others, 1981; Speer, 1984; Monier and Robert, 1986). This distinction was also observed in this study; texturally primary muscovite ranges from 0.3 to 1.0 weight percent TiO₂, whereas ragged secondary muscovite usually contains about 0.1 weight percent TiO₂ (Table 3). This difference is interpreted to be due to the combined effects of decreasing Ti solubility with decreasing temperature (Anderson and others, 1980; Anderson and Rowley, 1981) and changing effective bulk composition. No other systematic compositional differences as a function of inferred paragenesis have been noted in this study.

Composition of muscovite provides additional information concerning conditions of crystallization. Magmatic muscovite characteristically contains appreciable Fe and Mg and is silica enriched relative to end-member muscovite (Best and others, 1974; Guidotti, 1978; Davis and others, 1980; Anderson and others, 1980; Miller and others, 1981; Anderson and Rowley, 1981; Fig. 6). These compositional effects are loosely termed a celadonitic substitution, although the data in Figure 6 demonstrate an important ferrimuscovite component in the San Gabriel Mountains muscovites, as originally noted by Miller and others (1981). Velde (1965) and Massonne and Schreyer (1983) have demonstrated experimentally that Si in celadonitic muscovite increases with increasing pressure and decreasing temperature. The steep, subparallel dP/dT slopes of the granite solidus and muscovite-out reaction (Huang and Wyllie, 1981) indicate that late magmatic muscovite crystallizes over a restricted temperature range (less than 100 °C). Thus, the principal intensive variable affecting Si (celadonite) content of magmatic muscovite is likely to be pressure rather than temperature.

On the basis of these arguments, the relatively low-silica muscovites in plutons of the southern Cordilleran magmatic arc are consistent with shallow crustal emplacement inferred from field relations. Miller and others (1981) reported average Si contents of primary muscovites from 6.10 to 6.34 (per 22 oxygens) for plutons in the Mojave Desert and eastern Sierra Nevada regions. Similarly, Brand (1985) reported a range of 6.08 to 6.22 for Late Cretaceous(?) two-mica granites intruding the Joshua Tree terrane in the Pinto Mountains. In contrast, primary muscovite in San Gabriel Mountains Late Cretaceous plutons studied thus far has Si contents ranging from 6.19 to 6.55 (Table 3), suggestive of relatively higher pressures of equilibration at similar temperatures. A similar range (6.20 to 6.56) was found by Rowley (1981) and J. L. Anderson (1987, personal communication) in peraluminous members of a deep-seated Late Cretaceous intrusive suite of the Whipple Mountains core complex. Anderson (1985, 1989) estimated emplacement pressures of 7 to 9 kbar (25 to 35 km depth) for this suite based on garnet-biotite-muscovite-plagioclase-quartz equilibria and aluminum solubility in hornblende.

TABLE 3. REPRESENTATIVE MICROPROBE ANALYSES OF BIOTITE AND MUSCOVITE

Specimen*	J79			J44		J28		
Phase†	bt	mu(P)	mu(S)	bt	mu(P)	bt	mu(P)	mu(S)
SiO_2	37.37	48.94	49.35	35.08	46.47	35.47	48.78	47.39
Al_2O_3	16.49	30.44	30.46	17.04	33.01	15.77	29.68	32.73
$FeO‡$	20.26	5.76	4.99	23.59	3.87	23.06	5.79	5.28
MgO	7.86	1.69	1.61	6.56	0.65	8.25	1.58	0.84
CaO	0.16	0.04	0.06	0.15	0.02	0.18	0.13	0.29
Na_2O	0.07	0.25	0.15	0.08	0.41	0.09	0.41	0.40
K_2O	9.92	9.61	9.99	9.58	9.56	9.68	9.92	9.39
TiO_2	2.69	0.51	0.09	2.56	0.37	2.68	1.05	0.10
MnO	1.40	0.13	0.14	0.97	0.04	0.89	0.14	0.15
Sum	96.22	97.37	96.84	95.61	94.40	96.07	97.48	96.57

[cations per 22 oxygen formula unit]

Si	5.695	6.473	6.542	5.481	6.287	5.509	6.473	6.308
Al^{IV}	2.305	1.527	1.458	2.519	1.713	2.491	1.527	1.692
Al^{VI}	0.657	3.218	3.301	0.619	3.551	0.396	3.115	3.443
Fe	2.582	0.637	0.553	3.082	0.438	2.995	0.643	0.588
Mg	1.786	0.333	0.318	1.528	0.131	1.910	0.313	0.167
Mn	0.181	0.015	0.016	0.128	0.005	0.117	0.016	0.017
Ti	0.308	0.051	0.009	0.301	0.038	0.313	0.105	0.010
Ca	0.026	0.006	0.009	0.025	0.003	0.030	0.018	0.041
Na	0.021	0.064	0.039	0.024	0.108	0.027	0.105	0.103
K	1.929	1.622	1.690	1.909	1.650	1.918	1.679	1.595

*Specimen J79, aplite of Vetter Mountain Stock; J28 and J44, garnet two-mica granite and aplite of Josephine Mountain Intrusion; all samples also contain Al-Sp garnet, An_{10-15} plagioclase, orthoclase, and quartz.

†bt = biotite, mu = muscovite, (P) = texturally primary, (S) = texturally secondary.

‡Total Fe as FeO.

Two recent studies have attempted to quantify the barometric significance of compositional variability in muscovite. Powell and Evans (1983) utilized the experimental results of Velde (1965) to derive a theoretical barometer for the equilibrium

Mg-celadonite = phlogopite + K-feldspar + quartz + H_2O.

The left side of this reaction is favored (i.e., more celadonitic, Si-rich white mica) with increasing pressure and decreasing temperature. Contours of equal lnK_{eq} for this reaction as a function of pressure and temperature are shown in Figure 7. Values of lnK_{eq} for coexisting phases in the Josephine Mountain intrusion and Vetter Mountain stock were calculated using titaniferous muscovite as the closest approach to magmatic conditions. Ideal solution models were employed for calculation of phlogopite in biotite and Mg-celadonite in white mica (Powell, 1978), and unit activities were assumed for quartz and H_2O. Alkali feldspar activities were equated to mole fraction and varied from 0.6 to

0.8, consistent with the range of inferred temperatures and measured coexisting plagioclase compositions, based on the calibration of Stormer (1975). The resulting calculated pressures of 5 to 10 kbar, corresponding to equilibration at near-solidus conditions, are shown in Figure 7. Massonne and Schreyer (1983, 1985) have developed a separate barometer based on experimental results for this assemblage in the KMASH system; application to muscovite compositions from this study yields pressures in good agreement with the range shown in Figure 7 for the Josephine Mountain intrusion, and approximately 1 kbar lower for the Vetter Mountain stock. Overall, results are in good agreement with hornblende barometry in associated metaluminous portions of these intrusive complexes, in part overlapping and ranging to somewhat higher pressures (cf. Fig. 5).

Garnet

Magmatic garnets in plutonic rocks are typically almandine-spessartine solid solutions, with minor pyrope component

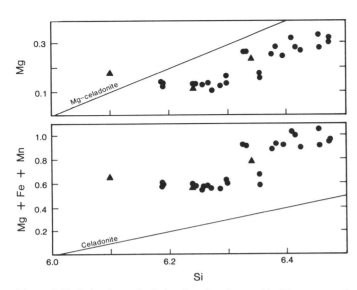

Figure 6. Variation in octahedral cation abundance with silica content of primary muscovites from Late Cretaceous two-mica granites. Solid triangles represent average muscovite compositions reported by Miller and others (1981). Ideal muscovite plots at the origin. Ideal celadonite substitution shown by solid lines.

(Wright, 1938; Miller and Stoddard, 1981, and references therein). This reflects the low MgO and Mg/Fe contents of granitic magmas that crystallize garnet and the affinity of garnet for manganese. Grossular and andradite contents of magmatic garnets typically total less than about 4 mole percent due to the reduced affinity of garnet for Ca at low pressures. Liquidus garnets produced in high-pressure crystallization experiments are significantly more calcic (e.g., Green, 1977; Stern and Wyllie, 1978). In addition, peraluminous melts that crystallize garnetiferous leucogranites, pegmatites, and aplites are typically depleted in Ca by differentiation involving fractionation of plagioclase.

Magmatic garnet occurs in the fractionated interior of the Mount Lowe intrusion and in leucogranites and aplites of the Josephine Mountain intrusion and Vetter Mountain stock. The field and textural relations of these rocks, as well as K_D^{Fe-Mg} values for coexisting ferromagnesian phases, are compatible with late supersolidus crystallization of garnet. In the Josephine Mountain intrusion and Vetter Mountain stock, the garnets are almandine-spessartine solid solutions, consistent with the relatively evolved nature of these plutons. Five-component garnets, containing up to 14 weight percent CaO in equilibrium with calcic oligoclase, occur in somewhat less evolved rocks in the fractionated interior of the Mount Lowe intrusion (Barth, 1984).

Coexisting garnet and plagioclase in the Mount Lowe intrusion show a positive correlation of calcium contents, suggestive of maintenance of the equilibrium

$$3CaAl_2Si_2O_8 = Ca_3Al_2Si_3O_{12} + SiO_2 + 2Al_2SiO_5.$$
$$\text{anorthite} \qquad \text{grossular} \qquad \text{quartz Al-silicate}$$

This equilibrium is the basis for well-tested barometers in SiO_2- and Al_2SiO_5-saturated metamorphic rocks (Ghent, 1976; Newton and Haselton, 1981), based on increasing grossular content of garnet at the expense of anorthite component in plagioclase with increasing pressure. For rocks of the Mount Lowe intrusion, barometry is hampered by the lack of an aluminum-saturating phase. Lack of aluminum saturation is in part reflected in the very calcic garnet compositions, the equilibria proceeding to the right with reduced $a_{Al_2SiO_5}$ in the melt.

Quantification of the activity of Al_2SiO_5 in the magma that crystallized garnet and plagioclase at known temperature allows pressure to be calculated in the absence of aluminum saturation. A rough estimate can be derived from the equilibrium

$$KFe_3AlSi_3O_{10}(OH)_2 + Al_2SiO_5 + 2SiO_2 =$$
$$\text{annite} \qquad \text{Al-silicate} \quad \text{quartz}$$
$$KAlSi_3O_8 + Fe_3Al_2Si_3O_{12} + H_2O,$$
$$\text{K-feldspar} \quad \text{almandine} \qquad \text{fluid}$$

using phase compositions inferred to be in equilibrium with each other and silicate liquid. Phillips (1980) used experimental data to derive an expression for K_{eq} for the sillimanite variant of this reaction as a function of temperature and pressure. Using an aplite dike sample containing garnet, biotite, plagioclase, alkali feldspar, sphene, epidote, and quartz, a temperature estimated at 610 to 650°C using the garnet-biotite thermometer of Ganguly and Saxena (1984), and a pressure of 6 kbar, K_{eq} was calculated. Because

$$K_{eq} = (a_{afs})(a_{alm})(a_{H_2O}) / (a_{ann})(a_{als})(a_{qtz}^2),$$

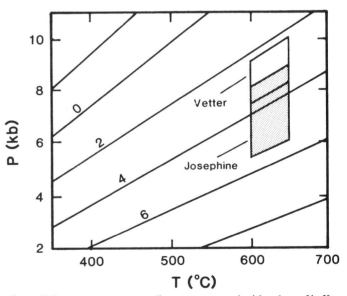

Figure 7. Pressure-temperature diagram contoured with values of ln K_{eq} for the Mg-celadonite barometer of Powell and Evans (1983). Boxes show range of calculated pressures at assumed temperatures of 600 to 650°C.

an approximation of $a_{Al_2SiO_5}$ (a_{als}) can be calculated, assuming sillimanite as the standard state for Al_2SiO_5. Quartz and a hydrous fluid phase were assumed to be pure. Values for a_{ann} and a_{alm} were derived from equilibrium mineral compositions assuming ideal mixing, and a_{afs} was estimated from coexisting plagioclase compositions using the calibration of Stormer (1975) and the assumption of ideal mixing. The calculated $a_{Al_2SiO_5}$ ranges from 0.20 to 0.30, which yields pressures of 8.5 to 10 kbar using the garnet-plagioclase-Al_2SiO_5-quartz barometer of Ghent (1976). The calculated activity of Al_2SiO_5 is relatively insensitive to the input pressure used in the model.

This technique provides an estimate of pressure that is probably a maximum for conditions of crystallization. Activities of H_2O and garnet components (grossular and almandine) estimated by the ideal approximation have substantial uncertainties. The fluid phase inferred to have been present during crystallization of the aplite and associated pegmatites was probably not pure H_2O, resulting in overestimation of pressure. No activity model is available for five-component garnets, and uncertainty as to mixing properties of the grossular-almandine and almandine-spessartine joins (e.g., Newton and Haselton, 1981; Ganguly and Saxena, 1984) introduce errors of uncertain magnitude. Thus, although this barometer cannot currently be applied quantitatively in these rocks, the results indicate that high calcium garnets are possible magmatic compositions at the inferred temperature and pressure of crystallization of the Mount Lowe intrusion.

CONTACT METAMORPHISM

Proterozoic gneisses that compose the wall rocks of Mesozoic plutons in the San Gabriel Mountains are dominantly biotite ± hornblende quartzofeldspathic gneisses and amphibolite, lithologies relatively insensitive to small changes in grade. Estimation of conditions attending pluton emplacement from contact metamorphic effects is only locally possible. One such locality is the eastern part of the Late Cretaceous Josephine Mountain intrusion. Wall rocks include a distinctive biotite + muscovite gneiss with relict alkali feldspar grains. Samples of this lithology collected less than 200 m from intrusive contacts with quartz diorite contain swirls of fibrolitic sillimanite in muscovite and fibrolite needles traversing grain boundaries and foliation. Rare small garnets are also observed in one sample. Field and textural relations suggest late prograde heating of these rocks proximal to intrusion of the quartz diorite.

Thermobarometric results for a sample of this aluminous gneiss collected about 50 m from the contact are shown in Figure 8. Temperatures were determined using garnet-biotite thermometry, and the Ganguly and Saxena (1984) calibration was found to yield the best agreement with experimental location of the muscovite + quartz breakdown reaction in the presence of a hydrous fluid phase. At the estimated temperature of 660 °C, biotite-muscovite-alkali feldspar-quartz (Massonne and Schreyer, 1983; Powell and Evans, 1983) and garnet-plagioclase-muscovite-quartz (Ghent and Stout, 1981; Hodges and Crowley, 1985)

barometry yield estimated pressures of 4.5 to 6 kbar. This result is in good agreement with hornblende barometry in the adjacent quartz diorite, which yields pressure estimates of 5 to 6.5 kbar.

TECTONIC IMPLICATIONS

Crystalline rocks of the San Gabriel Mountains are wedged between dextral slip faults of the San Andreas and San Gabriel fault zones (Fig. 1). Understanding the relation of these rocks to surrounding regions relies heavily on unraveling the effects of Neogene dismemberment of terranes in southern California by strike-slip faulting. A possible pre–late Miocene palinspastic reconstruction of southern California based on studies summarized by Ehlig (1981) and Powell (1982) is shown in Figure 9. The San Gabriel terrane in the San Gabriel Mountains is part of an extensive crystalline terrane underlying much of southeastern California. The terrane lies structurally above the Baldy and Joshua Tree terranes along thrust faults, referred to as the Vincent–Orocopia–Chocolate Mountains and Red Cloud thrusts, respectively. The relation, if any, of the San Gabriel terrane to autochthonous North America can only be discerned by unraveling the history of juxtaposition of these terranes.

In the San Gabriel Mountains (Fig. 1) and correlative basement exposures to the east across the San Andreas fault, Proterozoic rocks and Mesozoic plutons lie structurally above Pelona-Orocopia schists (Baldy terrane). Mid-crustal juxtaposition of these terranes in a Late Cretaceous–Paleocene subduction zone resulted in tectonic erosion of the base of the Mesozoic arc described above. Petrologic studies in lower plate schists indicate metamorphism synchronous with tectonic burial beneath a warm hanging wall at pressures of 8 to 10 kbar (Graham and England, 1976; Graham and Powell, 1984). Similar and slightly lower

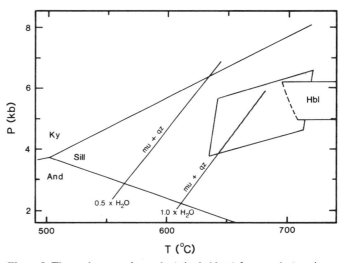

Figure 8. Thermobarometric results (stippled box) for sample (specimen J52) of contact metamorphic aureole of Late Cretaceous Josephine Mountain intrusion. Aluminum silicate phase diagram from Holdaway (1971); muscovite + quartz breakdown curves from Kerrick (1972). Field labeled hbl represents hornblende barometric results for nearby quartz diorite at magmatic temperatures.

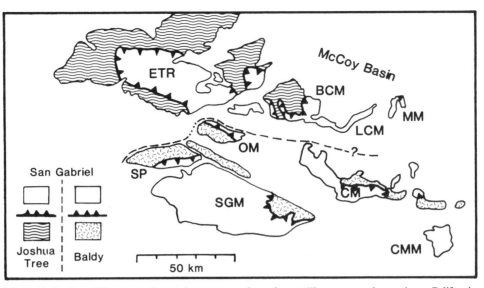

Figure 9. Pre-Late Miocene palinspastic reconstruction of crystalline terranes in southern California (modified from Ehlig, 1981). Dashed line separates northern and southern subterranes of the San Gabriel terrane discussed in text. BCM = Big Chuckwalla Mountains, CM = Chocolate Mountains, CMM = Cargo Muchacho Mountains, ETR = Eastern Transverse Ranges, LCM = Little Chuckwalla Mountains, MM = Mule Mountains, OM = Orocopia Mountains, SGM = San Gabriel Mountains, SP = Sierra Pelona.

pressures recorded by upper-plate plutons as young as Late Cretaceous (75 Ma) suggest that the geometry of this subduction event has been, for the most part, preserved in the San Gabriel Mountains. Farther east, however, the boundary between the San Gabriel terrane and structurally lower Baldy terrane has been modified by extensional faulting (e.g., Haxel and others, 1985; Jacobson and others, 1987), resulting in juxtaposition of upper crustal crystalline rocks or supracrustal rocks above high-pressure schists, thus accommodating significant local uplift of lower plate rocks subsequent to the subduction event.

The exact timing and vergence of juxtaposition of the San Gabriel and Baldy terranes are debated (Burchfiel and Davis, 1981; Crowell, 1981; Ehlig, 1981; Haxel and Tosdal, 1986). Vedder and others (1983) and Champion and others (1984) have suggested correlation of the San Gabriel terrane with the Salinian block, for which paleomagnetic data on Late Cretaceous marine sediments are interpreted to require 2,500 km or more of Late Cretaceous–early Tertiary northward translation relative to stable North America prior to accretion. However, the results of this study indicate that direct correlation of Salinia with the San Gabriel terrane is not possible. The San Gabriel terrane represents the mid-crustal roots of a continental margin magmatic arc as young as 75 Ma, and studies summarized by Ehlig (1981) indicate that mid-crustal juxtaposition with the Baldy terrane was synchronous with deposition of the Salinian block sediments from which the anomalous magnetic inclinations are reported. Thus, no direct correlation of the marine sediments with these mid-crustal terranes is yet possible, so implications of paleomagnetic data for the San Gabriel terrane are unknown. In addition, the suture required by the inferred pre-Eocene collision of the San

Gabriel terrane with North America has not been located in the Mojave Desert (Burchfiel and Davis, 1981). Rather, the close similarity in timing and chemistry of plutonism in the San Gabriel terrane with the Cordilleran magmatic arc of the Sierra Nevada and Mojave Desert regions is suggestive of a parautochthonous origin, regardless of the vergence of underthrusting of the Baldy terrane. Such an origin is further supported by preliminary neodymium isotopic studies (Bennett and DePaolo, 1986), which imply correlation of the San Gabriel terrane with the isotopically distinctive Mojave Desert region of cratonal North America.

Comparison of these results with studies by Powell (1982) and Tosdal (1984, 1986) suggests that the San Gabriel terrane, as depicted in Figure 9, is divisible into two subterranes with distinct Mesozoic structural and magmatic histories. These subterranes are referred to as the northern and southern subterranes in the discussion below. The boundary between these two inferred subterranes is shown as a dashed line in Figure 9, corresponding approximately to the present San Francisquito–Fenner–Clemens Well fault zone (Ehlig, 1981). South of this boundary, the southern subterrane is characterized by exposures of Proterozoic and Mesozoic rocks in the San Gabriel Mountains, where Mesozoic arc plutonism at mid-crustal depths preceded underthrusting by Pelona-type schists of the Baldy terrane. North of the inferred boundary, studies by Powell (1982) and Tosdal (1984, 1986) in the northern subterrane indicate that Mesozoic plutonism and deformation occurred at upper crustal levels. Thus, a significant contrast in exposed crustal depth is present across this boundary, yet Powell (1982) and Tosdal (1986) suggested that correlative Proterozoic and Triassic rocks of the San Gabriel terrane are present on both sides.

Powell (1982) suggested that the San Gabriel terrane in the northern subterrane lies structurally above the Joshua Tree terrane, composed of Precambrian crystalline basement and overlying late Precambrian and Paleozoic(?) supracrustal rocks. Metamorphism of the lower-plate Joshua Tree supracrustal sequence, in part coeval with thrust juxtaposition of the two terranes, occurred at pressures of 3 to 4 kbar (11 to 15 km). Studies of Mesozoic plutonic rocks in the northern part of the Joshua Tree terrane (Brand, 1985) are also suggestive of exposure of relatively shallow crustal levels (3 kbar, 11 km). The age of juxtaposition is pre–Middle Jurassic, and may be Late Triassic or Early Jurassic (R. E. Powell, 1987, personal communication). Structural studies (Powell, 1982; Postlethwaite and Jacobson, 1986) suggest west-vergent thrusting and associated folding. However, as originally noted by Powell (1982), no source region for the allochthon is present to the east in the present structural configuration. Powell suggested that this contradiction may reflect the presence of a strand or strands of the Mojave-Sonora megashear (Anderson and Silver, 1979) between the Joshua Tree terrane and cratonal rocks to the north, but has more recently suggested that the Joshua Tree terrane may be relatively autochthonous North American crust (R. E. Powell, 1987, personal communication). This suggestion requires a reevaluation of structural evidence bearing on vergence of the Red Cloud thrust; ongoing studies have not yet resulted in a definitive geologic history for this amalgamation event (C. E. Jacobson and C. Postlethwaite, 1987, personal communication).

Tosdal (1984, 1986) suggested that Middle Jurassic shallow-level plutonic and hypabyssal rocks intrude the northern subterrane of the San Gabriel terrane in the Mule and Trigo mountains regions along the California-Arizona border (Fig. 9). These same Middle Jurassic arc rocks form the basement for the McCoy Mountains Formation (Harding and Coney, 1985; Haxel and others, 1985; Tosdal and others, 1989), a weakly metamorphosed Jurassic(?)-Cretaceous supracrustal sequence with cratonal North American provenance affinities. The inference from this study, and that of Powell (1982) for the region to the west, is that the northern subterrane, perhaps at mid-crustal depths as late as Late Triassic time, was emplaced at shallow crustal levels, above Joshua Tree terrane and adjacent to North America, prior to Middle Jurassic arc magmatism.

The nature of the boundary between the northern and southern subterranes is uncertain. Ehlig (1981) suggested that it is principally a strike-slip fault of uncertain, but perhaps large displacement, separating terranes with distinct Mesozoic histories. This can be seen clearly in Figure 1, where Late Cretaceous–Paleocene marine sediments of the San Francisquito Formation are juxtaposed with contemporaneous Pelona Schist along the San Francisquito fault. This relation yields a minimum of 20 km apparent vertical displacement across this fault. A depth contrast of similar or somewhat smaller magnitude is suggested for the Clemens Well fault, although perhaps modified by later extensional faulting between upper- and lower-plate rocks (Jacobson and others, 1987). These relations led Ehlig (1981) to suggest that

this boundary may mark the suture between the San Gabriel terrane and North America. Alternatively, Powell (1982) correlated rocks on both sides with the Proterozoic suite of the San Gabriel terrane. If this correlation is valid, the boundary between the northern and southern subterranes may originally have been a gradational one, reflecting exposure of a range of crustal depths. The original structural relations could have been in part obscured by extensional faulting related to uplift of mid-crustal rocks during or following cessation of subduction, and subsequently modified by strike-slip faulting. The geometric relations of these two subterranes of the San Gabriel terrane are critical to understanding its accretion history, if any, but are not yet refined enough to choose between alternative models.

SUMMARY

The presence of magmatic epidote and aluminous hornblende in metaluminous rocks and calcic garnet and siliceous muscovite in peraluminous rocks suggest mid-crustal (5 to 8 kbar, 20 to 30 km) emplacement depths for Late Triassic and Late Cretaceous plutons in the San Gabriel Mountains. These rocks were subsequently underthrust by Pelona Schist in a Late Cretaceous–Paleocene subduction event. Similarities in timing and geochemical character suggest that upper-plate plutonic rocks represent mid-crustal levels of an arc similar to, if not the extension of, the eastern Cordilleran Mesozoic arc exposed to the north in the Mojave Desert and Sierra Nevada regions. The mid-crustal Mesozoic history documented here does not appear to characterize all the San Gabriel terrane, as defined on the basis of a distinctive suite of Proterozoic and Triassic rocks. The recognition of distinct differences in crustal depth and geologic history allows subdivision of the San Gabriel terrane into two subterranes. The southern subterrane is characterized by the mid-crustal Mesozoic history documented here. The northern subterrane, studied by Powell (1982) and Tosdal (1984, 1986), appears to have resided at significantly shallower levels throughout most, if not all, of Mesozoic time. A more refined understanding of the distinctions between these subterranes should result in significant clarification of the mechanism(s) of amalgamation of terranes in southeastern California and their mode and timing of juxtaposition with cratonal North America.

ACKNOWLEDGMENTS

This study was made possible through the support and encouragement of J. L. Anderson. Discussions with P. Ehlig, G. Haxel, T. Hoisch, C. Jacobson, R. E. Powell, W. Thomas, R. Tosdal, E. Young, and E-an Zen helped refine the arguments presented. R. Jones facilitated collection of microprobe data. I appreciate the reviews and suggestions of G. A. Davis, P. Ehlig, J. Hammarstrom, C. Jacobson, and W. Thomas. Financial support was provided by NSF Grant EAR-8618285, a Penrose grant from the Geological Society of America, and the Graduate Student Research Fund of the Department of Geological Sciences, University of Southern California.

REFERENCES CITED

Anderson, J. L., 1980, Mineral equilibria and crystallization conditions in the Late Precambrian Wolf River rapakivi massif, Wisconsin: American Journal of Science, v. 280, p. 289–332.

——, 1985, Contrasting depths of "core complex" mylonitization; Barometric evidence: Geological Society of America Abstracts with Programs, v. 17, p. 337.

——, 1989, Core complexes of the Mojave–Sonoran Desert; Conditions of plutonism, mylonitization, and decompression, in Ernst, W. G., ed., Metamorphism and crustal evolution of the western conterminous U.S., Rubey Volume 7: Englewood Cliffs, New Jersey, Prentice-Hall, (in press).

Anderson, J. L., and Rowley, M. C., 1981, Synkinematic intrusion of two-mica and associated metaluminous granitoids, Whipple Mountains, California: Canadian Mineralogist, v. 19, p. 83–101.

Anderson, J. L., Cullers, R. L., and Van Schmus, W. R., 1980, Anorogenic metaluminous and peraluminous granite plutonism in the mid-Proterozoic of Wisconsin, U.S.A.: Contributions to Mineralogy and Petrology, v. 74, p. 311–328.

Anderson, T. H., and Silver, L. T., 1979, The role of the Mojave–Sonora megashear in the tectonic evolution of northern Sonora: Geological Society of America Cordilleran Section Guidebook, p. 59–68.

Barth, A. P., 1984, Petrology of the Mount Lowe Intrusion, San Gabriel Mountains, California: Geological Society of America Abstracts with Programs, v. 16, p. 268.

Beckerman, G. M., Robinson, J. P., and Anderson, J. L., 1982, The Teutonia batholith; A large intrusive complex of Jurassic and Cretaceous age in the eastern Mojave Desert, California, in Frost, E. G., and Martin, D. L., eds., Mesozoic–Cenozoic tectonic evolution of the Colorado River region, California, Arizona, and Nevada: San Diego, California, Cordilleran Publishers, p. 205–221.

Bennett, V., and DePaolo, D. J., 1986, Implications of Nd isotopes for the crustal history of southern California: Geological Society of America Abstracts with Programs, v. 18, p. 84.

Best, M. G., Armstrong, R. L., Graustein, W. C., Embree, G. F., and Ahlborn, R. C., 1974, Mica granites of the Kern Mountains pluton, eastern White Pine County, Nevada; Remobilized basement of the Cordilleran miogeosyncline?: Geological Society of America Bulletin, v. 85, p. 1277–1286.

Brand, J. H., 1985, Mesozoic alkalic monzonites and peraluminous monzogranites of the northern portion of Joshua Tree National Monument, southern California [M.S. thesis]: Los Angeles, University of Southern California, 187 p.

Burchfiel, B. C., and Davis, G. A., 1981, Mojave Desert and environs, in Ernst, W. G., ed., The geotectonic development of California: Englewood Cliffs, New Jersey, Prentice-Hall, p. 217–252.

Carter, B., and Silver, L. T., 1971, Post-emplacement structural history of the San Gabriel anorthosite complex: Geological Society of America Abstracts with Programs, v. 3, p. 92–93.

Champion, D. E., Howell, D. G., and Gromme, C. S., 1984, Paleomagnetic and geologic data indicating 2,500 km of northward displacement for the Salinian and related terranes, California: Journal of Geophysical Research, v. 89, p. 7736–7752.

Chen, J. H., and Moore, J. G., 1979, Late Jurassic Independence dike swarm in eastern California: Geology, v. 7, p. 129–133.

Cox, B. F., Powell, R. E., Hinkle, M. E., and Lipton, D. A., 1983, Mineral resource potential of the Pleasant View roadless area, Los Angeles County, California: U.S. Geological Survey Miscellaneous Field Studies Map MF–1649–A, scale 1:62,500.

Crowell, J. C., 1962, Displacement along the San Andreas fault, California: Geological Society of America Special Paper 71, 61 p.

——, 1975, San Andreas fault in southern California, in Crowell, J. C., ed., San Andreas fault in Southern California: California Division of Mines and Geology Special Report 118, p. 7–27.

——, 1981, An outline of the geologic history of southeastern California, in Ernst, W. G., ed., The geotectonic development of California: Englewood Cliffs, New Jersey, Prentice-Hall, p. 583–600.

Czamanske, G. K., Ishihara, S., and Atkin, S. A., 1981, Chemistry of rockforming minerals of the Cretaceous–Paleocene batholith in southwestern Japan and implications for magma genesis: Journal of Geophysical Research, v. 86, p. 10431–10469.

Davis, G. A., Anderson, J. L., Frost, E. G., and Shackelford, T. J., 1980, Mylonitization and detachment faulting in the Whipple–Buckskin–Rawhide Mountains terrane, southeastern California and western Arizona, in Crittenden, M., Davis, G. H., and Coney, P. J., eds., Metamorphic core complexes: Geological Society of America Memoir 153, p. 79–129.

Dodge, F.C.W., Papike, J. J., and Mays, R. E., 1968, Hornblendes from granitic rocks of the central Sierra Nevada batholith, California: Journal of Petrology, v. 9, p. 378–410.

Ehlig, P. L., 1981, Origin and tectonic history of the San Gabriel Mountains, central Transverse Ranges, in Ernst, W. G., ed., The geotectonic development of California: Englewood Cliffs, New Jersey, Prentice-Hall, p. 254–283.

Ehlig, P. L., Ehlert, K. W., and Crowe, B. W., 1975, Offset of the Upper Miocene Caliente and Mint Canyon formations along the San Gabriel and San Andreas faults, in Crowell, J. C., ed., San Andreas fault in Southern California: California Division of Mines and Geology Special Report 118, p. 83–92.

Ganguly, J., and Saxena, S. K., 1984, Mixing properties of aluminosilicate garnets; Constraints from natural and experimental data, and applications to geothermo-barometry: American Mineralogist, v. 61, p. 88–97.

Ghent, E. D., 1976, Plagioclase–garnet–Al_2SiO_5–quartz; A potential geobarometer–geothermometer: American Mineralogist, v. 61, p. 710–714.

Ghent, E. D., and Stout, M. Z., 1981, Geobarometry and geothermometry of plagioclase–biotite–garnet–muscovite assemblages: Contributions to Mineralogy and Petrology, v. 76, p. 92–97.

Graham, C. M., and England, P. C., 1976, Thermal regimes and regional metamorphism in the vicinity of overthrust faults; An example of shear heating and inverted metamorphic zonation from southern California: Earth and Planetary Science Letters, v. 31, p. 142–152.

Graham, C. M., and Powell, R., 1984, A garnet–hornblende geothermometer; Calibration, testing, and application to the Pelona schist, southern California: Journal of Metamorphic Geology, v. 2, p. 13–31.

Green, T. H., 1977, Garnet in silicic liquids and its possible use as a P–T indicator: Contributions to Mineralogy and Petrology, v. 65, p. 59–67.

Guidotti, C. V., 1978, Muscovite and K-feldspar from two-mica adamellite in northwestern Maine; Compositions and petrogenetic implications: American Mineralogist, v. 63, p. 750–753.

Hammarstrom, J. M., and Zen, E-an, 1986, Aluminum in hornblende; An empirical igneous geobarometer: American Mineralogist, v. 71, p. 1297–1313.

Harding, L. E., and Coney, P. J., 1985, The geology of the McCoy Mountains Formation, southeastern California and southwestern Arizona: Geological Society of America Bulletin, v. 96, p. 755–769.

Hawthorne, F. C., 1981, Crystal chemistry of the amphiboles: Mineralogical Society of America Reviews in Mineralogy, v. 9A, p. 1–102.

Haxel, G. B., and Tosdal, R. M., 1986, Significance of the Orocopia schist and Chocolate Mountains thrust in the late Mesozoic tectonic evolution of the southeastern California–southwestern Arizona region [extended abstract]: Arizona Geological Society Digest, v. 16, p. 52–61.

Haxel, G. B., Tosdal, R. M., and Dillon, J., 1985, Tectonic setting and lithology of the Winterhaven Formation; A new Mesozoic stratigraphic unit in southeasternmost California and southwestern Arizona: U.S. Geological Survey Bulletin 1599, 19 p.

Hodges, K. V., and Crowley, P. D., 1985, Error estimation and empirical geothermobarometry for pelitic systems: American Mineralogist, v. 70, p. 702–709.

Holdaway, M. J., 1971, Stability of andalusite and the aluminum silicate phase diagram: American Journal of Science, v. 271, p. 97–131.

——, 1972, Thermal stability of Al-Fe epidote as a function of f_{O_2} and Fe content: Contributions to Mineralogy and Petrology, v. 37, p. 307–340.

Hollister, L. S., Grissom, G. C., Peters, E. K., Stowell, H. H., and Sisson, V. B., 1987, Confirmation of the empirical correlation of Al in hornblende with pressure of solidification of calc-alkaline plutons: American Mineralogist,

v. 72, p. 231–239.

Huang, W. L., and Wyllie, P. J., 1981, Phase relationships of S-type granite with H$_2$O to 35 kbar; Muscovite granite from Harney Peak, South Dakota: Journal of Geophysical Research, v. 86, p. 10515–10529.

Jacobson, C. E., 1983, Structural geology of the Pelona schist and the Vincent thrust, San Gabriel Mountains, California: Geological Society of America Bulletin, v. 94, p. 753–767.

Jacobson, C. E., Dawson, M. R., and Postlethwaite, C. E., 1987, Evidence for late stage normal slip on the Orocopia thrust and implications for the Vincent–Chocolate Mountains thrust problem: Geological Society of America Abstracts with Programs, v. 19, p. 714.

Joseph, S. E., Criscione, J. J., and Davis, T. E., 1978, Rb-Sr geochronology and geochemistry of the Lowe granodiorite, central San Gabriel Mountains, California: Geological Society of America Abstracts with Programs, v. 10, p. 111.

Kerrick, D. M., 1972, Experimental determination of muscovite + quartz stability with P(H$_2$O) ⩽ P(total): American Journal of Science, v. 272, p. 946–958.

Lindsley, D. H., 1973, Delimitation of the hematite-ilmenite miscibility gap: Geological Society of America Bulletin, v. 84, p. 657–662.

Liou, J. G., 1973, Synthesis and stability relations of epidote, Ca$_2$Al$_2$FeSi$_3$O$_{12}$ (OH): Journal of Petrology, v. 14, p. 381–413.

Massonne, H.-J., and Schreyer, W., 1983, A new experimental phengite barometer and its application to a Variscan subduction zone at the southern margin of the Rhenohercynicum: Terra Cognita, v. 3, p. 18.

——, 1985, Phengite barometry in assemblages with kyanite, Mg-rich silicates, and a SiO$_2$ phase: Terra Cognita, v. 5, p. 432.

Miller, C. F., 1977, Alkali-rich monzonites, California; Origin of near silica-saturated alkaline rocks and their significance in the calc-alkaline batholith belt of California [Ph.D. thesis]: Los Angeles, University of California, 283 p.

——, 1978, Early alkalic plutonism in the calc-alkaline batholithic belt of California: Geology, v. 5, p. 685–688.

Miller, C. F., and Bradfish, L. J., 1980, An inner Cordilleran belt of muscovite-bearing plutons: Geology, v. 8, p. 412–416.

Miller, C. F., and Stoddard, E. F., 1981, The role of manganese in the paragenesis of magmatic garnet; An example from the Old Woman–Piute Range, California: Journal of Geology, v. 89, p. 233–246.

Miller, C. F., Stoddard, E. F., Bradfish, L. J., and Dollasse, W. A., 1981, Composition of plutonic muscovite; Genetic implications: Canadian Mineralogist, v. 19, p. 25–34.

Miller, F. K., and Morton, D. M., 1980, Potassium-argon geochronology of the eastern Transverse Ranges and southern Mojave Desert, southern California: U.S. Geological Survey Professional Paper 1152, 30 p.

Monier, G., and Robert, J.-L., 1986, Titanium in muscovites from two-mica granites; Substitutional mechanism and partition with coexisting biotites: Neues Jarbuch für Mineralogie Abhandlungen, v. 153, p. 147–161.

Moore, J. G., and Hopson, C. A., 1961, The Independence dike swarm in eastern California: American Journal of Science, v. 259, p. 241–259.

Nabelek, C. R., and Lindsley, D. H., 1985, Tetrahedral Al in amphibole; A potential thermometer for some mafic rocks: Geological Society of America Abstracts with Programs, v. 17, p. 673.

Naney, M. T., 1983, Phase equilibria of rock-forming ferromagnesian silicates in granitic systems: American Journal of Science, v. 283, p. 993–1033.

Newton, R. C., and Haselton, H. T., 1981, Thermodynamics of the garnet-plagioclase–Al$_2$SiO$_5$–quartz geobarometer, *in* Newton, R. C., Navrotsky, A., and Wood, B. J., eds., Thermodynamics of minerals and melts: New York, Springer-Verlag, p. 129–145.

Noyes, H. J., Wones, D. R., and Frey, F. A., 1983, A tale of two plutons; Petrographic and mineralogic constraints on the petrogenesis of the Red Lake and Eagle Lake plutons, central Sierra Nevada, California: Journal of Geology, v. 91, p. 353–379.

Phillips, G. N., 1980, Water activity changes across an amphibolite-granulite facies transition, Broken Hill, Australia: Contributions to Mineralogy and Petrology, v. 75, p. 377–386.

Postlethwaite, C. E., and Jacobson, C. E., 1986, Structural analysis of the Red Cloud thrust system, eastern Transverse Ranges, California: Geological So-

ciety of America Abstracts with Programs, v. 18, p. 172.

Powell, R., 1978, Equilibrium thermodynamics in petrology: London, Harper and Row, 284 p.

Powell, R., and Evans, J. A., 1983, A new geobarometer for the assemblage biotite–muscovite–chlorite–quartz: Journal of Metamorphic Geology, v. 1, p. 331–336.

Powell, R. E., 1982, Crystalline basement terranes in the southern eastern Transverse Ranges, California, *in* Cooper, J. D., ed., Geologic excursions in the Transverse Ranges, southern California: Geological Society of America Cordilleran Section Guidebook, p. 109–136.

Rowley, M. C., 1981, Intrusion and synkinematic metamorphism of peraluminous and metaluminous granitoids in the autochthon of the central Whipple Mountains, southeastern California [M.S. thesis]: Los Angeles, University of Southeastern California, 144 p.

Silver, L. T., 1968, Pre-Cretaceous basement rocks and their bearing on large-scale displacements in the San Andreas fault system, *in* Dickinson, W. R., and Grantz, A., eds., Proceedings of a Conference on Geologic Problems of the San Andreas Fault System: Stanford, California, Stanford University Publications in the Geological Sciences, v. 11, p. 279–280.

——, 1971, Problems of crystalline rocks of the Transverse Ranges: Geological Society of America Abstracts with Programs, v. 3, p. 193–194.

——, 1982, Evolution of crystalline rock terrains of the Transverse Ranges, southern California: Geological Society of America Abstracts with Programs, v. 14, p. 234.

Speer, J. A., 1984, Micas in igneous rocks, *in* Bailey, S. W., ed., Micas: Mineralogical Society of America Reviews in Mineralogy, v. 13, p. 299–356.

Stern, C. R., and Wyllie, P. J., 1978, Phase compositions through crystallization intervals in basalt–andesite–H$_2$O at 30 kbar with implications for subduction zone magmas: American Mineralogist, v. 63, p. 641–663.

Stern, C. R., Huang, W., and Wyllie, P. J., 1975, Basalt–andesite–rhyolite–H$_2$O; Crystallization intervals with excess H$_2$O and H$_2$O undersaturated liquidus surfaces to 35 kilobars, with implications for magma genesis: Earth and Planetary Science Letters, v. 28, p. 189–196.

Stormer, J. C., 1975, A practical two feldspar geothermometer: American Mineralogist, v. 60, p. 667–674.

Tosdal, R. M., 1984, Tectonic significance of the late Mesozoic Mule Mountains thrust, southeast California and southwest Arizona: Geological Society of America Abstracts with Programs, v. 16, p. 676.

——, 1986, Mesozoic ductile deformations in the southern Dome Rock Mountains, northern Trigo Mountains, Trigo Peaks and Livingston Hills, southwestern Arizona, and Mule Mountains, southeastern California: Arizona Geological Society Digest, v. 16, p. 62–71.

Tosdal, R. M., Haxel, G. B., and Wright, J. E., 1989, Jurassic geology of the Sonoran Desert region, southern Arizona, southeastern California, and northernmost Sonora; Construction of a continental margin magmatic arc: Arizona Geological Society Digest (in press).

Vedder, J. G., Howell, D. G., and McLean, H., 1983, Stratigraphy, sedimentation, and tectonic accretion of exotic terranes, southern Coast ranges, California, *in* Watkins, J. S., and Drake, C. L., eds., Studies in continental margin geology: American Association of Petroleum Geologists Memoir 34, p. 471–496.

Velde, B., 1965, Phengitic micas; Synthesis, stability, and natural occurrence: American Journal of Science, v. 263, p. 886–913.

Wright, W. I., 1938, The composition and occurrence of garnets: American Mineralogist, v. 23, p. 436–449.

Zen, E-an, 1985, Implications of magmatic epidote-bearing plutons on crustal evolution in the accreted terranes of northwestern North America: Geology, v. 13, p. 266–269.

——, 1986, Magmatic epidote-bearing plutons in the western Cordillera and their tectonic significance; Abstracts, Rubey Symposium 7: Los Angeles, University of California.

Zen, E-an, and Hammarstrom, J. M., 1984, Magmatic epidote and its petrologic significance: Geology, v. 12, p. 515–518.

MANUSCRIPT SUBMITTED JULY 8, 1987
REVISED MANUSCRIPT SUBMITTED NOVEMBER 23, 1987
MANUSCRIPT ACCEPTED BY THE SOCIETY FEBRUARY 7, 1989

Printed in U.S.A.

Geological Society of America
Memoir 174
1990

Chapter 4

Middle to upper crustal plutonic construction of a magmatic arc; An example from the Whipple Mountains metamorphic core complex

J. Lawford Anderson
Department of Geological Sciences, University of Southern California, Los Angeles, California 90089-0740
Robert L. Cullers
Department of Geology, Kansas State University, Manhattan, Kansas 66506

ABSTRACT

Tectonic decompression of the Whipple Mountains core complex of southeastern California provides a unique window into contrasting crustal levels of magmatic arc development within the Cordilleran orogen. Before uplift of the complex, middle and Late Cretaceous lower plate plutons were emplaced into the crustal section when it resided in the middle crust (depths >27 to 33 km). More shallow emplaced Tertiary plutons, dikes, and sills were intruded as the crustal section was transported upward to a depth of 16 km at approximately 26 Ma, and to less than 6 km by 17 to 19 Ma during final stages of core complex mylonitic and detachment history. Thus, the Whipple crustal section exposes both middle and upper crustal plutonic elements of an evolving magmatic arc. Deep-seated Cretaceous plutons are composed of unusually calcic and Sr-enriched granitic magmas, including two-mica granites that have no compositional counterpart in this region of the Cordillera. Younger plutonism is characterized by more potassic felsic suites and mafic magmas.

The oldest plutons compose the 89-Ma Whipple Wash suite, a collection of eight or more granitic intrusions that are marginally metaluminous to moderately peraluminous and include a number of garnet-bearing, two-mica granites. All are low K, high Ca, and high Sr (>800 ppm), and are concluded to have been derived from a high degree of melting of a continental margin, arc-derived, calcic graywacke in equilibrium with an eclogitic residuum. Likewise, primitive members of the high-Sr (>1,000 ppm), 73-Ma Axtel quartz diorite are proposed to have been derived from an eclogitic basalt having an original composition of an altered and/or enriched mid-ocean ridge basalt. Subsequent fractional crystallization (48 percent) of plagioclase, hornblende, and biotite yielded the remainder of the Axtel series.

Coeval with core complex mylonitization at 26 Ma, the complex was pervaded by swarms of low-angle dikes and sills of biotite tonalite and trondhjemitic aplite. The tonalite is compositionally restricted and appears to image the same source as that which formed the Whipple Wash suite some 60 m.y. earlier. The aplites form a coherent group of leucocratic and sodic (Na_2O to 7.7 wt. %) intrusions that are strikingly depleted in rare earth elements (to subchrondritic values) and other compatible elements.

The 10-km-wide Chambers Well dike swarm intruded the western portions of the

Anderson, J. L., and Cullers, R. L., 1990, Middle to upper crustal plutonic construction of a magmatic arc; An example from the Whipple Mountains metamorphic core complex, *in* Anderson, J. L., ed., The nature and origin of Cordilleran magmatism: Boulder, Colorado, Geological Society of America Memoir 174.

complex during the Miocene and include an impressive suite of late kinematic andesite to dacite and postkinematic (ca. 21 Ma) diabase. The andesites are inferred to have been derived by partial melting of a partly eclogitized amphibolite; the dacites subsequently evolved by a combined fractionation and crustal assimilation process. The younger diabase dikes represent a separate magma system that formed from limited partial melting of enriched mantle.

The last major plutonic event is represented by the 19-Ma War Eagle complex, a composite intrusion consisting largely of clinopyroxene-hornblende diorite and hornblende-biotite quartz diorite. The most primitive rocks are olivine gabbro having a composition consistent with small degrees of partial melting (ca. 5 percent) of a chondritic mantle; the remainder of the complex formed by fractionation of a clinopyroxene, olivine, and plagioclase residue. The War Eagle complex was subsequently intruded by a biotite-hornblende granodiorite, the most potassic and least Sr-rich member of the compositionally evolving assemblage of magmas to be emplaced within the core complex.

Most of the plutonic complexes of the inner Cordillera were derived from crustal melting. However, the plutonism in the Whipple core complex is unlike the norm both in composition and inferred origin. Some crustal component is evident in the intermediate to felsic units, yet the inferred sources of calcic graywacke, eclogitic to amphibolitic basalt, and enriched to chondritic mantle signal a subduction setting for the origin of the magmatism.

INTRODUCTION

As in most metamorphic core complexes of the southwest U.S., the lower plate of the Whipple Mountains core complex of southeastern California is a regionally deformed Tertiary mylonitic terrane composed of Proterozoic crystalline rocks pervasively intruded by plutons, dikes, and sills ranging in age from Mesozoic to middle Tertiary. Recent thermobarometric studies (Anderson, 1985, 1988; Anderson and others, 1988) have demonstrated that the Whipple complex has Mesozoic mid-crustal roots; the older plutons represent deep-seated emplacement conditions that gave way to sequentially shallower crustal levels for younger stages of magmatism and deformation. The plutonic history has a wide range of emplacement depths. The older plutons, of middle to Late Cretaceous age, were emplaced at middle crustal levels more than 28 km deep, as evidenced by unusually calcic garnet and siliceous muscovite in the peraluminous two-mica granites and aluminous hornblende in metaluminous quartz diorites. Middle Tertiary pluton emplacement and regional development of a low-angle mylonitic fabric occurred at shallower levels at an estimated depth of 16 ± 5 km. Emplacement of postkinematic Miocene plutons occurred when the same crustal section was at upper crustal levels (ca. 5 to 6 km) in route to the near-surface conditions (<5 km) that characterized latest detachment faulting at 14 to 15 Ma. The implication is that the lower plate crystalline assemblages of the Whipple Mountains provide a rare view into the magmatic construction and tectonic evolution of both the middle and upper crust.

Whereas the Mesozoic intrusives are prekinematic to deformation-related core complex mylonitization, Tertiary plutons are both synkinematic and postkinematic to the deformation. In the Whipple Mountains, the age of mylonitization has been constrained by U-Pb (zircon) dating of synkinematic and postkinematic plutons (Wright and others, 1986) and $^{40}Ar/^{39}Ar$ dating of the mylonitic gneisses (DeWitt and others, 1986); the conclusion is that mylonitic deformation ongoing at 26 ± 5 Ma had ended by 19 ± 2 Ma. Subsequent detachment faulting, which produced the overlying and regionally extensive Whipple detachment fault, is considered to have occurred from 14 to 18 Ma (Davis and others, 1980, 1982, 1986). Although the Tertiary tectonic history seemingly dominates this core complex, the Phanerozoic evolution originated in the late Mesozoic. With ages provided by Wright and others (1986) and DeWitt and others (1986), the succession of plutonic and metamorphic events includes: (1) intrusion of the granitic Whipple Wash suite at 89 ± 3 Ma; (2) emplacement of the Axtel quartz diorite at 73 ± 3 Ma, (3) regional metamorphism and ductile deformation at 69 ± 8 Ma; (4) regional mylonitization intrusion of numerous synkinematic biotite tonalite and trondhjemitic aplite sills at 26 ± 5 Ma; (5) emplacement of the late synkinematic to postkinematic Miocene Chambers Well dike swarm, the younger members having an age of 21 ± 2 Ma; (6) emplacement of the postkinematic War Eagle gabbro-quartz diorite complex at 19 ± 2 Ma; and (7) intrusion of a post–War Eagle granodiorite at 16 to 19 Ma.

Descriptions of the regional and tectonic setting of the Whipple Mountains core complex were given in Anderson and others (1979), Davis and others (1980, 1982, 1986), and Davis (1988); the conditions of plutonism and mylonitization were reported in Anderson (1981, 1985, 1988), Anderson and Rowley (1981), and Anderson and others (1988).

The objective of this paper is to outline the petrogenetic evolution of the Mesozoic and younger magmatic suites as a

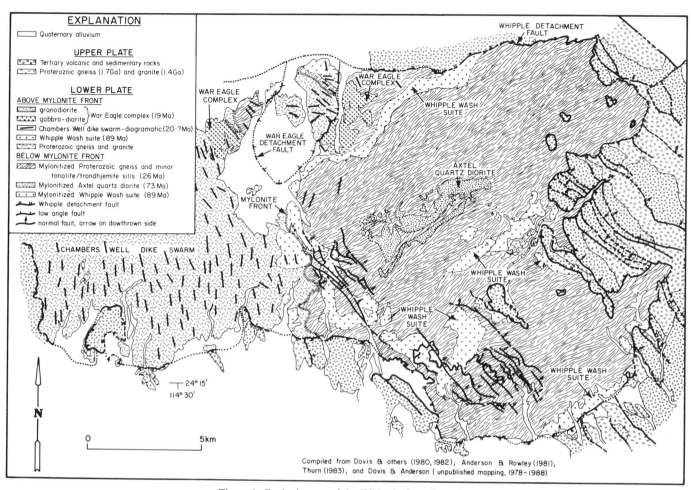

Figure 1. Geologic map of the Whipple Core Complex.

function of crustal depth. Anderson and Rowley (1981) previously described most of these intrusive events; this study builds on that work.

DESCRIPTION OF PLUTONIC SUITES

The host rocks for the Mesozoic and Tertiary intrusive units of the Whipple lower plate complex are a layered Proterozoic crystalline assemblage presumed to be approximately 1.7 b.y. old, based on U-Pb dating of similar rocks exposed elsewhere in southeastern California, including those of the upper plate of the Whipple detachment fault (J. Wright, personal communication, 1986; Anderson and others, in preparation). The most common lithology is a banded quartzo-feldspathic biotite gneiss that is locally migmatitic. The gneiss is interlayered with amphibolite and lesser amounts of pelitic gneiss containing garnet, biotite, muscovite, and aluminosilicate (kyanite at deeper structural levels, sillimanite at higher structural levels). Deformed sills of alkali feldspar–megacrystic granite (augen gneiss) locally intrude the section and have been dated by S. Bowring (personal communication, 1987) at 1.41 ± 0.01 Ga (U/Pb, zircon). All these units

are foliated and contain elements of the both steeply dipping, Mesozoic ductile fabric and the Tertiary mylonitic fabric.

Whipple Wash Suite

On the basis of field relations, Anderson and Rowley (1981) and Rowley (1981) defined two generations of marginally metaluminous to peraluminous granitic plutons, and concluded that the younger set was synkinematic to core complex mylonitization. Subsequent field and isotopic work has shown that all plutons of this suite are older than that deformation. Eight plutons have been recognized, which we collectively term the Whipple Wash suite after the usually dry wash that transects most of their exposures. Despite field evidence for two generations, all have an equivalent isotopic age of 89 ± 3 Ma. Moreover, the plutons, though not strictly comagmatic, are sufficiently similar in composition to allow treatment as one magmatic entity. The plutons occur in the upper two-thirds of the more than 3.9-km-thick mylonitic section of the Whipple lower plate (Fig. 1) as "sills" or low-angle intrusive sheets up to 0.5 km thick, and are compositionally stacked with (1) leucocratic, weakly metaluminous

intrusives of porphyritic biotite granodiorite, biotite-sphene granodiorite, and biotite leucotonalite composing the uppermost structural levels and (2) peraluminous intrusives (listed in descending
structural horizon) of two-mica granodiorite, garnet–two-mica
granodiorite, garnet-biotite granodiorite, and two-mica tonalite
occurring at deeper structural levels. All are mylonitically deformed, and parts of some of the intrusions also contain the
earlier Late Cretaceous metamorphic fabric. In addition to the
"sills," two small discordant plutons of leucocratic two-mica
monzogranite also occur, one structurally beneath the above-
described intrusions, and another above and marginal to the
upper limit of mylonitization (the "mylonite front" of Davis and
others, 1980) in the southwestern part of the range (Fig. 1).

Because Anderson and Rowley (1981) described these plutons in detail, the description presented here will focus on only
their intrinsic features. Compositionally, the suite spans a silica
range from 61.1 to 73.4 weight percent. Granodiorite is the dominant mode; the rocks range modally from calc-alkaline tonalite
to monzogranite (Fig. 2). Although mylonitization has affected
the composition of mineral phases in these plutons, relict igneous
compositions are preserved in most porphyroclasts. Compared to
other two-mica granites, the mineralogy of the Whipple Wash
suite is unusual in the siliceous nature of the plutonic muscovite
and the calcic character of the garnet (Anderson, 1988). Relict,
primary muscovite occurs as porphyroclasts and is conspicuously
high in Ti as is typical of other plutonic muscovites (Anderson
and Rowley, 1981). On an 11 oxygen formula basis, the mica
contains an average Si content of 3.16 ± 0.04 atoms, leading to
an average muscovite mole fraction of 0.58, the remainder being
mostly composed of Mg-celadonite, ferrimuscovite, and a Ti end
member. Garnet composes up to 4.0 percent of three of the
plutons and is uniformly enriched in grossular (18 to 24 mole
percent) and spessartine (21 to 32 mole percent) components.
The mineral compositions are consistent with crystallization at
pressures greater than 7.6 kbar (perhaps greater than 9 kbar by
some thermobarometric calibrations) at $746 \pm 55 \, °C$ (Anderson
and others, 1988). Such high pressures are suggestive of the occurrence of magmatic epidote (Zen and Hammarstrom, 1984),
and porphyroclasts of this phase, some containing cores of allanite, are common in most of the plutons. However, the severe
mylonitic deformation precludes any textural-based conclusion
that the epidote is magmatic in origin.

Axtel quartz diorite

The Axtel quartz diorite is the structurally deepest intrusion
in the Whipple complex, forming one to three coalescing sills that
underlie the highest elevations of the range, including Axtel Point,
the highest peak of the range after which the intrusion is named.
The composite thickness of the pluton is approximately 0.5 km.
The pluton is uniformly strongly mylonitized and contains distinctive, large tension gashes oriented near orthogonal to the low-
angle mylonitic foliation and lineation and infilled with
orthoclase and actinolitic hornblende. Modally, the pluton ranges

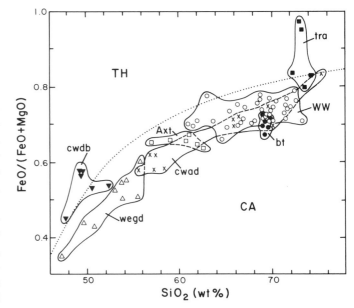

Figure 2. FeO/(FeO + MgO) versus silica for Mesozoic to Tertiary
intrusives of the Whipple core complex. Unit designations: WW =
Whipple Wash suite, Axt = Axtel quartz diorite, bt = biotite tonalite, tra
= trondhjemitic aplite, cwad = Chambers Well andesite to dacite, cwdb =
Chambers Well diabase, wegd = War Eagle gabbro/diorite. Calc-
alkaline and tholeiitic division from Miyashiro (1974).

from biotite-hornblende quartz diorite to granodiorite (Rowley,
1981), with a silica range of 57.0 to 62.6 weight percent.

Although Tertiary mylonitization has led to metamorphic
growth of new feldspars, amphibole, and biotite, relict igneous
compositions of these phases are well preserved. The original
amphibole, a pargasitic hornblende, is unusually aluminous (12.2
to 13.1 weight percent Al_2O_3), consistent with deep-seated conditions of crystallization which Anderson and others (1988) estimated to be at 7.9 ± 0.3 kbar. Epidote porphyroclasts are
common, but as in the Whipple Wash intrusions, any conclusion
as to this phase being of magmatic origin is not possible due to
subsequent recrystallization coincident with mylonitization.

Synkinematic intrusions

The entire 3.9-km-thick mylonitic section of the core complex is pervasively intruded by numerous, thin (usually <1 m)
low-angle dikes and sills of Oligocene-Miocene biotite tonalite
and trondhjemitic aplite. We call them synkinematic because
they locally crosscut the mylonitic foliation of the Cretaceous
plutons, but are mylonitized in their own plane of intrusion and
contain the same northeast-southwest–trending and shallow-
plunging lineation.

The tonalite is fine grained, gray, and contains porphyroclasts of relict, oscillatory zoned plagioclase (An_{22-27}) and biotite. The aplite is also fine grained, white, and contains
porphyroclasts of sodic plagioclase (An_{9-13}) and muscovite.

Chambers Well dike swarm

A north-trending, 10-km-wide swarm of steeply dipping dikes intrudes Proterozoic and Mesozoic crystalline rocks in the western part of the range. The swarm represents an impressive magnitude of east-west extension and, within the axial portions, the volume of dikes exceeds that of the host rock several fold. Most of the swarm consists of an andesite to dacite series intruded by a younger set of diabase and rare lamprophyre. Although much of the swarm occurs structurally above the mylonitic front, andesite and dacite dikes near or below the front exhibit a weak to strong mylonitic fabric. In contrast, diabase dikes are post-kinematic to mylonitic deformation. All members of the swarm are cut by the overlying Whipple detachment fault. The andesite-dacite dikes are not dated, but DeWitt and others (1987) have determined an Ar-Ar (hornblende) age from the diabase of 20 ± 1 Ma.

The andesite to dacite suite encompasses a broad silica range of 55.6 to 75.4 weight percent with a phenocryst assemblage changing from PLAG+HB to PLAG+HB+BIO to PLAG+BIO ±SAN with increasing silica. The younger diabase (SiO_2 = 47.6 to 52.5 weight percent) is fine grained, subophitic, and contains plagioclase, clinopyroxene, and late magmatic hornblende.

War Eagle Complex

In the southwestern part of the Whipple Mountains, a large complex of gabbro-diorite and younger granodiorite intrudes Proterozoic gneisses, Cretaceous two-mica granites, and all members of the Chambers Well swarm. Named for the nearby (abandoned) War Eagle Mine, the mafic intrusion is notable in its compositional range and textural variability. Rock types vary from OL(Fo_{75})-CPX-HB gabbro to CPX-HB-BIO diorite to HB-BIO quartz diorite with no apparent systematic zonation except that the gabbro phase occurs on the eastern margin (G. A. Davis, personal communication, 1986). All variants grade into each other with no sharp or crosscutting contacts. The complex is structurally overalin by the younger Whipple detachment fault and is disrupted by a lower plate detachment fault. The rock is undeformed, coarse grained, and changes from equigranular to seriate and porphyritic with increasing silica that ranges from 47.1 to 56.0 weight percent. Olivine occurs as an early phase in only the most mafic members, followed by clinopyroxene. Hornblende is ubiquotous and varies widely in texture, from coarse mantles on olivine and clinopyroxene (gabbroic members) to coarsely prismatic (dioritic members) and poikilitic phenocrysts (quartz diorite members). Some of the hornblende has Al-enriched cores, but all rims against quartz and alkali feldspar are low in alumina and indicative of low pressure during the final stages of emplacment. Crystallization thermobarometry (Anderson and others, 1988) has shown that the complex was emplaced at shallow depths (6 ± 2 km or 1.7 ± 0.5 kbar) over a temperature range of 752 °C (quartz diorite members) to 1040 °C (gabbroic members).

A small pluton of biotite-hornblende undeformed granodiorite cuts the gabbro-diorite complex and represents the youngest phase of plutonic activity in the Whipple core complex. Although not dated, the pluton is inferred to be between 16 and 19 m.y. old, the younger limit being the inferred age of last movement on the overlying Whipple detachment fault. At an average silica content of 69.5 weight percent, the granodiorite appears to be unrelated to the remainder of the War Eagle complex. The rock is medium grained, equigranular, and contains biotite, sphene, and minor hornblende as mafic minerals. Crystallization thermobarometry by Anderson and others (1988) are 739 ± 34 °C at 1.4 ± 0.6 kbar (5.2 ± 2.2 km).

GEOCHEMISTRY

Given that several members of the Whipple lower plate are orthogneisses that have undergone one or two periods of pre-detachment metamorphism and deformation (two periods for plutons of the Whipple Wash suite and the Axtel quartz diorite; one for the Oligocene-Miocene tonalites and trondjemitic aplites), an important consideration is whether their original magmatic compositions have been retained. Severe alteration (chloritization, epidotization) occurs in a chlorite-breccia zone (as described by Davis and others, 1980) that is adjacent to and below the Whipple detachment fault; rock samples from the zone were excluded from this study. Elsewhere the orthogneisses contain an abundance of igneous mineral phases that occur principally as porphyroclasts. Matrix recrystallization has led to the partial subsolidus reequilibration of some mineral phases, but most or all of these reactions can be attributed to closed-system behavior (Anderson, 1988). There is no petrographic evidence of significant chemical mobility, including that of net hydration, below the chlorite-breccia zone. Moreover, inspection of the elemental trends (Figs. 3 and 4) shows that each intrusive unit has a well-defined lineage for all elements, including those that are more prone to mobilization such as K and Rb. Specific exceptions occur for some samples, and those data points are shown with a question mark in Figures 3 and 4. The Rb-Sr isotopic system may be somewhat disturbed (see section on Rb and Sr isotopes), but any isotopic heterogeneity is not shared by the elemental data. Thus we conclude, with the exception of a few aberrant samples, that the data reflect magmatic conditions. Later sections serve to quantitatively test whether these trends are some form of magmatic process.

The entire Whipple intrusive complex is calc-alkaline (Fig. 2), with the exception of the marginally tholeiitic, 20-Ma diabases of the Chambers Well dike swarm. The most striking aspect of the complex is a systematic shift to less calcic and more potassic plutonism with decreasing age and depth of emplacement, indicating a fundamental change in the nature of magmatism at middle to upper crustal levels.

The oldest and most deep-seated part of the complex is represented by the Whipple Wash suite, which is composed of unusually calcic (alkali-lime index of 62), marginally metalumi-

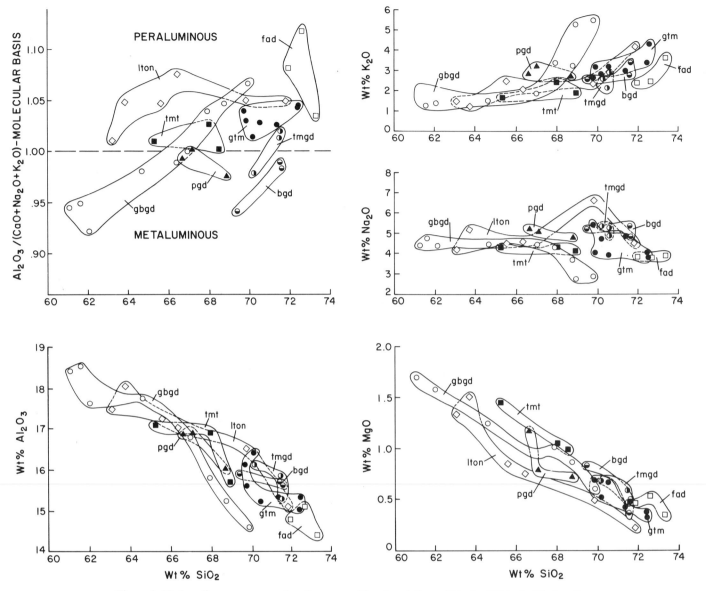

Figure 3. Harker diagrams representing the compositional variation within the Whipple Wash suite. Unit abbreviations: pgd = porphyritic biotite granodiorite, bgd = biotite-sphene granodiorite, tmgd = two-mica granodiorite, gtm = garnet–two-mica granodiorite, tmt = two-mica tonalite, gbgd = garnet-biotite granodiorite, fad = foliated, leucocratic monzogranite, lton = leucocratic biotite tonalite to monzogranite.

nous to peraluminous granitoids with Sr contents in excess of 800 ppm (and up to 1,270 ppm) in the more primitive members. At any level of SiO_2, they have the highest Sr, Na, and Ca and lowest Mg and K contents of the Whipple complex. Although garnet–two-mica granites are common in this region of the Cordillera, none match the unusual chemistry of these granites of the Whipple Mountains. The closest compositional analogs are the two-mica granites of the Idaho batholith (Hyndman, 1983), which were also emplaced at mid-crustal levels (Russell, 1987). Most of the Whipple Wash plutons are modestly peraluminous, with A/CNK values (molecular proportions of $Al_2O_3/CaO + Na_2O + K_2O$) less than 1.1 due to high levels of Na and Ca (Fig.

4). The garnet-biotite granodiorite has the widest range in composition. From 61.1 to 69.8 weight percent SiO_2, abundances of Al, Fe, Mg, Ca, and Na decrease and K and Rb increase. Sr remains elevated near 1,000 ppm (Table 1). The transition to peraluminous occurs at 66 weight percent SiO_2, signaled by the appearance of primary muscovite. Garnet is a conspicuous accessory mineral throughout the pluton.

The alkali-lime indices of subsequent intrusions shift to lower, calc-alkalic values, including ~59 for the Axtel quartz diorite, ~58 for the Chambers Well dike swarm, and ~57 for the War Eagle intrusion. Corresponding changes also occur for other elemental abundances. For a given silica content, Al, Ca, Na, and

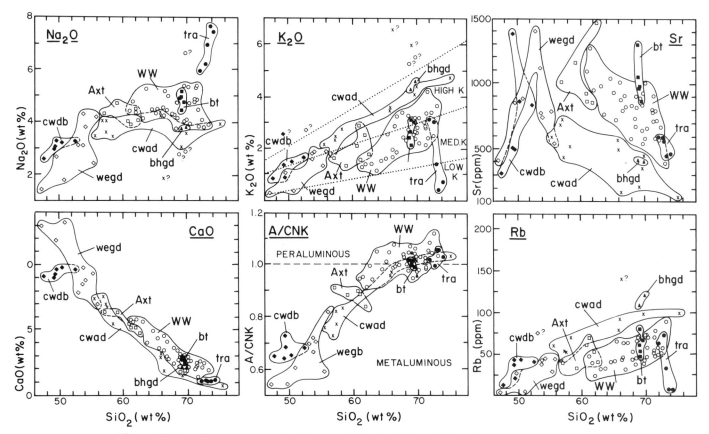

Figure 4. Harker diagrams representing the compositional variation of Mesozoic to Tertiary intrusions of the Whipple core complex. Unit designations as in Figure 2 except for bhgd, which is a biotite, hornblende granodiorite, the youngest pluton of the complex. Question marks designate data that fall outside the normal range of a given unit.

Sr decrease and Fe, Mg, K, and Rb increase from older, more deeply emplaced plutons to younger, more shallow emplaced plutons (Fig. 3 and Table 1).

The Axtel quartz diorite, spanning a silica range of 57.0 to 62.6 weight percent, is fundamentally metaluminous and exhibits a modest depletion in Fe, Mg, and Ca and enrichment in K, Rb, REE, and Th through its limited compositional range. Other elements exhibit no significant change, including the Sr content, which remains elevated at approximately 1,000 ppm.

The synkinematic biotite tonalites and trondhjemitic aplites deviate from the age-dependent trend noted above. The tonalites are compositionally similar to the Whipple Wash suite, and the aplites, being very evolved, have no counterpart elsewhere in the complex. The aplites are marginally peraluminous (muscovite-bearing with A/CNK of ~1.03), depleted in all compatible elements, and exhibit an enrichment in Na_2O (to 7.7 weight percent) and depletion in K_2O (to less than 0.5 weight percent), Sr, and Rb with increasing silica.

The most compositionally extended series (55.6 to 75.4 weight percent SiO_2) is represented by the andesite to dacite members of the Chambers Well dike swarm. Over a silica range of 55.6 to 75.4 weight percent, the dikes are consistently high in K. The dikes are principally metaluminous but become margi-

nally peraluminous in the most evolved members (at silica levels > 69 weight percent). Most elements analyzed in this study, including REE, decrease with increasing silica, except for K, Rb, Th (modest increase), and Ba (no change). Typical of younger members of the Whipple complex, Sr is low, the most primitive members having less than 600 ppm, rising to above 700 ppm (at 57.3 weight percent SiO_2), then decreasing below 500 ppm for more evolved members. Late intrusions of the swarm include medium- to high-K, olivine tholeiite diabase dikes that are compositionally distinct and presumably unrelated to the andesites and dacites. The diabase dikes show a modest increase in silica (47.6 to 52.5 weight percent SiO_2) with a concurrent depletion for only Fe, Mg, and Cr; most other elements increase, including Ti, Al, Na, K, Rb, Hf, and REE.

The War Eagle gabbro-diorite complex, though similar in age to the diabase of the Chambers Well swarm, differs in being calc-alkaline (due to lower Fe/Mg ratios) and depleted in Ti, Al, and alkalies. Most of the intrusion is olivine normative, although two of the nine analyses are marginally nepheline normative and the more felsic members become quartz normative (< 6 percent) at SiO_2 greater than 54 weight percent. From 47.1 to 56.0 weight percent SiO_2, abundances of Fe, Mg, Ca, Sc, and Cr decrease. Cr shows the greatest change, from greater than 1,000 to 44 ppm.

J. L. Anderson and R. L. Cullers

TABLE 1. MAJOR- AND TRACE-ELEMENT DATA

Unit:	pgd	pgd	pgd	bgd	bgd	bgd	tmgd	tmgd	tmgd	tmgd	gtm	gtm	gtm	gtm	gtm
Specimen:	78-53a	78-49b	78-49a	79-10	79-16	79-26	79-183	79-127b	79-43b	79-127a	MR-24	MR-47	WW-6	MR-118	MR-57
weight percent oxides															
SiO_2	66.65	67.08	68.78	69.43	71.62	71.58	66.37	70.20	71.50	71.51	69.72	69.82	70.17	70.51	71.36
TiO_2	0.51	0.37	0.42	0.72	0.25	0.23	0.38	0.36	0.27	0.31	0.36	0.27	0.17	0.31	0.25
Al_2O_3	16.86	16.87	15.97	15.86	15.60	15.66	16.93	16.12	15.82	15.28	16.13	15.59	16.39	15.19	15.30
FeO (total)	2.74	2.29	2.50	2.15	1.42	1.28	2.87	1.66	1.41	1.47	1.47	2.24	1.48	2.08	1.13
MgO	1.16	0.78	0.72	0.82	0.50	0.39	1.25	0.68	0.47	0.59	0.56	0.68	0.51	0.66	0.42
MnO	0.04	0.01	0.01	0.04	0.06	0.01	0.07	0.04	0.02	0.04	0.02	0.11	0.06	0.13	0.01
CaO	2.93	2.79	3.07	3.05	2.33	2.19	4.59	2.67	2.48	2.21	2.06	2.76	2.94	2.65	2.06
Na_2O	5.20	5.03	4.76	5.16	4.85	5.38	4.22	5.35	5.29	4.84	5.41	4.06	4.72	3.95	4.81
K_2O	2.86	3.25	2.73	2.59	3.37	2.77	1.71	2.61	2.12	2.87	2.65	3.18	2.82	3.19	3.00
LOI	0.61	0.62	0.45	0.80	0.38	0.59	0.70	0.49	0.58	0.47	0.70	0.52	0.80	0.45	0.56
Total	99.56	99.09	99.41	100.32	100.38	100.09	99.09	100.18	99.96	99.59	99.08	99.24	100.06	99.12	98.90
parts per million															
Rb	63.6	63.6	45.5	53.2	78.6	47.6	45.1	57.9	55.2	69.4	38.4	72.3	46.5	70.2	50.3
Sr	796	822	823	884	785	716	1017	1010	907	781	842	648	582	660	801
Ba	1114	1171	1344	1101	1458	1141	1066	1410	1242	1430	2909	936	1189	1651	1668

TABLE 1. MAJOR- AND TRACE-ELEMENT DATA
(continued)

Unit:	gtm	tmt	tmt	tmt	fad	fad	fad	gbgd	gbgd	gbgd	gbgd	gbgd	gbgd	gbgd	gbgd
Specimen:	79-241	WW-8	WW-19	79-129	78-47	78-46a	78-46b	MR-165	MR-162	MR-139	79-198	MR-195	MR-194	79-132	79-74
weight percent oxides															
SiO_2	72.45	65.27	67.99	68.51	71.93	72.66	73.37	61.09	61.60	62.05	64.65	66.93	67.90	68.75	69.89
TiO_2	0.17	0.42	0.28	0.28	0.16	0.14	0.16	0.56	0.44	0.51	0.47	0.34	0.52	0.28	0.37
Al_2O_3	14.98	17.08	16.87	15.69	14.78	15.07	14.37	18.42	18.53	17.61	17.73	16.78	15.80	15.25	14.47
FeO (total)	1.38	3.22	2.51	2.10	1.34	1.70	0.82	3.94	3.54	3.82	2.38	2.37	2.56	2.83	1.75
MgO	0.37	1.44	1.05	0.68	0.46	0.53	0.34	1.69	1.56	1.58	1.24	0.96	1.09	0.87	0.62
MnO	0.13	0.08	0.05	0.06	0.02	0.04	0.02	0.07	0.10	0.10	0.09	0.06	0.04	0.16	0.03
CaO	2.17	4.40	3.70	3.48	2.60	2.49	1.93	5.79	5.63	5.80	4.98	4.10	2.45	2.71	1.79
Na_2O	4.09	4.33	4.30	4.15	3.83	3.80	3.90	4.42	4.79	4.41	4.48	4.46	4.32	3.72	2.76
K_2O	3.39	1.65	2.43	2.33	2.43	2.49	3.66	1.57	1.31	1.41	1.54	1.86	3.39	3.26	5.30
LOI	0.30	1.16	0.59	0.72	0.97	1.02	0.74	0.97	1.07	1.01	0.99	0.68	0.69	0.50	0.61
Total	99.43	99.05	99.77	98.00	98.52	99.94	99.52	98.52	98.57	98.30	98.45	98.54	98.76	97.83	97.59
parts per million															
Rb	51.1	41.7	44.1	37.9	49.1	57.0	89.4	47.5	38.8	23.4	40.8	31.6	52.2	65.5	69.8
Sr	577	932	833	735	715	674	392	1096	1275	946	1037	908	580	679	905
Ba	1087	1077	1734	1374	777	968	783	892	636	1348	927	1488	2464	1464	3592

TABLE 1. MAJOR- AND TRACE-ELEMENT DATA
(continued)

Unit:	gbgd	lton	lton	lton	lton	lton	lmgr	axt	axt	axt	axt	axt	axt	bt	bt
Specimen:	79-74'	D-VK1	DV-21	LM12-5	GD-11	LM12-32	GD-21	79-302'	79-302	WW-17	MR-322	MR-322c	MR-292	MR-244	MR-277

weight percent oxides

SiO_2	69.80	63.08	63.73	65.57	67.38	69.82	71.82	57.03	59.12	60.82	61.13	61.99	62.62	68.99	69.14
TiO_2	0.43	0.59	0.50	0.29	0.25	0.28	0.10	0.72	0.81	0.66	0.67	0.63	0.74	0.38	0.29
Al_2O_3	14.81	17.46	18.03	17.43	17.01	16.49	15.09	18.74	18.22	16.87	16.82	16.33	17.08	16.49	16.34
FeO (total)	1.68	4.59	3.65	2.33	2.29	1.20	1.25	6.37	6.31	5.25	5.06	4.72	4.09	1.84	1.84
MgO	0.60	1.34	1.52	0.85	0.76	0.50	0.23	3.44	3.32	2.77	2.50	2.59	2.36	0.81	0.75
MnO	0.03	0.01	0.06	0.06	0.06	0.02	0.01	0.10	0.08	0.12	0.08	0.08	0.06	0.02	0.01
CaO	1.80	5.64	3.99	3.58	3.40	2.00	1.36	6.43	6.31	5.46	5.19	5.18	4.73	3.01	2.81
Na_2O	2.88	4.12	5.28	4.50	4.55	6.61	4.48	4.33	4.70	4.01	3.89	4.47	4.06	4.92	4.95
K_2O	5.51	1.42	1.15	2.54	1.97	2.38	4.18	1.65	1.34	2.11	2.89	2.53	1.74	2.44	2.65
LOI	0.68	nd	nd	nd	nd	nd	nd	nd	nd	0.93	nd	nd	0.95	0.59	0.58
Total	98.22	98.25	97.91	97.15	97.67	99.30	98.52	98.81	100.21	99.00	98.23	98.52	98.43	99.49	99.37

parts per million

Rb	72.4	32.0	32.0	66.0	44.0	41.0	57.0	39.5	32.8	60.0	68.8	51.9	38.4	61.0	53.2
Sr	930	981	763	724	881	539	584	1007	1155	919	860	853	1461	1300	1050
Ba	3605	903	1276	1086	1037	1607	3237	762	731	1065	1289	1067	1202	1336	1441

TABLE 1. MAJOR- AND TRACE-ELEMENT DATA
(continued)

Unit:	bt	bt	bt	tra	tra	tra	tra	tra	cwad	cwad	cwad	cwad	cwad	cwad	cwad
Specimen:	MR-D57	MR-57b	78-53c	MR-275	79-51c	79-43a	MR-273	79-63c	79255a	78-51a	78-51b	80-246	80-184	78-51c	79-254

weight percent oxides

SiO_2	69.19	69.24	69.62	72.06	72.92	73.20	73.62	74.27	75.39	69.99	69.76	69.20	66.37	66.01	65.92
TiO_2	0.43	0.41	0.35	0.02	0.05	0.05	0.06	0.07	0.18	0.31	0.28	0.42	0.38	0.66	0.57
Al_2O_3	15.68	16.08	15.57	15.57	15.60	15.73	15.98	15.79	13.33	14.74	14.94	14.49	14.72	16.09	15.79
FeO (total)	1.93	1.57	1.63	0.41	0.35	0.39	0.31	0.39	0.85	2.15	2.06	1.86	2.69	3.30	3.14
MgO	0.76	0.77	0.73	0.08	0.01	0.02	0.08	0.08	0.17	0.95	0.73	0.76	1.05	1.46	1.27
MnO	0.03	0.03	0.02	0.00	0.00	0.02	0.00	0.04	0.01	0.02	0.03	0.05	0.04	0.09	0.06
CaO	2.69	2.92	2.53	1.17	1.19	1.09	1.11	1.25	0.74	2.01	2.00	1.59	1.80	3.15	2.99
Na_2O	4.45	5.19	4.78	5.94	6.21	6.93	7.68	7.44	3.95	3.60	4.05	3.01	1.87	4.24	4.39
K_2O	3.12	2.12	3.03	3.13	3.04	1.43	0.46	0.76	4.73	4.44	4.09	5.97	6.59	3.62	3.48
LOI	0.70	0.57	0.50	0.35	0.38	0.28	0.30	0.28	0.47	1.34	0.85	2.17	2.74	0.55	0.78
Total	98.98	98.90	98.76	98.73	99.77	99.14	99.60	100.37	99.82	99.55	98.79	99.52	98.25	99.17	98.39

parts per million

Rb	80.2	46.9	66.5	63.6	73.0	33.7	8.1	8.2	99.5	73.4	98.2	207	141	93.0	79.1
Sr	961	977	867	582	590	563	451	462	136	454	354	214	173	792	574
Ba	1244	1281	781	989	960	926	203	633	964	1989	928	1176	1491	1144	1160

TABLE 1. MAJOR- AND TRACE-ELEMENT DATA
(continued)

Unit:	cwad	cwad	cwad	cwad	cwad	cwd	cwd	cwd	cwd	cwd	cwd	wegd	wegd	wegd	wegd
Specimen:	78-51d	78-52a	WSW201	79255b	79-253	WS104f	WS104h	79256a	78-52c	79256b	78-52b	WE-62	WE-38	WE-93a	WE-109

weight percent oxides

SiO_2	58.40	57.44	57.28	56.91	55.57	49.33	52.53	50.44	49.53	49.17	47.59	47.10	49.58	50.97	52.98
TiO_2	0.87	1.08	1.18	1.29	1.18	1.47	1.50	1.64	1.49	1.49	1.25	0.68	1.03	0.70	1.54
Al_2O_3	15.40	15.95	17.83	16.22	16.30	17.13	16.73	16.04	16.43	15.46	14.22	14.35	14.78	16.63	15.53
FeO (total)	5.85	6.71	5.96	6.83	6.65	9.65	7.73	8.14	9.48	9.01	9.53	7.03	7.27	6.48	8.02
MgO	4.25	4.16	4.34	4.22	4.84	7.40	6.66	7.20	6.95	6.55	11.56	13.32	9.35	8.79	7.25
MnO	0.08	0.10	0.09	0.08	0.10	0.17	0.01	0.13	0.16	0.13	0.15	0.12	0.12	0.13	0.12
CaO	5.40	6.66	6.91	7.53	7.41	9.29	9.61	9.79	9.66	9.07	9.15	12.98	11.85	13.23	7.85
Na_2O	3.45	3.60	4.06	4.06	3.45	3.08	3.23	3.19	3.29	3.00	2.60	1.46	2.71	1.79	3.14
K_2O	2.77	2.45	2.32	1.77	2.15	1.41	1.68	1.50	0.98	2.57	0.86	0.29	1.08	0.35	2.70
LOI	1.99	1.03	nd	0.83	1.95	nd	nd	1.51	1.51	1.05	1.62	nd	nd	nd	nd
Total	98.46	99.19	99.97	99.74	99.60	98.93	99.68	99.58	99.58	97.50	98.53	97.33	97.77	99.07	99.13

parts per million

Rb	70.9	51.9	52.8	41.4	60.8	38.1	40.7	43.3	21.6	43.0	13.3	5.1	27.9	5.8	75.2
Sr	523	435	730	684	588	502	834	871	495	1385	317	407	856	876	1408
Ba	1010	748	1168	844	1115	637	723	867	365	1306	450	244	812	112	813

TABLE 1. MAJOR- AND TRACE-ELEMENT DATA
(continued)

Unit:	wegd	wegd	wegd	wegd	wegd	bhgd	bhgd
Specimen:	WE-7	WE-164	WSW175	WSW185	WSW166	WSW181	WSW199

weight percent oxides

SiO_2	53.78	53.73	54.17	55.57	55.99	69.06	69.82	**Unit abbreviations:**
TiO_2	0.83	1.30	1.14	1.23	1.04	0.39	0.36	Whipple Wash suite
Al_2O_3	17.75	16.44	17.31	13.28	17.76	15.46	14.46	pgd = porphyritic biotite granodiorite
FeO (total)	6.15	7.17	5.97	7.90	6.22	2.40	2.12	bgd = biotite, sphene granodiorite
MgO	6.12	5.95	4.89	7.76	4.17	0.94	0.85	tmgd = two-mica granodiorite
MnO	0.10	0.12	0.10	0.17	0.19	0.04	0.04	gtm = garnet, two-mica granodiorite
CaO	9.79	8.53	8.86	9.35	6.98	2.20	2.16	tmt = two-mica tonalite
Na_2O	3.11	4.34	3.84	2.44	4.19	3.77	3.79	fad = foliated two-mica monzogranite
K_2O	1.63	1.85	1.91	1.38	1.95	4.25	4.58	gbgd = garnet, biotite granodiorite
LOI	nd	nd	nd	nd	nd	nd	nd	lton = leucocratic biotite tonalite
								lmgr = leucocratic biotite monzogranite
Total	99.26	99.43	98.19	99.08	98.49	98.51	98.18	axt = Axtel quartz diorite
								bt = biotite tonalite
								tra = trondhjemitic aplite
								cwad = Chambers Well andesite and dacite
	parts per million							cwdb = Chambers Well diabase
Rb	43.0	39.1	44.8	29.2	43.8	109	120	wegd = War Eagle gabbro/diorite
Sr	775	1118	743	789	548	419	401	bhgd = biotite, hornblende granodiorite
Ba	627	917	722	837	627	1042	1038	

Enrichment occurs for Ti, Al, Na, K, Rb, Ba, Hf, and all REE. Sr is low (ca. 410 ppm) in most primitive members, peaks at greater than 1,000 ppm at 53 percent SiO_2, and decreases to 550 ppm for the most evolved members.

The biotite-hornblende granodiorite, the youngest pluton in the complex, is also calc-alkaline but distinct in being the most potassic and enriched in Rb, and lowest in Sr (ca. 410 ppm) at its restricted silica range of 69.1 to 69.8 weight percent.

Rare earth elements

The REE patterns for most plutonic units of the complex are similar (Fig. 5). Europium anomalies are nonexistent and, for most samples, the light rare earth elements (LREE) (La and Ce) range from 45 to 100 × chondrite with a notable depletion of heavy rare earth elements (HREE) (Yb and Lu) down to 2 to 16 × chondrite. Most of the siliceous intrusives show a lowering of either LREE and/or total REE concentration with increasing silica, implying REE–rich accessory phase (allanite, apatite, sphene, and/or zircon) control during fractionation. Notably, a HREE increase occurs for some of the garnet-bearing members of the Whipple Wash suite, including the two-mica tonalite, two-mica granodiorite, and garnet-biotite granodiorite, indicating a lack of significant garnet fractionation. In contrast are the intermediate to mafic intrusions, including the Axtel quartz diorite, the diabase of the Chambers Well dike swarm, and the War Eagle gabbro-diorite complex, which exhibit an increase in REE abundance with increasing silica.

The trondhjemitic aplites are unique, being depleted in REE to near chondritic or subchondritic abundances. Arth (1979) has shown that the REE abundances for continental trondhjemites typically have LREE at 20 to 50 × chondrite and HREE at 2 to 3 × chondrite. We found the aplites to have REE abundances so low that the concentrations were close to or below the detection limit (see Table 2). Plotted in Figure 5 are approximate or maximum values (relative to chondrite), which range from 1 to 2 × chondrite for LREE and 0.05 to 0.1 × chondrite for HREE. To our knowledge, these are the most REE–depleted compositions that have ever been reported for trondhjemitic (see papers in Barker, 1979) or other granitic rocks.

Isotopic data

Isotopic data for the Whipple complex are incomplete and limited to whole-rock and mineral Rb and Sr data (from R. L. Armstrong, *in* Davis and others, 1982) and the U-Pb data of zircons (Wright and others, 1986, 1987).

Twenty-six Rb-Sr analyses from Davis and others (1982) are presented in Table 3, taken from five plutons of the Whipple Wash suite (13 whole-rock and mineral analyses), the biotite tonalite (2 whole-rock analyses), the trondhjemitic aplite (1 whole-rock analysis), and the Chambers Well dike swarm (10 whole-rock analyses). The data for the Whipple Wash suite exhibit considerable scatter. Meaningful whole-rock or whole-

rock–feldspar isochrons of 91 ± 24 and 80 ± 32 Ma are possible for only two plutons, a leucocratic tonalite (lton) and a leucocratic biotite monzogranite (lmgr). The most extensively sampled pluton is a porphyritic granodiorite (pgd) for which the model Sr initial (Sr_i) ratios range from 0.706 to 0.710, comparable to the total variation of the complete data set. The origin of the scatter in Sr_i remains uncertain. Perhaps the plutons were originally inhomogeneous with respect to initial Sr, but disturbance during any of the three subsequent deformation events (Cretaceous metamorphism, Tertiary mylonitization, and Miocene detachment faulting) could have contributed to the observed scatter. For our purposes we will assume that the average Sr initial (0.7077 ± .0013) is representative for the magma system. Similar ratios were obtained for the Tertiary biotite tonalite (0.708) and trondhjemitic aplite (0.707).

Initial Sr for the Chambers Well dike swarm also exhibits moderate variation. Two diabase dikes of the swarm yield equivalent Sr_i ratios of 0.706. For the older andesite-dacite members of the swarm, initial ratios range from 0.7077 to 0.7103 with a crude positive correlation with silica content. The intermediate to felsic members of the swarm appear to represent a fractionation sequence (see below), but the isotopic data imply that the fractionation also involved some level of crustal contamination. Inclusions of Proterozoic gneiss, though not abundant, have been observed in some members of the swarm.

Davis and others (1982) also reported the Rb-Sr isotopic composition of some of the country-rock Proterozoic units. At late Mesozoic to middle Tertiary time, amphibolitic portions had model $^{87}Sr/^{86}Sr$ ratios of 0.706, and the more abundant quartzofeldspathic gneisses and granitic units had ratios of 0.711 to 0.760. Their combined total Sr ranges from 200 to 520 ppm; thus, any incorporation of portions of these assemblages by assimilation could have variably elevated the isotopic ratios of affected intrusions.

That some older crustal component existed in the source regions for the Whipple magmas is clear from the U-Pb/zircon data of Wright and others (1987). Only the data for the War Eagle complex are concordant. Data for the Whipple Wash suite, the Axtel quartz diorite, and the 26-Ma tonalites are discordant, with upper intercepts at approximately 1.4, 1.65, and 1.5 Ma, respectively.

DEVELOPMENT OF MAGMA EVOLUTIONARY TRENDS

The individual plutonic suites of the Whipple complex exhibit a considerable range of magma composition, implying that some magmatic process, such as variable melting, differentiation, mixing, and/or assimilation, may have been an active mechanism during their separate evolutionary development. All the suites exhibit an increase in alumina saturation with increasing silica, but any further similarity is lacking. Each magma lineage clearly formed in a unique fashion, reflecting their different bulk compositions, mineral assemblages, and conditions of crystallization.

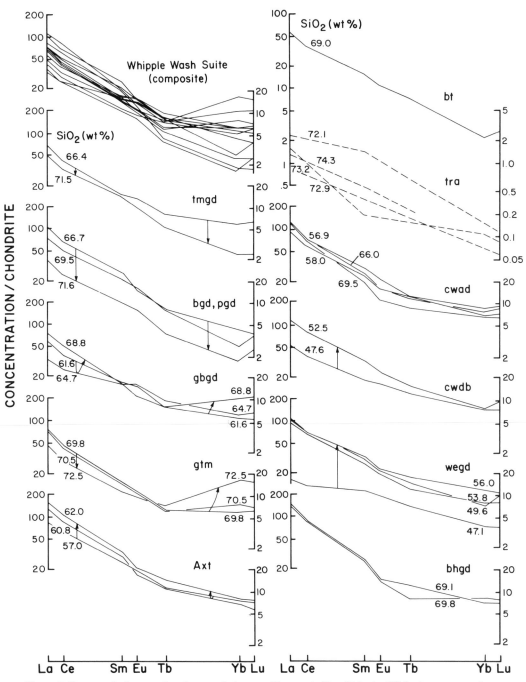

Figure 5. Rare earth element abundances of plutons, dikes, and sills within the Whipple core complex. SiO$_2$ (weight percent) values are designated where appropriate. Dashed trends of the trondhjemitic aplite reflect the near detection limit of those analyses. Arrows show consistent changes with increasing SiO$_2$.

TABLE 2. RARE EARTH AND OTHER TRACE-ELEMENT DATA*

Unit: Specimen:	pgd 78-53a	bgd 79-10	bgd 79-26	tmgd 79-183	tmgd 79-43b	gtm MR-47	gtm MR-118	gtm 79-241	tmt WW8	fad 78-47
La	35.1	25.0	13.1	23.7	17.3	25.2	23.7	15.0	29.5	38.5
Ce	63.0	46.6	22.5	40.8	30.2	42.3	40.5	26.5	54.9	75.4
Sm	5.12	4.30	2.0	3.0	2.8	2.89	2.86	2.2	3.91	3.97
Eu	1.12	1.13	0.61	1.01	0.73	0.83	0.77	0.70	1.0	0.9
Tb	0.40	0.38	0.19	0.37	0.26	0.30	0.29	0.35	0.35	0.20
Yb	0.98	0.60	0.38	1.37	0.53	1.37	1.71	3.60	1.14	0.39
Lu	0.14	0.13	0.082	0.22	0.083	0.21	0.24	0.52	0.20	0.06
Th	11.4	11.1	4.4	3.8	7.3	3.5	3.3	2.8	5.3	4.2
Sc	4.4	3.7	2.1	4.4	2.8	3.0	3.1	2.0	5.6	2.4
Cr	6.1	5.3	nd	8.4	2.0	3.0	3.0	4.8	8.8	5.4
Hf	4.8	4.7	3.5	2.8	3.9	3.2	2.7	2.9	3.6	3.5

Unit: Specimen:	gbgd MR162	gbgd 79-198	gbgd 79-132	axt MR302	axt WW17	axt MR322c	bt MR244	tra MR275	tra 79-51c	tra 79-43a
La	19.7	11.6	25.8	28.6	44.2	52.0	19.0	0.3	0.3	0.1
Ce	36.0	22.8	47.4	58.4	79.2	97.3	33.6	bd	bd	bd
Sm	3.28	3.02	3.2	4.87	5.82	6.94	3.1	0.2	bd	0.4
Eu	1.09	1.15	0.81	1.33	1.25	1.49	0.80	bd	bd	bd
Tb	0.36	0.45	0.36	0.53	0.52	0.67	0.35	bd	bd	bd
Yb	1.21	1.38	2.26	1.64	1.51	1.81	0.48	bd	bd	bd
Lu	0.18	0.22	0.36	0.24	0.20	0.27	0.089	0.004	0.002	0.003
Th	3.0	1.9	3.7	3.4	7.1	13.3	6.1	0.03	0.01	0.02
Sc	5.4	7.1	3.7	12.1	8.8	10.0	2.98	0.09	0.11	0.13
Cr	10.7	8.8	7.0	14.7	9.7	12.7	3.0	bd	bd	bd
Hf	4.3	3.5	3.4	4.6	4.4	5.9	4.0	1.9	1.8	2.0

Unit: Specimen:	tra MR273	tra 79-63	cwad 79255b	cwad 78-51d	cwad 78-51c	cwad 78-51b	cwdb 78-52b	cwdb WS104h	wegd WE-62	wegd WE-38
La	0.2	0.3	37.9	31.2	41.8	40.8	17.5	39.1	5.4	36.5
Ce	bd	bd	67.7	55.0	69.5	64.8	35.0	73.6	12.4	67.0
Sm	bd	0.09	5.8	4.52	4.89	3.70	3.86	6.44	2.23	5.97
Eu	bd	bd	1.6	1.17	1.17	0.80	1.19	1.71	0.73	1.53
Tb	bd	bd	0.59	0.57	0.55	0.41	0.57	0.74	0.33	0.70
Yb	bd	bd	1.88	1.51	1.67	1.44	1.60	1.70	0.84	1.58
Lu	bd	bd	0.31	0.25	0.28	0.22	0.26	0.32	0.13	0.33
Th	0.01	0.01	6.7	6.4	11.5	14.0	2.9	4.9	0.72	4.9
Sc	0.10	0.12	17.3	14.5	6.6	3.3	25.4	25.9	32.5	29.1
Cr	bd	bd	109	131	12.0	6.2	578	140	1090	265
Hf	2.1	1.8	4.9	4.1	5.4	5.6	2.7	4.2	1.3	3.8

Unit: Specimen:	wegd WE-7	wegd WSW166	bhgd WS181a	bhgd WS199
La	32.4	34.3	48.4	47.7
Ce	61.9	67.4	82.6	81.1
Sm	5.11	6.64	5.10	5.25
Eu	1.40	1.76	1.03	1.07
Tb	0.57	0.83	0.58	0.37
Yb	1.73	2.60	1.57	1.84
Lu	0.28	0.37	0.24	0.27
Th	5.4	4.4	12.0	16.2
Sc	22.2	16.5	4.1	4.7
Cr	65.4	43.6	12.2	12.9
Hf	3.6	4.9	5.0	5.3

*All data in ppm.
 bd = below detection limit
 nd = no data collected

Unit abbreviations as in Table 1.

TABLE 3. Rb AND Sr DATA*

Unit	Specimen	$^{87}Rb/^{86}Sr$	$^{87}Sr/^{86}Sr$	$^{87}Sr/^{86}Sr(i)$
Whipple Wash Suite				
pgd	GD3a-WR	0.501	0.7071	0.7065
	GD3d-WR	0.679	0.7087	0.7079
	GD3e-WR	0.801	0.7086	0.7076
	GD9-WR	0.188	0.7107	0.7105
	GD9-PL	0.126	0.7106	0.7104
	GD9-BIO	3.080	0.7112	0.7074
gtm	GD4b-WR	0.510	0.7074	0.7068
lton	GD1-WR	0.186	0.7064	0.7062
	GD1a-WR	0.881	0.7073	0.7062
lmgr	GD2-WR	0.376	0.7082	0.7077
	GD2-PL,QTZ	0.168	0.7079	0.7077
fad	GD6-WR	0.688	0.7085	0.7086
		0.148	0.7078	0.7076
Biotite tonalite and trondhjemitic aplite				
bt	GD3h-WR	0.303	0.7081	0.7080
	GD3g-WR	0.263	0.7082	0.7081
tra	GD3f-WR	0.786	0.7073	0.7070
Chambers Well dike swarm				
and	GD8a-WR	0.105	0.7077	0.7077
	78-52-WR	0.369	0.7079	0.7078
	78-51d-WR	0.372	0.7086	0.7085
dac	78-51a-WR	0.496	0.7105	0.7103
	78-51c-WR	0.558	0.7094	0.7092
	78-51d-WR	0.789	0.7086	0.7083
	GD10-WR	0.823	0.7105	0.7102
	GD7aWR	1.260	0.7105	0.7100
db	78-52b-WR	0.096	0.7063	0.7063
	78-52c-WR	0.121	0.7063	0.7063

*Data of R. L. Armstrong *in* Davis and others (1982); initial ratios based on U/Pb age of Wright and others (1986); unit symbols as in Figure 1.

This section attempts to quantify and model the different magma series. A working assumption is that the rock compositions correspond to melt, a limiting factor because any chosen plutonic rock composition could represent a mixture of melt plus incorporated solid of restitic, xenolithic, or cumulate origin. For purposes of quantification, the models presented below assume that the most primitive composition sampled is undifferentiated and serves as an estimate of the parental magma further evolved by one or more mechanisms. For all models, major-element mineral compositions were taken from the rock samples considered.

Elemental trends for the eight plutons of the Whipple Wash suite (Fig. 3) preclude their being comagmatic. Yet, their compositional features (high Ca, Na, and Sr; low K and Rb) are sufficiently similar that we infer they have evolved in a similar manner. The range of composition of the garnet-biotite granodiorite is the most extensive. The change from metaluminous to peraluminous (at approximately 66 to 67 percent SiO_2) indicates fractionation of phases such as hornblende, allanite, epidote,

and/or apatite. Hornblende (less felsic portions only) and allanite occur sporadically in trace amounts. Epidote and apatite are ubiquitous, although it is uncertain that the former is magmatic. Using microprobe data for compositional control of fractionating phases, we are able to model only two-thirds of this series. The results, given in Table 4, involve 38 percent separation of a residue consisting of plagioclase (An_{34}, 73 percent), hornblende (22 percent), biotite (2.3 percent), magnetite (1.4 percent), allanite, epidote, or apatite (0.7 percent) and garnet (0.7 percent). The more felsic portion of the pluton, from 68 to 70 percent SiO_2, involves sharp increases in K and Ba and a decrease in Na and Mg that cannot be explained by fractionation of the constituent phases. We attribute these changes to element mobility during metamorphism.

The seven other plutons of the Whipple Wash suite are more felsic than the garnet-biotite granodiorite and lack hornblende. Attempts to model their individual trends (Fig. 3), or even a general trend for the suite, consistently fail using mineral compositions derived from the plutons, including plagioclase + biotite + magnetite ± garnet ± ilmenite, which petrographically are the early crystallizing phases. Conspicuous errors include insufficient increases in K and decreases in Mg, both due to biotite being the prominent mafic phase. Assimilation may play a role, because the Proterozoic country-rock orthogneisses are potassic with low Mg/Fe ratios. The variation of Sr_i (0.706 to 0.710) for the plutons could be accounted for by as much as 22 percent assimilation of the gneisses, which had Mesozoic $^{87}Sr/^{86}Sr$ ratios ranging from 0.74 to 0.78 with 175 to 400 ppm Sr. Yet, field evidence for significant assimilation is lacking. The trends are compatible with equilibration with a higher Mg/Fe mafic mineral assemblage, such as one bearing hornblende and/or pyroxene. Ignoring the fact that the plutons lack these minerals, an artificial fractionation model using clinopyroxene, hornblende, and garnet works well for each of the individual trends. On the basis of this observation, we have considered an alternative model that accounts for the magmatic lineages based on partial melting. The next section addresses the source of the magmas; we conclude that the Whipple Wash suite was generated by partial melting of a calcic graywacke having an eclogite facies mineralogy. Using the major-element data from Bhatia (1985) for an arc-derived, calcic graywacke, we are able to approximate the Whipple Wash trends by a variable but high percentage of melting (47 to 65 percent), leaving a residue of clinopyroxene and garnet with lesser amounts of plagioclase (An_{55}); the plagioclase is more rapidly depleted during the progression of melting. Table 5 shows the parameters and model results for two percentages of partial melting, one at 47 and another at 65 percent. Average compositions of the Whipple Wash suite at comparable levels of silica are also shown. Melts produced by a lower percentage of melting will be more siliceous and peraluminous. At 47 percent melting, the derived liquid has 72.0 percent SiO_2 with an A/CNK ratio of 1.06. With increased melting, silica and K_2O decrease and the abundances of all compatible major elements increase. A/CNK decreases with increased melting, becoming

TABLE 4. FRACTIONAL CRYSTALLIZATION MODELS

Specimen:	A. Whipple Wash (partial)			B. Axtel quartz diorite			C. Chambers Well-Part 1			D. Chambers Well-Part 2			E. War Eagle		
	Parent (162)	Observed (195)	Model	Parent (302)	Observed (322/292)	Model	Parent (253)	Observed (254)	Model	Parent (254)	Observed (255A)	Model	Parent (62)	Observed (166)	Model
SiO_2	61.60	66.93	66.88	57.72	63.56	63.56	56.91	67.87	67.89	67.87	75.88	75.95	48.39	56.85	56.91
TiO_2	0.44	0.34	0.34	0.69	0.70	0.74	1.21	0.59	0.40	0.59	0.18	0.18	0.70	1.06	1.10
Al_2O_3	18.53	16.78	16.99	18.97	17.04	17.11	16.69	16.26	16.28	16.26	13.42	13.50	14.74	18.03	18.03
FeO	3.54	2.37	2.31	6.45	4.50	4.50	6.81	3.23	3.23	3.23	0.86	0.86	7.22	6.32	6.32
MgO	1.56	0.96	0.99	3.48	2.53	2.69	4.96	1.31	1.36	1.31	0.17	0.15	13.69	4.23	4.22
MnO	0.10	0.06	0.05	0.10	0.07	0.07	0.10	0.06	0.10	0.06	0.01	0.04	0.12	0.19	0.16
CaO	5.63	4.10	4.07	6.51	5.06	4.90	7.59	3.08	3.08	3.08	0.74	0.75	13.34	7.09	7.07
Na_2O	4.79	4.46	4.32	4.38	4.36	4.45	3.53	4.02	3.92	4.02	3.98	3.71	1.50	4.25	4.20
K_2O	1.31	1.86	1.86	1.67	2.08	1.92	2.20	3.58	3.58	3.58	4.76	4.68	0.30	1.98	1.89
XFe	0.69	0.71	0.70	0.65	0.64	0.63	0.58	0.71	0.70	0.71	0.83	0.85	0.35	0.60	0.60
A/CNK	0.95	1.00	1.03	0.91	0.91	0.93	0.76	1.01	1.02	1.01	1.03	1.07	0.55	0.82	0.83
%Fract		38.0			42.6			48.1			32.1			87.3	
%Solids: Plagioclase		73.4			58.1			35.1			68.2			37.3	
Hornblende		21.6			29.6			55.9			17.7			4.2	
Biotite		2.3			10.2			3.8			9.7			—	
Garnet		0.7			—			—			—			—	
Apatite		0.7			—			2.3			—			—	
Magnetite		0.9			2.2			3.0			3.6			1.0	
Ilmenite		0.5			—			—			0.7			—	
Clinopyroxene		—			—			—			—			38.4	
Olivine		—			—			—			—			21.1	

TABLE 5. VARIABLE MELTING MODEL—WHIPPLE WASH SUITE

	Model Source[*]	Low Silica		High Silica	
		Observed	Calculated[†]	Observed	Calculated
SiO_2	59.21	66.0 ± 1.0	66.1	72.0 ± 1.0	72.3
TiO_2	0.86	0.40 ± 0.15	0.37	0.18 ± 0.7	0.16
Al_2O_3	16.28	17.0 ± 0.4	16.97	15.3 ± 0.5	15.2
FeO	6.6	2.7 ± 0.5	2.86	1.4 ± 0.4	1.17
MgO	2.75	1.0 ± 0.3	1.12	0.4 ± 0.2	0.38
CaO	7.08	4.0 ± 0.8	4.41	2.1 ± 0.6	1.76
Na_2O	4.76	4.6 ± 0.6	5.08	4.5 ± 0.8	5.03
K_2O	1.16	2.1 ± 0.6	1.85	3.0 ± 0.7	2.66
FeO/(FeO + MgO)	0.708	0.72 ± 0.04	0.718	0.76 ± 0.3	0.755
A/CNK[‡]	0.74	0.99 ± 0.08	0.92	1.05 ± 0.06	1.06
% Melt			65.0		47.0
Residue Proportions:		Garnet	35.8		29.9
		Clinopyroxene	53.8		45.5
		Plagioclase (An^{55})	9.0		23.9
		Rutile	1.4		1.2

[*]Calcic, arc-derived graywacke from Bhatia (1985), recalculated to 100%.
[†]From equilibrium melting model: $Ci_L = (1/X_L)[Ci_{Source} - \Sigma (X_{Residue} Ci_{Residue})]$.
[‡]A/CNK = molecular proportions of $Al_2O_3/(CaO + Na_2O + K_2O)$.

less than unity at 55 percent melting with a corresponding SiO_2 of 69.6 weight percent.

If valid, this model requires that magma heterogeneity generated in the source region be approximately maintained during upward magma transport and emplacement. Preservation of primary magmatic variations may be unreasonable for upper crustal plutons. For the mid-crustal plutons, however, the vertical separation from the source region may not be large, and heterogeneities derived during progressive melting could well survive to emplacement.

The major-element variation within the Axtel quartz diorite constitutes a more simple lineage that can be explained by 42 percent fractional crystallization of plagioclase (An_{45}) with sequentially lesser amounts of hornblende, biotite, and magnetite (Table 4). Several of the trace elements increase in this differentiation series. Data for La exhibit the largest increase and imply 45 percent fractionation of solids having an assumed bulk distribution coefficient (D_0) approaching zero. This conclusion is based on the observation that as D_0 approaches zero for an incompatible element, the proportion of residual solid during perfect fractionation can be approximated as $1 - C_0/C_L$, where C_0/C_L represents the elemental ratio of the most primitive to most evolved compositions. Such a low D_0 is clearly a limiting case, and higher values would allow higher amounts of fractionation. For the same amount of fractionation, the bulk distribution coefficients controlling the variation of other elements are higher, ranging from 0.17 to 0.40 (Rb, Ba, Ce, Sm), 0.6 to 0.85 (Sc, Eu, Yb, Lu),

and 1.0 to 1.3 (Sr and Sc). These coefficients are consistent with plagioclase- and hornblende-dominated fractionation but also indicate an absence of LREE concentrating phases, such as allanite, in the removed fraction. Allanite occurs in the pluton, but is rare. Most of our thin sections of the quartz diorite lack this accessory phase.

Despite their widespread abundance, the biotite tonalite intrusives are homogeneous in composition, with a total SiO_2 range of 69.0 to 69.6 weight percent. Minor variation exists for only Fe, Mg, and Ca, all of which decrease slightly with the minor increase in silica (Table 1, Figs. 2 and 4).

The associated trondhjemitic aplites are peculiar in having chondritic to subchondritic REE abundances (Fig. 5). Hornblende-dominated fractionation or melting is often invoked for the evolution of trondhjemites (Arth, 1979). The Whipple aplites cannot be primary melts because the REE are too low. The rocks are undoubtedly very evolved but from what primary magma remains uncertain. Arth and others (1978) has described a gabbro-tonalite-trondhjemite fractionation suite with REE depletion accompanying the final (trondhjemite) portion of the evolved series. However, their trondhjemite REE abundances are an order of magnitude higher than what we report here. REE depletion during differentiation is not uncommon in felsic magma systems (see Mittlefehldt and Miller, 1983) due to fractionation of REE–concentrating accessory minerals. Thus, the low REE of the trondhjemitic aplites are best explained by significant separation of phases such as monazite and zircon. These minerals occur in trace amounts in the aplites. The rocks have a limited silica range (72.1 to 74.3 weight percent) through which there is a notable increase in Na and a depletion in K, Rb, Sr, and Ba. These changes are indicative of fractionation of muscovite and alkali feldspar, both of which occur as porphyroclasts.

The andesite to dacite series of the Chambers Well dike swarm composes a well-defined lineage from 55.5 to 75.4 weight percent SiO_2. Most elements decrease with increasing silica except for irregular increases for K, Rb, Th, and LREE. A model based on major-element variations shows that the lineage can be produced by 48 percent fractionation of HB > PLAG (An_{55}) > BIO > MT, AP up to 66 weight percent SiO_2 and an additional 32 percent fractionation of PLAG (An_{41}) > HB > BIO > MT, ILM for the remainder of the series (Table 4). All of these phases occur as phenocrysts and the above model proportions are also consistent with changes for the trace elements. Despite a good fit to the data, the increase in $^{87}Sr/^{86}Sr$ from 0.707 to 0.711 from intermediate to felsic members indicates some level of crustal enrichment. A more appropriate model is one of combined fractionation and contamination. Country-rock assemblages to the dike swarm are principally of Proterozoic crystalline rocks, including quartzo-feldspathic gneiss and lesser amounts of augen gneiss, potassic granite, and amphibolite. A general granitic composition, moderate Sr content (200 to 530 ppm), and range in Miocene $^{87}Sr/^{86}Sr$ ratios (0.704 to 0.763) of the Proterozoic units preclude a unique solution to the amount of contamination. An indication of the possible magnitude of contamination can be obtained from average $^{87}Sr/^{86}Sr$ and total Sr data for the gneissic and granitic Proterozoic units (Davis and others, 1982), which range from 0.738 at 400 ppm to 0.776 at 175 ppm. To increase a Sr isotopic ratio from 0.707 to 0.711, the contamination would be limited to 12.5 percent for andesites containing 600 ppm Sr and 6.5 percent for dacites with 300 ppm Sr. This conclusion is based on a mixing equation wherein the Sr isotopic ratio of a hybrid ($^{87}Sr/^{86}Sr_h$) is given by:

$$^{87}Sr/^{86}Sr_h = {^{87}Sr/^{86}Sr_1}(X_1 Sr_1/Sr_h) + {^{87}Sr/^{86}Sr_2}(Sr_2(1-X_1)/Sr_h),$$

where X is weight fraction, subscripts 1 and 2 refer to the end members to be mixed, and subscript h represents the contaminated hybrid.

The younger diabase dikes of the swarm may have undergone a modest level of assimilation, based on their elevated $^{87}Sr/^{86}Sr$ of 0.706. If the original initial ratio was 0.704, then the amount of contamination by the same Proterozoic crust would be less than 7.7 percent for an average diabase Sr content of 600 ppm.

The War Eagle gabbro-diorite complex is an unusual mafic intrusive unit. Presumably mantle derived, the magma was somewhat hydrous, including the most primitive gabbroic members, which contain the ubiquitous late occurrence of hornblende and titaniferous biotite overgrowing earlier olivine and clinopyroxene. The most evolved compositions are hornblende-biotite quartz diorite. Spanning 47.1 to 56.0 weight percent SiO_2, average major-element trends can be accounted for by 87 percent fractionation of CPX, PLAG (An_{77}), OL (Fo_{77}), and minor HB (Table 4). However, the elemental variations are irregular and indicate that the inferred phase proportions were not uniform. That the Sr abundance initially increases, peaks at an SiO_2 of 53 weight percent, and is followed by a systematic decrease requires that plagioclase had a prominent role in only the more evolved portions of the fractionation scheme. Likewise, the REE increase abruptly in the mafic portion of the series (47.1 to 49.6 percent SiO_2), but appear to be buffered for the remainder by an increased proportion of hornblende in the fractionated assemblage.

MAGMA GENERATION

The above sections have outlined the compositional variability of each of the Whipple intrusives, providing a basis for isolating the undifferentiated portions of the individual plutonic events. This section is directed at the nature of magma generation, based on the assumption that we have isolated the compositions that are direct imprints of the residual sources rather than being derived by differentiation from a more primitive magma or accumulation. Our sample suite is extensive and has been guided by detailed mapping. Cumulative structures and textures are lacking, and if more primitive components exist, they are not exposed. Moreover, the high Ca, Sr, Sc, and Eu/Sm of each plutonic suite serve as an argument that significant "hidden" accumulation has not occurred. Below, we address the origin of the major intrusions of the Whipple complex, namely the Whipple Wash suite, the Axtel quartz diorite, the synkinematic tonalite sills, the andesite and diabase of the Chambers Well dike swarm, and the War Eagle gabbro.

Whipple Wash suite

The numerous plutons of the Whipple Wash suite are intriguing. Comparable garnet–two-mica granites are lacking in this region of the Cordillera. High Ca, Na, Sr (>1000 ppm), marginal alumina saturation, low K and Rb, and lack of a europium anomaly characterize the most primitive members, which range in SiO_2 from 61 to 64 weight percent. Modeling to fit trace-element patterns often yields solutions that are not unique due to a number of unconstrained parameters, including the effects of accessory phases that preferentially incorporate certain elements. Yet, the unusual composition of the Whipple Wash suite allows few alternatives and eliminates derivation from many potential source rocks. Moreover, the high abundances of Ca and Sr and lack of a Eu anomaly require a high percentage of melting, and that all or most of the feldspar be eliminated by melting or by premelting metamorphism to eclogite facies conditions. A precursor history to increase the alumina saturation by weathering or alteration is also indicated. Separation from amphibole-bearing residua can also increase the alumina saturation level of a derived melt, but the process is not efficient (Zen, 1986). On the basis of the Sr isotopic data, the source should be relatively young and/or not too radiogenic.

The previous section has shown that much of the compositional variation of the Whipple Wash suite can be accounted for by variable partial melting of residual garnet, clinopyroxene, and minor plagioclase, the latter being rapidly depleted during the progression of melting. The preferred source composition should be one that is capable of yielding calcic, high-Sr, marginally peraluminous granodioritic melts with a Sr_i of approximately 0.707 to 0.709. A continental margin arc-derived graywacke that contains significant proportions of both volcanogenic and continental material is a good candidate. A more mature sediment is rejected because it is too peraluminous and is incapable of producing calcic granitoids. The Sr_i would also be too high. We also reject a purely arc-derived or oceanic metaigneous (basaltic to andesitic) source because large volumes of peraluminous melts would not be derived and the Sr_i would be too low unless this source was very old. Miller (1985) and Miller and others (this volume) present a convincing set of data indicating that the two-mica granites of the nearby Old Woman Mountains are derived from melting quartzo-feldspathic Proterozoic crust. The Old Woman granites are unlike those of the Whipple complex, however. They are more siliceous and have higher Sr_i (>0.71) and K and lower Sr and Ca normalized to any silica value. The REE patterns also consistently have a significant negative Eu anomaly.

We suggest that the volcanogenic sedimentary source is Mesozoic because exemplary materials of that age are common in the western portions of the Cordillera and could have been brought to the condition of partial melting coincident with subduction. Included are the Franciscan Formation of the coastal sections of northern California and Oregon, the Catalina-Pelona-Orocopia schists of southern California, and the Santa Monica Formation of the Santa Monica Mountains. These units have varying Mesozoic ages and compositions but share a common history of having both arc- and continent-derived detritus and containing significant portions of calcic graywacke that was shed into an active convergent margin system. Pre–San Andreas reconstruction allows only the Pelona-Catalina-Orocopia schists to have been in an appropriate geographic position to be subducted under this region of the Cordillera orogen. That the Pelona-Catalina-Orocopia schists and the Franciscan Formation were subducted and metamorphosed at depths of more than 30 km has been well characterized (Ernst, 1980; Blake and others, 1988; Sorenson, 1988; Peacock, 1988). Some of the more mature and/or siliceous components of these sections (i.e., those with SiO_2 contents greater than 68 weight percent; see Bailey and others, 1964) are not appropriate sources because they would be incapable of producing the more primitive compositions of the suite. We see two problems with the Pelona source model. The schist is graphitic, and any derived granitic melt would inherit low f_{O_2} conditions and be of the ilmenite series. The Whipple Wash magmas crystallized at moderate levels of f_{O_2} and are of the magnetite series (Anderson and Rowley, 1981). Second, the REE patterns of portions of the Orocopia schist have well-defined negative Eu anomalies (Haxel and others, 1987; G. Haxel, personal communication, 1987) and thus could not generate the Whipple Wash

magmas, all of which lack a Eu anomaly. If the Pelona or other equivalent units are representative of the Whipple Wash source, then that portion inferred to have been subducted and melted beneath the craton would have to have some basic differences from sections currently exposed. We are attracted to the model only because calcic graywackes (SiO_2 = 57 to 64 weight percent) occur abundantly in all these Mesozoic sections, and existing Rb-Sr isotopic data (Franciscan and Santa Monica Formations only; see Peterman and others, 1967; Criscione and others, 1977; Lanphere and others, 1978) show the rocks to be only moderately radiogenic and having $^{87}Sr/^{86}Sr$ at 89 Ma in the range observed for the Whipple Wash suite.

There are no isotopic data for the Catalina-Pelonia-Orocopia schists, and existing elemental data (Haxel and others, 1987) are limited. Thus, we are unable at this stage to thoroughly examine our preferred model. As an alternative test, we turn to the trace-element data for an arc-derived metagraywacke for which Bhatia (1985) and Bhatia and Crook (1986) have provided an extensive set of major- and trace-element data. This metagraywacke contains ~40 percent albitized plagioclase, <8 percent quartz, minor alkali feldspar, and 50 to 70 percent andesitic clasts. A comparison of model melt composition with the primitive composition range of the Whipple Wash suite is shown in Figure 6. Based on 40 percent partial melting, the fit is acceptable except for Sc, which is high in the predicted melt by a factor of two. The major-element model (previous section) and this trace-element model indicate differing levels of partial melting (maximum of 65 versus 40 percent, repsectively), but are consistent in requiring a high degree of melting of calcic graywacke with an eclogitic residue to produce these unusual peraluminous magmas.

Axtel quartz diorite

The 73-Ma Axtel quartz diorite is compositionally similar to high-Sr, medium-K andesites of modern continental arcs. As reviewed by Gill (1981), andesitic magmas can apparently be derived by several mechanisms, including fractionation from basalt, contamination of basalt with continental crust, and partial melting of amphibolitic to eclogitic basalt and hydrous peridotite. Anderson and Cullers (1987) have reviewed the compositional features of arc-type magmas produced by these various mechanisms. High-Sr andesitic melts fundamentally require derivation from a residual mineralogy that excludes Sr, such as an eclogitic source of basaltic composition. Peridotitic source materials, whether chondritic, enriched, or hydrous, lack an appropriate bulk composition to generate large volumes of high-Sr, intermediate melts. Magmas fractionated from a more mafic magma also do not lead to high Sr compositions. In addition, the Late Cretaceous was not a time of significant gabbro production in this region of the Cordillera, and no gabbros of this age are exposed in this region of the Cordilleran orogen. Echoing the conclusion of Apted (1981), Anderson and Cullers (1987) further emphasized the importance of high pressure on clinopyroxene- and garnet-

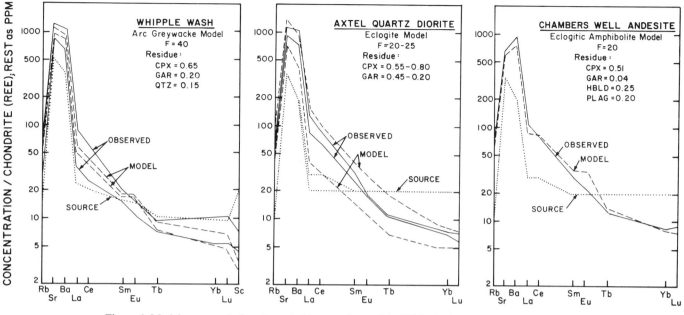

Figure 6. Model source solutions for primitive members of the Whipple Wash, Axtel, and Chambers Well intrusions. F = percent partial melting. Observed, model, and original source compositions are designated.

melt distribution coefficients and the effect of submarine alteration of basaltic crust, which generally leads to an enrichment in alkali, alkali earth, and rare earth elements. Although unaltered mid-ocean ridge basalt (MORB) oceanic crust is typically LREE depleted (to 4 to 6 × chondrite), alteration leads to flatter REE patterns with abundances greater than 10 and up to 30 × chondrite, with some LREE enrichment over HREE (Anderson and Cullers, 1987). We have excluded melting MORB-type oceanic crust as a potential source due to its intrinsic low abundance of REE. Our preferred model for the origin of the Axtel quartz diorite is derivation by 20 to 30 percent partial melting of an eclogite having the composition of altered and enriched oceanic basalt. Figure 6 compares the observed composition to that predicted from melting of eclogitic basalt having a range of original composition from 10 to 20 × chondrite.

Synkinematic dikes and sills

Of the tonalites and aplites that compose the synkinematic dikes and sills, the aplites are too evolved for use in gaining some information about their source. The tonalites may also represent a differentiated lineage, but one that is strikingly similar to the more evolved portions of the Whipple Wash suite, including low abundances of K and Rb, high Ca and Sr, fractionated and low REE, and a modest SR initial at 0.708. Thus, we suggest that their parental magmas also originated from a high degree of melting of an arc-derived calcic graywacke, despite the more than 60-m.y. difference in age.

Chambers Well dike swarm—andesites

The andesitic to dacitic portions of the Chambers Well dike swarm span a wide range of composition that has some affinity to

the Axtel quartz diorite. Obvious differences include higher K and Cr and lower Ca, Na, and Sr. The REE abundances are equivalent, with LREE at 70 to 110 × chondrite, HREE at 6 to 9 × chondrite, and no Eu anomaly. An earlier section has shown that the most primitive members are calc-alkaline andesites (SiO_2 = 55.6 to 57.3 weight percent). Evidence for derivation from more mafic magmas is lacking. Based on initial Sr_i values, the swarm has apparently undergone some modest degree of crustal assimilation, principally in the more felsic members. Assuming that the andesites are parental melts, we have investigated a range of probable origins. The modest level of undifferentiated Sr (590 to 730 ppm), like that of the Axtel quartz diorite, indicates a plagioclase-depleted residue. However, we have concluded a pure eclogitic basalt to be an inappropriate source because the calculated abundances of Sr are too high. A possible source model, also depicted in Figure 6, involves derivation by a minimum of 20 percent melting from a partially eclogitized, amphibolitic basalt source having an assumed original concentration at 30 (La, Ce) to 20 (other REE) × chondrite. At best, this result can only be viewed as an exemplary model, given the many unknowns in such melting calculations.

Chambers Well dike swarm—diabase

The numerous diabase dikes of the Chambers Well dike swarm have a narrow range of composition, and being the youngest component of the intrusive event, it is clear that they lack a comagmatic relation with the older andesites and dacites. The most primitive diabase (at 47.6 weight percent silica) has a Mg number of only 0.55, far less than the value of ~0.70 quoted by Frey and others (1978) for primary basaltic magmas. The large ion lithophile (LIL) element abundances, including REE,

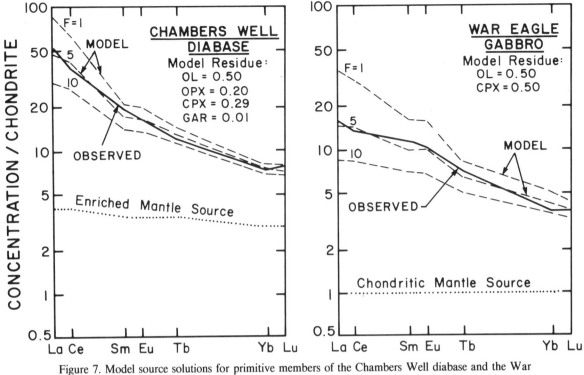

Figure 7. Model source solutions for primitive members of the Chambers Well diabase and the War Eagle complex. F = percent partial melting. Observed, model, and original source compositions are designated.

are also higher than most primitive basalts; it is probable that the magma system underwent fractionation at some depth prior to intrusion. However, the lack of an Eu anomaly precludes significant plagioclase separation, and the high Sc (25 ppm) and Cr (580 ppm) strongly limit the degree of olivine and/or pyroxene differentiation. Hammond (1986) has shown that continental diabases, like those of the Chambers Well, commonly have low Mg values and moderate REE abundances compatible with derivation by partial melting from an enriched, subcontinental mantle. Assuming the most mafic diabase (SiO_2 = 47.6 weight percent) to be the primary melt, we have modeled its composition by 5 percent melting of an enriched garnet peridotite having LREE at 4×, Eu to Tb at 3.5×, and HREE at 3× chondritic values (Fig. 7). If the parental magma is more mafic than our test sample, then the source could be less enriched.

War Eagle Gabbro

The most primitive member of the War Eagle complex is a hornblende-clinopyroxene-olivine gabbro (sample WE-62; SiO_2 = 47.1 weight percent) with low K, Sr (~410 ppm), and REE (16× chondrite for La to 4× chondrite for Lu). Although we have examined a vareity of potential mantle sources, the preferred, and simplest, model involves derivation by approximately 5 percent partial melting of a chondritic mantle, leaving a harzburgitic residue of olivine and orthopyroxene ± minor amounts of clinopyroxene and amphibole (Fig. 7).

TECTONIC SIGNIFICANCE

Magmatism within the Whipple core complex is fundamentally bimodal in age. Voluminous calcic peraluminous and intermediate magmas were emplaced when the Whipple lower plate crustal section was at middle crustal levels during the Late Cretaceous, considered to be a time of major plate convergence for the Cordilleran orogen. After a magmatic hiatus of nearly 50 m.y., renewed igneous activity began in the late Oligocene and continued until about 17 Ma, coincident with a time of regional crustal extension and evolution of core complexes. The later igneous activity occurred when the same crustal section resided in the upper crust and was coeval with a major period of explosive volcanism that is recorded in the upper plate in the Whipple Mountains as well as on a widespread basis throughout the southern Cordillera.

This Late Cretaceous–late Oligocene magmatic gap has regional significance; Coney and Reynolds (1977) attributed the gap to post-Cretaceous to Eocene shallowing followed by a post-Eocene steepening of subduction. Early Tertiary igneous activity lapsed in regions 100 to 500 km from the inferred trench, and the locus of magmatism migrated eastward at distances of up to 1,000 km. Although their compilation was based largely on K-Ar dates, the work presented here, based on the U-Pb dating by Wright and others (1986), supports their conclusion. Coney and Reynolds' interpretation further argues that subduction was continuously operative in southwestern North America from 130 to

15 Ma. The Whipple magmas have compositions consistent with a direct tie to a subducting plate. Modeled source materials include a continental margin arc-derived graywacke at 89 Ma, an eclogitic basalt at 73 Ma, more arc-derived graywacke at 26 Ma, a partially eclogitized amphibolite at 21 to 26 Ma, an enriched peridotite at 21 Ma, and a chondritic peridotite at 19 Ma. Hence, these inferred sources imply partial melting at various times of subducted arc sediments, oceanic slab, and overlying mantle wedge. An older continental component exists in some of these magmas, through either mixing in the source region or by contamination, but the striking aspect is the absence of magmas generated primarily from older crust.

CONCLUSION

Tectonic decompression of the Whipple core complex has provided an age-dependent, middle to upper crustal view of magmatic arc construction of the Cordilleran orogen. Middle crustal Ca- and Sr-enriched, peraluminous and metaluminous granitoids characterize the older components of the complex, which were subsequently intruded by more potassic granitic suites and enriched, mantle-derived magmas as the complex was transported to an upper crustal level by middle Miocene time.

The most deep-seated plutons (depths > 27 to 33 ± 4 km) compose the 89-Ma Whipple Wash suite, a collection of marginally metaluminous to peraluminous tonalites and granodiorites emplaced as low-angle sills and dikes throughout the upper 3 km of the complex. The most common rock types are two-mica $\pm$ garnet granitoids that are unlike any others in this region of the Cordillera. The suite is characterized by high Ca, Na, and Sr (>800 ppm) and low K, Mg, and Rb, with REE that are HREE depleted and lacking a Eu anomaly. A preferred model of origin is by a high degree of partial melting (approximately or greater than 40 percent) of a calcic, arc-derived graywacke with an eclogite facies mineralogy. Although fractional crystallization $\pm$ minor assimilation may have contributed to the compositional variation within the suite, the principal control appears to be the result of progressive melting of graywacke, leaving an eclogitic residue.

The 73-Ma Axtel quartz diorite intruded the structurally lower regions of the complex as one to three coalescing sills having a composite thickness greater than 0.5 km. The quartz diorite is metaluminous and contains pargasitic hornblende $\pm$ biotite, and sphene; it is less Ca-rich than the Whipple Wash suite, but has higher K and high Sr ($>1,000$ ppm). Partial melting (20 to 30 percent) of eclogite derived from altered and enriched MORB accounts for the more primitive components of the intrusion; up to 40 percent fractionation of dominantly hornblende and plagioclase ($\pm$ biotite, magnetite) yield the remainder of the differentiation series.

Coeval with mid-Tertiary core complex mylonitization (at approximately 26 Ma), swarms of low-angle sills of biotite tonalite and trondhjemitic aplite pervaded the complex, which during the middle Tertiary was at an average crustal level of 16 ± 5 km.

The tonalites and aplites are not comagmatic. The tonalites, despite the large age difference, appear to have been derived by a mechanism similar to that of the Whipple Wash suite. The aplites represent very evolved magmas that, being characterized by chondritic to sub-chondritic abundances of REE, apparently were derived by hornblende(?) fractionation from a magma system that is not exposed.

The more than 10-km-wide Chambers Well dike swarm intruded in two pulses. Late synkinematic (relative to core complex mylonitization) andesite to dacite dikes represent the most potassic magma system to intrude the complex by this time. Abundances of Ca and Sr (~600 ppm) are lower. Principally metaluminous, the more primitive andesites have compositions consistent with melting of a partially eclogitic, partly amphibolitic, enriched basaltic source. Differentiation to produce the dacitic portions of the swarm can be modeled by up to 80 percent fractionation of mineral phases that occur as phenocrysts (plagioclase, hornblende, biotite, magnetite $\pm$ apatite) plus up to 6 to 12 percent crustal assimilation. The second pulse of intrusives that make up the remainder of the swarm are of postkinematic diabase having a crystallization age of approximately 21 Ma. Their restricted compositional range can be accounted for by limited partial melting (~5 percent) of an enriched (from 3 to 4 $\times$ chondrite) mantle.

The 19-Ma, postkinematic War Eagle gabbro-diorite, the youngest large intrusive of the core complex, is inferred to have formed by limited partial melting (~5 percent) of a chondritic mantle. Dioritic members are modeled as having formed by fractionation of clinopyroxene, calcic plagioclase, olivine, and possible minor amounts of hornblende.

In summary, magmatism within the Whipple core complex is inferred to be derived from a variety of sources, all of which are consistent with magma production in a subduction setting. Melting of calcic graywacke and eclogitic basalt generated the Cretaceous plutons. The magmatic hiatus between 73 and 26 Ma may reflect a period when a shallowing of subduction angle carried the locus of subduction-related igneous activity eastward. The renewed magmatic activity at 26 Ma apparently again tapped a calcic graywacke source, and was followed by melting of a partially eclogitized amphibolite and a chondritic to enriched mantle. On a regional basis, the Whipple plutons are compositionally unique. Most inboard plutonic complexes of the region are principally crustal derived. Those reported here are not and differ in being less siliceous and less potassic with higher Ca and Sr and lower Sr_i.

ACKNOWLEDGMENTS

This research culminates twelve years of study of the Whipple core complex for the senior author, who benefited immeasurably from the collaborative effort with Greg Davis. The Masters thesis of Mark Rowley, who initially described the several magmatic entities composing the lower plate of the complex, contributed directly to this effort. This research has been funded by several grants (to JLA) from the National Science Foundation, including EAR-8618285. RLC thanks the Nuclear Engineering department, the reactor crew, and Doug Martin and Karen Shakelton at KSU for their aid in the INA analyses. Critical reviews by Andy Barth, Eric Christiansen, Joe Wooden, and Ed Young were helpful in the final preparation of this manuscript. Without the age control provided by Jim Wright and Ed DeWitt, our understanding of the Whipple magmatic history would have been severely limited.

REFERENCES CITED

Anderson, J. L., 1981, Conditions of mylonitization in a metamorphic core complex, Whipple Mountains, California, *in* Howard, K. A., Carr, M. D., and Miller, D. M., eds., Tectonic framework of the Mojave and Sonoran deserts, California and Arizona: U.S. Geological Survey Open-File Report 81-503, p. 1-3.

—— , 1985, Contrasting depths of "core complex" mylonitization; Barometric evidence: Geological Society of America Abstracts with Programs, v. 17, p. 337.

—— , 1988, Core complexes of the Mojave-Sonoran Desert; Conditions of plutonism, mylonitization, and decompression, *in* Ernst, W. G., ed., Metamorphic and crustal evolution of the western U.S., Rubey Volume 7: Englewood Cliffs, New Jersey, Prentice-Hall, p. 503-525.

Anderson, J. L., and Cullers, R. L., 1987, Crust-enriched, mantle-derived tonalites in the Early Proterozoic Penokean orogen of Wisconsin: Journal of Geology, v. 95, p. 139-154.

Anderson, J. L., and Rowley, M. C., 1981, Synkinematic intrusion of two-mica and associated metaluminous granitoids, Whipple Mountains, California: Canadian Mineralogist, v. 19, p. 83-101.

Anderson, J. L., Davis, G. A., and Frost, E. G., 1979, Field guide to regional Miocene detachment faulting and early Tertiary(?) mylonitization, Whipple-Buckskin-Rawhide mountains, southeastern California and western Arizona, *in* Abbott, P. L., ed., Geological excursions in the southern California area: San Diego, California, San Diego State University Publications, p. 109-133.

Anderson, J. L., Barth, A. P., and Young, E. D., 1988, Mid-crustal Cretaceous roots of Cordilleran metamorphic core complexes: Geology, v. 16, p. 366-369.

Apted, M. J., 1981, Rare earth element systematics of hydrous liquids from partial melting of basaltic eclogite; A re-evaluation: Earth and Planetary Science Letters, v. 52, p. 172-182.

Arth, J. G., 1979, Some trace elements in trondhjemites; Their implications to magma genesis and paleotectonic setting, *in* Barker, F., ed., Trondhjemites, dacites, and related rocks: New York, Elsevier, p. 123-132.

Arth, J. G., Barker, F., Peterman, Z. E., and Friedman, I., 1978, Geochemistry of the gabbro-diorite-tonalite-trondhjemite suite of southwest Finland and its implication for the origin of tonalitic and trondhjemitic magmas: Journal of Petrology, v. 19, part 2, p. 289-316.

Bailey, E. H., Irwin, W. P., and Jones, D. L., 1964, Franciscan and related rocks, and their significance in the geology of western California: California Division of Mines Geological Bulletin, v. 183, p. 89-112.

Barker, F., 1979, Trondhjemites, dacites, and related rocks: New York, Elsevier, 659 p.

Bhatia, M. R., 1985, Rare earth element geochemistry of Australian Paleozoic greywackes and mudrocks; Providence and tectonic control: Sedimentary Geology, v. 45, p. 97-113.

Bhatia, M. R., and Crook, K.A.W., 1986, Trace element characteristics of greywackes and tectonic setting discrimination of sedimentary basins: Contribution to Mineralogy and Petrology, v. 92, p. 181-193.

Blake, M. C., Jayko, A. S., McLaughlin, R. J., and Underwood, M. B., 1988, Metamorphic and tectonic evolution of the Franciscan complex, northern

California, *in* Ernst, W. G., ed., Metamorphism and crustal evolution of the western United States, Rubey Volume 7: Englewood Cliffs, New Jersey, Prentice-Hall, p. 1035-1060.

Coney, P. J., and Reynolds, S. J., 1977, Cordilleran Benioff zones: Nature, v. 270, p. 403-406.

Criscione, J. J., Davis, T. E., and Ehlig, P.J., 1978, The age of sedimentation/ diagenesis for the Bedford Formation and the Santa Monica Formation in southern California; A Rb/Sr evaluation, *in* Howell, D. G., and McDougall, K. A., eds., Mesozoic paleogeography of the western United States: Los Angeles, Society of Economic Paleontologists and Mineralogists, Pacific Coast Paleogeography Symposium 2, p. 385-396.

Davis, G. A., 1988, Rapid upward transport of mid-crustal mylonitic gneisses in the footwall of a Miocene detachment fault, Whipple Mountains, southeastern California: Geologische Rundschau, v. 77/1, p. 191-209.

Davis, G. A., Anderson, J. L., Frost, E. G., and Shackelford, T. J., 1980, Mylonitization and detachment faulting in the Whipple-Buckskin-Rawhide mountain terrane, southeastern California and western Arizona, *in* Crittenden, M. D., Coney, P. J., and Davis, G. H., eds., Cordilleran metamorphic core complexes: Geological Society of America Memoir 153, p. 79-130.

Davis, G. A., Anderson, J. L., Krummenacher, D., Frost, E. G., and Armstrong, R. L., 1982, Geologic and geochronologic relations in the lower plate of the Whipple detachment fault, Whipple Mountains, southeastern California; A progress report, *in* Frost, E. G., and Martin, D. L., eds., Mesozoioc-Cenozoic tectonic evolution of the Colorado River region, California, Arizona, and Nevada: San Diego, California, Cordilleran Publishers, p. 408-432.

Davis, G. A., Lister, G. S., and Reynolds, S. J., 1986, Structural evolution of the Whipple and South mountains shear zones, southwestern United States: Geology, v. 14, p. 7-10.

DeWitt, E., Sutter, J. F., Davis, G. A., and Anderson, J. L., 1986, ^{40}Ar/^{39}Ar age-spectrum dating of Miocene mylonitic rocks, Whipple Mountains, southeastern California: Geological Society of America Abstracts with Programs, v. 18, p. 584.

Ernst, W. G., 1980, Mineral paragenesis in Franciscan metagreywackes of the Nacimiento block, a subduction complex of the southern California Ranges: Journal of Geophysical Research, v. 85, p. 7045-7055.

Frey, F. A., Green, D. H., and Roy, S. D., 1978, Integrated models of basalt genesis; A study of quartz tholeiites to olivine melilites from southeastern Australia utilizing geochemical and experimental petrologic data: Journal of Petrology, v. 19, p. 463-513.

Gill, J. B., 1981, Orogenic andesites and plate tectonics: New York, Springer-Verlag, 390 p.

Hammond, J. G., 1986, Geochemistry and petrogenesis of Proterozoic diabase in the southern Death Valley region of California: Contributions to Mineralogy and Petrology, v. 93, p. 312-321.

Haxel, G. B., Budahn, J. R., Fries, T. L., King, B. W., White, L. D., and Aruscavage, P. J., 1987, Geochemistry of the Orocopia Schist, southeastern California; Summary: Arizona Geological Society Digest, v. 18, p. 49-64.

Hyndman, D. W., 1983, The Idaho batholith and associated plutons, Idaho and western Montana, *in* Roddick, J. A., ed., Circum-Pacific plutonic terranes: Geological Society of America Memoir 159, p. 213-240.

Lanphere, M. A., Blake, M. C., and Irwin, W. P., 1978, Early Cretaceous metamorphic age of the South Fork Mountain schist in the northern Coast Ranges of California: American Journal of Science, v. 278, p. 798-815.

Miller, C. F., 1985, Are strongly peraluminous magmas derived from pelitic sedimentary sources?: Journal of Geology, v. 93, p. 673-689.

Mittlefehldt, D. W., and Miller, C. F., 1983, Geochemistry of the Sweetwater Wash pluton, California; Implications for anomalous trace element behavior during differentiation of felsic magmas: Geochimica et Cosmochimica Acta, v. 47, p. 109-124.

Miyashiro, A., 1974, Volcanic rock series in island arcs and active continental margins: American Journal of Science, v. 274, p. 321-355.

Peacock, S. M., 1988, Inverted metamorphic gradients in the westernmost Cordillera, *in* Ernst, W. G., ed., Metamorphism and crustal evolution of the western United States, Rubey Volume 7: Englewood Cliffs, New Jersey,

Prentice-Hall, p. 953–975.

Peterman, Z. E., Hedge, C. E., Coleman, R. G., and Snavely, P. D., 1967, $^{87}Sr/^{86}Sr$ ratios in some eugeosynclinal sedimentary rocks and their bearing on the origin of granitic magma in orogenic belts: Earth and Planetary Science Letters, v. 2, p. 433–439.

Rowley, M. R., 1981, Intrusion and synkinematic metamorphism of peraluminous and metaluminous granitoids in the autochthon of the central Whipple Mountains, southeastern California [M.S. thesis]: Los Angeles, University of Southern California, 144 p.

Russell, C. W., 1987, Mafic complexes on the western margin of the Idaho batholith: Geological Society of America Abstracts with Programs, v. 19, p. 330.

Sorensen, S., 1988, Tectonometamorphic significance of the basement rocks of the Los Angeles Basin and the inner California continental borderland, *in* Ernst, W. G., ed., Metamorphism and crustal evolution of the western United States, Rubey Volume 7: Englewood Cliffs, New Jersey, Prentice-Hall, p. 198–1022.

Thurn, L. C., 1983, Geology of a portion of the southeastern Whipple Mountains, San Bernardino County, California [M.S. thesis]: Los Angeles, University of Southern California, 186 p.

Wright, J. E., Anderson, J. L., and Davis, G. A., 1986, Timing of plutonism, mylonitization, and decompression in a metamorphic core complex, Whipple Mountians, California: Geological Society of America Abstracts with Programs, v. 18, p. 201.

Wright, J. E., Howard, K. A., and Anderson, J. L., 1987, Isotopic systematics of zircons from Late Cretaceous intrusive rocks, southeastern California; Implications for a vertically stratified crustal column: Geological Society of America Abstracts with Programs, v. 19, p. 898.

Zen, E-an, 1986, Aluminum enrichment in silicate melts by fractional crystallization; Some mineralogic and petrographic constraints: Journal of Perology. v. 27, p. 1095–1117.

Zen, E-an, and Hammarstrom, J. M., 1984, Magmatic epidote and its petrologic significance: Geology, v. 12, p. 515–518.

MANUSCRIPT SUBMITTED AUGUST 5, 1988
REVISED MANUSCRIPT SUBMITTED SEPTEMBER 20, 1988
MANUSCRIPT ACCEPTED BY THE SOCIETY FEBRUARY 7, 1989

Chapter 5

Petrology and geochemistry of the metaluminous to peraluminous Chemehuevi Mountains Plutonic Suite, southeastern California

Barbara E. John*
U.S. Geological Survey, 345 Middlefield Road, Menlo Park, California 94025, and Department of Geological Sciences, University of California, Santa Barbara, California 93106
Joe Wooden
U.S. Geological Survey, 345 Middlefield Road, Menlo Park, California 94025

ABSTRACT

Structural relief resulting from middle Tertiary extensional deformation in the Chemehuevi Mountains exposes a unique cross section through a temporally and compositionally zoned (both vertically and horizontally), laccolith-shaped intrusion of Late Cretaceous age. The calc-alkalic, metaluminous to peraluminous Chemehuevi Mountains Plutonic Suite exhibits crude normal, vertical, and temporal zonation. The zones are progressively younger and more felsic away from the roof and walls; the most differentiated material is concentrated toward the center and floor of the intrusion. Hornblende-biotite- and biotite granodiorite are metaluminous and form the outer margin of the intrusion along the northern and southern walls, and sill-like bodies in an older suite of granitoids and Proterozoic basement rocks. Locally these rocks bear a subhorizontal, southwest-trending, mylonitic lineation, considered to be synchronous with regional mylonitic deformation. Later and more evolved units are subequigranular to porphyritic, metaluminous to weakly peraluminous biotite granodiorite to granite, and make up the greatest proportion of the intrusion. The youngest, most leucocratic members of the suite are undeformed, locally garnetiferous muscovite granite and granodiorite that form the central part of the intrusion.

Major, trace, and rare earth element data indicate that the magmas of the Chemehuevi Mountains Plutonic Suite became progressively enriched in Si, K, Rb, Mn, Y, U, and heavy rare earth elements (REE). Fractional crystallization of some REE–rich accessory minerals was important in producing some of these trends. Although modest compositional breaks occur across internal contacts, the general continuity of trends from field, modal, and chemical data suggests that these rocks constitute a comagmatic intrusive suite. Estimates for the pressure of emplacement of the suite vary from 4 to 6 kbar, or a minimum depth of 12 km. Preliminary Pb-, Sr-, and oxygen-isotopic data, together with the REE chemistry, suggest that the Chemehuevi Mountains Plutonic Suite was derived from a heterogeneous crustal source. Compositional variations within the plutonic suite are consistent with open-system fractionation, involving fractional crystallization of discrete batches of magma derived from the melting of a heterogeneous crustal source under H_2O-saturated conditions.

*Present address: Department of Earth Sciences, University of Cambridge, Downing Street, Cambridge CB2 3EQ, England.

John, B. E., and Wooden, J., 1990, Petrology and geochemistry of the Chemehuevi Mountains Plutonic Suite, southeastern California, *in* Anderson, J. L., ed., The nature and origin of Cordilleran magmatism: Boulder, Colorado, Geological Society of America Memoir 174.

INTRODUCTION

One problem of many zoned plutonic complexes is whether various intrusive members are genetically related to a single parent magma, and if so, what is the nature of the parental source rocks. Where exposure is limited, one can only infer the geometry and relations between vertical, horizontal, and temporal zonations. Structural relief resulting from middle Tertiary crustal extension in the Chemehuevi Mountains area provides a rare opportunity to document both the geometry of a mesozonal intermediate to silicic magma chamber and the nature of chemical zonation within the body. In this paper we document the field, petrographic, and chemical nature of compositional zonation in the Chemehuevi Mountains Plutonic Suite of southeast California, in order to evaluate the genetic relationship between the members, and the processes that occurred as the plutonic suite evolved. A more detailed description of the overall geometry of the suite is given in John (1988).

GEOLOGIC SETTING

The Chemehuevi Mountains Plutonic Suite is a part of the belt of calc-alkalic, metaluminous, and peraluminous granitoids (Miller, 1981) that are satellitic to the voluminous Sierra Nevada and Peninsular Ranges batholiths in southern California (Fig. 1). This suite of granitic rocks is here named the Chemehuevi Mountains Plutonic Suite, and includes the Chemehuevi Peak Granodiorite, which crops out over a broad area in the western portion of the Chemehuevi Mountains. The unit takes its name from its type locality, Chemehuevi Peak, the highest point in the range 972 m (3013 ft). A detailed description of the unit (Kpg) is given in Appendix 1. The suite represents the most areally extensive (>280 km^2) eastern exposure of the Late Cretaceous magmatic arc at lat 34° (Burchfiel and Davis, 1981; John, 1981). Although the rocks lie inboard of known exposures of the Mesozoic Cordilleran fold and thrust belt, the country rocks have undergone regional metamorphism and ductile deformation that are at least in part contemporaneous with shortening. Preliminary geochronologic data suggest that the plutonic suite was emplaced during the waning stages of Late Cretaceous compressional deformation and metamorphism, well exposed in the adjacent Old Woman–Piute and nearby Big Maria Mountains (Howard and others, 1987; Hoisch and others, 1988).

Subsequent to emplacement, the plutonic suite has been dissected by multiple middle Tertiary low-angle normal or detachment faults (John, 1987a, 1987b). Structural data (John, 1986, 1988) indicate a west-southwest tilt of the plutonic suite about 10° to 20° relative to its original orientation. The resulting structural relief, greater than 4 km, provides an excellent cross-sectional view through the temporally and compositionally zoned plutonic complex (Fig. 2). Tertiary extensional deformation unroofed the mid-crustal Chemehuevi Mountains Plutonic Suite and made it possible to document not only the chamber geome-

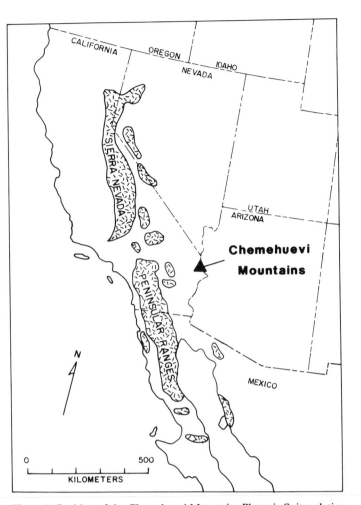

Figure 1. Position of the Chemehuevi Mountains Plutonic Suite relative to the Late Cretaceous Sierra Nevada and Peninsular Ranges batholiths.

try, but make inferences about the processes that occurred as the plutonic complex evolved.

Compositional trends and deformation styles, taken with the intrusive relations documented in the field and portrayed by John (1987b), suggest a minimum of three separate magma series in the Chemehuevi Mountains (Figs. 3, 4, and 5). The separate series include, from oldest to youngest, the Whale Mountain sequence, deformed metaluminous to peraluminous sheet-like intrusions, and the Chemehuevi Mountains Plutonic Suite. The older Whale Mountain sequence, named for exposures around Whale Mountain in the northern Chemehuevi Mountains, comprises sphene-bearing hornblende diorites, quartz diorites, quartz monzodiorites, and low-silica granites with alkalic affinities (Figs. 4 and 5). These rocks crop out along the northern and southern flanks of the range, and are spatially associated with both ductilely deformed and undeformed Proterozoic gneisses (Fig. 2). Granitic rocks intermediate in age between the Whale Mountain sequence and Chemehuevi Mountains Plutonic Suite are exposed in the structurally deepest part of the range, to the northeast and east, and are characterized by thin (a few tens of centimeters to about 30 m thick) sheet-like bodies that were intruded as dikes and have subsequently been rotated and ductilely deformed. Intrusive relations between these first two magma series have not been adequately established. In the northern and eastern parts of the range, both series have a well-developed ductile fabric; intrusion therefore predates mylonitic deformation. The Chemehuevi Mountains Plutonic Suite contains the youngest magmatic event and overlapped in time with a period of regional mylonitic deformation. The latter suite spans a compositional range from metaluminous to peraluminous, and underlies the western and central two-thirds of the range (Fig. 2). This paper will focus on the Chemehuevi Mountains Plutonic Suite. Preliminary data from the earlier two sequences are presented in Table 1 (Tables 1 through 6 are at end of chapter) and will be discussed briefly for comparative purposes.

A reconstruction of the pre-Tertiary (pre-tilt) configuration of the Chemehuevi Mountains Plutonic Suite by down-structure methods (John, 1986, 1988) is diagrammed in Figure 6. This reconstruction provides a useful framework for discussion of the chemical zonation within the suite and is outlined below. The complex had nearly vertical northwest and southeast walls, trending about 060°. The chamber was floored by subhorizontally foliated mylonitic gneisses. The floor was horizontal or very gently dipping, and defined by the lit par lit injection of phenocryst-poor biotite granodiorite, and by voluminous pegmatites. The suite was apparently intruded as two separate bodies. The first, smaller, body is a structurally deep granodiorite sill that intruded the upper part of the thick zone of mylonitic gneiss. The second body intruded into a structurally more favorable position at the upper margin of ductile deformation. Magma was fed into this chamber along at least three feeder dikes, oriented ~060°/vertical. At this structural level, the chamber was inflated laterally by three successively more fractionated pulses of magma before final cooling and solidification. Although the upper part of the suite and roof are not exposed, the presence of voluminous pegmatites and the zonation within the suite (Fig. 6) suggest that the roof zone lies a short distance to the west, beneath Chemehuevi Valley. The magma apparently ponded along the contact between undeformed Proterozoic basement above and subhorizontally foliated mylonitic gneisses below, and was therefore structurally controlled. This structural interface or discontinuity apparently acted as a trap for rising magma from a reservoir chamber at deeper structural levels.

Compositionally, the Chemehuevi Mountains Plutonic Suite is a metaluminous to peraluminous composite intrusion that exhibits a crude normal, vertical, and temporal zonation (Figs. 2 and 6), younging and becoming progressively more felsic away from the walls. The most differentiated material is concentrated toward the center and floor of the intrusion. The suite comprises five members. The older members are metaluminous, hornblende-biotite, and biotite-sphene granodiorites (Kgd and Kbg) that form the outer margin of the intrusion along the northern and

southern walls, and sill-like bodies in the Proterozoic basement. Intermediate in age are subequigranular to porphyritic, metaluminous to weakly peraluminous biotite granodiorite to granite (Kpg) that make up the greatest proportion of the body. The youngest, most leucocratic members are muscovite-bearing, locally garnetiferous granite and granodiorite (Kg and Kgg) that form the central part of the complex.

Preliminary U-Pb zircon data suggest that the Chemehuevi Mountains Plutonic Suite is Cretaceous in age. Zircon fractions from undeformed members of the suite (Kbg and Kpg) are variably discordant, but each define chords that yield Late Cretaceous crystallization ages (S. B. Mukasa, unpublished data; John and Mukasa, 1988). K-Ar cooling dates on biotite range 64.1 ± 2.2 Ma, from the Chemehuevi Peak Granodiorite in the southwestern part of range (John, 1982), to 57.3 ± 2.9 Ma from the same unit in the central part of the range (Frost and others, 1982). These minimum ages represent the time biotite passed through its blocking temperature of ~280° ± 40 °C (Harrison and McDougall, 1980). Granitic rocks in the Old Woman–Piute Mountains have U-Pb zircon ages of 72 and 76 Ma (J. Wright, *in* Miller and others, 1984). Similar rocks in the Whipple Mountains, south of the Chemehuevi Mountains, have U-Pb ages on zircon of 89 and 73 Ma (Wright and others, 1986). A late-stage aplite dike in the Iron Mountains has a K-Ar cooling age on muscovite of 62 Ma (Howard and others, 1982). These intrusive bodies have ranges in major-element, trace-element, and REE chemistry that are similar to those of the Chemehuevi Mountains (Miller and others, 1981; Miller and Mittlefehldt, 1982, 1984; Mittlefehldt and Miller, 1983; Miller and others, 1984). The preliminary U-Pb crystallization and K-Ar cooling ages, taken with these chemical similarities, suggest a Late Cretaceous age for intrusion of the suite.

STRUCTURE OF THE CHEMEHUEVI MOUNTAINS PLUTONIC SUITE

The reconstruction outlined above suggests that the Chemehuevi Mountains Plutonic Suite is a large, laccolith-shaped intrusion. Inferences about the chemical zonation of the suite are based on the reconstructed attitude of the suite (Fig. 6) combined with the orientation of igneous foliation, and textural and mineralogical changes (see Fig. 2).

Foliation

Igneous foliation within the Chemehuevi Mountains Plutonic Suite is defined by the planar orientation of biotite, muscovite, potassium-feldspar megacrysts, plagioclase crystals, and rare tabular mafic enclaves, country-rock xenoliths, and mafic schlieren. Igneous foliation is well developed along the eastern margin, where it is predominantly gently dipping, and has a northwest strike approximately parallel with the foliation in the bounding country rocks (John, 1987b). In the western part of the range, foliation is weak to absent. The majority of the Cheme-

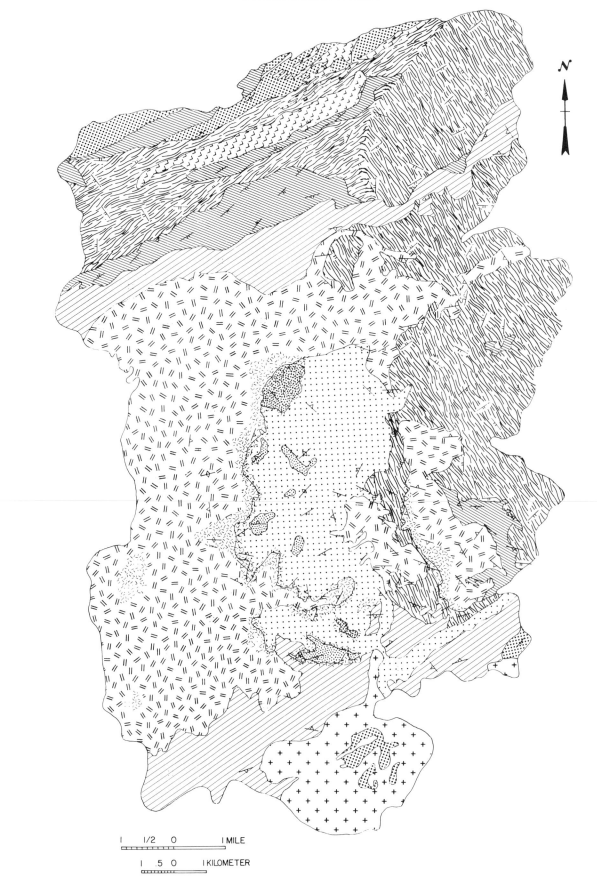

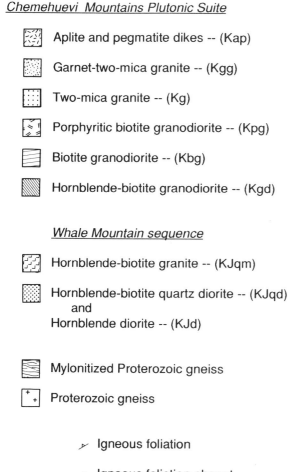

Chemehuevi Mountains Plutonic Suite

Aplite and pegmatite dikes -- (Kap)

Garnet-two-mica granite -- (Kgg)

Two-mica granite -- (Kg)

Porphyritic biotite granodiorite -- (Kpg)

Biotite granodiorite -- (Kbg)

Hornblende-biotite granodiorite -- (Kgd)

Whale Mountain sequence

Hornblende-biotite granite -- (KJqm)

Hornblende-biotite quartz diorite -- (KJqd)
and
Hornblende diorite -- (KJd)

Mylonitized Proterozoic gneiss

Proterozoic gneiss

↙ Igneous foliation

∷ Igneous foliation absent

↙ Mylonitic foliation

Figure 2 (facing page; explanation above). Generalized palinspastic map of the footwall to the Chemehuevi Mountains detachment fault, Chemehuevi Mountains and surrounding area (after John, 1986). The Chemehuevi Mountains Plutonic Suite lies in the west-central part of the range, and intrudes Proterozoic and older Mesozoic gneissic and granitic rocks.

huevi Peak Granodiorite is structureless and homogeneous, except for aplite and pegmatite dikes. Gently southwest-dipping schlieren characterize the eastern margin or floor of the porphyritic granodiorite. Igneous foliation in the two northern feeder dikes is concordant with the country-rock fabric. In outcrop, their contact is characterized by a lit par lit injection zone with interlayered granodiorite and Proterozoic gneiss, but at map scale defines steep feeder dikes. Igneous foliation in the hornblende-biotite granodiorite has been overprinted by the regionally developed mylonitic foliation and lineation, and is only rarely preserved.

Chemical data presented below suggest that the variation from biotite granodiorite (Kbg) to garnet-two-mica granite (Kgg) is a comagmatic sequence. As mentioned above, the early-formed hornblende-biotite granodiorite (Kgd) bears a mylonitic fabric,

and has been intruded at some later time by undeformed biotite granodiorite and more felsic members of the Chemehuevi Mountains Plutonic Suite. Although intrusion of the suite generally postdates metamorphism and ductile deformation, the early intrusive members were subjected to strain coaxial with that of the older plutonic and Proterozoic metamorphic rocks. The Chemehuevi Mountains Plutonic Suite is therefore late synkinematic to postkinematic.

Zonation

On the basis of textural, mineralogical, and geochemical arguments, the Chemehuevi Mountains Plutonic Suite is horizontally, vertically, and temporally zoned (Figs. 3, 6, 7). Intrusive relations indicate that undeformed members are more felsic and successively younger. Mylonitic hornblende-biotite granodiorite grades discontinuously inward along the northern boundary into undeformed biotite granodiorite and porphyritic granodiorite. In the southeastern part of the range, deformed hornblende-biotite granodiorite is clearly intruded by the Chemehuevi Peak Granodiorite, without the intermediate composition biotite granodiorite (Fig. 2).

The concentric pattern of rock types is evident from Figure 2 and John (1987b). Sharp internal contacts are common in the suite but are not present everywhere. Figure 2 shows discrete internal contacts; the boundaries are, however, marked by mineralogical and textural changes that may vary over a distance of tens of meters. The contact between two-mica granite and garnet–two-mica granite is gradational over about ten meters. The southernmost body of garnet–two-mica granite, however, has a sharp, fine-grained contact against the biotite granodiorite.

GEOCHEMISTRY

Introduction

The Chemehuevi Mountains Plutonic Suite forms a quartz-normative, calc-alkaline metaluminous to peraluminous suite. The plutonic units overlap in silica content and alumina saturation index, A/CNK (molar $Al_2O_3/[CaO+Na_2O+K_2O]$), and form a magma series from 60 to 75 percent SiO_2. Harker diagrams show nearly linear trends. Compositions cluster in the range 60 to 64 percent and 66 to 75 percent SiO_2.

Analytical methods

Forty samples, representing all stages of the plutonic suite and related aplite and pegmatite dikes, were collected from throughout the Chemehuevi Mountains. Brief petrologic and location descriptions are given in John (1986, Appendix 2). Major- and trace-element concentrations were determined by x-ray fluorescence techniques at the U.S. Geological Survey (USGS) Branch of Analytical Chemistry in Lakewood, Colorado, and Menlo Park, California, at Macquarie University, in the labora-

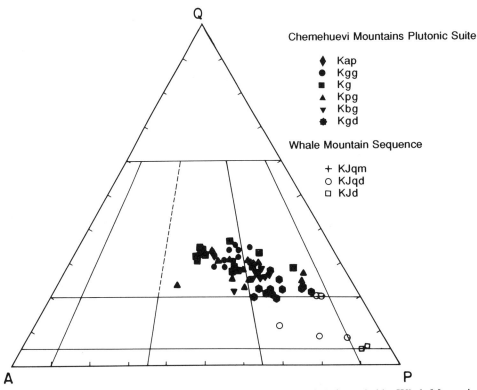

Figure 3. Modal composition of the Chemehuevi Mountains Plutonic Suite and older Whale Mountain sequence in terms of quartz (Q), alkali feldspar (A), and plagioclase (P). Modal composition based on a minimum count of 1,000 points on stained slabs. Modes of the strongly deformed sheetlike intrusions exposed in the eastern part of the range were not counted. Nomenclature taken from Streckeisen (1976). Abbreviations as in Figure 2.

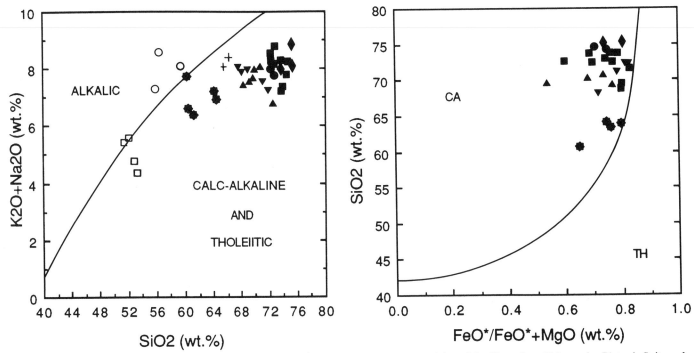

Figure 4. Composition of the Chemehuevi Mountains Plutonic Suite and older adjacent plutonic rocks in terms of weight percent of silica and total alkalies. Alkalic-subalkalic (calc-alkaline and tholeiitic) division is from Irvine and Baragar (1971).

Figure 5. Composition of the Chemehuevi Mountains Plutonic Suite and older adjacent plutonic rocks in terms of weight percent SiO_2 and FeO/(FeO+MgO). Calc-alkaline (CA) and tholeiitic (TH) division from Miyashiro (1974). Symbols as in Figure 3.

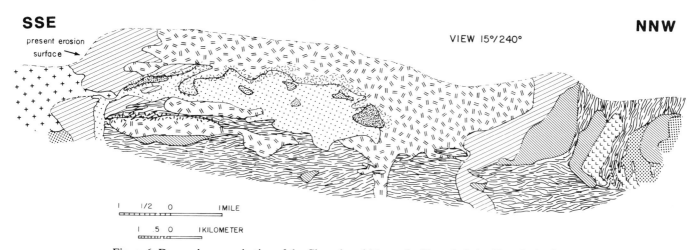

Figure 6. Down-plunge projection of the Chemehuevi Mountains Plutonic Suite. Note the horizontal, vertical, and temporal zonation, and concentration of aplite and pegmatite dikes along the top of both the lower intrusion and in the more voluminous chamber above. Patterns as in Figure 2.

tory of S. E. Shaw, and by neutron activation in the USGS analytical labs. The major-element data are estimated to be precise to relative ± 0.1 percent or absolute 0.01, whichever is larger, except for MgO, which is precise to relative ± 2 percent, and Na_2O, good to ±2.5 percent (J. C. Taggert, Jr., written communication, 1985). The rare earth elements, plus Co, Cr, Hf, Mn, Ba, Rb, Sr, Sb, Ta, Th, U, Zr, and Sc were determined by instrumental neutron activation analysis (INAA) at the U.S. Geological Survey in Lakewood, Colorado. INAA data are estimated to be precise to ±1 percent of the analyzed value for Ba, Co, Cr, Hf, Sr, Th, Sc, La, Sm, Eu, Fe, and Na, ±2 percent for Mn, Rb, Ce, Yb, and K, and ±3 to 20 percent for Cs, Sb, Ta, U, Gd, Dy, Tm, Zr, Nd, Tb, and Lu.

Initial Pb-, Sr-, and oxygen-isotopic compositions were determined for some samples of the plutonic suite and older igneous rocks. Sr-isotope analyses were performed by M. Lanphere, USGS Branch of Isotope Geology, Menlo Park. Whole-rock oxygen analyses were performed by G. C. Solomon at Cal Tech as part of a regional study of Mesozoic granitic rocks in the Mojave Desert area.

Analytical results

Major- and trace-element geochemistry. Rocks of the Chemehuevi Mountains Plutonic Suite have compositions typical of calc-alkaline magmatic suites (Irvine and Barager, 1971; Miyashiro, 1974), and are metaluminous to moderately peraluminous (Table 1 and Fig. 8). Silica contents range from 60 percent in the earliest, deformed hornblende-biotite granodiorite to 75 percent in the most silicic and leucocratic aplite dikes (Fig. 8). All major elements show fairly smooth, continuous variations with increasing silica between 67.5 and 75.3 percent (Fig. 9). The compatible elements Al, Ca, Fe, Mg, and Ti all decrease with increasing silica. Abundances for K_2O and Na_2O both show scatter, possibly due in part to postemplacement alteration and restricted alkali exchange.

Although the Harker variation diagrams (Fig. 9) show nearly linear trends, the data group into two clusters of points in the range 60 to 64.5 weight percent SiO_2, and 67 to 75 weight percent SiO_2, with an apparent silica gap between the mylonitized hornblende-biotite granodiorite and the undeformed biotite granodiorite. Although this may be simply due to samping bias or fundamental changes in whole-rock chemistry due to the mylonitic deformation, the occurrence of these two discrete compositions, with little or no overlap in silica, is not what would be expected if fractional crystallization controlled the composition of the magma. On the basis of arguments outlined below, it seems likely that the two clusters of points represent at least two batches of magma separated in time, yet derived from a similar source.

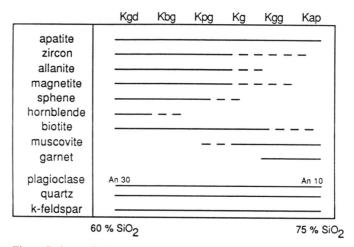

Figure 7. Crystallization sequences for the Chemehuevi Mountains Plutonic Suite (based on petrography). The length of each line indicates the duration of crystallization of each phase. Magmatic epidote occurs as overgrowths on allanite throughout the suite (see Fig. 17), except at the highest structural levels in the porphyritic biotite granodiorite (Kpg). Monazite is very rare and only recognized in one thin section of the garnet–two-mica granite (Kgg). Abbreviations as in Figure 2.

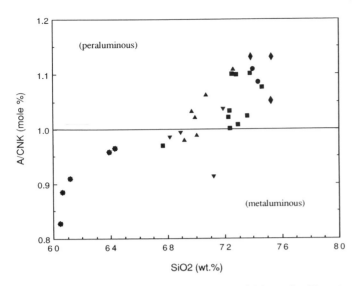

Figure 8. Chemical features of the Chemehuevi Mountains Plutonic Suite. SiO_2 vs. mole percent $(Al_2O_3/[CaO+K_2O+Na_2O])$, indicates the suite is compositionally expanded and metaluminous to weakly peraluminous (Shand, 1951).

Trace-element variation diagrams are shown in Figure 10, and indicate fairly smooth, continuous trends for most elements. Fractionation trends for the plutonic suite exhibit decreasing Sr, increasing Rb, and level to slightly decreasing Ba with progressive differentiation. The monotonic decrease in Sr is probably due to plagioclase fractionation.

Rare earth element chemistry. Chondrite-normalized (CN) rare earth element (REE) data for the plutonic suite are shown in Figure 11, and represent the full range of compositional and textural variation within the complex. Total REE contents in the suite are low to moderate, ranging from ≈140 to 260 ppm for the granodiorites, and ≈11 to 160 ppm for the granites and aplites. The most notable feature of the REE spectra is the steady decrease in light rare earth element (LREE) abundances and increase in the heavy rare earth element (HREE) concentration from the marginal hornblende-biotite granodiorite and biotite granodiorite, to the central two-mica and garnet–two-mica granite. There is an absolute increase in HREE with increasing silica throughout the Chemehuevi Mountains Plutonic Suite. Early, marginal members of the suite are moderately LREE–enriched, having CN LREE about 100 to 200 times condritic abundances and CN HREE values of 10 to 20. The inner, later part of the suite has nearly flat REE patterns between 50 and 100 times chondritic abundances. In contrast, rocks of the older Whale Mountain sequence have REE trends nearly parallel to, but with significantly higher LREE concentrations (200 to >500 times chondrite), and more depleted HREE, than the older members of the Chemehuevi Mountains Plutonic Suite (Fig. 12).

On the basis of the REE data, the plutonic suite can be divided into two subgroups with different trends, corresponding to compositions with <74% SiO_2, and >74% SiO_2. The

chondrite-normalized element ratio $(Ce/Yb)_{CN}$ provides a measure of the overall slope of the plot and the extent of fractionation of the LREE from the HREE. The intermediate and silicic rocks, those with <74% SiO_2, are moderately LREE enriched, with $1.0 < (Ce/Yb)_{CN} < 5.4$ (Fig. 11). These rocks have nearly linear REE patterns with a general decrease in slope with increasing silica, and little or no Eu anomaly. In contrast, the garnet–two-mica granites and aplite dikes with >74% SiO_2 exhibit little LREE to HREE fractionation, with $(Ce/Yb)_{CN}$ varying between 0.8 and 1.0. The pronounced LREE depletion of the granites relative to the granodiorites owes to fractionation of LREE-rich accessory minerals, including allanite and monazite (Fig. 7). Depletion of REE in the earlier members (hornblende-biotite granodiorite, biotite granodiorite, and the porphyritic biotite granodiorite) is probably controlled by other accessory minerals (allanite, zircon, apatite, and sphene), a feature typical of many evolved granitic systems (Dodge and Mays, 1972; Fourcade and Allegre, 1981; Mittlefehldt and Miller, 1983; Miller and Mittlefehldt, 1982, 1984).

Distribution coefficients for the LREE in most major minerals predict that these elements should behave incompatibly during crystallization, and therefore increase with fractionation (Mittlefehldt and Miller, 1983). REE patterns for the plutonic suite show a progressive decrease of LREE with increasing silica by a factor of 5 to 10 times. This "anomalous" behavior has been recognized in other felsic plutonic and volcanic suites (Hildreth, 1979, 1981; Miller and Mittlefehldt, 1982; Mittlefehldt and Miller, 1983). Mittlefehldt and Miller (1983) have shown that trace amounts of monazite in the Sweetwater Wash pluton in the Old Woman Mountains contain >75 percent of the LREE in the whole rock. Although monazite has only been recognized in one thin section, numerous other LREE–rich accessory minerals, including allanite, sphene, zircon, and apatite, are early crystallizing phases throughout the suite.

Isotope geochemistry. Samples of the Chemehuevi Mountains Plutonic Suite and adjacent rocks were analyzed for their isotopic compositions as part of broad regional studies of isotopic provinces in southern California (determined by J. Wooden, M. Lanphere, and G. C. Soloman). These isotopic studies were not keyed specifically to answering magma genesis questions in the Chemehuevi Mountains. However, the data reported here provide general constraints on the source and petrogenesis of the plutonic suite, although more isotopic data are needed to fully document their origin and evolution.

Initial Lead. Analyses for initial lead were performed on feldspar separates from the plutonic suite and adjacent Whale Mountain sequence. Pb-isotopic composition data are listed in Table 2, and plotted in Figures 13 and 14. Samples from the plutonic suite and adjacent intrusive rocks exhibit significant variation in initial Pb-isotopic composition. $^{206}Pb/^{204}Pb$ ratios vary from 18.01 to 18.79; $^{207}Pb/^{204}Pb$ from 15.58 to 15.67 and $^{208}Pb/^{204}Pb$ from 38.74 to 39.31. Because magmatic differentiation processes do not result in Pb-isotopic fractionation, the isotopic composition of all rocks derived by closed-system processes

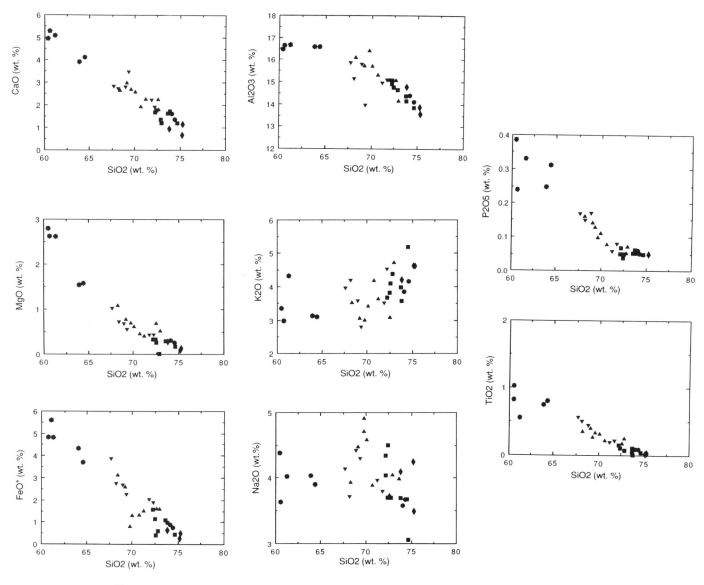

Figure 9. Selected Harker variation diagrams for the Chemehuevi Mountains Plutonic Suite. Symbols as in Figure 3.

from an isotopically homogeneous magma should be uniform (Gill, 1981, p. 149).

The variable initial lead data for the plutonic suite indicate that the intrusive members were not derived through closed-system fractionation of an isotopically homogeneous magma. In addition, there is no consistent correlation between Pb-isotopic composition and silica content (or any other index of fractionation) in the granitic rocks (Fig. 14). This relationship implies that the magmas were derived from, or interacted during fractionation with, crustal materials that had heterogeneous whole-rock and Pb-isotopic compositions. The feldspar Pb-isotopic data for samples Ch-139, Ch-141, Ch-142, Ch-143, and Ch-241 yield a $^{206}Pb/^{204}Pb$ vs. $^{207}Pb/^{204}Pb$ isochron with an age of 1,720 ± 89 Ma (1σ). Pb-isotopic data from all the samples analyzed in the Chemehuevi Mountains (Table 2) yield an isochron of 1,799 Ma

with a large uncertainty of ±300 Ma (1σ). The Pb-isotopic characteristics of the plutonic suite thus indicate that they were derived at least in part from an early Proterozoic terrane. These data are consistent with the regional Nd- and Sr-isotopic analyses of Farmer and DePaolo (1984) for Mesozoic and Tertiary intrusive rocks in eastern Nevada, north-central Utah, eastern California, and southern Arizona.

The $^{206}Pb/^{204}Pb$ ratios for the feldspars are much lower than predicted values from Stacey and Kramers (1975) or other Pb evolution curves. Two likely causes are either preferential assimilation of lead from the Proterozoic basement complex, or interaction with granulitic or other material with long-term low U/Pb. The fact that the $^{208}Pb/^{204}Pb$ ratios of the feldspars are higher than the values of Stacey and Kramers favors interaction with or derivation from granulites, because granulites are com-

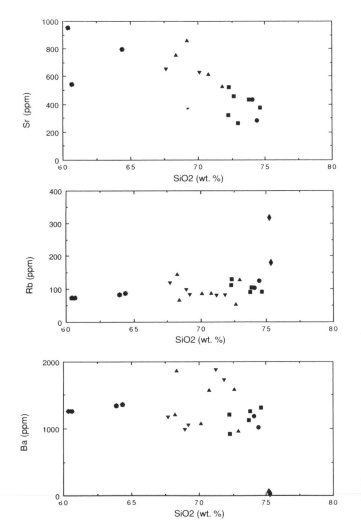

Figure 10. Variation diagrams of selected trace elements in rocks from the Chemehuevi Mountains Plutonic Suite. Symbols as in Figure 3.

monly more depleted in U with respect to Pb than Th with respect to Pb (Tilton and Barreiro, 1980). A suggestion of the lowering of the $^{206}Pb/^{204}Pb$ ratio with progressively more fractionated material in the suite (Fig. 14) indicates that the more highly evolved members may have interacted with or have been derived from granulitic material, the biotite and porphyritic biotite granodiorite being slightly more primitive, albeit with more radiogenic lead, than either the two-mica granite or the garnet–two-mica granite. With greater fractionation and therefore residence time in a reservoir chamber, potential contamination by or assimilation of depleted Proterozoic wall rocks could take place. To test this relation, further whole-rock initial lead analyses of exposed Proterozoic wall rocks to the suite are in progress.

The Pb-isotopic data for the plutonic suite are within the middle range of $^{206}Pb/^{204}Pb$ values reported by Wooden and others (1988) for Mesozoic intrusive rocks in southeastern California and western Arizona (Fig. 13). On the basis of the Pb-isotopic data, Wooden and others (1988) concluded that, on a regional basis, the Mesozoic intrusions in southeastern California and western Arizona were largely derived from the melting of and

interaction of magmas with the Proterozoic basement rocks. They further suggested that the Pb-isotopic compositions of the Mesozoic granitic rocks analyzed are not characteristic of igneous rocks generated purely by subduction (Church, 1976; Kay and others, 1978), but are more common in rock suites formed by the reworking of continental crust (Moorbath and Taylor, 1981).

Strontium. Values of $^{87}Sr/^{86}Sr_i$ for three samples from the Chemehuevi Mountains Plutonic Suite range from 0.7083 to 0.7097, and one analyzed from the Whale Mountain sequence yielded a ratio of 0.7083 (Table 3). These values are within the range found for other Late Cretaceous plutonic rocks in the eastern Mojave Desert (Miller and others, 1984; Davis and others, 1982; Howard and Lanphere, unpublished data), and within the range for continental arcs (Gill, 1981). The data scatter, with little correlation between initial ratios, whole-rock silica, Rb/Sr, and Sr content. The range of $^{87}Sr/^{86}Sr_i$ and high Sr content for the Chemehuevi Mountains Plutonic Suite are again indicative of either an isotopically heterogeneous source region or crustal contamination of an originally homogeneous source. There is no correlation between SiO_2 and $^{87}Sr/^{86}Sr$, or Sr and Rb/Sr (Fig. 15). The nonlinear strontium data ($^{87}Sr/^{86}Sr_i$ vs. $^{87}Rb/^{86}Sr$) for

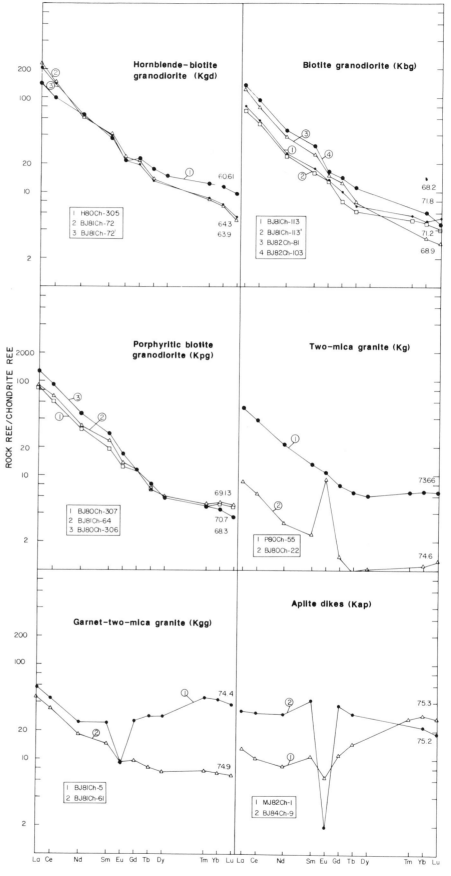

Figure 11. Chondrite normalized REE chemistry plotted with weight percent SiO$_2$ for the Chemehuevi Mountains Plutonic Suite. All data have been normalized against chondrite values listed in Haskin and others (1968). Chondritic values for Dy taken from Masuda and others (1973). Specimens BJ81 Ch-72 and 72′ (hornblende-biotite granodiorite), and BJ81Ch-113 and 113′ (biotite granodiorite) are duplicate analyses on splits from the same powders.

the plutonic suite indicate that the magma was isotopically very heterogeneous, and argue for significant two or more component mixing and/or assimilation. Initial strontium data, taken with the established intrusive relationships, older members (Kgd) having a ratio of 0.7083 and the younger members (Kbg and Kpg) having higher ratios of 0.7086 to 0.7097, suggest that Sr becomes more radiogenic with time. Although the data set is limited, it possibly represents an increasing contribution with time from a radiogenic crustal reservoir. In contrast, the initial Pb compositions for the youngest members of the suite apparently decrease in radiogenic Pb with time. The elevated $^{87}Sr/^{86}Sr$ initial ratio implies, however, that the suite was derived from a source of radiogenic quartzo-feldspathic crust.

Oxygen. Reconnaissance whole-rock oxygen-isotope data of Solomon (unpublished) for the Chemehuevi Mountains Plutonic Suite are listed in Table 4. The oxygen-isotopic compositions of the suite and leucocratic members of the Whale Mountain sequence are remarkably homogeneous; $\delta^{18}O$ values of each range from +7.0 to +7.8 ‰, well within normal values for unaltered granitic rocks (Taylor, 1978). Because these values lie within the "normal" range of oxygen isotopes (+6 < $\delta^{18}O$ < +10 ‰), it is difficult to conclude anything definitive about the origin of the suite on the basis of this data alone, except that there was little

interaction with meteoric water or hydrothermal fluids, such as might be expected from alteration associated with detachment faulting. Evidently, the suite was emplaced at a deep enough level in the crust to not set up a massive hydrothermal system. Taylor (1978) noted that granitoids at the low end of the normal range, with compositions similar to those reported here, could have been formed by direct differentiation from a basaltic or andesitic magma. This is not a unique interpretation of the data, however, because these values could also have been derived through partial melting of deep-seated rocks from the lower crust, or partial contamination or assimilation of high $\delta^{18}O$ metasedimentary rocks. Solomon (1986) suggested that rocks like the felsic two-mica granites in the Chemehuevi Mountains are nearly pure end-member melts of mid-crustal sialic material that comingled with melts from a deeper source, either from the upper mantle or lower crust.

The igneous values for the plutonic suite indicate little interaction with meteoric water or hydrothermal fluids. This suggests that fluids associated with the detachment faulting were restricted to zones along the faults, and that the suite was emplaced at a deep enough level in the crust to not drive a massive hydrothermal system.

Extreme variation of Pb-, Sr-, and O-isotopic values have

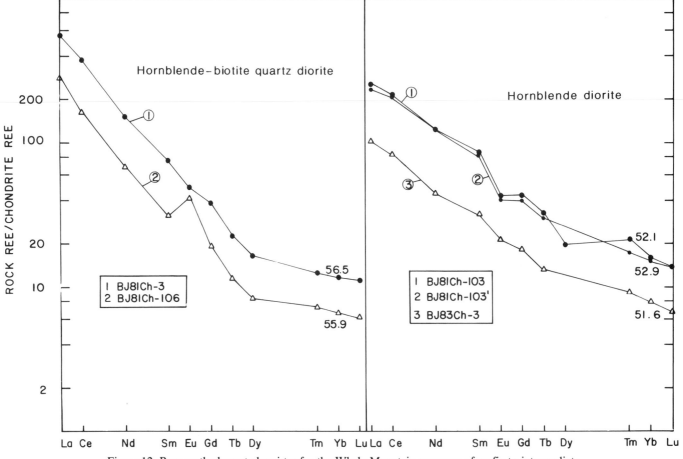

Figure 12. Rare earth element chemistry for the Whale Mountain sequence of mafic to intermediate plutonic rocks in the northern Chemehuevi Mountains. All data have been normalized as in Figure 11.

been noted for rhyolitic and shallow plutonic rocks from the Yellowstone Plateau, and indicate that processes other than wall-rock contamination/assimilation can influence isotopic ratios (Doe and others, 1986). Oxygen-isotopic data in particular indicate that aqueous fluids (meteoric and hydrothermal water) interacted with the evolving Yellowstone magmas. The few oxygen-isotope data from the plutonic suite retain their magmatic values, implying that the extreme variations in initial Pb ratios are not a function of hydrothermal circulation, but are probably primary magmatic or source-related features.

Conditions of emplacement of the Chemehuevi Mountains Plutonic Suite

A recurring problem in granite petrology is the development of reliable indictors of physical conditions during emplacement and crystallization. Reconstruction of a unique history of physical conditions may be very difficult except in unusual situations.

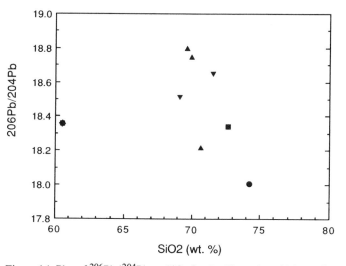

Figure 14. Plot of $^{206}Pb/^{204}Pb$ vs. SiO_2 for the Chemehuevi Mountains Plutonic Suite and associated rocks. Note that there is little overall correlation between composition and $^{206}Pb/^{204}Pb$.

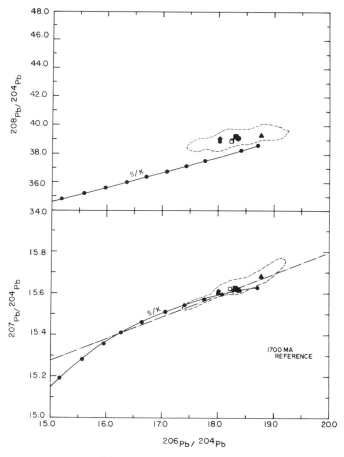

Figure 13. Plots of $^{206}Pb/^{204}Pb$ vs. $^{207}Pb/^{204}Pb$ and $^{206}Pb/^{204}Pb$ vs. $^{208}Pb/^{204}Pb$ for feldspars from the Chemehuevi Mountains Plutonic Suite and adjacent rocks. The lead evolution curve (S/K) represent average crust based on the model of Stacey and Kramers (1975). The dashed line outlines the field for all Mesozoic feldspar data from southeastern California, taken from Wooden and others (1988). Symbols as in Figure 3.

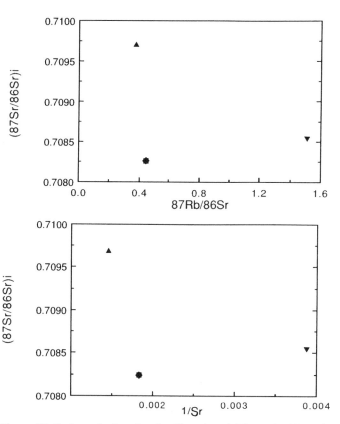

Figure 15. Sr isotopic data for the Chemehuevi Mountains Plutonic Suite. Symbols as in Figure 3.

Broad constraints on the conditions of emplacement of the Chemehuevi Mountains Plutonic Suite are outlined below.

Estimates of depth of emplacement. Pressure (depth) estimates of emplacement of the Chemehuevi Mountains Plutonic Suite based on structural and stratigraphic reconstructions of the cover rocks, granite minimum compositions, and a reconnaissance fluid-inclusion study indicate *minimum* emplacement pressures of approximately 4 kbar (12 to 15 km) in the southwestern or structurally highest part of the suite. The presence of magmatic epidote throughout most of the suite suggests that the emplacement pressure may be greater, a minimum of 5 to 6 kbar. Reconstruction of the suite as outlined above suggests that the intrusion is at least 4 km thick. An additional kilobar of pressure during emplacement is thus implied for the base of the intrusion. The suite was therefore emplaced in the middle crust, at depths of between 12 and 20 km.

(1) Minimum melt composition. A rough estimate of the pressure of emplacement and crystallization of the Chemehuevi Mountains Plutonic Suite can be based on the minimum melt composition of the suite plotted against the granite minimum, which varies with P_{H_2O}. The late, highly fractionated members of the suite were saturated with an aqueous vapor phase, as exemplified by voluminous aplite and pegmatite dikes, and by the highly variable pegmatitic textures in the garnet–two-mica granite. Pressure estimates of emplacement based on whole-rock chemical analyses of the aplite and pegmatite dikes and garnet–two-mica granite should therefore be valid if these rock samples actually represent total melt compositions. Figure 16 summarizes current experimental data as compiled in grid form by Anderson and Cullers (1978) and Anderson (1983) for the system quartz (Q), albite (A), anorthite (An), orthoclase (Or), and H_2O. Data from the garnet–two-mica granite and aplite dikes in the western and central part of the plutonic suite have been plotted on this grid. They indicate minimum crystallization pressures of about 4 kbar or an emplacement depth of 12 to 15 km.

(2) Stratigraphic overburden. Depth of emplacement can be crudely constrained by reconstructing the amount of stratigraphic cover present at the time of emplacement. This method is subject to large uncertainties arising from the complex late Mesozoic and Cenozoic structural history. Because the Paleozoic and Mesozoic sedimentary sequence that was most likely present during emplacement (Stone and others, 1983) has been removed by pre-Miocene erosion, it is not possible to directly measure the thickness of the overlying supracrustal sequence that existed during intrusion. The timing of unroofing of the cratonal strata is poorly constrained. The preservation of Paleozoic strata in ductile nappes in the Old Woman–Piute Mountains (Howard and others, 1987) implies that the sedimentary sequence was preserved until at least the inception of shortening deformation (Late Cretaceous time). Stone and others (1983) have estimated this sequence to have been as thick as 2 km over the entire region. Reconstruction of the pre-Tertiary extensional tilt blocks, composed exclusively of Proterozoic crystalline rocks that originally lay above the plutonic suite, adds a minimum of an additional 6

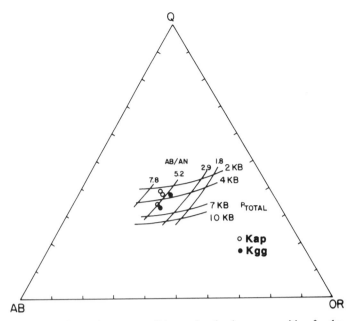

Figure 16. Normative quartz, albite, and orthoclase composition for the most fractionated members (Kgg and Kap) of the Chemehuevi Mountains Plutonic Suite compared to experimental minimum melt compositions over a range of P_{H_2O} (= P_{total}). Source data taken from Anderson and Cullers (1978). Abbreviations as in Figure 3.

to 8 km (John, 1987a). Combined, these estimates imply that the plutonic suite was emplaced at a minimum of 8 to 10 km depth, or about 3 kbar pressure. The overall texture of the suite (coarse-grained, equigranular to porphyritic), and the lack of a well-defined thermal metamorphic aureole around the body, implies that the country rocks were in thermal equilibrium with the intrusion. This relationship supports the inference of considerable depth based on the stratigraphic reasoning outlined.

(3) Magmatic epidote. Most members of the Chemehuevi Mountains Plutonic Suite contain conspicuous epidote, probably of two generations (Fig. 7). The majority of the epidote is secondary, related to fluid transport associated with detachment faulting (John, 1986, 1987a). An earlier generation of epidote includes large euhedra, commonly with allanite cores, enclosed or partially enclosed in magmatic biotite and muscovite, and rarely intergrown with hornblende (Fig. 17). Zen and Hammerstrom (1984) outlined textural relations characteristic of magmatic epidote, including those listed above, and suggested that epidote as a late-stage magmatic mineral in granitoid rocks must crystallize at pressures of greater than 8 kbar. Experimental studies on granitic and tonalitic compositions by Naney (1983) indicate that epidote becomes stable between 2 and 8 kbar. This study does not, however, indicate the low-pressure stability limit of magmatic epidote. Studies by Liou (1973) suggest that epidote is stable at a minimum of 5 to 6 kbar for granitic composition melts. If the epidote in the Chemehuevi Mountains Plutonic Suite is magmatic, as its texture implies, the suite was emplaced at depths

Figure 17. Photomicrograph of allanite-cored epidote (euhedral) surrounded by magmatic biotite in biotite granodiorite (Kbg—Specimen #BJ81Ch-241). Plane polarized light. Scale bar 1 mm.

greater than 5 kbar ($\approx$18 km), based on the magmatic stability of the phase.

Estimates of the pressures of emplacement of the Chemehuevi Mountains Plutonic Suite range from a minimum of >3 kbar, based on the minimum stratigraphic overburden, to 4 kbar, based on granite minimum compositions, to greater than 5 kbar, based on textural relations associated with primary magmatic epidote. The independent estimates of emplacement depth discussed above, although each is somewhat uncertain, together suggest that the plutonic suite crystallized at about 4 kbar pressure, or 12 to 15 km minimum depths.

Estimates of P_{H_2O}. Equilibrium experiments done by Naney (1983) show that the crystallization sequence of a granitic melt is strongly dependent on the water content. Estimates of the total H_2O content for the Chemehuevi Mountains Plutonic Suite can be made with reference to these experiments. It should be noted that this method can only provide an estimate of the relative amount of H_2O in the magma. Textures in the pluton indicate that hornblende crystallized before biotite in both the hornblende biotite granodiorite and, where present, in the biotite granodiorite. The experiments of Naney (1983) on synthetic granodiorite and granite compositions at 2 kbar and 8 kbar indicate that hornblende is only stable in systems with greater than about 3.5 weight percent H_2O at 2 kbar, and >3 weight percent H_2O at 8 kbar. Crystallization of hornblende before biotite, and both phases before vapor saturation, implies water contents between 3.5 and 5.0 weight percent at 2 kbar. The presence of magmatic epidote with hornblende and biotite suggests a minimum of 5 weight percent H_2O at 8 kbar. The maximum solubility of water in the granitic system is marked by the vapor saturation curve. These data constrain the relative amount of H_2O in the plutonic suite to about 4 to 5 weight percent, until saturation was reached in the late-stage aplite and pegmatite dikes.

ORIGIN AND EVOLUTION OF THE CHEMEHUEVI MOUNTAINS PLUTONIC SUITE

Overall similarities in mineralogy, major- and trace-element chemistry, and REE, taken with the preliminary U-Pb zircon data, allow a comagmatic origin for the felsic and intermediate members of the Chemehuevi Mountains Plutonic Suite. The spatial association of all members of the suite, and the textures and mineralogy, suggest similar histories. The three most probable hypotheses to account for the compositional variations within the suite are fractional crystallization of a common or similar parent magmas, variable contamination of a homogeneous parent magma by Proterozoic country rocks, and variable partial melting of a common source.

A model of fractional crystallization is supported by changes in major-element chemistry with time toward more felsic compositions. These changes are consistent with a liquid-line of descent toward the granite minimum, controlled initially by the crystallization of hornblende, biotite, and plagioclase, succeeded by muscovite, quartz, potassium feldspar, and garnet. This trend is inconsistent with sequential partial melting of a common source, which would yield progressively more mafic magmas with time. The relative abundance of rock types in the suite—mafic and intermediate rocks are more abundant than felsic rocks—is consistent with fractional crystallization. To test the hypothesis that fractional crystallization controlled the compositional variations in the plutonic suite, a least-squares model was run.

Least-squares fractional-crystallization model

Given a parent composition, the extent of fractional crystallization can be estimated by step-wise modeling of major-element changes through removal of constituent minerals. The simplest crystal fractionation model involves fractionating biotite granodiorite (Kbg), or hornblende-biotite granodiorite (Kgd) to produce the two-mica (Kg) or garnet–two-mica granites (Kgg). A least-squares mixing model, XLFRAC (Stormer and Nicholls, 1978), was used to test the model of fractional crystallization for major-element variations in the plutonic suite. End-member compositions used were averaged values of the two-mica granite and garnet–two-mica granite, considered to approximate the bulk composition of the "daughter," and the hornblende-biotite granodiorite (model I), and the biotite granodiorite (model II) as parent compositions (Table 5). The two parent compositions were modeled in an effort to see what relationship the deformed hornblende-biotite granodiorite has with the more felsic members of the plutonic suite. Mineral compositions used were based on microprobe analyses done by Shaw (reported in John, 1986) on mineral phases within the analyzed whole-rock chemistry samples, and phase chemistry of minerals in compositionally similar plutons of about the same age and emplacement depths from the nearby Old Woman Mountains and Teutonia batholith in the central Mojave Desert (Miller and Stoddard, 1981; Miller and others, 1981; Beckerman and others, 1982). Solutions were considered acceptable if the sum of the squares of the difference between the observed and calculated daughter was less than 1.

The model results (Table 6) indicate that the range in silica (69.88 to 74.20 percent—model II) and (62.08 to 74.20 percent—model I) and other elemental changes including increasing alumina saturation (Fig. 8) is due to 45 percent (model I) and 75 percent (model II), fractionation of plagioclase, hornblende, biotite, potassium feldspar, muscovite, garnet, and magnetite. In both models, fractionation of a magma of biotite granodiorite composition to one of porphyritic biotite granodiorite composition is of particular interest. Each model requires the input of between 1 and 10 percent new magma. This relationship implies that the chemical makeup of the suite is not wholly related to in situ fractionation. A further test of this model would be trace-element and REE modeling using mineral compositions, which are not available. The reconstruction of the suite outlined earlier (Fig. 6) indicates that the chamber was fed by at least three separate pulses of new, more fractionated magma with time. This relationship supports the numerical modeling. In conclusion, although the Chemehuevi Mountains Plutonic Suite forms a linearly correlative suite, fractional crystallization of an originally homogeneous parent was not the only mechanism producing chemical variation in the suite. The Sr- and Pb-isotopic data demand that there not be one uncontaminated liquid line of descent for the entire plutonic suite, assuming an isotopically homogeneous parent. The model of fractional crystallization is therefore too simple to accurately describe the processes involved in the formation of the suite.

Petrogenetic evidence, even on the scale of a single member within the suite, does not, however, point to a single process that is common to and dominant in the evolution of the entire suite. Any petrogenetic model must account for (1) the range in composition (60 to 75 weight percent SiO_2, with a silica gap between 64.3 and 67.5 percent SiO_2), (2) the major- and trace-element continuity among these rocks, (3) observed changes in the REE patterns over the silica range, (4) ductile deformation being restricted to the older mafic members of the suite, and (5) the isotopic compositions.

Major- and trace-element and isotopic data together broadly constrain the origin of the Chemehuevi Mountains Plutonic Suite. For the mafic and intermediate members of the suite, small or no Eu anomalies, low to moderate REE contents, and variable LREE/HREE ratios imply little or no residual plagioclase in their source. Alternatively, removal of subequal amounts of plagioclase and amphibole could have opposing effects on Eu anomalies, resulting in no net anomaly in the melt. Hornblende-bearing granulites are reasonable source rocks for the mafic and intermediate members of the suite (Cullers and Graf, 1984). The granodiorites could therefore be generated in large part by anatexis of mafic to intermediate lower crust. The youngest, most felsic rocks in the suite, however, require abundant plagioclase in their source to produce the negative Eu anomalies typical of these members. Possible source materials for these granitic rocks include metasedimentary rocks, siliceous granulites, quartzo-feldspathic gneisses,

and metamorphosed mafic plutonic rocks (diorites or tonalites). The REE data from the plutonic suite suggest the possibility of at least two different sources for the mafic and felsic members. At least some compositional variation in the suite could be a function of fractional crystallization. Earlier it was noted that absolute REE abundances can be controlled by fractional crystallization of small amounts of accessory monazite, allanite, sphene, zircon, or apatite. REE may decrease in the residual melts due to crystallization of these minerals (Mittlefehldt and Miller, 1983; Cullers and Graf, 1984).

Pb-, Sr-, and oxygen-isotopic trends characteristic of the Chemehuevi Mountains Plutonic Suite suggest that the Proterozoic crust played a significant role in determining the composition of the intrusion. The mechanism of this interaction, whether by assimilation or melting of a heterogeneous source, is not known. At least some granitoid source regions are undoubtedly heterogeneous, so a single fusion event might partially melt a variety of source rocks to produce a varying plutonic suite—magmas generated from the fusion event do not necessarily mix and so may be emplaced concentrically. Contamination by melting of country rock may have been an important process as well, as evidenced by the large number of country-rock xenoliths and schlieren concentrated in the feeder dikes and along the floor of the suite.

In an effort to explain isotopically heterogeneous metaluminous and peraluminous granitic rocks in the adjacent Old Woman Mountains, Miller and others (1982) suggested that a major Late Cretaceous thermal event caused anatexis at varying levels in the crust. Early metaluminous granodiorites were formed in the lower crust. At a slightly later time, heat had been transferred to a shallower and more silicic level in the crust, where the peraluminous granite magmas were generated. A similar case can be made for the Chemehuevi Mountains Plutonic Suite, and could help explain the apparent overlap in time of the plutonic suite and regional ductile deformation.

Intermediate to silicic magma chambers are often zoned with respect to chemical composition. Concentric zoning of tonalitic or granodioritic to granitic plutons, from mafic margin to felsic core, is well known from studies in the Sierra Nevada Batholith (Compton, 1955; Bateman and Nockelberg, 1978; Stephens and Halliday, 1980; Perfit and others, 1980), and reverse zoning, from felsic margin or roof to mafic core or floor, has been noted in upper levels of plutonic systems (Ludington and others, 1979; Fridrich and Mahood, 1984), as well as in relatively deep levels (Allen, 1986). Temporal zonation occurs in nested granitic intrusions, where each successive pulse of magma is progressively more felsic (e.g., Bateman and Chappell, 1979; Hirt, 1986). Direct evidence of vertical zonation in magma chambers is restricted to plutons that have been dissected by postemplacement deformation (Flood and Shaw, 1979; Barnes, 1983; Barnes and others, 1986; Dellinger and Hopson, 1986). Abundant indirect evidence from zoned ash flows summarized by Hildreth (1981) suggests that a cap of high-silica magma commonly develops at the top of magma chambers filled predominately with intermediate composition material (55–70 weight percent SiO$_2$). In contrast, the Chemehuevi Mountains Plutonic Suite is vertically zoned, but the high-silica material is concentrated near or at the floor of the chamber. The suite apparently fractionated from the walls and roof(?) inward after each of several pulses of new magma were intruded from a reservoir chamber at greater depth. The youngest, most highly differentiated material was isolated along the floor of the laccolith. The reason for this difference in chamber zonation may be the depth at which the intrusion was actually emplaced, its overall geometry, or country-rock temperatures. The depth of emplacement, estimated as ⩾12 km, and sill-like geometry may have allowed slow solidification of the magmas through efficient zoning processes, which allowed fractionation inward from the cooling walls and roof toward the warm floor.

The overall zonation in the Chemehuevi Mountains Plutonic Suite outlined above calls into question the need for liquid-state thermogravitational diffusion, as outlined by Shaw and others (1976) and championed by Hildreth (1981), to form vertical compositional zonation in intermediate to silicic magma chambers. The similarity in major-element, trace-element and REE trends between the felsic members of the Chemehuevi Mountains Plutonic Suite and the Bishop Tuff is remarkable (John, 1986). Hildreth (1981) proposed that these trends in the Bishop Tuff are the result of liquid-state thermogravitational diffusion. His model is commonly cited as a mechanism to form LREE–poor felsic rocks as a cap on other large magma chambers (Barnes and others, 1986; Lipman, 1984; Mahood, 1981). The critical problem with this hypothesis, as originally outlined by Mittlefehldt and Miller (1983) in the nearby Old Woman Mountains, is that these high-silica LREE–poor rocks did not form a cap to the Chemehuevi Mountains Plutonic Suite. Instead, these intrusions are found as dikes and small bodies concentrated near the floor of the intrusion, and clearly represent late-stage liquids formed by fractional crystallization.

CONCLUSIONS

Data presented above suggest that zonation in the Chemehuevi Mountains Plutonic Suite is in part the result of fractional crystallization of several discrete, yet cogenetic batches of magma derived predominantly from Proterozoic country rocks. The suite exhibits crude zonation, with progressively younger and more felsic material away from the walls, concentrated toward the center and floor of the intrusion. Hornblende-, biotite-, sphene-bearing members are metaluminous and form the outer margin along the northern and southern walls. Locally these units bear a subhorizontal southwest-trending mylonitic lineation, considered synchronous with regional Late Cretaceous ductile deformation. The silica gap and difference in deformation history between the hornblende-biotite granodiorite and younger biotite granodiorite and mineralogically equivalent porphyritic granodiorite suggest that these members represent at least two separate batches of cogenetic magma emplaced at slightly different times. Fresh

magma with a composition of two-mica granite was fractionated from a parental liquid similar to the biotite granodiorite and injected into the chamber at a slightly later time. The intrusion was structurally controlled, being trapped at the interface between the voluminous porphyritic granodiorite and the subhorizontally foliated gneissic floor. The restricted volume differentiates of this magma, the garnet–two-mica granite and aplite dikes, were concentrated in pods along the uppermost part of this smaller chamber and formed pockets of vapor-rich material. The final stage of solidification ended with the emplacement of aplitic and pegmatic dikes as the residual melt reached vapor saturation.

Preliminary Pb-, Sr-, and oxygen-isotopic data, taken with REE chemistry, suggest that the Chemehuevi Mountains Plutonic Suite was most likely derived from a heterogeneous (possibly granulitic) crustal source. Compositional trends for the suite are consistent with open-system fractionation involving further contamination and crystallization of discrete batches of magma derived from the melting of this source.

Radiogenic-isotopic compositions of a magma are unaffected by fractional crystallization, and are only slightly sensitive at plutonic temperatures. The variations in Pb- and Sr-isotopic composition within the plutonic suite must reflect either primary variations in a source region that was partially melted to produce the magmas, or a variable degree of contamination of melts before or during emplacement. Two important points are clear from the isotopic data. The magmas that crystallized to produce the Chemehuevi Mountains Plutonic Suite were not derived from a homogeneous source; the variations observed in chemical composition were not produced solely by magmatic differentiation. Second, the isotopic trends characteristic of the plutonic suite suggest the Proterozoic crust in southeastern California and western Arizona played a significant role in determining the isotopic composition of the magmas. The Sr- and Pb-isotopic data argue for an origin at least in part, if not totally, by crustal anatexis.

ACKNOWLEDGMENTS

The results reported in this paper are part of the Ph.D. dissertation by Barbara John at the University of California, Santa Barbara. Financial support for the project came from the U.S. Geological Survey Graduate Intern and BLM Wilderness assessment programs, and is gratefully acknowledged. Thanks are due to Lawford Anderson for his patience and enthusiasm in guiding the geochemical portion of this project, Marvin and Lanphere and Cleve Solomon for providing unpublished Sr- and O-isotopic data, respectively, Stirling Shaw for use of geochemical data, and B. John's long-term field companions, in particular Lindee Glick, Martha Pernokas, and Vicki Hansen, for their help in collecting and processing the granite samples. Numerous discussions with Paul Browning, David Dellinger, Gordon Haxel, Cliff Hopson, Keith Howard, Jim Mattinson, Calvin Miller, Steve Sparks, and George Tilton helped put the Chemehuevi Mountains data into perspective. Reviews by Gordon Haxell and Tom Frost are gratefully acknowledged.

TABLE 1. WHOLE-ROCK CHEMICAL ANALYSES

Chemehuevi Mountains Plutonic Suite

Specimen	Aplite Dikes (Kap)			Garnet-two-mica granite (Kgg)		Two-mica granite (Kg)			
	MJ82Ch-1	BJ84Ch-9	H79Ch-279	BJ81Ch-5	BJ81Ch-61	BJ81Ch-22	BJ81Ch-46	BJ80Ch-157	H79Ch-280
SiO_2	75.3	75.2	73.8	74.4	74.0	74.6	73.8	72.8	72.5
Al_2O_3	13.6	13.9	14.8	14.1	14.4	13.9	14.4	14.7	15.2
Fe_2O_3	0.40	0.08	0.64	0.45	0.45	0.20	0.52	0.62	0.39
FeO	0.17	0.19		0.31	0.45	0.25	0.46		
MgO	0.13	<0.10	0.29	0.26	0.30	0.19	0.31	0.02	0.26
CaO	1.17	0.68	0.98	1.35	1.64	1.24	1.71	1.4	1.8
Na_2O	3.49	4.25	4.1	3.67	3.57	3.06	3.70	3.7	3.7
K_2O	4.63	4.62	4.2	4.14	3.84	5.19	3.58	4.4	4.1
TiO_2	0.03	<0.02	0.01	0.08	0.09	0.03	0.10	0.07	0.03
P_2O_5	<0.05	<0.05	0.06	<0.05	0.06	<0.05	<0.05	0.05	0.04
MnO	0.04	0.30	0.27	0.07	<0.02	<0.02	<0.02	0.02	0.05
H_2O^+	0.19	0.09	0.42	0.41	0.43	0.42	0.46	0.70	3.8
H_2O^-	0.05	<0.01		0.01	0.01	0.02	<0.01		
CO_2	0.07	0.05	0.02	0.10	0.03	<0.01	0.05	0.05	0.04
Total	99.32	99.54	99.59	100.43	100.04	99.97	100.03	98.53	101.91
LOI @ 900°C	0.43	0.20		1.03	0.75	0.79	0.86		

X-ray Fluorescence Analyses (ppm)

Element	MJ82Ch-1	BJ84Ch-9	H79Ch-279	BJ81Ch-5	BJ81Ch-61	BJ81Ch-22	BJ81Ch-46	BJ80Ch-157	H79Ch-280
Y				46	14	9	22		
Sr				280	413	389	437		
Zr				100	112	55			
U									
Rb				127	106	108	106		
Th									
Pb									
Ga									
Zn									
Cu									
Ni									
Cr									
V									
Ba				1040	1190	1380	1260		
Nb				14	12	<5	10		

Instrumental Neutron Activation Analyses (ppm)

Element	MJ82Ch-1	BJ84Ch-9	H79Ch-279	BJ81Ch-5	BJ81Ch-61	BJ81Ch-22	BJ81Ch-46	BJ80Ch-157	H79Ch-280
Ba	267	59.5		1030	1190	1310			
Co	0.480	0.311		0.701	0.775	0.433			
Cr	1.74	<1.1		0.30	0.518	0.620			
Cs	1.39	1.19		0.301	0.375	0.263			
Hf	2.63	6.83		3.36	3.38	1.37			
Mn				530	200	79.5			
Rb	181	318		128	105	94.2			
Sb	0.0526	<0.046		0.0684	0.0763	0.0271			
Sr				283	433	370			
Ta	2.08	3.76		0.833	0.351	0.112			
Th	4.52	17.4		8.96	4.71	0.759			
U	7.14	7.65		1.42	0.41	0.325			
Zr	115	90		122	101	39.1			
Sc	3.46	11.1		2.34	1.72	0.876			
La	4.31	10.9		19.0	15.0	2.85			
Ce	9.02	27.8		38.7	30.2	5.66			
Nd	6.00	22.4		17.6	13.0	1.9			
Sm	1.95	7.78		4.38	2.68	0.426			
Eu	0.452	0.136		0.624	0.628	0.632			
Gd	2.76	9.23		6.33	2.41	0.340			
Tb	0.703	1.42		1.33	0.382	0.0430			
Dy				9.20	2.40	0.33			
Tm	0.810	0.00		1.37	0.230				
Yb	5.80	4.44		8.64	1.44	0.223			
Lu	0.912	0.631		1.31	0.232	0.0422			

TABLE 1. WHOLE-ROCK CHEMICAL ANALYSES (continued)

Chemehuevi Mountains Plutonic Suite (continued)

Specimen	Two-mica granite (Kg)				Porphyritic biotite granodiorite (Kpg)				
	BJ80Ch-302	P80Ch-55[1]	BJ80Ch-200[1]	H80Ch-308[1]	H80Mh-310[1]	BJ81Ch-64	BJ81Ch-306	BJ80Ch-241	BJ80Ch-241[1]
SiO_2	72.4	73.66	72.22	72.21	72.91	70.7	68.3	69.9	70.06
Al_2O_3	14.8	14.16	15.10	14.92	14.16	15.3	16.1	15.7	15.72
Fe_2O_3	1.1	0.77	0.77	0.49	0.91	0.76	1.40	1.3	1.06
FeO		0.35	0.57	1.05	0.68	0.74	1.29		0.78
MgO	0.34	0.31	0.33	0.45	0.54	0.47	0.71	1.5	0.62
CaO	1.8	1.62	1.91	1.69	1.27	1.92	2.68	2.6	2.56
Na_2O	4.5	3.98	4.34	4.04	4.04	3.88	3.92	4.9	4.59
K_2O	3.8	4.01	3.68	4.54	4.72	4.17	3.52	2.4	3.40
TiO_2	0.11	0.11	0.14	0.16	0.26	0.22	0.33	0.28	0.32
P_2O_5	0.04	0.05	0.05	0.07	0.07	0.08	0.15	0.15	0.11
MnO	0.07	0.03	0.03	0.03	0.05	<0.02	0.02	0.04	0.03
H_2O^+	0.62	1.25	1.08	0.39	0.00	0.43	0.33	0.46	0.63
H_2O^-		0.14	0.14	0.23	0.10	0.04	0.01		0.15
CO_2	0.07	0.03	0.04	0.02	0.06	0.14	0.05	0.08	0.01
Total	99.65	100.47	100.40	100.29	99.77	99.58	99.43	99.31	100.04
LOI @ 900°C						0.71	0.64		

X-ray Fluorescence Analyses (ppm)

	BJ80Ch-302	P80Ch-55[1]	BJ80Ch-200[1]	H80Ch-308[1]	H80Mh-310[1]	BJ81Ch-64	BJ81Ch-306	BJ80Ch-241	BJ80Ch-241[1]
Y		12	16	10	16	15	13		8
Sr		443	514	325	261	560	769		630
Zr		109	118	125	168	135	213		157
U		0	1	4	0				1
Rb		94	131	115	127	93	74		90
Th		4	7	7	10				6
Pb		22	21	39	16				19
Ga		0	0	0	0				0
Zn		22	29	37	27				46
Cu		2	5	2	2				5
Ni		1	1	0	3				1
Cr		3	1	3	4				3
V		10	18	9	18				30
Ba		1137	1212	931	953	1540	1950		1058
Nb		7	13	9	18	8	<5		9

Instrumental Neutron Activation Analyses (ppm)

	BJ80Ch-302	P80Ch-55[1]	BJ80Ch-200[1]	H80Ch-308[1]	H80Mh-310[1]	BJ81Ch-64	BJ81Ch-306	BJ80Ch-241	BJ80Ch-241[1]
Ba		1200			1000	1560	1870		
Co		54.7			63.4	2.05	3.42		
Cr		0.837			2.99	0.945	2.32		
Cs		0.241			0.667	0.239	0.176		
Hf		3.04			5.17	4.87	5.66		
Mn		151			305	230	256		
Rb		89.3			126	87.7	65.4		
Sb		0.0506			0.059	0.0376	<0.038		
Sr		539			325	621	763		
Ta		0.990			2.39	0.338	0.257		
Th		5.28			14.5	6.75	6.31		
U		0.686			2.26	0.93	0.570		
Zr		86.1			178	158	215		
Sc		2.79			2.42	3.13	2.95		
La		17.3			46.8	29.5	42.8		
Ce		33.7			83.1	60.6	82.1		
Nd		13.4			27.3	24.4	32.9		
Sm		2.41			3.90	4.19	5.04		
Eu		0.745			0.757	0.938	1.16		
Gd		1.97			3.94	2.90	2.87		
Tb		0.312			0.484	0.336	0.384		
Dy		1.99			2.93	2.00	1.90		
Tm		0.200				0.150	0.154		
Yb		1.36				1.04	1.02		
Lu		0.225			0.234	0.163	0.167		

TABLE 1. WHOLE-ROCK CHEMICAL ANALYSES (continued)

Chemehuevi Mountains Plutonic Suite (continued)

Specimen	Porphyritic biotite granodiorite (Kpg)				Biotite granodiorite (Kbg)				
	BJ80Ch-294	BJ80Ch-307[1]	H81Mh-61	BJ82Ch-103	BJ81Ch-113	BJ81Ch-113	BJ82Ch-81	BJ80Ch-322	H80Mh-287[1]
SiO_2	69.7	69.13	72.55	68.2	71.2	71.8	68.9	69.3	67.67
Al_2O_3	16.4	15.71	15.11	15.2	15.1	15.0	15.8	14.0	15.86
Fe_2O_3	1.3	1.01	0.39	1.82	0.93	0.73	1.62	0.82	1.63
FeO		1.20	1.21	1.29	1.10	1.18	0.98		1.15
MgO	0.70	0.80	0.69	1.09	0.42	0.43	0.69	0.56	1.03
CaO	2.7	2.97	2.28	2.73	2.25	2.24	2.80	3.5	2.87
Na_2O	4.7	4.46	3.72	3.58	3.96	3.80	4.22	4.3	4.16
K_2O	3.0	3.06	3.11	4.20	3.64	3.52	3.57	2.8	3.96
TiO_2	0.33	0.40	0.17	0.49	0.20	0.22	0.45	0.27	0.56
P_2O_5	0.10	0.14	0.05	0.16	0.06	0.08	0.17	0.13	0.17
MnO	0.07	0.03	0.01	0.03	0.03	0.04	<0.02	0.03	0.06
H_2O^+	0.43	1.00	0.90	0.45	0.36	0.37	0.37	1.06	0.18
H_2O^-		0.10	0	0.14	0.04	<0.01	0.02		0.10
CO_2	0.07	0.20	0	0.10	0.13	0.04	0.09	2.3	0.24
Total	99.57	100.21	100.19	99.48	99.42	99.75	99.70	99.07	99.64
LOI @ 900°C				0.64	0.49	0.29	0.44		

X-ray Fluorescence Analyses (ppm)

	BJ80Ch-294	BJ80Ch-307	H81Mh-61	BJ82Ch-103	BJ81Ch-113	BJ81Ch-113	BJ82Ch-81	BJ80Ch-322	H80Mh-287
Y		11	8						10
Sr		692	461						656
Zr		181	66						182
U		1	2						1
Rb		87	53						118
Th		4	3						8
Pb		23	22						13
Ga		0	15						
Zn		60	34						51
Cu		7	4						5
Ni		2	3						4
Cr		5	6						8
V		40	8						48
Ba		1019	1596						1179
Nb		9	5						10

Instrumental Neutron Activation Analyses (ppm)

	BJ80Ch-294	BJ80Ch-307	H81Mh-61	BJ82Ch-103	BJ81Ch-113	BJ81Ch-113	BJ82Ch-81
Ba		1050		1200	1880	1730	995
Co		67.5		5.86	1.90	1.88	3.64
Cr		2.23		5.53	0.715	<1.3	2.93
Cs		0.961		2.53	0.214	0.250	1.01
Hf		4.45		5.75	4.32	4.91	4.66
Mn		271				352	
Rb		83.9		146	80.9	83.1	100
Sb		0.0547		0.0645		0.057	0.104
Sr		860				521	
Ta		1.61		0.988	0.160	0.157	0.566
Th		7.01		13.4	4.67	5.14	9.65
U		1.36		2.83	0.648	0.590	2.05
Zr		158		182	149	161	158
Sc		287		4.54	4.36	4.86	2.47
La		28.2		44.6	23.7	26.5	39.9
Ce		54.2		82.1	46.4	50.9	68.9
Nd		20.1		32.5	18.0	18.2	27.5
Sm		3.51		5.71	3.07	3.25	4.51
Eu		0.863		1.12	0.900	0.930	1.03
Gd		2.74		3.58	1.98	2.53	3.10
Tb		0.337		0.521	0.293	0.338	0.372
Dy		1.99				2.00	
Tm					0.153	0.170	
Yb		0.890		1.24	0.939	0.995	0.659
Lu		0.127		0.158	0.138	0.181	0.0980

TABLE 1. WHOLE-ROCK CHEMICAL ANALYSES (continued)

| | Chemehuevi Mountains Plutonic Suite (continued) | | | | | Whale Mountain sequence | | |
| | Hornblende-biotite granodiorite (Kgd) | | | | | Hornblende biotite granite (KJqm) | | |
Specimen	BJ81Ch-72	BJ81Ch-72	BJ80Ch-194	H80Ch-305[1]	H80Ch-307[1]	BJ80Ch-198[1]	BJ80Ch-198	BJ80Ch-208[1]
SiO_2	63.9	64.3	61.2	60.61	60.41	66.18	66.5	65.47
Al_2O_3	16.6	16.6	16.7	16.68	16.48	15.37	16.5	16.48
Fe_2O_3	2.56	1.86	2.6	2.36	2.27	1.52	1.9	1.47
FeO	2.06	1.98		3.47	2.86	1.42		1.47
MgO	1.57	1.52	2.6	2.63	2.82	1.42	1.8	1.34
CaO	3.92	4.14	5.1	5.28	4.96	2.80	3.0	3.28
Na_2O	4.05	3.89	3.8	3.64	4.38	4.03	4.2	4.19
K_2O	3.15	3.11	2.6	2.98	3.38	4.34	3.9	3.87
TiO_2	0.79	0.75	0.52	0.83	1.01	0.54	0.45	0.53
P_2O_5	0.31	0.25	0.33	0.24	0.39	0.18	0.24	0.18
MnO	0.04	0.04	0.10	0.10	0.09	0.05	0.08	0.05
H_2O^+	0.68	0.65	1.27	0.48	0.76	1.39	0.59	0.64
H_2O^-	0.15	0.02		0.11	0.11	0.07		0.18
CO_2	0.06	0.18	0.09	0.00	0.07	0.05	0.11	0.32
Total	99.86	100.13	96.91	99.41	99.99	99.36	99.27	99.47
LOI @ 900°C	0.66	0.81						

X-ray Fluorescence Analyses (ppm)

Y		17		25	21	22		19
Sr		800		547	956	665		785
Zr		231		305	233	261		261
U				3	5	3		0
Rb		99		80	78	95		81
Th				8	15	7		11
Pb				16	33	25		20
Ga				0	0	0		0
Zn				81	69	55		48
Cu				83	35	8		3
Ni				15	39	16		17
Cr				24	51	21		21
V				132	102	53		54
Ba		1410		971	1270	1463		1484
Nb		11		14	20	19		18

Instrumental Neutron Activation Analyses (ppm)

Ba	1350	1360		1260				
Co	8.80	8.77		42.0				
Cr	8.16	7.93		22.8				
Cs	0.991	1.02		0.865				
Hf	7.93	7.21		7.62				
Mn		384		685				
Rb	84.0	87.9		74.4				
Sb	0.066	0.098		0.068				
Sr		801		675				
Ta	1.05	1.03		1.08				
Th	13.3	14.1		9.91				
U	2.2	1.88		1.41				
Zr	270	249		294				
Sc	6.36	5.97		12.6				
La	68.0	74.0		46.2				
Ce	124	128		87.6				
Nd	45.2	46.1		39.0				
Sm	7.42	7.39		6.78				
Eu	1.63	1.64		1.49				
Gd	4.93	5.27		5.64				
Tb	0.628	0.652		0.835				
Dy				4.85				
Tm	0.255	0.250		0.373				
Yb	1.44	1.43		2.31				
Lu	0.184	0.170		0.330				

TABLE 1. WHOLE-ROCK CHEMICAL ANALYSES (continued)

Whale Mountain sequence (continued)

	Hornblende-biotite quartz diorite (KJqd)				Hornblende diorite (KJd)		
Specimen	BJ81Ch-3	BJ81Ch-106	BJ80Ch-308	BJ83Ch-2	BJ81Ch-103	BJ81Ch-103	H80Mh-311[1]
SiO_2	56.5	55.9	59.4	52.9	52.1	51.6	53.15
Al_2O_3	18.9	20.4	17.9	16.5	15.8	15.9	13.59
Fe_2O_3	2.53	2.12	1.2	2.62	3.69	2.51	1.76
FeO	2.84	3.28	3.2	4.96	5.52	5.71	5.14
MgO	2.12	2.10	2.8	6.26	5.55	5.57	8.36
CaO	3.98	5.31	4.8	8.63	8.02	8.10	9.84
Na_2O	4.60	5.07	4.6	3.42	3.39	3.41	3.04
K_2O	4.00	2.25	3.5	1.39	2.21	2.05	1.32
TiO_2	1.08	1.18	0.79	0.98	1.38	1.43	0.96
P_2O_5	0.35	0.49	0.41	0.25	0.47	0.48	0.24
MnO	0.09	0.08	0.07	0.11	0.14	0.14	0.17
H_2O^+	0.60	0.78	0.78	1.77	1.51	1.46	1.43
H_2O^-	0.05	<0.01		0.31	0.30	0.24	0.23
CO_2	0.07	0.07	0.11	0.38	0.34	0.20	0.26
Total	98.33	99.49	99.56	100.47	100.42	100.24	99.49
LOI @ 900°C	0.62	0.45		1.91	1.43	1.44	

X-ray Fluorescence Analyses (ppm)

Y	22	12				28	20
Sr	1080	1560				853	583
Zr	571	722				269	125
U							0
Rb						33	31
Th							3
Pb							6
Ga							0
Zn							86
Cu							34
Ni							121
Cr							520
V							164
Ba	6720	3940				2080	898
Nb	8	<5				9	9

Instrumental Neutron Activation Analyses (ppm)

Ba	6370	3780		556	2170	1980	903
Co	9.94	8.96		31.2	25.9	26.8	51.2
Cr	16.2	10.1		31.1	159	154	472
Cs	0.275	0.24		<0.18	<0.43	0.12	0.352
Hf	17.8	19.5		4.05	8.57	8.51	3.53
Mn	747	677				1090	1050
Rb	59.6	38.0		24.1	31.9	32.1	31.9
Sb	<0.067	0.065		0.11	0.0754	<0.12	0.16
Sr	1090	1700				850	725
Ta	0.898	0.207		0.721	0.466	0.500	0.707
Th	11.5	5.33		3.55	4.04	4.43	3.48
U	3.30	0.906		1.05	0.717	1.3	0.718
Zr	709	840		170	370	346	158
Sc	8.53	5.26		22.2	25.2	24.6	32.7
La	181	93.3		33.9	77.7	84.1	24.3
Ce	333	144		72.9	189	188	46.3
Nd	110	49.4		32.1	91.1	91.2	22.3
Sm	13.7	5.85		5.75	14.8	15.6	4.46
Eu	3.41	2.84		1.50	2.85	2.96	1.39
Gd	9.53	4.83		4.57	10.1	10.7	3.70
Tb	1.06	0.536		0.627	1.44	1.53	0.52
Dy	5.38	2.70				<6.5	3.42
Tm	0.380	0.220		0.277	0.520	0.604	
Yb	2.35	1.33		1.58	3.05	3.20	1.54
Lu	0.377	0.207		0.231	0.463	0.462	0.252

Notes:

Major-element chemistry by x-ray spectroscopic analysis: J. Taggert, D. McKown (analysts), U.S. Geological Survey, Branch of Analytical Chemistry, Lakewood, Colorado.

Trace-element chemistry by x-ray spectroscopic analysis: R. Johnson, D. Burgi (analysts), U.S. Geological Survey, Branch of Analytical Chemistry, Reston, Virginia.

[1]S. Shaw, Macquarie University, Australia.

Instrumental neutron activation analysis; analysts: J. Taggert, D. McKown.

Emission spectrographic analysis: N. Elsheimer (analyst), U.S. Geological Survey, Branch of Analytical Chemistry, Menlo Park, California.

TABLE 2. FELDSPAR COMMON LEAD DATA FOR THE
CHEMEHUEVI MOUNTAINS PLUTONIC SUITE
AND ADJACENT WHALE MOUNTAIN SEQUENCE

Specimen*	Unit	$^{206}Pb/^{204}Pb$	$^{207}Pb/^{204}Pb$	$^{208}Pb/^{204}Pb$
BJ81Ch-143	Kgg	18.012	15.579	38.843
BJ81Ch-141	Kg	18.341	15.622	39.258
BJ80Ch-241	Kpg	18.743	15.649	39.254
BJ81Ch-142	Kpg	18.798	15.666	39.313
BJ81Ch-139	Kpg	18.219	15.593	39.135
BJ81Ch-145	Kbg	18.510	15.613	39.019
BJ82Ch-52	Kbg(ch)	18.656	15.643	39.279
BJ82Ch-54	Kgd	18.358	15.597	38.947
BJ81Ch-87	KJqm	18.333	15.615	39.125
BJ81Ch-140	KJqd	18.025	15.582	38.976
BJ81Ch-144	KJd	18.260	15.618	39.014
BJ81Ch-146	mgg	18.222	15.583	38.741

*Specimen descriptions and locations given in John (1986, Appendix 2).

TABLE 3. WHOLE-ROCK Sr-ISOTOPIC DATA FOR THE CHEMEHUEVI MOUNTAINS
PLUTONIC SUITE AND WHALE MOUNTAIN SEQUENCE*

Specimen[†]	Unit	Rb (ppm)	Sr (ppm)	$^{87}Rb/^{86}Sr$	$(^{87}Sr/^{86}Sr)m$	$(^{87}Sr/^{86}Sr)_i$[‡]
BJ80Ch-307	Kpg	90.4	692.2	0.378	0.70995 ± 27	0.70970 ± 27
H80Mh-310	Kbg	135.1	258.2	1.514	0.71028 ± 7	0.70856 ± 7
H80Ch-305	Kgd	84.4	550.2	0.444	0.70876 ± 11	0.70826 ± 11
H80Mh-311	KJd	34.2	605.5	0.163	0.70852 ± 5	0.70833 ± 5

*Data from M. Lanphere and K. Howard, U.S. Geological Survey (personal communication, 1984). Sr isotopic compositions by mass spectrometry. Rb and Sr concentrations by x-ray fluorescence (A. Berry-Tapay, analyst).

[†]Specimen descriptions and locations given in John (1986, Appendix 2).

[‡]$(^{87}Sr/^{86}Sr)_i$ based on an assumed 80-Ma age.

TABLE 4. WHOLE-ROCK OXYGEN ISOTOPIC DATA FOR THE CHEMEHUEVI MOUNTAINS PLUTONIC SUITE AND LEUCOCRATIC MEMBERS OF THE WHALE MOUNTAIN SEQUENCE*

Specimen[†]	Unit	$\delta^{18}O_{wr}$(‰)	SiO_2 (wt. %)
BJ80Ch-200	Kg	+7.8	72.22
H80Ch-307	Kgd	+7.4	60.41
H80Ch-305	Kgd	+7.0	60.61
BJ80Ch-200	KJqm	+7.4	65.47
BJ80Ch-198	KJqm	+7.7	66.18

*Data from G. C. Solomon, Cal Tech (personal communication, 1985).

[†]Specimen descriptions and locations given in John (1986, Appendix 2).

TABLE 5. PARENT-DAUGHTER COMPOSITIONS FOR CRYSTAL FRACTIONATION MODELING*

	Parent Composition		Daughter Composition	
	Kgd (n = 5)	Kbg (n = 5)	Kg (n = 8)	Kgg (n = 2)
SiO_2	62.08	69.88	73.03	74.2
Al_2O_3	16.61	15.02	14.65	14.25
Fe_2O_3	2.27	1.28	0.54	0.45
FeO	2.59	1.14	0.54	0.38
MgO	2.23	0.64	0.22	0.28
CaO	4.68	2.70	1.65	1.19
Na_2O	3.95	3.97	3.88	3.62
K_2O	3.04	3.55	4.16	3.99
TiO_2	0.78	0.59	0.09	0.08
P_2O_5	0.30	0.15	0.05	0.05
MnO	0.07	0.03	0.03	0.04
Total	98.63	97.92	98.85	98.78

*Values in weight percent.

TABLE 6. SUMMARY OF MINERAL PERCENTS USED IN DIFFERENTIAL CALCULATION GOING FROM HORNBLENDE-BIOTITE GRANODIORITE TO GARNET-TWO-MICA GRANITE (MODEL I), AND FROM BIOTITE TO GARNET-TWO-MICA GRANITE (MODEL II)

Model (I)	Model (II)
Kgd to Kbg	**Kbg to Kpg**
21.7 % plag	0.34 % plag
4.26 % ksp	0.23 % ksp
3.26 % bio	0.12 % bio
16.4 % hb	0.16 % hb
0.72 % mt	0.00 % mt
Kbg to Kpg	**Kpg to Kg**
43.4 % plag	9.86 % plag
22.0 % ksp	18.4 % ksp
18.3 % bio	4.15 % bio
14.5 % hb	0.00 % hb
4.6 % musc	2.04 % musc
Kpg to Kg	**Kg to Kgg**
11.7 % plag	1.04 % plag
2.4 % ksp	6.26 % ksp
3.3 % bio	0.45 % bio
0.58 % musc	2.12 % musc
0.00 % gar	0.16 % gar
Kg to Kgg	
5.78 % plag	
3.28 % ksp	
1.21 % bio	
2.51 % musc	
0.06 % gar	
Total % crystallization	
75.27 %	45.33 %

APPENDIX—LITHOLOGIC DESCRIPTIONS

Proterozoic metamorphic rocks

Heterogeneous amphibolite-facies Proterozoic crystalline rocks (including migmatites, granites, orthogneisses, and paragneisses) are the country rocks to the Chemehuevi Mountains Plutonic Suite (John, 1982). A layered gneiss, the most common unit, consists of garnet-bearing leucogneiss, subordinate coarse pegmatite, biotite schist, amphibolite to hornblendite, and laminated, and rare augen gneiss. In the central and eastern Chemehuevi Mountains, the layered gneiss has been overprinted by a Cretaceous-shallow-dipping, northwest-striking mylonitic foliation, and locally a subhorizontal mylonitic lineation (Fig. 2). Equivalent rocks in the northwestern part of the range have a steep, northeast-striking foliation and a subhorizontal, southwest-trending mylonitic lineation. Xenoliths of the mylonitized layered gneiss are abundant near the eastern contact or floor of the plutonic suite, and range up to 1 km in longest dimension (Fig. 6).

Lowlands along the south flank of the Chemehuevi Mountains expose a complex of garnet-bearing leucocratic granite gneiss, amphibolite, pegmatite, and fine-grained, laminated, biotite quartzo-feldspathic gneiss. In marked contrast to the gneissic rocks in the northern and central part of the range, these rocks are well foliated, but do not have a mylonitic fabric.

The age of the country rocks is uncertain. In the eastern Chemehuevi Mountains (John, 1987b), the gneisses are intruded by an undeformed coarse-grained granite porphyry with textural, compositional, and mineralogical similarities to 1.4 to 1.5 Ga plutons (Davis and others, 1980; Anderson, 1983). This relationship suggests that the gneissic country rocks to the plutonic suite are older than 1.4 to 1.5 Ga, and are probably ~1.7 Ga (Silver, 1968).

Plutonic rocks in the Chemehuevi Mountains

Rocks of the Chemehuevi Mountains Plutonic Suite are described in order of increasing silica and decreasing relative age. The older suite of hornblende-bearing granitic rocks of alkalic affinity, the Whale Mountain sequence, is described briefly. Rock names have been given to the plutonic rocks on the basis of modal compositions using the classification scheme of Streckeisen (1976). Detailed locations and sample descriptions are in John (1986).

Whale Mountain sequence. Members of the Whale Mountain sequence are relatively quartz poor and dissimilar in composition to the Chemehuevi Mountains Plutonic Suite. The sequence comprises three plutonic units that range in composition from mafic-rich diorite (KJd), quartz diorite and quartz monzodiorite (KJqd), and granodiorite and quartz-poor granite (KJqm) (Fig. 3). All three units are hornblende-rich, bear the regionally developed Cretaceous mylonitic foliation and lineation, and are characterized by the presence of numerous mafic enclaves. The oldest two members of the sequence (KJd and KJqd) overlap in composition from diorite to quartz diorite and quartz monzodiorite, with 5 to 10 percent modal quartz. These units are characterized by plagioclase phenocrysts in a matrix of 18 to 38 percent medium-grained, blue-green hornblende and blue-green biotite with interstitial alkali feldspar, and accessory sphene, magnetite, apatite, and zoned allanite with overgrowths of magmatic epidote. Similar rocks crop out in the lowlands along the south flank of the range. There they are relatively undeformed, and intrude nonmylonitic Proterozoic gneisses and amphibolites. The younger and more silica-rich member of the sequence KJqm ranges in composition from granodiorite to quartz-poor granite. This unit is characterized by microcline megacryst and 15 to 25 percent blue-green hornblende and biotite, with accessory sphene, magnetite, apatite, and zoned allanite/epidote. These rocks crop out as small concordant bodies up to 1 km by 4 km in plan view that are aligned parallel to the northeast-striking foliation in the northern part of the range (Fig. 2).

Chemehuevi Mountains Plutonic Suite. Modal composition of the Chemehuevi Mountains Plutonic Suite ranges from quartz-poor granodiorite (20 to 30 percent modal quartz) to monzogranite (Fig. 3). The order of crystallization of the minerals in all intrusive units of the Chemehuevi Mountains Plutonic Suite includes early plagioclase and quartz along with hornblende, biotite, and muscovite. The accessory phases—apatite, zircon, allanite/epidote and opaque minerals—are inclusions in plagioclase, and are inferred to have also crystallized early (Fig. 7). Perthitic alkali feldspar, despite its euhedral shape and large size in the porphyritic member, was the last mineral to crystallize. Secondary minerals include actinolitic amphibole after hornblende, epidote after mafic minerals and plagioclase, chlorite and sphene after biotite, sparse sericite after plagioclase, and hematite after magnetite.

(1) Hornblende-biotite granodiorite (Kgd). The oldest member of the suite is a relatively quartz-poor, variably porphyritic, hornblende-biotite granodiorite. The granodiorite contains small equant microcline phenocrysts (up to 1 cm), stubby blue-green hornblende (4 to 20 percent), euhedral biotite (2 to 5 percent), coarse sphene (1 to 3 percent), and accessory magnetite, allanite, epidote, and zircon. The epidote is considered to be late magmatic on the basis of textural relations.

(2) Biotite granodiorite (Kbg). The biotite granodiorite is subequigranular in texture. Biotite is the most abundant mafic mineral (as much as 10 to 12 percent) and is typically euhedral, with associated rare blue-green hornblende. Perthitic microcline and quartz are interstitial. Sphene (up to 2 percent) occurs as primary euhedral crystals and as secondary overgrowths on magnetite. Apatite and zircon occur in and near the magnetite. Metamict subhedral allanite grains are rare throughout this unit and commonly have euhedral magmatic epidote overgrowths. The margin of this member against the hornblende-biotite granodiorite and Proterozoic gneisses is fine to medium grained, and contains rare potassium feldspar megacrysts up to 4 cm long. Inward, and away from the external contacts, the phenocrysts increase in abundance, and primary igneous flow structures appear. Mineralogically, the biotite granodiorite is identical to the porphyritic biotite granodiorite, except for the rare occurrence of hornblende.

(3) Chemehuevi Peak Granodiorite (Kpg). The most voluminous member of the Chemehuevi Mountains Plutonic Suite is a variably porphyritic biotite granodiorite to granite (Fig. 2). Zoned microcline megacrysts, measuring up to 6 cm in greatest dimension, compose 20 to 40 percent of the rock, and are set in a medium-grained groundmass consisting of quartz, plagioclase, microcline, and biotite (5 to 12 percent). Coarse sphene, allanite-cored epidote euhedra, magnetite, apatite, zircon, and rare primary muscovite are accessory. Along the eastern margin or floor of the intrusion, the porphyritic granodiorite is characterized by mineralogic layering defined by 10- to 20-cm-wide discontinuous bands of plagioclase+potassium feldspar+quartz and 2- to 5-cm-thick biotite-rich bands. To the west, at structurally higher levels, only sparse phenocrysts occur, set in a matrix with large equant β-shaped quartz to 5 mm. At the highest structural levels in the suite, allanite occurs without epidote overgrowths.

(4) Two-mica granite (Kg). The central units of the plutonic suite are all hornblende free. They are texturally variable, but typically have a medium- to coarse-grained groundmass. Subequigranular to porphyritic two-mica granodiorite to granite is the youngest major member of the suite. The rocks contain microcline phenocrysts up to 1.5 cm in greatest dimension, in a coarse-grained groundmass of quartz, plagioclase, orthoclase (2 to 4 percent), biotite (1 to 2 percent), muscovite (1 to 2 percent), and accessory magnetite, apatite, allanite, epidote, zircon, and rare sphene and monazite. Locally, irregular blocks of the porphyritic granodiorite occur in the two-mica granite.

(5) Garnet-two-mica granite (Kgg). The most felsic rocks of the suite occur as dikes and small irregular bodies less than 2 km across. Leucocratic, subequigranular, garnet-bearing, muscovite granite occurs as small pods in the central part of the plutonic suite. Accessory minerals include euhedral muscovite (1 to 3 percent), biotite (less than 1 percent), garnet (1 to 2 percent), apatite, rare allanite, magnetite, zircon, and very rare monazite; no sphene is present. The unit is in gradational contact with the two-mica granite, but clearly intrudes the porphyritic biotite granodiorite. Locally, biotite-rich, schistose inclusions with large (1.5 to 3 cm) red-brown euhedral garnet define an igneous foliation.

(6) Aplite and pegmatite dikes (Kap). Complex and simple pegmatites and aplites are concentrated near the top of the two-mica granite (Figs. 2 and 6),

intruding the porphyritic biotite granodiorite, and in the interior of the two-mica granite associated with the garnet–two-mica granite bodies. The aplites are typically fine to medium grained, less than 10 cm thick, and consist of plagioclase, quartz, alkali feldspar, garnet, and trace amounts of muscovite, biotite, apatite, magnetite, and rare zircon.

Pegmatites are similar in occurrence to the aplites. They consist of alkali feldspar, quartz, plagioclase, muscovite and/or biotite, magnetite, and garnet. Grain size is highly variable; potassium feldspar crystals are as large as 5 cm in length, biotite and muscovite books are over 4 cm across, and garnets are as large as 1 to 2 cm. Compound aplite/pegmatite dikes and the garnet–two-mica granite have mutually crosscutting relations, suggesting a close temporal relation between these late-stage intrusions.

(7) Xenoliths and enclaves. Two types of enclaves are found in the plutonic suite; Proterozoic metasedimentary and/or metaigneous xenoliths, and hornblende, plagioclase-rich microgranitoid mafic enclaves. Mafic enclaves also occur rarely throughout the suite, but are common in the Whale Mountain sequence. The latter range from equigranular to porphyritic, fine- to coarse-grained, hypidiomorphic granular clots. Plagioclase and hornblende are the phenocryst phases and make up the majority of the groundmass. Biotite, quartz, and poikilitic potassium feldspar constitute the remainder of the enclaves.

REFERENCES CITED

Allen, C. M., 1986, Liquidus phases in granite to quartz diorite; A natural example from magma mixing: Geological Society of America Abstracts with Programs, v. 18, p. 525.

Anderson, J. L., 1983, Proterozoic anorogenic granite plutonism in North America, *in* Medaris, L. G., Jr., Byers, C. W., Mickelson, D. M., and Shanks, W. C., Proterozoic geology; Selected papers from an International Proterozoic Symposium: Geological Society of America Memoir 161, p. 133–154.

Anderson, J. L., and Cullers, R. L., 1978, Geochemistry and evolution of the Wolf River batholith, a late Precambrian rapakivi massif in North Wisconsin, USA: Precambrian Research, v. 7, p. 287–324.

Barnes, C. G., 1983, Petrology and upward zonation of the Wooley Creek batholith, Klamath Mountains, California: Journal of Petrology, v. 24, pt. 4, p. 495–537.

Barnes, C. G., Allen, C. M., and Saleeby, J. B., 1986, Open- and closed-system characteristics of a tilted plutonic system, Klamath Mountains, California: Journal of Geophysical Research, v. 91, p. 6073–6090.

Bateman, P. C., and Chappell, B. W., 1979, Crystallization, fractionation, and solidification of the Tuolumne Intrusive Series, Yosemite National Park, California: Geological Society of America Bulletin, v. 90, p. 465–482.

Bateman, P. C., and Nokleberg, W. J., 1978, Solidification of the Mount Givens granodiorite, Sierra Nevada, California: Journal of Geology, v. 86, p. 563–579.

Beckerman, G., Robinson, J. P., and Anderson, J. L., 1982, The Teutonia batholith; A large intrusive complex of Jurassic and Cretaceous age in the eastern Mojave Desert, California, *in* Frost, E. G., and Martin, D. L., eds., Mesozoic-Cenozoic tectonic evolution of the Colorado River region, California, Arizona, and Nevada: San Diego, California, Cordilleran Publishers, p. 205–220.

Burchfiel, B. C., and Davis, G. A., 1981, Mojave Desert and environs, *in* Ernst, W. G., ed., The geotectonic development of California: Englewood Cliffs, New Jersey, Prentice-Hall, p. 217–252.

Church, S. E., 1976, The Cascade Mountains revisited; A re-evaluation in light of new lead isotopic data: Earth and Planetary Science Letters, v. 29, p. 175–188.

Compton, R. R., 1955, Trondhjemite batholith near Bidwell Bar, California: Geological Society of America Bulletin, v. 66, p. 9–44.

Cullers, R. L., and Graf, J. C., 1984, Rare-earth elements in igneous rocks of the continental crust; Intermediate and silicic rocks-ore genesis, *in* Henderson, P., ed., Rare earth element geochemistry; Developments in geochemistry 2: New York, Elsevier, p. 275–316.

Davis, G. A., Anderson, J. L., Frost, E. G., and Shackelford, T. J., 1980, Mylonitization and detachment faulting in the Whipple-Buckskin-Rawhide Mountain terrane, southeastern California and western Arizona, *in* Crittenden, M. D., Jr., Coney, P. J., and Davis, G. H., eds., Cordilleran metamorphic core complexes: Geological Society of America Memoir 153, p. 79–129.

Davis, G. A., Anderson, J. L., Martin, D. L., Krummenacher, D., Frost, E. G., and Armstrong, R. L., 1982, Geologic and geochronologic relations in the lower plate of the Whipple detachment fault, Whipple Mountains, southeastern California; A progress report, *in* Frost, E. G., and Martin, D. L., eds., Mesozoic-Cenozoic tectonic evolution of the Colorado River region, California, Arizona, and Nevada: San Diego, California, Cordilleran Publishers, p. 409–432.

Dellinger, D. A., and Hopson, C. H., 1986, Age-depth compositional spectrum through the diapiric Duncan Hill pluton, North Cascades, Washington: Geological Society of America Abstracts with Programs, v. 18, p. 100.

Dodge, F.C.W., and Mays, R. E., 1972, Rare-earth element fractionation in accessory minerals, central Sierra Nevada batholith: U.S. Geological Survey Professional Paper 800-D, p. D165–D168.

Doe, B. R., Leeman, W. P., Christiansen, R. L., and Hedge, C. E., 1986, Lead and strontium isotopes and related trace elements as genetic tracers in the upper Cenozoic rhyolite-basalt association of the Yellowstone Plateau volcanic field: Journal of Geophysical Research, v. 87, p. 4785–4806.

Farmer, G. L., and DePaolo, D. J., 1984, Origin of Mesozoic and Tertiary granite in the western United States and implications for pre-Mesozoic crustal structure; 2, Nd and Sr isotopic studies of unmineralized and Cu- and Mo-mineralized granite in the Precambrian craton: Journal of Geophysical Research, v. 89, no. B12, p. 10141–10160.

Flood, R. H., and Shaw, S. E., 1979, K-rich cumulate diorite at the base of a tilted granodiorite pluton from the New England batholith, Australia: Journal of Geology, v. 87, p. 417–425.

Fourcade, S., and Allegre, C. J., 1981, Trace element behavior in granite genesis; A case study, The calc-alkaline plutonic association from the Querigut Complex (Pyrenees, France): Contributions to Mineralogy and Petrology, v. 76, p. 177–195.

Fridrich, C. J., and Mahood, G. A., 1984, Reverse zoning in the resurgent intrusions of the Grizzly Peak cauldron, Sawatch Range, Colorado: Geological Society of America Bulletin, v. 95, p. 417–425.

Frost, E. G., Cameron, T. G., and Krummenacher, D., 1982, Mid-Tertiary detachment related deformation in the Chemehuevi Mountains, and its implications for regional crustal extension: Geological Society of America Abstracts with Programs, v. 14, p. 164.

Gill, J. B., 1981, Orogenic andesites and plate tectonics: New York, Springer-Verlag, 390 p.

Harrison, T. M., and McDougall, I., 1980, Investigation of an intrusive contact, northwest Nelson, New Zealand; 1, Thermal, chronological, and isotopic constraints: Geochimica et Cosmochimica Acta, v. 44, p. 1985–2003.

Haskin, L. A., Haskin, M. A., Frey, F. A., and Wildeman, T. R., 1968, Relative and absolute terrestrial abundances of rare earths, *in* Akren, L. H., ed., Origin and distribution of the elements: New York, Pergamon Press, p. 889–912.

Hildreth, W., 1981, Gradients in silicic magma chambers; Implications for lithospheric magmatism: Journal of Geophysical Research, v. 86, p. 10153–10192.

Hirt, W. H., 1986, Petrologic and mineralogic constraints on the evolution of the Whitney intrusive series, southeastern Sierra Nevada, California: Geological Society of America Abstracts with Programs, v. 18, p. 117.

Hoisch, T. D., Miller, C. F., Heizler, M. T., Harrison, T. M., and Stoddard, E. F., 1988, Late Cretaceous regional metamorphism in southeastern California, *in* Ernst, W. G., ed., Metamorphism and crustal evolution of the western conterminous United States, Rubey Volume 8: Englewood Cliffs, New Jersey, Prentice-Hall, p. 538–571.

Howard, K. A., Miller, D. M., and John, B. E., 1982, Regional character of mylonitic gneiss in the Cadiz Valley area, southeastern California, *in* Frost, E. G., and Martin, D. L., eds., Mesozoic-Cenozoic tectonic evolution of the Colorado River region, California, Arizona, and Nevada: San Diego, California, Cordilleran Publishers, p. 441–447.

Howard, K. A., John, B. E., and Miller, C. F., 1987, Metamorphic core complexes, Mesozoic ductile thrusts, and Cenozoic detachments: Old Woman Mountains–Chemehuevi Mountains transect, California and Arizona and its margins; Excursions to choice areas: Arizona Bureau of Geology and Mineral Technology Special Paper 5, p. 365–382.

Irvine, T. N., and Baragar, W.R.B., 1971, A guide to chemical classification of the common igneous rocks: Canadian Journal of Earth Sciences, v. 8, p. 523–548.

John, B. E., 1981, Reconnaissance study of Mesozoic intrusive rocks in the Mojave Desert region, *in* Howard, K. A., Carr, M. D., and Miller, D. M., eds., Tectonic framework of the Mojave and Sonoran deserts, California and Arizona: U.S. Geological Survey Open-File Report 81-503, p. 48–50.

—— , 1982, Geologic framework of the Chemehuevi Mountains, southeastern California, *in* Frost, E. G., and Martin, D. L., eds., Mesozoic-Cenozoic tectonic evolution of the Colorado River region, California, Arizona, and Nevada: San Diego, California, Cordilleran Publishers, p. 317–325.

—— , 1986, Structural and intrusive history of the Chemehuevi Mountains area, southeastern California and western Arizona [Ph.D. thesis]: Santa Barbara, University of California, 295 p.

—— , 1987a, Geometry and evolution of a mid-crustal extensional fault system, Chemehuevi Mountains, southeastern California, *in* Coward, M., Dewey, J., and Hancock, P., eds., Continental extension tectonics: Geological Society of London Special Paper 28, p. 313–335.

—— , 1987b, Geologic map of the Chemehuevi Mountains area, San Bernardino County, California, and Mohave County, Arizona: U.S. Geological Survey Open-File Report 87-666, scale 1:24,000.

—— , 1988, Structural reconstruction and zonation of a tilted mid-crustal magma chamber; The felsic Chemehuevi Mountains plutonic suite: Geology, v. 16, p. 613–617.

John, B. E., and Mukasa, S. B., 1988, Structural and geochronologic evidence for the nature of Cretaceous plutonism and mylonitization in the Chemehuevi Mountains core complex, southeastern California: Geological Society of America Abstracts with Programs, v. 20, no. 7, p. A2171.

Kay, R. W., Sun, S. S., and Lee-Hu, C. N., 1978, Pb and Sr isotopes in volcanic rocks from the Aleutian Islands and Pribilof Islands, Alaska: Geochimica et Cosmochimica Acta, v. 42, p. 263–273.

Liou, J. G., 1973, Synthesis and stability relations of epidote, $Ca_2Al_2Fe-Si_3O_{12}(OH)$: Journal of Petrology, v. 14, p. 381–413.

Lipman, P. W., 1984, The roots of ash-flow calderas in western North America; Windows into the tops of granitic batholiths: Journal of Geophysical Research, v. 89, no. B10, p. 8801–8841.

Ludington, S., Sharp, W. N., McKowan, D., and Barker, F., 1979, The Redskin granite; A Proterozoic example of thermogravitational diffusion?: Geological Society of America Abstracts with Programs, v. 11, p. 469.

Mahood, G. A., 1981, A summary of the geology and petrology of the Sierra La Primavera, Jalisco, Mexico: Journal of Geophysical Research, v. 86, no. B11, p. 10137–10152.

Masuda, A., Nakamura, N., and Tanaka, T., 1973, Fine structures of mutually normalized rare-earth patterns of chondrites: Geochimica et Cosmochimica Acta, v. 37, p. 239–248.

Miller, C. F., 1981, Cordilleran peraluminous granites; An ancient quartzofeldspathic source, *in* Howard, K. A., Carr, M. D., and Miller, D. M., eds., Tectonic framework of the Mojave and Sonoran deserts, California and Arizona: U.S. Geological Survey Open-File Report 81-503, p. 70–72.

Miller, C. F., and Mittlefehldt, D. W., 1982, Light rare earth depletion in felsic magmas: Geology, v. 10, p. 129–133.

—— , 1984, Extreme fractionation in felsic magma chambers; A product of liquid-state diffusion or fractional crystallization?: Earth and Planetary Science Letters, v. 68, p. 151–158.

Miller, C. F., and Stoddard, E. F., 1981, The role of manganese in the paragenesis of magmatic garnet; An example from the Old Woman–Piute Range, California: Journal of Geology, v. 89, p. 233–246.

Miller, C. F., Howard, K. A., and Hoisch, T. D., 1982, Mesozoic thrusting, metamorphism, and plutonism, Old Woman–Piute Range, southern California, *in* Frost, E. G., and Martin, D. L., eds., Mesozoic-Cenozoic tectonic evolution of the Colorado River region, California, Arizona, and Nevada: San Diego, California, Cordilleran Publishers, p. 561–581.

Miller, C. F., Bennett, V., Wooden, J. L., Soloman, G. C., Wright, J. E., and Hurst, R. E., 1984, Origin of the composite metaluminous/peraluminous Old Woman–Piute batholith, southeast California: Isotopic constraints: Geological Society of America Abstracts with Programs, v. 16, p. 596.

Miller, D. M., Howard, K. A., and Anderson, J. L., 1981, Mylonitic gneiss related to the emplacement of a Cretaceous batholith, Iron Mountains, southern California, *in* Howard, K. A., Carr, M. D., and Miller, D. M., eds., Tectonic framework of the Mojave and Sonoran deserts, California and Arizona: U.S. Geological Survey Open-File Report 81-503, p. 73–75.

Mittlefehldt, D. W., and Miller, C. F., 1983, Geochemistry of the Sweetwater Wash Pluton, California; Implications for "anomalous" trace element behavior during differentiation of felsic magmas: Geochimica et Cosmochimica Acta, v. 47, p. 109–124.

Miyashiro, A., 1974, Volcanic rock series in island arcs and active continental margins: American Journal of Science, v. 274, p. 321–355.

Moorbath, S., and Taylor, P. N., 1981, Isotopic evidence for continental growth in the Precambrian, *in* Kroner, A., ed., Developments in Precambrian Geology, Volume 4, Precambrian plate tectonics: New York, Elsevier, p. 491–525.

Naney, M. T., 1983, Phase equilibria of rock-forming ferromagnesian silicates in granitic systems: American Journal of Science, v. 283, p. 933–1033.

Perfit, M. R., Brueckner, H., Lawrence, J. R., and Kay, R. W., 1980, Trace element and isotopic variations in a zoned pluton and associated volcanic rocks, Unalaska Island, Alaska; A model for fractionation in the Aleutian calc-alkaline suite: Contributions to Mineralogy and Petrology, v. 73, p. 69–87.

Silver, L. T., 1968, Precambrian batholiths of Arizona, *in* Abstracts for 1968: Geological Society of America Special Paper 121, p. 558–559.

Solomon, G. C., 1986, $^{18}O/^{16}O$ studies of Mesozoic-Cenozoic granites and their bearing on crustal evolution in southern California: Geological Society of America Abstracts with Programs, v. 18, p. 188.

Stacey, J. C., and Kramers, J. D., 1975, Approximation of terrestrial lead isotope evolution by two-stage model: Earth and Planetary Science Letters, v. 26, p. 207–221.

Stephens, W. E., and Halliday, A. N., 1980, Discontinuities in composition surface of a zoned pluton, Criffel, Scotland: Geological Society of America Bulletin, v. 91, p. 165–170.

Stone, P., Howard, K. A., and Hamilton, W., 1983, Correlation of metamorphosed Paleozoic strata of the southeastern Mojave Desert region, California and Arizona: Geological Society of America Bulletin, v. 54, p. 1135–1147.

Stormer, J. C., and Nicholls, J., 1978, XLFRAC; A program for the interactive testing of magmatic differentiation models: Computers and Geosciences, v. 4, p. 143–159.

Streckeisen, A. L., 1976, To each plutonic rock its proper name: Earth Science Reviews, v. 12, p. 1–33.

Taylor, H. P., Jr., 1978, Oxygen and hydrogen isotope studies of plutonic granitic rocks: Earth and Planetary Science Letters, v. 38, p. 177–210.

Tilton, G. R., and Barreiro, B. A., 1980, Origin of lead in Andean calc-alkaline lavas, southern Peru: Science, v. 210, p. 1245–1247.

Wooden, J., Stacey, J., Howard, K., and Miller, D., 1988, Pb isotopic evidence for the formation of Proterozoic crust in the southwestern United States, *in* Ernst, W. G., ed., Metamorphic and tectonic evolution of the western Cordillera, conterminous U.S.A.; Rubey Volume 7: Englewood Cliffs, New Jersey, Prentice-Hall, p. 68–86.

Wright, J. E., Anderson, J. L., and Davis, G. A., 1986, Timing of plutonism, mylonitization, and decompression in a metamorphic core complex, Whipple Mountains, California: Geological Society of America Abstracts with Programs, v. 18, p. 201.

Zen, E-an, and Hammarstrom, J. M., 1984, Magmatic epidote and its petrologic significance: Geology, v. 12, p. 515–518.

MANUSCRIPT SUBMITTED NOVEMBER 20, 1987
REVISED MANUSCRIPT SUBMITTED AUGUST 7, 1988
MANUSCRIPT ACCEPTED BY THE SOCIETY FEBRUARY 7, 1989

Geological Society of America
Memoir 174
1990

Chapter 6

Petrogenesis of the composite peraluminous-metaluminous Old Woman–Piute Range batholith, southeastern California; Isotopic constraints

Calvin F. Miller
Department of Geology, Vanderbilt University, Nashville, Tennessee 37235
Joseph L. Wooden
U.S. Geological Survey, 345 Middlefield Road, Menlo Park, California 94025
Victoria C. Bennett*
Department of Earth and Space Science, University of California at Los Angeles, Los Angeles, California 90024
James E. Wright
Department of Geology, Stanford University, Stanford, California 94305
G. Cleve Solomon
Department of Geological and Planetary Sciences, California Institute of Technology, Pasadena, California 91125
Richard W. Hurst
Department of Geology, California State University, Los Angeles, California 90032

ABSTRACT

The Late Cretaceous Old Woman–Piute Range batholith includes both metaluminous and strongly peraluminous granitoid series that intruded the reactivated craton of southeastern California shortly after the orogenic peak. Whole-rock Sr, Nd, and O, feldspar Pb, and zircon U-Pb isotopic compositions, in combination with major- and trace-element and petrographic data, indicate that although these series are not comagmatic, they both were generated primarily by anatexis of Proterozoic crust. Differences between the two rock types are functions of source compositions: peraluminous granitoids were apparently generated from an intermediate to felsic source, metaluminous granitoids from more mafic igneous material with a possible modest subcrustal contribution. No sedimentary input is required in production of the peraluminous granites, and in fact, chemically mature sedimentary material is ruled out as an important contributor— that is, these are not S-type granites. Lead-isotope data reveal that the crust that yielded both magma series had undergone an ancient high-grade uranium depletion event, but independent evidence indicates that at the time of anatexis this crust was by no means anhydrous.

*Present address: Research School of Earth Sciences, The Australian National University, Canberra, ACT 2600, Australia.

Miller, C. F., Wooden, J. L., Bennett, V. C., Wright, J. E., Solomon, G. C., and Hurst, R. W., 1990, Petrogenesis of the composite peraluminous-metaluminous Old Woman–Piute Range batholith, southeastern California; Isotopic constraints, *in* Anderson, J. L., ed., The nature and origin of Cordilleran magmatism: Boulder, Colorado, Geological Society of America Memoir 174.

INTRODUCTION

Granitoid magmas are generated from highly diverse sources in a wide variety of geologic settings. Broad similarity among granitoid rocks is a result of convergent evolution—quartz and feldspars dominate both crustal mineralogy and fractionating assemblages of intermediate to felsic magmas at crustal pressures. Thus, anatexis of, contamination by, and fractionation within the crust all lead to similar magmatic products. Granitoids have distinctive petrologic/petrochemical signatures, however, and these signatures allow both origins of the rocks and histories of the crust of which they are effective probes to be constrained. Isotopic studies are especially valuable in working out granite petrogenesis and in inferring the history of source regions. Such studies can suggest age, composition, and post-formation modifications of crust from which magmas were derived and may in some cases characterize and indicate proportions of distinct source components (e.g., Farmer and DePaolo, 1983, 1984; Solomon and Taylor, 1981). Each isotopic system constrains different aspects of source composition and/or history, so that data from multiple systems are far more petrogenetically precise than data from any single system.

Our purpose in this paper is to present and interpret whole-rock Nd, Sr, and O, feldspar Pb, and zircon U-Pb data, along with supporting major- and trace-element and petrographic data, for the Old Woman–Piute batholith of the eastern Mojave Desert, southeastern California. These data provide insights into the nature of plutonism in reactivated cratons, the origin of metaluminous and peraluminous magmas, and the history of continental crust of the southwestern United States.

REGIONAL SETTING OF THE OLD WOMAN–PIUTE RANGE BATHOLITH

The maximum ages of rocks in the eastern Mojave Desert determined by direct dating are generally in the range 1.7 to 1.8 Ga (Burchfiel and Davis, 1981; Bennett and DePaolo, 1987). Samarium-neodymium–depleted mantle model ages of 2.0 to 2.3 Ga for 1.4 to 1.8 Ga igneous and metamorphic rocks indicate the existence of a pre–1.8 Ga continental crustal component (Bennett and DePaolo, 1987; Nelson and DePaolo, 1985). Recent work by Wooden and co-workers verifies the presence of this ancient component, both through Pb isotopic data (Wooden and others, 1988b) and through direct U/Pb dating of zircons (ages ≥2.0 Ga; e.g., Wooden and others, 1986a, 1988a; Wooden, unpublished data). Cratonization of the region occurred after orogeny ceased about 1.6 Ga, and crustal stability persisted through the remainder of Proterozoic and Paleozoic time. Cratonal, carbonate-dominated sedimentation commenced at the beginning of Cambrian time and continued into the Triassic.

The craton was intensely reactivated during Mesozoic time and underwent thrust faulting, magmatism, and metamorphism. The foreland of the Cordilleran thrust belt passes through the eastern Mojave, where it is manifested by thick, ductile, basement-cored nappes, in contrast to the thin-skinned thrusts involving only miogeoclinal sediments that are exposed farther north (Burchfiel and Davis, 1981; Howard and others, 1980). Jurassic and Cretaceous plutonic belts extend southeastward from the Sierra Nevada into this area. In contrast to the Sierra Nevada, however, many Cretaceous granitoids are strongly peraluminous, muscovite-bearing rocks that form part of an extensive zone characterized by peraluminous granites; the zone extends through much of the interior of the Cordillera, near the present edge of Proterozoic crust (Miller and Bradfish, 1980; Miller and Barton, 1989).

The Old Woman–Piute Range (OWP; Fig. 1b) contains the Early Proterozoic basement and relatively thin Cambrian to Triassic stratigraphic sequence that typify the region (Miller and others, 1982; Stone and others, 1983). Here basement and Phanerozoic section are overturned in a large nappe and metamorphosed at grades as high as upper amphibolite facies. A maximum depth of tectonic burial of at least 15 km is indicated by metamorphic mineral assemblages (Hoisch and others, 1988). During the Late Cretaceous, apparently shortly after the culmination of metamorphism and deformation, the complex was intruded by two distinct magma series, the earlier comprising metaluminous to weakly peraluminous granodiorites (MG) and the latter comprising strongly peraluminous granites (PG). Together these granitoids form a 350-km^2 composite batholith. The entire crystalline complex was unroofed rapidly from mid-crustal levels during latest Cretaceous and earliest Tertiary time, immediately after (and perhaps beginning during) batholith emplacement (Knoll and others, 1985; Foster and others, 1989).

NATURE OF THE OLD WOMAN–PIUTE RANGE BATHOLITH

Nature of the granitoid rocks

Almost all granitoids of known or probable Cretaceous age fall clearly into either the MG or PG series. MG rocks are intermediate to felsic (57 to 69 weight percent SiO$_2$, with cognate(?) enclaves down to 50 weight percent); most are metaluminous, with more felsic and/or biotite-rich samples being slightly peraluminous (to 0.6 weight percent normative corundum). Granodiorite is by far the predominant rock type; tonalite and granite are subordinate. Hornblende is generally present in samples with less than about 65 weight percent SiO$_2$, but, except in some of the mafic enclaves, it is far less abundant than biotite. Sphene, apatite, and magnetite are relatively abundant, and zircon, allanite, and epidote (possibly in part magmatic) are present. PG rocks are uniformly felsic (70 to 76 wt% SiO$_2$) and peraluminous, as indicated by ubiquitous primary muscovite and normative corundum (typically 1 to 2 weight percent). The principal rock type is monzogranite, and felsic granodiorite is also common. Plagioclase is uniformly more abundant than potassium feldspar. Biotite is present in most samples, but in more felsic rocks it is joined by Fe and Mn-rich garnet, and in highly evolved dikes and pods it is

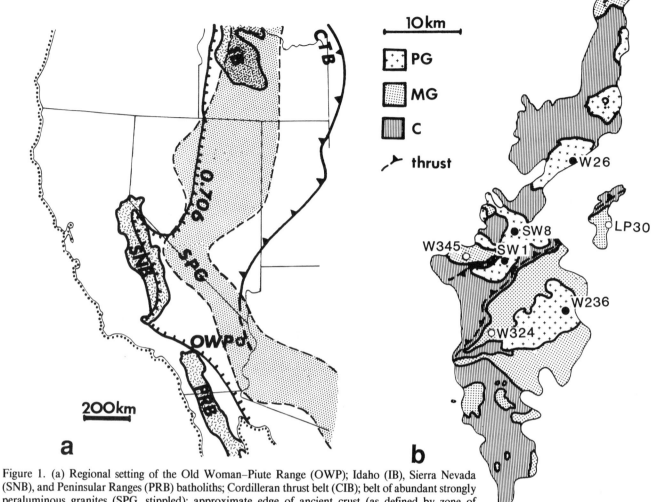

Figure 1. (a) Regional setting of the Old Woman–Piute Range (OWP); Idaho (IB), Sierra Nevada (SNB), and Peninsular Ranges (PRB) batholiths; Cordilleran thrust belt (CIB); belt of abundant strongly peraluminous granites (SPG, stippled); approximate edge of ancient crust (as defined by zone of Phanerozoic igneous rocks with initial $^{87}Sr/^{86}Sr > 0.706$) (hachured line). (b) Distribution of Cretaceous granitoids in OWP; PG: strongly peraluminous granitoids; MG: metaluminous granitoids; two small Cretaceous plutons in the northeastern OWP marked by question marks are distinct in fabric, petrography, and isotopic composition; they are omitted from Table 2 and discussion. C: Metamorphic country rock; thrust: thrust zone at base of nappe. Localities of specimens listed in Table 2 are shown.

absent (Miller and Stoddard, 1981). Zircon, apatite, and opaque minerals (primarily magnetite) are sparse. Monazite is present in all samples, and xenotime is very minor but widespread. Although the two series appear almost to merge on Harker diagrams (Fig. 2), they are clearly distinct in the field and in their mineral assemblages and paragenesis. The only exceptions to this distinctness occur at contacts between the two (discussed below). We interpret the merging of the compositional trends to be simply a manifestation of convergent granitoid evolution—many processes and many lineages lead toward a restricted range of minima.

Field relations

Regional tilting of the Old Woman–Piute Range exposes progressively deeper structural levels to the southeast (Howard and others, 1987). Figure 3 expresses in cartoon fashion the geometry of plutons that make up the batholith (excluding the smaller intrusions of uncertain affinity mentioned above) (cf. Young and Miller, 1983). PG and MG plutons are in all cases discrete. PG plutons lie at the highest level. Their roof contacts are sharp; roof zones are moderately injected by aplite/pegmatite dikes. Exposures of both roof and floor of the PG Sweetwater Wash pluton in the northern Old Woman Mounatins reveal this intrusion to be sheetlike. The upper part of the intrusion is relatively homogeneous with very sparse, 1 to 5 cm biotite + quartz ± muscovite enclaves, but the lower part grades into the floor through increasing proportions of country rock. Here, there is a continuum from inclusion-rich granite to heavily injected host rock. The injections, though crosscutting in detail, are generally sill-like in form and disrupt older structures remarkably little.

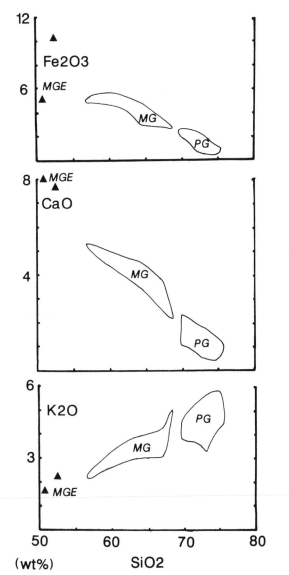

Figure 2. Harker diagrams showing fields of 30 MG and 70 PG samples. MG = field of metaluminous granitoids, MGE = mafic enclaves in MG, PG = peraluminous granitoids.

two plutons are extensive intrusive breccia zones, with massive blocks of MG engulfed by PG. Although sharp on outcrop scale, the block/host contacts are diffuse on a millimeter to centimeter scale, and PG undergoes changes in composition within meters of contacts, with muscovite diminishing in abundance or disappearing and rare sphene appearing. This suggests local interaction, possibly minor late-stage mixing with or small-scale assimilation of MG. Mingling may also be indicated by pillowlike inclusions of MG in PG in one area where the Sweetwater Wash pluton breaches the sheared gneiss zone and intrudes the Old Woman pluton. Numerous dikes that cut the Old Woman pluton above the Painted Rock pluton may represent feeders for the overlying Sweetwater Wash pluton.

Ages. Earlier Rb-Sr and K-Ar work has suggested a PG age of 70 to 80 Ma (Miller and others, 1982); MG was previously undated. Our U-Pb data indicate that MG is 71 ± 1 m.y. old and contains abundant zircons from a source with an average zircon age of about 1.6 to 1.7 Ga (Table 1; Fig. 4). PG zircons are even more discordant, with $^{207}Pb/^{206}Pb$ ages > 1.5 Ga. Because of this extreme discordance and the limited range of U/Pb, no meaningful PG crystallization age is defined, but the data are consistent with the same inheritance and emplacement ages as for MG. New ion microprobe and $^{40}Ar/^{39}Ar$ data corroborate our conclusions. Using zircon separates from our samples, Foster and others (1989) identified concordant grains from both PG (74 ± 6 Ma) and MG (73 ± 5 Ma). Ages are thus indistinguishable within ion probe uncertainty and are consistent with our 71 ± 1 Ma age. Furthermore, Foster and others (1989) show that all of the plutons had cooled through mica Ar closure by 70 Ma, again reinforcing the conclusion that emplacement (and subsequent rapid cooling) must have been almost simultaneous for PG and MG intrusions. Inherited zircons analyzed by ion probe on both PG and MG are diverse in age, ranging from 1.1 to 1.8 Ga.

GENESIS OF THE OLD WOMAN–PIUTE RANGE BATHOLITH

Petrochemical data

Isotope data presented in Table 2 and Figures 5 and 6 indicate considerable variability within both MG and PG series, but general intraseries, and to a lesser extent interseries, coherence is also apparent. Initial $^{87}Sr/^{86}Sr$ is high for both (MG 0.7095–0.7115, PG 0.714–0.719), and ϵ_{Nd} is uniformly low (MG –10 to –12, PG –16 to –17). Lead-isotope ratios are variable for both series and broadly overlapping. All samples fall in linear arrays on Pb/Pb plots extending down to values low in radiogenic Pb (especially ^{208}Pb: $^{206}Pb/^{204}Pb$ down to 17.7 for MG, 17.3 for PG). Values of $\delta^{18}O$ are intermediate and overlap considerably (MG 7.2 to 9.2, PG 8.2 to 9.3).

As noted previously, whole-rock chemistry of PG and MG rocks (summarized in Table 2) is broadly continuous from intermediate to felsic compositions. Incompatible elements are moderately abundant in both MG and PG; both are light rare earth

Beneath this injected zone, where the nappe structure is clearly preserved, lies a sheared, flattened, heterogeneous zone of gneisses and schists, and beneath this lies the large MG Old Woman pluton. This pluton is also sheetlike and extends well to the southwest of the Old Woman Mountains (e.g., Horringa, 1986). It contains widespread mafic enclaves with the same mineral assemblage as the host rock, and very large (to >1 km) local screens and blocks of orthogneiss. At deeper levels it becomes increasingly sheared, and its flat floor is underlain by flattened gneisses similar to those exposed at its roof (Howard and others, 1987). These gneisses are underlain by an extensive migmatite terrane. The Old Woman pluton is intruded by and almost totally encloses a large PG pluton (Painted Rock). Contacts between the

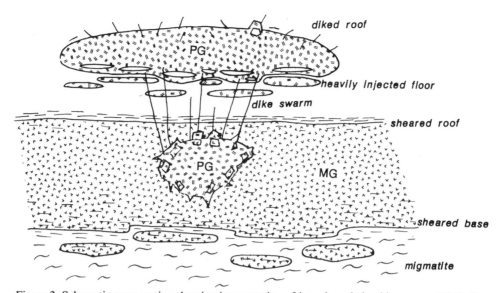

Figure 3. Schematic cross section showing interpretation of intrusive relationships among OWP Cretaceous granitoids.

TABLE 1. URANIUM-LEAD ISOTOPIC DATA

Specimen*	Wt. (mg)	U (ppm)	$^{206}Pb^{\dagger}$ (ppm)	Measured Ratios§			Atomic Ratios			Apparent Ages** (Ma)		
				$\frac{^{206}Pb}{^{204}Pb}$	$\frac{^{207}Pb}{^{206}Pb}$	$\frac{^{208}Pb}{^{206}Pb}$	$\frac{^{206}Pb^{\dagger}}{^{238}U}$	$\frac{^{207}Pb^{\dagger}}{^{235}U}$	$\frac{^{207}Pb^{\dagger}}{^{206}Pb^{\dagger}}$	$\frac{^{206}Pb^{\dagger}}{^{238}U}$	$\frac{^{207}Pb^{\dagger}}{^{235}U}$	$\frac{^{207}Pb^{\dagger}}{^{206}Pb^{\dagger}}$
ND-12>200	27.4	253.9	10.46	3,708	0.09250	0.10983	0.04794	0.58658	0.08874	301.9	468.7	1,399 ± 3
ND-12<200	20.9	417.4	11.26	5,804	0.08457	0.11118	0.03139	0.35552	0.08214	199.2	308.9	1,249 ± 2
ND-12<325	16.8	443.0	10.20	5,247	0.08164	0.11846	0.02682	0.29191	0.07895	170.6	260.1	1,171 ± 2
OW-1>100	16.8	603.1	52.69	12,394	0.09665	0.07784	0.10169	1.33951	0.09553	624.3	863.0	1,539 ± 2
OW-1<325	14.2	808.1	51.56	4,031	0.09933	0.08125	0.07426	0.98202	0.09590	461.8	694.6	1,546 ± 3

*100, <200, etc., refer to size fractions in mesh. All analyzed fractions were nonmagnetic at 1.7 amp with a 20° forward and a 1° side tilt on the Frantz magnetic separator.

†Denotes radiogenic Pb, corrected for common Pb using the isotopic composition of $^{206}Pb/^{204}Pb$ = 18.6 and $^{207}Pb/^{204}Pb$ = 15.6. Sample dissolution and ion exchange chemistry modified from Krogh (1973).

§Isotopic compositions corrected for a mass fractionation of 0.125% or 0.100%, depending on the mass spectrometer. Uncertainties in the $^{208}Pb/^{206}Pb$ ratios are on the order of 0.02 to 0.10%. $^{206}Pb/^{204}Pb$ errors range from about 1 to 7%, depending on the ratio (all uncertainties are at the two-sigma level).

**Ages calculated using the following constants: decay constants for ^{235}U and ^{238}U = 9.845E - 10 yr⁻¹ and 1.55125E - 10 yr⁻¹, respectively; $^{238}U/^{235}U$ = 137.88. Precisions on $^{206}Pb^{\dagger}/^{238}U$ ratios are about 0.2%, based on the replicate analysis of two "standard" zircon fractions. The two-sigma uncertainties in the $^{207}Pb^{\dagger}/^{206}Pb^{\dagger}$ ages were calculated from the combined uncertainties in mass spectrometry and an assumed uncertainty of ± 0.2 in the $^{207}Pb/^{204}Pb$ ratio used for the common Pb correction.

TABLE 2A. COMPOSITIONAL CHARACTERISTICS OF CRETACEOUS OWP GRANITOIDS

Approximate Mean Compositons of Granitoid Series

	SiO_2	Al_2O_3	CaO	Na_2O	K_2O	Fe_2O_3T +MgO	C*	Rb	Sr	Ba	La_N†	Sm_N†	Lu_N†	$\frac{Eu}{Eu}$§
MG (30)	63.5	16.5	3.8	4.2	3.3	6.0	0	90	800	1200	120	40	8	0.8
PG (70)	73.0	14.5	1.3	3.8	4.0	1.8	1.5	150	300	900	90	30	9	0.3

Ranges of Isotopic Compositions of Granitoid Series

	$^{87}Sr/^{86}Sr_t$	εNd_t	Feldspar			$\delta^{18}O$, %
			$^{206}Pb/^{204}Pb$	$^{207}Pb/^{204}Pb$	$^{208}Pb/^{240}Pb$	
MG	0.7095:0.7115	-10.3:-12.4	17.70:18.68	15.54:15.66	39.00:39.30	+7.2:+9.2
	(8)	(2)		(3)		(4)
PG	0.7143:0.7190	-16.0:-16.9	17.26:18.77	15.53:15.67	38.25:39.44	+8.2:+9.3
	(9)	(2)		(4)		(8)

Notes: MG = metaluminous to weakly peraluminous granitoids (30 samples analyzed).
PG = strongly peraluminous granitoids (70 samples analyzed).
Numbers in parentheses indicate number of samples analyzed.

*C = normative corundum (wt. %).

†Subscript ($_N$) indicates chondrite-normalized.

§Eu concentration interpolated from smooth normalized REE pattern.

t = 70 Ma.

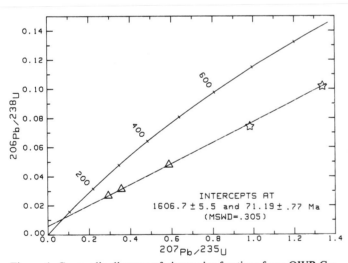

Figure 4. Concordia diagram of zircon size fractions from OWP Cretaceous granitoids. ND-12 (MG), triangles; OW-1 (PG, equivalent to SW-1), stars. Intercepts and errors (2 sigma) calculated using the program of Ludwig (1982). Only the data from ND-12 (MG) were used in the intercept calculation.

INTERCEPTS AT 1606.7 ± 5.5 and 71.19 ± .77 Ma (MSWD=.305)

element (LREE)–enriched (near 100 × chondrite) and have on the average moderate to high Rb and Ba. Negative Eu anomalies are absent to small in MG and uniformly large in PG. Sr concentrations in PG are mostly in the intermediate (200 to 400 ppm) range, whereas MG has high values (600 to 1000 ppm). K_2O is fairly high in MG for an intermediate rock (3 to 4 weight percent), and only slightly higher in PG (3.5 to 4.5 weight percent); K_2O/Na_2O is near unity in PG.

Petrochemical constraints on genesis

Implications of the data cited above for the origins of OWP granitoid magmas can be summarized briefly as follows.

(1) Sr-Nd (Fig. 5). The sources of both MG and PG were dominated by ancient crust older than 1.5 Ga; the age of the MG source may have been somewhat younger than that of PG, or it may have had a juvenile (young mantle-derived) contribution, or it may simply have had a somewhat higher Sm/Nd ratio. Probable average crustal residence time for PG source material was slightly more than 2 b.y. (cf. Bennett and DePaolo, 1987). Time-averaged Rb/Sr ratios of MG and PG sources were about 0.1 and 0.2, respectively, assuming a crustal age of near 2 Ga. This suggests a mafic to intermediate source for MG and an intermediate

TABLE 2B. COMPOSITIONS OF SELECTED SAMPLES

	SWl(PG)	SW8[1](PG)	W236(PG)	W26(PG)	W324(MG)	W345(MG)	LP30(MG)	BG(MG)
SiO_2	70.4	73.0	73.1	73.5	60.7	62.0	58.7	66.30
TiO_2	0.13	0.10	0.6	0.13	0.91	0.62	0.99	0.68
Al_2O_3	14.8	14.1	13.4	14.2	17.2	15.8	19.7	16.10
Fe_2O_3T	2.23	1.64	1.56	1.34	4.64	5.25	5.41	3.45
MnO	0.05	0.02	0.02	0.04	0.06	0.07	nd	0.06
MgO	0.25	0.18	0.12	0.18	1.62	2.13	1.89	1.17
CaO	1.72	1.24	0.78	1.02	4.37	4.17	4.79	3.15
Na_2O	3.93	3.46	3.85	3.26	4.50	3.66	4.96	4.30
K_2O	3.59	4.43	4.68	4.41	2.79	3.44	2.50	3.46
P_2O_5	0.06	0.08	0.05	0.05	0.30	0.25	nd	0.24
LOI	0.08	0.54	0.70	1.35	1.08	0.77	nd	0.74
Total	97.24	98.79	98.32	99.48	98.18	98.16	98.94	99.65
Rb	131	148	196	206	82	90	38	118
Sr	438	240	122	129	951	530	1014	589
Ba	1500	730	540	224	1210	1160	1200	1300
La	55	30	nd	12.0	nd	nd	59	40.8
Ce	110	58	nd	21.9	nd	nd	130	74.7
Nd	nd	18.05	16.79	nd	45.48	42.22	71	30.8
Sm	7.57	3.49	3.63	2.62	8.31	8.77	11	7.24
Eu	1.10	0.69	nd	0.54	nd	nd	3	1.57
Tb	0.89	0.62	nd	0.66	nd	nd	1	1.0
Yb	3.0	2.0	nd	1.86	nd	nd	1	2.27
Lu	0.43	0.28	nd	0.29	nd	nd	0.20	0.30
$^{143}Nd/^{144}Nd_o$	nd	0.51093 ± 24	0.510986 ± 51	nd	0.511275 ± 43	0.511163 ± 43	nd	nd
$^{143}Nd/^{144}Nd_i$	nd	0.51088	0.51093	nd	0.51122	0.51111	nd	nd
εNd_i	nd	-16.9	-16.0	nd	-10.3	-12.4	nd	nd
$^{87}Sr/^{86}Sr_o$	0.71514 ± 11	0.72007 ± 3	0.72127 ± 4	0.71988 ± 14	0.710774 ± 4	0.71136 ± 10	0.7059± 12	0.71204
$^{87}Sr/^{86}Sr_i$	0.71432	0.71838	0.71687	0.71599	0.71048	0.71089	0.70949	0.71149
εSr_i	+141	+198	+177	+158	+86	+92	+72	+101
Feldspar Pb[2]								
$^{207}Pb/^{206}Pb$	18.77	17.82	18.13	17.26	18.40	17.70	18.68	nd
$^{207}Pb/^{206}Pb$	15.67	15.56	15.61	15.53	15.68	15.54	15.66	nd
$^{207}Pb/^{206}Pb$	39.44	38.94	38.99	38.25	39.30	39.00	39.22	nd
$\delta^{18}O$	+9.0[3]	+9.1	+9.3[3]	nd	+7.2	+9.2	nd	nd

[1]Sr, Nd from Farmer and DePaolo (1983, their sample #W311); initial ratios calculated here for 70 Ma.
[2]2-sigma errors in Pb ratios are < ± 0.1%.
[3]Values for different samples, same locality.

Notes:
CHUR (chondritic reservoir) values: $^{143}Nd/^{144}Nd$ = 0.511836; $^{147}Sm/^{144}Nd$ = 0.1967.
Λ_{Sm} = 6.54 x 10^{12} yr^{-1}; UR (uniform reservoir) values: $^{87}Sr/^{86}Sr$ = 0.7045, $^{87}Rb/^{86}Sr$ = 0.0827,
Λ_{Rb} = 0.0142 x 10^{-11} yr^{-1}.
Rb, Sr, Sm, Nd by isotope dilution for samples for which isotope data are reported; major elements, Ba, other Rb,
Sr by XRF; REE (except Sm, Nd as noted) by INAA.
Sm-Nd data by methods described in DePaolo (1981); Rb-Sr as in Hurst and others (1975); Pb as in Ashwal and others
(1986); O modified from Taylor and Epstein (1962).
Major- and trace-element data for samples SW1 and SW8 from Mittlefehldt and Miller (1983).

to felsic source for PG; a mature sedimentary (S-type) source is ruled out for PG, unless it was strongly depleted in Rb by an ancient high-grade metamorphic event, or it was Phanerozoic in age. Potential Phanerozoic sedimentary sources are virtually nonexistent in the region (Stone and others, 1983).

(2) O. $\delta^{18}O$ values are too high to be dominated by a mantle component and too low to be dominated by a sedimentary component. Granulite facies metamorphism apparently can reduce $\delta^{18}O$ of sedimentary rocks (Longstaffe and Schwarcz, 1977), but even lower crustal metapelites of extreme grade have been reported to maintain isotopic distinctiveness ($\delta^{18}O > 10$; James and others, 1980).

(3) Pb (Fig. 6). The distribution of feldspar lead-isotope ratios in both MG and PG granitoids indicates that the Pb source materials had variable but characteristically low U/Pb ratios (compared with upper crust or mantle) for an extended period of

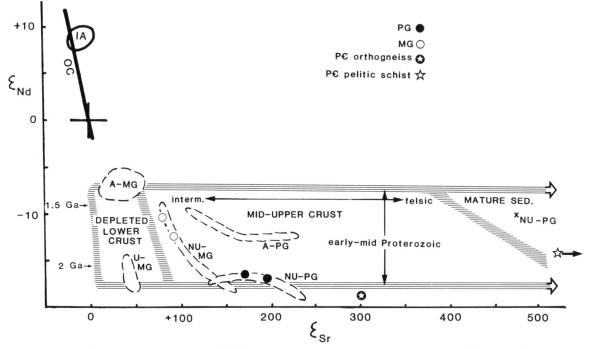

Figure 5. Initial ϵ_{Nd} vs. ϵ_{Sr} plot of OWP granitoids. Also shown are: $\epsilon_{70\ Ma}$ of OWP Proterozoic orthogneiss and pelitic schist (ϵ_{Sr} off scale) (Bennett and DePaolo, 1987); fields of initial ϵ of peraluminous (PG) and metaluminous (MG) granitoids from eastern Nevada and western Utah (NU; one high-ϵ_{Sr} specimen from Ruby Mountains, Nevada, plotted separately [x]), Arizona (A), and central Utah (U) (Farmer and DePaolo, 1983, 1984); estimates of present-day ϵ_{Nd} of "typical" 1.5 and 2 Ga crust (Farmer and DePaolo, 1983); approximate present-day fields of Early to Middle Proterozoic (approx. 1.5–2 Ga) Rb-depleted lower crust, intermediate to felsic middle and upper crust, mature sediment, and upper mantle (oceanic correlation line, OC) and immature island-arc (IA) ϵ values (Farmer and DePaolo, 1983).

time; Th/Pb ratio reduction was less pronounced. These data suggest that the sources of both series experienced an ancient, variable depletion in U, apparently accompanied by more modest depletion in Th; such depletion is generally attributed to very high-grade metamorphism with or without accompanying anatexis, and thus implies that the source was in part very high-grade (uppermost amphibolite to granulite facies) lower crust. The $^{207}Pb/^{204}Pb$ and $^{206}Pb/^{204}Pb$ ratios define a linear trend that indicates that this depletion event occurred at about 1.7 to 1.8 Ga. Time-averaged Th/U ratios calculated for the source rocks from these data are high (4.5 to 6.2), indicating stronger retention of Th than U. The data show no evidence for a primitive arc or mantle contribution to the MG and PG magmas (this would be anticipated, because Pb data show crustal far more clearly than mantle contributions due to much higher crustal Pb concentrations [Wooden and others, 1988b]).

(4) Other data. (a) MG has high Sr, Rb, and Ba, high total REE and LREE/HREE, relatively straight REE patterns (little middle REE depletion), and small negative Eu anomalies. The high incompatible-element concentrations rule out a depleted (mid-ocean ridge basalt [MORB]–like) mafic source, even if fraction of melting were to approach zero. The data further suggest that neither plagioclase, nor hornblende, nor garnet was left be-

hind as abundant residue or fractionating phases. Abundant residual plagioclase would result in Sr-depleted magma; hornblende, unless accompanied by subequal plagioclase, would induce a positive Eu anomaly and middle REE—and, to a lesser extent, heavy REE—depletion (concave-upward patterns) in the derived magma; large masses of residual garnet would result in extreme HREE depletion and positive Eu anomalies. (b) PG has rather high Ba (near 1,000 ppm) and low Rb/Ba (about 0.15), which are inconsistent with a pelitic source (Miller, 1985). Pelites have Rb/Ba typically >0.2 (Green, 1972) and at anatectic grade have stronger affinity for Ba than for Rb (see partition coefficients for K-feldspar and micas; Arth, 1976). Therefore, pelite-derived magmas should also have Rb/Ba > 0.2; that is, Rb/Ba is higher in derived magmas than in pelitic sources, and it will increase with fractionation. K_2O/Na_2O in the PG series is close to 1, lower than anticipated in pelite-derived magmas (e.g., Chappell and White, 1974; Miller, 1985; White and others, 1986). Furthermore, PG normative corundum of about 1.5 to 2 weight percent, although typical of strongly peraluminous rocks, is lower than expected in magmas with highly aluminous (pelitic) parentage (e.g., Clemens and Wall, 1981). (c) Large negative Eu anomalies of PG rocks indicate abundant residual feldspar; given the high Ba concentrations, the feldspar was presumably dominantly pla-

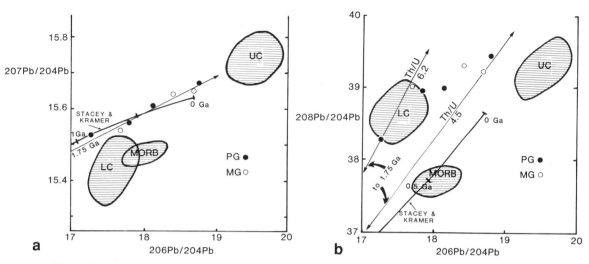

Figure 6. Feldspar Pb isotopic composition of OWP granitoids compared with present-day average lower crust (LC), mid-ocean ridge basalt (MORB; ca. depleted upper mantle), and upper crust (UC) (Zartman and Doe, 1981), and with Stacey and Kramer's (1975) two-stage model growth curves. 1.75 Ga isochrons for comparison. (a) $^{206}Pb/^{204}Pb$ vs. $^{207}Pb/^{204}Pb$. (b) $^{206}Pb/^{204}Pb$ vs. $^{208}Pb/^{204}Pb$. Isochrons originating from Stacey and Kramer's 1.75 Ga point shown for two elevated Th/U ratios (6.2, 4.5).

gioclase (K-feldspar would retain Ba). (d) Both MG and PG contain early hydrous minerals (micas and/or amphiboles), which demonstrates that the magmas were themselves moderately hydrous; this in turn implies either that the Proterozoic high-grade event affecting the source did not entirely dehydrate it, or that the source was subsequently rehydrated prior to or during anatexis.

Possible source materials

Attempting to identify specific source materials for most granitoid rocks is difficult at best. It is unlikely that crustal source regions for appreciable magma volumes are ever homogeneous—in fact, major lithologic variability is probable in source areas, and magmas will show the imprint of such diversity (cf. Miller and others, 1988). This complexity increases if there is material input from juvenile subcrustal magmas (probably not important in PG, but potentially appreciable in MG). Furthermore, even if a single homogeneous source could be assumed, it is rarely clear what if anything within a granitoid complex represents a liquid composition—and the best candidates are generally the most evolved and therefore the least useful in assessing source. The "least evolved" rocks are typically cumulate-rich, and thus also of limited usefulness. Nonetheless, it may be fruitful to use the available data to characterize what might be the average composition of the source of each magma series. (We consider the mean composition of each series to be the most useful composition to deal with, because it is the best available indicator of bulk magma composition intruding the study area; there are no good indicators of any primitive liquid compositions that might be more informative. Although some fractionation undoubtedly occurred

during ascent, the large volumes of magma involved and their similarity to their isotopically constrained crustal sources suggest that it was limited.)

The most probable origin for the MG series is by large-scale melting (with or without appreciable restite mobilization) of an intermediate-composition igneous source. This source was probably not a great deal more mafic than the average MG composition; note the close similarity of MG Rb/Sr to the time-averaged source Rb/Sr. As noted above, trace-element evidence requires that unless melting was extensive (probably more than 50 percent), the residue must have been relatively poor in plagioclase, hornblende, and garnet. If none of these minerals was abundant, a very mafic to ultramafic residue with abundant pyroxene and/or olivine seems required, and yet the isotopic data rule out a source material of this composition. The simplest way to explain this apparent paradox is by invoking large-scale melting of a source with a composition similar to the MG rocks, perhaps averaging quartz dioritic to tonalitic. Given source material of this sort, the nature of residual mineralogy is no longer a severe problem because the relatively small amount of restite left behind will not strongly influence derived magma composition. Depending on the extent of melting, pressure, temperature, and a_{H_2O}, it may have included plagioclase, pyroxenes, hornblende, and/or garnet.

The source of PG, as suggested above, was probably dominantly of igneous composition, and its high time-averaged Rb/Sr suggests that it was, on the average, moderately felsic, but in this case distinctly less felsic than the derived magma. The lower apparent Rb/Sr of the source than of the magma and the large negative Eu anomaly requires the influence of plagioclase, probably at least in part contained in plagioclase-rich residue; the high Ba indicates that K-feldspar was not abundant. A source whose average composition was granodioritic would be appropriate; unless the PG series was affected strongly by fractional crystallization prior to emplacement, the fraction of melting was probably less than 50 percent. A weakly peraluminous source composition would be simplest to reconcile with the peraluminous composition of PG, but slightly metaluminous materials are apparently capable of generating peraluminous magmas as well (cf. Miller, 1985).

CONCLUSIONS AND IMPLICATIONS

Magmas that formed the OWP batholith were derived primarily from a heterogeneous lower to mid-crustal region about 70 Ma. This region must have comprised a range of compositions, including mafic to intermediate metaigneous rocks (amphibolites?) and intermediate to felsic rocks (probably igneous, perhaps including ^{18}O-depleted chemically immature metasedimentary rocks). These conclusions demonstrate the problems inherent in applying the I- and S-type classification loosely (cf. Miller, 1985, 1986; White and others, 1986); superficially, the strongly peraluminous high initial $^{87}Sr/^{86}Sr$ PG series would appear to be S-type but, like MG, it is probably igneous-derived and therefore I-type. The MG series, on the other hand, demonstrates that even metaluminous, relatively mafic (<65 percent SiO_2) magmas can be generated largely or entirely from mature continental crust. Detailed investigations of granitoids and strict application of I and S terminology is likely to reveal that true S-type granitoids are very rare and that the problem facing petrologists is identification of contributions from a wide variety of crustal (and a perhaps lesser variety of mantle) materials.

Recent Nd isotopic studies have demonstrated that crust in a belt that extends from southeastern California northward through eastern Nevada and western Utah either formed at about 2.0 to 2.3 Ga or is a mix of Archean and 1.7 to 1.8 Ga (regional dominant zircon age) components (Bennett and DePaolo, 1987; Farmer and DePaolo, 1983; Bennett and DePaolo, 1984; Nelson and DePaolo, 1985). Nd isotopic studies specifically dealing with regional granitoid genesis have further suggested that this crust has not suffered a high-grade Rb-depleting event (Farmer and DePaolo, 1983). This province contrasts with the region to the east, extending from Arizona through Colorado, where zircon ages and Nd model ages are roughly coincident at about 1.8 Ga (above references plus Farmer and DePaolo, 1984). Wooden and coworkers (Wooden and others, 1986b, 1988b; Wooden, unpublished data) have demonstrated by using Pb isotopes that the crust in the southeastern California–eastern Nevada province formed prior to an Early Proterozoic high-grade U-depleting event. This crust is exposed at low-P granulite facies grade in southeastern California and adjacent southern Nevada (Wooden and others, 1986a; Elliott and others, 1986; Young and others, 1986; Thomas and Cargnelutti, 1986). Much higher P granulite xenoliths, which may also be derived from basement of the same age, have been discovered recently in Tertiary dikes in the OWP (Staude and Miller, 1987). OWP granitoids were clearly derived largely from the old (>2 Ga average crustal residence), U-depleted crust. The depletion event, which is clear from Pb isotopic data (Fig. 6), is not detectable in Nd-Sr data (Fig. 5); it may have been mild enough not to have affected Rb appreciably (or to have thoroughly dehydrated the lower crust). It is clear that depletion events of this sort do not render the lower crust permanently infertile as a source of granitoid magmas.

ACKNOWLEDGMENTS

We especially thank K. A. Howard and G. L. Farmer, whose insights into regional tectonic and isotopic problems stimulated this work. Reviews by Howard, E. D. Young, J. L. Anderson, and S. J. Reynolds helped us to clarify the manuscript and are appreciated. Research was supported in part by National Science Foundation Grant EAR 78-23694, the U.S. Geological Survey, and the Vanderbilt University Research Council.

REFERENCES CITED

Arth, J. G., 1976, Behavior of trace elements during magmatic processes; A summary of theoretical models and their applications: U.S. Geological Survey Journal of Research, v. 4, p. 41–47.

Ashwal, L. D., Wooden, J. L., and Emslie, R. F., 1986, Sr, Nd, and Pb isotopes in Proterozoic intrusives astride the Grenville Front in Labrador; Implications for crustal contamination and basement mapping: Geochimica et Cosmochimica Acta, v. 50, p. 2571–2585.

Bennett, V. C., and DePaolo, D. J., 1984, The distribution of 2.0–2.3 b.y. neodymium model-age rocks in the western United States: Geological Society of America Abstracts with Programs, v. 16, p. 442.

—— , 1987, Proterozoic history of the western United States as determined by neodymium isotopic mapping: Geological Society of America Bulletin, v. 99, p. 674–685.

Burchfiel, B. C., and Davis, G. A., 1981, Mojave Desert and environs, *in* Ernst, W. G., ed., The geotectonic development of California, Rubey Volume I: Englewood Cliffs, New Jersey, Prentice-Hall, Inc., p. 217–252.

Chappell, B. W., and White, A.J.R., 1974, Two contrasting granite types: Pacific Geology, v. 8, p. 173–174.

Clemens, J. D., and Wall, V. J., 1981, Origin and crystallization of some peraluminous (S-type) granitic magmas: Canadian Mineralogist, v. 19, p. 111–131.

DePaolo, D. J., 1981, A neodymium and strontium isotopic study of the Mesozoic calc-alkaline batholiths of the Sierra Nevada and Peninsular Ranges, California: Journal of Geophysical Research, v. 86, p. 10470–10488.

Elliott, G., Wooden, J., Miller, D., and Miller, R., 1986, Lower-granulite grade Early Proterozoic supracrustal rocks, New York Mountains, SE California: Geological Society of America Abstracts with Programs, v. 18, p. 352.

Farmer, G. L., and DePaolo, D. J., 1983, Origin of Mesozoic and Tertiary granite in the western United States and implications for pre-Mesozoic crustal structure; 1, Nd and Sr isotopic studies in the geocline of the northern Great Basin: Journal of Geophysical Research, v. 88, p. 3379–3401.

—— , 1984, Origin of Mesozoic and Tertiary granite in the western United States and implications for pre-Mesozoic crustal structure; 2, Nd and Sr isotopic studies of unmineralized and Cu-Mo mineralized granite in Precambrian craton: Journal of Geophysical Research, v. 89, p. 10141–10161.

Foster, D. A., Harrison, T. M., and Miller, C. F., 1989, Age, inheritance, and uplift history of the Old Woman–Piute batholith, California, and implications for K-feldspar age spectra: Journal of Geology, v. 97, p. 232–243.

Green, J., 1972, Elements; Planetary abundances and distribution, *in* Fairbridge, R. W., ed., Encyclopedia of geochemistry and environmental science: New York, Van Nostrand-Reinhold, p. 268–300.

Hoisch, T. D., Miller, C. F., Heizler, M. T., Harrison, T. M., and Stoddard, E. F., 1988, Late Cretaceous regional metamorphism in southeastern California, *in* Ernst, W. G., ed., Metamorphism and crustal evolution of the western United States, Ruby Volume 7: Englewood Cliffs, New Jersey, Prentice-Hall, p. 538–571.

Horringa, E. D., 1986, Mesozoic tectonism in the northern Kilbeck Hills, southeastern California: Geological Society of America Abstracts with Programs, v. 18, p. 118.

Howard, K. A., Miller, C. F., and Stone, P., 1980, Mesozoic thrusting in the eastern Mojave Desert, California: Geological Society of America Abstracts with Programs, v. 12, p. 112.

Howard, K. A., John, B. E., and Miller, C. F., 1987, Metamorphic core complexes, Mesozoic ductile thrusts, and Cenozoic detachments; Old Woman Mountains–Chemehuevi Mountains transect, California and Arizona, *in* Davis, G. J., and Vanderwolder, E. M., eds., Geologic diversity of Arizona and its margins: Excursions to choice areas: Arizona Bureau of Geology and Mineral Technology, Special Paper 5, p. 365–382.

Hurst, R. W., Bridgwater, D., and Collerson, K. D., 1975, 3600-m.y. Rb-Sr ages from very early Archean gneisses from Saglek Bay, Labrador: Earth and Planetary Science Letters, v. 27, p. 393–403.

James, D. E., Padovani, E. R., and Hart, S. R., 1980, Preliminary results on the oxygen isotopic composition of the lower crust, Kilbourne Hole Maar, New Mexico: Geophysical Research Letters, v. 7, p. 321–324.

Knoll, M. A., Harrison, T. M., Miller, C. F., Howard, K. A., Duddy, I. R., and Miller, D. S., 1985, Pre-Peach Springs Tuff (18 m.y.) unroofing of the Old Woman Mountains crystalline complex, southeastern California; Implications for Tertiary extensional tectonics: Geological Society of America Abstracts with Programs, v. 17, p. 365.

Krogh, T. E., 1973, A low-contamination method for hydrothermal decomposition of zircon and extraction of U and Pb for isotopic age determinations: Geochimica et Cosmochimica Acta, v. 37, p. 485–494.

Longstaffe, F. J., and Schwarcz, H. P., 1977, $^{18}O/^{16}O$ of Archean clastic metasedimentary rocks; A petrogenetic indicator for Archean gneisses?: Geochimica et Cosmochimica Acta, v. 41, p. 1303–1312.

Ludwig, K. R., 1982, A computer program to convert raw Pb-U-Th isotope ratios to blank-corrected isotope ratios and concentrations, with associated errors and error correlations: U.S. Geological Survey Open-File Report 82–0820, 16 p.

Miller, C. F., 1985, Are strongly peraluminous magmas derived from pelitic metasedimentary sources?: Journal of Geology, v. 93, p. 673–689.

——, 1986, Comment *on* "S-type granites and their probable absence in southwestern North America": Geology, v. 14, p. 804–805.

Miller, C. F., and Barton, M. D., 1989, Phanerozoic plutonism in the Cordilleran interior, western USA, *in* Kay, S. M., and Rapela, D. W., eds., Plutonism from Alaska to Antarctica: Geological Society of America Special Paper 241 (in press).

Miller, C. F., and Bradfish, L. J., 1980, An inner Cordilleran belt of muscovite-bearing plutons: Geology, v. 8, p. 412–416.

Miller, C. F., Howard, K. A., and Hoisch, T. D., 1982, Mesozoic thrusting, metamorphism, and plutonism, Old Woman–Piute Range, southeastern California, *in* Frost, E. G., and Martin, D. L., eds., Mesozoic–Cenozoic tectonic evolution of the Colorado River region, California-Arizona-Nevada: San Diego, California, Cordilleran Publishers, p. 561–581.

Miller, C. F., and Stoddard, E. F., 1981, The role of manganese in the paragenesis of magmatic garnet: an example from the Old Woman–Piute Range, California: Journal of Geology, v. 89, p. 233–246.

Miller, C. F., Watson, E. B., and Harrison, T. M., 1988, Perspectives on the source, segregation, and transport of granitoid magmas: Transactions of the Royal Society of Edinburgh, v. 79, p. 135–156.

Mittlefehldt, D. W., and Miller, C. F., 1983, Geochemistry of Sweetwater Wash pluton, California; Implications for "anomalous" trace element behavior during differentiation of felsic magmas: Geochimica et Cosmochimica Acta, v. 47, p. 109–124.

Nelson, B. K., and DePaolo, D. J., 1985, Rapid production of continental crust 1.7–1.9 b.y. ago; Nd isotopic evidence from the basement of the North American mid-continent: Geological Society of America Bulletin, v. 96, p. 746–754.

Solomon, G. C., and Taylor, H. P., Jr., 1981, Oxygen isotope study of Mesozoic batholithic rocks in southwestern California and southern Arizona, *in* Howard, K. A., Carr, M. D., and Miller, D. M., eds., Tectonic framework of the Mojave and Sonoran deserts, California and Arizona: U.S. Geological Survey Open File Report 81-503, p. 100.

Stacey, J. S., and Kramers, J. D., 1975, Approximation of terrestrial lead isotope evolution by a two-stage model: Earth and Planetary Science Letters, v. 26, p. 207–221.

Staude, J.-M., and Miller, C. F., 1987, Lower crustal xenoliths from a Tertiary composite dike, Piute Mountains, SE California: Geological Society of America Abstracts with Programs, v. 19, p. 454.

Stone, P., Howard, K. A., and Hamilton, W., 1983, Correlation of metamorphosed Paleozoic strata of the southeastern Mojave Desert region, California and Arizona: Geological Society of America Bulletin, v. 94, p. 1135–1147.

Taylor, H. P., Jr., and Epstein, S., 1962, Relationship between O^{18}/O^{16} ratios in coexisting minerals of igneous and metamorphic rocks; Part 1, Principles and experimental results: Geological Society of America Bulletin, v. 73, p. 461–480.

Thomas, W., and Cargnelutti, D. H., 1986, Granulite facies metamorphism in the Gold Butte area, Clark Co., Nevada: Geological Society of America Abstracts with Programs, v. 18, p. 192.

White, A.J.R., Clemens, J. D., Holloway, J. R., Silver, L. T., Chappell, B. W., and Wall, V. J., 1986, S-type granites and their apparent absence in southwestern North America: Geology, v. 14, p. 115–118.

Wooden, J., Miller, D., and Elliott, G., 1986a, Early Proterozoic geology of the northern New York Mountains, southeastern California: Geological Society of America Abstracts with Programs, v. 18, p. 424.

Wooden, J., Stacey, J., Howard, K., and Miller, D., 1986b, Crustal evolution in southeastern California: constraints from Pb isotopic evidence: Geological Society of America Abstracts with Programs, v. 18, p. 200.

Wooden, J. L., Miller, D. M., and Howard, K. A., 1988a, Early Proterozoic chronology of the eastern Mojave Desert: Geological Society of America Abstracts with Programs, v. 20, p. 243.

Wooden, J. L., Stacey, J. S., Doe, B. R., Howard, K. A., and Miller, D. M., 1988b, Pb isotopic evidence for the formation of Proterozoic crust in the southwestern United States, *in* Ernst, W. G., ed., Metamorphism and crustal evolution of the western United States, Ruby Volume 7: Englewood Cliffs, New Jersey, Prentice-Hall, p. 69–86.

Young, E. D., and Miller, C. F., 1983, The geology of the Florence pluton area, and implications for pluton emplacement, Old Woman Mountains, SE California: Geological Society of America Abstracts with Programs, v. 15, p. 421.

Young, E. D., Clarke, H. S., and Anderson, J. L., 1986, Proterozoic low-pressure hornblende-granulite facies migmatites, McCullough Range, southern Nevada: Geological Society of America Abstracts with Programs, v. 18, p. 202.

Zartman, R. E., and Doe, B. R., 1981, Plumbotectonics; The model: Tectonophysics, v. 75, p. 135–162.

MANUSCRIPT SUBMITTED MAY 15, 1987
REVISED MANUSCRIPT SUBMITTED DECEMBER 29, 1987
MANUSCRIPT ACCEPTED BY THE SOCIETY FEBRUARY 7, 1989

Geological Society of America
Memoir 174
1990

Chapter 7

Jurassic granitoids and related rocks of the southern Bristol Mountains, southern Providence Mountains, and Colton Hills, Mojave Desert, California

Lydia K. Fox
Department of Geological Sciences, University of California, Santa Barbara, California 93106, and U.S. Geological Survey, MS 975, 345 Middlefield Road, Menlo Park, California
David M. Miller
U.S. Geological Survey, MS 975, 345 Middlefield Road, Menlo Park, California 94025

ABSTRACT

Jurassic plutons in the east-central Mojave Desert region are markedly different from older and younger Mesozoic plutons in the region. They form a chemically and texturally heterogeneous group that ranges in composition from diorite to syenogranite; some phases are alkalic. Igneous rocks in the southern Bristol Mountains, southern Providence Mountains, and Colton Hills are subdivided into five broadly defined groups on the basis of field relations and geochemistry: mafic intrusive rocks; mixed intrusive rocks, consisting of subequigranular and porphyritic subgroups; felsic intrusive rocks; metavolcanic and hypabyssal rocks; and dikes. There is a general trend from older, more mafic and heterogeneous rocks to younger, more felsic and homogeneous plutonic phases. Extreme spatial variations in composition and texture and other field relations indicate that the plutons were intruded during a relatively short time span. Field relations also indicate that the plutons were intruded at upper crustal levels. The plutons were affected by extensive late- or early post-magmatic sodium metasomatism (albitization), which resulted from the introduction and circulation of predominantly meteoric fluids. We propose that the plutons in this region were derived from compositionally heterogeneous but genetically related magmas generated from an upper mantle/lower crustal amphibolitic source. Similar Jurassic rocks are found elsewhere in the southern Cordillera, indicating that the genesis of these unusual rocks is a regional phenomenon.

INTRODUCTION

Jurassic plutons occur throughout the southern Cordillera where they make up part of a continental-margin magmatic arc that was constructed on the truncated southwestern margin of the North American craton (Burchfiel and Davis, 1981). This arc was constructed as a result of oblique subduction of the Kula and/or Farallon plates under the North American plate. Within California's Mojave Desert region, plutons representing this Cor-

dilleran magmatic arc (Fig. 1) range in age from Late Permian–Early Triassic to Late Cretaceous and are widespread and abundant. The majority of these bodies are Jurassic and Cretaceous in age. On the whole, the Jurassic plutonic rocks in the eastern Mojave Desert region have been less well studied than the Cretaceous plutons (Beckerman and others, 1982; C. F. Miller and others, 1982; John, 1981, 1986; Anderson, 1988), although they have been studied in the adjacent Sonoran Desert region of southern Arizona, southeasternmost California, northern Sonora

Fox, L. K., and Miller, D. M., 1990, Jurassic granitoids and related rocks of the southern Bristol Mountains, southern Providence Mountains, and Colton Hills, Mojave Desert, California, *in* Anderson, J. L., ed., The nature and origin of Cordilleran magmatism: Boulder, Colorado, Geological Society of America Memoir 174.

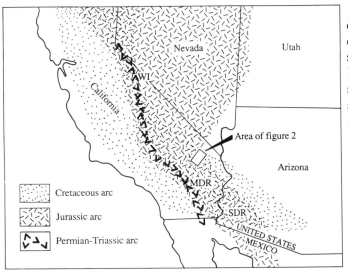

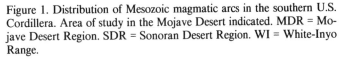

Figure 1. Distribution of Mesozoic magmatic arcs in the southern U.S. Cordillera. Area of study in the Mojave Desert indicated. MDR = Mojave Desert Region. SDR = Sonoran Desert Region. WI = White-Inyo Range.

(Tosdal and others, 1989), and in the central Mojave Desert (Karish and others, 1987). The purpose of this paper is to describe Jurassic intrusive rocks in the east-central Mojave Desert region and speculate on their origin. We focus on plutons and related rocks exposed in the southern Bristol Mountains, southern Providence Mountains, and Colton Hills (Fig. 2).

Regional Setting

Granitoids in the southern U. S. Cordillera can be divided into three major age groups: Late Permian–Early Triassic, Jurassic, and Cretaceous. These groups form distinct, approximately northwest-trending magmatic belts that cut obliquely across Paleozoic depositional trends (Burchfiel and Davis, 1981) and are part of larger swaths of arc magmatism that extend throughout the Cordillera (Fig. 1) (Davis and others, 1978; Monger and Price, 1979; Anderson and Silver, 1979; Burchfiel and Davis, 1981; Damon and others, 1981).

Late Permian to Triassic plutonic rocks are best known in the western and southern Mojave Desert region (Miller, 1978; Miller, 1981; Carr and others, 1984; Tosdal, 1988), where they form two distinct suites (John, 1981): (1) alkalic monzonites and (2) foliated calc-alkaline monzodiorites to granodiorites. Both suites contain hornblende, clinopyroxene, and garnet. A monzonitic pluton (suite 1) in the Victorville area yielded a U-Pb zircon age of 242 ± 2 Ma (J. E. Wright, unpublished, quoted *in* Walker, 1987), and a calc-alkaline granodioritic to tonalitic pluton (suite 2) in the El Paso Mountains yielded K-Ar cooling ages of 239 ± 7 Ma and 230 ± 7 on hornblende and biotite, respectively (Cox and Morton, 1980). These sparse data suggest an intrusive event spanning the Permian-Triassic boundary.

Jurassic plutonic rocks are exposed in a broad belt that extends from the central to eastern Mojave Desert region and is continuous with similar rocks in the Sonoran Desert region of southwestern Arizona. Similar rocks also occur from west of Death Valley to the Inyo Mountains. Most of the Jurassic intrusive rocks in the Mojave Desert region are texturally and compositionally heterogeneous, but they are typically quartz-poor, sphene-bearing, potassium-rich, mesocratic rocks. In many places they contain anhedral to subhedral pale reddish to purple potassium feldspars and mafic phases that tend to display clotted textures (D. M. Miller and others, 1982). Many of the Jurassic plutons are epizonal to hypabyssal and have associated (comagmatic?) volcanic rocks, but some deeper seated Jurassic plutons occur in the region (Howard and others, 1987b; Young and Wooden, 1988). In many places the shallow-level plutons are spatially and temporally(?) associated with magnetite skarn deposits and zones of extensive albitization. Jurassic plutons mainly yield K-Ar dates of 160 to 150 Ma and U-Pb dates of 165 to 160 Ma (Calzia and Morton, 1980, and references therein), although data are sparse.

Cretaceous plutonic rocks are exposed as large composite batholiths throughout the Mojave Desert region. Examples of these batholiths are the Teutonia batholith (Beckerman and others, 1982), the Cadiz Valley batholith (John, 1981), and a plutonic suite exposed in the Old Woman, Turtle, and Riverside mountains (Howard and others, 1987a). The Cretaceous plutons are more homogeneous than the Jurassic plutons and range in composition from granodiorite to monzogranite. All are calc-alkaline and include both metaluminous and peraluminous variations. They typically have a low color index, subhedral to euhedral buff-colored potassium feldspars (commonly with zonally arranged mineral inclusions), and disseminated mafic minerals (D. M. Miller and others, 1982). Many of the Cretaceous plutons were intruded at deeper levels than the Jurassic plutons (Anderson and others, 1988). On the basis of U-Pb dating of zircon, Cretaceous plutons appear to belong to two age groups, 99 to 95 Ma and 75 to 70 Ma (Wright and others, 1987; J. L. Wooden and Ed DeWitt, 1987, oral communications).

Jurassic plutons have been described in other regions of the southwestern Cordillera: the Sierra Nevada batholith (Saleeby, 1981, and references therein); the White-Inyo Range (Sylvester and others, 1978; Ross, 1969; Crowder and Ross, 1973); and the Sonoran Desert region (Tosdal and others, 1989), but many known or inferred Jurassic plutons have not been studied. Despite the gaps in studies of these plutons, unifying features such as alkalic affinities and low quartz content appear to be common in Jurassic plutons.

Jurassic plutonic rocks on the west side of the Sierra Nevada batholith are similar in character to the Cretaceous rocks in that region. Plutonic rocks of both age groups contain subequal amounts of gabbro-diorite, quartz diorite and tonalite, and lesser amounts of granodiorite (Saleeby, 1981). The plutons tend to be homogeneous, with distinct contacts between intrusions. However, some of the markedly different Jurassic plutons on the

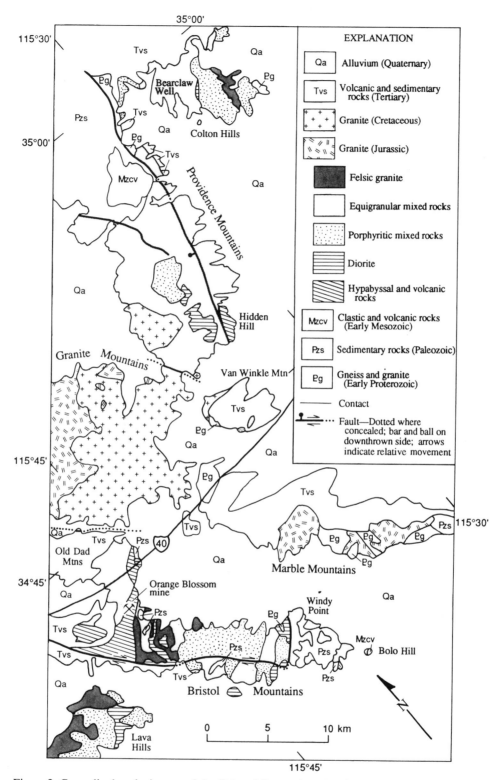

Figure 2. Generalized geologic map of the Colton hills, southern Providence Mountains, and Bristol Mountains area. Map based on unpublished mapping by D. M. Miller (1980–1983) and L. K. Fox (1985–1988); Miller and others (1985); Goldfarb and others (1988); and Howard and others (1988).

eastern side of the batholith are syenodioritic to quartz monzonitic in composition and locally have an alkalic affinity. Schweickert (1976) described two such quartz monzonite bodies that are syenodioritic to quartz monzonitic in composition, one of which is clinopyroxene-bearing.

Plutonic rocks of the White-Inyo Mountains, immediately east of the Sierra Nevada, are generally similar in character to their calc-alkaline Sierran counterparts. However, some of the Jurassic plutons are monzonitic with alkalic affinities (Sylvester and others, 1978), and range in composition from monzodiorite and monzonite to quartz monzodiorite and quartz monzonite. These alkalic plutons contain up to 20 modal percent clinopyroxene and, in some instances, nepheline.

Middle(?) to Late Jurassic plutons in the Sonoran Desert region of southern Arizona, southeastern California, and northernmost Sonora, described by Tosdal and others (1989), also contain a group of more alkali-enriched rocks. A calc-alkaline superunit, Kitt Peak–Trigo Peaks, is made up of homogeneous plutons that range from diorite to syenogranite in composition. In contrast, the slightly younger Ko Vaya superunit is texturally and compositionally heterogeneous, and has alkalic components. The Ko Vaya is compositionally bimodal; it consists of leucocratic monzogranite, syenogranite, and monzodiorite, with only minor amounts of quartz monzonite and granodiorite. In several mountain ranges, plutons of this superunit intrude coeval volcanic and hypabyssal rocks (Tosdal and others, 1989).

Our studies of some of the Jurassic granites in the east-central Mojave Desert show that they bear chemical, petrographic, and textural similarities to the alkalic plutons in the Inyo Mountains and the Sonoran Desert region. The plutons we studied range from mafic (diorite) to felsic (syenogranite), but the majority are composed of complexly mixed low-silica rocks, including quartz syenite and quartz monzonite.

GEOLOGIC SETTING

In the east-central Mojave region the Jurassic plutons intrude Proterozoic gneiss, granite, and diorite; variably deformed and metamorphosed Paleozoic epicontinental strata; and rare Mesozoic supracrustal rocks (Fig. 2). Although intrusive relations are in many places obscured by overlying deposits, examples of contacts with Proterozoic, Paleozoic, and Mesozoic wall rocks occur in the Bristol and Providence Mountains. Paleozoic carbonate rocks are metamorphosed to marble and bear considerable exoskarn adjacent to the Jurassic plutons. Mesozoic strata of the region may display subaerial records of magmatic arc evolution. In the Providence Mountains, the lower part of a thick sequence of early Mesozoic clastic and carbonate rocks consists of red sandstone and nodular and shaley limestone; it was assigned by Hazzard (1954) to the Moenkopi Formation of Triassic age. Overlying the Moenkopi Formation is up to 365 m (1,200 ft) of conglomerate and volcaniclastic rocks (Goldfarb and others, 1988) that conformably underlie the Fountain Peak Rhyolite of Hazzard (1954). The Fountain Peak Rhyolite was fed by dikes

that have yielded a Jurassic U-Pb zircon crystallization age (J. D. Walker, 1988, oral communication), indicating that underlying volcaniclastic rocks are probably also Jurassic in age. A possibly equivalent sequence of cross-bedded arenitic metaquartzite (possibly correlative with the Aztec Sandstone of Triassic and Early Jurassic age) overlain by massive intermediate metavolcanic rocks is exposed at Bolo Hill at the southeastern tip of the Bristol Mountains. Elsewhere in the Mojave Desert region, the Aztec and correlative formations commonly are intercalated with and overlain by volcanic rocks. Burchfiel and Davis (1981) interpreted this relation as representative of the transgression of the Jurassic magmatic arc over the craton. However, the voluminous Jurassic plutons of the eastern Mojave Desert region are distinctly younger than volcanic rocks associated with the Aztec.

Jurassic plutons and associated hypabyssal and volcanic rocks make up about 50 percent of the area we studied (Fig. 2). These and other plutons in the east-central Mojave Desert region of California have been described on a reconnaissance basis by John (1981), Beckerman and others (1982), D. M. Miller and others (1982), Allen and others (1983), Howard and John (1983), Miller and others (1985), Goldfarb and others (1988), and Howard and others (1987b). These studies established many of the general characteristics described above (low silica content, purple to pink potassium feldspars, mesocratic, complexly heterogeneous), and have placed initial age estimates of late Middle to early Late Jurassic for the rocks.

The Jurassic plutons are intruded by leucocratic Cretaceous plutons (Miller and others, 1985; Howard and others, 1987b) and are overlain by Miocene volcanic and volcaniclastic rocks and Quaternary deposits. Tertiary normal faults and strike-slip faults (D. M. Miller and others, 1982) cut the Jurassic plutons in places, but the total separation along these latter faults is generally less than 10 km.

DESCRIPTION OF THE ROCK UNITS

The Jurassic igneous rocks discussed in this paper are exposed in the Colton Hills, southern Providence Mountains, and southern Bristol Mountains (Fig. 2). Similar rocks in the adjacent Lava Hills, Marble Mountains, Van Wrinkle Mountain, and Granite Mountains (Fig. 2) have been studied only in reconnaissance. The rocks display extreme variations in composition, texture, and degree of alteration on the scale of meters to tens of meters within each mountain range, but broadly similar suites in the three ranges can be divided into five groups, primarily on the basis of field relations and geochemistry. Modal compositions and geochemical variations are summarized in Table 1 (A–D) and Figures 3 through 7.

General Description

The five groups of Jurassic igneous rocks include three groups of plutonic rocks that compose most of the igneous complexes, and two groups of related rocks that are much less exten-

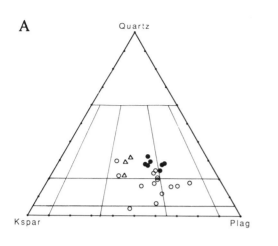

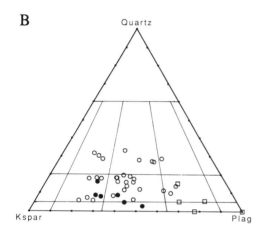

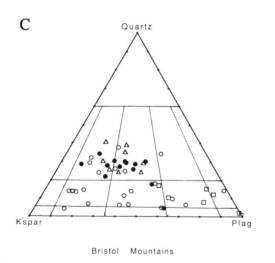

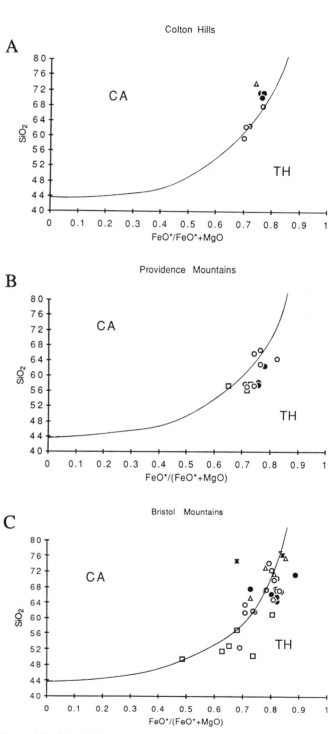

Figure 3. Modal compositions of Jurassic plutons in the (A) Colton Hills, (B) southern Providence Mountains and (C) southern Bristol Mountains. Symbols as follows: squares = mafic intrusives; open circles = subequigranular mixed subgroup; closed circles = porphyritic mixed subgroup; triangles = felsic intrusives. Petrographic classification nomenclature used in text is that of Streckeisen (1976).

Figure 4. FeO*/(FeO*+MgO) and SiO_2 data from Jurassic plutons and associated rocks of the (A) Colton Hills, (B) southern Providence Mountains, and (C) southern Bristol Mountains. Calc-alkaline-tholeiitic boundary from Miyashiro (1974). Symbols as in Figure 3; addition; stars = hypabyssal rocks; bar = aplite dike. All data are in weight percent and FeO* is total Fe calculated as FeO.

sive. The groups are: (1) mafic intrusive rocks; (2) mixed (heterogeneous) intrusive rocks of intermediate to felsic composition, which are generally potassium-rich and quartz-poor and range in texture from fine-grained, equigranular to coarsely porphyritic; (3) felsic intrusive rocks of relatively quartz-rich, leucocratic monzogranite; (4) highly altered metavolcanic and hypabyssal rocks; and (5) dikes that are mafic to felsic and aphanitic to porphyritic.

In our description of the mineralogic and chemical characteristics of the different groups, we highlight the similarities and differences among members of these groups in the different mountain ranges. The data we present are those we consider relevant to the question of the origin of these rocks.

Mafic intrusive rocks

Mafic intrusive rocks occur in all three ranges, including the monzodiorite and porphyritic quartz monzonite to diorite (Miller and others, 1985) in the southern Providence Mountains, diorite to quartz monzodiorite in the southern Bristol Mountains, and

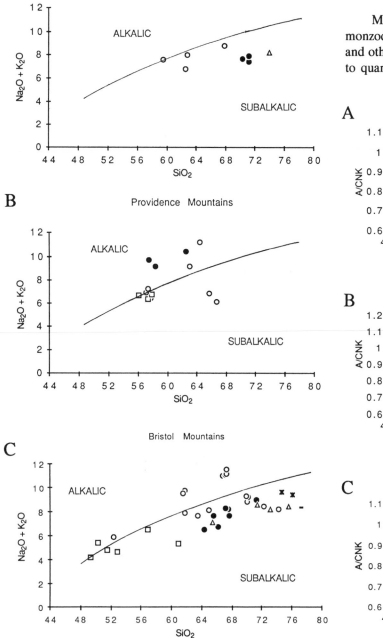

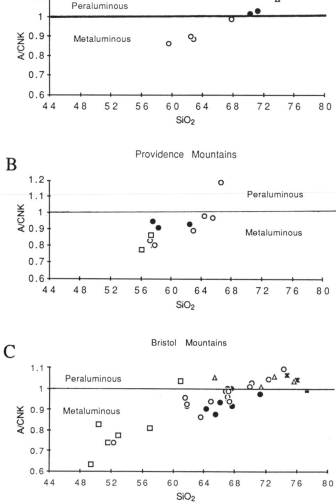

Figure 5. Na_2O+K_2O and SiO_2 data from Jurassic plutons and associated rocks of the (A) Colton Hills, (B) southern Providence Mountains, and (C) southern Bristol Mountains. Alkalic-subalkalic boundary from Irvine and Baragar (1971). Symbols as in Figures 3 and 4. All data are in weight percent.

Figure 6. $Al_2O_3/(CaO+Na_2O+K_2O)$ or A/CNK (molecular proportions) and SiO_2 for Jurassic plutons and associated rocks of the (A) Colton Hills, (B) southern Providence Mountains, and (C) southern Bristol Mountains. Symbols as in Figures 3 and 4.

gabbro-diorite in the Colton Hills. These rocks range from fine to coarse grained and vary widely in composition, but are more mafic than rocks in other groups, and appear in most places to be the oldest intrusive rocks. Similar diorite-gabbro and quartz diorite, exposed as several small plutons in the Lava Hills (Fig. 2), have gradational contacts with one another and with surrounding granites.

The diorite-gabbro of the Colton Hills is medium to coarse grained and pervasively altered, including plagioclase completely pseudomorphed by sausserite. Clinopyroxene, the major ferromagnesian phase, has reaction rims of hornblende. The rock also contains twinned remnants of orthopyroxene. Biotite is partially altered to chlorite, and hornblende crystals are partially altered to actinolitic masses.

The mafic intrusive rocks in the southern Providence Mountains consist of dark gray to black, fine- to medium-grained hornblende-biotite quartz monzodiorite, monzodiorite, and diorite (Fig. 3B). The rock has a foliation defined by a preferred alignment of mafic minerals, which compose 20 to 30 percent of the rock. Abundant pale green hornblende is present as both poikilitic prisms and an intergranular phase, along with brown biotite. Subhedral plagioclase and potassium feldspar grains are present as inclusions within the hornblende. Clinopyroxene, Fe-Ti oxides, zircon, sphene, and apatite all occur as accessory phases.

In the southern Bristol Mountains, fine- to medium-grained diorite occurs in the southern part of the area, and fine-grained monzodiorite is exposed in the northern part. In both places the rocks range in composition from diorite to quartz monzodiorite, although the fine-grained monzodiorite includes rare quartz monzonite (Fig. 3C). Both units contain subhedral to euhedral plagioclase (An_{45-50}) with sericitized cores. In the diorite unit, biotite and hornblende usually occur in subequal amounts, with brown biotite as distinct crystals and as felted masses. Olive-green hornblende often has pyroxene cores. Xenocrystic clinopyroxene is present in a few samples, and some samples contain skeletal blue-green uralitic hornblende as a replacement product. Hornblende exceeds biotite in abundance in the monzodiorite unit. Minor interstitial potassium feldspar and quartz and accessory phases of apitite, sphene, and Fe-Ti oxides occur in the mafic rocks.

The chemical characteristics of the mafic intrusive rocks are best known for the Bristol Mountains and less so for the southern Providence Mountains (Table 1A). The mafic plutonic rocks are metaluminous and subalkaline, and they straddle the boundary between the calc-alkaline and tholeiitic fields on a $FeO/FeO+MgO$ vs. SiO_2 diagram as defined by Miyashiro (1974) (Figs. 4, 5, and 6). SiO_2 content ranges from 49 to 60 weight percent, and MgO content varies from 3.3 to 8.7 weight percent (Fig. 7). These rocks have high large ion lithophile element (LILE) abundances. Mafic intrusive rocks from the southern Providence Mountains have higher Sr, Ba, and other LILE values than those of the southern Bristol Mountains. The abundances of

"compatible" (Ni, Cr) trace elements are lower in the southern Providence Mountains.

The mafic plutonic phases are, in general, the oldest of the intrusive rocks in the three areas. With the exception of the fine- to medium-grained mafic intrusive phase in the northern part of the southern Bristol Mountains, the mafic rocks are intruded by all the other plutonic phases in the ranges. However, in many places, the mafic rocks are mixed with or grade into adjacent felsic rocks, suggesting broadly contemporaneous intrusion.

Mixed intrusive rocks

The mixed intrusive rocks are by far the most abundant plutonic rocks. The group consists of extremely heterogeneous rocks ranging texturally from fine grained and equigranular to coarsely porphyritic, and compositionally from quartz monzodiorite to syenite and syenogranite. Rocks of this group are distinguished in the field by having a lower color index than those of the mafic group and by being markedly more heterogeneous than those of the felsic group. Contacts between all phases are gradational, and the grain size, color index, and quartz content of these rocks vary on the scale of meters to tens of meters. In order to simplify the description of these rocks, we have subdivided them on a textural basis into a porphyritic subgroup of relatively restricted composition, and a subequigranular subgroup of highly variable composition. These subgroups are broadly distinguishable, but texturally transitional rocks almost always form a gradation between the subgroups.

Porphyritic subgroup. The plutonic rocks of the porphyritic subgroup consist of three fairly discrete plutons that are internally heterogeneous: the monzogranite of Colton Hills (hereafter termed the Colton Hills monzogranite), monzogranite to syenogranite in the southern Bristol Mountains, and the quartz syenite of Winston Basin in the southern Providence Mountains (Miller and others, 1985). Rocks similar to those described here occur in adjacent ranges including the Marble Mountains, the Lava Hills, and Van Winkle Mountain (Fig. 2).

The Colton Hills monzogranite is quartz rich (>25 modal % quartz) and ranges in composition from granodiorite to monzogranite (Fig. 3A). This pluton has a weak to strong tectonic foliation. Biotite is the only ferromagnesian mineral present. Accessory phases are apatite, sphene, and Fe-Ti oxides. Potassium feldspar occurs both as anhedral grains in the matrix and as subhedral phenocrysts, indicating intermediate and late crystallization. The phenocrysts (up to 5 × 10 cm) are zoned and exhibit microcline twinning and contain inclusions of euhedral plagioclase, biotite, apatite, and Fe-Ti oxides.

The quartz syenite of Winston Basin is the most quartz poor of the porphyritic rocks. It consists of markedly porphyritic, coarse-grained, melanocratic, augite-hornblende-biotite quartz syenite to mesocratic quartz monzonite and monzonite (Fig. 3B). The rock contains much more brown biotite than hornblende or augite. Quartz generally makes up less than 10 modal percent of these rocks and mafic mineral contents range from 8 to 18 modal percent. Orthoclase phenocrysts are locally perthitic, faintly zoned, purple to pink, contain plagioclase and biotite, and are 1 to 4 cm in greatest dimension. Orthoclase is rare as a matrix phase. Sphene is a common accessory phase in addition to magnetite and zircon.

The monzogranite to syenogranite in the southern Bristol Mountains is texturally similar to the quartz syenite of Winston Basin but generally has a higher quartz content (20 to 25 percent) (Fig. 3C). This pluton is locally strongly foliated; the foliation is irregular (both in intensity and orientation) and appears to be magmatic rather than of regional tectonic origin. Potassium feldspar is found predominantly as phenocrysts (up to 10 cm), although it occurs to a lesser degree as a matrix phase. Mafic minerals (biotite > hornblende) tend to clot together. Accessory phases are magnetite, sphene, zircon, and apatite. In most outcrops the phenocrysts are pale purple in color, although locally they are brick red. In all instances the potassium feldspar phenocrysts are coarsely perthitic and contain inclusions of the other mineral phases in a fairly random distribution.

Chemically, the three porphyritic plutonic phases are differ-

ent. The quartz syenite of Winston Basin (Providence Mountains) and the monzogranite in the Bristol Mountains are metaluminous, whereas the Colton Hills monzogranite is marginally peraluminous (Fig. 6). The quartz syenite of Winston Basin is alkalic (based on total K_2O+Na_2O; Fig. 5) and has the lowest silica content (58 to 63 wt%), whereas the Colton Hills monzogranite and the monzogranite in the Bristol Mountains are calc-alkaline and have higher silica contents of 70 to 71 weight percent and 62 to 67 weight percent, respectively (Fig. 7, Table 1B). In all three phases, alkali contents are high (K_2O+Na_2O = 6 to 10 wt%); K_2O is about twice as abundant as Na_2O. Trace elements also differ between the plutons (Fig. 7, Table 1B): Sr varies from 154 to 240 ppm (Bristol Mountains) to 348 to 468 ppm (Providence Mountains) to 427 to 515 ppm (Colton Hills), and Rb varies from 99 to 142 ppm (Providence Mountains) to 108 to 121 ppm (Colton Hills) to 170 to 360 ppm (Bristol Mountains). Other significant variations occur in uranium, thorium, and niobium (Table 1B).

In all three mountain ranges, the porphyritic plutonic phases intrude rocks of the mafic intrusive group with sharp, distinct contacts. Contacts with subequigranular phases of the mixed

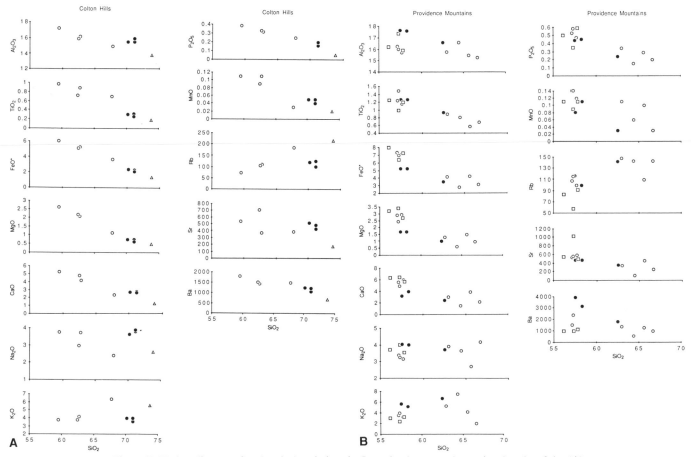

Figure 7. Harker diagrams for chemical variations in Jurassic plutons and associated rocks of the (A) Colton Hills, (B) southern Providence Mountains, and (C, facing page) southern Bristol Mountains. Symbols as follows: squares = mafic intrusives; open circles = subequigranular mixed intrusives; closed circles = porphyritic mixed intrusives; triangles = felsic intrusives; stars = hypabyssal rocks. Major oxide data are in weight percent. Trace element data are in parts per million.

group are gradational over tens or hundreds of meters and commonly are defined by change in phenocryst size. Where the contacts are relatively sharp, the rocks are generally mutually intrusive. However, contacts with the felsic intrusives group indicate that the felsic rocks are younger, as described below.

Subequigranular subgroup. Rocks of the subequigranular subgroup are the most abundant as well as the most texturally and compositionally variable of the Jurassic intrusive rocks. Grain size, color index, and quartz content vary complexly on the scale of meters to tens of meters; there are no distinct contacts separating different rock types. Map units within this subgroup are difficult to define and generally are based on differences in texture or composition over kilometer-scale distances. Similar

subequigranular, mixed-composition rocks occur in the neighboring Marble Mountains and Van Winkle Mountain.

The subequigranular subgroup underlies much of the Colton Hills area. There is a gradation from more mafic and less quartz-rich rocks in the north to monzogranite in the central part of the area. Rocks in the north are extensively altered and mineralized spatially coincident with a magnetic anomaly, possibly indicating the presence of subsurface skarn mineralization (Goldfarb and others, 1988). Most of the rocks are fine- to medium-grained quartz monzonite to monzogranite, but in the northwest Colton Hills the rocks span a broad compositional range from tonalite to quartz monzodiorite to monzonite and monzogranite (Fig. 3A). These rocks are locally subporphyritic with scattered phenocrysts

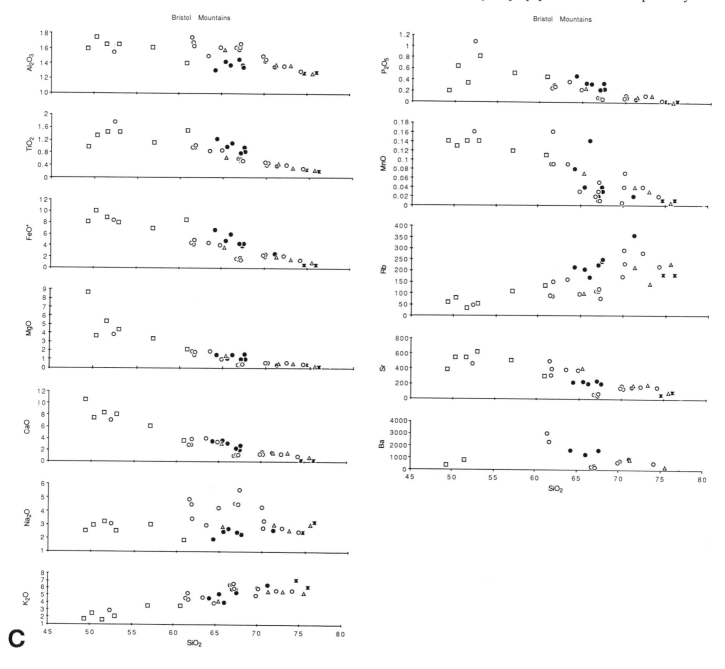

C

L. K. Fox and D. M. Miller

TABLE 1A. MAJOR- AND TRACE-ELEMENT DATA
FOR MAFIC INTRUSIVE ROCKS GROUP

	Providence Mountains			Bristol Mountains					
	M83SP-15	M83SP-43	M83SP-49	M80BR-53	M83BR-131	F87BR-37	F86BR-135	F87BR-67	F86BR-105
SiO_2	57.31	56.16	57.83	51.51	49.32	60.90	56.90	50.30	52.90
TiO_2	0.98	1.25	1.19	1.45	0.98	1.49	1.11	1.33	1.44
Al_2O_3	17.37	16.20	15.89	16.54	15.96	14.10	16.20	17.50	16.50
Fe_2O_3	2.89	4.82	4.40	3.95	3.03	3.40	3.29	5.30	4.06
FeO	3.75	3.66	3.31	5.39	5.47	5.46	4.04	5.31	4.44
MgO	3.41	3.20	2.69	5.38	8.70	2.09	3.30	3.66	4.35
MnO	0.09	0.11	0.11	0.14	0.14	0.11	0.12	0.13	0.14
CaO	6.39	6.34	5.72	8.38	10.60	3.69	6.16	7.45	8.16
Na_2O	3.99	3.72	3.54	3.24	2.53	1.85	3.02	2.98	2.54
K_2O	2.38	2.98	3.23	1.61	1.69	3.53	3.49	2.46	2.14
P_2O_5	0.35	0.50	0.59	0.35	0.20	0.46	0.53	0.65	0.83
LOI	nd	nd	nd	nd	nd	1.96	0.50	1.90	1.50
Total	98.91	98.94	98.50	97.94	98.62	99.04	98.66	98.97	99.00
H_2O+	1.08	1.10	1.01	1.83	0.79	1.97	0.64	1.82	1.49
H_2O-	0.07	0.16	0.11	0.23	0.09	0.19	0.06	0.19	0.26
CO_2	0.03	0.02	0.12	0.06	0.07	0.08	<0.01	0.14	<0.01
FeO*	6.35	8.00	7.27	8.94	8.20	8.52	7.00	10.08	8.09
A/CNK[†]	0.836	0.775	0.805	0.740	0.631	1.037	0.811	0.828	0.772
FeO*/ FeO*+MgO	0.651	0.714	0.730	0.624	0.485	0.803	0.680	0.734	0.650
Ba[§]	971	1003	1134	787	399	nd	nd	nd	nd
Nb	8	18	22	nd	14	24	21	18	17
Rb	57	83	91	36	62	134	110	80	54
Sr	1026	541	491	557	393	305	510	550	630
Zr	178	321	400	205	109	345	340	200	190
Y	16	44	49	47	47	68	47	62	40
U	nd	3	4	2	nd	nd	nd	nd	nd
Th	3	12	8	9	nd	nd	nd	nd	nd
Zn	101	52	53	171	72	nd	nd	nd	nd
Cu	55	69	47	129	117	nd	nd	nd	nd
Ni	29	33	24	92	108	nd	nd	nd	nd
Cr	46	37	10	130	465	nd	nd	nd	nd

*All Fe as FeO.

[†]A/CNK = mole ratio of $Al_2O_3/(CaO + Na_2O + K_2O)$.

[§]Trace elements as ppm.

of potassium feldspar or plagioclase and poikilitic biotite. The plutonic rocks on the eastern and western flanks of the range have a strong penetrative foliation; elsewhere in the range the plutonic rocks are variably foliated. Dark brown to red-brown biotite and olive-green hornblende are the major ferromagnesian minerals and are present in varying ratios. Biotite is more abundant than hornblende in the more felsic varieties, whereas they are subequal in the more mafic rocks. The biotite, and in some cases hornblende, poikilitically encloses plagioclase, pyroxene, Fe-Ti oxides, and apatite. Hornblende contains clinopyroxene cores. Along the eastern and western flanks of the Colton Hills, this plutonic phase

has its highest potassium feldspar content (~42 percent by volume); potassium feldspar grains are zoned and contain inclusions of most of the other mineral phases. Subhedral plagioclase (An_{24-38}) is variably sericitized. Quartz is generally anhedral and interstitial and myrmekite is locally present. Apatite, sphene, zircon, and Fe-Ti oxides are the accessory phases. Locally, this plutonic phase has a "spotted" appearance due to the presence of poikilitic and composite grains of biotite and/or hornblende.

The subequigranular subgroup underlies most of the southern Providence Mountains area. Included are the syenogranite of Quail Spring and the quartz monzonite of Goldstone, which were

TABLE 1B. MAJOR- AND TRACE-ELEMENT DATA
FOR MIXED PORPHYRITIC INTRUSIVE ROCKS GROUP

	Colton Hills			Providence Mountains			Bristol Mountains						
	M83CH-116	F83CH-33	H80Co-424	M82SP-58	M82SP-82	M83SP-37	M80BR-17	M80BR-62	N86BR-129	F87BR-46A	F87BR-64A	F87BR-89A	F87BR-90A
SiO_2	71.20	71.20	70.22	58.30	62.50	57.52	71.26	66.09	67.50	64.30	67.60	65.50	67.10
TiO_2	0.32	0.26	0.31	1.27	0.93	1.27	0.37	1.08	0.95	1.22	0.82	0.97	0.78
Al_2O_3	15.50	15.90	15.46	17.60	16.60	17.65	13.61	13.74	13.80	13.10	13.50	14.20	14.50
Fe_2O_3	1.26	1.11	1.29	2.99	1.96	2.97	1.08	3.17	1.03	3.77	1.64	2.34	2.48
FeO	1.20	1.10	1.26	2.51	1.70	2.55	1.58	3.13	3.07	3.32	2.83	2.79	2.14
MgO	0.75	0.63	0.76	1.68	0.99	1.68	0.33	1.48	1.51	1.48	0.963	1.09	0.94
MnO	0.05	0.04	0.05	0.11	0.03	0.08	0.02	0.14	0.04	0.08	0.03	0.04	0.02
CaO	2.75	2.61	2.68	3.94	2.41	3.23	1.51	3.20	1.96	3.46	2.80	3.58	2.25
Na_2O	3.78	3.89	3.63	4.01	3.71	4.03	2.60	2.72	2.36	1.92	2.27	2.50	2.45
K_2O	3.58	3.96	3.99	5.10	6.70	5.66	6.40	4.04	5.85	4.63	5.40	5.14	5.83
P_2O_5	0.16	0.20	0.18	0.45	0.24	0.44	0.06	0.33	0.34	0.47	0.24	0.35	0.23
LOI	nd	nd	nd	0.50	1.15	nd	nd	nd	0.50	1.45	0.98	0.94	0.72
Total	100.55	100.90	99.83	98.46	98.92	97.08	98.82	99.12	98.91	99.20	99.07	99.44	99.44
H_2O+	0.35	0.48	0.20	0.62	0.99	1.70	0.79	1.13	0.35	1.13	0.62	0.60	0.46
H_2O-	0.20	0.19	0.16	0.04	0.01	0.06	0.27	0.23	0.10	0.20	0.21	0.17	0.15
CO_2	0.02	0.03	0.03	0.01	0.28	0.48	0.06	0.03	<0.01	0.09	0.04	0.03	0.03
FeO*	2.34	2.10	2.42	5.20	3.46	5.22	2.55	5.98	4.00	6.71	4.31	4.90	4.37
A/CNK†	1.026	1.029	1.018	0.912	0.935	0.946	0.974	0.936	1.000	0.904	0.919	0.876	1.003
FeO*/ FeO*+MgO	0.757	0.769	0.761	0.756	0.778	0.757	0.885	0.802	0.726	0.819	0.818	0.818	0.823
Ba§	1160	1210	1240	3140	1810	3917	904	1260	nd	1593	1600	nd	nd
Nb	10	9	14	17	14	16	nd	nd	30	34	28	28	24
Rb	100	126	120	98.7	142	116	360	170	240	215	250	205	225
Sr	479	427	515	468	348	468	154	205	210	220	198	230	240
Zr	137	128	155	982	655	886	329	628	610	440	425	560	435
Y	20	17	14	47	30	38	57	81	46	100	82	98	66
U	1.36	1.83	1	1.6	1.87		13	3	nd	2.88	5.12	nd	nd
Th	9.98	10.9	12	7.16	nd	5	171	58	nd	46.9	51	nd	nd
Zn	43.6	38.3	62	48.2	nd	50	39	64	nd	nd	nd	nd	nd
Cu	nd	nd	6	nd	nd	15	10	11	nd	nd	nd	nd	nd
Ni	nd	nd	3	nd	nd	7	12	10	nd	15.8	10.5	nd	nd
Cr	3.29	1.74	0	nd	nd	3	5	6	nd	15.9	10	nd	nd

*All Fe as FeO

†A/CNK = mole ratio of $Al_2O_3/(CaO + Na_2O + K_2O)$

§Trace elements as ppm.

divided by Miller and others (1985) to express a general southward increase in quartz content. These rocks host extensive sericitic and albitic alteration. The northern, low-silica rocks range in composition from quartz monzonite to quartz monzodiorite, quartz diorite, and quartz syenite (Fig. 3B), and the color index ranges from 8 to 16. These northern rocks contain purplish anhedral orthoclase set in a medium to coarse matrix of quartz, brown biotite, subhedral to euhedral plagioclase that typically contains abundant mafic mineral inclusions, and hornblende. Uncommon textural variations include zoned plagioclase, perthite, and myrmekite. Clinopyroxene is a minor phase, and accessory phases are sphene, zircon, apatite, and magnetite. The more quartz-rich rocks in the southern part of the mountain range share many features with those in the north, but differ in having more quartz, fewer mafic minerals (generally 2 to 10 percent), less hornblende, and no pyroxene. These rocks range in composition from quartz monzodiorite to quartz syenite and syenogranite (Fig. 3B).

Two extremely heterogeneous units occur in the southern Bristol Mountains: one of generally quartz syenitic composition and another of fine-grained granite. The quartz syenite unit underlies much of the southern part of the area and also occurs

TABLE 1C. MAJOR- AND TRACE-ELEMENT DATA
FOR MIXED SUBEQUIGRANULAR INTRUSIVE ROCKS GROUP

	Colton Hills				Providence Mountains							Bristol Mountains		
	M83CH-113B	M83CH-115	F83CH-32	F83CH-40	M82SP-63	M82SP-75	M83SP-41	M83SP-48	M83SP-59	M84SP-98	M84SP-99	M80BR-34	M80BR-46	M83BR-132
SiO_2	62.80	62.50	67.80	59.50	64.40	57.70	66.65	62.95	57.16	57.30	65.60	61.73	61.49	74.23
TiO_2	0.89	0.72	0.70	0.97	0.80	1.15	0.68	0.89	1.24	1.49	0.57	0.96	0.95	0.28
Al_2O_3	16.20	15.90	14.90	17.20	16.60	15.70	15.29	15.77	16.25	16.00	15.50	16.86	17.55	12.96
Fe_2O_3	2.62	2.54	2.21	3.11	1.75	3.26	1.79	2.59	3.41	3.87	2.25	2.56	2.82	1.27
FeO	2.90	2.85	1.70	3.20	1.16	4.27	1.53	1.79	4.25	3.50	2.15	1.97	1.95	0.30
MgO	2.08	2.16	1.13	2.59	0.59	2.93	0.97	1.28	2.89	2.43	1.46	1.48	1.87	0.38
MnO	0.11	0.09	0.03	0.11	0.06	0.12	0.03	0.11	0.14	0.14	0.10	0.16	0.09	0.02
CaO	4.16	4.78	2.34	5.27	1.49	5.96	2.12	3.04	5.55	4.87	3.86	2.92	2.94	0.84
Na_2O	3.74	2.97	2.40	3.77	3.65	3.17	4.16	3.92	3.39	3.27	2.71	4.49	4.85	2.52
K_2O	4.21	3.75	6.34	3.79	7.53	3.24	4.98	5.24	3.53	3.95	4.11	5.25	4.64	5.70
P_2O_5	0.32	0.33	0.25	0.39	0.15	0.47	0.20	0.34	0.53	0.58	0.29	0.30	0.26	0.04
LOI	nd	0.47	nd	nd	0.49	0.79	nd	nd	nd	1.29	0.90	nd	nd	nd
Total	100.03	99.06	99.80	99.90	97.95	98.76	95.40	97.92	98.34	98.69	99.50	98.68	99.41	98.54
H_2O+	0.40	0.56	0.56	0.47	0.39	0.90	0.41	0.80	0.97	1.07	0.68	0.53	0.75	0.69
H_2O-	0.20	0.09	0.12	0.26	0.03	0.03	0.39	0.15	0.13	0.10	0.11	0.19	0.21	0.07
CO_2	0.03	0.069	0.02	0.02	0.01	0.01	0.02	0.01	0.04	0.06	0.09	0.00	0.06	0.12
FeO^*	5.26	5.14	3.69	6.01	2.74	7.20	3.14	4.12	7.32	6.98	4.18	4.27	4.49	1.44
A/CNK[†]	0.885	0.900	0.987	0.864	0.983	0.802	1.190	0.892	0.833	0.863	0.972	0.916	0.955	1.093
FeO^*/FeO^*+MgO	0.717	0.704	0.766	0.699	0.823	0.711	0.764	0.763	0.717	0.742	0.741	0.743	0.706	0.791
Ba[§]	1440	1510	1480	1800	529	1140	997	1387	1521	2380	1250	2352	3026	570
Nb	<5	13	6	6	23	10	25	22	17	20	<10	nd	nd	19
Rb	110	105	185	73.8	13	99.4	143	148	107	115	109	87	91	219
Sr	369	710	387	535	113	582	253	338	526	550	448	311	500	154
Zr	332	284	640	303	817	376	402	620	346	533	171	786	838	228
Y	25	30	43	30	46	35	40	41	45	54	21	54	44	36
U	1.95	1.76	3.47	1.7	1.8	1.87	5	2	4	2.69	1.05	2	1	5
Th	9.95	7.75	10.8	6.86	11.2	14.1	15	18	11	15.1	8.88	9	9	55
Zn	56.2	49	40	54.6	33.9	nd	26	69	98	70.9	54.9	81	69	16
Cu	nd	nd	nd	nd	nd	nd	9	11	52	nd	nd	7	8	5
Ni	nd	nd	nd	nd	nd	nd	5	7	25	nd	nd	5	3	6
Cr	8.56	7.67	3.87	17.6	0.5	26.4	nd	nd	27	6.65	4.14	2	6	2

*All Fe as FeO.

[†]A/CNK = mole ratio of $Al_2O_3/(CaO + Na_2O + K_2O)$.

[§]Trace elements as ppm.

locally in the central part of the area and in the adjacent Old Dad Mountains. This unit ranges in composition from quartz monzodiorite to quartz syenite and syenogranite, but most of the unit is quartz syenitic in composition (Fig. 3C). This plutonic phase is medium to coarse grained for the most part and texturally is equigranular to subporphyritic. Potassium feldspar (up to 70 modal percent) is anhedral to subhedral and coarsely perthitic. Subhedral to euhedral plagioclase is mildly to pervasively sericitized. Quartz is present as anhedral grains and as an interstitial phase, and in some samples myrmekite embayments into potas-

sium feldspar are present. Brown biotite is the major ferromagnesian mineral present. Olive-green hornblende, present in lesser amounts than biotite, generally has clinopyroxene cores. Sphene is an abundant accessory phase. Other accessory minerals are apatite, allanite, and Fe-Ti oxides. The fine-grained granite unit exposed in the northern part of the area is extremely heterogeneous, variations in quartz content range from 10 to 38 percent, and the color index varies from 2 to 8. The texture of this unit varies also, but it is most commonly fine grained. It ranges in composition from quartz monzonite to syenogranite. Potassium feldspar is

**TABLE 1C. MAJOR- AND TRACE-ELEMENT DATA
FOR MIXED SUBEQUIGRANULAR ROCKS GROUP (continued)**

	Bristol Mountains (continued)													
	F84BR-43-1	F84BR-43-6	F84BR-43-7	F84BR-44-4	F85BR-07A	F85BR-52A	F86BR-28A	F87BR-14	F87BR-39	F86BR-84A**	F86BR-103**	F86BR-121A**	F87BR-99A**	F87BR-99B**
SiO_2	66.80	67.10	67.10	67.20	67.30	61.80	52.30	69.80	64.90	72.30	70.10	63.50	70.20	69.90
TiO_2	0.59	0.53	0.57	0.52	0.54	144.03	1.77	0.72	0.87	0.04	0.40	0.84	0.46	0.49
Al_2O_3	16.20		16.00	15.90	16.20	16.60	16.40	15.50	13.70	16.20	13.70	14.30	15.00	14.50	15.00
Fe_2O_3	1.41	1.31	1.47	1.47	1.35	2.66	5.38	2.16	2.36	1.19	1.09	2.76	1.51	1.62
FeO	0.45	0.23	0.53	0.581	0.18	2.63	3.59	2.57	1.97	1.09	1.13	1.96	1.08	0.90
MgO	0.34	0.31	0.53	0.38	0.39	1.80	3.85	1.05	0.98	0.54	0.50	1.85	0.54	0.55
MnO	0.02	<0.02	0.03	0.05	<0.02	0.09	0.16	0.02	0.03	0.04	0.04	0.09	0.07	<0.02
CaO	1.06	1.29	1.15	0.96	1.13	3.95	7.07	1.02	3.37	1.32	1.64	4.03	1.25	1.31
Na_2O	4.57	4.56	4.51	4.50	5.55	3.46	3.09	6.00	4.22	2.77	2.76	3.00	3.28	4.30
K_2O	6.40	6.40	6.51	6.66	5.97	4.96	2.84	1.21	3.88	5.64	6.06	4.70	5.93	4.97
P_2O_5	0.08	0.07	0.07	0.07	0.06	0.28	1.09	0.25	0.23	0.12	0.12	0.37	0.08	0.07
LOI	0.52	0.64	0.61	0.69	0.73	0.44	1.50	0.88	0.62	0.63	0.50	0.75	0.55	0.45
Total	98.44	98.44	98.98	99.21	99.80	99.50	98.14	99.38	99.63	99.74	98.64	98.85	99.45	99.56
H_2O+	0.31	0.34	0.23	0.25	0.23	0.469	1.44	0.61	0.39	0.41	0.30	0.60	0.34	0.26
H_2O-	0.16	0.11	0.17	0.13	0.17	0.12	0.16	0.13	0.12	0.10	0.11	0.08	0.08	0.11
CO_2	0.09	0.22	<0.02	0.07	0.11	0.12	0.18	0.01	0.04	<0.01	<0.01	<0.01	0.01	0.02
FeO*	1.72	1.41	1.85	1.83	1.39	5.02	8.43	4.51	4.09	2.16	2.11	4.44	2.44	2.36
A/CNK[†]	0.988	0.953	0.959	0.989	0.940	0.898	0.737	1.050	0.937	1.047	1.014	0.863	1.028	1.010
FeO*/ FeO*+MgO	0.835	0.820	0.777	0.828	0.781	0.736	0.686	0.811	0.807	0.800	0.808	0.706	0.819	0.811
Ba[§]	303	367	323	221	nd	nd	nd	nd	nd	nd	nd	nd	714	596
Nb	30	27	27	23	22	24	18	38	20	24	26	22	26	32
Rb	110	100	105	110	78	150	47	122	96	280	290	160	230	172
Sr	60	70	60	40	72	400	470	128	385	160	170	390	130	146
Zr	750	630	660	670	1000	490	390	750	340	460	490	510	600	660
Y	120	100	95	100	95	60	62	70	64	58	59	57	70	88
U	1.32	1.58	1.11	1.16	nd	nd	nd	nd	nd	nd	nd	nd	1.72	2.13
Th	16.3	18	15.1	13.9	nd	nd	nd	nd	nd	nd	nd	nd	33.4	34.4
Zn	25.7	21.2	30.8	38.8	nd	nd	nd	nd	nd	nd	nd	nd	nd	nd
Cu	nd	nd	nd	nd	nd	nd	nd	nd	nd	nd	nd	nd	nd	nd
Ni	nd	nd	nd	nd	nd	nd	nd	nd	nd	nd	nd	nd	1.45	4.74
Cr	9.35	1.71	0.5	<1.9	nd	nd	nd	nd	nd	nd	nd	nd	3.95	4.36

*All Fe as FeO.

[†]A/CNK = mole ratio of $Al_2O_3/(CaO + Na_2O + K_2O)$.

[§]Trace elements as ppm.

**Samples of fine-grained granite unit. Remaider of Bristol Mountains samples are of quartz syenite unit.

perthitic and in some samples exhibits microcline twinning. Subhedral to euhedral plagioclase is mildly to pervasively sericitized. Brown biotite is the principal ferromagnesian mineral present. Hornblende, when present, has clinopyroxene cores. Accessory phases are sphene and Fe-Ti oxides.

Granitoids in this subgroup exhibit wide variations in chemistry. In a general sense the quartz syenite of the southern Bristol Mountains is alkalic, whereas the other granitoids of the Bristol Mountains and the Colton Hills are subalkalic; the subequigranu-

lar plutonic phases of the southern Providence Mountains have both alkalic and subalkalic constituents (Fig. 5). Silica contents in the southern Bristol Mountains show a more expanded range (52.3 to 74.2 wt%) as compared to those from the Colton Hills and southern Providence Mountains (59.5 to 67.8 wt% and 57.2 to 66.7 wt%, respectively) (Table 1C, Fig. 7). The mixed subequigranular plutonic phases in the Colton Hills are metaluminous, whereas those in the southern Bristol Mountains and the southern Providence Mountains range from metaluminous to marginally

TABLE 1D. MAJOR- AND TRACE-ELEMENT DATA
FOR FELSIC INTRUSIVE ROCKS GROUP AND HYPABYSSAL ROCKS GROUP

	Felsic Intrusive Rocks Group					Hypabyssal Rocks Group	
	Colton Hills	Bristol Mountains				Bristol Mountains	
	F84CH-	F86BR-	F86BR-	F87BR-	F87BR-	F85BR-	F85BR-
	12	74	123	78A	91A	16C	42A
SiO_2	73.84	73.10	65.40	75.60	71.40	74.70	76.10
TiO_2	0.19	0.30	0.65	0.23	0.45	0.25	0.20
Al_2O_3	13.77	13.80	15.90	12.70	13.90	12.70	12.80
Fe_2O_3	0.94	0.96	2.24	0.90	1.32	0.44	0.55
FeO	0.52	0.73	1.72	0.28	0.94	0.22	0.09
MgO	0.48	0.45	1.41	0.19	0.50	0.29	0.11
MnO	0.02	0.03	0.07	<0.02	0.04	<0.02	<0.02
CaO	1.23	1.47	3.14	0.79	1.49	0.12	0.18
Na_2O	2.62	2.63	2.89	3.03	3.04	2.43	3.21
K_2O	5.58	5.55	4.22	5.38	5.57	7.14	6.16
P_2O_5	0.05	0.12	0.26	<0.05	0.10	<0.05	<0.05
LOI	nd	0.75	1.75	0.61	0.69	0.79	0.47
Total	99.24	99.89	99.65	99.71	99.44	99.08	99.87
H_2O+	0.55	0.39	1.13	0.27	0.25	0.43	0.20
H_2O-	0.15	0.14	0.18	0.15	0.17	0.14	0.07
CO_2	0.04	<0.01	0.24	0.03	0.11	0.15	0.08
FeO*	1.37	1.59	3.73	1.09	2.13	0.61	0.58
A/CNK[†]	1.092	1.059	1.056	1.036	1.010	1.062	1.041
FeO*/							
FeO*+MgO	0.695	0.779	0.726	0.852	0.810	0.678	0.841
Ba[§]	697	nd	nd	248	850	nd	nd
Nb	14	16	15	24	24	32	35
Rb	216	140	100	230	215	180	180
Sr	170	190	410	88	184	48	85
Zr	147	290	330	280	580	220	340
Y	24	33	30	46	70	47	47
U	4	nd	nd	1.08	2.31	nd	nd
Th	38	nd	nd	26.7	27.9	nd	nd
Zn	nd	nd	nd	nd	nd	nd	nd
Cu	nd	nd	nd	nd	nd	nd	nd
Ni	nd	nd	nd	1.86	3.42	nd	nd
Cr	5	nd	nd	1.42	2.7	nd	nd

*All Fe as FeO.

[†]A/CNK = mole ratio of $Al_2O_3/(CaO + Na_2O + K_2O)$.

[§]Trace elements as ppm.

peraluminous (Fig. 6). In general, it is the most felsic portions of these plutonic phases that are peraluminous. As a group, the subequigranular plutonic phases define vaguely linear trends on Harker diagrams (Fig. 7). These trends are less well defined for the alkalis, which is probably due to the pervasive alkali metasomatism that affected the region (see below). As will be discussed below, the main chemical effects of the metasomatism were changes in alkalic concentrations; the other major oxides were largely unaffected. Thus, decreases of CaO, MgO, TiO_2, and FeO* with increasing SiO_2 are considered to be valid magmatic trends. Trace-element concentrations show similar variations (Table 1C, Fig. 7). Rb varies less in the Providence Mountains and Colton Hills than in the Bristol Mountains, whereas Sr and Zr vary widely in all three areas.

As was discussed above, these subequigranular mixed plutonic phases are extremely heterogeneous, and thus a large degree of "lumping" was used in defining units. Most contacts between these units are gradational. In the Colton Hills, all contacts are gradational within this subgroup, but in places, strongly foliated subequigranular monzogranite grades into slightly foliated porphyritic monzogranite, indicating that the porphyritic phase is slightly younger. The contact between the subequigranular porphyritic monzogranite phases is gradational over tens of meters and is defined by increasing size and abundance of phenocrysts and decreasing color index. The subequigranular, mixed plutonic phases in the southern Providence Mountains grade into the porphyritic mixed phases in most places, but locally intrude the porhyritic rocks. In the southern Bristol Mountains the quartz syenite locally intrudes the diorite of the mafic intrusives group, but in places the contact is gradational and is defined by an increasing color index and decreasing abundances of potassium feldspar and, to some extent, quartz. Contacts with the porphyritic mixed plutonic phase are gradational over meters to tens of meters and defined by increasing phenocryst size and abundance. In the northern part of the Bristol Mountains, the quartz syenite unit is intruded by a relatively quartz-rich homogeneous biotite granite of the felsic intrusives group. However, at least part of the fine-grained granite unit of the subequigranular mixed group appears to be the youngest intrusive phase in the southern Bristol Mountains because some phases cut all of the other major plutonic phases.

Felsic intrusive rocks

The group of felsic intrusive rocks is characterized by higher silica content and by more compositional and textural homogeneity than other rock groups. The group includes a body of leucocratic granite in the Colton Hills and biotite granite in the southern Bristol Mountains. No high-silica homogeneous plutons of Jurassic age are exposed in the southern Providence Mountains. Rocks resembling the biotite granite of the Bristol Mountains occur widely in the adjacent Lava Hills (Fig. 2).

The leucogranite of the Colton Hills is a monzogranite (Fig. 3A) that is nonfoliated to weakly foliated and cuts strongly foliated rocks of the mixed intrusive group. It is a subequigranular, fine-to medium-grained monzogranite, and is characterized in hand specimen by clear quartz, white feldspars, and low color index (0.4 to 2.9). Locally it contains minor amounts of interstitial muscovite. Plagioclase is normally zoned, and the more calcic cores have been pervasively sericitized. Perthitic potassium feldspar is anhedral to subhedral with inclusions of euhedral plagioclase and anhedral quartz. Dark brown biotite is interstitial to the other major mineral phases. Apatite and Fe-Ti oxides are the accessory phases.

The biotite granite of the southern Bristol Mountains is medium grained and ranges in composition from monzogranite to syenogranite (Fig. 3C). Potassium feldspar is anhedral to subhedral, perthitic, and commonly exhibits microcline twinning. Subhedral plagioclase has moderately to pervasively sericitized cores. Quartz is anhedral and locally appears to be recrystallized. Dark brown biotite is the principal ferromagnesian mineral present. Accessory phases are sphene, allanite, zircon, and Fe-Ti oxides.

Similar granite occurs in the western and northern Lava Hills, where it ranges in composition from monzogranite to granodiorite.

All the felsic plutonic phases are subalkalic and generally mildly peraluminous (Figs. 5 and 6). SiO_2 contents are higher, in general, than for the other intrusive groups; most of the rocks in this group have $SiO_2 > 70$ wt% (Fig. 7, Table 1D). Rb contents vary from 100 to 290 ppm, Sr from 88 to 410 ppm, and Ba 248 to 850 ppm with most >600 ppm. Cr and Ni values are low. For both of these elements, values for the leucogranite of Colton Hills are higher than those for the Bristol Mountains samples (Table 1D). Zr and Y values for the leucogranite of Colton Hills are low relative to those for the Bristol Mountains rocks (Table 1D).

In almost all cases, the felsic intrusives are the youngest of the plutonic rocks. In the Colton Hills, the leucocratic granite intrudes foliated monzogranite of the mixed intrusives group along clearly defined and nearly vertical contacts. Foliation in all rocks, including a slight foliation in the leucocratic granite, favors a broadly synchronous intrusive history for all rocks, however. In many places in the southern Bristol Mountains, the biotite granite intrudes other rock units along sharp contacts. However, important local exceptions are contacts that are less distinct, with rounded patches of the mafic monzodiorite unit within the granite. We take these relations to indicate that the two phases are broadly comagmatic and that the diorite was still hot and "soft" at the time of granite intrusion. The biotite granite is locally intruded by the most felsic portions of the subequigranular fine-grained granite of the mixed group. These units are texturally and mineralogically distinct, even though they overlap in compositional space (Fig. 7C). The most notable difference is the lack of hornblende in the biotite granite.

Metavolcanic and hypabyssal rocks

Metavolcanic and hypabyssal rocks that may be comagmatic with the intrusive rocks are exposed in the southern Providence and southern Bristol Mountains (Fig. 2). In the Providence Mountains, this group is represented by dark-weathering, highly propylitically altered, quartz-poor hypabyssal rocks and dark colored, foliated, fine-grained, intermediate to silicic metavolcanic rocks that retain ghosts of feldspar phenocrysts. Hypabyssal rocks have altered feldspar and biotite phenocrysts set in a granophyric groundmass. The highly altered hypabyssal rocks appear to grade into subequigranular mixed plutonic rocks, and probably grade into the volcanic rocks as well, although intense alteration obscures relations.

The hypabyssal and volcanic rocks in the southern Bristol Mountains are also intensely propylitically altered, making relations difficult to distinguish in the field. Flow banding suggestive of volcanic origin is present in some of the siliceous rocks, but numerous nondescript varieties of dark aphanitic to fine-grained rocks predominate. These rocks have a porphyritic texture with subhedral to euhedral phenocrysts of potassium feldspar, plagioclase, and quartz set in a granophyric groundmass. These rocks, which we interpret as hypabyssal, are intruded by the biotite granite of the felsic intrusive rocks group and the fine-grained granite of the mixed intrusive rocks group. Limited sampling of the hypabyssal rocks show that some are rhyolitic; the SiO_2 content is 75 to 76 weight percent, and the total alkali content (Na_2O+K_2O) is greater than 9 weight percent; K_2O is two to three more times abundant than Na_2O (Table 1D, Fig. 7C).

Dikes

In the southern Providence Mountains and Colton Hills, plutons are cut by extensive north-northwest–trending dike swarms. Along the western side of the southern Providence Mountains these dikes form a sheeted complex (Miller and others, 1985) that ranges in composition from felsic to intermediate. These and other dikes in the range vary from dark dacite porphyry to flinty light green aphanitic rock to light bluish-gray fine-grained quartzofeldspathic rock and pink aplite. These dikes are cut by Cretaceous plutons.

In the Colton Hills the dikes are rhyodacitic in composition, range in thickness from 2 to 15 m, and have chilled borders. They are composed of plagioclase and potassium feldspar phenocrysts and laths of hornblende and biotite that are set in a very fine-grained matrix. Isotopic dates (summarized below) suggest that they may be time-correlative with the Independence dike swarm described by Moore and Hopson (1961), although Hopson (1988) suggested that these dike systems are products of Jurassic arc magmatism and that they are genetically related to the plutons. Similar dikes are found in the central Mojave Desert (Karish, 1983; Karish and others, 1987) and Sonoran Desert region (Tosdal and others, 1989).

Dikes are much less common in the southern Bristol Mountains, where scattered lamprophyric and diabase dikes of uncertain age intrude all of the plutonic phases. Rare aplitic dikes locally intrude the quartz syenite and other granitic phases.

ALBITIZATION

Many of the plutonic and hypabyssal rocks in these three mountain ranges have undergone extensive late- or early post-magmatic albitization. This alteration, which provides clues to the emplacement history of the plutons, was most intense in the southernmost Providence Mountains and throughout the southern Bristol Mountains (Miller and others, 1985; Fox, 1986, 1987a, 1987b). Pronounced albitic alteration occurs as linear white zones in the normally mesocratic plutonic rocks, and is characterizd by the replacement of potassium feldspar by albite. More widespread but less pronounced albitization produced mottled textures consisting of 2- to 5-cm albitized patches; this "spotted" albitization is ubiquitous and affects all plutonic phases.

We interpret the roughly planar zones of white altered rock as the result of albitizing fluids channelized in a fracture system. The pervasive "spotted" albitization suggests that there was extensive fluid flow along microcracks and grain boundaries that gave way to more channelized flow with time.

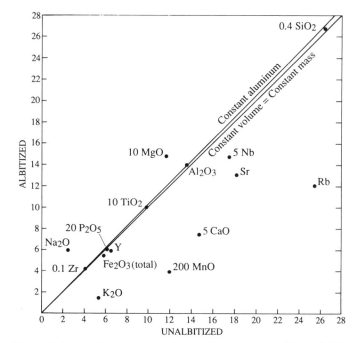

Figure 8. Isocon diagram comparing whole-rock compositions of albitized and unalbitized quartz syenite of the subequigranular mixed group near Windy Point in the southern Bristol Mountains. Best-fit isocon (= constant alumina) shown in comparison to constant volume isocon (which is equal to constant mass isocon for this unit). Major oxide data scaled in weight percent, trace element data scaled in 0.1 ppm.

The primary mineralogic effect of the albitization process was the replacement of potassium feldspar by albite with little or no change in abundances of quartz or mafic minerals. Plagioclase and primary accessory phases such as sphene were generally unaffected. Biotite was locally partially to completely altered to chlorite. The metasomatic albite is very turbid and is twinned in a distinctive discontinuous chess-board pattern.

Chemically, the albitization produced a strong increase in Na_2O (from 4.5 to 8.5 wt%) accompanied by an almost total loss of K_2O (from 6.5 to <1.0 wt%). Where albitization was accompanied by a chloritization of biotite there is also a net loss in total alkalies. Changes in Fe, Mg, and Ca abundances depend on the extent of alteration of the mafic phases. Trace (Y, Zr) and rare earth elements, as well as Al and Ti, were immobile on hand-specimen scale. This alteration appears to have essentially conserved volume and mass, as is illustrated in an isocon diagram (after Grant, 1986) comparing albitized and unalbitized compositions of the quartz syenite at Windy Point (Fig. 8).

The albitization results in a strong depletion in whole-rock $\delta^{18}O_{SMOW}$ from about $+8^0/_{00}$ to about $+4^0/_{00}$. Feldspar alteration is responsible for the bulk of this depletion, because quartz shows only a mild $\delta^{18}O$ depletion (<$1^0/_{00}$). Biotite from albitized rocks shows $\delta^{18}O_{SMOW}$ depletions similar to those for feldspar, and is depleted in δD_{SMOW} ($-106°$ to $-160^0/_{00}$) as well. These data suggest that the fluids responsible for the alteration were predominantly meteoric in origin.

Hall and others (1988) suggested, on the basis of fluid inclusion and stable isotope data, that pervasive albitization of Jurassic granitic rocks and felsic dikes in the nearby Marble Mountains (Fig. 2) occurred penecontemporaneously with contact skarn and dike skarn development. They concluded that the fluid responsible for the albitization had a large magmatic component or that it equilibrated isotopically with the pluton at temperatures ≤600 °C. They also reported a low-temperature (200 to 250 °C) meteoric overprint on the albitization. The study of Hall and others (1988) suggests that the albitization in the Marble Mountains was a late magmatic event. The larger role of meteoric fluids in the albitization process in the Bristol Mountains may indicate that the alteration continued there into early post-magmatic stages.

Similar zones of albitization have been recognized in Jurassic rocks throughout the southern Cordillera, including the Yerington district (Carten, 1986), White-Inyo Mountains (Anderson, 1937; Crowder and Ross, 1973), central Mojave Desert (Karish, 1983; Cox and others, 1987), and Sonoran Desert region (Tosdal and others, 1989).

AGE OF THE GRANITOIDS

The ages of the Jurassic intrusive rocks in this region are as yet poorly constrained. In the Colton Hills, porphyritic granite yields K-Ar cooling ages on biotite of 159 ± 6 Ma and 152 ± 4.0 Ma (K. A. Howard, 1984, written communication), and a dacite dike cutting the plutons yields a K-Ar cooling age on biotite of 145.7 ± 3.6 Ma (J. K. Nakata, analyst). In the southern Providence Mountains the quartz monzonite of Goldstone of the mixed-subequigranular group yielded a U-Pb zircon crytallization age of approximately 164 to 162 Ma (J. S. Stacey, 1985, written communication) and a K-Ar biotite cooling age of 157.0 ± 3.9 Ma (M. A. Pernokas, analyst). The Providence Mountains plutons and dikes are cut by Cretaceous granites yielding K-Ar biotite cooling ages of about 74 Ma (Miller and others, 1985). In the southern Bristol Mountains, the quartz syenite of the mixed-subequigranular group has yielded K-Ar biotite cooling ages of 154 ± 2 and 139 ± 4.2 Ma (Armstrong and Suppe, 1973; Calzia and Morton, 1980).

We take these K-Ar and U-Pb data as indicating late Middle to early Late Jurassic intrusion ages for these plutons of the Colton Hills, Providence Mountains, and Bristol Mountains. The U-Pb dates are the only firm estimate for emplacement age. The 157-Ma K-Ar cooling age for the same rock unit may be used to infer similar emplacement ages for other units in the Bristol Mountains dated at ~155 Ma by K-Ar. Thus, all data can be interpreted as indicating a short, widespread intrusive event, although this interpretation is not unique. In the Colton Hills, post-plutonic dikes were evidently emplaced during the Late Jurassic. Similar dikes in the other ranges may have similar emplacement ages.

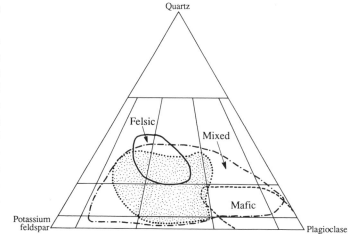

Figure 9. Modal compositions of Jurassic plutons included in this study compiled by intrusive group, irrespective of location. Patterned portion of mixed group is porphyritic subgroup.

SUMMARY

A general mafic to felsic compositional variation is documented in all three ranges studied (Fig. 9), suggesting that all igneous rocks can be viewed as broadly related, despite geographic separations. In general, the dioritic rocks are the oldest units, and the most silica-rich granites are the youngest intrusive phases. However, there are striking variations within the individual plutonic phases and exceptions to the generality that mafic are oldest and felsic are youngest, especially within the mixed subequigranular group. The compositional variations within each group or subgroup tend to be wider within a specific mountain range than between ranges, and thus the subdivision of the units into the various textural/compositional groups is valid on a regional basis.

Parallel to the mafic to felsic change with time is a change from being compositionally heterogeneous to homogeneous with time. Mafic rocks and subequigranular mixed-group rocks are strongly variable compositionally and texturally, typically on a scale of meters. Within the subequigranular mixed subgroup, the more felsic rocks in places can be shown to be the youngest, and they are generally more homogeneous. Rocks of the porphyritic mixed subgroup are less heterogeneous and form fairly discrete plutonic phases with gradational margins. Rocks of the felsic group are homogeneous and form discrete plutonic phases that in many cases display sharp contacts with other phases.

The continuous compositional spectrum and linear trends in Harker diagrams (especially for the Bristol Mountain where the sample density is greatest) suggest a broadly related suite of magmas; this is supported by field evidence showing that all rocks are closely related. Contact relations (no chill margins, paucity of sharp contacts) suggest that the intrusive rocks were continuously hot and probably intruded over a relatively short time span, from about 165 to 160 Ma. The presence of contemporaneous (?) hypabyssal and volcanic rocks indicates that the plutonic complexes were intruded at a shallow level. Field evidence indicates that the alkalic and subalkalic intrusive phases were contemporaneous. The plutons were affected by late- or early post-magmatic hydrothermal circulation, which resulted in extensive sodium metasomatism.

DISCUSSION

A model for the generation, evolution, and emplacement of the Jurassic plutonic complexes must account for unusual features of these complexes, including the overall breadth in chemistry, the extreme small-scale spatial variations in texture and mineralogy, the alkalic nature of some of the plutonic phases, and the widespread presence of albitization. In the following sections we attempt to quantify important parameters such as depth of emplacement and water content of the magma, and then derive a model explaining the unusual features.

Estimates of depths of emplacement

Estimates of the depths of emplacement of granitic rocks are generally crude, especially in the absence of precise compositional data for pressure-sensitive mineral phases. In the absence of useful contact metamorphic assemblages or precise hornblende compositional data, depths of emplacement can be estimated from field evidence such as the reconstruction of the thickness of overlying strata and/or the presence or absence of late-magmatic meteoric hydrothermal circulation systems.

Shallow depths of emplacement for the intrusive rocks we have studied are indicated by geologic relations. Although it is impossible to reconstruct the overlying strata due to the paucity of Mesozoic supracrustal rocks in the region and uncertainties in the pre-plutonism structural history of the area, in several locations the plutons intruded approximately coeval volcanic and hypabyssal rocks, suggesting shallow emplacement levels. In addition, the Paleozoic strata they intrude lack significant pre-intrusion metamorphism. The presence of extensive albitization that resulted from the late- or early post-magmatic hydrothermal circulation of predominantly meteoric fluids indicates depths of emplacement of less than 10 km for the exposed intrusives. These shallow depths of emplacement are consistent with barometric studies of the quartz monzonite of Goldstone in the northern part of the southern Providence Mountains, from which Young and Wooden (1988) reported a pressure of about 3 kbar, based on hornblende geobarometry (Hammarstrom and Zen, 1986; Hollister and others, 1987). The mineralogic data and field relations together point to an upper crustal emplacement for these Jurassic plutonic complexes.

Estimates of water content

Experimental data of Naney (1983) indicate that the crystallization sequence of granitic magmas is strongly dependent on water content. At 2 kbar, hornblende is stable only if the system has at least 4 weight percent H_2O (2.5 wt% at 8 kbar), whereas biotite is stable in more water-poor systems. Hornblende is present in most of the plutonic groups described above, and textural evidence indicates that it crystallized concurrently with or just prior to biotite. These data indicate a minimum water content of approximately 4 weight percent for these magmas at the time of crystallization. The paucity of pegmatitic and aplitic phases combined with the presence of hornblende indicates that the water content of the magma probably did not greatly exceed 4 wt% and that much of the crystallization of the magmatic suites was at a subsaturation level. The lack of hornblende in the more felsic phases probably reflects the low calcium contents of these granitic melts and lower temperatures of crystallization.

Origin of spatial heterogeneities

The spatial variations in grain size, color index, and, in some cases, quartz content can best be explained by nearly contemporaneous pulses of magmas that are at different stages of evolution. The requirement of contemporaneity stems from the lack of distinct contacts between the texturally and compositionally different phases, suggesting that successive small intrusive pulses of crystal-rich magma intermixed at their contacts and did not impose foliations on still-hot intrusive pulses. Because the rock compositions and textures vary on scales of meters to tens of meters, the magmas in successive pulses were apparently highly heterogeneous. Intrusive pulses in any given area were derived from a single evolving source or closely related magma sources.

Chemical variation trends for rocks in the Bristol Mountains (for which the data set is the most extensive) suggest that the intrusive groups are comagmatic (Fg. 7C). These trends also indicate an extensive amount of fractionation. Compatible major elements, Sr, and Ba decrease with increasing SiO_2, accompanied by an increase in A/CNK. These trends can be explained by fractionation of clinopyroxene, hornblende, plagioclase, and potassium feldspar.

We consider the spatial heterogeneities to be best explained by repeated intrusion of small magma pulses tapping different portions of a fractionating system of one or more parent bodies. These pulses may have had varying liquid:crystal ratios. The pulses possibly tapped magma systems generated from different sources in the lower crust and upper mantles, further accentuating compositional heterogeneities.

Origin of alkalic phases

Several models have been proposed for the origin of granitoids with alkalic affinities. Among these is a model by Miller (1978) for the early Mesozoic alkali-rich monzonitic plutons of California, proposing that they originated from the melting of a moderately potassic eclogite source within the newly initiated subduction zone. Rocks derived from such a protolith would be metaluminous and strongly enriched in LILE, including the

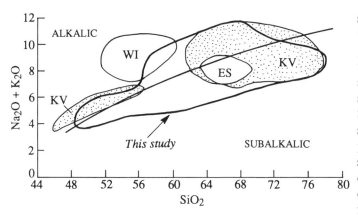

Figure 10. Comparison of intrusive rocks from this study to other Jurassic plutons of the southern Cordillera using Na_2O+K_2O and SiO_2 data. Sources of data: WI = White–Inyo Range, from Sylvester and others (1978); ES = Eastern Sierra Nevada, from Schweickert (1976); KV = Ko Vaya superunit, Sonoran Desert region of Tosdal and others (1989).

lighter rare earth elements (LREE). The monzonitic plutons included in Miller's (1978) model are characterized by high Na_2O+K_2O (~10 wt%) and Sr (1,000 to 2,000 ppm), moderate SiO_2 (53 to 63 wt%), and steep negatively sloping REE patterns (from >100 to <10 x chondrite). The plutonic phases with alkalic affinities in the Bristol and Providence mountains area display similarly high total alkalies and moderate SiO_2 contents, but the Sr concentrations are much lower (<1,000 ppm) than those discussed by Miller (1978). Despite the lower Sr, the potassic eclogite source model could apply to the Mojave Desert granites.

Another possible explanation for the origin of the alkalic plutons in this region is extensive hornblende fractionation, which would enrich the magma in alkalis and aluminum while depleting it in iron, magnesium, and calcium. Appropriate fractionation trends are seen in the alkalic rocks of the subequigranular mixed intrusive group of the Bristol Mountains (Fig. 7C). If the spatial heterogeneities are explained by tapping different portions of a fractionating system, then the magma pulses that resulted in alkalic rocks may have tapped a portion of the system that had undergone extensive hornblende fractionation.

The plutons we have studied may have been generated by the partial melting of a source that was chemically similar to the phlogopite-bearing quartz eclogite proposed by Miller (1978). A possible source for the slightly silica-oversaturated, alkali-enriched melt suggested by the data from this study is a partially eclogitized amphibolite, perhaps from an altered subducted oceanic slab. The strong alkali enrichment of some of the plutonic units is probably due to tapping a level of the magma system that was fractionating hornblende.

REGIONAL SIGNIFICANCE

Jurassic plutons with alkalic affinities and strongly heterogeneous compositions have been described in other parts of the

southern Cordillera. Schweickert (1976) described Jurassic plutons with alkalic affinities in the eastern Sierra Nevada. These plutons are more texturally and compositionally homogeneous than those of this study, but they display heterogeneous hypabyssal marginal facies. Alkalic Jurassic plutons have also been described in the White-Inyo Mountains by Miller (1978) and Sylvester and others (1978). Tosdal and others (1989) have described texturally and compositionally heterogeneous Jurassic plutons of the Ko Vaya superunit (Sonoran Desert region of southern Arizona). These plutons also show variations in quartz content, color index, and grain size on the scale of meters to tens of meters. The chemical characteristics of these Jurassic plutons from elsewhere in the region are compared with those from this study in Figure 10. The intrusive suites from the area discussed here span a wider compositional range than those reported elsewhere, but data from other areas are limited.

The distribution of known texturally and compositionally heterogeneous Jurassic plutons with alkalic affinities appears to be spatially restricted to the eastern edge of the Jurassic magmatic arc, where it was constructed across continental crust. Farther north, the crust intruded by this margin of the arc was transitional to, or wholly oceanic, in character. In addition, heterogeneous and alkalic Jurassic plutons are known primarily from locations where they are among the first intrusive phases, with no Triassic plutonism documented. Early melting in the continental lower crust and upper mantle below the eastern margin of the Jurassic arc (and probably the first arc-generated magma in that crust) was probably conducive to producing compositionally heterogeneous magmas, either as a result of initial crustal heterogeneities, or as a result of successive events of melting and movement of magmas. Along the eastern side of the arc the crust was probably cooler and thicker and thus more conducive to multiple feeders to a shallow magma inflation zone rather than a crustal-scale magma system. Perhaps an extensional tectonic regime in the relatively cool and brittle crust along the eastern side of the arc facilitated rapid, repeated emplacement of small magma pulses rather than less frequent, large plutons, as seen in the arc batholiths farther west.

Dilles and Wright (1988), in a discussion of Jurassic magmatism in the Yerington district of western Nevada, proposed that the Middle Jurassic magmatism associated with the Yerington batholith was restricted to a 4 m.y. interval (169 to 165 Ma). Magmatic activity began with the eruption of a volcanic sequence that was followed by intrusion of the comagmatic(?) 250-km^2 Yerington batholith, which was differentiated, emplaced, and crystallized within 1 m.y. (169.4 to 168.5 Ma). Successive pulses of this batholith were volumetrically smaller and emplaced in deeper, more central parts of the batholith and are interpreted to have tapped deeper levels of the parent magma chamber (Dilles, 1984). This model may apply to other parts of the southern Cordillera, because it accounts for the widespread compositional and textural heterogeneity of plutons. Generation and emplacement of voluminous magmas over a short time span would maintain the hot emplacement environment necessary to explain gradational contacts between successively emplaced pulses without significant cooling. In addition, continued emplacement deep in the batholith would provide the heat necessary to drive late meteoric-hydrothermal circulation systems seen as pervasive albitization in the upper parts.

CONCLUSIONS

Jurassic plutons in the southern Bristol Mountains, southern Providence Mountains, and Colton Hills are extremely heterogeneous in texture and composition, and display alkalic affinities. The plutons have been subdivided into three major compositional and/or textural groups that were emplaced in overlapping pulses. The oldest of these consists of diorite to quartz monzodiorite. The most voluminous group is the most heterogeneous and consists of mixed porphyritic and mixed subequigranular subgroups that range from quartz monzodiorite to syenogranite. The youngest of the intrusive phases is the most felsic, consisting of biotite granite, and is also the most homogeneous. These plutons appear to have intruded broadly contemporaneous hypabyssal and volcanic cap rocks. The plutonic, hypabyssal, and minor aplitic phases were affected by extensive late or early post-magmatic sodium metasomatism (albitization) as a result of the introduction and circulation of predominantly meteoric fluids. The plutons are cut by a series of Late Jurassic mafic to felsic dikes that may be correlative with the Independence dike swarm.

Field relations, compositional data, and hornblende geobarometry indicate that these plutons were intruded at upper crustal levels. Comparisons of petrographic observations with experimental data indicate water contents of approximately 4 weight percent for the majority of the plutonic phases. The extreme textural and compositional variations and lack of sharp contacts between units suggest continuous intrusion of small magma pulses over a short period of time in a hot environment. A mafic to felsic trend with time was probably controlled by differentiation of the magmatic system; the spatial heterogeneities and local

alkalic character most likely resulted from tapping different portions of the fractionating system.

These rocks are similar to other plutons from the eastern edge of the Jurassic magmatic arc and appear to differ from those in the western part of the arc. In general, the unifying characteristics of these plutons are: epizonal setting; strong compositional and textural variations; and alkalic affinities.

We propose that the plutons in the southern Bristol Mountains, Colton Hills, and southern Providence Mountains were derived from compositionally heterogeneous but genetically related magmas that were rapidly emplaced as numerous small magma pulses at a shallow level in the crust, but in a continuously hot environment. The repeated emplacement produced long-standing or numerous recyclings of hydrothermal systems that are manifested as widespread albitization. The plutons were emplaced during a fairly short period during Middle to Late Jurassic time.

ACKNOWLEDGMENTS

Discussions with Keith Howard contributed a great deal to the development of this manuscript. His lead in studying granites of the region focused us on many of the problems we studied and elucidated the regional relations. Some of the whole-rock chemical data presented here were provided by Stirling Shaw of McQuarie University, New South Wales, and we gratefully acknowledge this contribution. John Stacey, John Nakata, and Martha Pernokas provided much of the geochronologic data presented here. Lindee Glick assisted in field mapping in the Providence Mountains and Colton Hills. Support for work in the Bristol Mountains by Fox was provided through a Graduate Intern Fellowship from the U.S. Geological Survey. Reviews by Dave Dellinger, Howard Wilshore, and Ed Young are greatly appreciated. Lawford Anderson, Steve Richard, Jim Wright, and Michael Ort critiqued the manuscript at various stages of completion, and their suggestions contributed to its evolution to its present form.

REFERENCES CITED

Allen, C. M., Miller, D. M., Howard, K. A., and Shaw, S. E., 1983, Field, petrologic, and chemical characteristics of Jurassic intrusive rocks, eastern Mojave Desert, southeastern California: Geological Society of America Abstracts with Programs, v. 15, p. 410–411.

Anderson, G. H., 1937, Granitization, albitization, and related phenomena in the northern Inyo Range of California–Nevada: Geological Society of America Bulletin, v. 48, p. 1–74.

Anderson, J. L., 1988, Core complexes of the Mojave–Sonora Desert; Conditions of plutonism, mylonitization, and decompression, in Ernst, W. G., ed., Metamorphic and crustal evolution of the western U.S.: Englewood Cliffs, New Jersey, Prentice-Hall, p. 503–525.

Anderson, J. L., Barth, A. P., Young, E. D., Davis, M. J., Farber, D., Hayes, E. M., and Johnson, K. A., 1988, Contrasting depth of Mesozoic arc emplacement across the Tnjunga–North American terrane boundary: Geological Society of America Abstracts with Programs, v. 20, p. 139.

Anderson, T. H., and Silver, L. T., 1979, The role of the Mojave Sonora megashear in the tectonic evolution of northern Sonora, in Anderson, T. H., and Roldan-Quintana, J., eds., Geology of northen Sonora (Geological Society of America guidebook, field trip no. 27): Instituto de Geologia, U.N.A.M., Hermosillo, Sonora, Mexico, and the University of Pittsburgh, Pittsburgh, Pennsylvania, p. 59–68.

Armstrong, R. L., and Suppe, J., 1973, Potassium-argon geochronometry of Mesozoic igneous rocks in Nevada, Utah, and southern California: Geological Society of America Bulletin, v. 84, p. 1375–1392.

Beckerman, G. M., Robinson, J. P., and Anderson, J. L., 1982, The Teutonia batholith; A large intrusive complex of Jurassic and Cretaceous age in the eastern Mojave Desert, California, in Frost, E. G., and Martin, D. M., eds., Mesozoic-Cenozoic tectonic evolution of the Colorado River region, California, Arizona, and Nevada: San Diego, California, Cordilleran Publishers, p. 205–220.

Burchfiel, B. C., and Davis, G. A., 1981, Mojave Desert and environs, *in* Ernst, W. G., ed., The geotectonic development of California: Englewood Cliffs, New Jersey, Prentice-Hall, p. 217–252.

Calzia, J. P., and Morton, J. L., 1980, Compilation of isotopic ages within the Needles 1° by 2° Quadrangle, California and Arizona: U.S. Geological Survey Open-File Report 80–1303, scale 1:250,000.

Carr, M. D., Poole, F. G., and Christenson, R. L., 1984, Pre-Cenozoic geology of the El Paso Mountains, southwestern Great Basin; A summary, *in* Lintz, J., ed., Western geological excursions, Volume 4: Reno, Nevada, MacKay School of Mines, p. 84–93.

Carten, R. B., 1986, Sodium-calcium metasomatism; Chemical, temporal, and spatial relationships at the Yerington, Nevada, porphyry copper deposit: Economic Geology, v. 81, p. 1495–1519.

Cox, B. F., and Morton, J. L., 1980, Late Permian plutonism, El Paso Mountains, California: Geological Society of America Abstracts with Programs, v. 12, p. 103.

Cox, B. F., Griscom, A., Kilburn, J. E., Raines, G. L., Knepper, D. H., Jr., Sabine, C., and Kuizon, L., 1987, Mineral resources of the Newberry Mountains and Rodman Mountains Wilderness study areas, San Bernardino County, California: U.S. Geological Survey Bulletin 1712–A, 28 p.

Crowder, D. F., and Ross, D. C., 1973, Petrography of some granitic bodies in the northern White Mountains, California–Nevada: U.S. Geological Survey Professional Paper 775, 28 p.

Damon, P. E., Shafiqullah, M., and Clark, K. F., 1981, Age trends of igneous activity in relation to metallogenesis in the southern Cordillera: Arizona Geological Society Digest, v. 14, p. 137–153.

Davis, G. A., Monger, J.W.H., and Burchfiel, B. C., 1978, Mesozoic construction of the Cordilleran "collage," central British Columbia to central California, *in* Howell, D. G., and McDougall, K. A., eds., Mesozoic paleogeography of the western United States: Los Angeles, Society of Economic Paleontologists and Mineralogists, Pacific Coast Paleogeography Symposium 2, p. 1–32.

Dickinson, W. R., 1970, Relations of andesites, granites, and derivative sandstones to arc-trench tectonics: Reviews of Geophysics and Space Physics, v. 8, no. 4, p. 813–860.

Dilles, J. H., 1984, The petrology and geochemistry of the Yerington batholith and the Ann-Mason porphyry copper deposit, western Nevada [Ph.D. thesis]: Stanford, California, Stanford University, 389 p.

Dilles, J. H., and Wright, J. E., 1988, The chronology of early Mesozoic arc magmatism in the Yerington district of western Nevada and its regional implications: Geological Society of America Bulletin, v. 100, p. 644–652.

Fox, L. K., 1986, Sodium metasomatism of a Jurassic quartz syenite, Bristol Mountains, California [abs.]: EOS Transactions of the American Geophysical Union, v. 67, no. 44, p. 1269.

—— , 1987a, Sodium metasomatism of Jurassic plutons, east-central Mojave Desert, California: Geological Society of America Abstracts with Programs, v. 19, p. 379.

—— , 1987b, Mineralogic and chemical effects of late-magmatic albitization of Jurassic plutons, Bristol Mtns, CA: Implications for fluid composition: Geological Society of America Abstracts with Programs, v. 19, p. 667.

Goldfarb, R. J., Miller, D. M., Simpson, R. W., Hoover, D. B., Moyle, P. R., Olson, J. E., and Gaps, R. S., 1988, Mineral resources of the Providence Mountains Wilderness study area, San Bernardino County, California: U.S. Geological Survey Bulletin 1712, p. D1–D70.

Grant, J. A., 1986, The isocon diagram; A simple solution to Gressen's equation for metasomatic alteration: Economic Geology, v. 81, p. 1976–1982.

Hall, D. J., Cohen, L. H., and Schiffman, P., 1988, Hydrothermal alteration associated with the Iron Hat iron skarn deposit, eastern Mojave Desert, San Bernardino County, California: Economic Geology, v. 81, p. 586–605.

Hammarstrom, J. M., and Zen, E-an, 1986, Aluminum in hornblende; An empirical igneous geobarometer: American Mineralogist, v. 71, p. 1297–1313.

Hazzard, J. C., 1954, Rocks and structures of the northern Providence Mountains, San Bernardino County, California: California Division of Mines Bulletin 170, p. 27–35.

Hollister, L. S., Grissom, G. C., Peters, E. K., Stowell, H. H., and Sisson, V. B., 1987, Confirmation of the empirical correlation of Al in hornblende with pressure of solidification of calc-alkaline plutons: American Journal of Science, v. 72, p. 231–239.

Hopson, C. A., 1988, Independence dike swarm; Origin and tectonic significance [abs.]: EOS Transactions of the American Geophysical Union, v. 69, no. 44, p. 1479.

Howard, K. A., and John, B. E., 1983, Geologic map of the Sheep Hole–Cadiz Wilderness study area (CDCA–305), San Bernardino County, California: U.S. Geological Survey Miscellaneous Field Investigations Map MF–1615A, scale 1:62,500.

Howard, K. A., John, B. E., and Miller, C. F., 1987a, Metamorphic core complexes, Mesozoic ductile thrusts, and Cenozoic detachment; Old Woman Mountains–Chemehuevi Mountains transect, California and Arizona, *in* Davis, G. H., and VandenDolder, E. M., eds., Geologic diversity of Arizona and its margins; Excursions to choice areas (Geological Society of America Annual Meeting field-trip guidebook): Arizona Bureau of Geology and Mineral Technology, Geological Survey Branch Special Paper 5, p. 365–382.

Howard, K. A., Kilburn, J. E., Simpson, R. W., Fitzgibbon, T. T., Detra, D. E., Raines, G. L., and Sabine, C., 1987b, Mineral resources of the Bristol/Granite Mountains Wilderness study area, San Bernardino County, California: U.S. Geological Survey Bulletin 1712–C, 18 p.

Irvine, T. N., and Baragar, W.R.A., 1971, A guide to the chemical composition of the common volcanic rocks: Canadian Journal of Earth Sciences, v. 8, p. 523–548.

John, B. E., 1981, Reconnaissance study of Mesozoic plutonic rocks in the Mojave Desert region, *in* Howard, K. A., Carr, M. D., and Miller, D. M., eds., Tectonic framework of the Mojave and Sonoran deserts, California and Arizona: U.S. Geological Survey Open-File Report 81–503, p. 49–51.

—— , 1986, Structural and intrusive history of the Chemehuevi Mountains area, southeastern California and western Arizona [Ph.D. thesis]: Santa Barbara, University of California, 295 p.

Karish, C. F., 1983, Mesozoic geology of the Ord Mountains, Mojave Desert; Structure, igneous petrology, and radiometric dating of a failed incipient intra-arc rift [M.S. thesis]: Stanford, California, Stanford University, 112 p.

Karish, C. R., Miller, E. L., and Wright, J. E., 1987, Mesozoic tectonic and magmatic history of the central Mojave Desert, *in* Dickinson, W. R., and Klute, M. A., eds., Mesozoic rocks of southern Arizona and adjacent areas: Tucson, Arizona Geological Society Digest, v. 18, p. 15–32.

Miller, C. F., 1978, An early Mesozoic alkalic magmatic belt in western North America, *in* Howell, D. C., and McDougall, D. A., eds., Mesozoic paleogeography of the western United States: Society of Economic Paleontologists and Mineralogists, Pacific Section, Pacific Coast Paleogeography Symposium 2, p. 163–174.

Miller, C. F., Howard, K. A., and Hoisch, T. D., 1982, Mesozoic thrusting, metamorphism, and plutonism, Old Woman–Piute Range, southeastern California, *in* Frost, E. G., and Martin, D. L., eds., Mesozoic–Cenozoic tectonic evolution of the Colorado River region, California, Arizona, and Nevada: San Diego, California, Cordilleran Publishers, p. 561–581.

Miller, D. M., Howard, K. A., and John, B. E., 1982, Preliminary geology of the Bristol Lake region, Mojave Desert, California, *in* Cooper, J. D., compiler, Geologic excursions in the California desert (Geological Society of America Cordilleran Section meeting guidebook): Shoshone, California, Death Valley Publishing Company, p. 91–100.

Miller, D. M., Glick, L. L., Goldfarb, R. J., Simpson, R. W., Hoover, D. B., Detra, D. E., Dohrenwend, J. C., and Munts, S. R., 1985, Mineral resources and resource potential map of the South Providence Mountains Wilderness study area, San Bernardino County, California: U.S. Geological Survey Miscellaneous Field Studies Map MF–1780–A, 29 p., scale 1:62,500.

Miller, E. L., 1981, Geology of the Victorville region, California: Geological Society of America Bulletin, pt. 2, v. 92, p. 554–608.

Miyashiro, A., 1974, Volcanic rock series in island arcs and active continental margins: American Journal of Science, v. 274, p. 324–355.

Monger, J.W.H., and Price, R. A., 1979, Geodynamic evolution of the Canadian Cordillera; Progress and problems: Canadian Journal of Earth Sciences, v. 16, p. 770–772.

Moore, J. G., and Hopson, C. A., 1961, The Independence dike swarm in eastern California: American Journal of Science, v. 259, p. 241–259.

Naney, M. T., 1983, Phase equilibria of rock-forming ferromagnesian silicates in granitic systems: American Journal of Science, v. 285, p. 993–1033.

Ross, D. C., 1969, Descriptive petrography of three large granitic bodies in the Inyo Mountains, California: U.S. Geological Survey Professional Paper 601, 47 p.

Saleeby, J., 1981, Ocean floor accretion and volcanoplutonic arc evolution of the Mesozoic Sierra Nevada, *in* Ernst, W. G., ed., The geotectonic evolution of California: Englewood Cliffs, New Jersey, Prentice-Hall, p. 132–181.

Schweikert, R. A., 1976, Shallow-level plutonic complexes in eastern Sierra Nevada, California, and their tectonic implications: Geological Society of America Special Paper 176, 58 p.

Streckeisen, A. L., 1976, To each plutonic rock its proper name: Earth Science Reviews, v. 12, p. 1–33.

Sylvester, A. G., Miller, C. F., and Nelson, C. A., 1978, Monzonites of the White–Inyo Range, California, and their relation to the calc-alkaline Sierra Nevada batholith: Geological Society of America Bulletin, v. 89, p. 1677–1687.

Tosdal, R. M., 1988, Mesozoic rock units along the Late Cretaceous Mule Mountains thrust system, southeastern California and southwestern Arizona [Ph.D. thesis]: Santa Barbara, University of California, 365 p.

Tosdal, R. M., Haxel, G. B., and Wright, J. E., 1989, Jurassic geology of the Sonoran Desert region, southern Arizona, southeastern Californa, and northernmost Sonora; Construction of a continental-margin magmatic arc, *in* Jenny, J. P., and Reynolds, S. J., eds., Geologic evolution of Arizona: Tucson, Arizona Geological Society Digest, v. 17 (in press).

Walker, J. D., 1987, Permian to Middle Triassic rocks of the Mojave Desert: Arizona Geological Society Digest, v. 18, p. 1–14.

Wright, J. E., Howard, K. A., and Anderson, J. L., 1987, Isotopic systematics of zircons from Late Cretaceous intrusive rocks, southeastern California; Implications for a vertically stratified crust: Geological Society of America Abstracts with Programs, v. 19, p. 898.

Young, E. D., and Wooden, J. L., 1988, Mid-crustal emplacement of Mesozoic granitoids, eastern Mojave Desert; Evidence from crystallization barometry: Geological Society of America Abstracts with Programs, v. 20, p. 244.

MANUSCRIPT SUBMITTED SEPTEMBER 8, 1988
REVISED MANUSCRIPT OCTOBER 13, 1988
MANUSCRIPT ACCEPTED BY THE SOCIETY FEBRUARY 7, 1989

Geological Society of America
Memoir 174
1990

Chapter 8

Extension-related Miocene volcanism
in the Mopah Range volcanic field,
southeastern California

Richard W. Hazlett
Department of Geology, Seaver Laboratory South, Pomona College, 609 North College Avenue, Claremont, California 91711-6339

ABSTRACT

The Mopah Range volcanic field lies near the western edge of the Whipple detachment fault terrane in southeastern California. The volcanic field formed in early Miocene time. In the Central Mopah Range, a lower succession of basalt-to-rhyolite lavas and tuffs, at least 700 m thick, is capped unconformably by a stack of basalt and andesite flows with a maximum thickness of 70 m. Sedimentary units, which thicken westward toward the crystalline highland of the Turtle Mountains, interfinger with volcanic units.

Normal faults with primarily down-to-the-east sense of motion dissect the Mopah Range. The concentration of faults is greater in the lower succession than in the capping succession. Dikes and faults are subparallel in mean surface trend, and show crosscutting relations indicating coeval development. These and other observations demonstrate that the Mopah Range volcanic field formed during detachment faulting. The type of volcanism is most likely to have been low-volume explosive eruptions, dome and dome-fed flow growth, and cinder cone activity at many small vents—similar to the activity described by Bacon and others (1981) in the Quaternary Coso Hills.

INTRODUCTION

One of the most extensive and best preserved volcanic terrains of the eastern Mojave Desert region is exposed in the Mopah Range, a part of the Turtle Mountains in southeastern California (Fig. 1). Volcanic activity in the Mopah Range occurred from 22.5 to 14.5 Ma, coeval with an episode of intensive magmatism that took place throughout the southern Cordillera in mid-Tertiary time (Keith, 1978; Glazner and Supplee, 1982). The Mopah Range volcanic field lies within the structural terrane of the Whipple detachment fault, which dips eastward and may die out under the Colorado Plateau (Davis and others, 1980; Howard and others, 1982). The Whipple detachment fault is exposed almost 15 km east of the volcanic field, along the margin of the Whipple Mountains core complex. The headwall of the detachment terrane lies under alluvium probably 10 to 30 km west of the volcanic field (Okaya and Frost, 1989). Evidence for synchronous formation of the detachment fault and volcanic activity

in the Mopah Range is presented below, together with a general overview of the stratigraphy, petrology, and character of this detachment-related volcanism.

The study area lies in the central Mopah Range, within an approximately 10-km radius of Mopah Peaks, a pair of topographically prominent plugs that dominate the skyline of the range. Near the northwestern base of the northernmost peak is Mopah Spring, a tiny oasis readily accessible by foot from the end of Mopah Spring Road (Figs. 1 and 2). These locations will be mentioned frequently in this article.

Mapping and sampling in the study area was done over a period of four months in 1983–1984, and was described in detail by Hazlett (1986). Not included in the study area are the northern and southern ends of the Mopah Range. Chesterman (1949), Embree (1967), and Nielson and Turner (1986) studied volcanic and intrusive rocks of the northern Mopah Range. Carr and

Hazlett, R. W., 1990, Extension-related Miocene volcanism in the Mopah Range volcanic field, southeastern California, *in* Anderson, J. L., ed., The nature and origin of Cordilleran magmatism: Boulder, Colorado, Geological Society of America Memoir 174.

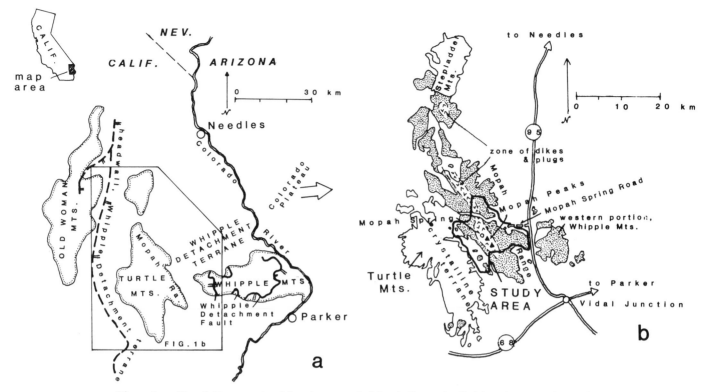

Figure 1. a: Mopah Range regional location map. b: Mopah Range detailed location map. Areas of mountainous basement rock exposure are outlined. Stippled pattern shows Miocene rocks, predominantly volcanic. "v" pattern shows zone of dikes and plugs at the core of the Mopah Range and in the adjoining Stepladder Mountains.

others (1980) mapped the southern end of the range in great detail. Howard and others (1982) provided a summary discussion of structure in the Turtle Mountains within the context of regional detachment faulting.

OBSERVATIONS

Dikes and plugs of the Mopah Range volcanic field are exposed in a zone trending about 25 km north-northwesterly along the eastern edge of the Turtle Mountains. This zone reaches a maximum width of about 3 km in the vicinity of Mopah Peaks (Fig. 2). Volcanic rocks that may be directly associated with the Mopah Range volcanic field cover an area of about 170 km². These volcanic rocks are deposited on a basement comprising Proterozoic intrusive and metamorphic rocks, intruded by small Cretaceous granitoid plutons (Howard and others, 1982; Allen, 1986). Paleozoic and Mesozoic sedimentary rocks are found elsewhere in the region, but none are preserved in the Mopah Range. A nonconformity found at the base of a Tertiary volcanic section, as seen in the Mopah Range, is a common relation throughout much of southern California.

The base of the Mopah Range volcanic section is exposed only at the northern end of the volcanic field. There the section has a total thickness of between 700 and 1,000 m (Embree, 1967;

Nielson and Turner, 1986). Near Mopah Spring, about 800 m of section is exposed, representing a minimum stratigraphic thickness for this area (Fig. 3). Carr and others (1980) estimated the volcanic section in the southern Mopah Range to be as much as 500 m thick.

Most of the volcanic section comprises dacitic and andesitic lava flows, flow breccias, pyroclastic deposits, and related volcaniclastic rocks, with minor alkali olivine-basalt and rhyolite lavas, arkoses, and nonvolcanic breccia conglomerates. This mix of rock types, hereafter referred to as the "lower section," is capped unconformably by a homogeneous-appearing stack of andesite and basalt lavas, hereafter referred to as the "capping section."

Stratigraphy of the Mopah Range volcanic section is very complex, and only generalized in the description to follow. Many rock units are of irregular geometry. Breccias and stacks of lava flows, in particular, show great lateral variation in thickness. Small, isolated sedimentary and volcanic bodies that cannot be correlated stratigraphically with larger units are common throughout the section. A complex network of faults greatly disrupts the volcanic field, further complicating the interpretation of its stratigraphy. These features are illustrated in Figure 2, which portrays the geology in the central Mopah Range. The volcanic section is exposed most completely in the western part of this area, especially around Mopah Spring.

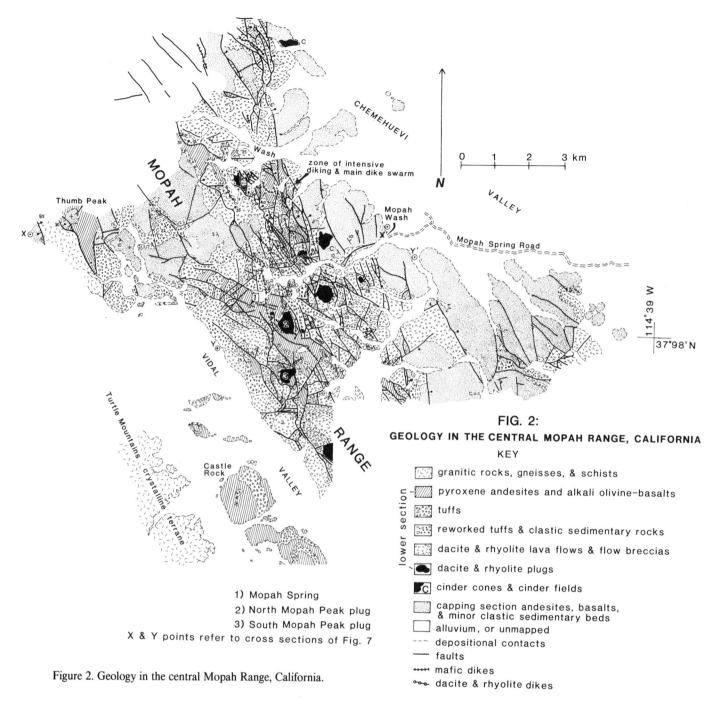

FIG. 2:

GEOLOGY IN THE CENTRAL MOPAH RANGE, CALIFORNIA

KEY

lower section

- granitic rocks, gneisses, & schists
- pyroxene andesites and alkali olivine–basalts
- tuffs
- reworked tuffs & clastic sedimentary rocks
- dacite & rhyolite lava flows & flow breccias
- dacite & rhyolite plugs
- cinder cones & cinder fields
- capping section andesites, basalts, & minor clastic sedimentary beds
- alluvium, or unmapped
- - - depositional contacts
- —— faults
- ++++ mafic dikes
- ooo dacite & rhyolite dikes

1) Mopah Spring
2) North Mopah Peak plug
3) South Mopah Peak plug

X & Y points refer to cross sections of Fig. 7

Figure 2. Geology in the central Mopah Range, California.

Description of units

Figure 3 portrays major stratigraphic units exposed in the Mopah Spring area, divided into lower and capping sections. The lowermost exposed unit is a white pumiceous tuff of a few meters minimum thickness. The tuff is overlain by a 300-m-thick stack of lava flows composed primarily of andesite, but also including alkali olivine-basalt flows. The andesite is characterized by conspicuous, abundant, blocky phenocrysts of black augite and randomly oriented laths of plagioclase that range in size from a few

millimeters to as much as a half centimeter in diameter. Vesicles and veins are common, and many are filled with blue to clear agate or dark-green secondary celadonite. Some celadonitic masses enclose cores of bluish silica. Alkali olivine-basalt flows are nearly aphyric, with sparse olivine phenocrysts that rarely exceed a few millimeters in size.

Stacks of andesite and basalt flows similar to those seen in outcrop at Mopah Spring are widespread in the terrane of the lower section. At some localities, the exposed lower section consists almost entirely of these lavas. A flow stack at least 280 m

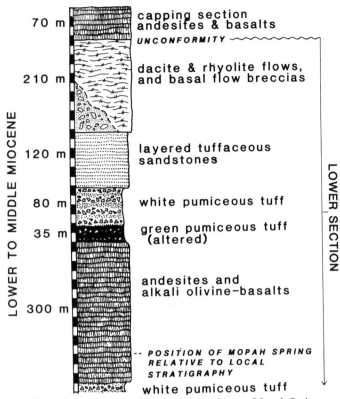

Figure 3. Stratigraphy of nonintrusive units near Mopah Spring.

thick forms the lower slopes of Thumb Peak (Fig. 2). A section of similar thickness crops out along Gary Wash, near the western limit of the study area. The andesitic flow stack forming the base of Castle Rock (Fig. 2) is at least 170 m thick. A thick stack of flows, some of which are lithologically indistinguishable from those at Mopah Spring, also crops out as a Tertiary erosional remnant in Fortification Canyon, at the southern end of the Turtle Mountains. This erosional outlier lies about 22 km from the section at Mopah Spring.

Overlying the andesite and basalt flows near Mopah Spring is poorly welded, white to green crystal-lithic pumiceous tuff of dacitic composition (Fig. 3). This pyroclastic unit has undergone secondary celandonitic mineralization near its contact with the subjacent lavas. The basal altered zone is green; celadonitization is concentrated in the matrix of the tuff. Clasts of both mafic and silicic lavas, as much as several meters across, are entrained within the tuff. The tuff is about 115 m thick in the section at Mopah Spring. This is the thickest pyroclastic layer yet reported in the Mopah Range. Nielson and Turner (1986) mentioned a 50- to 75-m-thick deposit of similar appearance in the northern Mopah Range. Carr and others (1980) described a crystal-lithic tuff layer "a few tens of meters" thick at the southern end of the range. Because multiple tuff units of similar lithology occur throughout the Mopah Range, it is possible that not all these documented thicknesses pertain to the same stratigraphic unit.

The upper contact of the tuff exposed near Mopah Spring is gradational with overlying tuffaceous sandstones, showing evidence of sedimentary reworking. The overlying layered tuffaceous sandstones contain rare clasts of basement crystalline rock. The concentrations and sizes of basement clasts in the tuffaceous sandstones increase westward from Mopah Spring, in the direction of the Turtle Mountains crystalline terrane (Fig. 2). Near the western edge of the volcanic field, the sandstones grade into a breccia conglomerate several hundred meters thick and rich in clasts of granitic rock, gneisses, and schists. Many of these clasts bear close resemblance to locally occurring basement rocks.

Overlying the tuffaceous sedimentary beds near Mopah Spring is a set of pinkish-red to gray, cliff-forming dacitic lava flows. Flows of similar composition compose most of the exposures where the lower section crops out in the eastern and northern parts of the study area (Fig. 2). Individual lava flows range in thickness from 10 m to as much as 100 m. Each flow is divided into two components; a solid core underlain by a pad of flow breccia. Any given flow breccia is usually less regular in thickness and thinner than its associated overlying flow core. A conspicuous layer of black vitrophyre less than a few meters thick typically lies at the base of each flow core.

Throughout the central Mopah Range, the dacitic and much less abundant rhyolitic lavas and tuffs share a common phenocryst mineralogy, typically including, in order of abundance, plagioclase, hornblende, biotite, zircon, apatite, and sphene. Vitrophyres may also contain spherulites. Together with the stratigraphically associated andesites and basalts, these lower section rocks compose a suite that ranges from as low as 45 wt.% silica to more than 75 wt.% (Table 1, Fig. 4). There is no evident "silica gap" as observed in other coeval volcanic suites of the southern Basin and Range (e.g., Smith, 1982; Suneson and Luchitta, 1983). Although the augite-bearing andesitic and hornblende-biotite phyric dacitic-rhyolitic rocks of the lower section are petrographically distinct, they overlap slightly in composition. Hence, as shown in Figure 5, some rocks identifiable on the basis of phenocrysts, color, texture, and structure as part of the dacitic suite lie in the high-silica portion of the andesite field. One sample (#26, Table 1) associated with the augite-bearing andesites at Mopah Spring lies within the dacite compositional field.

On a plot of SiO_2 vs. $FeO^*/FeO^* + MgO$, the lower-section volcanics straddle the boundary between tholeiitic and calc-alkalic (Fig. 6). The Peacock index is around 55, which characterizes the section as alkali calcic. The section is also highly potassic (Fig. 5). Whereas K-metasomatism is a common form of alteration in Tertiary volcanics throughout this region (Glazner, 1986), there is no strong petrographic evidence that it occurred in the Mopah Range: flows are not coursed with reddened, potassium-enriched veins, and electron microprobe analyses of plagioclase from dacites and rhyolites show no replacement by secondary potassic phases, including sericite or adularia (Hazlett, 1986). K_2O/Na_2O is close to 1 for most samples of siliceous lavas (Table 1), a value Suneson and Luchitta (1983) considered typical for unaltered rhyolites in this region. Low-grade K-metasomatism could explain the high potash content (3.7 wt.%)

Figure 4. Table 1 specimen location map (base map from U.S. Geological Survey Rice 15-minute topographic quadrangle).

of one analyzed alkalic basalt from the lower section (Sample 23, Table 1).

Capping-section andesites and basalts occur as dark stacks of flows forming flat mesa surfaces, steplike mountainsides, or dip slopes on fault-bounded cuestas. The remnants of at least two cinder cones are preserved within these flows (Flow 2). In hand sample, capping-section lavas tend to be darker, more vesicular, less weathered, and much finer grained than the andesites found at Mopah Spring. Celadonitic mineralization does not occur in capping-section flows, although calcite is a widespread product of hydrothermal activity. Phenocrysts are inconspicuous in many hand samples. A typical assemblage of phenocrysts, in order of abundance, includes plagioclase, forsteritic olivine, clinopyroxene, apatite, sparse opaque oxides, and sparse altered hydrous

TABLE 1. WHOLE-ROCK COMPOSITIONS OF VOLCANIC ROCKS FROM THE MOPAH RANGE
(Specimen localities given in Fig. 4)

A. LAVAS ASSOCIATED WITH LOWER SECTION BASALTIC AND ANDESITIC FLOW STACKS

Specimen	23	48	37	27	35	39	54	26
SiO_2	45.24	53.1	55.69	55.9	56.86	61.3	62.2	64.4
Al_2O_3	15.9	15.9	18.2	15.7	17.7	15.4	16.8	16.0
Fe_2O_3	0.91	0.34	0.67	0.36	0.53	0.5	0.41	0.39
FeO	8.18	3.03	5.97	2.97	4.75	4.2	3.68	3.47
MgO	6.7	4.15	3.2	3.44	3.1	1.07	1.05	1.17
CaO	10.65	8.12	6.23	6.24	5.45	3.87	4.42	3.01
Na_2O	3.03	3.37	4.94	3.33	4.37	4.12	4.09	3.68
K_2O	3.71	1.64	3.28	3.4	3.36	3.64	2.87	4.28
TiO_2	1.63	1.55	1.15	1.21	0.88	0.9	0.73	0.7
P_2O_5	1.0	0.34	0.42	0.59	0.39	0.36	0.32	0.21
MnO	0.13	0.14	0.11	0.1	0.08	0.08	0.02	0.06
Total	97.08	91.68	99.86	93.24	97.47	95.44	96.59	97.37
A/CNK	0.560	0.719	0.790	0.765	0.8526	0.866	0.939	0.989
$Fe^*/(Fe^*+Mg)$	0.576	0.448	0.675	0.492	0.630	0.815	0.796	0.767

B. ROCKS FROM AREAS DOMINATED BY LOWER SECTION DACITES AND RHYOLITES

Specimen	36	47	49	38	32	30	31	3	19	13	53	40
SiO_2	60.5	61.5	62.0	62.17	62.25	62.25	63.0	64.9	65.0	65.2	65.3	65.9
Al_2O_3	14.5	16.9	16.1	17.0	17.3	17.2	14.9	15.6	14.7	16.0	15.3	14.5
Fe_2O_3	0.39	0.27	0.31	0.36	0.35	0.35	0.32	0.38	0.35	0.40	0.24	0.25
FeO	3.53	2.42	2.74	3.27	3.26	3.15	2.87	3.46	3.15	3.55	2.17	2.21
MgO	1.68	1.06	1.21	0.85	0.86	1.06	1.44	0.88	0.87	0.88	0.87	1.00
CaO	3.99	1.91	3.15	2.96	3.19	3.47	4.9	3.47	2.91	3.26	3.12	2.89
Na_2O	2.29	4.48	4.21	4.98	5.13	4.75	3.39	3.95	4.12	4.47	3.99	3.11
K_2O	3.99	4.48	4.59	4.75	4.6	4.36	4.37	3.8	3.56	3.7	4.73	4.29
TiO_2	0.66	0.43	0.49	0.65	0.61	0.59	0.54	0.65	0.72	0.86	0.38	0.39
P_2O_5	0.15	0.18	0.35	0.34	0.27	0.32	0.21	0.35	0.32	0.24	0.12	0.13
MnO	0.03	0.04	0.06	0.04	0.06	0.05	0.05	0.04	0.04	0.03	0.05	0.04
Total	91.71	94.67	95.21	97.37	97.81	97.55	95.09	97.48	95.86	98.59	96.27	94.71
A/CNK	0.944	0.964	0.912	0.908	0.899	0.911	0.816	0.921	0.922	0.925	0.880	0.965
$Fe^*/(Fe^*+Mg)$	0.700	0.717	0.716	0.810	0.808	0.781	0.689	0.814	0.806	0.818	0.735	0.711

TABLE 1. WHOLE-ROCK COMPOSITIONS OF VOLCANIC ROCKS FROM THE MOPAH RANGE* (continued)

B. ROCKS FROM AREAS DOMINATED BY LOWER SECTION DACITES AND RHYOLITES (continued)

Specimen	45	51	22	52	10	20	42	29	43	8	12
SiO_2	66.15	66.5	66.6	66.7	66.8	66.8	66.90	67.0	67.3	68.0	68.2
Al_2O_3	16.1	15.5	13.5	13.5	15.1	14.8	13.8	14.5	14.1	15.0	14.8
Fe_2O_3	0.25	0.35	0.23	0.18	0.25	0.24	0.21	0.36	0.24	0.26	0.22
FeO	2.20	3.14	2.06	1.60	2.27	2.15	1.91	3.19	2.11	2.33	1.99
MgO	0.89	0.61	0.81	0.72	0.96	0.90	0.75	1.05	0.88	0.66	0.76
CaO	2.46	2.96	1.99	2.24	2.57	2.68	2.03	2.64	2.53	2.91	2.12
Na_2O	4.14	3.40	3.52	2.37	3.50	3.22	3.55	3.55	3.04	4.19	3.51
K_2O	5.21	3.99	4.36	5.25	4.11	4.46	4.25	3.81	4.47	3.89	4.72
TiO_2	0.38	0.57	0.37	0.30	0.45	0.41	0.34	0.42	0.36	0.53	0.40
P_2O_5	0.21	0.17	0.23	0.09	0.12	0.13	0.24	0.14	0.12	0.14	0.10
MnO	0.04	0.02	0.04	0.03	0.04	0.04	0.04	0.04	0.04	0.04	0.03
Total	98.03	97.21	94.11	92.98	96.17	95.83	94.02	96.70	95.19	97.96	96.85
A/CNK	0.950	1.012	0.955	0.987	1.013	0.986	0.975	0.982	0.975	0.913	1.003
$Fe^*/(Fe^*+Mg)$	0.734	0.851	0.739	0.712	0.724	0.724	0.774	0.755	0.728	0.797	0.744

Specimen	14	11	10	41	7	9	46	15	5
SiO_2	68.5	68.5	68.6	68.70	69.1	69.9	70.4	71.5	75.7
Al_2O_3	1.42	15.2	15.4	13.7	14.0	14.4	14.3	14.0	11.1
Fe_2O_3	0.18	0.26	0.25	0.23	0.17	0.18	0.18	0.14	0.14
FeO	1.65	2.33	2.27	2.03	1.50	1.58	1.66	1.25	1.28
MgO	0.70	0.67	0.67	0.80	0.67	0.57	0.41	0.41	0.61
CaO	1.73	2.60	2.41	2.04	2.41	1.60	1.58	1.18	1.47
Na_2O	3.13	3.98	4.17	3.46	4.17	3.59	4.10	3.12	2.75
K_2O	4.96	3.87	3.94	4.37	3.94	4.66	4.48	5.56	3.12
TiO_2	0.34	0.46	0.52	0.38	0.52	0.32	0.35	0.26	0.27
P_2O_5	0.097	0.13	0.13	0.17	0.06	0.07	0.08	0.05	0.06
MnO	0.03	0.02	0.02	0.05	0.03	0.03	0.05	0.03	0.02
Total	95.49	98.02	98.38	95.93	96.57	96.90	97.59	97.50	96.52
A/CNK	1.034	0.982	0.992	0.968	0.902	1.038	0.988	1.052	1.047
$Fe^*/(Fe^*+Mg)$	0.723	0.795	0.788	0.737	0.714	0.755	0.818	0.772	0.700

TABLE 1. WHOLE-ROCK COMPOSITIONS OF VOLCANIC ROCKS FROM THE MOPAH RANGE* (continued)

C. CAPPING SECTION LAVAS

Specimen	16	24	4	2	25	34	33	18	17	1	21	50	44	28
SiO_2	44.5	45.65	46.31	47.1	49.9	50.3	50.7	53.5	54.5	54.9	56.0	56.6	57.2	57.78
Al_2O_3	13.0	18.24	17.0	16.7	17.52	14.5	15.6	16.3	15.3	15.3	15.7	16.5	15.0	18.3
Fe_2O_3	1.01	1.11	1.05	0.97	0.92	0.86	0.87	0.78	0.73	0.69	0.73	0.68	0.68	0.55
FeO	8.17	9.99	9.45	8.71	8.24	7.74	7.77	6.97	6.53	6.23	6.58	6.15	6.05	4.97
MgO	6.02	5.62	7.37	7.70	5.18	5.29	5.84	4.34	4.60	4.68	4.26	3.14	2.91	2.02
CaO	13.4	10.96	10.2	9.04	9.8	9.89	9.06	7.46	7.74	8.11	7.29	6.24	6.41	4.82
Na_2O	2.50	3.68	3.57	3.40	3.56	2.95	2.93	3.25	3.02	3.42	3.03	3.98	3.69	4.89
K_2O	2.00	1.24	1.42	1.51	2.18	2.14	2.08	2.58	2.63	2.23	2.92	2.85	3.16	4.05
TiO_2	1.59	1.58	1.65	1.56	1.32	1.27	1.47	1.38	1.25	1.11	1.28	1.22	1.27	1.05
P_2O_5	0.93	0.28	0.12	0.54	0.58	0.71	0.53	0.49	0.46	0.53	0.48	0.50	0.56	0.50
MnO	0.13	0.16	0.05	0.14	0.14	0.14	0.12	0.11	0.10	0.11	0.10	0.11	0.11	0.10
Total	93.15	98.51	98.19	97.37	99.34	95.79	96.97	97.16	96.86	97.31	98.37	97.97	97.03	99.03
A/CNK	0.424	0.667	0.665	0.707	0.679	0.573	0.662	0.753	0.698	0.670	0.733	0.789	0.708	0.860
Fe*/(Fe*+Mg)	0.601	0.664	0.588	0.554	0.639	0.619	0.597	0.641	0.612	0.597	0.632	0.685	0.698	0.732

D. SPECIMEN TRACE ELEMENT CHEMISTRY

Specimen Number	Ba	Nb	Rb	Sr	Zr	Y
23 (lsm)*	2021	13	46	1324	267	27
37 (lsm)	1660	15	58	626	301	24
35 (lsm)	1346	14	87	984	249	19
47 (lsf)	1571	5	100	812	189	12
49 (lsf)	1189	13	117	565	209	19
38 (lsf)	1430	14	108	486	323	20
32 (lsf)	1565	18	110	494	325	20
30 (lsf)	1207	8	95	616	239	17
53 (lsf)	1038	12	131	443	187	20
45 (lsf)	1027	12	134	408	184	19
24 (cs)	582	4	13	566	158	31
4 (cs)	523	7	24	456	183	26
2 (cs)	604	14	25	577	206	28
25 (cs)	1277	5	31	971	182	25
28 (cs)	1264	15	73	706	273	33

*lsm = lower section andesites and basalts.

lsf = lower section dacites and rhyolites.

cs = capping section lavas.

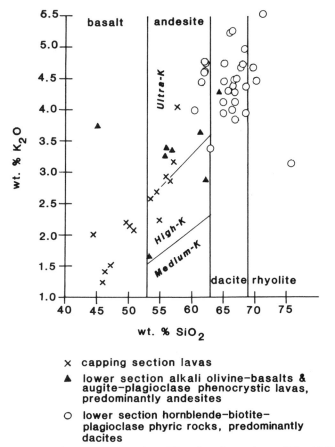

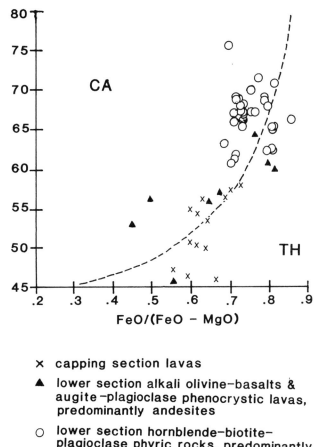

x capping section lavas

▲ lower section alkali olivine–basalts &
   augite–plagioclase phenocrystic lavas,
   predominantly andesites

○ lower section hornblende–biotite-
   plagioclase phyric rocks, predominantly
   dacites

(andesite K-classification based on Gill, 1981)

Figure 5. SiO$_2$ vs. K$_2$O, Mopah Range volcanic suite (analyses given in Table 1).

x capping section lavas

▲ lower section alkali olivine–basalts &
   augite–plagioclase phenocrystic lavas,
   predominantly andesites

○ lower section hornblende–biotite-
   plagioclase phyric rocks, predominantly
   dacites

Figure 6. SiO$_2$ vs. FeO/(FeO+MgO), Mopah Range volcanic suite (analyses given in Table 1).

silicates, especially biotite. Capping section lavas span a silica range of 45.6 to 57.8 wt.% SiO$_2$ (Table 1), and are potassium rich, like the lower section volcanics. The elevated K$_2$O + Na$_2$O content of the lavas may be characterized as alkalic to subalkalic.

All seven plugs exposed in the lower section of the central Mopah Range, including Mopah Peaks (Fig. 2), are petrographically similar to the dacitic and rhyolitic extrusive rocks of the lower section, and therefore may be associated with their eruption. The northern Mopah Peak shows a joint pattern that may be primary and characteristic of other, less well-exposed plugs in the Mopah Range. Near the base of the plug this jointing is crudely displayed and nearly vertical. The joint pattern is more easily discerned in the upper part of the plug, where it gradually fans outward (Fig. 7).

Whereas most plugs are intermediate to siliceous in composition, about 75% of the approximately 12 km of exposed dikes in the central Mopah Range is made up of mafic rock similar in composition to capping-section lavas (Fig. 2). The continuation of these dikes to high levels in the stratigraphic section, up to but not through the capping section, is further evidence for their association with capping-section volcanism. Most dikes strike

north-northwesterly in a crudely linear swarm, coincident with the overall trend of the volcanic field (Fig. 2). Small, short radial dikes feed off the northern Mopah Peak and a few other plugs, but most plugs lack sets of radial dikes.

Structure

The pattern of faults shown in Figure 2 seems to represent a structurally chaotic terrane, though one significant feature may be clearly seen; the density of faulting is greater in the landscape of the lower section relative to areas underlain by the capping section. Fault traces, like dikes, generally bear northwesterly, subparallel to the overall trend of the volcanic field (Fig. 8).

Because of erosion and poor exposure, dips could be measured directly on only a few fault planes. Three-point solutions were attempted on other faults, the majority in a zone of intensive faulting between Mopah and Gary washes. Only ten complete attitudes could be measured with certainty (Fig. 8). These show a consistent pattern of eastward-dippling slip surfaces. Displacements on certainly most, and probably all of these faults are normal.

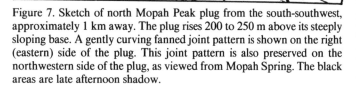

Figure 7. Sketch of north Mopah Peak plug from the south-southwest, approximately 1 km away. The plug rises 200 to 250 m above its steeply sloping base. A gently curving fanned joint pattern is shown on the right (eastern) side of the plug. This joint pattern is also preserved on the northwestern side of the plug, as viewed from Mopah Spring. The black areas are late afternoon shadow.

ers, 1982; Okaya and Frost, 1989). Hence, faulting in the Mopah Range may be attributed to brittle extension of an upper plate during extensional faulting. Down-to-the-east normal faulting and southwestward rotation of strata in fault blocks are consistent with upper-plate deformation observed elsewhere in the Whipple detachment fault terrane. Attitudes of faults in the Mopah Range are also consistent with the original azimuth of extension, defined as the bearings of lines drawn at right angles to upper-plate normal faults of the Whipple detachment fault in the Whipple Mountains (Fig. 8; Davis and others, 1980).

The greater density of faults in the lower section than in the capping section of the volcanic field indicates that much of the fault pattern must have formed during or after deposition of the lower section, but before deposition of the capping section. New faults continued to form for an unknown time after capping-section volcanism ended. Also significant is the fact that almost as many dikes cut faults as faults displace dikes in the central Mopah Range. This evidence supports a history of volcanism (22.5 to 14.5 Ma) occurring simultaneously with detachment faulting. The angular unconformity separating lower- and capping-section volcanics represents a hiatus in deposition during progressive, primarily southwestward tilting of faulted strata. The lower sec-

Figure 9 shows east-west cross-sections through the volcanic field, illustrating a pattern of faults that is largely inferred from truncation of strata. The general sense of fault movement appears to be down-to-the-east. In the zone of intensive faulting, shown in the right portion of the lower cross section, this displacement amounts to about 500 m across a distance of less than 2 km.

This fault zone (Fig. 9) also corresponds to the area of the main dike swarm transecting the volcanic field. The means of the surface trends of dikes and faults are roughly similar throughout the volcanic field (cf. Figs. 6 and 10). About 10 percent of the total length of exposed dikes is intruded along faults. Elsewhere, of some 60 mapped dike-fault intersections, about half are dikes crossing faults, and half are faults displacing dikes (Hazlett, 1986).

Also represented in Figure 9 is the general attitude of bedding throughout the volcanic field. Capping-section lavas and units of the lower section west of the crest of the Mopah Range dip southwestward. Furthermore, the lower and capping sections are separated by angular unconformity. This unconformity may be plainly seen in the crestal area of the Mopah Range (lower cross section, Fig. 9). There, lower-section strata dip as much as 25°, whereas capping-section flows dip at most only 5 to 10°. East of the crest of the Mopah Range, bedding-plane orientations in the lower section are highly variable (Figs. 2 and 9). This variability could be a result of deposition of bedding, especially of air-fall or pyroclastic flow ejecta, as mantle layers across an irregular initial topography.

DISCUSSION

The Whipple detachment fault and/or related décollements underlie the Mopah Range at unknown depth (Howard and oth-

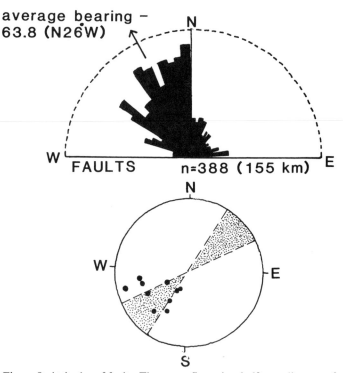

Figure 8. Attitudes of faults. The upper figure is a half-rose diagram of the trends of fault traces throughout the central Mopah Range. Three hundred eighty-eight bearings were taken by averaging the trend of each fault visually along 0.4-km-long segments. About 155 km of faults, virtually the entire network in the study area, were measured in this way. The lower figure shows lower-hemisphere pole projections of faults for which strike and dip could be measured, either directly or by rule of v's. The hachured zone shows the approximate regional azimuth of extension, inferred from the trends of normal fault traces in the upper plate of the Whipple detachment fault in the Whipple Mountains.

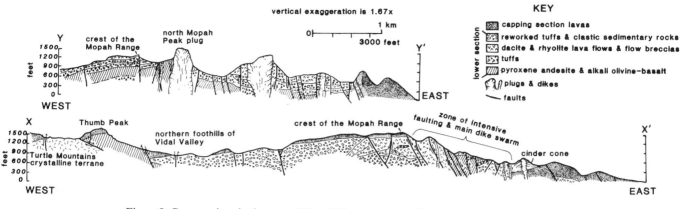

Figure 9. Cross sections in the central Mopah Range (endpoint locations are given in Fig. 3).

tion dips more steeply than the capping section because it was subjected to a longer interval of strain.

The same extensional stresses that led to faulting should have influenced the pattern by which magma reached the surface, and perhaps even the style of volcanism to follow. In an ideal situation, dikes in an extensional regime should develop in a plane parallel to the maximum principal stress direction, and normal to the direction of greatest principal strain (Anderson, 1942; Nakamura and Uyeda, 1980). Faults should form in a conjugate or single set at a constant acute angle to the dike plane. This ideal case is not well illustrated in the Mopah Range. Surface trends of faults and dikes generally coincide, however, although most dikes are high-angle intrusions, some dip eastward, and in many outcrops, contacts are irregular or curviplanar. Faults also show a wide variation in dips (Fig. 6). A complex relation between stress, faults, and dikes is indicated; individual localities show evidence for somewhat unique conditions in this relation. Nevertheless, because of the evidence for coeval origin and the similar surface trends of dikes and faults, it is reasonable to assume that the regional stresses that led to faulting influenced the pattern of intrusion in the volcanic field as well.

The coincidence of the dike swarm in the central Mopah Range with a zone of intensive faulting (Figs. 2 and 9) suggests at least two possibilities: (1) the dikes may have selectively reached the surface through a previously formed and still developing zone of intensive faulting. In other words, the dikes found a ready path to the surface through an extensional fault system that would have shown the same level of structural complexity had no magmatism occured. This is a form of the "passive upwelling" model, favored by many workers in the Basin and Range (e.g., Lachenbruch and Sass, 1978). (2) The dike swarm may have served to thermally weaken "ordinary" previously faulted crust in such a way that additional faulting occurred there more easily than elsewhere in the region. In other words, much of the structural complexity and offset of the zone of intensive faulting shown in Figures 2 and 9 resulted from the intrusion of the dikes. Intensive faulting may have continued in the area of the dikes after their emplacement as a function of the time it took for the crust to cool.

This model may be favored because of the observation that fracturing and normal faulting often accompany the intrusion of dike swarms; for example, in Iceland and Hawaii. Walker (1986) showed evidence for the occurrence of normal faulting due to slip along active dikes in a rift zone of Koolau volcano. If such fracturing occurred in the stress environment of regional, subvolcanic detachment faulting, the result might closely resemble that of the faulting dike swarm in the Mopah Range.

The mechanics for eruption in the Mopah Range volcanic field can be inferred by looking at the pattern of dikes and faults from a different perspective. No concentric ring-fracture system, suggestive of caldera collapse, is evident in the Mopah Range. The dikes there do not occur in great radial arrays, as is typical of large composite cones eroded deeply enough to expose their plugs (Hyndman and Alt, 1987). Stratigraphically, evidence of these two types of volcanic structures is also lacking. The thickest tuff beds in the Mopah Range are much thinner than the pyroclastic infill sequences of Tertiary calderas seen elsewhere in the southern Cordillera (Lipman, 1984). No pyroclastic outflow or caldera wall breccia units have been identified. The thinly interbedded flow, cinder, and tuff sequences characteristic of composite cones are also lacking. Though impressively large, the north Mopah Peak plug, if an eruptive conduit, probably fed a dome. The

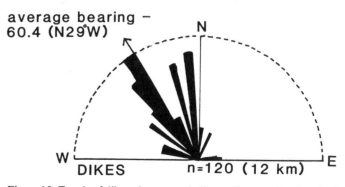

Figure 10. Trends of dikes, shown as a half-rose diagram. One hundred twenty bearings were taken by visually averaging the map trend of each dike along 100 m segments. About 12 km of dikes, virtually the entire network in the study area, were measured in this way.

fanned joint pattern (Fig. 7) at the top of the plug is observed in many endogenous domes viewed in cross section (Macdonald, 1972).

The development of domes may be conceived as a three-stage process, beginning with explosive clearing of a vent as magma first reaches the surface. This stage is accompanied by pyroclastic eruptions, which may form a low cone around a vent. In the second stage, after initial loss of volatiles, a dome is extruded into the crater, enclosing the vent. The third stage consists of lateral spreading of the dome; in an advanced form, feeding lengthy coulee lava flows such as at Mono Craters and in the Medicine Lake Highland of California. In the Mopah Peaks and Mopah Spring are, tuffs and tuff breccias underlie thick flows of dacitic lava. Perhaps these tuffs originated during initial stages of dome development in this area, to be overlain by the dacite flows as dome growth progressed.

If most plugs in the Mopah Range represent the roots of domes, then the Mopah Range volcanic field during the time of lower-section volcanism may be pictured as a field of domes and coulee flows and related pyroclastic ejecta and breccias. Mafic to intermediate volcanism occurred in the volcanic field throughout lower-section times, and exclusively during eruptions of the capping section. Partial preservation of cinder cones in the capping section indicate the character of at least some of the venting that accompanied the last stage of mafic activity.

A contemporary analog of the Mopah Range volcanic field might be the volcanism described by Bacon and others (1981) in the Coso Hills, 350 km northwest of the Mopah Range. There, rhyolitic and dacitic domes and basaltic cinder cones are concentrated in an area measuring approximately 25 × 30 km, evidently a much larger volcanic field than once existed in the Mopah Range. Bacon and others (1981) postulated that the extensional crustal regime in the Coso Hills inhibits development of a large magma chamber at shallow depth with a structurally simple conduit extending to the surface, as might underlie a large composite cone or incipient caldera. Instead, deep normal faulting and other forms of extension trigger injection of magma into shallow crustal levels as numerous dikes. Volatile pressures in the magma supply are reduced through diking events, many of which feed relatively small-volume eruptions, including the extrusion of isolated domes. Not only are volatile pressures reduced through dikes, but Bacon and others (1981) believed that the main volume of intermediate to silicic magma lies so deep beneath the Coso Hills that levels of volatile supersaturation required for catastrophic, caldera-forming ash-flow eruption are unattainable; hence this magma is extruded principally as lava flows. Certainly intermediate to silicic lava flows are more abundant than tuffs in the Mopah Range, consistent with this line of reasoning.

Major-element compositional data and lithology, discussed above, and trace-element analyses, discussed in Hazlett (1986), suggest that at least three or four magma lineages are represented in the volcanic rocks of the Mopah Range. At least two discrete magmas erupted coevally during the time of formation of the lower section, developing the augite-bearing andesitic and hornblende-biotite dacitic to rhyolitic suites. Lower-section alkali olivine-basalts may represent their own melt—a third lower-section lineage—unrelated to the parent magma of the andesites with which they are interbedded. The capping-section lavas represent the last eruptive magma type. Of course, much additional work is required to develop a detailed petrogenetic model.

The nonvolcanic sedimentary rocks in the western part of the Mopah Range volcanic field are almost certainly derived from the adjoining basement terrane. Hence, a high area probably existed in the crystalline part of the Turtle Mountains in early Miocene time, perhaps persisting there continuously ever since. The wedgelike shape, coarse clastic texture, and massive structure of the sedimentary strata at the western edge of the volcanic field may represent talus cones and small steep fans, probably related to an active range-front fault bounding the basement highland. Several northwesterly striking faults are exposed in the basement terrane (Howard and others, 1980), but due to erosion, none of these can be related explicitly to Miocene sedimentation.

CONCLUSIONS

Volcanic activity in the Mopah Range from 22.5 to 14.5 Ma produced a succession of potassium-rich alkali-calcic andesites, dacites, and rhyolites, with interbedded alkali olivine-basalts, capped unconformably by alkalic to subalkalic andesites and basalts. These volcanic rocks were probably erupted from many small vents; no evidence exists to suggest the development of a large caldera or composite cone during volcanism. Sedimentary units within the volcanic pile were derived locally. Numerous faults of northwest-southeast mean orientation dissect the volcanic pile. Normal faults predominate, dropping strata down to the east. The concentration of faults and westward tilting of strata are greater in the lower section of the volcanic sequence than in the capping section. The surface trends of dikes and faults suggest that both sets of structures formed under the same conditions of stress. Crosscutting relations demonstrate that dikes and faults are coeval. These observations indicate that the Mopah Range volcanic field is an example of mid-Tertiary magmatism occurring during a time of crustal extension attributed to low-angle detachment faulting.

ACKNOWLEDGMENTS

Support for this study was provided by the U.S. Geological Survey Branch of Western Regional Geology, Menlo Park, especially through J. E. Nielson, and by National Science Foundation Grant EAR 81-20880 (to J. Lawford Anderson). Stan Keith of Magmachem Incorporated provided trace-element analyses given in Table 1, Part D. Work was completed both as part of a wilderness study for the Bureau of Land Management, and as a Ph.D. dissertation at the University of Southern California. I acknowledge J. Lawford Anderson, James Lee Anderson, K. A. Howard, and J. E. Nielson for helpful initial reviews and discussions pertaining to this manuscript, and Gerhard Ott of Pomona College for his valuable technical assistance.

REFERENCES CITED

Allen, C. M., 1986, Rb-Sr pseudochron; The result of mixing in a reversely-zoned, calc-alkaline pluton, Turtle Mountains, S. E. California: Geological Society of America Abstracts with Programs, v. 18, p. 81.

Anderson, E. M., 1942, Dynamics of faulting and dyke formation with application to Britain: Edinburgh, Oliver and Boyd, 206 p.

Bacon, C. R., Macdonald, R., Smith, R. L., and Baedecker, P. A., 1981, Pleistocene high-silica rhyolites of the Coso volcanic field, Inyo County, California: Journal of Geophysical Research, v. 86, p. 10223–10241.

Carr, W. J., Dickey, D. D., and Quinlivin, W. D., 1980, Geologic map of the Vidal NW, Vidal Junction, and parts of the Savahia Peak quadrangles, San Bernardino County, California: U.S. Geological Survey Miscellaneous Investigations Series Map I–1126, scale 1:24,000.

Chesterman, C. W., 1949, Dike complex in the Turtle Mountains, eastern San Bernardino County, California [abs.]: Geological Society of America Bulletin, v. 60, p. 1927.

Davis, G. A., Anderson, J. L., Frost, E. G., and Shackelford, T. J., 1980, Mylonitization and detachment faulting in the Whipple–Buckskin–Rawhide mountains terrane, southeastern California: Geological Society of America Memoir 153, p. 79–129.

Embree, G., 1967, Geology of a portion of the Turtle Mountains Quadrangle, San Diego County, California [Senior thesis]: San Diego, California, San Diego State College, 40 p.

Glazner, A. F., 1986, Stratigraphy, structure, and potassic alterations of Miocene volcanic rocks in the Sleeping Beauty area, central Mojave Desert, *in* Nielson, J. E., and Glazner, A. F., eds., Cenozoic stratigraphy in the Mojave Desert; Trip 5, Geological Society of America Cordilleran Section Meeting Fieldtrip Guidebook: Los Angeles, California State University Department of Geology, p. 51–64.

Glazner, A. F., and Supplee, J. A., 1982, Migration of Tertiary volcanism in the southwestern United States and subduction of the Mendocino fracture zone: Earth and Planetary Science Letters, v. 60, p. 429–436.

Hazlett, R. W., 1986, Geology of a Tertiary volcanic center, Mopah Range, San Bernardino County, California [Ph.D. thesis]: Los Angeles, University of Southern California, 303 p.

Howard, K. A., Stone, P., Pernokas, M. A., and Marvin, R. F., 1982, Geologic and geochronologic reconnaissance of the Turtle Mountains area, California; West border of the Whipple Mountains detachment terrane, *in* Frost, E. G., and Martin, D. L., eds., Mesozoic–Cenozoic tectonic evolution of the Colorado River region, California, Arizona, and Nevada: San Diego, California, Cordilleran Publishers, p. 341–349.

Hyndman, D. W., and Alt, D., 1987, Radial dikes, laccoliths, and gelatin models: Journal of Geology, v. 95, p. 763–774.

Keith, S. B., 1978, Paleosubduction geometries inferred from Cretaceous and Tertiary magmatic patterns in southwestern North America: Geology, v. 6, p. 516–521.

Lachenbruch, A. H., and Sass, J. H., 1978, Models of an extending lithosphere and heat flow in the Basin and Range province, *in* Smith, R. B., and Eaton, C. P., eds., Cenozoic tectonics and regional geophysics of the western Cordillera: Geological Society of America Memoirs 152, p. 209–250.

Lipman, P. W., 1984, The roots of ash flow calderas in western North America; Windows into the tops of granitic batholiths: Journal of Geophysical Research, v. 89, p. 8801–8841.

Macdonald, G. A., 1972, Volcanoes: Englewood Cliffs, New Jersey, Prentice-Hall, 510 p.

Nakamura, K., and Uyeda, S., 1980, Stress gradient in arc-back arc regions and plate subduction: Journal of Geophysical Research, v. 85, p. 6419–6428.

Nielson, J. E., and Turner, R., 1986, Miocene rocks of the northern Turtle Mountains, San Bernardino County, California, *in* Nielson, J. E., and Glazner, A. F., eds., Cenozoic stratigraphy, structure, and mineralization in the Mojave Desert, Trip 5 (82nd Annual Geological Society of America Cordilleran Section Meeting Guidebook): Los Angeles, California State University, p. 25–32.

Okaya, D. A., and Frost, E. G., 1989, Seismic profiling in the Mojave–Sonoran extensional terrane; CALCRUST reprocessing and interpretation of industry seismic profiles: Tectonics (in press).

Smith, E. I., 1982, Geology and geochemistry of the volcanic rocks in the River Mountains, Clark County, Nevada, and comparisons with volcanic rocks in nearby areas, *in* Frost, E. C., and Martin, D. L., eds., Mesozoic–Cenozoic tectonic evolution of the Colorado River region, California, Arizona, and Nevada: San Diego, California, Cordilleran Publishers, p. 41–54.

Suneson, N. H., and Lucchita, I., 1983, Origin of bimodal volcanism, southern Basin and Range province, west-central Arizona: Geological Society of America Bulletin, v. 94, p. 1005–1019.

Walker, G. W., 1986, Koolau dike complex, Oahu; Intensity and origin of a sheeted-dike complex high in a Hawaiian volcanic edifice: Geology, v. 14, p. 310–313.

MANUSCRIPT SUBMITTED JULY 3, 1987
REVISED MANUSCRIPT SUBMITTED MARCH 8, 1988
MANUSCRIPT ACCEPTED BY THE SOCIETY FEBRUARY 7, 1989

Geological Society of America
Memoir 174
1990

Chapter 9

Recycling of continental crust in Miocene volcanic rocks from the Mojave block, southern California

Allen F. Glazner
Department of Geology, Mitchell Hall, CB 3315, University of North Carolina, Chapel Hill, North Carolina 27599

ABSTRACT

Tertiary volcanism in the Mojave Desert region of southern California followed a long early Tertiary hiatus in volcanism and sedimentation. Volcanism began simultaneously across the region, producing a broad belt of volcanoes that stretched at a high angle to the continental margin from the western tip of the Mojave Desert eastward into Arizona, a distance of more than 500 km. This band of volcanoes was part of a northward-moving wave of volcanism that passed through the southwestern United States in the Tertiary, inland of the migrating Mendocino triple junction. Volcanism coincided (at the temporal resolution of present data) with crustal extension and with the change from subduction to transform-fault tectonics.

Although the suite includes rocks ranging from alkali basalt to high-silica rhyolite, petrologic data indicate that volcanism was caused by large-scale injection of the crust by high-alumina basalt magma. Basalt magmas were probably trapped in the crust owing to low crustal density. Intermediate rocks are hybrids produced by mixing of silicic crustal material into mafic magma. Evidence for mixing includes (1) ubiquitous disequilibrium phenocryst textures (e.g., quartz xenocrysts in mafic rocks; reverse-zoned, spongy plagioclase), and (2) positive correlations of $^{87}Sr/^{86}Sr$ and $\delta^{18}O$ with SiO_2. Major-element, trace-element, and isotopic trends from rocks with <65 weight percent SiO_2 are consistent with a simple mixing model involving addition of rhyolite and minor fractionation of olivine. Above 65 weight percent SiO_2, addition of rhyolite alone can explain observed chemical trends.

The tectonic significance of Mojave volcanism remains obscure. The hybrid nature of intermediate rocks and lack of a clear connection to subduction rule out the possibility of using the rocks to make inferences about paleosubduction geometries. The basalt magmas that triggered the volcanic outburst may represent the release, during lithospheric extension, of partial melts of sub-Mojave lithosphere, which was significantly metasomatized by the long period of early Tertiary nonvolcanic subduction.

INTRODUCTION

Importance of Tertiary volcanism

The Oligocene and Miocene epochs were times of great geologic reorganization in the southwestern United States. During this period, subduction was replaced by transform faulting along the west coast of North America (Atwater, 1970). Throughout the region, Oligocene-Miocene time was characterized by crustal extension, voluminous volcanism, and coarse-clastic sedimentation. Volcanic rocks provide one of our main sources of knowledge of this important period because they are volumetrically dominant in most areas, are amenable to isotopic dating, and are influenced by tectonic events.

Glazner, A. F., 1990, Recycling of continental crust in Miocene volcanic rocks from the Mojave block, southern California, *in* Anderson, J. L., ed., The nature and origin of Cordilleran magmatism: Boulder, Colorado, Geological Society of America Memoir 174.

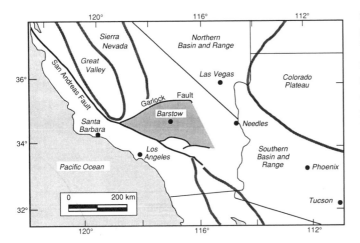

Figure 1. Map showing location of the Mojave block. Eastern boundary is the south-southeastern extension of the Death Valley fault zone.

Oligocene and Miocene volcanic rocks are scattered across most of the southwestern United States. In southern California, significant concentrations occur in the California Coast Ranges, near the San Andreas fault (Johnson and O'Neil, 1984; Weigand, 1982); in southeasternmost California and adjacent Arizona (Crowe and others, 1979; Hazlett, this volume); in the Las Vegas area (Smith and others, this volume); and in the Mojave Desert. This chapter is concerned with the petrology and significance of the last group.

The tectonic significance of Tertiary volcanism in the southwestern United States has been debated for decades. Hamilton and Myers (1966) considered most volcanism in the Basin and Range province to be related to crustal extension. In the early 1970s a variety of authors (e.g., Lipman and others, 1971; McKee, 1971; Lipman and others, 1972; Christiansen and Lipman, 1972), using newly developed models of plate tectonics, proposed that Tertiary volcanic rocks in the southwestern United States can be divided into two groups: an earlier group of intermediate rocks that was generated by subduction of the Farallon plate beneath western North America, and a later group of basaltic or bimodal basaltic-rhyolitic rocks related to late Cenozoic crustal extension. In their model the character of volcanism in the southwestern United States changed from intermediate, subduction-related to dominantly basaltic, extension-related in concert with the change from subduction to transform-fault tectonics.

Miocene volcanic rocks of the Mojave Desert and surrounding regions have proven to be a tempting target for tectonic classification. Most authors consider them to be subduction related (e.g., Snyder and others, 1976; Coney and Reynolds, 1977; Pilger and Henyey, 1979; Moseley and others, 1982); others have suggested that they record a period of post-subduction, fundamentally basaltic volcanism (Christiansen and Lipman, 1972; Nason and others, 1979). A lack of fundamental petrologic and age data has hampered efforts to characterize the suite.

Part of this confusion may result from the transitional tec-

tonic setting under which the rocks were erupted. Current plate reconstructions indicate that volcanism in the southwestern United States occurred during the changeover from subduction to transform-fault tectonics off the coast of southern California (Glazner and Bartley, 1984). Thus, if these reconstructions are accurate, volcanism was not clearly "arc"-related, nor did it occur in a clearly post-subduction setting. Moreover, Glazner and Richardson (1983) showed that post-subduction volcanic suites in western North America are generally calc-alkaline and often include abundant intermediate-composition rocks. Thus, a volcanic suite cannot be characterized as "subduction-related" merely because it has calc-alkaline chemical characteristics or because it includes andesites and dacites. The common equation of andesites with subduction is too simplistic.

Scope

The purpose of this paper is to present and synthesize new chemical, isotopic, and petrographic data for a regional suite of volcanic rocks from the central and western Mojave Desert. These data complement more detailed studies of individual volcanic areas, such as those of Smith (1964), Moseley (1978), Nason and others (1979), Williamson (1980), Casey (1981), and Glazner (1988).

This chapter is mainly concerned with Tertiary volcanism within the Mojave volcanic belt, a northwest-trending zone of volcanic rocks that cuts across the center of the Mojave Desert (Figs, 1, 2). The belt is terminated on the northwest by the Garlock fault, although Tertiary volcanic rocks in the southern Sierra Nevada (Dibblee, 1967d) align with it when left-lateral slip on the Garlock fault is restored. To the southeast the belt merges with a broad zone of Tertiary volcanic rocks that extends along the southern Colorado River trough.

Rocks discussed in this chapter were collected from within the Mojave block, a wedge-shaped region bounded by the Garlock fault on the north, the San Andreas fault on the southwest, and by the northern bounding fault of the San Bernardino Mountains on the south (Fig. 1). The eastern boundary of the Mojave block is not sharply defined; following Hewett (1954), I use the south-southeastern extension of the Death Valley fault zone, the "Mojave-Sonoran tectonic boundary" of Fuis (1981). This line separates an eastern terrane of linear, north-trending ranges with abundant Paleozoic and Precambrian rocks from a western region that lacks these features. It also coincides with an abrupt westward thickening of the crust (Fuis, 1981), a gravity high (Eaton and others, 1978), a westward decrease in heat flow (Lachenbruch and others, 1978), and a proposed major fault zone (Hamilton and Myers, 1966). Darton and others (1915, p. 149) noted that the Providence Mountains, which lie just east of the boundary, are "the south end of a great north-south divide which separates the Las Vegas and Colorado valleys on the east from the deserts on the west and seems to be an important but little understood geologic boundary in this region." Much the same could be said today.

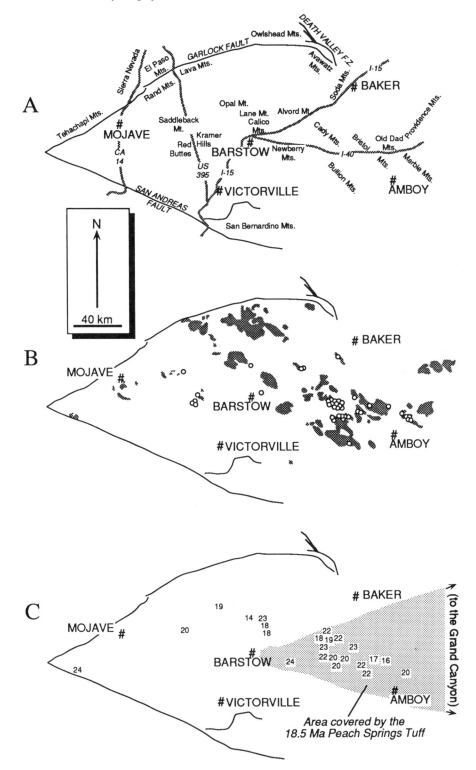

Figure 2. A: Geographic features of the Mojave block. B: Outcrops of Tertiary volcanic rocks. Dots give locations of analyzed specimens (also see Appendix 1). C: K-Ar ages of volcanic rocks from the Mojave block. Ages taken from sources in text (recalculated to new decay constants where necessary). In the region marked in the eastern part of the Mojave block, the Peach Springs Tuff, which is 18 to 19 Ma (Glazner and others, 1986), is the stratigraphically highest volcanic unit. Ages from the Peach Springs Tuff and from basalt flows and air-fall tuffs within the predominantly clastic Barstow Formation, which has been extensively studied because of its rich mammalian fauna, are omitted in order to avoid biasing the data.

Locations of samples discussed herein are shown in Figure 2B, and specific location data are given in Appendix 1. The only major occurrence of Tertiary volcanic rocks in the Mojave block not sampled as part of this study lies within the military reservations in the north-central Mojave block. Outcrops within the Twentynine Palms Marine Base were sampled during a reconnaissance survey in July 1981.

GEOLOGIC SETTING OF THE MOJAVE VOLCANIC BELT

Introduction

Recent models of continental magmatism (e.g., Eichelberger, 1978; Hildreth, 1981) suggest that magmatic systems are driven by basalt magmas derived from the mantle, and that intermediate and silicic rocks are usually hybrids that contain both crustal and mantle components. If these models are correct, then the crust through which magmas ascend plays an important role in the evolution of a given magmatic system. In particular, the isotopic composition of a crustally derived magma such as rhyolite is controlled largely by the isotopic composition of its crustal source region. A summary of current knowledge of the crustal composition and structure of the Mojave block is presented below.

Pre-Tertiary geology

Burchfiel and Davis (1981) summarized the pre-Tertiary geology of the Mojave Desert and surrounding areas. Within the Mojave block, Tertiary volcanic rocks rest upon a pre-Tertiary basement complex composed of (1) Mesozoic and late Paleozoic granitoids, metavolcanic rocks, and minor metasedimentary rocks, and (2) Paleozoic and Precambrian Z marine sedimentary rocks. As shown below, this pre-Tertiary basement formed a heterogeneous source region for the silicic Tertiary rocks.

Documented outcrops of Precambrian basement rocks are rare within the Mojave block, although such rocks crop out extensively to the east (Lanphere, 1964; Jennings, 1977) and are present in the San Bernardino Mountains to the south (Cameron, 1982). Several outcrops of alleged Precambrian rocks north and west of Barstow (Jennings, 1977) are apparently Paleozoic or younger, on the basis of stratigraphic correlation (Kiser, 1981) and Rb/Sr model ages (Glazner and others, 1988). This apparent lack of Precambrian basement in the Mojave block has important implications for the isotopic composition of silicic rocks derived from the crust.

Late Proterozoic and Paleozoic sedimentary rocks in the Mojave block consist of two groups: (1) late Proterozoic and Paleozoic platformal sedimentary rocks, and (2) allochthonous Paleozoic eugeoclinal rocks. These two groups are apparently juxtaposed along a poorly defined boundary that extends southwest from the north-central Mojave block to near Victorville (Burchfiel and Davis, 1981). The nature of this proposed boundary (e.g., thrust, strike slip, etc.) is unclear.

Most pre-Tertiary rocks in the Mojave block are Mesozoic plutonic and volcanic rocks. Few geochronologic studies of these rocks exist, and K-Ar systems have been extensively reset (Miller and Morton, 1980). The oldest dated plutons are Triassic, but most are Jurassic and Cretaceous (Burchfiel and Davis, 1981). Mesozoic metavolcanic rocks crop out in the central and northeastern parts of the block. These Mesozoic units apparently represent a well-developed but fluctuating Andean-type magmatic belt (Hamilton, 1969).

Scattered bodies of mafic and quartzofeldspathic schist (the Rand, Pelona, and Orocopia schists) compose a small but potentially important part of the pre-Tertiary basement complex. These bodies, which apparently represent Mesozoic ocean-floor assemblages (Haxel and Dillon, 1978), crop out in the southwestern Mojave block (along the San Andreas fault) and in the Rand Mountains. Although they compose but a small fraction of surface exposures, tectonic and isotopic studies indicate that they may constitute a large proportion of the crust in the western Mojave block (Burchfiel and Davis, 1981; Glazner and O'Neil, 1989).

The juxtaposition of platform and eugeoclinal facies in the central Mojave block is one of several zones of proposed pre-Tertiary dislocation that have been postulated to run through the region. Others include a large left-lateral fault extending from Sonora into the Mojave Desert (the "Mojave-Sonora megashear" of Silver and Anderson, 1974) and an ancient northwest-trending rift in the central Mojave block (Kistler and Peterman, 1978). Recent work has shown that these latter two features probably do not pass through the Mojave block. For example, Cameron (1982), Stewart (1982), and Walker (1988) used facies trends in late Proterozoic and Paleozoic rocks to show that the Mojave-Sonora megashear must extend south of the Mojave block, if it exists in southern California, and Glazner and O'Neil (1989) showed, on the basis of Sr-isotopic data, that there is no evidence for a pre-Tertiary rift in the center of the block.

Early Tertiary quiescence

Tertiary volcanism and sedimentation followed a profound early Tertiary hiatus that began with the waning of Cretaceous plutonism (Hewett, 1954; Armstrong and Higgins, 1973). No post-Cretaceous, pre–latest Oligocene rocks are known from within the Mojave block. Lack of early Tertiary units and patchy occurrence of Paleozoic rocks within the Mojave block led Hewett (1954) to propose that the block was actively uplifted and eroded during the early Tertiary. The cause of this hiatus in magmatism and sedimentation is unknown. It is generally ascribed to shallow subduction (Lipman and others, 1971; Lowell, 1974), with analogy to parts of modern-day South America. The shallow-subduction model explains both lack of volcanism and rapid uplift (Damon, 1979; Glazner and Schubert, 1985).

Tertiary units

Tertiary rocks in the Mojave block are dominantly volcanic and nonmarine clastic rocks. No coarse-grained plutons of Tertiary age have been identified. The only reported Tertiary marine rocks within the area are a small patch at the western tip of the Mojave Desert (Dibblee, 1967d).

Correlation of Tertiary units is difficult because of rapid lateral facies changes and restricted environments of deposition. In most areas deposition commenced with eruption of a thick stack of volcanic rocks which was followed by fluvial and lacustrine deposition and scattered volcanism. Where depositional contacts between Tertiary rocks and basement are found, the volcanic sequence sits directly on weathered basement rocks with little (<5 m) or no sedimentary cover in between. No deep, early Tertiary, prevolcanic basins have been found. This puzzling observation implies that the Mojave Desert was extremely well drained in the early Tertiary and that sediments were efficiently carried out of the area by a river system that left no trace of its existence (Hewett, 1954).

Most volcanic rocks in the Mojave block were erupted as flows and domes. No large ignimbrites have been found, although small, unwelded ignimbrites derived from dome eruptions are common. The Peach Springs Tuff, an enormous ignimbrite that blankets much of the eastern Mojave block, was erupted from a source well east of the Mojave block (Glazner and others, 1986). Basalt cinder cones are common. Intermediate and silicic rocks were generally erupted from domes, although one large stratovolcano has been identified in the Cady Mountains (Glazner, 1988).

Age and plate-tectonic setting

The Mojave volcanic belt comprises two belts of different ages. The main belt of rocks discussed here (Fig. 2, B and C), which extends through the central Mojave block from the town of Mojave eastward to the Marble Mountains and thence on to the Whipple and Mohave Mountains and western Arizona, was erupted in the early Miocene, 18 to 22 Ma (Armstrong and Higgins, 1973; Woodburne and others, 1974; Nason and others, 1979; Moseley and others, 1982; Howard and others, 1982; D. M. Miller, 1984, written communication; Nielson, 1986; Glazner, 1988). Rocks in the northern Mojave block and adjacent areas are poorly dated but appear to be younger. For example, eight isotopic ages determined by Cox and Diggles (1986) in the El Paso Mountains, immediately north of the Garlock fault, range from 14.0 to 18.1 Ma. In the Castle Mountains, south of Las Vegas, volcanism occurred from 13 to 18 Ma (Turner, 1985). In the Lava Mountains, immediately south of the Garlock fault, dacite flow overlie nonmarine sedimentary rocks, which are dated by fossils as late Miocene (mid-Hemphillian; C. A. Repenning and G. I. Smith, 1981, oral communications). In the Owlshead Mountains, north of the Garlock fault, volcanism occurred 12 to 14 Ma (Davis and Fleck, 1977). Volcanism in the area north of Barstow overlapped both belts; Burke et al. (1982) reported ages ranging from 23.1 to 13.5 Ma, excluding the Pliocene Black Mountain Basalt.

In several areas, K-Ar dating indicates that the entire Miocene volcanic section was erupted within a span of a few million years. For example, in the Cady Mountains, andesite from the base of a 3-km section of volcanic rocks is dated at 19.8 Ma, and the section is capped by the Peach Springs Tuff, which is approximately 18.5 m.y. old (Glazner, 1988). In the Marble Mountains, dacite from the base of a several-hundred meter section of volcanic rocks is dated at 19.6 Ma; this section is also capped by the Peach Springs Tuff (Glazner and Bartley, 1988). East of the Mojave block, in the Turtle Mountains, K-Ar dating indicates that most of the volcanic section was erupted between 18 and 20 Ma (Howard and others, 1982).

These relations indicate that the Mojave block experienced a brief but intense period of volcanism which peaked about 20 Ma. At this time, a belt of active volcanoes extended at a high angle to the continental margin from the western tip of the Mojave Desert eastward into Arizona. This belt moved northward into the northern Mojave block about 15 Ma. Glazner and Bartley (1984) showed that this outburst was part of a wave of volcanism that swept northward with time, inland of the calculated position of the Mendocino triple junction. They related this correspondence to extensional tectonism at the unstable Mendocino triple junction and to deformation of the continental margin above the subducted Mendocino fracture zone.

PETROLOGY

Introduction

Recent work has shown that magma mixing plays a dominant role in the genesis of many calc-alkaline magma series in both subduction-zone (e.g., Eichelberger, 1978; Sakuyama, 1981; Koyaguchi, 1986) and extensional (e.g., Nielsen and Dungan, 1985; McMillan and Dungan, 1986; Novak and Bacon, 1986) settings. A major point of the discussion below is that Tertiary volcanic rocks from the Mojave block are hybrids consisting of both mantle-derived and crust-derived components. In this chapter, I use "mixing" as a general term to encompass both mixing of discrete magmas and assimilation of crustal material by basalt magma.

Hydrothermal alteration, both argillic and potassic, is widespread in Tertiary volcanic rocks from the Mojave Desert. Potassic alteration is prevalent in extensional, volcanic terranes throughout the southwestern United States (Chapin and Glazner, 1983). The 42 analyses reported here were culled from a study of approximately 150 samples from across the Mojave block. Samples were rejected from the study if they showed evidence of potassic metasomatism (secondary adularia combined with abnormally high K_2O values; Glazner, 1988), significant argillic alteration, or abundant calcite. During the course of this study, rocks showing extreme potassic metasomatism were discovered in the southeastern and central Cady Mountains, at Sunshine Peak, and in the Waterman Hills near Barstow.

Rock names used in this paper are based on weight percent SiO_2, expressed on a volatile-free basis with all Fe as Fe_2O_3 ($Fe_2O_3^t$) and analyses recalculated to total 100 percent. Follow-

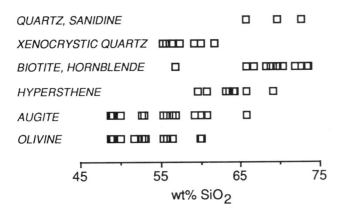

Figure 3. Phenocryst assemblages of analyzed specimens plotted against silica. All specimens except 15 and 16 also contain plagioclase phenocrysts. Note that olivine is present in specimens with as much as 60 wt% SiO_2, a feature that is characteristic of mixed-magma suites (Ussler and Glazner, 1989). Quartz xenocrysts are present in several specimens and usually coexist with olivine.

ing Novak and Bacon (1986), rocks with <53 wt% SiO_2 are designated as basalt, 53 to 63 wt% andesite, 63 to 68 wt% dacite, 68 to 71 wt% rhyodacite, and >71 wt% rhyolite.

Petrography: textural disequilibrium

Petrographic characteristics of the suite are illustrated in Figure 3 and Table 1. As a function of silica content, phenocryst assemblages follow the general pattern: plagioclase + olivine + augite (<55 wt% SiO_2), plagioclase + augite + xenocrystic quartz ± olivine (55 to 62 wt% SiO_2), plagioclase + hypersthene (63 to 65 wt% SiO_2), and plagioclase + biotite and/or hornblende (>66 wt% SiO_2). Phenocrystic quartz and sanidine are uncommon in analyzed samples from this study, although hydrothermally altered rhyolites from the western Mojave Desert commonly contain phenocrystic quartz. Opaque minerals (chiefly magnetite) are present in nearly all samples, but only rarely do they exceed 0.5 mm in diameter.

Most samples, especially the andesites and dacites, show prominent textural disequilibrium. The most common disequilibrium textures are (1) xenocrystic, augite-rimmed quartz, (2) reverse-zoned, spongy plagioclase, and (3) two populations of plagioclase.

Quartz. Xenocrystic quartz is present in most andesites (Fig. 4, A and B) as anhedral, blob-like masses that range up to 3 mm in diameter in thin section. Radiating coronas of augite are ubiquitous. Most grains contain brown rhyolitic glass (Figs. 4, A and B; Table 2) both as rounded inclusions or reentrants and as a thin layer between the quartz and its augite corona. This glass is broadly rhyolitic in composition, although depleted in alkalis (cf. Eichelberger, 1978).

The interpretation of xenocrystic quartz in andesites and basalts has puzzled petrologists for a century or more. Popular

interpretations include: (1) derivation from assimilated basement rocks (Lacroix, 1893, p. 43–48; Sato, 1975); (2) an origin as high-pressure phenocrysts (Diller, 1891; Nicholls and others, 1971; Best and Brimhall, 1974); and (3) an origin as phenocrysts from rhyolitic magma that mixed with basaltic magma (Eichelberger, 1978). The ubiquitous association of brown rhyolitic glass with xenocrystic quartz (including at such classic localities as Lassen Volcanic National Park and the western Grand Canyon; Glazner, W. Ussler, and M. G. Best, unpublished data), coupled with the lack of experimental evidence for high-pressure stability of quartz, rules out the high-pressure phenocryst origin. Eichelberger (1978) proposed that quartz xenocrysts with rhyolitic glass inclusions must have originated as phenocrysts in rhyolite, reasoning that the rhyolitic glass was trapped during rapid growth of the phenocryst. However, Mies and Glazner (1987) noted the textural similarity between quartz xenocrysts and anhedral quartz produced by natural partial melting of granite by basalt (Fig. 4C). They found that rhyolitic inclusions can form by melting of feldspar inclusions in quartz, and concluded that assimilation is the simplest process that can account for the textural features of quartz xenocrysts.

Quartz in rhyolites from the Mojave volcanic belt is generally anhedral and deeply embayed (Fig. 4D), as is the quartz in most rhyolites worldwide. This texture is generally ascribed to rapid growth or to resorption of the quartz by the liquid. However, Mies and Glazner (1987) found that relict quartz in partially melted granite has the anhedral, deeply embayed character of rhyolitic quartz (cf. Fig. 4, C and D). Deep embayments and concave morphology occur because quartz is a late-crystallizing phase and fills intergranular voids in a crystallizing granite. These observations indicate that quartz phenocrysts in many rhyolites are probably incompletely melted relics of the rhyolite's source material.

Plagioclase. Reverse-zoned, spongy plagioclase phenocrysts (Fig. 4E) are another prominent indicator of textural disequilibrium. This texture has been given a number of names, including dusty, clouded, honeycomb, spongy, fritted, fingerprint-like, and sieve. "Spongy" will be used here. "Sieve" implies an analogy with poikiloblastic or poikilitic texture, where a growing crystal engulfs crystal or liquid material in the matrix. Although some spongy plagioclase may originate this way, Tsuchiyama and Takahashi (1983) and Tsuchiyama (1985) produced similar textures by partially melting plagioclase crystals.

In Mojave rocks the spongy texture results from a fine network of light brown glass channels that pervades the spongy zone (Fig. 4E). Optical and scanning-electron microscope study of the spongy zone (S. B. Dent and W. Ussler, unpublished data) indicates that it contains minute grains of ferromagnesian phases. The glass channels are tabular parallel to (010). This spongy texture is distinct from crystals in which blebs of rhyolitic glass, interpreted as liquid trapped during rapid growth, are arranged zonally (Fig. 4F; Table 2).

In Table 1, the spongy vs. glass-bearing nature of plagioclase phenocrysts is noted. A striking feature is that the two textures are

TABLE 1. PETROGRAPHY

#	SiO_2	gm	plag	ol	aug	hyp	hbl	bio	x qtz	qtz	san	opaq
1	48.7		62.8	11.9	16.2							9.1
2	48.9	75.4	11.6	12.2	0.8							
3	49.1		65.0	14.3	18.6							2.1
4	50.0		48.0	19.0	22.4							10.6
5	51.7		x	x								
6	52.7		x	x								
7	52.7	69.9	21.9s	1.5	4.6							2.1
8	53.0		x	x	x							
9	53.1	92.2	4.6s	3.2								
10	53.1	75.6	12.8s	8.0								
11	55.3		xs	x	x				x			
12	55.7	85.8	3.0	11.0	x				1.2			
13	56.4	85.6	10.8s	x	2.4				1.2			
14	56.9	86.1	6.2s		1.0		6.8					
15	57.4								x			
16	57.7											
17	59.3	81.6	13.8s	x	2.0				2.6			
18	59.7	76.6	22.8s			0.6						
19	59.9		xs	x								
20	60.0		xs						x			
21	60.1	81.6	17.4s	x	1.0							
22	60.8		xs		x	x						
23	61.7		xs						x			
24	63.2		xgs			x						
25	63.6		x			x						
26	64.1	33.0g			2.6	7.0						2.2
27	64.3		xg		x							
28	64.3		xg			x						
29	65.8	72.2	17.8		1.2		3.0	1.2		4.0		
30	65.8	64.0	24.4s			1.0	3.6	7.0				
31	66.2		x									
32	66.8	67.8	26.6g				5.6					
33	68.3	69.0	20.6				6.4	2.2				1.8
34	68.8		xg				x	x				
35	69.1	71.8	19.6g			0.6	5.8	2.2				
36	69.5	70.0	22.6gs				3.8	1.8				1.8
37	69.7		xg				x	x			x	
38	70.4		xgs				x	x				
39	71.9	73.0	21.8g				1.2	2.8				1.2
40	72.8	71.6	10.6g				4.6	8.0		0.2	5.0	
41	73.5	62.4	29.2g				5.5	2.9				
42	73.6	70.0	23.6g				1.0	4.2				1.2

Notes:
　Numbers give area percent based on 500 points per thin section.
　x = phase present as phenocryst.
　s = abundant spongy plagioclase.
　g = abundant glass inclusions in plagioclase.

Column heads:

# = specimen number	aug = augite	x qtz = xenocrystic quartz
SiO_2 = wt% SiO_2	hyp = hypersthene	qtz = quartz
gm = groundmass	hbl = hornblende (oxidized in	san = sanidine
plag = plagioclase	some specimens)	opaq = opaque phases
ol = olivine (altered to	bio = biotite (oxidized in	
iddingsite in many specimens)	some specimens)	

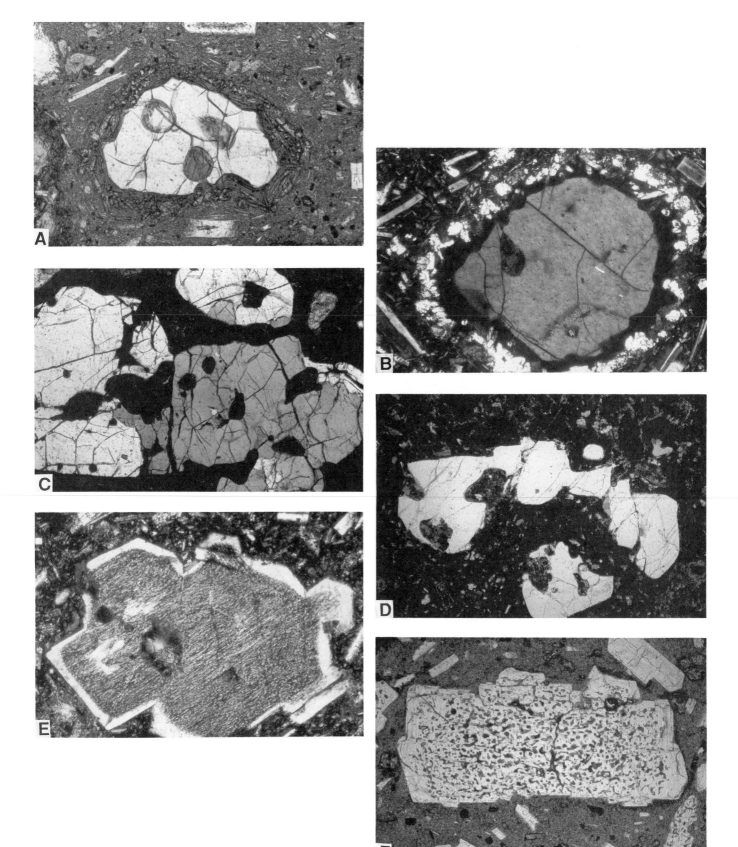

TABLE 2. ELECTRON MICROPROBE ANALYSES OF GLASS INCLUSIONS

Specimen: Host	17 Quartz	26 Plag.	35 Plag.	97 Quartz
SiO_2	76.3	77.1	79.4	76.0
TiO_2	0.7	0.5	0.06	0.3
Al_2O_3	10.8	11.7	8.7	7.4
FeO^t	0.9	2.1	0.8	2.1
MnO	0.02	0.02	0.0	0.02
MgO	0.06	0.4	0.8	1.4
CaO	0.3	0.5	1.9	0.9
Na_2O	1.3	0.8	0.3	0.5
K_2O	4.4	4.2	0.6	2.0
Total	94.8	97.3	92.5	90.6
n	13	3	6	4

Notes:
plag. = plagioclase
n = number of analyses
Analyses by electron microprobe, using defocused beam
(approximately 20 µm), expressed as wt.% oxides.
Specimen 97 is an andesite from the Kramer Hills.
Low totals may reflect unanalyzed volatiles in the glass.

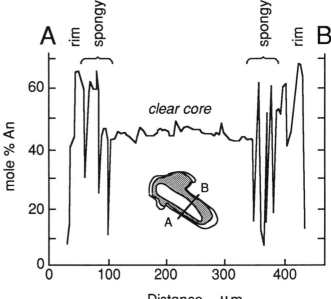

Figure 5. Electron microprobe traverse of a spongy plagioclase phenocryst from specimen 17 (an andesite from the Kramer Hills), showing reverse zoning. Inset diagram shows form of grain and location of traverse. High- and low-CaO spikes within the spongy zone may represent analysis of phases other than plagioclase and therefore may not be directly translatable into An content.

Figure 4. Photomicrographs of textural features of rocks from the Mojave volcanic belt. A: Anhedral quartz grain in andesite with three glass inclusions and a corona consisting of brown glass and prismatic augite crystals (specimen CS-126-T of Turner, 1985; plane-polarized light; width of field 1.4 mm). Glass inclusions at bottom center and upper right are brown; inclusion at upper left is clear. B: Anhedral quartz grain in andesite, showing thin zone of brown glass (black in photograph) adhering to quartz grain and surrounded by blocky, bright-white augite crystals (andesite from the Kramer Hills; crossed polarizers; width of field 0.7 mm). Quartz grain contains a dark inclusion of partially melted plagioclase in which albite twinning is visible. Devitrified, eutectic glass is present at the quartz-plagioclase contact. Melting of feldspar inclusions may produce glass inclusions such as those in Figure 4A. C: Anhedral quartz (gray) and glass (black) from partially melted granite north of Mono Lake, California (see Mies and Glazner, 1987; crossed polarizers; width of field 3.5 mm). Glass forms by eutectic melting between quartz and feldspar. Fusion of feldspar inclusions forms glass inclusions. D: Quartz in hydrothermally altered rhyolite from the Waterman Hills, near Barstow (crossed polarizers; width of field 3.5 mm). Note similarity to C, indicating that quartz phenocrysts in some rhyolites may be partially digested remnants of the source material instead of primary precipitates. E: Spongy, reverse-zoned plagioclase in andesite, showing a large spongy zone, a clear, calcic rim, and remnants of a clear, sodic core (specimen 17; crossed polarizers; width of field 1.4 mm). Compare analyses in Figures 5 and 6. Grain of spongy zone parallels (010). F: Plagioclase with abundant inclusions of brown glass (specimen 26; plane-polarized light; width of field 3.5 mm). This texture is clearly distinct from spongy texture. Glass analysis in Table 2.

nearly mutually exclusive. Rocks with <53 wt% SiO_2 have clear plagioclase. From 53 to 64 wt% SiO_2, most rocks contain spongy plagioclase. Rocks with >64 wt% SiO_2 generally have glass-bearing plagioclase. Only a few samples contain both spongy and glass-bearing plagioclase.

Spongy crystals commonly comprise a clear, relatively sodic ($\approx An_{45}$) core surrounded by a spongy zone and a thin, clear, relatively calcic ($\approx An_{70}$) rim. In some crystals the clear core is absent, although this may be an artifact of the thin-section cut. A zoning profile across a typical spongy plagioclase phenocryst is shown in Figure 5. For this sample (#17, an andesite with 59.3 wt% SiO_2), the composition of the rims of spongy plagioclase phenocrysts matches the composition of plagioclase tablets in the groundmass (Fig. 6A). This rim composition is also similar to the compositions of clear phenocrysts in basalts, whereas the core composition is similar to the composition of clear phenocrysts in dacites (Fig. 6B). These data support the interpretation that reverse zoning and the spongy zone form by incorporation of sodic crystals from a relatively silicic assimilant (rock or magma) into a mafic magma. In this interpretation, the spongy zone results from partial melting of a sodic plagioclase phenocryst by an engulfing mafic magma.

Some samples show two or more distinct populations of plagioclase. For example, in an altered andesite dike from the Castle Mountains (sample CS-126-T of Turner, 1985), spongy plagioclase coexists with clear, rounded plagioclase. The clear phenocrysts are compositionally similar to the sodic cores of the

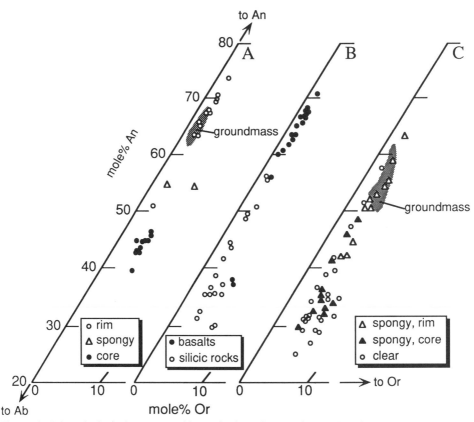

Figure 6. Selected plagioclase compositions. A: Andesite (specimen 17) with spongy phenocrysts, showing prominent reverse zoning and compositional similarity between phenocryst rims and groundmass plagioclase. B: Selected basalts (specimens 1, 2, 3, 4, and 7) and silicic rocks (specimens 26, 34, 35, 36, and a dacite from the southeastern Cady Mountains). Note the similarity between the core compositions in A and the silicic-rock phenocrysts of B, and the similarity between the rim compositions in A and the basalt phenocrysts of B. These relations support a mixing model. C. Andesite (specimen CS-126-T of Turner, 1985) showing both spongy and clear plagioclase phenocrysts. Clear phenocrysts are similar in composition to the cores of spongy phenocrysts, indicating that they were introduced into the magma a relatively short time before the rock was frozen.

spongy phenocrysts (Fig. 6C). This implies that the clear phenocrysts were introduced into the magma a short enough time before the rock was quenched that there was insufficient time for a spongy zone to grow. Kinetic data of Tsuchiyama (1985) indicate that a spongy zone can grow to visible thickness (≈ 10 μm) at magmatic temperatures (≈ 1150 °C) in hours to years, depending on the choice of rate constant.

Chemistry

Introduction. In the discussion below the sample set is treated as a whole for modeling purposes. This approach can be criticized because the samples are clearly not comagmatic in the classical sense of being derived by fractionation of a common parent magma. However, the classical definition of "comagmatic" is not applicable to hybrid magma suites, because such suites are not formed by fractionation of a single parent magma. Even in studies of single volcanoes or small areas, where the mafic end member of the mixing suite can be assumed to be

homogeneous, hybrid magmas can show scattered chemical trends owing to incorporation of a variety of crustal melts. Given the heterogeneous nature of Mojave crust, it is unreasonable to assume that anatectic melts derived from even a small region of the crust will be homogeneous.

The general trends discussed below are similar to trends displayed by smaller areas of the Mojave Desert. For example, trends of 45 analyses of Miocene volcanic rocks from the Old Woman Mountains region of the eastern Mojave Desert (Miller, 1989) are identical to the trends discussed here. Similarly, other, smaller data sets from restricted areas within the Mojave Desert (e.g., Newberry Mountains, Nason, 1978; Bristol Mountains, Casey, 1981; Castle Mountains, Turner, 1985; southeastern Cady Mountains, this study) show trends similar to those defined below. Therefore, I conclude that modeling of the suite as a whole is justified.

Major elements. Chemical data for rocks from the Mojave volcanic belt are presented in Tables 3 and 4 and in Figures 7, 8, and 9. Major-element data (Fig. 7) define trends that are broadly

TABLE 3. MAJOR-ELEMENT, TRACE-ELEMENT, AND Sr-ISOTOPE DATA

#	SiO_2	TiO_2	Al_2O_3	$Fe_2O_3^t$	MgO	CaO	Na_2O	K_2O	P_2O_5	LOI	orig. tot.	Rb	Sr	Y	Zr	Ba	Ni	Nb	$^{87}Sr/^{86}Sr_i$
1	48.7	1.63	17.1	11.80	7.94	8.88	2.78	0.91	0.27	3.14	99.3	15	483	28	122	194	175	23	0.7058
2	48.9	1.88	16.7	10.36	8.66	8.43	3.53	1.16	0.43	2.41	98.3	28	556	26	195	374	183	22	0.7055
3	49.1	1.23	17.4	10.97	6.91	10.74	3.03	0.49	0.20	0.26	99.6	9	287	28	103	382	36	0	0.7046
4	50.0	2.65	16.2	12.50	4.55	8.29	3.69	1.54	0.55	-1.12	98.1	31	557	30	202	500	99	28	0.7055
5	51.7	1.60	16.6	9.21	6.30	8.92	3.82	1.56	0.33	0.32	100.4	34	641	27	181	473	113	12	——
6	52.7	2.13	19.2	8.55	3.27	8.03	4.09	1.77	0.22	0.26	99.4	33	920	28	158	748	4	10	——
7	52.7	1.20	16.2	9.37	5.86	9.05	3.28	1.91	0.34	0.37	100.2	47	730	32	178	687	63	2	0.7080
8	53.0	1.18	17.1	9.34	5.65	8.79	3.38	1.21	0.26	0.82	100.1	46	528	31	164	529	45	3	——
9	53.1	2.25	16.2	10.67	3.83	7.55	3.83	2.09	0.50	0.70	99.0	56	526	30	217	583	70	21	0.7057
10	53.1	1.14	16.8	9.04	5.59	9.27	3.25	1.52	0.25	0.47	99.9	33	533	32	146	548	50	0	——
11	55.3	1.35	15.8	7.99	2.38	9.61	3.42	3.74	0.44	——	101.0	169	828	26	211	1128	68	12	——
12	55.7	1.33	16.6	7.39	5.34	7.27	3.61	2.46	0.39	0.39	99.5	51	899	28	205	1279	93	13	——
13	56.4	1.41	16.1	7.80	3.61	7.54	3.88	2.72	0.45	0.53	101.3	60	922	31	222	1041	22	13	0.7075
14	56.9	1.29	18.9	7.07	2.76	6.41	4.01	2.26	0.35	0.81	99.0	63	891	28	227	1018	26	0	——
15	57.4	1.28	16.3	7.72	5.11	6.37	3.47	2.15	0.24	1.36	98.4	32	399	23	187	571	120	32	——
16	57.7	1.53	17.8	7.78	1.99	6.10	4.58	2.15	0.34	0.37	98.1	63	598	23	206	580	3	11	0.7055
17	59.3	0.75	16.2	6.36	4.70	6.86	3.22	2.32	0.19	0.67	99.9	82	356	21	145	599	56	5	0.7069
18	59.7	1.03	16.6	6.76	2.94	5.82	4.30	2.68	0.23	1.18	99.3	70	532	26	240	782	17	19	——
19	59.9	0.87	16.7	8.84	1.30	4.21	4.40	3.26	0.49	0.39	100.2	73	607	55	565	1024	—	—	——
20	60.0	1.14	15.8	7.29	3.74	5.53	3.45	2.82	0.24	0.77	98.8	97	387	25	184	700	79	25	0.7051
21	60.1	0.79	16.5	6.98	2.83	5.30	3.98	3.34	0.22	0.51	100.0	82	412	28	255	748	32	20	——
22	60.8	1.09	17.4	5.72	2.89	5.66	3.55	2.68	0.21	0.00	100.2	99	646	23	174	762	18	8	——
23	61.7	0.96	15.6	5.88	3.71	5.66	3.56	2.69	0.20	1.45	100.4	84	313	22	172	586	66	24	0.7054
24	63.2	0.76	16.4	5.85	1.49	3.70	5.01	3.20	0.33	0.34	100.3	115	450	35	339	981	1	—	0.7086
25	63.6	0.67	15.9	6.22	0.92	3.59	4.36	4.49	0.27	——	101.1	107	419	31	352	1019	10	—	0.7087
26	64.1	0.86	16.2	4.44	2.21	4.62	4.13	3.24	0.19	0.83	98.9	109	618	21	193	1221	3	14	0.7074
27	64.3	0.98	17.6	4.76	1.45	4.48	4.68	1.49	0.22	1.95	98.3	141	630	20	209	944	19	—	——
28	64.3	0.94	16.5	4.40	1.94	4.42	4.28	2.98	0.21	0.69	100.5	104	694	21	177	956	4	14	0.7078
29	65.8	0.71	16.2	4.04	1.71	4.49	4.27	2.65	0.14	0.78	100.4	79	784	19	166	898	38	2	——
30	65.8	0.59	16.5	3.78	1.76	3.75	4.13	3.45	0.23	1.20	98.2	96	752	25	240	1158	18	12	0.7078
31	66.2	0.60	17.0	3.48	0.39	4.33	4.45	3.37	0.17	0.95	98.7	106	661	18	175	863	0	0	——
32	66.8	0.43	16.0	2.87	1.15	5.35	3.54	3.60	0.29	1.88	101.3	73	1015	22	163	1064	3	0	——
33	68.3	0.40	15.6	2.86	1.12	3.45	4.09	4.09	0.14	0.90	101.0	128	710	20	178	901	0	0	0.7071
34	68.8	0.44	16.1	2.51	1.19	3.04	4.18	3.64	0.09	1.68	98.4	117	558	15	151	808	11	2	0.7070
35	69.1	0.50	15.8	3.17	1.59	3.94	3.96	1.80	0.13	1.77	98.4	203	737	21	185	782	1	10	0.7075
36	69.5	0.41	15.8	2.75	0.71	3.29	4.00	3.36	0.11	0.88	98.3	88	579	26	162	830	0	4	0.7069
37	69.7	0.57	15.9	2.65	0.65	2.97	4.35	3.05	0.11	0.57	98.6	94	680	16	146	1030	9	0	0.7080
38	70.4	0.50	14.9	2.84	0.68	2.54	3.97	4.03	0.16	0.58	98.1	110	497	20	189	940	9	29	——
39	71.9	0.37	15.3	2.08	0.64	2.08	3.89	3.63	0.07	2.92	101.3	336	462	18	188	952	2	33	0.7079
40	72.8	0.06	14.1	2.08	0.25	1.48	3.79	5.46	0.02	0.81	99.4	178	135	39	211	970	8	—	0.7076
41	73.5	0.00	12.9	1.16	0.97	1.64	4.16	5.67	0.00	1.23	101.3	78	733	13	157	914	8	19	——
42	73.6	0.36	13.5	2.24	0.40	1.90	3.90	3.94	0.10	0.43	99.3	111	420	18	178	925	2	40	——

Notes:

Analyses recalculated to sum to 100 wt% on an anhydrous basis with all Fe calculated as ferric iron.

"orig. tot." gives original analysis total (including LOI).

Na_2O and MgO analyses by atomic absorption spectrophotometry; other elements by x-ray fluorescence analysis of fused glass discs (Norrish and Hutton, 1969) for oxides and rock powders for metals.

Oxides in wt %, metals in parts per million by weight.

LOI indicates loss on ignition at 1000 °C.

Initial Sr ratios calculated from data of Glazner and O'Neil (1989), assuming an age of 20 Ma.

TABLE 4. NEUTRON-ACTIVATION ANALYSIS DATA FOR SELECTED SPECIMENS

	1	2	4	13	17	22	Specimen 24	25	36	39	40	98	99
La	13	33	26	60	25	30	44	43	30	61	41	28	77
Ce	18	56	53	98	43	50	81	81	54	95	74	47	135
Nd	bd	bd	13	30	bd	15	19	18	29	34	26	17	48
Sm	4	6.5	6.5	9	4.9	5.3	6.8	7.1	5.1	5.9	6.9	4.6	10.2
Eu	1.44	1.99	2.29	2.21	1.19	1.46	1.91	2.07	1.09	1.13	1	1.25	0.76
Tb	1.75	1.47	1.07	1.01	1.26	0.49	0.85	0.87	0.37	0.52	0.77	0.34	0.95
Yb	1.7	2.2	2.7	1.6	1.4	1.4	2.4	2.1	1.8	2.1	3.3	1.2	4
Lu	0.46	0.38	0.37	0.32	0.33	0.22	0.37	0.35	0.3	0.26	0.49	0.15	0.62
Cs	1.2	8.2	1.5	1.2	3.7	2.5	19.6	4.9	2.8	64.1	5.2	18.5	14.7
Th	1.2	3.3	3.3	7	6.6	6.3	9.3	9.1	6.7	15.8	17	7.6	30.9
U	bd	bd	0.9	0.8	1.7	1	2.2	2.5	1.5	2.4	3.4	1.7	4.2
Hf	2.8	4.3	5.6	5.4	3.4	4.8	7.9	8.4	4.2	5.6	5.8	4.7	8.5
Sc	29.49	25.11	21.4	18.83	21.6	12.96	6.63	7.24	6.05	3.21	1.99	8.49	3.91
Sb	bd	bd	bd	bd	0.3	0.3	bd	bd	0.3	0.4	0.6	0.5	0.9
Ta	0.7	1.5	bd	0.9	0.6	0.9	bd	bd	0.8	2.2	1.7	1	2.4
Co	51.4	46.1	bd	26.6	27.6	20	bd	bd	5.3	9.9	1.1	13.3	1.7
Cr	295	324	bd	84	251	22	bd	bd	11	5	2	58	11
Zn	bd	93	bd	63	43	72	bd	bd	58	30	57	69	85

Notes:

bd indicates below detection limit for that sample.

Concentrations in parts per million by weight.

Specimens 4, 24, and 25 analyzed at the University of California, Los Angeles; other specimens analyzed by E. I. Smith, University of Nevada at Las Vegas.

Specimens 98 and 99 are a dacite and Peach Springs Tuff from the southeastern Cady Mountains (Glazner, 1988).

linear for all oxides except Al_2O_3 and P_2O_5 and, to a lesser extent, MgO. Alumina exhibits a pronounced kink at about 65 wt% SiO_2, and MgO exhibits a slight upward concavity. Similar trends in Al_2O_3 and MgO curves are seen in variation diagrams from several other calc-alkaline suites (e.g., Bacon and Metz, 1984; Gunderson and others, 1986). For all oxides the major-element trends point at the average composition of high-silica rhyolite from the Pliocene-Pleistocene Coso volcanic field (Bacon and others, 1981). This young, fresh, well-analyzed rhyolitic suite, which lies just north of the Mojave block, was chosen as a model of the sort of high-silica mixing component that can be derived by anatexis of Mojave crust.

The major-element trends of Figure 7 can be explained by a simple mixing–fractional crystallization (MFC) model involving olivine and high-silica rhyolite or its crystallized equivalent. An MFC model for rocks with less than 65 wt% SiO_2 (the point at which the bend in the Al_2O_3 trend occurs), is given in Table 5. In this model, the parent and daughter are average compositions at 48 and 60 wt% SiO_2. Average compositions were used instead of discrete rock compositions in order to minimize the effects of analytical variability. Average compositions were determined from cubic curves of the form $X = a+bS+cS^2+dS^3$, where S is weight percent SiO_2 and X is weight percent other oxides (third-order curves were used because they are the simplest curves that

reproduce the general trends of the data; statistical significance is not claimed). Coefficients (Table 6) were determined by a robust fitting technique (iteratively reweighted least squares; Phillips and Eyring, 1983) in order to minimize the effects of outliers. The simple MFC model reproduces the observed trends remarkably well. Predicted compositions at 60 wt% SiO_2 (Δ symbols of Fig. 7) lie sensibly within the bands of data for all oxides.

Flatness of the Al_2O_3 trend at low silica values results from the vector-addition effect of olivine subtraction coupled with rhyolite addition. Slight upward concavity of the MgO trend results from minor olivine fractionation, and most rocks plot between a linear mixing trend and the olivine fractionation line (Fig. 7). In rocks with >65 wt% SiO_2, it is evident from Figure 7 that all trends can be adequately explained by rhyolite addition alone. The absence of major-element evidence for crystal fractionation at silica values above the Al_2O_3 kink can be explained by two processes: (1) absence of dense ferromagnesian phases such as olivine, augite, and hypersthene, and (2) increased liquid viscosity. Figure 10 shows calculated liquid viscosity vs. silica along a basalt-rhyolite mixing line. Viscosities increase dramatically at approximately 65 wt% SiO_2 because of increased polymerization of the liquid (the sharp bend in the curve is masked when viscosity is plotted on a logarithmic scale; however, dynamic properties such as settling velocity depend linearly on the

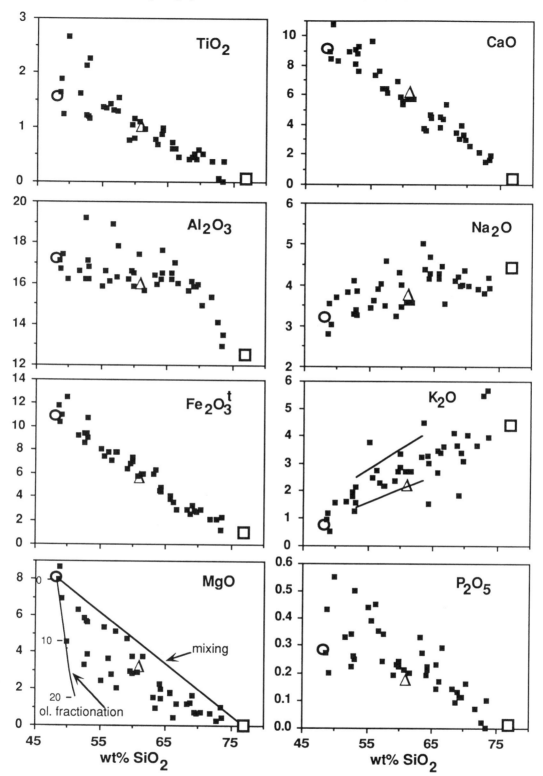

Figure 7. Major-element Harker diagrams for the Mojave volcanic belt. Solid squares are analyses; open square is average Coso rhyolite (Bacon and others, 1981); circle and delta are parent and predicted daughter compositions from MFC model (see text). Depicted on MgO plot are (1) a mixing line between basalt specimen 1 and Coso rhyolite and (2) an olivine-fractionation curve, calculated assuming all Fe as FeO and an olivine-liquid K_D of 0.3. Numbered tic marks give weight percent olivine removed. Lines on K_2O plot give boundaries of high-K andesite field of Gill (1981).

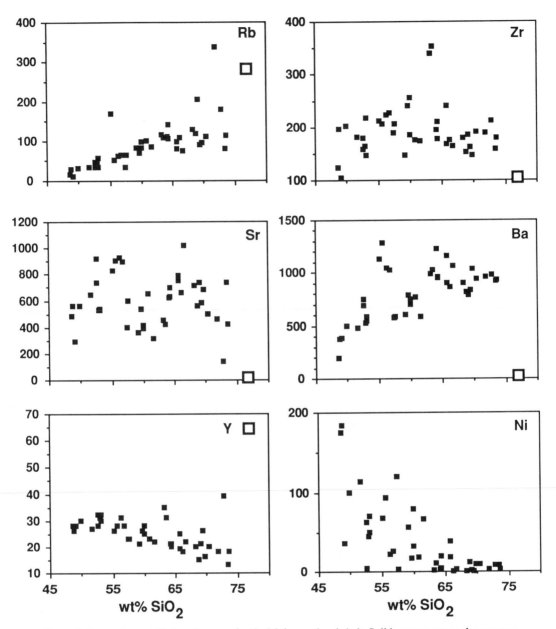

Figure 8. Trace-element Harker diagrams for the Mojave volcanic belt. Solid squares are analyses; open square is average Coso rhyolite (Bacon and others, 1981). Ni data for Coso field are not available.

viscosity, not on its logarithm). Increased viscosity greatly inhibits crystal fractionation.

Trace elements. In contrast to the relatively smooth trends exhibited by major elements, many trace elements show little correlation with silica (Fig. 8). Rb and Ba show a general increase with silica, and Y and Ni show crude decreases, but Sr and Zr show no correlation. For example, Sr varies between 200 and 1,000 ppm across the entire spectrum from basalt to rhyolite. Coso rhyolite is clearly an inadequate model for the trace-element signature of a silicic mixing component, especially for Y and Ba.

Rare-earth element (REE) patterns for the Mojave suite are shown in Figure 9. Patterns across the compositional spectrum

are similar, although silicic rocks are somewhat enriched in light REE and slightly depleted in heavy REE relative to mafic rocks, resulting in a slight clockwise rotation of the patterns from basalt to rhyolite. Only one sample (Peach Springs Tuff) shows a significant negative Eu anomaly.

Sr-isotopic composition. Nason and others (1979) made the first determinations of $^{87}Sr/^{86}Sr$ in volcanic rocks from the Mojave block. Their data show that $^{87}Sr/^{86}Sr_i$ (calculated initial $^{87}Sr/^{86}Sr$) is elevated in silicic rocks from the Newberry Mountains (0.706 to 0.707), implying a crustal source. Initial $^{87}Sr/^{86}Sr$ ratios measured as part of this study increase with increasing silica, although the trend is scattered (Fig. 11). Silicic rocks generally have $^{87}Sr/^{86}Sr_i$ ranging from 0.707 to 0.709, whereas most basalts and andesites have $^{87}Sr/^{86}Sr_i < 0.706$. Glazner and O'Neil (1989), in a study of Tertiary volcanic rocks from the Mojave volcanic belt and surrounding areas, showed that $^{87}Sr/^{86}Sr_i$ correlates positively with both silica and with distance inland. Thus, in a given area, $^{87}Sr/^{86}Sr_i$ correlates positively with SiO_2, and $^{87}Sr/^{86}Sr_i$ is elevated across the entire basalt-rhyolite spectrum in areas to the east (e.g., Colorado River trough) relative to areas in the west. When the correlation with distance inland is filtered out, the correlation with silica is significantly strengthened.

These data are consistent with a contamination model in which the silicic end member had a $^{87}Sr/^{86}Sr$ ratio of approximately 0.708 to 0.709 20 m.y. ago. Although few $^{87}Sr/^{86}Sr$ ratios have been measured on granitic rocks from the Mojave block, existing data generally fall around these values (Kistler and Peterman, 1978). An alternative source rock is Pelona-type schist, which has present-day $^{87}Sr/^{86}Sr$ ratios of 0.704 to 0.710 (Glazner and O'Neil, 1989). Involvement of a schist source for silicic rocks in the western Mojave is consistent with $\delta^{18}O$ values of silicic rocks, which are high in the western Mojave block and decrease to the east (Glazner and O'Neil, 1989).

Discussion

The simple MFC model presented above is consistent with major-element, textural, and Sr-isotopic data from the Mojave volcanic belt. Although it is possible to obtain reasonable fits to the major-element data with a pure crystal-fractionation model, such a model (1) does not explain the general increase in $^{87}Sr/^{86}Sr$ with SiO_2, and (2) requires significant fractionation of magnetite, a phase that is not a prominent phenocryst in any of the studied samples. The MFC model cannot distinguish between the two end-member cases of mixing of a silicic liquid with mafic liquid and assimilation of silicic rocks by mafic liquid, although the textural data presented above indicate that assimilation of solid material was at least locally important.

The poor correlation between many trace elements and silica stands in stark contrast to the relatively coherent patterns displayed by the major elements. This dichotomy probably results from the differing behavior of trace elements and major elements during anatexis and assimilation. For example, the trace-element content of a rhyolitic liquid produced by anatexis of a granitoid is controlled by the percentage of melting and by the phases present in the residue (presence or absence of zircon, etc.), whereas the major-element composition is controlled by the phase equilibria of the granitoid. A liquid produced by 5 wt% melting of a granitoid source region will have significantly different trace-element signature than a liquid produced by 20 wt% melting of the same source region, yet both liquids will be rhyolitic. Thus, major elements and trace elements are decoupled during anatexis and mixing.

Similarly, present-day $^{87}Sr/^{86}Sr$ ratios of Precambrian granitoids in the Mojave Desert commonly exceed 0.78 (Lanphere

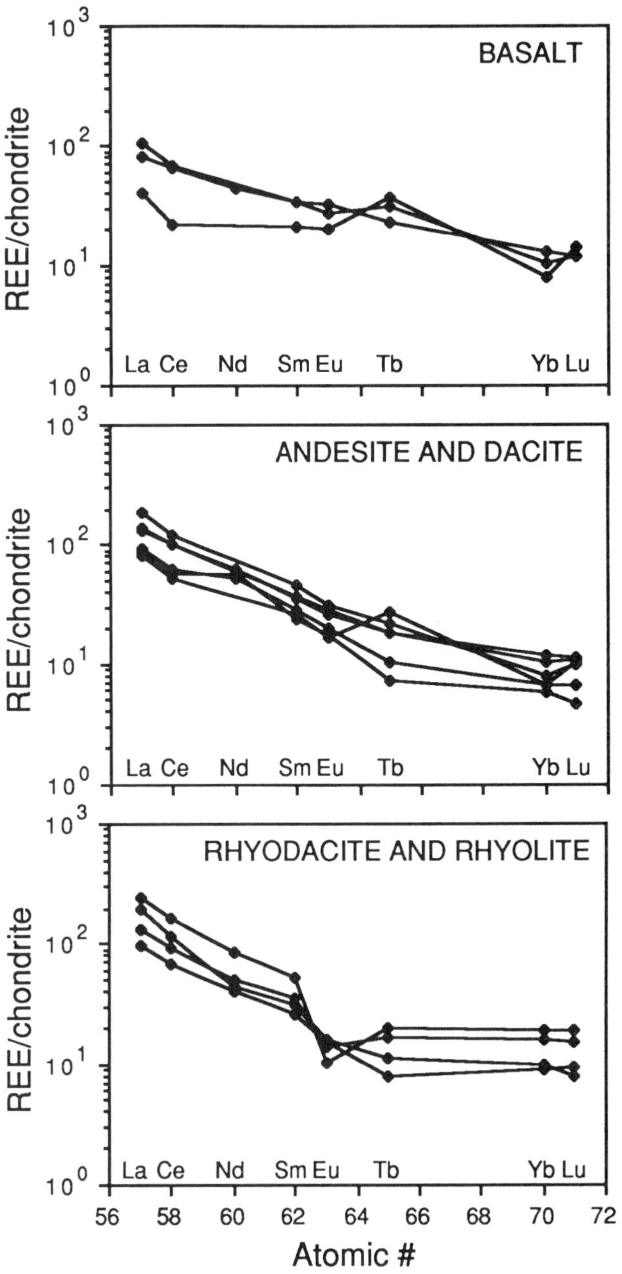

Figure 9. Rare-earth element patterns of rocks from this study and the Peach Springs Tuff (rhyolite specimen with deep Eu anomaly; see Table 4).

and others, 1964; C. A. Allen, 1987, written communication; Glazner and others, 1988) and are far greater than present-day $^{87}Sr/^{86}Sr$ ratios from Mesozoic granitoids (≈ 0.710), yet both will yield a rhyolitic liquid upon anatexis. Thus, major elements and isotopic ratios are also decoupled during anatexis and mixing.

Therefore, because silicic mixing components derived from the crust cannot avoid being heterogeneous, especially in their isotopic and trace-element compositions, coherency of major-element trends and scatter in trace-element and isotopic trends

TABLE 5. MIXING-FRACTIONAL CRYSTALLIZATION MODEL FOR MEAN TREND OF MOJAVE VOLCANIC BELT, 48 TO 60 WT% SiO2
MODEL: DAUGHTER = a(PARENT) + b(RHYOLITE) + c(OLIVINE)

Oxide	Parent	Rhyolite	Olivine	Daughter	Predicted	Residual
SiO_2	48.00	77.04	37.33	60.00	60.07	-0.07
TiO_2	1.59	0.06	0.00	1.04	1.05	-0.01
Al_2O_3	17.31	12.54	0.00	16.47	16.27	0.20
FeO^t	9.89	0.93	26.40	5.68	5.29	0.39
MgO	8.21	0.02	36.28	3.06	3.28	-0.22
CaO	9.35	0.38	0.00	5.90	6.22	-0.32
Na_2O	3.23	4.42	0.00	3.96	3.88	0.09
K_2O	0.79	4.38	0.00	2.73	2.28	0.45
P_2O_5	0.29	0.01	0.00	0.27	0.19	0.08
coeff.	0.648	0.403	-0.056			
t value	0.0001	0.0001	0.0015			

Model: daughter = 0.648(parent) + 0.403(rhyolite) - 0.056(olivine)

Standard deviation of error about regression hyperplane: 0.282
Root-mean-square of residuals: 0.250
Degrees of freedom (# oxides - # coeffs): 6
Condition number of correlation matrix: 57.6

Notes:

Olivine composition used is the mean of 23 olivine analyses from Mojave volcanic belt rocks (Glazner, unpublished data), and the rhyolite composition is the mean of analyses reported by Bacon and others (1981).

Condition number is ratio of largest and smallest eigenvalues of correlation matrix.

TABLE 6. COEFFICIENTS OF THE CUBIC TREND CURVES
$$X = a + bS + cS^2 + dS^3$$

Oxide	a	b	$c \times 10^2$	$d \times 10^4$
TiO_2	-3.24	0.281	-0.481	0.221
Al_2O_3	246.10	-11.810	20.149	-11.408
$Fe_2O_3^t$	-28.32	2.648	-5.250	2.997
MgO	37.25	-0.487	-0.676	0.898
CaO	-11.46	1.459	-2.885	1.558
Na_2O	18.76	-0.983	1.962	-1.223
K_2O	-32.90	1.372	-1.794	0.827
P_2O_5	-5.50	0.273	-0.408	0.190

Notes:

S = wt% SiO_2.

X = wt% other oxides.

Coefficients determined by robust regression of data from Table 3.

TABLE 7. CALCULATED END-MEMBER COMPOSITIONS AND AVERAGE COMPOSITIONS OF YOUNG MOJAVE ALKALI BASALTS AND RHYOLITES

Oxide	1	2	3	4
SiO_2	48.0	48.12	75.0	77.1
TiO_2	1.59	2.40	0.06	0.06
Al_2O_3	17.3	15.8	12.5	12.6
$Fe_2O_3^t$	10.99	10.8	1.43	1.03
MgO	8.21	6.9	0.54	0.02
CaO	9.35	9.6	1.45	0.38
Na_2O	3.23	3.6	3.77	4.43
K_2O	0.79	1.67	4.01	4.39
P_2O_5	0.29	0.53	0.01	0.01

Column heads:

1 = calculated basalt composition at 48 wt% SiO_2.

2 = average of 45 basalts from Pisgah and Amboy Craters (Hughes, 1986).

3 = calculated rhyolite composition at 75 wt% SiO_2.

4 = average of 36 high-silica rhyolites from the Coso volcanic field (Bacon and others, 1981).

are predicted by a generalized mixing model. Two-component mixing is too simplistic a model to apply in all but the simplest cases.

The general compositional characteristics of the mixing components can be estimated from the coefficients of Table 6. Calculated compositions of the major-element trends at 48 and 75 wt% SiO_2 are given in Table 7. The calculated model basalt is a high-alumina olivine basalt with a trace of normative nepheline. Scatter at the mafic end of the spectrum (e.g., large ranges in TiO_2, P_2O_5, and Al_2O_3) indicates that this model basalt may be an average of more than one basalt type, but existing data are too sparse to define these characteristics. Miller's (1989) study of volcanism in the Old Woman Mountains region also indicates evidence for multiple basalt parents.

The calculated model basalt is similar to many of the subduction-related basalts tabulated by Hughes (1982, p. 378) except for its significantly higher TiO_2 content. Elevated TiO_2 is often associated with "nonorogenic" basalts (e.g., Chayes, 1964; Martin and Piwinskii, 1972). However, Glazner and Richardson (1983) showed that TiO_2 cannot be used to discriminate syn- and post-subduction basalts in western North America. They found that P_2O_5 is the best single discriminant; syn-subduction basalts generally have less than 0.5 wt% P_2O_5, whereas post-subduction basalts generally have more than 0.5 wt% P_2O_5. By this criterion the model basalt would be classified as syn-subduction.

The model basalt differs in composition from alkali basalts from two Pliocene-Holocene volcanoes in the Mojave Desert (Table 7). The younger alkali basalts are significantly lower in

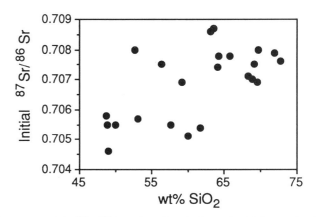

Figure 11. Initial $^{87}Sr/^{86}Sr$ ratios of rocks from the Mojave volcanic belt, calculated from measured $^{87}Sr/^{86}Sr$ and Rb/Sr ratios and assuming an age of 20 Ma. The general, albeit scattered, increase with silica is consistent with a mixing model in which the isotopic composition of the silicic end member is highly variable. Much of the scatter also results from regional variability in the isotopic composition of the mixing components (see text).

Al_2O_3 and higher in TiO_2, K_2O, and P_2O_5 than the model basalt. The model basalt cannot be related to the younger basalts by crystal-fractionation or mixing models.

TECTONIC SIGNIFICANCE

Despite the data reported herein, the Mojave volcanic belt defies tectonic interpretation. All that can be said with certainty is that volcanism commenced in the early Miocene in response to invasion of the crust by high-alumina, slightly alkalic basalt magma. The reason for this sudden influx of magma is not well understood. Its timing indicates that it is probably related to lithospheric extension near the Mendocino triple junction (Dickinson and Snyder, 1979; Glazner and Bartley, 1984). Plate reconstructions indicate that subduction continued throughout the early Tertiary hiatus, until the early Miocene transition to strike-slip faulting. It is possible that nonvolcanic subduction under the area modified the composition of the sub-Mojave lithosphere by addition of water and other volatiles, and that early Miocene extension-related volcanism tapped this modified, "juiced-up" mantle.

The simultaneous onset of volcanism across a belt that stretched more than 500 km inland, nearly perpendicular to the continental margin, is difficult to explain by invoking rapid steepening of the Farallon plate, as postulated by Coney and Reynolds (1977). In addition, because intermediate rocks from the Mojave Desert and many other areas are hybrids, methods for inferring the depth to the subduction zone based on K_2O-depth relations are invalid. Potassium contents of hybrid volcanic rocks are determined by the K_2O contents of the end members involved in mixing and by the extent of crystal fractionation. Crustal thickness and composition probably play an important role (Elston, 1984; Meen and Hartley, 1986).

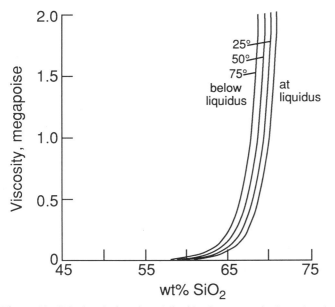

Figure 10. Calculated viscosity of liquids along an anhydrous basalt-rhyolite mixing line at one atmosphere (Ussler and Glazner, 1989). Note the extremely rapid increase in viscosity at about 65 wt% SiO_2. Curves show calculated viscosities (using the method of Shaw, 1972) at 0, 25, 50, and 75 °C below the liquidus, and do not take into account the increase in viscosity caused by the presence of crystals. Assuming 3 wt% water in the rhyolite displaces the curves to slightly higher viscosities because the liquidus temperatures are significantly lowered.

Tertiary volcanic rocks from the Mojave block are calc-alkaline and resemble many subduction-related suites in composition. However, many other suites that are clearly unrelated to subduction also resemble subduction-related suites. For example, Pliocene rocks from the Coso field, which were erupted 7 to 10 m.y. after subduction ceased at that latitude, exhibit chemical trends identical to those displayed by Mojave rocks (Novak and Bacon, 1986). Other post-subduction suites of the western United States show similar subduction-like trends (e.g., Luft, 1964; Wenrich-Verbeek, 1979). Because mixing produces the trends that make a suite calc-alkaline, calc-alkaline rocks can form in any environment in which basalt can mix with silicic material.

SUMMARY

Volcanism began in the Mojave block in latest Oligocene and early Miocene time, following a long early Tertiary hiatus. Volcanism commenced in an east-west band that extended from the westernmost tip of the Mojave Desert eastward to the Colorado River and beyond. This band was part of a northward-moving wave of volcanism and extensional deformation that passed through southernmost California about 25 Ma, through the central Mojave Desert about 20 Ma, and through the northern Mojave-Les Vegas region about 15 Ma. The cause of this intense resumption of volcanism is unknown, but it may be related to lithospheric extension and deformation near the Mendocino triple junction.

Volcanic rocks in the Mojave block are hybrids that were produced by mixing of mafic magmas derived from the mantle with continental crust and anatectic crustal liquids. Thus, although volcanism was driven by mantle-produced basalts, the spectrum of rocks produced contains a significant component of recycled continental crust. Evidence for mixing includes: (1) ubiquitous disequilibrium phenocryst assemblages (xenocrystic, armored quartz in mafic rocks; spongy, reverse-zoned plagioclase); (2) a positive correlation between $^{87}Sr/^{86}Sr$ and SiO_2; (3) elevated $\delta^{18}O$ in silicic rocks (Glazner and O'Neil, 1989); and (4) chemical trends that can be explained by a simple mixing-fractional crystallization model. Even relatively primitive basalts show evidence of crustal contamination. In hybrid suites of this type, the term "comagmatic" loses it meaning.

Most major elements show coherent variations with SiO_2, but patterns for many trace elements and $^{87}Sr/^{86}Sr_i$ are highly scattered. These variations are consistent with a mixing model in which the silicic end member is broadly rhyolitic in composition but is highly variable in trace-element and isotopic composition. The basalt end member is similar in composition to subduction-related basalts from other regions and differs from Pliocene-Holocene alkali basalts from the Mojave Desert. Scatter at the mafic end of the spectrum indicates that more than one basalt end member may have been involved.

Regional isotopic trends indicate that the silicic end member increases in $^{87}Sr/^{86}Sr$ and decreases in $\delta^{18}O$ from west to east. These trends may reflect decreasing involvement of Pelona-type schist and/or increasing involvement of Proterozoic basement from west to east. Distinguishing these possibilities will require studies of other isotopic systems.

ACKNOWLEDGMENTS

This work was supported by National Science Foundation Grant EAR-8219032, U.S. Department of Energy Grant 85ER13414, the Petroleum Research Fund, which is administered by the American Chemical Society, and the University of North Carolina Research Council. This paper is dedicated to my former teachers Alexander K. Baird and Donald B. McIntyre. Donald's interest in the connections between plate tectonics and magmatism led to this study; Alex's skepticism of tectonic models and careful criticism were a constant source of inspiration. M. A. Dungan, W. P. Leeman, and P. W. Weigand provided thorough and constructive reviews. Support from the U.S. Geological Survey (in particular, K. A. Howard, D. M. Miller, and J. E. Nielson) greatly aided the research. G. I. Smith first pointed out to me the curious nature of the simultaneous inception of volcanism over such a large area. The commanding officer of the Twentynine Palms Marine Base graciously offered access to important outcrops in the Bullion Mountains, and the U.S. Geological Survey provided logistical support. B. O. Richardson, J. P. Kurtz, S. N. Ehrenberg, R. D. Turner, and R. L. Jones aided the analytical work, and E. I. Smith provided INAA analyses. J.J.W. Rogers and W. Ussler III provided constructive reviews of an early version of the manuscript.

APPENDIX 1. ROCK SPECIMEN INFORMATION

For each specimen, information is given in the order: specimen number; latitude; longitude; general location; field sample name; geologic unit (if any).

#	Description
1	35.0640; 116.5454; Alvord Mountains; ALVO-3; basalt flow in Barstow Formation (Byers, 1960).
2	34.4957; 116.1492; Noble Pass area, Bullion Mountains; NBPS-6; unnamed, unit Tb of Dibblee (1967c).
3	35.0595; 117.6253; Saddleback Mountain; SADL-1; Saddleback Basalt of Gale (1946).
4	34.7817; 116.2442; southeastern Cady Mountains; 12-3; formation of Argos Station of Glazner (1988).
5	34.7063; 116.2106; northern Bullion Mountains; LUDL-C; unnamed, unit QTb of Dibblee (1967a).
6	34.7670; 116.2840; southeastern Cady Mountains; 11-90; formation of Argos Station of Glazner (1988).
7	34.6801; 115.6390; northern Marble Mountains; MARB-522-23; unnamed.
8	34.6810; 115.6381; northern Marble Mountains; MARB-522-22; unnamed.
9	34.7724; 116.2432; southeastern Cady Mountains; 13-22; formation of Argos Station of Glazner (1988).
10	34.6822; 115.6424; northern Marble Mountains; MARB-522-9; unnamed.
11	34.7550; 116.2186; southeastern Cady Mountains; 77032; formation of Argos Station of Glazner (1988).
12	34.8070; 116.0060; northern Bristol Mountains; BRST-11; unnamed, unit QTb of Dibblee (1967b).
13	34.6717; 116.2901; northern Bullion Mountains; LVLK-2; unnamed, unit QTb of Dibblee (1966).
14	34.7431; 115.7548; Old Dad Mountains; OLDD-2; unnamed.
15	34.8188; 117.5378; Red Buttes; A5-2; quartz andesite of Bowen (1954).
16	35.0705; 116.5735; Alvord Mountains; ALVO-1A; Alvord Peak Basalt of Byers (1960).
17	34.8994; 117.5116; Kramer Hills; KRMR-1; quartz andesite of Bowen (1954).
18	34.7036; 116.2075; northern Bullion Mountains; LUDL-B; unnamed, unit Tt of Dibblee (1967a).
19	34.8507; 116.0930; northern Bristol Mountains; BRST-2; unnamed, unit Tb of Dibblee (1967b).
20	34.8209; 117.5346; Red Buttes; A5-3; quartz andesite of Bowen (1954).
21	34.6890; 116.1783; northern Bullion Mountains; A2-5; unnamed, unit Tb of Dibblee (1967a).
22	34.8307; 116.3154; southeastern Cady Mountains; 82-16; formation of Argos Station of Glazner (1988).
23	34.8182; 117.5325; Red Buttes; A5-1; quartz andesite of Bowen (1954).

#	Description
24	34.7745; 116.2424; southeastern Cady Mountains; AG-2; dacite of Cady Mountains of Glazner (1988).
25	34.7607; 116.2310; southeastern Cady Mountains; AG-13; dacite of Cady Mountains of Glazner (1988).
26	34.8250; 116.3085; southeastern Cady Mountains; 82-22A; formation of Sleeping Beauty ridge of Glazner (1988).
27	34.7900; 116.2401; southeastern Cady Mountains; 10-5; formation of Sleeping Beauty ridge of Glazner (1988).
28	34.7841; 116.2161; southeastern Cady Mountains; 22-10A; formation of Sleeping Beauty ridge of Glazner (1988).
29	34.6450; 115.9625; Bristol Mountains; LVHL-2; unnamed.
30	35.1438; 116.2085; Soda Mountains; SODA-2; unnamed.
31	34.6615; 115.9726; Bristol Mountains; LVHL-1; unnamed.
32	34.5895; 116.3079; Lavic Lake; LVLK-1; unnamed, unit QTr of Dibblee (1966).
33	34.8098; 116.3182; southeastern Cady Mountains; 82-25; formation of Sleeping Beauty ridge of Glazner (1988).
34	34.7868; 116.3021; southeastern Cady Mountains; 25-13; formation of Sleeping Beauty ridge of Glazner (1988).
35	34.8055; 116.6698; Newberry Mountains; A4-2; unnamed, unit Tt of Dibblee and Bassett (1966).
36	34.8768; 116.8900; Barstow; BARS-2; unnamed, unit Tai of Dibblee (1970).
37	34.6925; 116.2007; northern Bullion Mountains; LUDL-D; unnamed, unit Tap of Dibblee (1967a).
38	34.7036; 115.6766; northern Marble Mountains; MARB-5; unnamed.
39	34.6683; 115.6412; northern Marble Mountains; MARB-2; unnamed.
40	35.0880; 116.9426; Lane Mountain; LNMT-2; Lane Mountain Quartz Latite of Burke and others (1982).
41	34.6938; 116.1906; northern Bullion Mountains; A2-3; unnamed, unit Ta of Dibblee (1967a).
42	34.6854; 115.6498; northern Marble Mountains; MARB-522-24; unnamed.

REFERENCES CITED

Armstrong, R. L., and Higgins, R. E., 1973, K-Ar dating of the beginning of Tertiary volcanism in the Mojave Desert, California: Geological Society of America Bulletin, v. 84, p. 1095–1100.

Atwater, T., 1970, Implications of plate tectonics for the Cenozoic tectonic evolution of western North America: Geological Society of America Bulletin, v. 81, p. 3513–3536.

Bacon, C. R., and Metz, J., 1984, Magmatic inclusions in rhyolites, contaminated basalts, and compositional zonation beneath the Coso volcanic field, California: Contributions to Mineralogy and Petrology, v. 85, p. 346–365.

Bacon, C. R., MacDonald, R., Smith, R. L., and Baedecker, P. A., 1981, Pleistocene high-silica rhyolites of the Coso volcanic field, Inyo County, California: Journal of Geophysical Research, v. 86, p. 10223–10241.

Best, M. G., and Brimhall, W. H., 1974, Late Cenozoic alkalic basaltic magmas in the western Colorado Plateaus and the Basin and Range transition zone, U.S.A., and their bearing on mantle dynamics: Geological Society of America Bulletin, v. 85, p. 1677–1690.

Bowen, N. L., 1928, The evolution of the igneous rocks: Princeton, New Jersey, Princeton University Press, 333 p.

Bowen, D. E., Jr., 1954, Geology and mineral deposits of Barstow quadrangle, San Bernardino County, California: California Division of Mines and Geology Bulletin 165, 185 p.

Burchfiel, B. C., and Davis, G. A., 1981, Mojave Desert and environs, in Ernst, W. G., ed., The geotectonic development of California: Englewood Cliffs, New Jersey, Prentice-Hall, p. 217–252.

Burke, D. B., Hillhouse, J. W., McKee, E. H., Miller, S. T., and Morton, J. L., 1982, Cenozoic rocks in the Barstow Basin area of southern California; Stratigraphic relations, radiometric ages, and paleomagnetism: U.S. Geological Survey Bulletin, v. 1529-E, p. 1–16.

Byers, F. M., Jr., 1960, Geology of the Alvord Mountain Quadrangle, San Bernardino County, California: U.S. Geological Survey Bulletin, v. 1089-A, 71 p.

Cameron, C. S., 1982, Stratigraphy and significance of the upper Precambrian Big Bear Group, in Cooper, J. D., Troxel, B. W., and Wright, L. A., eds., Geology of selected areas in the San Bernardino Mountains, western Mojave Desert, and southern Great Basin, California (Geological Society of America, Cordilleran Section Meeting, field trip number 9): Shoshone, California, Death Valley Publishing Co., p. 5–20.

Casey, B. J., 1981, The geology of a portion of the northwestern Bristol Mountains, Mojave Desert, California [M.S. thesis]: University of California at Riverside, 128 p.

Chapin, C. E., and Glazner, A. F., 1983, Widespread K2O metasomatism of Cenozoic volcanic and sedimentary rocks in the southwestern United States: Geological Society of America Abstracts with Programs, v. 15, p. 282.

Chayes, F., 1964, A petrographic distinction between Cenozoic volcanics in and around the open oceans: Journal of Geophysical Research, v. 69, p. 1573–1588.

Christiansen, R. L., and Lipman, P. W., 1972, Cenozoic volcanism and plate-tectonic evolution of the western United States; 2, Late Cenozoic: Royal Society of London Philosophical Transactions, ser. A, v. 271, p. 249–284.

Coney, P. J., and Reynolds, S. J., 1977, Cordilleran Benioff zones: Nature, v. 270, p. 403–406.

Cox, B. F., and Diggles, M. F., 1986, Geologic map of the El Paso Mountains wilderness study area, Kern County, California: U.S. Geological Survey Miscellaneous Field Studies Map MF–1827, scale 1:24,000.

Crowe, B. M., Crowell, J. C., and Krummenacher, D., 1979, Regional stratigraphy, K-Ar ages, and tectonic implications of Cenozoic volcanic rocks, southeastern California: American Journal of Science, v. 279, p. 186–216.

Damon, P. E., 1979, Continental uplift at convergent boundaries: Tectonophysics, v. 61, p. 307–319.

Darton, N. H., and others, 1915, Guidebook of the western United States; Part C, The Santa Fe route: U.S. Geological Survey Bulletin, v. 613, 194 p.

Davis, G. A., and Fleck, R. J., 1977, Chronology of Miocene volcanic and

structural events, central Owlshead Mountains, eastern San Bernardino County, California: Geological Society of America Abstracts with Programs, v. 9, p. 409.

Dibblee, T. W., Jr., 1966, Geologic map of the Lavic Quadrangle, San Bernardino County, California: U.S. Geological Survey Map I–472, scale 1:62,500.

——, 1967a, Geologic map of the Ludlow Quadrangle, San Bernardino County, California: U.S. Geological Survey Map I–477, scale 1:62,500.

——, 1967b, Geologic map of the Broadwell Lake Quadrangle, San Bernardino County, California: U.S. Geological Survey Map I–478, scale 1:62,500.

——, 1967c, Geologic map of the Deadman Lake Quadrangle, San Bernardino County, California: U.S. Geological Survey Miscellaneous Geologic Investigations Map I–488, scale 1:62,500.

——, 1967d, Areal geology of the western Mojave Desert, California: U.S. Geological Survey Professional Paper, v. 522, 153 p.

——, 1970, Geologic map of the Daggett Quadrangle, San Bernardino County, California: U.S. Geological Survey Map I–592, scale 1:62,500.

Dibblee, T. W., Jr., and Bassett, A. M., 1966, Geologic map of the Newberry Quadrangle, San Bernardino County, California: U.S. Geological Survey Miscellaneous Geologic Investigations Map I–461, scale 1:62,500.

Dickinson, W. R., and Snyder, W. S., 1979, Geometry of subducted slabs related to San Andreas transform: Journal of Geology, v. 87, p. 609–627.

Diller, J. S., 1891, A late volcanic eruption in northern California and its peculiar lava: U.S. Geological Survey Bulletin, v. 79, 33 p.

Eaton, G. P., Wahl, R. R., Prostka, H. J., Mabey, D. R., and Kleinkopf, M. D., 1978, Regional gravity and tectonic patterns; Their relation to late Cenozoic epeirogeny and lateral spreading in the western Cordillera: Geological Society of America Memoir 152, p. 51–91.

Eichelberger, J. C., 1978, Andesitic volcanism and crustal evolution: Nature, v. 275, p. 21–27.

Elston, W. E., 1984, Subduction of young oceanic lithosphere and extensional orogeny in southwestern North America during mid-Tertiary time: Tectonics, v. 3, p. 229–250.

Fuis, G. S., 1981, Crustal structure of the Mojave Desert, California: U.S. Geological Survey Open-File Report 81–503, p. 36–38.

Gale, H. S., 1946, Geology of the Kramer borate district, Kern County, California: California Journal of Mines and Geology, v. 42, p. 325–378.

Gill, J., 1981, Orogenic andesites and plate tectonics: New York, Springer-Verlag, 390 p.

Glazner, A. F., 1988, Stratigraphy, structure, and potassic alteration of Miocene volcanic rocks in the Sleeping Beauty area, central Mojave Desert, California: Geological Society of America Bulletin, v. 100, p. 424–435.

Glazner, A. F., and Bartley, J. M., 1984, Timing and tectonic setting of Tertiary low-angle normal faulting and associated magmatism in the southwestern United States: Tectonics, v. 3, p. 385–396.

——, 1988, Early Miocene dome emplacement, diking, and faulting in the Marble Mountains, eastern Mojave Desert: Geological Society of America Abstracts with Programs, v. 20, p. 163–164.

Glazner, A. F., and O'Neil, J. R., 1989, Crustal structure of the Mojave Desert, California: Inferences from Sr and O isotope studies of Miocene volcanic rocks: Journal of Geophysical Research, v. 94 (in press).

Glazner, A. F., and Richardson, B. O., 1983, Major-element differences between syn- and post-subduction volcanic rocks in the western U.S.: Geological Society of America Abstracts with Programs, v. 15, p. 280.

Glazner, A. F., and Schubert, G., 1985, Flexure of the North American lithosphere above the subducted Mendocino fracture zone and the formation of east-west faults in the Transverse Ranges: Journal of Geophysical Research, v. 90, p. 5405–5409.

Glazner, A. F., Nielson, J. E., Howard, K. A., and Miller, D. M., 1986, Correlation of the Peach Springs Tuff, a large-volume Miocene ignimbrite sheet in California and Arizona: Geology, v. 14, p. 840–843.

Glazner, A. F., Walker, J. D., Bartley, J. M., and Dent, S. B., 1988, Distribution and relations of Precambrian and Paleozoic rocks in the central Mojave Desert, California: Geological Society of America Abstracts with Programs, v. 20, p. 163.

Gunderson, R., Cameron, K., and Cameron, M., 1986, Mid-Cenozoic high-K calc-alkalic and alkalic volcanism in eastern Chihuahua, Mexico; Geology and geochemistry of the Benavides–Pozos area: Geological Society of America Bulletin, v. 97, p. 737–753.

Hamilton, W., 1969, Mesozoic California and the underflow of Pacific mantle: Geological Society of America Bulletin, v. 80, p. 2409–2430.

Hamilton, W., and Myers, W. B., 1966, Cenozoic tectonics of the western United States: Reviews of Geophysics, v. 4, p. 509–549.

Haxel, G., and Dillon, J., 1978, The Pelona–Orocopia schist and Vincent–Chocolate Mountain thrust system, southern California, *in* Howell, D. G., and McDougall, K. A., eds., Mesozoic paleogeography of the western United States; Pacific Coast Paleogeography Symposium 2: Los Angeles, California, Society of Economic Paleontologists and Mineralogists, p. 453–469.

Hewett, D. F., 1954, General geology of the Mojave Desert region, California: California Division of Mines and Geology Bulletin, v. 170, p. 5–20.

Hildreth, W., 1981, Gradients in silicic magma chambers; Implications for lithospheric magmatism: Journal of Geophysical Research, v. 86, p. 10153–10192.

Howard, K. A., Stone, P., Pernokas, M. A., and Marvin, R. F., 1982, Geologic and geochronologic reconnaissance of the Turtle Mountains area, California; West border of the Whipple Mountains detachment terrane, *in* Frost, E. G., and Martin, D. L., eds., Mesozoic–Cenozoic tectonic evolution of the Colorado River region, California, Arizona, and Nevada: San Diego, California, Cordilleran Publishers, p. 341–354.

Hughes, C. J., 1982, Igneous petrology: New York, Elsevier, 551 p.

Hughes, W. T., 1986, Geochemical evolution of basalts from Amboy and Pisgah lava fields, Mojave Desert, California [M.S. thesis]: Chapel Hill, University of North Carolina, 113 p.

Jennings, C. W., 1977, Geologic map of California: California Division of Mines and Geology, scale 1:750,000.

Johnson, C. M., and O'Neil, J. R., 1984, Triple junction magmatism; A geochemical study of Neogene volcanic rocks in western California: Earth and Planetary Science Letters, v. 71, p. 241–262.

Kiser, N. L., 1981, Stratigraphy, structure and metamorphism in the Hinkley Hills, Barstow, California [M.S. thesis]: Palo Alto, California, Stanford University, 70 p.

Kistler, R. W., and Peterman, Z. E., 1978, Reconstruction of crustal blocks of California on the basis of initial strontium isotopic compositions of Mesozoic granitic rocks: U.S. Geological Survey Professional Paper 1071, 17 p.

Koyaguchi, T., 1986, Textural and compositional evidence for magma mixing and its mechanism, Abu volcano group, southwestern Japan: Contributions to Mineralogy and Petrology, v. 93, p. 33–45.

Lachenbruch, A. H., Sass, J. H., and Galanis, S. P., Jr., 1978, New heat flow results from southern California [abs.]: EOS Transactions of the American Geophysical Union, v. 59, p. 1051.

Lacroix, A., 1893, Les Enclaves des Roches Volcaniques: Paris, Masson.

Lanphere, M. A., 1964, Geochronologic studies in the eastern Mojave Desert, California: Journal of Geology, v. 72, p. 381–399.

Lanphere, M. A., Wasserburg, G.J.F., Albee, A. L., and Tilton, G. R., 1964, Redistribution of strontium and rubidium isotopies during metamorphism, World Beater complex, Panamint Range, California, *in* Craig, H., Miller, S. L., and Wasserburg, G. J., eds., Isotopic and cosmic chemistry: Amsterdam, North-Holland, p. 269–320.

Lipman, P. W., Prostka, H. J., and Christiansen, R. L., 1971, Evolving subduction zones in the western United States, as interpreted from igneous rocks: Science, v. 174, p. 821–825.

—— , 1972, Cenozoic volcanism and plate-tectonic evolution of the western United States; 1, Early and middle Cenozoic: Royal Society of London Philosophical Transactions, ser. A, v. 271, p. 217–248.

Lowell, J. D., 1974, Plate tectonics and foreland basement deformation: Geology, v. 2, p. 275–278.

Luft, S. J., 1964, Mafic lavas of Dome Mountain, Timber Mountain caldera, southern Nevada: U.S. Geological Survey Professional Paper 501–D, p. 14–21.

Martin, R. F., and Piwinskii, A. J., 1972, Magmatism and tectonic settings: Journal of Geophysical Research, v. 77, p. 4966–4975.

McKee, E. H., 1971, Tertiary igneous chronology of the Great Basin of western United States; Implications for tectonic models: Geological Society of America Bulletin, v. 82, p. 3497–3502.

McMillan, N. J., and Dungan, M. A., 1986, Magma mixing as a petrogenetic process in the development of the Taos Plateau volcanic field, New Mexico: Journal of Geophysical Research, v. 91, p. 6029–6045.

Meen, J. K., and Hartley, P., 1986, Control of potash contents of arc volcanics by pressure of fractionation of parental basalts; Experimental evidence: Geological Society of America Abstracts with Programs, v. 18, p. 692.

Mies, J. W., and Glazner, A. F., 1987, Quartz xenocrysts with rhyolite glass inclusions in andesite as evidence of assimilated granite [abs.]: EOS Transactions of the American Geophysical Union, v. 68, p. 434–435.

Miller, F. K., and Morton, D. M., 1980, Potassium-argon geochronology of the eastern Transverse Ranges and southern Mojave Desert, southern California: U.S. Geological Survey Professional Paper 1152, 30 p.

Miller, J. S., 1989, The Tertiary volcanic history and petrology of the Old Woman Mountains area, eastern Mojave Desert, California [M.S. thesis]: Nashville, Tennessee, Vanderbilt University, 160 p.

Moseley, C. G., 1978, The geology of a portion of the northern Cady Mountains, Mojave Desert, California [M.S. thesis]: Riverside, University of California, 131 p.

Moseley, C. G., Williamson, D. A., and Miller, S. T., 1982, The stratigraphy of the northeastern Cady Mountains and its implications for the Cenozoic volcanic evolution of the Mojave Desert, *in* Ingersoll, R. V., and Woodburne, M. O., eds., Cenozoic nonmarine deposits of California and Arizona: Society of Economic Paleontologists and Mineralogists, p. 75–81.

Nason, G. W., 1978, Geology of a portion of the northern Newberry Mountains, San Bernardino County, California [M.S. thesis]: California State University at Los Angeles, 70 p.

Nason, G. W., Davis, T. E., and Stull, R. J., 1979, Cenozoic volcanism in the Newberry Mountains, San Bernardino County, California, *in* Armentrout, J. M., Cole, M. R., and TerBest, H., Jr., eds., Cenozoic paleogeography of the western United States: Society of Economic Paleontologists and Mineralogists Pacific Coast Paleogeography Symposium 3, p. 89–95.

Nicholls, J., Carmichael, I.S.E., and Stormer, J., 1971, Silica activity and P_{total} in igneous rocks: Contributions to Mineralogy and Petrology, v. 33, p. 1–20.

Nielsen, R. L., and Dungan, M. A., 1985, The petrology and geochemistry of the Ocate volcanic field, north-central New Mexico: Geological Society of America Bulletin, v. 96, p. 296–312.

Nielson, J. E., 1986, Miocene stratigraphy of the Mohave Mountains, Arizona, and correlation with adjacent ranges, *in* Nielson, J. E., and Glazner, A. F., eds., Cenozoic stratigraphy, structure, and mineralization in the Mojave Desert: Geological Society of America Cordilleran Section Guidebook and Volume, p. 15–24.

Norrish, K., and Hutton, J. T., 1969, An accurate X-ray spectrographic method for the analysis of a wide range of geological samples: Geochimica et Cosmochimica Acta, v. 33, p. 431–453.

Novak, S. W., and Bacon, C. R., 1986, Pliocene volcanic rocks of the Coso Range, Inyo County, California: U.S. Geological Survey Professional Paper 1383, 44 p.

Phillips, G. R., and Eyring, E. M., 1983, Comparison of conventional and robust regression in analysis of chemical data: Analytical Chemistry, v. 55, p. 1134–1338.

Pilger, R. H., Jr., and Henyey, T. L., 1979, Pacific–North American plate interaction and Neogene volcanism in coastal California: Tectonophysics, v. 57, p. 189–209.

Sakuyama, M., 1981, Petrological study of the Myoko and Kurohime volcanoes, Japan; Crystallization sequence and evidence for magma mixing: Journal of Petrology, v. 22, p. 553–583.

Sato, H., 1975, Diffusion coronas around quartz xenocrysts in andesite and basalt from Tertiary volcanic region in northeastern Shikoku, Japan: Contributions to Mineralogy and Petrology, v. 50, p. 49–64.

Shaw, H. R., 1972, Viscosities of magmatic silicate liquids; An empirical method of prediction: American Journal of Science, v. 272, p. 870–893.

Silver, L. T., and Anderson, T. H., 1974, Possible left-lateral early to middle Mesozoic disruption of the southwestern North American craton margin: Geological Society of America Abstracts with Programs, v. 6, p. 955.

Smith, G. I., 1964, Geology and volcanic petrology of the Lava Mountains, San Bernardino County, California: U.S. Geological Survey Professional Paper 457, 97 p.

Snyder, W. S., Dickinson, W. R., and Silberman, M. L., 1976, Tectonic implications of space-time patterns of Cenozoic magmatism in the western United States: Earth and Planetary Science Letters, v. 32, p. 91–106.

Stewart, J. H., 1982, Regional relations of Proterozoic Z and Lower Cambrian rocks in the western United States and northern Mexico, *in* Cooper, J. D., Troxel, B. W., and Wright, L. A., eds., Geology of selected areas in the San Bernardino Mountains, western Mojave Desert and southern Great Basin, California (Geological Society of America Cordilleran Section Meeting, field trip number 9): Shoshone, California, Death Valley Publishing Co., p. 171–186.

Tsuchiyama, A., 1985, Dissolution kinetics of plagioclase in the melt of the system diopside-albite-anorthite, and origin of dusty plagioclase in andesites: Contributions to Mineralogy and Petrology, v. 89, p. 1–16.

Tsuchiyama, A., and Takahashi, E., 1983, Melting kinetics of a plagiocase feldspar: Contributions to Mineralogy and Petrology, v. 84, p. 345–354.

Turner, R. D., 1985, Miocene folding and faulting of an evolving volcanic center in the Castle Mountains, southeastern California and southern Nevada [M.S. thesis]: Chapel Hill, University of North Carolina, 56 p.

Ussler, W., III, and Glazner, A. F., 1989, Phase equilibria along a basalt-rhyolite mixing line: Implications for the origin of calc-alkaline intermediate magmas: Contributions to Mineralogy and Petrology, v. 101, p. 232–244.

Walker, J. D., 1988, Permian and Triassic rocks of the Mojave Desert and their implications for the timing and mechanism of continental truncation: Tectonics, v. 7, p. 685–709.

Weigland, P. W., 1982, Middle Cenozoic volcanism of the western Transverse Ranges, *in* Fife, D. L., and Minch, J. A., eds., Geology and mineral wealth of the California Transverse Ranges: Santa Ana, California, South Coast Geological Society, p. 170–188.

Wenrich-Verbeek, K. J., 1979, The petrogenesis and trace-element geochemistry of intermediate lavas from Humphreys Peak, San Francisco volcanic field, Arizona: Tectonophysics, v. 61, p. 103–129.

Williamson, D. A., 1980, The geology of a portion of the eastern Cady Mountains, Mojave Desert, California [M.S. thesis]: Riverside, University of California, 148 p.

Woodburne, M. O., Tedford, R. H., Stevens, M. S., and Taylor, B. E., 1974, Early Miocene mammalian faunas, Mojave Desert, California: Journal of Paleontology, v. 48, p. 6–26.

MANUSCRIPT SUBMITTED 7/31/87
REVISED MANUSCRIPT SUBMITTED 1/19/88
MANUSCRIPT ACCEPTED BY THE SOCIETY FEBRUARY 7, 1989

Geological Society of America
Memoir 174
1990

Chapter 10

Mid-Miocene volcanic and plutonic rocks in the Lake Mead area of Nevada and Arizona; Production of intermediate igneous rocks in an extensional environment

Eugene I. Smith, Daniel L. Feuerbach, and Terry R. Naumann
Department of Geoscience, University of Nevada, Las Vegas, Nevada 89154
James G. Mills
Department of Geology, Monmouth College, Monmouth, Illinois 61462

ABSTRACT

Middle Tertiary volcanic rocks of the Lake Mead field are calc-alkalic to alkalic-calcic and vary continuously in composition from basalt to rhyolite. These volcanic rocks formed during Basin-and-Range extension and are spatially and genetically associated with diorite-to-granite intrusions of the Wilson Ridge pluton. Locally, igneous rocks were subjected to potassium metasomatism.

Field relations and petrography provide evidence of disequilibrium mineral assemblages and liquid-liquid mixing of basalt and granite magmas to form the intermediate rock types of the Lake Mead volcanic field. Evidence of mixing includes incompatible phase assemblages of euhedral olivine, embayed quartz, and sodic plagioclase within andesite flows. Plagioclase occurs in rounded and partially resorbed clusters of equant crystals and commonly displays oscillatory zoning and outer glass-charged zones (fretted texture). Quartz phenocrysts are commonly surrounded by rims of prismatic augite and glass. Fine-grained spheroidal to ellipsoidal inclusions of basalt are common in dacite flows and dikes. Thus, various mixing ratios of olivine basalt and granite end members may be responsible for the textural variations observed in volcanic rocks of the Lake Mead field.

The evolution of the igneous rocks of the Lake Mead field was evaluated by petrogenetic models involving both crystal fractionation and magma mixing. These processes may have operated together to produce the compositional range in volcanic and plutonic rocks of the Lake Mead area. Open-system models provide estimates of the relative importance of the two processes and suggest that mixing was more important in the derivation of andesite and diorite (mass mixed component/mass crystallizing phase R = 0.8 to 2.2) than dacite, quartz monzonite, or granite (R = 0.1 to 0.65).

The calc-alkaline–alkalic-calcic nature of the igneous rocks of the Lake Mead field, and possibly other similar rock suites that formed in the Great Basin during regional extension, may result from magma mixing. Basalts and rhyolites may mechanically mix in various proportions to produce intermediate rock types. The classic bimodal assemblages may only occur where mixing is incomplete or in structural situations where different magma types cannot mix.

Smith, E. I., Feuerbach, D. L., Naumann, T. R., and Mills, J. G., 1990, Mid-Miocene volcanic and plutonic rocks in the Lake Mead area of Nevada and Arizona; Production of intermediate igneous rocks in an extensional environment, *in* Anderson, J. L., ed., The nature and origin of Cordilleran magmatism: Boulder, Colorado, Geological Society of America Memoir 174.

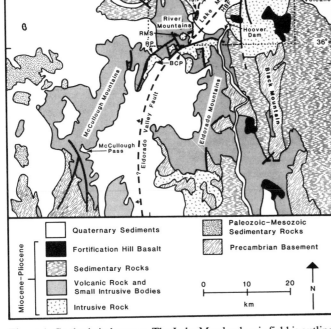

Figure 1. Geologic index map. The Lake Mead volcanic field is outlined by the box and shown in detail in Figure 4. WRP = Wilson Ridge pluton, RMS = River Mountains stock, BCP = Boulder City pluton, RP = Railroad Pass, BSVF = Bitter Spring Valley fault, HBF = Hamblin Bay fault.

INTRODUCTION

In the Lake Mead area of southern Nevada and northwestern Arizona, structural and topographic relief provides a cross section of a mid-Miocene (20 to 12 Ma) volcanic sequence and related subjacent plutons emplaced during Basin-and-Range extension (Fig. 1). Volcanic rocks vary continuously in composition from basalt (47 percent SiO_2) to rhyolite (75 percent SiO_2). Stratovolcanoes in the River, McCullough, Eldorado, and northern Black Mountains are composed mainly of andesite and dacite (56 to 68 percent SiO_2). Basalt and rhyolite are rare and erupted during the last episode of volcanism in the River Mountains (Smith, 1984; Smith and others, 1986). Volcanic rocks are associated with cogenetic diorite to granite intrusions, the Boulder City and Wilson Ridge plutons.

Our approach involves an integrated field, petrographic, and geochemical study of a suite of rocks in the River Mountains–Hoover Dam, and Boulder Wash–Wilson Ridge areas. Petrogenetic models involving both crystal fractionation and magma mixing were developed using the least-squares mass-balance equation of Stormer and Nicholls (1978). Models were refined using techniques proposed by Langmuir and others (1978) and

DePaulo (1981) and recently applied to petrologic problems by McMillan and Dungan (1986) and Thompson and others (1986). This suite of rocks, herein named the Lake Mead field, was previously interpreted by Weber and Smith (1987) as a cogenetic suite that evolved independent from volcanic rocks in the McCullough and Eldorado Mountains and the Boulder City pluton.

REGIONAL SETTING

The Lake Mead area of southern Nevada and northwestern Arizona is at the northern end of the Colorado River detachment terrane, a region that was subjected to large-scale extension during mid-Miocene time (Anderson, 1971; Frost and others, 1982; Spencer, 1985; Weber and Smith, 1987) (Fig. 1). Volcanism began in the Lake Mead area at about 20 Ma and continued until about 12 Ma. Basalt at Fortification Hill and at scattered localities near Lake Mead is dated between 4 and 6 Ma and represents the youngest volcanism in the region (Anderson and others, 1972; Feuerbach and Smith, 1987). Tilting, faulting, and detachment of the volcanic section related to the main phase of extension occurred mainly after 14.7 Ma; however, faulting began earlier (15 to 21 Ma) in the River Mountains (Smith, 1982) and in the Hoover Dam area (Mills, 1985).

On the basis of geochemical correlation and geometric reconstructions, Weber and Smith (1987) proposed a model for the prefaulting configuration of volcanoes near Lake Mead. Their model suggested that the River, McCullough, and Eldorado Mountains lie in the upper plate of a west-dipping detachment zone and that prior to mid-Tertiary extensional faulting the Lake Mead area contained three compound stratovolcanoes. These are (1) the River Mountains–Hoover Dam–Boulder Wash volcanoes associated with the Wilson Ridge Pluton (Smith, 1982, 1984; Mills, 1985; Naumann, 1987); (2) the McCullough-Eldorado volcanoes related to the Boulder City and Nelson plutons (Anderson, 1971; Smith and others, 1986); and (3) the Hamblin-Cleopatra volcano associated with an unnamed pluton (Anderson, 1973; Thompson, 1985) (Fig. 2). The stratovolcanoes were assigned to specific plutons on the basis of similarities in trace and rare earth element (REE) distributions (Weber and Smith, 1987). The River Mountains–Hoover Dam–Boulder Wash–Wilson Ridge suite (the Lake Mead field) is characterized by low Ta contents and a negative correlation between total REE concentration and SiO_2 content. The McCullough–Eldorado–Boulder City suite displays high Ta concentrations and a positive correlation between total REE and SiO_2. These characteristics suggest that the two volcanic-plutonic suites formed and evolved independently (Weber and Smith, 1987).

VOLCANIC STRATIGRAPHY AND PETROLOGY

River Mountains

In the River Mountains an andesite-dacite stratovolcano is surrounded by a field of dacite domes and flows. Volcanic activity occurred in four pulses, each characterized by the eruption of andesite and dacite flows. Flows of the first episode (volcanic rocks of River Mountains; Bell and Smith, 1980) formed the River Mountains stratovolcano at about 13.5 Ma (Fig. 3). Andesite flows cut by dikes and sills of plagioclase-biotite dacite (Table 1 [Tables 1 through 4 located at end of chapter.]) form the flanks of the volcano. A complex pluton of quartz monzonite containing quartz, plagioclase, biotite, and hornblende occupies the core of the stratovolcano (River Mountains stock; Bell and Smith, 1980) (Fig. 4). Volcanic rocks of the second episode (volcanic rocks of Bootleg Wash; Bell and Smith, 1980) exposed only in the southern part of the River Mountains just to the northwest of Boulder City (Fig. 4) contain a basal andesite overlain by a thin volcaniclastic unit that is in turn overlain by plagioclase-, biotite-, and sphene-bearing dacite flows. Dacite contains scattered grains of highly resorbed quartz. The third episode of volcanism formed a broad field of dacite and andesite domes and flows that are associated with thick deposits of breccia and volcaniclastic debris (volcanic rocks of Powerline Road; Bell and Smith, 1980). The last episode of volcanism is characterized by rhyolite and alkali basalt dated at 12 Ma (Anderson and others, 1972).

These volcanic rocks erupted from separate centers in the northern part of the River Mountains and mark the first appearance of rhyolite and basalt.

Field evidence for magma mixing and assimilation in the River Mountains includes dacite and quartz monzonite that contain inclusions of pyroxene basalt(?) and/or hornblende andesite, a flow within the Powerline Road section that contains 20 to 40 percent basaltic inclusions, and basaltic inclusions within the River Mountains stock that reach 1 m in diameter.

Hoover Dam

At Hoover Dam, a dacite ash-flow tuff (the tuff of Hoover Dam; Smith, 1984) separates a lower sequence of andesite flows and conglomerate from an upper sequence of dacite flows and breccia, andesite flows, and conglomerate (Fig. 3). The tuff may have erupted from a northwest-trending sag-graben caldera to the northwest of Hoover Dam (Mills, 1985). Because of structural disruption and the Lake Mead reservoir, the form and size of this source area is difficult to document. The following evidence, however, is supportive of a source area for the tuff in the vicinity

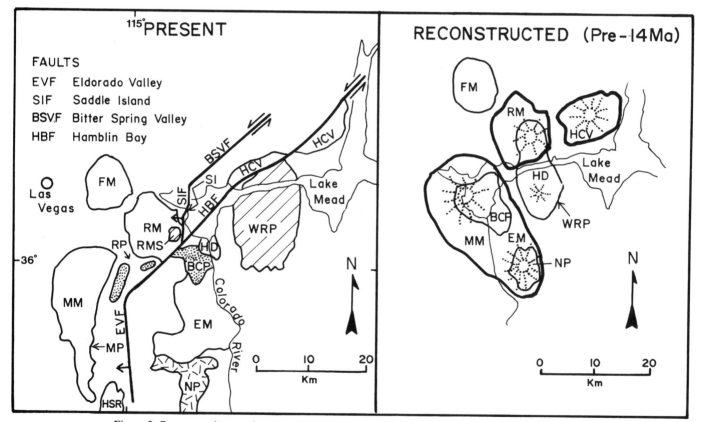

Figure 2. Present geology and proposed reconstruction of the Lake Mead area prior to mid-Miocene extension. In reconstruction, thick solid lines = boundaries of volcanic piles, and thin solid lines = possible extent of subjacent plutons. HSR = Highland Spring Range, FM = Frenchman Mountain, RM = River Mountains, MM = McCullough Mountains, EM = Eldorado Mountains, HD = Hoover Dam volcanic section, HCV = Hamblin-Cleopatra volcano, NP = Nelson Pluton, SI = Saddle Island. Other abbreviations are defined in the caption to Figure 1.

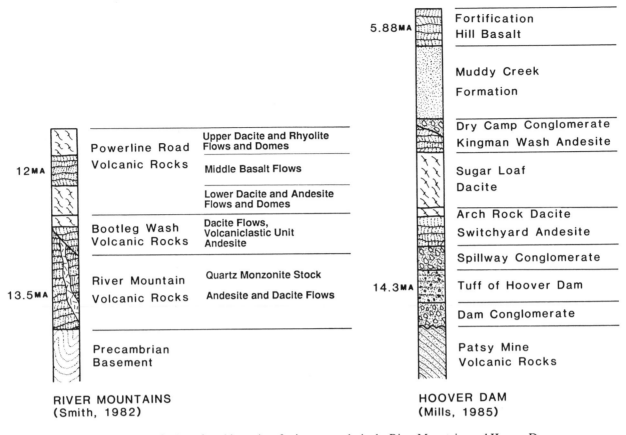

Figure 3. Generalized stratigraphic sections for igneous rocks in the River Mountains and Hoover Dam area.

of Hoover Dam. (1) The tuff of Hoover Dam is restricted in outcrop to a 3-km radius about Hoover Dam (Fig. 4). It is more than 185 m thick at Hoover Dam, but pinches out 1.5 km to the south. (2) To the north and northwest of Hoover Dam, along the south shore of Lake Mead, the tuff is rich in xenoliths of lower-sequence andesite. At Promontory Point (Fig. 4), xenoliths as much as 1 m in diameter compose 75 percent of the tuff. This deposit may represent a megabreccia unit near the west wall of the caldera. (3) Upper-sequence dacite is chemically related to the tuff and may represent post-caldera domes and flows. We envision the eruption of the tuff from a sag-graben or trap-door style caldera. The tuff of Hoover Dam is mineralogically and chemically zoned from dacite (68 percent SiO_2) at its stratigraphic top to andesite (56 percent SiO_2) at its base.

Upper-sequence rocks include a section of dacite flows, breccia, and andesite flows interbedded with conglomerate. The Arch Rock dacite (Mills, 1985) is a flow breccia containing rounded clasts of devitrified dacite. The hornblende-, biotite-, and plagioclase-bearing Sugarloaf dacite (Mills, 1985) has a well-developed basal vitrophyre. The dacite erupted from a large complex dome 1 km south of Hoover Dam. Mafic flows in the upper sequence include the olivine-bearing Switchyard and Kingman Wash andesites (Mills, 1985).

Wilson Ridge pluton

The Wilson Ridge pluton (Anderson, 1978), interpreted as a subvolcanic intrusion related to volcanic centers in the River Mountains and at Hoover Dam (Feuerbach and Smith, 1986), varies in composition from diorite to granite. The mid-Tertiary pluton (13.6 and 15.1 Ma; Anderson and others, 1972) is now exposed in a series of horsts and grabens in the northern Black Mountains (Figs. 1 and 4). During faulting the pluton was tilted 2° to 3° to the north (Feuerbach, 1986). Structural relief provides excellent exposures of a complex composite intrusion composed of at least four intrusive and hypabyssal phases and numerous felsic and mafic dikes (Fig. 4), listed as follows. (1) A *medium-grained phase* is composed of medium- to coarse-grained quartz monzonite to granite, the dominant phase of the Wilson Ridge pluton. This phase contains plagioclase, microcline, orthoclase, quartz, biotite, and hornblende, and minor amounts of sphene, apatite, and zircon (Table 1). (2) A *hypabyssal phase* is formed by monzonite to quartz monzonite containing phenocrysts of plagioclase, orthoclase, quartz, and biotite with subordinate hornblende and zircon. Rocks of this phase crop out in the northern part of the Gilbert Canyon graben and in the Boulder Wash area (Fig. 4). (3) A *diorite phase* is dominated by plagioclase, hornblende, and biotite with subordinate amounts of orthoclase and trace amounts of sphene, quartz, apatite, and zircon. Diorite is commonly intruded by quartz monzonite along the margins of the pluton, and occurs as inclusions within the pluton (sample 57d). (4) A *red-feldspar granite phase* crops out on Fortification Ridge (Fig. 4) and contains phenocrysts of red to pink orthoclase in a matrix of medium-grained plagioclase, quartz, biotite, microcline, and trace amounts of apatite and zircon (Table 1).

Dikes of granite, granite porphyry, aplite, basalt, and biotite lamprophyre intruded the pluton. Feuerbach (1986) estimated that at least 400 north-trending dikes with an average width of 7 m intruded the core of the pluton and resulted in about 20 percent east-west extension.

Boulder Wash

The Boulder Wash area in the northern Black Mountains (Fig. 4) consists of multiple sheet-like intrusions of quartz monzonite of the Wilson Ridge pluton cut by dikes of dacite, basalt, and biotite lamprophyre. Volcanic rocks in the Boulder Wash area consist of a highly faulted 700-m-thick secton of biotite-plagioclase dacite flows and flow breccias interbedded with flows of pyroxene-olivine andesite containing xenocrysts of quartz and orthoclase. A dacite flow in the eastern part of the volcanic field was dated at 14.2 Ma (Thompson, 1985).

Petrographic and textural evidence of magma mixing is spectacularly developed in the Wilson Ridge pluton and in associated volcanic rocks in the Boulder Wash area (Naumann and Smith, 1987; Naumann, 1987). Evidence includes incompatible phase assemblages of euhedral olivine, embayed quartz, and sodic plagioclase within andesite flows (Naumann and Smith, 1987; Naumann, 1987). Plagioclase occurs in rounded and partially resorbed clusters of equant crystals and commonly displays oscillatory zoning and outer glass-charged zones (fretted texture) (Fig. 5). Quartz phenocrysts are commonly surrounded by rims of prismatic augite and glass (Fig. 5). Dacites contain an identical disequilibrium phenocryst asemblage, but contain biotite rather than olivine. Fine-grained inclusions of basalt are common in dacite flows and dacite dikes within the Wilson Ridge pluton. The inclusions range in size from 2 mm to more than 50 cm and contain phenocrysts of olivine and plagioclase (5 percent total phenocrysts) set in matrix of plagioclase microlites and glass. Elliptical to spherical inclusions commonly have crenulated margins (Fig. 6). Some inclusions have fine-grained margins and coarse-grained vesicular cores (Fig. 6). The presence of fine-grained rims (quench rims) and crenulated margins suggests that these inclusions are quenched "blobs" of mafic magma that crystallized after mixing with the host dacite liquid (Bacon, 1986; Koyaguchi, 1986; Mattison and others, 1986). A continuum of mixing textures exists in the Boulder Wash lavas and related dikes. As the proportion of mafic inclusions decreases, the modal abundance of quartz and sodic plagioclase phenocrysts increases. On the basis of a model by Koyaguchi (1986), we concluded that various mixing ratios of olivine basalt and granite end members are responsible for the textual variations (Naumann and Smith, 1987; Naumann, 1987).

INSTRUMENTAL TECHNIQUES

Whole-rock major-element concentrations were determined by Inductively Coupled Plasma techniques (ICP) at Chemex Labs, Inc. (Sparks, Nevada) and by x-ray fluorescence (XRF) analysis in the Rock Chemistry Laboratory at the University of Nevada, Las Vegas, and in the Department of Geology, Michigan State University. Cr, Ni, Cu, Zn, Rb, Sr, Y, Zr, Nb, and Ba were analyzed by XRF. Rare-earth elements and Sc, Rb, Sr, Ba, Ta, Hf, Zr, U, and Th were analyzed by Instrumental Neutron Activation Analysis (INAA) at the Phoenix Memorial Laboratory, University of Michigan. The multielement standards G-2, GSP-1, BHVO-1, and RGM-1 were used as internal standards. Precision for REE with concentrations of less than 1,000 ppm is 5 percent, except for Nd, Tb, and Yb, which is 10 percent.

MAJOR- AND TRACE-ELEMENT CHEMISTRY

Representative major- and trace-element analyses are shown in Table 2. Harker variation plots show a continuous range of SiO_2 contents from 46 to 77 percent (Fig. 7). Volcanic rocks in the River–Hoover Dam–Boulder Wash sections are mainly calc-alkalic or alkalic-calcic andesites and dacites (Fig. 8), with SiO_2 content varying between 54 and 67 percent. Plutonic rocks have the same geochemical affinities, but are generally more highly evolved (SiO_2 contents up to 77 percent) than their volcanic counterparts (Feuerbach, 1986).

Rocks of the Lake Mead field show decreasing total REE content with increasing SiO_2, and in the River Mountains, each of the four episodes of andesite-dacite volcanism is accompanied by a decrease in total REE content (Figs. 9, 10). Chondrite-normalized REE distribution plots (Fig. 11) in general show light REE depletion with increasing SiO_2. Several curves show small negative Eu anomalies. Distribution curves for samples of the tuff of Hoover Dam are stacked with lower REE contents in the dacitic top of the ash-flow sheet and higher contents at the andesitic base of the unit (Fig. 11C).

METASOMATISM AND ALTERATION

Some samples of igneous rock of the Lake Mead field were strongly affected by K-metasomatism (Table 2). Metasomatism mainly produced changes in the abundances of Na_2O, K_2O, Ba, and Rb (Fig. 7 and Table 2), but did not cause any noticeable lithologic or petrographic changes. Therefore, metasomatized rocks cannot be easily recognized by field or petrographic examination, but must be identified by evaluation of chemical data. A plot of Na_2O vs K_2O (Fig. 9) was used to evaluate the degree of metasomatism for volcanic and plutonic rocks in the Lake Mead field with SiO_2 more than 60 percent. "Normal" unmetasomatized rocks fall within the solid box (Carmichael and others,

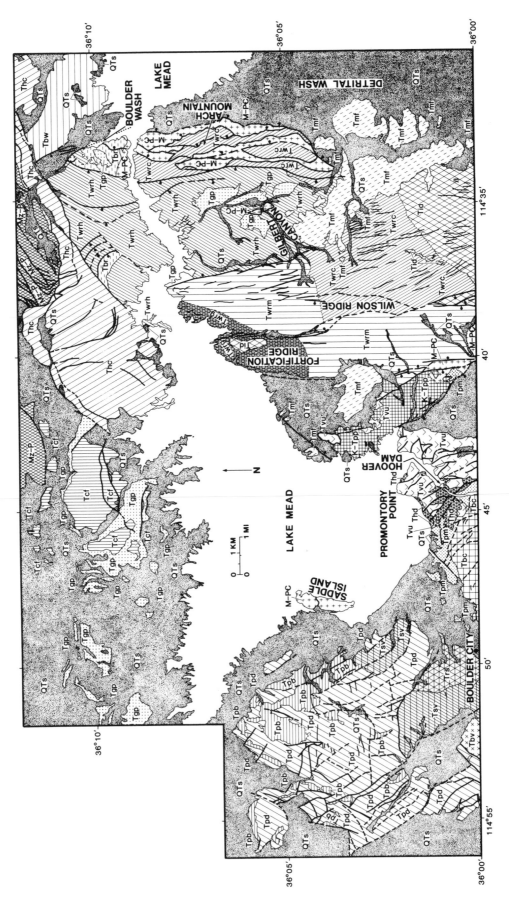

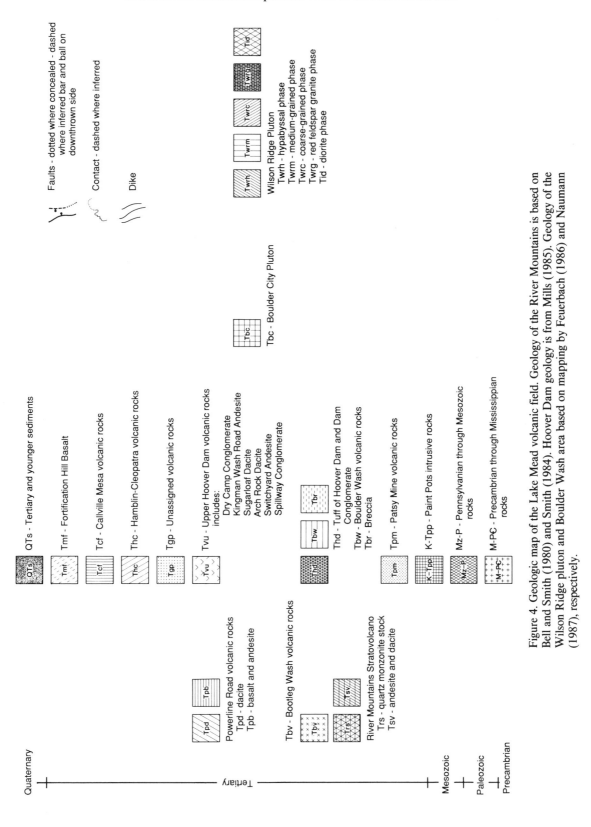

Figure 4. Geologic map of the Lake Mead volcanic field. Geology of the River Mountains is based on Bell and Smith (1980) and Smith (1984). Hoover Dam geology is from Mills (1985). Geology of the Wilson Ridge pluton and Boulder Wash area based on mapping by Feuerbach (1986) and Naumann (1987), respectively.

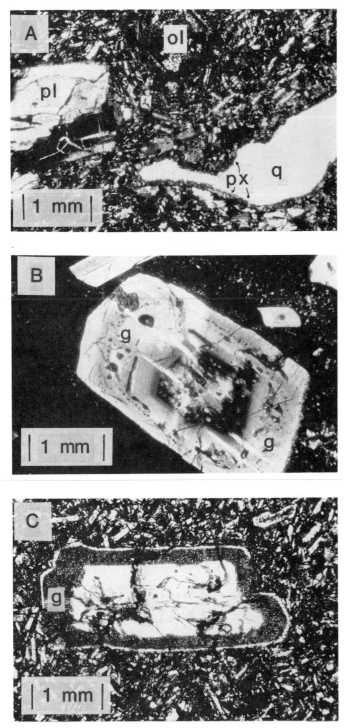

Figure 5. Photomicrographs of disequilibrium phenocrysts in Boulder Wash andesites (polarized light) (Naumann, 1987). A: Euhedral olivine (ol), rounded and partially resorbed sodic plagioclase (pl), and embayed quartz (q) with a rim of granular clinopyroxene (px) in specimen BW1. B: Rounded and partially resorbed, oscillatory zoned, sodic plagioclase with glass-charged zones (g) in specimen BW3. C: Rounded and partially resorbed plagioclase with well-developed glass-charged zones (g) (fretted texture) in specimen BW4.

1974). Note that 74 percent of the rocks of the Lake Mead field plot within the range of "normal" intermediate and felsic igneous rocks. Altered rocks are both high in K_2O and low in Na_2O, and high in Na_2O and low in K_2O. Also note the apparent negative correlation between Na_2O and K_2O contents for metasomatized rocks of the Wilson Ridge pluton. Perhaps this relation indicates that the pluton was, for all practical purposes, a closed system during metasomatism, so that K metasomatism and Na expulsion in one area resulted in Na metasomatism in another, and vice versa. Alteration is also likely in samples with loss on ignition (LOI) values more than 2 percent.

Whenever possible, unaltered samples were used to develop petrogenetic models involving the major elements. However, all samples of the tuff of Hoover Dam and Bootleg Wash volcanic rocks in the River Mountains were strongly affected by K-metasomatism, so the use of altered rocks in modeling differentiation processes for these volcanic suites was unavoidable. Major-element models that use altered rocks should be applied with caution (models 4, 5, 6, 14, and 21; Table 3).

An important concern in the application of REE and trace elements to petrogenetic studies is their mobility during hydrothermal alteration and low-grade metamorphism. Among others, Condie and others (1977), Martin and others (1978), Herrmann and others (1974), Vocke and others (1979), and Ludden and Thompson (1979) concluded that unless alteration or metamorphism was severe, they do not produce significant changes in either the abundances or distributions of the REE. Also, Hildreth and Mahood (1985) indicated that Sc, Ti, REE, Zr, Hf, Nb, Ta, and Th are relatively immobile during the alteration of volcanic rocks and are useful elements for correlating strongly altered tuffs. The relative immobility of Sc and the REE in igneous rocks of the Lake Mead field is demonstrated by their moderate to high correlation with SiO_2 on Harker variation diagrams (Fig. 7), and by REE patterns and distributions that lack selective enrichment or depletion of specific REE elements or element groups (light vs. heavy REE) (Fig. 11). Therefore, igneous rocks of the Lake Mead field should have REE and Sc abundances indicative of the original unaltered rock. Models that use these elements realistically constrain evolutionary trends and are probably not affected by secondary processes.

DIFFERENTIATION MODELS

Introduction

We evaluate open-magma system evolutionary paths for the River Mountains and Hoover Dam volcanics and Wilson Ridge pluton using both Rayleigh fractionation and magma mixing.

Major elements were modeled by using the program XLFRAC (Stormer and Nicholls, 1978). XLFRAC solves a series of linear least-squares mass-balance equations to determine the proportions of added or subtracted phases required to produce a fractionated rock from a given parent. Distribution coefficients for basalts and rhyolites are average values reported in Arth (1976). Mineral compositions used in models are from Deer and others (1972) and Thompson (1985) (Table 4). Mineral analyses from Thompson are from andesites and dacites of the Hamblin-Cleopatra volcano. These mineral analyses were used for major-element models, because the rocks of the Hamblin-Cleopatra volcano are petrographically and chemically similar to volcanic rocks of the Lake Mead field. Also, the Hamblin-Cleopatra volcano is temporally and spatially related to igneous rocks of the Lake Mead field (Weber and Smith, 1987).

Parent rocks

Our major- and trace-element open-system mixing models use compositions of basalt from the northern River Mountains (218) and high-silica granite of the Wilson Ridge pluton (WR57 and WR59) as parental compositions. The basalt and high-silica granites were chosen because they are the most mafic and felsic rocks, respectively, in the Lake Mead area, and lack obvious mixing textures. Also, basalt is similar in mineralogy to basalt inclusions within dikes that cut the Wilson Ridge pluton.

River Mountains

Six models provided reasonable matches between the observed and calculated compositions of differentiated andesitic magma (Table 3). Because many samples showed evidence of K-metasomatism and/or alteration, models were accepted if the value of the sum of squares of the residuals (r) was less than 10. Models 10 to 15 involve both mixing of Wilson Ridge granite and fractionation to produce andesite from basalt. Fractionation of plagioclase and clinopyroxene as well as mixing are required in models 10–12. Models 14 and 15 involve olivine, clinopyroxene, and plagioclase, as well as the addition of Wilson Ridge granite. Note that fractionation alone produces unacceptably high r values (Model 13). Between 20 and 58 percent fractionation is required by models that involve mixing, whereas 52 percent fractionation is required without mixing. R values (mass mixed-component/mass crystallizing phase) vary between 0.76 and 2.24.

Three models provided reasonable matches for the evolution of dacite from andesite. Models 1 and 2 require 41 percent fractionation of hornblende and plagioclase and the addition of 19.8 to 30.1 percent Wilson Ridge magma (WR57 or WR59) (R = 0.48–0.73). Forty-five percent fractionation is required without mixing (model 3). In the Bootleg Wash suite, models 4 and 5, which derive dacite from andesite, require 29 percent fractionation of hornblende and plagioclase and the addition of Wilson Ridge pluton (R = 0.30–0.46). Derivation of dacite from andesite in the Powerline Road section (models 7–9) also requires removal of hornblende and plagioclase (41 to 44 percent) and the addition of Wilson Ridge pluton (R = 0.24–0.69). These models are consistent with modal differences between parent and daughter, except that clinopyroxene is a phase in the andesite (1 percent), but in models that include clinopyroxene as a fractionating phase, XLFRAC requires that it be added to, not subtracted from, the andesite to form dacite.

Figure 6. Basalt inclusions in Boulder Wash dacite flows and dikes within the Wilson Ridge pluton (Naumann, 1987). A: Cut surface of an ellipsoidal basalt inclusion in dacite showing fine-grained rim and coarser-grained core. B: Ellipsoidal basalt inclusions in dacite dikes within the Wilson Ridge pluton. C: Basalt inclusion with crenulate margins in a Boulder Wash dacite flow.

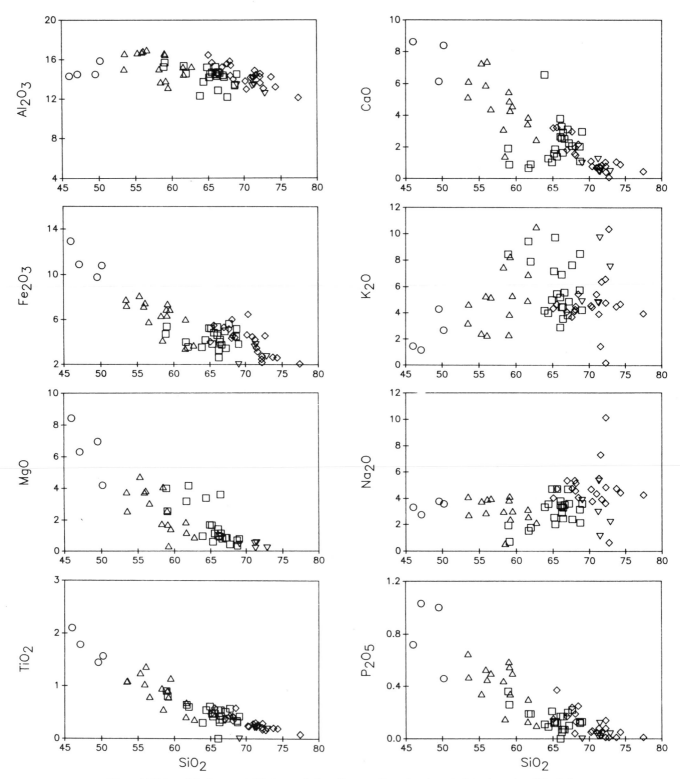

Figure 7 (this and facing page). Harker variation diagrams for volcanic and plutonic rocks of the Lake Mead field. Concentrations of oxides are in weight percent and elements in parts per million. Triangle = andesite, diamond = granite, circle = basalt, downward-pointing triangle = rhyolite, box = dacite.

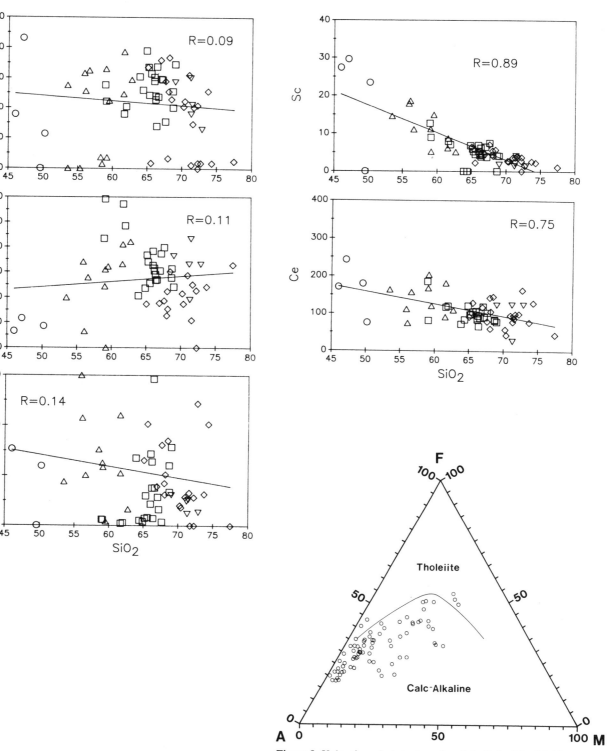

Figure 8. Volcanic and plutonic rocks of the Lake Mead field are calc-alkalic based on an AFM plot. The boundary line between tholeiitic and calc-alkalic fields is from Irvine and Baragar (1971).

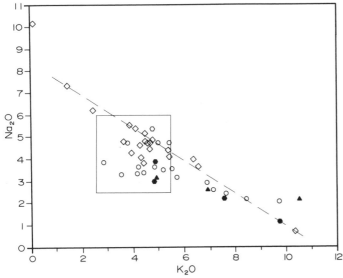

Figure 9. Na$_2$O vs. K$_2$O plot for volcanic and plutonic rocks of the Lake Mead field with SiO$_2$ > 60 percent. Rocks with "normal" alkali (Na$_2$O and K$_2$O) contents should fall within the box. The box was constructed from chemical data for unaltered rocks with SiO$_2$ > 60 percent listed in Carmichael and others (1974). The dashed line represents a possible metasomatic mixing line between rocks with high K and rocks with high Na. Filled upward-pointing triangles = andesite, circles = dacite, diamonds = granite, and filled hexagons = rhyolite.

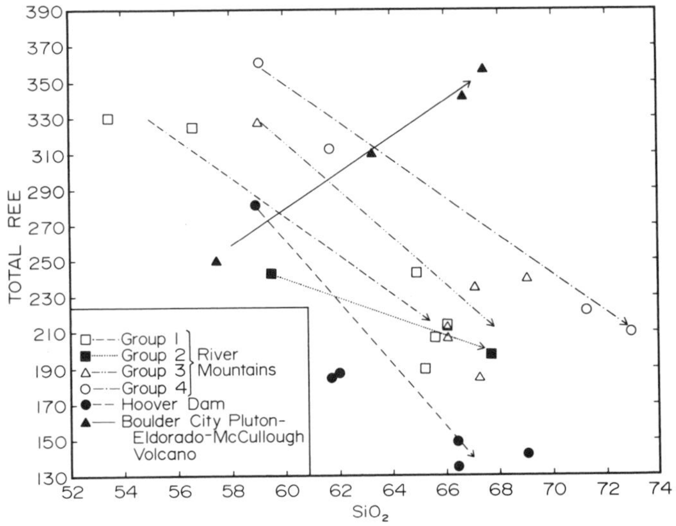

Figure 10. Total REE (La, Ce, Nd, Sm, Eu, Tb, Yb, Lu) vs. SiO$_2$ plot for volcanic rocks of the River Mountains and Hoover Dam. Each of the four episodes of andesite-dacite volcanism in the River Mountains was accompanied by a decrease in total REE content. Volcanic rocks in the Hoover Dam area also show a negative correlation between total REE content and SiO$_2$. For comparison, igneous rocks of the McCullough–Eldorado–Boulder City area display a positive correlation between total REE content and SiO$_2$ concentration.

Hoover Dam

No fractionation or mixing models were successful in modeling the range of compositions observed within the Hoover Dam Tuff or between andesite and dacite flows. Even though extreme K-metasomatism contributes to the large errors, the lack of success of these models cannot be attributed entirely to the effect of this alteration. Trace-element models (discussed below) suggest that processes other than fractional crystallization may be responsible for the observed compositional range in the tuff. The differentiation path between dacite representing the most evolved part of the tuff of Hoover Dam and Sugarloaf dacite were successfully modeled by fractionation of plagioclase, biotite, and hornblende (F = 0.23) (Model 21, Table 3).

Wilson Ridge

We tested two evolutionary paths using XLFRAC for the Wilson Ridge pluton. First, we evaluated the possibility that diorite (57d) was produced by fractionation of plagioclase, olivine, and clinopyroxene from basalt (218) and the addition of Wilson Ridge granite. About 30 percent fractionation is required with mixing (R = 1.04). Second, we evaluated the derivation of Wilson Ridge granite (WR33) from diorite (57d). Models involving mixing provided the best fit but required the subtraction of quartz, a requirement that is not supported by rock modes. Fractionation of hornblende, biotite, orthoclase, and quartz from dio-

rite to form granite without mixing provides a model that agrees with the modal difference between rock types (Model 16, Table 3).

Trace-element models

Models derived from the major elements were refined by use of REE and Sc. If magma mixing is an important differentiation process, samples will fall on a hyperbolic curve on a ratio-ratio plot and on linear trends on companion plots (plots of the ratios of the denominators against one of the original ratios; Langmuir and others, 1978). In addition, each sample should maintain its position relative to adjacent samples regardless of the elements plotted. End-member compositions can be approximated on ratio-ratio plots because the hyperbola will become asymptotic to the X and Y coordinates at ratios that approximate the elemental ratios of the end members (Langmuir and others, 1978). Differentiation processes were evaluated using the trace elements La, Sc, Ce, and Yb.

Samples from the River Mountains, Hoover Dam, and Boulder Wash plot close to a hyperbolic mixing curve on a Ce/Yb-La/Sc plot (Fig. 12), calculated by using two widely separated points (218-basalt and 226-dacite) and applying the equations in Langmuir and others (1978). The hyperbolic trend on this diagram is suggestive of magma mixing, but data scatter indicates that other processes such as fractionation are involved in magmatic evolution. For example, crystal fractionation may ex-

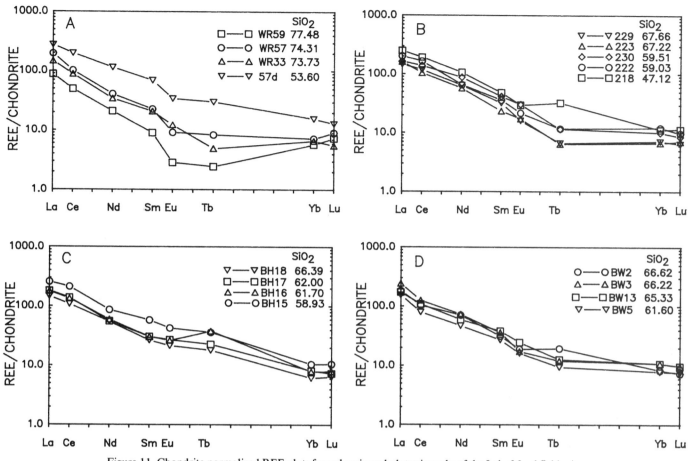

Figure 11. Chondrite normalized REE plots for volcanic and plutonic rocks of the Lake Mead field. A: Wilson Ridge pluton. B: River Mountains. C: Tuff of Hoover Dam. D: Boulder Wash. Note that REE contents in general decrease with increasing SiO_2.

plain higher Ce/Yb than predicted by the mixing line, because fractional crystallization of observed phases results in lower bulk distribution coefficients for Ce than for Yb.

To evaluate the relative importance of mixing and fractionation, Ce and Yb were modeled using Rayleigh fractionation and techniques that determine the change of the concentration of an element as a system undergoes concurrent mixing and fractionation (Depaulo, 1981; Thompson and others, 1986). This element pair was chosen because distribution coefficients are readily available (Arth, 1976). Each area within the Lake Mead field was considered separately. Major-element models were refined to account for the presence of sphene (<1 percent) in the mode of most andesites, dacites, and granites. Bulk distribution coefficients used for each model were calculated using proportions of phenocryst phases determined from the major-element models (Table 3).

For the River Mountains, samples fall on a crude linear trend between basalt (218) and high-silica granite (WR57) (Fig. 13). Note that andesite end members of each River Mountain suite fall below a mixing curve drawn between 218 and WR57; dacite end members fall above or just below this curve. We first

evaluated models that derive the andesites from basalt (218). Neither fractionation nor mixing models alone predict the Ce/Yb ratio of the andesites. Evolution paths calculated using the equations of DePaulo (1981) radiate from the basalt end member and were calculated by assuming certain values of R (mass of mixed component/mass of crystallized component) and allowing F (mass of magma/initial mass of magma) to vary. The evolution paths for R = 1.5 provide the best fit to the differentation path between basalt (218) and andesite (226 and 222). R = 1.5 to 2.0 is required to match the differentiation path from basalt (218) to Bootleg Wash andesite (230). These values agree well with R values of 0.76 to 2.12 predicted by major-element models (Table 3).

Models deriving the River Mountain and Powerline Road dacites (227 and 223) from andesites 226 and 222, respectively, indicate that R = 0.6 for the River Mountain section and 0.9 for the Powerline Road section (Fig. 13). These values are similar to those predicted by the major-element models. The Bootleg Wash differentiation path shows a sharp increase in Ce/Yb. The evolution path calculated using Rayleigh fractionation models is essentially identical to the differentiation path, suggesting that the

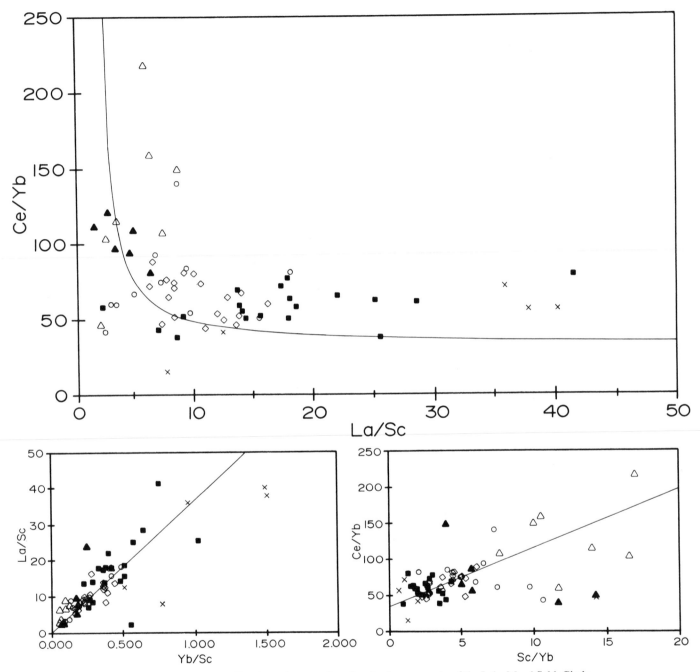

Figure 12. Ce/Yb vs. La/Sc plot and companion plots for igneous rocks of the Lake Mead field. Circle = andesite, X = rhyolite, open triangle = basalt, filled triangle = diorite, diamond = dacite, and filled box = granite.

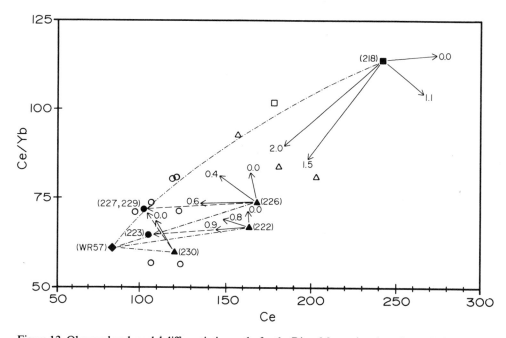

Figure 13. Observed and model differentiation paths for the River Mountains plotted on a Ce/Yb vs. Ce diagram. Filled symbols are rocks used in models. Open symbols represent other specimens. Square = basalt, diamond = Wilson Ridge pluton specimen WR57, triangles = andesites, circles = dacite. Dash-dot curves are two-component mixing curves calculated by using the equations in Langmuir and others (1978). Dashed lines are observed differentiation paths. Solid lines with arrows are differentiation paths calculated using the equations of DePaulo (1981). The number at the tip of each arrow is the R value for each model (R = mass of mixed component/mass crystallizing phase).

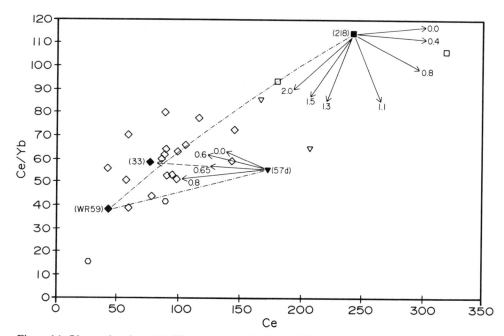

Figure 14. Observed and model differentiation paths for the Wilson Ridge pluton plotted on a Ce/Yb vs. Ce diagram. Filled symbols are rocks used in models. Open symbols represent other specimens. Diamonds = granite, downward-pointing triangles = diorite. Other symbols are defined in the caption to Figure 13.

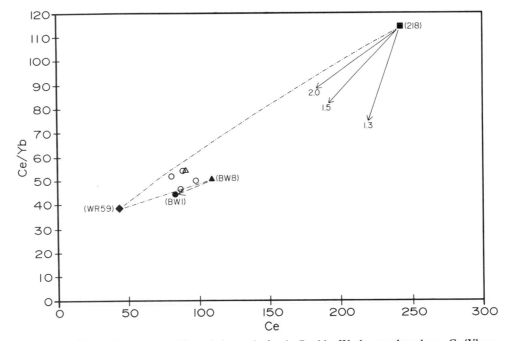

Figure 15. Observed and model differentiation paths for the Boulder Wash area plotted on a Ce/Yb vs. Ce diagram. Filled symbols are rocks used in models. Open symbols represent other specimens. Symbols and lines are defined in the caption to Figure 13.

dacite formed by 34 percent fractionation of hornblende, plagioclase, and sphene from andesite (230).

Models for the Wilson Ridge pluton suggest that diorite (57d) can be derived by 30 percent fractionation of clinopyoxene and plagioclase from basalt magma having the composition of sample 218 and mixing with high-silica granite (WR59) (R = 1.5) (Fig. 14). Modeling suggests that granite represented by sample WR33 may be produced from diorite (sample 57d) by 40 percent fractionation and mixing with high-silica granite (R = 0.65). Models for the Wilson Ridge pluton and related volcanic rocks in the Boulder Wash area produce similar results, except that mixing alone may have formed the Boulder Wash dacites (Fig. 15).

Rayleigh fractionation was unsuccessful in modeling the compositional variation observed within the tuff of Hoover Dam. Evolution paths trended toward higher Ce/Yb and higher Ce. Successful models involving fractionation and mixing with high-silica granite magma (WR57) (R = 0.8) were only obtained by using sphene as a fractionated phase. Sphene is not found in the mode, so these models are invalid. On the other hand, because both andesite and dacite of the tuff fall close to the mixing line, mixing of high-silica magma with andesite may be the dominant differentiation process. Other differentiation processes such as Soret diffusion (Hildreth, 1981) may also be operating. A more detailed study of the tuff of Hoover Dam is required to resolve problems regarding its evolution.

Summary

Magma evolution in the Lake Mead field was complex and probably involved episodic and/or coeval fractional crystallization, magma mixing, crustal assimilation, and partial melting. Models based on trace element confirm that concurrent and/or episodic mixing and fractionation are the dominant differentiation processes. Open-system models provide estimates of the relative importance of the two processes and suggest that mixing was more important in the derivation of the andesites and diorites (R = 0.8 to 2.2) than in the formation of dacite, quartz monzonite, or granite (R = 0.1 to 0.65).

PRODUCTION OF INTERMEDIATE COMPOSITION IGNEOUS ROCKS IN AN EXTENSIONAL ENVIRONMENT

Lipman and others (1972) and Christiansen and Lipman (1972) suggested that the change from calc-alkalic intermediate volcanism to a bimodal rhyolite-basalt suite marked the change from regional compression to extension. Even though bimodal suites form during periods of extension in the Basin and Range province (e.g., Suneson and Lucchitta, 1983), recent work suggests that volcanism before and during the main pulses of extension is mainly calc-alkalic or alkalic-calcic with basaltic-andesite, andesite, and dacite predominating (Eaton, 1982; Anderson,

1973; Elston and Bornhorst, 1979; Smith, 1982; Otton, 1982). The tectonic transition between regional compression and extension may pass without affecting the nature of magmatic activity. Our observations suggest that the combined effect of mixing of basalt and granite parental magmas and crystal fractionation results in magma compositions with many of the characteristics of a calc-alkalic or alkalic-calcic suite (Fig. 8) formed during plate convergence. In the Lake Mead area, basalt and high-silica granite (rhyolite) are inferred to be parental magmas, so, if mixing was prevented, a bimodal suite may have resulted. The occurrence of a bimodal suite may therefore be more a function of the tectonic "state" of the crust rather than some primary petrogenetic process. If fractures dip steeply and penetrate to deep levels of the crust, magma may rise to the surface along these zones of weakness without mixing, and bimodal or dominantly basaltic volcanism may predominate. Alternately, if extension results in shallow faults (e.g., detachment structures), magma may rise until encountering a low-angle fault zone, where it may spread laterally and accumulate. In this structural scenario, the opportunity for magma mixing may be high, and intermediate volcanism may predominate.

In the Lake Mead field, basalt and high-silica granite (rhyolite) mixed to produce intermediate calc-alkalic igneous rocks prior to detachment faulting (20 to 13.4 Ma), but did not erupt until 4 to 12 Ma, when deeply penetrating high-angle faults tapped unmixed magma (Smith and others, 1987; Feuerbach and Smith, 1987). Basaltic volcanism occurred mainly in the northern River Mountains, in the Fortification Hill area, and to the southeast of Hoover Dam (Campbell and Schenk, 1950; Anderson, 1973; Feuerbach and Smith, 1987). Therefore, in the Lake Mead field, there was a delay of as long as 8 m.y. between the initial generation of bimodal magmas and bimodal volcanism. The transition from calc-alkalic to dominantly basaltic volcanism in the Lake Mead area reflects a change in structural style during regional extension, and not a fundamental change from regional compression to extension.

ACKNOWLEDGMENTS

We thank the staff of the Phoenix Memorial Laboratory, University of Michigan for completing the REE analyses. Financial support by the Department of Energy to the Phoenix Memorial Laboratory through the University Research Reactor Assistance Program and Reactor Facility Cost Sharing Program made this work possible. Much of our mapping covered areas studied earlier by R. E. Anderson and C. E. Longwell. We especially thank R. E. Anderson for his continuing help and encouragement of our studies in the Lake Mead area. R. Cullers, R. E. Anderson, and R. Scott provided helpful reviews. We thank Allen Glazner for providing us with a manuscript based on a thesis by R. Turner describing magma mixing in a mid-Tertiary volcanic section in the Castle Mountains, California. Their work provided the stimulus for our evaluation of the importance of mixing process in the petrogenesis of the volcanic and plutonic rocks of the Lake Mead field.

TABLE 1. MODAL COMPOSITIONS OF REPRESENTATIVE PHENOCRYSTS OF VOLCANIC ROCKS AND MODAL COMPOSITIONS OF PLUTONIC ROCKS, LAKE MEAD VOLCANIC FIELD

	Number of Specimens	Quartz	Plag.	Microcline	Kspar	Biotite	Hn	Cpx	Ol	Ap	Zircon	Sphene	Opaque	Matrix
Hoover Dam volcanic rocks (Mills, 1985)														
Tuff of Hoover Dam														
Top	3	-	31	-	-	7	2	tr	-	-	-	-	-	54
Base	2	-	26	-	-	3	-	2	-	-	-	-	-	63
Switchyard Basalt	3	-	5-15	-	-	-	-	3-5	-	-	-	-	-	80-92
Arch Rock Dacite	2	-	5-15	-	-	3	1-2	-	-	-	-	-	-	80-91
Surgarloaf Dacite	2	-	3-15	-	-	2-4	2	-	-	-	-	-	-	79-93
Wilson Ridge Pluton (Feuerbach, 1986)														
Quartz Monzonite (WR57)	1	17	41	8	22	7	3	-	-	tr	tr	tr	tr	-
Red-feldspar Granite	2	26	34	2	32	4	-	-	-	tr	tr	tr	2	-
Diorite (33d)	1	1	30	-	4	7	1	-	-	tr	tr	1	2	-
Granite (WR59)	1	49	24	2	22	1	-	-	-	-	tr	-	tr	-
Diorite (57d)	1	-	61	-	4	10	23	-	-	tr	tr	tr	2	-
Boulder Wash volcanic rocks (Naumann, 1987)														
Dacite (BW1)	1	5	24	-	-	6	-	-	-	tr	-	tr	1	64
Andesite (BW6)	1	tr	31	-	1	-	-	14	4	tr	-	-	-	50
River Mountains igneous rocks (Smith, unpublished data)														
River Mountains stock	5	18	22	-	-	8	2	-	-	-	-	-	5	45
River Mountains dacite	18	-	35	-	-	2	-	-	-	tr	-	tr	1	62
River Mountains andesite	13	-	35	-	-	-	3	-	-	-	-	tr	1	61
Bootleg Wash dacite	5	tr	30	-	-	9	-	-	-	-	-	1	tr	60
Powerline Rd dacite	24	-	37	-	-	15	5	-	-	-	-	-	tr	55
Powerline Rd basalt (218)	1	-	5	-	-	-	-	10	2	-	-	-	tr	83

Notes: The top of the tuff of Hoover dam contains 4% andesite and basalt xenoliths, and base 6%. Modes are average values. Hn = hornblende, cpx = clinopyroxene, ol = olivine, ap = apatite, Kspar = K-feldspar, and tr = trace. Point counts based on at least 500 points per slide.

TABLE 2. CHEMICAL ANALYSES OF REPRESENTATIVE VOLCANIC AND PLUTONIC ROCKS FROM THE LAKE MEAD VOLCANIC FIELD

Oxide	Hoover Dam Volcanics				Hoover Dam Tuff			
	DHD 84-3	DHD 84-4	AHD 84-2	AHD 84-5	THD BH-15	THD BH-16	THD BH-17	THD BH-18
SiO_2	66.4	69.0	55.9	56.1	58.9	61.7	62.0	66.4
Al_2O_3	14.7	14.5	16.7	16.8	15.2	15.4	14.6	12.9
Fe_2O_3	4.2	3.8	7.2	7.5	4.7	4.0	3.6	4.0
CaO	2.9	3.0	5.9	7.4	1.9	0.7	0.9	1.6
MgO	1.1	0.8	3.7	3.8	4.0	3.2	4.2	3.6
Na_2O	3.3	3.6	2.9	3.9	1.9	1.5	1.8	2.5
K_2O	3.6	4.2	5.3	2.3	8.5	9.4	7.9	4.5
TiO_2	0.4	0.4	1.0	1.4	0.9	0.6	0.6	0.5
MnO	0.1	0.0	0.2	0.1	0.1	0.3	0.1	0.1
P_2O_5	0.1	0.1	0.5	0.5	0.4	0.2	0.2	0.2
LOI	3.4	0.5	1.2	0.8	2.4	2.6	2.4	1.7
Total	100.8	100.3	100.9	100.8	99.2	99.6	99.4	98.1

Trace elements in ppm

La	62.7	56.0	54.9	47.5	84.4	58.1	59.2	47.9
Ce	66.1	77.9	111.3	73.6	185.8	117.4	120.9	94.3
Nd	33.6	30.5	29.7	13.2	51.6	35.5	33.3	32.8
Sm	4.9	7.2	4.5	1.3	10.4	5.5	5.5	4.8
Eu	1.0	1.0	2.0	1.7	2.9	1.8	1.9	1.5
Tb	0.8	1.0	4.4	3.4	1.7	1.8	1.1	0.8
Yb	1.1	1.5	1.8	1.8	2.1	1.6	1.6	1.2
Lu	0.3	0.4	0.3	0.2	0.4	0.3	0.3	0.2
U	14.9	7.8	12.1	22.5	4.6	3.6	3.0	2.6
Th	13.5	15.3	11.3	6.9	19.8	17.0	16.3	12.8
Hf	4.2	4.6	5.8	5.2	8.1	5.8	6.5	5.1
Ba	1690	1730	1580	1280	1384	901	1024	699
Rb	134	121	170	32	217	296	242	145
Sr	1170	630	1200	860	50	18	24	59
Ta	1.2	1.2	1.1	1.4	1.3	1.2	1.3	1.0
Sc	3.9	4.1	17.9	18.6	12.7	7.9	7.1	6.2

Major elements in weight percent.
Total iron as Fe_2O_3
AHD = Hoover Dam andesite
DHD = Hoover Dam dacite
s = Specimen used in models

NA = not analyzed or not detected.
THD = Tuff of Hoover Dam

TABLE 2. CHEMICAL ANALYSES OF REPRESENTATIVE VOLCANIC AND PLUTONIC ROCKS FROM THE LAKE MEAD VOLCANIC FIELD (continued)

Oxide	Wilson Ridge Pluton GWR WR368	GWR WR46	GWR WR53	GWR WR55	s GWR WR57	GWR WR58	GWR WR62	GWR WR63	GWR WR67	GWR WR56	GWR WR71	GWR WR65	GWR WR72	GWR WR36
SiO_2	68.2	68.5	72.3	68.1	74.3	67.0	70.2	71.3	72.7	65.6	71.7	71.3	71.6	71.0
Al_2O_3	15.4	14.0	14.6	14.4	13.2	15.2	13.8	14.2	13.1	15.7	14.4	14.2	14.9	14.2
Fe_2O_3	4.6	4.4	2.8	6.0	2.6	5.3	4.7	4.2	4.6	5.5	3.1	3.6	3.5	4.5
CaO	1.5	2.2	0.4	2.0	0.9	1.8	1.1	0.8	0.1	3.2	0.8	0.5	0.7	0.7
MgO	1.0	1.1	0.6	1.0	0.4	0.9	0.5	1.0	0.2	1.5	0.3	0.2	0.7	0.6
Na_2O	5.2	4.1	10.1	4.6	4.4	5.4	4.7	5.5	0.6	4.7	3.9	5.3	7.3	4.4
K_2O	4.5	5.5	0.2	4.3	4.7	4.1	4.6	3.9	10.4	4.7	6.4	4.8	1.5	5.4
TiO_2	0.4	0.6	0.3	0.3	0.2	0.4	0.2	0.3	0.2	0.6	0.3	0.2	0.3	0.3
MnO	0.0	0.1	0.0	0.0	0.0	0.0	0.0	0.0	0.0	0.0	0.0	0.0	0.0	0.0
P_2O_5	0.1	0.3	0.1	0.2	0.1	0.2	0.1	0.1	0.0	0.4	0.1	0.0	0.0	0.1
LOI	0.1	0.2	0.4	0.1	0.1	0.0	0.0	0.7	0.3	0.2	1.1	0.2	0.7	0.1
Total	101.0	100.8	101.7	101.0	100.9	100.3	99.9	102.0	102.1	102.1	102.1	100.3	101.1	101.2
Trace elements in ppm														
La	88.9	97.9	66.7	46.6	64.2	80.9	48.2	49.7	62.6	64.2	58.3	17.4	54.0	55.8
Ce	105.7	145.8	90.3	59.8	88.6	117.0	57.6	59.3	89.8	88.6	98.6	26.7	89.8	95.4
Nd	41.0	61.0	21.2	26.2	24.4	34.2	19.0	18.3	25.1	24.4	37.9	10.5	18.7	38.1
Sm	6.5	8.6	4.4	4.7	4.1	6.5	3.4	4.0	4.4	4.1	5.6	2.1	4.5	5.0
Eu	1.4	1.6	0.8	1.0	0.6	1.3	0.7	0.8	0.7	0.6	1.1	0.4	1.0	1.0
Tb	0.5	1.1	0.5	0.4	0.4	0.5	0.9	0.8	0.3	0.4	0.5	0.3	0.4	0.4
Yb	1.5	2.0	1.4	1.6	1.4	1.5	1.1	0.9	1.1	1.4	1.9	1.7	1.5	1.8
Lu	0.4	0.4	0.3	0.3	0.3	0.3	0.2	0.3	0.2	0.3	0.3	0.3	0.3	0.2
U	16.9	15.2	17.2	11.1	18.8	11.9	10.3	11.3	20.5	18.8	1.6	2.4	0.8	2.4
Th	20.1	18.9	16.8	11.7	21.0	15.4	16.3	17.2	19.1	21.0	16.0	17.2	12.2	16.9
Hf	5.9	8.1	5.4	4.8	4.9	5.5	3.6	5.3	4.1	4.9	4.9	5.5	4.3	4.9
Ba	1840	1146	1989	1274	811	1796	1021	1702	975	811	1008	903	736	1554
Rb	77	151	NA	112	129	89	108	78	164	129	125	96	54	143
Sr	410	680	NA	249	NA	314	163	NA	NA	NA	NA	99	264	230
Ta	1.7	1.9	1.4	1.3	2.2	1.4	1.5	1.5	1.3	2.2	1.5	1.2	1.1	1.4
Sc	4.0	5.7	3.7	5.4	2.3	4.5	2.7	3.6	1.5	2.3	4.1	2.2	3.9	3.6

Major elements in weight percent.   NA = not analyzed or not detected.
Total iron as Fe_2O_3.   THD = Tuff of Hoover Dam
AHD = Hoover Dam andesite.   GWR = Wilson Ridge granite or quartz monzonite
DHD = Hoover Dam dacite.   DWR = Wilson Ridge diorite
s = Specimen used in models.

TABLE 2. CHEMICAL ANALYSES OF REPRESENTATIVE VOLCANIC AND PLUTONIC ROCKS FROM THE LAKE MEAD VOLCANIC FIELD (continued)

Oxide	Wilson Ridge Pluton GWR WR57	GWR WR67	s GWR WR33	s GWR WR59	GWR WR106	GWR WR114	GWR WR120	DWR WR74	s DWR 57d	DWR 39d	DWR WR107	GWR WR121
SiO_2	67.6	71.5	73.7	77.5	68.0	72.2	65.1	59.7	53.6	57.0	55.9	53.3
Al_2O_3	15.6	13.4	14.2	12.1	15.8	14.3	16.5	19.1	15.4	15.6	17.4	17.6
Fe_2O_3	5.2	3.8	2.7	2.1	4.4	2.5	4.0	6.2	8.9	6.6	6.4	7.6
CaO	3.0	0.4	1.1	0.4	1.6	1.0	3.2	4.7	5.5	6.7	4.2	6.7
MgO	1.2	0.6	0.6	0.1	1.0	0.5	1.5	1.7	4.5	6.5	2.8	3.5
Na_2O	4.8	1.1	4.8	4.3	5.4	3.6	4.0	6.1	4.6	4.7	5.2	3.7
K_2O	3.7	9.7	4.5	4.0	4.1	6.6	4.4	2.6	3.0	2.2	4.2	3.3
TiO_2	0.4	0.2	0.2	0.1	0.4	0.2	0.5	0.7	1.1	0.7	0.8	1.4
MnO	0.0	0.0	0.0	0.0	0.0	0.0	0.1	0.1	0.2	0.1	0.1	0.1
P_2O_5	0.2	0.1	0.0	0.0	0.0	0.0	0.2	0.2	0.8	0.3	0.5	0.4
LOI	0.0	0.6	0.3	0.2	0.4	0.2	0.2	0.4	1.8	1.5	1.6	0.4
Total	101.8	101.5	102.0	100.7	101.2	101.2	99.5	101.4	99.4	101.8	99.0	98.0

Trace elements in ppm

La	49.7	51.9	47.9	28.8	10.3	69.8	58.6	206.5	90.5	50.3	105.0	54.0
Ce	79.0	89.5	77.1	43.6	143.2	99.2	91.2	328.1	173.2	79.0	167.1	76.4
Nd	31.9	35.2	20.5	12.6	43.4	24.5	38.1	101.0	68.2	39.0	52.7	NA
Sm	5.9	5.1	3.8	1.6	0.8	4.5	6.1	13.6	12.5	7.3	11.2	8.4
Eu	1.4	1.0	0.8	0.2	1.6	0.9	1.4	3.5	2.4	2.0	2.6	2.1
Tb	0.5	0.5	0.2	0.1	0.5	0.4	0.7	1.3	1.4	1.2	1.3	1.1
Yb	1.8	2.1	1.3	1.2	2.4	1.6	1.7	2.2	3.1	1.6	2.0	2.0
Lu	0.3	0.3	0.2	0.3	0.0	0.3	0.3	0.3	0.4	0.2	0.3	0.4
U	1.4	2.2	1.9	4.2	0.2	2.1	1.0	NA	2.4	NA	2.0	1.0
Th	10.0	13.7	13.5	25.1	18.9	18.9	8.8	17.0	14.4	4.5	11.0	7.0
Hf	5.1	4.6	4.3	3.3	7.7	5.2	5.0	10.4	7.8	4.0	6.0	5.0
Ba	1448	1063	1281	123	166	1045	1679	2830	1339	1055	1883	1632
Rb	93	217	121	164	64	113	87	63	126	77	70	54
Sr	646	212	254	NA	339	227	524	1660	415	778	663	505
Ta	1.3	1.2	1.1	1.7	1.4	1.3	1.0	0.9	1.8	0.6	0.9	1.3
Sc	7.1	4.2	2.6	1.1	4.4	2.8	6.4	8.7	17.9	22.7	11.1	22.7

Major elements in weight percent.
Total iron as Fe_2O_3.
AHD = Hoover Dam andesite.
DHD = Hoover Dam dacite.
s = Specimen used in models.

NA = not analyzed or not detected.
THD = Tuff of Hoover Dam.
GWR = Wilson Ridge granite or quartz monzonite.
DWR = Wilson Ridge diorite.

TABLE 2. CHEMICAL ANALYSES OF REPRESENTATIVE VOLCANIC AND PLUTONIC ROCKS FROM THE LAKE MEAD VOLCANIC FIELD (continued)

River Mountains

Oxide	PB 218	s PB 219	DP 220	s DP 223	DP 271	RP 348	RP 349	AP 346	AP 347	s AP 222	s DB 229	s AB 230	s AB 226	MR 231	DR 229	DR 272
SiO$_2$	47.1	46.0	67.1	67.2	66.0	72.9	71.2	59.1	61.7	59.0	67.7	59.5	53.5	64.9	65.2	56.6
Al$_2$O$_3$	14.5	14.3	14.4	14.2	14.5	12.6	13.3	16.5	14.5	16.6	12.2	13.1	15.0	15.2	14.2	17.0
Fe$_2$O$_3$	10.9	12.9	5.0	3.5	4.6	2.7	1.8	6.4	6.0	6.9	5.6	6.9	7.8	5.3	5.2	5.8
CaO	11.2	8.6	3.1	2.3	3.8	0.5	1.3	4.9	3.9	5.5	2.1	4.6	5.2	1.0	1.6	4.4
MgO	6.3	8.4	0.9	0.9	1.0	0.2	0.5	1.7	1.2	2.6	0.4	1.4	3.8	1.7	1.7	3.0
Na$_2$O	2.8	3.3	4.7	3.6	3.5	2.2	3.0	4.2	2.6	3.9	2.4	3.0	4.1	4.7	2.5	4.0
K$_2$O	1.2	1.5	3.8	4.9	5.2	7.5	4.8	3.9	6.9	2.3	7.7	5.3	3.2	5.0	7.2	5.2
TiO$_2$	1.8	2.1	0.5	0.4	0.5	0.2	0.2	0.9	0.7	0.9	0.6	1.1	1.1	0.6	0.5	0.8
MnO	0.1	0.2	0.1	0.1	0.1	0.0	0.1	0.1	0.1	0.1	0.0	0.1	0.1	0.1	0.1	0.1
P$_2$O$_5$	1.0	0.7	0.2	0.1	0.2	0.0	0.0	0.6	0.3	0.6	0.2	0.5	0.7	0.2	0.1	0.5
LOI	2.3	1.7	0.3	3.0	1.0	0.1	4.4	0.2	1.7	1.0	0.8	3.3	4.7	0.8	1.3	1.4
Total	99.2	99.8	100.0	100.0	100.4	99.0	100.8	98.8	99.8	99.4	99.6	98.9	99.1	99.4	99.5	98.8
Trace elements in ppm																
La	107.6	75.9	64.7	52.4	55.0	55.6	59.5	93.5	82.1	81.7	47.7	53.6	74.5	63.0	49.9	75.9
Ce	242.4	170.9	119.3	90.7	105.4	124.5	124.5	203.5	181.5	167.9	102.6	120.3	163.6	121.6	97.6	157.2
Nd	117.7	44.2	41.3	34.2	37.0	22.4	29.1	50.6	37.6	63.3	38.5	56.5	75.5	49.3	35.6	77.9
Sm	15.5	9.1	5.6	4.2	5.6	3.7	4.6	7.5	7.2	8.7	5.8	7.5	10.6	5.6	4.5	9.1
Eu	3.9	2.7	1.4	1.2	1.3	1.0	1.0	1.9	1.9	2.0	1.1	2.1	2.5	1.4	1.1	2.2
Tb	3.0	2.0	0.9	0.3	1.2	0.4	0.4	0.9	0.4	1.5	0.3	0.5	0.7	0.1	0.2	1.1
Yb	2.1	1.7	1.5	1.3	1.6	2.2	2.2	2.5	2.2	2.3	1.4	2.0	2.4	1.5	1.4	1.7
Lu	0.4	0.3	0.3	0.2	0.3	0.3	0.3	0.4	0.3	0.4	0.2	0.3	0.4	0.3	0.3	0.3
U	6.4	8.7	9.9	9.1	7.6	3.9	3.6	2.1	2.0	4.6	3.0	2.6	2.0	NA	1.3	1.3
Th	13.2	7.7	18.5	17.6	15.4	31.2	26.3	19.3	18.6	14.9	14.8	10.8	20.7	14.2	15.8	15.7
Hf	8.1	6.4	4.7	4.8	4.7	4.9	4.5	9.2	6.7	7.3	4.1	5.1	6.6	5.5	4.5	5.8
Ba	2155	891	1484	1477	1517	650	1510	2740	1930	1650	774	1121	1376	1950	1683	1625
Rb	58	33	152	187	163	166	166	155	205	121	199	161	99	118	184	139
Sr	1205	614	230	131	175	110	200	470	420	504	30	33	351	33	60	405
Ta	1.5	1.6	0.9	1.2	1.1	15.3	14.6	15.1	11.1	1.0	1.2	1.1	0.9	1.0	0.9	1.1
Sc	29.6	27.4	6.5	3.8	6.9	1.5	1.5	5.2	8.7	11.2	7.5	14.9	14.6	6.9	5.9	11.0

Major elements in weight percent.
Total iron as Fe$_2$O$_3$.
PB = Powerline Road basalt.
DP = Powerline Road dacite.
s = Specimen used in models.
DR = Dacite of the River Mountains stratavolcano.

NA = not analyzed or not detected.
AP = Powerline Road andesite.
DB = Bootleg Wash dacite.
AB = Bootleg Wash andesite.
MR = Quartz monzonite of the River Mountains stock.
AR = Andesite of the River Mountains stratovolcano.

**TABLE 2. CHEMICAL ANALYSES OF REPRESENTATIVE VOLCANIC AND PLUTONIC ROCKS
FROM THE LAKE MEAD VOLCANIC FIELD** (continued)

Boulder Wash

Oxide	s ABW BW5	ABW BW8	ABW BW4	ABW BW10	ABW BW6	BBW BW12	s DBW BW1	DBW BW2	DBW BW3	DBW BW13	DBW BW27
SiO_2	61.6	62.8	55.3	53.6	50.2	47.9	66.2	66.6	66.2	65.3	68.8
Al_2O_3	15.2	15.3	16.7	16.6	15.9	16.1	14.3	14.6	14.5	14.5	13.4
Fe_2O_3	3.4	3.7	8.1	7.3	10.8	4.5	3.3	3.8	2.6	3.8	5.2
CaO	3.5	2.5	7.3	6.1	8.4	10.0	3.3	2.5	2.6	1.9	1.1
MgO	1.8	0.9	4.7	2.5	4.2	1.2	0.9	0.8	0.9	0.6	0.3
Na_2O	3.2	2.1	3.8	2.7	3.6	3.4	2.9	3.5	3.4	2.0	2.1
K_2O	5.0	10.5	2.4	4.7	2.7	7.4	6.9	5.6	4.5	9.7	8.5
TiO_2	0.4	0.4	1.2	1.1	1.6	1.1	0.4	0.4	0.3	0.4	0.3
MnO	0.1	0.1	0.1	0.1	0.1	0.2	0.1	0.1	0.1	0.1	0.1
P_2O_5	0.1	0.1	0.3	0.5	0.5	0.4	0.1	0.1	0.1	0.1	0.1
LOI	5.7	1.4	1.7	3.5	0.4	7.5	1.5	0.2	4.3	0.9	0.1
Total	99.9	99.6	101.7	98.6	98.3	99.7	99.8	98.1	99.3	99.3	100.0
Trace elements in ppm											
La	59.3	79.0	NA	NA	50.2	69.3	53.1	54.2	57.6	65.5	34.6
Ce	90.6	109.3	NA	NA	75.3	109.2	84.1	88.7	87.8	98.4	81.5
Nd	42.3	43.5	NA	NA	53.2	40.4	29.7	33.4	29.4	32.0	5.2
Sm	5.7	6.5	NA	NA	8.4	8.4	6.1	5.6	5.3	6.3	1.0
Eu	1.3	1.2	NA	NA	2.1	2.0	1.2	1.2	1.1	1.2	0.4
Tb	0.9	0.6	NA	NA	1.4	1.1	1.0	0.5	0.5	0.4	1.6
Yb	1.7	2.2	NA	NA	1.7	1.8	1.9	1.6	1.9	2.0	0.2
Lu	0.3	0.3	NA	NA	0.4	0.4	0.3	0.3	0.3	0.3	1.8
U	1.1	1.9	NA	NA	1.1	1.4	1.8	2.1	1.5	2.3	NA
Th	13.9	18.0	NA	NA	5.1	9.3	13.7	14.6	13.5	16.4	13.1
Hf	4.9	5.7	NA	NA	4.5	4.8	5.1	5.4	4.8	5.5	4.1
Ba	1232	1472	NA	NA	569	1067	1140	1187	1206	1216	1006
Rb	166	211	NA	NA	43	113	158	135	153	170	157
Sr	883	132	NA	NA	479	351	303	304	513	241	270
Ta	1.6	1.2	NA	NA	1.6	1.4	1.4	1.3	1.3	1.6	1.0
Sc	6.1	5.1	NA	NA	23.4	21.5	4.9	4.5	4.3	5.3	4.1

Major elements in weight percent.
Total iron as Fe_2O_3.
ABW = Boulder Wash andesite.
DBW = Boulder Wash dacite.
s = Specimen used in models.

NA = not analyzed or not detected.
BBW = Boulder Wash basalt.

TABLE 3. MAJOR ELEMENT MODELS

Model Number	Phases added or subtracted*							mixed component	R	T	r
	cpx	hn	plag	ol	kspar	qtz	biotite				
1 RM(226-227)	....	28.70	12.30	....	....	....	....	30.1(WR57)	0.73	0.41	1.69
2	....	29.30	12.00	....	....	....	....	19.8(WR59)	0.48	0.41	1.90
3	....	32.90	12.10	....	....	....	....	....	....	0.45	3.37
4 RM(230-229)	....	16.10	13.60	....	....	....	....	13.3(WR57)	0.46	0.29	1.94
5	....	16.30	12.60	....	....	....	....	8.7(WR59)	0.30	0.29	2.02
6	....	18.50	12.10	....	....	....	....	....	....	0.31	2.40
7 RM(222-223)	....	22.80	19.20	....	....	....	....	28.1(WR57)	0.69	0.41	5.29
8	....	23.90	20.40	....	....	....	....	10.4(WR59)	0.24	0.44	5.45
9	....	25.70	22.60	....	....	....	....	....	....	0.48	5.57
10 RM(218-226)	19.45	....	0.54	....	....	....	....	42.4(WR57)	2.12	0.20	7.26
11	16.58	....	5.7 An +15.7 Ab	....	....	....	....	28.9(WR57)	0.76	0.38	2.71 ....
12	26.70	+32.3	3.6 An +21.4 Ab	....	....	....	....	48.0(WR57)	0.83	0.58	1.37 ....
13	33.00	....	18.50	....	....	....	....	....	....	0.52	55.70
14 RM(218-230)	7.30	....	22.60	18.40	....	....	....	53.3(WR59)	1.11	0.48	11.57
15 RM(218-222)	23.20	....	....	0.96	....	....	....	53.8(WR57)	2.24	0.24	3.84
16 WR(57-33)	....	34.60	....	....	+10.52	+22.9	....	....	....	0.40	3.61
17	....	25.70	....	....	+13.2	2.40	....	188 (WR59)	4.95	0.38	3.52
18 WR(218-57)	20.30	....	25.90	9.90	....	....	....	....	....	0.56	34.40
19	21.70	....	8.47	....	....	....	....	....	....	0.32	6.85
20	20.80	....	8.90	....	....	....	....	31.3(WR57)	1.04	0.30	6.14
21 HD(BH10–84-4)	....	5.00	15.00	....	....	....	3.00	....	....	0.23	2.10

R = mass ratio of the mixed component/crystallizing phase
T = total phenocrysts relative to initial mass of magma
r = sum of squares of the residuals
*All numbers are negative except those values preceded by + sign.

TABLE 4. MINERAL COMPOSITIONS USED IN MAJOR ELEMENT MODELS

Oxides in weight percent	Hornblende*	Biotite[†]	Biotite*	Andesite[†]	Labradorite[†]	Orthoclase[†]	Quartz[†]	Clinopyroxene*	Olivine*
SiO_2	43.5	39.14	36.14	58.1	52.96	64.46	99.99	51.83	38.00
Al_2O_3	11.29	13.1	12.88	26.44	29.72	18.55	0	2.29	0.02
Fe_2O_3	13.05	17.99	16.38	0	0	0.14	0	7.75	22.12
CaO	11.17	1.64	0.00	7.84	13.28	0.17	0	20.28	0.12
MgO	12.77	12.65	13.77	0	0	0.00	0	16.40	39.11
MnO	2.65	0.7	0.98	6.7	4.21	0.49	0	0.35	0.01
K_2O	0.73	6.55	8.39	1.1	0.1	16.07	0	0.00	0.00
TiO_2	3.55	4.27	7.27	0.00	0	0.00	0	0.63	0.00

*Mineral analyses from volcanic rocks of the Hamblin-Cleopatra volcano (Thompson, 1985).
[†]Mineral analyses from Deer and others (1972).

REFERENCES CITED

Anderson, R. E., 1971, Thin skin distension in Tertiary rocks of southeastern Nevada: Geological Society of America Bulletin, v. 82, p. 42–58.

——, 1973, Large-magnitude late Tertiary strike-slip faulting north of Lake Mead, Nevada: U.S. Geological Survey Professional Paper 794, 18 p.

Anderson, R. E., 1978, Geologic map of the Black Canyon 15° quadrangle, Arizona and Nevada: U.S. Geological Survey map GQ-1394.

Anderson, R. E., Longwell, C. R., Armstrong, R. L., and Marvin, R. F., 1972, Significance of K-Ar ages of Tertiary rocks from the Lake Mead region, Nevada–Arizona: Geological Society of America Bulletin, v. 83, p. 273–287.

Arth, J. G., 1976, Behavior of trace elements during magmatic processes; A summary of theoretical models and their applications: U.S. Geological Survey Journal of Research, v. 4, no. 1, p. 41–47.

Bacon, C. R., 1986, Magmatic inclusions in silicic and intermediate volcanic rocks: Journal of Geophysical Research, v. 91, no. B6, p. 6091–6112.

Bell, J. W., and Smith, E. I., 1980, Geological map of the Henderson Quadrangle, Clark County, Nevada: Nevada Bureau of Mines and Geology Map 67, scale 1:24,000.

Campbell, I., and Schenk, E. T., 1950, Camptonite dikes near Boulder Dam, Arizona: American Mineralogist, v. 35, no. 9–10, p. 671–692.

Carmichael, I.S.E., Turner, F. J., and Verhoogen, J., 1974, Igneous petrology: New York, McGraw Hill Book Company, 739 p.

Christiansen, R. L., and Lipman, P. W., 1972, Cenozoic volcanism and plate-tectonic evolution of the western United States; 2, Late Cenozoic: Philosophical Transactions of the Royal Society of London, series A, v. 271, p. 249–284.

Condie, K. C., Viljoen, M. J., and Kable, E.J.D., 1977, Effects of alteration on element distributions in Archaean tholeiites from the Barberton greenstone belt, South Africa: Contributions to Mineralogy and Petrology, v. 64, p. 75–89.

Deer, W. A., Howie, R. A., and Zussman, J., 1972, An introduction to the rock forming minerals: London, Longman Group Limited, 528 p.

DePaulo, D. J., 1981, Trace element and isotopic effects of combined wall-rock assimilation and fractional crystallization: Earth and Planetary Science Letters, v. 53, p. 189–202.

Eaton, G. P., 1982, The Basin and Range Province; Origin and tectonic significance: Annual Review of Earth and Planetary Sciences, v. 10, p. 409–440.

Elston, W. E., and Bornhorst, T. J., 1979, The Rio Grande rift in context of regional post-40 m.y. volcanic and tectonic events, *in* Riecker, R. E., ed., Rio Grande Rift; Tectonics and magmatism: Washington, D.C., American Geophysical Union, p. 418–438.

Feuerbach, D. L., 1986, Geology of the Wilson Ridge pluton; A mid-Miocene quartz monzonite intrusion in the northern Black Mountains, Mohave County, Arizona and Clark County, Nevada [M.S. thesis]: Las Vegas, University of Nevada, 79 p.

Feuerbach, D. L., and Smith, E. I., 1986, The mid-Miocene Wilson Ridge pluton; A subvolcanic intrusion in the Lake Mead region, Arizona and Nevada: EOS (Transactions of the American Geophysical Union), v. 67, no. 44, p. 1262.

——, 1987, Late Miocene Fortification Hill basalt, Lake Mead area, Nevada and Arizona; Source area and conduit geometry: Geological Society of America Abstracts with Programs, v. 19, p. 376–377.

Herrmann, A. G., Potts, M. J., and Knake, D., 1974, Geochemistry of the rare earth elements in spillites from the oceanic and continental crust: Contributions to Mineralogy and Petrology, v. 44, p. 1–16.

Hildreth, W., 1981, Gradients in silicic magma chambers; Implications for lithospheric magmatism: Journal of Geophysical Research, v. 86, p. 10153–10192.

Hildreth, W., and Mahood, G., 1985, Correlation of ash-flow tuffs: Geological Society of America Bulletin, v. 96, p. 968–974.

Irvine, T. N., and Baragar, W.R.A., 1971, A guide to the chemical classification of the common volcanic rocks: Canadian Journal of Earth Sciences, v. 8, p. 523–548.

Koyaguchi, T., 1986, Textural and compositional evidence for magma mixing and its mechanism, Abu volcano group, southwestern Japan: Contributions to Mineralogy and Petrology, v. 93, p. 33–45.

Langmuir, C. H., Vocke, R. D., Jr., Hanson, G. H., and Hart, S. H., 1978, A general mixing equation with applications to Icelandic basalts: Earth and Planetary Science Letters, v. 37, p. 380–392.

Lipman, P. W., Prostka, H. J., and Christiansen, R. L., 1972, Cenozoic volcanism and plate-tectonic evolution of the western United States; 1, Early and middle Cenozoic: Philosophical Transactions of the Royal Society of London, series A, v. 271, p. 217–248.

Ludden, J. N., and Thompson, G., 1979, An evaluation of the behaviour of the rare-earth elements during weathering of sea-floor basalt: Earth and Planetary Science Letters, v. 43, p. 85–92.

McMillan, N. J., and Dungan, M. A., 1986, Magma mixing as a petrogenetic process in the development of the Taos Plateau Volcanic Field, New Mexico: Journal of Geophysical Research, v. 91, no. B6, p. 6029–6045.

Martin, R. F., Whitley, J. E., and Wooley, A. R., 1978, An investigation of rare-earth mobility; Fenitized quartzite Borralan complex, N.W. Scotland: Contributions to Mineralogy and Petrology, v. 66, p. 66–73.

Mattison, S. R., Vogel, T. A., and Wilband, J. T., 1986, Petrochemistry of the silicic-mafic complexes at Vesturhorn and Austurhorn, Iceland; Evidence for zoned/stratified magma: Journal of Volcanology and Geothermal Research, v. 28, p. 197–223.

Mills, J. G., 1985, The geology and geochemistry of volcanic and plutonic rocks in the Hoover Dam 7½ Quadrangle, Clark County, Nevada, and Mohave County, Arizona [M.S. thesis]: Las Vegas, University of Nevada, 119 p.

Naumann, T. R., 1987, Geology of the central Boulder Canyon Quadrangle, Clark County, Nevada [M.S. thesis]: Las Vegas, University of Nevada, 68 p.

Naumann, T. R., and Smith, E. I., 1987, Evidence for magma mixing in Mid-Tertiary volcanic rocks, Lake Mead region, southern Nevada: Geological Society of America Abstracts with Programs, v. 19, p. 435–436.

Otton, J. K., 1982, Tertiary extensional tectonics and associated volcanism in west-central Arizona, *in* Frost, E. G., and Martin, D. L., eds., Mesozoic-Cenozoic tectonic evolution of the Colorado River region, California, Arizona, and Nevada: San Diego, California, Cordilleran Publishers, p. 143–157.

Smith, E. I., 1982, Geology and geochemistry of the volcanic rocks in the River Mountains, Clark County, Nevada, and comparisons with volcanic rocks in nearby areas, *in* Frost, E. G., and Martin, D. L., eds., Mesozoic-Cenozoic tectonic evolution of the Colorado River region, California, Arizona, and Nevada: San Diego, California, Cordilleran Publishers, p. 41–54.

——, 1984, Geological map of the Boulder Beach Quadrangle, Nevada: Nevada Bureau of Mines and Geology Map 81, scale 1:24,000.

Smith, E. I., Schmidt, C. S., and Weber, M. E., 1986, Mid-Tertiary volcanic rocks of the McCullough Range, Clark County, Nevada: Geological Society of America Abstracts with Programs, v. 18, p. 187.

Smith, E. I., Eschner, E., Feuerbach, D. L., Naumann, T. R., and Sewall, A., 1987, Mid-Tertiary extension in the eastern Basin and Range Province, Nevada and Arizona; The Las Vegas Valley–Detrital Wash transect: Geological Society of America Abstracts with Programs, v. 19, p. 848–849.

Stormer, J. C., Jr., and Nicholls, J., 1978, XLFRAC; A program for the interactive testing of magmatic differentiation models: Computers and Geoscience, v. 4, p. 143–159.

Suneson, N. H., and Lucchitta, I., 1983, Origin of bimodal volcanism, southern Basin and Range province, west-central Arizona: Geological Society of America Bulletin, v. 94, p. 1005–1019.

Thompson, K. G., 1985, Stratigraphy and petrology of the Hamblin-Cleopatra volcano, Clark County, Nevada [M.S. thesis]: Austin, University of Texas, 306 p.

Thompson, R. A., Dungan, M. A., and Lipman, P. W., 1986, Multiple differentiation processes in early-rift calc-alkalic volcanics, northern Rio Grande Rift, New Mexico: Journal of Geophysical Research, v. 91, no. B6, p. 6046–6058.

Vocke, R. D., Hanson, G. N., and Gruenenfelder, M., 1979, The effects of low temperature metasomatism on REE distributions in the Roffna Gneiss, Switzerland: EOS (Transactions of the American Geophysical Union), v. 60, p. 425.

Weber, M. E., and Smith, E. I., 1987, Structural and geochemical constraints on the reassembly mid-Tertiary volcanoes in the Lake Mead area of southern Nevada: Geology, v. 15, p. 553–556.

Manuscript Submitted August 26, 1987.
Revised Manuscript Submitted January 4, 1988
Manuscript Accepted by the Society February 7, 1989

Geological Society of America
Memoir 174
1990

Chapter 11

Late Cretaceous–Tertiary magmatism in the Colorado Mineral Belt; Rare earth element and samarium-neodymium isotopic studies

Holly J. Stein
Central Mineral Resources, U.S. Geological Survey, MS 905, Box 25046, Denver Federal Center, Denver, Colorado 80225
James G. Crock
Branch of Geochemistry, U.S. Geological Survey, MS 973, Box 25046, Denver Federal Center, Denver, Colorado 80225

ABSTRACT

Rare earth element concentrations for 52 granitoid stocks, plutons, laccoliths, and volcanic rocks, together with neodymium isotopic data for 30 of these units, indicate a dominantly crustal origin for Late Cretaceous–Tertiary magmatism in the Colorado Mineral Belt (COMB). This comprehensive data set is summarized in the table below where igneous rocks of the COMB have been grouped according to age, composition, and their REE and ^{143}Nd/^{144}Nd (epsilon Nd) characteristics.

Age	Rock Suite	Sm-Nd Model Age[†]	Epsilon Nd	(La/Yb)$_N$	Eu Anomaly (Eu/Eu*)$_N$	REE Pattern
Late Cretaceous-early Tertiary (Laramide) 45 to 75 Ma	Monzonite Suite	662 to 1318 Ma (DM) 145 to 875 Ma (CHUR)	-1.0 to -9.3	10 to 53 Avg = 24 La$_N$ = 117 to 382 Yb$_N$ = 2 to 15	very small to absent 0.65 to 0.95 Avg = 0.87	linear, with steep slopes
Middle Tertiary 29 to 45 Ma	Granodiorite-Quartz Monzonite Suite	1042 to 1377 Ma (DM) 581 to 957 Ma (CHUR)	-6.7 to -10.6	11 to 24 Avg = 16 La$_N$ = 103 to 215 Yb$_N$ = 6 to 13	very small to absent 0.73 to 0.95 Avg = 0.86	linear, with moderately steep slopes
Oligocene-Miocene 10 to 29 Ma	Granite Suite	1099 to 1542 Ma (DM) 715 to 1093 Ma (CHUR)	-8.0 to -14.0	2 to 65 Avg = 13 La$_N$ = 46 to 207 Yb$_N$ = 3 to 22	extremely large 0.07 to 0.65 Avg = 0.35	U-shaped

[†]First range is calculated source age assuming depleted mantle (DM); second assumes chnodritic uniform reservoir (CHUR).

Rare earth element abundances in COMB granitoids are significantly higher than bulk continental crust abundances. The sources for COMB granitoids might have be-

Stein, H. J., and Crock, J. G., 1990, Late Cretaceous–Tertiary magmatism in the Colorado Mineral Belt; Rare earth element and samarium-neodymium isotopic studies, *in* Anderson, J. L., ed., The nature and origin of Cordilleran magmatism: Boulder, Colorado, Geological Society of America Memoir 174.

come enriched in rare earth elements (REE), particularly light REE, (1) early in their history, possibly by metamorphic events associated with the formation of Proterozoic batholiths, and/or (2) at a later time, possibly by degassing of metasomatized mantle or devolatilization of oceanic slab at the base of the continental crust during Laramide subduction and/or Tertiary extension. The latter requires a component of Archean detritus in Colorado Proterozoic units to accommodate distinctly negative epsilon Nd values in Laramide-Tertiary intrusions. A mixing model involving both felsic and mafic Proterozoic lower crust ($\pm$ mantle) can explain COMB Late Cretaceous–Tertiary magma compositions. Older, Laramide age (Late Cretaceous–early Tertiary) alkaline monzonites probably were predominantly derived from highly metasomatized mafic crust (amphibolite to granulite) with a possible mantle component, whereas younger (Oligocene-Miocene) quartz monzonites, granodiorites, and highly evolved topaz rhyolites and Climax-type granites were probably predominantly derived from intermediate to felsic crust that underwent episode(s) of dehydration-dominated, melt-absent metamorphism (granulite). Alkali- and CO_2-rich fluids were probably instrumental in mobilizing and concentrating REE in the lower and middle crust. The REE patterns for Laramide-Tertiary alkaline and calc-alkalic intrusions may in part reflect the history of their source rocks. The distinct U-shaped REE patterns for evolved granites and rhyolites, however, are largely the product of upper crustal mineral-melt and melt-vapor fractionation processes.

INTRODUCTION

Igneous rocks of the Colorado Mineral Belt (COMB) (Tweto and Sims, 1963) represent the most interior zone of Cordilleran magmatic activity. These rocks formed about 1,000 km inland from the plate margin during Late Cretaceous–Tertiary time. Intrusive and extrusive rocks of the COMB record nearly continuous Cordilleran magmatism over a 70-m.y. time period, which includes an initial phase of Laramide compression, followed by tectonic relaxation, and the subsequent development of the Rio Grande rift system.

The COMB has been the subject of several isotopic studies in recent years (Stein, 1985). Isotopic investigations were designed to help characterize and distinguish sources for intrusions associated with belts of economic mineral occurrences, in particular Climax-type granites and their stockwork molybdenum deposits. In an effort to better understand Late Cretaceous–Tertiary magmatism and ore deposits in the COMB, these previous investigations also addressed the problem of why other chemically and temporally similar granitoid intrusions lack mineral deposits. This chapter presents new rare earth element (REE) data and samarium-neodymium isotopic data for COMB Laramide-Tertiary igneous rocks. This new data is considered in the context of earlier obtained isotopic and geochemical data (Stein, 1985).

Proposed sources for Late Cretaceous–Tertiary magmatism in the COMB include both mantle and crust (Lipman and others, 1978; Isaacson and Smithson, 1976; White and others, 1981; Bookstrom, 1981; Mutschler and others, 1981a; Westra and Keith, 1981). However, radiogenic and stable isotopic studies (Stein, 1983, 1985, 1988a; Stein and Huebner, 1984; Stein and Hannah, 1982, 1985; Stein and Fullagar, 1985; Hannah and Stein, 1986; Stein and others, 1987; Stein and Crock, 1987) and a Nd isotopic and REE study on a suite of alkaline monzonite

samples from the northern COMB by Musselman (1987) show that Cordilleran magmatic activity, including older Laramide-age monzonites and young Climax-type granites, was largely the product of lower-crustal melting. This extensive lower-crustal melting need not be tied to subduction-related processes (Isaacson and Smithson, 1976; Larson and others, 1987).

This chapter gives a broad overview of the REE and Nd isotopic characteristics for three compositionally and temporally distinct Late Cretaceous–Tertiary igneous rock suites in the COMB. These characteristics can be related to changing magma sources as the tectonic environment evolved from compression to extension in Colorado. Other isotopic and geochemical data, particularly Pb and Sr isotopes (Stein 1985; Stein and Fullagar, 1985; Stein and others, 1987), have been used successfully to characterize different Late Cretaceous–Tertiary magma sources. Although Nd isotopic data in this study support earlier conclusions based on Pb and Sr isotopic data, the Sm-Nd system alone does not produce differences in data sets that are as distinct as those generated by the U-Th-Pb system.

GEOLOGIC SETTING

The COMB is defined by a northeast-trending zone of Late Cretaceous–Tertiary plutonic rocks and associated mineral deposits (Tweto and Sims, 1963). The belt contains an array of granitoids that includes (1) Late Cretaceous–early Tertiary alkaline monzonites and syenites (**Laramide Monzonite Suite**), mostly middle Tertiary calc-alkalic granodiorites and quartz monzonites (**Middle Tertiary Granodiorite–Quartz Monzonite Suite**), and (3) Oligocene-Miocene highly evolved granites and topaz rhyolites (**Oligocene-Miocene Granite Suite**). Ore occur-

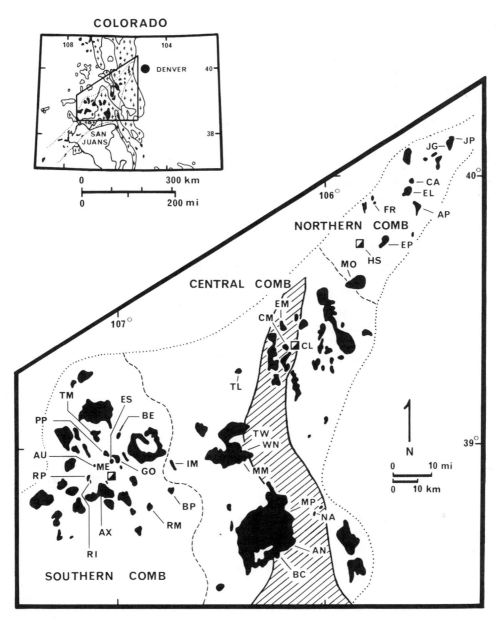

Figure 1. Map showing study area (outlined by quadrilateral), Colorado Mineral Belt (abbreviated COMB and outlined by dotted line), Precambrian outcrops which generally correspond to cores of major mountain ranges (plus signs), Late Cretaceous–Tertiary intrusions (solid black), fields of San Juan and other Tertiary volcanic rocks (no pattern), northern extension of Rio Grande rift (diagonal pattern), northern, central, and southern COMB geographic divisions (separated by dashed lines) as defined by lead isotopic studies of Late Cretaceous–Tertiary intrusions (Stein, 1985), Climax-type granites and their associated stockwork molybdenum deposits (half-filled squares), and intrusive and volcanic rocks used in this study (two letter abbreviations which correspond to samples listed in Tables 1, 2, and 3).

rences in the COMB range from Au, Ag, Pb, Zn, Cu, and F vein and replacement deposits associated with older alkalic and calc-alkalic rocks to high-grade stockwork molybdenum deposits associated with young, highly evolved, silicic-felsic, composite Climax-type granites. Other notable young, silicic-felsic igneous rocks in the COMB include occurrences of topaz rhyolite. Eruption of alkalic basalt flows and lamprophyre dikes accompanied young felsic magmatism in the COMB. The study area is

bounded on the south by the San Juan Mountains (Lipman and others, 1978; Doe and others, 1979), and extends about 300 km to the northeast (Fig. 1). This region of the COMB has been subdivided on the basis of geological, geochemical, and isotopic considerations (Stein, 1982, 1985, 1988a) into a northern, central, and southern part (Fig. 1).

The **northern** COMB contains numerous Late Cretaceous–early Tertiary intrusions of alkaline affinity. The major volume of intrusive rock in this region is in the **Laramide Monzonite Suite.** A Late Cretaceous–early Tertiary (Laramide) age, 45 to 75 Ma, is the principal criterion for classification in this suite. The monzonite label is intended to portray an alkalic rock suite whose total $Na_2O + K_2O$ is high relative to SiO_2 (Table 1 [Tables 1, 2, and 3 are at the end of the chapter.]). Rock types are variable and include mafic hornblende-pyroxene monzonites and pink syenites. Laramide monzonitic rocks typically occur as stocks (Fig. 1) and are commonly dark in color (Fig. 2). Some granodiorites and quartz monzonites from the calc-alkalic **Middle Tertiary Granodiorite–Quartz Monzonite Suite,** which dominates the central and southern COMB, are also present in the northern COMB (Table 1). Rocks belonging to the **Oligocene-Miocene Granite Suite** in this northern region are rare (Table 1), and are represented almost exclusively by those associated with the Climax-type molybdenum deposit at Urad-Henderson.

The **central** COMB is characterized largely by middle Tertiary, calc-alkalic plutons and batholiths of granodiorite and quartz monzonite (Fig. 1). Although several older Laramide monzonites are also present (Table 1), the major volume of intrusive rock in the central COMB belongs to the **Middle Tertiary Granodiorite–Quartz Monzonite Suite.** Classification in this suite requires both a granodiorite or quartz monzonite composition and a middle Tertiary (29 to 45 Ma) age. Oligocene granite stocks, rhyolite plugs and flows, and topaz rhyolites, including the well-known composite granite stocks and associated molybdenum deposit at Climax and the topaz rhyolite at Chalk Mountain (Fig. 2), are present in the central COMB (Table 1); these are included in the **Oligocene-Miocene Granite Suite.**

The **southern** COMB contains numerous Oligocene-Miocene intrusions, 10 to 29 Ma, and is mainly characterized by large laccoliths and immense sills of Oligocene quartz monzonite (Fig. 1). These calc-alkalic intrusions are remarkably uniform in age, about 29 Ma, and form the West Elk and Elk Mountains (Table 1). Intrusions appear homogeneous in the field, displaying porphyritic textures, which feature twinned, 1 to 3 cm, euhedral K-feldspar and plagioclase megacrysts (Fig. 2). These laccoliths, plutons, and sills form a major part of the **Middle Tertiary Granodiorite–Quartz Monzonite Suite.** Several small granite stocks and rhyolite plugs of Miocene age are present in the southern COMB (Table 1), including the Mount Emmons–Redwell granites and associated Climax-type molybdenum deposits (Fig. 2); these small, highly evolved, intrusive and volcanic rocks compose a major portion of the **Oligocene-Miocene Granite Suite.** Older Laramide age intrusions are not known in the main southern COMB region.

Late Cretaceous–Tertiary intrusions in the COMB are hosted by a highly variable Proterozoic crust (Hedge and others, 1986) that formed in a composite back-arc basin bounded by magmatic arc complexes to the immediate north and south (Reed and others, 1987). Metasedimentary and metavolcanic sequences beneath the COMB represent this tectonically complex region of backarc basin sandwiched by very different magmatic-arc ter-

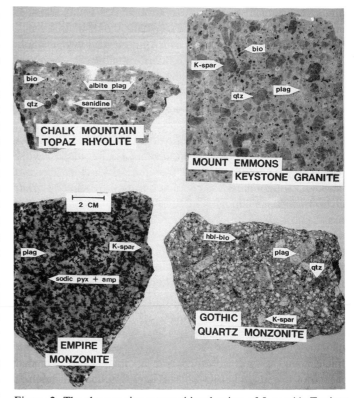

Figure 2. The three major compositional suites of Laramide-Tertiary rocks in the Colorado Mineral Belt (COMB). Empire is a mafic alkalic stock (northern COMB) from the Laramide Monzonite Suite. Gothic is a laccolith (southern COMB) representing the Middle Tertiary Granodiorite–Quartz Monzonite Suite. Mount Emmons is a Climax-type granite stock (southern COMB) and Chalk Mountain is a topaz rhyolite (central COMB); both represent the Oligocene-Miocene Granite Suite.

rains. The oldest Proterozoic sequences (1,750 to 1,950 Ma), referred to as Idaho Springs Formation (ISF), consist of lower amphibolite- to granulite-grade metasedimentary and less abundant metavolcanic rocks whose precursors include siliceous graywackes and shales, and tholeiitic basalt and rhyodacite tuffs and lavas, respectively.

Three major Proterozoic plutonic events are known in Colorado. Foliated, 1,670-Ma, predominantly intermediate composition intrusions, including the extensive Boulder Creek Granodiorite, are present as batholiths and plutons of the Routt Plutonic Suite (Tweto, 1987), and appear to be associated with the waning stages of metamorphism and deformation of ISF units. Crosscutting the 1,750- to 1,950-Ma ISF sequences are several 1,430-Ma granites of considerable lateral and vertical extent, including the Sherman, Eolus, and Silver Plume Granites of the Berthoud Plutonic Suite (Tweto, 1987). The two-mica Silver Plume Granite (SPG) is the rock standard GSP-1, and has unusual trace-element characteristics such as $Th/U = 50$ and $(La/Yb)_N = 84$. The youngest Proterozoic magmatic event is represented by the highly potassic and pegmatitic, 1,015-Ma Pikes Peak Batholith, located mostly southeast of the COMB (Barker and others, 1975).

RESULTS AND DISCUSSION OF REE CONCENTRATION DATA

This section contains a discussion of REE data for sample groups by rock composition, in geographic order (Table 1). The geographic divisions in Figure 1, largely established by lead isotopic data (Stein, 1985), also correlate well with granitoid age (Table 2) and chemical composition (Table 3). Thus, the group subheadings in Tables 1, 2, and 3 emphasize the correlation between geographic location, age, and intrusion composition.

Sample selection, analytical methods, and data representation are discussed in the appendices of this paper. Other information on samples, analyses, errors, and calculations is presented in the tables.

Northern COMB

Laramide monzonite suite intrusions, compared to all other Late Cretaceous–Tertiary igneous rocks in the COMB, contain higher light REE (LREE) concentrations (Table 2, Fig. 3) yielding REE patterns with steep negative slopes (La/Yb_N = 10 to 53). Europium anomalies are very small to absent ($Eu/Eu*_N$ = 0.65 to 0.95). The generally straight-line REE patterns tend to be concave up at the heavy REE (HREE) end. Two samples from the central COMB have been included in this alkaline monzonite suite: (1) the Elk Mountain Porphyry, a 67-Ma quartz monzonite intrusion that is visibly lacking phenocrystic quartz and is characterized by abundant plagioclase and K-feldspar phenocrysts, and (2) the Twin Lakes Granodiorite, a locally layered, zoned, quartz monzonite pluton (Wilshire, 1969), now believed to be of Laramide age (63.8 ± 0.7 Ma) on the basis of $^{40}Ar/^{39}Ar$ dating of hornblende (Shannon and others, 1987a). The Twin Lakes pluton was previously dated at 40 to 45 Ma (Obradovich and others, 1969; Marvin and others, 1974). Although the Montezuma stock is included in the northern COMB (Fig. 1) on the basis of its lead isotopic character (Stein, 1985), this pluton is discussed in the central COMB section of this paper because of its middle Tertiary age (39 Ma). The REE patterns that characterize Laramide monzonite rocks in the COMB are typical of other patterns for alkalic, SiO_2-saturated rocks around the world (Henderson, 1984; Nelson and others, 1987; Morris and Pasteris, 1987). Their chondrite normalized LREE/HREE far exceed average values of about 3.9 and 9.5 for lower- and upper-crustal rocks, respectively (Taylor and McLennan, 1985).

Many workers have suggested that alkalic magmas are the result of small amounts of partial melting of garnet peridotite mantle; this model generally involves a prior metasomatic event within the mantle, whereby certain regions become enriched in REE and achieve high LREE/HREE (Henderson, 1984; Wilshire, 1984, 1987; Menzies and Wass, 1983). Indeed, Laramide monzonite rocks in the COMB were most likely derived from a source that was LREE–enriched, but this source need not be mantle. The source probably does not contain much residual plagioclase, given typical Sr concentrations of 1,000 to 3,000

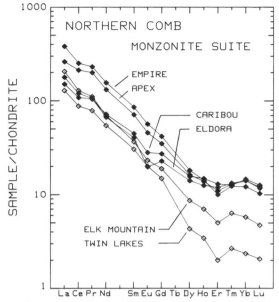

Figure 3. REE patterns for the Laramide Monzonite Suite. This alkalic rock suite is located mainly in the northern COMB (solid diamonds), and is characterized by steep REE patterns which have very small, negative Eu anomalies. Two quartz monzonite plutons from the central COMB (open diamonds) are included in this figure because of their Laramide age.

ppm (Stein, 1985, Appendix B) and the lack of significant Eu anomalies in the rocks of the Laramide alkaline suite (Fig. 3). High LREE/HREE may indicate garnet in the residue. The small negative Eu anomalies might simply reflect minor removal of plagioclase ± clinopyroxene ± hornblende during crystallization at higher crustal levels.

Rather than calling on a mantle source, we suggest that Laramide alkaline rocks in the COMB were largely derived from a metasomatized, amphibolitic to granulitic, mafic lower crust enriched in K, Na, and LREE. This interpretation is consistent with lead isotopic data, which do not permit direct and complete derivation of Laramide monzonites from a simple mantle source (Stein and Hannah, 1985; Stein, 1985). Migration of CO_2-rich fluids, derived from (1) repeated high-grade Proterozoic metamorphism in a sediment-laden, back-arc basin, (2) Proterozoic and/or Phanerozoic mantle degassing, and/or (3) Laramide devolatilization of oceanic slab beneath the COMB, may have played an important role in metasomatism, mobilizing and concentrating alkalies and LREE in regions of the lower crust. The apparent mobility of alkalies, LREE, and other components in CO_2-rich fluids permits contamination of the lower continental crust (Glassley, 1983; Newton, 1986), either by penetration of supercritical fluids derived from below or by generation of metamorphic fluids from within. Strontium isotopic data (Stein and Fullagar, 1985; Simmons and Hedge, 1978; Musselman, 1987) indicate that source(s) for Late Cretaceous–early Tertiary intrusions in the northern COMB must have had low Rb/Sr throughout their history. Depletion of Rb relative to Sr might have been accomplished by high-grade Proterozoic metamorphic event(s). Alternatively, low $^{87}Sr/^{86}Sr$ may have been maintained if much of the original crust in the northern COMB was composed of mantle-derived, mafic units with initially low Rb/Sr. Direct involvement of upper mantle is not necessary to explain alkalic magmatism in Laramide time, although we do not exclude this possibility. A REE study of granodiorites and monzonites in the northern COMB (Simmons and Hedge, 1978) and a subsequent, more detailed modeling study of REE and Nd isotopic data for a small group of mafic alkalic rocks in the northern COMB (Musselman, 1987; Musselman and Simmons, 1987) also suggested a lower crustal source consisting of plagioclase + pyroxene + garnet + apatite ± alkali feldspar ± quartz ± olivine, with pyroxene + accessory garnet and apatite largely confined to the restite. Lower crustal xenoliths in kimberlites on the Colorado-Wyoming border include hypersthene-augite and garnet granulites, gabbros, and norites (Smith and others, 1982; Bradley and McCallum, 1982). Such rock types may also provide potential source(s) for northern COMB intrusions, but additional study is needed before this can be established.

Granodiorites are uncommon in the northern COMB, although one large granodiorite body is spatially associated with a younger, pink-gray syenite stock at Jamestown, Colorado. The syenite has been explored for economic molybdenum deposits (Threlkeld, 1982), and peripheral to this syenite stock is a discontinuous ring of mined fluorite deposits (Goddard, 1954; Nash and Cunningham, 1973). The Late Cretaceous granodiorite at Jamestown is not as enriched in REE (Table 2), and its REE pattern is not as steep (La/Yb_N = 14.8) as some of the alkalic monzonites in the northern COMB (Fig. 4). The early Tertiary syenite at Jamestown is also less REE enriched (Table 2); its REE pattern is like that of the granodiorite (Fig. 4). The similar REE patterns for these two very different rock types at Jamestown indicate that, although spatially associated, the syenite cannot be a differentiate of the older granodiorite magma nor of its source. Removal of plagioclase in quantity large enough to differentiate a granodiorite with ($K_2O + Na_2O$)/CaO = 2 to a syenite with ($K_2O + Na_2O$)/CaO = 10 (data in Table 1 and Stein, 1985, Appendix A) presumably would have produced a large negative Eu anomaly in the REE pattern for the syenite. Therefore, the similarity in the two patterns is probably fortuitous, and the syenite stock at Jamestown must have its own unique source.

Granites in the northern COMB are also uncommon. Two examples are the 29-Ma rhyolite tuff at Fraser, and the 26-Ma granite of the Seriate intrusive center at Henderson. The Seriate is a small fingerlike stock that is part of a multiple sequence of granite stocks composing the Urad-Henderson intrusive system (Carten and others, 1988). The Urad-Henderson granite intrusions are related to two stacked Climax-type molybdenum ore bodies, separated vertically by about 1,000 m. The Urad units breached the surface through a volcanic vent that eventually filled and became plugged with porphyritic rhyolites. Subsequent pulses of granite magma formed the Henderson units, located

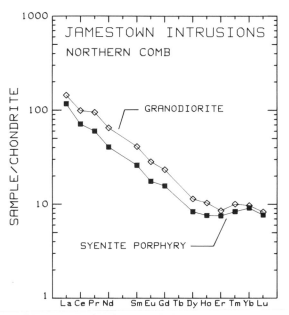

Figure 4. REE patterns for the granodiorite and syenite at Jamestown, northern COMB. On the basis of REE and other geochemical data, the syenite, although spatially associated with the older granodiorite, cannot be a differentiate of the granodiorite or its source.

some 600 m at depth and accessed only by underground workings and drill holes. The lower grade Urad ore body is near the surface in the volcanic neck, and the deeper, higher grade Henderson ore body has a broader, cuplike shape near the top of the widening magma chamber (Wallace and others, 1978). The REE patterns for these granites contrast sharply with patterns for all other Late Cretaceous–Tertiary intrusions in the northern COMB (Fig. 5); they display deep negative Eu anomalies ($Eu/Eu*_N$ = 0.14 and 0.19), U shapes with depletions of the heavier middle REE (MREE), moderate (La/Yb)$_N$ ratios (La/Yb_N = 6.1 and 6.7), and markedly lower REE concentrations (Table 2). Although located about 14 km to the north, the rhyolite tuff at Fraser appears to be related to the Urad-Henderson system. This has been documented by lead isotopic data (Stein, 1985) and is consistent with the similar REE data for Fraser and Urad; three REE patterns for the rhyolite porphyry at Urad (H. Stein, unpublished data) exactly overlie the pattern shown for the rhyolite tuff at Fraser in Figure 5. If the volcanic rocks at Fraser were not extruded directly from the Urad vent, then there must be unrecognized or buried vents for the rhyolite tuffs at Fraser that tapped the same magma source as the Urad-Henderson granites.

Central COMB

The central COMB middle Tertiary granodiorite–quartz monzonite suite is represented by three major calc-alkalic intrusions: Montezuma, Mount Princeton, and Turquoise Lake (Table 1). The REE patterns for these intermediate composition intrusions are typical of patterns displayed by other granodiorites and quartz monzonites developed on continental crust (Henderson, 1984). All have moderate LREE/HREE ratios (La/Yb$_N$ = 16 to 23), display small but distinct negative Eu anomalies (Eu/Eu*$_N$ = 0.73 to 0.79), and flatten to curve slightly upward at their HREE end (Fig. 6). The REE concentrations and LREE/HREE are not quite as high as those for Laramide monzonites in the northern COMB (Table 2). The lower HREE concentrations for the Turquoise Lake stock may reflect local removal of HREE by F- and CO$_2$-bearing fluids (Michard and others, 1987; Koch, 1983; Strong and others, 1984) associated with the development of a subeconomic stockwork molybdenum system. Such fluids were present because both fluorite and carbonate have been documented petrographically in the Turquoise Lake stock (Stein, 1985, Appendix A). On the basis of REE and isotopic data, the middle Tertiary granodiorites and quartz monzonites in the central COMB were most likely derived largely from lower crust containing abundant plagioclase + quartz + amphibole ± pyroxene ± garnet ± K-feldspar. In the broadest sense, these source rocks may have been dominated by metagraywackes, now present as metasomatized, high-grade metamorphic rocks at lower crustal depths.

Granites from the central COMB discussed in this study include those from the Winfield–Middle Mountain, Mount Antero, and Climax–Chalk Mountain areas, all of which are associated with stockwork molybdenum or vein molybdenum occurrences.

Exposures of the granite at Middle Mountain (37 to 38 Ma) in the Winfield area exhibit many textural features displayed in Climax-type granites. These features reflect the cyclic crystallization of eutectic or near-eutectic melts in an H$_2$O-saturated envi-

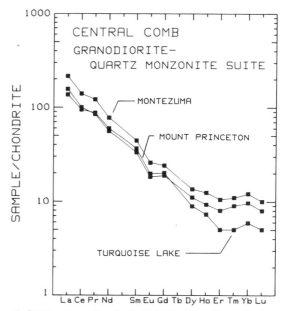

Figure 6. REE patterns for the Middle Tertiary Granodiorite–Quartz Monzonite Suite, central COMB. These large, calc-alkalic intrusions have moderately steep REE patterns with small, but well-defined, negative Eu anomalies.

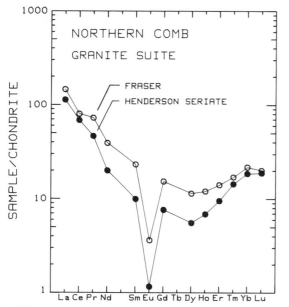

Figure 5. REE patterns for the granite of the Seriate intrusive center at Hendersen and the rhyolite tuff at Fraser, Oligocene-Miocene Granite Suite, northern COMB. Note contrast between granite REE patterns and patterns for older, Laramide alkaline monzonites (Fig. 3).

ronment (Shannon and others, 1982; Carten and others, 1988). In fact, Middle Mountain intrusives may well have produced a molybdenum deposit that was subsequently eroded. The remaining lobes of an upsidedown, cup-shaped shell of stockwork molybdenum ore attest to the earlier existence of a much larger Climax-type ore body (Ranta, 1974). The REE patterns associated with the rhyolite porphyry at Middle Mountain and underlying granite porphyry stock, and the nearby, slightly younger granite at Winfield Peak (Fig. 7) are quite similar, and display moderately negative Eu anomalies (Eu/Eu*$_N$ = 0.38 to 0.65) and minor upward tailing in HREE (La/Yb$_N$ = 9.7 to 14.4). Major- and trace-element compositions for the Middle Mountain–Winfield stocks, however, indicate granite systems that are not nearly as evolved as Climax types (Stein, 1985, Appendix B).

The Mount Antero region is well known for its mineral-collecting localities where spectacular beryl and fluorite crystals and molybdenum rosettes can be found in pegmatites, veins, and greisens developed within several highly evolved, 29-Ma granites (Sharp, 1976). Northeast of the Mount Antero region (Fig. 1), similar-age topaz rhyolites at Nathrop (Christiansen and others, 1986) are prospected for garnet and topaz in lithophysae. The Antero granites occur along the western margin, and the topaz rhyolites at Nathrop occur along the eastern margin of the northward-narrowing Rio Grande rift in central Colorado. The Antero granites and Nathrop Volcanics may represent epizonal and vent facies equivalents of the same evolved granite system; differential uplift and erosion along the margins of this graben segment of the Rio Grande have exhumed the western and eastern parts of the rift to different crustal levels (Shannon and others,

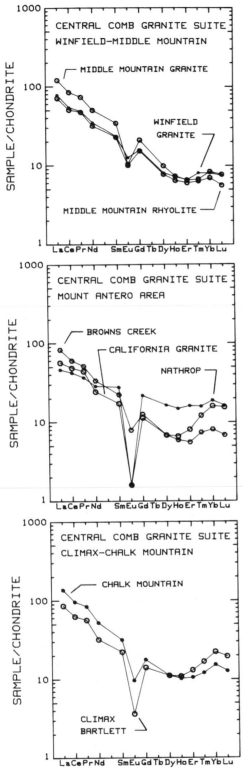

Figure 7. REE patterns for the Oligocene-Miocene Granite Suite, central COMB. The U shape and very large negative Eu anomaly is most pronounced in younger, highly evolved, strongly silicic-felsic granites (Antero California and Climax Bartlett stocks). REE patterns for granites, rhyolites, and topaz rhyolites are easily distinguished from patterns for older granodiorites and quartz monzonites in the central COMB (Fig. 6).

1987b). Examples of REE patterns for the granites and rhyolites in the Mount Antero–Nathrop area are given in Figure 7 to illustrate the distinct REE characteristics displayed by Oligocene granites in the COMB. These patterns are for the California granite stock (Shannon and others, 1987b) and the Browns Creek rhyolite plug, both of which have been prospected for economic molybdenum deposits. The Browns Creek plug may be an extrusive rhyolite related to Mount Antero granites (Coolbaugh, 1985). Though no topaz was noted, the groundmass in the analyzed Browns Creek rhyolite sample contained ubiquitous fluorite (Stein, 1985, Appendix A).

The REE patterns for the California granite stock and Browns Creek rhyolite plug show that REE concentrations are somewhat variable for chemically similar, essentially contemporaneous, evolved granite intrusions in the Mount Antero area (Fig. 7). These seemingly large differences may be controlled by chemical and/or mineral fractionation processes at shallow crustal levels. The REE patterns for both intrusions are marked by more pronounced U shapes (La/Yb_N = 3.5 and 10.3) and have large to moderate negative Eu anomalies ($Eu/Eu*_N$ = 0.12 and 0.47). These granite and rhyolite REE patterns contrast sharply with pattern shapes for older granodiorites and quartz monzonites (Fig. 6), including the nearby Mount Princeton batholith (Fig. 1), and REE concentrations in Mount Antero area silicic rocks are less than those in older, intermediate-composition rocks (Table 2). The REE pattern for the nearby topaz rhyolite at Nathrop is also shown in Figure 7. The Nathrop pattern is typical of REE patterns for topaz rhyolites in the western United States (Christiansen and others, 1983, 1984, 1986), displaying the characteristic flat pattern (La/Yb_N = 2.5) and very large negative Eu anomaly ($Eu/Eu*_N$ = 0.07). The data for Nathrop in this study (Table 2) agree well with earlier REE analyses of this topaz rhyolite by Zielinski and others (1977). If topaz rhyolites are indeed surface manifestations of buried A-type granites, as has been suggested by several workers (Burt and others, 1982; Christiansen and others, 1986), then the lower, flattened, and Eu-depleted REE pattern for Nathrop might be attributed to fractionation of feldspar and LREE–concentrating minerals such as allanite and/or monazite from a less evolved granite melt.

The 29-Ma Climax Bartlett stock (previously called the Central Mass) is part of a small granite intrusion associated with the formation of the upper molybdenum ore body at the Climax mine (Wallace and others, 1968, 1978; White and others, 1981). A topaz rhyolite porphyry on Chalk Mountain (Fig. 2), about 1.5 km west of the Climax mine, is presumably related to the granites at Climax, on the basis of geophysical, structural, and geochemical evidence (Christiansen and others, 1986; Burt and others, 1982). Isotopic data, particularly Pb, also support a genetic relation between the Chalk Mountain Rhyolite and Climax Bartlett stock (Stein, 1985). Chalk Mountain, however, has 290 ppm Sr and a Rb/Sr ratio of 2.6, very high and very low, respectively, compared to granite stocks at Climax. If Chalk Mountain is related to Climax, it might represent an earlier, less-evolved version of a Climax-type granite in which Climax-type chemical and accessory mineral fractionation was less complete, and concentration of strontium-bearing plagioclase, a major phenocrystic phase at Chalk Mountain (Stein, 1985, Appendix A), was more extensive. This difference in plagioclase abundance is reflected in the much larger $Eu/Eu*_N$ for Chalk Mountain compared to Climax (Table 2). The REE data for the Climax Bartlett stock and the topaz rhyolite at Chalk Mountain (Fig. 7) are typical of highly evolved Oligocene-Miocene granites in the COMB. Their total REE concentrations are lower than those for older intermediate composition rocks in the region, and patterns are distinctly U shaped (La/Yb_N = 3.9 and 8.9), swing upward at the HREE ends, and display pronounced negative Eu anomalies ($Eu/Eu*_N$ = 0.20 and 0.41). The deeper Climax Bartlett granite stock has a REE pattern reflecting more extensive differentiation than Chalk Mountain, its possible higher level equivalent (Fig. 7). The source for Climax-type granites and other evolved Oligocene-Miocene rhyolites and granites is discussed in a later section.

A suite of central COMB granodiorite-quartz monzonite from the Italian Mountain Intrusive Complex includes, from oldest to youngest, separate bodies of quartz diorite, granodiorite, and quartz monzonite (Cunningham, 1976). The 33-Ma quartz monzonite is the only dated unit. The presence of an isolated quartz diorite in this area is somewhat unusual, because most older, more mafic rocks are located in the northern COMB. On the basis of its lead isotopic composition (Stein, 1985) and neodymium isotopic composition (this study, discussed in a later

section), the undated quartz diorite could be of Larmaide age. In fact, numerous COMB intrusions south of Italian Mountain have been dated recently as Late Cretaceous (E. H. DeWitt, U.S. Geological Survey, Denver, 1987, oral communication). It is interesting that the REE data for the quartz diorite at Italian Mountain are similar to the REE data for other Laramide monzonites, particularly the hornblende monzonite at Caribou in the northern COMB (Table 2). The Italian Mountain Intrusive Complex illustrates that, near the southern COMB border (Fig. 1), slopes for REE patterns characterizing intermediate-composition rocks decrease (La/Yb_N = 11.7 to 12.9), the result of lower LREE contents (Fig. 8). The quartz monzonite at Italian Mountain may reflect a general transition from strongly LREE–enriched central COMB granodiorite–quartz monzonite to somewhat less LREE–enriched southern COMB quartz monzonite. The REE data for the granodiorite at Italian Mountain are generally intermediate between the quartz diorite and quartz monzonite (Fig. 8). Like the Jamestown intrusives in the northern COMB, the REE data do not indicate a genetic relation between intrusions forming the Italian Mountain Intrusive Complex.

Southern COMB

Eight REE patterns for 29-Ma quartz monzonite laccoliths, plutons, and sills of the West Elk and Elk Mountains display moderate slopes (La/Yb_N = 12.4 to 22.3), slight negative Eu anomalies ($Eu/Eu*_N$ = 0.88 to 0.95), and very similar REE concentrations (Fig. 9) for intrusions that are distributed over a large geographic area (Fig. 1). This implies that the source for these voluminous intermediate composition rocks might have

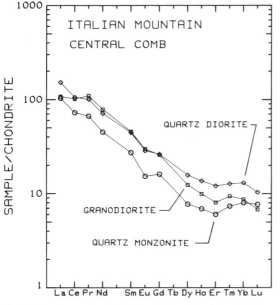

Figure 8. REE patterns for the Italian Mountain Intrusive Complex, central COMB (near southern COMB border, see Fig. 1). The REE pattern for the undated, more mafic, quartz diorite unit is reminiscent of some patterns for Laramide monzonites in the northern COMB. The oldest quartz diorite unit at Italian Mountain may represent a Laramide stock in the central-southern region of the COMB. Decreased REE abundances in the quartz monzonite at Italian Mountain, compared to other granodiorites and quartz monzonites in the central COMB (Fig. 6), may reflect a general transition to lower REE concentrations in southern COMB quartz monzonites (Fig. 9).

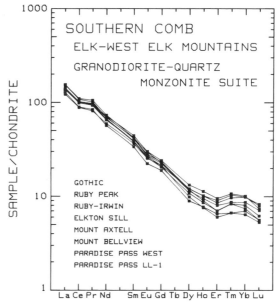

Figure 9. REE patterns for quartz monzonites of the Elk and West Elk Mountains, Middle Tertiary Granodiorite-Quartz Monzonite Suite, southern COMB. The nearly identical REE patterns indicate that all of these intermediate intrusions may be related to a laterally homogeneous batholith underlying a large geographic region (Fig. 1).

been a large batholith beneath the entire southern COMB. On the basis of a major negative gravity anomaly (minimum = −325 mgal), Isaacson and Smithson (1976) postulated that an 8- to 25-km-thick quartzofeldspathic batholith is present in the upper crust in the southern and central COMB region. They suggested that the numerous Oligocene laccoliths, plutons, and sills in this southern COMB region are protrusions off the top of this batholith, which, on the basis of the gravity anomaly, does not follow Precambrian structural trends. The REE data (Table 2 and Fig. 9) demonstrate similar REE fractionation within and between individual intrusions, and indicate a mineralogically and chemically (REE) homogeneous source over a large geographic region.

The proposed homogeneous batholith source for the southern COMB quartz monzonites is further supported by isotopic data (Stein, 1985; Stein and Fullagar, 1985; Hannah and Stein, 1986; Stein and others, 1987). Lead and strontium isotopic data for these eight Oligocene quartz monzonites are compatible with an intermediate-composition, extremely homogeneous, predominantly lower-crustal source; $^{87}Sr/^{86}Sr$, $^{206}Pb/^{204}Pb$, and $^{208}Pb/^{204}Pb$ for these intrusions are very consistent, averaging about 0.7073 ± 0.0002, 17.7 ± 0.1 and 37.9 ± 0.1, respectively. Neodymium isotopic data, presented in a later section of this chapter, are also very uniform, yielding $^{143}Nd/^{144}Nd$ that average 0.512183 ± 0.00007. Corresponding Sm/Nd vary less than 5 percent. However, variation in Rb/Sr within this group of southern COMB quartz monzonites exceeds 200 percent, indicating some chemical heterogeneity among more readily fractionated elements.

Compared to proposed sources for Laramide monzonites and middle Tertiary granodiorites and quartz monzonites in the northern and central COMB, potential differences in the source for this more homogeneous group of southern COMB quartz monzonites might be (1) less felsic parent material, (2) greater amount of partial melting, (3) small quantity of plagioclase, hornblende, apatite, sphene, and/or garnet in the residuum, and/or (4) reduced metasomatism in southern COMB lower crust. These potential differences in the source for southern COMB Oligocene quartz monzonites are consistent with the slight decrease in La/Yb$_N$ in intermediate rocks as the COMB is traversed from northeast to southwest.

Several of the southern COMB intermediate-composition intrusions, including the Paradise Pass, Mount Bellview, and Augusta stocks, contain molybdenite-bearing quartz + sericite + pyrite veins. The Augusta stock, like Italian Mountain in the central COMB, is an example of a localized sequence of presumably Tertiary-age intrusions. The sequence includes quartz monzodiorite, granodiorite, and quartz monzonite (Stein, 1985, Appendix A). On the basis of geologic mapping (Gaskill and others, 1967) and the concentric nature of the outcrops at Augusta, the outlying quartz monzodiorite is probably the oldest unit and does not appear to be related to the other two intrusions. The centrally located mass of quartz monzonite is the youngest unit and is rimmed by a thin border of granodiorite. Isolated quartz + molybdenite veins cut the Augusta stock, and ruby silver ores occur

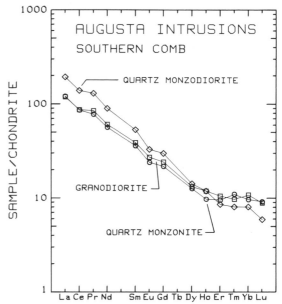

Figure 10. REE patterns for the intrusive sequence of Augusta, southern COMB. The undated quartz monzodiorite has a steeper REE pattern, much like patterns for Laramide monzonites in the northern COMB. The granodiorite and quartz monzonite at Augusta have patterns very similar to REE patterns for other southern COMB quartz monzonites. Although intrusions older than about 35 Ma are unknown in the immediate area, the quartz monzodiorite may be Late Cretaceous in age.

peripherally to the stock (Mutschler and others, 1981b). The REE patterns for the granodiorite and quartz monzonite at Augusta (Fig. 10) are like those for other quartz monzonite intrusions in the Elk and West Elk Mountains. The quartz monzodiorite, however, has a steeper REE pattern (La/Yb$_N$ = 24.1) and a more pronounced negative Eu anomaly (Eu/Eu*$_N$ = 0.83), similar to patterns for Laramide monzonites. Laramide-age intrusions are not known in this region. Although the quartz monzodiorite at Augusta has not been dated, its REE pattern suggests that it may be an older pluton of Laramide affinity.

The granite suite is well represented in the southern COMB. Without exception, all the southern COMB granite suite members are Miocene, possibly reflecting progressively younger magmatism associated with a subsurface, westward-migrating margin of the northern end of the Rio Grande rift system (Fig. 1 and Stein, 1982). Miocene granites in the southern COMB include the 17-Ma Mount Emmons–Redwell Basin composite granite stock, which is associated with a major Climax-type molybdenum ore body (Thomas and Galey, 1982; Dowsett and others, 1981; Sharp, 1978; Stein and Hannah, 1982), and the 10-Ma topaz rhyolite at Boston Peak (Ernst, 1980), 12-Ma rhyolite at Round Mountain (Mutschler and others, 1981b), and 12-Ma granite at Treasure Mountain (Mutschler, 1976).

The composite granite stock at Mount Emmons–Redwell Basin, somewhat similar to the Urad-Henderson stock, explosively breached the surface and has several associated ore bodies, including two low-grade ore blankets within the Redwell volcanic pipe, and a high-grade ore shell associated with the small cupola of Mount Emmons intrusions. The Redwell pipe, however, is not located directly above the stacked Mount Emmons stock phases, but is a volcanic vent about 300 m to the northwest. The Redwell pipe and composite Mount Emmons stock are connected in the subsurface, and it appears that the Redwell pipe sampled magma from near the base of the Mount Emmons cupola (Stein and Hannah, 1982; Stein, 1985). The geometry of the composite stock at Mount Emmons–Redwell Basin is such that the Redwell sample of granite porphyry, taken from drill core at a depth of 1,545 m (5,100′), is actually deeper in the magmatic system than the Mount Emmons sample of Keystone stock (Table 1, Fig. 2). The REE patterns (Fig. 11) for the Mount Emmons–Redwell Basin are similar to the Urad-Henderson and Climax REE patterns, except that REE concentrations (Table 2) are somewhat higher, U shapes are not as spectacular (La/Yb_N = 11.8 and 20.5), and negative Eu anomalies are not as pronounced ($Eu/Eu*_N$ = 0.38 and 0.39). Although the source for Climax-type granites is probably similar in all three geographic regions of the COMB, differing degrees of partial melting, the timing and extent of mineral fractionation, and minor variations in volatile composition or vapor volume relative to melt could easily produce the slight differences in REE patterns at Mount Emmons–Redwell Basin, Urad-Henderson, and Climax.

The highly evolved rhyolite at Boston Peak is not spatially or temporally associated with a known Climax-type system, although it has been prospected for molybdenum because of its intriguing major- and trace-element chemistry. Its REE pattern displays a strong U shape and pronounced negative Eu anomaly (Fig. 11), very similar to patterns for the granites at Mount Emmons–Redwell Basin (La/Yb_N = 7.7, $Eu/Eu*_N$ = 0.29). However, its REE concentrations are distinctly lower than those from the Mount Emmons–Redwell Basin (Table 2). The rhyolite at Boston Peak, with its much lower REE concentrations, could be an economically unimportant occurrence of felsic volcanic rock that lost REE and possibly ore-bearing volatile phases during crystallization.

The granite at Treasure Mountain is not as chemically evolved as Climax-type granites, and its equigranular texture is uncharacteristic of the well-developed porphyritic textures in COMB Climax-type stocks (Stein, 1985). However, minor showings of fracture-coating molybdenite, the ubiquitous presence of fluorite, and the extensive development of skarn-related minerals peripheral to the Treasure Mountain stock have enticed mining companies to periodically explore for economic molybdenum deposits. Although the REE pattern (Fig. 11) for the granite at Treasure Mountain is similar to Mount Emmons–Redwell Basin patterns, lead isotopic data (Stein, 1985) suggest that Treasure Mountain is probably related to the voluminous quartz monzonites in the southern COMB and/or their source. The granite at Treasure Mountain may have formed from local melting of the Oligocene southern COMB batholith during Miocene extension.

The REE pattern for the rhyolite at Round Mountain is

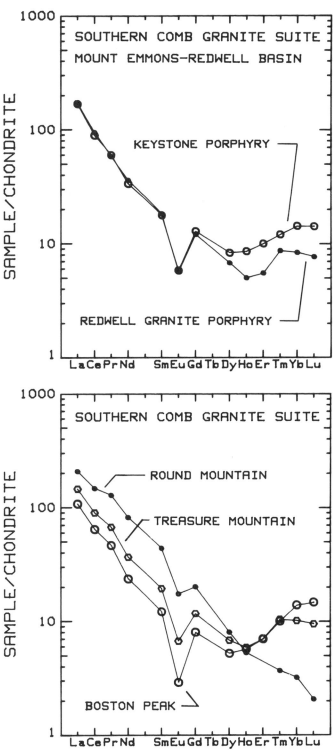

Figure 11. REE patterns for the Oligocene-Miocene Granite Suite, southern COMB. REE concentrations are somewhat higher, and negative Eu anomalies are not as pronounced in southern COMB granites (Miocene) compared to northern and central COMB granites (Oligocene). In the southern COMB, Miocene granite REE patterns contrast sharply with Oligocene quartz monzonite patterns (Fig. 9).

anomalous (Fig. 11) because it does not have the typical U shape for rhyolites and granites throughout the northern, central, and southern COMB. Its relatively high LREE concentrations (Table 2), steep REE pattern (La/Yb$_N$ = 64.7), and only moderate negative Eu anomaly (Eu/Eu*$_N$ = 0.59) indicate a source and/or a chemical, mineral, and/or vapor fractionation history different from all other COMB Oligocene-Miocene granites. Major- and trace-element and isotopic data indicate that Round Mountain is not an evolved A-type rhyolite (Stein, 1985).

Origin of Oligocene-Miocene COMB granites

The REE patterns for Oligocene-Miocene granites in the northern, central, and southern COMB are markedly different from patterns for all older calc-alkalic and alkalic rocks. Granite REE characteristics include lower REE concentrations, patterns with U shapes, and pronounced negative Eu anomalies. Because these granites have undergone variable but extensive chemical and crystal fractionation, and because most of these granites exsolve H_2O-, F-, Cl-, and CO_2-bearing vapors and possibly immiscible F- and Cl-rich liquid fractions at upper crustal levels, it is very difficult to constrain initial magma source(s) using REE data. Given our limited knowledge of distribution coefficients for the REE in high-temperature fluids (particularly volatile phases), it is probably impossible to distinguish the effects of source composition, mineral-melt fractionation, and melt-vapor fractionation on the final REE patterns for COMB Oligocene-Miocene granites. We conclude that little information on source can be gained using REE patterns for evolved Oligocene-Miocene granites in the COMB .

Mineral-melt fractionation was probably important in creating the pronounced concave-upward U shapes and large negative Eu anomalies in Oligocene-Miocene granite REE patterns. The removal of MREE–enriched phases such as apatite, sphene, or hornblende could have contributed to the pronounced U shapes. Although an assortment of LREE– and HREE–rich accessory minerals, common in highly evolved silicic rocks, are also present in COMB granites, the low LREE abundances probably reflect fractionation of LREE–rich accessory phases such as allanite or monazite (Cameron and Cameron, 1986; Miller and Mittlefehldt, 1982; Sawka and others, 1984). The large negative Eu anomalies in granite REE patterns almost certainly indicate some fractionation of feldspar from the melt. Candela (1987), however, has shown that at high but reasonable conditions of f_{O_2}, near the hematite-magnetite buffer, a near-minimum granite melt with 2 percent initial H_2O (6 percent H_2O at vapor saturation) and 2,000 ppm Cl will lose 50 percent of its Eu to the vapor phase.

The evolution of vapor phases or "ore liquids" (Carten, 1987) in the final stages of granite crystallization may also drastically alter REE patterns for granite melts. Experimental data on REE transport in high-temperature ore fluids are limited, but CO_2-rich hydrothermal fluids carrying complexed elements such as Al, Be, Fe, Zr, and the ligands F, Cl, and CO_2 appear to be very effective in mobilizing REE (Humphris, 1984; Cullers and

Graf, 1984). A preferential solubility of HREE over LREE in F-rich volatile phases associated with large ion lithophile element–rich silicic magmas has been experimentally demonstrated by London and Hervig (1986) and London and others (1987). Likewise, extreme HREE enrichments in F-rich, peraluminous rhyolites in the Trans-Pecos region in Texas have been attributed to F-rich vapor phase crystallization (Rubin and others, 1987; Price and others, 1987). The distinct U-shaped REE patterns in Climax-type granites may partly result from the presence of F-bearing vapor phases during crystallization; fluorite is ubiquitous in stockwork veinlets and as an accessory mineral in the groundmass of Climax-type granites. The vein and groundmass presence of fluorite and calcite in several other COMB granites may also indicate concentration of REE, particularly HREE, by late-stage F- and CO_2-rich fluids.

Isotopic data are far more useful than REE data in constraining source-rock compositions for Oligocene-Miocene granites. Lead isotopic data (Stein, 1985) indicate that granite sources had lower than average U/Pb ($\mu = {}^{238}U/{}^{204}Pb$ = 4 to 7) and somewhat elevated Th/U (5.5 to 7.5). Initial ${}^{87}Sr/{}^{86}Sr$ range from 0.708 to 0.710 (Stein and Fullagar, 1985; Stein, 1985), indicating sources with only moderate Rb/Sr. Neodymium isotopic data for Oligocene-Miocene granites yield low initial ${}^{143}Nd/{}^{144}Nd$, which generally suggest sources that had or obtained low Sm/Nd early in their Proterozoic history and maintained low Sm/Nd into the Phanerozoic. Collectively, these isotopic data are consistent with a lower-crustal source of felsic to intermediate composition.

Collins and others (1982) and Clemens and others (1986) called on previously melt-depleted I-type source rocks in the lower crust for the origin of A-type granites. Although this may be true in some cases, we suggest that in the case of COMB Proterozoic lower crust which produced highly evolved Oligocene-Miocene granites, a prior, moderately high to high-grade, dehydration-dominated, essentially melting-absent metamorphic history may be just as effective in preparing the granite source(s). This suggestion is compatible with a source that may have lost H_2O relative to CO_2, U relative to Th and Pb, and Rb relative to Sr (assuming some breakdown of K[Rb]-rich micas). Thus, the isotopic data are accommodated. A near–granulite-grade metasedimentary (± metavolcanic) lower crust dominated by quartz and feldspar, particularly K-feldspar, and containing some remaining F- and Cl-rich hydrous phases such as biotite or phlogopite, is an attractive potential source for evolved COMB Oligocene-Miocene granites. Partial melting of moderate- to high-grade Proterozoic rocks that contain slightly different volatile proportions would stabilize different phases and produce different melt structures, perhaps accounting for much of the observed variation in trace-element chemistry among these COMB granites (Stein, 1985, Appendix B). Density contrast with the surrounding residuum, and a high temperature and low viscosity associated with vapor-absent melting, would allow the Oligocene-Miocene granite melt to ascend in relatively small volume.

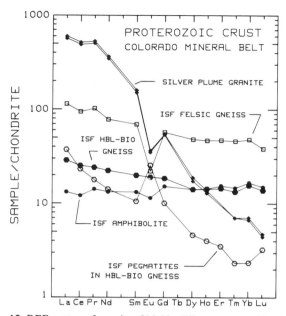

Figure 12. REE patterns for units of highly different composition in the Idaho Springs Formation (ISF), central COMB, and the Silver Plume Granite, northern COMB. Extreme variation in the REE geochemistry of Proterozoic rocks at the surface is apparent. Similar chemical variation might also be expected in COMB Proterozoic source rocks in the middle and lower crust.

Precambrian rocks

Proterozoic basement in the COMB, including four units from the Idaho Springs Formation (ISF) and two examples of Silver Plume Granite (SPG), was sampled to examine variability in REE concentrations and patterns in rocks possibly related to lower crustal source rocks. Meager sampling of surface exposures of Colorado Precambrian rocks in no way guarantees information on lower crustal sources for Late Cretaceous–Tertiary magmas (Stein and Hannah, 1988). The four ISF units (Xf, Xh, Xb, Xb pegs, Table 1, Appendix 1) were taken from a typical exposure of complexly folded, steeply dipping gneisses and amphibolites mapped by Bergendahl (1963). Pegmatitic dikes and segregations (ISF Xb pegs) that crosscut banded hornblende-biotite gneisses (ISF Xb) almost certainly represent local migmatization during peak thermal metamorphism.

Not surprisingly, REE concentrations and pattern shapes for COMB Proterozoic rocks are extremely variable (Table 2 and Fig. 12), ranging from flat lines (La/Yb$_N$ = 0.79) with REE concentrations of only 11 to 17 times chondrite for ISF amphibolite to steep, negative-sloping lines (La/Yb$_N$ = 84), with La$_N$ values of nearly 600 for SPG. The positive Eu anomaly and HREE depletion in ISF Xb pegmatites, relative to hosting ISF Xb hornblende-biotite gneiss (Fig. 12), reflect plagioclase concentration in the pegmatite and amphibole in the gneiss.

The variation in REE concentrations and patterns for COMB Proterozoic rocks suggests that a potentially complimen-

tary and equally complex assortment of rock types might be expected in the middle and lower crust. This variation probably reflects both highly varying precursors and differing magmatic, metamorphic, and metasomatic histories in Proterozoic units.

RESULTS AND DISCUSSION OF SAMARIUM-NEODYMIUM ISOTOPIC DATA

This section contains a general discussion of Sm-Nd isotopic data for Late Cretaceous–Tertiary COMB granitoids, again grouping samples by age and composition, both of which correlate well with geographic location (Fig. 1 and Table 3). Previous Sm-Nd isotopic analyses for two COMB intrusions (Farmer and DePaolo, 1984) agree well with data in this study.

Source model ages using CHUR (Chondritic Uniform Reservoir) and DM (Depleted Mantle) are tabulated in Table 3. However, the usefulness of such model age calculations is limited unless the rock suite in question was derived directly from CHUR or DM (Arndt and Goldstein, 1987). Although DM model ages yield values that are closer to COMB basement ages than CHUR model ages, this is purely the outcome of assumptions inherent in the DM model; these DM values still fall far short of known ages for major segments of Proterozoic crust in Colorado and the western United States. Given the available geochemical and isotopic data, the derivation of Late Cretaceous–Tertiary plutonic and volcanic rocks in the COMB undoubtedly involved Proterozoic lower-crustal rocks whose Precambrian history was very complex (Stein, 1985). Because Sm/Nd ratios in Proterozoic rocks change with episodes of crust modification, the Sm/Nd for COMB Proterozoic source rocks cannot be directly represented by CHUR or DM values. Knowledge of these Sm/Nd ratios in lower-crustal rocks, established during metamorphic and plutonic events in the Proterozoic, is needed to calculate correct model ages.

The histograms in Figure 13 display ^{143}Nd/^{144}Nd for COMB samples, illustrating the correlation between Nd isotopic ratio, rock type, and geographic location. The ^{143}Nd/^{144}Nd for all samples are less than present-day ^{143}Nd/^{144}Nd for CHUR (0.512638) and are much less than ^{143}Nd/^{144}Nd for rocks developing in DM island-arc or oceanic-ridge environments (0.5128 to 0.5131). Although there is substantial overlap in the three data sets, the ^{143}Nd/^{144}Nd are somewhat lower for central and southern COMB granodiorites, quartz monzonites, and granites relative to northern COMB monzonites (Fig. 13). This may indicate lower Sm/Nd in central and southern COMB sources, possibly the result of (1) initially more felsic parent material and/or (2) more intense or widespread Precambrian metasomatism; both possibilities could result in increased LREE enrichment (Nd >>Sm) in the central and southern COMB lower crust. Assuming that some Archean detritus is present in COMB Proterozoic crust (Stein, 1985; Patchett and Arndt, 1986; Nelson and DePaolo, 1984; Bennett and DePaolo, 1987), and that the same general magma-generating processes persisted throughout the Late Cretaceous and Tertiary, the most negative ϵ_{Nd} values

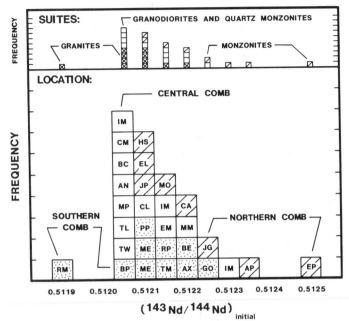

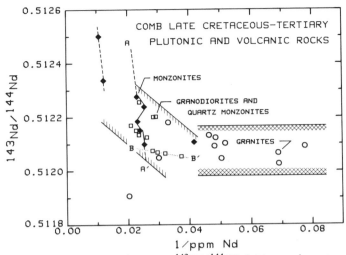

Figure 14. Nd concentration versus $^{143}Nd/^{144}Nd$ plot to examine potential contamination of lower crustal sources by mantle-type rocks. Monzonite, granodiorite, and quartz monzonite $^{143}Nd/^{144}Nd$ compositions may reflect minor contamination of lower crustal intermediate to felsic sources by a LREE-rich, mantle-like component (mafic lower crust and/or fertile mantle). Granite sources could be uncontaminated lower crust. Varying Nd concentrations within the granite suite reflect differing mineral-melt and melt-vapor fractionation of REE. From bottom to top of figure, data connected by dashed line A-A' are from stocks EL, EM, CA, JG, and IM-Tqd; from left to right, data connected by dotted line B-B' are from plutons or batholiths TL, MP, TW, and IM-Tpqm.

Figure 13. Histograms showing the range and frequency of initial $^{143}Nd/^{144}Nd$ for Late Cretaceous–Tertiary plutonic and volcanic rocks in the Colorado Mineral Belt (COMB). The Oligocene-Miocene Granite Suite (cross pattern) has the lowest $^{143}Nd/^{144}Nd$, and the Laramide Monzonite Suite, prevalent in the northern COMB (diagonal pattern), has the highest $^{143}Nd/^{144}Nd$. The Middle Tertiary Granodiorite–Quartz Monzonite Suite of the central (no pattern) and southern (stipple pattern) COMB is characterized by intermediate $^{143}Nd/^{144}Nd$. The skewed-to-the-left shape of the histograms may indicate variable, but small amounts of mixing between a mafic lower crustal (± mantle) component ($^{143}Nd/^{144}Nd$ >0.5125) and a dominant, intermediate to felsic, lower crustal granulite component ($^{143}Nd/^{144}Nd$ = 0.51205).

(lowest $^{143}Nd/^{144}Nd$) would be expected in the northern COMB, nearest the Wyoming craton. However, the observed trend of $^{143}Nd/^{144}Nd$ is not consistent with this simple model, suggesting that different sources and tectonic processes were involved in magma generation from northern to central to southern COMB. The skewed-to-the-left shape of the histograms may have been created by the mixing of two isotopically distinct sources: (1) a dominant source of $^{143}Nd/^{144}Nd$ at about 0.51205 and (2) a subordinate source of $^{143}Nd/^{144}Nd$ greater than 0.5125. A similar histogram for $^{206}Pb/^{204}Pb$ shows exactly the same correlation between geographic location, rock type, and lead isotopic ratios (Stein, 1985). The U-Th-Pb system, however, yields much more distinct data sets (less overlap) than the Sm-Nd system.

The possibility of contamination of lower-crustal magmas by mantle-derived or mantle-like melts is shown in Figure 14. The granites plot along a horizontal band of highly variable Nd concentration, but uniform $^{143}Nd/^{144}Nd$ composition. This suggests that granite sources have not been contaminated by mantle-type material, and that variation in granite Nd concentrations is created during chemical and mineral fractionation and vapor evolution accompanying granite ascent and crystallization. The

monzonites, granodiorites, and quartz monzonites, in contrast, trend along moderately to steeply dipping, negative-sloping trends, suggesting that initially low $^{143}Nd/^{144}Nd$ values could have been slightly raised by adding Nd from metasomatized mantle-type sources with higher Nd and higher Sm/Nd (dashed line A-A' in Fig. 14). An alternative argument could call upon variable contamination of magmas with initially high $^{143}Nd/^{144}Nd$ (CHUR-like ratios) by material with very low $^{143}Nd/^{144}Nd$ (Archean-like ratios). The relatively flat trend (dotted line B-B' in Fig. 14), which connects data from four major middle Tertiary plutons to batholiths in the central COMB, demonstrates that there is little variation in $^{143}Nd/^{144}Nd$ despite the potential for addition of mantle-type $^{143}Nd/^{144}Nd$ compositions to large crustal reservoirs.

All the data from Late Cretaceous–Tertiary plutonic and volcanic rocks in the COMB fall in the lower right quadrant on an ϵ_{Nd} versus ϵ_{Sr} diagram (Fig. 15), strongly indicating involvement of old crustal sources. The three major Laramide-Tertiary rock suites are somewhat separated in ϵ_{Nd}-ϵ_{Sr} space. Ranges in ϵ_{Nd} are –1.0 to –9.3, –6.7 to –10.6, and –8.0 to –14.0 for Laramide monzonites, middle Tertiary granodiorites and quartz monzonites, and Oligocene-Miocene granites, respectively; similarly, ranges for ϵ_{Sr} are 6.8 to 46, 32 to 83, and 40 to 432 (Table 3). The ϵ_{Nd}-ϵ_{Sr} field for Colorado Proterozoic granulites (DePaolo, 1981a) is essentially coincident with that of major Late Cretaceous and middle Tertiary plutons and batholiths of the

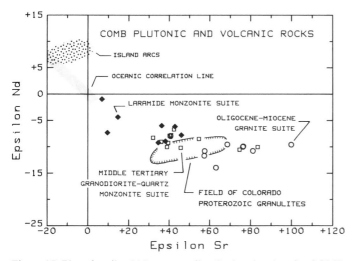

Figure 15. Plot of epsilon Nd versus epsilon Sr showing data for COMB Late Cretaceous–Tertiary igneous rocks. Field showing Colorado Proterozoic granulites is from DePaolo (1981a). Fields for MORB and OIB are represented by the upper and lower parts of the oceanic correlation line, respectively. The confinement of data points to the lower-right quadrant suggests major involvement of crustal sources, particularly for the Oligocene-Miocene Granite Suite and Middle Tertiary Granodiorite–Quartz Monzonite Suite. Some of the more mafic, highly alkaline members of the Laramide Monzonite Suite, however, have epsilon Nd values that approach the lower end of the oceanic correlation line, suggesting that mafic crust and/or some lithospheric mantle could be involved in their generation.

northern and central COMB. The three data points for Laramide monzonites located well left of the Colorado Proterozoic granulite field (Fig. 15) represent very mafic alkalic plutons (EP, AP, CA in Table 1). The granite suite is characterized by relatively uniform ϵ_{Nd} and highly variable ϵ_{Sr} values, reflecting parent material with uniform Sm/Nd, but possibly variable Rb/Sr; this is consistent with the suggestion of a Proterozoic metasedimentary (± metavolcanic), lower crustal source that underwent periods of dehydration-dominated, melting-absent metamorphism during which local breakdown of Rb-rich micas may have occurred. Some variation in ϵ_{Sr} among young granites could have resulted from the use of incorrect granite ages in isotopic calculations; ages reported in this paper, however, are generally well established by modern dating methods. Alternatively, some of the variation in ϵ_{Sr} in these small granite stocks could have resulted from contamination by Proterozoic country rocks either during ascent or at the site of stock emplacement.

To examine the contamination explanation for variable ϵ_{Sr} in the granite suite, the Oligocene Urad-Henderson intrusive system and Proterozoic Silver Plume Granite host together provide an ideal stock–country-rock pair. For the purpose of calculations, it is assumed that isotopic values for Mount Emmons and Climax represent uncontaminated Climax-type granites. Data for calculations are in Tables 2 and 3 unless otherwise noted. The Seriate granite stock at Henderson (5 ppm Sr) has an ϵ_{Sr} value of +432,

which is so high that it is not shown in Figure 15; host Silver Plume Granite (250 ppm Sr) has present-day ϵ_{Sr} values that range from +2,300 to +5,500 (Peterman and others, 1968). Calculations show that potential SPG contamination of the Seriate is less than 0.5 percent. Contamination of the Seriate stock (12 ppm Nd) by Nd from SPG (210 ppm Nd), whose ϵ_{Nd} value is very low (present-day ϵ_{Nd} values = –24.60 and –24.41, or $^{143}Nd/^{144}Nd$ = 0.511377 and 0.511386, $^{147}Sm/^{144}Nd$ = 0.07668; H. Stein, unpublished data), is negligible (<0.06 percent). This is supported by the very similar ϵ_{Nd} values (–9.64 to –10.04) in geographically separated, variably hosted, COMB Climax-type granites; in fact, the ϵ_{Nd} values for these Climax-type granites are almost within analytical error of one another. Lead isotopic data (Stein, 1985; Stein and Hannah, 1985), however, indicate up to 7 percent possible contamination of the Tertiary Seriate granite stock at Henderson by lead from Precambrian SPG. The calculated variable amounts of potential contamination (0.5, 0.06, and 7 percent) of Seriate by host SPG probably reflect different element mobility within this Climax-type magmatic-hydrothermal system. Differences in ϵ_{Sr} and ϵ_{Nd} among other COMB Oligocene-Miocene granites are more likely attributable to heterogeneity in the source.

Climax-type granites reflect a unique, though not necessarily unusual source, with uniform Sm/Nd and possibly variable Rb/Sr. The granite at Middle Mountain, included with the Oligocene-Miocene granite suite because of its associated Climax-type stockwork molybdenum ore shell, contains the lowest ϵ_{Sr} and highest ϵ_{Nd} in the granite suite, which complements its unevolved major- and trace-element chemistry and older age (Stein, 1985, Appendix B). The rhyolite at Round Mountain contains the lowest ϵ_{Nd} (–14.0) in the granite suite, suggesting a slightly different origin, perhaps involving Proterozoic crustal rocks with lower Sm/Nd and/or Archean detritus; alternatively, its original ϵ_{Nd} value may have been decreased by contamination from low ϵ_{Nd} SPG-type rocks at depth, although no SPG crops out in the Round Mountain region. Lead isotopic data (Stein, 1985), however, support derivation of Round Mountain from a slightly different, granulitic lower crust having very low U/Pb, rather than basement contamination.

Mixing of Proterozoic crustal sources *could* alone explain COMB Laramide-Tertiary magma types (Fig. 16). It appears that metasomatized mafic lower-crustal rocks, with or without enriched lithospheric mantle, are most likely the dominant source for Late Cretaceous monzonites, whereas 1,800-Ma granulites are most likely the dominant source for Tertiary granodiorites, quartz monzonites, and granites. Crustal sources for Late Cretaceous–Tertiary magmas could include (1) mafic, metasomatized, amphibolitic to granulitic, mantle-derived lower crust (ϵ_{Nd} = +1 to –2) and (2) intermediate to felsic, possibly metasomatized, granulitic, metasedimentary (± metavolcanic) lower crust (ϵ_{Nd} = –10 to –14). DePaolo (1981a) reported present-day ϵ_{Nd} values of +0.6 and +0.9 for 1,800-Ma metatholeiites and +4.6 for a 1,800-Ma metadacite in Colorado. The ISF amphibolite (Table 2 and Fig. 12) might represent a nonmetasomatized variety of potential

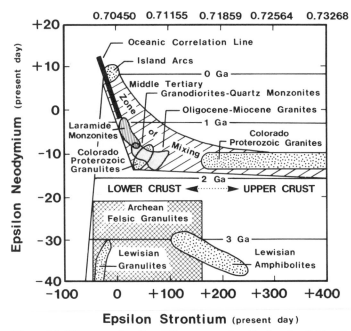

Figure 16. Diagram of epsilon Nd versus epsilon Sr showing fields of data for Late Cretaceous–Tertiary igneous rocks in the COMB. Fields for present-day compositions of Colorado Proterozoic granites and granulites are also shown (data in DePaolo, 1981a). The zone of mixing (diagonal pattern) includes epsilon Nd-epsilon Sr values for 1670, 1430, and 1015 Ma Colorado Proterozoic granites to the right, and enriched and depleted mantle to the left. The mixing zone is centered on Colorado Proterozoic granulites. For reference, broad fields for Archean felsic granulites (Jacobsen and Wasserburg, 1978; Collerson and others, 1983; McCulloch and Black, 1984) and Lewisian amphibolites and granulites (Hamilton and others, 1979) are plotted. Horizontal lines indicate expected epsilon Nd values at 1 b.y. time intervals using a depleted mantle model for crust formation. Diagram modified from DePaolo (1981b).

mafic members in the Proterozoic COMB lower crust. Intermediate to felsic members could be countless combinations of REE-enriched, low Sm/Nd, dehydrated granulitic rocks in lower-crustal ISF-type Proterozoic sequences. These granulites, whose protoliths developed in a complex Proterozoic back-arc basin environment, may have been largely immature sedimentary and/or volcanic rocks. The extension of the data field for Tertiary intrusions toward the elongate field for Colorado Proterozoic granites (Fig. 16) suggests that Oligocene-Miocene granites in particular might have a small component similar to these Proterozoic plutonic rocks in their source. The 1,430-Ma Silver Plume and Sherman granite batholiths, which have ϵ_{Nd} values between –15.0 and –24.1 (DePaolo, 1981a), are not shown in Figure 16 because their ϵ_{Sr} values exceed +400 and are as high as +5,500 (Peterman and others, 1968). However, the incorporation of extremely minor amounts of 1,430-Ma granites is still permissible in this mixing model. Clearly, Laramide, middle Tertiary, and Oligocene-Miocene magmatism in this geographically broad region of the COMB did not originate solely from lithospheric mantle or oceanic slab; however, mantle and/or slab may have

played an important role, particularly in the generation of Laramide monzonites.

Mantle involvement

Modeling Laramide-Tertiary magma sources requires knowledge of or assumptions about the chemical and isotopic nature of mantle beneath the COMB. Eggler and others (1987), in a study of mantle nodules from Devonian kimberlite pipes on the Colorado-Wyoming border, documented enriched and infertile peridotite and websterite xenoliths. They noted that the ratio of enriched to infertile xenoliths (enriched = high Na_2O and low $Mg/[Mg + Fe]$) is unusually high, and they suggested that 80 percent of the lithosphere sampled between the crust and 100 km depth in this region is occupied by enriched mantle rocks. They determined that this enrichment in the shallow lithosphere must have occurred during Precambrian time. If somewhat enriched lithosphere was (is) also present beneath the nearby COMB, it may have played a critical role in chemically preparing Proterozoic sources for Late Cretaceous–Tertiary magmatism by providing alkali-, CO_2-, and LREE–rich fluids that invaded COMB lower crust.

Isotopic and geochemical data permit total derivation of Laramide-Tertiary magmas from COMB Proterozoic lower crust. However, melts from enriched mantle (or oceanic slab) ponding at the base of Colorado continental crust during Laramide time may have produced extreme thermal perturbations in heterogeneous ISF–type lower crust. Mantle-derived melts may have eventually invaded overlying lower crust and, in a compressional tectonic environment (Laramide orogeny), communication between mantle-derived melts and Proterozoic lower crust could have been particularly prolonged. Alkalic monzonites generated during Laramide compression might represent hybrid mixtures of mantle and lower crust (Fig. 16). Alternatively, the source for Laramide monzonites could simply be metasomatized, mafic lower crust or possibly enriched mantle. It is difficult to distinguish isotopically between mantle and mantle-derived Proterozoic mafic lower crust, particularly because the mantle beneath this region of Colorado may be atypically fertile (Eggler and others, 1987). The very steep REE patterns indicate strong LREE enrichment in alkaline monzonites, and this generally argues against significant contribution from a depleted mantle source. Lower-crustal sources for middle Tertiary granodiorites and quartz monzonites could also have a minor component of mantle-derived melt, very slightly raising their distinctly negative ϵ_{Nd} and reducing their distinctly positive ϵ_{Sr} values (Fig. 15).

During Oligocene-Miocene tectonic extension in the COMB, mantle-derived melts penetrating lower crust have a higher likelihood of ascending to upper-crustal levels where they may form the mafic component in bimodal magma suites. If communication between mantle-derived basaltic magmas and lower crust is minimized, then contemporaneous silicic magmatism may approximate the isotopic composition of pure lower crust, uncontaminated by mantle-derived melts. This lower crust, of course, may have been affected by previous metasomatic event(s) involving mantle. The most crustal isotopic signatures (lowest ϵ_{Nd}) in COMB granites are associated with Oligocene-Miocene silicic rocks that developed during Rio Grande rifting.

SUMMARY

1. Late Cretaceous–Tertiary intrusions in the COMB may be grouped by their REE geochemistry and $^{143}Nd/^{144}Nd$ isotopic composition, as well as by age, geographic location, and rock type. They are broadly divided into three major compositional suites: **Laramide Monzonite Suite, Middle Tertiary Granodiorite–Quartz Monzonite Suite,** and **Oligocene-Miocene Granite Suite.** Base- and precious-metal deposits are associated with some Laramide and middle Tertiary rocks, and Climax-type stockwork molybdenum deposits are associated with several highly evolved granites from the Oligocene-Miocene suite.

2. The Proterozoic lower crust in the COMB that largely produced Laramide-Tertiary intrusions may have been modified by one or both of the following:

(a) *Archean detritus* shed southward from the Archean craton in Wyoming and incorporated in developing Proterozoic crust in Colorado.

(b) *Metasomatic fluids* (1) generated in the lower crust during Proterozoic metamorphism, (2) associated with subduction and dehydration of oceanic slab during the Laramide orogeny, and/or (3) emanating from enriched lithospheric mantle during Proterozoic and/or Phanerozoic time.

3. A lower-crust mixing spectrum with a major contribution from Proterozoic intermediate to felsic granulitic rocks and a subordinate contribution from Proterozoic metasomatized mafic lower crust can explain the isotopic and chemical character of Late Cretaceous–Tertiary igneous rock suites. Metasomatized mantle could substitute for mafic lower crust.

(a) The source for the **Laramide Monzonite Suite** was most likely dominated by rather mafic, highly metasomatized amphibolitic to granulitic lower crust (± mantle) enriched in alkalies and REE, particularly the LREE.

(b) The source for the **Middle Tertiary Granodiorite-Quartz Monzonite Suite** was probably largely intermediate composition, granulitic lower crust.

(c) The source for the **Oligocene-Miocene Granite Suite** was probably moderately felsic, granulitic lower crust that may have undergone episode(s) of melt-absent, dehydration-dominated metamorphism.

4. Upper crustal processes have modified COMB granitoid REE patterns, particularly where F- and CO_2-rich vapor phases were present during crystallization. Oligocene-Miocene granites have REE patterns that may have been almost exclusively shaped during melt-mineral and mineral-vapor fractionation.

ACKNOWLEDGMENTS

We thank the following mining companies for allowing us to sample drill cores and/or collect samples underground: Climax Molybdenum Company (Henderson, Climax, Mount Emmons, Treasure Mountain, Winfield–Middle Mountain, Ruby Peak–Ruby Irwin, Mount Axtell), Noranda Exploration, Inc. (Jamestown, Mount Bellview), Duvall Corporation (Paradise Pass), and Bear Creek Mining Company (Turquoise Lake). The many company geologists who helped with sample collection, provided field trips, and supplied much stimulating discussion during this project are also thanked for their interest and encouragement. We especially acknowledge Will White, Reese Ganster, Art Bookstrom, Arne Ward, Jim Shannon, Sandy Gunow, Rick Carten, Bruce Walker, Don Ranta, Willy Lynch, Bill Threlkeld, Steve Craig, and Fred Reisback. Thanks also to the U.S. Geological Survey, Branch of Isotope Geology, Denver, especially M. Tatsumoto and K. Ludwig for providing lab space and mass spectrometer time. The manuscript benefitted from insightful reviews by Judy Hannah, Eric Christiansen, Jon Patchett, Ken Ludwig, Ted Armbrustmacher, Paul Sims, David Lindsey, and David Kelley. A special thanks to Steve Kish for the use of his computer program for corrected ratio, epsilon, and model age calculations. Work was supported in part by National Science Foundation Grant EAR 81-20925 to Paul Fullagar and Holly Stein.

TABLE 1. LOCATION AND ABBREVIATED PETROGRAPHIC AND GEOCHEMICAL CLASSIFICATION FOR THE 40 COLORADO MINERAL BELT SAMPLES USED IN REE AND Sm-Nd STUDIES

Sample Number*		Sample Site	Rock Type†	Age§	SiO_2† (wt%)	$Na_2O + K_2O$† (wt%)	Latitude	Longitude	Comments
Northern COMB (9 samples)									
HS-82-10	JP	Jamestown	Syenite	45	65.3	10.7	40°07'11"	105°23'08"	core, JT-3, 3123', Tt l
HS-82-41	JG	Jamestown	Granodiorite	72	61.1	8.5	40°07'03"	105°23'28"	surface sample
HS-82-19	EP	Empire	Hbl-Pyx Monzonite	68	52.0	7.4	39°45'48"	105°43'14"	surface sample
HS-82-38	AP	Apex	Hbl Alkali Syenite	60	62.0	10.5	39°51'54"	105°33'19"	surface sample, Dakota Hill Porphyry
HS-82-39	CA	Caribou	Hbl Monzonite	60	56.1	8.2	39°58'37"	105°34'28"	surface sample
HS-82-40	EL	Eldora	Quartz Monzonite	62	66.9	8.5	39°57'07"	105°35'11"	surface sample
HS-82-08	MO	Montezuma	Quartz Monzonite	39	68.1	7.1	39°36'20"	105°54'55"	surface sample
HS-82-45	FR	Fraser	Rhyolite Tuff	29	82.7	5.6	39°54'10"	105°45'49"	surface sample
HS-82-61	HS	Henderson	Granite	26	75.4	8.5	39°45'37"	105°50'32"	core, H-480, 1062'; Seriate Stock
Central COMB (15 samples)									
HS-82-35	AN	Mount Antero	Granite	29	75.2	8.6	38°39'06"	106°14'59"	surface sample, California Stock
HS-82-24	BC	Browns Creek	Rhyolite	29	75.5	10.5	38°38'27"	106°16'27"	surface sample
HS-82-31	CL	Climax	Granite	29	76.3	8.2	39°22'15"	106°09'54"	core, DDH-1300, 665'; Bartlett Stock
HS-82-47	CM	Chalk Mountain	Topaz Rhyolite	27	71.6	7.9	39°21'52"	106°12'45"	surface sample
HS-82-34	NA	Nathrop	Topaz Rhyolite	29	73.8	8.5	38°45'40"	106°04'30"	surface sample
HS-82-26	MM	Middle Mountain	Rhyolite	38	74.3	8.5	38°58'43"	106°25'55"	core, MM-1, 970', Trp
HS-82-27	MM	Middle Mountain	Granite	37	73.8	7.6	38°58'43"	106°25'55"	core, MM-1, 2160', Tg
HS-82-50	WN	Winfield Peak	Granite	34+	69.9	8.0	38°58'35"	106°27'33"	core, WIN-8, 1565', Tgp
HS-82-07	TW	Twin Lakes	Quartz Monzonite	64	70.0	7.6	38°59'24"	106°25'23"	surface sample
HS-82-36	MP	Mount Princeton	Granodiorite	40	68.9	7.8	38°42'54"	106°15'27"	surface sample
HS-82-46	EM	Elk Mountain	Quartz Monzonite	67	64.4	6.9	39°25'27"	106°11'02"	surface sample
HS-82-55	TL	Turquoise Lake	Granodiorite	36	65.2	7.6	39°16'38"	106°24'21"	core, DDH-BL-2A, 2447'
HS-82-21	IM	Italian Mountain	Quartz Diorite	33++	61.8	6.6	38°56'54"	106°45'43"	surface sample, oldest unit, Tqd
HS-82-22	IM	Italian Mountain	Granodiorite	33+	64.5	7.3	38°55'12"	106°44'17"	surface sample, intermediate unit, Tgc
HS-82-23	IM	Italian Mountain	Quartz Monzonite	33	70.9	7.5	38°56'59"	106°45'45"	surface sample, youngest unit, Tpqm
Southern COMB (16 samples)									
HS-82-01	ME	Mount Emmons	Granite	17	75.7	7.3	38°52'56"	107°03'05"	underground, 2000 level, Keystone Stock
HS-82-29	ME	Mount Emmons	Granite	16	76.0	8.5	38°53'14"	107°03'23"	core, RW-13, 5100'; Redwell Stock
HS-82-04	TM	Treasure Mountain	Granite	12	73.6	8.2	39°01'56"	107°04'53"	core, CP-1, 2018'; Crystal Peak
HS-82-17	RM	Round Mountain	Rhyolite	12	71.1	8.4	38°46'40"	106°52'00"	surface sample
HS-82-37	BP	Boston Peak	Topaz Rhyolite	10	78.0	8.0	38°50'34"	106°43'00"	surface sample
HS-82-05	RP	Ruby Peak	Quartz Monzonite	31	64.2	7.0	38°54'02"	107°07'25"	core, RP-2, 778'
HS-82-11	RI	Ruby-Irwin	Quartz Monzonite	30	61.3	7.5	38°53'18"	107°06'38"	core, RI-5, 1676'
HS-82-12	PP	Paradise Pass	Quartz Monzonite	29	67.2	8.0	38°59'26"	107°03'54"	surface sample, west side
HS-82-44	PP	Paradise Pass	Quartz Monzonite	29	66.1	7.9	38°59'24"	107°03'56"	core, LL-1, 1620'
HS-82-13	AX	Mount Axtell	Quartz Monzonite	29	64.4	7.6	38°50'14"	107°01'39"	core, MAC-2, 1890'

TABLE 1. LOCATION AND ABBREVIATED PETROGRAPHIC AND GEOCHEMICAL CLASSIFICATION FOR THE 40 COLORADO MINERAL BELT SAMPLES USED IN REE AND Sm-Nd STUDIES (continued)

Sample Number*		Samples Site	Rock Type[†]	Age[§]	SiO$_2$[†] (wt%)	Na$_2$O + K$_2$O[†] (wt%)	Latitude	Longitude	Comments
Southern COMB (16 samples)(continued)									
HS-82-16	GO	Gothic	Quartz Monzonite	29	66.0	7.9	39°57'13"	106°59'40"	surface sample
HS-82-20	ES	Elkton Sill	Quartz Monzonite	29	62.1	6.7	38°58'20"	107°02'47"	surface sample, Tqmp
HS-82-30	BE	Mount Bellview	Quartz Monzonite	24+	66.6	8.7	39°00'59"	107°01'07"	core, MB-4, 2902'
HS-82-18	AU	Augusta	Quartz Monzonite	29	65.6	7.2	38°57'36"	107°06'05"	surface sample, youngest unit, Tqm
HS-82-52	AU	Augusta	Granodiorite	29+	67.3	7.3	38°57'34"	107°06'03"	surface sample, older unit, Tg
HS-82-63	AU	Augusta	Quartz Monzodiorite	29++	61.9	6.6	38°57'33"	107°05'53"	surface sample, older unit, Tgp
Precambrian Samples (6 samples)									
HS-82-53	SPG	Silver Plume	Granite	1430	66.1	8.4	39°41'49"	105°44'28"	surface sample, quarry
HS-82-69	SPG	Silver Plume	Granite	1430	66.1	8.2	39°41'49"	105°44'28"	surface sample, quarry
HS-82-70	ISF	Idaho Springs	Felsic Gneiss	1800	65.4	5.0	39°34'14"	106°07'02"	surface sample, Xf unit
HS-82-71	ISF	Idaho Springs	Amphibolite	1800	47.4	4.7	39°34'08"	106°07'13"	surface sample, Xh unit
HS-82-72	ISF	Idaho Springs	Hbl-Bio Gneiss	1800	54.5	5.0	39°33'17"	106°07'58"	surface sample, Xb unit
HS-82-73	ISF	Idaho Springs	Pegmatite	1800	72.0	6.2	39°33'22"	106°07'53"	surface sample, Xb unit pegmatites

*Two letter sample abbreviations correspond to those in Figure 1.

[†]Detailed petrographic descriptions, leading to rock type, and geochemical data for the HS-82 samples are in Stein (1985, Appendixes A and B).

[§]References for ages are in Stein (1985, Appendix A).

TABLE 2. REE CONCENTRATION DATA (PPM) AND SELECTED CHONDRITE NORMALIZED DATA FOR 40 COLORADO MINERAL BELT GRANITOID AND PRECAMBRIAN ROCK SAMPLES BY AGE

Sample Name*	COMB Location	La	Ce	Pr	Nd	Nd†	Sm	Sm†	Eu	Gd	Dy	Ho	Er	Tm	Yb	Lu	(La)N	(Yb)N	(La/Yb)N	(Eu/Eu*)N
Late Cretaceous–Early Tertiary (Laramide) 45 to 75 Ma (8 samples)																				
JP Jamestown Syenite	Northern	38.5	62.7	6.7	24.3	24.08	4.7	4.369	1.21	3.9	2.7	0.53	1.5	0.25	1.82	0.26	116	9.1	12.8	0.87
JG Jamestown Granodiorite	Northern	47.4	86.9	10.6	38.9	39.42	7.4	7.272	1.95	5.8	3.7	0.72	1.7	0.30	1.93	0.28	143	9.7	14.8	0.92
EP Empire	Northern	126	221	25.8	93.5	93.90	15.5	15.03	3.91	10.4	5.9	1.00	2.0	0.37	2.43	0.35	381	12.2	31.3	0.95
AP Apex	Northern	86.2	187	22.4	79.1	82.62	12.9	13.03	3.15	8.7	5.3	0.97	2.2	0.39	2.82	0.41	261	14.1	18.5	0.92
CA Caribou	Northern	49.8	95.5	11.7	43.2	43.19	8.1	7.843	1.94	6.8	5.1	1.04	2.6	0.38	2.93	0.43	150	14.7	10.3	0.80
EL Eldora	Northern	59.0	106	11.9	40.4	39.44	7.3	6.768	1.37	5.7	4.6	0.88	2.4	0.40	2.85	0.40	178	14.3	12.5	0.65
TW Twin Lakes	Central	42.3	77.2	8.8	32.6	31.15	5.5	4.930	1.38	3.7	1.4	0.24	0.4	0.08	0.47	0.07	128	2.4	53.4	0.94
EM Elk Moutain	Central	67.7	113	12.4	41.7	41.77	6.6	6.245	1.60	4.7	2.8	0.49	1.0	0.19	1.15	0.16	205	5.8	35.4	0.88
Middle Tertiary 29 to 45 Ma (20 samples)																				
MM Middle Mountain Trp	Central	23.4	44.4	5.3	18.9	n.d.	4.1	n.d.	0.69	3.8	2.5	0.45	1.2	0.19	1.39	0.19	70.9	7.0	10.1	0.54
MM Middle Mountain Tg	Central	39.5	74.2	8.2	30.0	30.21	6.2	5.955	0.71	5.2	3.2	0.51	1.3	0.20	1.66	0.26	119	8.3	14.4	0.38
WN Winfield	Central	25.6	47.7	5.4	20.8	n.d.	4.2	n.d.	0.86	3.9	2.6	0.50	1.3	0.24	1.60	0.25	77.6	8.0	9.7	0.65
MO Montezuma	Central	70.9	123	13.6	46.6	44.16	8.0	7.317	1.78	6.0	4.4	0.87	2.1	0.33	2.42	0.34	214	12.1	17.8	0.79
MP Mount Princeton	Central	51.7	88.1	9.5	33.5	33.79	6.0	5.718	1.26	4.7	3.6	0.65	1.6	0.27	1.93	0.27	156	9.7	16.2	0.73
TL Turquoise Lake	Central	45.1	83.2	9.8	35.8	35.72	6.6	6.409	1.36	5.0	2.9	0.51	1.0	0.15	1.18	0.17	136	59	23.2	0.73
IM Italian Mountain Tqd	Central	50.0	92.4	11.2	42.4	43.55	8.0	7.946	1.96	6.5	5.1	0.95	2.4	0.38	2.59	0.35	151	13.0	11.7	0.84
IM Italian Mountain Tgc	Central	35.4	89.0	12.2	46.8	47.76	8.2	8.115	2.04	6.4	4.0	0.69	1.6	0.28	1.73	0.23	107	8.7	12.3	0.87
IM Italian Mountain Tpqm	Central	34.0	63.4	7.4	26.9	26.75	4.9	4.749	1.05	4.0	2.5	0.48	1.2	0.22	1.59	0.26	103	8.0	12.9	0.73
RP Ruby Peak	Southern	44.9	89.4	10.9	42.8	42.43	8.0	7.473	2.07	6.0	4.3	0.79	1.9	0.32	2.01	0.25	136	10.1	13.5	0.92
RI Ruby-Irwin	Southern	51.0	96.6	11.8	43.9	n.d.	7.6	n.d.	2.03	5.7	3.8	0.63	1.4	0.25	1.48	0.19	154	7.4	20.9	0.95
PP Paradise Pass West	Southern	47.0	89.5	10.6	39.8	38.21	7.0	6.601	1.83	5.3	3.2	0.53	1.2	0.20	1.28	0.18	142	6.4	22.3	0.92
PP Paradise Pass LL-1	Southern	45.1	86.8	10.4	38.9	n.d.	6.9	n.d.	1.78	5.1	3.5	0.60	1.4	0.25	1.60	0.21	136	8.0	17.1	0.92
AX Mount Axtell	Southern	40.2	77.6	9.1	35.5	35.33	6.6	6.244	1.75	5.3	3.9	0.71	1.8	0.31	1.96	0.28	121	9.8	12.4	0.91
GO Gothic	Southern	50.4	94.5	11.3	41.8	42.12	7.4	7.065	1.87	5.6	3.7	0.66	1.6	0.26	1.73	0.24	152	8.7	17.6	0.89
ES Elkton Sill	Southern	46.1	89.0	10.7	41.4	n.d.	7.5	n.d.	1.93	5.8	3.9	0.71	1.7	0.29	1.98	0.27	139	9.9	14.1	0.90
BE Mount Bellview	Southern	42.2	78.5	9.4	33.9	34.31	6.1	5.820	1.54	4.7	2.9	0.54	1.3	0.20	1.40	0.19	127	7.0	18.3	0.88

TABLE 2. REE CONCENTRATION DATA (PPM) AND SELECTED CHONDRITE NORMALIZED DATA FOR 40 COLORADO MINERAL BELT GRANITOID AND PRECAMBRIAN ROCK SAMPLES BY AGE (continued)

Sample Name*	COMB Location	La	Ce	Pr	Nd	Nd†	Sm	Sm†	Eu	Gd	Dy	Ho	Er	Tm	Yb	Lu	(La)$_N$	(Yb)$_N$	(La/Yb)$_N$	(Eu/Eu*)$_N$
Middle Tertiary 29 to 45 Ma (20 samples) (continued)																				
AU Augusta Tqm	Southern	39.8	75.8	8.7	33.8	n.d.	6.5	n.d.	1.65	5.4	4.1	0.68	1.9	0.33	1.92	0.31	120	9.6	12.6	0.86
AU Augusta Tg	Southern	39.2	76.3	9.5	36.4	n.d.	7.0	n.d.	1.87	6.0	4.3	0.83	2.1	0.29	2.16	0.30	118	10.8	11.0	0.89
AU Augusta Tgp	Southern	63.6	122	14.5	53.7	n.d.	9.6	n.d.	2.26	7.4	4.6	0.83	1.7	0.24	1.60	0.20	192	8.0	24.1	0.83
Oligocene-Miocene 10 to 29 Ma (12 samples)																				
FR Fraser	Northern	48.0	70.2	8.1	23.5	n.d.	4.2	n.d.	0.25	3.8	3.7	0.84	2.8	0.51	4.34	0.68	145	21.7	6.7	0.19
HS Henderson Seriate	Northern	37.3	60.1	5.2	12.4	12.90	1.8	1.791	0.08	1.9	1.8	0.48	1.9	0.43	3.71	0.64	113	18.6	6.1	0.14
CL Climax Bartlett	Central	28.3	55.0	6.3	19.1	20.81	4.0	4.036	0.25	3.5	3.6	0.76	2.6	0.50	4.43	0.66	85.8	22.2	3.9	0.20
CM Chalk Mountain	Central	44.8	84.5	9.4	31.2	33.33	5.7	5.931	0.66	4.4	3.6	0.71	2.1	0.36	3.04	0.43	135	15.2	8.9	0.41
AN Mount Antero California	Central	18.6	42.6	4.9	14.5	14.55	3.1	2.883	0.11	2.8	2.2	0.46	1.6	0.36	3.17	0.52	56.4	15.9	3.5	0.12
BC Browns Creek	Central	27.1	52.5	5.7	20.0	19.89	4.0	3.822	0.54	3.1	2.2	0.41	1.1	0.22	1.60	0.23	82.1	8.0	10.3	0.47
NA Nathrop	Central	15.2	37.4	4.1	17.1	n.d.	5.0	n.d.	0.11	5.4	5.3	1.03	3.2	0.47	3.75	0.55	46.1	18.8	2.5	0.07
ME Mount Emmons Keystone	Southern	55.6	78.1	6.7	20.1	19.42	3.2	3.006	0.40	3.2	2.7	0.60	2.0	0.36	2.85	0.48	168	14.3	11.8	0.38
ME Mount Emmons Redwell	Southern	56.7	83.1	6.5	21.6	20.65	3.3	3.034	0.39	3.0	2.2	0.35	1.1	0.26	1.67	0.26	171	8.4	20.5	0.39
TM Treasure Mountain	Southern	47.7	78.8	7.5	21.9	21.60	3.5	3.298	0.46	2.9	2.2	0.41	1.4	0.31	2.01	0.32	144	10.1	14.3	0.45
RM Round Mountain	Southern	68.3	129	14.3	49.0	49.53	7.9	7.528	1.20	5.0	2.6	0.37	0.5	0.11	0.64	0.07	207	3.2	64.7	0.59
BP Boston Peak	Southern	35.5	56.7	5.2	14.2	14.51	2.2	2.036	0.20	2.0	1.7	0.40	1.4	0.30	2.78	0.50	107	13.9	7.7	0.29
Precambrian (6 samples)																				
SPG Silver Plume	Northern	197	453	59.3	218	192	28.8	24.39	2.50	13.6	6.1	0.96	0.6	0.21	1.41	0.16	597	7.1	84.1	0.39
SPG Silver Plume	Northern	187	429	56.4	207	n.d.	27.2	n.d.	2.40	13.3	5.6	0.90	0.6	0.21	1.33	0.15	566	6.7	84.6	0.39
ISF Idaho Springs Xf	Central	37.8	83.4	11.5	47.0	n.d.	12.6	n.d.	1.52	14.2	15.6	3.27	9.4	1.38	9.57	1.30	114	47.9	2.4	0.35
ISF Idaho Springs Xh	Central	4.4	10.7	1.6	8.0	n.d.	2.4	n.d.	0.79	3.8	4.6	1.01	3.1	0.44	3.35	0.51	13.3	16.8	0.79	0.80
ISF Idaho Springs Xb	Central	9.5	22.2	2.7	13.4	n.d.	3.6	n.d.	1.31	4.6	4.6	1.00	2.9	0.40	3.12	0.47	28.8	15.6	1.8	0.99
ISF Idaho Springs Xb pegs	Central	12.3	20.4	2.0	8.5	n.d.	1.9	n.d.	1.75	2.5	1.5	0.28	0.7	0.07	0.47	0.11	37.3	2.4	15.5	2.49

TABLE 2. REE CONCENTRATION DATA (PPM) AND SELECTED CHONDRITE NORMALIZED DATA FOR 40 COLORADO MINERAL BELT GRANITOID AND PRECAMBRIAN ROCK SAMPLES BY AGE (continued)

Sample Name*	COMB Location	La	Ce	Pr	Nd	Nd†	Sm	Sm†	Eu	Gd	Dy	Ho	Er	Tm	Yb	Lu	$(La)_N$	$(Yb)_N$	$(La/Yb)_N$	$(Eu/Eu^*)_N$
Normalization Values (Hanson, 1980)																				
Composite of 9 chondrites		0.330	0.88	0.112	0.60		0.181		0.069	0.249	0.325	0.070	0.200	0.030	0.200	0.034				

*Two letter sample abbreviations correspond to those in Figure 1.

†Analyses by isotope dilution for comparison; all others are by ICAP-AES method.

N = Chondrite normalized value of ratio.

$Eu^* = [log (Sm)_N + log (Gd)_N]/2$

$(La)_N$, $(Yb)_N$, $(La/Yb)_N$, $(Eu/Eu^*)_N$ for the three MM and WN granite samples are included with the Oligocene–Miocene granite suite in abstract summary.

Analytical errors discussed in text.

n.d. = no data

TABLE 3. SAMARIUM–NEODYMIUM AND STRONTIUM ISOTOPIC DATA FOR 30 SELECTED COLORADO MINERAL BELT GRANITOID SAMPLES ARRANGED BY AGE AND COMPOSITIONAL SUITE

Sample Name*		COMB Location	Age (Ma)	(^{143}Nd/^{144}Nd) measured	(^{143}Nd/^{144}Nd) initial	(^{147}Sm/^{144}Nd) measured	(Sm/Nd)†	(^{87}Sr/^{86}Sr) initial	Epsilon Nd	Epsilon Sr	Model Age (CHUR)	Model Age (DM)
Laramide Monzonites (8 samples)												
JP	Jamestown Syenite	Northern	45	0.512138	0.512106	0.10953	0.1814	0.70688	-9.25	34.51	875	1318
JG	Jamestown Granodiorite	Northern	72	0.512290	0.512238	0.11137	0.1845	0.70697	-6.01	36.22	622	1119
EP	Empire	Northern	68	0.512543	0.512500	0.09665	0.1601	0.70490	-0.98	6.80	145	662
AP	Apex	Northern	60	0.512373	0.512336	0.09523	0.1577	0.70546	-4.39	14.62	399	866
CA	Caribou	Northern	60	0.512226	0.512183	0.10964	0.1816	0.70510	-7.37	9.51	722	1193
EL	Eldora	Northern	62	0.512140	0.512098	0.10361	0.1716	0.70711	-8.98	38.08	816	1245
EM	Elk Mountain	Central	67	0.512190	0.512150	0.09027	0.1495	0.70766	-7.83	45.91	642	1053
IM	Italian Mountain Tqd	Central	33++(36)	0.512301	0.512275	0.11017	0.1825	0.70747	-6.18	42.76	594	1090
				Avg =0.512236		Avg=0.10331	Avg=0.1711					
Middle-Tertiary Granodiorites and Quartz Monzonites (11 samples)												
TW	Twin Lakes	Central	64(45)	0.512092	0.512064	0.09555	0.1583	0.70718	-10.07	38.85	823	1223
MO	Montezuma	Central	39	0.512175	0.512149	0.10005	0.1657	0.70830	-8.55	54.59	731	1161
MP	Mount Princeton	Central	40(36)	0.512092	0.512068	0.10217	0.1692	0.70767	-10.22	45.60	881	1294
TL	Turquoise Lake	Central	36	0.512100	0.512074	0.10833	0.1794	0.71033	-10.09	83.40	928	1357
IM	Italian Mountain Tgc	Central	33+	0.512191	0.512168	0.10258	0.1699	0.70671	-8.32	31.93	725	1166
IM	Italian Mountain Tpqm	Central	33	0.512076	0.512053	0.10721	0.1775	0.70971	-10.59	74.50	957	1377
RP	Ruby Peak	Southern	31	0.512154	0.512133	0.10634	0.1761	0.70700	-9.08	36.02	816	1257
PP	Paradise Pass West	Southern	29	0.512144	0.512124	0.10430	0.1728	0.70724	-9.30	39.42	816	1248
AX	Mount Axtell	Southern	29	0.512220	0.512200	0.10671	0.1767	0.70735	-7.82	40.89	709	1169
GO	Gothic	Southern	29	0.512275	0.512255	0.10128	0.1677	0.70744	-6.74	42.28	581	1042
BE	Mount Bellview	Southern	24+	0.512217	0.512201	0.10242	0.1696	0.70730	-7.92	40.13	681	1129
				Avg=0.512135		Avg=0.10336	Avg=0.1711					

H. J. Stein and J. G. Crock

TABLE 3. SAMARIUM–NEODYMIUM AND STRONTIUM ISOTOPIC DATA FOR 30 SELECTED COLORADO MINERAL BELT GRANITOID SAMPLES ARRANGED BY AGE AND COMPOSITIONAL SUITE (continued)

Sample Name*		COMB Location	Age (Ma)	($^{143}Nd/^{144}Nd$) measured	($^{143}Nd/^{144}Nd$) initial	($^{147}Sm/^{144}Nd$) measured	(Sm/Nd)†	($^{87}Sr/^{86}Sr$) initial	Epsilon Nd	Epsilon Sr	Model Age (CHUR)	Model Age (DM)
Oligocene–Miocene Granites (11 samples)												
HS	Henderson Seriate	Northern	26(27)	0.512105	0.512090	0.08379	0.1388	0.73488	-10.00	431.68	720	1099
AN	Mount Antero California	Central	29(26)	0.512085	0.512065	0.11961	0.1981	n.d.	-10.53	n.d.	1093	1542
BC	Browns Creek	Central	29(30)	0.512068	0.512045	0.11601	0.1922	0.71018	-10.81	81.06	1076	1512
CL	Climax Bartlett	Central	29	0.512113	0.512091	0.11708	0.1939	0.70984	-9.95	76.34	1005	1458
CM	Chalk Mountain	Central	27	0.512067	0.512048	0.10743	0.1779	0.70851	-10.83	57.43	975	1392
MM	Middle Mountain Tg	Central	37	0.512208	0.512179	0.11902	0.1971	0.70731	-8.02	40.55	844	1337
ME	Mount Emmons Keystone	Southern	17	0.512112	0.512101	0.09347	0.1548	0.70984	-10.04	76.15	778	1177
ME	Mount Emmons Redwell	Southern	16(16.4)	0.512132	0.512122	0.08872	0.1469	0.71151	-9.64	99.77	715	1109
TM	Treasure Mountain	Southern	12(12.4)	0.512138	0.512131	0.09218	0.1527	0.70931	-9.59	68.46	729	1132
RM	Round Mountain	Southern	12	0.511913	0.511906	0.09175	0.1520	0.70892	-13.98	62.94	1053	1405
BP	Boston Peak	Southern	10(9.8)	0.512030	0.512025	0.08470	0.1403	0.70852	-11.72	57.24	828	1194
					Avg=0.512073	Avg=0.10125	Avg=0.1677					

*Two letter sample abbreviations correspond to those in Figure 1.

†Calculated from Sm and Nd concentration data by isotope dilution (Table 2).

Age shown is that used to calculate initial ($^{143}Nd/^{144}Nd$) and initial ($^{87}Sr/^{86}Sr$); parentheses give alternative pluton ages.

Epsilon values calculated relative to CHUR at time of pluton formation.

Model age calculations relative to CHUR and DM after DePaolo and Wasserburg (1976) and DePaolo (1981a, 1981b); model ages are in Ma.

Strontium isotopic data from Stein and Fullagar (1985; in preparation) and Stein (1985) except MO, EP, IM, MP, AP, CA, and EL which are from Simmons and Hedge (1978).

Analytical methods and errors discussed in text.

n.d. = no data

APPENDIX I: SAMPLE SELECTION

A total of 52 Late Cretaceous–Tertiary granitoid samples from within the COMB, as defined in Figure 1, were collected for analytical work. Six reconnaissance samples of Proterozoic basement, including four units in the Idaho Springs Formation near Frisco, Colorado, and two samples of the Silver Plume Granite from a quarry near Silver Plume, Colorado, were also collected. Although the summary table in the abstract includes the results and ranges for all 52 granitoid samples, only 40 of these samples are actually discussed in this paper. These 40 samples include all 30 samples for which Sm-Nd isotopic data were obtained. The 12 samples whose REE characteristics are not discussed in this paper are either (1) part of a sample suite collected for a more detailed study of REE variations within composite Climax-type granites and their interaction with host rocks, or (2) part of a more detailed study of igneous rocks in the Mount Antero area (Shannon and others, 1987b). Only one or two representative patterns from stocks containing each Climax-type granite are included in this paper. The 40 granitoid samples and the 6 Proterozoic basement samples whose REE patterns are discussed in this paper are listed in Table 1. The 30 granitoid samples for which Sm-Nd isotopic data were obtained are listed in Table 3. Samples used in this study are the same as those used in previous Pb and Sr isotopic studies (Stein, 1985; Stein and Fullagar, 1985).

The freshest samples of selected granitoids were collected for chemical and isotopic analyses. Though some plutons are characteristically altered, previous isotopic studies have shown that, in general, isotopic disturbances in selected mineral phases from visibly altered stocks are no greater than minor isotopic deviations seen in fresh-looking intrusive rocks (Hannah and Stein, 1986; Stein and Hannah, 1985). Alteration is variable, depending on intrusion composition and hydrothermal history, but typically ranges from chloritization of mafic minerals in intermediate-composition rocks to sericitization of feldspars and quartz ± potassic flooding in evolved granites. Samples with obvious veining of any kind were avoided. Complete hand specimen and thin section descriptions, and detailed information on sample location and major- and trace-element geochemistry, are given in Stein (1985, Appendix A).

APPENDIX II: ANALYTICAL METHODS

Routine clean lab procedures were used during sample preparation and dissolution. A multi-acid medium of concentrated HF, HNO_3, and $HClO_4$ was used to digest 1.000 g samples of –200 mesh whole-rock powder in open Teflon beakers for determination of REE concentrations. For Sm-Nd isotopic studies, PFE Savillex vessels were used in a 6-day $HF-HNO_3$ sample digestion at 150 °C. Depending on Sm-Nd concentrations, known from earlier REE concentration work by ICAP-AES (Inductively Coupled Argon Plasma-Atomic Emission Spectrometry), between 10 and 130 mg of whole-rock powder was dissolved for isotopic determinations. Sample dissolution was carefully monitored.

The REE concentrations were determined at the U.S. Geological Survey, Branch of Geochemistry, Denver, using the ICAP-AES method (Crock, 1981; Crock and Lichte, 1982). Analytical uncertainties in measured REE concentrations range from 1 to 4 percent at the 95 percent confidence level (Crock and Lichte, 1982), and duplicate determinations on samples and standards yielded excellent results. The negative Er spike in REE patterns is the result of electronic problems in the Er channel. Because the Er spike is especially pronounced in samples with low HREE abundances, Er was not plotted in the REE patterns for two units. The Sm and Nd concentrations determined by the ICAP-AES method are in good agreement with Sm and Nd determined by isotope dilution (Table 2).

Samarium-neodymium isotopic analyses were performed at the U.S. Geological Survey, Branch of Isotope Geology, Denver, using a VG Micromass 54E thermal-ionization, single-collector mass spectrometer controlled by software written by Ludwig (1986). Samples were spiked before acid digestion with a single solution containing a ^{149}Sm-^{150}Nd mixed spike. Spike volume was calculated for each sample so that all runs had $^{144}Nd_{SAMPLE}/^{150}Nd_{SPIKE}$ and $^{147}Sm_{SAMPLE}/^{149}Sm_{SPIKE}$ of approximately 10 and 1.5, respectively. Routine clean-column chemistry was used for initial concentration of REE, and Sm and Nd were separated subsequently using calibrated and cleaned high-pressure columns equilibrated in alpha-hydroxyisobutryic acid of known pH. After evaporation of Sm- and Nd-bearing solutions, a second clean-up column was used to eliminate any organic compounds remaining from the alpha-hydroxyisobutryic acid. Sample loads, in a 2 percent H_3PO_4 medium, ranged from 200 to 800 ng for Sm and 500 to 1000 ng for Nd, and were placed on the side filaments of a Re triple filament configuration. The Nd runs were virtually free of any interfering masses of Sm and similarly, Sm runs were free of potentially interfering masses of Nd. Blank levels, less than 0.2 ng for Nd and 0.01 ng for Sm, were negligible.

All analytical errors reported in this paper are at the 95 percent confidence level. Errors in determining Sm and Nd concentrations by isotope dilution range from 0.01 to 0.05 percent. Within-run uncertainties in $^{143}Nd/^{144}Nd$ are less than ±1.8E-5 (0.0035 percent) or ±0.35 epsilon units. Between-run agreement on eight duplicate sample analyses is within ±0.5 epsilon units; some duplicate sample analyses were made using two different VG Micromass 54E mass spectrometers. Measured Sm and Nd ratios were fractionation corrected during the run using $^{147}Sm/^{149}Sm = 1.08507$ and $^{144}Nd/^{146}Nd = 1.3852$ ($^{146}Nd/^{144}Nd = 0.7219$).

Six runs of the Cal Tech Nd Standard (CIT) were made during this study. Sample loads of the CIT standard varied from 300 to 1000 ng. The weighted average for the CIT $^{143}Nd/^{144}Nd$ is 0.5119010 ±6.8E-6 (0.0013 percent). One run of USGS rock standard BCR-1 yielded a $^{143}Nd/^{144}Nd$ of 0.512651 ±1.2E-5 (0.0023 percent). Comparative $^{143}Nd/^{144}Nd$ ratios for the CIT and the BCR-1 standards are found in Wasserburg and others (1981) and O'Nions and others (1977).

APPENDIX III: DATA REPRESENTATION

Isotopic data for Nd (this paper) and Sr (unpublished data, Stein and Fullagar, used in Figures 15 and 16) are presented using the epsilon Nd and epsilon Sr notation as defined by DePaolo and Wasserburg (1976, 1977). Epsilon (ϵ) is a measure of the relative enrichment (positive values) or depletion (negative values) in initial $^{143}Nd/^{144}Nd$ in a sample relative to Chondrite Uniform Reservoir (CHUR) and in initial $^{87}Sr/^{86}Sr$ in a sample relative to Uniform Reservoir (UR). The UR is not a chondritic reservoir, but a model reservoir that represents bulk earth. Epsilon values represent the departure in the initial ratio for a rock sample, in parts per 10^4, from the isotopic ratio for CHUR or UR at the time that rock formed (equations 1 and 2).

By definition:

$$(1) \qquad \epsilon_{Nd_{T_o}} = 10^4 \left[\frac{(^{143}Nd/^{144}Nd_{ROCK})_{T_o}}{(^{143}Nd/^{144}Nd_{CHUR})_{T_o}} - 1 \right],$$

and

$$(2) \qquad \epsilon_{Sr_{T_o}} = 10^4 \left[\frac{(^{87}Sr/^{86}Sr_{ROCK})_{T_o}}{(^{87}Sr/^{86}Sr_{UR})_{T_o}} - 1 \right],$$

where T_o represents some time in the past, for example the age of a particular Late Cretaceous–Tertiary COMB pluton.

The ^{143}Nd/^{144}Nd and ^{87}Sr/^{86}Sr for CHUR and UR at a time in the past (T_o) may be calculated using the Sm-Nd and Rb-Sr age equations (3 and 4), where:

(a) ^{147}Sm/^{144}Nd present-day ratio for CHUR = 0.1966
(b) ^{143}Nd/^{144}Nd present-day ratio for CHUR = 0.512638
(c) decay constant for ^{147}Sm (λ) = 6.54 × 10^{-12}/yr
(d) ^{87}Rb/^{86}Sr present-day ratio for UR = 0.0839
(e) ^{87}Sr/^{86}Sr present-day ratio for UR = 0.7045
(f) decay constant for ^{87}Rb (λ) = 1.42 × 10^{-11}/yr
(g) age of a COMB pluton = T_o in Ma

$$(3) \quad (^{143}\text{Nd}/^{144}\text{Nd}_{\text{CHUR}})_{T_o} = 0.512638 - 0.1966 \, [\text{EXP}(6.54{\cdot}10^{-12}{\cdot}T_o) - 1],$$

and

$$(4) \quad (^{87}\text{Sr}/^{86}\text{Sr}_{\text{UR}})_{T_o} = 0.7045 - 0.0839 \, [\text{EXP}(1.42{\cdot}10^{-11}{\cdot}T_o) - 1].$$

Present-day $(^{147}\text{Sm}/^{144}\text{Nd})_M$, $(^{143}\text{Nd}/^{144}\text{Nd})_M$, $(^{87}\text{Rb}/^{86}\text{Sr})_M$, and $(^{87}\text{Sr}/^{86}\text{Sr})_M$ were directly measured from COMB rock samples. Inserting these measured or known ratios (M) into fundamental age equations (5 and 6), and knowing the value for T_o, $(^{143}\text{Nd}/^{144}\text{Nd}_{\text{ROCK}})_{T_o}$ and $(^{87}\text{Sr}/^{86}\text{Sr}_{\text{ROCK}})_{T_o}$ for a particular time in the past (T_o) are calculated.

$$(5) \quad (^{143}\text{Nd}/^{144}\text{Nd}_{\text{ROCK}})_{T_o} = (^{143}\text{Nd}/^{144}\text{Nd}_{\text{ROCK}})_M - (^{147}\text{Sm}/^{144}\text{Nd}_{\text{ROCK}})_M \, [\text{EXP}(6.54{\cdot}10^{-12}{\cdot}T_o) - 1],$$

and

$$(6) \quad (^{87}\text{Sr}/^{86}\text{Sr}_{\text{ROCK}})_{T_o} = (^{87}\text{Sr}/^{86}\text{Sr}_{\text{ROCK}})_M - (^{87}\text{Rb}/^{86}\text{Sr}_{\text{ROCK}})_M \, [\text{EXP}(1.42{\cdot}10^{-11}{\cdot}T_o) - 1].$$

The calculated ratios from equations 3, 4, 5, and 6 are used in equations 1 and 2 to determine ϵ_{Nd} and ϵ_{Sr}, the enrichment or depletion in the source for each COMB granitoid relative to CHUR and UR, respectively, at time T_o when the granitoid formed. Because all epsilon calculations for Late Cretaceous–Tertiary COMB granitoids yield negative values for ϵ_{Nd} and positive values for ϵ_{Sr} (Table 3), sources for all varieties of COMB plutons may be described as having lower Sm/Nd and higher Rb/Sr than CHUR and UR at time T_o. The ratios for CHUR and UR at the time of formation of each Late Cretaceous–Tertiary COMB granitoid, based on pluton age (T_o), have been calculated. The measured ^{143}Nd/^{144}Nd for each granitoid has been corrected for added radiogenic ^{143}Nd produced by decay of ^{147}Sm from time T_o to present day. Although these corrections are relatively small for young granitoid samples with low Sm/Nd, they were nonetheless made so that ϵ_{Nd} values are as accurate as possible. Corrections for measured ^{87}Sr/^{86}Sr are somewhat larger because some COMB granitoids, for example, young Climax-type granites and topaz rhyolites, have very high Rb/Sr.

Model source ages using both a CHUR and a DM (depleted mantle) source were calculated (Table 3). A CHUR model age represents the time in the past when a rock sample, whose ^{147}Sm/^{144}Nd and ^{143}Nd/^{144}Nd have been determined, would have the same ϵ_{Nd} as chondritic mantle. Similarly, a DM model age represents the time in the past when a rock sample would have the same ϵ_{Nd} as depleted upper mantle. The isotopic character of a DM source is adjusted to account for previous depletion(s) in Nd relative to Sm.

Equations for model age calculations based on DM are discussed in DePaolo (1981a, 1981b). Model age calculations of any type simplistically assume a single-stage origin. Lead and other isotopic data (Stein, 1985) demonstrate that sources for Late Cretaceous–Tertiary COMB intrusions do not have a single-stage history. In other words, Laramide-Tertiary intrusions in the COMB were not derived directly from either CHUR or DM. Although in theory both CHUR and DM are equally inappropriate sources for Late Cretaceous–Tertiary COMB intrusions (Arndt and Goldstein, 1987; Stein, 1988b), calculated DM model ages are more in line with known ages of potential Proterozoic source material in the COMB.

REFERENCES CITED

Arndt, N. T., and Goldstein, S. L., 1987, Use and abuse of crust-formation ages: Geology, v. 15, p. 893–895.

Barker, F., Wones, D. R., Sharp, W. N., and Desborough, G. A., 1975, The Pikes Peak batholith, Colorado Front Range, and a model for the origin of the gabbro-anorthosite-syenite-potassic granite suite: Precambrian Research, v. 2, p. 97–160.

Bennett, V. C., and DePaolo, D. J., 1987, Proterozoic crustal history of the western United States as determined by neodymium isotopic mapping: Geological Society of America Bulletin, v. 99, p. 674–685.

Bergendahl, M. H., 1963, Geology of the northern part of the Tenmile Range, Summit County, Colorado: U.S. Geological Survey Bulletin 1162-D, 19 p.

Bookstrom, A. A., 1981, Tectonic setting and generation of Rocky Mountain porphyry molybdenum deposits, *in* Dickinson, W. R., and Payne, W. D., eds., Relations of tectonics to ore deposits in the southern Cordillera: Arizona Geological Society Digest, v. 14, p. 213–226.

Bradley, S. D., and McCallum, M. E., 1982, Lower crustal xenoliths from Colorado-Wyoming state line kimberlites: Terra Cognita, v. 2, no. 3, p. 236.

Burt, D. M., Sheridan, M. F., Bikun, J. V., and Christiansen, E. H., 1982, Topaz rhyolites; Distribution, origin, and significance for exploration: Economic Geology, v. 77, p. 1818–1836.

Cameron, K. L., and Cameron, M., 1986, Whole-rock/groundmass differentiation trends of rare earth elements in high-silica rhyolites: Geochimica et Cosmochimica Acta, v. 50, p. 759–769.

Candela, P. A., 1987, Theoretical constraints on the chemistry of the magmatic aqueous phase: Geological Society of America Abstracts with Programs, v. 19, p. 610.

Carten, R. C., 1987, Evolution of immiscible Cl- and F-rich liquids from ore magmas, Henderson porphyry molybdenum deposit, Colorado: Geological Society of America Abstracts with Programs, v. 19, p. 613.

Carten, R. C., Geraghty, E. P., Walker, B. M., and Shannon, J. R., 1988, Cyclic development of igneous features and their relationship to high-temperature hydrothermal features in the Henderson porphyry molybdenum deposit, Colorado: Economic Geology, v. 83, p. 266–296.

Christiansen, E. H., Burt, D. M., Sheridan, M. F., and Wilson, R. T., 1983, The petrogenesis of topaz rhyolites from the western United States: Contributions to Mineralogy and Petrology, v. 83, p. 16–30.

Christiansen, E. H., Bikun, J. V., Sheridan, M. F., and Burt, D. M., 1984, Geochemical evolution of topaz rhyolites from the Thomas Range and Spor Mountain, Utah: American Mineralogist, v. 69, p. 223–236.

Christiansen, E. H., Sheridan, M. F., and Burt, D. M., 1986, The geology and geochemistry of Cenozoic topaz rhyolites from the western United States: Geological Society of America Special Paper 205, 82 p.

Clemens, J. D., Holloway, J. R., and White, A.J.R., 1986, Origin of an A-type granite; Experimental constraints: American Mineralogist, v. 71, p. 317–324.

Collerson, K. D., Reid, E., Millar, D., and McCulloch, M. T., 1983, Lithological and Sr-Nd isotopic relationships in the Vestfold Block; Implications for Archean and Proterozoic crustal evolution in the East Antarctic, *in* Oliver, R. J., James, P. R., and Jago, J. B., eds., Antarctic earth science: Cambridge, Cambridge University Press, 697 p.

Collins, W. J., Beams, S. D., White, A.J.R., and Chappell, B. W., 1982, Nature and origin of A-type granites with particular reference to southeastern Australia: Contributions to Mineralogy and Petrology, v. 80, p. 189–200.

Coolbaugh, M., 1985, Geology and economic mineral potential of upper Browns Creek basin, Chaffee County, Colorado [M.S. thesis]: Tucson, University of Arizona, 241 p.

Crock, J. G., 1981, The determination of selected rare earth elements in geological materials by inductively coupled argon plasma-optical emission spectroscopy [Ph.D. thesis]: Golden, Colorado School of Mines, 169 p.

Crock, J. G., and Lichte, F. E., 1982, Determination of rare earth elements in geological materials by inductively coupled argon plasma/atomic emission spectrometry: Analytical Chemistry, v. 54, no. 8, p. 1329–1332.

Cullers, R. L., and Graf, J. L., 1984, Rare earth elements in igneous rocks of the continental crust; Intermediate and silicic rocks–ore petrogenesis, *in* Henderson, P., ed., Rare earth element geochemistry: Amsterdam, Elsevier Science Publishers, p. 275–316.

Cunningham, C. G., Jr., 1976, Petrogenesis and post-magnetic geochemistry of the Italian Mountain intrusive complex, eastern Elk Mountains, Colorado: Geological Society of America Bulletin, v. 87, p. 897–908.

DePaolo, D. J., 1981a, Nd in the Colorado Front Range and crust-mantle evolution in the Proterozoic: Nature, v. 291, p. 193–196.

—— , 1981b, A neodymium and strontium isotopic study of the Mesozoic calc-alkaline granitic batholiths of the Sierra Nevada and Peninsular Ranges, California: Journal of Geophysical Research, v. 86, p. 10470–10488.

DePaolo, D. J., and Wasserburg, G. J., 1976, Nd isotopic variations and petrogenetic models: Geophysical Research Letters, v. 3, p. 249–252.

—— , 1977, The sources of island arcs as indicated by Nd and Sr isotopic studies: Geophysical Research Letters, v. 4, p. 465–468.

Doe, B. R., Steven, T. A., Delevaux, M. H., Stacey, J. S., Lipman, P. W., and Fisher, F. S., 1979, Genesis of ore deposits in the San Juan volcanic field, southwestern Colorado; Lead isotope evidence: Economic Geology, v. 74, p. 1–26.

Dowsett, F. R., Ganster, M. W., Ranta, D. E., Baker, D. J., and Stein, H. J., 1981, Geology of the Mount Emmons molybdenite deposit, Crested Butte, Colorado: New Mexico Geological Society 32nd Field Conference Guidebook, p. 325–331.

Eggler, D. H., McCallum, M. E., and Kirkley, M. B., 1987, Kimberlite-transported nodules from Colorado–Wyoming: A record of enrichment of shallow portions of an infertile lithosphere, *in* Morris, E. M., and Pasteris, J. D., eds., Mantle metasomatism and alkaline magmatism: Geological Society of America Special Paper 215, p. 77–90.

Ernst, D. R., 1980, Petrography and geochemistry of Boston Peak and Tomichi Dome, and relation to other plutons in Gunnison County, Colorado [M.S. thesis]: Cheney, Eastern Washington University, 52 p.

Farmer, G. L., and DePaolo, D. J., 1984, Origin of Mesozoic and Tertiary granite in the western United States and implications for pre-Mesozoic crustal structure; 2, Nd and Sr isotopic studies of unmineralized and Cu- and Mo-mineralized granite in the Precambrian craton: Journal of Geophysical Research, v. 89, p. 10141–10160.

Gaskill, D. L., Godwin, L. H., and Mutschler, F. E., 1967, Geologic map of the Oh-Be-Joyful Quadrangle, Gunnison County, Colorado: U.S. Geological Survey Map GQ-578, scale 1:24,000.

Glassley, W. E., 1983, The role of CO_2 in the chemical modification of deep continental crust: Geochimica et Cosmochimica Acta, v. 47, p. 597–616.

Goddard, E. N., 1954, The influence of Tertiary intrusive structural features on mineral deposits at Jamestown, Colorado: Economic Geology, v. 30, p. 370–386.

Hamilton, P. J., Evenson, N. M., and O'Nions, R. K., 1979, Sm-Nd systematics of Lewisian gneisses; Implications for the origin of granulites: Nature, v. 277, p. 25–28.

Hannah, J. L., and Stein, H. J., 1986, Oxygen isotope compositions of selected Laramide–Tertiary granitoid stocks in the Colorado Mineral Belt and their bearing on the origin of Climax-type granite-molybdenum systems: Contributions to Mineralogy and Petrology, v. 93, p. 347–358.

Hanson, G. N., 1980, Rare earth elements in petrogenetic studies of igneous systems: Annual Review of Earth and Planetary Sciences, v. 8, p. 371–406.

Hedge, C. E., Houston, R. S., Tweto, O. L., Peterman, Z. E., Harrison, J. E., and Reid, R. R., 1986, The Precambrian of the Rocky Mountain region: U.S. Geological Survey Professional Paper 1241-D, 17 p.

Henderson, P., editor, 1984, Rare earth element geochemistry: Amsterdam, Elsevier Science Publishers, 510 p.

Humphris, S. E., 1984, The mobility of the rare earth elements in the crust, *in* Henderson, P., ed., Rare earth element geochemistry: Amsterdam, Elsevier Science Publishers, p. 317–342.

Isaacson, L. B., and Smithson, S. B., 1976, Gravity anomalies and granite emplacement in west-central Colorado: Geological Society of America Bulletin, v. 87, p. 22–28.

Jacobsen, S. B., and Wasserburg, G. J., 1978, Interpretation of Nd, Sr, and Pb isotope data from Archean migmatites in Lofoten–Vesteralen, Norway: Earth and Planetary Science Letters, v. 41, p. 245–253.

Koch, C. F., 1983, Evidence for rare-earth element mobility in two S.E. Arizona porphyry-copper systems: Geological Society of America Abstracts with Programs, v. 15, p. 275.

Larson, E. E., Mutschler, F. E., and Bruce, R. N., 1987, Nagging questions concerning the model of Laramide flat-plate subduction; A need for an alternative model: Geological Society of America Abstracts with Programs, v. 19, p. 740.

Lipman, P. W., Doe, B. R., Hedge, C. E., and Steven, T. A., 1978, Petrologic evolution of the San Juan volcanic field, southwestern Colorado; Pb and Sr isotope evidence: Geological Society of America Bulletin, v. 89, p. 59–82.

London, D., and Hervig, R. L., 1986, Trace element partitioning in the system macusanite-H_2O at 200 MPA (H_2O): EOS (Transactions of the American Geophysical Union), v. 67, no. 44, p. 1258.

London, D., Morgan, G. B., and Hervig, R. L., 1987, Differentiation of peraluminous, volatile-rich granites; An experimental study of Macusani glass: Geological Society of America Abstracts with Programs, v. 19, p. 749.

Ludwig, K. R., 1986, User's manual for *Analyst,* a computer program for control of an isomass 54E thermal-ionization, single-collector mass-spectrometer (Revision D): U.S. Geological Survey Open-File Report 85–141, 95 p.

Marvin, R. F., Young, E. J., Mehnert, H. H., and Naeser, C. W., 1974, Summary of radiometric age determinations on Mesozoic and Cenozoic igneous rocks and uranium and base metal deposits in Colorado: Isochron/West, no. 11, p. 1–41.

McCulloch, M. T., and Black, L. P., 1984, Sm-Nd isotope systematics of Enderby Land granulites and evidence for the redistribution of Sm and Nd during metamorphism: Earth and Planetary Science Letters, v. 71, p. 46–58.

Menzies, M. A., and Wass, S. Y., 1983, CO_2- and LREE-rich mantle below eastern Australia; A REE and isotopic study of alkaline magmas and apatite-rich mantle xenoliths from the Southern Highlands Province, Australia: Earth and Planetary Science Letters, v. 65, p. 287–302.

Michard, A., Beaucaire, C., and Michard, G., 1987, Uranium and rare earth elements in CO_2-rich waters from Vals-les-Bains (France): Geochimica et Cosmochimica Acta, v. 5, p. 901–909.

Miller, C. F., and Middlefehldt, D. W., 1982, Depletion of light rare-earth elements in felsic magmas: Geology, v. 10, p. 129–133.

Morris, E. M., and Pasteris, J. D., editors, 1987, Mantle metasomatism and alkaline magmatism: Geological Society of America Special Paper 215, 383 p.

Musselman, T. E., 1987, A modified crustal source for the Colorado Mineral Belt; Implications for REE buffering in CO_2-rich fluids [M.S. thesis]: Golden, Colorado School of Mines, 127 p.

Musselman, T. E., and Simmons, E. C., 1987, Crustal source for a mafic alkalic suite from the Colorado Mineral Belt, with evidence for regional metamorphism: Geological Society of America Abstracts with Programs, v. 19, p. 783.

Mutschler, F. E., 1976, Crystallization of a soda granite, Treasure Mountain Dome, Colorado, and the genesis of stockwork molybdenite deposits, *in* Northrup, S. A., and Woodward, L. A., eds., Regional tectonics and mineral resources of southwestern North America; A volume honoring V. C. Kelly: New Mexico Geological Society Special Paper 6, p. 199–205.

Mutschler, F. E., Wright, E. G., Ludington, S., and Abbott, J. T., 1981a, Granite molybdenum systems: Economic Geology, v. 76, p. 874–897.

Mutschler, F. E., Ernst, D. R., Gaskill, D. L., and Billings, P., 1981b, Igneous rocks of the Elk Mountains and vicinity, Colorado; Chemistry and related ore deposits, *in* Epis, R. C., and Callender, J. F., eds., Western Slope, Colorado: New Mexico Geological Society 32nd Field Conference Guidebook, p. 317–324.

Nash, T. J., and Cunningham, C. G., 1973, Fluid inclusion studies of the fluorspar

and gold deposits, Jamestown district, Colorado: Economic Geology, v. 68, p. 1247–1262.

Nelson, B. K., and DePaolo, D. J., 1984, 1,700-Myr greenstone volcanic successions in southwestern North America and isotopic evolution of Precambrian mantle: Nature, v. 311, no. 5990, p. 143–146.

Nelson, D. O., Nelson, K. L., Reeves, K. D., and Mattison, G. D., 1987, Geochemistry of Tertiary alkaline rocks of the eastern Trans-Pecos magmatic province, Texas: Contributions to Mineralogy and Petrology, v. 97, p. 72–92.

Newton, R. C., 1986, Late Archean/Early Proterozoic CO_2 streaming through the lower crust and geochemical segration: EOS Transactions of the American Geophysical Union, v. 67, no. 16, p. 387.

Obradovich, J. D., Mutschler, F. E., and Bryant, B., 1969, Potassium-argon ages bearing on the igneous and tectonic history of the Elk Mountains and vicinity, Colorado; A preliminary report: Geological Society of America Bulletin, v. 80, p. 1749–1756.

O'Nions, R. K., Hamilton, P. J., and Evensen, N. M., 1977, Variations in $^{143}Nd/^{144}Nd$ and $^{87}Sr/^{86}Sr$ ratios in oceanic basalts: Earth and Planetary Science Letters, v. 34, p. 13–22.

Patchett, P. J., and Arndt, N. T., 1986, Nd isotopes and tectonics of 1.9–1.7 Ga crustal genesis: Earth and Planetary Science Letters, v. 78, p. 329–338.

Peterman, Z. E., Hedge, C. E., and Braddock, W. A., 1968, Age of Precambrian events in the northeastern Front Range, Colorado: Journal of Geophysical Research, v. 73, no. 6, p. 2277–2296.

Price, J. G., Henry, C. D., and Rubin, J. N., 1987, Peraluminous rhyolites in a continental arc, Trans-Pecos Texas; Chemical modification by vapor-phase crystallization: Geological Society of America Abstracts with Programs, v. 19, p. 810.

Ranta, D. E., 1974, Geology, alteration, and mineralization of the Winfield (La Plata) district, Chaffee County, Colorado [Ph.D. thesis]: Golden, Colorado School of Mines, 261 p.

Reed, J. C., Jr., Bickford, M. E., Premo, W. R., Aleinikoff, J. N., and Pallister, J. S., 1987, Tectonic evolution of the Early Proterozoic Colorado province; Constraints from U-Pb geochronology: Geology, v. 15, p. 861–865.

Rubin, J. N., Price, J. G., Henry, C. D., and Koppenaal, D. W., 1987, Cryolite-bearing and rare metal-enriched rhyolite, Sierra Blanca Peaks, Hudspeth County, Texas: American Mineralogist, v. 72, p. 1122–1130.

Sawka, W. N., Chappell, B. W., and Norrish, K., 1984, Light-rare-earth-element zoning in sphene and allanite during granitoid fractionation: Geology, v. 12, p. 131–134.

Shannon, J. R., Walker, B. M., Carten, R. B., and Geraghty, E. P., 1982, Unidirectional solidification textures and their significance in determining relative ages of intrusions at the Henderson mine, Colorado: Geology, v. 10, p. 293–297.

Shannon, J. R., Naeser, C. W., DeWitt, E. H., and Wallace, A. R., 1987a, Timing of Cenozoic magmatism and tectonism in the Sawatch uplift and northern Rio Grande rift, Colorado: Geological Society of America Abstracts with Programs, v. 19, p. 839.

Shannon, J. R., Stein, H. J., and Smith, R. P., 1987b, Geology and geochemistry of Oligocene topaz rhyolites, northern Rio Grande rift, Colorado: Geological Society of America Abstracts with Programs, v. 19, p. 841.

Sharp, J. E., 1978, A molybdenum mineralized breccia pipe complex, Redwell Basin, Colorado: Economic Geology, v. 73, p. 369–392.

Sharp, W. N., 1976, Geologic map and details of the beryllium and molybdenum occurrences, Mount Antero, Chaffee County, Colorado: U.S. Geological Survey Map MF–810, 2 sheets, scale 1:24,000.

Simmons, E. C., and Hedge, C. E., 1978, Minor-element and Sr-isotope geochemistry of Tertiary stocks, Colorado Mineral Belt: Contributions to Mineralogy and Petrology, v. 67, p. 379–396.

Smith, C. B., McCallum, M. E., and Hedge, C. E., 1982, Rb/Sr isotopic ratios in selected lower crustal-upper mantle nodules from Colorado-Wyoming kimberlites: U.S. Geological Survey Open-File Report 82–178, 21 p.

Stein, H. J., 1982, The timing and tectonic setting of molybdenum mineralization in the southern Rocky Mountains: Geological Society of America Abstracts with Programs, v. 14, p. 236–237.

—— , 1983, A lower crustal origin for molybdenum porphyry systems; Lead isotope evidence from southern Cordilleran deposits: Geological Association of Canada, Mineralogical Association of Canada, and Canadian Geophysical Union Program with Abstracts, v. 8, p. A64.

—— , 1985, A lead, strontium, and sulfur isotope study of Laramide-Tertiary intrusions and mineralization in the Colorado Mineral Belt with emphasis on Climax-type porphyry molybdenum systems plus a summary of other newly acquired isotopic and rare earth element data [Ph.D. thesis]: Chapel Hill, University of North Carolina, 493 p.

—— , 1988a, Genetic traits of Climax-type granites and molybdenum mineralization, Colorado Mineral Belt, *in* Taylor, R. P., and Strong, D. F., eds., Recent advances in the geology of granite-related mineral deposits: Canadian Institute of Mining and Metallurgy Special Volume 39, p. 394–401.

—— , 1988b, Comment *on* "Use and abuse of crust-formation ages": Geology, v. 16, p. 376.

Stein, H. J., and Crock, J. G., 1987, Colorado Mineral Belt Lake Cretaceous–Tertiary magmatism; Neodymium isotopic and rare earth element data: Geological Society of America Abstracts with Programs, v. 19, p. 454.

Stein, H. J., and Fullagar, P. D., 1985, Origin of Colorado Mineral Belt Laramide-Tertiary magmatism; Lead and strontium isotope evidence: Geological Society of America Abstracts with Programs, v. 17, p. 727.

Stein, H. J., and Hannah, J. L., 1982, The Mount Emmons porphyry molybdenum deposit; A lower crustal origin; Lead and oxygen isotope evidence: Geological Society of America Abstracts with Programs, v. 14, p. 625.

—— , 1985, Movement and origin of ore fluids in Climax-type systems: Geology, v. 13, p. 460–474.

—— , 1988, Comment *on* "Molybdenum distribution in Precambrian rocks of the Colorado Mineral Belt": Mineralium Deposita, v. 23, p. 222–226.

Stein, H. J., and Huebner, M., 1984, A heavy isotope enriched sulfur source for Climax-type porphyry molybdenum deposits; Molybdenite compositions: Geological Society of America Abstracts with Programs, v. 16, p. 667.

Stein, H. J., Fullagar, P. D., and Hannah, J. L., 1987, Source of Colorado Mineral Belt Late Cretaceous–Tertiary intrusions; Regional Pb, Sr, and O isotopic studies: Geological Society of American Abstracts with Programs, v. 19, p. 336.

Strong, D. F., Fryer, B. J., and Kerrich, R., 1984, Genesis of the St. Lawrence fluorspar deposits as indicated by fluid inclusion, rare earth element, and isotopic data: Economic Geology, v. 79, p. 1142–1158.

Taylor, S. R., and McLennan, S. M., 1985, The continental crust; Its composition and evolution: Oxford, England, Blackwell Scientific Publications, 312 p.

Thomas, J. A., and Galey, J. T., Jr., 1982, Exploration and geology of the Mount Emmons molybdenite deposits, Gunnison County, Colorado: Economic Geology, v. 77, p. 1085–1104.

Threlkeld, W. E., 1982, Geology of the stockwork molybdenite occurrence, Jamestown, Colorado [M.S. thesis]: London, Ontario, Canada, University of Western Ontario, 108 p.

Tweto, O. L., 1987, Rock units of the Precambrian basement in Colorado: U.S. Geological Survey Professional Paper 1321–A, 54 p.

Tweto, O. L., and Sims, P. K., 1963, Precambrian ancestry of the Colorado Mineral Belt: Geological Society of America Bulletin, v. 74, p. 991–1014.

Wallace, S. R., Muncaster, N. D., Jonson, D. C., MacKenzie, W. B., Bookstrom, A. A., and Surface, V. E., 1968, Multiple intrusion and mineralization at Climax, Colorado, *in* Ridge, J. D., ed., Ore deposits of the United States, 1933–1967; Graton-Sales, v. 1: American Institute of Mining, Metallurgy, and Petroleum Engineers, p. 605–640.

Wallace, S. R., MacKenzie, W. B., Blair, R. G., and Muncaster, N. K., 1978, Geology of the Urad and Henderson molybdenite deposits, Clear Creek County, Colorado, with a section on a comparison of these deposits with those at Climax, Colorado: Economic Geology, v. 73, p. 325–368.

Wasserburg, G. J., Jacobsen, S. B., DePaolo, D. J., McCulloch, M. T., and Wen, T., 1981, Precise determination of Sm/Nd ratios; Sm and Nd isotopic abundances in standard solutions: Geochimica et Cosmochimica Acta, v. 45, p. 2311–2323.

Westra, G., and Keith, S. B., 1981, Classification and genesis of stockwork molybdenum deposits: Economic Geology, v. 76, p. 844–873.

White, W. H., Bookstrom, A. A., Kamilli, R. J., Ganster, M. W., Smith, R. P., Ranta, D. R., and Steininger, R. C., 1981, Character and origin of Climax-type molybdenum deposits: Economic Geology, 75th Anniversary Volume, p. 270–316.

Wilshire, H. G., 1969, Mineral layering in the Twin Lakes granodiorite, Colorado, *in* Larson, L., ed., Igneous and metamorphic geology: Geological Society of America Memoir 115, p. 235–261.

—— , 1984, Mantle metasomatism; The REE story: Geology, v. 12, p. 395–398.

—— , 1987, A model of mantle metasomatism, *in* Morris, E. M., and Pasteris, J. D., eds., Mantle metasomatism and alkaline magmatism: Geological Society of America Special Paper 215, p. 47–60.

Zielinski, R. A., Lipman, P. W., and Millard, H. T., Jr., 1977, Minor-element abundances in obsidian, perlite, and felsite of calc-alkalic rhyolites: American Mineralogist, v. 62, p. 426–437.

Manuscript Submitted December 18, 1987
Revised Manuscript Submitted October 24, 1988
Manuscript Accepted by the Society February 7, 1989

Printed in U.S.A.

Geological Society of America
Memoir 174
1990

Chapter 12

Geochemistry of the garnet-bearing Tharps Peak granodiorite and its relation to other members of the Lake Kaweah intrusive suite, southwestern Sierra Nevada, California

David L. Liggett
Department of Geological Sciences, California State University, Northridge, California 91330

ABSTRACT

The garnet-bearing Tharps Peak granodiorite, located along the southwestern margin of the Sierra Nevada batholith, is the most chemically evolved pluton in a suite of intrusions with typical Sierran chemical characteristics. A genetic relation between the Tharps Peak granodiorite and the surrounding metaluminous granitoids is suggested by (1) continuity of chemical trends within the suite, (2) a Rb-Sr isochron age of 109 ± 8 Ma, which indicates that the Tharps Peak granodiorite and the surrounding metaluminous granitoids were emplaced during the same intrusive event, and (3) an initial $^{87}Sr/^{86}Sr$ ratio of 0.7049 for the metaluminous granitoids and the Tharps Peak granodiorite, which suggests they were derived from the same source.

Systematic chemical variations between the metaluminous rocks and the Tharps Peak granodiorite, including the progressive increase in the A/CNK ratio, are due primarily to the removal of hornblende and plagioclase. The low initial $^{87}Sr/^{86}Sr$ ratio indicates that the suite was derived from a mantle or lower-crustal source or from materials derived from them. The presence of elevated oxygen isotopic values, xenocrystic zircons, and biotite-rich inclusions with high $^{87}Sr/^{86}Sr$ ratios indicates assimilation of metasedimentary rocks.

The composition and distribution of garnets in the Tharps Peak granodiorite indicate that these garnets are of igneous origin. They are inferred to have formed in response to an elevated molar $Mn/(Fe+Mg)$ ratio and low oxygen fugacity in the magma. Partitioning of Fe and Mg between biotite and garnet indicates decreasing *P-T* conditions during garnet crystallization of 4.5 kbar and 653 °C for garnet cores and 3.2 kbar and 521 °C for garnet rims.

Liggett, D. L., 1990, Geochemistry of the garnet-bearing Tharps Peak granodiorite and its relation to other members of the Lake Kaweah intrusive suite, southwestern Sierra Nevada, California, *in* Anderson, J. L., ed., The nature and origin of Cordilleran magmatism: Boulder, Colorado, Geological Society of America Memoir 174.

INTRODUCTION

Peraluminous garnet-bearing granitoids are distributed sporadically throughout the Sierra Nevada batholith. Typically, they are small plutons (<25 km^2), with more than 70 percent SiO$_2$, and where field relations permit relative age determinations, they are younger than the surrounding metaluminous plutons (Hamilton, 1956; Ross, 1958; Wones and others, 1969; Liggett, 1987). Most commonly they either intrude or are in close proximity to metasedimentary country rocks (Durrell, 1940; Ross, 1958, 1989; Moore and others, 1979).

The occurrence of garnet-bearing granitoids within the predominantly metaluminous Sierra Nevada batholith contrasts with occurrences of peraluminous granitoids in regions such as southeastern Australia and the inner Cordillera of western North America. S-type granitoids in the Lachland fold belt, southeastern Australia, occur in batholiths largely devoid of metaluminous intrusions (White and others, 1974). Similarly, peraluminous granitoids in the inner Cordillera, described by Miller and Bradfish (1980), are also not commonly associated with more mafic metaluminous intrusions. This investigation was initiated to determine the field and geochemical characteristics of the garnet-bearing Tharps Peak granodiorite, and its relations with the surrounding metaluminous granitoids and metasedimentary wall rocks. In addition, *P-T* conditions, possible source material, and the origin of garnet in the Tharps Peak granodiorite were studied.

The Tharps Peak granodiorite and associated granitoids are located at Lake Kaweah in the western Sierra Nevada foothills (Fig. 1). For ease of discussion, the granitoids in this area have been assigned informal names and are separated into peraluminous and metaluminous groups. The Tharps Peak granodiorite is the largest intrusion in the peraluminous group. Intimately comingled with this pluton is the garnet-bearing Wukchumni granodiorite. It is finer grained and chemically distinct from the Tharps Peak granodiorite. Also included in the peraluminous group is a garnet-bearing aplite dike, which intrudes the Tharps Peak granodiorite, and a medium-grained, garnet-free granodiorite dike. The metaluminous group comprises three intrusions with compositions more typical of Sierran granitoids; the Pierce Drive and Greasy Creek tonalites and the Horse Creek granodiorite. Collectively, the above metaluminous and peraluminous intrusions are referred to as the Lake Kaweah intrusive suite (Liggett, 1987).

The age of the Lake Kaweah intrusive suite is Early Cretaceous. Rb-Sr isotopic data indicate an age of 109 Ma for the Tharps Peak granodiorite (Liggett, 1987). U-Pb systematics on zircon fractions give an age of 108 Ma for the Pierce Drive tonalite and <112 Ma for the Horse Creek granodiorite (Chen and Moore, 1982). K-Ar dating has yielded ages of 102 Ma (biotite) and 103 Ma (hornblende) for the Horse Creek granodiorite (Everden and Kistler, 1970). The age difference between the K-Ar and U-Pb methods does not preclude all these intrusions from being coeval. The age differences may be due either to differences in blocking temperatures of the analyzed minerals or

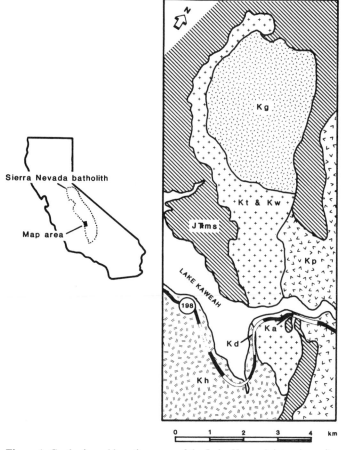

Figure 1. Geologic and location map of the Lake Kaweah intrusive suite, Tulare County, California. Outcrop rock types are abbreviated as follows. The peraluminous group: Kt & Kw (undivided) = Tharps Peak granodiorite and Wukchumni granodiorite; Ka = aplite dike; Kd = garnet-free granodiorite dike. The metaluminous group: Kp = Pierce Drive tonalite; Kg = Greasy Creek tonalite; and Kh = Horse Creek granodiorite. Metasedimentary rocks of the Kings Sequence are designated J℞ ms. Ka and Kd, too small to be shown at this map scale, are located at the intersections of the indicator lines and highway 198.

resetting of K-Ar ages from a later thermal event (Chen and Moore, 1982).

The Lake Kaweah intrusive suite intrudes quartz-mica schist, quartzite, marble, and calc-silicate hornfels of the Lower Kaweah River roof pendants. These prebatholithic metasedimentary rocks have been assigned to the Late Triassic to Early Jurassic Kings Sequence on the basis of lithologic similarities with rocks farther east (Saleeby and others, 1978). The Kings Sequence is, in part, a submarine fan complex composed of former clays, sands, and silts deposited in deep water along the continental margin of western North America (Saleeby and others, 1978). These rocks attained greenschist to amphibolite grades of metamorphism during the emplacement of the Sierra Nevada batholith (Durrell, 1940; Goodin, 1978).

METHODS

Thirty-two samples, fused and cast into glass disks, were analyzed for major-element concentrations using x-ray fluorescence at California State University, Northridge. Replicate analyses of U.S. Geological Survey standards yielded standard deviations of 1 to 2 relative percent. Strontium and oxygen isotopic determinations on 14 samples were provided by R. W. Kistler of the U.S. Geological Survey, Menlo Park, California. Standard deviations are ±0.00003 for $^{87}Sr/^{86}Sr$ (R. Kistler, unpublished data) and ±0.3 for ^{18}O (I. Barnes, unpublished data). Selected samples were analyzed by X-Ray Assay Laboratories, Ltd., Ontario, Canada, for trace-element and rare earth element concentrations. Uncertainties for these analyses will be provided by X-Ray Assay Laboratories, Ltd., upon request.

Microprobe analyses on polished thin sections were used to determine garnet compositions. Selected biotite, plagioclase, and muscovite grains were also analyzed for thermobarometry. Spot analyses were done on cores and rims of mineral grains using the MAC 5-SA3 electron microprobe at California Institute of Technology. Data were reduced using the ULTIMATE program, which utilizes the concentration corrections of Bence and Albee (1968). Reproducibility of data is 3 percent for elemental abundances of 0.1 percent to 1.0 percent, and 1.5 percent for abundances more than 1 percent.

PERALUMINOUS INTRUSIONS

Tharps Peak granodiorite

The Tharps Peak granodiorite is predominantly medium-grained, allotriomorphic seriate, and locally porphyritic. The principal mineral phases, in order of crystallization, are plagioclase (oligoclase), biotite, quartz, and potassium feldspar. Accessory minerals include garnet, muscovite, apatite, and zircon. Opaque oxide minerals are notably rare. Chlorite and sphene are present as alteration products of biotite.

Small pink garnets occur throughout the pluton. They are not spatially related to either the country rocks or the metasedimentary xenoliths. Two populations of garnets are distinguished on the basis of their sizes, morphologies, and occurrences. The most common type are anhedral, isolated grains, typically 1 to 2 mm across and usually fractured or fragmented. Biotite and muscovite are commonly adjacent or in close proximity to these garnets, and zircon is sometimes included within them. The second type of garnet is smaller (0.05 to 0.5 mm), anhedral to subhedral, usually free of inclusions, and is less commonly associated with biotite or muscovite. This type of garnet commonly occurs in tiny, macroscopic, pink veinlets that locally cut the foliation of the host rock at high angles. The foliation is defined by oriented biotite-rich inclusions, trains of biotite flakes, and parallel, elongate aggregates of feldspar and quartz.

Contacts between the Tharps Peak granodiorite and the metamorphic wall rocks are typically sharp, steeply dipping, and subparallel to the foliation planes in the metasedimentary rocks. Hornfels are developed locally along these contacts. In some outcrops the invading granodiorite partially or completely surrounds meter-sized blocks of metamorphic rocks, suggesting that local stoping occurred.

Contacts between the Tharps Peak granodiorite and adjacent plutons are sharp and lack chilled margins. Crosscutting relations indicate that the Tharps Peak granodiorite is the youngest of the major intrusions. The relative ages between the metaluminous intrusions could not be determined because the intrusions are not in contact. Due to their comingled nature, contacts between the Tharps Peak and Wukchumni granodiorites are abundant. These contacts are typically sharp, highly irregular, and are locally demarcated by centimeter-wide zones with high concentrations of biotite. In some outcrops, the Wukchumni granodiorite forms straight-sided dikes that crosscut and contain inclusions of Tharps Peak granodiorite.

Three principal types of inclusions occur in the Tharps Peak granodiorite: (1) xenoliths that have metasedimentary structures, textures, and compositions; (2) xenoliths of igneous rocks often derived from an adjacent intrusion; and (3) small, fine-grained, biotite-rich inclusions. The first two types of inclusions consist mainly of angular blocks and fragments, typically less than a meter across and in sharp contact with the enclosing granodiorite. These two types of inclusions occur almost exclusively in close proximity to the margin of the pluton. Metasedimentary inclusions that occur away from the margin of the pluton have undergone extensive reaction with the enclosing granodiorite. Felsic constituents in these xenoliths appear to have been preferentially replaced, disaggregated, and/or assimilated by the granodiorite while refractory biotite was left behind. In some places this process apparently spawned small biotite-rich inclusions.

Steeply dipping, layered schlieren, composed of alternate bands of light and dark minerals, are present in a discontinuous zone near the western margin of the pluton. Individual layers are relatively constant in thickness and composition. Felsic layers average about 7 to 10 cm in thickness and have the same grain size and abundances of minerals as the host rock. Mafic layers are finer grained, thinner, and contain higher concentrations of biotite than the felsic layers. In some outcrops, sets of 10 to 30 mafic-felsic layers with common orientation were partially scoured out and unconformably overlain by "younger" layer sets with a different orientation. The juxtaposition of these adjacent sets resembles cross-bedding in sedimentary rocks. The orientation of the cross-beds indicates that the layers were first emplaced near the contact with the metasedimentary rocks, then progressively toward the interior of the pluton. Scouring and emplacement of subsequent layer sets with different orientations suggest that each set of layers was the result of a separate pulse of magma.

Wukchumni granodiorite

The Wukchumni granodiorite is distributed discontinuously throughout the mapped part of the Tharps Peak granodiorite and makes up less than 20 percent of the exposed outcrops. It is intimately comingled with the Tharps Peak granodiorite, except along the south shore of Lake Kaweah where it forms meter-wide dikes that crosscut and contain inclusions of the Horse Creek granodiorite. The small size and random distribution of the Wukchumni granodiorite prevents it from being mapped separately from the Tharps Peak granodiorite. The Wukchumni granodiorite is similar in texture and mineral content to the Tharps Peak granodiorite, including the presence of garnet, but is distinguished primarily by its finer grain size.

Peraluminous dikes

A few widely scattered aplite dikes, typically less than a meter across and a few tens of meters long, intrude the Tharps Peak granodiorite. The aplite dikes are commonly associated with, and locally grade into, pegmatite dikes. Both contain the same minerals as the Tharps Peak granodiorite, but in different proportions. One of the aplite dikes was sampled for chemical analysis and is included in the peraluminous group.

A small granodiorite dike that intrudes the Horse Creek granodiorite is similar in grain size and outcrop appearance to the Wukchumni granodiorite, but lacks garnet. The garnet-free dike can be distinguished from the Wukchumni granodiorite in thin section by the presence of allanite, which is commonly rimmed by epidote.

METALUMINOUS INTRUSIONS

Pierce Drive tonalite

The Pierce Drive tonalite, the most mafic member of the suite, is in contact with the Tharps Peak granodiorite north of Lake Kaweah, but is separated by a metasedimentary screen farther south (Fig. 1). The tonalite contains hypersthene and augite, that are often mantled and replaced by hornblende. Biotite, subhedral plagioclase, quartz, and a trace of potassium feldspar make up the remainder of the rock. Opaque oxide minerals occur as inclusions in the ferromagnesian minerals and in some samples poikilitically enclose pyroxene.

Greasy Creek tonalite

The Greasy Creek tonalite is bounded on the north and east by the metasedimentary rocks of the Lower Kaweah River roof pendant and on the south and west by the Tharps Peak granodiorite (Fig. 1). In a few exposures a thin screen of metasedimentary rocks separates the two intrusions. The screen is only a few meters thick and has not been depicted on the map (Fig. 1). The Greasy Creek tonalite is medium grained, and contains plagioclase, quartz, hornblende, biotite, sphene, apatite, and opaque oxides.

Horse Creek granodiorite

The Horse Creek granodiorite, which lies along the southwestern margin of the Tharps Peak granodiorite, extends an undetermined distance to the south and west and is bounded on the southeast by metasedimentary wall rocks (Fig. 1). The Horse Creek granodiorite is a medium-grained, biotite-hornblende granodiorite composed principally of plagioclase, quartz, biotite, hornblende, and potassium feldspar. Minor phases include sphene, apatite, and zircon; alteration minerals include chlorite, muscovite, and calcite (trace). Potassium feldspar exhibits a wide variation in modal percentage and occurs as interstitial fillings and anhedral grains up to 5 mm across. A characteristic feature of this intrusion is the presence of abundant mafic inclusions.

GEOCHEMISTRY

Major-element concentrations

Thirty-two samples of the Lake Kaweah intrusive suite, collected mainly from an east-west traverse along highway 198 (Fig. 1), were analyzed for major-element concentrations (Table 1). As SiO_2 increases from 56 percent in the Pierce Drive tonalite to 75 percent in the Wukchumni granodiorite, Al_2O_3, total Fe, CaO, MgO, TiO_2, and P_2O_5 decrease, and K_2O and Na_2O increase. These trends reflect decreasing abundances of hornblende, biotite, and calcic plagioclase and increasing proportions of quartz and K-feldspar from the metaluminous to peraluminous rocks. Systematic chemical and mineralogical variations of this type and magnitude are typical of Sierran intrusive suites and are usually ascribed to fractional crystallization processes (Presnall and Bateman, 1973; Bateman and Nokleberg, 1978; Bateman and Chappell, 1979).

The Pierce Drive tonalite has a mafic margin and a more felsic interior. Variations in major-oxide concentrations from the margin inward are the most pronounced for SiO_2 (56.9 to 61.2 percent), Al_2O_3 (16.6 to 15.3 percent), CaO (8.99 to 6.63 percent), and K_2O (0.85 to 2.04 percent). In contrast, the Greasy Creek tonalite and the Horse Creek granodiorite are more chemically homogeneous. On silica variation diagrams, samples from these plutons form separate, coherent groups that lie along smooth trend lines from the Pierce Drive tonalite to the Tharps Peak granodiorite (Liggett, 1987).

Despite their narrow range of SiO_2 (71 to 75 percent), the peraluminous rocks generally have distinctive chemical identities. The Wukchumni granodiorite and the garnet-free granodiorite dike have less evolved chemical signatures than the Tharps Peak grdanodiorite, on the basis of their lower averages of K_2O, MnO, and P_2O_5, and higher total Fe content. Of the two finer grained granodiorites, the garnet-free dike appears least evolved, and has higher Al_2O_3, total Fe, CaO, and MgO.

The garnet-bearing aplite dike has a composition that is

distinctly different from the other peraluminous rocks. It has low concentrations of total Fe, TiO_2, MgO, CaO, Na_2O, high MnO, and very high K_2O (6.88 percent). These differences in major-oxide concentrations, as well as Sr isotopic data presented later, suggest that the aplite dike was either strongly contaminated by the surrounding metamorphic rocks, or it was derived as an anatectic melt from them.

One of the biotite-rich inclusions from the Tharps Peak granodiorite was analyzed to determine its relation to the rest of the suite. Its high concentrations of Al_2O_3, total Fe, K_2O, Na_2O, MnO, and low SiO_2, CaO, and MgO suggest it was not derived from the Tharps Peak granodiorite or any adjacent intrusions (Table 1). Strontium isotopic data indicate that this inclusion probably was derived from a metasedimentary source.

The A/CNK in the Lake Kaweah intrusive suite progressively increases from 0.7 in the Pierce Drive tonalite to 1.2 in the Wukchumni granodiorite (Table 1). Most Tharps Peak granodiorite samples have values of 1.1. The increase in A/CNK from the metaluminous to peraluminous rocks is a result of a progressive decrease in CaO due primarily to the removal of hornblende. Relatively low Na_2O in the aplite dike, and low K_2O in the Wukchumni granodiorite and garnet-free granodiorite dike further contribute to their elevated A/CNK ratios.

The Lake Kaweah samples plot within the calcic field on the Peacock alkali-lime index (Peacock, 1931). The Peacock index of approximately 64 is similar to other western Sierra Nevada intrusions (Ross, 1972), and slightly higher than values for the southernmost Sierra (Ross, 1989).

Minor elements

With increasing SiO_2, abundancs of Rb and Ba increase and Sr decreases. These variations are not as smooth as those of the major elements. Strontium shows the greatest variability (Table 2). Rubidium varies in a manner similar to K_2O, as might be expected because of their similar chemical characteristics. Both Rb and Sr contents are lower in the Lake Kaweah intrusive suite than in most other Sierran intrusive suites (Kistler and Peterman, 1973; Dodge and others, 1982). The low Rb may reflect the progressive east-west decrease across the batholith (Dodge, 1972). The low Sr is puzzling, especially in view of the calcic nature of the suite. Low Sr in the Tharps Peak granodiorite and aplite dike can be attributed to the fractionation of plagioclase (Liggett, 1987).

Barium exhibits a marked increase from 360 ppm in the Pierce Drive tonalite to 1,400 ppm in the Wukchumni granodiorite. The metaluminous rocks of the suite have Ba concentrations that reflect a progressive east to west decrease suggested by Dodge and others (1982). The peraluminous rocks, except for the aplite dike, have Ba concentrations comparable to eastern Sierran granitoids.

The K/Ba ratio can be useful in evaluating whether groups of intrusions are genetically related. During differentiation or partial melting this ratio should remain relatively constant in genetically related suites. Except for the aplite dike, the K/Ba ratio for the Lake Kaweah intrusive suite has a narrow range of 13 to 31. Established comagmatic intrusive sequences within the Sierra Nevada batholith have comparable ranges, but higher ratios (Dodge and others, 1982). These higher ratios are the result of lower K_2O in the Lake Kaweah intrusive suite. The K/Ba in the aplite dike is an order of magnitude greater than this range and provides further support that the aplite dike is not a simple differentiate of any of the other intrusions in the suite.

Rare earth elements

Rare earth element (REE) distribution patterns for the Lake Kaweah intrusive suite fall into three distinct groups: (1) the metaluminous intrusions, (2) the Wukchumni granodiorite and garnet-free granodiorite dike, and (3) the Tharps Peak granodiorite and aplite dike (Fig. 2). The metaluminous rocks have moderate LREE enrichment, slight negative Eu anomalies, and relatively flat HREE patterns at 10× chondritic values. The Wukchumni granodiorite and the garnet-free granodiorite dike have nearly parallel, steeply sloping REE distribution patterns. Their LREE abundances are enriched compared to those of the metaluminous rocks, and their HREEs have a concave-upward pattern. The garnet-free granodiorite dike has the lowest HREE concentrations, with abundances approaching chondrite values. In the Tharps Peak granodiorite and the aplite dike, LREE concentrations are lower and HREE are significantly higher than the finer grained granodiorites, but are similar to those in the metaluminous rocks. In addition, the Tharps Peak granodiorite and the aplite dike have prominent negative Eu anomalies.

REE patterns in the Lake Kaweah intrusive suite, like REE patterns in other Sierran granitoid suites, appear to be influenced, in part, by the fractionation of hornblende and plagioclase (Frey and others, 1978; Dodge and others, 1982). In Sierran granitoids with 55 percent to about 70 percent SiO_2, hornblende dominates fractionation (Dodge and others, 1982). Rocks of this composition commonly have REE patterns similar to the metaluminous group of the Lake Kaweah suite (Frey and others, 1978; Dodge and others, 1982; Ross, 1989). In Sierran granitoids with SiO_2 more than 72 percent, hornblende is no longer present, and the fractionation of plagioclase is manifested by the presence of prominent negative Eu anomalies. The absence of a prominent negative Eu anomaly in the Wukchumni granodiorite, atypical of REE patterns in garnet-bearing granitoids of the Sierra Nevada (Moore and others, 1979; Dodge and others, 1982; Griffis, 1987; Ross, 1989) indicates that plagioclase fractionation, although common, is not a necessary requirement in the development of these garnet-bearing intrusions.

Strontium isotopes

Fourteen whole-rock samples from the Lake Kaweah intrusive suite were analyzed for Rb-Sr isotopic contents; the results of these analyses are plotted on an isochron diagram (Fig. 3). A

D. L. Liggett

TABLE 1. MAJOR-ELEMENT CONCENTRATIONS FOR SPECIMENS FROM THE LAKE KAWEAH INTRUSIVE SUITE

Specimen	PDT 24	PDT 25	PDT 26	PDT 27	GCT 30	GCT 31	GCT 32	HCG 1
SiO_2	56.92	57.81	59.77	61.24	63.90	64.11	63.48	67.25
Al_2O_3	16.59	16.14	16.02	15.25	15.69	16.94	15.53	15.15
Fe_2O_3	3.36	3.02	3.00	2.61	2.25	2.00	2.22	1.95
FeO	5.38	4.83	4.81	4.18	3.61	3.21	3.56	3.12
MgO	4.20	3.72	3.56	3.17	2.21	2.86	2.31	1.91
CaO	8.99	7.93	7.60	6.63	5.13	4.98	5.16	4.45
Na_2O	3.44	3.80	3.67	3.31	3.86	4.42	3.76	3.68
K_2O	0.85	1.25	1.28	2.04	1.83	2.22	1.78	2.71
TiO_2	0.89	0.88	0.86	0.74	0.77	0.69	0.80	0.57
P_2O_5	0.19	0.21	0.19	0.17	0.20	0.17	0.20	0.13
MnO	0.15	0.13	0.13	0.12	0.10	0.09	0.09	0.09
SUM	100.96	99.72	100.89	99.46	99.55	101.69	98.89	101.01
LOI	0.31	0.43	0.43	0.52	0.56	0.57	0.52	0.39
A/CNK	0.72	0.73	0.75	0.77	0.89	0.90	0.89	0.89

Specimen	HCG 2	HCG 3	HCG 4	GFGD 5	GFGD 6	GFGD 7	BI 29	AD 19
SiO_2	64.43	66.57	67.85	73.58	73.71	73.02	60.61	73.52
Al_2O_3	15.44	15.11	15.52	15.11	14.84	14.64	17.95	14.42
Fe_2O_3	1.99	2.03	2.09	1.25	0.81	1.12	3.23	0.53
FeO	3.18	3.25	3.34	2.01	1.29	1.79	5.16	0.86
MgO	2.59	1.89	1.95	0.63	0.66	0.56	2.61	0.08
CaO	4.67	4.31	4.44	2.77	2.73	2.70	2.51	0.43
Na_2O	4.11	3.53	4.01	4.35	4.12	4.15	4.30	3.42
K_2O	1.57	2.81	2.60	4.35	4.12	4.15	3.30	6.88
TiO_2	0.63	0.57	0.61	0.24	0.16	0.23	0.78	0.01
P_2O_5	0.10	0.12	0.13	0.03	0.02	0.02	0.18	0.04
MnO	0.08	0.09	0.10	0.05	0.03	0.04	0.18	0.08
SUM	101.79	100.28	102.64	102.00	100.58	100.26	100.81	100.27
LOI	0.69	0.70	0.71	0.41	0.32	0.43	0.82	0.10
A/CNK	0.91	0.91	0.89	1.05	1.05	1.05	1.18	1.04

Specimen	TPG 8	TPG 9	TPG 11	TPG 12	TPG 15	TPG 16	TPG 17	TPG 18
SiO_2	71.71	72.33	72.88	73.14	72.26	73.56	72.57	72.29
Al_2O_3	14.89	14.37	14.43	14.57	14.62	15.24	14.43	14.06
Fe_2O_3	1.19	1.10	0.96	0.74	1.27	1.36	0.95	0.85
FeO	1.91	1.76	1.54	1.19	2.03	2.17	1.52	1.37
MgO	0.55	0.56	0.46	0.50	0.49	0.65	0.42	0.47
CaO	2.01	2.01	1.91	2.06	1.90	2.32	1.63	1.73
Na_2O	4.50	3.99	4.69	4.38	4.41	4.39	4.32	3.83
K_2O	2.55	2.52	2.73	2.84	2.62	1.98	2.99	3.01
TiO_2	0.19	0.19	0.17	0.20	0.17	0.20	0.15	0.14
P_2O_5	0.08	0.06	0.06	0.08	0.06	0.04	0.06	0.06
MnO	0.08	0.07	0.08	0.07	0.06	0.07	0.07	0.05
SUM	99.74	98.96	99.91	99.77	99.89	101.98	99.11	97.86
LOI	0.44	0.40	0.39	0.47	0.49	0.44	0.38	0.35
A/CNK	1.08	1.11	1.02	1.04	1.08	1.12	1.08	1.11

TABLE 1. MAJOR-ELEMENT CONCENTRATIONS FOR SPECIMENS FROM THE LAKE KAWEAH INTRUSIVE SUITE (continued)

Specimen	TPG 20	TPG 21	TPG 22	TPG 23	TPG 38	WG 10	WG 13	WG 14
SiO_2	72.24	72.04	71.97	73.83	72.44	75.16	74.98	75.92
Al_2O_3	14.71	14.64	14.22	14.34	14.50	13.59	14.29	13.95
Fe_2O_3	1.00	0.96	1.16	1.26	0.99	1.01	0.98	0.99
FeO	1.59	1.54	1.85	2.01	1.59	1.62	1.57	1.59
MgO	0.51	0.50	0.41	0.45	0.45	0.36	0.51	0.40
CaO	1.81	1.65	1.54	1.60	1.68	1.76	1.99	1.86
Na_2O	4.12	3.94	3.92	4.28	4.24	4.15	4.38	4.06
K_2O	2.90	3.39	3.24	3.48	3.25	1.60	1.71	1.95
TiO_2	0.16	0.17	0.16	0.18	0.16	0.11	0.12	0.12
P_2O_5	0.04	0.04	0.04	0.09	0.07	0.03	0.03	0.04
MnO	0.05	0.07	0.08	0.07	0.11	0.04	0.06	0.06
SUM	99.13	98.94	98.59	101.59	99.48	99.43	100.62	100.94
LOI	0.36	0.41	0.36	0.31	0.43	0.34	0.25	0.27
A/CNK	1.11	1.11	1.11	1.05	1.07	1.16	1.13	1.15

Note: Concentrations are in weight percent.
Abbreviations are same as Figure 2.

TABLE 2. MINOR-ELEMENT, Rb-Sr ISOTOPIC AND $\delta^{18}O$ VALUES FROM THE LAKE KAWEAH INTRUSIVE SUITE

Specimen		Ba (ppm)	Rb (ppm)	Sr (ppm)	$^{87}Rb/^{86}Sr$	$^{87}Sr/^{86}Sr$	$\delta^{18}O$
PDT	24	360	26.9	411	0.189	0.70528	+7.5
PDT	26	....	45.6	355	0.372	0.70550	+8.0
GCT	30	....	45.4	138	0.952	0.70516	+8.8
GCT	32	660	43.4	455	0.276	0.70516	+9.4
HCG	2	1000	40.6	290	0.405	0.70478	+8.2
HCG	3	750	85.8	250	0.993	0.70580	+8.4
GFGD	6	900	45.6	368	0.358	0.70535	+9.2
GFGD	7	....	49.1	368	0.386	0.70543	+9.5
WG	13	1000	41.9	260	0.466	0.70558	+9.9
WG	14	1400	44.4	246	0.522	0.70560	+9.8
TPG	12	1400	81.3	175	1.34	0.70680	+10.1
TPG	20	1000	62.6	167	1.08	0.70675	+10.8
AD	19	180	90.6	24	11.1	0.72991	+9.9
BI	29	....	88.8	239	0.372	0.71206	+9.5

Abbreviations are same as Figure 2.

York regression on nine of these samples yields an age of 109 ± 8 Ma and an initial $^{87}Sr/^{86}Sr$ ratio of 0.7049 ± 0.00008. The initial $^{87}Sr/^{86}Sr$ ratio correlates well with data of Kistler and Peterman (1973) for this geographic position in the batholith, and the age matches closely with the 108-Ma U-Pb (zircon) age of the Pierce Drive tonalite (Chen and Moore, 1982). Scatter about the

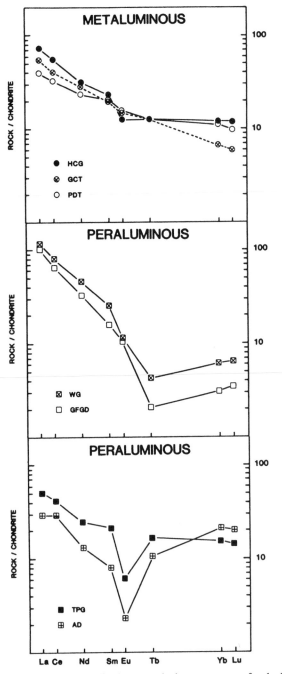

Figure 2. Chondrite-normalized rare earth element patterns for the Lake Kaweah intrusive suite. PDT = Pierce Drive tonalite; GCT = Greasy Creek tonalite; HCG = Horse Creek granodiorite; WG = Wukchumni granodiorite; GFGD = garnet-free granodiorite dike; TPG = Tharps Peak granodiorite; AD = aplite dike. Chondritic values are from Haskin and others (1968).

isochron suggests that the Sr isotopic composition of the magma was not uniform at the time of emplacement.

The Horse Creek samples form a slightly steeper isochron with an indicated age of 120 Ma. This conflicts with previous age dates for this intrusion of 102 Ma (K-Ar on biotite), 103 Ma (K-Ar on hornblende; Everden and Kistler, 1970) and <112 Ma (U-Pb on zircon; Chen and Moore, 1982) and suggests that this steeper isochron is not well constrained. Contamination is suspected for the Greasy Creek tonalite sample that plots away from the other samples.

The biotite-rich inclusion and aplite dike both plot significantly above the isochron and are therefore not compatible with an origin from the same source. At the time the mafic inclusion was incorporated into the Tharpes Peak granodiorite, the $^{87}Sr/^{86}Sr$ ratio of the inclusion would have been approximately 0.710, which is significantly higher than its host. If the aplite intruded about the same time as the rest of the suite, its $^{87}Sr/^{86}Sr$ ratio would have been 0.713 when it was emplaced. Values for both samples are comparable to those of metasedimentary material elsewhere in the Sierra Nevada (Kistler and Peterman, 1973; Collins, 1988).

Oxygen isotopes

Oxygen isotopic values for the suite range from $\delta^{18}O$ = +7.5 to +10.8 (Table 2). In general, the $\delta^{18}O$ values increase with increasing SiO_2, and no distinctive break in continuity occurs between the metaluminous and peraluminous groups. A sample collected along the eastern margin of the Tharps Peak granodiorite, near the contact with the metasedimentary rocks, has the highest $\delta^{18}O$ of the suite (+10.8). Its oxygen isotopic composition is elevated above the rather restricted range of the other peraluminous samples (+9.2 to +10.1). Proximity to the contact with the metasedimentary rocks and the elevated $\delta^{18}O$ value, relative to the $\delta^{18}O$ value in a sample from the center of the pluton, may indicate possible oxygen isotopic exchange with the country rocks.

The $\delta^{18}O$ values for the Lake Kaweah suite fall within the range of most samples from the Sierra Nevada batholith but are higher than the few known values on other granitoids in the Kaweah River drainage (Masi and others, 1981). The $\delta^{18}O$ values for the suite are all above mantle values ($\delta^{18}O$ = +6.0 ± 0.5 maximum; Masi and others, 1981), which indicates that partial melting, assimilation, or isotopic exchange with crustal material has occurred. The elevated ^{18}O for the Tharps Peak granodiorite indicates a significant contribution of metasedimentary rock (Taylor, 1978).

Garnet chemistry

Microprobe analyses indicate distinctly different chemical compositions for garnets in each intrusion (Fig. 4). Variability is seen in MnO, FeO, and MgO; FeO is distinct for each intrusion (Liggett, 1987). The Tharps Peak granodiorite has the highest

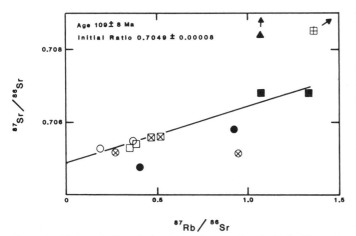

Figure 3. Rb-Sr whole-rock isochron diagram for the Lake Kaweah intrusive suite. The aplite dike and biotite-rich inclusion plot above the diagram. Symbols are the same as for Figure 2 with the addition of the solid triangle for the biotite-rich inclusion (BI).

range of MnO (6.6 to 12.2 percent) and the lowest range of FeO (29.7 to 36.4 percent). Concentrations of MgO in the Tharps Peak garnets are lower than those in garnets from the aplite dike, but they overlap with those of the Wukchumni granodiorite. Concentrations of MnO in the Wukchumni granodiorite are similar to those in the aplite garnets but their MgO is lower. Chemical compositions of both garnet types from the Tharps Peak granodiorite are essentially the same except that the MnO content is slightly higher in cores of the type that occurs in veins (Liggett, 1987). The higher MnO in the cores of this garnet type suggests that they may have formed later.

Manganese is thought to be a primary controlling factor in the genesis of garnets in peraluminous rocks (Hall, 1965; Miller and Stoddard, 1981; Abbott, 1981). Experimental data indicate that high Mn in garnet (>10 percent spessartine content) enhances its stability in Al-rich magma (Green, 1977) and allows the garnet to crystallize as a primary phase. The high Mn content in garnets from the Tharps Peak granodiorite suggests that the magma was highly evolved (White and others, 1986).

In all but one of the analyzed garnets, Mn is higher in the rims than in the cores. This type of zoning, most pronounced in the Tharps Peak garnets, is common in garnets from peraluminous intrusions (Miller and Stoddard, 1981) and may result from an increase in the molar Mn/(Fe+Mg) ratio in the magma due to decreasing temperature and fractional crystallization (Miller and Stoddard, 1981; Clarke, 1981; Abbott, 1981). The molar Mn/(Fe+Mg) ratio in the suite progressively increases from the mafic to felsic rocks (Liggett, 1987). Despite having an A/CNK ratio similar to the other garnet-bearing intrusions, the molar Mn/(Fe+Mg) is lower in the granodiorite dike than in the other peraluminous intrusions. This lower ratio may provide an explanation for the lack of garnets in the garnet-free granodiorite dike.

P-T *conditions*

The thermodynamic equilibrium equations of Ferry and Speer (1978) and Ghent and Stout (1981) were utilized to estimate the *P-T* conditions during crystallization of the Tharps Peak granodiorite. These equations were derived from equilibrium reactions in which the partitioning of Fe and Mg between coexisting garnet and biotite is temperature dependent, and the changes in Al (6 to 4) and Fe-Mg (8 to 6) coordination are pressure dependent (Ghent and Stout, 1981). Solutions of these equations, using the electron microprobe data from the Tharps Peak granodiorite (Liggett, 1987), yield a pressure of 4.5 kbar and a temperature of 653 °C based on garnet core composition. Both *P* and *T* decrease to 3.2 kbar and 521 °C based on garnet rim composition.

Two factors impose a certain amount of analytical uncertainty on the above results. The first is possible deviation from binary solid solution of garnet, biotite, muscovite, and plagioclase. Ferry and Spear (1978) indicated that their equation could be used without correction for minor elements as long as the ratio (Ca+Mn)/(Ca+Mn+Fe+Mg) in the garnet does not exceed 0.15. These limits are exceeded by the garnet rim (0.25) and biotite (0.26). The second uncertainty results from analyzing biotite grains that are in contact with garnet instead of matrix biotite. During cooling, late Fe-Mg exchange may take place between garnet rims and adjacent biotite, resulting in a lower temperature than in garnet cores and matrix biotite. Both factors suggest that some adjustment to the above *P-T* determinations may be necessary. Minimum estimates of standard deviation for the equations are ±800 bar and ±50 °C (Ferry and Spear, 1978; Ghent and Stout, 1981).

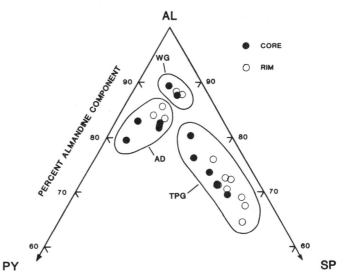

Figure 4. Garnet composition diagram for the Tharps Peak granodiorite (TPG), Wukchumni granodiorite (WG), and aplite dike (AD). End-member compositions of almandine, spessartine, and pyrope are normalized to 100 percent. Open circles are from garnet rims, and solid circles are from garnet cores.

DISCUSSION

Close spatial, temporal, and chemical relations between the Tharps Peak granodiorite and the adjacent metaluminous plutons suggest a genetic relation between them. The regular chemical trends of the major oxides and regular variations in A/CNK, and ^{18}O all suggest chemical continuity between the two groups. The Rb-Sr isochron that is defined by the nine metaluminous and peraluminous samples (Fig. 3) indicates that these intrusions were emplaced during the same magmatic event, and provides compelling evidence that they are genetically related.

The evolved nature of the Tharps Peak pluton, as shown by the Mn-rich compositions of the garnets and the chondrite-normalized REE patterns, suggests that this intrusion is a late-stage differentiate (Miller and Stoddard, 1981; Miller and Mittlefehldt, 1984; White and others, 1986; Calk and Dodge, 1986). This is supported by the contact relations, which show that the Tharps Peak granodiorite has the youngest relative age of the major intrusions in this area.

The systematic chemical variations between the metaluminous and peraluminous intrusions, which culminate in the Tharps Peak granodiorite, seem best explained by a model of hornblende and plagioclase fractionation. This model has been used to explain similar chemical variations in other Sierran intrusive sequences (Cawthorn and Brown, 1976; Dodge and others, 1982). The progressive removal of hornblende with increasing SiO_2 in these suites is indicated by (1) the systematic decrease in TiO_2, which is partitioned preferentially into amphibole relative to the melt (Cawthorn, 1976); (2) a decrease in Fe, V, Cr, Mn, Co, and Ni, which are similarly partitioned into amphibole (Dodge and others, 1982); (3) a decrease in the hornblende/biotite ratio (Hamilton, 1956); and (4) the absence of hornblende in intrusions with more than 70 to 72 percent SiO_2 (Dodge and others, 1982). The presence of these same features in the Lake Kaweah intrusive suite suggests that hornblende fractionation may account for many of the observed chemical trends. Plagioclase fractionation is indicated by the marked negative europium anomaly and concommitant decrease in Sr in the Tharps Peak granodiorite.

The initial $^{87}Sr/^{86}Sr$ ratio of 0.7049 for the Lake Kaweah intrusive suite indicates it was derived from a mantle, a possible lower-crustal source, or from materials from these sources. The suite is in a region of the Sierra Nevada batholith that consists predominantly of mafic metaluminous plutons that have quartz diorite as the dominant composition (Durrell, 1940). Regional investigations of granitoids in the batholith indicate that plutons in the western Sierra Nevada have been derived from a mantle or lower crustal source (Kistler and Peterman, 1973; DePaolo, 1981).

The Tharps Peak granodiorite could not have been derived entirely from a partial melt of Kings Sequence rocks. If it were, the initial $^{87}Sr/^{86}Sr$ and ^{18}O would be expected to be the same as the Kings Sequence. Although isotopic data from the Lower Kaweah River roof pendants are not available, similar lithologies in the Kings Sequence at Lake Isabella have significantly higher strontium and oxygen isotopic values (Collins, 1988).

Contamination by metasedimentary material, however, was a factor in the development of the Tharps Peak granodiorite. The intrusive suite was emplaced into what probably was once a continuous roof of metamorphic rocks (Durrell, 1940); remnant metasedimentary septa, screens, and partly digested xenoliths within and adjacent to the granitoids substantiate this hypothesis (Liggett, 1987). Evidence that the intrusive suite actually contains metasedimentary material is indicated by (1) the presence of inherited or entrained "old" zircons in the Horse Creek granodiorite and Pierce Drive tonalite (Chen and Moore, 1982); (2) $\delta^{18}O$ values that are elevated and have too great a spread to be accounted for by crystal fractionation alone; (3) abundant, widespread, biotite-rich inclusions in the Tharps Peak granodiorite with high strontium and oxygen isotopic values; and (4) biotite composition in the Tharps Peak granodiorite (see below).

In a recent regional investigation of California granitoids, Ague and Brimhall (1987), on the basis of biotite composition, identified a class of granitoids that is composed of mantle-derived I-type magmas that have been strongly contaminated and reduced by assimilation of pelitic metasedimentary material. These I-SCR type intrusions are most abundant in the western Sierra Nevada, where they are in close spatial association with roof pendants of the Kings Sequence.

Whole-rock chemistry, close spatial proximity to the Kings Sequence, and the mineral assemblage in the Tharps Peak granodiorite are comparable to these same characteristics in I-SCR–type intrusions (Liggett, 1987; Ague and Brimhall, 1987). More important, biotite compositions in the Tharps Peak granodiorite (Liggett, unpublished data) plot within the I-SCR field of Ague and Brimhall (1987), indicating probable contamination by sedimentary rocks and reducing magmatic conditions. The paucity of opaque mineral phases and the absence of primary sphene in the Tharps Peak granodiorite further indicate a reduced magma (Ishihara, 1977). The reduced nature of the magma may have been the result of the incorporation of graphite, which is a common constituent in the metasedimentary rocks of the Lower Kaweah River roof pendants (Durrell, 1940).

Contamination by metasedimentary rocks, accompanied by a decrease in oxygen fugacity, may have played a role in the occurrence of garnet in the Tharps Peak granodiorite. The stability of almandine garnet, the dominant composition of garnets present in the Tharps Peak granodiorite, is much greater at low oxygen fugacity (Wood, 1974). Furthermore, Calk and Dodge (1986) have accounted for the presence of garnet in the Sherman Thomas tonalite in the western Sierra Nevada as being a result of the reduced magmatic conditions. The observation that garnet-bearing granitoids in the Sierra are spatially related to metasedimentary wall rocks supports this assertion.

SUMMARY AND CONCLUSIONS

The garnet-bearing Tharps Peak granodiorite is a felsic end member of a suite of Late Cretaceous metaluminous and peraluminous granitoids. Systematic chemical variations between the metaluminous and peraluminous intrusions, including an increasing A/CNK ratio, can be accounted for by crystal fractionation of hornblende and plagioclase from a mantle-derived, I-type magma followed by assimilation of metasedimentary rock.

The composition and distribution of garnets in the Tharps Peak granodiorite, Wukchumni granodiorite, and the aplite dike indicate that the garnets had an igneous origin. They are inferred to have formed in response to an elevated $Mn/(Fe+Mg)$ ratio and low oxygen fugacity in the magma. *P-T* conditions determined from the partitioning of Fe and Mg in garnet-biotite pairs from the Tharps Peak granodiorite indicate a decrease in both pressure and temperature during garnet crystallization.

The above evidence suggests that the origin of the Tharps Peak granodiorite differs from the proposed models for other garnet-bearing granitoids such as the S-type granites of southeastern Australia and the inner Cordilleran muscovite granites of western North America. S-type granitoids are thought to have been derived from partial melting of quartzofeldspathic graywackes with a minor shale component (White and others, 1986). Peraluminous intrusions from the inner Cordillera muscovite belt of Miller and Bradfish (1980) have a probable source of Precambrian mid- to upper-crustal material. The chemical characteristics, geologic setting, and spatial association with more mafic, metaluminous rocks in the Tharps Peak granodiorite set it apart from the peraluminous intrusions in these other regions.

Available data from other garnet-bearing granitoids from the Sierra Nevada batholith indicate that they, like the Tharps Peak granodiorite, are evolved end members of metaluminous to peraluminous sequences (Liggett, 1987). The above model for the development of the Tharps Peak granodiorite may be applicable to these other garnet-bearing granitoids.

ACKNOWLEDGMENTS

This paper represents part of my research toward a Master of Science degree at California State University, Northridge. Critical reviews by L. G. Collins, G. H. Girty, W. H. Hirt, R. J. Stull, and P. W. Weigand improved the manuscript considerably. I am grateful to R. W. Kistler for providing strontium and oxygen isotopic data. This work was supported by the Department of Geological Sciences and the Foundation Students Project Committee, both at California State University, Northridge.

REFERENCES CITED

Abbott, R. N., Jr., 1981, AFM liquidus projections for granitic magmas, with special reference to hornblende, biotite, and garnet: Canadian Mineralogist, v. 19, p. 103–110.

Ague, J. J., and Brimhall, G. H., 1987, Granites of the batholiths of California; Products of local assimilation and regional-scale crustal contamination: Geology, v. 15, p. 63–66.

Bateman, P. C., and Chappell, B. W., 1979, Crystallization, fractionation, and solidification of the Tuolumne Intrusive Series, Yosemite National Park, California: Geological Society of America Bulletin, v. 90, Part 1, p. 465–482.

Bateman, P. C., and Nokleberg, W. J., 1978, Solidification of the Mount Givens Granodiorite, Sierra Nevada, California: Journal of Geology, v. 86, p. 563–579.

Bence, A. E., and Albee, A. L., 1968, Empirical correction factors for the electron microanalysis of silicates and oxides: Journal of Geology, v. 76, p. 382–403.

Calk, L. C., and Dodge, F.C.W., 1986, Garnet in granitoid rocks of the Sierra Nevada batholith, California: Stanford, California, 14th International Mineralogical Association Abstracts, p. 69.

Cawthorn, R. G., 1976, Some chemical controls on igneous amphibole compositions: Geochimica et Cosmochimica Acta, v. 40, p. 1319–1328.

Cawthorn, R. G., and Brown, P. A., 1976, A model for the formation and crystallization of corundum-normative calc-alkaline magmas through amphibole fractionation: Journal of Geology, v. 84, p. 467–476.

Chen, J. H., and Moore, J. G., 1982, Uranium-lead isotopic ages from the Sierra Nevada batholith, California: Journal of Geophysical Research, v. 87, p. 4761–4784.

Clarke, D. B., 1981, The mineralogy of peraluminous granites: A review: Canadian Mineralogist, v. 19, p. 3–17.

Collins, L. G., 1988, Hydrothermal differentiation and myrmekite; A clue to many geologic puzzles: Athens, Theophrastus Publications S.A., 382 p.

DePaolo, D. J., 1981, A neodymium and strontium isotopic study of Mesozoic calc-alkaline granitic batholiths of the Sierra Nevada and Peninsular Ranges, California: Journal of Geophysical Research, v. 86, p. 10470–10488.

Dodge, F.C.W., 1972, Trace-element contents of some plutonic rocks of the Sierra Nevada batholith: U.S. Geological Survey Bulletin 1314-F, p. F1–F13.

Dodge, F.C.W., Millard, H. T., Jr., and Elsheimer, H. N., 1982, Compositional variations and abundances of selected elements in granitoid rocks and constituent minerals, central Sierra Nevada batholith, California: U.S. Geological Survey Professional Paper 1248, 24 p.

Durrell, C., 1940, Metamorphism in the southern Sierra Nevada northeast of Visalia, California: University of California Publications in Geological Sciences, v. 25, p. 1–118.

Everden, J. F., and Kistler, R. W., 1970, Chronology of emplacement of Mesozoic batholithic complexes in California and western Nevada: U.S. Geological Survey Professional Paper 623, 42 p.

Ferry, J. M., and Spear, F. S., 1978, Experimental calibration of the partitioning of Fe and Mg between biotite and garnet: Contributions to Mineralogy and Petrology, v. 66, p. 113–117.

Frey, F. A., Chappell, B. W., and Roy, S. D., 1978, Fractionation of rare-earth elements in the Tuolumne intrusive series, Sierra Nevada batholith, California: Geology, v. 6, p. 239–242.

Ghent, E. D., and Stout, M. Z., 1981, Geobarometry and geothermometry of plagioclase-biotite-garnet-muscovite assemblages: Contributions to Mineralogy and Petrology, v. 76, p. 92–97.

Goodin, S. E., 1978, Metamorphic country rocks of the southern Sierra Nevada, California; A petrologic and structural study to determine their early Mesozoic paleotectonic and paleogeographic setting [M.S. thesis]: Berkeley, University of California, 75 p.

Green, T. H., 1977, Garnet in silicic liquids and its possible use as a P-T indicator: Contributions to Mineralogy and Petrology, v. 65, p. 59–67.

Griffis, R. A., 1987, Kern Knob pluton and other highly-evolved granitoids in east-central California [M.S. thesis]: Northridge, California State University, 305 p.

Ishihara, S., 1977, The magnetite-series and ilmenite-series rocks: Mining Geology, v. 27, p. 293–305.

Hall, A., 1965, The origin of accessory garnet in the Donegal granite: Mineralogy Magazine, v. 35, p. 628–633.

Hamilton, W. B., 1956, Geology of the Huntington Lake area, Fresno County, California: California Division of Mines Special Report 46, 25 p.

Haskin, L. A., Haskin, M. A., Frey, F. A., and Wildeman, T. R., 1968, Relative and absolute terrestrial abundances of the rare earths, *in* Ahrens, L. H., ed., Origin and distribution of the elements: New York, Pergamon, p. 889–912.

Kistler, R. W., and Peterman, Z. E., 1973, Variations in Sr, Rb, K, Na, and initial Sr^{87}/Sr^{86} in Mesozoic granitic rocks and intruded wall rocks in central California: Geological Society of America Bulletin, v. 84, p. 3489–3512.

Liggett, D. L., 1987, Geology and geochemistry of a garnet-bearing granitoid in the southwestern Sierra Nevada, Tulare County, California [M.S. thesis]: Northridge, California State University, 143 p.

Masi, U., O'Neil, J. R., and Kistler, R. W., 1981, Stable isotope systematics in Mesozoic granites of central and northern California and southwest Oregon: Contributions to Mineralogy and Petrology, v. 76, p. 116–126.

Miller, C. F., and Bradfish, L. J., 1980, An inner Cordilleran belt of muscovite-bearing plutons: Geology, v. 8, p. 412–416.

Miller, C. F., and Mittlefehldt, D. W., 1984, Extreme fractionation in felsic magma chambers; A product of liquid-state diffusion or fractional crystallization?: Earth and Planetary Science Letters, v. 68, p. 151–158.

Miller, C. F., and Stoddard, E. F., 1981, The role of manganese in the paragenesis of magmatic garnet; An example from the Old Woman–Piute Range, California: Journal of Geology, v. 89, p. 233–246.

Moore, J. G., Nokleberg, W. J., Chen, J. H., Girty, G. H., and Saleeby, J. B., 1979, Geologic guide to the Kings Canyon Highway, central Sierra Nevada, California, Geological Society of America Cordilleran Section Meeting Fieldtrip Guidebook: Los Angeles, California State University, 33 p.

Peacock, M. A., 1931, Classification of igneous rock series: Journal of Geology, v. 39, p. 54–67.

Presnall, D. C., and Bateman, P. C., 1973, Fusion relations in the system $NaAlSi_3O_8$-$CaAl_2Si_2O_8$-$KAlSi_3O_8$-SiO_2-H_2O and generation of granitic magmas in the Sierra Nevada batholith: Geological Society of America Bulletin, v. 84, p. 3181–3202.

Ross, D. C., 1958, Igneous and metamorphic rocks of parts of Sequoia and Kings Canyon National Parks, California: California Division of Mines and Geology Special Report 53, 24 p.

——— , 1972, Petrographic and chemical reconnaissance study of some granitic and gneissic rocks near the San Andreas fault from Bodega Head to Cajon Pass, California: U.S. Geological Survey Professional Paper 698, 92 p.

——— , 1989, The metamorphic and plutonic rocks of the southernmost Sierra Nevada, California, and their tectonic framework: U.S. Geological Survey Professional Paper 1381, 183 p.

Saleeby, J. B., Goodin, S. E., Sharp, W. D., and Busby, C. J., 1978, Early Mesozoic paleotectonic-paleogeographic reconstruction of the southern Sierra Nevada region, *in* Howell, D. G., and McDougall, K. A., eds., Mesozoic paleogeography of the western United States: Pacific Section, Society of Economic Paleontologists and Mineralogists Paleogeography Symposium 2, p. 311–336.

Taylor, H. P., 1978, Oxygen and hydrogen isotope studies of plutonic granitic rocks: Earth and Planetary Science Letters, v. 38, p. 177–210.

White, A.J.R., Chappell, B. W., and Cleary, J. R., 1974, Geologic setting and emplacement of some Australian Paleozoic batholiths and implications for intrusive mechanisms: Pacific Geology, v. 8, p. 159–171.

White, A.J.R., Clemens, J. D., Holloway, J. R., Silver, L. T., Chappell, B. W., and Wall, V. J., 1986, S-type granites and their probable absence in southwestern North America: Geology, v. 14, p. 115–118.

Wood, C. P., 1974, Petrogenesis of garnet-bearing rhyolites from Canterbury, New Zealand: New Zealand Journal of Geology and Geophysics, v. 17, p. 759–787.

Wones, D. R., Hon, R., and Bateman, P. C., 1969, Depth of crystallization of a garnet-bearing quartz monzonite of the Sierra Nevada batholith: EOS (American Geophysical Union Transactions), v. 50, p. 329.

MANUSCRIPT SUBMITTED MAY 15, 1987
REVISED MANUSCRIPT SUBMITTED MARCH 30, 1988
MANUSCRIPT ACCEPTED BY THE SOCIETY FEBRUARY 7, 1989

Geological Society of America
Memoir 174
1990

Chapter 13

Petrogenesis and evolution of the Salinian magmatic arc

James M. Mattinson
Department of Geological Sciences, University of California, Santa Barbara, California 93106

ABSTRACT

Granitic rocks ranging in age from Early Cretaceous (about 100 to 110 Ma, and perhaps as old as 120 Ma) to Late Cretaceous (76 Ma) make up the "Salinian magmatic arc" of California. These granitoids, along with a variety of metamorphic country rocks, constitute the pre-Cenozoic basement of the Salinian block or Salinian composite terrane (SCT), an important, but somewhat enigmatic element in the Mesozoic tectonic evolution of the California Cordillera. The ages of magmatic emplacement, based on interpretation of zircon data, reveal a systematic younging to the east across the axis of the arc. The locus of active intrusion migrated eastward at an average rate of about 3 to 4 mm per year, presumably in response to an evolving continental-margin subduction system. Initial Pb, Sr, and Nd isotopic ratios also vary systematically across the arc. The oldest and westernmost intrusions are the most "primitive" in their isotopic characteristics; however, with $^{87}Sr/^{86}Sr$ ratios of 0.7055 to 0.7070, ϵ_{Nd} values of –4.4, and fairly radiogenic Pb isotopic ratios, their sources are much more highly evolved or "continental" than the sources of, for example, western Sierra Nevada plutons. Younger SCT plutons, emplaced farther east (and, presumably, farther "inboard"), have even more "continental" signatures, with higher Sr ratios, more negative ϵ_{Nd} values, more "crustal" Pb signatures, and clear evidence for inheritance of Precambrian zircons from their sources. Overall, most of the SCT initial isotopic data appear to define a main mixing trend between more primitive or "oceanic" end members (never observed in the SCT) and a continental crustal end member. The latter may be of metasedimentary origin, perhaps similar to the schist of the Sierra de Salinas, into which some of the plutons intrude. The youngest and easternmost plutons show mixing between the main trend and a distinctive end member with high $^{208}Pb/^{204}Pb$ and $^{87}Sr/^{86}Sr$ ratios, a low $^{206}Pb/^{204}Pb$ ratio, and a low ϵ_{Nd} value. This end member may be the Barrett Ridge gneiss, or similar rocks at depth with a Precambrian history of high-grade metamorphism. Evidently the Salinian magmatic arc straddled the margin of the craton, and the plutons were derived, in part, by anatexis and hybridization of the preexisting basement rocks.

INTRODUCTION

The Salinian block or "Salinian composite terrane" (SCT) of western California (Vedder and others, 1983) is a large, allochthonous terrane underlain by a basement complex comprising Cretaceous granitic rocks and a variety of high-grade metamorphic rocks. The SCT is an elongate tectonic slice, bounded on both sides by major fault systems; the San Andreas system on the northeast, and the Sur-Nacimiento system on the southwest (Fig. 1). These faults "sandwich" the granitic and high-grade metamorphic rocks of the SCT between two essentially identical belts of "oceanic" Franciscan-assemblage rocks. Apart from well-documented Neogene San Andreas fault offsets of about 305 km, the details of the tectonic transport and emplace-

Mattinson, J. M., 1990, Petrogenesis and evolution of the Salinian magmatic arc, *in* Anderson, J. L., ed., The nature and origin of Cordilleran magmatism: Boulder, Colorado, Geological Society of America Memoir 174.

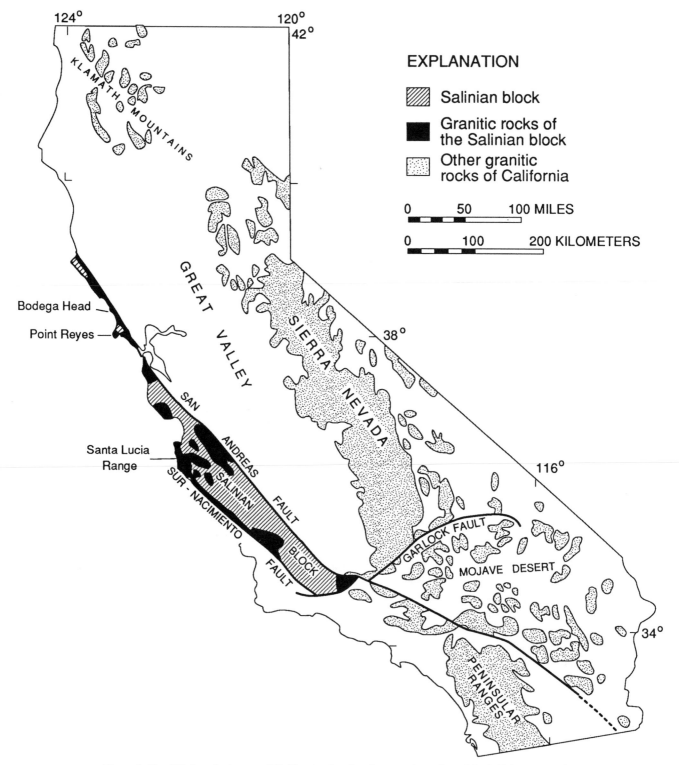

Figure 1. Simplified geologic map of California, showing the tectonic setting of the Salinian composite terrane.

ment history of the SCT have been the subject of considerable controversy, as discussed in more detail later.

This chapter focuses on the petrogenesis of the Cretaceous granitic rocks of the SCT. The granitic rocks, and the metamorphic rocks they intrude, are well suited for a variety of geochronologic and isotope tracer studies, including U-Pb geochronology of zircon, sphene (titanite), and apatite, and the initial isotopic compositions of Pb, Sr, and Nd. These studies yield important clues about the origins of the granitic magmas, and the evolution of the "Salinian magmatic arc" in space and time. As detailed in this chapter, the Salinian magmatic arc is a typical Cordilleran magmatic system. Granitoid magmas were emplaced during a span of about 30 to 40 m.y. in the Cretaceous, with the locus of magmatic activity migrating eastward during this time. The granitoids show systematic variations in various isotopic parameters with age and location suggesting that magmatic migration straddled the cratonal margin. The isotopic characteristics of the youngest and most inboard granitoids are dominated by Precambrian crustal signatures, indicating that melting of such ancient crust, or melting of metasedimentary rocks, derived in part from such ancient crust, contributed a large proportion of the magma from which the SCT granitoids crystallized.

BACKGROUND

Tectonic setting

As noted above, the details of the pre-Neogene tectonic history of the SCT are highly controversial. Inasmuch as the tectonic history bears directly on the ancestry of the SCT—that is, the original setting for Salinian magmatism and metamorphism—it is essential to briefly examine current interpretations (a more detailed discussion can be found in Mattinson and James, 1985).

There are currently two major schools of thought regarding the pre-Neocene tectonics of the SCT. One school, relying almost exclusively on recent paleomagnetic evidence, holds that the SCT has been displaced northward a total of 2,100 to 5,600 km since Late Cretaceous time. The second school, relying on a variety of geologic and isotopic evidence, rejects the paleomagnetic data and holds that the SCT is allochthonous "only" to the extent of several hundred kilometers.

Clearly, the well-documented Neogene movement history of the San Andreas fault system is only the latest manifestation of the extensive translations associated with Pacific (Pacific-Kula-Farallon) plate–North American plate interactions throughout the Mesozoic and Cenozoic eras. This is made apparent by the mounting paleomagnetic, paleontologic, and geologic evidence for northward translations of thousands of kilometers for the "Wrangellia" terranes (e.g., Jones and others, 1977) and some parts of the Franciscan complex (Blake and Jones, 1978; Alvarez and others, 1980), and for the assembly of much of the western margin of the North American continent by wholesale accretion of such far-traveled allochthonous terranes. It remains to be determined whether the SCT has participated in these extensive

pre-Neogene northward translations, or is only a much more recent (late Neogene) Pacific plate passenger. Perhaps more subtly, within the context of accretionary tectonics, what is the significance of the present-day San Andreas fault, if any, beyond the fact that it has been the Pacific–North American plate boundary for the past few millions of years? Must we look much farther inboard (east) to find autochthonous North American basement with which to compare the basement rocks of the SCT?

It has long been clear that well-demonstrated Neogene offsets of only about 305 km along the San Andreas fault zone do not explain fully the apparent offsets of at least 500 to 600 km of parts of the SCT, relative to the Sierran batholithic belt. The "extra" offset has been explained in various ways by a number of workers. Some have proposed pre-Neogene movement along a proto- or ancestral San Andreas fault (e.g., Suppe, 1970; Silver and others, 1971; Gastil and others, 1972; Garfunkel, 1973; Armstrong and Suppe, 1973). Others have documented slivering and extension of the SCT by internal faults (Johnson and Normark, 1974; Ross and Brabb, 1973; Howell, 1975; Dibblee, 1976); for example, the Rinconada fault with 40 to 60 km of right slip (Dibblee, 1976; Graham, 1978), and the San Gregorio–Hosgri fault with 80 to 115 km of right slip (Silver, 1974; Hall, 1975; Graham and Dickinson, 1978). Figure 2 shows the major areas of crystalline basement exposure in the SCT with the Rinconada and San Gregorio–Hosgri slip restored. The west-to-east cross section in this figure is used later for projection of age and isotopic parameters. Silver (1982, 1983) has suggested major west-directed thrusting of an SCT "flake" prior to San Andreas movement.

Most of the above hypotheses are based on the premise that the SCT, at least during the Cretaceous, was a part of the Sierran-Peninsular ranges Cordilleran system, and that it could be restored to its "rightful place" by unslipping Neogene San Andreas movement plus a modest amount of pre-Neogene movement, as discussed above. Recent geological and isotopic support for this premise has been presented by Ross (1984) and Silver and Mattinson (1986). Ross suggests some possible strong correlations between granitic rocks of the Gabilan Range and those of the Sierran tail, and also a possible correlation between the schist of Sierra de Salinas in the SCT, and the schist of Portal-Ritter Ridge (a possible correlative of the Pelona-Orocopia-Rand suite) east of the Sierran tail, on the northeast side of the San Andreas fault. Silver and Mattinson (1986) noted that, with removal of 305 km of right slip on the San Andreas fault system, Pb isotope patterns in Cretaceous plutonic rocks appear to continue unbroken across the SCT, the Sierran tail, and the Mojave.

An entirely different hypothesis is suggested by paleomagnetic work over the past several years in the SCT and adjacent terranes. This work reveals that some sedimentary rocks and granitic rocks of the SCT exhibit low apparent paleomagnetic inclinations, suggesting that they have acquired their magnetic signatures at low latitudes, and raising the possibility of pre-Neogene translations of thousands of kilometers. Kanter and Debiche (1985) provided a summary of recent studies; a few salient

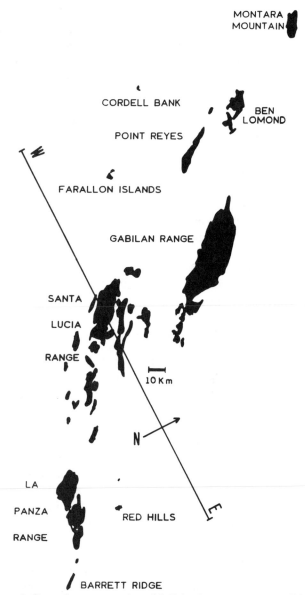

Figure 2. Tectonic reconstruction of Salinian basement outcrops. Right slip of 110 km removed from the San Gregorio–Hosgri fault trend, and 60 km removed from the Rinconada fault (after Mattinson and James, 1985). West to east line of section 100 km long is used for projection of age and isotopic data in several of the following figures.

results are noted here. Studies of the Late Cretaceous sedimentary rocks at Pigeon Point (Champion and others, 1980; Wilson and others, *in* Page, 1982) suggest 2,500 to 5,600 km of post-Late Cretaceous northward translation. Studies of the Paleocene sedimentary rocks at San Pedro Point (Champion and others, 1984, and *in* McWilliams and Howell, 1982) suggest about 2,100 km of northward translation since the Paleocene. Some caution is in order, however, because these interpretations involve major structural corrections, and many of the original data points were discarded due to severe overprinting by secondary magnetization. Moreover, the tectonic relation of the Pigeon Point area to the

SCT is not entirely clear. Nevertheless, additional supporting evidence for large translations comes from preliminary paleomagnetic work on Salinian plutonic rocks (Kanter and others, 1982), paleomagnetic work on the Stanley Mountain terrane, which lies outboard of the SCT and may have been amalgamated with it as early as the Late Cretaceous (McWilliams and Howell, 1982), and preliminary results from the spilites of the Gualala basin (Kanter and Engebretson, 1982; Kanter and others, 1982).

To summarize, the most recent phase of tectonic emplacement of the SCT is related to opening of the Gulf of California in the past few million years, and the accompanying few hundreds of kilometers of right-lateral offset along the San Andreas fault zone. There is considerable controversy regarding the timing, extent, and nature of earlier phases of emplacement of the SCT, however. Current (and conflicting) tectonic models for the emplacement of the SCT in its present position invoke additional north-northwestward translations of a few hundred to a few thousand kilometers, or major westward-directed thrusting (e.g., compare Dickinson, 1983; Page 1982; and Silver, 1982, 1983). Further evaluation of these opposing tectonic schemes is beyond the scope of this brief tour of SCT tectonic setting. The controversy is likely to persist until much more paleomagnetic, geologic, and isotopic work is completed and critically evaluated.

Summary of basement geology

Metamorphic country rocks. The older country rocks into which the Cretaceous granitoids were emplaced comprise three distinct metamorphic suites (Ross, 1977): (1) "Sur-Series" type metamorphic rocks of the central, western, and northern SCT (subdivisions of the SCT follow Ross, 1978); (2) high-grade gneisses, migmatites, and schists of the southeastern SCT (including the Barrett Ridge slice); and (3) the schist of the Sierra de Salinas in the central SCT. The significance of these country rocks is twofold. First, they provide clues to the pre-intrusive tectonic history of the SCT, with the potential for correlation with similar units elsewhere in southern California (e.g., see the earlier discussion of the possible Sierra de Salinas Schist correlation with the Pelona-Orocopia-Rand suite). Second, and of particular interest to this study, the metamorphic host rocks exposed at the surface may have equivalents at greater depth. Thus, they may provide a glimpse of the type of material through which the granitic magmas have ascended (with the possibility for contamination), or of materials at still greater depth where, by anatexis and mixing, they have contributed directly to granite genesis. Each suite is discussed briefly below.

The "Sur Series" rocks of the Santa Lucia Range (Trask, 1926) and their presumed equivalents elsewhere in the SCT, are chiefly quartzo-feldspathic granofels and gneiss, biotite-feldspar quartzite, aluminous and graphitic schists, marble, para(?)-amphibolite, and calc-silicate rocks. These metasedimentary rocks evidently were derived from a shallow, platformal sequence of continental-margin origin. Limited Sr and U-Pb isotopic evidence suggests a Paleozoic depositional age and indicates derivation, in part, from a Precambrian cratonal source (James and Mattinson, 1988). Metamorphism of the suite is essentially synplutonic (Compton, 1966; Weibe, 1970) and thus is about mid-Cretaceous in age (Mattinson, 1978).

Metamorphic rocks from the southeastern SCT are predominantly high-grade gneisses, migmatites, and schists, with local thin-bedded amphibolite, marble, calc-hornfels, and quartzite. The metamorphic rocks crop out in a large block in the Mt. Pinos–Mt. Abel area, the southeasternmost basement in the Salinian block, and in two very small areas at Barrett Ridge and Red Hills. Mattinson (1983) reported a U-Pb zircon concordia intercept age of about 1.7×10^9 yr for the Barrett Ridge gneiss. Ross (1977) suggested that the high-grade rocks of the Barrett Ridge slice correlate with the high-grade rocks of the San Gabriel Mountains.

The schist of the Sierra de Salinas in the central SCT is a homogeneous biotite quartzo-feldspathic rock with minor quartzite, marble, and amphibolite. On the basis of chemistry, Ross (1976) suggested that the schist was derived from a thick, uniform pile of graywacke. The schist crops out on both sides of the Salinas Valley, and has been penetrated by wells as far south as the San Ardo oil field (Ross, 1976). The Sierra de Salinas schist is unlike any other metamorphic rock in the SCT. Its closest relatives may be the Pelona and Orocopia schists in the Mojave Desert, especially the Pelona schist of Portal and Ritter Ridge and Quartz Hill (Ross, 1976). The Sierra de Salinas schist is intruded by unmetamorphosed 80- to 85-Ma plutons (Mattinson, 1982a). Thus the metamorphism of the schist is mid–Late Cretaceous or older. The schist contains abundant Precambrian zircon grains, indicating derivation from an ancient cratonal source; however, direct evidence for the age of deposition is sparse. On the basis of limited Rb/Sr data, James and Mattinson (1988) suggested that the protolith of the schist was deposited in the Mesozoic.

Plutonic rocks. Plutonic rocks are exposed throughout the SCT, but are concentrated in the central part, which includes the Gabilan Range, the Ben Lomond area, the La Panza Range, and the eastern part of the Santa Lucia Range. Granitoids of the SCT are, for the most part, typical of the Cordilleran batholith belt in a general way. They are calc-alkalic to calcic; variation diagram trends are in the range of those for the Sierra Nevada and the Peninsular Ranges. A few bear garnet as an accessory mineral (Ross, 1972). Most appear to have been emplaced at mesozonal depths. The SCT plutons contrast with those from the western parts of the Sierra Nevada and Peninsular Ranges batholiths in that diorite and true trondhjemite are rare to absent, as are plutons with "oceanic" initial Sr, Nd, and Pb isotopic signatures (discussed in more detail later). Thus, by contrast with the "intact" parts of the California cordilleran magmatic belt (Sierra Nevada and Peninsular Ranges batholithic belt), the western part of the "Salinian magmatic arc" appears to be missing (see Page, 1982, for discussion).

Two suites of rocks in the SCT are anomalous. Anorthositic and quartz gabbros of possible ophiolitic affinities crop out at Logan as a fault sliver at the eastern margin of the SCT, and

"charnokitic" plutonic rocks crop out in the western SCT south of Monterey. The rocks at Logan have been correlated with gabbro at Eagle Rest Peak in the San Emigdio Mountains by Ross (1970). They are Jurassic in age (James and others, 1986, and in prep.) and are unrelated to the granitoids of the SCT. The suite of deep-seated granitoids from the western SCT includes synmetamorphic charnokitic tonalite and cumulate ultramafites that are associated with granulite-grade wall rocks (Compton, 1960; Wiebe, 1970). These rocks are distinctive in terms of their metamorphic history and their thermal history (Mattinson, 1978) compared with other SCT granitoids. These differences appear to relate primarily to the present level of exposure, because the crystallization ages and the isotopic signatures of the charnokitic rocks are essentially identical to those for mesozonal plutons to the north (see Mattinson, 1978, and discussions below).

METHODS AND RESULTS

Granitic rocks and selected metamorphic rocks have been collected from throughout the SCT, from onland outcrops, the Farallon Islands, and sub-sea outcrops from Cordell Bank over a number of years. Minerals for U-Pb, Rb-Sr, and Sm-Nd isotopic analyses have been separated and purified by conventional techniques. Emphasis in earlier phases of this study has been primarily on U-Pb geochronology (Mattinson, 1978, 1982a, 1983, 1986; Mattinson and James, 1985, 1986; James, 1984, 1986). In this chapter, the geochronologic data are summarized graphically (Figs. 3, 4, 5) and discussed briefly.

This study concentrates on the results of isotope tracer work, using initial Pb, Sr, and Nd data. The detailed analytical results are too bulky to present here, so the data are summarized in a series of figures and one table of selected samples (Table 1). The

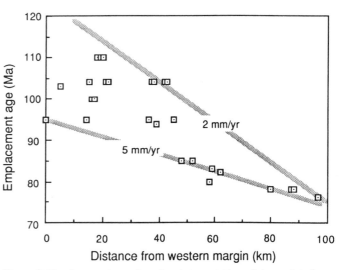

Figure 3. Emplacement ages based on interpretation of zircon data from SCT granitic rocks plotted along west to east cross section from Figure 2. Trend of ages indicates a west to east migration for the locus of magmatic activity. Heavy stippled lines bracket migration rate at 2 and 5 mm per year; average rate is about 3 to 4 mm per year.

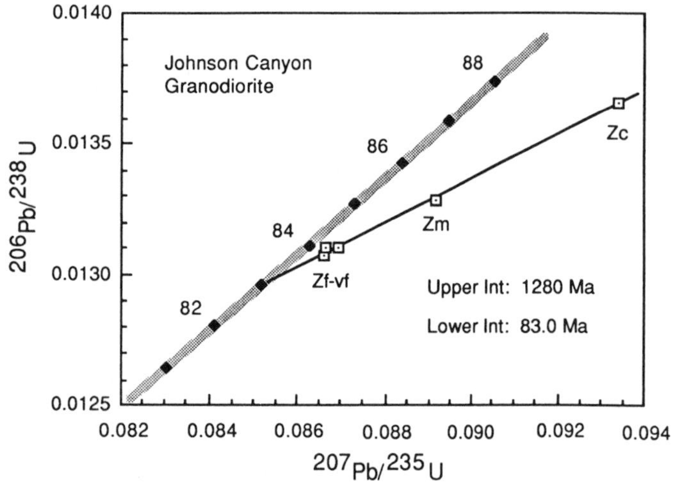

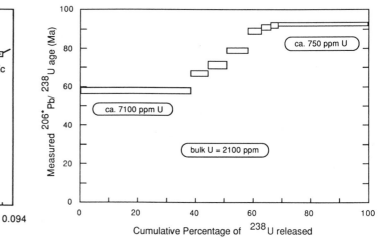

Figure 4. Concordia diagram showing a pattern of "micro-discordance" from the Johnson Canyon granodiorite, southern Gabilan Range. Five fractions of zircon define an emplacement age (lower intercept on concordia) of 83 Ma. The three lowest points represent fine- to very fine-grained zircon fractions that contain a very small inherited component, but are dominated by newly crystallized igneous zircon. Medium- and coarse-grained zircon fractions contain progressively more important inherited components, probably in the form of cores with igneous overgrowths. The upper intercept of about 1,300 Ma reflects inheritance of Precambrian zircons of about this age, older zircons that were already discordant prior to incorporation in the Cretaceous granodiorite, or a mixture of older and younger zircons (Mattinson, 1982a, and in preparation).

Figure 5. Results of a stepwise dissolution experiment (Mattinson, 1984, and in prep.) on a high-uranium zircon fraction from granodiorite of Gloria Road, southern Gabilan Range. These high-U zircons commonly show the effects of recent Pb loss superimposed on the "primary" patterns due to inheritance and magmatic crystallization. This "incremental U release" diagram is analogous to $^{39}Ar/^{40}Ar$ incremental release patterns. High-U, radiation damaged, and readily soluble zircon is dissolved in the early steps (left side of the diagram). The U-Pb system associated with these steps is highly discordant, as indicated by the low apparent $^{206*}Pb/^{238}U$ ages. Much more refractory zircon, digested in later, much longer dissolution steps, and finally, in a total dissolution step (identical to conventional zircon analysis, right side of diagram), is an order of magnitude lower in U concentration. The U-Pb system associated with these steps is either concordant, or plots on "primary" discordia trajectories so that the magmatic crystallization age of the granitoid can be obtained.

isotopic composition of initial Pb for the granitoids has been determined directly by analyzing feldspar separates. Feldspars in the granitoids have very low U/Pb ratios, and corrections for in situ decay of U are not necessary. Initial Pb is plotted in Figures 6, 7, 8, and 9.

Initial Sr isotopic ratios have been approximated closely by analyzing Sr from apatite separates. The apatites have very low Rb/Sr ratios; therefore, as in the case of the feldspar Pb, no in situ decay corrections are necessary. U/Pb systematics of apatite from a wide range of SCT samples reveal that while most of the apatites became isotopically closed systems shortly after magmatic crystallization, some have remained open with respect to Pb migration (and, thus, possibly Sr migration) for as much as 20 m.y. after initial crystallization (i.e., the apatites record cooling ages rather than primary crystallization ages; Mattinson, 1978, 1982b). In such cases, the apatites yield upper limits on the initial Sr ratios. Nevertheless, whole-rock Rb/Sr ratios for most samples tend to be fairly low (see Evernden and Kistler, 1970; Ross, 1972; Kistler and Peterman, 1973), and only very small errors are introduced by measuring the initial ratios in this way. In fact, the errors are possibly smaller than those that would be introduced by correcting present-day whole-rock data using measured Rb/Sr ratios from the all too commonly deeply weathered SCT grani-

toids. Initial Sr ratios for selected samples are plotted in Figure 10, and the correlation between initial Sr and initial $^{208}Pb/^{204}Pb$ in Figure 11.

Initial Nd ratios have been determined by analyzing Nd and Sm from apatite separates, and correcting the Nd ratio for in situ decay of Sm over the age of the rock. The apatites concentrate the rare earth elements strongly relative to whole-rock samples. As in the case of Sr, any evolution of the Nd ratio between the time of primary crystallization and the time of closure of apatite as indicated by the U/Pb cooling ages would be negligible. Nd data for selected samples are plotted in Figure 12, and the correlation between Nd and Sr is plotted in Figure 13.

Analytical methods for all the isotopic systems are fairly conventional, and are discussed only briefly. Zircons were digested, and U and Pb isolated by methods modified after Krogh (1973). Smaller dissolution vessels were used, and a double digestion procedure followed (Mattinson, 1987). Some high-uranium zircons were subjected to a stepwise dissolution procedure (Mattinson, 1984, and in prep.) in order to "see through" the effects of recent Pb losses. U and Pb separation followed Krogh (1973), except for miniaturization (150 μl resin volume columns). Sr and Nd were isolated using procedures similar to those described in Kwon (1986).

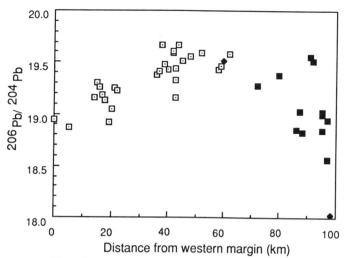

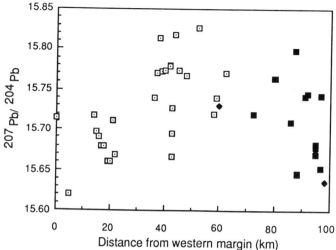

Figure 6. $^{206}Pb/^{204}Pb$ for SCT granites projected onto the west to east line of section from Figure 2. Granitic rocks from Cordell Bank, Montara Mtn., the Farallon Islands, Point Reyes, Bodega Head, Ben Lomond, the Gabilan Range, and the Santa Lucia Range are plotted as open squares. Granitic rocks from Adelaida, the La Panza Range, Red Hills, and Barrett Ridge are plotted as filled squares. The schist of Sierra de Salinas (at 60 km) and the Barrett Ridge gneiss (near the eastern end of the section) are plotted as filled diamonds.

Figure 7. $^{207}Pb/^{204}Pb$ for SCT granites projected onto the west to east line of section from Figure 2. Symbols as described in caption for Figure 6.

TABLE 1. SELECTED ISOTOPIC DATA FROM SCT GRANITOIDS AND METAMORPHIC ROCKS

Specimen*	Location†	Dist.§	Pb isotopes**			Sr‡ 87/86	Nd‡ Epsil.	Ref.§§
			206/204	207/204	208/204			
1G	Cordell Bank	0	18.94	15.71	38.86	....	....	3
2G	Montara Mtn.	5	18.86	15.62	38.50	0.70565	....	2
3G	Farallon Is.	14	19.16	15.72	38.90	0.70616	-4.4	3
4G	Bodega Head	15	19.30	15.70	38.87	0.70683	....	1
5G	Point Reyes	22	19.22	15.67	38.79	0.70705	....	1
6G	N. Gabilan	36	19.37	15.74	39.06	0.70690	-4.9	3
7G	Santa Lucias	44	19.67	15.82	39.49	0.70864	....	3
8G	S. Gabilan	58	19.43	15.72	39.18	0.70875	-8.6	3
9G	S. Gabilan	59	19.47	15.74	39.21	0.70839	-7.0	3
10SdS	S. Gabilan	60	19.52	15.73	39.30	0.71033	-7.6	3
11G	Red Hills	88	19.03	15.80	39.69	0.70917	-9.6	3
12G	La Panza	91	19.55	15.74	39.19	0.70903	-8.6	3
13G	Barrett Ridge	95	19.00	15.68	40.88	0.75094	....	3
14BRG	Barrett Ridge	95	18.84	15.68	41.54	0.76072	-20.6	3
15G	Barrett Ridge	97	18.95	15.74	39.66	0.71533	-11.4	3
16BRG	Barrett Ridge	98	18.02	15.64	40.05	0.74864	-20.0	3

*G = granitoid; SdS = Sierra de Salinas Schist; BRG = Barrett Ridge Gneiss.
†Detailed specimen locations available from the author on request.
§Approximate distances from western edge of section shown on Figure 2.
**Pb isotopic compositions corrected for mass fractionation based on replicate analyses of NBS Pb standards.
‡For granitoids, these are initial ratios; for metamorphic rocks, these are ratios at the time of granitoid emplacement.
§§1 = Mattinson (1978); 2 = James (1986); 3 = Mattinson (unpublished data)

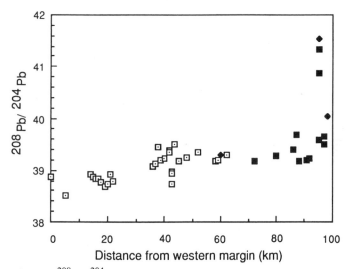

Figure 8. $^{208}Pb/^{204}Pb$ for SCT granites projected onto the west to east line of section from Figure 2. Symbols as described in caption for Figure 6.

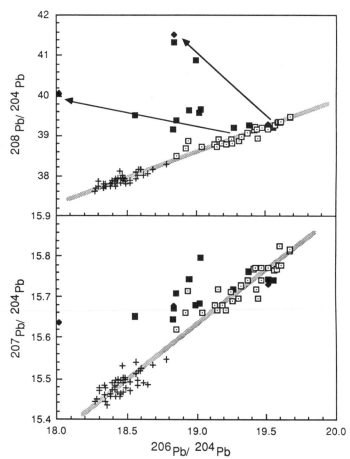

Figure 9. $^{207}Pb/^{204}Pb$ and $^{208}Pb/^{204}Pb$ versus $^{206}Pb/^{204}Pb$ evolution diagram for SCT granitoids and metamorphic rocks. Symbols as described in caption for Figure 6, except that the crosses represent the field of MORB from the Gorda–Juan de Fuca Ridge (Church and Tatsumoto, 1975) and from the East Pacific Rise at 21°N (Vidal and Clauer, 1981). The heavy stippled line represents a possible mixing trend between primitive, MORB-like sources and evolved, crustal sources to generate a "main trend" on which most of the northwestern and central granitoids lie. Southeastern granitoids appear to be pulled off this trend by mixing with a third source, possibly the Barrett Ridge Gneiss. This is shown most clearly in the $^{208}Pb/^{204}Pb$ versus $^{206}Pb/^{204}Pb$ diagram, where the secondary mixing trends are suggested by the solid arrows.

Early U and Pb determinations were run on the University of California, Santa Barbara (UCSB) Avco single collector instrument, running Pb by the conventional silica gel-phosphoric acid method, and U by using graphite and phosphoric acid on a single rhenium filament. More recent U and Pb determinations and all Sr and Sm-Nd determinations were run on the UCSB Finnigan-MAT 261 multicollector instrument. Pb was run by the silica gel-phosphoric acid method, U in part by using graphite and phosphoric acid or graphite and nitric acid, and in part by using silica gel and phosphoric acid. Sr was run using tantalum oxide powder and phosphoric acid on a single rhenium filament. Sm and Nd were run as metal by double filament techniques.

DISCUSSION

Zircon geochronology

Magmatic crystallization ages of SCT granitoids as inferred from zircon data are summarized in Figure 3. Before discussing these ages and their tectonic and petrogenetic significance, it is important to note that most individual ages are based on interpretation of several fractions of zircon. Depending on the complexity of the isotopic history of the individual sample, this interpretation can range from straightforward and well constrained to only weakly constrained. Although detailed analytical results of SCT samples will be presented elsewhere, it is useful to examine a few examples.

The isotopic systematics of zircon populations from most SCT granitoids can be described with a single word: discordant. Discordance in these zircon populations stems primarily from inheritance of older zircons of a variety of ages. In "well-behaved" discordant populations, the patterns of discordance or

"micro-discordance" can be interpreted with some confidence to yield the primary crystallization age of the granitoid; and to give some idea about the age range of the inherited component, see, for example, Figure 4. If the inherited zircons include a range of ages, scatter in the observed data may preclude a precise interpretation of the intercept ages. Some high-uranium populations of zircon are even more complex. For those zircons, the "primary" discordance patterns are overprinted by relatively recent, post-crystallization Pb loss. In some of these cases, step-wise dissolution techniques can successively strip away the individual zones within each zircon crystal that are highest in U, and hence the most damaged by radiation and susceptible to Pb loss (Mattinson,

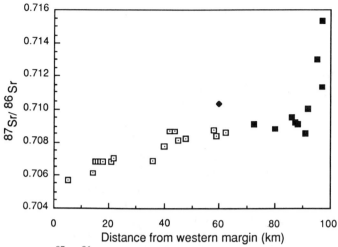

Figure 10. ^{87}Sr/^{86}Sr initial ratios for SCT granites projected onto the west to east line of section from Figure 2. Symbols as described in caption for Figure 6. Two specimens of the Barrett Ridge Gneiss and two specimens of southeastern granitoid with Sr$_i$ > 0.74 and which would plot at 95 to 98 km have been omitted.

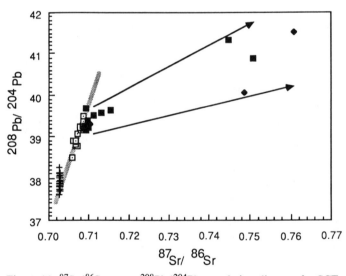

Figure 11. ^{87}Sr/^{86}Sr versus ^{208}Pb/^{204}Pb correlation diagram for SCT granites. Symbols as described in caption for Figure 6, except that the crosses represent the field of MORB from the Gorda–Juan de Fuca Ridge (Church and Tatsumoto, 1975) and from the East Pacific Rise at 21°N (Vidal and Clauer, 1981). Sr ratios are only available for a few of these samples, so "typical" MORB values in the range of 0.7025 to 0.7030 have been used. As in Figure 9, the heavy stippled line represents a possible mixing trend between primitive, MORB-like sources and evolved, crustal sources to generate a "main trend" for the SCT granitoids, and the solid arrows represent mixing with a third source, possibly the Barrett Ridge Gneiss.

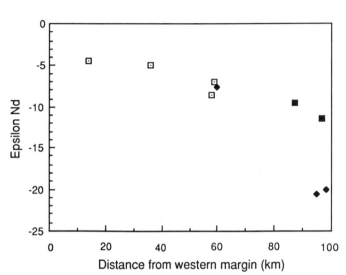

Figure 12. ϵ_{Nd} for selected SCT granitoids and metamorphic rocks projected onto the west to east line of section from Figure 2. Symbols as described in caption for Figure 6.

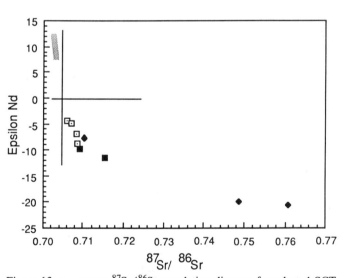

Figure 13. ϵ_{Nd} versus ^{87}Sr/^{86}Sr correlation diagram for selected SCT granitoids and metamorphic rocks. Symbols as described in caption for Figure 6. Epsilon values and Sr ratios are initial values for granitoids and values at time of granitoid emplacement for metamorphic rocks. Stippled area is field of MORB and intersecting lines represent "bulk earth" values (e.g., see Fig. 13.6 of Faure, 1986).

1984, and in prep.). It is then possible to "see through" the recent discordance, and interpret the "primary" discordance; see, for example, Figure 5.

Despite these complexities, it is now possible to discuss with some confidence the ages and trends of ages throughout most of the SCT. This is most readily done with reference to a simple model: (1) the granitoids of the SCT were generated in a single magmatic arc (referred to herein as the "Salinian magmatic arc"); (2) the present SCT represents an inboard segment of this arc system; and (3) removal of slip along major, known fault systems within the SCT adequately restores the granitoids to their original positions relative to one another.

For the purposes of this chapter, emplacement ages of the granitoids are projected onto an east-west line of section across a palinspastic reconstruction of the SCT (Fig. 3). From this it becomes clear that the axis of magmatic activity migrated from west to east, across the SCT. The most westerly (and northerly) granitoids with well-determined ages were emplaced at about 100 to 110 Ma. Some are possibly older or younger (in the range of 120 or 95 Ma; see James 1984, 1986; Mattinson and James, 1985), but these determinations are less certain owing to complex mixtures of inheritance and discordance in the zircon populations. The ages become systematically younger to the east and south; ages are as low as 76 to 78 Ma in the La Panza Range, Red Hills, and Barrett Ridge. The age progression can be interpreted either as a continuum (with considerable scatter), or as a "static arc" from about 110+ Ma to 95 Ma (0 to about 45 km) and a migrating arc (5 mm per year) from about 85 Ma to 75 Ma (45 to 100 km). More data would be required to choose confidently between these two possibilities, but the latter interpretation is very similar to that of Silver and others (1979) for part of the Peninsular Ranges batholith. Nevertheless, from the overall trend of west-to-east migration, two conclusions follow: first, as pointed out by Mattinson and James (1985), this age "polarity" indicates that the Salinian magmatic arc was west-facing; that is, the subduction zone was to the west of the arc. This may seem trivial in light of the present setting of the SCT along the western margin of North America, but it is important to recall that, based on paleomagnetic interpretations, the SCT may or may not be indigenous to North America. Second, the age progression of the granitoids suggests an *average* rate of eastward migration of about 3 to 4 mm per year, with bounding limits at about 2 and 5 mm per year. This estimate is subject to the uncertainties about the upper age limit for the westernmost granitoids, and to uncertainty about the true direction of "petrologic" cross-section across the tectonically slivered SCT, but is probably accurate within a factor of two. The SCT magmatic migration rate can be compared with a magmatic migration rate of 2.7 mm per year determined by Chen and Moore (1982) for part of the Sierran magmatic arc, and must be related to the evolution of the subduction system, with age, thermal state, or subduction rates.

Another major result emerges from the zircon data. As noted earlier, and as discussed in Mattinson and James (1985), zircon upper intercept ages on concordia diagrams reveal impor-

tant Precambrian contributions to the zircon populations in many of these Cretaceous granites. Zircons of appropriate age (up to about 1.7 Ga) and isotopic characteristics are present in the schist of the Sierra de Salinas, the Santa Cruz schist, and the Barrett Ridge gneiss (Mattinson, 1982a, 1983; Mattinson and James, 1985; James, 1984, 1986).

Common Pb

Initial or "common" Pb isotopic compositions of igneous rocks provide information about the long-term U/Pb and U/Th ratios in their source rocks. "Depleted" mantle, especially the source of mid-ocean ridge basalts (MORB), is characterized by low U/Pb ratios early in the Earth's history, and thus by relatively nonradiogenic Pb isotopes, especially $^{207}Pb/^{204}Pb$ (e.g., see Church and Tatsumoto, 1975). Highly differentiated continental crustal rocks are characterized by high U/Pb ratios, and thus, if sufficiently old, by relatively radiogenic Pb isotopes. Continental crustal rocks that have evolved radiogenic Pb early in their histories, then have been subjected to U-depleting high-grade metamorphism, have distinctive low $^{206}Pb/^{204}Pb$ ratios with relatively high $^{207}Pb/^{204}Pb$ and $^{208}Pb/^{204}Pb$ ratios (e.g., Tilton and Barreiro, 1980). Magmas derived by the melting or partial melting of such rocks, or contaminated by them, will bear distinctive Pb isotopic fingerprints that implicate their sources.

Compared with depleted mantle Pb, and even "average crustal Pb" (e.g., Stacey and Kramers, 1975), most of the SCT granitoids show a highly evolved Pb signature (Mattinson and James, 1985) suggesting at least partial derivation from old continental crustal rocks. From west to east, the initial Pb values for both uranogenic ^{206}Pb and ^{207}Pb (Figs. 6 and 7, respectively) and thorogenic ^{208}Pb (Fig. 8) show systematic increases across most of the SCT. Over the last 30 to 40 km, the ratios appear to level off; then, at the eastern end of the section, the $^{206}Pb/^{204}Pb$ and $^{207}Pb/^{204}Pb$ values drop, and the $^{208}Pb/^{204}Pb$ values increase sharply. A sample of the schist of the Sierra de Salinas collected from the southern Gabilan Range plots in the field of SCT granitoid Pb, near the end of the zone of systematic increase in all the Pb ratios. Pb from feldspar in the schist is approximately representative of total-rock Pb at the time of metamorphism or the last isotopic homogenization. Partial isotopic homogenization may have occurred around the time of pluton emplacement, according to U-Pb apatite ages for the schist (Mattinson, 1982a). Thus, the measured Pb isotopic composition of the schist reflects the isotopic composition in local country rock at the time of pluton generation and emplacement, and constitutes a possible end member for mixing via contamination or anatexis. Samples of the Barrett Ridge Gneiss, into which some of the southeasternmost SCT granitoids intrude, show low $^{206}Pb/^{204}Pb$ ratios, along with moderately low $^{207}Pb/^{204}Pb$ ratios and relatively high $^{208}Pb/^{204}Pb$ ratios (Mattinson, 1983; Mattinson and James, 1985). This is strongly suggestive of an early moderate U (but not Th) depletion as a result of high-grade metamorphism of the gneiss. As in the case of the schist of the Sierra de Salinas, U-Pb apatite ages for the gneiss (Mattinson, 1983) indicate isotopic equilibration at the time of pluton emplacement. Thus, the plotted gneiss values are possible mixing end members, as discussed below.

A plot of $^{207}Pb/^{204}Pb$ and $^{208}Pb/^{204}Pb$ versus $^{206}Pb/^{204}Pb$ (Fig. 9) is particularly revealing. Most of the SCT granitoids, along with the schist of the Sierra de Salinas, plot along a rather tightly constrained trend, especially in the $^{208}Pb/^{204}Pb$ versus $^{206}Pb/^{204}Pb$ plot. This trend suggests mixing between less radiogenic sources (to the lower left in the diagram)—for example, MORB—and more evolved crustal sources, perhaps similar to the schist or some more radiogenic composition along the trend. Isotopic compositions from the more easterly SCT samples form a separate array, distinct from the "main trend." They appear to lie on mixing lines between the upper (more radiogenic) end of the main SCT trend and end members with low $^{206}Pb/^{204}Pb$, high $^{208}Pb/^{204}Pb$ ratios like those that characterize the Barrett Ridge gneiss.

Initial Sr

Initial $^{87}Sr/^{86}Sr$ ratios (Sr_i) for SCT granitoids closely parallel the Pb data in both petrogenetic indications and age and geographic trends (Fig. 10). The Sr ratios show a systematic increase across the western and much of the central part of the SCT, then a possible leveling out, and finally a sharp increase in the easternmost part of the section. Sr_i from the western part of the cross section (the westernmost *exposed* part of the arc) is in the range of 0.7055 to 0.7070, still high relative to depleted mantle values (<0.7035) or western Sierran values (0.7040 to 0.7060; Kistler and Peterman, 1973). Younger and more easterly plutons have still higher Sr_i; 0.7075 to 0.7090. The schist of the Sierra de Salinas had an $^{87}Sr/^{86}Sr$ ratio of 0.71033 at the time of pluton emplacement, slightly higher than that for many of the plutons in the central part of the SCT where the schist is exposed. The easternmost plutons reach Sr_i values of 0.715, and small dikes and pegmatitic stringers within the Barrett Ridge gneiss are as high as 0.750. The latter must represent total or near total melts of the gneiss itself, which had Sr ratios of about 0.75 to 0.76, based on data from apatites which reequilibrated their U-Pb systems at the time of pluton emplacement.

A correlation diagram of $^{87}Sr/^{86}Sr$ versus $^{208}Pb/^{204}Pb$ (Fig. 11) confirms the trends noted in the plot of $^{206}Pb/^{204}Pb$ versus $^{208}Pb/^{204}Pb$. Most of the SCT data plot along a "main" trend that is linear and suggests mixing between a nonradiogenic (for example, MORB) end member and a more radiogenic, crustal end member. The easterly SCT samples are evidently "pulled off" the more radiogenic end of this main trend, by mixing with high $^{208}Pb/^{204}Pb$, high $^{87}Sr/^{86}Sr$ sources, similar in isotopic character to the Barrett Ridge gneiss.

Initial Nd

Limited $^{143}Nd/^{144}Nd$ data for SCT plutons and metamorphic rocks (Fig. 12) reflect the patterns seen in the other isotopic systems almost perfectly, except that Nd and its parent element, Sm, show the well-known opposite sense of fractionation from the U-Pb and Rb-Sr systems. Thus, the westernmost samples have the most radiogenic $^{143}Nd/^{144}Nd$ ratios (the least negative in the ϵ_{Nd} notation), and the easternmost samples have the least radiogenic or most negative values. As with Sr and Pb, the westernmost plutons are still quite "crustal," with ϵ_{Nd} values only as high as –4.4. Central plutons range from –7 to –8.6; the Sierra de Salinas schist is in the same range (–7.6). The easternmost plutons range from –8.6 to –11.4; the Barrett Ridge gneiss is at –20.0 to –20.6. As with the other isotopic data, the Nd results reveal that even the westernmost exposed plutons of the SCT contain substantial crustal contributions, and that the proportion of crustal material increases systematically to the east.

A plot of ϵ_{Nd} versus Sr (Fig. 13), like the Pb-Pb and Pb-Sr plots (Figs. 9 and 11, respectively), strongly suggests that the granites of the SCT crystallized from magmas derived by mixing varying proportions of mantle materials and crust. The Nd data are too sparse at present to fully define such a mixing curve, but the similarities to the more complete data of DePaolo (1981) for the Sierra Nevada and Peninsular Ranges and the data of McCulloch and Chappell (1982) for granitoids from southeastern Australia are striking. The chief difference is that the Barrett Ridge gneiss, at –20 ϵ_{Nd}, is much more negative than the probable crustal end member in the McCulloch and Chappell (1982) study.

SUMMARY AND CONCLUSIONS

U-Pb geochronology of zircons and measurements of initial Pb, Sr, and Nd isotopic ratios from SCT granitic rocks and their associated metamorphic country rocks suggest that the granitic rocks were emplaced as a part of a coherent system—dubbed herein the "Salinian magmatic arc." By comparison with the better-known Sierra Nevada and Peninsular Ranges magmatic arcs, the present exposures of SCT granitic rocks, including those from the submerged Cordell Bank, may represent only the eastern part of the original arc (e.g., Page, 1982). Nevertheless, the age data reveal that the exposed part of the arc was active in Cretaceous time, from about 100 to 110 Ma (or perhaps 120 Ma) to about 76 Ma. During this time, the axis of active magmatism migrated to the east at an average rate of about 3 to 4 mm per year, comparable to the rate of migration in the central Sierra Nevada batholith as documented by Chen and Moore (1982).

The isotopic "signatures" of the SCT granitic rocks show marked and systematic variations with time and geographic position, providing important clues about the petrogenesis of magmas that fed the arc. The earliest (and most westerly) of the granitic rocks are the least radiogenic in terms of Pb and Sr isotopes and the most radiogenic in terms of Nd isotopes. These characteristics are relative, however; even the most westerly rocks have Sr_i in the range of 0.7055 to 0.7070, and ϵ_{Nd} values of –4.4 compared to 0.7025 to 0.7030 and +8 to +12, respectively, for MORB. The SCT values indicate the significant involvement of old continental crustal rocks, perhaps as anatectic mixtures with, or as wall-rock contamination of, more primitive arc magmas. Toward the central part of the arc, the proportion of crustal material evidently increases, as indicated by rather smooth increases in all the initial Pb isotopic ratios and Sr_i, and more negative ϵ_{Nd} values. The proportion of inherited zircon in the granitic rocks also increases (Mattinson and James, 1985).

Pb, Sr, and Nd isotopic ratios of the schist of the Sierra de Salinas are very similar to those for the central arc granites. Moreover, the schist contains abundant detrital zircons of Precambrian age, similar to those that occur as inherited cores in many of the granitic zircon populations. Thus it is tempting to suggest that equivalents of the schist at greater depth have melted and mixed with more mafic, subduction-derived magmas to give rise to the granitic rocks presently exposed at the surface in the northwestern and central parts of the SCT. The youngest (and most easterly) granitic rocks deviate from this simple mixing trend. Instead, their isotopic ratios are pulled toward a very distinctive third component: an old, high-grade metamorphic source characterized by high $^{208}Pb/^{204}Pb$ ratios, very high $^{87}Sr/^{86}Sr$ ratios, and very negative ϵ_{Nd} values. These same isotopic characteristics are seen in the Barrett Ridge gneiss. Thus the gneiss, or similar rocks at depth, appears to be a likely candidate for the third end member.

The west-to-east trends in isotopic ratios displayed by the granitic rocks could be explained in two ways. In one alternative, migration of the locus of magmatism to the east with time would result in the interaction of the rising magmas with progressively thicker parts of a continental-margin wedge of metasedimentary rocks. Thus, the oldest granitic rocks would be only moderately contaminated by the thin end of the wedge. The younger magmas would rise into the thicker part of the wedge, with extensive anatexis and hybridization, such that the isotopic systematics of the granites would be dominated by the metasedimentary signature. The Barrett Ridge gneiss, or similar rocks at depth, possibly representing the edge of the old craton (as opposed to the younger metasedimentary wedge derived from the old craton), may have become involved in anatexis and mixing as the axis of magma-tism finally migrated across this edge. The sharpness of this isotopic boundary and the fact that the distinctive high-grade isotopic signature of the gneiss is not shared by the metasedimentary rocks of the Sierra de Salinas suggest that the gneiss is separated from the rocks to the west by a significant pre–Late Cretaceous tectonic boundary.

An alternative possibility for the isotopic gradients, at least in the western and central parts of the arc, is that the younger (and coincidentally more easterly) magmas incorporated a greater proportion of crustal material because earlier melts rising through the crust had already raised regional temperatures. This would permit more anatexis to take place with time in the arc system. Possibly some combination of the geographic and thermal effects is responsible for the overall pattern across the Salinian magmatic arc.

ACKNOWLEDGMENTS

This work was supported in part by National Science Foundation Grant EAR 80-08215, and by a University of California, Santa Barbara, faculty research grant. Thanks are due Eric James for many discussions of Salinian geochronology and tectonics, and to Leon Silver, Benjamin Page, and Clifford Hopson, who have provided much encouragement for my Salinian work over several years. Mark Stein assisted with maintaining the mass spectrometers. Special thanks to Robert Schmieder of the Cordell Bank Expedition, who kindly provided a specimen of granite from current-swept sub-sea exposures at Cordell Bank, and to Sung-Tack Kwon, who performed the separations and mass spectrometry for the Nd and Sm work. Thoughtful reviews by George Tilton, Joe Wooden, Virgil Frizzell, and an anonymous reviewer reviewer improved the final manuscript. However, it is to Donald Ross that I dedicate this attempt at synthesis of SCT granite petrogenesis. Without his many years of work on the SCT, this study would have been much more difficult, if not impossible. Don also has supplied much encouragement and advice, and difficult to obtain specimens from the Farallon Islands.

REFERENCES CITED

Alvarez, W., Kent, D. V., Premoli Silva, I., Schweickert, R. A., and Larson, R. L., 1980, Franciscan limestone deposited at 17° south paleolatitude: Geological Society of America Bulletin, v. 91, p. 476–484.

Armstrong, R. L., and Suppe, J., 1973, Potassium-argon geochronometry of Mesozoic igneous rocks in Nevada, Utah, and southern California: Geological Society of America Bulletin, v. 84, p. 1375–1392.

Blake, M. C., Jr., and Jones, D. L., 1978, Allochthonous terranes in northern California? A reinterpretation, *in* Howell, D. G., and McDougall, K. A., eds., Mesozoic paleogeography of the western United States: Society of Economic Paleontologists and Mineralogists, Pacific Section, Pacific Coast Paleogeography Symposium 2, p. 397–400.

Champion, D., Gromme, S., and Howell, D. G., 1980, Paleomagnetism of the Cretaceous Pigeon Point Formation and the inferred northward displacement of 2,500 km for the Salinian block, California: EOS (Transactions of the American Geophysical Union), v. 61, p. 948.

——— , 1984, Paleomagnetic and geologic data indicating 2,500 km northward displacement for the Salinian and related terranes, California: Journal of Geophysical Research, v. 89, p. 7736–7752.

Chen, J. H., and Moore, J. G., 1982, Uranium-lead isotopic ages from the Sierra Nevada batholith, California: Journal of Geophysical Research, v. 87, p. 4761–4784.

Church, S. E., and Tatsumoto, M., 1975, Lead isotope relations in oceanic ridge basalts from the Juan de Fuca–Gorda Ridge area, N.E. Pacific Ocean: Contributions to Mineralogy and Petrology, v. 53, p. 253–279.

Compton, R. R., 1960, Charnockitic rocks of the Santa Lucia Range, California: American Journal of Science, v. 58, p. 609–636.

——— , 1966, Granitic and metamorphic rocks of the Salinian block, California Coast Ranges: California Division of Mines and Geology Bulletin 190, p. 277–287.

DePaolo, D. J., 1981, A neodymium and strontium isotopic study of the Mesozoic calc-alkaline batholiths of the Sierra Nevada and Peninsular Ranges, California: Journal of Geophysical Research, v. 86, p. 10470–10488.

Dibblee, T. W., Jr., 1976, The Rinconada and related faults in the southern Coast Ranges, California, and their tectonic significance: U.S. Geological Survey Professional paper 981, 55 p.

Dickinson, W. R., 1983, Cretaceous sinistral strike slip along Nacimiento fault in coastal California: American Association of Petroleum Geologists Bulletin, v. 67, p. 624–645.

Evernden, J. F., and Kistler, R. W., 1970, Chronology of emplacement of Mesozoic batholithic complexes in California and western Nevada: U.S. Geological Survey Professional Paper 623, 42 p.

Faure, G., 1986, Principles of isotope geology: New York, John Wiley and Sons, 589 p.

Garfunkel, Z., 1973, History of the San Andreas fault as a plate boundary: Geological Society of America Bulletin, v. 84, p. 2409–2430.

Gastil, G. G., Phillips, R. P., and Rodriquez-Torres, R., 1972, The reconstruction of Mesozoic California: 24th International Geologic Congress, Montreal, 1972, Proceedings, Section 3, p. 217–229.

Graham, S. A., 1978, Role of the Salinian block in the evolution of the San Andreas fault system: American Association of Petroleum Geologists Bulletin, v. 62, p. 2214–2231.

Graham, S. A., and Dickinson, W. R., 1978, Evidence for 115 kilometers of right slip on the San Gregorio-Hosgri fault trend: Science, v. 199, p. 179–181.

Hall, C. A., Jr., 1975, San Simeon-Hosgri fault system, coastal California; Economic and environmental implications: Science, v. 190, p. 1291–1294.

Howell, D. G., 1975, Hypothesis suggesting 700 km of right slip in California along northwest-oriented faults: Geology, v. 3, p. 81–84.

James, E. W., 1984, U/Pb ages of plutonism and metamorphism in part of the Salinian block, Santa Cruz and San Mateo counties, California: Geological Society of America Abstracts with Programs, v. 16, p. 291.

——, 1986, Geochronology, isotopic characteristics and paleogeography of parts of the Salinian block of California [Ph.D. thesis]: Santa Barbara, University of California, 176 p.

James, E. W., and Mattinson, J. M., 1988, Metamorphic history of the Salinian block; An isotopic reconnaissance, *in* Ernst, W. G., ed., Metamorphism and crustal evolution of the western United States, Rubey Volume 7: Englewood Cliffs, New Jersey, Prentice-Hall, p. 938–952.

James, E. W., Kimbrough, D. L., and Mattinson, J. M., 1986, Evaluation of pre-Tertiary piercing points along the northern San Andreas fault using U/Pb dating, initial Sr, and common Pb isotopic ratios: Geological Society of America Abstracts with Programs, v. 18, p. 121.

Johnson, J. D., and Normark, W. R., 1974, Neogene tectonic evolution of the Salinian block, west-central California: Geology, v. 2, p. 11–14.

Jones, D. L., Silberling, N. J., and Hillhouse, J., 1977, Wrangellia; A displaced terrane in northwest North America: Canadian Journal of Earth Sciences, v. 14, p. 2565–2577.

Kanter, L. R., and Debiche, M., 1985, Modeling the motion histories of the Point Arena and central Salinia terranes, *in* Howell, D., ed., Tectonostratigraphic terranes of the Circum-Pacific region: Circum-Pacific Council for Energy and Mineral Resources, Earth Science Series 1, p. 227–238.

Kanter, L. R., and Engebretson, D. C., 1982, Preliminary paleomagnetic results from the Gualala block, northern California: Geologica Society of America Abstracts with Programs, v. 14, p. 177.

Kanter, L. R., Engebretson, D. C., and Cox, A., 1982, Paleomagnetism of continental and oceanic terranes of coastal California: EOS (Transactions of the American Geophysical Union), v. 63, no. 45, p. 915.

Kistler, R. W., and Peterman, Z. E., 1973, Variations in Sr, Rb, K, Na, and initial Sr^{86}/Sr^{86} in Mesozoic granitic rocks and intruded wall rocks in central California: Geological Society of America Bulletin, v. 84, p. 3489–3512.

Krogh, T. E., 1973, A low contamination method for hydrothermal decomposition of zircon and extraction of U and Pb for isotopic age determinations: Geochimica et Cosmochimica Acta, v. 37, p. 485–494.

Kwon, S.-T., 1986, Pb-Sr-Nd isotope study of the 100 to 2,700 Ma old alkalic rock-carbonatite complexes in the Canadian shield; Inferences on the geo-

chemical and structural evolution of the mantle [Ph.D. thesis]: Santa Barbara, University of California, 242 p.

Mattinson, J. M., 1978, Age, origin, and thermal histories of some plutonic rocks from the Salinian block of California: Contributions to Mineralogy and Petrology, v. 67, p. 233–245.

——, 1982a, Granitic rocks of the Gabilan Range; U-Pb isotopic systematics and implications for age and origin: Geological Society of America Abstracts with Programs, v. 14, p. 184.

——, 1982b, U-Pb "blocking temperatures" and Pb loss characteristics in young zircon, sphene, and apatite: Geological Society of America Abstracts with Programs, v. 14, p. 558.

——, 1983, Basement rocks of the southeastern Salinian block, California; U-Pb isotopic relationships: Geological Society of America Abstracts with Programs, v. 15, p. 414.

——, 1984, Labile Pb in young, high-uranium zircons: Geological Society of America Abstracts with Programs, v. 16, p. 559.

——, 1986, Nature of granitic crust of the Salinian block of California; Isotopic evidence for the recycling of old continental crust: Geological Society of America Abstracts with Programs, v. 18, p. 154.

——, 1987, U-Pb ages of zircons; A basic examination of error propagation: Chemical Geology, v. 66, p. 151–162.

Mattinson, J. M., and James, E. W., 1985, Salinian block age and isotopic variations; Implications for origin and emplacement of the Salinian terrane, *in* Howell, D., ed., Tectonostratigraphic terranes of the Circum-Pacific region: Circum-Pacific Council for Energy and Mineral Resources, Earth Science Series 1, p. 215–226.

——, 1986, The Sierra de Salinas schist, Salinian block, California; Isotopic constraints on age and origin: Geological Society of America Abstracts with Programs, v. 18, p. 154.

McCulloch, M. T., and Chappell, B. W., 1982, Nd isotopic characteristics of S- and I-type granites: Earth and Planetary Science Letters, v. 58, p. 51–64.

McWilliams, M. O., and Howell, D. G., 1982, Exotic terranes of western California: Nature, v. 297, p. 215–217.

Page, B. M., 1982, Migration of Salinian composite block, California, and disappearance of fragments: American Journal of Science, v. 282, p. 1694–1734.

Ross, D. C., 1970, Quartz gabbro and anorthositic gabbro; Markers of offset along the San Andreas fault in the California Coast Ranges: Geological Society of America Bulletin, v. 81, p. 3647–3662.

——, 1972, Petrographic and chemical reconnaissance study of some granitic and gneissic rocks near the San Andreas fault from Bodega Head to Cajon Pass, California: U.S. Geological Survey Professional Paper 698, 92 p.

——, 1976, Metagraywacke in the Salinian block, central Coast Ranges, California, and a possible correlative across the San Andreas fault: U.S. Geological Survey Journal of Research, v. 4, no. 6, p. 683–696.

——, 1977, Pre-intrusive metasedimentary rocks of the Salinian block, California; A tectonic dilemma, *in* Stewart, J. H., Stevens, C. H., and Fritsche, A. E., eds., Paleozoic paleogeography of the western United States: Society of Economic Paleontologists and Mineralogists, Pacific Section, Pacific Coast Paleogeography Symposium 1, p. 371–380.

——, 1978, The Salinian block; A Mesozoic granitic orphan in the California Coast Ranges, *in* Howell, D. G., and McDougall, K. A., eds., Mesozoic paleogeography of the western United States: Society of Economic Paleontologists and Mineralogists, Pacific Section, Pacific Coast Paleogeography Symposium 2, p. 509–522.

——, 1984, Possible correlations of basement rocks across the San Andreas, San Gregorio–Hosgri, and Rinconada–Reliz–King City faults, California: U.S. Geological Survey Professional Paper 1317, 37 p.

Ross, D. C., and Brabb, E. E., 1973, Petrography and structural relations of granitic basement rocks in the Monterey Bay area, California: U.S. Geological Survey Journal of Research, v. 1, p. 273–282.

Silver, E. A., 1974, Structural interpretation from free-air gravity on the California continental margin, 35°–40°N: Geological Society of America Abstracts with Programs, v. 6, p. 253.

Silver, E. A., Curray, J. R., and Cooper, A. K., 1971, Tectonic development of the continental margin off central California, *in* Lipps, J. H., and Moores, E. M., eds., California geologic guide to the northern California Coast Ranges, Point Reyes region, California: Geological Society of Sacramento Annual Field Trip Guidebook, p. 1–10.

Silver, L. T., 1982, Evidence and a model for west-directed early to mid-Cenozoic overthrusting in southern California: Geological Society of America Abstracts with Programs, v. 14, p. 617.

——, 1983, Paleogene overthrusting in the tectonic evolution of the Transverse Ranges, Mojave, and Salinian regions, California: Geological Society of America Abstracts with Programs, v. 15, p. 438.

Silver, L. T., and Mattinson, J. M., 1986, "Orphan Salinia" has a home: EOS (Transactions of the American Geophysical Union), v. 67, p. 1215.

Silver, L. T., Taylor, H. P., and Chappell, B., 1979, Some petrological, geochemical, and geochronological observations of the Peninsular Ranges batholith near the international border of the U.S.A. and Mexico, *in* Abbott, P. L., and Todd, V. R., eds., Mesozoic crystalline rocks: Peninsular Ranges batholith and pegmatites, Point Sal Ophiolite; San Diego, California, Department of Geological Sciences, San Diego State University, p. 84–110.

Stacey, J. S., and Kramers, J. D., 1975, Approximation of terrestrial lead isotopic evolution by a two-stage model: Earth and Planetary Science Letters, v. 26, p. 207–221.

Suppe, J. E., 1970, Offset of late Mesozoic basement terranes by the San Andreas fault system: Geological Society of America Bulletin, v. 81, p. 3253–3258.

Tilton, G. R., and Barreiro, B. A., 1980, Origin of lead in Andean calc-alkaline lavas, southern Peru: Science, v. 210, p. 1245–1247.

Trask, P. D., 1926, Geology of the Point Sur Quadrangle, California: California University Department of Geological Science Bulletin, v. 16, no. 6, p. 119–186.

Vedder, J. G., Howell, D. G., and McLean, H., 1983, Stratigraphy, sedimentation, and tectonic accretion of exotic terranes, southern Coast Ranges, California, *in* Watkins, J. S., and Drake, C. L., eds., Studies in continental margin geology: American Association of Petroleum Geologists Memoir 34, p. 471–496.

Vidal, Ph., and Clauer, N., 1981, Pb and Sr isotopic systematics of some basalts and sulfides from the East Pacific Rise at 21°N (project RITA): Earth and Planetary Science Letters, v. 55, p. 237–246.

Wiebe, R. A., 1970, Relations of granitic and gabbroic rocks, northern Santa Lucia Range, California: Geological Society of America Bulletin, v. 81, p. 105–116.

MANUSCRIPT SUBMITTED JULY 20, 1987
REVISED MANUSCRIPT SUBMITTED JANUARY 22, 1988
MANUSCRIPT ACCEPTED BY THE SOCIETY FEBRUARY 7, 1989

Geological Society of America
Memoir 174
1990

Chapter 14

Middle Cretaceous silicic metavolcanic rocks in the Kings Canyon area, central Sierra Nevada, California

Jason B. Saleeby
Division of Geological and Planetary Sciences, California Institute of Technology, Pasadena, California 91125
Ronald W. Kistler
U.S. Geological Survey, 345 Middlefield Road, Menlo Park, California 94025
Samuel Longiaru
Earth Sciences, University of California, Santa Cruz, California 95064
James G. Moore and Warren J. Nokleberg
U.S. Geological Survey, 345 Middlefield Road, Menlo Park, California 94025

ABSTRACT

Metamorphosed silicic volcanic and hypabyssal rocks of middle Cretaceous (110 to 100 Ma) age occur in two roof pendants in the Kings Canyon area of the central Sierra Nevada. The metavolcanic remnants are similar in age to or are only slightly older than the voluminous enclosing batholithic rocks. Thus, high to surface levels of the batholith are implied for this region. This is interesting considering that deep-level ($\sim$25 km) batholithic rocks of the same age as the metavolcanic rocks occur at the southern end of the range. Apparent structural continuity between these two regions suggests that the southern half of the range offers an oblique section through young ($\sim$100 Ma) sialic crust.

The middle Cretaceous ages of the two volcanic sequences are indicated by U/Pb zircon and Rb/Sr bulk-rock isochron data. The two isotopic systems agree very closely with one another. Some of the U/Pb systems within the Boyden Cave pendant are discordant due to the inheritance or entrainment of Proterozoic zircon. This is a common phenomenon in volcanic or plutonic rocks erupted or emplaced within the Kings sequence metamorphic framework, a belt of distinct pendants with abundant continent-derived sedimentary protoliths. In conjunction with other petrochemical parameters, lavas and magmas of this framework domain are shown to be contaminated with sedimentary admixtures. The contaminated domain of the batholith reflects the bounds of the Kings sequence framework, which along its eastern margin probably represents a major pre-batholith to early batholith tectonic break.

The middle Cretaceous metavolcanic sequences were apparently built on two distinctly different early Mesozoic substrates separated by a major tectonic break. In the Boyden Cave pendant, the substrate may be represented by the shallow to deep-marine Kings sequence; to the east in the Oak Creek pendant, the substrate consists of a thick silicic ignimbrite sequence. In both areas the middle Cretaceous rocks and adjacent sequences share intense ductile deformation fabrics. Earlier views that considered these fabrics as an expression of Jurassic orogenic deformation are in error. Structural and age relations indicate that the fabrics developed between 105 and 100 Ma and during the medial phases of Cretaceous composite batholith growth.

Saleeby, J. B., Kistler, R. W., Longiaru, S., Moore, J. G., and Nokleberg, W. J., 1990, Middle Cretaceous silicic metavolcanic rocks in the Kings Canyon area, central Sierra Nevada, California, *in* Anderson, J. L., ed., The nature and origin of Cordilleran magmatism: Boulder, Colorado, Geological Society of America Memoir 174.

INTRODUCTION

Sequences of silicic metavolcanic rock occur in the central and southern Sierra Nevada as parts of roof pendants within the eastern and axial zones of the Sierra Nevada batholith (Rinehart and Ross, 1957, 1964; Peck, 1980; Christensen, 1963; Moore, 1963; Huber and Rinehart, 1965; Kistler, 1966; Fiske and Tobisch, 1978; Saleeby and others, 1978). Metamorphic recrystallization and penetrative deformation have led most workers to interpret the metavolcanic rocks as part of the pre-Cretaceous wall-rock framework for the voluminous Cretaceous composite batholith. In particular, much of the deformation has been interpreted as a direct expression of the Late Jurassic Nevadan orogeny (Nokleberg and Kistler, 1980; Schweickert and others, 1984). Recent work, however, has revealed the widespread existence of strongly deformed Early and middle Cretaceous metavolcanic rocks (Nokleberg, 1981; Kistler and Swanson, 1981; Tobisch and others, 1986; Saleeby and Busby-Spera, 1986). The existence of such metavolcanic remnants, particularly those of middle Cretaceous age, carry important information on the crustal structure, tectonics, and petrogenesis of the Cretaceous Sierra Nevada batholith.

The Sierra Nevada batholith comprises chiefly Cretaceous age granitoid plutons that are arranged in a north-northwest–trending belt with almost continuous exposure for a length of ~500 km (Fig. 1). Metamorphic wall rocks for the batholith consist of the near-continuous western metamorphic belt, and steeply dipping screens, or roof pendants, which are most abundant in the central and southern segments of the range. Late Triassic and Jurassic plutons constitute part of the pre-batholithic framework, and are accordingly concentrated within, or in proximity to, the metavolcanic and metasedimentary wall rocks. In this chapter we focus on wall-rock remnants from the central part of the range that are well exposed near and at the headwaters of the Kings River. In this region and throughout regions to the south, the wall-rock remnants strongly reflect the primary structure of the Cretaceous batholith. Such remnants have traditionally been termed roof pendants. Structural configurations of the pendants, however, rarely resemble the roof of a given pluton. More commonly the pendants occur as steeply dipping screens or septa separating different plutons of the composite batholith. Throughout this paper we will refer to such screens as pendants.

The internal structures of the axial pendants commonly reflect transposition of primary features. The eastern pendants are likewise penetratively deformed, but primary features and stratigraphic relations are more commonly preserved. The traditional view of such pendant deformation as having resulted from pre-batholithic regional tectonic events is now shown to be only locally applicable (Nokleberg and Kistler, 1980; Saleeby and Busby-Spera, 1986; Tobisch and others, 1986; Longiaru, 1987; Saleeby and others, 1987, and this study). These studies have revealed that penetrative deformation in numerous pendants occurred in close conjunction with batholith emplacement. In some cases such synbatholithic deformation can be shown to have

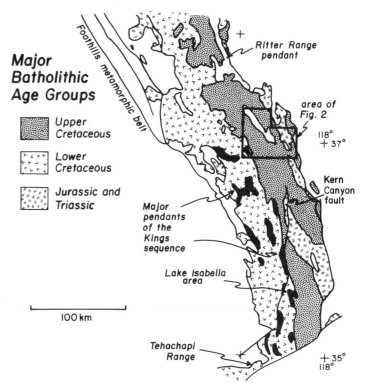

Figure 1. Regional map of the central and southern Sierra Nevada showing major age groupings of the batholith, major metamorphic wall-rock exposures, and areas referred to in text. Major pendants of Kings sequence shown in dark pattern in order to accentuate Kings sequence wall-rock domain of batholith (after Bateman and Clark, 1974; Saleeby and others, 1978). Other major metamorphic units are nondifferentiated in clear pattern.

been superposed over pre-batholithic regional structures. In other cases, however, little- or non-deformed primary features were strongly deformed during the emplacement interval of adjacent non- to strongly deformed batholithic plutons. The documentation of such deformation as having been imparted on silicic volcanic rocks only slightly predating the enclosing batholithic rocks is one of the main contributions of this chapter.

The documentation of virtually synbatholithic silicic volcanic rocks in the central part of the range augments recent efforts in geobarometry of the Cretaceous batholith (Sharry, 1981; Domenick and others, 1983; Elan, 1985; Dodge and others, 1986; Sams and Saleeby, 1988; Saleeby, 1989). The geobarometric studies, in conjunction with petrologic and geochronological studies, have revealed and placed constraints on the nature of mid- to lower-crustal batholithic rocks of mid-Cretaceous age throughout a number of areas in the southern Sierra. The work presented in this chapter sheds light on uppermost crustal phenomena for the same mid-Cretaceous phase of batholith petrogenesis. Additional remnants of mid-Cretaceous silicic metavolcanic rocks have been reported from the Ritter Range, Strawberry Mine, and Merced Peak areas to the north of the study area (Fiske and others, 1977; Peck, 1980; Kistler and Swanson, 1981; Nokleberg, 1981) and from the Lake Isabella area to the south (Saleeby and Busby-Spera, 1986). Consideration of the shallow and deep-level rocks and their regional map relations yields insight into batholith crustal structure, material transport patterns, and petrogenesis (Saleeby and others, 1986, 1987; Saleeby, 1989). This study provides an important link in the chain of information that will refine our crustal-scale view of the composite batholith.

GEOLOGIC SETTING

Silicic metavolcanic rocks occur primarily in three pendants in the upper drainages of the Kings River (Fig. 2). These consist of the Boyden Cave, Mount Goddard, and Oak Creek pendants. The Boyden Cave pendant contains a substantial sequence of pre-Cretaceous metasedimentary rock, whereas the Mount Goddard and Oak Creek pendants are nearly entirely metavolcanic. The pendants are separated by a series of batholithic plutons which in general show a north-northwest pattern in maximum dimension. Thus the pendants are grossly concordant with the structure of the host batholith, although fine-scale discordant contacts between pendants and plutons are common.

The batholithic plutons range from gabbroids to granitoids; granodioritic compositions are by far the most abundant. The gabbroidal plutons of the study area for the most part occur as small screens or clots between larger granitoid masses (Fig. 2). Likewise, a number of very narrow screens of metasedimentary and metavolcanic rock can be seen separating adjacent batholithic plutons. Jurassic-age plutons are shown in close association with the Oak Creek pendant.

Pb/U zircon ages on the batholithic plutons from Chen and Moore (1982) and sample locations from this study are plotted in Figure 2. The Cretaceous ages range from 110 to 85 Ma, a range that is typical for the axial and eastern zones of the central segment of the Sierra Nevada batholith. Ages ranging back to ~125 Ma occur along the western zone of the batholith (Saleeby and Sharp, 1980; Stern and others, 1981; Chen and Moore, 1982). The west-to-east age progression in the Cretaceous batholith is semicontinuous at a regional scale, a pattern noted earlier by K/Ar age patterns (Evernden and Kistler, 1970). Pre-Cretaceous plutons are spatially related to pendants and, as discussed below, are probably genetically related to the older pre-Cretaceous metavolcanic sequences.

The Cretaceous batholithic belt shows a pronounced geochemical zonation pattern in addition to the age zonation. In the field, this pattern is clearly expressed by a concentration of gabbroidal and tonalitic rocks in the west and granodioritic rocks in the east. Initial $^{87}Sr/^{86}Sr$ (Sr_i) values reflect this pattern; values between 0.703 and 0.704 occur along the western margin of the batholith, and values of >0.706 are typical of the axial and eastern zones (Kistler and Peterman, 1973, 1978; Saleeby and Chen, 1978). Initial Pb (Pb_i) isotopes show an analogous pattern to Sr_i with the least radiogenic in the west; however, a reversal occurs along the axial to eastern zones of the batholith, yielding an axial radiogenic high (Chen and Tilton, 1978, and 1984,

written communication). The eastern edge of the radiogenic ridge in general corresponds to pronounced changes in the oxygen isotopic composition of the batholith, Rb/Sr relative abundance patterns, and the oxidation state of the batholith. The significance of these patterns is discussed below in conjunction with tectonic considerations.

The geochemical zonation patterns in the Cretaceous batholith are considered here and in Kistler (this volume) to represent contrasting lithosphere types within the pre-batholithic framework. Pertinent to our discussions are the structural and stratigraphic settings of middle Cretaceous metavolcanic sequences which appear to reflect these lithosphere types. In terms of stratigraphic settings, the Boyden Cave silicic rocks belong to a distinct framework domain termed the Kings sequence (Bateman and Clark, 1974; Saleeby and others, 1978). The Kings sequence consists of shelf and basin metasedimentary rocks with subordinate metavolcanic rocks. The Kings sequence is of early Mesozoic and possibly Paleozoic age, and constitutes the axial to western pendants along the southern half of the Sierra Nevada (Fig. 1). In contrast, the Oak Creek pendant Cretaceous rocks were built on a thick early Mesozoic silicic to intermediate metavolcanic sequence that probably included the Mount Goddard pendant as well as the Ritter Range pendant to the north (Fig. 1). The Ritter Range metavolcanic sequence was built unconformably across complex Paleozoic marine basin strata. Remnants of such strata may be preserved in small pendants consisting of hornfels, schist, and marble in the region of the Oak Creek pendant (Fig. 2; Moore, 1963). Similar metasedimentary rocks are dispersed along the high Sierra crest between the Oak Creek and Ritter Range areas. We now turn to the more detailed geologic relations within the Boyden Cave and Oak Creek pendants.

Boyden Cave pendant

The Boyden Cave pendant underlies ~100 km^2 of the deeply incised canyons of the South and Middle forks of the Kings River. The pendant, as well as its internal contacts and structures, trends northwest and is generally subvertical. Metasedimentary rocks of the Kings sequence constitute the western exposures of the pendant, and metamorphosed silicic volcanic, hypabyssal, and metaplutonic rocks constitute the eastern exposures. The metasedimentary rocks consist of an ~5-km-thick structural sequence of metamorphosed quartzite, marble, calcareous mudstone, pelite, and turbiditic strata. Structural-metamorphic units are shown in Figure 2. Direct age constraints for most units are lacking, while Early Jurassic marine fossils have been recovered from the eastern unit (Moore and Dodge, 1962; Jones and Moore, 1973; Saleeby and others, 1978). Facing data and internal stratigraphic relations are equivocal throughout the pendant due to intense polyphase deformation (Moore and Marks, 1972; Saleeby and others, 1978; Moore and others, 1979; Moore and Nokleberg, 1989).

Metamorphosed silicic volcanic and intrusive rocks constituting the eastern part of the Boyden Cave pendant were interpreted as the upper levels of the lower Mesozoic section (Moore

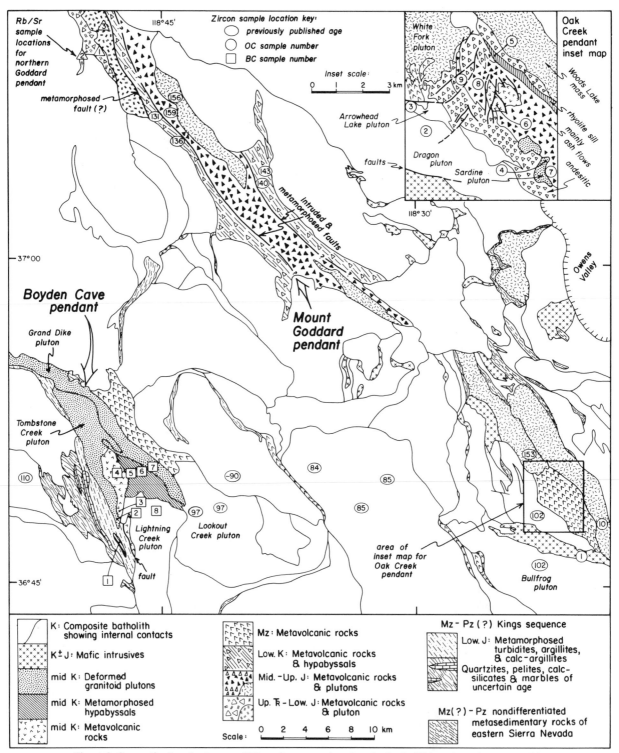

Figure 2. Generalized geologic map of Kings Canyon region showing batholithic units and metamorphic pendants. Major contacts are from Moore and Sisson (1987). Zircon ages on batholithic plutons are from Chen and Moore (1982) and for Goddard pendant from Tobisch and others (1986). Zircon samples for this study are coded as BC = Boyden Cave pendant and adjacent plutons, and OC = Oak Creek pendant and adjacent plutons. Inset shows a more detailed geological map of the Oak Creek pendant with locations of U/Pb zircon samples (after Moore, 1963; Longiaru, 1987).

and Marks, 1972; Saleeby and others, 1978). This study, however, shows that these rocks are middle Cretaceous in age and consist, from west to east, of: (1) schistose granodiorite of Tombstone Creek and the metamorphosed dacite porphyry of Boulder Creek; (2) an ~1-km-thick sequence dominated by rhyolitic ash-flow tuff; (3) an additional 1- to 2-km-thick sequence dominated by subvolcanic intrusives including metamorphosed hypersthene dacite; (4) the protomylonitic granitic pluton of the Grand Dike; and (5) an eastern sequence of mixed silicic to intermediate volcanic and volcaniclastic rocks.

Intrusion of the middle Cretaceous hypabyssal and plutonic rocks into the Boyden Cave metasedimentary rocks is indicated by the intrusive contacts of the granodiorite of Tombstone Creek and the metadacite porphyry of Boulder Creek. These intrusive relations, however, do not clearly indicate deposition of the metavolcanic rocks on the metasedimentary rocks. Only remnants of a fault contact are observed between the metavolcanic and metasedimentary sequences (Moore and Nokleberg, 1989). In most places the schistose granodiorite of Tombstone Creek intervenes.

Metasedimentary and metavolcanic rocks of the Boyden Cave pendant are pervaded by a strong planar north-northwest–trending deformation fabric, which in metasedimentary rocks is locally seen to be axial planar to tight and steeply southeast-plunging folds and to be superposed on earlier structures (Saleeby and others, 1978; Nokleberg and Kistler, 1980). This deformation fabric is expressed in metavolcanic protoliths by flattening of pumice lapilli, rare clasts and phenocrysts, and the development of a fine schistosity in groundmass materials. The middle Cretaceous hypabyssal rocks are inhomogeneously deformed; fabrics range from protomylonitic or highly schistose to weakly schistose with incipient phenocryst deformation. Strong deformation fabrics also occur in the schistose granodiorite of Tombstone Creek and the protomylonite granite of the Grand Dike. Deformation of the metavolcanic-metaplutonic sequence occurred under upper greenschist- to lower amphibolite-facies conditions.

The strong north-northwest–trending fabric that pervades the Boyden Cave pendant metavolcanic and metasedimentary rocks is observed to overprint earlier deformation fabrics and structures in the metasedimentary sequence (Nokleberg and Kistler, 1980; Moore and Nokleberg, 1989). The earlier structures are absent in the metavolcanic sequence. The general structural chronology for the pendant can be summarized in four stages. (1) Prior to eruption of the volcanic rocks, the metasedimentary sequence was deformed under amphibolite-facies conditions and intruded by Early Cretaceous (~110 Ma) batholithic rocks. (2) Immediately following the eruption of the volcanic rocks (~105 Ma), the volcanic and metasedimentary sequences were faulted into contact with one another and pervasively deformed together. (3) During the later stages of deformation (~103 Ma), tabular bodies of granodiorite and granite (Tombstone Creek and Grand Dike units) were syntectonically intruded parallel to the north-northwest–trending deformation fabric. (4) Post-deformational plutonism commenced at ~100 Ma.

Oak Creek pendant

The Oak Creek pendant underlies ~22 km² of the high, rugged crest of the eastern Sierra Nevada at the head of the South Fork of the Kings River. In addition, an area of greater size is underlain by several Jurassic plutons that are closely associated with the pendant, and that constitute part of the pre-batholithic framework of the region. The Oak Creek pendant, as well as many of its internal contacts and structures, trends northwest. It consists exclusively of silicic to subordinate mafic metavolcanic and subvolcanic intrusive rocks. Some of the more detailed relations within the metavolcanic rocks are shown in the inset map of Figure 2 (Moore, 1963; Longiaru, 1987).

Metavolcanic rocks of the Oak Creek pendant include two stratigraphic sequences separated by a complex angular unconformity. The older uppermost Middle Jurassic rocks consist of a steeply dipping, apparently westward-facing sequence of rhyolitic to dacitic ash-flow tuffs overlain by andesitic to basaltic pyroclastic and flow deposits. Although broken by faults, the sequence appears to be depositionally conformable.

Rhyolitic to dacitic volcanic rocks dominate the older sequence. Lithic and nonlithic quartz-porphyritic ash-flow tuffs are by far the most common rocks, but flow rocks and felsic volcanic breccias occur locally. Ash-flow tuffs dominate the eastern and stratigraphically lower two-thirds of the sequence, but are also present as minor constituents within higher parts of the sequence to the west, where they are interbedded with andesitic to basaltic pyroclastic deposits and flows. Typically, the ash-flow deposits are rich in quartz and feldspar phenocrysts (as much as 30 or more percent volume), and most outcrops contain up to 5 percent lapilli-sized lithic fragments of andesite and rhyolite. All the ash flows possess a foliation defined either as a fine, penetrative cleavage or as the preferred alignment of elongate phenocrysts or lithic fragments. Deformation and metamorphism took place under upper greenschist-facies conditions (Longiaru, 1987).

A high degree of homogeneity in the Middle Jurassic ash-flow sequence suggests that the entire 2 km of exposed section was derived from a single eruptive source and therefore may have been deposited within a relatively brief period of time. The restricted compositional range, as well as limited variation in the concentration, composition, and size of the phenocryst and lithic populations suggests that there was no substantive change in the eruptive source or distance from the eruptive center throughout the depositional history of the sequence. As shown below, zircon populations from three widely spaced ash-flow exposures yield very similar ages.

Andesitic and basaltic volcaniclastic and flow rocks overlie the ash-flow tuffs and dominate the western part of the Oak Creek pendant. Rocks of this composition also occur within the lowermost part of the Middle Jurassic sequence near the eastern edge of the pendant. In most areas the intermediate to mafic rocks are massive; contacts between individual flows or sills are only locally resolved. Most of the flows are andesitic in composition; basaltic-andesites are less abundant. Volcaniclastic rocks are also locally abundant and consist of andesitic and basaltic tuffs, lapilli tuffs and agglomerates, minor tuff breccias, accretionary lapilli tuffs, and probable epiclastic deposits. Bedding within the volcaniclastic rocks is generally well developed with sparse facing data indicating up to the west.

Mineral assemblages in the intermediate to mafic rocks indicate upper greenschist- and locally lower amphibolite-facies conditions (Longiaru, 1987). Most of the rocks possess moderate to strong foliation, except for basaltic flow rocks which are commonly only weakly foliated. Metamorphic grade and textural reconstitution increase toward intrusive contacts.

As demonstrated below, samples from the intermediate to mafic rocks lie on the same Rb/Sr isochron as the zircon ash-flow samples and yield an isochron age identical to that determined by U/Pb techniques on the zircon. This indicates the eruption of the entire silicic to mafic sequence over a geologically short time interval, and either derivation of the respective magmas from a common source or, alternatively, multiple sources with similar time-integrated Sr-isotopic evolutions.

A middle Cretaceous volcanic sequence overlies the Middle Jurassic sequence with pronounced angular unconformity, and consists of a moderately northeastward-dipping series of well-bedded rhyolitic to basaltic tuffs, lapilli tuffs, minor tuff breccias, flows, and volcanic-related sills. The contact between the Jurassic and Cretaceous volcanic sequences is visible only locally due to extensive rotational block faulting and scree cover. The Cretaceous sequence is divided into two major units on the basis of overall composition. The first unit consists of rhyolitic to dacitic ash-flow tuffs, lapilli tuffs, minor breccias, and probable volcanic-related sills, and the second unit consists of andesitic tuffs, lapilli tuffs, and andesitic to basaltic flows.

Tuffs and lapilli tuffs are the most common rock types within the silicic unit, although locally coarse breccias are present. Tuffs are commonly less porphyritic than those within the Middle Jurassic sequence, but like the Jurassic rocks they commonly contain mafic lithic fragments. A moderate foliation is developed within the silicic volcanic rocks and is defined by either a penetrative microfoliation or by the elongation and alignment of lithic fragments. In thin section, the foliation is defined by the alignment of slightly deformed, elliptical quartz grains or by a preferred orientation of micaceous minerals.

The intermediate and mafic volcanic rocks of the Cretaceous sequence are generally well bedded and consist of fine tuffs, lapilli tuffs, and thin flows. Locally, small zones of accretionary lapilli tuff are present. Coarser volcaniclastic rocks such as agglomerates, volcanic breccias, or volcanic conglomerates are rare. A metamorphic foliation is commonly defined by the alignment of biotite flakes within the matrix and within lithic fragments. Metamorphic mineral assemblages within the intermediate to mafic volcanic rocks as well as the silicic rocks are in the greenschist facies (Longiaru, 1987).

Intrusive rocks that on the basis of age data and field relations are likely to be closely related to the middle Cretaceous sequence cut the Jurassic sequence. These consist of a 300-m-wide rhyolitic sill that extends along strike for at least 3.5 km and the small alaskite granite Sardine pluton. Both were deformed with their Jurassic metavolcanic host rocks, but the Sardine pluton is observed to have cut an earlier fabric in its Jurassic host rocks. As discussed below, plutons with slightly younger ages are nondeformed and cut the deformation fabrics that pervade the pendant.

Granitoid plutons of Late Jurassic age are also closely associated with the Oak Creek pendant (Moore, 1963; Chen and Moore, 1982). These consist of the Woods Lake mass of the Tinemaha granodiorite, and the White Fork pluton. The former is a pervasively foliated porphyritic granodiorite; the latter is an inhomogeneously foliated and sheared granodiorite. Both plutons are cut by a myriad of basaltic to granodioritic dikes of the Late Jurassic Independence dike swarm. The plutons and the dike swarm intrude the Middle Jurassic metavolcanic sequence, and share the north-northwest–trending foliation that pervades both the Jurassic and overlying Cretaceous metavolcanic rocks.

Detailed mapping within the Oak Creek pendant and finite strain studies on a variety of the volcanic rocks from both the Jurassic and Cretaceous sequences (Moore, 1963; Longiaru, 1987), in conjunction with age data discussed below, indicate the following sequence of structural events following the eruption of the Middle Jurassic volcanic rocks: (1) rotation and moderate deformation of the Jurassic volcanic sequence along north-northwest trends followed closely by the intrusion of the Woods Lake pluton, all at ~165 Ma; (2) intrusion of the White Fork pluton at ~153 Ma with further deformation along north-northwest trends; (3) intrusion of the Independence dike swarm at ~148 Ma along the north-northwest–trending deformation fabrics (Chen and Moore, 1982); (4) erosion of the Jurassic rocks between ~148 and ~110 Ma; (5) eruption and deposition of the middle Cretaceous volcanic sequence at ~110 Ma in conjunction with block faulting; (6) penetrative ductile deformation of both the Jurassic and Cretaceous volcanic rocks together between 110 and 105 Ma; and (7) initiation of the emplacement of post-deformational batholithic plutons possibly as early as 105 Ma, but definitely by 102 Ma. Based on the finite strain studies of Longiaru (1987), the 110- to 105-Ma deformation event is shown to have imposed the greatest strain on the entire metavolcanic sequence.

GEOCHRONOLOGICAL DATA

Samples of ash-flow tuffs, subvolcanic intrusives, and intrusive rocks carrying important structural relations were collected from or adjacent to the Boyden Cave and Oak Creek pendants for U/Pb zircon studies. A number of the zircon samples, as well as additional samples covering as wide a compositional range as possible, were also analyzed by Rb/Sr bulk-rock techniques. Appendix 1 gives sample locations and brief petrographic data for the samples. Table 1 gives the U/Pb data and information on analytical techniques and uncertainties; Table 2 gives the same for the Rb/Sr data. The primary aim of the isotopic studies was to establish protolith ages for the main volcanic sequences of the Boyden Cave and Oak Creek pendants, and to place absolute age constraints on the major deformational features. As shown below, the Pb/U and Rb/Sr data are in close agreement, so the two isotopic systems will be discussed together. The petrogenetic and structural implications of the isotopic data will be discussed below.

Discussion of the isotopic data centers on the graphic representations presented in strontium evolution and U/Pb concordia diagrams. The U/Pb systematics are represented by $^{207}Pb/^{206}U$-$^{238}U/^{206}Pb$ concordia diagrams (after Tera and Wasserburg, 1972). Internal concordance is used here to denote agreement of U-Pb and Pb-Pb ages of a given analysis within analytical uncertainty expressed graphically by the intersection of concordia with the error bars. External concordance is defined as agreement, or graphic overlap, in internally concordant ages from multiple fractions of a given sample or multiple samples from a given rock unit.

An in-depth zircon geochronological transect was published for the Sierra Nevada batholith along the general latitude of the Kings River (Chen and Moore, 1982). Intercalibration data between Chen and Moore's study and this study are presented in Table 3. The intercalibrations include work performed on the same zircon separates, or on separates from different samples of the same map unit. There is a clear pattern to the data of Table 3. Those samples that are externally concordant yield reasonable agreement (at 1 percent or analytical uncertainty levels) between the two labs. This includes the Mt. Whitney, Dragon, western Foothills, and Woods Lake units. Discordant samples yield more complex results. The JS data for the Goddard pendant unit were reported in Tobisch and others (1987). The discordance patterns are clearly indicative of minor inheritance or entrainment of Proterozoic zircon (Saleeby, 1987; Tobisch and others, 1986). Replicate analyses of the medium size fraction are in agreement (Table 3), but the JS data on fine and coarse fractions reveal an inheritance or entrainment discordance mechanism.

Replicate work performed on the Tombstone Creek and Lightning Creek units (Table 3) are highly pertinent to this study. Samples 13, 14, and BC2 were taken from the schistose granodiorite of Tombstone Creek. The initial results in Chen and Moore (1982) were difficult to interpret, and in conjunction with the detailed field study of Moore and Nokleberg (1989), a more suitable sample was selected for this study (BC2). The BC2 results are externally concordant yet slightly older than Chen and Moore's internally concordant sample (14). The sample 14 population is relatively enriched in U and may have undergone minor disturbance. Sample 13 clearly shows the effects of inheritance or entrainment. As discussed below, the geological setting of the Tombstone Creek unit in conjunction with the other age data are consistent with the externally concordant ages of sample BC2 representing the igneous age of the unit.

The data from the Lightning Creek unit are also complex. Chen and Moore (1982) reported an internally concordant age of 108 Ma on a single intermediate size fraction. Three size fractions

of the same population yield a discordant and two externally concordant ages. As discussed below, the coarse discordant fraction shows the effects of inheritance or entrainment. Unlike the Goddard sample, however, Chen and Moore's data do not fall on the discordia mixing line. This is not surprising considering the heterogeneity observed in the coarser fraction(s) of the population, which includes a wide array of colors, morphologies, and inclusion densities. As discussed below, the geologic setting of the Lightning Creek unit in conjunction with the other age data and discordance patterns are consistent with the externally concordant ages representing the igneous age of the unit.

Boyden Cave pendant

Two ash-flow tuffs (BC 3 and 4), three small hypabyssal intrusives (BC 1, 5, and 6), and two deformed tabular plutons (BC 2 and 7) were sampled for U/Pb zircon age determination. The ash-flow tuffs and one of the hypabyssal intrusive samples (BC1) are notably contaminated with Middle Proterozoic zircon, and yield significant discordances. The other samples are concordant, or very slightly discordant, probably due to minor inheritance or entrainment.

Concordia plots for the ash-flow tuffs are given in Figure 3A. Sample BC3 yielded four fairly homogeneous size fractions that define a chord with a 104 ± 2 Ma lower intercept and a 1,630 ± 30 Ma upper intercept (r factor = 0.9979 where 1 = perfect linear array). The 45 to 62 μm fraction from BC4 is highly discordant and heterogeneous; the other two fractions are uniform and plot near concordia at 106 Ma, which is also the lower intercept age. The upper intercept derived from the aberrant fraction is 1,488 ± 15 Ma. The BC3 ash-flow tuff appears to have inherited Early Proterozoic zircon from its magmatic source, such that the older zircon components were overgrown by substantial cognate zircon prior to the 104-Ma eruption event. The derivative systematics show a strong relation between grain size and proportion of inherited component (Saleeby, 1987). In contrast, the sample BC4 population is dominated by cognate zircon crystallized just prior to the ~106-Ma eruption event. The highly discordant fraction probably reflects entrainment of detrital Middle Proterozoic zircon at relatively high levels prior to eruption. Such entrainment results in poor grain-size proportion of contaminant relations due to the relatively short time interval of magma residence for the contaminants (Saleeby, 1987).

The likelihood for the contamination of the Cretaceous magma systems by Proterozoic detrital zircon from Kings sequence metasedimentary rocks is demonstrated by detrital zircon analyses performed by J. H. Chen (*in* Moore and others, 1979). Boyden Cave quartzite unit detrital zircon ages of t $^{206}Pb/^{238}U$ = 1,511 Ma and t $^{207}Pb/^{206}Pb$ = 2,000 Ma, and turbidite unit ages of t $^{206}Pb/^{238}U$ = 542 Ma and t $^{207}Pb/^{206}Pb$ = 1,310 Ma are reported. Such detrital zircon ages are similar to comparable Kings sequence rock units from the southernmost Sierra Nevada (Saleeby and others, 1987). Chords projected from a 100-Ma lower intercept through the Boyden Cave detrital zircon data

TABLE 1. ZIRCON ISOTOPIC AGE DATA

Specimen	Fraction† (µm)	Amount Analyzed (mg)	Concentrations		206Pb/204Pb	Atomic ratios			Isotopic ages (Ma)§		
			238U (ppm)	206Pb* (ppm)		206Pb*/238U	207Pb*/235U	207Pb*/206Pb*	206Pb*/238U	207Pb*/235U	207Pb*/206Pb*
BC 1	<45	10.5	206	4.5	490	0.02502(18)	0.1956	0.05674(26)	159	181	481 ± 9
	45-80	6.8	247	6.1	247	0.01694(13)	0.1146	0.04908(41)	108	110	151 ± 20
	>80	10.8	257	8.5	2,028	0.03812(26)	0.4271	0.08130(22)	241	361	1,229 ± 5
BC 2	<45	7.5	773	10.7	385	0.01605(12)	0.1062	0.04804(26)	103	103	101 ± 13
	45-80	10.5	838	11.6	748	0.01602(11)	0.1059	0.04799(15)	102	102	99 ± 5
BC 3	<45	3.2	715	10.1	4,680	0.01683(13)	0.1153	0.04968(08)	108	111	180 ± 4
	45-62	3.5	603	9.6	2,113	0.01837(14)	0.1375	0.05432(07)	117	131	384 ± 4
	60-80	2.9	535	8.9	2,037	0.01931(15)	0.1520	0.05711(08)	123	143	495 ± 4
	80-120	2.2	607	11.4	1,498	0.02164(15)	0.1838	0.06163(08)	138	171	661 ± 3
BC 4	<45	5.7	412	5.9	503	0.01653(12)	0.1106	0.04855(17)	106	107	126 ± 8
	45-62	12.9	229	6.1	1,391	0.03088(21)	0.2998	0.07043(25)	196	266	941 ± 7
	62-80	6.5	387	5.6	774	0.01677(12)	0.1120	0.04831(13)	107	108	115 ± 6
BC 5	<45	8.6	1,198	16.8	8,934	0.01621(11)	0.1079	0.04829(10)	104	104	113 ± 5
	45-80	9.3	564	7.9	7,985	0.01614(11)	0.1077	0.04830(06)	103	104	113 ± 4
BC 6	45-62	12.8	779	10.7	3,863	0.01583(11)	0.1050	0.04813(13)	101	101	105 ± 7
	62-80	12.2	810	11.2	3,437	0.01604(11)	0.1068	0.04829(11)	103	103	113 ± 6
BC 7	<45	7.6	901	12.6	1,948	0.01617(16)	0.1080	0.04842(15)	103	104	120 ± 7
	45-80	16.7	836	11.8	2,248	0.01635(16)	0.1087	0.04829(14)	105	105	113 ± 7
BC 8	<45	7.4	825	11.2	4,181	0.01565(13)	0.1036	0.04803(08)	100	100	100 ± 5
	45-62	6.6	523	7.1	4,168	0.01572(10)	0.1041	0.04806(13)	101	101	102 ± 7
	62-100	3.9	336	4.7	6,591	0.01614(10)	0.1079	0.04851(09)	103	104	124 ± 5

TABLE 1. ZIRCON ISOTOPIC AGE DATA (continued)

Specimen	Fraction† (µm)	Amount Analyzed (mg)	Concentrations		206Pb/204Pb	Atomic ratios			Isotopic ages (Ma)§		
			238U (ppm)	206Pb* (ppm)		$\frac{206Pb*}{238U}$	$\frac{207Pb*}{235U}$	$\frac{207Pb*}{206Pb*}$	$\frac{206Pb*}{238U}$	$\frac{207Pb*}{235U}$	$\frac{207Pb*}{206Pb*}$
OC 1	<45	2.4	665	9.2	2,703	0.01601(13)	0.1059	0.04798(17)	102	102	99 ± 8
OC 2	<45	11.6	362	5.0	3,221	0.01587(11)	0.1053	0.04814(12)	102	102	105 ± 6
	45-80	17.3	263	3.6	1,965	0.01595(12)	0.1054	0.04803(14)	102	102	101 ± 6
OC 3	<45	10.0	1,639	23.3	2,438	0.01644(13)	0.1093	0.04823(12)	105	105	110 ± 7
	45-80	11.8	1,462	20.8	1,414	0.01646(11)	0.1092	0.04815(15)	105	105	106 ± 8
OC 4	<45	25.2	967	13.5	3,958	0.01614(11)	0.1069	0.04806(12)	103	103	102 ± 7
	45-80	19.3	732	10.5	4,102	0.01659(11)	0.1103	0.04821(07)	106	106	109 ± 5
OC 5	45-62	11.9	396	5.8	188	0.01682(15)	0.1118	0.04821(32)	108	108	109 ± 16
	62-80	7.9	303	4.5	1,793	0.01728(12)	0.1143	0.04799(51)	110	109	99 ± 24
OC 6a	<45	5.9	912	13.4	6,818	0.01692(11)	0.1124	0.04823(09)	108	108	110 ± 5
OC 6b	<45	2.6	490	7.2	252	0.01702(18)	0.1126	0.04801(63)	109	108	100 ± 30
	45-80	7.5	400	6.0	142	0.01724(20)	0.1145	0.04820(25)	110	110	109 ± 13
OC 7	<45	6.0	433	9.6	440	0.02571(21)	0.1752	0.04946(20)	164	164	169 ± 10
	45-80	11.2	590	13.1	919	0.02574(21)	0.1763	0.04969(17)	164	165	180 ± 9
	80-120	15.7	485	10.9	1,732	0.02587(21)	0.1766	0.04952(15)	165	165	172 ± 8
OC 8	<45	8.6	675	15.1	2,174	0.02580(17)	0.1756	0.04939(11)	164	164	166 ± 6
	45-60	10.7	661	14.8	2,059	0.02587(18)	0.1768	0.04938(10)	165	165	165 ± 6
OC 9	<62	12.1	625	14.2	923	0.02621(18)	0.1786	0.04945(11)	167	167	169 ± 6
	62-100	8.4	476	10.8	1,534	0.02615(18)	0.1777	0.04932(14)	166	166	163 ± 7
OC 10	<100	9.0	974	21.9	3,308	0.02593(21)	0.1764	0.04936(15)	165	165	165 ± 7

*Radiogenic; nonradiogenic correction based on 40 picogram blank Pb (1:18.78:15.61:38.50) and initial Pb approximations: 1:19.34:15.68:38.97 for BC suite and 1:18.7:15.6:38.7 for OC suite (after Chen and Moore, 1982, and written communication, 1985, specimens 14, 15, 24, 25, and 26 of their Table 1.)

†Fractions separated by grain size and magnetic properties. Magnetic properties are given as non-magnetic split at side/front slopes for 1.7 amps on Franz Isodynamic Separator. Samples hand-picked to 99.9% purity prior to dissolution. Dissolution and chemical exraction techniques modified from Krogh (1973).

§Decay constants used in age calculation: λ238U = 1.55125 x 10⁻10, λ235U = 9.8485 x 10⁻10 Jaffey and others, 1971); 238U/235U atom = 137.88. Uncertainties in 206Pb*/206Pb* are given as (±) in last two figures. Uncertainties calculated by quadratic sum of total derivatives of 238U and 206Pb* concentration and 207Pb*/206Pb* equations with error differentials defined as: 1. Isotope ratio determinations from standard errors (σ/√n) of mass spectrometer runs plus uncertainties in fractionation corrections based on multiple runs of NBS 981, 982, 983, and U500 standards; 2. Spike concentrations from range of deviations in multiple calibrations with normal solutions; 3. Spike compositions from external precisions of multiple isotope ratio determinations; 4. Uncertainty in natural 238U/235U from Chen and Wasserburg (1981); and 5. Nonradiogenic Pb isotopic compositions from uncertainties in isotope ratio determinations of blank Pb and uncertainties in composition of initial Pb from estimates of regional variations based on references given above and consideration of rock type.

TABLE 2. RUBIDIUM AND STRONTIUM ABUNDANCE AND ISOTOPIC DATA

Specimen Number	Rb (ppm)	Sr (ppm)	Rb/Sr (wt)	$^{87}Rb/^{86}Sr$ Atom	$^{87}Sr/^{86}Sr$ Measured
Boyden Cave Pendant					
A	112	336	0.333	0.964	0.70814 ± 5
B	173	223	0.726	2.24	0.71027 ± 3
C	148	246	0.602	1.74	0.70951 ± 5
D	166	423	0.392	1.13	0.70845 ± 7
E	293	17.3	16.94	49.33	0.77810 ± 5
F	199	82	2.43	7.04	0.71720 ± 6
G	118	329	0.359	1.039	0.70827 ± 8
H	111	343	0.324	0.938	0.70811 ± 6
I	82.8	718	0.115	0.333	0.70731 ± 7
J	183	339	0.540	1.56	0.70900 ± 4
K	162	268	0.604	1.75	0.70930 ± 4
L	210	92.2	2.28	6.60	0.71630 ± 2
M	133	240	0.554	1.60	0.70909 ± 3
N	107	371	0.228	0.833	0.70785 ± 6
O	146	223	0.655	1.90	0.70953 ± 5
P	124	218	0.569	1.65	0.70915 ± 8
Q	102	118	0.864	2.50	0.71042 ± 8
R	140	264	0.530	1.53	0.70898 ± 9
S	117	198	0.591	1.71	0.70935 ± 6
T	121	112	1.08	3.13	0.71134 ± 5
U	85	364	0.234	0.677	0.70826 ± 4
BC1	31.3	797	0.039	0.114	0.70378 ± 5
BC2	145	162	0.895	2.591	0.71112 ± 2
BC7	253	21.9	11.5	33.58	0.75665 ± 4
Oak Creek Pendant–younger unit					
OC2	63.2	475	0.133	0.384	0.70622 ± 2
OC3	126	46.9	2.69	7.790	0.71676 ± 2
OC4	114	150	0.760	2.199	0.70882 ± 3
OC5	113	107	1.06	3.068	0.70993 ± 2
OC6a	74.2	343	0.216	0.625	0.70799 ± 2
OC6b	133	156	0.853	2.469	0.71001 ± 2
Oak Creek Pendant –older unit					
OC7	250	190	1.32	3.822	0.71559 ± 2
OC8	149	235	0.634	1.835	0.71123 ± 2
OC9	254	186	1.37	3.968	0.71588 ± 1
V	106	529	0.200	0.579	0.70818 ± 4
W	78.4	644	0.122	0.353	0.70739 ± 2
X	54.3	569	0.095	0.274	0.70737 ± 2
Y	142	374	0.380	1.100	0.70933 ± 2
Mount Goddard Pendant					
1	108	173	0.622	1.80	0.71151 ± 5
2	109	97	1.12	3.24	0.71560 ± 3
3	110	417	0.264	0.763	0.70808 ± 2

Rb and Sr concentrations were determined by X-ray dispersive techniques; uncertainties in the Rb/Sr values determined by this method are ± 3 percent or less. Sr isotope ratios were measured with a 90°sector, 46 cm mass spectrometer using double rhenium filament mode of ionization, and with automated data collection and reduction. Replicate analyses of the Eimer and Amend, and NBS $SrCO_3$ standards yielded $^{87}Sr/^{86}Sr$ values respectively of 0.708000 ± 0.00003 and 0.71023 ± 0.00003. All Sr isotopic ratios are normalized to a $^{86}Sr/^{88}Sr$ value of 0.1194.

TABLE 3. COMPARISON OF U/Pb ZIRCON AGE DETERMINATIONS PERFORMED DURING THIS STUDY
ON SPECIMENS ORIGINALLY REPORTED IN CHEN AND MOORE (1982)

Unit name	Specimen Number*	Fraction Properties	^{238}U ppm	$\dfrac{^{206}Pb}{^{204}Pb}$	Isotopic ages (Ma)[†]		
					$^{206}Pb/^{238}U$	$^{207}Pb/^{235}U$	$^{207}Pb/^{206}Pb$
Mt. Whitney	49	45-80μ	1064	10000	83.4	83.5	88
	49(JS)	45-62μ	1331	13324	83.4	83.5	89
	49(JS)	62-80μ	910	13428	83.9	83.9	84
Dragon	25	45-80μ	838	1563	102.5	102.8	112
	OC2	<45μ	362	3221	101.5	101.6	105
	OC2	45-80μ	263	1965	102.0	101.9	101
Western Foothills	1	45-80μ	176	1501	114.2	114.1	113
	1(JS)	74-180μ	376	3738	115.0	115.6	126
Tombstone Creek	13	45-80μ	886	5882	115.7	117.2	149
	14	45-80μ	1076	4762	99.1	99.4	105
	BC2	<45μ	773	385	102.7	102.5	101
	BC2	45-80μ	838	748	102.4	102.3	99
Lightning Creek	15	45-80μ	897	901	108.0	107.9	106
	BC8	<45μ	825	4181	100.1	100.1	100
	BC8	45-62μ	523	4168	100.6	100.6	102
	BC8	62-100μ	336	6591	103.2	104.0	124
Goddard pendant	75	45-80μ	315.7	1852	157.0	158.8	186
	75(JS)	<45μ	396	2140	155.8	155.7	155
	75(JS)	45-80μ	304	1509	158.3	159.2	176
	75(JS)	80-120μ	171	1010	160.6	163.1	208
Woods Lake mass	26	45-80μ	1007	5556	164.4	165.1	176
	26	<45μ	1155	5882	165.2	165.5	171
	OC10	<100μ	974	3308	165.0	165.0	165

*Specimen numbers refer to those reported in Chen and Moore (1982). JS refers to replicate analyses performed on zircon separates obtained from J. H. Chen (see Chen and Moore, 1982, for field locations). Additionally, BC8 and OC10 data reported in this study were performed on Chen's separates, whereas OC2 and BC2 were recollected for this study.
[†]Blanket analytical uncertainties of ±0.7 m.y. and ±12 m.y. are reported for $^{206}Pb/^{238}U$ and $^{207}Pb/^{206}Pb$ ages, respectively, in Chen and Moore (1982). Comparable or smaller uncertainties for work done in this study are given for each specimen as uncertainties in radiogenic ratios in Table 2.

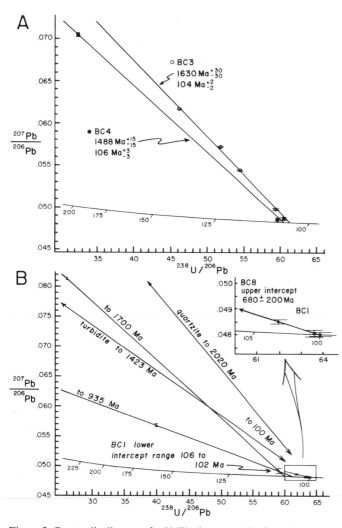

contaminant. The medium size fraction is nearly concordant, whereas coarse and fine fractions are dispersed off concordia along highly divergent trajectories. Chords passed from the nearly concordant fraction through the highly discordant coarse and fine fractions yield 1,700-Ma and 935-Ma upper intercepts, respectively. The fine fraction is likely to represent a Middle-Proterozoic and early Mesozoic polygenetic detrital suite. The range of lower intercepts derived from the two chords is 106 Ma to 102 Ma. The most reasonable igneous age for the porphyry is 105 ± 3 Ma. A high-level entrainment mechanism for the BC1 discordance is also suggested by the Rb/Sr data (Table 2). This sample yields a distinct and unique Sr_i for the Boyden Cave suite of 0.7033. This low value indicates ascent of the magma from the mantle without equilibration with preexisting continental crustal materials, leaving high-level entrainment as the only viable mechanism for contamination of the zircon population. The zircon systematics and the Sr_i data for BC1 are in sharp contrast to those of the BC3 ash-flow tuff. As noted above, BC3 appears to have incorporated its Proterozoic component early in its petrogenetic history. Such source-level contamination is consistent with an Sr_i value of 0.7074 calculated for a 104-Ma igneous age from the data of Table 2.

The clustering of igneous ages for the Boyden Cave pendant between 105 and 100 Ma is also suggested by the concordant to slightly discordant samples. Relations between the data points of these samples and concordia are summarized in Figure 4A. This figure shows the pertinent segments of concordia stacked in such a way as to facilitate direct comparison of error bar–concordia relations between the various samples. Sample BC2 (schistose granodiorite of Tombstone Creek) shows external concordance at 102 Ma. This is considered the best approximation for the igneous age of the schistose intrusion based on it crosscutting the ~105 Ma metavolcanics, and it being cut by the ~100 Ma granodiorite of Lightning Creek. Sample BC5 (metamorphosed hornblende porphyry intrusion) data points cluster tightly above concordia. The position of the data points in conjunction with a lack of dispersion along concordia strongly suggests very minor inheritance or entrainment of Proterozoic zircons. Consideration of the discordia trajectories shown in Figure 3 leads to an age assignment of 103 ± 2 Ma for BC5. Sample BC6 (metamorphosed hypersthene dacite intrusion) is slightly more complex due to minor dispersion along the trend of concordia. Such dispersion can be accounted for by the indicated errors, or alternatively represent minor disturbance superposed over minor inheritance or entrainment. The interpreted igneous age is therefore 102 +5/–2 Ma. Sample BC7 (protomylonitic granite of Grand Dike) shows moderate overlap between two nearly concordant fractions, but with a pattern mimicking that of sample BC6. Considerations similar to those used for the BC6 data in conjunction with its intrusive relations with the metavolcanics and hypabyssals lead to a 103 ± 2 Ma age assignment. Additionally, sample BC7 and a second sample from the Grand Dike intrusion (number 21, Table 2) yield a two point Rb/Sr isochron age of 103.5 ± 3 Ma with $Sr_i = 0.70725$.

Figure 3. Concordia diagrams for U/Pb zircon samples from the Boyden Cave pendant that show significant discordance (after Tera and Wasserburg, 1972). Linear regressions and intercept errors are adapted from York (1969). A: Plots and intercept solutions for samples BC3 and BC4. B: Reference chords for Boyden Cave pendant detrital zircon from quartzite and turbidite units (after J. H. Chen *in* Moore and others, 1979) with fixed 100 Ma lower intercept, and concordia solutions for highly divergent data points of BC1 and for concordant and slightly discordant points of BC8. Inset shows details of lower intercept for BC8.

points are shown in Figure 3B. The 100-Ma lower intercept is chosen to represent the thermal maxima for the region. The quartzite chord yields a 2,020-Ma upper intercept, and the turbidite unit yields a 1,423-Ma upper intercept. The turbidite detrital population in particular may be polygenetic with an early Mesozoic silicic volcanic component. The wide variation observed within the Kings sequence detrital zircon makes it difficult to give specific age significance to the BC3 and 4 upper intercepts.

The possibility for inheritance or entrainment of polygenetic detrital suites is shown clearly in the BC1 data from the dacite porphyry of Boulder Creek. These data reflect entrainment where there is no relation between grain size and proportion of the

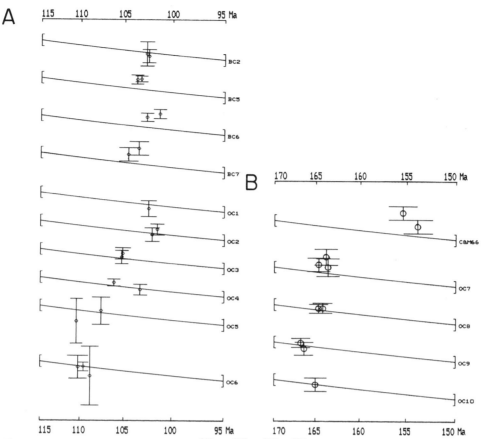

Figure 4. Stacked segments of concordia ($^{207}Pb/^{206}Pb$-$^{238}U/^{206}Pb$ coordinates not shown) with corresponding ages projected onto abscissa lines at bottom and top of diagram. Each segment contains data points and error bars for indicated sample. Bars at ends of concordia segments show uncertainty in $^{207}Pb/^{206}Pb$ values of concordia based on uncertainties in ^{238}U and ^{235}U decay constants from Mattinson's (1987) treatment of Jaffey and others (1971) data. A: Middle Cretaceous specimens from Boyden Cave (BC) and Oak Creek (OC) pendants. B: Jurassic specimens from Oak Creek pendant. Specimen C&M66 is White Fork pluton data from Chen and Moore (1982).

The granodiorite of Lightning Creek crosscuts the Boyden Cave metavolcanic and hypabyssal rocks as well as the schistose granodiorite of Tombstone Creek (Fig. 2). The Lightning Creek unit is in turn cut by the 97 Ma Lookout Creek pluton (Chen and Moore, 1982). Data points for sample BC8 (Lightning Creek unit) are plotted on the Figure 3B concordia diagram. The two finer fractions are externally concordant at 100 Ma. The third fraction is dispersed off concordia along a chord with a 680 ± 200 Ma upper intercept. As discussed above, and shown in Figure 3B, the upper intercept probably represents inheritance or entrainment of an inhomogeneous contaminant. The 100-Ma concordant fractions best approximate the igneous age of the granodiorite, which places a 100-Ma limit on penetrative deformation of the metavolcanics and related intrusives.

The igneous ages derived from the U/Pb zircon data outlined above are strongly supported by a 20 point Rb/Sr isochron on samples collected from a wide variety of rocks scattered throughout the Boyden Cave volcanic-hypabyssal sequence (samples 1–20, Table 2). The isochron is shown on a strontium evolution diagram (Fig. 5A) with an age of 103.3 ± 2.6 Ma and an Sr_i value of 0.70677 (r factor = 0.99998). The high Sr_i value indicates strong interaction between magmas and preexisting continental crustal materials, a relation also implied by the U/Pb zircon systematics. The strong linear array further suggests that the various magma batches were highly homogenized relative to one another in terms of their Rb/Sr and Sr isotopic and trace-element chemistry. In summary, both the Rb/Sr bulk rock and U/Pb zircon isotopic data strongly point to the construction and penetrative deformation of the Boyden Cave volcanic-hypabyssal sequence between 108 and 101 Ma.

Oak Creek pendant

The isotopic data for the Oak Creek pendant are treated in two groups, that of the older sequence and that of the younger. U/Pb zircon age data for the older sequence are summarized in Figure 4B. Three ash-flow tuff samples collected from widely spaced localities throughout the older sequence (OC7, 8 and 9) yield externally concordant ages clustered at 165 Ma. Specific age

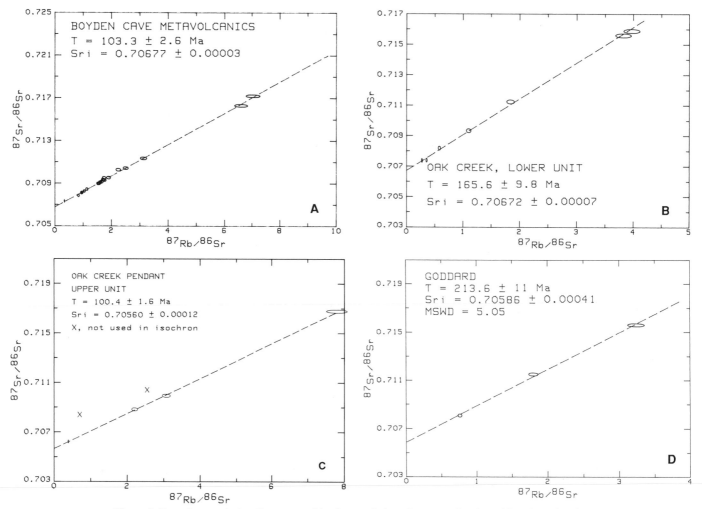

Figure 5. Strontium evolution diagrams and isochron solutions for metavolcanic and hypabyssal rocks from Boyden Cave, Mount Goddard, and Oak Creek pendants. Linear regressions after York (1969). A: Boyden Cave metamorphosed volcanic and hypabyssal rocks. B: Oak Creek pendant older sequence. C: Oak Creek pendant intrusives. The x's denote ash-flow samples omitted from isochron solution. D: Metavolcanic rocks and subvolcanic pluton from the northern Mount Goddard pendant.

assignments for the samples are as follows: OC7: 165 ± 2 Ma; OC8: 165 ± 1 Ma; and OC9: 166 ±2 Ma. These samples along with four additional andesite and basaltic-andesite samples yield a 165.6 ± 9.8 Ma Rb/Sr bulk-rock isochron age. Sr_i for the isochron is 0.7067 and the r factor of the linear array is 0.9995. It thus appears that much of, or the entire, older sequence was derived from a common source. The Rb/Sr and U/Pb data clearly point to a major pulse of silicic with subordinate andesitic to basaltic volcanism at ~165 Ma in the Oak Creek pendant. A similar pulse of silicic ash-flow volcanism, with subordinate andesites, occurred at 163 ± 5 Ma in the Ritter Range pendant to the north (Kistler and Swanson, 1981).

Two significant granitoid intrusive masses are closely associated with the 165-Ma volcanic sequences. The Woods Lake mass of the Tinemaha granodiorite intruded the eastern lower part of the volcanic sequence, and the White Fork pluton intruded the northwestern edge of the sequence. U/Pb zircon ages

for both plutons were reported in Chen and Moore (1982). As noted above, the Woods Lake mass yields an internally concordant age of 165 Ma (Chen and Moore, 1982; sample OC10 of Table 1 and Fig. 4B). These data, in conjunction with the age data presented above for the volcanic sequence, demonstrate that the Woods Lake mass was closely related to the volcanic sequence. The White Fork pluton data are more complex. Chen and Moore (1982) interpreted slightly discordant ages of this pluton as indicative of minor disturbance of a population with an igneous age of ~156 Ma. Chen and Moore's (1982) work was completed prior to the development of a broad data base documenting widespread minor to significant inheritance or entrainment phenomena within Sierran igneous rocks (Saleeby, 1987). Chen and Moore's (1982) White Fork pluton data are plotted in Figure 4B (sample C&M66). The dispersion pattern of the data points is much more suggestive of minor inheritance or entrainment than post-crystallization disturbance. Following the rationale used above for the interpretation of such discordance patterns, a revised igneous age of 153 ± 3 Ma is suggested for the White Fork pluton.

The White Fork pluton, Woods Lake mass of the Tinemaha granodiorite and the older metavolcanic sequence are cut by a major swarm of mafic to felsic dikes (Independence dike swarm of Moore and Hopson, 1981). The dikes were emplaced preferentially along a north-northwest–trending deformation fabric within the Jurassic rocks. Concordant zircon ages of 148 Ma were reported for the dike swarm from areas to the south of the study area (Chen and Moore, 1979). Dikes of the swarm are not present in the younger volcanic sequence of the Oak Creek pendant.

U/Pb zircon age data for samples from the younger volcanic sequence as well as those for closely related intrusive rocks are summarized in Figure 4A. Most important is sample OC6, which consists of two adjacent ash-flow sheets. Single and multiple fractions from the two sheets are externally concordant at 109 ± 2 Ma. Sample OC5 is a large rhyolitic sill that cuts the older sequence, and from its apparent age probably fed the upper sequence. The data points show minor dispersion along concordia suggestive of minor disturbance of at least the finer fraction. The coarse fraction is interpreted not to be significantly disturbed, yielding an ∼110 Ma age for the sill.

Samples OC1 through 4 are a series of small plutons that may have formed in the subvolcanic environment of the younger section. The plutons all cut the older section, and were emplaced during or shortly after the last phase of ductile deformation, which affected both the older and younger volcanic sequences. Sample OC4 is from the syn-deformational Sardine plutons. Two internally concordant data points are dispersed along concordia making the population externally discordant. The pattern is suggestive of minor disturbance, and the upper data point is considered to approximate the igneous age taken as 106 +3/−1 Ma. Sample OC3 is from the post-deformational granite of Arrowhead Lake. The externally concordant data points indicate a 105 ± 1 Ma igneous age.

Samples OC1 and 2 are from a post-deformational gabbrodiorite mass of Dragon Peak and the closely related mafic granodioritic Dragon pluton. Internally and externally concordant ages on these samples yield a 102 ± 1 Ma igneous age. As noted above, a similar age (103 ± 2 Ma) was reported for a different sample location within the Dragon pluton by Chen and Moore (1982). A major alaskite granite pluton, the Bullfrog pluton, is closely associated and may be synplutonic with the Dragon pluton. The Bullfrog pluton yielded slightly discordant zircon ages of 100 to 103 Ma (Chen and Moore, 1982).

The zircon sample suite from the younger volcanic sequence and the felsic intrusives discussed above were analyzed by Rb/Sr bulk-rock techniques. The results are summarized in a strontium evolution diagram (Fig. 5C). The felsic intrusives (OC2 through 5) form a strong linear array with an isochron age of 100.4 ± 1.6 Ma (r factor = 0.9999) and Sr_i = 0.7056. These data are in general agreement with the U/Pb zircon data, although slightly older ages

were resolved for three of the samples. The two ash-flow tuff samples are not age diagnostic and plot well above the pluton linear array, suggesting that the parent magma was enriched in a high Sr_i component relative to the intrusives.

The isotopic pattern displayed in Figure 5C is perhaps analogous to Sr_i gradients discovered in large ash-flow sequences where the higher level, lower overall temperature silicic magmas were enriched in high Sr_i components, whereas the deeper, higher temperature magmas were isotopically homogenized and show lower overall Sr_i values (Hildreth, 1981). Such a view assumes that the Oak Creek intrusives are broadly cogenetic with the volcanics, calling for an ∼10 m.y. lifespan of the silicic magma system. Furthermore, this view calls on the ductile deformation event, which pervaded the Oak Creek pendant, to have occurred during the life span of the silicic center. Alternatively, the ash-flow samples as well as the rhyolite sill and Sardine pluton composed a distinct, isotopically heterogeneous magma system that predated the deformation event. The distinct magma system of the post-deformational intrusives shared similar time-integrated Sr evolution patterns as the intrusive phases of the predeformational system.

In summary, both the U/Pb zircon data and Rb/Sr bulk rock data clearly resolve the two volcanic sequences that make up the Oak Creek pendant. The lower sequence formed abruptly at 165 Ma and included a large subvolcanic granitoid pluton. The upper sequence formed at 110 Ma and was penetratively deformed with its Jurassic substrate prior to 105 Ma. Voluminous post-deformational plutonism intruded and disrupted the Jurassic and middle Cretaceous volcanic section at ∼102 Ma.

GEOLOGIC IMPLICATIONS OF THE ISOTOPIC DATA

The isotopic age data presented above for metavolcanic rocks of the Boyden Cave and Oak Creek pendants carry a number of important implications for the structural and petrogenetic development of the Sierra Nevada batholith and its wall rocks. By study of Figure 2 it is evident that the middle Cretaceous volcanic sequences of these two pendants are only slightly older than a significant volume of the enclosing batholithic material. Furthermore, a significant tract of Early Cretaceous batholithic material had been emplaced along the western zones of the composite batholith prior to the eruption of the middle Cretaceous sequence (Fig. 1). Thus the tectonics responsible for both the deformation and preservation of the middle Cretaceous sequence operated within the confines of the Cretaceous batholithic belt. This is critical in our consideration of the deformation fabrics present within the middle Cretaceous sequences, inasmuch as the fabrics must be a reflection of the dynamics within the batholithic belt. In the discussions below we focus first on topics related to such intra-batholithic tectonics, and then we consider some of the regional petrogenetic implications of the tectonics as well as the isotopic patterns.

Regional structural chronology

Middle Cretaceous metavolcanic rocks of the Boyden Cave and Oak Creek pendants contain strong penetrative deformation fabrics that affect the pre-Cretaceous strata as well. Such deformation fabrics are for the most part absent in ~100 Ma and younger plutons which encase the pendants. Thus, significant deformation of these pendants occurred between 110 and 100 Ma. The tectonic setting of this middle Cretaceous deformation event is poorly understood. It is also recognized in the Ritter Range pendant to the north of the study area (Kistler and Swanson, 1981; Tobisch and Fiske, 1982), and in the Lake Isabella and southernmost Sierra-Tehachapi Range areas to the south (Saleeby and Busby-Spera, 1986; Saleeby and others, 1987). It is thus regional in extent, and future studies will probably reveal additional localities.

It is generally assumed that the Cretaceous Sierra Nevada batholith formed coherently as a continental or Andean-type arc along the North American margin. There are, however, no strong ties between eastern and western Sierra metamorphic wall rocks for pre-middle Cretaceous time. Nor are there any strong ties between the western zone of Early Cretaceous batholithic rocks and the eastern metamorphic wall rocks. Thus, a major tectonic break may have extended along the axis of the batholith, and the break may have been active as late as the middle Cretaceous.

The intra-batholithic tectonic break hypothesized above is reflected in wall-rock geology and batholith petrochemistry. In terms of wall-rock geology it corresponds to a cryptic (intruded) boundary between the early Mesozoic Kings sequence and thick sediment-poor sections of early Mesozoic ignimbrites—the Ritter Range, Mount Goddard, and Oak Creek pendants. Whether the middle Cretaceous deformation event represents the juxtaposition of these two Jurassic terranes, or remobilization of an earlier (Jurassic) structure is unknown. Alternatively, such a preexisting structure may have behaved passively during Cretaceous batholithic activity, leaving the middle Cretaceous event as a reflection of regional magma emplacement dynamics alone (Saleeby and Busby-Spera, 1986; Saleeby and others, 1987; Saleeby, 1989).

The available data do not permit us to favor or dismiss any of the tectonic mechanisms presented above for the middle Cretaceous deformation event. A much fuller understanding of the wall-rock structure and stratigraphy as well as the batholith structure and petrochemistry are required to begin to discriminate between these and possible additional mechanisms. Below we focus on some of the implications of our data on these more basic topics.

Regional correlations of early Mesozoic metavolcanic sequences

The Ritter Range pendant contains the most complete record of silicic volcanism in the Sierra Nevada (Fiske and others, 1977; Fiske and Tobisch, 1978; Kistler and Swanson, 1981; Tobisch and others, 1986). The grossly west-facing volcanic section

of the Ritter Range is ~10 km thick, records a number of pulses of silicic volcanism between ~230 and ~130 Ma, and is capped unconformably by a middle Cretaceous caldera-fill sequence. The Ritter Range sequence extends continuously for 60 km as a north-northwest–trending belt, and additional remnants of the belt appear to extend southward as smaller pendants. Study of Figure 1 raises the question that perhaps the Mount Goddard and Oak Creek pendants are the southward continuation of the Ritter Range sequence.

Field and geochronological data discussed for the Mount Goddard pendant (Tobisch and others, 1986) reveal strong similarities with the Upper Jurassic–Lower Cretaceous interval of the Ritter Range pendant. Additionally, we present here new Rb/Sr bulk-rock data from the northern Goddard Range pendant which suggest that Late Triassic volcanic and plutonic rocks similar to those of the Ritter Range occur in the Goddard Range pendant as well (Figs. 2 and 5D; Table 3). As noted above, distinct voluminous pulses of silicic volcanism are recognized at ~165 Ma in both the Ritter Range and Oak Creek lower section. Like the Ritter Range pendant, both the Mount Goddard and the Oak Creek pendants are grossly west-facing sections. Each of the sections is complexly faulted and intruded by Middle and Late Jurassic plutons. Thus a number of lines of evidence suggest that the Mount Goddard and Oak Creek pendants were once the southern continuation of the Ritter Range sequence. Furthermore, small highly disrupted screens of schist, marble, and hornfels that extend along the high Sierra crest near and to the east of the Oak Creek and Mount Goddard pendants may represent vestiges of the Paleozoic marine section which underlies the Ritter Range section, and by analogy once lay beneath the Oak Creek and Mount Goddard pendants. The Paleozoic marine sequence and its thick, early Mesozoic ignimbrite cover constitute a distinct pre-batholithic terrane of the Sierra Nevada, and this terrane may typify much of the eastern wall of the batholith.

Batholithic petrochemical patterns and the distribution of pre-batholithic terranes

The early Mesozoic metavolcanic sequence of the Ritter Range, Mount Goddard, and Oak Creek pendants contrasts sharply with early Mesozoic marine strata of the Kings sequence. Petrochemical variations within the central and southern segments of the batholith reflect these contrasts. The wall-rock and batholithic contrasts are consistent with the existence of a pre-batholith tectonic break between the two terranes, and the subsequent petrochemical fingerprinting of the terranes by the batholithic magmas.

The most notable petrochemical variations are seen in Sr_i and Pb_i values, which become more radiogenic eastward across the batholith, although the Pb_i values drop off abruptly in areas to the east of the Kings sequence pendants (Chen and Tilton, 1984, written communication). Such a pattern is not widely observed in Sr_i, although the contrast in Sr_i intercepts of 0.7068 and 0.7073 in the Boyden Cave samples versus 0.7056 in the middle Cretaceous samples of the Oak Creek pendant mimics the pattern. Furthermore, at given Sr concentration levels, Rb concentrations are systematically higher in plutons with $Sr_i < 0.706$ to the east of the Kings sequence pendants (Kistler and Peterman, 1978; Kistler, 1987; this volume). Delta ^{18}O values for plutons emplaced within the Kings sequence are systematically higher, commonly greater than +10, than for plutons emplaced elsewhere in the Sierra Nevada (Masi and others, 1981; Ross, 1983; Kistler, 1987; Saleeby and others, 1987).

The petrochemical distinctiveness of batholithic magmas emplaced into the Kings sequence metamorphic framework was also noted by Ague and Brimhall (1987). Primarily on the basis of biotite phase chemistry, these workers distinguished many of these magmas as I-type, but strongly contaminated by reducing pelite rich metasedimentary materials. Migmatization of major sections of Kings sequence psammite-pelite, and the intermixing of melt products with the invading magmas is well documented in the more southerly pendants of the range (Saleeby and Busby-Spera, 1986; Saleeby and others, 1987; Saleeby, 1989). As discussed below, the southerly pendants represent a deeper level of exposure than those of the study area. Ague and Brimhall's (1987) suggestion that the distinctiveness of the Kings sequence domain of the batholith arises from such contamination is consistent with general patterns in zircon systematics. Batholithic plutons and silicic volcanic rocks emplaced or erupted within the Kings sequence framework are commonly contaminated with Proterozoic zircon (Saleeby and Busby-Spera, 1986; Saleeby and others, 1987, and unpublished data; and this study). Such distinctness is clearly seen in this study by comparing the Boyden Cave sample suite with the Oak Creek pendant suite. Close to half of the Boyden Cave (Kings sequence framework) samples are strongly contaminated, whereas samples from the more eastern framework are only locally, and typically faintly, contaminated.

The Rb/Sr concentration patterns coupled with the other petrochemical patterns suggest that the magmas emplaced into and contaminated within the Kings sequence framework entered the framework without prior significant interaction with old sialic crust. The Sr_i data on sample BC1 discussed above indicate that this sample represents a rare instance of mantle-derived material ascending to high levels without undergoing significant contamination from melted sediments. Mixing models for southern Sierra batholithic rocks based on Nd, Sr, and O isotopes are also consistent with much of the Kings sequence domain batholith being highly contaminated melted sediments (DePaolo, 1981; Saleeby and others, 1987). In terms of Rb/Sr isotopic systematics, large volumes of both highly and poorly homogenized magma are shown to have resulted from the melting and mixing phenomena.

As noted by Saleeby and others (1987), there is no direct evidence for the Kings sequence having been deposited on crystalline sialic crust. The Kings sequence sedimentary prism may thus have been built on oceanic lithosphere, a relation that is at least locally observed with its more western basinal facies (Saleeby and

others, 1978). The eastern (Ritter Range section and underlying Paleozoic marine strata) wall-rock sequence may have been deposited on, or at an early stage emplaced tectonically above, North American Proterozoic sial (Kistler and Peterman, 1973, 1978; Saleeby and others, 1986). The petrochemical boundary within the axial zone of the Sierra Nevada batholith may thus coincide with a tectonic boundary between fundamentally different lithosphere types (Kistler, 1987; this volume).

Batholithic crustal structure

The results of this study, in conjunction with work in adjacent regions to the northwest (Fiske and others, 1977; Peck, 1980; Nokleberg, 1981; Kistler and Swanson, 1981), show that middle Cretaceous volcanic rocks are widespread in the central Sierra Nevada. In contrast, similar-age plutonic rocks exposed ~200 km to the south at the southern termination of the range crystallized at depths corresponding to perhaps as much as 8 kbar pressure (Sharry, 1981; Ross, 1985; Saleeby and others, 1987; Sams and Saleeby, 1988; Saleeby, 1989). The transition from surficial volcanic rock to contemporaneous deep-level plutonic rock is broad and apparently continuous. Metamorphic mineral assemblages developed at ~3 kbar in conjunction with 100-Ma plutonism occur in the Lake Isabella region, yielding some quantitative intermediate depth-time control on the transition zone (Elan, 1985; Saleeby and Busby-Spera, 1986).

The increase in depth of exposure southward from the study area occurs almost totally within the Kings sequence framework domain of the batholith. Throughout this domain the pre-batholithic rocks occur only as steeply dipping screens, commonly with steep-plunging constrictional fabrics. The steep linear fabrics are more pervasive southward where they are shown to have developed in conjunction with the middle Cretaceous deformation event (Saleeby and Busby-Spera, 1986; Saleeby and others, 1987). Of particular interest here are leucosomes within Kings sequence migmatites that were synplutonically deformed with the steep linear fabric. Middle Cretaceous silicic metavolcanic rocks of the Lake Isabella region were also transposed with this fabric element, and in conjunction with the ~3 kbar thermobarometric constraints, a significant downward flow component is implied for the wall rocks of this region. Similar fabrics occur in the Boyden Cave rocks, but they are not as intense nor as penetrative as those of the Lake Isabella region. The fabrics developed in the Boyden Cave pendant may represent a higher level, less intense analogue to those developed to the south.

At the southern termination of the range, where the deepest level of exposure is observed, the deformation fabrics noted above are shared equally by middle Cretaceous batholithic rocks as well as vestiges of Kings sequence framework rocks (Saleeby and others, 1987; Sams and Saleeby, 1988). The batholithic rocks have affinities to granulites and/or charnockites, but they are middle Cretaceous in age, and are primarily mantle derived. Thus, no vestiges of a crystalline basement for the Kings sequence are observed in the deep-level terrane, nor are there significant volumes of crustal-level residues.

The map relations, age data, and paleodepth constraints for batholithic and framework rocks between the deep-level terrane and the study area suggest that an ~25-km-thick crustal column was created by the emplacment of middle Cretaceous mantle-derived magmas with moderate to locally strong contamination by Kings sequence partial-melt products. Geophysical data synthesized across the central Sierra Nevada suggest an ~30-km-thick felsic to intermediate composition batholithic layer underlain by a 20-km-thick mafic lower crustal layer (Saleeby and others, 1986). The map view between the study area and the deep-level terrane may thus resemble a cross-sectional view through the felsic to intermediate layer encompassing volcanic to granulitic levels.

ACKNOWLEDGMENTS

Support for field and laboratory studies was provided by National Science Foundation (NSF) Grants EAR-8218460 and EAR-8419731 (to Saleeby) and the U.S. Geological Survey, Menlo Park. Funding for work in the Oak Creek pendant was provided for Longiaru by NSF Grants EAR-8318212 and EAR-8503882 (to O. T. Tobisch). Funding for instrumental facilities (Saleeby) was provided by NSF Grant AEO-8415114 and the Weingart Foundation. Patience and expertise in hand-sorting of zircon by Cherilyn Saleeby is gratefully acknowledged. Special thanks to J. H. Chen for supplying zircon separates for replicate analysis. Caltech Division of Geological & Planetary Science Contribution Number 4611.

Appendix 1. Specimen locations and protolith name.

BC1	36°47.2'	118°47.7'	porphyritic hornblende dacite
BC2	36°48.5'	118°47.6'	schistose hornblende granodiorite
BC3	36°48.6'	118°47.4'	crystal-lithic rhyolite tuff
BC4	36°50.3'	118°47.5'	crystal-lithic rhyolite tuff
BC5	36°50.5'	118°47.5'	porphyritic hornblende dacite
BC6	36°50.7'	118°46.5'	porphyritic hypersthene dacite
BC7	36°51.1'	118°46.1'	protomylonitic granite
BC8	36°46.4'	118°20.5'	hornblende biotite granodiorite
OC1	26°46.4'	118°20.5'	hornblende quartz gabbro
OC2	36°48.7'	118°23.8'	mafic granodiorite
OC3	36°49.4'	118°24.4'	alaskite granite
OC4	36°48.1'	118°20.3'	foliated alaskite granite
OC5	36°50.0'	118°21.3'	rhyolite vitrophyre
OC6	36°49.3'	118°21.4'	a. crystal-lithic rhyolite tuff
			b. crystal-lithic rhyolite tuff
OC7	36°48.1'	118°20.0'	crystal rhyolite tuff
OC8	36°49.9'	118°22.1'	crystal rhyolite tuff
OC9	36°49.9'	118°22.2'	crystal-lithic rhyolite tuff
OC10	36°47.1'	118°18.9'	foliated prophyritic granodiorite
A	36°50.6'	118°45.9'	hypersthene porphyry
B	36°48.5'	118°47.5'	rhyolite
C	36°48.5'	118°47.5'	dacite
D	36°49.4'	118°47.2'	dacite
E	36°51.6'	118°48.2'	dacite
F	36°50.9'	118°45.7'	protomylonitic granite
G	36°50.7'	118°46.6'	dacite tuff
H	36°49.5'	118°45.8'	dacite tuff
I	36°50.4'	118°47.2'	basalt
J	36°49.7'	118°46.7'	dacite tuff
K	36°50.3'	118°47.5'	rhyolite tuff
L	36°50.3'	118°47.4'	rhyolite tuff
M	36°50.5'	118°47.2'	rhyolite tuff
N	36°50.4'	118°47.3'	dacite tuff
O	36°50.4'	118°47.3'	rhyolite tuff
P	36°50.3'	118°47.7'	rhyolite tuff
Q	36°50.2'	118°47.8'	rhyolite flow
R	36°50.2'	118°48.0'	dacite flow
S	36°50.6'	118°47.9'	dacite flow
T	36°50.6'	118°47.9'	rhyolite flow
U	36°51.6'	118°47.2'	protomylonitic granite
V	36°54.4'	118°22.0'	basaltic andesite flow
W	36°49.2'	118°20.0'	andesite flow
X	36°48.9'	118°22.3'	andesite flow
Y	36°49.7'	118°20.5'	dacite flow
1	37°09.2'	118°47.2'	rhyodacite tuff
2	37°09.3'	118°49.6'	rhyodacite tuff
3	37°11.6'	118°48.3'	sheared granodiorite

REFERENCES CITED

Ague, J. J., and Brimhall, G. H., 1987, Granites of the batholiths of California: Products of local assimilation and regional-scale crustal contamination: Geology, v. 15, p. 63–66.

Bateman, P. C., and Clark, L. D., 1974, Stratigraphic and structural setting of the Sierra Nevada batholith: Pacific Geology, v. 8, p. 78–89.

Chen, J. H., and Moore, J. G., 1979, Late Jurassic Independence dike swarm in eastern California: Geology, v. 7, p. 129–133.

——, 1982, Uranium-lead isotopic studies of the southern Sierra Nevada batholith, California: Geological Society of America Abstracts with Programs, v. 10, p. 99–100.

Chen, J. H., and Tilton, G. R., 1978, Lead and strontium isotopic studies of the southern Sierra Nevada batholith, California: Geological Society of America Abstracts with Programs, v. 10, p. 99–100.

Christensen, M. N., 1963, Structure of metamorphic rocks at Mineral King, California: University of California Publications in the Geological Sciences, v. 42, p. 159–198.

DePaolo, D. J., 1981, A neodymium and strontium isotopic study of the Mesozoic calc-alkaline granitic batholiths of the Sierra Nevada and Peninsular Ranges, California: Journal of Geophysical Research, v. 86, p. 10470–10485.

Dodge, F.C.W., Calk, L. C., and Kistler, R. W., 1986, Lower crustal zenoliths, Chinese Peak lava flow, central Sierra Nevada: Journal of Petrology, v. 27, p. 1277–1304.

Domenick, M. A., Kistler, R. W., Dodge, R.C.W., and Tatsumoto, M., 1983, Nd and Sr isotopic study of crustal and mantle inclusions from the Sierra Nevada and implications for batholith petrogenesis: Geological Society of America Bulletin, v. 94, p. 713–719.

Elan, R., 1985, High grade contact metamorphism at the Lake Isabella north shore roof pendant, southern Sierra Nevada, California [M.S. thesis]: Los Angeles, University of Southern California, 202 p.

Evernden, J. F., and Kistler, R. W., 1970, Chronology of emplacement of Mesozoic batholithic complexes in California and western Nevada: U.S. Geological Survey Professional Paper 623, 67 p.

Fiske, R. S., and Tobisch, O. T., 1978, Paleogeographic significance of volcanic rocks of the Ritter Range pendant, central Sierra Nevada, California, *in* Howell, D. G., and McDougall, K. A., eds., Mesozoic paleogeography of the western United States: Pacific Section, Society of Economic Paleontologists and Mineralogists, Pacific Coast Paleogeography Symposium 2, p. 209–222.

Fiske, R. S., Tobisch, O. T., Kistler, R. W., Stern, T. W., and Tatsumoto, M., 1977, Minarets Caldera; A Cretaceous volcanic center in the Ritter Range pendant, central Sierra Nevada, California: Geological Society of America Abstracts with Programs, v. 9, p. 975.

Girty, G. H., 1985, Shallow marine deposits in Boyden Cave roof pendant, west-central Sierra Nevada: California Geology, v. 38, no. 3, p. 51–55.

Hildreth, W., 1981, Gradients in silicic magma chambers: Implications for lithospheric magmatism: Journal of Geophysical Research, v. 86, p. 10153–10192.

Huber, N. K., and Rinehart, C. D., 1965, Geologic map of the Shuteye Peak Quadrangle, Sierra Nevada, California: U.S. Geological Survey Geological Quadrangle Map GQ-728, scale 1:62,500.

Jaffey, A. H., Flynn, K. F., Glendenin, L. E., Bentley, W. C., and Essling, A. M., 1971, Precision measurement of the half-lives and specific activities of ^{235}U and ^{238}U: Physics Review, v. C4, p. 1889–1906.

Jones, D. L., and Moore, J. G., 1973, Lower Jurassic ammonite from the south-central Sierra Nevada, California: U.S. Geological Survey Journal of Research, v. 1, p. 453–458.

Kistler, R. W., 1966, Structure and metamorphism in the Mono Craters Quadrangle, Sierra Nevada, California: U.S. Geological Survey Bulletin 1221-E, p. E-1–E53.

——, 1987, Lithosphere types in the Sierra Nevada: Geological Society of America Abstracts with Programs, v. 19, p. 395.

Kistler, R. W., and Peterman, Z. E., 1973, Variations in Sr, Rb, K, Na, and initial $^{87}Sr/^{86}Sr$ in Mesozoic granitic rocks and intruded wall rocks in central California: Geological Society of America Bulletin, v. 84, p. 3489–3512.

——, 1978, Reconstruction of crustal blocks of California on the basis of initial strontium isotopic compositions of Mesozoic granitic rocks: U.S. Geological Survey Professional Paper 1071, 17 p.

Kistler, R. W., and Swanson, S. E., 1981, Petrology and geochronology of metamorphosed volcanic rocks and a Middle Cretaceous volcanic neck in the east-central Sierra Nevada, California: Journal of Geophysical Research, v. 86, no. B11, p. 10489–10501.

Longiaru, S., 1987, Tectonic evolution of Oak Creek volcanic roof pendant, eastern Sierra Nevada, California [Ph.D. thesis]: Santa Cruz, University of California, 242 p.

Masi, U., O'Neil, J. R., and Kistler, R. W., 1981, Stable isotope systematics in Mesozoic granites of central and northern California and southwestern Oregon: Contributions to Mineralogy and Petrology, v. 76, p. 116–126.

Mattinson, J. M., 1987, U-Pb ages of zircons; A basic examination of error propagation: Chemical Geology, v. 66, p. 151–162.

Moore, J. G., 1963, Geology of the Mount Pinchot Quadrangle, southern Sierra Nevada, California: U.S. Geological Survey Bulletin 1130, 152 p.

Moore, J. G., and Dodge, F. C., 1962, Mesozoic age of metamorphic rocks in the Kings River area, southern Sierra Nevada, California, *in* Short papers in geology, hydrology, and topography, 1962: U.S. Geological Survey Professional Paper 450-B, p. B19–B21.

Moore, J. G., and Hopson, C. A., 1961, The Independence dike swarm in eastern California: American Journal of Science, v. 259, p. 241–259.

Moore, J. G., and Marks, L. Y., 1972, Mineral resources of the High Sierra Primitive Area, California: U.S. Geological Survey Bulletin 1371-A, p. A1–A40.

Moore, J. G., and Nokleberg, W. J., 1989, Geological map of the Tehipite Dome Quadrangle, Fresno County, California: U.S. Geological Quadrangle Map GQ-1676, scale 1:62,500.

Moore, J. G., and Sisson, T. W., 1987, Preliminary geologic map of Sequoia and Kings Canyon National Parks and vicinity, California: U.S. Geological Map N-3615, scale 1:62,500.

Moore, J. G., Nokleberg, W. J., Saleeby, J. B., Girty, G., and Chen, J. C., 1979, Field guide and roadlog for the Kings Canyon Highway, central Sierra Nevada, California: Geological Society of America 75th Annual Meeting, Cordilleran Section: San Jose, 55 p.

Nokleberg, W. J., 1981, Stratigraphy and structure of the Strawberry Nine roof pendant, central Sierra Nevada, California: U.S. Geological Survey Professional Paper 1154, 18 p.

Nokleberg, W. J., and Kistler, R. W., 1980, Paleozoic and Mesozoic deformations, central Sierra Nevada, California: U.S. Geological Survey Professional Paper 1145, 24 p.

Rinehart, C. D., and Ross, D. C., 1957, Geology of the Casa Diablo Mountain Quadrangle, California: U.S. Geological Survey Geological Quadrangle Map GQ-99, scale 1:62,500.

——, 1964, Geology and mineral deposits of the Mount Morrison Quadrangle, Sierra Nevada, California, with a section on a gravity study of Long Valley by L. C. Pakiser: U.S. Geological Survey Professional Paper 385, 106 p.

Peck, D. L., 1980, Geologic map of the Merced Peak Quadrangle, central Sierra Nevada, California: U.S. Geological Survey Geological Quadrangle Map GQ-1531, scale 1:62,500.

Ross, D. C., 1985, Mafic gneisses complex (batholithic root?) in the southernmost Sierra Nevada, California: Geology, v. 13, p. 288–291.

Saleeby, J. B., 1987, Discordance patterns in Pb/U zircon ages of the Sierra Nevada and Klamath Mountains: EOS Transactions of the American Geophysical Union, v. 14.

——, 1989, Progress in tectonic and petrogenetic studies in an exposed cross-section of young (~100 Ma) continental crust, southern Sierra Nevada, California, *in* Salisbury, M. H., ed., Exposed cross-sections of the continental crust: Dordrecht, Holland, Reidel Publishing Co. (in press).

Saleeby, J. B., and Busby-Spera, C. V., 1986, Fieldtrip guide to the metamorphic framework rocks of the Lake Isabella area, southern Sierra Nevada, California; Mesozoic and Cenozoic structural evolution of selected areas, east-central California: Geological Society of America Cordilleran Section Meeting Guidebook: p. 81–94.

Saleeby, J. B., and Chen, J. H., 1978, Preliminary report on initial lead and strontium isotopes from ophiolitic and batholithc rocks, southwestern foothills Sierra Nevada, California: U.S. Geological Survey Open-File Report 78-701, p. 375-376.

Saleeby, J. B., and Sharp, W. D., 1980, Chronology of the structural and petrologic development of the southwest Sierra Nevada foothills, California: Geological Society of America Bulletin, v. 91, part 2, p. 1416–1535.

Saleeby, J. B., Busby, C., Goodin, W. D., and Sharp, W. D., 1978, Early Mesozoic paleotectonic-paleogeographic reconstruction of the southern Sierra Nevada region, California, *in* Howell, ed., Mesozoic paleogeography of the western United States: Pacific Section, Society of Economic Paleontologists and Mineralogists, p. 311–336.

Saleeby, J. B., and 12 others, 1986, Central California offshore to Colorado Plateau: Boulder, Colorado, Geological Society of America Continent/ Ocean Transect C-2, scale 1:500,000.

Saleeby, J. B., Sams, D. B., and Kistler, R. W., 1987, U/Pb zircon, strontium, and oxygen isotopic and geochronological study of the southernmost Sierra Nevada batholith, California: Journal of Geophysical Research, v. 92, p. 10443–10446.

Sams, D. B., and Saleeby, J. B., 1988, Geology and petrotectonic significance of crystalline rocks of the southernmost Sierra Nevada, California, *in* Ernst, W. G., ed., Metamorphism and crustal evolution of the western United States; Rubey Volume 7: Englewood Cliffs, New Jersey, Prentice-Hall, p. 865–893.

Schweickert, R. A., Bogen, N. L., Girty, G. H., Hanson, R. E., and Merguerian, C., 1984, Timing and structural expression of the Nevadan orogeny, Sierra Nevada, California: Geological Society of America Bulletin, v. 95, p. 967–979.

Sharry, J., 1981, The geology of the western Tehachapi Mountains, California [Ph.D. thesis]: Cambridge, Massachusetts Institute of Technology, 215 p.

Stern, T. W., Bateman, P. C., Morgan, B. A., Newell, M. F., and Peck, D. L., 1981, Isotopic U-Pb ages of zircon from granitoids of the central Sierra Nevada, California: U.S. Geological Survey Professional Paper 1185, 17 p.

Tera, F., and Wasserburg, G. J., 1972, U/Pb systematics in lunar basalts: Earth and Planetary Science Letters, v. 17, p. 65–78.

Tobisch, O. T., and Fiske, R. S., 1982, Repeated parallel deformation in part of the eastern Sierra Nevada, California, and its implications for dating structural events: Journal of Structural Geology, v. 4, p. 177–195.

Tobisch, O. T., Saleeby, J. B., and Fiske, R. S., 1986, Structural history of continental volcanic arc rocks along part of the eastern Sierra Nevada, California: A case for extensional tectonics: Tectonics, v. 5, p. 65–94.

York, D., 1969, Least-squares fitting of a straight line with correlated error: Earth and Planetary Science Letters, v. 5, p. 320–324.

MANUSCRIPT SUBMITTED OCTOBER 23, 1987
REVISED MANUSCRIPT SUBMITTED APRIL 22, 1988
MANUSCRIPT ACCEPTED BY THE SOCIETY FEBRUARY 7, 1989

Geological Society of America
Memoir 174
1990

Chapter 15

Two different lithosphere types
in the Sierra Nevada, California

Ronald W. Kistler

U.S. Geological Survey, MS 937, 345 Middlefield Road, Menlo Park, California 94025

ABSTRACT

Chemical and isotopic characteristics of plutons in the western United States reflect compositions and protoliths of subjacent source materials. A discontinuously exposed shear zone that extends along the length of the Sierra Nevada in California marks a boundary between two areas manifested geologically by wall-rock and roof-pendant lithologies of different ages, depositional environments, and structural histories. In addition, plutons on either side of the boundary have different chemical and isotopic compositions, which indicate that their source regions are of two fundamentally different lithosphere types. The western lithosphere type is called Panthalassan, whereas the eastern type is called North American.

Isotopic investigations of plutons have defined an initial $^{87}Sr/^{86}Sr$ (Sr_i) = 0.706 line in each lithosphere type. However, $\delta^{18}O$ more than +9 per mil in plutons with Sr_i greater than 0.706 in the Panthalassan lithosphere indicates a significantly greater sedimentary component in the source materials for these plutons than for those plutons with similar Sr_i but $\delta^{18}O$ less than +9 per mil intruded into North American lithosphere. In contrast to the North American lithosphere, there is no evidence that a Proterozoic crystalline sialic basement exists where plutons have Sr_i greater than 0.706 in the Panthalassan lithosphere. Instead, the plutons with Sr_i greater than 0.706 intruded into Panthalassan lithosphere probably acquired that characteristic by assimilation of sediments derived from a Proterozoic sialic crust.

Plutons with Sr_i less than 0.706 have chemical and Nd isotopic characteristics that indicate time-integrated depletion in large ion lithophile elements in their source regions in the Panthalassan lithosphere relative to their sources in the North American lithosphere.

The tectonic contact between the two lithosphere types may be the extension of the Sonora-Mojave megashear into northern California.

INTRODUCTION

The isotopic compositions of Sr, O, Nd, and Pb in igneous rocks are sensitive indicators of the source materials of magmas and of the type of crust underlying these rocks in the western United States (Kistler and Peterman, 1973, 1978; Doe and Delevaux, 1973; Masi and others, 1981; Taylor and Silver, 1978; DePaolo, 1981; Farmer and DePaolo, 1983; Armstrong and others, 1977; Fleck and Criss, 1985). The (Sr_i) isopleth of 0.706 is a geographic marker of paleogeographic, paleotectonic, and geo-chemical significance. The region where Sr_i values of plutons are greater than 0.706 is apparently underlain by Precambrian sialic crust or by sediments derived from Precambrian sialic crust about 1,700 m.y. old, whereas the region where Sr_i values of plutons are less than 0.706 is underlain by transitional or oceanic crust of Phanerozoic age (Kistler and Peterman, 1973, 1978).

Sr_i values of plutons in California, Nevada, Idaho, and Washington have now been determined with sufficient numbers (several thousand) and geographic coverage (Fleck and Criss, 1985; Kistler, 1983, and unpublished data; Kistler and Lee, 1989)

Kistler, R. W., 1990, Two different lithosphere types in the Sierra Nevada, California, *in* Anderson, J. L., ed., The nature and origin of Cordilleran magmatism: Boulder, Colorado, Geological Society of America Memoir 174.

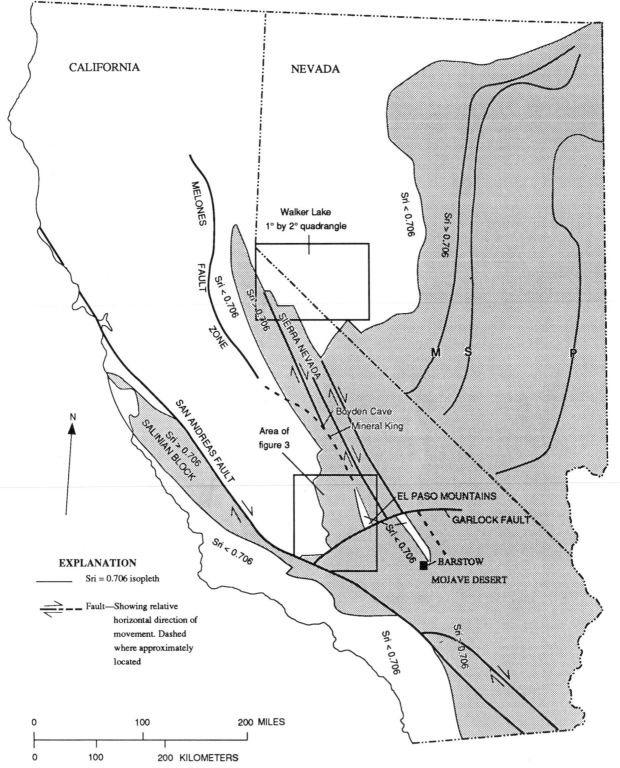

Figure 1. Outline map of California and Nevada showing the $Sr_i = 0.706$ isopleth for plutonic rocks in the region. Facies boundaries: belt of Permian rugose corals (P) is from Stevens (1982), Silurian shelf-slope break (S) is from Sheehan (1980), and belt of thickest Lower Mississippian foreland clastic deposits (M) is from Poole and Sandberg (1977). Shaded area has plutons with $Sr_i > 0.706$.

to accurately draw the 0.706 isopleth through those states. In Nevada, the strontium isotopic 0.706 isopleth is parallel to facies boundaries in the Cordilleran miogeocline that range in age from early to late Paleozoic (Fig. 1). This indicates that the present configuration of the edge of Precambrian sialic crust in the state, approximated by the 0.706 isopleth, has been little modified since its formation by rifting in latest Precambrian and Early Cambrian time (Speed, 1983; Heck and Speed, 1987). However, in east-central California along the eastern margin of the Sierra Nevada, the 0.706 isopleth is abruptly offset by faulting (Kistler and others, 1980; Fig. 1), from a southwest trend to a northwest trend, in a right-lateral sense for about 300 km. Triassic plutons (215 to 200 Ma) offset by the faults, folds associated with development of the faults in 185-Ma, but not in 163-Ma, metavolcanic rocks in the Ritter Range pendant, and geometric control of the locus of the Middle Jurassic (177 ± 5 Ma) plutons (Fig. 2) in the Sierra Nevada, constrain the time of this modification of the trend of the continental margin to between 185 and 177 Ma.

In the western Sierra Nevada the edge of sialic crust trends southeastward and, as in Nevada, is apparently unmodified from its latest Precambrian configuration north of about lat 37° N. South of this latitude, the 0.706 isopleth changes trend to southwestward in several steps, the last step being approximately coincident with the Garlock fault (Fig. 1). The southwestward trend of the 0.706 isopleth along the Garlock fault probably was caused by oroclinal flexure of the crust in the southwestern Sierra Nevada in the early Tertiary (Kanter and McWilliams, 1982; McWilliams and Li, 1985). At the west end of the Garlock fault, the 0.706 isopleth has a final modification to a northwestward trend because of displacement along the Neogene and currently active San Andreas fault system (Fig. 1).

A MAJOR TECTONIC BOUNDARY IN THE SIERRA NEVADA

Plutons in the Sierra Nevada were emplaced during an interval of approximately 160 m.y., from 240 to 80 Ma. The age distribution of plutons, modified from Kistler and others (1971), along with the locations of geographic features discussed in this report, are shown in Figure 2.

In the southern Sierra Nevada, in the vicinity of Walker Pass, and to the south in the El Paso Mountains, a narrow northwest-trending belt of 240-Ma plutons crop out. In this area, their Sr_i values, less than 0.7060, mark a conspicuous hiatus in the regional pattern of isotopic values that are greater than 0.706 (Fig. 1; Kistler and Ross, 1989). The eastern parts of these plutons are strongly sheared, and where not engulfed by Cretaceous plutons they are in tectonic contact with wall rocks in roof pendants and with other sheared plutons that were intruded during the Middle Jurassic Inyo Mountains intrusive epoch, about 177 ± 5 Ma (Fig. 3; Kistler and Ross, 1989).

On the basis of the age of faulted strata, this zone of shear can be projected discontinuously northward as a fault zone that includes a mylonitic dacite with Sr_i of 0.7046 and with a U/Pb

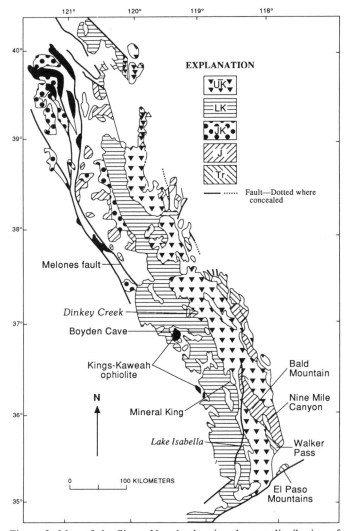

Figure 2. Map of the Sierra Nevada showing the age distribution of plutonic rocks and locations of features mentioned in the text. Solid black pattern is for ophiolites in western Sierra Nevada. Pluton ages: UK, Late Cretaceous (92–77 Ma); LK, Early Cretaceous (123–100 Ma); JK, latest Jurassic and Early Cretaceous (152–127 Ma); J, Middle Jurassic (180–165 Ma); Tr, Triassic (240–200 Ma).

zircon date of 240 Ma (Busby-Spera, 1983) in the Mineral King pendant, and as another fault zone that includes thoroughly deformed Triassic and Jurassic fossils in the Boyden Cave roof pendant (Moore and Dodge, 1962; Girty, 1985).

South of the Garlock fault, the belt of 240-Ma plutons with Sr_i less than 0.706 extends southeastward into the central Mojave Desert to the vicinity of Barstow (Fig. 1). These plutons with Sr_i less than 0.706 define a boundary between two terranes, each characterized by plutons with Sr_i greater than 0.706, and called the Sierran and Salinian–western Mojave terranes (Kistler, 1978; Kistler and Peterman, 1978). The more extensive data of Kistler and Ross (1989) indicate that the Salinian–western Mojave terrane extends much farther north into the Sierra Nevada than

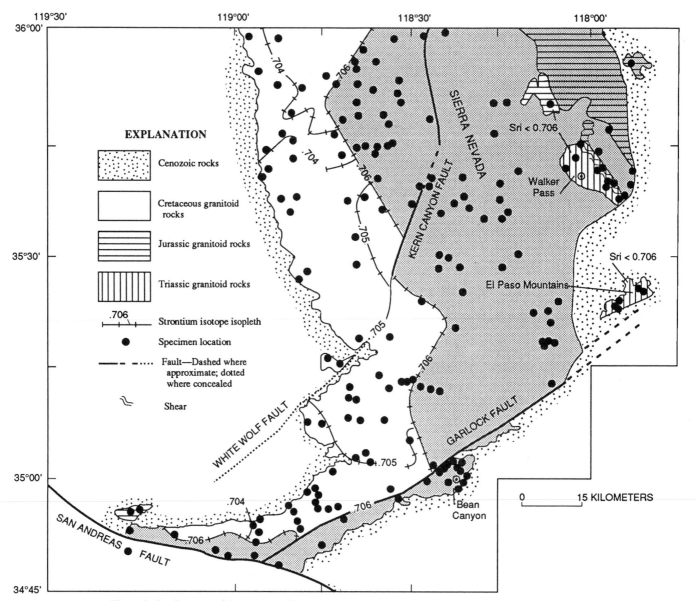

Figure 3. Outline map of the southern Sierra Nevada and El Paso Mountains showing strontium isotope isopleths and the three age groups of plutons that crop out in the area (Kistler and Ross, 1989). In places the strontium 0.706 isopleth coincides with and is offset by the Kern, Garlock, and San Andreas fault systems. Shaded area has plutons with $Sr_i > 0.706$.

shown by Kistler and Peterman (1978), and it is bounded on the east by the shear zone and 240-Ma plutons (Fig. 3). The wall rocks of the plutons in the Salinian–western Mojave terrane in the southern Sierra Nevada are predominantly metamorphosed sedimentary rocks of early Mesozoic age, and sedimentary and volcanic rocks of middle Cretaceous age, called the Kings sequence and the Erskine Canyon sequence, respectively, in the vicinity of Lake Isabella (Saleeby and Busby-Spera, 1986).

The Kings sequence was first defined for Late Triassic and Early Jurassic metamorphosed sedimentary rocks exposed in the Kings River Canyon in the Boyden Cave roof pendant (Bateman and Clark, 1974), and metamorphosed sedimentary rocks of sim-

ilar age and lithology (Christensen, 1963) are known to occur in the Mineral King roof pendant located between the Boyden Cave pendant and the Lake Isabella area (Fig. 2). The region in the Sierra Nevada batholith that contains metamorphosed sedimentary rocks of the Kings sequence has been called the Kings terrane by Nokleberg (1983). However, rocks in roof pendants in the eastern part of the southern Sierra Nevada assigned to the Kings sequence (Saleeby and others, 1978) that are east of the shear zone have lithologic and structural histories different from the Kings sequence to the west of the shear zone. The rocks in roof pendants to the east of the shear zone are excluded from the Kings sequence in this chapter.

Other metamorphosed wall rocks of the batholith to the west of the shear zone in the southern Sierra Nevada and just north of the Garlock fault are called the Pampa Schist. These rocks consist of sillimanite- and andalusite-bearing graphitic pelite interlayered with psammitic schist and local lenses of amphibolitic mafic to intermediate volcaniclastic rocks (Dibblee and Chesterman, 1953). This assemblage strongly resembles lower Mesozoic slaty rocks that lie depositionally above the Paleozoic Kings-Kaweah ophiolite belt about 50 km to the north of the Garlock fault (Saleeby, 1979). Blocks of quartzite and stratified sequences of quartz-rich turbidites intermixed with the Kings-Kaweah slaty strata suggest these rocks and the Pampa Schist are a western facies of the Mesozoic Kings sequence (Saleeby and others, 1978).

Basement rocks for the Kings sequence are unknown, except for the apparent westward overlap relation with Paleozoic ophiolitic rocks (Saleeby and others, 1978). This basement includes plagiogranite dikes, 285 ± 45 Ma, that intruded the early Paleozoic (485 ± 21 Ma) Kings-Kaweah ophiolite (Shaw and others, 1984, 1987). Rocks mapped as Kings sequence in the Tule River pendants (Saleeby and others, 1978) to the east of the Kaweah ophiolite include 300-Ma volcanic rocks that may be part of the basement for these sediments (Kistler and Sawlan, 1986, unpublished data).

Metamorphosed sedimentary rocks, assigned to the Kings sequence by Saleeby and others (1978), in the Bald Mountain and Nine Mile Canyon roof pendants are east of the shear zone and along the western margin of the Sierran terrane in the southern Sierra Nevada (Fig. 2). These rocks are excluded from the Kings sequence in this chapter because they are lithologically similar to some found to the north in the western Sierra Nevada foothills (Weber, 1963), and include bedded barite, indicating a protolith of Paleozoic age (Taylor, 1984; Diggles and others, 1985). To the south in the El Paso Mountains and along the western margin of the Sierran terrane into the central Mojave desert near the vicinity of Barstow, other metamorphic rock sequences crop out that are of both early and late Paleozoic age and are lithologically similar to the western facies rocks of west-central Nevada (Carr and others, 1981).

Quartzites, schists, and marbles in the Dinkey Creek roof pendant assigned to the Kings sequence (Bateman and Clark, 1974; Saleeby and others, 1978) are also excluded from the Kings sequence in this chapter. Stratigraphy and structure in the Dinkey Creek pendant are the same as in fossiliferous lower Paleozoic metamorphosed sedimentary rocks exposed in roof pendants in the eastern Sierra Nevada (Kistler, 1966; Kistler and Bateman, 1966). Structural studies in the Mineral King pendant (Christensen, 1963) show that the early Mesozoic metamorphosed sedimentary rocks in the Kings sequence have a less complex deformational history than the rocks in the Dinkey Creek roof pendant and correlative lower Paleozoic rocks of the eastern Sierra Nevada.

The cryptic shear zone in the southern Sierra Nevada must pass to the west of the Dinkey Creek pendant in a projection to the north of the Boyden Cave roof pendant. The Melones fault zone in the western foothills of the northern Sierra Nevada is picked as the next exposed segment of this shear zone because, as in the southern Sierra Nevada, it marks the western tectonic contact of Middle Jurassic plutons in this area. Late Jurassic to Late Cretaceous plutons have engulfed the shear zone along most of its length, and constrain the time of shearing to between about 160 and 150 Ma.

To summarize, a discontinuously exposed shear zone extends along the length of the Sierra Nevada batholith and marks a boundary between wall-rock and roof-pendant lithologies of different ages, depositional environments, and structural histories. The shear zone is a tectonic western limit to plutons of Middle Jurassic age intruded during the Inyo Mountains intrusive epoch of Evernden and Kistler (1970). In addition, plutons on either side of the boundary have different chemical and isotopic characteristics that indicate their source regions are of two fundamentally different lithosphere types. The western lithosphere type is called Panthalassan, whereas the eastern lithosphere type is called North American (Kistler, 1987). The next section documents the different chemical and isotopic characteristics of plutons intruded into these two lithosphere types.

ISOTOPIC AND CHEMICAL CHARACTERISTICS OF PLUTONS INTRUDED INTO THE PANTHALASSAN AND NORTH AMERICAN LITHOSPHERES

A northwest-trending belt of plutons that have been described as strongly contaminated and reduced (Ague and Brimhall, 1987), mostly because of low Fe_2O_3 in ilmenite, and that lack hornblende and sphene in their mineral assemblages was intruded into the Panthalassan lithosphere. The chemical characteristics of the plutons, believed unique in the Sierra Nevada, have been interpreted to be due to assimilation of highly reduced pelites in the sediments of the Kings sequence (Ague and Brimhall, 1987). These plutons correspond to those called the western foothills rocks and the Shaver sequence by Dodge (1972) and have low oxidation ratios relative to plutons intruded into North American lithosphere. Dodge (1972) suggested that the lower oxidation ratios of plutons of the western foothills rocks and Shaver sequence resulted from low water contents in these plutons at the inception of crystallization of the magmas. These contaminated and reduced plutons are known to occur predominantly in the restricted area of the Kings sequence, as defined in this paper, and their sources were in Panthalassan lithosphere.

Plutons intruded into Panthalassan lithosphere have $\delta^{18}O$ values (Masi and others, 1976, 1981; Ross, 1983; Saleeby and others, 1987; Kistler, unpublished data) consistently greater than +9 per mil in those with Sr_i greater than 0.706 and often greater than +9 per mil in those with Sr_i less than 0.706. The ^{18}O-enriched characteristic of these plutons also indicates that a significant sedimentary component was in the sources of their parent magmas (Fig. 4). In contrast, $\delta^{18}O$ values of plutons intruded

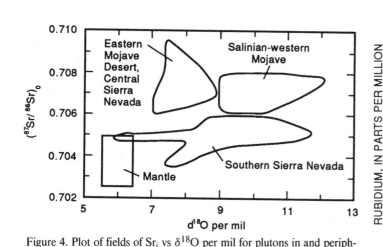

Figure 4. Plot of fields of Sr$_i$ vs δ^{18}O per mil for plutons in and peripheral to the Salinian–western Mojave terrane in the southern Sierra Nevada and for plutons in the central Sierra Nevada and eastern Mojave Desert.

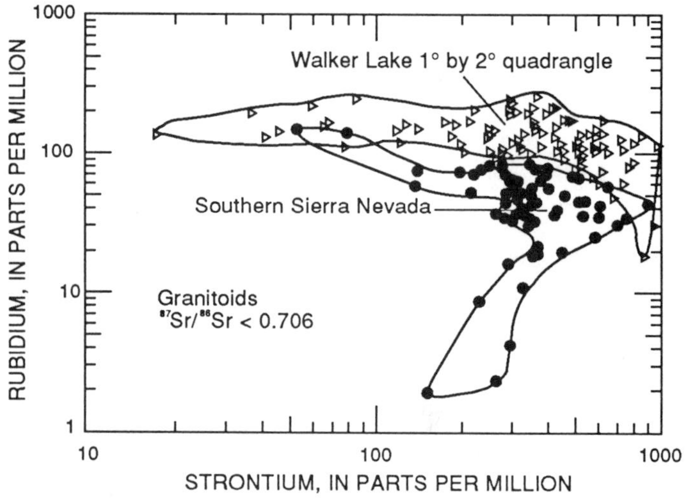

Figure 5. Plot of Rb vs. Sr for plutons with Sr$_i$ less than 0.706 peripheral to the Salinian–western Mojave terrane in Panthalassan lithosphere and peripheral to the Sierran terrane in North American lithosphere in the Walker Lake 1° × 2° quadrangle. Solid circles are for specimens from the southern Sierra Nevada (Kistler and Ross, 1989) and open triangles are for specimens from the Walker Lake 1° × 2° quadrangle (Robinson and Kistler, 1986).

into the North American lithosphere are consistently less than +9 per mil (Fig. 4), a characteristic indicating igneous source materials for these granitoid rocks.

Concentrations of Rb in plutons with Sr$_i$ less than 0.706 in Panthalassan lithosphere are consistently less than the concentrations of Rb in plutons with similar Sr$_i$ in North American lithosphere. Rb is plotted against Sr (Fig. 5) for plutons with Sr$_i$ less than 0.706 intruded into the North American lithosphere in the Walker Lake 1°×2° quadrangle (Robinson and Kistler, 1986) and into the Panthalassan lithosphere in the southern Sierra Nevada (Kistler and Ross, 1989). Granitoids with these Sr$_i$ values have Rb concentrations less than 100 ppm or greater than 100 ppm in Panthalassan and North American lithospheres, respectively. Also, in plutons with Sr$_i$ less than 0.706, Sm and Nd have generally lower concentrations in plutons intruded into the Panthalassan lithosphere than in plutons intruded into North American lithosphere. The ϵ_{Nd} values of plutons intruded into North American lithosphere are less positive (DePaolo, 1981) than those for plutons with the same Sr$_i$ (i.e., 0.704) intruded into Panthalassan lithosphere. These chemical and isotopic characteristics indicate that the source region for plutons with Sr$_i$ less than 0.706 have a time-integrated depletion in large ion lithophile elements in the Panthalassan lithosphere relative to the North American lithosphere. The extremely low heat production from granitic rocks intruded into Panthalassan lithosphere and cored in drill holes for heat-flow studies (locations ST and SJ; Lachenbruch, 1968) is also consistent with these plutons having sources that are depleted in large ion lithophile elements.

The sum of the isotopic and chemical data discussed here indicates that, by itself, Sr$_i$ greater than 0.706 in plutons in the western United States does not characterize everywhere the basement beneath the plutons as crystalline Precambrian sialic crust, as suggested by Kistler and Peterman (1973). For example,

the combination of strontium and oxygen isotopes and mineral chemistry in plutons with Sr$_i$ greater than 0.706 that intruded the Panthalassan lithosphere indicates that the material that caused the radiogenic Sr isotopic signature was sedimentary in nature. This observation is supported by the characteristics of distinctive gneisses exposed in the southernmost Sierra Nevada, which represent the deepest exposed levels of the Cretaceous batholithic belt (Sharry, 1981; Ross, 1985; Sams, 1986; Saleeby and others, 1987). Thermo-barometric estimates of up to 8 kbar for mineral equilibration in the gneiss complex and the enclosing granitoid rocks indicate that mid-crustal levels of the batholith are exposed here (Sharry, 1981; Sams, 1986). These paragneisses, characterized by radiogenic strontium and detrital Proterozoic zircons, were formed during an Early Cretaceous metamorphism (110–120 Ma), and no direct remnants of Proterozoic sialic crystalline basement have been found at this level of the Panthalasan lithosphere (Sams, 1986; Saleeby and others, 1987).

On the other hand, Sr$_i$ greater than 0.706 in Mesozoic plutons intruded into the North American lithosphere in the Sierra Nevada are interpreted to indicate that source materials for the plutons were from predominantly crystalline Proterozoic lower crust (Kistler and Peterman, 1973; Kistler and others, 1986). In support of this are δ^{18}O values consistently less than +9 in these plutons and the observation that xenoliths entrained in Tertiary volcanic rocks that were derived in the North American lithosphere in the central Sierra Nevada include garnet granulites that represent a direct sample of the Proterozoic lower crust in that area (Domenick and others, 1983).

THE GRAVITY FIELD AND TWO LITHOSPHERE TYPES

A crustal model that compares near-surface geology with residual gravity, assuming perfect Airy-type isostasy, along a traverse from Visalia to Lone Pine across the southern Sierra Nevada (Oliver and Robbins, 1982), crosses the tectonic boundary between the Panthalassan and North American lithospheres in the Mineral King roof pendant. In their model, the depth to Moho increases abruptly by 4 km, from about 30 km to 34 km, across the subsurface projection of the lithosphere boundary. If this model is correct, it indicates that not only chemical and isotopic characteristics, but also the thickness of the crust is different in the two lithosphere types, the Panthalassan crust being thinner.

IMPLICATIONS FOR THE TECTONIC ASSEMBLY OF CALIFORNIA

Figure 6 is an outline map of the granitoid rock exposures in the Sierra Nevada and southern California with the Tertiary displacements along the San Andreas and Garlock fault systems restored. This reconstruction places granitoid rocks of the central Salinian block of Ross (1972) adjacent to and correlative with granitoid rocks with identical Sr_i (Kistler and others, 1973) of the northwestern Mojave Desert (the Salinian–western Mojave terrane of Kistler and Peterman, 1978). This reconstruction also aligns, and brings into proximity, wall rocks of plutons in the Salinian–western Mojave terrane with the metamorphic rocks of the Kings sequence in the western Sierra Nevada. The basement of the Kings sequence seems to be polygenetic ophiolite mélange that has yielded limestone olistoliths with an exotic Late Permian Tethyan fauna (Schweickert and others, 1977). The Late Triassic and Early Jurassic fossils that date the metamorphosed sedimentary rocks of the Kings sequence are not exotic to North America, however, and require that the combined Salinian–western Mojave and Kings terranes were adjacent to North America as long ago as the Late Triassic. These observations are not compatible with paleomagnetic data that have been interpreted to require that the Salinian terrane originated far to the south of its present position and only accreted to the southern California region in latest Paleocene or earliest Eocene time (Vedder and others, 1982; Champion and others, 1984; Kanter and Debiche, 1985).

The Panthalassan lithosphere includes oceanic crust of early Paleozoic age (Shaw and others, 1984, 1987) that encroached on and subducted beneath western North America in the early Mesozoic. The sedimentary and volcanic rocks of the Kings sequence were deposited on this crust in a fore-arc basin of the Late Triassic–Early to Middle Jurassic magmatic arc component of the Sierra Nevada (see also Saleeby and others, 1978). The original position and configuration of the fore-arc–arc pair have been modified, as evidenced by the tectonic nature of their contact along the western margin of the Middle Jurassic plutons. Figure 7 is a palinspastic outline map of the western United States that has Tertiary Basin and Range extension and San Andreas and Garlock fault displacements removed (modified after Armstrong and Suppe, 1973; Armstrong and others, 1978). The outcrops of Middle Jurassic plutons of the Inyo Mountains intrusive epoch (Evernden and Kistler, 1970), which extend from the Klamath Mountains in northwestern California southeastward through the central Sierra Nevada to southern Arizona (Kistler and others, 1971), are shown in Figure 7. Also shown on the diagram (Fig. 7) are the tectonic boundary between the Panthalassan and North American lithospheres along the western margin of this locus of plutons, the outline around the combined Salinian–western Mojave and Kings terranes, the outcrop areas of the Pelona-Orocopia schist bodies in southern California and southwestern Arizona, and the projection of the Sonora-Mojave megashear of Silver and Anderson (1974) in the southeastern corner of California. If the oroclinal flexure of the southern Sierra Nevada and the Salinian-western Mojave terrane in the northwestern Mojave Desert were removed, the tectonic boundary between the two lithosphere types would line up nicely with the Sonora-Mojave megashear. The estimate of timing of motion along the megashear (about 160 Ma) by Anderson and Schmidt (1983) agrees very well with the constraints of timing of displacement along the lithosphere boundary in the Sierra Nevada. These observations support the suggestion of Kistler (1978) and Kistler and Peterman (1978) that the Melones fault zone and the eastern margin of the Salinian–western Mojave terrane mark the extension of the Sonora-Mojave megashear through California.

SUMMARY AND CONCLUSIONS

Chemical and isotopic compositions of plutons in the Sierra Nevada reflect source materials from two distinctly different lithosphere types. The two lithosphere types are in tectonic contact along a fault zone that may be the extension of the Sonora-Mojave megashear through California. Rocks of the North American lithosphere have apparently undergone some displacements along lateral faults during the Jurassic. However, the continuity of trends of geologic features of intruded rocks as old as early Paleozoic with the chemical and isotopic trends mapped in the Mesozoic granitoid rocks suggest there are no far-traveled exotic terranes in this lithosphere type. Late Paleozoic, Tethyan fossils have been known to occur to the west of the Melones fault zone since the work of Douglass (1967). These, and the Tethyan fusulinids in the Kaweah mélange (Schweikert and others, 1977) suggest an exotic origin for all exposed rocks older than Late Triassic for the Panthalassan lithosphere. Late Triassic fossils with North American affinities in the Kings sequence, which was deposited on Panthalassan lithosphere, require a site of deposition near North America for these rocks.

The time of juxtaposition of the two lithosphere types is constrained to be younger than the sheared Middle Jurassic plutons of the Inyo Mountains intrusive epoch along the western

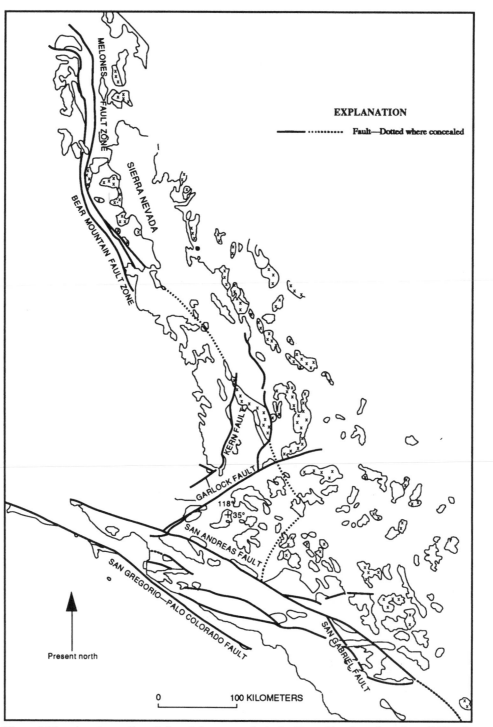

Figure 6. Map showing outline of plutonic igneous rocks in the Sierra Nevada and southern California. Cenozoic displacements on the Garlock, San Andreas, San Gabriel, and San Gregorio–Palo Colorado faults have been removed. Plutons patterned with x range in age from 215 to about 160 Ma. Modified from Kistler and Peterman (1978). The boundary between the Panthalassan and North American lithospheres is shown as the Melones fault and a continuation to the south as a dotted line that extends across the Garlock fault to the central Mojave Desert, where it bends sharply to the southwest to intersect the San Andreas fault.

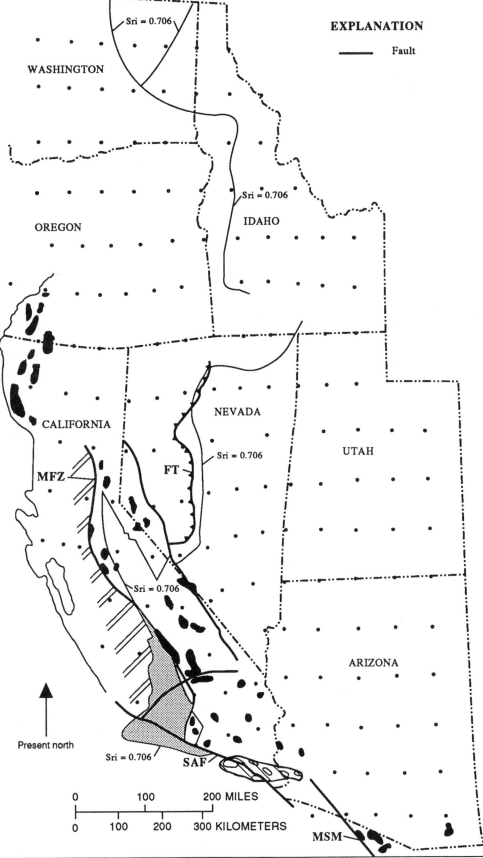

Figure 7. Palinspastic map of the western United States with Cenozoic extension in the Basin and Range removed and displacements along the San Andreas and Garlock fault zones restored. MFZ, Melones fault zone; SAF, San Andreas fault zone; FT, Fencemaker thrust zone; MSM, Mojave-Sonora megashear. Outcrops of plutons emplaced during the Lee Vining and Inyo Mountains intrusive epochs (Evernden and Kistler, 1970) are shown in black. The Salinian–western Mojave terrane is patterned gray, whereas the rest of the Panthalassan lithosphere is patterned with northeast-trending diagonal lines. Pelona-Orocopia schist belt is patterned with northwest-trending diagonal lines. The boundary between the Panthalassan and North American lithospheres is the Melones fault zone, the eastern boundary of the Salinian–western Mojave terrane, and the east-trending belt of Pelona-Orocopia schist exposures. Dots represent palinspastically restored 1° latitude and longitude markers.

margin of the North American lithosphere and older than Late Jurassic and Early Cretaceous plutons of the Yosemite intrusive epoch (150 to 135 Ma) that transect the Melones fault in the northern Sierra Nevada (Evernden and Kisteler, 1970). This time of faulting agrees with that suggested for the left-lateral Sonora-Mojave megashear by Anderson and Schmidt (1983). Slip-sense indicators along the exposed parts of the shear zone in the Sierra Nevada are unknown or ambiguous (e.g., Saleeby, 1979; Girty, 1985; Nokleberg, 1983), however, and a correspondence with the Sonora-Mojave megashear is only permissive.

REFERENCES CITED

Ague, J. J., and Brimhall, G. H., 1987, Granites of the batholiths of California; Products of local assimilation and regional-scale crustal contamination: Geology, v. 15, p. 63–66.

Anderson, T. H., and Schmidt, V. A., 1983, The evolution of middle America and the Gulf of Mexico–Caribbean Sea region during Mesozoic time: Geological Society of America Bulletin, v. 94, p. 941–966.

Armstrong, R. L., and Suppe, J., 1973, Potassium-argon geochronometry of Mesozoic granitic rocks in Nevada, Utah, and southern California: Geological Society of America Bulletin, v. 84, p. 1375–1392.

Armstrong, R. L., Taubeneck, W. H., and Hales, P. O., 1977, Rb-Sr and K-Ar geochronometry of Mesozoic granitic rocks and their Sr isotopic composition, Oregon, Washington, and Idaho: Geological Society of America Bulletin, v. 88, p. 397–411.

Bateman, P. C., and Clark, L. D., 1974, Stratigraphic and structural setting of the Sierra Nevada batholith, California: Pacific Geology, v. 8, p. 78–89

Busby-Spera, C. J., 1983, Paleogeographic reconstruction of a submarine volcanic center; Geochronology, volcanology, and sedimentology of Mineral King roof pendant, Sierra Nevada, California [Ph.D. thesis]: Princeton, New Jersey, Princeton University, 290 p.

Carr, M. D., Poole, F. G., Harris, A. G., and Christiansen, R. L., 1981, Western facies Paleozoic rocks in the Mojave Desert, California: U.S. Geological Survey Open-File Report 81–503, p. 15–17.

Champion, D. E., Howell, D. G., and Gromme, C. S., 1984, Paleomagnetic and geologic data indicating 2,500 km of northward displacement for the Salinian and related terranes, California: Journal of Geophysical Research, v. 89, p. 7736–7752.

Christensen, M. N., 1963, Structure of the metamorphic rocks at Mineral King, California: Berkeley, California University Publications in the Geological Sciences, v. 42, no. 4, p. 159–198.

DePaolo, D. J., 1981, A neodymium and strontium isotopic study of the Mesozoic calc-alkaline granitic batholiths of the Sierra Nevada and Peninsular ranges, California: Journal of Geophysical Research, v. 86, no. B11, p. 10470–10488.

Dibblee, T. W., Jr., and Chesterman, C. W., 1953, Geology of the Breckenridge Mountain Quadrangle, California: California Division of Mines and Geology Bulletin 168, 56 p.

Diggles, M. F., Tucker, R. E., Griscom, A., Causey, J. D., and Gaps, R. S., 1985, Mineral resources of the Owens Peak and Little Lake Canyon wilderness study area, Inyo and Kern counties, California: U.S. Geological Survey Bulletin 1708–B, 14 p.

Dodge, F.C.W., 1972, Variation of ferrous-ferric ratios in the central Sierra Nevada batholith, U.S.A.: 24th International Geological Congress, Section 10, p. 12–19.

Doe, B. R., and Delevaux, M. H., 1973, Variations in lead isotopic compositions in Mesozoic granitic rocks of California; A preliminary investigation: Geological Society of America Bulletin, v. 84, no. 11, p. 3513–3526.

Domenick, M. R., Kistler, R. W., Dodge, F.C.W., and Tatsumoto, M., 1983, Nd and Sr isotopic study of crustal and mantle inclusions from the Sierra Nevada and implications for batholith petrogenesis: Geological Society of America Bulletin, v. 94, p. 713–719.

Douglass, R. C., 1967, Permian Tethyan fusulinids from California: U.S. Geological Survey Professional Paper 593A, 13 p.

Evernden, J. F., and Kistler, R. W., 1970, Chronology of emplacement of Mesozoic batholithic complexes in California and western Nevada: U.S. Geological Survey Professional Paper 623, 42 p.

Farmer, G. L., and DePaolo, D. J., 1983, Origin of Mesozoic and Tertiary granite in the western United States and implications for pre-Mesozoic crustal structure; 1, Nd and Sr isotopic studies in the geocline of the northern Great Basin: Journal of Geophysical Research, v. 88, no. B4, p. 3379–3401.

Fleck, R. J., and Criss, R. E., 1985, Strontium and oxygen isotopic variations in Mesozoic and Tertiary plutons in central Idaho: Contributions to Mineralogy and Petrology, v. 90, p. 291–308.

Girty, G. H., 1985, Boyden Cave roof pendant, west-central Sierra Nevada, Madera and Tulare counties: California Geology, no. 3, p. 51–55.

Heck, F. R., and Speed, R. C., 1987, Triassic olistostrome and shelf-basin transition in the western Great Basin; Paleogeographic implications: Geological Society of America Bulletin, v. 99, p. 539–551.

Kanter, L. R., and Debiche, M., 1985, Modeling the motion histories of the Point Arena and central Salinian terranes, in Howell, D. G., ed., Tectonostratigraphic teranes of the circum-Pacific region: Circum-Pacific Council for Energy and Mineral Resources, Earth Science Series no. 1, p. 227–238.

Kanter, L. R., and McWilliams, M. O., 1982, Tectonic rotation of the southernmost Sierra Nevada, California: Journal of Geophysical Research, v. 87, p. 3819–3830.

Kistler, R. W., 1966, Structure and metamorphism in the Mono Craters Quadrangle, Sierra Nevada, California: U.S. Geological Survey Bulletin 1221–E, p. E1–E53.

—— , 1978, Mesozoic paleogeography of California; A viewpoint from isotope geology, in Howell, D. G., and McDougall, K. A., eds., Mesozoic paleogeography of the western United States: Society of Economic Paleontologists and Mineralogists Pacific Coast Paleogeography Symposium 2, p. 75–84.

—— , 1983, Isotope geochemistry of plutons in the northern Great Basin: Geothermal Resources Council Special Report 13, p. 3–8.

—— , 1987, Lithosphere types in the Sierra Nevada: Geological Society of America Abstracts with Programs, v. 14, no. 6, p. 395.

Kistler, R. W., and Peterman, Z. E., 1973, Variations in Sr, Rb, K, Na, and initial $^{87}Sr/^{86}Sr$ in Mesozoic granitic rocks and intruded wall rocks in central California: Geological Society of America Bulletin, v. 84, p. 3489–3512.

—— , 1978, Reconstruction of crustal blocks of California on the basis of initial strontium isotopic compositions of Mesozoic granitic rocks: U.S. Geological Survey Professional Paper 1071, 17 p.

Kistler, R. W., and Lee, D. E., 1989, Rubidium strontium and strontium isotopic data for a suite of granitoid rocks from the Basin and Range Province, Arizona, California, Nevada, and Utah: U.S. Geological Survey Open-File Report 89–199, 13 p.

Kistler, R. W., and Ross, D. C., 1989, A strontium isotopic study of plutons of the southern Sierra Nevada: U.S. Geological Survey Bulletin (in press).

Kistler, R. W., Evernden, J. F., and Shaw, H. R., 1971, Sierra Nevada plutonic cycle; Part 1, Origin of composite granitic batholiths: Geological Society of America Bulletin, v. 82, p. 853–868.

Kistler, R. W., Peterman, Z. E., Ross, D. C., and Gottfried, D., 1973, Strontium isotopes and the San Andreas fault, in Kovach, R. L., and Nur, A., eds., Proceedings of the conference on tectonic problems of the San Andreas fault system: Stanford, California, Stanford University Publications in Geological Sciences, v. 13, p. 339–347.

Kistler, R. W., Robinson, A. C., and Fleck, R. J., 1980, Mesozoic right-lateral fault in eastern California: Geological Society of America Abstracts with Programs, v. 12, p. 115.

Kistler, R. W., Chappell, B. W., Peck, D. L., and Bateman, P. C., 1986, Isotopic variation in the Tuolumne Intrusive Suite, central Sierra Nevada, California:

Contributions to Mineralogy and Petrology, v. 94, p. 205–220.

Lachenbruch, A. H., 1968, Preliminary geothermal model of the Sierra Nevada: Journal of Geophysical Research, v. 73, p. 6977–6990.

Masi, U., O'Neil, J. R., and Kistler, R. W., 1976, Stable isotope systematics in Mesozoic granites near the San Andreas and Garlock fault systems, California: Geological Society of America Abstracts with Programs, v. 8, p. 998

——, 1981, Stable isotopes in Mesozoic granites of central and northern California and southwestern Oregon: Contributions to Mineralogy and Petrology, v. 76, p. 116–126.

McWilliams, M., and Li, Y., 1985, Oroclinal bending of the southern Sierra Nevada batholith: Science, v. 230, p. 172–175.

Moore, J. G., and Dodge, F. C., 1962, Mesozoic age of metamorphic rocks in the Kings River area, southern Sierra Nevada, California; Geological Survey Research 1962: U.S. Geological Survey Professional Paper 450–B, p. B19–B21.

Nokleberg, W. J., 1983, Wall rocks of the central Sierra Nevada batholith, California; A collage of accreted tectono-stratigraphic terranes: U.S. Geological Survey Professional Paper 1255, 28 p.

Oliver, H. W., and Robbins, S. L., 1982, Bouger gravity map of California, Fresno sheet: California Division of Mines and Geology, 23 p.

Poole, F. G., and Sandberg, C. A., 1977, Mississippian paleogeography and tectonics of the western United States, *in* Stewart, J. H., Stevens, C. H., and Fritsche, R. E., eds., Paleozoic paleogeography of the western United States, Pacific Coast Paleogeography Symposium 1: Pacific Section, Society of Economic Paleontologists and Mineralogists, p. 67–84.

Robinson, A. C., and Kistler, R. W., 1986, Maps showing isotopic dating in the Walker Lake 1° by 2° Quadrangle, California and Nevada: U.S. Geological Survey Map MF–1382N, scale 1:250,000.

Ross, D. C., 1972, Petrographic and chemical reconnaissance of some granitic and gneissic rocks near the San Andreas fault from Bodega Head to Cajon Pass, California: U.S. Geological Survey Professional Paper 698, 92 p.

——, 1983, δ^{18}O in the southern Sierra Nevada: U.S. Geological Survey Open-File Report 83–904, scale 1:250,000.

——, 1985, Mafic gneissic complex (batholithic root?) in the southernmost Sierra Nevada, California: Geology, v. 13, p. 288–291.

——, 1987, Generalized geologic map of the basement rocks of the southern Sierra Nevada: U.S. Geological Survey Open-File Report 87-276, scale 1:250,000.

Saleeby, J. B., 1979, Kaweah serpentinite melange, southwest Sierra Nevada foothills, California: Geological Society of America Bulletin, v. 90, p. 29–46.

Saleeby, J. B., and Busby-Spera, C. J., 1986, Field trip guide to the metamorphic framework rocks of the Lake Isabella area, southern Sierra Nevada, California, *in* Dunne, G. C., compiler, Mesozoic and Cenozoic structural evolution of selected areas, east-central California, Geological Society of America Cordilleran Section meeting guidebook: Santa Fe Springs, California, Comet Reproduction Service, p. 81–94.

Saleeby, J. B., Goodin, S. E., Sharp, W. D., and Busby, C. J., 1978, Early Mesozoic paleotectonic-paleogeographic reconstruction of the southern Sierra Nevada region, *in* Howell, D. G., and McDougall, K. A., eds., Mesozoic paleogeography of the western United States: Society of Economic Paleontologists and Mineralogists Pacific Coast Paleogeography Symposium 2, p. 311–336.

Saleeby, J. B., Sams, D. B., and Kistler, R. W., 1987, U/Pb zircon, strontium, and oxygen isotopic and geochronological study of the southernmost Sierra

Nevada batholith, California: Journal of Geophysical Research, v. 92, no. B10, p. 10443–10466.

Sams, D. B., 1986, U/Pb geochronology, petrology, and structural geology of the crystalline rocks of the southernmost Sierra Nevada and Tehachapi Mountains, Kern County, California [Ph.D. thesis]: Pasadena, California Institute of Technology, 315 p.

Schweickert, R. A., Saleeby, J. B., Tobisch, D. T., and Wright, W. H., III, 1977, Paleotectonic and paleogeographic significance of the Calaveras Complex, western Sierra Nevada, California, *in* Stewart, J. H., Stevens, C. H., and Fritsche, R. E., eds., Paleozoic paleogeography of the western United States: Pacific Section, Society of Economic Paleontologists and Mineralogists, p. 381–394.

Sharry, J., 1981, The geology of the western Tehachapi Mountains, California [Ph.D. thesis]: Boston, Massachusetts, Massachusetts Institut of Technology, 215 p.

Shaw, H. F., Chen, J. H., Wasserburg, G. J., and Saleeby, J. B., 1984, Nd-Sr-Pb systematics and age of the Kings-Kaweah ophiolite, California: EOS (Transactions of the American Geophysical Union), v. 65, no. 45, p. 1147.

Shaw, H. F., Chen, J. H., Saleeby, J. B., and Wasserburg, G. J., 1987, Nd-Sr-Pb systematics and age of the Kings River ophiolite, California; Implications for depleted mantle evolution: Contributions to Mineralogy and Petrology, v. 96, p. 281–290.

Sheehan, P. M., 1980, Paleogeography and marine communities of the Silurian carbonate shelf in Utah and Nevada, *in* Fouch, T. D., and Magathan, E.E.R., eds., Paleozoic paleogeography of the west-central United States; Rocky Mountain Paleogeography Symposium no. 1: Society of Economic Paleontologists and Mineralogists, p. 19–37.

Silver, L. T., and Anderson, T. H., 1974, Possible left-lateral early to middle Mesozoic disruption of the southwestern North American craton margin: Geological Society of America Abstracts with Programs, v. 6, p. 955–956.

Speed, R. C., 1983, Pre-Cenozoic tectonic evolution of northeastern Nevada: Geothermal Resources Council Special Report 13, p. 11–24.

Stevens, C. H., 1982, The Early Permian thysanophyllum coral belt; Another clue to Permian plate-tectonic reconstructions: Geological Society of America Bulletin, v. 93, p. 798–803.

Taylor, G. C., 1984, Rockhouse Basin Wilderness study area, Kern and Tulare counties: California Geology, v. 37, no. 12, p. 263–272.

Taylor, H. P., Jr., and Silver, L. T., 1978, Oxygen isotope relationships in plutonic igneous rocks of the Peninsular Ranges batholith, southern and Baja California, *in* Zartman, R. E., ed., Short papers of the 4th international conference on geochronology, cosmochronology, and isotope geology: U.S. Geological Survey Open-File Report 78–701, p. 423–426.

Vedder, J. G., Howell, D. G., and McLean, H., 1982, Stratigraphy, sedimentation, and tectonic accretion of exotic terranes, southern Coast Ranges, California, *in* Watkins, J. S., and Drake, C. L., eds., Studies in continental margin geology: American Association of Petroleum Geologists Memoir 34, p. 471–496.

Weber, H. F., Jr., 1963, Barite in California: California Division of Mines and Geology Mineral Information Service, v. 16, no. 10, p. 1–10.

MANUSCRIPT SUBMITTED JUNE 30, 1987
REVISED MANUSCRIPT SUBMITTED NOVEMBER 25, 1987
MANUSCRIPT ACCEPTED BY THE SOCIETY FEBRUARY 7, 1989

Geological Society of America
Memoir 174
1990

Chapter 16

Cretaceous magmatism, metamorphism, and metallogeny in the east-central Great Basin

Mark D. Barton
Department of Earth and Space Sciences, University of California, Los Angeles, California 90024

ABSTRACT

Compilation of published and new data on the distribution, timing, and composition of igneous rocks, ore deposits, and metamorphic rocks in the east-central Great Basin reveals systematic relations among Cretaceous magmatism, mineralization, metamorphism, and deformation. Magmatic compositions change with time from Early Cretaceous (~125 to 100 Ma) quartz diorite, monzonite, and quartz monzonite, to mid-Cretaceous metaluminous (± hornblende) granodiorite and granite, and ultimately to Late Cretaceous (~90 to 70 Ma) strongly peraluminous (two-mica) granite and granodiorite. Sr, O, and Nd isotopic data indicate a concomitant increasing crustal component, with a significant (meta)sedimentary component in the later plutons. Style and type of mineralization closely correlate with intrusion compositions. Porphyry Cu and Cu skarn deposits associated with the early plutons give way to porphyry Mo-Cu, polymetallic W skarn, and base-metal replacement mineralization associated with the metaluminous granodiorites and granites. F-rich, lithophile-element skarns and greisen mineralization are characteristic of the Late Cretaceous two-mica granites. Ar-Ar and U-Pb studies in the Snake and Ruby ranges and clustering of metamorphic K-Ar dates elsewhere are compatible with a Late Cretaceous (90 to 70 Ma) metamorphic culmination. Major tectonic subsidence in the foreland basin in central Utah, reflecting Sevier thrusting, began at about the same time (~90 Ma).

These observations are interpreted in the following way: increased deep (conductive) heat input accompanied renewal of magmatism, leading to increasing incorporation of crustal components with time in subduction-related magmas. Metallogeny followed the systematic changes in magma compositions. The metamorphic (thermal) culmination occurred simultaneously with maximum incorporation of crustal components in the magmas. Progressive thermal weakening of the crust was enhanced by wholesale assimilation or anatexis at this stage; thus major thrusting and the metamorphic culmination were synchronous with emplacement of two-mica granites. Simple one-dimensional thermal models are consistent with this scenario. Alternative interpretations that depend on crustal thickening as the primary mechanism are inconsistent with thermal considerations and the geologic record, although thickening probably played some role.

Similarities between the Cretaceous history in the east-central Great Basin and other areas in the western United States suggest analogous processes elsewhere, modified by local factors. Magmatic and metallogenic differences among the Cretaceous, Jurassic, and Tertiary periods in the eastern Great Basin, and between the Great Basin Cretaceous events and collisional orogens may reflect differences in the thermal evolution and magmatic fluxes.

Barton, M. D., 1990, Cretaceous magmatism, metamorphism, and metallogeny in the east-central Great Basin, *in* Anderson, J. L., ed., The nature and origin of Cordilleran magmatism: Boulder, Colorado, Geological Society of America Memoir 174.

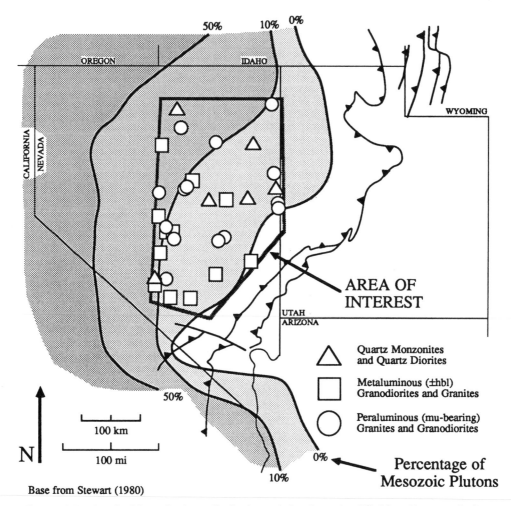

Figure 1. Map showing Mesozoic pluton distribution and abundance (modified from Barton and others, 1988) and the Sevier thrust belt, with the area and localities discussed here.

INTRODUCTION

The relations among magmatism, metamorphism, and deformation have received considerable attention in the Cordillera and other orogenic belts. Each process records a facet of the redistribution of energy and mass in an orogenic belt. Some relations among Cretaceous magmatism, metamorphism, attendant deformation, and related mineralization in the east-central Great Basin have been investigated previously, but little effort has been made to synthesize both physical and chemical information in a temporal framework.

The study area lies in the hinterland of the Sevier thrust belt (Armstrong, 1968), on the eastern edge of the Cretaceous magmatic arc along the Cordilleran miogeocline (Figs. 1, 2). The crust is transitional from the craton on the east to eugeoclinal terranes on the west. The area is part of the "eastern Cordilleran metamorphic belt"—easternmost of the two generalized Mesozoic metamorphic culminations in the western United States (Armstrong, 1982). Systematic investigation of the regional metamorphic and structural history of the eastern Great Basin began with the work

of Misch (1960; Misch and Hazzard, 1962). Recent reviews by Miller and others (1988), Snoke and Miller (1988), and Speed and others (1988) cover many aspects of the Mesozoic and Cenozoic tectonic, metamorphic, and igneous history of the eastern and central Great Basin. Farmer and DePaolo (1983, 1984), Kistler (1983; Kistler and others, 1981), and Lee (1984; Lee and Christiansen, 1983; Lee and others, 1981, 1984), among others, have studied and discussed aspects of Mesozoic magmatism. The studies of plutonism have emphasized regional (spatial) variations and petrogenetic characteristics, and have identified petrogenetic inheritance reflecting the nature of the crust (e.g., Farmer and DePaolo, 1983; Kistler, 1974) or the inferred effects of depth to and angle of the subducting slab (e.g., Keith, 1978). Temporal and smaller scale spatial changes in magmatism and their relation to metamorphism and other processes are not well known.

The relations between Cordilleran magmatism and regional deformation have been explored by many workers (e.g., Armstrong, 1974, 1983; Burchfiel and Davis, 1975; and Coney and Harms, 1984). There is widespread agreement that deformation is related to crustal softening during major magmatic episodes, but

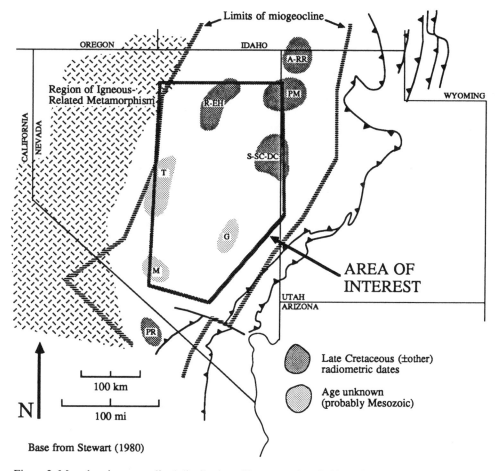

Figure 2. Map showing generalized distribution of known and probable regions of Mesozoic metamorphism in the Great Basin. Also shown are the Sevier thrust belt and the general extent of the Cordilleran miogeocline (modified from Stewart, 1980). Metamorphism in the Grant and Quinn Canyon ranges is pre-70 Ma. The abbreviations are: A-RR = Albion Mountains–Raft River Range; G = Grant and Quinn Canyon ranges; M = Mineral Ridge; PM = Pilot Mountains, PR = Panamint Range–Funeral Mountains; R-EH = Ruby Mountains–East Humboldt Range; S-SC-DC = Snake, Schell Creek, and Deep Creek ranges; T = Toiyabe Range.

the details of the mechanisms and driving forces remain uncertain (e.g., Armstrong, 1982, 1974; Burchfiel and Davis, 1975; Hamilton, 1978, 1988). Likewise, the relation between metamorphism and deformation has long been recognized (Misch, 1960; Misch and Hazzard, 1962), but timing and mechanisms are still controversial (e.g., Allmendinger and Jordan, 1981; Armstrong, 1982; Miller and others, 1988; Snoke and Miller, 1988).

Regional variations in mineralization (e.g., metal content and alteration associations) are commonly compositionally dependent on and relate to magmatism developed under different tectonic settings (e.g., Guild, 1978; Mitchell and Garson, 1981). Early attempts at correlating mineralization with timing of intrusion in the Great Basin (e.g., Jerome and Cook, 1967) were largely unsuccessful because of the poor geochronological and petrological data base. Keith (1983) developed a classification scheme relating metal contents to magma compositions in the Great Basin, but placed little emphasis on the timing. Other attempts to relate distribution of mineralization styles to magmatic distribution through time (e.g., Westra and Keith, 1982) have not focused on area-specific magmatic evolution as a key to metallogenesis. The relative importance in metallogenic provinces of original (lithospheric) enrichment (e.g., Noble, 1970; Titley and Beane, 1981) versus regional or temporal variations in the petrogenetic processes has rarely been examined.

Study of magmatic and associated mineralizing processes within a laterally homogeneous segment of crust removes one potentially important but indeterminable variable in magma evolution: the effect of variable crustal protolith on melt petrology. The east-central Great Basin offers such an opportunity because it contains a reasonably well-documented record of magmatism and other features over a large, fairly uniform region. A long period of stable subduction during the Cretaceous has been inferred by a number of workers and is consistent with reconstructions of plate motions (Engebretson and others, 1985). Response of this relatively uniform region under different tectonic environment in the Jurassic and the middle Tertiary provides additional constraints on the crust's nature and on Phanerozoic magmatic evolution.

This chapter examines timing, petrology, geochemistry, and energy budget of interrelated deformation, metamorphism, plutonism, and metallogeny. A unifying model, involving the energy and mass transfer that takes place within an evolving Andean-type continental margin, integrates the disparate processes. The conclusions presented here build on many earlier investigations, but differ substantially from previous interpretations. The scheme resembles that presented by Haxel and others (1984) for Laramide orogenesis in southern Arizona. It differs in downplaying the importance of thrusting in the thermal evolution and in emphasizing the differences between the geological environments and timing in Arizona and the Great Basin.

REGIONAL METAMORPHISM AND DEFORMATION

Regionally extensive Mesozoic metamorphism is documented in many areas in the east-central Great Basin and adjoining areas (Fig. 2; e.g., Armstrong, 1982; DeWitt and others, 1984; Labotka and others, 1985; Miller and others, 1988; Snoke and Miller, 1988). Available dates on metamorphic minerals cluster in the Late Jurassic, the Late Cretaceous, and the middle Tertiary, suggesting three metamorphic or cooling episodes (cf. Miller and others, 1987). In a few areas, such as the Snake Range and environs, integrated field and detailed Ar-Ar and other geochronometric studies suggest that all three general ages represent regionally significant metamorphism with associated, extensively developed structural fabrics (Miller and others, 1988). In some areas, such as the northern Snake Range, extensive high T/P metamorphic gradients require mid- or upper-crustal heat sources, almost certainly intrusions, to provide the energy for the localized metamorphic highs. A Jurassic metamorphic maximum is more clearly recognized in the northern Great Basin than one in the Cretaceous (e.g., DeWitt and others, 1984; Miller and others, 1988; Snoke and Miller, 1988).

Although its timing and character are poorly known, a regionally significant Late Cretaceous metamorphic culmination seems likely. Many metamorphic rocks from the Albion Mountains on the Utah-Idaho border to the Panamint Range in eastern California yield Late Cretaceous radiometric dates (Figs. 2 and 3). In many cases, this Cretaceous event appears to be an overprint or retrogression of higher grade Jurassic metamorphism (e.g., in the Panamint Range; Labotka and others, 1985; parts of northeastern Nevada; Snoke and Miller, 1988). In other areas, the Cretaceous metamorphism is related to a superimposed penetrative fabric (e.g., Schell Creek Range; Miller and others, 1988). Metamorphic dates cluster in the Late Cretaceous; mid- and Early Cretaceous dates are less common (see histogram, Fig. 9, in Miller and others, 1987).

Metamorphism ranges from subgreenschist to amphibolite facies and is commonly synkinematic. Petrologic constraints, in-

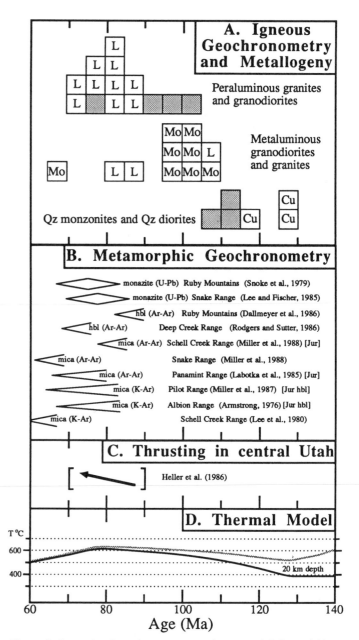

Figure 3. Synopsis of geochronometry and two model thermal histories. A: Histogram of best age estimates for the plutons of Figure 1 and Table 1 organized by composition. Associated mineralization is indicated by the abbreviations: L = lithophile element (Be, F, W, Mo) veins, greisens, and skarns; Mo = porphyry-style Mo-Cu, base-metal replacement, and/or polymetallic W skarns; and Cu = porphyry Cu, Cu skarns, Au-bearing jasperoids. Shading indicates no reported alteration or mineralization. B: Geochronometry on probable Cretaceous metamorphism in the Great Basin. The "crescendi" indicate the approximate ranges of dates (for K-Ar and Ar-Ar dates); they are open to the old end to show that they are cooling ages. Also indicated are areas with Jurassic dates on metamorphic micas ± hornblende [Jur] or just hornblende [Jur hbl]. C: Time of movement on the Sevier thrust system in central Utah. D: Model thermal histories at 20 km depth; the solid line is for Cretaceous heating only; the shaded line indicates a maximal Jurassic heating event (cf. Fig. 5; see text for discussion).

cluding the occurrence of kyanite in several areas, and the considerable sratigraphic depth to the beginning of greenschist facies metamorphism in many areas indicate medium-pressure facies series, Barrovian-type metamorphism (Barton and others, 1988; Miller and others, 1988; Snoke and Miller, 1988). Andalusite-bearing rocks appear to be restricted to narrow contact aureoles developed around major plutons. These inferences are consistent with estimates based on conodont maturation, which also show local thermal highs around Mesozoic plutons but a 30 to 40 °C/km maximum background gradient (Gans and others, 1987; Harris and others, 1980).

The Late Cretaceous clustering of radiometric dates could reflect an independent Cretaceous metamorphic event or regional cooling caused by uplift. Several reasons support the idea of a Late Cretaceous thermal maximum, although uplift probably contributed to the geochronometric systematics. The dated minerals have closure temperatures from about 300 °C (micas) to greater than 500 °C (hornblende and monazite), indicating that isotopic signatures were likely retained close to the metamorphic maximum; otherwise, one might expect a greater spread in ages. Local evidence for Early Cretaceous orogenesis (e.g., the Newark Canyon Formation; Stewart, 1980) could have provided some uplift, yet comparatively few Early Cretaceous dates are known. Extensive uplift and erosion in eastern Nevada did not begin until the middle Tertiary (Armstrong, 1968; Gans and Miller, 1983). Possible Late Cretaceous removal of the 1 to 3 km of Carboniferous to Triassic cover rocks, coeval with thrusting in the foreland fold and thrust belt (Fig. 3), would not be sufficient to permit adequate, regionally extensive cooling. Cooling following an earlier metamorphic event (Early Cretaceous or older) would take 10 to 30 m.y. (see Thermal Model, below) and would not yield the observed multiple-maximum geochronometric signature. These arguments leave cessation of an independent thermal event as the most plausible mechanism for the clustering of dates.

Deformation

Contraction along the Sevier thrust belt in central Utah is now thought to be Late Cretaceous (Heller and others, 1986; Figs. 2 and 3), roughly contemporaneous with the inferred metamorphic maximum. To the north, in northern Utah and western Wyoming, shortening began earlier, in the Middle or Late Jurassic, and ended with a major episode in the Late Cretaceous and early Paleogene (Wiltschko and Dorr, 1983; Heller and others, 1986). There is little surface expression of Mesozoic brittle deformation in eastern Nevada. Broad folds and local thrust faults beneath the middle Tertiary unconformity may be related to Sevier contraction (e.g., Armstrong, 1968), but most major pre-Tertiary structures are related to ductile deformation in the metamorphic infrastructure, as in the Ruby Mountains (of uncertain age[s], probably mainly Jurassic; Snoke and Miller, 1988). However, Miller and others (1988) argued that, in the Schell Creek Range, increasing strain down-section recorded by Late Cretaceous fabrics may indicate approach to a thrust zone related to the Sevier deformation.

It is possible that Cretaceous compression began in the western or central Great Basin and moved eastward with time, bypassing a large area in eastern Nevada. Speed and others (1988) propose a belt of Early Cretaceous deformation in central Nevada, indicated by thrust faults of uncertain age in the Eureka area and by the occurrence of Early Cretaceous Newark Valley Formation clastic rocks. Thrust faults in metamorphosed miogeoclinal rocks south of Eureka in the Fish Creek, Quinn Canyon, and Grant ranges that are cut by Late Cretaceous two-mica granite (Bartley and others, 1985) or related mineralization (Barton, 1982) may also reflect pre–Late Cretaceous Mesozoic deformation in central Nevada.

MAGMATISM AND METALLOGENY

Magmatism in the east-central Great Basin falls broadly into three episodes: late Middle to early Late Jurassic, Early to Late Cretaceous, and middle Tertiary (Armstrong and Suppe, 1973; Barton and others, 1988; Stewart, 1980). Cretaceous plutonism changed temporally from early, comparatively silica-poor, metaluminous plutons to late silicic, strongly peraluminous granitoids. Oxygen, neodymium, and strontium isotope ratios also vary systematically (indicating larger proportions of crustal material in the later phases), as does the metallogeny (from early chalcophile element–dominated deposits to late lithophile element–dominated deposits). The tripartite igneous divisions shown in Figure 1 are not mutually exclusive; gradations exist at all scales.

Timing and composition of plutons

About one-third of the more than 100 plutons in the east-central Great Basin have Cretaceous radiometric dates (Table 1, Fig. 1). Nearly all are K-Ar dates on micas; thus they represent cooling ages rather than emplacement ages. For several plutons, available dates are markedly discordant; in such cases the most reasonable (generally the oldest) date was selected to represent the age. Some radiometric dates, however, clearly were reset, and some "Cretaceous" ages may turn out to be Jurassic upon widespread application of U-Pb techniques (e.g., as in the Pilot Range; Miller and others, 1987). Furthermore, the sparse modal data for plutons in this region make some of the assignments to compositional groups tentative. Nonetheless, the systematics discussed below suggest that the data indicate meaningful trends.

The geochronometry on the igneous and metamorphic rocks is imperfect, but several lines of evidence suggest that the clustering of dates is significant. Although it takes several million years for the thermal anomaly associated with a large pluton to dissipate (Jaeger, 1964), K-Ar dates for intrusions emplaced into regions cooler than 250 to 300 °C should be close to emplacement ages, if there is no later reheating. Available evidence and thermal models (Lachenbruch and Sass, 1978; also see below) suggest that temperatures did not exceed these values at depths less than 8 to 10 km.

It is unlikely that the covariation of radiometric dates with

TABLE 1. ROCK TYPE, AGE, AND MINERALIZATION OF CRETACEOUS PLUTONS

Name	Dominant rock type	Age (methods) Ma*	Age of youngest host[†]	Alteration/ mineralization[§]	Recent references and d/ or sources
Elko County					
Dawley Canyon	2-mica monzogranite	84 (Rb-Sr)	Cambrian	LE pegmatites	Kistler and others (1981), Olson and Hinrichs (1960)
Dolly Varden	Quartz monzonite	125-154 (K-Ar)	Permian	Cu skarn/Cu porph.	Atkinson and others (1982), Granger and others (1957)
Toano Range	2-mica monzogranite	76 (K-Ar)	Cambrian	—	Lee and others (1981, 1984)
Esmeralda County					
Klondyke	Mu(?) monzogranite	104 (K-Ar)	Ordovician	Greisen, BM veins	Bonham and Garside (1979)
Lone Mountain	Granodiorite	71-86 (K-Ar; Rb-Sr)	Cambrian	Mo-Cu porph/BM repl.	Bonham and Garside (1979), John (1987)
Lone Mountain	Hornblende gabbro	113 (K-Ar)	Cambrian	—	Bonham and Garside (1979), John (1987)
Eureka County					
Eureka	Granodiorite	101 (K-Ar)	Cambrian	BM repl./W skarn/ Mo porph.	Nolan and Hunt (1968), Nolan and others (1973)
Gold Strike	Quartz diorite (?)	78-134 (K-Ar)	Silurian	porph.(?) and skarn(?)	Evans (1980), Hausen and Kerr (1968)
McCullough Butte	2-mica monzogranite	84 (K-Ar)	Ordovician	LE greisen and skarn	Barton (1982, 1987)
Richmond	Bi(-Mu?) monzogranite	108 (K-Ar)	Silurian	W-BM skarn/"Deuteric"	Evans (1980)
Rocky Canyon	2-mica monzogranite	84 (Rb-Sr)	Cambrian	LE greisen and skarn	Barton (1987)
Lander County					
Birch Creek	Bi(-Mu?) monzogranite	75-89 (K-Ar; U-Pb)	Ordovician	LE veins/skarn	Stewart and others (1977), D. L. Smith (1987, personal communication)
Gold Acres	Monzogranite	84-98 (K-Ar)	Devonian	Mo-qz veins/ BM-Mo skarn	Stewart and others (1977)
Lincoln County					
Pioche	Granodiorite (?)	95 (K-Ar)	Cambrian	BM repl./Mo skarn/ sericitic	Tschanz and Pampeyan (1970), Johnston (1972), Barton (unpublished data)
Tempiute	Granodiorite	96 (K-Ar)	Mississippian	Mo porph./W skarn	Tschanz and Pampeyan (1970), Buseck (1967), Barton (unpublished data)

TABLE 1. ROCK TYPE, AGE, AND MINERALIZATION OF CRETACEOUS PLUTONS (continued)

Name	Dominant rock type	Age (methods) Ma*	Age of youngest host†	Alteration/ mineralization§	Recent references and d/ or sources
Nye County					
Belmont	Monzogranite	79-85 (K-Ar; Rb-Sr)	Ordovician	W-qz veins/BM veins	Kleinhampl and Ziony (1984), Shawe and others (1986)
Climax	Granodiorite	105 (fis. trk.; K-Ar)	Ordovician	Mo-Cu porph./W skarn	Cornwall (1972)
Gold Meadow	Monzogranite	94 (fis. trk.)	Cambrian	?	Cornwall (1972)
Hall	Monzogranite	66-70 (K-Ar; U-Pb)	Ordovician	Mo-Cu porph./BM veins	Shaver (1984)
Ophir	Granodiorite	100 (Rb-Sr)	Ordovician	W skarn	John (1987)
Pipe Spring	2-mica (?) monzogranite	80 (K-Ar)	Ordovician	Greisen W-Be-F veins	Shawe and others (1986), Tingley and Maldonado (1983)
Shoshone granite	Monzogranite	95 (K-Ar; U-Pb)	Ordovician	Mo porph./Mo-W skarn	Kleinhampl and Ziony (1984; Shawe and others (1986)
Round Mountain	2-mica aplite/pegmatite	80 (K-Ar)	[K granite]	Greisen W veins	Shawe and others (1986)
Troy Canyon	2-mica monzogranite	70 (Rb-Sr)	Cambrian	W, Be, BM skarn/veins	Kleinhampl and Ziony (1984), Fryxell (1988)
White Pine County					
Ely	Quartz monzonite	116 (K-Ar; fis. trk.)	Permian	Cu porph./Au, BM repl.	Bauer and others (1966), James (1976), Hose and others (1976)
Tungstonia	2-mica monzogranite	69-75 (U-Pb, Ar-Ar)	Mississippian	Greisen veins/LE skarn	Lee and Christiansen (1983), Barton (1987), P. B. Gans (personal communication, 1986)
Lexington Creek	2-mica monzogranite	86 (K-Ar)	Ordovician	Greisen veins/LE skarn	Lee and Christiansen (1983), Barton (1987)
Monte Cristo	Granodiorite	94-140 (K-Ar)	Cambrian	Porph. Mo/W-BM skarn	Hose and others (1976), Sonnevil (1979)
N. Snake Range	Bi(-mu-hbl) metatonalite	100 (102-108) (U-Pb)	Cambrian	—	Miller and others (1988)
Pancake Range	Quartz monzodiorite	110 (K-Ar)	Mississippian	—	Hose and others (1976), Marvin and Dobson (1979)
Pole Canyon	2-mica monzogranite	79 (Rb-Sr)	Cambrian	Mo-qz veins/LE skarn	Lee and Christiansen (1983), Barton (1987)

*The ages have not been systematically corrected for the new decay constants (makes ~+3% difference in ages published before ~1978).
†Determined from present exposures.
§Abbreviations are: LE = lithophile element; Porph = porphyry style; Qz = quartz; BM = base metal (Zn, Pb, Cu); repl. = replacement.

TABLE 2. SUMMARY OF SOME GEOCHEMICAL CHARACTERISTICS OF CRETACEOUS GRANITOIDS AND OTHER PHANEROZOIC IGNEOUS ROCKS, EAST-CENTRAL GREAT BASIN*

Magma Type	K_2O (wt %)	SiO_2 (wt %)	Rb/Sr	ε_{Nd}	$^{87}Sr/^{86}Sr_i$	$\delta^{18}O_{SMOW}$ (‰)
Cretaceous						
Quartz monzonites and quartz diorites	3.4 (2.8-4.6)	59 (56-64)	0.2 (0.14-0.4)	-4 (+0.7- -7.3)	0.706 (0.7042-0.7089)	8.7 (8.2-9.2)
Metaluminous granites and granodiorites	3.3 (2.7-4.4)	69 (62-74)	0.2 (0.11-0.25)	-7 (-5.4- -8.6)	0.708 (0.7065-0.7089)	10.8 (9.5-11.6)
Peraluminous granites and granodiorites	4.0 (3.2-4.7)	73 (71-74)	0.5 (0.17-3.0)	-14 (-9.7- -19.2)	0.719 (0.711-0.737)	11.2 (9.5-13.4)
Jurassic						
Metaluminous quartz mon- zonites and granodiorites	....	....	0.2 (0.11-0.4)	-6 (-4.2- -8.6)	0.707 (0.705-0.710)	10.5 (9.8-11.1)
Peraluminous granites	4.4 (4.1-4.7)	73 (72-74)	1 (0.5-6)	-12 (-6.6- -17.3)	0.712 (0.710-0.714)	10.3 (9.9-10.6)
Tertiary						
Metaluminous inter- mediate volcanics	3.3 (2.4-4.1)	63 (60-67)	0.3 (0.14-0.44)	-16 (-15.1- -16.8)	0.712 (0.712-0.713)	....
Metaluminous felsic volcanics and granitoids	4.8 (3.1-5.2)	73 (67-76)	0.8 (0.3-1.7)	-17 (-13.7- -18.7)	0.714 (0.711-0.716)	9

*Data are from: Farmer and DePaolo (1983, 1984), Gans and others (1989), Lee and others (1981), Kistler and others (1981), compilation for Cretaceous peraluminous granitoids in Barton (1987), and unpublished data of M. D. Barton, J. N., Grossman, and G. L. Farmer. Values given are averages for main phase of igneous rocks. The range of averages is given in parentheses.

composition simply reflects regional cooling (i.e., that the two-mica granitoids are generally deeper than other compositions; see Tables 1 and 3). An important example, Tungstonia, the shallowest and best-dated of the two-mica granites, is the youngest. Resetting K-Ar systematics by mid-Tertiary events occurred in some places, particularly for some of the deeper two-mica granites; nonetheless, these yield Late Cretaceous dates by other methods (Table 1; Lee and others, 1984). Commonly, isotopic systematics are either clearly reset or retain Cretaceous values; there are many fewer Paleocene or Eocene than Cretaceous or Oligocene dates. Furthermore, dates tend to be crudely concordant where multiple determinations have been done on Mesozoic plutons (within 10 to 15 m.y.; e.g., Miller and others, 1988, for the Snake Range). Although the Cretaceous geochronometry of the eastern Great Basin plutons is not simple, the best estimates for the plutons' ages indicate that a stable but complex regime of Cretaceous plutonism was established, comprising plutons of differing character and metallogeny (Fig. 1), contrary to the simplified notion of the eastward sweep of Laramide magmatism (e.g., Hamilton, 1988; Keith and Reynolds, 1981).

The overall abundance of intrusions and the magmatic flux is difficult to estimate given the relatively small number of plu-

tons. This is a consequence of the limited exposure. Pre-Cenozoic rocks compose approximately 20 percent of the surface exposure in the east-central Great Basin, and about half of those are Carboniferous or younger (Stewart and Carlson, 1978). More than three-quarters of the Cretaceous intrusions occur in rocks of Devonian age or older (Table 1); thus, the sampling area is proportionately quite small. This is illustrated by the fact that nearly every range that exposes Cambrian rocks has at least one, and generally several, plutons. Cenozoic extension further complicates flux estimates (~100 percent extension regionally, locally >250 percent; Gans, 1987).

Cretaceous intrusions are felsic, contain moderate amounts of K_2O (2.7 to 4.7 wt %), and become increasingly silicic with time (Table 2). Early intrusions are quartz-poor (quartz diorite, quartz monzonite, local monzonite, and syenite), and contain hornblende, abundant biotite, and clinopyroxene. Magnetite, sphene, apatite, and zircon are common accessory phases. Where evident, differentiation trends within an intrusion appear to go from early quartz monzonite or monzodiorite to later monzogranite. The quartz monzonites and related rocks at Ely are the best example (Bauer and others, 1966). Geochronometry indicates that the quartz-poor plutons were emplaced between 130 and

100 Ma (Fig. 3, Table 1). The rocks more closely resemble the relatively less silicic, slightly alkaline rocks of the Jurassic, than the subsequent quartz-rich calc-alkalic granitoids of the mid- and Late Cretaceous. The Dolly Varden and Ely intrusions are strongly discordant and crosscut Permian rocks. The deeper Smith Creek metatonalite in the Snake Range metamorphic core complex appears more nearly concordant; however, the original intrusive relations have been obscured by intense Tertiary deformation (Miller and others, 1988). Several plutons in the region described as quartz diorites or quartz monzonites (e.g., the Mineral Hill pluton, Eureka district; Nolan, 1962) are instead part of the medial metaluminous granodiorite and monzogranite suite.

Metaluminous to weakly peraluminous biotite ± hornblende granodiorites and rarer monzogranites dominate the mid-Cretaceous (110 to 90 Ma; Fig. 3). A few of these intrusions are Late Cretaceous, mostly in southern Nevada (e.g., the Hall stock; Shaver, 1984). Widespread accessory minerals include magnetite, zircon, apatite, and sphene; monazite and ilmenite occur locally. They contain abundant large quartz phenocrysts or glomeroporphyritic aggregates (quartz "eyes") and late-crystallizing potassium feldspar megacrysts. Myrmekite is widespread, and locally abundant. These intrusions discordantly intrude Late Proterozoic to Mississippian rocks and contain common aplitic dikes. In contrast to the less siliceous intrusions (including the Jurassic), none appear to have risen to high stratigraphic levels (Pennsylvanian or younger).

Strongly peraluminous granodiorites and monzogranites, distinguished by the presence of magmatic muscovite, dominate Late Cretaceous magmatism (90 to 70 Ma; Fig. 3). Monazite and apatite are the most abundant accessory phases; ilmenite, magnetite, and zircon are uncommon; sphene is absent. These intrusions vary greatly in size and geometry. Where prominently exposed they tend to form broadly concordant plutons, commonly with evidence for forceful emplacement (e.g., the Tungstonia pluton; Best and others, 1974). In other areas, such as McCullough Butte and the Round Mountain area, Late Cretaceous muscovite-bearing granitoids crop out only in small dikes and pods, although evidence exists for much greater masses at depth (Barton, 1982; Shawe and others, 1986). Two-mica granitoids are largely confined to the deeper part (Ordovician or older) of the section, suggesting a deeper level of emplacement. An exception is the Tungstonia granite, the largest of these bodies, which intruded as high in the section as the Mississippian—apparently within 4 km or less of the paleosurface (Gans and others, 1986). Aplites and pegmatites are abundant, even more so than in the metaluminous plutons. The rarity of oxide minerals, especially magnetite, the high iron contents of the biotites, and evidence for associated reduced fluids (near CH_4-CO_2 buffer; Barton, 1987) demonstrate that these intrusions were rather reduced and wet compared to the earlier metaluminous suites.

Isotopic compositions vary systematically with the Phanerozoic magma type and geochemical trends (Table 2), but are limited. Initial Sr isotopic values and $\delta^{18}O$ increase and ϵ_{Nd} decreases with time and the compositional changes in the Cretaceous intrusions. The isotopic and major-element changes indicate increasing involvement of an ancient crustal component with time in the Cretaceous magmas. This temporal trend complements the spatial trends from west to east across the Sierra Nevada and the northern Great Basin (Farmer and DePaolo, 1983; Kistler, 1983). The compositional systematics could be interpreted as reflecting different isolated sources for the magmas, rather than changing contributions from several reservoirs. The paucity of data on the probable sources (cf. Farmer and DePaolo, 1983) permits either interpretation, but hinders quantitative modeling of relative contributions from different sources. Separate sources, however, seem less likely to explain the relatively continuous and systematic geochemical and petrological changes.

Systematic changes in trace-element contents with time and composition are less dramatic (M. D. Barton and J. N. Grossman, unpublished data; Barton, 1987; Lee, 1984; Table 2). Main phases of nearly all analyzed plutons have low Rb/Sr ratios, strong LREE enrichment with minor or absent Eu anomalies, and high Ba and Sr contents. Much of the observed trace-element variation can be attributed to late-stage differentiation and local deuteric alteration. These rocks have continental magmatic-arc affinities (e.g., Pearce and others, 1984; Harris and others, 1986; Fig. 4). They differ from collision-related felsic plutons, although the trend with time is toward more collision-like compositions. The latter point contrasts with the common interpretation of peraluminous magmas as pure crustal melts, triggered by crustal thickening (e.g., Armstrong, 1983; Best and others, 1974; Farmer and DePaolo, 1983). Neither the isotopic nor the elemental compositions confine the source of the magmas to the crust; indeed, the systematic variations outlined here, and the differences between peraluminous granitoids from the Cordillera and those from collisional orogens may reflect subcrustal components in the former (cf., Brown and others, 1984; Miller and Barton, 1989).

Oxidation state and volatile contents of the magmas also decrease and increase, respectively, with time and greater crustal involvement. Increasingly reduced compositions are implied by increasing Fe/Mg in igneous biotites that vary from subequal values in the metaluminous rocks to higher values (0.7 to 0.8) in the strongly peraluminous rocks (Barton, unpublished data; Keith and others, 1985; Lee and others, 1981; Kistler and others, 1981) concomitantly with increasing whole-rock FeO/Fe_2O_3. Changing minor-mineral abundances parallel these shifts; abundant magnetite and sphene and lesser ilmenite are replaced by oxide-poor assemblages bearing ilmenite, subordinate magnetite, and monazite. The crude correlation of depth with composition (as indicated by the age of the country rocks; Table 1), the changing mineral assemblages (biot + hbl ± cpx to biot ± hbl to biot + musc), and the greater abundance of aplites and pegmatites in the granitic rocks (especially the peraluminous rocks) are consistent with increasing magmatic water contents with time. This follows from magmatic phase equilibria which imply that drier magmas can reach higher levels, and that mica-rich, especially muscovite-rich magmas contain higher water contents than typical amphibole ± pyroxene–bearing magmas (e.g., Wyllie, 1977). The

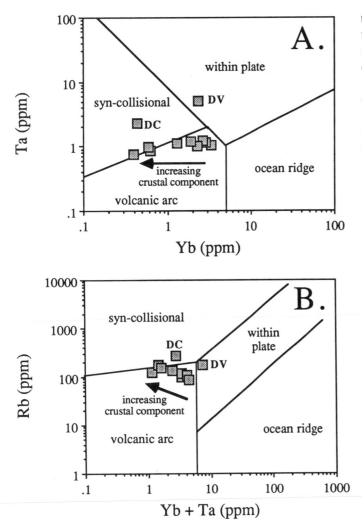

Figure 4. Rb vs. Yb+Ta and Ta vs. Yb discriminant diagrams with fields for various classes of granitoids (Pearce and others, 1984) showing available data for Cretaceous granitoids from the east-central Great Basin. DC indicates Dawley Canyon; DV indicates Dolly Varden. Data for DC are from Kistler and others (1981), the remainder are from unpublished analyses of J. N. Grossman and M. D. Barton.

volume fraction of demonstrably volatile-saturated intrusive phases (pegmatites and aplites) is an additional qualitative indication of original water content.

Metallogeny

Metals and hydrothermal alteration are associated with most of the intrusions where they vary systematically with igneous composition (Fig. 3, Table 3). Several of the areas contain major mining districts, including Ely (Bauer and others, 1966), Eureka (Nolan and Hunt, 1968), Pioche (Westgate and Knopf, 1932), and Tempiute (Tschanz and Pampeyan, 1970). Little production has been made from deposits associated with the two-mica grani-

toids, but several have abundant associated mineralization (Barton, 1987). The mineralization is divided for convenience into three categories based on metal contents and alteration characteristics.

Copper-dominated porphyry and skarn mineralization occurs with monzonitic intrusions in the Ely (Bauer and others, 1966; James, 1976; Westra, 1982) and Dolly Varden districts (Atkinson and others, 1982; Granger and others, 1957). Similar alteration is reported from several other localities (Table 1). Other metals are much less abundant: molybdenum is scarce to absent; minor Pb-Zn replacement bodies occur in carbonates; and precious metals, principally gold, are locally important in quartz veins and silicified sedimentary rocks. Early potassic alteration (biotitization of hornblende, development of secondary orthoclase) and abundant sericitic alteration are prominent at Ely. Sericitic alteration is common elsewhere in this association, with local evidence for potassic alteration. These alteration types are intimately associated with the copper mineralization. Oxidized skarns (indicated by andraditic garnet, diopsidic pyroxene, common magnetite) are prominently developed, generally with copper minerals. Abundant siliceous replacement of carbonate rocks and clay alteration of silicate rocks postdate skarn and hornfels formation (James, 1976; Westra, 1982).

Varied mineralization occurs within and around the metaluminous granodiorites and monzogranites. It is typically of quartz-monzonite porphyry molybdenum type (Shaver, 1984; Westra and Keith, 1982) and polymetallic skarn and replacement ores. Abundant quartz veins, some with greisen envelopes, and prominent pink hydrothermal potassium feldspar are characteristic of the intrusion-hosted alteration (e.g., Hall; Shaver, 1984; Monte Cristo; Sonnevil, 1979). Albitization is locally present, but appears to be a minor, late-magmatic phenomenon. Molybdenum with or without accessory copper is the main ore metal in the intrusions. Fluorine is commonly, but not always, concentrated in these systems, typically as fluorite and fluorine-bearing micas in the greisen-style veins. Oxidized, polymetallic skarns associated with these systems consist of diopsidic pyroxene, andraditic garnet, and a widespread hydrous overprint of amphibole, chlorite, epidote, quartz, and sporadic fluorite (e.g., Tempiute; Buseck, 1967; Einaudi and others, 1981). Economically significant W, Mo, and base metals occur in the intrusions and skarns, but the historically dominant ores are Pb-Zn-Cu-Ag-Au carbonate-replacement deposits with or without introduced silicate-carbonate gangue.

Distinctive lithophile-element (Be, F, W, Mo, Sn, Zn) mineralization occurs with the Late Cretaceous two-mica granitoids (Barton, 1987). Alteration in intrusions consists of quartz veins, greisen (muscovite ± fluorite) zones, and local albitization with variable, generally small amounts of W, Mo, and Be minerals. Secondary potassium feldspar has not been recognized. Carbonate rocks host complex, reduced (grossularitic to subcalcic garnet, hedenbergitic clinopyroxene), fluorine-rich stockwork skarns. Late, widespread aluminum- and fluorine-rich hydrous skarns containing abundant fluorite, muscovite, and albitic plagioclase

TABLE 3. TYPES AND CHARACTERISTICS OF MINERALIZATION

Type	Igneous rocks and Alteration	Mineralization in Country Rocks	Emplacement Depth*	Examples
Cu-Mo	- Quartz monzonites, quartz diorites, granodiorites; oxidized - Potassic/sericitic/porpylitic with Cu±Mo in porphyry	- Oxidized Cu skarns and gold-bearing jasperoids; minor sulfide replacement ores	1-5 km	Ely, Dolly Varden
Mo-Cu-W-Zn-Pb	- Granodiorites, granites; oxidized - Potassic/greisen/abundant large quartz veins in intrusion (Mo±Cu mineralization)	- Oxidized polymetallic skarns (W, Mo, Cu, Bi, F) and base-metal, precious-metal sulfide replacement bodies; less jasperoid	3-9 km	Eureka, Pioche, Tempiute, Hall
Lithophile	- Two-mica granites and granodiorites; reduced - Greisen/quartz veins, no potassic, W+Mo+Be	- Reduced F- and Al-rich stockwork skarns (F, Be, Zn, W, Mo, Sn); jasperiod absent, metal-bearing quartz carbonate veins	5-12 km	McCullough Butte, Pole Canyon

*Variously estimated from stratigraphic level and, locally, petrological indicators.

distinguish these occurrences. Clastic rocks contain limited mineralization, largely quartz veins with minor pyrite, sericite, and fluorite, and trace beryl and wolframite.

Systematic changes in the oxidation state, metasomatic components, and fluid compositions of the mineralization parallel the magmatic changes described above. Early Cretaceous mineralization is dominated by base metals, especially copper, and occurs in oxidized systems. There is no evidence for significant concentration of lithophile elements, including F, in these early rocks. Increasingly lithophile and decreasingly chalcophile element associations and decreasing oxidation state accompany the increasing crustal component in the magmas (Fig. 3, Table 1). Reconnaissance examination of the fluid inclusions indicates that moderately to highly saline fluids accompanied the Early Cretaceous Cu-rich systems and that salinities systematically decrease to low values (<5 wt % NaCl equivalent) in the lithophile-element–rich systems. Such trends are consistent with increasing water/Cl (= wetter magmas?) and the decreasing Ca and mafic contents of the magmas (cf. Barton, 1987). These changes resemble metallogenic changes associated with "magnetite series" and "ilmenite series" granitoids (Burnham and Ohmoto, 1980; Einaudi and others, 1981; Ishihara, 1981). Ishihara (1981) and others emphasized the spatial variation in these series, analogous to spatial variation in plutonic elemental and isotopic compositions (e.g., Farmer and DePaolo, 1983), in contrast to the temporal variation emphasized here.

AN INTERPRETIVE SYNTHESIS

The systematics of magmatism, metallogeny, metamorphism, and deformation are interpreted as interrelated manifestations of crustal warming during an extended period of stable

Cretaceous subduction. Permissive, one-dimensional thermal modeling corroborates the inferred thermal histories.

Two model Cretaceous thermal histories are shown with the geochronometric summaries in Figure 3, and in greater detail in Figure 5. Scattered but continuous Cretaceous (70 to 130 Ma) plutonism in eastern Nevada was coeval with coastal batholith emplacement (Armstrong and Suppe, 1973; cf. Figs. 3 and 6) during a period of active, stable convergence between North America and the Farallon plate (Engebretson and others, 1985). Magmatism postdates a period of minimum convergence in the Early Cretaceous, and predates the Laramide orogeny when the subducted slab is inferred to have been flat beneath the Great Basin (e.g., Bird, 1988; Dickinson and Snyder, 1978). The metamorphic dates indicate a thermal maximum and/or cooling event

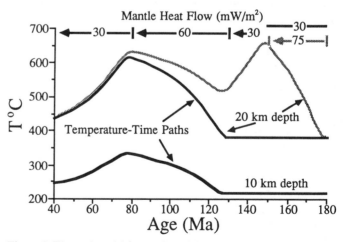

Figure 5. Thermal model for heating of the Cretaceous crust. The solid lines are for Cretaceous heating only; the shaded line includes a maximal Jurassic heating event. See text for discussion.

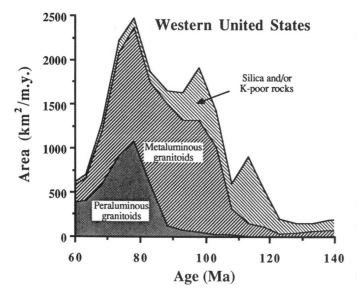

Figure 6. Apparent magmatic flux for the Cretaceous in the western United States (modified from Barton and others, 1988; based on plutons whose ages are probably known within ±10 m.y.). Compositional categories are equivalent to those in Figures 1 and 3.

near the end of this period, contemporaneous with shortening in the Sevier orogenic belt.

Progressive heating of the crust began with the reinitiation of subduction in the Early Cretaceous. Armstrong (1982) suggested that Mesozoic regional metamorphism to the east of the main batholiths could be related to subduction-induced counter flow in the mantle wedge. Calculations of such flow to model the development of back-arc basins and continental plateaus indicate that higher heat flow and erosion of the lithosphere occur over a considerable width behind the magmatic arc (Andrews and Sleep, 1974; Toksoz and Bird, 1977). Although additional work needs to be done to evaluate the importance of this mechanism (Peter Bird, 1987, personal communication), elevated heat flows in back-arc regions are well known (Henry and Pollack, 1988). For the purpose here, any of several mechanisms that increase heat flow to the middle crust would be adequate, provided that they correlate with plate motions and constraints on subcontinental mantle.

Isotopic evidence favors the presence of geochemically distinctive, old (>1 Ga) subcontinental mantle beneath large parts of the southwestern United States, including parts of the Great Basin (Farmer, 1988). Farmer interpreted this as subcontinental lithosphere present since the formation of the overlying crust. Such a "keel" of distinct old lithosphere would preclude shallow Laramide subduction and large-scale Mesozoic asthenospheric upwelling. It would also significantly change allowable time scales for Cretaceous thermal events by requiring conductive heat transfer through a much greater distance. An alternative interpretation consistent with the presence of distinct subcontinental mantle (but perhaps lacking the specific regional variations suggested by

Farmer) is that the materials flowing in behind the steepening slab in the middle Tertiary had continental lithosphere isotopic characteristics, consistent with their derivation from the east beneath central North America.

The regional thermal gradient increased as long as the elevated heat source persisted—until the Latest Cretaceous. This heating caused progressive, regionally extensive metamorphism of lower grade rocks and resetting of isotopic systematics in previously (Jurassic) metamorphosed rocks. Decreased mantle heat flow at about 80 Ma, correlated with changes in subduction, led to rapid cooling (see below) and the resulting Late Cretaceous maximum in radiometric dates for the metamorphic minerals. Similarly, deformation peaked in the Late Cretaceous when the crust was hottest and softest (cf. Armstrong, 1974; Burchfiel and Davis, 1975), 30 to 40 m.y. after the reinitiation of magmatism. Foreland deformation increased as the crust heated, dramatically so when the basal miogeocline and the materials beneath it reached near-anatectic temperatures. This may have been aided by partial melting (Hollister and Crawford, 1986) and is reflected by the syn-thrusting, crust-dominated, strongly peraluminous granites. It is interesting that the amount of shortening and the shortening rates in the foreland thrust belt are approximately balanced by the Cretaceous magmatic flux (Allmendinger and Jordan, 1981; cf. Fig. 6). Thrusting ceased as the crust stiffened on cooling at the beginning of the Laramide orogeny, or alternatively, with the possible elimination of the driving force.

Great Basin magmatism revived with renewed subduction in the Early Cretaceous. Early in the sequence, dry and relatively hot mantle-derived magmas rose to fairly high levels with comparatively little incorporation of crustal components. Assimilation of crustal materials increased with time as the crust heated and became easier to assimilate (e.g., roughly half as much energy is required for crust at 650 °C rather than 400 °C; DePaolo, 1981). Other changes, such as decreasing density and rheological contrasts and increasing crustal thickness, may also have promoted assimilation. Compositions changed to quartz-rich granitoids in the mid-Cretaceous, and ultimately to strongly peraluminous granitoids in the Late Cretaceous. These later, cooler(?) magmas crystallized at somewhat deeper levels, reflecting their higher water contents and lower heat contents (except the Tungstonia pluton, whose higher level emplacement is consistent with its large size). An important aspect of this model is that even the Late Cretaceous, crust-dominated magmas might also have significant lower crust and/or mantle components. As pointed out above, uncertainty in reservoir compositions and evolutionary paths makes quantification of sources uncertain, but many features point to a more complex petrogenesis than simple anatexis.

Magmatism ended in the northern Great Basin at 70 to 80 Ma following the changes in subduction accompanying the beginning of the Laramide orogeny. Early Laramide plutons in southern Nevada mark the transition from the abrupt shut-off of magmatism in the north to the more gradual eastward sweep of magmatism in southern California, Arizona, and New Mexico (e.g., Coney and Reynolds, 1977).

Thermal model

Simple dynamic heat-flow calculations support the proposed model. These calculations are based on the described chronology and an assumed increase in heat input to the base of the crust. The calculations do not depend on the particulars of the heat source (e.g., subduction-induced counter flow in the mantle wedge), only that an increase in heat transfer to the lower crust occurred and is correlated with the timing of subduction. The model successfully accommodates the time scale and magnitude of a developing Mesozoic thermal anomaly culminating in a late Cretaceous thermal maximum to account for variations in plutonism, metallogeny, and deformation.

The thermal effects of induced mantle flow are modeled as an increase in mantle heat flow from 30 mW/m^2 to 60 mW/m^2. A one-dimensional model is adequate because the horizontal length scale (100 to 300 km) is several times the likely thickness of the Cretaceous crust (35 to 50 km; Gans, 1987). A 40-km-thick crust with plausible radiogenic heat production (declining exponentially with depth, with a length scale of 10 km and a surface heat production of 3 $\mu W/m^3$) was chosen. Initial surface heat flow (~1.2 HFU) is cratonal in magnitude; after increasing the mantle heat input the heat flow evolves to values more characteristic of back-arc regions (~2 HFU in the steady state). These values are compatible with, but at the upper end of the range of increases obtained from geophysical modeling of subcrustal flow (Andrews and Sleep, 1974; Toksoz and Bird, 1977; Peter Bird, 1987, personal communication). The higher heat flow is added as a 50-m.y. pulse (130 to 80 Ma) corresponding to the time of "normal" subduction along the Cretaceous continental margin (Engebretson and others, 1985). At 80 Ma, basal heat flow is reduced to initial values; it may have fallen even farther if the (relatively cool) subducted slab lay immediately beneath the crust, as is widely postulated (Bird, 1988; Dickinson and Snyder, 1978).

No account is made for advective transport of heat within the crust. The Cretaceous magmatic flux, as evidenced by exposed intrusions, was unquestionably more than an order of magnitude too low to have had a significant (i.e., >10 percent) effect on the regional heat flux. There is no evidence for widespread magmatic underplating. If it had occurred, underplating would have had a similar thermal effect to advective heat transport within the subcontinental mantle. Changing crustal thickness during heating would affect the results in detail, but the amounts of thickening that can be inferred from the geologic history would not grossly change the thermal evolution. Temperatures in the upper crust would increase somewhat more slowly in a thickening crust than in one of constant thickness.

Figure 5 shows results for depths of 10 and 20 km. At 10 km depth the model predicts temperature increases equivalent to a change from sub-greenschist to greenschist facies conditions, consistent with observed metamorphism in the Lower Cambrian and Late Proterozoic rocks that were at this stratigraphic depth. Near the base of the crust, temperatures exceed 1,000 °C. At levels corresponding to <15 to 20 km beneath the Cretaceous surface (approximately the base of the miogeocline), temperatures reach amphibolite facies metamorphic conditions, and the thermal gradients are about 50 percent higher than original values. These conditions approach those needed for anatexis in water-saturated quartzofeldspathic rocks; they should promote large degrees of assimilation in rising magmas and possibly bulk anatexis or lower crustal convection. There is little evidence for bulk anatexis in the Great Basin, but northward, in Idaho, where the eastward Laramide magmatic shift was somewhat later and less abrupt, the voluminous latest Cretaceous and Paleocene peraluminous Idaho batholith might reflect the culmination of this process. Lower crustal convection, in a solid or partially molten state, would reduce the upper-mantle temperatures required to cause crustal anatexis. A modified case for 20 km (shaded line) includes the maximum effect of an earlier, somewhat more intense Jurassic thermal pulse. Its timing is based on plate motions and the western U.S. magmatic record (Engebretson and others, 1985; Barton and others, 1988); its intensity is based on the likelihood of a neutral or extensional regime during that time (Karish and others, 1987).

The time scale for heating from the base of the crust is about 40 to 50 m.y. With cessation of the elevated heat source, the upper-crustal thermal anomaly decayed rapidly. At the mid- and upper-crustal levels depicted in Figure 5, significant cooling began within a few million years. Temperatures fell about halfway to background values within the first 20 m.y. This decrease is consistent with the time and spread of the Late Cretaceous metamorphic geochronometry; it rules out simple cooling from a pre–Late Cretaceous thermal event—cooling is too fast. This can also be seen from the shaded line in Figure 5, which includes a Jurassic heating event. The Jurassic thermal maximum, peaking at 150 Ma (roughly the time indicated by metamorphic dates and magmatic fluxes, but constrained by plate motions) had half decayed by the Early Cretaceous inception of reheating. Erosion accompanying Late Cretaceous uplift could contribute to observed dates, but as discussed above, the geologic evidence seems incompatible with the requisite amounts of erosion (>4 to 6 km) for uplift alone to be the cause.

ALTERNATIVE MECHANISMS

Alternative mechanisms have been proposed to explain Cretaceous magmatism and metamorphism, particularly the Great Basin peraluminous plutonism and metamorphism: crustal thickening (Armstrong, 1983; Coney and Harms, 1984; Miller and others, 1988), direct melting of the subducted slab (Keith, 1978; Keith and Reynolds, 1981), fluid fluxing (Hoisch and others, 1988; Wickham and others, 1987), higher mantle heat flow (Armstrong, 1982; Best and others, 1974; Farmer and DePaolo, 1983; Haxel and others, 1984), and magmatic underplating or pluton emplacement in the lower crust (Speed and others, 1988; Haxel and others, 1984).

The preferred mechanism is one that conducts heat into the middle crust from below. This could be increased mantle heat flow (by any of several mechanisms) and/or underplating or intrusion of the lower crust by mafic magmas. Negative evidence exists for underplating and/or deep intrusion: the low abundance of Cretaceous plutons in present exposures (⩽5 percent, Fig. 1) seems inconsistent with the need for large amounts of underplated magma to heat the whole crust (Wells, 1980). Such a mechanism may be more plausible where magmatic fluxes are higher (e.g., Arizona; Haxel and others, 1984), or along the coastal batholiths, but even there, fluxes appear inadequate to maintain regional thermal gradients near maximum values for the duration of the regional magmatic events (Barton and Hanson, 1989), unless there is an effective way to make room for continued deep intrusion (e.g., by return flow or extension) without drastically thickening the crust.

Crustal thickening (Armstrong, 1983; Coney and Harms, 1984) probably fails as an *independent* mechanism for producing either the presently exposed regional metamorphism or the magmatism. The timing of deformation and the lack of significant cover provide the key evidence against this mechanism. The youngest plutons, the two-mica granitoids, were largely contemporaneous with thrusting rather than later, as would be expected from thermal considerations (England and Thompson, 1986). The lack of evidence for deep burial at present exposure levels in the east-central Great Basin precludes thickening as a cause of most of the exposed metamorphism (excepting the high-grade, probably Jurassic, structures in the Ruby and East Humboldt ranges), pointing instead to an increased geothermal gradient. Pre–Late Cretaceous thickening is quite possible in the middle or lower crust, but any surface expression must have been to the west. The need for increased Cretaceous heat flow into the upper crust, the geochemical characteristics of the magmas (e.g., differences with collision-related granitoids), and the continuous variation in regime require an alternative mechanism.

Crustal thickening, although insufficient by itself to cause these features, probably was important in other ways. The increasing crustal component in the magma granites might reflect a longer travel path and longer residence time if they rose through crust of increasing thickness. This would be aided if the crust thickened to 50 to 60 km in the Late Cretaceous (as suggested by Coney and Harms, 1984; see Gans, 1987, for an alternative view). Continental underthrusting might have placed relatively low-grade, wet upper crust at considerable depths beneath the east-central Great Basin, leading to anatexis, perhaps analogous to the Himalayan leucogranites (e.g., Le Fort, 1986). Timing relations (Fig. 3) are permissible for the latter, but the amount of shortening in the Sevier belt (~60 to 100 km; Armstrong, 1968) appears inadequate; the small amount of material eroded from the top of the section prior to the middle Tertiary is incompatible with Himalayan-like thickening, and the geochemistry of the two-mica granitoids is questionably anatectic.

Keith and Reynolds (1981) suggested direct melting of Franciscan-like sediments during low-angle subduction as one possibility for the generation of Late Cretaceous peraluminous magmas; however, neither the timing of low-angle subduction nor the isotopic compositions of Franciscan rocks (Nelson, 1985) are compatible with this mechanism in the Great Basin. Large fluid fluxes into the base of the crust during low-angle subduction in southeastern California are postulated to have provided the heat for Late Cretaceous low-pressure facies series metamorphism and perhaps the flux for some of the magmatism (Hamilton, 1988; Hoisch and others, 1988). On the basis of isotopic evidence, Wickham and others (1987) inferred the involvement of large quantities of fluid during high-grade metamorphism and anatexis in the Ruby Mountains, similar to Hercynian metamorphism and magmatism in the Pyrenees (Wickham and Taylor, 1985). High fluid fluxes, however, are incompatible with the Cretaceous magmatic and metamorphic record in the Great Basin. The thermal balance, igneous compositions (isotopic and otherwise), and tectonic regime all preclude large fluid fluxes from the subducted slab. Surface-derived fluids are incompatible with stable-isotope compositions of the granitoids, their related mineralization, and estimated Cretaceous meteoric waters (Barton, 1987, and unpublished data).

COMPARISON WITH OTHER AREAS AND TIMES

Comparison of the Cretaceous evolution, discussed above, with other times and areas demonstrates broadly similar patterns in Cretaceous to early Tertiary orogeny and metallogeny in the western United States, but different patterns for other times and tectonic regimes. Cretaceous–early Tertiary events throughout the western U.S. show broadly similar patterns, notably synkinematic peraluminous plutonism postdating metaluminous plutonism. This contrasts with the shorter-lived, more intense, metaluminous middle Tertiary and Jurassic magmatism in the Great Basin, and the postkinematic, strongly peraluminous to later metaluminous magmatic patterns of collisional orogenic belts.

Western United States

Temporal changes in Cretaceous magmatism in the western U.S. and, to a large measure, Canada, resemble those in the eastern Great Basin (e.g., Barton and others, 1988; Burchfiel and Davis, 1975; Armstrong, 1989; Hamilton, 1978). Systematic differences exist from region to region, particularly in the Cordilleran interior, but the broad pattern of increasingly felsic and crustally dominated magmatism with time seems to hold (Miller and Barton, 1989; Fig. 6). Metamorphism and deformation are also broadly similar from the Canadian Cordillera to southern Arizona. Although a general correspondence exists between the timing of magmatism and foreland thrusting elsewhere (e.g., Armstrong, 1974; Burchfiel and Davis, 1975; Hamilton, 1978), the relations are seemingly not as straightforward as in the Great Basin. Late Cretaceous movement in the foreland thrust belt occurs along the arc from Canada south and is contemporaneous with crustally dominated magmatism. To both the north and south of the Great Basin, these events continued into the Paleogene, whereas in the middle latitudes they vanished with the onset of the Laramide orogeny and the shift of magmatism far to the east (Lawton, 1985; Heller and others, 1986).

Analogous relations in magmatism and mineralization are documented in Arizona, southeastern California, and Colorado, where the differences are attributable to the differences in tectonic regimes. Laramide magmatism in Arizona began in the Late Cretaceous with metaluminous hornblende-bearing quartz monzonites and granodiorites and changed during the early Tertiary to predminantly two-mica granitoids that are syn- to post-kinematic with early Tertiary thrusting and metamorphism in southern and central Arizona (Bykerk-Kauffman and Janecke, 1987; Haxel and others, 1984; Miller and Barton, 1989). The porphyry Cu province of Arizona and New Mexico is associated with the older, shallowly emplaced intrusions, whereas minor greisen-style tungsten mineralization occurs with the younger, strongly peraluminous magmas. Haxel and others (1984) interpreted this scenario analogously to the story in the Great Basin, although they placed a greater emphasis on the thermal consequences of crustal thickening. They suggested the superposition of two "more or less independent causes" (external compression and conductive + magmatic heat input into the crust). Thermal considerations indicate that, even in Arizona with 5- to 10-km thrust sheets, the geochronology and heating rates for the lower crust preclude crustal thickening from contributing significantly to anatexis.

In southeastern California, formation of ductile nappes and thrusts preceded the formation of Late Cretaceous granitoids (Hamilton, 1982; Miller and others, 1982; Hoisch and others, 1988). Field relations and Ar-Ar geochronometry suggest that metamorphism was syn- to post-kinematic and overlapped with emplacement of Late Cretaceous metaluminous granitoids and slightly younger, crosscutting two-mica granites. Timing and field relations preclude crustal thickening and probably high-level magmatism as causes of the observed medium- to low-pressure facies series metamorphism (Hoisch and others, 1988). Plutonism in southeastern California and Arizona is part of the latest Cretaceous to early Tertiary eastward sweep of magmatism (e.g., Coney and Reynolds, 1977). The rapid Laramide compositional changes in these areas ($\leqslant$20 m.y.; contrast Fig. 6) could reflect the consequences of arc migration eastward through crust preheated by earlier Cretaceous mantle counterflow.

In the Colorado Tertiary, older, relatively quartz poor alkalic intrusions are associated with base-metal precious-metal deposits (e.g., porphyry Mo-Cu, base-metal precious-metal replacements and lodes). Younger, less alkalic, more silica-rich compositions (granodiorites and quartz monzonites), ultimately give way to high-silica granites. Lithophile-element mineralization in the later metaluminous granitoids is prominent, expressed by Climax-type porphyry Mo(-F-W) deposits. ϵ_{Nd} decreases with time and increasing silica content (from -2 to -14), analogous to the inferred variation in the Cretaceous of the Great Basin (Stein and Crock, this volume). Stein and Crock interpret this variation as reflecting the character of the Proterozoic crustal sources, perhaps with some mantle component in the earlier intrusions. Alternatively, this could reflect progressive changes in the proportions of mantle versus crustal sources as inferred for the Great Basin.

Comparison with Jurassic and Tertiary in the Great Basin

The Jurassic metamorphic and magmatic episode broadly resembles the Cretaceous, although there are systematic differences. Felsic magmatism in the eastern Great Basin was of shorter duration ($\sim$170 to 150 Ma; Allmendinger and Jordan, 1981; Wright and Miller, 1986) and concentrated in northern Nevada and northwestern Utah. Related metamorphism was apparently more intense, also mainly in northern Nevada (DeWitt and others, 1984; Miller and others, 1988; Snoke and Miller, 1988). Jurassic intrusions are more alkalic and less siliceous than the Cretaceous; quartz monzonites dominate in contrast to the granodiorites of the Cretaceous (cf. Miller and Barton, 1989). Strongly peraluminous granitoids are less common and concentrated in deep, migmatitic exposures in the Ruby Range (Dallmeyer and others, 1986; Kistler and others, 1981). The few isotopic and whole-rock data for the metaluminous Jurassic plutons (Table 2) resemble the less siliceous Early Cretaceous suite. Jurassic plutons are more commonly composite, ranging from hornblende quartz diorite to granite, a sequence interpreted as due to fractional crystallization (e.g., Snake Creek pluton; Lee and Christiansen, 1983). Some evidence suggests that Jurassic magmatism reflects a different tectonic regime, perhaps a static or weakly extensional regime (particularly to the west and south; Karish and others, 1987; Oldow and Bartel, 1987). Such a neutral or extensional regime might be more suited to the generation and rise of magmas that undergo less interaction with the crust, thus retaining a more primitive character than Cretaceous magmas that rose through crust under compression.

In contrast to the long-lived, low-magmatic flux conditions prevailing during the Mesozoic, Tertiary magmatism in the east-central Great Basin was short-lived and intense (Stewart and Carlson, 1976; Gans and others, 1989). Tertiary magmatism correlates with dramatic extension (Gans and others, 1989), perhaps related in part to coeval rapid steepening of the subducting Farallon plate that placed hot mantle (and probably basaltic magma) near the base of the crust (Bird, 1988). Voluminous volcanic rocks, mostly erupted in less than 5 m.y., were accompanied by many large granitoid stocks (biot $\pm$ hbl granodiorites and monzogranites). Estimates based on exposure area and geochronometry indicate that the middle Tertiary magmatic flux was 10 to 50 times greater than the Cretaceous flux. Sr and Nd isotopic compositions indicate that a larger contribution of crust was involved in the Tertiary magmas (even the relatively mafic compositions) than in all but the strongly peraluminous Mesozoic magmas (Table 2). Larger degrees of crustal melting would be a plausible consequence of intense heating of the lower crust immediately following asthenospheric upwelling. Steady-state thermal models for extension in the Great Basin (Lachenbruch and Sass, 1978) indicate that during rapid extension accommodated by basaltic underplating or diking, the temperature of the lower crust can rise above the dry solidus, leading to large amounts of crustal melting. These crustal melts need not necessarily hybridize extensively (by mixing or assimilation) with basaltic magmas, and thus could retain crust-dominated geochemical signatures. This rapid, intense, but short-duration heating of the lower crust contrasts with the slower, less intense, much longer-lived heating postulated for the Cretaceous. The low-flux magmas intruding slowly warming crust during the Cretaceous would have been less able to incorporate crustal materials. Only in the Late Cretaceous was the crust warm enough to allow large degrees of assimilation and/or significant anatexis, leading to the strongly peraluminous, "pure crystal" melts.

Mineral deposits are common with both Jurassic and Tertiary plutonism; they more resemble those related to the metaluminous intrusions of the Early and mid-Cretaceous than the lithophile-element–rich, crustally dominated magmatic systems of the Late Cretaceous. Jurassic magmas are associated with various base-metal and Fe-rich replacements, and locally some tungsten mineralization (e.g., Cortez district and many iron-rich replacements in Eureka County, Nevada; Roberts and others, 1967; parts of the Snake Range tungsten belt; Hose and others, 1976). Tertiary-age districts in eastern Nevada are dominated by porphyry Mo-Cu ("quartz monzonite" type) and Mo (transitional to Climax type) mineralization in the intrusions, and composite W and/or base-metal skarns and replacement bodies (e.g., Westra and Keith, 1982; Hose and others, 1976). Epithermal precious-metal systems associated with Tertiary volcanic centers, may also be directly related to the magmatic systems, even though stable-isotope data indicate a preponderance of meteoric waters (summary in Field and Fifarek, 1985). Epithermal systems, if originally present in the Mesozoic, are not preserved in this region.

Collisional orogens

Magmatic and metallogenetic aspects of collisional orogens (e.g., the Himalaya, the European Hercynian) differ significantly from Cordilleran phenomena: early (postcollision) magmas are dominantly peraluminous, rather than metaluminous (Harris and others, 1986; Pitcher, 1987), and have been interpreted as due to thermal relaxation following crustal thickening (e.g., England and Thompson, 1986), or anatexis in the base of continental materials in a hot upper plate following subduction and devolatilization of low-grade, water-rich materials (e.g., Le Fort, 1986). Later magmas are commonly metaluminous, interpreted as resulting from continued thermal relaxation leading to intense heating of the underthrust continental plate (Harris and others, 1986). Collisional peraluminous magmas also tend to have features even more distinctive of continental crust than Cordilleran two-mica granites (e.g., higher K_2O/Na_2O, $Sr_{initial}$, $\delta^{18}O$, Rb/Sr; lower

CaO, MgO; numerous trace-element characteristics; Reynolds and Keith, 1982; Harris and others, 1986; Brown and others, 1984; cf. Fig. 4). The metaluminous granitoids from the two settings also differ, but less distinctly so (Harris and others, 1986). These differences between collisional leucocratic granitoids and mature continental-arc leucocratic granitoids may reflect different modes of origin, the former being pure crustal melts, perhaps largely of metasedimentary sources, whereas the latter may contain a substantial deep-seated metaigneous and/or mantle component, but with a weathered component (probably metasediments) dominating aspects of the major-element and isotopic chemistry.

Metallogenic differences probably reflect the differences in the magmatic compositions. Peraluminous systems in the western United States, although showing a number of similarities with those elsewhere in the world, apparently lack the high-grade mineralization associated with other weakly to strongly peraluminous systems (Barton, 1987; Reynolds and Keith, 1982). The differences must reflect some combination of differences in original metal contents, postmagmatic processes, and magmatic volatile and major-element compositions. Relatively low contents of lithophile elements in Cordilleran two-mica granites (Reynolds and Keith, 1982) may have inhibited formation of ore-grade mineralization. Higher water contents in Cordilleran systems may have lowered ore-forming capacity both by increasing the probable depth of crystallization, disfavoring concentration of postmagmatic solutions (cf. Burnham and Ohmoto, 1980), and by decreasing the concentration of the components (e.g., Cl) necessary for metal transport. This possibility is supported by the low fluid salinities found in high-temperature primary fluid inclusions from the Cretaceous two-mica systems (Barton, unpublished data). Major-element compositions may also play a role in suppressing the formation of the halogen-rich, acid solutions needed for ore formation in two-mica granitoids (cf., Barton, 1987).

SUMMARY

Cretaceous magmatism, metamorphism, deformation, and related mineralization are related in a systematic manner in the eastern Great Basin (Fig. 7). The variation is readily interpreted as the consequence of progressive conductive heating of the crust. Great Basin Cretaceous magmatism was contemporaneous with stable convergence between North America and the Farallon plate and generation of the coastal batholiths. The changing character of plutonism from low-silica metaluminous to high-silica metaluminous to strongly peraluminous granitoids is paralleled by isotopic changes, indicating an increasing crustal component in the magmas with time. Metallogeny (metal content and alteration associations) changes predictably with plutonic compositions, from Cu to Mo to lithophile-element–dominated deposits.

Metamorphic geochronometry is best interpreted as reflecting a Late Cretaceous metamorphic maximum, followed by fairly rapid cooling. Deformation in the foreland fold and thrust belt is contemporaneous with this culmination; it may reflect the pro-

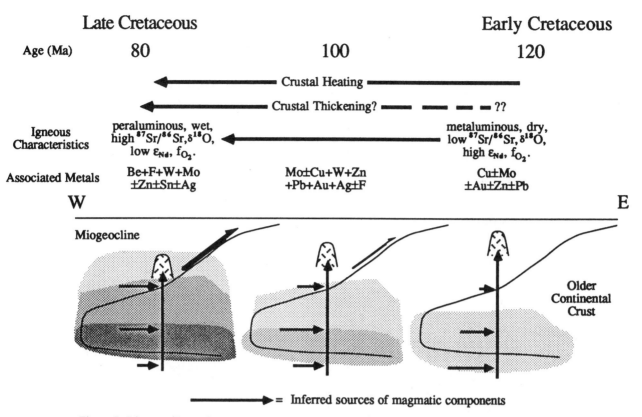

Figure 7. Diagram illustrating the principal features of and proposed model for the Cretaceous east-central Great Basin. Increasing temperature and progressive regional metamorphism are indicated by increasingly dark shading. See text for discussion.

gressive weakening of the crust during the thermal event. The simultaneity of peraluminous magmatism and deformation rule out crustal thickening as the primary cause of the changes in magmatism, in favor of an underlying cause for the regional thermal event reflected by the metamorphism.

This model minimizes the number of special events that must be invoked, while systematically unifying the observations in a way consistent with physical reality (magnitude and time scales of likely thermal events; regional tectonic history, geochemical environment). The same constraints eliminate other hypotheses, such as crustal thickening or high-level plutonism, as dominant causes of regional metamorphism in the area. A key point is that the Cretaceous variations and, in a larger time frame, the Phanerozoic variations occur within the same crust, one that apparently has undergone relatively little major addition or subtraction of material (possibly until the early and mid-Tertiary; cf., Bird, 1988; Gans and others, 1989). The causes of temporal variability must be sought in external factors such as changes in the thermal regime, crustal thickness, subcrustal magma source(s), and state of stress.

ACKNOWLEDGMENTS

Stimulating discussions and field excursions with Peter Bird, Eric Seedorff, Elizabeth Miller, and Phil Gans helped formulate and clarify various aspects of this project. Brooks Hanson was largely responsible for developing the computer programs used in the thermal models. Helpful reviews of the manuscript by Hanson, Miller, Seedorff, J. L. Anderson, J. D. Keith, and especially R. G. Anderson are much appreciated. This study was supported by grants from the National Science Foundation (EAR 86-07452) and the Academic Senate Committee on Research (University of California).

REFERENCES CITED

Allmendinger, R. W., and Jordan, T. E., 1981, Mesozoic evolution of the Sevier orogenic belt: Geology, v. 9, p. 308–313.

Andrews, D. J., and Sleep, N. H., 1974, Numerical modeling of tectonic flow behind island arcs: Royal Astronomical Society Geophysical Journal, v. 38, p. 237–251.

Armstrong, R. L., 1968, The Sevier orogenic belt in Nevada and Utah: Geological Society of America Bulletin, v. 79, p. 429–458.

—— , 1974, Magmatism, orogenic timing, and orogenic diachronism in the Cordillera from Mexico to Canada: Nature, v. 247, p. 348–351.

—— , 1976, The geochronometry of Idaho: Isochron/West, v. 15, p. 1–33.

—— , 1982, Cordilleran metamorphic core complexes—From Arizona to southern Canada: Annual Review of Earth and Planetary Sciences, v. 10, p. 129–154.

—— , 1983, Cordilleran S- and I-type granites; Indicators of lithosphere thickness: Geological Association of Canada Program with Abstracts, v. 8, p. A3.

—— , 1989, Mesozoic and early Cenozoic magmatic evolution of the Canadian

Cordillera, *in* Rodgers Symposium Volume: American Journal of Science (in press).

Armstrong, R. L., and Suppe, J., 1973, Potassium-argon geochronometry of Mesozoic igneous rocks in Nevada, Utah, and southern California: Geological Society of America Bulletin, v. 84, p. 1375–1392.

Atkinson, W. W., Jr., Kaczmarowski, J. H., and Erickson, A. J., Jr., 1982, Geology of a skarn-breccia orebody at the Victoria Mine, Elko County, Nevada: Economic Geology, v. 77, p. 899–918.

Bartley, J. M., Murray, M. E., and Wright, S. D., 1985, Mesozoic thrusts and folds in the northern Quinn Canyon Range, Nye County, Nevada: Geological Society of America Programs with Abstracts, v. 17, p. 340.

Barton, M. D., 1982, Some aspects of the geology and mineralogy of the fluorine-rich skarn at McCullough Butte, Eureka Co., Nevada: Carnegie Institution of Washington Year Book, v. 81, p. 324–328.

—— , 1987, Lithophile-element mineralization associated with Late Cretaceous two-mica granites in the Great Basin: Geology, v. 15, p. 337–340.

Barton, M. D., and Hanson, R. B., 1989, Magmatism and the development of low-pressure metamorphic belts; Implications from thermal modeling and the western United States: Geological Society of America Bulletin, p. 1051–1065.

Barton, M. D., and 8 others, 1988, Mesozoic contact metamorphism in the western United States, *in* W. G. Ernst, ed., Metamorphism and crustal evolution, western conterminous United States; Rubey Volume 7: Englewood Cliffs, New Jersey, Prentice-Hall, p. 110–178.

Bauer, H. L., Jr., Beitrick, R. A., Cooper, J. J., and Swinderman, J. N., 1966, Porphyry copper deposits in the Robinson mining district, *in* Titley, S. R., and Hicks, C. L., eds., Geology of the porphyry copper deposits, southwestern North America: Tucson, University of Arizona Press, p. 232–244.

Best, M. G., Armstrong, R. L., Graustein, W. C., Embree, G. F., and Ahlborn, R. C., 1974, Two-mica granites of the Kern Mountains pluton, eastern White Pine County, Nevada; Remobilized basement of the Cordilleran miogeosyncline?: Geological Society of America Bulletin, v. 85, p. 1277–1286.

Bird, G. P., 1988, Formation of the Rocky Mountains, western United States; A continuum computer model: Science, v. 239, p. 1501–1507.

Bonham, H. F., Jr., and Garside, L. J., 1979, Geology of the Tonopah, Lone Mountain, Klondike and northern Mud Lake quadrangles, Nevada: Nevada Bureau of Mines and Geology Bulletin 92, 142 p.

Brown, G. C., Thorpe, R. S., and Webb, P. C., 1984, The geochemical characteristics of granitoids in contrasting arcs and comments on magma sources: Geological Society of London Journal, v. 141, p. 369–377.

Burchfiel, B. C., and Davis, G. A., 1975, Nature and controls of Cordilleran orogenesis, western United States; Extensions of an earlier synthesis: American Journal of Science, v. 275-A, p. 393–396.

Burnham, C. W., and Ohmoto, H., 1980, Late-stage processes of felsic magmatism, *in* Ishihara, S., and Takenouchi, S., eds., Granitic magmatism and related mineralization: Mining Geology Special Issue 8, p. 1–11.

Buseck, P. R., 1967, Contact metasomatism and ore deposition; Tempiute, Nevada: Economic Geology, v. 62, p. 331–353.

Bykerk-Kauffman, A., and Janecke, S. U., 1987, Late Cretaceous to early Tertiary ductile deformation; Catalina-Rincon metamorphic core complex, southeastern Arizona: Geology, v. 15, p. 462–465.

Coney, P. J., and Harms, T. A., 1984, Cordilleran metamorphic core complexes; Cenozoic extensional relics of Mesozoic compression: Geology, v. 12, p. 550–554.

Coney, P. J., and Reynolds, S. J., 1977, Cordilleran Benioff zones: Nature, v. 270, p. 403–406.

Cornwall, H. R., 1972, Geology and mineral deposits of southern Nye County, Nevada: Nevada Bureau of Mines and Geology Bulletin 77, 49 p.

Dallmeyer, R. D., Snoke, A. W., and McKee, E. H., 1986, The Mesozoic-Cenozoic tectonothermal evolution of the Ruby Mountains, East Humboldt Range, Nevada; A Cordilleran metamorphic core complex: Tectonics, v. 5, p. 931–954.

DePaolo, D. J., 1981, Trace element and isotopic effects of combined wall-rock assimilation and fractional crystallization: Earth and Planetary Science Letters, v. 53, p. 189–209.

DeWitt, E., Miller, D. M., and Snoke, A. W., 1984, Mesozoic regional metamorphic terranes, western U.S.: Geological Society of America Abstracts with Programs, v. 16, p. 487.

Dickinson, W. R., and Snyder, W. S., 1978, Plate tectonics of the Laramide orogeny: Geological Society of America Memoir 151, p. 355–366.

Einaudi, M. T., Meinert, L. D., and Newberry, R. J., 1981, Skarn deposits: Economic Geology 75th Anniversary Volume, p. 327–391.

Engebretson, D. C., Cox, A., and Gordon, R. G., 1985, Relative motions between oceanic and continental plates in the Pacific basin: Geological Society of America Special Paper 206, 59 p.

England, P. C., and Thompson, A. B., 1986, Some thermal and tectonic models for crustal melting in collision-zone metamorphism, *in* Coward, M. P., and Ries, A. C., eds., Collision tectonics: Geological Society of London Special Publication 19, p. 83–94.

Evans, J. G., 1980, Geology of the Rodeo Creek NE and Welches Canyon quadrangles, Eureka County, Nevada: U.S. Geological Survey Bulletin 1473, 81 p.

Farmer, G. L., 1988, Isotope geochemistry of Mesozoic and Tertiary igneous rocks in the western U.S. and implications for the structure and composition of the deep continental lithosphere, *in* Ernst, W. G., ed., Metamorphism and crustal evolution, western conterminous United States; Rubey Volume 7: Englewood Cliffs, New Jersey, Prentice-Hall, p. 87–109.

Farmer, G. L., and DePaolo, D. J., 1983, Origin of Mesozoic and Tertiary granite in the western United States and implications for pre-Mesozoic crustal structure; 1, Nd and Sr isotopic studies in the geocline of the northern Great Basin: Journal of Geophysical Research, v. 88, p. 3379–3401.

—— , 1984, Origin of Mesozoic and Tertiary granite in the western United States and implications for pre-Mesozoic crustal structure; 2, Nd and Sr isotopic studies of unmineralized and Cu- and Mo-mineralized granite in the Precambrian craton: Journal of Geophysical Research, v. 89, p. 10141–10160.

Field, C. W., and Fifarek, R. H., 1985, Light stable-isotope systematics in the epithermal environment, *in* Berger, B. R., and Bethke, P. M., eds., Geology and geochemistry of epithermal systems: Reviews in Economic Geology, v. 2, p. 99–128.

Fryxell, J. E., 1988, Geologic map and descriptions of stratigraphy and structure of the west-central Grant Range, Nye County, Nevada: Boulder, Colorado, Geological Society of America, Map Chart Series MCH064.

Gans, P. B., 1987, A two-layer crustal stretching model for the eastern Great Basin: Tectonics, v. 6, p. 1–12.

Gans, P. B., and Miller, E. L., 1983, Style of mid-Tertiary extension in east-central Nevada, *in* Geologic excursions in the overthrust belt and metamorphic core complexes of the intermountain region, Nevada; Geological Society of American field trip guidebook: Utah Geological and Mineral Survey Special Studies 59, p. 107–160.

Gans, P. B., Clark, D. H., Miller, E. L., and Wright, J. E., 1986, Structural development of the Kern Mountains and northern Snake Range: Geological Society of America Abstracts with Programs, v. 18, p. 108.

Gans, P. B., Clark, D., and Repetski, J. E., 1987, Conodont geothermometry of supracrustal rocks in the eastern Great Basin: Geological Society of America Abstracts with Programs, v. 19, p. 380.

Gans, P. B., Mahood, G., and Schermer, E., 1989, Synextensional magmatism from the Basin and Range Province; A case study from the eastern Great Basin: Geological Society of America Special Paper 233, 60 p.

Granger, A. E., Bell, M. M., Simmons, G. C., and Lee, F., 1957, Geology and mineral resources of Elko County, Nevada: Nevada Bureau of Mines Bulletin 54, 190.

Guild, P. W., 1978, Metallogenesis in the western United States: Geological Society of London Journal, v. 135, p. 355–376.

Hamilton, W., 1978, Mesozoic tectonics of the western United States: Pacific Section, Society of Economic Paleontologists and Mineralogists, Pacific Coast Paleogeography Symposium 2, p. 33–70.

—— , 1982, Structural evolution of the Big Maria Mountains, northeastern Riverside County, southeastern California, *in* Frost, E. G., and Martin, D. L., eds., Mesozoic-Cenozoic tectonic evolution of the Colorado River region, California, Arizona, and Nevada: San Diego, California, Cordilleran Publishers, p. 1–28.

—— , 1988, Tectonic setting and variations with depth of some Cretaceous and Cenozoic strucural and magmatic systems of the western United States, *in* Ernst, W. G., ed., Metamorphism and crustal evolution, western conterminous United States; Rubey Volume 7: Englewood Cliffs, New Jersey, Prentice-Hall, p. 1–40.

Harris, A. G., Wardlaw, B. R., Rust, C. C., and Merrill, G. K., 1980, Maps for assessing thermal maturity (conodont color alteration index maps) in Ordovician through Triassic rocks in Nevada and Utah and adjacent parts of Idaho and California: U.S. Geological Survey Miscellaneous Investigations Map I–1249, scale 1:2,500,000.

Harris, N.B.W., Pearce, J. A., and Tindle, A. G., 1986, Geochemical characteristics of collision-zone granites, *in* Coward, M. P., and Ries, A. C., eds., Collision tectonics: Geological Society of London Special Publication 19, p. 67–81.

Hausen, D. M., and Kerr, P. F., 1968, Fine gold occurrence at Carlin, Nevada, *in* Ridge, J. D., ed., Ore deposits of the United States, Volume 1: American Institute of Mining, Metallurgical, and Petroleum Engineers, p. 908–940.

Haxel, G. B., Tosdal, R. M., May, D. J., and Wright, J. E., 1984, Latest Cretaceous and early Tertiary orogenesis in south-central Arizona; Thrust faulting, regional metamorphism, and granitic plutonism: Geological Society of America Bulletin, v. 95, p. 631–653.

Heller, P. L., and 7 others, 1986, Time of initial thrusting in the Sevier orogenic belt, Idaho-Wyoming and Utah: Geology, v. 14, p. 388–391.

Henry, S. G., and Pollack, H. N., 1988, Terrestrial heat flow above the Andean subduction zone in Bolivia and Peru: Journal of Geophysical Research, v. 93, p. 15,153–15,162.

Hoisch, T. D., Miller, C. F., Heizler, M. T., Harrison, T. M., and Stoddard, E. F., 1988, Late Cretaceous regional metamorphism in southeastern California, *in* Ernst, W. G., ed., Metamorphism and crustal evolution, western conterminous United States; Rubey Volume 7: Englewood Cliffs, New Jersey, Prentice-Hall, p. 538–571.

Hollister, L. S., and Crawford, M. L., 1986, Melt-enhanced deformation; A major tectonic process: Geology, v. 14, p. 558–561.

Hose, R. K., Blake, M. C., Jr., and Smith, R. M., 1976, Geology and mineral resources of White Pine County, Nevada: Nevada Bureau of Mines and Geology, v. 85, 105 p.

Ishihara, S., 1981, The granitoid series and mineralization: Economic Geology 75th Anniversary Volume, p. 458–484.

Jaeger, J. C., 1964, Thermal effects of intrusions: Reviews in Geophysics, v. 2, p. 443–466.

James, L. P., 1976, Zoned alteration in limestone at porphyry copper deposits, Ely, Nevada: Economic Geology, v. 71, p. 488–512.

Jerome, S. E., and Cook, D. R., 1967, Relation of some metal mining districts in the western United States to regional tectonic environments and igneous activity: Nevada Bureau of Mines Bulletin, v. 69, 35 p.

John, D. A., 1987, Map showing the distribution and characteristics of plutonic rocks in the Tonopah 1° by 2° Quadrangle, central Nevada: U.S. Geological Survey Miscellaneous Field Studies Map MF–1877-J, scale 1:250,000.

Johnston, W. P., 1972, K-Ar ages of the Blind Mountain stock and Yuba dike, Lincoln County, Nevada: Isochron/West, no. 3, p. 30.

Karish, C. R., Miller, E. L., and Sutter, J. F., 1987, Mesozoic tectonic and magmatic history of the central Mojave Desert: Arizona Geological Society Digest, v. 18, p. 15–32.

Keith, J. D., Clark, A. H., and Hodgson, C. J., 1985, Characterization of granitoid rocks associated with tungsten skarn deposits of the North American Cordillera: Geological Survey of Canada, 129 p. (unpublished).

Keith, S. B., 1978, Paleosubduction geometries inferred from Cretaceous and Tertiary magmatic patterns in southwestern North America: Geology, v. 6, p. 515–521.

—— , 1983, Distribution of fossil metallogenic systems and magma geochemical belts in the Great Basin and vicinity from 145 million years ago to present:

Geothermal Resources Council Special Report 13, p. 285–286.

Keith, S. B., and Reynolds, S. J., 1981, Low-angle subduction origin for paired peraluminous-metaluminous belts of mid-Cretaceous to early Tertiary Cordilleran granitoids: Geological Society of America Abstracts with Programs, v. 13, p. 63–64.

Kistler, R. W., 1974, Phanerozoic batholiths in western North America; A summary of some recent work on variations in time, space, chemistry, and isotopic compositions: Annual Review of Earth and Planetary Sciences, v. 2, p. 403–418.

—— , 1983, Isotope geochemistry of plutons in the northern Great Basin: Geothermal Resources Council Special Report 13, p. 3–8.

Kistler, R. W., Ghent, E. D., and O'Neil, J. R., 1981, Petrogenesis of two-mica granites in the Ruby Mountains, Nevada: Journal of Geophysical Research, v. 86, p. 10591–10606.

Kleinhampl, F. J., and Ziony, J. I., 1984, Mineral resources of northern Nye County, Nevada: Nevada Bureau of Mines and Geology Bulletin 99B, 243 p.

Labotka, T. C., Warasila, R. L., and Spangler, R. R., 1985, Polymetamorphism in the Panamint Mountains, California; An ^{40}Ar-^{39}Ar study: Journal of Geophysical Research, v. 90, p. 10359–10371.

Lachenbruch, A. H., and Sass, J. H., 1978, Models of an extending lithosphere and heat flow in the Basin and Range province, *in* Smith, R. B., and Eaton, G. P., eds., Cenozoic tectonics and regional geophysics of the Western Cordillera: Geological Society of America Memoir 152, p. 209–250.

Lawton, T. F., 1985, Style and timing of frontal structures, thrust belt, central Utah: American Association of Petroleum Geologists Bulletin, v. 69, p. 1145–1159.

Lee, D. E., 1984, Analytical data for a suite of granitoid rocks from the Basin and Range Province: U.S. Geological Survey BUlletin 1602, 54 p.

Lee, D. E., and Christiansen, E. H., 1983, The granite problem as exposed in the southern Snake Range, Nevada: Contributions to Mineralogy and Petrology, v. 83, p. 99–116.

Lee, D. E., and Fischer, L. B., 1985, Cretaceous metamorphism in the northern Snake Range, Nevada; A metamorphic core complex: Isochron/West, no. 42, p. 3–7.

Lee, D. E., Marvin, R. F., and Mehnert, H. H., 1980, A radiometric study of Mesozoic-Cenozoic metamorphism in eastern White Pine County, Nevada and adjacent Utah: U.S. Geological Survey Professional Paper 1158C, p. C17–C28.

Lee, D. E., Kistler, R. W., Friedman, I., and Van Loenen, R. E., 1981, Two-mica granites of northeastern Nevada: Journal of Geophysical Research, v. 86, p. 10607–10616.

Lee, D. E., Friedman, I., and Gleason, J. D., 1984, Modification of δD values in eastern Nevada granitoid rocks spatially related to thrust faults: Contributions to Mineralogy and Petrology, v. 88, p. 288–298.

Le Fort, P., 1986, Metamorphism and magmatism during Himalayan collision, *in* Coward, M. P., and Ries, A. C., Collision tectonics: Geological Society of London Special Publication 19, p. 159–172.

Marvin, R. F., and Dobson, S. W., 1979, Radiometric ages; Compilation B, U.S. Geological Survey: Isochron West, v. 26, p. 3–32.

Miller, C. F., and Barton, M. D., 1989, Phanerozoic plutonism in the Cordilleran interior, U.S.A., *in* Kay, S. M., and Rapela, C. W., Plutonism from Antartica to Alaska: Geological Society of America Special Paper 241 (in press).

Miller, C. F., Howard, K. A., and Hoisch, T. D., 1982, Mesozoic thrusting, metamorphism, and plutonism, Old Woman–Piute Range, southeastern California, *in* Frost, E. G., and Martin, D. L., eds., Mesozoic–Cenozoic tectonic evolution of the Colorado River region, California, Arizona, and Nevada: San Diego, California, Cordilleran Publishers, p. 561–581.

Miller, D. M., Hillhouse, W. C., Zartman, R. E., and Lanphere, M. A., 1987, Geochronology of intrusive and metamorphic rocks in the Pilot Range, Utah and Nevada, and comparison with regional patterns: Geological Society of America Bulletin, v. 99, p. 866–879.

Miller, E. L., Gans, P. B., Wright, J. E., and Sutter, J. F., 1988, Metamorphic history of the east-central Basin and Range province; Tectonic setting and relationship to magmatism, *in* Ernst, W. G., ed., Metamorphism and crustal evolution, western conterminous United States; Ruby Volume 7: Englewood Cliffs, New Jersey, Prentice-Hall, p. 649–682.

Misch, P., 1960, Regional structural reconnaissance in central-northeast Nevada and some adjacent areas; Observations and interpretations: Intermountain Association of Petroleum Geologists 11th Annual Field Conference Guidebook, p. 17–42.

Misch, P., and Hazzard, J. C., 1962, Stratigraphy and metamorphism of the late Precambrian rocks in central northeastern Nevada and adjacent Utah: American Association of Petroleum Geologists Bulletin, v. 46, p. 289–343.

Mitchell, A.H.G., and Garson, M. S., 1981, Mineral deposits and global tectonic settings: New York, Academic Press, 405 p.

Nelson, B. K., 1985, Samarium-neodymium and rubidium-strontium isotopic studies of the origin and evolution of continental crust [Ph.D. thesis]: Los Angeles, University of California, 174 p.

Noble, J. A., 1970, Metal provinces of the western United States: Geological Society of America Bulletin, v. 81, p. 1607–1624.

Nolan, T. B., 1962, The Eureka mining district, Nevada: U.S. Geological Survey Professional Paper 406, 78 p.

Nolan, T. B., and Hunt, R. N., 1968, The Eureka mining district, Nevada, *in* Ridge, J. D., ed., Ore deposits of the United States, Volume 1: American Institute of Mining, Metallurgical, and Petroleum Engineers, p. 966–991.

Nolan, T. B., Merriam, C. W., and Blake, M. C., Jr., 1973, Geologic map of the Pinto Summit Quadrangle, Eureka and White Pine counties, Nevada: U.S. Geological Survey Miscellaneous Investigations Map I–793, scale 1:31,680.

Oldow, J. S., and Bartel, R. L., 1987, Early to Middle(?) Jurassic extensional tectonism in the western Great Basin; Growth faulting and synorogenic deposition of the Dunlap Formation: Geology, v. 15, p. 740–743.

Olson, J. C., and Hinrichs, E. N., 1960, Beryl-bearing pegmatites in the Ruby Mountains and other areas in Nevada and northwestern Arizona: U.S. Geological Survey Bulletin 1082–D, p. 135–200.

Pearce, J. A., Harris, N.B.W., and Tindle, A. G., 1984, Trace element discrimination diagrams for the tectonic interpretation of granitic rocks: Journal of Petrology, v. 25, p. 956–983.

Pitcher, W. S., 1987, Granites and yet more granites forty years later: Geologische Rundschau, v. 76, p. 51–79.

Reynolds, S. J., and Keith, S. B., 1982, Geochemistry and mineral potential of peraluminous granitoids: Arizona Bureau of Geology and Mineral Technology Field Notes, v. 12, p. 4–6.

Roberts, R. J., Montgomery, K. M., and Lehner, R. E., 1967, Geology and mineral resources of Eureka County, Nevada: Nevada Bureau of Mines Bulletin, v. 64, 152 p.

Rodgers, D. W., and Sutter, J. F., 1986, Thermal history of the Deep Creek Range, Nevada-Utah, and implications for Cordilleran tectonics: Geological Society of America Programs with Abstracts, v. 18, p. 177.

Shaver, S. A., 1984, The Hall (Nevada Moly) molybdenum deposit, Nye County, Nevada; Geology, alteration, mineralization, and geochemical dispersion [Ph.D. thesis]: Stanford, California, Stanford University, 261 p.

Shawe, D. R., Marvin, R. J., Andriessen, P.A.M., Mehnert, H. H., and Merritt, V. M., 1986, Ages of igneous and hydrothermal events in the Round Mountain and Manhattan gold districts, Nye County, Nevada: Economic Geology, v. 81, p. 388–407.

Snoke, A. W., and Miller, D. M., 1988, Metamorphic and tectonic history of the northeastern Great Basin, *in* Ernst, W. G., ed., Metamorphism and crustal evolution, western conterminous United States; Ruby Volume 7: Englewood Cliffs, New Jersey, Prentice-Hall, p. 606–648.

Snoke, A. W., McKee, E. H., and Stern, T. W., 1979, Plutonic, metamorphic, and structural chronology in the northern Ruby Mountains, Nevada; A preliminary report: Geological Society of America Programs with Abstracts, v. 11, p. 520–521.

Sonnevil, R. A., 1979, Evolution of skarn at Monte Cristo, Nevada [M.S. thesis]: Stanford, California, Stanford University, 84 p.

Speed, R. C., Elison, M. W., and Heck, F. R., 1988, Phanerozoic tectonic evolution of the Great Basin, *in* Ernst, W. G., ed., Metamorphism and crustal evolution, western conterminous United States; Ruby Volume 7: Englewood Cliffs, New Jersey, Prentice-Hall, p. 572–605.

Stewart, J. H., 1980, Geology of Nevada: Nevada Bureau of Mines and Geology Special Publication 4, 136 p.

Stewart, J. H., and Carlson, J. E., 1976, Cenozoic rocks of Nevada; Four maps and brief description of distribution, lithology, age, and centers of volcanism: Nevada Bureau of Mines Geological Map 52, scale 1:1,000,000.

—— , 1978, Geologic map of Nevada: U.S. Geological Survey, scale 1:500,000.

Stewart, J. H., McKee, E. H., and Stager, H. K., 1977, Geology and mineral deposits of Lander County, Nevada: Nevada Bureau of Mines and Geology Bulletin, v. 88, 106 p.

Tingley, J. V., and Maldonado, F., 1983, Investigation of the mineral potential of the Clipper Gap, Lone Mountain–Weepah, and Pipe Spring plutons, Nevada: Nevada Bureau of Mines and Geology Open-File Report 83–8, 103 p.

Titley, S. R., and Beane, R. E., 1981, Porphyry copper deposits; Part 1, Geologic settings, petrology, and tectogenesis: Economic Geology 75th Anniversary Volume, p. 214–235.

Toksoz, M. N., and Bird, P., 1977, Formation and evolution of marginal basins and continental plateaus, *in* Talwani, M., and Pitman, W. C., III, eds., Island arcs, deep-sea trenches, and back-arc basins: American Geophysical Union, Maurice Ewing Series, v. 1, p. 379–393.

Tschanz, C. M., and Pampeyan, E. H., 1970, Geology and mineral deposits of Lincoln County, Nevada: Nevada Bureau of Mines Bulletin, v. 73, 188 p.

Wells, P.R.A., 1980, Thermal models for the magmatic accretion and subsequent metamorphism of continental crust: Earth and Planetary Science Letters, v. 46, p. 253–265.

Westgate, L. G., and Knopf, A., 1932, Geology and ore deposits of the Pioche District, Nevada: U.S. Geological Survey Professional Paper 171, 79 p.

Westra, G., 1982, Alteration and mineralization in the Ruth porphyry copper deposit near Ely, Nevada: Economic Geology, v. 77, p. 950–970.

Westra, G., and Keith, S. B., 1982, Classification and genesis of stockwork molybdenum deposits: Economic Geology, v. 76, p. 844–873.

Wickham, S. M., and Taylor, H. P., Jr., 1985, Stable isotope evidence for large scale seawater infiltration in a regional metamorphic terrane; The Trois Seigneurs Massif, Pyrenees, France: Contributions to Mineralogy and Petrology, v. 91, p. 122–137.

Wickham, S. M., Taylor, H. P., Jr., and Snoke, A. W., 1987, Fluid-rock-melt interaction in core complexes; A stable isotope study of the Ruby Mountains–East Humboldt Range, Nevada: Geological Society of America Abstracts with Programs, v. 19, p. 463.

Wiltschko, D. V., and Dorr, J. A., Jr., 1983, Timing of deformation in overthrust belt and foreland of Idaho, Wyoming, and Utah: American Association of Petroleum Geologists Bulletin, v. 67, p. 1304–1322.

Wright, J. E., and Miller, E. L., 1986, An expanded view of Jurassic orogenesis for the western U.S. cordillera: Geological Society of America Abstracts with Programs, v. 18, p. 201.

Wyllie, P. J., 1977, Crustal anatexis; An experimental review: Tectonophysics, v. 43, p. 41–71.

MANUSCRIPT SUBMITTED OCTOBER 6, 1987
REVISED MANUSCRIPT SUBMITTED AUGUST 20, 1988
MANUSCRIPT ACCEPTED BY THE SOCIETY FEBRUARY 7, 1989

Geological Society of America
Memoir 174
1990

Chapter 17

Partial melting of metabasites in the contact aureoles of gabbroic plutons in the Smartville Complex, Sierra Nevada, California

James S. Beard
Virginia Museum of Natural History, 1001 Douglas Avenue, Martinsville, Virginia 24112

ABSTRACT

Metamorphosed volcanic and hypabyssal rocks (metabasites) have been partially melted in the contact aureoles of gabbroic plutons in the Smartville Complex of northern California. The melting occurred in the upper crust of an active arc at pressures of less than 3 kbar and temperatures that may have exceeded 900 °C. The resultant rocks resemble intrusive breccias and consist of pyroxene hornfels of metamorphic origin and clearly igneous diorite. Coexisting hornfels and diorite appear to be in mineralogical equilibrium. The bulk compositions of the hornfels and of the hornfels-diorite mixed rocks as a whole are depleted in alkalis and silica and enriched in Fe and Mg (restitic) with respect to their inferred greenstone protoliths. The diorite veins and layers in the mixed rocks are unlike any other intrusive rocks in the Smartville Complex in that they have refractory bulk compositions, but evolved mineral compositions. A partial melt origin for the mixed rocks is consistent with their high temperatures of formation, the inferred equilibrium between hornfels and diorite, and the estimated major-element chemistry of the hornfels. The refractory chemistry of the diorite veins and layers and the restitic character of the mixed rocks as a whole suggest that a melt has been extracted from the mixed rocks. Although the mixed rocks physically resemble intrusive breccias, they are by most definitions migmatites. Some Smartville Complex tonalites may be related to melts extracted from these rocks.

INTRODUCTION

Partial melting has been documented within the contact aureoles of intrusions, but in most of these cases, melting occurred either within a larger regional metamorphic context (Barr, 1985) or involved low-melting-temperature rocks (e.g., granites; Kovach and Marsh, 1981). The rocks described in this chapter occur in the contact aureoles of gabbroic plutons in the upper levels of the crust of a Jurassic ensimatic arc (Smartville Complex; Beard and Day, 1987). Although these igneous and metamorphic mixed rocks have the appearance of intrusive breccias, evidence will be presented that suggests that they formed by partial melting more or less in situ.

SETTING, OCCURRENCE, AND DESCRIPTION

Evidence for partial melting can be found in contact-metamorphosed volcanic and hypabyssal rocks in the Smartville Complex, a Late Jurassic rifted ensimatic arc located in the northwestern foothills of the California Sierra Nevada. The Smartville Complex consists of a carapace of tholeiitic to calc-alkalic basalts, andesites, and dacites that is intruded by diabase, gabbro, diorite, and tonalite of the arc core (Moores, 1972; Xenophontos and Bond, 1978; Menzies and others, 1980; Day and others, 1985; Beard and Day, 1987). The oldest rocks in the Smartville Complex are the volcanic rocks and an intrusive unit consisting largely of massive diabase. All the oldest rocks were

Beard, J. S., 1990, Partial melting of metabasites in the contact aureoles of gabbroic plutons in the Smartville Complex, Sierra Nevada, California, *in* Anderson, J. L., ed., The nature and origin of Cordilleran magmatism: Boulder, Colorado, Geological Society of America Memoir 174.

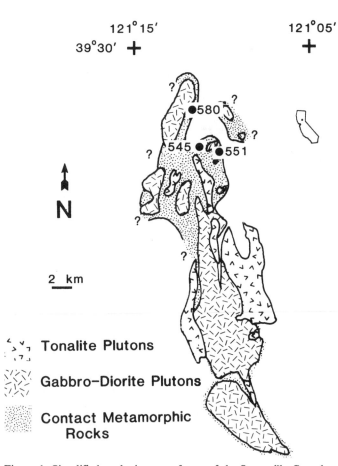

121°15'   121°05'
39°30' +   +

●580

545 ● ● 551

N

2 km

Tonalite Plutons

Gabbro–Diorite Plutons

Contact Metamorphic
Rocks

Figure 1. Simplified geologic map of part of the Smartville Complex showing the gabbro and tonalite plutons that intrude the arc core. Contact-metamorphic rocks shown are those interpreted as having formed in response to the intrusion of high-temperature gabbroic magmas. Protoliths include older diabases and volcanic rocks. The contact metamorphism overprints a regional prehnite-pumpellyite or greenschist facies assemblage. Unpatterned areas include a variety of volcanics and hypabyssal greenstones.

regionally metamorphosed to prehnite-pumpellyite and lower greenschist facies (Beiersdorfer and Day, 1983; Xenophontos, 1984) and then intruded by a series of tonalite and gabbro-diorite plutons during continued arc magmatism (Beard and Day, 1987). The gabbro-diorite intrusions include large, mostly dioritic intrusions and smaller plutons that consist mostly or entirely of olivine gabbro and gabbronorite. Rocks that show evidence of partial melting occur in pyroxene hornfels in the inner regions of the extensive contact aureoles associated with the smaller, more mafic gabbroic plutons (Fig. 1). Protoliths for the contact-metamorphosed and partially melted rocks include both diabasic and volcanic greenstones.

Most of the mixed rocks have brecciated structure similar to typical intrusive breccias (Fig. 2b), but weakly to strongly layered structure is locally developed (Fig. 2, a and c). The proportion of diorite to metabasite varies on an outcrop scale; some exposures are dominated by diorite and others by metabasite. The dioritic

material consists of ortho- and clinopyroxene (opx > cpx), reversely zoned andesine to labradorite plagioclase, magnetite, ilmenite, and 1 to 6 percent interstitial quartz. A single grain of altered biotite occurs in one thin section (551). The diorite is a hypidiomorphic granular rock containing idiomorphically zoned plagioclase (Fig. 2d). Such textures indicate an igneous origin for the diorite (e.g., Ashworth and McLellan, 1985). The composition of the diorite veins and layers in the mixed rocks is very different from the composition of the pluton (usually olivine gabbro) that generated the contact aureole.

In contrast to the diorite, the host rock has well-developed hornfelsic texture (Fig. 2, b and c). The mineral assemblage of the hornfels resembles that of the diorite except that the plagioclase is unzoned labradorite and quartz (and biotite) and lacking. Unlike the diorites, the hornfels contains more clinopyroxene than orthopyroxene.

Sieve-textured amphibole grains straddle the contacts between the diorite and hornfels. Amphiboles are typically zoned from greenish-brown cores to brownish-green rims. The amphibole has interstitial to poikolitic texture and is a late crystallizing phase that postdates the formation of hornfelsic texture in the hornfels.

MINERAL CHEMISTRY

Four samples were selected for microprobe study. The compositions of all major phases in diorite and hornfels occurring in a single thin section were determined for three of the samples. Only mafic silicate compositions were determined for sample 580a. Samples 580a and 580c are layered rocks that were collected from adjacent outcrops in the contact aureole of a zoned olivine gabbro-gabbronorite pluton. Samples 551 and 545 have brecciated structure and are from the contact aureole of an olivine gabbro plug (Fig. 1).

Clinopyroxene. Clinopyroxene compositions are En_{35-37}, Fs_{19-23}, Wo_{42-44} in the hornfelses and En_{33-38}, Fs_{18-23}, Wo_{43-44} in the diorites (Fig. 3; Table 1). Within the range of intra-sample variation, clinopyroxene compositions are virtually identical in coexisting hornfels and diorite, except for sample 551. Al_2O_3 (0.6–1.2 wt.%), TiO_2 (0.1–0.3 wt.%), and Na_2O (0.2–0.25 wt.%) concentrations are low, and Cr_2O_3 is at or near or at detection limits. MnO ranges from 0.4 to 0.7 wt.% and increases with Fe.

Orthopyroxene. Orthopyroxene compositions are En_{46-54}, Fs_{43-51}, $Wo_{2.1-3.0}$ in the hornfelses and En_{43-54}, Fs_{43-54}, $Wo_{2.7-3.2}$ in the diorites (Fig. 3; Table 2). Like clinopyroxene, orthopyroxene from coexisting diorite and hornfels have compositions that are essentially identical within the range of intra-sample variability, again except for sample 551. Al_2O_3 and TiO_2 contents are low. MnO varies from 0.7 to 1.3 wt.% and increases with iron.

Amphibole. The amphiboles are hornblendes with a limited compositional range (Fig. 3; Table 3). Most of the variation in amphibole chemistry within single samples reflects core-to-rim

Figure 2. Photograph and photomicrographs of the mixed rocks. a: Typical mixed rock outcrop. b: Brecciated mixed rock. c: Layered mixed rock. d: Dioritic material in mixed rock.

zoning, with Fe, Al, Ti, and alkalis enriched in the amphibole cores.

Fe-Ti oxides. Coexisting magnetite and ilmenite were analyzed in three of the four samples and results are given in Table 4. Titanomagnetite compositions are Uv_{19-32}. The concentration of Al_2O_3 ranges from 0.3 to 1.9 wt.%, that of Cr_2O_3 from 0.2 to 0.8 wt.%, and that of MnO from 0.3 to 1.2 wt.%. Ilmenite compositions range from Il_{91-96}. MnO concentration in the ilmenite is as high as 3 wt.%, but other minor constituents are at or near detection limits.

Plagioclase. The plagioclase crystals in coexisting hornfels and diorite in the mixed rocks have systematic differences in zoning and composition. Plagioclase in the hornfels is very weakly, normally, or irregularly zoned. Compositions range from An_{50-59} (Table 5). In contrast, nearly every plagioclase grain in the dioritic veins and layers is reversely zoned (Fig. 4). Average

plagioclase compositions in the diorites range from An_{47-57}. Rims average An_{48-59} and are always more calcic than the plagioclase as a whole (Table 5). There are none of the disequilibrium features typical of reversed zoning that results from magma mixing (e.g., corroded cores or abrupt or discontinuous compositional changes; Eichelberger, 1975) in the diorite plagioclases. Diorite plagioclase rim compositions are similar to the bulk compositions of relatively weakly zoned plagioclase in the hornfels (Table 5).

WHOLE-ROCK CHEMISTRY

Major-element concentrations for three of the mixed rocks were determined by x-ray fluorescence. The compositions of the diorites were estimated by combining mineral chemistry with mineral mode (recalculated to a weight basis). Hornfels composi-

TABLE 1. CLINOPYROXENE

	d545•	h545	d551	h551	d580c	h580c	d580a	h580a
Wt.% Oxides								
SiO$_2$	52.44	52.37	52.53	52.18	52.69	52.52	52.44	52.56
TiO$_2$	0.21	0.24	0.13	0.32	0.24	0.31	0.31	0.29
Al$_2$O$_3$	0.98	0.98	0.62	1.07	1.08	1.16	1.14	1.10
FeO	12.33	12.81	14.29	14.04	11.37	11.64	11.99	11.69
MnO	0.61	0.56	0.70	0.62	0.46	0.42	0.46	0.46
MgO	12.43	12.56	11.30	11.98	13.17	13.07	12.90	13.20
CaO	21.45	20.98	21.21	20.32	21.38	21.33	21.29	21.11
Na$_2$O	0.22	0.24	0.20	0.22	0.23	0.24	0.23	0.24
Cr$_2$O$_3$	0.01	0.01	0.02	0.03	0.01	0.02	0.02	0.04
Total	100.69	100.75	100.99	100.78	100.64	100.72	100.79	100.70
Cations/6 Oxygens								
SI	1.973	1.970	1.988	1.971	1.972	1.966	1.966	1.968
TI	0.006	0.007	0.003	0.009	0.007	0.009	0.009	0.008
AL	0.043	0.043	0.026	0.048	0.048	0.051	0.050	0.049
FE	0.388	0.403	0.452	0.443	0.356	0.364	0.376	0.366
MN	0.020	0.018	0.022	0.020	0.015	0.013	0.015	0.015
MG	0.697	0.704	0.637	0.674	0.734	0.730	0.721	0.737
CA	0.865	0.846	0.859	0.822	0.857	0.856	0.855	0.847
NA	0.016	0.017	0.014	0.016	0.017	0.018	0.017	0.017
CR	0.000	0.000	0.001	0.001	0.000	0.001	0.001	0.001
Total	4.007	4.009	4.003	4.004	4.005	4.008	4.008	4.007
Wo	44.3	43.3	44.1	42.4	44.0	43.9	43.8	43.4
En	35.8	36.1	32.7	34.8	37.7	37.4	36.9	37.8
Fs	19.9	20.6	23.2	22.9	18.3	18.7	19.3	18.8

*In this and all subsequent tables, d = diorite and h = hornfels.

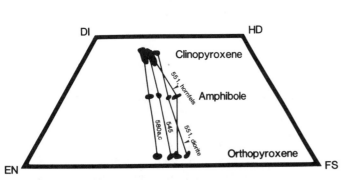

Figure 3. Quadrilateral projection for clinopyroxene, orthopyroxene, and amphibole. Fields enclose the range of analyses for each specimen and tie lines connect average compositions. Mafic silicates in 580a and 580c hornfels and diorite and in 545 diorite and hornfels have indistinguishable compositions and are not separated. Hornfels and diorite fields are shown for specimen 551.

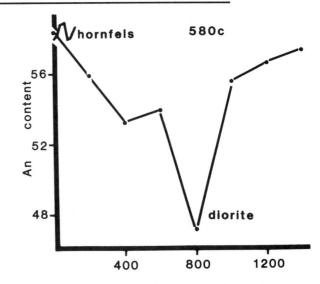

Figure 4. A representative diorite plagioclase zoning profile; rim to rim distance is in microns. See text for discussion.

TABLE 2. ORTHOPYROXENE

	d545	h545	d551	h551	d580c	h580c	d580a	h580a
Wt.% Oxides								
SiO_2	50.99	51.05	50.25	50.63	51.75	51.72	51.91	51.72
TiO_2	0.26	0.17	0.22	0.25	0.21	0.18	0.23	0.23
Al_2O_3	0.56	0.52	0.49	0.49	0.62	0.67	0.59	0.64
FeO	29.34	29.41	32.12	30.58	26.62	27.11	26.96	26.83
MnO	1.20	1.25	1.34	1.19	0.79	0.85	0.82	0.85
MgO	16.70	16.94	14.54	15.71	18.93	19.06	18.94	18.71
CaO	1.43	1.04	1.50	1.41	1.28	1.03	1.29	1.36
Total	100.49	100.38	100.45	100.25	100.20	100.63	100.74	100.33
Cations/6 Oxygens								
SI	1.969	1.972	1.971	1.972	1.972	1.966	1.970	1.971
TI	0.007	0.005	0.007	0.007	0.006	0.005	0.007	0.007
AL	0.026	0.024	0.023	0.023	0.028	0.030	0.026	0.029
FE	0.948	0.950	1.053	0.996	0.849	0.862	0.856	0.855
MN	0.039	0.041	0.044	0.039	0.026	0.027	0.026	0.027
MG	0.962	0.975	0.850	0.912	1.075	1.080	1.071	1.063
CA	0.059	0.043	0.063	0.059	0.052	0.042	0.052	0.056
Total	4.010	4.010	4.011	4.009	4.007	4.013	4.009	4.008
Wo	3.0	2.2	3.2	3.0	2.7	2.1	2.6	2.8
En	48.9	49.5	43.2	46.4	54.4	54.4	54.1	53.9
Fs	48.1	48.3	53.6	50.6	42.9	43.4	43.2	43.3

TABLE 3. AMPHIBOLES

	d545	h545	d551	h551	d580c	h580c	d580a
Wt.% Oxides							
SiO_2	46.35	47.09	46.07	45.70	46.80	47.06	47.97
TiO_2	1.13	1.09	1.34	1.13	1.07	0.92	0.74
Al_2O_3	6.71	6.41	6.99	6.68	6.55	6.22	5.75
FeO	17.76	17.37	19.53	20.55	15.67	16.13	15.74
MnO	0.46	0.42	0.45	0.52	0.29	0.37	0.32
MgO	12.30	12.51	11.49	10.44	13.58	13.41	14.25
CaO	11.30	11.59	11.71	11.04	11.34	11.49	11.62
Na_2O	1.00	0.78	1.29	1.00	0.95	0.79	0.61
K_2O	0.33	0.28	0.39	0.50	0.30	0.26	0.21
Total	97.33	97.53	98.70	97.53	96.53	96.62	97.21
Cations/23 Oxygens							
Si	6.964	7.032	6.889	6.952	7.007	7.051	7.115
Ti	0.126	0.121	0.150	0.129	0.120	0.103	0.082
Al	1.188	1.129	1.232	1.199	1.156	1.098	1.006
Fe	2.232	2.170	2.443	2.614	1.962	2.022	1.952
Mn	0.059	0.053	0.058	0.067	0.037	0.046	0.040
Mg	2.753	2.785	2.561	2.366	3.030	2.995	3.150
Ca	1.818	1.854	1.789	1.799	1.819	1.844	1.846
Na	0.290	0.224	0.372	0.295	0.275	0.231	0.177
K	0.062	0.054	0.074	0.096	0.057	0.050	0.040
Total	15.490	15.420	15.567	15.515	15.461	15.438	15.408

J. S. Beard

TABLE 4. OXIDES

	d545	h545	d551	h551	d580c	h580c		d545	h545	d551	h551	d580c	h580c
			Magnetite							Ilmentite			
SiO_2	0.05	0.05	0.11	0.05	0.11	0.05		0.07	0.03	0.02	0.05	0.04	0.02
TiO_2	8.39	10.48	10.72	10.27	6.40	10.77		50.13	48.98	49.25	48.18	48.93	45.62
Al_2O_3	1.21	1.90	0.48	0.28	1.26	1.27		....	....	....	....	....	....
Fe_2O_3	50.13	44.99	45.89	46.92	53.51	43.38		4.19	5.55	5.61	6.41	4.92	9.55
FeO	38.04	38.86	39.68	38.79	36.17	38.93		42.91	42.07	41.04	39.67	41.76	37.91
MnO	0.47	0.50	0.70	1.05	0.30	1.18		2.03	1.92	3.11	3.13	2.06	2.90
MgO	0.01	0.08	0.01	0.01	0.05	0.02		0.07	0.03	0.01	0.02	0.06	0.04
Cr_2O_3	0.10	0.16	0.29	0.20	0.21	0.81		0.04	0.04	0.04	0.04	0.02	0.14
Total	98.40	97.02	97.88	97.57	98.01	96.41		99.44	98.62	99.08	97.50	97.79	96.18
Cations/4 Oxygens										Cation/3 Ox.			
Si	0.002	0.002	0.004	0.002	0.004	0.002		0.002	0.001	0.001	0.001	0.001	0.001
Ti	0.243	0.303	0.313	0.301	0.186	0.218		0.958	0.945	0.946	0.937	0.952	0.905
Al	0.055	0.086	0.022	0.013	0.058	0.059		....	....	....	....	....	....
Fe^{+3}	1.452	1.301	1.338	1.377	1.559	1.278		0.080	0.107	0.108	0.126	0.096	0.190
Fe^{+2}	1.228	1.282	1.288	1.265	1.172	1.277		0.912	0.906	0.878	0.867	0.906	0.838
Mn	0.015	0.016	0.023	0.035	0.010	0.039		0.044	0.042	0.068	0.070	0.046	0.067
Mg	0.001	0.004			0.003	0.001		0.003	0.001	0.001	0.001	0.002	0.002
Cr	0.003	0.005	0.009	0.006	0.007	0.025		0.001	0.001	0.001	0.001	0.001	0.003
Total	2.999	2.999	2.997	2.999	2.999	2.999		2.000	2.003	2.003	2.003	0.004	0.006
Uv/Il	24.3	30.3	31.3	30.1	18.6	31.8		95.8	94.5	94.6	93.7	95.2	90.5

TABLE 5. PLAGIOCLASE

	d545	h545	d551	h551	d580c	h580c
Wt.% Oxide						
SiO_2	55.62	54.17	56.28	55.83	53.60	53.38
Al_2O_3	28.36	28.71	27.19	27.66	28.76	29.00
FeO	0.28	0.38	0.24	0.37	0.36	0.38
CaO	10.81	11.37	9.41	10.08	11.37	11.71
Na_2O	5.47	5.08	5.99	5.60	4.79	4.54
K_2O	0.19	0.17	0.27	0.27	0.18	0.16
Total	100.73	99.80	99.38	99.81	99.06	99.17
Cations/8 Oxygens						
Si	2.491	2.453	2.544	2.518	2.445	2.433
Al	1.497	1.532	1.449	1.470	1.546	1.557
Fe	0.011	0.014	0.009	0.014	0.014	0.015
Ca	0.519	0.552	0.456	0.487	0.556	0.572
Na	0.475	0.446	0.525	0.490	0.424	0.402
K	0.011	0.010	0.016	0.016	0.010	0.010
Total	4.004	5.007	4.999	4.995	4.995	4.989
An (ave.)	52.2	55.3	46.5	49.9	56.7	58.7
An (rim)	56.0	56.0	47.5	49.8	58.8	59.1
An (min.)	46.3	50.0	43.6	48.4	47.0	57.3

tions were estimated by proportionally subtracting the estimated diorite composition from the bulk mixed-rock composition (Table 6).

Differences in composition among the mixed rocks appear to reflect compositional differences in the greenstone protolith. Samples 551 and 545, from the eastern Smartville Complex, are associated with Fe-rich, tholeiitic greenstones (Table 6). Sample 580 is from a more central locality and is associated with more typical calc-alkalic rocks (Table 6). In both cases, the hornfels and the mixed rocks as a whole are depleted in alkalis and silica and enriched in MgO relative to the greenstones (Fig. 5). In addition, whereas the hornfels and mixed rocks are largely anhydrous, the hydrous mineralogy (epidote, chlorite, actinolite) of the greenstones is reflected by their bulk analyses (Table 6).

The estimated diorite compositions are similar to andesite or basaltic andesite in having high alumina, 53 to 56 wt.% SiO_2, 4 to 5 wt.% MgO, and 3 to 4% total alkalis. Estimated K_2O contents, however, are lower than most andesites, even assuming that all K_2O in the mixed-rock analysis is in the dioritic portion.

DISCUSSION

Equilibrium between hornfels and diorite

Despite textural (Fig. 2), mineralogical, and geochemical (Table 6) differences, the chemistry of mineral phases in the coexisting hornfels and diorites of the mixed rocks is similar, suggesting that the two rock types have equilibrated (Fig. 3, Tables 1–5). For three of the four samples, mafic silicate phases in coexisting hornfels and diorite have compositions that are identical within the range of intrasample variation. Plagioclase rim compositions in the diorites are similar to the bulk compositions of weakly zoned plagioclase in the hornfels. This last observation suggests an approach to equilibrium over time (assuming that the outer portions of the crystals were the last to form). The continuous nature of the reversely zoned profiles is unlike those typical of mixing phenomena (Eichelberger, 1975).

Pressure-temperature conditions of mixed-rock formation

On the basis of mineralogy and mineral chemistry, it appears that the mixed rocks formed at temperatures that were at least as high as 750 °C, and probably exceeded 900 °C.

The two-pyroxene thermometer of Lindsley (1983) was applicable to two of the diorites and three of the hornfelses. The thermometer yields equilibration temperatures ranging from 705 to 765 °C (Table 7). Two-pyroxene temperatures of diorite and hornfels average 730 °C and 727 °C, respectively. The similarity in calculated temperature is not surprising given that pyroxene compositions in coexisting hornfels and diorite are virtually identical. The same thermometer applied to olivine gabbros like those in the aureole-forming plutons yields temperatures of approximately 1,000 °C (Beard and Day, 1986).

Fe-Ti oxide thermometry (Buddington and Lindsley, 1964;

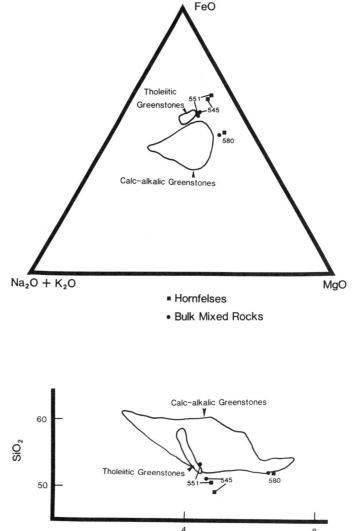

Figure 5. Whole-rock chemistry for Smartville greenstones, hornfelses, and mixed rocks. Specimens 551 and 545 are depleted in SiO_2 and alkalics and enriched in MgO and FeO (restitic) with respect to the tholeiitic greenstones of the eastern Smartville complex. Specimen 580 is similarly depleted and enriched with respect to calc-alkalic greenstones. Note that both the hornfels and the bulk mixed rocks have restitic compositions.

Lindsley, 1976) yields a wider temperature range (650 to 800 °C; Table 7), with a greater discrepancy between diorite (range 650 to 740 °C, average 687 °C) and hornfels (range 740 to 792 °C, average 758 °C) temperatures. Sample 551 is the only one for which diorite and hornfels yield the same temperature. All samples yielding temperatures of less than 750 °C closely follow the FMQ buffer (Fig. 6). Similar behavior is observed during subsolidus reequilibration in many plutonic igneous systems (Haggerty, 1976).

It is known from a variety of paragenetic studies that pyroxene and oxide temperatures yielded by intrusive rocks tend to be

TABLE 6. MAJOR ELEMENT CHEMISTRY (A) AND MODES OF MIXED ROCK DIORITE (B)

A. Major Element Chemistry

Wt.% Oxides	545	551	580	d545	d551	d580
	Mixed Rocks, Bulk Analysis			Diorites*		
SiO_2	51.16	53.05	52.10	54.25	55.65	53.08
TiO_2	0.88	0.98	0.46			
Al_2O_3	17.08	16.83	16.34	17.60	16.89	18.95
FeO	11.22	10.89	9.60	9.47	9.43	8.50
MnO	0.31	0.30	0.26			
MgO	4.71	4.53	6.60	4.42	4.24	5.37
CaO	10.23	9.82	12.34	8.92	8.74	9.73
Na_2O	2.26	2.43	1.93	3.36	3.69	3.13
K_2O	0.12	0.28	0.08	0.25	0.30	0.25
P_2O_5	0.27	0.30	0.17			
Volatiles	†	†	†			
Total	98.24	99.43	99.88	98.27	98.94	99.01

	h545	Hornfels* h551	h580	Smartville Greenstones ave. Tholelite	ave Ca	Average Smartville Diorite
SiO_2	49.10	50.46	51.99	53.97	53.86	54.60
TiO_2				1.31	1.03	0.89
Al_2O_3	16.56	16.82	16.04	15.25	15.97	16.04
FeO	12.38	12.36	9.72	11.22	7.97	8.36
MnO				0.28	0.16	0.19
MgO	4.90	4.82	6.73	3.99	4.68	3.93
CaO	11.10	10.90	12.63	7.29	7.35	9.00
Na_2O	1.53	1.17	1.80	3.43	3.53	3.23
K_2O				0.22	0.83	1.16
P_2O_5				0.23	0.16	0.20
Volatiles				1.66	3.58	1.81
Total	95.57	96.53	98.91	98.85	99.12	99.41

B. Modes of Mixed Rock Diorites§

	Quartz	Plag.	Opx	Cpx	Hbl	Oxides
d545	5	66	13	9	5	2
d551	6	64	13	9	7	1
d580	2	70	18	9	tr.	1

*Diorite compositions estimated from mode (Table 6B) and mineral chamistry. All K_2O given to diorite. Hornfels chemistry estimated by proportionally subtracting the diorite composition from the bulk analysis. 545 is 40% diorite, 551 is 50% diorite, 580 is 10% diorite.

†No loss on ignition.

§Quartz, plagioclase, and color index determined by 1,000 counts on slabs stained for potassium feldspar. Mafic minerals estimated from petrography.

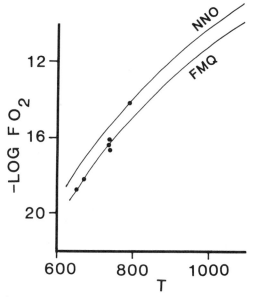

Figure 6. f_{O_2}-temperature plot based on the compositions of coexisting magnetite and ilmenite. See text. NNO = Nickel Nickel Oxide buffer curve; FMQ = Fayalite-Magnetite-Quartz buffer curve.

TABLE 7. TEMPERATURE AND PRESSURE CONSTRAINTS

	Temperature	
Pyroxene Thermometry:		
Diorite	ave. 730 °C	range 725-735 °C
Hornfels	ave. 727 °C	range 705-765 °C
Oxide Thermometry:		
Diorite	Ave. 687 °C	range 650-740 °C
Hornfels	Ave. 758 °C	range 740-792 °C
Phase Assemblage:		
Lack of prograde		
amphibole in hornfels	T >900 °C	
	Pressure	
Al in Amphibole, Smartville Plutons:		
Diorites	ave. 2.6 kbar	range 2.2-2.0 kbar
Tonalites	ave. 0.8 kbar	range 0.5-1.0 kbar
Granodiorites	ave. 0.8 kbar	range 0.8-0.8 kbar
Lack of lawsonite in		
metamorphic rocks	P <3 kbar	

lower than temperatures yielded by extrusive rocks of equivalent composition (e.g., Haggerty, 1976; Lindsley, 1976, 1983). This is due to equilibration during the long cooling history of the intrusive rocks. Therefore, the temperatures given by nonvolcanic systems, including this one, must be regarded as minima.

The absence of amphibole, except as a retrograde mineral, from the hornfels is an indication of high temperature. Spear (1981) found that in olivine tholeiite compositions at 1 kbar P_{H_2O} and oxygen fugacity ranging between the WM and HM buffers, amphibole was stable to at least 900 °C. Spear (1981) suggested that lower temperatures for amphibole breakdown could result from dilution of the vapor phase by CO_2. For the rocks examined here, however, this seems unlikely because the greenstones typically contain much more H_2O than CO_2 (Xenophontos, 1984), and carbonate rocks are absent.

The Al-in-amphibole geobarometer of Hammarstrom and Zen (1986) as modified and refined by Hollister and others (1987) can be applied to a variety of plutonic rocks in the Smartville Complex (Table 7). Pressure estimates range from 0.5 to 3.0 kbar. Pressure estimates for mixed-rock amphibole are invalid because the amphibole does not coexist with the proper phase assemblage (Hollister and others, 1987). Nevertheless, these pressure estimates are bracketed by the range of pressures given by other rocks in the Smartville Complex.

The metamorphic petrology of the Smartville Complex suggests pressures of less than 3 kbar. Lawsonite does not occur in Smartville metabasites, although appropriate bulk compositions apparently exist. The lack of garnet and amphibole in the pyroxene hornfelses also suggests low pressure.

The geology of the Smartville Complex as a whole suggests

an upper crustal setting. Qualitative indications of the low-pressure nature of the Smartville Complex include the widespread occurrence of granophyric rocks (Beard and Day, 1987; Barker, 1971), the close association between plutonic and hypabyssal rocks in the arc core, and the observation that plutonic rocks intrude volcanic rocks yielding essentially the same U-Pb Zircon ages (Saleeby, 1982; Saleeby and Moores, 1984). The mixed rocks appear to have formed in an upper crustal setting at pressures below 3 kbar.

Comparison of mixed-rock diorites and other Smartville Complex diorites

Diorites in the mixed rocks are unlike any other plutonic rocks in the Smartville complex. In particular, they are dissimilar to diorites that occur in several of the larger zoned gabbroic plutons (described in Beard and Day, 1987). Both types of diorite have SiO_2 (53 to 56 wt.%) and MgO (4 to 6 wt.%) contents that are similar to those of mafic to intermediate andesites (e.g., Gill, 1981) (Table 6). However, the mixed-rock diorites are low in K_2O and have high Na_2O/K_2O relative to other Smartville Complex diorites. Mineralogical differences between the plutonic and mixed-rock diorites are particularly striking. Biotite is abundant and ubiquitous and potassium feldspar is always present in the plutonic diorites, but both are lacking in the mixed-rock diorites. Amphibole is a major constituent of the plutonic diorites, commonly 10 to 30% by mode, but a minor, late-crystallizing phase in the mixed-rock diorites. Plagioclase in the plutonic diorites is normally zoned, and cores that are as calcic as An_{70-90} are common. Zoning ranges of 30 to 50 mol% An are common. This contrasts with the weakly and reversely zoned andesine-labradorite found in the mixed-rock diorites. There is no indication of any petrogenetic relation between the plutonic and the mixed-rock diorites in the Smartville Complex.

Partial melting and mixed-rock formation

The juxtaposition of igneous and metamorphic rock types in the hornfels-diorite mixed rocks represents either the injection of unrelated melt into metamorphosed rocks or the separation and movement of melt locally derived by partial melting of the host metabasites. An injection or intrusive breccia origin for the rocks is suggested first by their close association with plutonic contacts, and second because the brecciated structure that characterizes the rocks is typically associated with melt injection along intrusive contacts. Despite this resemblance to intrusive breccia, the mineralogical, thermometric, and geochemical characteristics of the mixed rocks are better explained by a partial melting origin.

The apparent mineralogical equilibrium between diorite and hornfels of differing bulk composition is an expected consequence of equilibrium partial melting. The high temperatures yielded by various geothermometers also suggest that partial melting may have occurred. In fact, if the 900 °C and higher temperatures suggested by the lack of prograde amphibole in the mixed rocks is accurate, then most Smartville greenstones would have begun to melt, even at P_{H_2O} as low as 1 kbar (Beard and Lofgren, 1987).

The estimated composition of the restite in a melting model (the hornfels) is enriched in Fe and Mg and depleted in Si, alkalics, and volatiles with respect to typical Smartville greenstones (Table 6, Fig. 5). These are the sort of chemical changes that would result from the extraction of a silicic melt from a greenstone. Recent work on metamorphosed dikes in the Stillwater Complex (Helz, 1987) has shown that mosaic textures like those in the hornfels can develop during melt extraction. Finally, the dioritic veins and layers in the mixed rocks are mineralogically and compositionally unlike any other intrusive rocks in the Smartville Complex. As discussed earlier, they are particularly unlike the gabbroic rocks in the aureole-forming plutons and the diorites associated with them. Although the mixed rocks physically resemble intrusive breccias, they are better described as migmatites (e.g., Mehnert, 1968).

A problem with this interpretation is that liquidus temperatures for compositions like those estimated for the diorites in the mixed rocks would almost certainly exceed 1,100 °C, even at elevated P_{H_2O} (Wyllie, 1977; Huang and Wyllie, 1986). These high apparent liquidus temperatures suggest that the diorites themselves may be "residual"—i.e., largely crystalline material left behind after partial crystallization of a melt followed by melt extraction. The extraction of a silicic melt would account for the observation that not only the hornfels, but the mixed rocks as a whole have compositions that appear to be refractory (high Mg, Fe, and low alkalics, silica, and volatiles) with respect to typical Smartville greenstones (Table 6). Melt extraction could also explain why the diorites have relatively refractory bulk compositions, while their mineralogy is relatively differentiated (e.g., andesine cores in plagioclase, Fe-rich mafic phases).

The ultimate disposition of any melt extracted from the mixed rocks is not known with any degree of certainty. Numerous silicic plutons, mostly tonalite and trondhjemite, were being emplaced into the core of the Smartville arc close to the areas where the mixed rocks occur and at approximately the same time that the mixed rocks were being formed (Beard and Day, 1987). These tonalite-trondhjemite plutons are chemically diverse and, like most tonalite suites, polygenetic (Malpas, 1979; Menzies and others, 1980; Spulber and Rutherford, 1983; Xenophontos, 1984; Johnston, 1986). It seems plausible that some portion of this silicic melt is related to the formation of the mixed zones. An experimental test of this hypothesis is underway, and preliminary results indicate that 1 kbar melting of Smartville greenstones at temperatures of between 900 °C and 1,000 °C will generate melts of tonalitic to trondhjemitic composition (Beard and Lofgren, 1987).

SUMMARY

Mixed hornfels-diorite rocks occur in the contact aureoles of gabbroic intrusions in the Smartville Complex. Although these rocks closely resemble intrusive breccias, geothermometry, geochemistry, and mineral chemistry support the interpretation that the mixed rocks represent partially melted rocks from which a silicic melt has been extracted. These rocks are, by definition, migmatites. This implies that silicic melts can form as a result of the emplacement of mafic magmas at relatively shallow levels in the crust of an active arc. The close physical resemblance of the mixed rocks to intrusive breccias suggests that they may have been overlooked in other localities and that the importance of medium- to low-pressure crustal partial melting in arcs has been underestimated.

ACKNOWLEDGMENTS

Overall support for this project was provided by a National Research Council Fellowship to work at Johnson Space Center and by a Smithsonian Institution Fellowship. Microprobe analyses of plagioclase were done at the Department of Mineral Sciences, Smithsonian. Other microprobe work was done at Johnson Space Center. Thanks to Gene Jarosevich and Vincent Yang for help with the microprobe work. Don Elthon (University of Houston) provided the XRF analyses. Russ Colson, Gary Lofgren, and Peter Thy provided helpful comments on early versions of the manuscript. The manuscript was greatly improved by conscientious and thorough reviews by Sorena Sorensen, Peter Schiffman, and Pat Bickford.

REFERENCES CITED

Ashworth, J. R., and McLellan, E. L., 1985, Textures, *in* Ashworth, J. R., ed., Migmatites: New York, Chapman and Hall, p. 180–203.

Barker, D. S., 1971, Compositions of granophyre, myrmekite, and graphic granite: Geological Society of America Bulletin, v. 81, p. 339–350.

Barr, D., 1985, Migmatites in the Moines, *in* Ashworth, J. R., ed., Migmatites: New York, Chapman and Hall, p. 225–264.

Beard, J. S., and Day, H. W., 1986, Origin of gabbro pegmatite in the Smartville intrusive complex, northern Sierra Nevada, California: American Mineralogist, v. 71, p. 1085–1099.

—— , 1987, The Smartville intrusive complex, northern Sierra Nevada, California: The core of a rifted volcanic arc: Geological Society of America Bulletin, v. 99, p. 779–791.

Beard, J. S., and Lofgren, G. E., 1987, Experimental melting of greenstones; Implications for tonalite genesis [abs.]: EOS (Transactions of the American Geophysical Union), v. 68, p. 1519.

Beiersdorfer, R. E., and Day, H. W., 1983, Pumpellyite-actinolite facies metamorphism in the Smartville ophiolite complex, northern Sierra Nevada: Geological Society of America Abstracts with Programs, v. 15, p. 436.

Buddington, A. F., and Lindsley, D. H., 1964, Iron-titanium oxide minerals and synthetic equivalents: Journal of Petrology, v. 5, p. 310–357.

Day, H. W., Moores, E. M., and Tuminas, A. C., 1985, Structure and tectonics of the northern Sierra Nevada: Geological Society of America Bulletin, v. 96, p. 436–450.

Eichelberger, J. C., 1975, Origin of andesite and dacite; Evidence of mixing at Glass Mountain in California and at other circum-Pacific volcanoes: Geological Society of America Bulletin, v. 86, p. 1381–1391.

Gill, J. B., 1981, Orogenic andesites and plate tectonics: New York, Springer-Verlag, 391 p.

Haggerty, S. E., 1976, Oxidation of opaque minerals in basalts, *in* Rumble, D., ed., Reviews in mineralogy; Volume 3, Oxide minerals: Mineralogical Society of America, p. Hg1–Hg100.

Hammarstrom, J. M., and Zen, E-an, 1986, Aluminum in hornblende; An empirical igneous geobarometer: American Mineralogist, v. 71, p. 1297–1313.

Helz, R. T., 1987, Evidence for melt extraction from the sills and dikes associated with the Stillwater Complex, Montana: Geological Socioety of America Abstracts with Programs, v. 19, p. 699.

Hollister, L. S., Grissom, G. C., Peters, E. K., Stowell, H. H., and Sisson, V. B., 1987, Confirmation of the empirical correlation of Al in hornblende with pressure of solidification of calc-alkaline plutons: American Mineralogist, v. 72, p. 231–239.

Huang, W.-L., and Wyllie, P. J., 1986, Phase relationships of gabbro-tonalite-granite-water at 15 kbar with applications to differentiation and anatexis: American Mineralogist, v. 71, p. 301–316.

Johnston, A. D., 1986, Anydrous P-T phase relations of near-primary high-alumina basalt from the South Sandwich islands; Implications for the origin of island arc and tonalite-trondhjemite series rocks: Contributions to Mineralogy and Petrology, v. 92, p. 368–382.

Kovach, L. A., and Marsh, B. A., 1981, Magma flow rate and partial fusion of wall rock, Huntington Lake, California: Geological Society of America Abstracts with Programs, v. 13, p. 490.

Lindsley, D. H., 1976, Experimental studies of oxide minerals, *in* Rumble, D., Reviews in Mineralogy; Volume 3, Oxide minerals: Mineralogical Society of America, p. L61–L88.

—— , 1983, Pyroxene thermometry: American Mineralogist, v. 68, p. 477–493.

Malpas, J., 1979, Two contrasting trondhjemite associations from transported ophiolites in western Newfoundland; Initial report, *in* Barker, F., ed., Trondhjemites, dacites, and related rocks: New York, Elsevier, p. 465–488.

Mehnert, K. R., 1968, Migmatites and the origin of granitic rocks: New York, Elsevier, 405 p.

Menzies, M. D., Blanchard, D., and Xenophontos, X., 1980, Genesis of the Smartville arc-ophiolite, Sierra Nevada foothills, California: American Journal of Science, v. 280a, p. 329–344.

Moores, E. M., 1972, Model for the Jurassic island arc-continental margin collision in California: Geological Society of America Abstracts with Programs, v. 4, p. 202.

Saleeby, J. B., 1982, Polygenetic ophiolite belt of the California Sierra Nevada; Geochronological and tectonostratigraphic development: Journal of Geophysical Research, v. 87, p. 1803–1824.

Saleeby, J. B., and Moores, E. M., 1984, Continent-ocean transect; Geochronological and structural profiles across the northern (C1) and southern (C2) Sierra Nevada metamorphic belt (SNMB): Geological Society of America Abstracts with Programs, v. 16, p. 642.

Spear, F. S., 1981, An experimental study of hornblende stability and compositional variability in amphibolite: American Journal of Science, v. 271, p. 697–734.

Spulber, S. D., and Rutherford, M. J., 1983, The origin of rhyolite and plagiogranite in oceanic crust; An experimental study: Journal of Petrology, v. 24, p. 1–25.

Wyllie, P. J., 1977, Crustal anatexis; An experimental review: Tectonophysics, v. 43, p. 41–72.

Xenophontos, C., 1984, Geology, petrology, and geochemistry of part of the Smartville Complex, northern Sierra Nevada foothills, California [Ph.D. thesis]: Davis, University of California, 446 p.

Xenophontos, C., and Bond, G. C., 1978, Petrology, sedimentation, and paleogeography of the Smartville terrane (Jurassic) bearing on the genesis of the Smartville ophiolite, *in* Howell, D. G., and MacDougall, K. A., eds., Mesozoic paleogeography of the western United States: Society of Economic Paleontologists and Mineralogists, Pacific Coast Paleogeography Symposium 2, p. 291–302.

MANUSCRIPT SUBMITTED JULY 8, 1987
REVISED MANUSCRIPT SUBMITTED DECEMBER 18, 1987
MANUSCRIPT ACCEPTED BY THE SOCIETY FEBRUARY 7, 1989

Geological Society of America
Memoir 174
1990

Chapter 18

High-K, continental-arc volcanism in the Kettle Rock sequence of the eastern Mesozoic belt, northern Sierra Nevada, California; Implications for lower Mesozoic Cordilleran tectonics

Geoff Christe and Judith L. Hannah
Department of Geology, University of Vermont, Burlington, Vermont 05405

ABSTRACT

Lower Mesozoic volcanic rocks exposed in an 8- to 15-km-wide belt between Westwood and Taylorsville, northern California, are the northernmost exposures of a volcanic sequence that originally spanned the eastern flank of the present-day Sierra Nevada batholith. The northwest-striking, southwest-dipping, west-facing, homoclinal volcanic section is only weakly metamorphosed and deformed. The more than 11-km-thick volcanic sequence records at least four episodes of subaerial, alkalic to calc-alkalic, andesitic to dacitic volcanism punctuated by intervals of clastic deposition. Rock types include monolithic intrusive breccia, porphyritic flow rock, tuff breccia, and hypabyssal intrusive rock. The interbedded clastic rocks consist of fluvial to shallow-water bedded volcanic arenites, conglomerates, laharic breccias, debris flows, siltstones, and shales. Major- and trace-element abundances for the volcanic rocks, including rare earth elements (REE), are similar to those in modern continental arc sequences. Ce/Y:Y, La:Ba, La:Th, $K_2O:Na_2O$, and $Ba:K_2O$ resemble those in volcanic rocks from high-K provinces. On the basis of $K_2O:SiO_2$ relations, most of the volcanic rocks are classified as latites or toscanites.

The morphology, stratigraphy, and major- and trace-element chemistry of the lower Mesozoic rocks exposed in northeastern California resemble those of other mildly alkalic, lower Mesozoic volcanic sequences along the eastern flank of the Sierra Nevada, California, in western Arizona, and western Nevada. It is proposed that this belt of high-K volcanic rock (the high-K magmatic province) represents postorogenic magmatic activity associated with a phase of long-lived extensional tectonics following the Permian-Triassic Sonoma orogeny.

INTRODUCTION

The lower Mesozoic volcanic and sedimentary rocks exposed north and east of Mount Jura constitute one of the least understood pre-Nevadan stratigraphic sequences in the Sierra Nevada. More well known, apparently correlative early Mesozoic belts are exposed in northwestern Nevada (Russell, 1984; Maher and Saleeby, 1986), the northern Sierra (D'Allura, 1977), the central Sierra (D'Allura, 1977; Schweickert, 1978; Schweickert and others, 1984a, 1984b), and along the southeastern flank of the Sierra (Grose, 1959; Abbott, 1972; Dunne and others, 1978; Kistler, 1978; Miller, 1978; Fates and Hanson, 1985; Cole and others, 1986; Schneidereit, 1987). The present study was undertaken to provide the first detailed geochemical analysis of the intermediate felsic to silicic lower Mesozoic volcanic rocks north of Taylorsville, California.

Christe, G., and Hannah, J. L., 1990, High-K, continental-arc volcanism in the Kettle Rock sequence of the eastern Mesozoic belt, northern Sierra Nevada, California; Implications for early Mesozoic Cordilleran tectonics, *in* Anderson, J. L., ed., The nature and origin of Cordilleran magmatism: Boulder, Colorado, Geological Society of America Memoir 174.

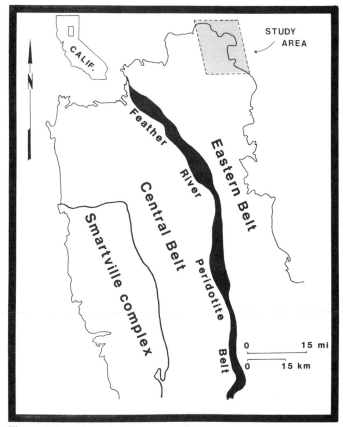

Figure 1. Location of study area, indicated by dashed box within the Eastern Belt, on the simplified geo-tectonic map of the northern Sierra Nevada (modified from Moores and Day, 1984).

The study area is located along the eastern margin of the Eastern Belt, as delineated by Moores and Day (1984), in a belt of lower Mesozoic volcanic and sedimentary rock designated the Eastern Mesozoic Belt (EMB; Fig. 1). The EMB, the easternmost occurrence of pre-Cretaceous rocks in the northern Sierra Nevada, is bound to the west by deformed Paleozoic island-arc volcanic and sedimentary rocks, to the north by Tertiary volcanic rocks, and to the south and east by Cretaceous granites of the Sierra Nevada batholith and Tertiary basalts.

The EMB consists of two separate, opposite-facing stratigraphic sections of uncertain relations (Fig. 2). The westernmost, overturned and east-facing section consists of lower early Mesozoic, fossiliferous, shallow-marine clastic, volcaniclastic, and carbonate rocks, which are associated with a number of andesitic to dacitic flows and rhyolitic plugs (Diller, 1892, 1908; Hyatt, 1892; G. Christe, 1989, unpublished field data). These rocks are herein referred to as the Mount Jura Sequence (MJS) after the early stratigraphic work of Diller. The easternmost, upright, and west-facing section consists of subaerial to shallow-water, slightly alkalic volcanic rocks and minor clastic rocks (Christe and Hannah, 1987) herein referred to as the Kettle Rock sequence (KRS) after the highest topographic point in the region. The two

opposite-facing sections are in fault contact with each other north and east of Mount Jura (Christe, 1987).

Rocks of the EMB have been previously studied by Diller (1892, 1908), Crickmay (1933), McMath (1958, 1966), Hannah (1980), Christe (1987), and Christe and Hannah (1987). Diller lumped all of the volcanic rocks of the KRS into one "catch-all" unit, his Carboniferous Kettle meta-andesite. Later workers only partially modified Diller's definition of the unit. Christe (1987) recognized that the volcanic rocks of the KRS represent multiple phases of continental-arc, alkalic, andesitic to dacitic, subaerial volcanism and associated fluvial to shallow-marine clastic sedimentation. The age of the KRS is poorly constrained. A Callovian age for the upper part of the KRS was established by McMath (1958) on the basis of a single Jurassic ammonite locality. The age of the lower part of the sequence can only be broadly established as post-Sonoman, pre-Callovian. The thickness of the KRS, artificially increased to some degree by numerous hypabyssal volcanic bodies, ranges from 6,600 m west of Taylor Lake to 3,300 m west of Moonlight Peak; although major faults form the western boundary of the KRS, no major structures have been identified that repeat the stratigraphy within the sequence.

LITHOLOGY OF THE KETTLE ROCK SEQUENCE

The west-facing KRS consists of a variety of porphyritic, intermediate to silicic, slightly alkalic, subaerial volcanic flow rocks, monolithic intrusive breccias, tuff breccias, lapilli tuffs, and hypabyssal intrusive rocks. Significant concentrations of these rock types in distinct parts of the study area have been taken to represent facies changes around proposed vent complexes (Christe, 1987). The minor amounts of laharic breccia, coarse-grained volcanic arenite, conglomerate, laminated fine-grained sandstone, and mudstone within the predominantly volcanic sequence represent intervals of clastic sedimentation, the result of erosion of dormant or extinct vent complexes. In total, volcanic rocks account for more than 80 percent of the stratigraphy preserved in the KRS.

Description of rock types

Flows of andesitic to dacitic composition make up a significant portion of the KRS. The moderately to coarsely porphyritic flows are regionally restrictive and discontinuous along strike. Although autobreccias and flow banding are locally developed, most are massive, structureless, and 5 to more than 50 m thick. Euhedral, sericitized plagioclase is the dominant phenocryst, commonly composing 5 to 25 percent of the flow rock. Other phenocrysts include hornblende, clinopyroxene, magnetite, biotite, and rare quartz.

Large masses of coarse, monolithic intrusive breccia are located west of Taylor Lake, around Wheeler Peak, in the south-central KRS near Bobeck Peak, and in the Moonlight Creek vicinity. (see locations in Fig. 2) In all three locations the breccia is characterized by abundant angular porphyritic volcanic clasts,

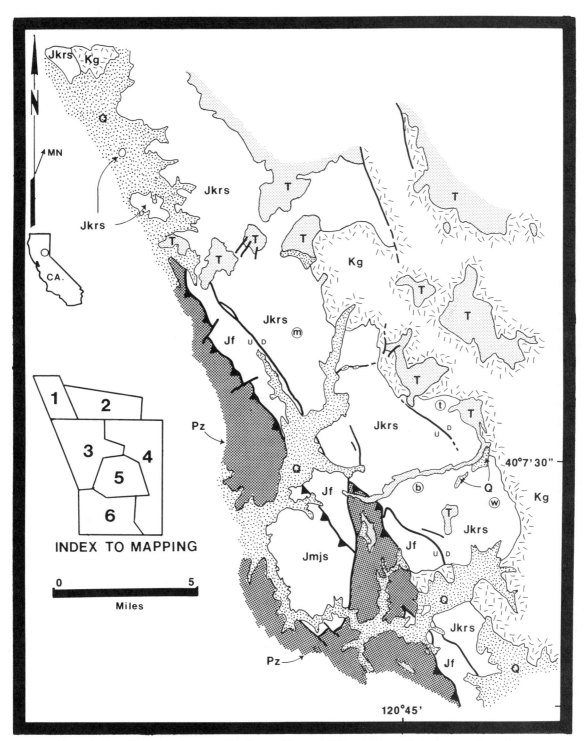

Figure 2. Simplified geologic map of the Eastern Mesozoic Belt and surrounding region, northern Sierra Nevada, California. Q = Quaternary undivided; T = Tertiary undivided; Kg = Cretaceous granitic rocks; Jf = Foreman Formation; Jmjs = Mount Jura sequence; Jkrs = Kettle Rock sequence; Pz = Paleozoic undivided. Locations mentioned in the text: t = Taylor Lake; w = Wheeler Peak; b = Bobeck Peak, m = Moonlight Creek. Index to mapping: 1, Hannah and Christe, reconnaissance; 2, L. T. Gross, 1987, written communication; 3, J. L. Hannah, unpublished field data; 4, modified from Lydon and others (1960); 5, Christe (1987); 6, McMath (1958).

some up to 0.3 m in diameter, enclosed in a porphyritic volcanic matrix. At the Taylor Lake and Bobeck Peak localities, small sills and plug-like volcanic masses intrude, or are associated with, the breccia. Elsewhere in the KRS, intrusive breccia composes a small percentage of the volcanic section or is totally absent.

Tuff breccia is the most common extrusive fragmental rock type in the KRS and locally accounts for as much as 75 percent of the volcanic section. The breccia is typically heterolithic, poorly sorted, and of pyroclastic origin. Excellent examples of this type of breccia occur immediately west of Kettle Rock, where it dominates the volcanic section and locally contains carbonized wood fragments and subvolcanic, plutonic clasts. More rarely, the tuff breccia is monolithic, pumice-rich, and locally graded. The best examples of the latter breccia type are restricted to the western shore of Taylor Lake. Lapilli tuffs are exposed sporadically throughout the central part of the KRS east of Moonlight Creek, and locally in the section west of Taylor Lake where they overlie the tuff breccias.

Hypabyssal intrusive rocks in the form of sills, dikes, and small, quartz-bearing, plug-like masses make up the smallest portion of KRS volcanic rock. They are widely scattered throughout the section but are most commonly found near centers of intrusive breccia such as the Taylor Lake and Bobeck Peak localities. Elsewhere in the KRS, quartz-bearing plugs of uncertain age intrude a wide variety of rock types. These small volcanic bodies may be correlative with the rhyodacitic plugs noted by Diller (1892, 1908) that intrude the rocks of the Mount Jura sequence. Dikes are most commonly found in the breccia and flow-dominated section south and east of Moonlight Creek, where they are green, sulfide-bearing, and of andesitic composition.

Mineralogy and textures

Phenocrystic feldspar, either albitic plagioclase or less common potassium feldspar, is present in 99 percent of the KRS volcanic rocks. Plagioclase phenocrysts occur as euhedral laths, 5 to 15 mm in length, frequently glomerophyric with hornblende or clinopyroxene. Relict albite twinning, rare carlsbad twinning, and complex zoning are preserved in plagioclase phenocrysts that have not been completely saussuritized. Potassium feldspar is present in roughly 40 percent of KRS volcanic rock. The K-spar occurs as euhedral to subhedral, square or blocky, generally untwinned, 10 to 15 mm phenocrysts. The phenocrysts are easily recognized in thin section by their turbid interiors or rare cross-hatched twinning.

Quartz, which is restricted to the more felsic rocks, occurs as euhedral or embayed, clear, beta-habit crystals. The highest concentration of quartz-bearing rocks occurs around Bobeck Peak in the south-central KRS. Elsewhere in the KRS, quartz-bearing volcanic rocks are rare or absent.

Hornblende in both oxidized and unoxidized varieties is found in almost 40 percent of the KRS volcanic rocks as small (2 to 8 mm in length) euhedral to subhedral laths, some of which display corroded margins. The larger hornblende phenocrysts are

commonly glomerophyric with plagioclase or, rarely, clinopyroxene. In some cases plagioclase has crystallized into the corroded margins of the amphibole.

Clinopyroxene and biotite are relatively rare in KRS volcanic rock. Clinopyroxene is restricted to the more andesitic end members, where it occurs as small, simple twinned, euhedral phenocrysts. Biotite occurs with quartz in the more silicic rocks, and with albitic plagioclase in the more felsic sills that intrude volcaniclastic rocks west of Taylor Lake.

The groundmass of the aphanitic extrusive rocks of the KRS consists of random, or aligned, albitic plagioclase microlites and ubiquitous, small, euhedral Fe-Ti oxides, set in a finely crystalline devitrified mesostasis.

METAMORPHISM

All pre-Cretaceous rocks in the KRS have undergone lowest greenschist facies metamorphism believed to be the result of the Nevadan orogeny (McMath, 1958; D'Allura, 1977; Hannah and Verosub, 1980; Schweickert and others, 1984b). The rocks adjacent to the Cretaceous Sierra Nevada batholith have undergone a subsequent contact-metamorphic event.

The regional metamorphic episode is responsible for the partial to complete replacement of phenocrysts and recrystallization of groundmass in the volcanic rocks. Phenocrysts of feldspar have been partially replaced by sericite, epidote, albite, and, rarely, calcite. Hornblende phenocrysts have been partially replaced by actinolite, albite, sphene, or chlorite. Biotite phenocrysts have been partially replaced by calcite, and clinopyroxene phenocrysts have been partially altered to chlorite and Fe-Ti oxides. The groundmass in the volcanic rocks has been recrystallized to a microcrystalline aggregate of albite and quartz, which generally preserves original volcanic textures.

Contact metamorphism has overprinted the effects of the regional metamorphic event in volcanic rocks along the eastern margin of the KRS adjacent to the Sierra Nevada batholith. The effect of this metamorphic event has been the post-tectonic crystallization of randomly oriented, platy chlorite, needles of andalusite, radial bundles of albite, quartz, epidote, ilmenite, and specular hematite, in a band of hornfelsed volcanic and volcaniclastic rock exposed east and southeast of Taylor Lake.

GEOCHEMISTRY

Eighteen samples of unaltered porphyritic flow rock, four of porphyritic or aphanitic dike rock, three of coarsely porphyritic hypabyssal intrusive rock, and one of a metasomatized dacitic flow rock were selected for whole-rock major- and trace-element analysis in order to define the magmatic characteristics of the lower Meszoic KRS volcanic suite (Table 1). All analyzed samples were plagioclase-phyric andesites or dacites; sparse hornblende, Fe-Ti oxide, clinopyroxene, biotite, K-spar, and quartz accompany plagioclase as phenocrystic phases (see Appendix for descriptions). Major elements were determined on fused samples

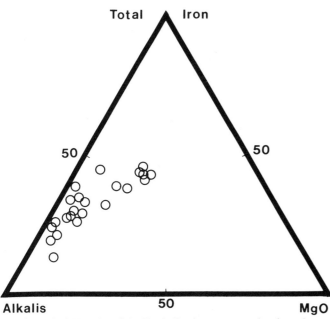

Figure 3. AFM plot of the Kettle Rock sequence volcanic rocks.

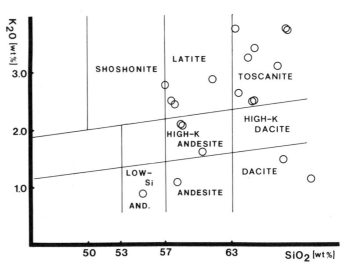

Figure 4. Classification scheme for potassium-rich volcanic rocks (MacKenzie and Chappell, 1972); circles indicate compositions of KRS volcanic rocks.

by x-ray fluorescence at the Branch of Analytical Chemistry, U.S. Geological Survey (USGS), Denver. Dissolved samples were analyzed for REE and other trace elements by inductively coupled plasma spectroscopy, also at the USGS, following methods outlined by Crock and Lichte (1982) and Crock and others (1983). Concentrations of additional trace elements were determined by x-ray fluorescence of pressed powders by S. T. Ahmedali at the Geochemical Laboratories, McGill University, Montreal.

Major-element abundances in KRS volcanic rocks reveal intermediate to silicic compositions typical of mature, calc-alkalic volcanic arc complexes. SiO_2 contents range from 55 to 70 percent, and compositions plotted on an AFM diagram (Fig. 3) fall within the normal range of calc-alkalic sequences. Nevertheless, the rocks are atypical of other magmatic belts in the Sierra Nevada. Mafic end members of the calc-alkalic series are not represented, and phenocrystic pyroxene, common in volcanic rocks of virtually all other Mesozoic belts in the northern Sierra, is rare. In addition, moderately high alkalic contents, especially K_2O, disclose a mildly alkalic character more typical of high-K andesites or toscanites (Figs. 4 and 5). These rock suites are commonly found in mature arcs constructed well inboard of the trench or over thickened sialic crust. K_2O/Na_2O ratios are intermediate between normal calc-alkalic and high-K suites. The average K_2O/Na_2O of 0.66 for the KRS is significantly greater than the ratio of 0.28 reported for Mount St. Helens (Smith and Leeman, 1987), but somewhat less than those documented in high-K to shoshonitic suites (0.73 to 1.16; Innocenti and others, 1982; Barberi and others, 1974; Keller, 1974).

Because the alkalic elements may be mobile during secondary processes, strict reliance on elevated K_2O/Na_2O and total

alkalic to document a mildly alkalic character is unwise. Concentrations of trace elements, some notably immobile during secondary processes, can aid in recognition of rock suites and understanding of petrogenesis. Large ion lithophile (LIL) elements (e.g., Rb, K, Ba, Sr, Th, La, and Ce) may be selectively transferred to the mantle wedge overlying the subduction zone during slab dehydration (Keller, 1983; Peccerillo, 1985); magmas may also be enriched in LIL by contributions from subducted sediments or by crustal contamination. High field strength (HFS) elements (e.g., Ti, Zr, and Nb) are commonly depleted in the upper mantle as a result of previous melting events (Mitropoulos

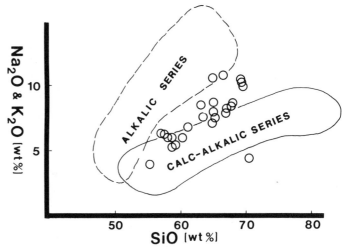

Figure 5. Comparison of KRS volcanic rocks with common alkalic and calc-alkalic series. (Field boundaries after Morrison, 1980, as adapted from Kuno, 1966, and Irvine and Baragar, 1971.)

TABLE 1. ANALYSES OF VOLCANIC AND INTRUSIVE ROCKS FROM THE KETTLE ROCK SEQUENCE

				PORPHYRITIC FLOW ROCKS					
Specimen	TL-8	TL-9	TL-16	TL-17	TL-19	TL-42	TL-200	KR-CR	KR-BR
SiO_2	57.48	57.78	65.05	67.09	63.43	63.34	70.40	61.19	58.91
TiO_2	1.11	1.07	0.67	0.75	0.78	0.57	0.54	0.83	1.22
Al_2O_3	17.57	17.19	16.43	15.68	16.43	16.62	14.55	16.62	16.06
FeO	7.21	6.82	4.37	3.37	4.63	5.02	3.73	5.66	6.82
MnO	0.17	0.13	0.11	0.09	0.18	0.13	0.31	0.11	0.16
MgO	3.32	3.81	1.14	1.18	2.16	0.73	1.44	2.82	3.81
CaO	6.72	6.99	3.92	3.36	4.76	4.89	4.62	5.88	7.42
Na_2O	3.51	3.52	4.58	4.72	4.72	4.72	3.11	3.64	3.12
K_2O	2.53	2.41	3.37	3.13	2.65	3.73	1.17	2.89	2.17
P_2O_5	0.41	0.31	0.34	0.27	0.27	0.25	0.18	0.37	0.34
La	26.30	26.70	28.40	25.20	23.70	27.00	25.20	32.40	22.30
Ce	55.00	54.00	58.30	57.20	44.00	54.60	57.20	65.40	44.40
Pr	6.50	6.80	6.80	5.60	5.00	6.40	5.60	7.50	4.50
Nd	28.20	29.50	28.60	24.50	20.20	24.60	24.50	32.30	21.70
Sm	5.90	6.10	5.70	5.00	3.80	4.80	5.00	5.90	4.00
Eu	1.66	1.72	1.53	1.28	1.05	1.26	1.28	1.70	1.56
Gd	5.60	5.70	5.80	5.00	4.80	5.60	5.00	5.60	4.80
Dy	3.80	4.20	4.80	3.90	3.70	3.90	3.90	3.30	3.20
Ho	0.85	0.84	0.98	0.83	0.69	0.77	0.83	0.81	0.72
Er	2.20	2.20	2.80	2.40	1.70	2.00	2.40	2.20	1.90
Tm	0.33	0.32	0.38	0.33	....	....	0.33	0.34	0.24
Yb	2.00	1.90	2.70	2.30	1.40	1.90	2.30	2.00	1.60
Lu	0.29	0.27	0.42	0.35	0.27	0.32	0.35	0.32	0.23
Ba	740.00	750.00	960.00	1000.00	1300.00	890.00	800.00	130.00	590.00
Zr	174.00	174.00	....	....	....	192.00	193.00	....	169.00
Nb	15.00	18.00	....	....	....	16.00	21.00	....	25.00
Th	....	8.00	7.00	7.00	4.00	6.00	9.00	....	....
Y	20.00	20.00	25.00	21.00	13.00	18.00	19.00	18.00	16.00
Sc	18.00	17.00	9.00	10.00	11.00	12.00	7.00	13.00	17.00
Ni	44.00	40.00	7.00	14.00	31.00	25.00	8.00	28.00	30.00
Rb	68.00	43.00	....	....	....	71.00	33.00	....	34.00
Sr	622.00	630.00	500.00	380.00	560.00	473.00	356.00	570.00	586.00

and others, 1987). Thus, high LIL/HFS ratios, such as high La/Yb, are hallmarks of subduction-related magmatic sequences (Saunders and others, 1980). Similarly, low TiO_2 is characteristic of arc volcanic rocks. Independent behavior of elements within these groups reflect unique petrogenetic processes (e.g., Mitropoulos and others, 1987; Arculus, 1987). Ewart (1982) documented unusually high concentrations of Ba, Sr, Zr, Pb, and LREE in subduction-related high-K volcanic suites.

Trace-element characteristics of the KRS volcanic rocks support classification of the KRS rocks as high-K orogenic andesites. In particular, concentrations of Ba, Zr, and LREE are higher than normal calc-alkalic suites, but similar to those of high-K andesites. High Zr/Nb ratios and low TiO_2 concentrations resemble those listed for high-K andesite suites by Gill (1981). Steep chondrite-normalized REE patterns reflect the high average chondrite-normalized La/Yb ratio of 15 (Fig. 6), typical of arc suites constructed on thickened crust (Bailey, 1981). Elevated concentrations of both Th and Ba with respect to La, and Ce/Y greater than 2 over a wide range of Ce concentrations are all characteristic of high-K andesite suites. Whereas Ba/K_2O ratios of KRS samples overlap those of both calc-alkalic and shoshonitic series volcanic rocks from the Aeolian arc of southern Italy and Sicily (Fig. 7), Ba/SiO_2 and K_2O/SiO_2 ratios show the random scatter typical of shoshonitic and high-K volcanic suites (Hatherton and Dickinson, 1969; Abbott, 1972; Meen, 1987).

Although the influences of thickened sialic crust or subducted sediment are difficult to quantify even in modern arc complexes, particularly without supporting isotopic data, several trace element indicators provide clues and suggest avenues for further research. For example, relatively high Ni and low MgO concentrations reflect eruption through thickened crust (Gill, 1981). Similarly, comparison of La/Yb (10 to 35) with Sc/Ni (0.4 to 3) suggests an Andean-type setting (Bailey, 1981). The implied 35 to 60 km crustal thickness could arise either from

TABLE 1. ANALYSES OF VOLCANIC AND INTRUSIVE ROCKS FROM THE KETTLE ROCK SEQUENCE (continued)

Specimen	PORPHYRITIC FLOW ROCKS								
	KR-BRQ	KR-KP2	KR-KP3	KR-KP4	JR-AR	JR-5	JR-13	JR-19	JHFC
SiO_2	69.29	69.54	64.89	69.21	64.48	65.09	60.13	67.58	58.41
TiO_2	0.42	0.36	0.47	0.42	0.91	0.62	0.85	0.77	0.81
Al_2O_3	15.49	15.11	15.11	15.58	17.02	18.13	17.95	15.87	16.43
FeO	2.57	2.71	3.22	2.83	4.76	3.47	7.72	4.37	7.98
MnO	0.13	0.05	0.11	0.07	0.92	0.04	0.17	0.11	0.16
MgO	0.50	0.65	0.63	0.22	0.35	0.58	3.32	0.41	3.65
CaO	1.18	1.68	4.22	1.54	4.06	3.36	5.74	2.52	7.28
Na_2O	4.85	4.45	4.44	4.72	3.91	5.93	4.72	6.47	3.12
K_2O	5.42	5.32	2.53	5.18	3.25	2.53	1.14	1.57	2.03
P_2O_5	0.16	0.16	0.21	0.16	0.39	0.25	0.31	0.34	0.16
La	49.00	34.10	24.30	47.80	35.20	59.10	43.00	28.80	11.20
Ce	93.50	60.00	46.50	93.70	70.70	117.00	91.50	56.10	25.70
Pr	11.00	6.10	4.70	10.70	7.90	13.50	11.50	6.20	3.00
Nd	42.20	23.00	19.10	40.40	35.10	55.20	48.50	27.00	15.60
Sm	7.30	4.00	3.50	6.40	6.40	9.30	9.60	5.00	3.90
Eu	1.62	0.96	0.92	1.54	1.87	2.54	2.71	1.37	1.05
Gd	6.10	4.30	3.20	5.20	5.90	7.60	8.30	5.30	4.70
Dy	4.70	2.90	2.50	3.40	4.20	5.20	5.70	4.10	47.00
Ho	1.00	0.61	0.50	0.69	0.75	0.97	1.13	0.84	1.00
Er	2.90	1.80	1.40	1.70	1.90	2.40	2.80	2.40	3.00
Tm	0.43	0.30	0.23	0.25	0.27	0.34	0.42	0.34	0.43
Yb	3.10	2.00	1.50	1.80	1.60	2.20	2.50	2.30	2.90
Lu	0.49	0.31	0.24	0.27	0.25	0.34	0.38	0.37	0.45
Ba	1200.00	1200.00	1000.00	1200.00	1300.00	940.00	820.00	620.00	700.00
Zr	....	....	168.00	....	205.00	....	....	203.00	106.00
Nb	....	....	13.00	....	13.00	....	....	14.00	8.00
Th	9.00	9.00	10.00	4.00	5.00	6.00	5.00	10.00	....
Y	21.00	15.00	13.00	16.00	16.00	22.00	22.00	17.00	18.00
Sc	4.00	4.00	5.00	4.00	13.00	8.00	15.00	9.00	32.00
Ni	....	5.00	7.00	3.00	15.00	....	7.00	8.00	12.00
Rb	....	....	72.00	....	71.00	....	....	72.00	18.00
Sr	380.00	270.00	474.00	360.00	448.00	500.00	810.00	504.00	459.00

construction of the arc on cratonic crust or, more likely, on imbricated arc and/or microcontinental terranes. Finally, the KRS samples all have high Ba/Th ratios, and many show slight negative Ce anomalies on chondrite-normalized REE plots. These chemical signatures have been interpreted as indicators of involvement of subducted pelagic sediment during magma genesis (Dixon and Batiza, 1979; Hole and others, 1984).

Chemical effects of secondary processes

Correct interpretation of ancient volcanic suites depends on recognition and understanding of the degree of posteruptive alteration. In the KRS, lower greenschist facies metamorphism affected all pre-Cretaceous volcanic rocks. Despite local replacement of feldspar and biotite phenocrysts by calcite, indicating an open system in some areas, there is no evidence that regional metamorphism is responsible for the high-K signature of the en-

tire 11-km-thick sequence (see also Rogers and others, 1974). The entire suite is systematically enriched in K, Ba, Rb, Sr, Zr, P, Pb, and LREE relative to normal calc-alkalic rocks. Available data on elemental mobility in volcanic rocks during greenschist facies metamorphism (e.g., Condie and others, 1977) indicate, however, that these elements do not vary systematically. More specifically, greenschist facies metamorphism cannot account for the high Ba contents of KRS samples because metamorphism tends to lower Ba concentrations. In addition, Zr and LREE are widely accepted as immobile except under extreme conditions or in highly permeable rocks. Thus, it is highly unlikely that the high-K character of the KRS volcanic suite, observed in massive flow and hypabyssal rocks, is the result of regional metamorphism.

Extreme potassic metasomatism has been described recently for a number of Tertiary volcanic sequences in California and Arizona (Chapin and Glazner, 1983; Brooks, 1986; Glazner,

TABLE 1. ANALYSES OF VOLCANIC AND INTRUSIVE ROCKS FROM THE KETTLE ROCK SEQUENCE (continued)

Specimen	Dikes				Other Intrusives			Metasomatite
	JHMC	VR-5	TL-11	TL-34	BMI	BM	KR-4	JR-3
SiO_2	55.01	58.19	68.04	67.79	66.57	64.69	56.89	65.50
TiO_2	0.83	0.77	0.47	0.57	0.23	0.33	0.92	0.47
Al_2O_3	17.95	17.95	15.31	15.68	15.30	16.25	17.38	16.06
FeO	8.88	7.72	3.09	3.61	3.47	4.25	7.33	4.63
MnO	0.19	0.17	0.09	0.13	0.09	0.17	0.16	0.13
MgO	4.31	3.32	1.13	0.73	0.27	1.41	3.65	0.38
CaO	8.67	5.74	2.38	2.81	3.08	2.24	6.99	0.25
Na_2O	3.11	4.72	4.72	4.72	5.66	5.79	3.37	0.46
K_2O	0.86	1.14	3.74	3.74	5.18	4.70	2.77	11.93
P_2O_5	0.21	0.31	0.21	0.25	0.16	0.18	0.55	0.21
La	9.10	16.40	25.60	46.70	11.70	15.60	28.90	12.30
Ce	20.30	34.30	46.50	72.80	23.80	29.00	59.50	24.00
Pr	2.20	3.80	4.90	7.10	2.40	2.80	6.60	3.40
Nd	12.40	20.80	19.00	27.90	13.10	15.30	30.80	15.00
Sm	3.30	3.90	3.30	4.60	2.80	2.80	5.60	3.50
Eu	1.05	1.39	0.89	1.30	0.84	0.94	1.73	0.95
Gd	3.90	4.30	3.90	5.50	2.80	3.00	5.40	3.40
Dy	3.70	3.50	2.20	2.60	1.90	21.00	4.00	2.40
Ho	0.76	0.67	0.53	0.81	0.41	0.45	0.78	0.43
Er	2.10	1.90	1.40	2.20	1.10	1.20	2.10	1.20
Tm	0.33	0.30	0.22	0.38	0.14	0.18	0.30	0.16
Yb	2.00	1.70	1.50	2.20	1.00	1.00	1.90	1.00
Lu	0.31	0.25	0.24	0.36	0.16	0.16	0.20	0.15
Ba	490.00	510.00	1000.00	1000.00	1300.00	1200.00	880.00	1900.00
Zr	134.00	....	....	....	....	93.00	160.00	....
Nb	9.00	....	....	....	....	5.00	14.00	....
Th	13.00	....	10.00	8.00	....	7.00	5.00	....
Y	25.00	15.00	13.00	21.00	10.00	11.00	18.00	12.00
Sc	29.00	13.00	5.00	6.00	6.00	8.00	14.00	7.00
Ni	17.00	11.00	5.00	4.00	2.00	14.00	17.00	
Rb	45.00	....	....	....	....	117.00	49.00	....
Sr	268.00	500.00	430.00	400.00	170.00	196.00	824.00	77.00

1988). The main effects of this type of alteration are extreme enrichment of K and Rb and associated depletion of Sr, Na, Ca, and MgO (Glazner, 1988). Alteration of this type is apparently best developed adjacent to fault zones, and has been tied to extensional tectonic processes (Rehrig and others, 1980; Glazner, 1988).

There is evidence that some of the volcanic rocks of the uppermost KRS have undergone potassic metasomatism. In the field, these altered "metasomatites" are associated with a number of intraformational fault zones, some of which are traceable up to 2 km along strike (H. Rose, 1985, personal communication). A feature common to these fault zones is abundant jasper, which acts as cement for the associated fault breccias. The close association of jasper-filed fault zones and fault breccias with adjacent K-metasomatized volcanic rock has been noted in Miocene volcanic rocks of the Mojave Desert region (Glazner, 1988).

One sample of apparently metasomatized KRS dacite has been included in Table 1 for comparison with unaltered samples. The sample shows all the characteristics of potassic metasomatism: high $K_2O:Na_2O$ ratios (about 26), extremely high K_2O content (11.93 wt.%), low MgO, CaO, and Na_2O contents (0.38, 0.25, and 0.46 wt.%, respectively), and elevated Ba content (1,900 ppm). Nevertheless, just as the presence of K-metasomatism in some Miocene volcanic rocks of southeastern California does not account for the original high-K characteristics of the unaltered lavas (see Table 2 of Glazner, 1988), the presence of "metasomatites" in the upper part of the KRS cannot explain the high-K characteristics of the entire volcanic suite. In fact, the relatively low K_2O/Na_2O ratios of the unaltered KRS samples listed in Table 1 (0.24 to 1.19) are far below the values suggesting incipient (2.00) or thorough (>3.00) potassic metasomatism (Rehrig and others, 1980; Brooks, 1986).

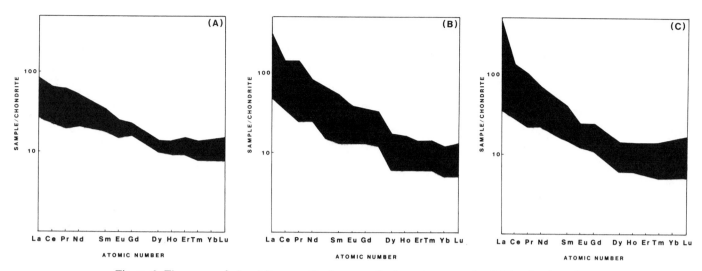

Figure 6. The range of chondrite-normalized rare earth element patterns for KRS volcanic rocks, grouped by weight percent SiO_2; A = 55–59%, B = 60–64%, and C = 65–70%.

Taken together, the geochemical data strongly suggest that the high-K characteristics of KRS volcanic rock reflect an original magmatic signature, and were not produced by regional metamorphism or localized metasomatism.

REGIONAL CORRELATIONS

Lower Mesozoic volcanic rocks with high-K or alkalic characteristics have been widely reported along the eastern flank of the Sierra Nevada in both California and westernmost Nevada. Many of these reported sequences are exposed in southeastern California in the Death Valley region (Johnson, 1957), the Soda Mountains (Grose, 1959), the Slate, Argus, and Panamint Ranges (Dunne and others, 1978, and references within), and in the northern White and southern Inyo Mountains (Merriam, 1963; Abbott, 1972; Ross, 1967; Fates and Hanson, 1985; Cole and others, 1986; Hanson and Saleeby, 1986). The only available chemical data for these volcanic rocks suggest a high-K or alkalic character (Abbott, 1972; Rogers and others, 1974). Miller (1978) recognized a number of lower Mesozoic, alkalic (monzonitic) plutons in the southeastern Sierra Nevada, which he included in his early Mesozoic alkalic magmatic province (AMP) in order to distinguish them from the later, typically calc-alkalic granitic rocks of the Sierra Nevada batholith.

In Nevada, north of the examples noted above, lower Mesozoic volcanic sequences with alkalic characteristics are present in the Gillis Range (Talukdar, 1972; Speed, 1973), the Pine Nut Range (Noble, 1962), the Yerington district (Dilles and Wright, 1988), and northwest of the Lake Tahoe–Reno area (Peavine sequence of Bonham, 1969). Northwest of these locations, the high-K volcanic rocks of the KRS and their probable correlatives south and east of Mount Jura (McMath, 1958; D'Allura, 1977) form the northernmost exposures of high-K volcanic rock recognized in the Sierra Nevada. No chemically similar lower Meso-

zoic volcanic rocks have been recognized in the eastern Klamath Mountains to the northwest (Lapierre and others, 1987). However, Maher and Saleeby (1986) mentioned mildly alkalic lower Mesozoic volcanic rocks in the Jackson Mountains of northwestern Nevada (see also Russell, 1984).

In light of the recent recognition of high-K volcanic rocks north of Miller's (1978) original AMP, it is proposed that the AMP be extended from southern California northward through northwestern Nevada (Fig. 8). Because the term "alkalic" can refer to a wide variety of igneous rock types, it is also proposed that the AMP be renamed the high-K magmatic province (HKMP) in keeping with recent volcanic terminology applied to

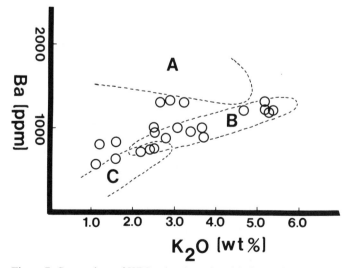

Figure 7. Comparison of KRS volcanic rocks with those of the Aeolian arc of the Mediterranean and Absaroka igneous province of North America; A = Absaroka Province shoshonitic series; B = Aeolian shoshonitic series; C = Aeolian calc-alkalic series. (Absaroka data from Meen, 1987; Aeolian fields modified from Keller, 1983.)

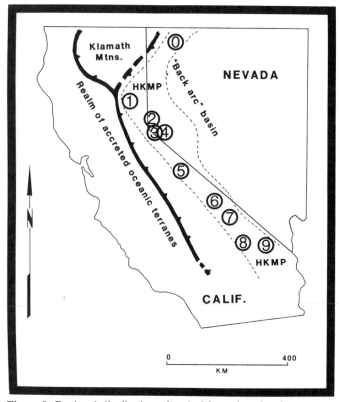

Figure 8. Regional distribution of early Mesozoic volcanic sequences with high-K characteristics along the eastern Sierra Nevada, California, and western Nevada. HKMP = High-K Magmatic Province. Locality key: 0 = Jackson Mountains, 1 = Eastern Mesozoic Belt, 2 = Peavine sequence, 3 = Pine Nut Range, 4 = Yerington district, 5 = White Mountains, 6 = Inyo Mountains, 7 = Panamint Range, 8 = Soda Mountains, 9 = Old Dad Mountain (references for each locality found in text).

igneous rocks of this type (see Innocenti and others, 1982; Keller, 1983; Mortimer, 1986; Lapierre and others, 1987).

PLATE TECTONIC IMPLICATIONS

The presence of high-K volcanic rocks such as those of the KRS in the northern Sierra Nevada limits the possible plate tectonic setting of the region during the early Mesozoic. Earlier workers suggested that the present-day Sierra Nevada was the site of an Andean-type continental arc associated with an eastward-dipping subduction zone that developed across the truncated margin of western North America following the culmination of the Permian-Triassic Sonoma orogeny (Burchfiel and Davis, 1975; Schweickert and Cowan, 1975; Schweickert, 1981). We suggest, however, that the early Mesozoic HKMP developed in a complex extensional regime reflecting postorogenic plate reorganization.

In modern environments, high-K volcanic suites are re-

stricted to the following four types of tectonic environments: (1) behind normal calc-alkalic arc fronts (Kuno, 1959; Foden and Varne, 1980; Varne, 1985; Varekamp and others, 1986); (2) above deep subduction zones in evolved arc systems (Caputo and others, 1972; Ballance, 1975; Morrison, 1980); (3) in intracontinental extensional regions such as the East African Rift (Thompson, 1985), West Kimberly Province of Australia (Varne, 1985), or the Tertiary Province of New South Wales (Nelson and others, 1986); and (4) in areas that are currently or have just recently undergone a complex transition in tectonic environment such as deepening of the subduction zone, slab fragmentation, reversal of polarity, or postorogenic extension (Morrison, 1980; Innocenti and others, 1982; Beccaluva and others, 1982, 1985; Thompson and Fowler, 1986; Peccerillo, 1985; Luhr and others, 1985; Varne, 1985; Zhou, 1985; MacDonald and others, 1985).

The first three environments can be ruled out on stratigraphic and petrologic grounds. There is no preserved stratigrahic evidence to suggest that the volcanic rocks of the HKMP formed behind a coeval, normal calc-alkalic front. Lower Mesozoic volcanic rocks to the west are dominantly intraoceanic arc and ophiolitic sequences, and are not tied to the North American continental margin (e.g., Saleeby, 1981; Day and others, 1985). Similarly, the earliest, Mesozoic high-K eruptive products in the Sierra Nevadas are dated at 230 Ma (Rogers and others, 1974; Miller, 1978; Marzolf, 1987; Dilles and Wright, 1988), indicating that magmatic activity began soon after the close of the Permian-Triassic Sonoma orogeny. That is, the HKMP was not yet a mature, long-lived arc system when high-K magmatism was initiated. Finally, a purely intracontinental-extensional environment can be ruled out because of the uniformly low TiO_2 contents and Nb/Zr ratios of KRS volcanic rock (see Keller, 1983; Leat and others, 1986, for comparative field boundaries).

There is some evidence that suggests the volcanic rocks of the HKMP erupted in a complex tectonic environment following the Sonoma orogeny. Recent data from volcanic, plutonic, and sedimentary rocks of early Mesozoic age in the southwestern Cordillera suggest that much of the southern HKMP was undergoing extensional tectonics and related high-K or silicic volcanism (Fates and Hanson, 1985; Krebs and others, 1986; Tosdal and Haxel, 1987; Klute and Dickinson, 1987; Busby-Spera and others, 1987; Ague and Brimhall, 1988). High-angle faulting and basin development in the Happy Creek Volcanic complex of the Jackson Mountains in northwestern Nevada (Maher and Saleeby, 1986) suggest that extensional tectonism also occurred in the northern HKMP.

Harper and others (1985) suggested that the lower Mesozoic rhyolite-dominated, marine pyroclastic sequence of the Mineral King and related southern Sierra Nevada roof pendants (see Fiske and Tobisch, 1978; Saleeby and others, 1978; Busby-Spera, 1984) developed over fragmenting continental crust. Oldow and Bartel (1987) recently proposed that the rapid facies changes east of the HKMP in western Nevada, preserved in the shallow-marine to subaerial sedimentary rocks of the Early to Middle Jurassic Dunlap Formation, were the result of deposition in a series of discontinuous, extensional basins.

That examples of early Mesozoic extensional tectonics are preserved throughout the HKMP, as well as to the west in the southern Sierra Nevada ignimbrite province and to the east in the "back-arc" region of western Nevada, suggests extensional tectonics played an important role in the structural development of the region during post-Sonoma, pre-Nevadan time.

The association between early Mesozoic extensional tectonics and high-K volcanism preserved in the southwestern Cordillera is similar to that of other recent high-K magmatic provinces such as the Aegean region (Angelier and others, 1981; Sengor and Yilmaz, 1981; Keller, 1983), western Anatolia (Keller and Villari, 1972; Innocenti and others, 1982), Tibet (Zhou, 1985), Fiji (Dickinson and others, 1968; Gill, 1970; Gill and Gorton, 1973), and Papua, New Guinea (Ruxton, 1966; MacKenzie and Chappell, 1972). In all the above examples, high-K volcanic activity is distinctly postorogenic and is associated with uplift, block, and/or transcurrent faulting. In all cases, the high-K volcanism began soon after the peak orogenic phase. In the HKMP, the earliest volcanic products have been dated near 230 Ma (Rogers and others, 1974; Miller, 1978), placing them within 10 to 15 m.y. of the close of the Sonoma orogeny. Alkalic rocks immediately postdating the Sonoma orogeny are present in west-central Nevada in the Koipato Group (Muller and others, 1951), but it is not certain whether these volcanic rocks can correctly be considered part of the HKMP.

Whereas the whole-rock chemistry, structural setting, and postorogenic nature of the HKMP resemble those of other recent high-K magmatic provinces, the apparent duration of volcanic activity within the HKMP remains a problem. In the Jackson Mountains of Nevada, the youngest high-K volcanism associated with the Happy Creek Volcanic complex has been dated as Oxfordian (Maher and Saleeby, 1988). Near the southern section of the HKMP, high-K rocks of the northern White Mountains may be as young as Kimmeridgian (Hanson and Saleeby, 1986; Hanson and others, 1987). Between the Jackson Mountains and northern White Mountains localities, terminal dates for high-K magmatism range from Toarcian (Peavine sequence—Bonham, 1969) to Callovian (KRS—McMath, 1966; Yerington district—Dilles and Wright, 1988; Eastern Mojave region—Marzolf, 1987). The data therefore suggest that high-K volcanism was ongoing in the region during the entire length of time between the Sonoma and Nevadan orogenies, or about 95 m.y. Certainly no modern examples of such long-lived, postorogenic, potassic magmatic provinces exist today.

CONCLUSIONS

Major- and trace-element characteristics of the volcanic rocks within the Kettle Rock Sequence of the northern Sierra Nevada of California classify the volcanic sequence as a high-K magmatic suite generated along a convergent margin. Negative Ce anomalies and high Ba versus Th ratios indicate a contribution from subducted pelagic sediment during magma genesis. La/Yb vs. Sc/Ni and Ni vs. MgO ratios suggest eruption through thick crust. The chemical characteristics of KRS volcanic rock resemble those of other lower Mesozoic volcanic sequences located along the eastern flank of the Sierra Nevada batholith, as well as in western Nevada and Arizona. It is proposed that these scattered outcrops of potassium-rich, intermediate felsic to silicic volcanic rock are the remnants of a once more continuous, high-K magmatic province that spanned the western Cordillera in the Late Triassic and Early Jurassic.

On the basis of the scattered occurrences of lower Mesozoic blueschist facies metamorphic rocks east of the Sierra Nevada and eastern Klamaths (Schweickert, 1976; Hotz and others, 1977; Schweickert and others, 1980; Miller, 1987), past workers have tied volcanism in the HKMP to normal (to oblique) eastward subduction. However, the numerous examples of Late Triassic to Early Jurassic extensional tectonics preserved in the HKMP, western Nevada, and Arizona, when combined with the unique characteristics of the associated volcanic rocks, suggest a tectonic environment which more resembles that of areas undergoing postorogenic extensional tectonics. It is probable that the igneous rocks within the HKMP were emplaced during a period of extensional tectonics in response to reorganization of plate motions west of the North American margin following the Permian-Triassic Sonoma orogeny.

ACKNOWLEDGMENTS

Assistance, ideas, and support in the field were provided by Hugh Rose, Richard Markey, Sara Kirby, Thomas Homza, Gita Mazumdar, and Thomas Taylor. Pamela Steele assisted with the sample preparation for chemical analysis. We are grateful for the help of James G. Crock and Paul H. Briggs of the U.S. Geological Survey for guidance and assistance in the laboratory. The manuscript benefited from the critical reviews of David S. Harwood, Richard S. Fiske, and Eldridge M. Moores. Field studies were supported in part by the U.S. Geological Survey. Additional support was provided by grants from the American Chemical Society and Research Corporation to Hannah, and the Geological Society of America to Christe.

APPENDIX. HAND-SPECIMEN DESCRIPTIONS OF ROCKS LISTED IN TABLE 1.

Specimens from porphyritic flows

TL-8 and TL-9
Black, porcelaneous, moderately porphyritic dacite, 2 to 4 mm plagioclase laths, rare 1 mm hornblende in TL-8.

TL-16 and TL-17
Black, pink-weathering, moderately porphyritic dacite, 2 to 4 mm plagioclase laths, rare 3 to 5 mm blocky K-spar laths.

TL-19
Gray-green, pink-weathering, sparsely porphyritic dacite, 1 to 4 mm plagioclase laths, rare 2 to 4 mm cloudy K-spar laths and 1 to 2 mm hornblende.

TL-42
Black, sparsely porphyritic dacite, 1 to 3 mm plagioclase laths and rare 1 to 2 biotite.

TL-200
Green, moderately porphyritic dacite, 1 to 4 mm plagioclase laths, rare <1 mm opaques.

KR-CR
Black, sparsely porphyritic andesite, 1 to 3 mm plagioclase laths, rare 1 mm clinopyroxene.

KR-BR
Black, porcelaneous, sparsely porphyritic dacite, 1 to 4 mm plagioclase laths.

KR-BRQ
Green, vesicular, sparsely porphyritic dacite, 1 to 2 mm beta-quartz.

KR-KP2
Green, moderately porphyritic dacite, 1 to 3 mm plagioclase laths, rare 1 mm hornblende and <1 mm opaques.

KR-KP3
Gray-green, sparsely porphyritic dacite, 1 to 4 mm plagioclase laths, rare 1 to 2 mm hornblende.

KR-KP4
Black, porcelaneous, flow-banded, sparsely porphyritic dacite, 2 to 3 mm plagioclase, rare 1 mm hornblende.

JR-AR
Gray-green, sparsely porphyritic andesite, 1 to 3 mm plagioclase laths, sparse 1 mm hornblende.

JR-5
Red, flow-banded, sparsely porphyritic dacite, 1 to 3 mm plagioclase laths, rare <1 mm opaques.

JR-13
Brick red, porcelaneous, sparsely porphyritic dacite, 1 to 3 mm plagioclase laths, rare 1 mm hornblende.

JR-19
Green, pink-weathering, moderately porphyritic dacite, 1 to 4 mm plagioclase laths.

JHFC
Green, sparsely porphyritic andesite, 5 percent 1 to 2 mm plagioclase laths, sparse clear green pyroxene.

Specimens from dikes

JHMC
Green, blocky, moderately porphyritic andesite, 10 percent, 1 to 2 mm plagioclase laths, 5 percent, 1 to 2 clear clinopyroxene.

VR-5
Green, sulfide-bearing, aphanitic andesite.

TL-11
White, coarsely porphyritic dacite, 25 percent, 1 to 3 mm plagioclase laths, 5 percent, 1 to 2 mm biotite and 1 percent <1 mm magnetite.

TL-34
Gray, moderately porphyritic dacite, 2 to 4 mm plagioclase laths, rare 1 mm hornblende and <1 mm opaques.

Specimens from other intrusive rocks

KR-BMI
Red and gray, sparsely porphyritic intrusive dacite breccia, 1 to 2 mm plagioclase laths, rare <1 mm opaques.

KR-BM
Brick red, coarsely porphyritic hypabyssal dacite, 20 percent, 1 to 3 mm plagioclase laths, 15 percent, 2 to 4 mm biotite, 8 percent, 1 to 2 mm subhedral quartz.

KR-4
Dark green, finely crystalline, phaneritic andesitic plug sample with 1 to 2 mm plagioclase, hornblende, clinopyroxene and rare magnetite.

Specimens of metasomatite

JR-3
Red, banded, moderately porphyritic dacite, 1 to 3 mm plagioclase laths, rare 1 mm hornblende.

Notes:

- Except as noted, all phenocrysts are euhedral.
- Except as noted, groundmass is sphanitic or microcrystalline.
- Descriptive terms rare, sparsely, moderately, and coarsely refer to phenocryst percentages of 0 to 1, 2 to 5, 6 to 20, and 20 to 30, respectively.

REFERENCES CITED

Abbott, E., 1972, Stratigraphy and petrology of the Mesozoic volcanic rocks of southeastern California [Ph.D. thesis]: Houston, Texas, Rice University, 196 p.

Ague, J. J., and Brimhall, G. H., 1988, Regional variations in bulk chemistry, mineralogy, and the compositions of mafic and accessory minerals in the batholiths of California: Geological Society of America Bulletin, v. 100, p. 891–911.

Angelier, J., Dumont, J. F., Karamanderesi, H., Poisson, A., Simsek, S., and Uysal, S., 1981, Analysis of fault mechanism and expansion of southwestern Anatolia since the late Miocene: Tectonophysics, v. 75, p. 1–9.

Arculus, R. J., 1987, The significance of source versus process in the tectonic controls of magma genesis: Journal of Volcanology and Geothermal Research, v. 32, p. 1–12.

Bailey, J. C., 1981, Geochemical criteria for a refined tectonic discrimination of orogenic andesites: Chemical Geology, v. 32, p. 139–154.

Ballance, P., 1975, Evolution of the upper Cenozoic magmatic arc and plate boundary in northern New Zealand: Earth and Planetary Science Letters, v. 28, p. 356–370.

Barberi, F., Innocenti, F., Ferrara, G., Keller, J., and Villari, L., 1974, Evolution of the Aeolian Arc volcanism (southern Tyrrhenian Sea): Earth and Planetary Science Letters, v. 21, p. 269–276.

Beccaluva, L., Rossi, P. L., and Serri, G., 1982, Neogene to Recent volcanism of the southern Tyrrhenian–Sicilian area; Implications for the geodynamic evolution of the Calabrian arc: Earth Evolution Science, v. 3, p. 222–238.

Beccaluva, L., Gabbianelli, G., Lucchini, F., Rossi, P. L., and Savelli, C., 1985, Petrology and K/Ar ages of volcanics dredged from the Eolian seamounts; Implications for the geodynamic evolution of the southern Tyrrhenian basin: Earth and Planetary Science Letters, v. 74, p. 187–208.

Bonham, H. F., 1969, Geology and mineral deposits of Washoe and Storey counties, Nevada: Nevada Bureau of Mines Bulletin, v. 70, 140 p.

Brooks, W. E., 1986, Distribution of anomalously high K_2O volcanic rocks in Arizona; Metasomatism at the Picacho Peak detachment fault: Geology, v. 14, p. 339–342.

Burchfiel, B. C., and Davis, G. A., 1975, Nature and controls of Cordilleran orogenies of the western United States; Extensions of an earlier synthesis: American Journal of Science, v. 275a, p. 363–396.

Busby-Spera, C. J., 1984, Large volume rhyolite ash flows, eruptions, and submarine caldera collapse in the lower Mesozoic Sierra Nevada, California: Journal of Geophysical Research, v. 89, p. 8417–8427.

Busby-Spera, C. J., Mattison, J. M., and Riggs, N. R., 1987, Lower Mesozoic extensional continental arc, Arizona and California; A depocenter for craton derived quartz arenites: Geological Society of America Abstracts with Programs, v. 19, p. 662.

Caputo, M., Panza, G. F., and Postpischl, D., 1972, New evidence about the deep structure of Lipari arc: Tectonophysics, v. 15, p. 219–231.

Chapin, C. E., and Glazner, A. F., 1983, Widespread K_2O metasomatism of Cenozoic volcanic and sedimentary rocks in the southwestern United States: Geological Society of America Abstracts with Programs, v. 15, p. 282.

Christe, G., 1987, The geology and petrology of the Eastern Mesozoic Belt, northern Sierra, California [M.S. thesis]: Burlington, University of Vermont, 350 p.

Christe, G., and Hannah, J. L., 1987, Continental arc volcanism in the Eastern Mesozoic Belt, northern Sierra Nevada, California; Implications for a revision of Jurassic paleogeography: Geological Society of America Abstracts with Programs, v. 19, p. 366.

Cole, R. D., Marzolf, J. E., and Avent, J., 1986, The transition from shallow marine sedimentation to orogenic arc volcanism; The Triassic Butte Valley and Warm Springs formations, southern Panamint Range; Another piece of the puzzle: Geological Society of America Abstracts with Programs, v. 18, p. 96.

Condie, K. C., Viljoen, M. J., and Kable, E.J.D., 1977, Effects of alteration on element distributions in Archean tholeiites from the Barberton Greenstone Belt, South Africa: Contributions to Mineralogy and Petrology, v. 64, p. 75–89.

Crickmay, C. H., 1933, Mount Jura investigation: Geological Society of America Bulletin, v. 44, p. 895–926.

Crock, J. G., and Lichte, F. E., 1982, Determination of rare earth elements in geological materials by inductively coupled argon plasma/atomic emission spectrometry: Analytical Chemistry, v. 54, p. 1329–1332.

Crock, J. G., Lichte, F. E., and Briggs, P. H., 1983, Determination of elements in National Bureau of Standards' Geological Reference Materials SRM 278 Obsidian and SRM 688 Basalt by inductively coupled argon plasma/atomic emission spectrometry: Geostandards Newsletter, v. 7, p. 335–340.

D'Allura, J., 1977, Stratigraphy, structure, petrology, and regional correlations of metamorphosed upper Paleozoic volcanic rocks in portions of Plumas, Sierra, and Nevada counties, California [Ph.D. thesis]: Davis, University of California, 338 p.

Day, H. W., Moores, E. M., and Tuminas, A. C., 1985, Structure and tectonics of the northern Sierra Nevada: Geological Society of America Bulletin, v. 96, p. 436–450.

Dickinson, W. R., Rickard, M. J., Coulson, F. I., Smith, J. C., and Lawrence, R. L., 1968, Late Cenozoic shoshonitic lavas in northwestern Viti-Levu, Fiji: Nature, v. 219, p. 148.

Diller, J. S., 1892, Geology of the Taylorsville region of California: Geological Society of America Bulletin, v. 3, p. 369–394.

—— , 1908, Geology of the Taylorsville region, California: U.S. Geological Survey Bulletin 353, 128 p.

Dilles, J. H., and Wright, J. E., 1988, The chronology of early Mesozoic arc magmatism in the Yerington district of western Nevada and its regional implications: Geological Society of America Bulletin, v. 100, p. 644–652.

Dixon, T. H., and Batiza, R., 1979, Petrology and chemistry of recent lavas in the northern Marianas; Implications for the origin of island arc basalts: Contributions to Mineralogy and Petrology, v. 70, p. 167–181.

Dunne, G. C., Gulliver, R. M., and Sylvester, A. G., 1978, Mesozoic evolution of the rocks of the White, Inyo, Argus, and Slate ranges, eastern California, *in* Howell, D., and McDougall, K., eds., Mesozoic paleogeography of the western United States: Pacific Section, Society of Economic Paleontologists and Mineralogists Pacific Coast Paleogeography Symposium 2, p. 189–207.

Ewart, A., 1982, The mineralogy and petrology of Tertiary-recent orogenic volcanic rocks with special reference to the andesitic-basaltic compositional range, *in* Thorpe, R., ed., Andesites: New York, John Wiley and Sons, p. 25–95.

Fates, D. G., and Hanson, R. B., 1985, Mesozoic (?) metavolcanic rocks, northern White Mountains, California; Lithology, depositional setting, and paleogeographic significance: Geological Society of America Abstracts with Programs, v. 17, p. 354.

Fiske, R. S., and Tobisch, O. T., 1978, Paleogeographic significance of the volcanic rocks of the Ritter Range Pendant, central Sierra Nevada, California, *in* Howell, D., and McDougall, K., eds., Mesozoic paleogeography of the western United States: Pacific Section, Society of Economic Paleontologists and Mineralogists Pacific Coast Paleogeographphy Symposium 2, p. 209–221.

Foden, J. D., and Varne, R., 1980, The petrology and tectonic setting of Quaternary-Recent volcanic centers of Lombok and Sumbawa, Sunda Arc: Chemical Geology, v. 30, p. 201–226.

Gill, J. B., 1970, Geochemistry of Viti-Levu, Fiji, and its evolution as an island arc: Contributions to Mineralogy and Petrology, v. 27, p. 179–203.

—— , 1981, Orogenic andesites and plate tectonics: Heidelberg, Springer-Verlag, 390 p.

Gill, J. B., and Gorton, M., 1973, A proposed geological and geochemical history of eastern Melanesia, *in* Coleman, P. J., ed., The western Pacific; Island arcs, marginal seas, geochemistry: Nedlands, University of Western Australia Press, p. 453–566.

Glazner, A. F., 1988, Stratigraphy, structure, and potassic alteration of Miocene volcanic rocks in the Sleeping Beauty area, central Mojave Desert, California: Geological Society of America Bulletin, v. 100, p. 424–435.

Grose, L. T., 1959, Structure and petrology of the northeast part of Soda Mountains, San Bernardino County, California: Geological Society of America Bulletin, v. 70, p. 1509–1548.

Hannah, J. L., 1980, Stratigraphy, petrology, paleomagnetism, and tectonics of Paleozoic arc complexes, northern Sierra Nevada [Ph.D. thesis]: Davis, University of California, 323 p.

Hannah, J. L., and Verosub, K. L., 1980, Tectonic implications of remagnetized late Paleozoic strata of the northern Sierra Nevada: Geology, v. 8, p. 520–524.

Hanson, R. B., and Saleeby, J. B., 1986, Mesozoic metavolcanic and metasedimentary rocks, northern White Mountains, California; U/Pb age, stratigraphy, and timing of westward-vergent structures: Geological Society of America Abstracts with Programs, v. 18, p. 113.

Hanson, R. B., Saleeby, J. B., and Fates, D. G., 1987, Age and tectonic setting of Mesozoic metavolcanic and metasedimentary rocks, northern White Mountains, California: Geology, v. 15, p. 1074–1078.

Harper, G. D., Saleeby, J. S., and Norman, E., 1985, Geometry and tectonic setting of sea floor spreading for the Josephine ophiolite and implications for Jurassic accretionary events along the California margin, *in* Howell, D., ed., Tectonostratigraphic terranes of the circum-Pacific region; Earth Science Series 1: Houston, Texas, Circum-Pacific Council for Energy and Mineral Resources, p. 239–258.

Hatherton, T., and Dickinson, W. R., 1969, The relationship between andesitic volcanism and seismicity in Indonesia, the Lesser Antilles, and other island arcs: Journal of Geophysical Research, v. 74, p. 5301–5328.

Hole, M. J., Saunders, A. D., Marriner, G. F., and Tarney, J., 1984, Subduction of pelagic sediments; Implications for the origin of Ce-anomalous basalts from the Mariana Islands: Geological Society of London Journal, v. 141, p. 453–472.

Hotz, P. E., Lanphere, M. A., and Swanson, D. A., 1977, Triassic blueschist from northern California and north-central Oregon: Geology, v. 5, p. 659–663.

Hyatt, A., 1892, Jura and Trias at Taylorsville, California: Geological Society of America Bulletin, v. 3, p. 395–412.

Innocenti, F., Manett, P., Mazzouli, R., Pasquare, G., and Villari, L., 1982, Anatolia and northwestern Iran, *in* Thorpe, R. S., ed., Andesites: New York, John Wiley and Sons, p. 327–349.

Irvine, T. N., and Baragar, W.R.A., 1971, A guide to the chemical classification of common volcanic rocks: Canadian Journal of Earth Sciences, v. 8, p. 523–548.

Johnson, B. K., 1957, Geology of a part of the Manley Peak Quadrangle, southern Panamint Range, California: University of California Publications in the Geological Sciences, v. 30, p. 353–423.

Keller, J., 1974, Petrology of some volcanic rock series of the Aeolian Arc, southern Tyrrhenian Sea; Calc-alkaline and shoshonitic associations: Contributions to Mineralogy and Petrology, v. 46, p. 29–47.

—— , 1983, Potassic lavas in the orogenic volcanism of the Mediterranean area: Journal of Volcanology and Geothermal Research, v. 18, p. 321–335.

Keller, J., and Villari, L., 1972, Rhyolitic ignimbrites in the region of Afyon (central Anatolia): Bulletin of Volcanology, v. 36, p. 342–358.

Kistler, R., 1978, Mesozoic paleogeography of California; A viewpoint from isotope geology, *in* Howell, D., and McDougall, K., eds., Mesozoic paleogeography of the western United States: Pacific Section, Society of Economic Paleontologists and Mineralogists Pacific Coast Paleogeography Symposium 2, p. 75–84.

Klute, M. A., and Dickinson, W. R., 1987, Tectonostratigraphic evolution of the late Mesozoic rifted Bisbee Basin in southeastern Arizona: Geological Society of America Abstracts with Programs, v. 19, p. 729.

Krebs, C. K., Ruiz, J., and Dickinson, W. R., 1986, Geochemistry of the Canelo Hills volcanics and Glance conglomerate and implications for the Mesozoic tectonic history of southeastern Arizona: Geological Society of America Abstracts with Programs, v. 18, p. 662.

Kuno, H., 1959, Origin of Cenozoic petrographic provinces of Japan and surrounding areas: Bulletin of Volcanology, v. 11, p. 37–57.

—— , 1966, Lateral variation of basalt magma type across continental margin and island arcs: Bulletin of Volcanology, v. 29, p. 195–222.

Lapierre, H., Brouxel, M., Albarede, F., Coulon, C., Lecuyer, C., Martin, P., Mascle, G., and Rover, O., 1987, Paleozoic and lower Mesozoic magmas from the eastern Klamath Mountains (northern California) and the geodynamic evolution of northwestern America: Tectonophysics, v. 140, p. 155–177.

Leat, P. T., Thompson, R. N., Morrison, M. A., Hendry, G. L., and Trayhorn, S. C., 1986, Geodynamic significance of post-Variscan intrusive and extrusive potassic magmatism in SW England: Royal Society of Edinburgh Transactions, Earth Sciences, v. 77, p. 349–360.

Luhr, J. F., Nelson, S. A., Allan, J. F., and Carmichael, I.S.E., 1985, Active rifting in southwestern Mexico; Manifestations of an incipient eastward spreading-ridge jump: Geology, v. 13, p. 54–57.

Lydon, P. A., Gay, T. E., Jr., and Jennings, C. W., 1960, Geologic atlas of California, Westwood Sheet: California State Division of Mines and Geology, scale 1:250,000.

MacDonald, R., Thorpe, R. S., Gaskarth, J. W., and Grindrod, A. R., 1985, Multicomponent origin of lamprophyres of northern England: Mineralogical Magazine, v. 49, p. 485–494.

MacKenzie, D. E., and Chappell, B. W., 1972, Shoshonitic and calc-alkaline lavas from the Highlands of Papua, New Guinea: Contributions to Mineralogy and Petrology, v. 35, p. 50–62.

Maher, K., and Saleeby, J. B., 1986, Geology of the Jackson Mountains, northwestern Nevada: Geological Society of America Abstracts with Programs, v. 18, p. 679.

—— , 1988, Age constraints on the geologic evolution of the Jackson Mountains, NW Nevada: Geological Society of America Abstracts with Programs, v. 20, p. 177.

Marzolf, J. E., 1987, Lower Jurassic overstep of Triassic depositional sequences; Implications for the timing of Cordilleran arc development: Geological Society of America Abstracts with Programs, v. 19, p. 762.

McMath, V., 1958, Geology of the Taylorsville area, northern Sierra Nevada, California [Ph.D. thesis]: Los Angeles, University of California, 180 p.

—— , 1966, Geology of the Taylorsville area, northern Sierra Nevada, California: California Division of Mines and Geology Bulletin 190, p. 173–183.

Meen, J. K., 1987, Formation of shoshonites from calc-alkaline basalt magmas; Geochemical and experimental constraints from the type locality: Contributions to Mineralogy and Petrology, v. 97, p. 333–351.

Merriam, C. W., 1963, Geology of the Cerro Gordo mining district, Inyo County, California: U.S. Geological Survey Professional Paper 408, 83 p.

Miller, C. F., 1978, An Early Mesozoic alkalic magmatic belt in the western United States, *in* Howell, D., and McDougall, K., eds., Mesozoic paleogeography of the western United States: Pacific Section, Society of Economic Paleontologists and Mineralogists Pacific Coast Paleogeography Symposium 2, p. 163–174.

Miller, M. M., 1987, Dispersed remnants of a northeast Pacific fringing arc; Upper Paleozoic terranes of Permian McCloud faunal affinity, western U.S.: Tectonics, v. 6, p. 807–830.

Mitropoulos, P., Tarney, J., Saunders, A. D., and Marsh, N. G., 1987, Petrogenesis of Cenozoic volcanic rocks from the Aegean island arc: Journal of Volcanology and Geothermal Research, v. 32, p. 177–193.

Moores, E. M., and Day, H. W., 1984, Overthrust model for the Sierra Nevada: Geology, v. 12, p. 416–419.

Morrison, G. W., 1980, Characteristics and tectonic setting of the shoshonitic rock association: Lithos, v. 13, p. 97–108.

Mortimer, N., 1986, Late Triassic, arc-related, potassic igneous rocks in the North American Cordillera: Geology, v. 14, p. 1035–1038.

Muller, S. W., Ferguson, H. G., and Roberts, R. J., 1951, Geology of the Mount Tobin Quadrangle, Nevada: U.S. Geological Survey Map GQ–7, scale 1:125,000.

Nelson, D. R., McCulloch, M. J., and Sun, S. S., 1986, The origins of ultrapotassic rocks as inferred from Sr, Nd, and Pb isotopes: Geochimica et Cosmochimica Acta, v. 50, p. 231–245.

Noble, D. C., 1962, Mesozoic geology of the southern Pine Nut Range, Douglas County, Nevada [Ph.D. thesis]: Stanford, California, Stanford University, 251 p.

Oldow, J. S., and Bartel, R. L., 1987, Early to Middle Jurassic extensional tectonism in the Western Great Basin; Growth faulting and synorogenic deposition of the Dunlap Formation: Geology, v. 15, p. 740–743.

Peccerillo, A., 1985, Roman co-magmatic province (central Italy); Evidence for subduction-related magma genesis: Geology, v. 13, p. 103–106.

Rehrig, W. A., Shafiqullah, M., and Damon, P. E., 1980, Geochronology, geology, and listric normal faulting of the Vulture Mountains, Maricopa County, Arizona: Arizona Geological Society Digest, v. 12, p. 89–110.

Rogers, J. J., Burchfiel, B. C., Abbott, E. W., Anepohl, J. K., Ewing, A. H., Koeknken, P. J., Novitsky-Evans, J. M., and Talukdar, S. C., 1974, Paleozoic and lower Mesozoic volcanism and continental growth in the western United States: Geological Society of America Bulletin, v. 85, p. 1913–1924.

Ross, D. C., 1967, Generalized geologic map of the Inyo Mountains region, California: U.S. Geological Survey Map I–506, scale 1:62,500.

Russell, B. J., 1984, Mesozoic geology of the Jackson Mountains, northwestern Nevada: Geological Society of America Bulletin, v. 95, p. 313–323.

Ruxton, B. P., 1966, A late Pleistocene to recent rhyodacite trachybasalt-basaltic-latite volcanic association in northeast Papua: Bulletin of Volcanology, v. 29, p. 347–373.

Saleeby, J. B., 1981, Ocean floor accretion and volcano-plutonic arc evolution in the Mesozoic Sierra Nevada, California, *in* Ernst, W. G., ed., The geotectonic development of California, Rubey Volume 1: Englewood Cliffs, New Jersey, Prentice-Hall, p. 132–181.

Saleeby, J. B., Goodin, S. E., Sharp, C. J., and Busby, C. J., 1978, Early Mesozoic paleotectonic-paleogeographic reconstruction of the southern Sierra Nevada region, *in* Howell, D., and McDougall, K., eds., Mesozoic paleogeography of the western United States: Pacific Section, Society of Economic Paleontologists and Mineralogists Pacific Coast Paleogeography Symposium 2, p. 311–336.

Saunders, A. D., Tarney, J., Marsh, N. G., and Wood, D. A., 1980, Ophiolites as ocean crust or marginal basin crust; A geochemical approach, *in* Panayiotou, A., ed., Ophiolites; Proceedings, International Ophiolite Symposium, Cyprus, 1979: Republic of Cyprus Geological Survey Department, Nicosia, Cyprus, Printco Ltd., p. 193–204.

Schneidereit, D. C., 1987, Stratigraphy of Mesozoic volcanic and sedimentary rocks, Inyo Mountains, California: Geological Society of America Abstracts with Programs, v. 19, p. 448.

Schweickert, R. A., 1976, Lawsonite blueschist within the Melones fault zone, northern Sierra Nevada: Geological Society of America Abstracts with Programs, v. 8, p. 409.

—— , 1978, Triassic and Jurassic paleogeography of the Sierra Nevada and adjacent regions, California and Nevada, *in* Howell, D., and McDougall, K., eds., Mesozoic paleogeography of the western United States: Pacific Section, Society of Economic Paleontologists and Mineralogists Pacific Coast Paleogeography Symposium 2, p. 361–384.

—— , 1981, Tectonic evolution of the Sierra Nevada Range, *in* Ernst, W. G., ed., The geotectonic development of California; Rubey Volume 1: Englewood Cliffs, New Jersey, Prentice-Hall, p. 87–131.

Schweickert, R. A., and Cowan, D. S., 1975, Early Mesozoic tectonic evolution of the western Sierra Nevada, California: Geological Society of America Bulletin, v. 86, p. 1329–1336.

Schweickert, R. A., Armstrong, R. L., and Harakal, J. E., 1980, Lawsonite blueschist in northern Sierra Nevada, California: Geology, v. 8, p. 27–31.

Schweickert, R. A., Girty, G., Hansen, R., and Harwood, D., 1984a, Tectonic development of the northern Sierra Nevada; An accreted Late Paleozoic island arc and its basement, *in* Lintz, J. J., ed., Western geological excursions (Geological Society of America annual meeting field trip guidebook): Reno, University of Nevada, Mackay School of Mines, p. 1–66.

Schweickert, R. A., Bogen, N. L., Girty, G., Hansen, R. E., and Merguerian, C., 1984b, Timing and structural expression of the Nevadan orogeny, Sierra Nevada, California: Geological Society of America Bulletin, v. 95, p. 967–979.

Sengor, A.M.C., and Yilmaz, Y., 1981, Tethyan evolution of Turkey; A plate tectonic approach: Tectonophysics, v. 75, p. 181–241.

Smith, D. R., and Leeman, W. P., 1987, Petrogenesis of Mount St. Helens dacitic magmas: Journal of Geophysical Research, v. 92, p. 10313–10334.

Speed, R. C., 1973, Excelsior and Pablo formations, western Nevada; Problems and progress in analysis: Geological Society of America Abstracts with Programs, v. 5, p. 109–110.

Talukdar, S. C., 1972, Implications of petrological study of Paleozoic and Mesozoic volcanic rocks of Mineral County, Nevada [Ph.D. thesis]: Houston, Texas, Rice University, 121 p.

Thompson, R. N., 1985, Asthenospheric source of Ugandan ultra-potassic magma: Journal of Geology, v. 13, p. 603–608.

Thompson, R. N., and Fowler, M. B., 1986, Subduction related shoshonitic and ultra-potassic magmatism; A study of Siluro–Ordovician syenites from the Scottish Caledonides: Contributions to Mineralogy and Petrology, v. 94, p. 507–522.

Tosdal, R. M., and Haxel, G. B., 1987, Late Jurassic regional metamorphism and deformation, southeastern California and southwestern Arizona: Geological Society of America Abstracts with Programs, v. 19, p. 870.

Varekamp, J., Van Bergen, M., Poorter, R., Vroon, P., Wirakusumah, A., Erfan, R., Sriwana, T., and Suharyono, K., 1986, Subduction related potassic volcanism: Geological Society of America Abstracts with Programs, v. 18, p. 778.

Varne, R., 1985, Ancient subcontinental mantle; A source for K-rich orogenic volcanics: Geology, v. 13, p. 405–408.

Zhou, J., 1985, The timing of calc-alkaline magmatism in parts of the Alpine–Himalayan collisional zone and its relevance to the interpretation of Caledonian magmatism: Geological Society of London Journal, v. 142, p. 309–317.

MANUSCRIPT ACCEPTED JUNE 25, 1987
REVISED MANUSCRIPT SUBMITTED SEPTEMBER 11, 1988
MANUSCRIPT ACCEPTED BY THE SOCIETY FEBRUARY 7, 1989

Geological Society of America
Memoir 174
1990

Chapter 19

Magmatic components of a tilted plutonic system, Klamath Mountains, California

Calvin G. Barnes
Department of Geosciences, Texas Tech University, Lubbock, Texas 79409
Charlotte M. Allen*
Department of Geological Sciences, Virginia Polytechnical Institute and State University, Blacksburg, Virginia 24061
James D. Hoover
Westinghouse Hanford Co., P.O. Box 1970, Richland, Washington 99352
Robert H. Brigham*
U.S. Geological Survey, 345 Middlefield Road, Menlo Park, California 94025

ABSTRACT

The Slinkard pluton (SP) and Wooley Creek batholith (WCB) are the lower and upper parts, respectively, of a tilted Middle Jurassic magma system. The SP and lower WCB intruded structurally lower ophiolitic mélange of the Marble Mountain terrane; the upper WCB intruded successively structurally higher metavolcanic and metasedimentary rocks of the western and eastern Hayfork terranes. The predominant volume of the system comprised a two-layer chamber in which an upper dacitic magma crystallized to form tonalite to granite in the upper WCB and a lower andesitic magma crystallized to form gabbro to tonalite in the lower WCB and SP. The upper part of the system had Sr_i = 0.7043 and a range of $\delta^{18}O$ from +8.7 to +11.2$^0/_{00}$; the lower part had average Sr_i = 0.7046 and $\delta^{18}O$ from +8.1 to +8.8$^0/_{00}$. The two layers of the system are separated by a transition zone that is intermediate in isotopic composition. The compositional differences between upper and lower parts of the system can be explained as (1) the result of intrusion of two separate pods of noncogenetic magma, or (2) the product of in situ assimilation-fractional crystallization. The second explanation requires that a relatively ^{87}Sr-rich contaminant such as the structurally lower Marble Mountain terrane was assimilated in the lower part of the system, whereas an ^{18}O-rich, generally ^{87}Sr-poor contaminant such as the structurally intermediate western Hayfork terrane was assimilated by the upper part. Trace-element evidence suggests that gradational upward zoning (from gabbro to granite) resulted from an upward decrease in the efficiency of crystal-melt segregation and crystal accumulation. H_2O-rich basaltic magma preceded development of the two-layer system, and basaltic pulses into the lower part of the system continued during most of its solidification history. Most basaltic rocks display evidence of some degree of fractional crystallization and interaction with crustal rocks; however, a few have low Sr_i and high concentrations of Cr and Ni, characteristics of undifferentiated mantle melts. Two-mica granite of the western Slinkard pluton cannot be related to the remainder of the system by fractional crystallization. High $\delta^{18}O$, high Ba, and low Sr abundances suggest that the two-mica granite is probably a partial melt of crustal material.

*Present addresses: Allen, Department of Geology, University of Kentucky, Lexington, Kentucky, 40506; Brigham, Charles Evans and Associates, 301 Chesapeake Drive, Redwood City, California 94063.

Barnes, C. G., Allen, C. M., Hoover, J. D., and Brigham, R. H., 1990, Magmatic components of a tilted plutonic system, Klamath Mountains, California, *in* Anderson, J. L., ed., The nature and origin of Cordilleran magmatism: Boulder, Colorado, Geological Society of America Memoir 174.

INTRODUCTION

Mesozoic plutonic rocks of the Klamath Mountain province of northern California and southern Oregon have long been considered to be examples of convergent margin magmatism in which the principal magmatic component was derived from the mantle (e.g., Lanphere and others, 1968; Farmer and DePaolo, 1983). This view was supported by isotopic studies (Kistler and Peterman, 1973; Masi and others, 1981), which showed that Klamath plutons display relatively primitive $^{87}Sr/^{86}Sr$. As more detailed studies of individual Klamath plutons have been made (e.g., Charlton, 1979; Barnes, 1983; Vennum, 1980), it has become apparent that many of the large plutons of the province have complex magmatic histories that involve several magmatic components. The Slinkard pluton and Wooley Creek batholith compose one such system. Previous studies (Barnes, 1983; Barnes and others, 1986b) have shown that the Slinkard pluton and Wooley Creek batholith represent the lowest and highest exposed parts, respectively, of a tilted Middle Jurassic magmatic system with at least 9 km of original structural relief. Extreme upward compositional zonation (gabbro to granite; Barnes, 1983), geochemical evidence for magma mixing (Barnes and others, 1986a), and isotopic evidence for combined assimilation and fractional crystallization and local crustal melting (Barnes and others, 1987) demonstrate the complexity of the system and suggest that it may provide an analogue for modern vertically extensive magma chambers. The purpose of this paper is to identify the various magmatic components in the Wooley Creek–Slinkard system and to evaluate their effect on its petrologic history.

GEOLOGIC SETTING

The Wooley Creek batholith and Slinkard pluton intruded the lowermost terranes of the composite western Paleozoic and Triassic belt at about 162 Ma (U-Pb, zircon; Barnes and others, 1986a). The plutons and host terranes were thrust westward during the Nevadan orogeny, and subsequent post-Nevadan domal uplift tilted the entire section toward the southwest (Jachens and others, 1986; Barnes and others, 1986b).

From structurally lowest to highest, the host terranes of the Wooley Creek and Slinkard are the Marble Mountain terrane, which is the high-grade equivalent of the Rattlesnake Creek terrane (Donato, 1987), the western Hayfork terrane, and the eastern Hayfork terrane (Fig. 1). The Rattlesnake Creek terrane is a Late Triassic ophiolitic mélange (e.g., Irwin, 1972; Gray, 1986) that increases in metamorphic grade from south to north (Gray and Petersen, 1982). The western Hayfork terrane is a Middle Jurassic arc sequence (Harper and Wright, 1984) that ranges from metamorphosed basaltic and andesitic volcaniclastic rocks to argillitic rocks (Donato and others, 1982). The eastern Hayfork terrane (as defined by Wright, 1982) is a chert and argillite matrix mélange of Triassic age with blocks of peridotite, marble, ribbon chert, and metabasalt. The location of the contact between the eastern and western Hayfork terranes east of the Wooley

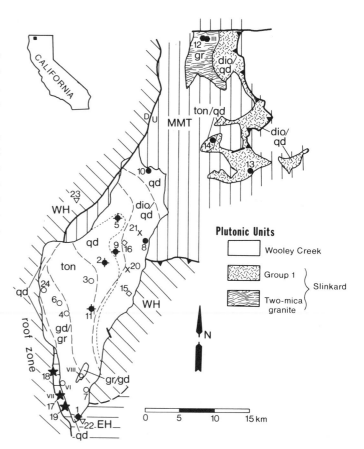

Figure 1. Simplified geologic map of Slinkard pluton and Wooley Creek batholith. Dashed lines represent gradational contacts between rock types, dotted line represents gradational contact between pyroxene-bearing lower rocks (to the east and northeast) and pyroxene-free rocks (to the southwest) and generally corresponds to boundary between groups 1 and 2. Faults shown by heavy solid lines. WH, western Hayfork terrane; EH, eastern Hayfork terrane; MMT, Marble Mountain terrane (the high-grade equivalent of the Rattlesnake Creek terrane). Symbols show sample localities, numbered to correspond to Table 4; open circles, upper Wooley Creek batholith (Group 3); dots with cross, central Wooley Creek (Group 2); dots, Slinkard and lower Wooley Creek (Group 1); hexagons, two-mica granite; stars, roof-zone dikes; inverted triangle, wall rocks; X, xenoliths; diamonds, synplutonic mafic dikes. Modified after Barnes et al. (1987).

Creek batholith (Fig. 1) is uncertain; however, recent work by M. M. Donato (personal communication) indicates that the eastern Hayfork is not as extensive as has been shown on earlier maps (e.g., Barnes and others, 1986b). In addition, reinterpretation of field and petrographic data indicates that the mélange unit that crops out on the northwestern side of the Wooley Creek batholith (Fig. 1) is part of the Marble Mountain terrane, as is evident from the grade of metamorphism (lower amphibolite facies), discordant foliation directions relative to bedding in adjacent Hayfork rocks, and the relative abundance of marble (cf., Donato and others, 1982; Donato, 1987). Note that all the Slinkard pluton and much of the lower part of the Wooley Creek

TABLE 1. COMPOSITIONAL GROUPS OF WOOLEY CREEK AND SLINKARD

TABLE 1. COMPOSITIONAL GROUPS OF WOOLEY CREEK AND SLINKARD

Wooley Creek and Slinkard	Location	Lithology	Equivalent Roof-Zone Dikes	Timing*
Group 1	Slinkard and lower WCB	2-px gabbro to bio-hnbl tonalite; xeno-liths of MMT locally abundant	2-px andesite	2 and 4
Group 2	central WCB, transitional between 1 and 2	bio-cpx-hnbl diorite and qtz diorite	?	?
Group 3	upper WCB	bio-hnbl tonalite to granite; includes late granite plug	cpx-hnbl andesite to dacite	3 and 5
2-mica granite	northwestern Slinkard	muscovite-biotite granite and granodio.	none	?
gabbroic blocks and selvages	Slinkard, lower WCB, and roof zone	hnbl-px gabbro	basalt	1
synplutonic dikes	central WCB primarily in Group 2	hnbl-phyric and fine-grained gabbro	basalt	1 and continuous

*1 = earliest event

batholith intruded the Marble Mountain terrane, whereas the upper (southwestern) part of the Wooley Creek intruded the western Hayfork and eastern Hayfork terranes.

COMPOSITIONAL GROUPS AMONG THE PLUTONIC ROCKS AND THEIR EQUIVALENT ROOF-ZONE DIKES

The Wooley Creek–Slinkard system consists of four principal groups of coarse-grained rocks (Table 1) that have been distinguished on the basis of major-element concentrations (Barnes and others, 1986a). In general, the system is zoned upward from two-pyroxene gabbro through tonalite (Group 1) to biotite-hornblende tonalite through granite (Group 3). The compositions of Group 2 samples are intermediate between Groups 1 and 3. The area underlain by Group 2 rocks is also characterized by an abundance of mafic microgranitoid enclaves and basaltic dikes in various stages of disruption (Barnes and others, 1986a). The fourth major group consists of two-mica granite that underlies the northwestern part of the Slinkard pluton (Fig. 1).

Porphyritic and aphyric dikes intrude the roof rocks of the Wooley Creek batholith. These dikes were interpreted by Barnes and others (1986a) to represent samples of the batholithic magmas that can be correlated with coarse-grained cumulate equivalents in the subjacent plutons (Table 1). The dikes thus provide insight into the compositions of magmas in the subjacent system.

Detailed study of the mineralogy of the Wooley Creek batholith, Slinkard pluton, and related synplutonic and roof-zone dikes (Barnes, 1987) indicated that the majority of plutonic rocks crystallized from a two-layer magmatic sequence. The lower layer (now Groups 1 and 2) was predominantly andesitic and received abundant basaltic input. Mixing of basaltic magma acted as a buffer to counteract effects of fractional crystallization on major-element concentrations (Barnes, 1987). The upper layer (now Group 3) consisted of dacitic (and some rhyolitic?) magma and was liquid at the same time as the lower layer. Thus, the volumetrically predominant *magmas* of the Wooley Creek and Slinkard plutons can be described in terms of three compositional groups: basalt (synplutonic and roof-zone dikes) that rose into the system from greater depth, andesite (roof-zone dikes) from which Groups 1 and 2 crystallized, and dacite (roof-zone dikes) from which Group 3 crystallized.

CRUSTAL COMPONENTS

Local abundance of crustal xenoliths in the Slinkard and lower Wooley Creek suggests that assimilation of the Marble Mountain terrane and Hayfork terranes contributed to the chemical characteristics of the system. Xenoliths in the lower part of the pluton are hornfelsic and are primarily basaltic in composition, but encompass a wide range of lithologies, including gabbro, peridotite, and rare calc-silicates (Barnes, 1987). Sparse semipe-

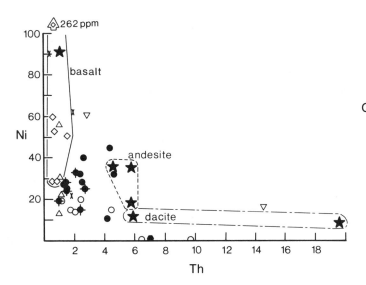

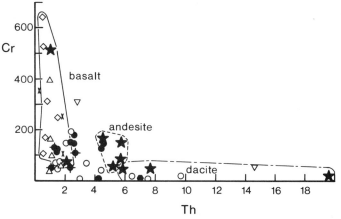

Figure 2. Ni vs. Th (ppm). Symbols as in Figure 1. Enclosed fields for basalt (roof-zone and synplutonic dikes), roof-zone andesite, and roof-zone dacite dikes. Note range of Ni contents in basalts to as much as 262 ppm in sample 201 and higher Th in roof-zone dikes relative to corresponding cumulate rocks.

Figure 3. Cr vs. Th (ppm). Symbols and fields as in Figure 2. Note range in Cr composition of basalts.

litic to pelitic layers occur in some xenoliths of basaltic composition, attesting to the apparent volcaniclastic nature of the mafic xenoliths. The xenolith lithologies are most similar to lithologies exposed in the adjacent Marble Mountains terrane (e.g., Donato, 1987).

Although xenoliths of the western and eastern Hayfork terranes are rare, assimilation of these rocks must also be considered, especially in view of field evidence for emplacement of the upper Wooley Creek batholith by stoping (Barnes, 1983). The western Hayfork terrane in contact with the Wooley Creek batholith consists predominantly of metamorphosed mafic volcanic and volcaniclastic rocks. Siliceous argillite and feldspathic wacke are locally abundant. Eastern Hayfork terrane rocks intruded by the Wooley Creek batholith are siliceous chert-argillite breccia with sparse marble pods and rare lenses of serpentinite.

ANALYTICAL RESULTS

Methods

Rb, Sr, and Zr data were obtained by x-ray fluorescence analysis (Norrish and Chappell, 1967), and the remaining trace elements were analyzed using INAA (Gordon and others, 1968). Precision was equivalent to, or better than, that reported by Barnes (1983). Sr isotopic analyses were obtained by using the procedure reported by Myers and others (1984), and the average value of the E and A standard over the period these samples were run was 0.70812. $^{87}Sr/^{86}Sr$ was normalized to an E and A standard value of 0.70800. Initial $^{87}Sr/^{86}Sr$ was calculated using an age of 162 Ma (U-Pb on zircon; Barnes and others, 1986a)

and a decay constant for ^{87}Rb of 1.42×10^{-11} y. $^{87}Sr/^{86}Sr$ (hereinafter Sr_i) is precise to less than ±0.0001. All quoted uncertainties reflect a 2-sigma confidence level. Oxygen was extracted using the ClF_3 method (Borthwick and Harmon, 1982) and converted to CO_2 over hot graphite. $^{18}O/^{16}O$ was measured on a Nier-type mass spectrometer and is reported in the standard delta notation in parts per mil relative to SMOW. $\delta^{18}O$ values are precise to $\pm 0.1^0/_{00}$.

Major and trace elements

Basaltic component. The basaltic component of the Wooley Creek batholith and Slinkard pluton occurs as pyroxene- and hornblende-bearing roof-zone dikes, as hornblende-phyric and fine-grained synplutonic dikes (with relict clinopyroxene) in the central part of the Wooley Creek batholith (Barnes et al., 1986a), and as pyroxenitic and gabbroic cumulate blocks (Barnes, 1983, 1987; Table 1). The basaltic dikes range in composition from olivine to quartz normative (Table 2). Olivine is rarely present; instead, dikes with olivine-normative compositions are typically clinopyroxene or hornblende rich. Most of the olivine-normative basaltic dikes are fine grained to sparsely porphyritic, an indication that crystal accumulation is not responsible for their silica-deficient nature. In fact, obvious cumulates (pyroxenitic and gabbroic blocks and dikes) are typically quartz normative. Some fine-grained synplutonic dikes (e.g., samples 192, 201, 776; Table 2) have values of Mg/(Mg+Fe^{2+}) (0.67 to 0.72), and Ni and Cr abundances (Figs. 2 and 3; Table 3) are within the range of compositions considered to be in equilibrium with the mantle (e.g., Basaltic Volcanism Study Project, 1981). In

**TABLE 2. MAJOR ELEMENT COMPOSITIONS AND MOLECULAR NORMS
MAFIC SYNPLUTONIC DIKES AND MAFIC MICROGRANITOID ENCLAVES**

Sample	Dikes						Enclaves			
	776	775A	771	201	188	368*	681B	154B	683E	686B
SiO_2	47.98	49.34	49.97	50.61	53.45	54.55	48.78	50.40	55.51	56.00
TiO_2	0.77	1.05	0.92	0.81	0.73	0.52	0.90	0.83	0.74	1.20
Al_2O_3	12.04	13.43	17.42	14.45	14.82	7.58	16.22	14.24	16.73	16.97
Fe_2O_3	2.53	1.91	2.02	8.68	8.93	0.8	12.36	10.98	0.00	5.05
FeO	8.77	8.77	7.84	n.d.	n.d.	7.31	n.d.	n.d.	10.06	2.81
MnO	0.20	0.19	0.19	0.14	0.15	0.17	0.21	0.21	0.13	0.16
MgO	11.19	9.64	6.24	10.11	6.94	12.88	7.11	8.55	4.77	4.94
CaO	11.45	10.87	10.04	7.88	9.29	12.33	9.52	10.34	6.97	7.27
Na_2O	1.27	2.08	2.68	3.06	2.45	1.36	2.65	2.42	3.04	3.16
K_2O	0.60	0.43	0.67	0.50	0.90	0.65	1.04	0.71	1.32	1.29
P_2O_5	0.25	0.28	0.24	0.16	0.18	0.07	0.21	0.21	0.22	0.22
LOI	1.31	0.91	0.98	3.29	1.39	1.45	1.38	0.99	1.20	0.96
Total	98.36	98.90	99.21	99.69	99.23	99.67	100.38	99.88	100.69	100.03
Mg'	0.67	0.65	0.56	0.72	0.63	0.76	0.56	0.63	0.49	0.57
Molecular Norms										
Q	0.00	0.00	0.00	0.00	4.61	3.64	0.00	0.00	5.67	7.01
OR	3.67	2.60	4.05	3.04	5.49	3.89	6.29	4.28	7.90	7.75
AB	11.79	19.09	24.59	28.23	22.70	12.37	24.36	22.17	27.66	28.83
AN	26.24	26.62	34.27	24.88	27.64	12.82	29.99	26.43	28.49	28.77
DI	24.64	21.32	12.04	11.37	14.97	38.94	13.57	19.62	4.08	5.14
HY	22.14	20.70	18.52	22.78	22.04	26.35	9.47	19.24	23.33	19.34
OL	8.35	6.14	3.40	7.12	0.00	0.00	13.05	5.28	0.00	0.00
MT	1.56	1.48	1.35	1.11	1.15	1.11	1.57	1.39	1.39	1.02
IL	1.11	1.50	1.31	1.16	1.05	0.73	1.28	1.18	1.05	1.70
AP	0.51	0.56	0.48	0.32	0.36	0.14	0.42	0.42	0.44	0.44
Total	100.00	100.00	100.00	100.00	100.00	100.00	100.00	100.00	100.00	100.00

Note: Mg' calculated according to Basaltic Volcanism Study Project (1981) recommended procedure.
*Specimen is a clinopyroxene- and hornblende-rich cumulate

general, the basalts display trace-element concentrations typical of island-arc tholeiites (Figs. 4, 5, and 6; Basaltic Volcanism Study Project, 1981). These include relatively high Ba, low Nb, and rare earth element (REE) patterns with shallow negative slopes (Figs. 4 and 6a; Table 3). The wide range in Ni and Cr contents over a small range of Th concentration (Figs. 2 and 3) suggests that batches of basic magma underwent olivine or spinel fractionation prior to emplacement (see below). The composition of the basaltic group varies widely with respect to both Rb and Sr abundances (Fig. 5; note that mafic microgranitoid enclaves were not included in the basaltic group). Sr contents are low in cumulates that are mineralogically compatible with accumulation from basaltic magma (Sr <150 ppm).

The paucity of olivine (or relict olivine) combined with the variation of Ni and Cr in SiO_2-undersaturated samples can be explained by crystallization at elevated P_{H2O}. For example, experiments on Hawaiian tholeiite (Allen and others, 1975; Allen

and Boettcher, 1978; Yoder and Tilley, 1962) indicate that clinopyroxene and an oxide phase are on the liquidus at $P_{H2O} = P_{total}$ above about 10 kbar. If some of the basaltic magmas injected into the Wooley Creek–Slinkard system experienced high-pressure fractionation of clinopyroxene and spinel, they would have become depleted in Ni and Cr, as is observed among synplutonic and roof-zone basaltic dikes.

Andesitic component. Andesitic roof-zone dikes include early two-pyroxene andesite and later two-pyroxene and hornblende-pyroxene andesite that postdates emplacement of granodiorite in the upper Wooley Creek batholith (Barnes and others, 1986a). In general, pre- and post-granodiorite andesites have similar trace-element contents. Zr, Sr, and Hf are more abundant in roof-zone andesite than in roof-zone dacite (Table 3), although Ba concentrations in the two groups are similar (Fig. 4). Sc, Ni, and Cr contents of roof-zone andesite overlap the compositional ranges of basaltic dikes and the coarse-grained

TABLE 3. REPRESENTATIVE TRACE ELEMENT DATA

Sample	La	Ce	Nd	Sm	Eu	Tb	Yb	Lu	Sc	Cr
In ppm					SLINKARD PLUTON					
642A	23.8	44.8	15.9	2.4	0.68	0.22	1.13	0.19	1.6	2.4
645A	3.9	7.8	5.2	1.3	0.52	0.32	1.40	0.18	32.1	97
				WOOLEY CREEK LATE-STAGE PLUG (374 AND 377) AND PEGMATITE						
374	22.0	42.5	15.7	2.8	0.95	0.31	1.40	0.15	4.0	4
377	14.9	29.4	18.4	2.9	0.85	n.d.	1.07	0.13	2.4	4
350B	13.8	27.6	8.6	1.4	0.53	n.d.	0.45	0.05	0.05	b.d.
				SYNPLUTONIC BASALTIC DIKES						
188	10.8	25.1	16.0	3.5	1.14	0.55	1.55	0.25	39.9	252
201	7.3	18.4	9.9	2.8	0.92	0.53	1.49	0.22	24.0	643
639	16.2	39.7	21.8	5.3	1.59	0.77	2.63	0.41	42.5	172
771	11.0	28.8	14.2	3.7	1.21	0.61	2.18	0.29	31.8	109
775A	5.6	14.9	8.3	2.6	0.88	0.55	1.51	0.21	36.9	314
776	7.5	19.0	11.5	2.7	0.93	0.47	1.55	0.18	36.5	527
				ROOF-ZONE DIKES						
555	11.1	24.5	14.0	3.4	1.06	0.57	1.79	0.29	0.38	71
590	5.7	12.6	8.2	1.9	0.72	0.44	1.75	0.23	41.5	512
554	21.3	44.4	23.0	4.8	1.28	0.65	1.96	0.31	27.1	147
704	18.5	41.0	21.0	4.3	1.14	0.70	1.97	0.27	26.4	84
164B	18.4	39.0	19.6	4.6	1.25	0.67	2.06	0.28	29.1	166
548	19.4	34.8	17.6	3.3	0.97	0.44	1.77	0.23	18.2	46
551	19.8	34.6	14.0	2.8	0.75	0.33	1.39	0.20	12.3	46
579	26.9	39.8	11.3	2.3	0.64	0.32	1.00	0.14	6.2	16
693	18.3	36.4	21.1	3.9	1.20	0.58	1.84	0.27	24.2	55

Note: Slinkard pluton specimen 642A is two-mica granite, specimen 645A is two-pyroxene gabbro.
Roof-zone dikes 555 and 590 are basalt; 554, 704, 1648, and 693 are andesite; and
548, 551, and 579 are dacite.

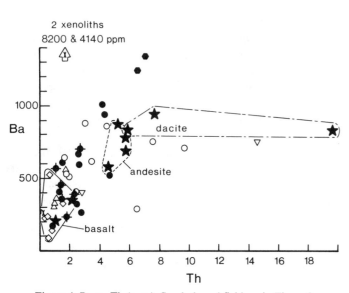

Figure 4. Ba vs. Th (ppm). Symbols and fields as in Figure 2.

rocks of Groups 1 and 2 (Slinkard pluton, lower and central Wooley Creek batholith; Figs. 2 and 3; Table 3). Andesitic roof-zone dikes are richer in Sr than are roof-zone dacites and span a considerable range of Rb content. Groups 1 and 2 (cumulates from the andesitic magma) typically have lower Sr contents than the roof-zone andesite, an indication that the bulk partition coefficient of Sr was less than unity (Barnes and others, 1986a). Enrichment of Sr and Rb in the andesite relative to basalt and dacite is in accord with trace-element enrichment due to combined magma mixing and fractional crystallization (DePaolo, 1981).

LREE in the andesites are similar to the dacites and enriched relative to the basalts by factors of 1.5 to 3.0. In contrast, HREE in the andesites are similar to those in to the basalts and elevated relative to the dacites (Fig. 6, a–c). The andesitic rocks display a slight but distinct Eu anomaly. REE patterns of the roof-zone andesites are subparallel to those of Groups 1 and 2 (Fig. 6b), although La/Lu of the dikes is slightly higher than is La/Lu of the corresponding coarse-grained rocks.

TABLE 3. REPRESENTATIVE TRACE ELEMENT DATA (continued)

Sample	Co	Ni	Rb	Sr	Zr	Ba	Cs	Hf	Th	Ta
In ppm				SLINKARD PLUTON						
642A	42.1	n.d.	75	327	94	1346	2.83	3.63	7.02	3.69
645A	32.7	n.d.	2	250	n.d.	251	n.d.	1.18	n.d.	0.84
		WOOLEY CREEK LATE-STAGE PLUG (374 AND 377) AND PEGMATITE								
374	3.5	n.d.	100	398	121	755	3.56	2.97	7.54	0.44
377	3.0	n.d.	61	530	153	886	2.04	3.55	3.01	n.d.
350B	0.4	n.d.	56	243	42	2299	0.69	1.81	6.13	n.d.
			SYNPLUTONIC BASALTIC DIKES							
188	31.7	51	24	294	78	336	n.d.	n.d.	1.53	n.d.
201	40.2	262	10	365	68	231	n.d.	1.73	0.54	n.d.
639	48.5	53	25	n.d.	n.d.	526	0.64	2.09	0.70	1.18
771	30.6	29	14	485	98	242	n.d.	2.27	0.56	0.85
775A	34.5	29	13	303	51	151	n.d.	1.39	0.85	0.60
776	40.3	60	21	250	38	92	0.47	1.30	0.59	0.63
			ROOF-ZONE DIKES							
555	32.1	n.d.	39	417	74	353	2.88	2.10	2.13	0.57
590	46.9	91	11	236	42	206	1.46	1.11	1.06	0.66
554	40.1	35	72	426	135	687	4.28	3.78	5.76	1.07
704	47.9	18	61	450	137	784	4.67	3.70	5.74	2.51
164B	34.5	35	83	403	122	575	6.98	3.47	4.58	0.93
548	28.5	11.7	65	405	109	830	3.16	3.48	5.87	1.22
551	24.7	n.d.	64	384	82	941	1.55	3.15	7.69	1.29
579	39.7	8.9	135	265	190	832	3.33	3.23	19.62	2.56
693	33.4	n.d.	54	437	125	871	4.40	3.30	5.23	1.65

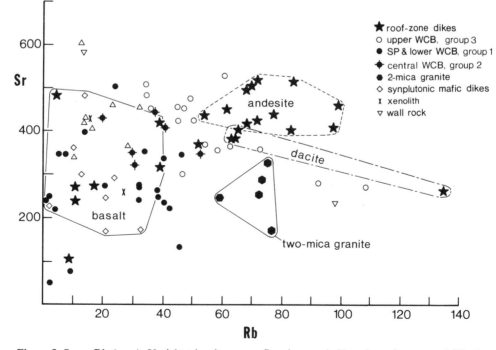

Figure 5. Sr vs. Rb (ppm). Upright triangles are mafic microgranitoid enclaves from central Wooley Creek batholith. Low-Sr samples (<150 ppm) are cumulate blocks in Wooley Creek and cumulate roof-zone dike.

Dacitic component. Dacitic roof-zone dikes contain abundances of Ni, Cr, Sc, Th, and U that are typical of fractional crystallization from andesite (Table 3). However, roof-zone dacite dikes have Hf, Zr, Rb, and Sr concentrations that are similar to or lower than roof-zone andesites (e.g., Fig. 5; Table 3), except for a single Rb-rich sample that approaches rhyodacitic composition. If the dacitic magmas were related to the andesitic magmas by a differentiation process, then that process must allow for enrichment of Zr, Rb, and Sr in the andesites relative to the dacite. Cumulates of the dacite (Group 3; upper Wooley Creek) typically have higher Sr contents than the dacite (Fig. 5), an indication that the bulk partition coefficient of Sr was greater than unity in the upper part of the system. The change in bulk partition coefficient of Sr from less than one in the lower part of

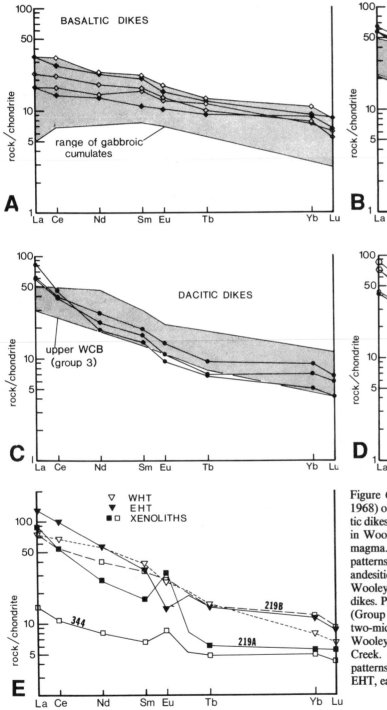

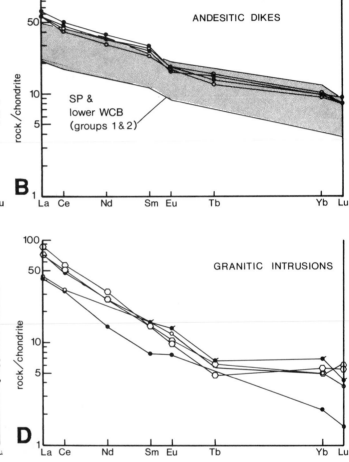

Figure 6. a: Chondrite-normalized REE patterns (Haskin and others, 1968) of roof-zone basaltic dikes (filled symbols) and synplutonic basaltic dikes (unfilled symbols). Patterned area represents range of cumulates in Wooley Creek batholith thought to have accumulated from basaltic magma. Note similar shallow slope and lack of Eu anomaly. b: REE patterns of early (filled symbols) and late (unfilled symbols) roof-zone andesitic dikes. Patterned area represents range of REE patterns of lower Wooley Creek batholith (Group 1). c: REE patterns of roof-zone dacite dikes. Patterned area represents range of upper Wooley Creek batholith (Group 3). d: REE patterns of granitic compositions. Hexagon, Slinkard two-mica granite; circles and dots with tick mark, granitic plug in upper Wooley Creek (see Fig. 1); dots, pegmatite dike in upper Wooley Creek. e: REE patterns of xenolith and wall-rock samples. Xenolith patterns labeled by sample number. WHT, western Hayfork terrane; EHT, eastern Hayfork terrane.

the system to greater than one in the upper part is attributed to a combination of upward increase in SiO_2 and decrease in temperature.

Figure 6c demonstrates that the REE concentrations of roof-zone dacites are similar to those of the upper Wooley Creek batholith (Group 3). The coarse-grained Group 3 samples tend to be slightly enriched in HREE relative to the dike rocks, an effect that is typical of hornblende accumulation (e.g., Arth and Barker, 1976).

Granitic components. Two-mica granite of the Slinkard pluton is chemically distinct from the rest of the system. The compositional distinction is apparent in the Sr- and Rb-poor (Fig. 5) and Ba-rich (Fig. 4) nature of the two-mica granite and in its peraluminous rather than metaluminous bulk composition and mineralogy (e.g., 1 to 2 percent normative corundum, aluminous biotite; Barnes and others, 1986a; Barnes, 1987). Therefore, this granite is interpreted to be comagmatic but not cogenetic with the rest of the Wooley Creek and Slinkard magmas. It is interesting to note that no distinction between dacite and two-mica granite can be made on the basis of REE concentrations (Figs. 6, c and d).

The late-stage biotite-hornblende granitic body in the southern Wooley Creek batholith (Fig. 1) is a second granitic component. This intrusion appears to be comagmatic with the upper part of the system, but mineralogical evidence (e.g., primary titanite and magnetite) indicates that it cooled under relatively oxidizing conditions compared with the main Wooley Creek–Slinkard magma (Barnes, 1987). The biotite-hornblende granite has trace-element concentrations that are intermediate between andesitic and dacitic compositions, except for the REE, which are nearly identical to the dacitic dikes (Fig. 6d).

Wall rocks and xenoliths. Major-element data indicate that the eastern Hayfork chert-argillite breccia is siliceous and, with the exception of low Na_2O, approaches rhyodacite in composition. The eastern Hayfork terrane sample is Th rich and has concentrations of Ni, Cr, Ba, and Rb that are similar to Group 3 samples (Figs. 2–5). Sr is slightly less abundant and LREE more abundant in the eastern Hayfork sample than in Group 3. The sample displays a steep negative slope among the LREE, a negative Eu anomaly, and a shallow slope among HREE (Fig. 6e). The prominent negative Eu anomaly is in contrast to dacitic dikes, which display little or no anomaly.

The analyzed sample of the western Hayfork is basaltic in composition and is similar to samples of the western Hayfork terrane analyzed by Donato (1987). It is similar to the basaltic roof-zone dikes in Ni, Cr, Ba, and Rb concentrations. Th, Sr, and the LREE are enriched in the western Hayfork sample relative to basalts in the plutonic system. LREE in this sample are distinctive in that they display a concave-downward pattern (Fig. 6e).

Basaltic xenoliths plot near the compositional range of basaltic dikes with regard to Th, Rb, Sr, Cr, and Ni (Figs. 2–5). The xenoliths are characterized by concave upward LREE patterns, and two samples have positive Eu anomalies (Fig. 6e). Ba is

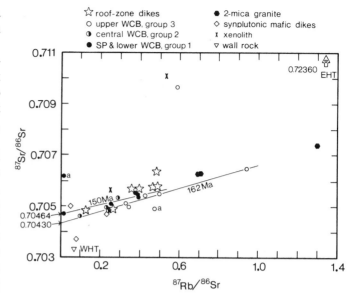

Figure 7. Rb-Sr isochrons for Slinkard pluton and lower Wooley Creek (Group 1) and upper Wooley Creek (Group 3). Note that isochrons have distinct initial $^{87}Sr/^{86}Sr$.

anomalously rich in two xenoliths (Fig. 4) and is in relatively low abundance in the third.

RB-SR ISOTOPIC DATA

Rb and Sr isotopic data are plotted in Figure 7. Chert-argillite breccia of the eastern Hayfork terrane (sample 236C; Table 4) is enriched in ^{87}Sr relative to all other samples. Conversely, the sample of western Hayfork terrane (sample 672D; Table 1) is ^{87}Sr poor. Mafic hornfels xenoliths (samples 219A and 219B) show a range in $^{87}Sr/^{86}Sr$, although both are more radiogenic than the enclosing plutonic rocks.

Coarse-grained rocks from Group 1, the Slinkard pluton and lower Wooley Creek batholith (exclusive of the two-mica granite), define an isochron (calculated according to Model II of York, 1969) with an age of 150 ± 30 Ma and initial $^{87}Sr/^{86}Sr$ of 0.70464 ± 0.00014 (Table 5; Fig. 7). One sample of the Slinkard pluton (sample 645B) plots above the isochron; this sample has undergone high-temperature hydrothermal alteration and was not used in the isochron calculation. Synplutonic basaltic dikes sampled from the lower part of the Wooley Creek batholith (samples 188 and 201; Table 4) have lower Sr_i than their host rocks, an indication that they are not in isotopic equilibrium with their host rocks. The same is true for mafic hornfels xenoliths in the lower Wooley Creek (see above). Too few samples are available to determine the extent to which individual xenoliths exchanged Sr (or oxygen) isotopes with their host, but the overall effect is discussed below.

Samples of the upper Wooley Creek batholith (Group 3) form an isochron with an apparent age of 162 ± 20 Ma and initial

TABLE 4. Rb, Sr, AND OXYGEN ISOTOPIC DATA, WOOLEY CREEK BATHOLITH AND SLINKARD PLUTON

Map Number	Field Number	$^{87}Sr/^{86}Sr$	$^{87}Rb/^{86}Sr$	Rb	Sr	Sr(i)	$\delta^{18}O$
		SLINKARD PLUTON TWO-MICA GRANITE					
12	642A	0.70629	0.709	59	253	0.7047	11.8
12	642B	0.70740	1.300	77	171	0.7044	12.2
III	SL III	0.70623	0.698	59	246	0.7046	*12.0
		SLINKARD PLUTON AND LOWER WOOLEY CREEK BATHOLITH (GROUP 1)					
8	111	0.70535	0.394	35	252	0.7044	8.1
8	111	0.70546	0.397	35	252	0.7046	n.d.
10	293	0.70545	0.387	34	255	0.7046	8.7
14	SL117A	0.70559	0.373	45	348	0.7047	10.7
14	SL149A	0.70507	0.253	48	545	0.7045	12.2
13	645A	0.70469	0.012	1	250	0.7047	8.0
13	645B[†]	0.70618	0.012	1	240	0.7062	8.0
		CENTRAL WOOLEY CREEK BATHOLITH (GROUP 2)					
11	379	0.70532	0.289	41	409	0.7047	n.d.
9	777B	0.70464	0.096	16	480	0.7044	8.2
5	342	0.70472	0.245	30	352	0.7042	7.8
1	236A	0.70490	0.243	37	445	0.7043	8.2
2	194	0.70497	0.230	36	454	0.7044	8.8
		UPPER WOOLEY CREEK BATHOLITH (GROUP 3)					
3	317	0.70495	0.343	51	427	0.7042	8.7
4	320	0.70548	0.495	63	367	0.7043	9.9
24	321[†]	0.70488	0.474	58	357	0.7038	n.d.
7	361	0.70645	0.942	92	283	0.7043	9.6
6	394	0.70539	0.423	54	370	0.7044	n.d.
VI	471[§]	0.70963	0.587	73	360	0.7083	9.2
VIII	377a	0.70509	0.332	61	530	0.7043	11.2
		ROOF-ZONE DIKES					
17	548	0.70574	0.467	65	405	0.7047	10.3
VII	551	0.70632	0.484	64	384	0.7052	11.3
17	554	0.70577	0.487	72	426	0.7047	9.5
17	555	0.70487	0.269	39	417	0.7043	8.5
18	590	0.70479	0.129	11	236	0.7045	8.9
17	693	0.70564	0.357	54	437	0.7048	11.8
19	704	0.70566	0.395	61	450	0.7058	10.7
		SYNPLUTONIC BASALTIC DIKES					
15	188	0.70469	0.234	24	294	0.7042	8.4
9	192	0.70498	0.053	14	436	0.7049	n.d.
16	201	0.70369	0.082	10	365	0.7035	n.d.

$^{87}Sr/^{86}Sr$ of 0.70430 ± 0.00016 (Table 5; Fig. 7). Isochron ages for both Group 1 and Group 3 are in accord with the U-Pb zircon) age of 162 Ma (Barnes and others, 1986a).

Group 2 samples from the central Wooley Creek batholith cannot be fitted to an isochron using York's (1969) Model II procedure. On the isochron diagram (Fig. 7), Group 2 samples plot on or between isochrons for Groups 1 and 3.

The unpredictable effects of isotopic exchange with wall rocks are also apparent in Figure 7 and Table 4. Samples 236A

and 471 were collected near the Wooley Creek batholith–eastern Hayfork terrane contact (Fig. 1). $^{87}Sr/^{86}Sr$ in sample 471 is elevated relative to the rest of the upper Wooley Creek batholith, whereas sample 236A plots near other samples of Group 2. Slightly saussuritized sample 321 was collected near the contact with western Hayfork rocks. It plots below the isochron for Group 3 and probably has undergone loss of radiogenic Sr. Andesitic and dacitic roof-zone dikes are enriched in ^{87}Sr relative to the underlying plutonic rocks (Fig. 7). All the analyzed andesitic

TABLE 4. Rb, Sr, AND OXYGEN ISOTOPIC DATA, WOOLEY CREEK BATHOLITH AND SLINKARD PLUTON
(continued

Map Number	Field Number	$^{87}Sr/^{86}Sr$	$^{87}Rb/^{86}Sr$	Rb	Sr	Sr(i)	$\delta^{18}O$
			XENOLITHS				
20	219A	0.71007	0.531	70	387	0.7089	9.0
20	219B	0.70560	0.252	14	164	0.7050	10.9
21	344	n.d.	n.d.	n.d.	n.d.		9.4
			WALL ROCKS				
22	236C	0.72360	1.334	98	234	0.7205	15.0
23	672D	0.70331	0.068	14	580	0.7032	10.2

Note: N.d. = not determined; wall-rocks samples are from the eastern Hayfork (236C) and western Hayfork (672D) terranes. Rb concentrations in samples 645A, 645B, and 236C measured by isotope dilution.
*Estimated from quartz separate with $\delta^{18}O$ = 13.0
†Altered samples omitted from isochron claculations
§Fresh samples omitted from isochron calculation (see text)

and dacitic roof-zone dikes analyzed were emplaced into chert-argillite breccia of the eastern Hayfork terrane. Thus, it is probable that the increased $^{87}Sr/^{86}Sr$ in roof-zone dikes is due to isotopic exchange with the eastern Hayfork terrane.

OXYGEN ISOTOPES

Figure 8 shows the variation of $\delta^{18}O$ as a function of Sr_i. The chert-argillite breccia from the eastern Hayfork terrane has $\delta^{18}O$ = +15‰, and the western Hayfork sample has $\delta^{18}O$ = +10.2‰. Xenoliths range from 9.0‰ to 10.9‰ (Table 4). Among the coarse-grained plutonic rocks, the effects of oxygen isotopic exchange near contacts are only apparent in two samples

TABLE 5. REGRESSION ANALYSIS OF Rb-Sr ISOTOPIC DATA MODEL II (York, 1969)

Slinkard pluton and lower Wooley Creek batholith (Group 1)

Samples used in regression: 111, 293, 645A, SL117, SL149

initial $^{87}Sr/^{86}Sr$ = 0.70464 ± 0.00014
apparent age = 150 ± 30 Ma
SRMSRS = 1.70

Upper Wooley Creek batholith (Group 3)

Samples used in regression: 317, 320, 361, 377A, 394

initial $^{87}Sr/^{86}Sr$ = 0.70430 ± 0.00016
apparent age = 162 ± 20 Ma
SRMSRS = 1.54

Note: SRMSRS = square root of mean sum of residuals squared. Errors are quoted at the 2 sigma confidence level.

from the southwestern margin of the Slinkard pluton (location 14, Fig. 1). The samples were collected in a lit par lit contact zone with siliceous and calcareous metasediments of the Marble Mountain terrane and have apparently exchanged oxygen with them. Some roof-zone dike samples appear to have undergone ^{18}O exchange with the host chert-argillite breccia.

$\delta^{18}O$ in Groups 1 and 2 (lower and central Wooley Creek batholith and Slinkard pluton, exclusive of the two samples from the lit par lit contact zone) displays a narrow compositional range between +7.8 and +8.8‰. In the upper Wooley Creek batholith, $\delta^{18}O$ ranges from +8.7 to +11.2‰. The increase in $\delta^{18}O$ from the central to the upper Wooley Creek batholith correlates with an increase in SiO_2 content and a decrease in structural level (Barnes and others, 1987).

Slinkard pluton two-mica granite has $\delta^{18}O$ of about +12‰. The high $\delta^{18}O$ values support the conclusion that this granite was not a differentiate of the main Wooley Creek/Slinkard magmas.

DISCUSSION

The origin of mineralogically, chemically, and isotopically distinct andesitic and dacitic layers in the Slinkard pluton and Wooley Creek batholith can be explained in at least two ways: as the result of emplacement of two "pods" of internally uniform, possibly noncogenetic magma, one andesitic and the other dacitic, or as the product of efficient side-wall crystal/liquid fractionation (see McBirney, 1980; McBirney and others, 1985; Barnes and others, 1986a) accompanied by contamination. Either explanation must also be in accord with the sequence of intrusion in the roof zone as determined by Barnes and others (1986a; Table 1): (1) early basalt, (2) two-pyroxene andesite, (3) biotite-hornblende dacite and granodiorite, (4) two-pyroxene andesite and hornblende-pyroxene andesite, (5) late granitic dikes and

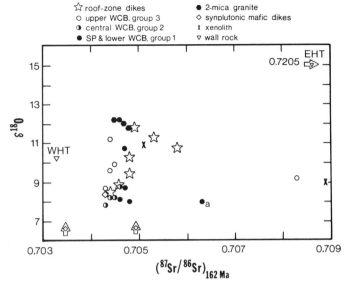

Figure 8. $\delta^{18}O$ vs. Sr_i (calculated at 162 Ma). Lower-case a adjacent to sample indicates an altered sample. Increase in $\delta^{18}O$ and Sr_i in roof-zone dikes is probably caused by hydrothermal exchange with host (see text).

plugs (Barnes and others, 1986a). The intrusive relations indicate that andesitic and dacitic magma coexisted in the system and andesitic magma was present in deeper levels after at least some of the dacite had crystallized to form roof-zone granodiorite (Barnes and others, 1986a).

In a geochemical sense, the first explanation is the most straightforward. Each of the andesitic and dacitic components would have been derived from an isotopically distinct source. If this scenario is correct, then the sequence of roof-zone dike emplacement requires that dacitic magma rose through (or around) preexisting andesitic magma, then cooled below its solidus prior to solidification of the underlying andesite.

$\delta^{18}O$ values (Table 4) indicate that each compositional group contains a component of Klamath crust and that the dacitic group could be a partial melt of that crust (e.g., White and Chappell, 1977). However, increase of $\delta^{18}O$ with SiO_2 content and with decreasing structural level in the upper Wooley Creek batholith (Barnes and others, 1987) is best explained as the result of crustal assimilation rather than partial melting (see below). It seems to us that the most likely crustal melt in the system is the two-mica granite of the Slinkard pluton. Its peraluminous nature, high $\delta^{18}O$, and apparent low f_{O_2} (see above and Barnes, 1987) are all indicative of partial melting of metasedimentary rocks (White and Chappell, 1983), although the low Sr_i and low K/Na of these rocks are suggestive of a relatively primitive sedimentary source.

In a geologic sense, derivation of a two-layer magmatic system by crystal/liquid fractionation appears to be an equally reasonable explanation. This model for the Wooley Creek batholith and Slinkard pluton has been presented in detail by Barnes (1983) and Barnes and others, 1986a), and is briefly summarized below.

Initial growth of the chamber involved influx of basaltic magmas followed by either influx of andesite or in situ fractionation to andesite. The relative lack of cumulates with mineralogy typical of a basaltic parent suggests that the former is most likely. If so, fractionation of basalt to andesite probably occurred deeper in the crust, and could have provided the heat needed for partial melting of the source rocks of the Slinkard two-mica granite. The andesitic magma then underwent a protracted history of side-wall crystallization accompanied by influx and mixing of basaltic magma. Mixing tended to buffer the andesitic magma so as to maintain a relatively uniform bulk composition over time. Some of the magma that underwent side-wall fractionation rose by boundary-layer flow due to its lower density. The denser parts of this boundary layer were probably mixed back into the andesitic magma (e.g., Christiansen, 1984). The lighter fraction continued to differentiate as it rose, ultimately collecting as a dacitic capping magma. As the basaltic flux to the lower part of the chamber diminished, the loss of heat resulted in crystallization from the roof inward, leaving a pocket of H_2O-rich andesitic magma deep in the system. The gradational upward zonation of the system (Barnes, 1983) is, according to this model, the result of an upward decrease in the efficiency of crystal accumulation rather than a gradual change in magmatic composition. This magmatic history explains the order of intrusion of roof-zone dikes without requiring emplacement of dacitic magma through andesitic magma and is in accord with the apparently equivalent f_{O_2} values in both upper and lower parts of the system (Barnes, 1987).

This model cannot explain the isotopic differences between andesitic and dacitic magmas (as determined from the coarse-grained rocks of Groups 1 to 3) solely by crystal fractionation. If the model is correct, then crustal assimilation must be called on to modify the isotopic composition of both magma types. The lower part of the system is predominantly in contact with rocks of the Marble Mountain terrane (Fig. 1). The upper part of the system is predominantly in contact with rocks of the western Hayfork terrane and, in structurally highest exposures, with rocks of the eastern Hayfork terrane. If crustal assimilation were responsible for the isotopic differences between the two magma types, then one would expect corresponding isotopic differences in the wall rocks. The following section presents an expanded version of the preceding model. This expanded version explains the isotopic variation in the system as the result of combined crustal assimilation, magma mixing, and fractional crystallization.

IN SITU ASSIMILATION MODEL

Attempts to model isotopic and trace-element variation in the lower part of the system by combined assimilation-fractional crystallization (AFC; DePaolo, 1981; Taylor, 1980) are complicated by the need to consider two types of "contaminant": injected basaltic magma, and wall-rock xenoliths (or partial melts therefrom). The choice of contaminant composition is further complicated by the range of $\delta^{18}O$, Sr_i, and Sr content among the basaltic dikes and the xenoliths (Table 4) and by the fact that the Sr content of a partial melt of a xenolith is not likely to be equivalent to the bulk Sr content of the xenolith. It is clear that even without consideration of the variables inherent in AFC calculations, a unique solution to the isotopic variation of the Wooley Creek and Slinkard magmas is not possible.

Major-element concentrations of more than 20 synplutonic mafic dikes (Table 2; Barnes, 1983, 1987, and unpublished data) indicate that the "average" basaltic composition in the system is approximately silica saturated. Such dikes appear to have Sr_i of about 0.7042 and $\delta^{18}O$ of about 8.0$^0/_{00}$. We have used these values and Sr = 400 ppm, Rb = 30 ppm (Barnes and others, 1986a) as representative of the basaltic end member in our models. We then calculated the range of compositions produced by simple mixing of the basaltic end member with each of the measured xenolith and wall-rock compositions (Fig. 9a). Points along these mixing curves represent possible contaminants that can be used in AFC calculations. The isotopic composition of the "initial" lower magma was taken to be the same as the average basalt, and the mass proportion of contaminant to crystals removed was assumed to be 0.5, in accord with earlier models (Barnes and others, 1986a). The bulk partition coefficient for Sr in the lower part of the system was taken to be approximately 0.6 (Barnes and others, 1986a). Figure 9b shows the result of AFC calculations for the lower part of the system. Mix 1 used xenolith sample 219A as the contaminant. Mix 2 used a 70/30 mixture of the basaltic "parent" and xenolith 219A (see Fig. 9a). The bulk of the variation in both Groups 1 and 2 can be explained by AFC mixing of this type. The range of Sr_i (Fig. 4) and the lack of correlation among Sr_i, $\delta^{18}O$, SiO_2, and structural level in the lower part of the system suggest that the contamination process was not uniform in the andesitic zone, as would be expected in a magma stirred by mixing.

In contrast, Group 3 samples from the upper Wooley Creek batholith display little or no variation in Sr_i, but have a somewhat wider range of $\delta^{18}O$ that is correlated with SiO_2 content and with decrease in structural level (Barnes and others, 1987).

Simple end-member mixing among the assumed parent (Sr_i = 0.7042, $\delta^{18}O$ = +8.0$^0/_{00}$, Sr = 400 ppm) and either of the wall-rock (Hayfork) compositions (Fig. 9a) will not account for the observed variation. Simple end-member mixing or AFC mixing among the assumed parent and the Slinkard two-mica granite (calculations not shown) can explain the range of $\delta^{18}O$ values in the upper Wooley Creek batholith; however, such mixing is incompatible with Ba, Rb, and Sr abundances (Tables 3 and 4; Figs. 4 and 5) and with the higher oxidation state of the upper Wooley Creek batholith.

Inasmuch as the upper Wooley Creek batholith intruded both western and eastern Hayfork terranes, it seems appropriate to use a contaminant composition that is some combination of both units. Figure 9c shows part of the curve that results from

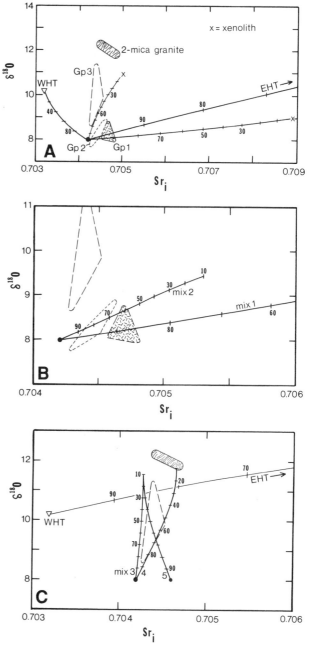

Figure 9. a: Two-component mixing curves among average basalt (dot) and possible contaminants. Compositional groups among Slinkard and Wooley Creek shown by fields. See text for further explanation. b: Mixing calculations for Groups 1 and 2. AFC mixes in which mass of contaminant/mass of crystals formed is 0.5 and bulk partition coefficient for Sr = 0.6. Mix 1 with assumed basaltic parent and xenolith 219A. Mix 2 with assumed basaltic parent and a combination of 70 percent basalt and 30 percent xenolith 219A. c: Mixing calculations for upper Wooley Creek (Group 3). Curve between WHT and EHT is simple end-member mixing line between western Hayfork sample 672D and eastern Hayfork sample 236C (off scale). Curves 3 and 4 are AFC mixes in which Sr(parent) is 400 ppm and Sr, Sr_i, $\delta^{18}O$ of contaminant defined by the simple combination of wall-rock types. Proportions of western to eastern Hayfork are 85 and 80 percent for mixes 3 and 4, respectively. Mix 5 is an AFC mix similar to mix 3 except with parent Sr_i of 0.7046.

simple end-member mixing of western Hayfork sample 672D with eastern Hayfork sample 236C. The $\delta^{18}O$ value of the western Hayfork sample is probably low relative to the majority of the unit because the western Hayfork terrane locally contains siliceous arenite and interbedded lithic to feldspathic wacke (Donato and others, 1982, 1983). Higher $\delta^{18}O$ in the western Hayfork component would have the effect of lowering the mass of contaminant necessary to raise $\delta^{18}O$ in the upper Wooley Creek batholith magma. If the measured western Hayfork terrane values of Sr_i and $\delta^{18}O$ are used, AFC calculations indicate that mixing of the assumed parent with a western Hayfork–eastern Hayfork combination in the range of 85/15 (Mix 3, Fig. 9c) to 80/20 (Mix 4, Fig. 9c) can explain the variation of $\delta^{18}O$ in the upper Wooley Creek batholith. Such a process is compatible with the correlation among SiO_2 and $\delta^{18}O$. The upward increase in $\delta^{18}O$ may be due in part to the fact that the eastern Hayfork terrane is the predominant wall-rock type in the uppermost part of the system (Fig. 1).

We now turn to the origin of the assumed parent of the upper magma. Major-element mass-balance calculations demonstrate that either basaltic or andesitic magma can be fractionated, by removal of plagioclase, hornblende, and oxide phases, to yield the dacitic composition (Barnes, 1983). Such models are in agreement with the decrease in Sr content in dacite relative to andesite, because in the andesite-to-dacite fractionation step the bulk partition coefficient of Sr is greater than one (Barnes, 1983). The models are also consistent with the increase in the slopes of REE patterns because of hornblende fractionation (e.g., Arth and Barker, 1976). If a basaltic parent is called on, then the fact that the dacite and typical basalt have identical Sr_i requires that the dacitic cap formed relatively early in the history of the system and that fractionated liquid from the lower andesitic magma did not rise into the cap (or was not sampled in this study). However, if an andesitic parent is called on, the fact that the andesite was generally richer in radiogenic Sr must be accounted for. This possibility is explored in Figure 9c. Mix 5 presents an AFC trajectory similar to Mix 3 but with a starting value of Sr_i in the range of the andesitic lower part of the system. Inasmuch as the mixing curve depends on the proportions of western and eastern Hayfork rocks in the contaminant, it is apparent that many such curves could be calculated. Nevertheless, it indicates that contamination of the products of fractionation of the andesitic magma by Hayfork lithologies could result in lowered Sr_i and increased $\delta^{18}O$.

SUMMARY AND CONCLUSIONS

Trace-element and mineralogical study of the Slinkard pluton, Wooley Creek batholith, and roof-zone dikes strongly indicates that during much of its magmatic history the system had a two-layer geometry comprising a lower convecting andesitic magma that was repeatedly recharged by basalt and an upper dacitic unit that is now characterized by an upward increase in $\delta^{18}O$ and SiO_2. A small two-mica granite emplaced in the deepest part of the system was not a differentiate of the adjacent magma: rather, it was the result of crustal anatexis at a deeper level. Anatexis may have been aided by heat derived from the passage of basaltic magma through the lower crust and from basalt trapped in the lower crust.

Gradational upward compositional zonation in the system is apparently due to more efficient crystal segregation and accumulation in deeper levels, input and mixing of mafic magma at deeper levels, and initial development of the dacitic cap by sidewall crystallization and boundary-layer flow. The REE display the effects of accumulation particularly well (Figs. 6, a–c). Rocks that crystallized from basaltic and andesitic magma have lower REE abundances than corresponding roof-zone dikes, an indication of clinopyroxene and plagioclase accumulation in the coarse-grained plutonic samples. However, REE abundances in dacitic roof-zone dikes are generally similar to those in the most siliceous samples from the underlying Wooley Creek batholith (Group 3). Taken together, these data suggest that crystal accumulation was less effective at shallower levels and more siliceous bulk composition, and that hornblende was an important part of the accumulating crystal assemblage.

The andesitic part of the system is isotopically distinct from the dacitic part, even though a broad gradational zone (Group 2) is observed in the field (Barnes, 1983) and the two units share similar T-f_{O_2} histories (Barnes, 1987). The isotopic distinction could be the product of generation and intrusion of separate magma batches (andesite followed by dacite) along with more or less continuous influx of basalt to the lower part of the system. The requirement that the structurally higher dacite intruded through or around the structurally lower andesitic magma suggests emplacement of the dacite as a diapir. *There is no evidence for diapiric emplacement of the dacitic magma;* in fact, contact relations indicate that the dacite intruded primarily by stoping (Barnes, 1983).

An alternative explanation for the isotopic heterogeneity involves in situ assimilation of host rocks combined with fractional crystallization and, in the lower part of the system, mixing of isotopically heterogeneous basaltic magmas. Isotopic differences among wall-rock units provided structural control necessary for enrichment of ^{87}Sr in the lower part of the system (with little variation in $\delta^{18}O$) and enrichment of $\delta^{18}O$ in the upper part (with no variation in Sr_i).

The latter explanation better fits intrusive relations in the roof zone. In the former, it is difficult to reconcile the presence of relatively radiogenic andesitic magma with less radiogenic dacite. This is contrary to most documented examples of isotopic heterogeneity in granitoid intrusions, in which felsic compositions are more radiogenic than are more mafic compositions (e.g., Stephens and Halliday, 1979; Halliday, 1983; Kistler and others, 1986).

Basaltic magmas were the first to be intruded, and basaltic input into the lower part of the system continued for most, if not all, of its crystallization history. Some basalts display clear Sr isotopic evidence of crustal interaction and fractional crystallization; others have Sr_i, $Mg/(Mg+Fe^{2+})$, and Cr and Ni contents that indicate a mantle origin with little or no differentiation. The clinopyroxene- or amphibole-rich nature of most roof-zone and synplutonic basaltic dikes implies a significant H_2O content, and is similar to observations by Anderson (1979, 1980) and Beets and others (1984) of high H_2O content in arc-related lavas. Influx of basaltic magma had important implications for evolution of the system. Basalt provided the chemical and thermal input that buffered the bulk composition of the andesitic magma (e.g., Hill and others, 1985, 1986) but allowed significant enrichment in excluded trace elements such as Rb and the LREE (Barnes and others, 1986a). The basaltic heat flux also permitted the dacitic cap to remain liquid long enough to develop the upward increase in $\delta^{18}O$ through assimilation of roof rocks.

ACKNOWLEDGMENTS

We are deeply grateful to A. K. Sinha for the use of laboratory facilities at Virginia Polytechnic Institute and State University and to M. A. Barnes for assistance in the field and laboratory. M. M. Donato's discussions of regional geology and her thorough review are greatly appreciated, as are reviews by A. N. Halliday, N. J. McMillan, J. McMurry, and J. L. Anderson. This work was supported by National Science Foundation Grant EAR-8408319 to Barnes.

REFERENCES CITED

Allen, J. C., and Boettcher, A. L., 1978, Amphiboles in andesite and basalt; 2, Stability as a function of P-T-f (H_2O)-f(O_2): American Mineralogist, v. 63, p. 1074–1087.

Allen, J. C., Boettcher, A. L., and Marland, G., 1975, Amphiboles in andesite and basalt; 1, Stability as a function of P-T-f(O_2): American Mineralogist, v. 60, p. 1069–1085.

Anderson, A. T., Jr., 1979, Water in some hypersthenic magmas: Journal of Geology, v. 87, p. 509–531.

—— , 1980, Significance of hornblende in calc-alkaline andesites and basalts: American Mineralogist, v. 65, p. 837–851.

Arth, J. G., and Barker, F., 1976, Rare-earth partitioning between hornblende and dacitic liquid and implications for the genesis of trondhjemitic-tonalitic magmas: Geology, v. 4, p. 534–536.

Barnes, C. G., 1983, Petrology and upward zonation of the Wooley Creek batholith, Klamath Mountains, California: Journal of Petrology, v. 24, p. 495–537.

—— , 1987, Mineralogy of the Wooley Creek batholith, Slinkard pluton, and related dikes, Klamath Mountains, northern California: American Mineralogist, v. ;72, p. 879–901.

Barnes, C. G., Allen, C. M., and Saleeby, J. B., 1986a, Open- and closed-system characteristics of a tilted plutonic system, Klamath Mountains, California: Journal of Geophysical Research, v. 91, p. 6073–6090.

Barnes, C. G., Rice, J. M., and Gribble, R. F., 1986b, Tilted plutons in the Klamath Mountains of California and Oregon: Journal of Geophysical Research, v. 91, p. 6059–6071.

Barnes, C. G., Allen, C. M., and Brigham, R. H., 1987, Isotopic heterogeneity in a tilted plutonic system, Klamath Mountains, California: Geology, v. 15, p. 523–527.

Basaltic Volcanism Study Project, 1981, Basaltic volcanism on the terrestrial planets: New York, Pergamon Press, 1286 p.

Beets, D. J., Maresch, W. V., Klaver, G. T., Mottana, A., Bocchio, R., Beunk, F. F., and Monen, H. P., 1984, Magmatic rock series and high-pressure metamorphism as constraints on the tectonic history of the southern Caribbean, *in* Bonini, W. E., Hargraves, R. B., and Shagam, R., eds., The Caribbean–South American plate boundary and regional tectonics: Geological Society of America Memoir 162, p. 95–130.

Borthwick, J., and Harmon, R. S., 1982, A note regarding ClF_3 as an alternative to BrF_5 for oxygen isotope analysis: Geochimica et Cosmochimica Acta, v. 46, p. 1665–1668.

Charlton, D. W., 1979, Geology of part of the Ironside Mountain Quadrangle, northern California Klamath Mountains [Ph.D. thesis]: Santa Barbara, University of California, 542 p.

Christiansen, E. H., 1984, Geochemical evolution of a magmatic system open to self-contamination; An examination of fractionation in a double-diffusive

magma system, *in* Dungan, M. A., Grove, T. L., and Hildreth, W., eds., Proceedings of the Conference on Open Magmatic Systems: Dallas, Texas, Southern Methodist University Institute for the Study of Earth and Man, p. 26–28.

DePaolo, D. J., 1981, Trace element and isotopic effects of combined wallrock assimilation and fractional crystallization: Earth and Planetary Science Letters, v. 53, p. 189–202.

Donato, M. M., 1987, Evolution of an ophiolitic tectonic mélange, Marble Mountains, northern California Klamath Mountains: Geological Society of America Bulletin, v. 98, p. 448–464.

Donato, M. M., Barnes, C. G., Coleman, R. G., Ernst, W. G., and Kays, M. A., 1982, Geologic map of the Marble Mountain wilderness, Siskiyou County, California: U.S. Geological Survey Miscellaneous Field Studies Map MF–1452-A, scale 1:48,000.

Donato, M. M., Barnes, C. G., and Gray, G. G., 1983, Geologic map of the Orleans Mountain roadless area, Humboldt and Siskiyou counties, California: U.S. Geological Survey Miscellaneous Field Studies Map MF–1526–A, scale 1:48,000.

Farmer, G. L., and DePaolo, D. J., 1983, Origin of Mesozoic and Tertiary granite in the western United States and implications for pre-Mesozoic crustal structure; 1, Nd and Sr isotopic studies in the geocline of the northern Great Basin: Journal of Geophysical Research, v. 88, p. 3379–3401.

Gordon, G. E., Randle, K. R., Goles, G. G., Corliss, J. B., Beeson, M. H., and Oxley, S. S., 1968, Instrumental activation analysis of standard rocks with high-resolution gamma-ray detectors: Geochimica et Cosmochimica Acta, v. 32, p. 369–396.

Gray, G. G., 1986, Native terranes of the central Klamath Mountains, California: Tectonics, v. 5, p. 1043–1054.

Gray, G. G., and Petersen, S. W., 1982, Northward continuation of the Rattlesnake Creek terrane, west-central Klamath Mountains, California: Geological Society of America Abstracts with Programs, v. 14, p. 167.

Halliday, A. N., 1983, Crustal melting and the genesis of isotopically and chemically zoned plutons in the Southern Uplands of Scotland, *in* Atherton, M. P., and Gribble, C. D., eds., Migmatites, melting, and metamorphism: Cheshire, Shiva Publishing Ltd., p. 54–61.

Harper, G. D., and Wright, J. E., 1984, Middle to Late Jurassic tectonic evolution of the Klamath Mountains, California-Oregon: Tectonics, v. 3, p. 759–772.

Haskin, L. A., Haskin, M. A., Frey, F. A., and Wildeman, T. R., 1968, Relative and absolute terrestrial abundances of the rare earths, *in* Ahrens, L. H., ed., Origin and distribution of the elements: Oxford, Pergamon, p. 889–912.

Hill, R. I., Silver, L. T., Chappell, B. W., and Taylor, H. P., Jr., 1985, Solidification and recharge of SiO_2-rich plutonic magma chambers: Nature, v. 313, p. 643–646.

Hill, R. I., Silver, L. T., and Taylor, H. P., Jr., 1986, Coupled Sr-O isotope variations as an indicator of source heterogeneity for the northern Peninsular Ranges batholith: Contributions to Mineralogy and Petrology, v. 92, p. 351–361.

Irwin, W. P., 1972, Terranes of the western Paleozoic and Triassic belt in the southern Klamath Mountains, California: U.S. Geological Survey Professional Paper 800-C, p. 103–111.

Jachens, R. C., Barnes, C. G., and Donato, M. M., 1986, Subsurface configuration of the Orleans fault; Implications for deformation in the western Klamath Mountains, California: Geological Society of America Bulletin, v. 97, p. 388–395.

Kistler, R. W., and Peterman, Z. E., 1973, Variations in Sr, Rb, K, Na, and initial $^{87}Sr/^{86}Sr$ in Mesozoic granitic rocks and intruded wall rocks in central California: Geological Society of America Bulletin, v. 84, p. 3489–3512.

Kistler, R. W., Chappell, B. W., Peck, D. L., and Bateman, P. C., 1986, Isotopic variation in the Toulumne Intrusive Suite, central Sierra Nevada, California: Contributions to Mineralogy and Petrology, v. 94, p. 205–220.

Lanphere, M. A., Irwin, W. P., and Hotz, P. E., 1968, Isotopic age of the Nevadan orogeny and older plutonic and metamorphic events in the Klamath Mountains, California: Geological Society of America Bulletin, v. 79, p. 1027–1052.

Masi, U., O'Neil, J. R., and Kistler, R. W., 1981, Stable isotope systematics in Mesozoic granites of central and northern California and south western Oregon: Contributions to Mineralogy and Petrology, v. 76, p. 116–126.

McBirney, A. R., 1980, Mixing and unmixing of magmas: Journal of Volcanology and Geothermal Research, v. 7, p. 357–371.

McBirney, A. R., Baker, B. H., and Nilson, R. H., 1985, Liquid fractionation; Part 1, Basic principles and experimental simulations: Journal of Volcanology and Geothermal Research, v. 24, p. 1–24.

Myers, J. D., Sinha, A. K., and Marsh, B. D., 1984, Assimilation of crustal material by basaltic magma; Strontium isotopic and trace element data from the Edgecumbe volcanic field, SE Alaska: Journal of Petrology, v. 25, p. 1–26.

Norrish, K., and Chappell, B. W., 1967, X-ray fluorescence spectrography, *in* Zussman, J., ed., Physical methods in determinative mineralogy: London, Academic Press, p. 171–214.

Stephens, W. E., and Halliday, A. N., 1980, Discontinuities in the composition surface of a zoned pluton, Criffell, Scotland: Geological Society of America Bulletin, v. 91, p. 165–170.

Taylor, H. P., Jr., 1980, The effects of assimilation of country rocks by magmas on $^{18}O/^{16}O$ and $^{87}Sr/^{86}Sr$ systematics in igneous rocks: Earth and Planetary Science Letters, v. 47, p. 243–254.

Vennum, W. R., 1980, Petrology of the Castle Crags pluton, Klamath Mountains, California: Geological Society of America Bulletin, v. 91, p. 1332–1393.

White, A.J.R., and Chappel, B. W., 1977, Ultrametamorphism and granitoid genesis: Tectonophysics, v. 43, p. 7–22.

—— , 1983, Granitoid types and their distribution in the Lachlan Fold Belt, southeastern Australia, *in* Roddick, J. A., ed., Circum-Pacific plutonic terranes: Geological Society of America Memoir 159, p. 21–34.

Wright, J. E., 1982, Permo-Triassic accretionary subduction complex, southwestern Klamath Mountains, northern California: Journal of Geophysical Research, v. 87, p. 3805–3818.

Yoder, H. S., Jr., and Tilley, C. E., 1962, Origin of basalt magmas; An experimental study of natural and synthetic rock systems: Journal of Petrology, v. 3, p. 342–532.

York, D., 1969, Least-squares fitting of a straight line with correlated errors: Earth and Planetary Science Letters, v. 5, p. 320–324.

Manuscript Submitted May 15, 1987
Revised Manuscript Submitted February 26, 1988
Manuscript Accepted by the Society February 7, 1989

Geological Society of America
Memoir 174
1990

Chapter 20

Magma mixing and mingling between synplutonic mafic dikes and granite in the Idaho-Bitterroot batholith

David A. Foster* and Donald W. Hyndman
Department of Geology, University of Montana, Missoula, Montana 59812

ABSTRACT

Intruded into the granites of the Idaho-Bitterroot batholith is a suite of mafic rocks dominated by basaltic andesite to dacite dikes, but also including angular to rounded andesite inclusions and quartz diorite complexes. Mutually intrusive relations suggest that these rocks were intruded while the granite was still partially fluid and thus are synplutonic. Magma interactions between the mafic and felsic rocks can be divided into three broad groups: magma mingling, magma mixing, and mingling combined with mixing. Magma mingling was important in composite dikes that contain andesite masses surrounded and cut by leucogranite veins and pods. Mixing below the present level of exposure resulted in hybrid dike rocks with disequilibrium phenocrysts. Mingling combined with mixing produced quartz diorite complexes that contain mafic, felsic, and hybrid rocks complexly swirled together. Mixing has resulted in the production of hybrid rocks that plot between end members of basaltic andesite and granite on Harker diagrams. The dominance of dikes over inclusions suggests that the mafic magma was intruded late in the crystallization history of the granite and/or that the granites were quite viscous throughout their history.

INTRODUCTION

The Late Cretaceous Idaho-Bitterroot batholith consists of mainly medium-grained, massive to moderately foliated biotite $\pm$ muscovite granite and granodiorite in the central and eastern portions and foliated, hornblende- and biotite-rich tonalite and quartz diorite in a 12- to 16-km western border zone (Fig. 1) (Hyndman, 1983, 1984; Hyndman and Foster, 1988). Emplaced into the granite and granodiorite are numerous mafic synplutonic dikes and small quartz diorite complexes. A detailed summary of the relation between the main-phase granites, western tonalites, and synplutonic dikes and their tectonic implications can be found in Hyndman and Foster (1988). The synplutonic dikes range in composition from basaltic andesite to dacite and show evidence for both magma mingling and magma mixing with the

host granite. Following definitions summarized by Frost and Mahood (1987), magma mixing refers to magma interactions that produce "homogeneous hybrid magmas" of intermediate composition. Magma mingling refers to magma interactions that produce "heterogeneous banded or enclave-bearing rocks."

Synplutonic mafic dikes are common in many granitoid terranes throughout the world, including the Sierra Nevada batholith (Moore and Hopson, 1961; Bateman and others, 1963; Chen and Moore, 1979; Reid and others, 1983; Furman and Spera, 1985; Reid and Hamilton, 1987; Frost and Mahood, 1987), the Coast plutonic complex, British Columbia (Roddick and Armstrong, 1959; Roddick, 1965), the Coastal batholith of Peru (Cobbing and Pitcher, 1972; Cobbing and others, 1981), plutons in the Klamath Mountains, California (Barnes and others, 1986), the Idaho batholith (Williams, 1977; Hyndman, 1985; Foster, 1986; Hyndman and Foster, 1988), the southern Califor-

---

*Present address: Department of Geological Sciences, State University of New York at Albany, Albany, New York 12222.

Foster, D. A., and Hyndman, D. W., 1990, Magma mixing and mingling between synplutonic mafic dikes and granite in the Idaho-Bitterroot batholith, *in* Anderson, J. L., ed., The nature and origin of Cordilleran magmatism: Boulder, Colorado, Geological Society of America Memoir 174.

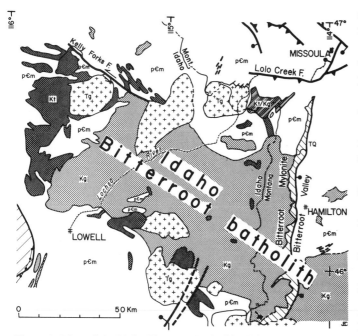

Figure 1. Map of the Idaho-Bitterroot batholith. Kt = Late Cretaceous mafic plutonic rocks (tonalite and quartz diorite); Kg = Late Cretaceous main-phase felsic plutonic rocks (granite and granodiorite); Tg = Tertiary granite; PЄm = Proterozoic Belt metamorphic rocks; TQ = Tertiary and Quaternary valley-fill deposits. After Hyndman and Foster (1988).

nia batholith (G. Gastil, 1981, personal commun. to Hyndman), the Topsails igneous terrane, Newfoundland (Whalen and Currie, 1984), Mount Desert Island, Maine (Taylor and others, 1980), and the Wadi Um-Mara area, Sinai (Eyal, 1980).

Mafic dikes are widely distributed along the entire well-exposed Lochsa River canyon cross section through the Bitterroot batholith (Fig. 1) and are spatially confined to the batholith (Hyndman, 1985; Foster, 1986). They make up about 20 percent by volume of the batholithic rocks, as measured over a 10-km section in the Lochsa canyon. Mafic dikes have also been examined in reconnaissance in widespread areas of the batholith by Williams (1977), Toth (1983, 1985, 1987), Reid (1987), and Hyndman and Foster (1988). For example, they are well exposed in the Bitterroot Range near the head of Bear Creek, in the canyons of Sweathouse and Blodgett Creeks, and in scattered areas west of the Bitterroot Range crest.

GENERAL DESCRIPTION OF ROCK TYPES

The two-mica granites and granodiorites of the Lochsa River section of the Bitterroot batholith have been described in some detail by Hyndman (1984), so the reader is referred to that paper for an overview. Mafic dikes of the Bitterroot batholith are black to grayish or greenish-black basaltic andesites, andesites, and dacites that average 2.5 m and are as much as 10 m thick. Numerous mutually intrusive relations indicate that the mafic

dikes are synplutonic with the main-phase granites, including the following.

1. Mafic dikes cut the granite as tabular bodies and, less commonly, as small plutons which in turn are cut by tabular or ptygmatic dikes of the host granite.

2. Dikes grade into angular to rounded mafic enclaves and/or schlieren.

3. The granite contains early intruded mafic rock, including isolated angular to rounded mafic inclusions, inclusion trains, and schlieren of rock petrographically similar to the dikes.

4. Leucogranites and andesite in composite dikes show small-scale mingling textures (Fig. 2).

5. Granite near some of the dikes is contaminated and more mafic than normal Bitterroot batholith granite.

6. Intermediate-composition dikes contain rounded and angular inclusions of granite and basalt.

7. Mafic dike–pegmatite or aplite contacts contain intergrown, poikilitic crystals that bridge the contacts.

The mafic dikes show a wide range in degree of metamorphism and deformation, the result of dike minerals equilibrating to the granite temperatures and postemplacement movements of the granite magma. Moderately deformed and metamorphosed dikes are foliated and/or lineated; the foliation in many of these dikes is asymmetric and oblique to the walls, suggesting that it was imposed by movements of the host granite and is not a flow foliation. Strongly deformed and metamorphosed dikes are very fine grained and schistose; they pinch and swell, are folded, and have irregular to diffuse borders. Some of the most deformed dikes are S-C mylonites (Fig. 3). Dikes deformed more than these are boudinaged and broken into inclusion trains. All of these occur in nearly unfoliated, undeformed granite. This chapter concentrates on the less metamorphosed dikes because they retain the primary igneous textures important in this discussion.

Figure 2. Photo of composite dike with small-scale magma mingling, angular to rounded masses of basaltic andesite to quartz diorite, surrounded by andesite to dacite. Highway U.S. 12, milepost 134.3.

Figure 3. Photo of dike with foliation, lineation, and mylonitic textures imposed by postemplacement movements of the granite. Highway U.S. 12, milepost 124.95.

The unmetamorphosed dikes are massive, very fine- to fine-grained, porphyritic basaltic andesite, andesite, dacite, and less commonly, medium-grained, hornblende-biotite quartz diorite to granodiorite. Some dikes have fine-grained border zones. These dikes generally contain phenocrysts of normal and reverse zoned plagioclase ranging from An_{75-30}, hornblende, and biotite ± augite and pigeonite in a fine-grained matrix of plagioclase, hornblende, and biotite, ± quartz. Accessory minerals include apatite, sphene, zircon, and iron oxides. Primary augite phenocrysts are commonly partly to fully pseudomorphically replaced by fine-grained hornblende and biotite intergrowths. Many contain 1- to 2-cm gabbroic inclusions and xenocrysts consisting of medium-grained, euhedral, oscillatory zoned and partially resorbed plagioclase, and augite replaced by hornblende. In addition, the dikes contain rounded, very fine-grained black inclusions of basaltic rock of various sizes. Some andesitic dikes are compositionally and texturally intermediate between enclosed fine-grained basaltic inclusions and the medium-grained granite intruded by the dike (Fig. 4).

A number of dikes are composite, consisting of various proportions of mingled granitic and mafic material (Fig. 2). Typically, these dikes contain angular to rounded masses of mafic rock (3 to 50 cm) surrounded by thin rims (0.1 to 1 cm) of fine-grained granitic rock, all in a matrix andesite. From the centers of the veinlets to the andesite there is a full spectrum of rock types intermediate between granite and andesite. Granitic streaks and dikelets in the composite dikes are typically aplitic with slightly zoned, anhedral to blocky plagioclase (An_{38-18}); interstitial quartz ± alkali feldspar, and myrmekitic and graphitic textures are common. Biotite and hornblende increase in the direction of the andesite-granite interfaces and are probably xenocrysts from the andesite.

Composite dikes and other synplutonic dikes are concentrated in foliated quartz diorite to granodiorite complexes that are extremely heterogeneous and contain both granite and andesite end members, as well as hybrid intermediate-composition rocks. All rock types are complexly swirled together, forming "marble cake"–like banding, each rock type existing as inclusions in all others. Synplutonic dikes in these complexes commonly grade into mafic inclusions and schlieren (Fig. 4a).

Disequilibrium textures exist in rocks of intermediate composition such as the dacite dikes, hornblende-biotite quartz diorites, and composite dikes. For example, a population of disequilibrium plagioclase phenocrysts from a single dike contains adjacent grains with dissimilar cores and zoning histories.

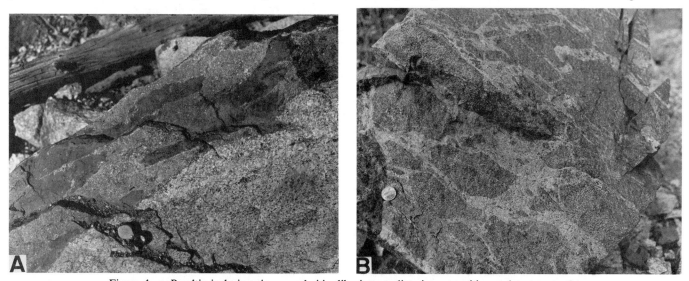

Figure 4. a. Basaltic inclusions in an andesitic dike intermediate in composition and texture to the intruded granite—apparently mixing of mafic and felsic magmas. Highway U.S. 12, milepost 124.75.
b. Photo of mafic dike separated into a swarm of mafic inclusions. Highway U.S. 12, milepost 139.2

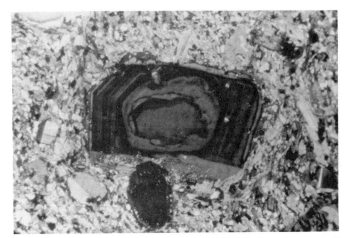

Figure 5. Photomicrograph of a strongly zoned plagioclase phenocryst (2 mm in length) with a resorbed core; from sample 135-2A.

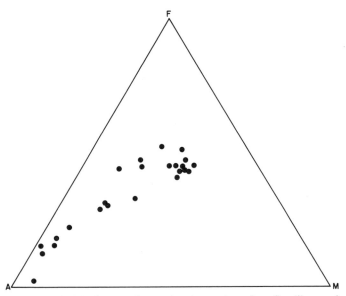

Figure 6. AFM diagram for analyzed samples of mafic dikes and granitoids.

Some have normal, reverse, or oscillatory zoning with large oscillations from core to rim and large changes in An content (Fig. 5) (e.g., core to rim: An_{70} to An_{25}; core to rim: An_{25} to An_{65}), and many have partly resorbed cores with euhedral rims. Resorbed clumps of euhedral phenocrysts of both gabbroic and granitic character also occur in andesite and dacite dikes.

CHEMICAL ANALYSES

Chemical analyses for the most mafic to dacitic dikes, granitoids of the quartz diorite complexes, and main-phase granite were produced by the commercial lab at Washington State University. Major elements were analyzed by x-ray spectrometry, trace elements by ICP.

The most mafic dikes are similar in composition to high-K basaltic andesites (Table 1). The more felsic dikes have compositions in the range of hornblende andesite to dacite. Silica contents range from 54 to 72 percent. The basaltic andesites are hypersthene and quartz normative; some have high alumina (as much as 17 percent). They have high large ion lithophile (LIL) contents for their percent SiO_2. K_2O ranges from 1.4 to 2.8 percent, and Sr from 477 to 681 ppm with an average of 580 ppm. FeO/MgO is less than 2.3 at 57 percent SiO_2. A calc-alkalic "differentiation" trend is shown when rocks of this suite are plotted on an AFM diagram (Fig. 6). All the above suggest the mafic rocks are a subduction-generated, calc-alkalic series arc suite.

Granitoids sampled from the dike complexes (e.g., no. 134.3C, 139.3B, 139.3A) are similar in composition to tonalite or quartz diorite, granodiorite, and granite. The granites are similar to typical main-phase Bitterroot batholith compositions as found by Hyndman (1984) throughout this same cross-section.

Harker diagrams for the suite from basaltic andesite to granite show linear trends for major elements (Fig. 7). All rock types have relatively similar rare earth element (REE) trends (Fig. 8). As a suite, these rocks are enriched in LREE, depleted in HREE,

and lack a Eu anomaly. All rocks of the suite have similar magnitude LREE, and the variation in one rock type is as large as the entire suite (Fig. 9a). There are slight differences in HREE (Fig. 9b). When two HREE are plotted against each other, the granitic rocks plot separate from the andesites and intermediate rocks.

MIXING OF MAGMA

Magma mixing and the production of intermediate rock types is important in many granitic systems that contain both mafic and felsic rocks (e.g., Eichelberger, 1975; Vogel, 1982; Sparks, 1983; Bell, 1983; Vogel and others, 1984; Whalen and Currie, 1984; Barnes and others, 1986; Hildreth and others, 1986), especially in areas where synplutonic mafic dikes and inclusions are emplaced in granitic batholiths (e.g., Taylor and others, 1980; Reid and others, 1983; Frost and Mahood, 1987).

In the Bitterroot batholith, evidence for mingling and mixing between end members of basaltic andesite and granite is found at outcrop, hand sample, and thin-section scales, and is reflected in chemical compositions. Frost and Mahood (1987) suggested that magma mixing is only effective for magmas of similar SiO_2. Vogel (1982) noted that in mixing systems, magma homogenization is a function of the efficiency of mechanical mixing, whereas the presence of disequilibrium phenocrysts is a function of residence time in the hybrid magma. Thus the mechanical breakdown and incorporation of material is an important means of mixing even though diffusion of chemical constituents across an interface is slow (Watson, 1982). In many cases, mixing in and around the dikes is dominated by the mechanical breakdown of mafic dikes and inclusions by shearing to form hydrid rocks.

Convective velocities in granitic magma chambers are quite large (e.g., Spera and others, 1984; Mahon and others, 1988),

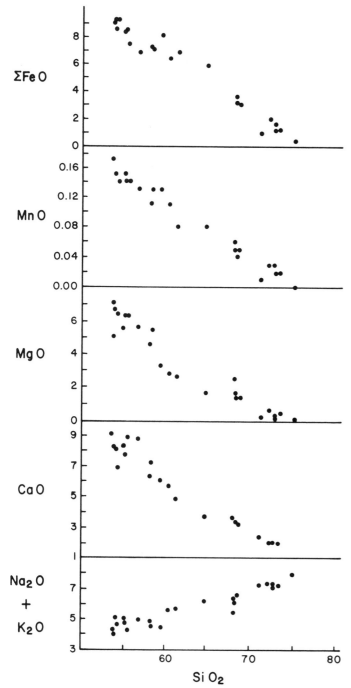

Figure 7. Harker variation diagrams for analyzed samples of mafic dikes and granitoids. Linear correlation coefficients against SiO₂ are ΣFeO = –0.98; MnO = –0.98; MgO = –0.96; CaO = –0.98; Na₂O = 0.47; K₂O = 0.78.

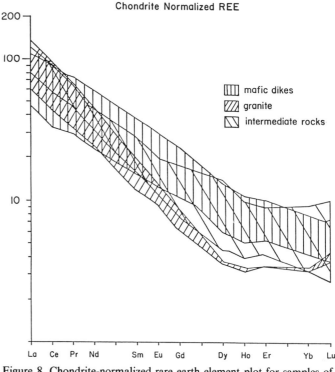

Figure 8. Chondrite-normalized rare earth element plot for samples of mafic dikes and granitoids.

root batholith were injected late in the history of the batholith; they thereby preserve the best evidence of magma mixing.

A range in degree and style of magma interactions is shown by the Bitterroot batholith rocks. These interactions can be grouped into three broad types: mingling, mixing, and mingling combined with mixing. Mixing in this case involves the mechanical mixing of mafic and felsic magmas and the formation of a hybrid magma of intermediate composition. This process was responsible for the formation of nearly homogeneous dacitic dikes with microscopic disequilibrium textures and xenocrysts, and coarser grained granodiorite dikes with streaks and round inclusions of mafic material. This more complete form of mixing must have taken place below the present level of exposure.

The composite dikes portray classic magma mingling textures where andesite is surrounded by thin rims of leucogranite. To attribute all the textures in composite dikes to mingling would be oversimplifying, because some hybridization has taken place. The dikes contain areas that exhibit a complete series of compositions across contacts between leucogranite and andesite. Contacts between the granitic and basaltic andesite components in the composite dikes are cuspate and sharp on both a megascopic and microscopic scale, suggesting that two fluids were in contact. These textures are common in other igneous systems that are considered to have formed by mingling of magmas (e.g., Taylor and others, 1980; Reid and others, 1983; Vogel and others, 1984; Mezeger and others, 1985; Frost and Mahood, 1987). The preservation of mingling magmas is due to the failure of two miscible

except later in the crystallization history when the magma viscosity is high; thus the outcrop-scale evidence for magma mixing should be rare. Only mixing that occurred when a pluton was nearly solidified, and had slow convection, will be preserved (Furman and Spera, 1985). Thus, dikes preserved in the Bitter-

TABLE 1. CHEMICAL ANALYSIS OF MAFIC DIKES, INTERMEDIATE ROCKS, AND GRANITES FROM THE IDAHO BATHOLITH

	124.95B	141.95	136.05A	135.9A	125.05	136.05B	134.3A1	134.3A2	139.3C
				BASALTIC ANDESITE DIKES				ANDESITE DIKES	
In wt.%									
SiO_2	53.61	53.75	53.89	54.19	54.94	55.07	55.43	56.72	58.08
TiO_2	0.91	1.36	0.82	2.28	0.93	0.82	0.75	0.66	0.98
Al_2O_3	14.89	17.28	15.88	15.21	15.77	15.92	16.19	16.49	17.29
Fe_2O_3	4.42	4.56	4.19	4.53	4.11	4.15	3.67	3.34	3.56
FeO	5.06	5.22	4.80	5.19	4.71	4.75	4.20	3.83	4.08
MnO	0.17	0.15	0.15	0.14	0.15	0.14	0.14	0.13	0.11
MgO	7.15	5.08	6.70	6.46	5.58	6.32	6.35	5.63	4.60
CaO	9.12	8.26	8.18	6.87	8.35	7.79	8.82	8.08	6.36
Na_2O	2.62	2.61	2.56	2.64	2.21	2.45	2.17	2.39	3.19
K_2O	1.62	1.39	2.49	1.94	2.78	2.28	2.04	2.49	1.57
P_2O_5	0.440	0.334	0.346	0.545	0.457	0.324	0.244	0.249	0.185
In ppm									
Ba				645		673	778	957	535
Rb				56		85			56
Co				38		35	35	35	35
Cr				211		188	307	247	134
Cu				54		83	19	21	42
Li				24		32	12	13	39
Nb				42		10	15	13	13
Ni				146		36	25	25	44
Sc				17		22	28	22	16
Sr				681		584	477	529	536
V				152		155	194	147	102
Y				23		17	16	16	17
Zn				97		71	73	65	80
Zr				106		21	21	20	17
Norms									
AN	52.07	58.65	53.89	52.00	57.11	55.36	60.74	57.10	51.11
Q	5.13	8.78	3.97	8.98	7.63	7.32	8.61	9.22	12.58
or	9.57	8.21	14.72	11.46	16.43	13.47	12.06	14.72	9.28
ab	22.17	22.09	21.66	22.34	18.70	20.73	18.36	20.22	26.99
an	24.09	31.33	24.49	23.92	24.90	25.71	28.41	26.91	28.22
C	0.00	0.00	0.00	0.00	0.00	0.00	0.00	0.00	0.00
di	14.57	5.97	11.03	5.21	10.81	8.63	10.94	9.19	1.69
hy	15.33	13.65	15.71	15.92	12.73	15.83	14.32	13.07	13.79
mt	6.41	6.61	6.08	6.57	5.96	6.02	5.32	4.84	5.16
il	1.73	2.58	1.56	1.26	1.77	1.56	1.42	1.25	1.86
ap	1.02	0.77	0.80	0.00	1.06	0.75	0.57	0.58	0.43
FeO*	9.04	9.32	8.57	9.27	8.41	8.49	7.50	6.84	7.28
Rare earth elements									
La				37.98		13.41	14.38	15.94	18.60
Ce				79.10		29.67	28.29	30.49	35.68
Pr				9.01		4.00	3.58	3.66	6.30
Nd				37.15		17.87	14.34	14.38	16.89
Sm				7.42		4.07	3.22	3.09	3.52
Eu				2.27		1.30	1.08	1.03	1.14
Gd				6.38		3.53	3.13	2.98	3.26
Dy				4.57		2.72	2.67	2.50	2.85
Ho				0.82		0.52	0.53	0.51	0.56
Er				2.31		1.51	1.43	1.35	1.64
Yb				1.77		1.34	1.48	1.44	1.54
Lu				0.24		0.20	0.25	0.25	0.22

TABLE 1. CHEMICAL ANALYSIS OF MAFIC DIKES, INTERMEDIATE ROCKS, AND GRANITES FROM THE IDAHO BATHOLITH (cont'd).

	132.9	134.3C	116.7	116.0	124.0	124.95A	118.6	139.3B	135.0
	ANDESITE	QUARTZ DIORITE	ANDESITE DIKES		——————DACITE DIKES——————			GRANODIORITE	DACITE
In wt.%									
SiO_2	58.33	59.37	60.43	61.32	64.82	68.22	68.24	68.36	68.72
TiO_2	0.82	0.89	1.11	1.23	1.17	0.52	0.57	0.53	0.58
Al_2O_3	15.94	17.15	17.32	16.85	15.88	15.84	16.05	16.65	16.08
Fe_2O_3	3.47	3.95	3.14	3.34	2.87	1.77	1.57	1.55	1.49
FeO	3.98	4.52	3.60	3.82	3.29	2.02	1.80	1.78	1.71
MnO	0.13	0.13	0.11	0.08	0.08	0.06	0.05	0.04	0.05
MgO	5.49	3.32	2.79	2.56	1.71	2.55	1.70	1.50	1.49
CaO	7.17	6.07	5.71	4.88	3.79	3.62	3.61	3.45	3.27
Na_2O	2.25	2.45	2.94	2.91	2.96	3.32	2.68	3.20	2.72
K_2O	2.18	1.93	2.56	2.69	3.11	1.95	3.57	2.77	3.71
P_2O_5	0.247	0.247	0.285	0.331	0.323	0.131	0.174	0.176	0.187
In ppm									
Ba		1002	513	944			619	1148	
Rb			89	96			147	94	
Co		35	29	23			33	37	
Cr		78	42	32			60	71	
Cu		33	25	23			17	14	
Li		21	21	31			27	38	
Nb		19	16	19			13	11	
Ni		26	12	16			18	22	
Sc		17	12	10			7	6	
Sr		571	404	616			320	586	
V		147	71	114			49	46	
Y		25	18	17			10	9	
Zn		92	73	75			58	70	
Zr		7	63	90			45	6	
Norms									
AN	58.61	57.89	51.55	47.24	39.99	37.84	42.52	37.09	39.46
Q	14.04	18.74	16.85	19.68	25.08	29.57	28.68	29.47	29.52
or	12.88	11.41	15.13	15.90	18.38	11.52	21.10	16.37	21.93
ab	19.04	20.73	24.88	24.62	25.05	28.09	22.68	27.08	23.02
an	26.96	28.50	26.47	22.05	16.69	17.10	16.77	15.97	15.00
C	0.00	0.59	0.01	1.07	1.53	2.00	1.63	2.54	2.09
di	5.57	0.00	0.00	0.00	0.00	0.00	0.00	0.00	0.00
hy	14.35	12.08	9.34	8.75	6.15	7.85	5.39	4.92	4.75
mt	5.03	5.73	4.55	4.84	4.16	2.57	2.28	2.25	2.16
il	1.56	1.69	2.11	2.34	2.22	0.99	1.08	1.01	1.10
ap	0.57	0.57	0.66	0.77	0.75	0.30	0.40	0.41	0.43
FeO*	7.10	8.08	6.43	6.83	5.87	3.61	3.21	3.18	3.05
Rare earth elements									
La		30.92	29.05	39.84			38.72	34.42	
Ce		58.63	57.80	77.69			72.81	61.85	
Pr		6.62	6.56	8.60			7.67	6.30	
Nd		27.20	26.45	32.64			28.52	23.18	
Sm		5.50	5.25	5.58			4.75	3.72	
Eu		1.52	1.46	1.64			1.09	1.00	
Gd		4.86	4.50	4.38			3.28	2.60	
Dy		3.91	3.55	3.10			2.05	1.59	
Ho		0.76	0.68	0.60			0.39	0.30	
Er		2.10	2.00	1.72			1.20	0.94	
Yb		1.07	1.72	1.40			0.96	0.74	
Lu		0.35	0.25	0.19			0.13	0.10	

TABLE 1. CHEMICAL ANALYSIS OF MAFIC DIKES, INTERMEDIATE ROCKS, AND GRANITES FROM THE IDAHO BATHOLITH (cont'd).

	139.3A	135.9B	134.38	125.0	134.15	139.3D
			GRANODIORITE			
In wt.%						
SiO_2	71.18	72.22	72.79	72.80	73.38	75.09
TiO_2	0.21	0.47	0.24	0.22	0.26	0.15
Al_2O_3	17.70	15.14	16.39	15.57	15.29	15.01
Fe_2O_3	0.49	1.02	0.58	0.79	0.63	0.24
FeO	0.56	1.17	0.67	0.91	0.72	0.28
MnO	0.01	0.03	0.02	0.03	0.02	0.00
MgO	0.28	0.70	0.21	0.43	0.57	0.20
CaO	2.42	1.96	2.15	1.98	1.97	1.17
Na_2O	4.78	2.81	3.63	2.59	2.80	2.49
K_2O	2.31	4.35	3.27	4.61	4.25	5.27
P_2O_5	0.054	0.146	0.060	0.070	0.090	0.084
In ppm						
Ba	610	975	1477			1406
Rb	57	179				109
Co	35	26	29			45
Cr	31	33	32			17
Cu	11	13	8			7
Li	23	33	12			15
Nb	9	15	10			7
Ni	7	11	8			7
Sc	2	4	2			2
Sr	932	352	1050			645
V	12	26	17			9
Y	6	10	5			6
Zn	42	60	45			35
Zr	4	49	4			4
Norms						
AN	22.37	26.95	25.07	29.94	27.94	19.96
Q	28.95	34.13	34.23	35.08	35.82	37.84
or	13.65	25.71	19.32	27.24	25.12	31.14
ab	40.45	23.78	30.72	21.92	23.69	21.07
an	11.65	8.77	10.27	9.37	9.19	5.26
C	3.07	2.60	3.11	2.89	2.72	3.28
di	0.00	0.00	0.00	0.00	0.00	0.00
hy	0.99	2.33	0.92	1.78	1.83	0.57
mt	0.71	1.48	0.84	1.15	0.91	0.35
il	0.40	0.89	0.46	0.42	0.49	0.28
ap	0.13	0.34	0.14	0.16	0.21	0.19
FeO*	1.00	2.09	1.19	1.62	1.29	0.50
Rare earth elements						
La	27.08	36.48	45.96			19.75
Ce	50.21	69.91	81.34			37.20
Pr	5.58	7.33	8.19			4.18
Nd	19.21	27.19	28.43			14.84
Sm	3.19	4.60	3.84			2.38
Eu	0.85	0.95	1.00			0.73
Gd	2.08	3.13	2.35			1.70
Dy	1.55	1.90	1.26			1.23
Ho	0.33	0.35	0.26			0.26
Er	1.22	1.05	0.78			0.79
Yb	0.96	0.81	0.75			0.72
Lu	0.13	0.10	0.15			0.09

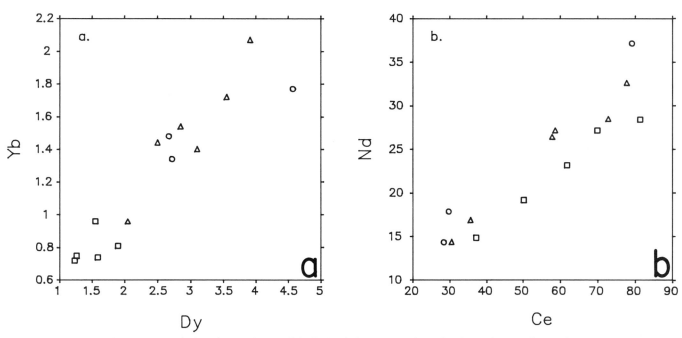

Figure 9. a. Variation diagram for two light REE; circles are andesites, triangles are intermediate rocks, and squares are granites. b. Variation diagram for two heavy REE; symbols same as 9a.

magmas to mix because of high viscosities and to thermal disequilibrium causing rapid crystallization (Taylor and others, 1980).

The quartz diorite complexes described above are an example of mingling combined with mixing. The biotite-rich granodiorite and hornblende-biotite quartz diorites are hybrid rocks. They are restricted spatially to the areas near synplutonic and composite dikes, contain rounded and angular inclusions of both andesite and granite, and are very inhomogeneous at all scales, even though they are themselves hybrid compositions. Dikes grading into inclusions and schlieren and isolated inclusions and schlieren in the intermediate granitoids of the quartz diorite complexes were frozen in the process of disaggregation, causing the granitoids of the complexes to become more mafic.

TEXTURAL AND CHEMICAL EVIDENCE FOR MAGMA MIXING

As discussed above, plagioclase phenocrysts from individual intermediate rocks have a range of core compositions and zoning histories suggesting different origins and supporting a mixing process (e.g., Bell, 1983; Hibbard and Watters, 1985). The discontinuous nature of plagioclase zoning and irregular shapes of the cores imply resorption and a secondary origin of the rims; this suggests that some phenocrysts in the mixed rocks originated in the andesite, while others were present in the granite at the time of intrusion. The outer rims may be the result of partial equilibrium with the hybrid following intrusion.

In hornblende-biotite quartz diorites and granodiorites, which are interpreted to be mixed rocks, compositions of biotite and plagioclase are different even in the same thin section. These

rocks also contain small, inhomogeneous rounded inclusions of mafic material, and alkali feldspar megacrysts similar to those in the nearby granite. The alkali feldspar megacrysts have resorbed borders, suggesting that they, too, are out of equilibrium and were incorporated from the granite. These features are all evidence for incomplete mixing (e.g., Taylor and others, 1980). In granodiorite dike rocks, mixing of a hotter mafic magma with cooler felsic magma has caused rapid crystallization of relatively calcic plagioclase. This calcic plagioclase occurs as many small crystals and as calcic growth zones ("mega-oscillations" of Hibbard and Watters, 1985) on more sodic plagioclase present at the time of mixing. An example of this is plagioclase phenocrysts from a granodiorite dike with cores of An_{30}, a zone of An_{60}, and a rim of An_{25}.

Other geologists report that in mixing systems, augite phenocrysts in the mafic rocks are partly to fully pseudomorphically replaced by fibrous hornblende and biotite (e.g., Taylor and others, 1980; Reid and others, 1983; Hibbard and Watters, 1985; Mezeger and others, 1985). Whalen and Currie (1984) suggested that the replacement of augite by amphibole and biotite indicates the late introduction of potassium and water from the granite. Experimental work by Watson (1982) and Watson and Jurawicz (1984) indicates that potassium diffuses rapidly across an interface from granite into basaltic liquid, making the liquid more andesitic. This replacement phenomenon is widespread in the mafic dikes of the Bitterroot batholith, and with the available data, it can only be speculated that potassium diffusion was responsible. Dikes that appear to have interacted to a great extent below the present level of exposure have no remaining pyroxene. However, the composite dikes that predominantly show magma mingling still contain augite in various stages of breakdown to hornblende and biotite.

Chemical compositions of the dikes and associated granitoids support a mixing origin for the intermediate rock types. As discussed, most of this mixing was mechanical, but some component of it must have been the result of diffusion of mobile constituents for short distances across contacts. That these dikes, which were probably originally basaltic andesite, or possibly basalt, have higher K_2O and SiO_2 than the original magmas suggests that there has been some contamination of basalt or basaltic andesite to produce andesite and dacite. Experimental work by Watson (1982) and Watson and Jurewicz (1984) indicates that the uptake of SiO_2 by a well-mixed basalt is moderately rapid and that K_2O and Na_2O are extremely mobile, resulting in considerable uptake of potassium by the basaltic melt and the eventual loss of sodium from the basalt to the granite by up-gradient diffusion. The rate of uptake of SiO_2 by the basalt is slower than potassium, causing potassium contamination well beyond the zone of SiO_2 contamination (Watson and Jurewicz, 1984). This presents a possible explanation for why the more highly deformed dikes, which have been in the batholith longer than undeformed dikes, have somewhat higher SiO_2 and much higher K_2O contents, and why the Na_2O and K_2O contents of this suite are highly variable and lack the linear trends on variation diagrams.

Mixing of mafic and felsic magmas will produce linear trends on element-element variation plots (e.g., Vogel and others, 1983). The major-element compositions of the dikes and the granitic rocks plot as linear trends against SiO_2 (Fig. 7). For most elements, the compositions of the intermediate rocks lie on straight mixing lines between mafic and felsic rocks. Correlation coefficients are high for all elements, except K_2O and Na_2O, which are extremely mobile. Some nonlinearity in Harker diagrams could be due to the very wide area of sampling, a section greater than 50 km, and thus different end members to mixing could be important in different areas. Trace-element variation diagrams for the suite of samples are ambiguous; no trends, linear or nonlinear, can be recognized. This may be due to local contamination of the trace elements by variable country-rock material, mixing of different end-member magmas, or analytical error for some elements. Evidence for or against mixing from REE is also ambiguous because all rock types have similar REE patterns (Fig. 8). This is especially evident for LREE, where the range in one rock type is as large as that of the suite.

The mingling of leucogranite and andesite in the composite dikes might suggest that the leucogranite evolved through liquid immiscibility. However, there is no independent evidence for liquid immiscibility, and it is more likely that this texture was produced by magma mingling. If the composite dikes evolved by immiscibility, the mafic components should show an enrichment in REE over the felsic components by a factor of five to ten (Watson, 1982).

PHYSICAL ASPECTS OF MAFIC MAGMA INJECTION

The mutually intrusive relations described above demonstrate that the mafic dikes were injected into the batholith when it was still partly fluid. Most of the mafic rocks are preserved as dikes, intruded along fractures; evidently they were intruded late in the development of the batholith when the proportion of crystals in the granite was large enough to sustain a fracture. Experimental studies and mathematical models agree that sometime before it becomes about 60 percent crystalline, a magma behaves as a ductile solid and may be fractured (e.g., Walker, 1969; Murrell and Ismail, 1976; Arzi, 1978; van der Molen and Peterson, 1979; Auar and others, 1981; Marsh, 1981; Paquet and others, 1981; McBirney and Murase, 1984; Frost and Mahood, 1987). Actual values of viscosity and strength of partially molten rocks are uncertain because experiments have not been performed at equilibrium melt fractions and melt distributions; in addition, mathematical models have not taken into consideration processes such as contiguity (Miller and others, 1988). Even without actual values, approximate trends of viscosity can be assumed; somewhere above a melt fraction of 0.5 (or as high as 0.6 if contiguity is important [Miller and others, 1988]), the viscosity of the magma rises to values equivalent to a somewhat brittle solid. At low melt fractions, all solid grains are in contact and the rheological properties of the magma are dominated by the mechanical properties of the grains: brittle behavior at high strain rates and ductile behavior at low strain rates (Wickham, 1987).

After mafic magma is injected into a granitic magma, it is deformed and, to a variable extent, mixed with the granite due to convective movements in the pluton. The efficiency of mixing is partly dependent on the mass fraction of mafic magma and crystal content of the granite (Frost and Mahood, 1987). Convection in the pluton acts to redistribute dikes and inclusions as well as to mechanically break down masses of solidified mafic material, thereby enhancing magma mixing. This is documented by the occurrence of deformed inclusions, and synplutonic dikes, which are rotated, sheared, and drawn out into inclusion trains and streaky schlieren (Cobbing and Pitcher, 1972; Furman and Spera, 1985; Foster, 1986; Hyndman and Foster, 1988).

The efficiency of mechanical magma mixing depends on the rates of convection and thus on the crystal content and associated viscosity of the host granite at the time of mafic magma intrusion (Furman and Spera, 1985). Rapid convection rates (up to about 1 km/yr) at low host-magma crystal contents (0 to 13 percent) results in dispersal of mafic material and produces textures such as disequilibrium xenocrysts and mineral assemblages, schlieren banding, and rounded inclusions. Slow convection rates (0 to a few cm/yr) at higher crystal contents (30 to 50 percent) result in deformed synplutonic dikes, dike trains, and large inclusion swarms. Mafic magma injected after convection has ended (sometime after 50 percent crystals), results in undeformed synplutonic dikes and composite dikes cut by late-stage dikes of the host granite.

In addition to synplutonic dikes, the Bitterroot batholith contains less common rounded mafic igneous inclusions (Foster, 1986) similar to inclusions described in other bodies by Reid and others (1983) and Vernon (1984). In some cases it can be documented that these inclusions are dismembered synplutonic dikes, but commonly they are isolated or in swarms with no associated dikes. The dominant physical process responsible for the formation of rounded magmatic inclusions is somewhat unclear. Plausible processes include (1) quenching of hot mafic magma into pillows against cooler granitic magma (Reid and others, 1983; Vernon, 1984); (2) mechanical breakup of dikes and small intrusions followed by rounding in the pluton due to abrasion similar to the rounding of country-rock xenoliths; or (3) vesiculation of basaltic magma at a basalt-granite interface and subsequent floating of basalt (Eichelberger, 1980).

Rounded blobs of "mafic magma" in "felsic magma" have been formed by strictly fluid processes in experiments that have questionable relevance to this problem (Huppert and others, 1983; Kouchi and Sunagawa, 1985). The mafic magma is not intruding a highly fluid host as in the experiments, suggesting that simple fluid processes are oversimplified. The mafic magma is actually intruding a granitic magma which has a very high viscosity late in its crystallization history (probably near brittle), when these features are preserved. The basalt also acts brittlely because it is undercooled by contact with the cooler granitic magma (Vernon, 1984). Probably the only time "pillows" can be formed is early in the crystallization history of a granitic pluton when the pluton is quite far above its solidus and has a lower viscosity.

The main-phase granites of the Bitterroot batholith were intruded deep in the crust and were never far above their solidus (Hyndman, 1981). This suggests that the granites were highly viscous for most of their history and may explain the predominance of dikes and angular inclusions from dismembered dikes over round magmatic inclusions. This contrasts with other plutons, such as those in the Sierra Nevada batholith, which intruded higher levels of the crust and were significantly above their soli- dus at times in their histories. Plutons of this type were less viscous, and mafic magma intruded into them was able to form "pillows" (e.g., Reid and others, 1983).

CONCLUSIONS

The evidence presented is interpreted as outcrop-scale mixing and mingling of basaltic andesite and granite magmas in the Idaho-Bitterroot batholith. Three types of magma interactions are observed: magma mingling in composite dikes and pods, magma mixing and the production of hybrid rocks such as dacite and granodiorite dikes, and mingling combined with mixing in heterogeneous quartz diorite complexes.

The predominant mode of mafic magma injection in the batholith is by synplutonic dikes, which are far more common than mafic magmatic inclusions and schlieren. Thus, it can be inferred that most of the synplutonic mafic magma at the present level of exposure must have been intruded relatively late in the crystallization history of the granite. The lack of numerous mafic inclusions is also related to the fact that the Bitterroot batholith granites were never far above their solidus and thus had high viscosities throughout their histories. The only large-scale exceptions to this are the quartz diorite complexes, which must have resulted from larger mass fractions of mafic magma (e.g., Frost and Mahood, 1987) and probably some remelting of the granite.

ACKNOWLEDGMENTS

A small grant from the University of Montana to Hyndman made available the chemical analyses. This manuscript was greatly improved by careful reviews by J. B. Reid, Jr., T. A. Vogel, and F. J. Spera.

REFERENCES CITED

Arzi, A. A., 1978, Critical phenomena in the rheology of partially melted rocks: Tectonophysics, v. 44, p. 173–184.

Auer, F., Berckhemer, H., and Oehlschehel, G., 1981, Steady state creep of fine grain granite at partial melting: Journal of Geophysics, v. 49, p. 89–92.

Barnes, C. G., Allen, C. M., and Saleeby, J. B., 1986, Open- and closed-system characteristics of a tilted plutonic system, Klamath Mountains, California: Journal of Geophysical Research, v. 91, p. 6073–6090.

Bateman, P. C., Clark, L. D., Huber, N. K., Moore, J. G., and Rinehart, C. D., 1963, The Sierra Nevada batholith; A synthesis of recent work across the central part: U.S. Geological Survey Professional Paper 414-D, 46 p.

Bell, B. R., 1983, Significance of ferrodiorite liquids in magma mixing processes: Nature, v. 306, p. 323–327.

Chen, J. H., and Moore, J. G., 1979, Late Jurassic Independence dike swarm in eastern California: Geology, v. 7, p. 129–133.

Cobbing, E. J., and Pitcher, W. S., 1972, The Coastal batholith of central Peru: Journal of the Geological Society of London, v. 128, p. 421–460.

Cobbing, E. J., Pitcher, W. S., Wilson, J. J., Baldcock, J. W., Taylor, W. P., McCourt, W., and Snelling, N. J., 1981, The geology of the western Cordillera of northern Peru: Institute of Geological Sciences Overseas Memoir 5, 143 p.

Eichelberger, J. C., 1975, Origin of andesite and dacite; Evidence of mixing of Glass Mountain in California and at other circum-Pacific volcanoes: Geological Society of America Bulletin, v. 86, p. 1381–1391.

Eichelberger, J. C., 1980, Vesiculation of mafic magma during replenishment of silica magma reservoirs: Nature, v. 288, p. 446–450.

Eyal, Y., 1980, Synplutonic dikes in the Wadi Um-Mara Area, Sinai: Tectonophysics, v. 67, p. 35–44.

Foster, D. A., 1986, Synplutonic dikes of the Idaho batholith: Geological Society of America Abstracts with Programs, v. 18, p. 355.

Frost, T. P., and Mahood, G. A., 1987, Field, chemical, and physical constraints on mafic-felsic interactions in the Lamarck Granodiorite, Sierra Nevada, California: Geological Society of America Bulletin, v. 99, p. 272–291.

Furman, T., and Spera, F. J., 1985, Co-mingling of acid and basic magma with implications for the origin of mafic I-type xenoliths; Field and petrochemical relations of an unusual dike complex at Eagle Lake, Sequoia National Park, California, USA: Journal of Volcanology and Geothermal Resources, v. 24, p. 151–178.

Hibbard, M. J., and Watters, R. J., 1985, Fracturing and diking in incompletely crystallized granitic plutons: Lithos, v. 18, p. 1–12.

Hildreth, W., Groves, T. L., and Dungan, M. A., 1986, Introduction to special section on open magmatic systems: Journal of Geophysical Research, v. 91, p. 5887–5889.

Huppert, H. E., Sparks, R.S.J., and Turner, J. S., 1983, Laboratory investigations of viscous effects in replenished magma chambers: Earth and Planetary Science Letters, v. 65, p. 377–381.

Hyndman, D. W., 1981, Controls on source and depth of emplacement of granitic magma: Geology, v. 9, p. 244–249.

—— , 1983, The Idaho batholith and associated plutons, Idaho and western Montana *in* Roddick, J. A., ed., Circum-Pacific plutonic terranes: Geological Society of America Memoir 159, p. 213–240.

—— , 1984, A petrographic and chemical section through the northern Idaho batholith: Journal of Geology, v. 92, p. 83–102.

—— , 1985, Source and formation of the Idaho batholith: Geological Society of America Abstracts with Programs, v. 17, p. 226.

Hyndman, D. W., and Foster, D. A., 1988, The role of tonalites and mafic dikes in the generation of the Idaho batholith: Journal of Geology, v. 96, p. 31–46.

Kouchi, A., and Sunagawa, I., 1985, A model for mixing basaltic and dacitic magmas as deduced from experimental data: Contributions to Mineralogy and Petrology, v. 89, p. 17–23.

Mahon, K. I., Harrison, T. M., and Drew, D. A., 1988, Ascent of a granitoid diapir in a temperature varying medium: Journal of Geophysical Research, v. 93, p. 1174–1188.

Marsh, B. D., 1981, On the crystallinity, probability of occurrence and rheology of lava and magma: Contributions to Mineralogy and Petrology, v. 78, p. 85–96.

McBirney, A. R., and Muruse, T., 1984, Rheological properties of magmas: Annual Reviews of Earth and Planetary Science, v. 12, p. 337–357.

Mezeger, K., Alterr, R., Okrusch, M., Henjes-Kurst, F., and Kreuzer, H., 1985, Genesis of acid/basic rock associations; A case study the Kallithea intrusive complex, Samos, Greece: Contributions to Mineralogy and Petrology, v. 90, p. 353–366.

Miller, C. F., Watson, E. B., and Harrison, T. M., 1988, Perspective on the source, segregation, and transport of granitoid magmas: Transactions of the Royal Society of Edinburgh: Earth Sciences, v. 79, 135–156.

Moore, J. G., and Hopson, C. A., 1961, The Independence dike swarm in eastern California: American Journal of Science, v. 259, p. 241–259.

Murrell, S.A.F., and Ismail, I.A.H., 1976, The effect of temperature on the strength at high confining pressure of granodiorite containing free and chemically-bound water: Contributions to Mineralogy and Petrology, v. 55, p. 317–330.

Paquet, J., Francois, P., and Nedelec, A., 1981, Effect of partial melting on rock deformation; Experimental and natural evidence on rocks of granitic compositions: Tectonophysics, v. 78, p. 545–565.

Reid, R. R., 1987, Structural geology and petrology of a part of the Bitterroot lobe of the Idaho batholith, *in* Vallier, T. L., ed., The Idaho batholith: U.S. Geological Survey Professional Paper 1436, p. 37–58.

Reid, J. B., and Hamilton, M. A., 1987, Origin of Sierra Nevadan granite; Evidence from small-scale composite dikes: Contributions to Mineralogy and Petrology, v. 96, p. 441–454.

Reid, J. B., Evans, O. C., and Fates, D. G., 1983, Magma mixing in granitic rocks of the central Sierra Nevada, California: Earth and Planetary Science Letters, v. 66, p. 243–261.

Roddick, J. A., 1965, Vancouver North, Coquitlum and Pit Lake map-area, British Columbia, with special emphasis on the evolution of the plutonic rocks: Geological Survey of Canada Memoir 335, 276 p.

Roddick, J. A., and Armstrong, J. E., 1959, Relict dikes in the Coast Mountains near Vancouver, B.C.: Journal of Geology, v. 67, no. 6, p. 603–613.

Sparks, R.S.J., 1983, Mixed-up magmas: Nature, v. 306, p. 315–316.

Spera, F. J., Yuen, D. A., and Kemp, D. V., 1984, Mass transfer along vertical walls in magma chambers and marginal upwelling: Nature, v. 310, p. 764–767.

Taylor, T. R., Vogel, T. A., and Wilband, J. T., 1980, The composite dikes at Mount Desert Island, Maine; An example of coexisting acidic and basic magmas: Journal of Geology, v. 88, p. 433–444.

Toth, M. I., 1983, Reconnaissance geologic map of the Selway–Bitterroot Wilderness, Idaho, and Missoula and Ravalli counties, Montana: U.S. Geological Survey Map MF–1495-B, scale 1:125,000.

—— , 1985, Petrology and evolution of the Bitterroot Lobe of the Idaho batholith: Geological Society America Abstracts with Programs, v. 17, p. 269.

—— , 1987, Petrology and origin of the Bitterroot lobe of the Idaho batholith, *in* Vallier, T. L., ed., The Idaho batholith: U.S. Geological Survey Professional Paper 1436, p. 9–35.

van der Molen, I., and Peterson, M. S., 1979, Experimental deformation of partially-melted granite: Contributions to Mineralogy and Petrology, v. 70, p. 299–318.

Vernon, R. H., 1984, Microgranitoid enclaves in granites; Globules of hybrid magma quenched in a plutonic environment: Nature, v. 309, p. 438–439.

Vogel, T. A., 1982, Magma mixing in the acidic-basic Complex of Ardnamurchan; Implications on the evolution of shallow magma chambers: Contributions to Mineralogy and Petrology, v. 79, p. 411–423.

Vogel, T. A., Noble, D. C., and Younker, L. W., 1983, Chemical evolution of a high-level magma system; The Black Mountain volcanic center southern Nevada: Livermore, California, Lawrence Livermore National Laboratory, 49 p.

Vogel, T. A., Younker, L. W., Wilband, J. T., and Kampmueller, E., 1984, Magma mixing; The Marsco suite, Isle of Skye, Scotland: Contributions to Mineralogy and Petrology, v. 87, p. 231–241.

Walker, G.P.L., 1969, The breaking of magma: Geological Magazine, v. 106, p. 166–173.

Watson, E. B., 1982, Basalt contamination by continental crust; Some experiments and models: Contributions to Mineralogy and Petrology, v. 80, p. 73–87.

Watson, E. B., and Jurawicz, S. R., 1984, Behavior of alkalies during diffusive interaction of granitic xenoliths with basaltic magma: Journal of Geology, v. 92, no. 2, p. 121–131.

Whalen, J. B., and Currie, K. L., 1984, The Topsails igneous terrane, Western Newfoundland; Evidence for magma mixing: Contributions to Mineralogy and Petrology, v. 87, p. 319–327.

Wickman, S. M., 1987, The segregation and emplacement of granitic magmas: Journal of the Geological Society of London, v. 144, p. 281–297.

Williams, L. D., 1977, Petrology and petrography of a section across the Bitterroot lobe of the Idaho batholith [Ph.D. thesis]: Missoula, University of Montana, 221 p.

MANUSCRIPT SUBMITTED MAY 26, 1987
REVISED MANUSCRIPT SUBMITTED FEBRUARY 5, 1988
MANUSCRIPT ACCEPTED BY THE SOCIETY FEBRUARY 7, 1989

Geological Society of America
Memoir 174
1990

Chapter 21

Neodymium, strontium, and trace-element evidence of crustal anatexis and magma mixing in the Idaho batholith

Robert J. Fleck
U.S. Geological Survey, 345 Middlefield Road, Menlo Park, California 94025

ABSTRACT

Variations in initial $^{143}Nd/^{144}Nd$ in Late Cretaceous plutonic rocks along the South Fork of the Clearwater River (SFCR) supplement results of Sr and O studies, which demonstrate large-scale mixing in magmas forming the western margin of the Idaho batholith. These marginal or border phases of the batholith span the terrane boundary between Proterozoic crust of North America and late Paleozoic–Mesozoic intraoceanic arc terranes (WSD terranes), delineated by the Western Idaho suture zone (or WISZ). $\epsilon_{Nd}(t)$ values in Early Cretaceous and older, pre-accretionary plutons of the WSD range from +3 to +7.6, and average +5.7. Proterozoic orthogneisses and metasedimentary rocks range from –7.4 to –13.7 and –10.45 to –15.7, respectively. $\epsilon_{Nd}(t)$ in Late Cretaceous plutons of the SFCR decreases abruptly from west to east near the WISZ, varying inversely with $\epsilon_{Sr}(t)$. Although Sr isotopic evidence (Fleck and Criss, 1985) is consistent with a binary mixing model, Sm-Nd results modify those conclusions, suggesting that SFCR plutons may be divided into three groups. Group 1 plutons occur in a narrow zone (<4 km width) along the suture zone (WISZ). These bodies probably represent at least three-component mixtures of very high-Sr, arc-type magmas, one or more Proterozoic crustal components that may include lower crust, and a high-Nb, high-Zr component. Group 2 plutons are characterized by high $\epsilon_{Sr}(t)$ and nearly constant, low $\epsilon_{Nd}(t)$. These bodies are thought to represent mixtures of deep-seated partial melts of two different Proterozoic lithospheric types, possibly representing upper and lower crust. Plutons belonging to Group 3 have $\epsilon_{Nd}(t)$ values <–14 and probably incorporated substantial amounts of Proterozoic metasedimentary rocks, but mixing components are poorly defined.

Trace-element variations in SFCR rocks also reflect the arc terrane–continental crustal boundary as Nb, Zr, and Nd increase dramatically, whereas Sr, Rb/Nb, and Sm/Nd exhibit coincident decreases east of the WISZ. Modeling of these variations with the isotopic variations in Nd and Sr supports mixing, but precludes contamination–bulk-assimilation models. Correlated ϵ_{Nd}, ϵ_{Sr}, and $\delta^{18}O$ within the SFCR favors mixing of crustal and subcrustal magmas rather than derivation of the melts entirely from subcontinental lithosphere.

Fleck, R. J., 1990, Neodymium, strontium, and trace element evidence of crustal anatexis and magma mixing in the Idaho batholith, *in* Anderson, J. L., ed., The nature and origin of Cordilleran magmatism: Boulder, Colorado, Geological Society of America Memoir 174.

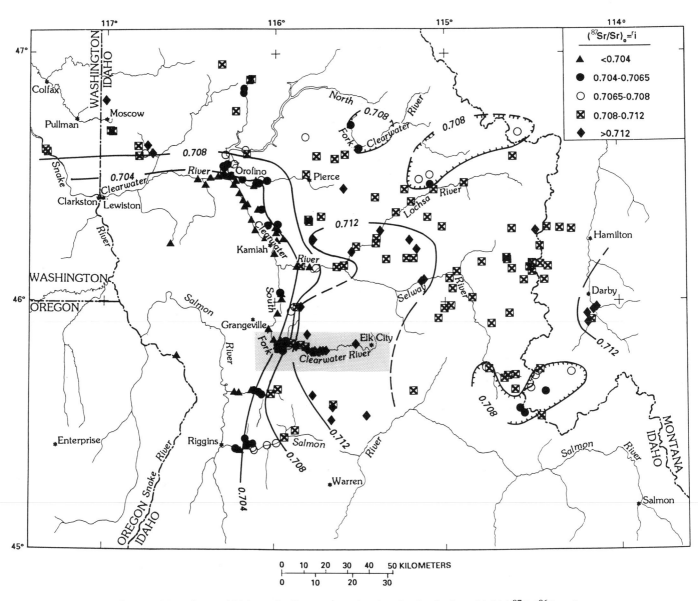

Figure 1. Map of central Idaho and adjacent areas, showing the distribution of initial $^{87}Sr/^{86}Sr$ ratios (Sr_i) of Mesozoic and Tertiary plutons (from Fleck and Criss, 1985) and the location (shaded) of the sample suite along the South Fork Clearwater River (SFCR). The Western Idaho Suture Zone, or WISZ (not shown), is located between the 0.704 and 0.708 Sr_i contours.

INTRODUCTION

Chemical and isotopic studies of plutonic rocks exposed in the canyon of the South Fork Clearwater River (SFCR) in central Idaho by Fleck and Criss (1985) provided Sr and O isotopic evidence of large-scale crustal involvement in the Late Cretaceous magmas responsible for this westernmost part of the Idaho batholith. Regional studies (Armstrong and others, 1977; Fleck and Criss, 1985; Criss and Fleck, 1987) document a dramatic increase in initial $^{87}Sr/^{86}Sr$ ratios (Sr_i) from values uniformly below 0.704 in Oregon and western Idaho to values uniformly above 0.708 in the western part of the Idaho batholith (Fig. 1). The current study utilizes the samples of plutonic, metasedimentary,

and orthogneissic rocks from the SFCR studied by Fleck and Criss (1985) to examine Nd isotopic variations in these rocks and to evaluate the petrogenetic model of mixing of anatectic melts of Precambrian wall rocks with high-Sr orogenic magmas. In addition to the isotopic and related trace-element studies, Nb, Y, and Zr were analyzed to characterize further the compositional variations in the plutonic suite.

The suite of Late Cretaceous (85 to 70 Ma) plutons exposed along the SFCR ranges in composition from tonalite-trondhjemite to granite and crosses the terrane boundary between the late Paleozoic and Mesozoic accreted terranes and Precambrian sialic crust in western Idaho (Fig. 1). A summary of the geologic setting of the region was presented by Fleck and Criss (1985), but studies by Vallier and others (1977), Myers (1982), Taubeneck (1971), Armstrong and others (1977), Brooks and Vallier (1978), and a volume edited by Vallier and Brooks (1987) provide more detailed geological and geochronological discussions. For the present study, only a brief description of the rock types of the two terranes is necessary.

The accreted terranes, referred to here as the Wallowa–Seven Devils (or WSD) terrane, occur west of about long 116°W and south of lat 46°30′N in western Idaho, eastern Oregon, and southern Washington (Fig. 1). Composed of at least three accreted crustal units of late Paleozoic and Mesozoic age (Vallier and others, 1977), the WSD terrane represents a suite of tectonically juxtaposed crustal blocks of marine-sedimentary and volcanic-arc origin. The WSD terrane was sutured to cratonal North America between about 130 and 80 Ma (Fleck and Criss, 1985; Criss and Fleck, 1987) along a highly deformed zone (Myers, 1982), referred to here as the Western Idaho suture zone (or WISZ). Rocks of the Precambrian terrane (called here the Belt-Yellowjacket terrane), including strata of the Belt Supergroup, the Lemhi Group, the Yellowjacket Formation, and a variety of orthogneisses, migmatites, and high-grade metasedimentary rocks, are the primary hosts of the Idaho batholith. The majority of the batholith is granodiorite to monzogranite in composition and latest Cretaceous to Eocene (about 72 to 45 Ma) in age. Along its western margin, however, a border or "transition" zone of gradationally more mafic and less siliceous plutons older than 80 Ma spans the terrane boundary defined by the WISZ and extends westward into the WSD terrane. Some older bodies also occur along the eastern margin of the batholith (Armstrong, 1975; Armstrong and others, 1977), but these are unrelated to known terrane boundaries. The SFCR suite characterizes the transition zone on the west, extending from tonalites of the WSD terrane 7 km west of the WISZ to granodiorites and granites 23 km east of the suture, intruding Precambrian schist and gneiss. In addition to the plutons of the SFCR, samples of plutons that intruded the WSD terrane prior to accretion to North America and samples of schists and gneisses of Middle Proterozoic age from along and east of the SFCR were analyzed as part of this study. All samples analyzed are splits of powders analyzed for Rb, Sr, ^{87}Sr/^{86}Sr, and oxygen isotopes (Fleck and Criss, 1985; Criss and Fleck, 1987).

ANALYTICAL TECHNIQUES

Samples analyzed were whole-rock powders (–200 mesh) split from 1 to 3 kg of crushed and powdered rock. Many of the samples were also studied by K-Ar or ^{40}Ar/^{39}Ar techniques for age, but different aliquants of each sample were utilized for those mineral separations to avoid any potential mechanical fractionation of the whole-rock powders. Nd isotopic analyses were performed by double-collection techniques on a Finnigan-MAT 261, thermal-ionization mass spectrometer, utilizing fully automatic operation. Analysis of USGS standard BCR-1 during the period of SFCR analyses yielded a ^{143}Nd/^{144}Nd of 0.512627 ± 25 (2σ

mean) and concentrations of Nd = 29.3 ppm and Sm = 6.55 ppm. Concentrations and isotopic compositions were obtained on the same aliquant of each sample by splitting of solutions after digestion. Separate ion-exchange and mass-spectrometric procedures were performed on the spiked and unspiked solutions, eliminating increased uncertainties due to underspiking or corrections for ^{143}Nd/^{144}Nd in the tracer solutions. Uncertainties on the ^{143}Nd/^{144}Nd ratio based on replicate chemistry and within-run statistics are similar at about ±35 ppm (2σ mean); these correspond to an uncertainty of ±0.35 ϵ_{Nd} units. Constants used for Nd include: λ_{Sm} = 6.54 × 10^{-12} yr^{-1}, (^{143}Nd/^{144}Nd$_{CHUR}$ = 0.51264, and (^{147}Sm/^{144}Nd)$_{CHUR}$ = 0.1967. Constants used for Rb-Sr systematics are: λ_{Rb} = 1.42 × 10^{-11} yr^{-1}, (^{87}Sr/^{86}Sr)$_{CHUR}$ = 0.7045, and (^{87}Rb/^{86}Sr)$_{CHUR}$ = 0.0839. ϵ values for Nd and Sr initial ratios, $\epsilon_{Nd}(t)$ and $\epsilon_{Sr}(t)$, are calculated in the usual manner relative to CHUR, an undisturbed chondritic reservoir (e.g., DePaolo and Wasserburg, 1976, 1979).

Trace-element analyses were done by standard techniques of isotope dilution (Rb, Sr, Sm, Nd) or by energy-dispersive x-ray fluorescence (XRF) (Zr, Y, Nb). Rb and Sr spikes were calibrated against gravimetrically prepared, high-purity RbCl and SrCO$_3$ solutions, and uncertainties in these determinations were commonly between 0.3 and 1 percent (2σ mean) (Fleck and others, 1980). Sm and Nd tracers were calibrated against normal solutions prepared from high-purity rare earth element (REE) metals. XRF analyses were performed using techniques similar to those of Norrish and Chappell (1967), modified slightly to correct for short-term instrumental drift. International standards were analyzed with the SFCR suite and used to prepare XRF calibration curves after routine corrections were made for elemental interferences. Uncertainties in absolute abundances of Zr, Y, and Nb may be as large as 5 to 10 percent, but relative abundances between samples are probably better than ±3 percent (2σ mean), based on replicate analyses.

NEODYMIUM ISOTOPIC VARIATIONS

In addition to 25 samples of SFCR plutons, Nd isotopic compositions and Sm and Nd concentrations were determined on 17 samples of Precambrian gneisses and metasedimentary rocks and on 15 samples from plutons of the WSD terrane (Table 1). The suite of SFCR samples represents the same suite for which Sr and O isotopic results were reported by Fleck and Criss (1985). The Nd initial ratios of the plutons, calculated as $\epsilon_{Nd}(t)$ where t = 80 Ma, decrease from about +6 west of the suture (WISZ) to less than –15 east of the zone (Fig. 2a). Sr initial ratios (Sr$_i$) exhibit a concurrent increase (Fig. 2b), rising from values of about 0.7035 ($\epsilon_{Sr}(t)$ = –14.2) in the west to greater than 0.730 (+362) where emplaced in the 1800- to 1500-Ma gneisses and schists of the Middle Proterozoic craton (Fleck and Criss, 1985; Criss and Fleck, 1987). Oxygen isotopic fractionations, expressed as δ^{18}O, increase with $\epsilon_{Sr}(t)$ from values of about +8.5 west of the WISZ to greater than +12 in plutons intruding Precambrian metasedimentary rocks east of the suture (Fleck and Criss, 1985; Criss and

R. J. Fleck

TABLE 1. Sm-Nd AND Sr RESULTS
FOR ROCKS OF THE SOUTH FORK CLEARWATER RIVER AREA (SFCR), IDAHO

Specimen Number	Nd	Sm	$^{143}Nd/^{144}Nd$	$\varepsilon_{Nd(t)}$	$\varepsilon_{Sr(t)}$	$\delta^{18}O$
PLUTONS OF THE SFCR						
797-26D	2.1	0.51	0.512872	+5.11	-10.1	9.0
797-26E	10.5	2.08	0.512730	+2.59	-9.12	8.5
797-26H	16.3	2.88	0.512008	-11.49	162	10.2
797-26I	31.2	5.06	0.512192	-7.74	48.7	9.6
807-27A	4.07	0.81	0.512924	+6.32	-10.6	10.4
807-27C	18.1	2.68	0.512469	-2.17	5.31	9.1
807-28B	31.3	5.24	0.512475	-2.18	3.79	8.5
807-28F	32.6	5.20	0.512308	-5.38	18.3	9.8
807-28G	19.4	2.71	0.512383	-3.79	16.8	10.2
807-28H	14.6	2.05	0.512169	-7.97	29.8	10.4
807-28I	36.0	5.43	0.512196	-7.51	43.5	9.2
807-29A	14.0	2.58	0.511814	-15.25	122	11.2
807-29B	18.6	3.24	0.512078	-10.04	95.8	10.2
807-29C	20.7	3.28	0.512047	-10.62	92.1	11.6
807-29D	13.5	2.25	0.512068	-10.19	77.6	9.9
807-29F	25.6	5.32	0.511960	-12.55	161	12.1
807-29H	26.0	4.68	0.511860	-14.33	265	11.5
807-29I	26.0	5.28	0.511806	-15.52	199	10.9
807-29J	23.1	3.92	0.512044	-10.67	93.2	10.4
807-30A	30.7	5.08	0.512017	-11.17	127	10.9
807-30B	22.4	4.25	0.512036	-10.95	146	10.0
807-30C	10.4	2.01	0.512059	-10.53	139	10.9
807-30D	28.7	5.17	0.512029	-11.03	154	11.5
807-30I	20.2	4.10	0.512030	-11.16	392	9.1
807-30J	25.4	3.57	0.512008	-11.19	219	10.4
837-28H	32.9	5.69	0.512179	-8.05	59.6	9.8
PLUTONS OF WSD TERRANE						
797-25F	15.9	3.27	0.512895	5.70	-14.7	6.7
797-25I	7.4	2.22	0.512943	6.07	-7.35	6.6
797-26A	9.8	2.93	0.512953	6.26	-9.99	5.5
797-26B	21.0	3.39	0.512860	5.30	-17.3	7.8
818-10F	9.9	1.12	0.512798	4.39	-5.65	8.7
818-10G	28.3	6.33	0.512934	6.35	-9.45	6.8
818-11C	13.9	3.96	0.512885	5.02	-14.2	6.2
818-11D	16.4	3.53	0.512907	5.88	-14.1	6.7
818-11E	4.1	0.57	0.512894	6.08	-12.5	7.5
818-11F	14.9	3.20	0.512914	6.02	-14.3	6.7
818-11G	12.6	2.40	0.512885	5.61	-13.3	6.0
827-28D	8.1	2.30	0.513015	7.57	-16.5	6.4
827-28E	13.5	3.00	0.512902	5.74	-13.7	6.4
827-28F	16.2	3.58	0.512921	6.11	-14.2	6.6
827-28G	20.9	4.44	0.512767	3.16	-12.8	6.3
PRECAMBRIAN METASEDIMENTARY ROCKS						
797-25C	48.7	9.30	0.511795	-15.67	1561	10.8
797-26F	38.3	6.87	0.511863	-14.27	1087	11.3
807-31J	38.9	8.23	0.512069	-10.45	405	10.3
808-1C	24.0	4.25	0.511951	-12.54	853	9.4
837-28G	85.6	14.8	0.511812	-15.22	272	10.4

**TABLE 1. Sm-Nd AND Sr RESULTS
FOR ROCKS OF THE SOUTH FORK CLEARWATER RIVER AREA (SFCR), IDAHO (continued)**

Specimen Number	Nd	Sm	$^{143}Nd/^{144}Nd$	$\varepsilon_{Nd}(t)$	$\varepsilon_{Sr}(t)$	$\delta^{18}O$
PRECAMBRIAN ORTHOGNEISSES						
807-30E	32.4	6.72	0.512091	-9.99	685	10.8
807-30F	50.2	10.8	0.512225	-7.43	662	10.9
807-30G	32.4	7.62	0.512126	-9.48	666	12.0
807-30H	34.5	7.56	0.512143	-9.05	561	9.5
807-30K	61.7	12.8	0.511913	-13.46	3266	8.9
808-1D	43.9	9.09	0.512080	-10.20	727	9.8
808-1E	43.9	9.36	0.512117	-9.52	1249	10.0
808-1F	38.4	8.23	0.512034	-11.15	1669	9.9
808-1G	38.3	8.12	0.512032	-11.17	1619	9.3
808-1H	43.1	9.23	0.512101	-9.84	793	9.7
808-1J	39.7	8.64	0.512041	-11.03	1111	9.2
808-1K	47.2	9.28	0.511960	-12.48	570	10.3
808-1L	49.2	9.40	0.511897	-13.68	384	10.2

Fleck, 1987). This correlation of $\delta^{18}O$ with the radiogenic isotope ratios in SFCR plutons contrasts sharply with the reported absence of such correlations in basaltic rock types thought to be derived from enriched subcontinental mantle (Menzies and others, 1983; Hart, 1985).

The correlation of $\delta^{18}O$ with $\varepsilon_{Nd}(t)$ (Fig. 3) demonstrates the systematic nature of isotopic variations within the SFCR suite. High ε_{Nd} plutons of the suite west of the WISZ generally have $\delta^{18}O$ values of +8.5 to +10, whereas the low $\varepsilon_{Nd}(t)$ rocks commonly have $\delta^{18}O$ above +10.5 (Fig. 3). As with Sr-O results, the dispersion of Nd-O data is significant, but the general trend reflects the systematic covariations: $\delta^{18}O$ and $\varepsilon_{Sr}(t)$ increase with decreasing $\varepsilon_{Nd}(t)$.

The isotopic covariation of Nd and Sr, displayed in an $\varepsilon_{Nd}(t)$ versus $\varepsilon_{Sr}(t)$ plot in Figure 4, reproduces much of the trend expected if separation of the magmas from the mantle actually occurred sporadically from Middle Proterozoic through Cretaceous time. Because the SFCR plutons have been shown to be Late Cretaceous in age (Criss and Fleck, 1987), the observed hyperbolic covariation strongly supports a mixing relation such as presented for the correlations of Rb, Sr, $\delta^{18}O$, and $^{87}Sr/^{86}Sr$ in these samples by Fleck and Criss (1985). However, the three lowest $\varepsilon_{Nd}(t)$ samples fall well below a smooth, two-end-member mixing curve through the bulk of the data and suggest a complexity not apparent in Rb-Sr data. For this reason a two-component mixing of wall-rock melts and arc magma cannot be the only process operative in the petrogenesis of SFCR plutons. Because many of these plutons conform to a hyperbolic curve from $\varepsilon_{Nd}(t)$ of –12 to +6, however, mixing of Mesozoic arc-like and Proterozoic crustal components is clearly a primary factor.

In contrast, plutons of the WSD terrane, sampled between Grangeville and Orofino, Idaho (Fig. 1), define a narrow field on the $\varepsilon_{Nd}(t)$ versus $\varepsilon_{Sr}(t)$ diagram (Fig. 4) and fall within that field defined by ocean-island basalts (OIB) (e.g., De Paolo and Was-

serburg, 1976, 1979; O'Nions and others, 1977; Zindler and others, 1979). The distribution of data in the unaltered OIB field and at lower $\varepsilon_{Nd}(t)$ than most mid-ocean ridge basalts (MORB) is not unexpected for oceanic-arc intrusive rocks (e.g., DePaolo and Wasserburg, 1977; Nye and Reid, 1986).

The distribution of data for all analyzed plutons (both from the SFCR and the WSD terranes) and Precambrian metasedimentary rocks and orthogneisses is displayed in Figure 4. WSD plutons group tightly at the high-$\varepsilon_{Nd}(t)$ end of the curve, whereas Proterozoic wallrocks exhibit a significant scatter at the high-$\varepsilon_{Sr}(t)$ end. Plutons of the SFCR fill much of the space between these fields and overlap parts of each. The distribution of the 1500-Ma orthogneisses suggests that bulk assimilation of these wall rocks alone cannot model the origin of SFCR magmas, because the gneiss data are at substantially higher $\varepsilon_{Nd}(t)$ than any simple hyperbolic mixing curve through SFCR pluton data. Data for metasedimentary samples are more favorably distributed relative to a best-fit hyperbola, but exhibit significant scatter. The three lowest $\varepsilon_{Nd}(t)$ plutonic samples, however, are most similar to one of the metasedimentary rock samples, but seem to require source materials different from those of the main suite of plutons (Fig. 4).

Correlated ε_{Nd}, ε_{Sr}, and $\delta^{18}O$ variations within the SFCR plutons require a petrogenesis involving systematic contributions of magmatic components from two or more sources of significantly different chemical and isotopic compositions. The high-$\varepsilon_{Nd}(t)$, low-$\varepsilon_{Sr}(t)$ magmas west of the WISZ indicate a younger and/or much higher Sm/Nd source than the low-$\varepsilon_{Nd}(t)$, high-$\varepsilon_{Sr}(t)$ melts emplaced in Proterozoic schists and gneisses east of the suture. The correlation of $\delta^{18}O$ with $\varepsilon_{Sr}(t)$ (Fleck and Criss, 1985) and with $\varepsilon_{Nd}(t)$ (Fig. 3) also may reflect source-related isotopic variations. Because these variations are unaffected by closed-system magmatic processes, all viable petrogenetic models for the SFCR suite must involve mixing of two or more

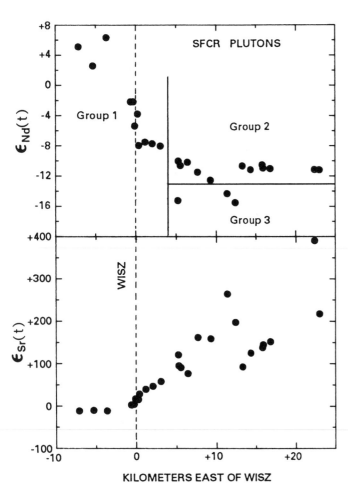

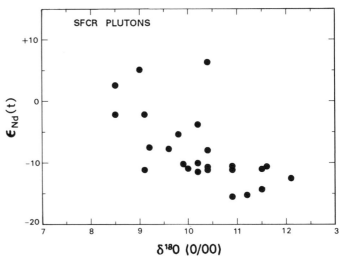

Figure 3. Plot of $\delta^{18}O$ versus $\epsilon_{Nd}(t)$ showing a general increase in $\delta^{18}O$ with decreasing $\epsilon_{Nd}(t)$ and distance into the Precambrian terrane (note location of $\epsilon_{Nd}(t)$ in Fig. 2). Samples with $\epsilon_{Nd}(t) > 0$ intrude the Wallowa–Seven Devils (WSD) terrane and may have interacted with altered volcanic or marine sedimentary rocks of the accreted arc terrane.

Figure 2. Variation diagrams of $\epsilon_{Nd}(t)$ and $\epsilon_{Sr}(t)$ with distance eastward from the suture zone (WISZ) along the east-west course of the South Fork Clearwater River (Fig. 1). Plutons west of the WISZ intrude rocks of the Paleozoic-Mesozoic accreted terranes; to the east wall rocks are referred to the Precambrian Belt–Yellowjacket terrane and may range in age from 1900 to 1300(?) Ma. Both isotopic variations are consistent with an eastward increase in Proterozoic crustal components in the magmas, although a small (lithologically controlled?) offset is apparent in each trend about 13 km east of the WISZ. Note that whereas $\epsilon_{Sr}(t)$ continues to increase, with the exception mentioned, $\epsilon_{Nd}(t)$ is nearly constant or even less negative at distances greater than about 5 km east of the suture. Grouping of plutons on the $\epsilon_{Nd}(t)$ plot is based entirely on Sm/Nd systematics and will be discussed later (see Fig. 5 and text).

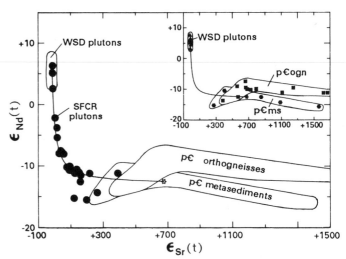

Figure 4. Variation of ϵ_{Nd} with ϵ_{Sr} in SFCR plutons (circles), WSD plutons (triangles), and samples of Precambrian orthogneisses (squares) and metasediments (hexagons) at 80 Ma. Orthogneisses fit a 1500–1400 Ma distribution, whereas metasedimentary samples appear to fit a 1900–1700 Ma trend. Simple mixtures of an oceanic or continental-marginal arc magma (ϵ_{Nd} = 5.5, ϵ_{Sr} = –11) with a Middle Proterozoic component (ϵ_{Nd} = –12, ϵ_{Sr} = 675) define a hyperbolic trend (solid line) that fits higher ϵ_{Nd} samples well, but no single model accommodates all data.

compositionally distinct end members. These models may include simple mixing of melts ("magma mixing"), assimilation of wall rock by intrusive magmas ("contamination"), or melting of varying proportions of enriched (metasomatized) and normal subcontinental lithosphere ("source mixing"). Unless specified, the term "mixing" is used here in a general sense to include any of a variety of mechanisms by which systematically variable amounts of two or more components are incorporated in SFCR magmas.

TRACE-ELEMENT CONSTRAINTS

The generally hyperbolic covariation of $\epsilon_{Nd}(t)$ and $\epsilon_{Sr}(t)$ (Fig. 4) is strong evidence for a cogenetic relation commonly associated with some form of mixing. To evaluate potential petrogenetic models and define mixing parameters for SFCR plutons, combined trace-element and isotopic compositional variations were examined for correlations predicted by such a model. Because SFCR Rb and Sr relations were reported by Fleck and Criss (1985) and Criss and Fleck (1987), these are not described in detail, but are included in discussions.

Sm and Nd

Because the REE reside primarily in accessory phases, measured concentrations of Nd or Sm, although precisely determined by isotope dilution, are subject to enormous sampling inhomogeneities. For this reason, element ratios are much more reliable measures of REE relations. A correlation of Sm/Nd with $\epsilon_{Nd}(t)$ may be produced by natural radioactive decay (a Sm-Nd isochron) or by a mixing process during petrogenesis. Although mixing may occur during partial melting or fractional crystallization, these latter processes do not themselves produce correlated isotopic–trace-element variations (Allegre and Minster, 1978; Briqueu and Lancelot, 1979; Taylor, 1980; DePaolo, 1981). As discussed by DePaolo (1981) and Fleck and Criss (1985), mixing processes may produce "pseudoisochrons" that may, but do not necessarily, have age significance. As shown in Figure 5, variation of $\epsilon_{Nd}(t)$ with Sm/Nd in plutons of the SFCR is unquestionably related to mixing, but these data reveal significantly more information about the process than was evident in Sr data (Fleck and Criss, 1985). If all SFCR pluton data are considered together, the resulting data array forms a "crescent moon" pattern with a negative slope at low $\epsilon_{Nd}(t)$ and a positive slope for higher values. On the diagram this difference occurs between $\epsilon_{Nd}(t) = -8$ and -10 and is located geographically 3 to 5 km east of the WISZ (Fig. 2). No values of $\epsilon_{Nd}(t)$ greater than -9 occur east of this point, which represents the eastern margin of a north-south–trending septum of Proterozoic quartzite, schist, and migmatite. Samples west of this point and spanning the suture zone have $\epsilon_{Nd}(t) > -9$ and are assigned to Group 1 for discussion here.

Samples east of the Proterozoic septum fall into two groups in Figure 5: one with a nearly constant $\epsilon_{Nd}(t)$ between -12.6 and -10, assigned here to Group 2, and the other with $\epsilon_{Nd}(t) < -14$, assigned to Group 3. One could argue that by varying the bulk

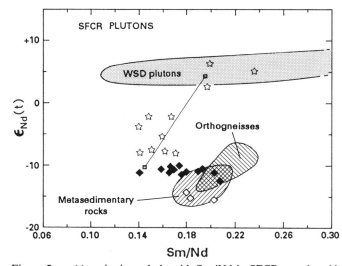

Figure 5. $\epsilon_{Nd}(t)$ varies irregularly with Sm/Nd in SFCR samples. Although plutons with the lowest $\epsilon_{Nd}(t)$ coincide with measured values for Precambrian orthogneiss and metasedimentary rock samples, the distribution of the remaining SFCR samples is difficult to achieve with a two-end-member mixture. If samples are grouped geographically, more regular trends appear in the data: Group 1 (stars) includes all SFCR plutons within 1 km west of the WISZ and up to 4 km east; Group 2 (solid diamonds) includes all remaining samples east of Group 1 except the three lowest $\epsilon_{Nd}(t)$ rocks (Group 3—open diamonds), which appear to be related to metasedimentary wall-rocks. Squares locate end members of Group 1 plutons discussed later. The limited variation of $\epsilon_{Nd}(t)$ in Group 2 is consistent with partial melting of Proterozoic crust, but also could be produced by mixtures of melts from sources of similar age.

distribution coefficients and invoking assimilation–fractional crystallization models, two endmembers might be mixed to produce the SFCR Nd systematics. As discussed in detail by Fleck and Criss (1985), however, such a model is either unnecessary or insignificant in explaining ϵ_{Sr} and Rb-Sr variations. These data argue strongly for a minimum of three distinct end members to produce the observed variations in the SFCR suite.

Group 1 plutons intrude both the WSD and Belt-Yellowjacket terranes, extending as much as 3 km east of the Western Idaho Suture Zone. Samples of these bodies vary in composition, ranging from biotite hornblende tonalite to biotite muscovite monzogranite. Their distribution in Figure 5, although exhibiting significant scatter, falls along a trend compatible with binary mixing between magmatic arc melts, such as the average WSD plutons, and a LREE-enriched Proterozoic source. Group 2 samples have Sm/Nd ratios ranging from highly LREE-enriched values of 0.14 to about 0.2, where values fall in the field of measurements of the wall-rock orthogneisses (Fig. 5). In view of the nearly constant $\epsilon_{Nd}(t)$ of Group 2 at a value nearly identical to the average orthogneiss sampled, partial melting (anatexis), with its resultant LREE enrichment, represents an attractive model. All three Group 3 samples lie in the field of measured metasedimentary wall rocks. Because these three samples were

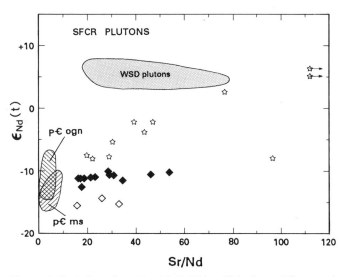

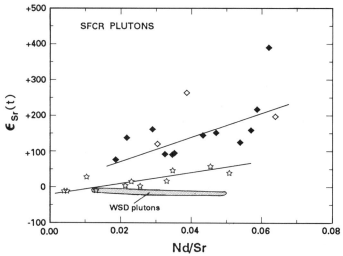

Figure 6. Variation of ϵ_{Nd}(t) with Sr/Nd exhibits large differences in ϵ_{Nd}(t) in Group 1, consistent with mixing of a high Sr, volcanic-arc melt (ϵ_{Nd}(t) = +3 to +6) with a Proterozoic component with intermediate Sr/Nd. Note that groups 1 and 2 define trends intersecting at a point within the fields of Proterozoic wall rocks, whereas Sm/Nd variations (Fig. 5) intersect at Group 2 values most *different* from the wall rocks. This paradox requires a process more complex than two-end-member mixing and demonstrates that isotope ratio plots, such as $\epsilon_{Nd}/\epsilon_{Sr}$, may be misleading. Group 3 data indicate no clear trend. Symbols and patterned fields as in Figure 5.

Figure 7. Plot of ϵ_{Sr}(t) versus Nd/Sr permits identification of strong trends for Groups 1 and 2, which clearly have different end members. As discussed by Fleck and Criss (1985), only the highest Sr (lowest Nd/Sr here) WSD plutons (shaded area) could represent lower end members for SFCR magmas. Geographic groupings here show that Group 2 plutons are incompatible with such a source and are more consistent with an older, possibly lower-crust source. The high Sr, low Nd/Sr members of these trends argue for incorporation of a Sr-rich component such as plagioclase from sources with significantly different ϵ_{Sr}(t) values. Precambrian wall rocks plot well off the diagram (see Table 1). Group 3 data are poorly constrained. Symbols as in Figure 5.

collected adjacent to Proterozoic migmatites and metasedimentary units, a metasedimentary component in the magmas is not improbable. In fact, sample 807-29A is from the same outcrop of muscovite biotite granite studied by Hoover (1987), which, on the basis of REE studies, she concluded was contaminated by metasedimentary wall rock.

Sr and Nd

ϵ_{Sr} and ϵ_{Nd} correlations (Fig. 4) suggest that Sr and Nd concentrations would reveal similar covariations. Although those relations are present, the complexities noted in Figures 4 and 5 are especially apparent in Sr/Nd versus ϵ_{Nd} (Fig. 6) and Nd/Sr versus ϵ_{Sr} (Fig. 7) diagrams. The data groups defined by geographic, ϵ_{Nd}, and Sm/Nd parameters exhibit distinctly different linear correlations. These variation trends indicate at least three and probably five different end members for the suite, but support binary mixing between geographically restricted groups. Consequently, SFCR plutons within about 3 km of the suture (Group 1) reflect mixing between a Mesozoic or late Paleozoic, high-Sr, marginal-arc component (Sr/Nd = 70 to 75, ϵ_{Sr} = –10 to –15, ϵ_{Nd} = +3 to +5) and a lower-Sr, Proterozoic crustal component (Sr/Nd = 15 to 20, ϵ_{Sr} = 60 to 100, ϵ_{Nd} = –8 to –11) (Figs. 6 and 7).

Sr/Nd data from Group 2 plutons indicate little or no direct involvement with Mesozoic arc-related magmas (Fig. 6). For ϵ_{Nd}

values of the high-Sr end member of this group to be greater than –8 would require Sr/Nd ratios greater than 90, and to approach the +6 values of WSD plutons would require impossibly high Sr/Nd. As with Sm/Nd variations, Sr/Nd systematics are not inconsistent with a partial-melting trend (constant ϵ_{Nd}) for Group 2 samples; ϵ_{Sr} results are not constant, but are correlated with Rb, Sr, and Rb/Sr (Fleck and Criss, 1985; Table 1) and cannot accommodate such a model. Therefore, components of Group 2 plutons must have similar ϵ_{Nd} and Sm/Nd, but significantly different Rb, Sr, and ϵ_{Sr}. Regression of Group 2 data yields a small, negative slope with ϵ_{Nd}(t) end members at about –10.4 and –11.3 for reasonable Sr/Nd values.

The number of data and limited variation of ϵ_{Nd} and Sr/Nd in Group 3 provide little insight into magmatic components (Fig. 6). Rb/Sr and ϵ_{Sr} are equally inconclusive because of enormous scatter. The degree of scatter and absence of systematic element–isotope trends would be consistent with local variations in metasedimentary contaminants, but open-system behavior of magma systems would provide an equally valid explanation.

Zr, Y, and Nb

Concentrations of Nb, Zr, and Y were measured as part of this study to evaluate mixing models and potential source materials (Table 2). Similar isotopic and chemical (including trace element) studies of volcanic rocks of the western Snake River

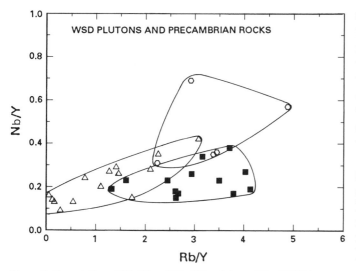

Figure 8. Covariation of Rb/Y and Nb/Y in plutons of the WSD terrane (open triangles), Precambrian orthogneisses (solid squares), and Precambrian metasedimentary rocks (open hexagons) defines different fields, but with overlap at Rb/Y values above 1.2 and at Nb/Y values less than 0.4 (most of the measured Nb/Y values).

Plain and areas to the west reveal a strong correlation of isotopic variations as a function of position relative to the southern extension of the WISZ (Hart, 1985; Leeman and Hawksworth, 1986). However, Hart (1985), Leeman and Hawksworth (1986), and other authors reported the absence of a strong correlation of $\delta^{18}O$ and elemental ratios with the radiogenic isotope ratios in petrologically uniform groups of basalts. They argued that this indicates an absence of crustal contamination of the volcanic rocks. Leeman and Hawksworth (1986) demonstrated the useful constraints placed on source materials by combined trace-element and isotopic studies. As in the examples discussed by the above authors, Nb, Zr, and Y variations in SFCR samples and potential source materials clarify trends suggested by isotopic variations.

Variations of Rb/Y and Nb/Y ratios in the WSD and Precambrian wall-rock samples are shown in Figure 8. WSD samples reveal a linear array (correlation coefficient, r = 0.88), the slope of which indicates an average Rb/Nb ratio of 9.65, but measured Rb/Nb values average 4.75. Precambrian metasediments and orthogneisses yield less linear variations (r = 0.38 and 0.31, respectively), reflecting the heterogeneity expected in these materials. Orthogneisses yield an average Rb/Nb of 13.6, consistent with the higher ratios expected in continental crustal materials (Pearce and others, 1984; Leeman and Hawksworth, 1986). Metasedimentary rocks yield an average Rb/Nb of only 7.9 due to some high Nb values. In spite of the somewhat different trends of the data, significant overlap in Rb/Y and Nb/Y ratios occurs between the accreted arc plutons (WSD) and Precambrian upper crust (combined wall-rock data).

Plutons of the SCFR, considered as a single group, exhibit a wide variation in Rb and Nb values (Table 2). Such a range

should be expected if mixing of materials of widely different ratios is the primary control in petrogenesis. If the three-group model suggested by Sm/Nd variations (Fig. 5) is used in grouping the plutons, however, a significantly better correlation is observed within Groups 2 and 3 (Fig. 9). Group 1 plutons exhibit a wide and unsystematic variation (Fig. 9A). An average Rb/Nb for these plutons is about 6, suggesting a significant amount of noncrustal material, but is of little consequence numerically due to the wide scatter.

Group 2 plutons, with $-10.0 > \epsilon_{Nd}(t) > -12.6$, form a much more systematic array (r = 0.75) in Rb/Y versus Nb/Y, corresponding to an average Rb/Nb of 10.35 (Fig. 9b). This high Rb/Nb ratio suggests an evolved (crustal) component, and the more uniform Rb/Nb is consistent with either a relatively uniform crustal source or binary mixing. The Group 3 Rb/Y versus Nb/Y trend shows low dispersion and an Rb/Nb ratio of about 14 (Fig. 9c). These results are also consistent with significant melting of a crustal source, but one different from that of Group 2. Wall-rock averages of Rb/Nb = 13.6 for orthogneisses and 7.9 for metasedimentary rocks suggest that neither Group 2 nor 3 plutons were derived solely from either of these exposed Proterozoic rock groups, but that some mixture of crustal sources is necessary. This also supplements ϵ_{Nd} and Sm/Nd evidence that the primary components of Group 2 melts were derived from Proterozoic crust. The linearity of the Group 2 data (Fig. 9b) and intercepts with x and y axes near the origin are most consistent with a two-component mixing model in which both components have similar Rb/Nb ratios, but quite different Rb/Y and Nb/Y values.

One of the most important aspects of the Rb/Y versus Nb/Y variations in SFCR plutons relates to the significantly higher Rb/Y ratios of all three groups when compared to the WSD and Precambrian rock samples (Fig. 9). All but a few of the SFCR pluton samples have Rb/Y and Nb/Y values above the range of the WSD, metasedimentary, and orthogneiss samples (Figs. 8 and 9). Comparing these variations to Rb versus Nb arrays (Fig. 10), however, reveals that Rb and Nb values of the plutons generally fall between those of WSD and Precambrian samples. The only exceptions are the Nb values of Group 1 plutons, which are clearly above the binary mixing array of all remaining samples. The Rb/Y and Nb/Y ratios of all pluton groups (Fig. 9) are above Precambrian wall-rock values solely because Y values in SFCR plutons are very low. If Precambrian wall rocks reflect compositions of the source of high-Rb, high-$\epsilon_{Sr}(t)$ components in these plutons, Y was strongly partitioned from the magmas. Hoover (1987) reported HREE values of Precambrian rocks significantly higher than any SFCR plutons, in agreement with observed Y relations. These observations indicate a magmatic or fluid history for the high-$\epsilon_{Sr}(t)$ component, from which Y and HREE were partitioned prior to mixing.

Elevated Nb in Group 1 plutons, diverging from the trend of WSD, Precambrian rocks, and Group 2 and 3 plutons (Fig. 10), supports the presence in near-suture zone magmas of a component not represented by either arc magmas or exposed (i.e.,

R. J. Fleck

TABLE 2. TRACE ELEMENT RESULTS FOR
ROCKS OF THE SOUTH FORK CLEARWATER RIVER AREA (SFCR), IDAHO

Specimen Number	Rb	Sr	Zr	Y	Nb
PLUTONS OF THE SFCR					
797-26E	26.2	806	107	12.6	8.42
797-26H	114	562	147	16.5	10.1
797-26I	46.5	901	227	20.9	13.2
807-27A	23.2	832	123	5.17	2.89
807-27C	38.2	852	158	4.62	7.73
807-28B	33.3	1228	186	19.5	21.9
807-28F	54.8	988	155	11.8	14.3
807-28G	45.6	842	156	4.07	8.42
807-28H	29.9	1406	268	11.8	9.11
807-28I	41.7	709	152	12.9	31.2
807-29A	110	461	98.7	12.9	9.11
807-29B	104	529	125	11.8	9.11
807-29C	96.8	599	140	9.57	9.11
807-29D	65.5	726	164	7.92	7.73
807-29F	98.5	449		21.1	13.2
807-29H	62.9	672	144	13.4	5.31
807-29I	108	407	135	10.1	8.07
807-29J	97.8	710	167	15.1	14.6
807-30A	72.7	570	118	9.02	8.07
807-30B	66.0	517	136	16.2	6.34
807-30C	88.3	479	92.9	19.5	10.1
807-30D	59.2	610	129	17.8	6.69
807-30I	113	326	86.7	14.0	9.80
807-30J	83.7	433	135	9.57	6.00
837-28H	97.0	724	277	25.8	15.3
PLUTONS OF THE WSD TERRANE					
797-25F	23.1	615	123	20.9	4.27
797-25I	9.48	334	43.8	17.6	2.20
797-26A	7.14	269	60.8	25.3	2.20
797-26B	15.4	635	126	12.1	3.23
818-10F	23.7	756	183	7.7	3.23
818-10G	46.6	587	282	33.0	9.45
818-11C	3.68	661	104	23.1	2.89
818-11D	12.8	682	94.9	16.5	3.93
818-11E	8.3	864	89.0		2.20
818-11F	25.7	629	68.5	17.6	4.62
818-11G	21.1	773	70.4	9.35	3.23
827-28D	0.67	280	63.5	13.8	2.20
827-28E	2.76	764	72.8	22.6	3.23
827-28F	32.3	467	131	18.7	2.89
827-28G	42.8	535	129	20.4	5.65
PRECAMBRIAN METASEDIMENTARY ROCKS					
797-25C	180	112	216	53.3	18.4
797-26F	96.9	88.2	220	28.1	10.1
807-31J	84.1	298	221	37.6	11.5
808-1C	62.8	60.6	257	12.9	7.38
837-28G	182	548	631	62.1	42.6

TABLE 2. TRACE ELEMENT RESULTS FOR
ROCKS OF THE SOUTH FORK CLEARWATER RIVER AREA (SFCR), IDAHO (continued)

Specimen Number	Rb	Sr	Zr	Y	Nb
PRECAMBRIAN ORTHOGENEISSES					
807-30E	117	163	245	44.8	8.07
807-30F	114	167	285	70.6	16.4
807-30G	67.3	189	217	50.8	9.45
807-30H	106	192	280	39.8	6.69
807-30K	284	94.3	260	75.0	12.9
808-1D	123	203	251	50.2	11.5
808-1E	196	124	211	48.6	12.9
808-1F	194	93.7	230	47.0	9.11
808-1G	178	88.3	242	50.8	11.9
808-1H	143	176	254	54.7	8.07
808-1J	154	130	217	52.4	13.6
808-1K	117	194	283	37.1	12.6
808-1L	158	247	369	42.6	16.4

sampled) wall rocks. Considering Group 1 samples alone, Nb exhibits no significant correlation with Sr or $\epsilon_{Sr}(t)$, which vary inversely with each other (Fleck and Criss, 1985). This absence of correlation with Sr suggests that the high Nb, low Rb/Nb component has neither high Sr nor high $\epsilon_{Sr}(t)$, because large contributions of either from this highly variable "third" component are inconsistent with the well-defined Sr-$\epsilon_{Sr}(t)$ covariation of Group 1 plutons (Fleck and Criss, 1985).

Concentrations of Zr and Y (Fig. 11) illustrate most clearly the inadequacy of bulk wall-rock assimilation as a model of mixing in SFCR magmas. Significant overlap in Zr and Y contents exists between the three groups of plutons and those of the WSD. Precambrian samples, however, are significantly higher in both Zr and Y and do not lie along any trend in SFCR data. In addition, Group 2 plutons, which contain larger contributions of Proterozoic components (high ϵ_{Sr}, low ϵ_{Nd}) than Group 1 plutons, have even lower Zr. Even if Y contents of a Proterozoic component were reduced prior to mixing, if this component were also the primary source of Zr, Group 2 plutons should have more Zr than Group 1. Even more critically, Group 2 rocks exhibit a surprisingly strong positive correlation between Sr and Zr (r = 0.77), rather than the expected inverse if Zr were derived from the low-Sr Precambrian components. These relations indicate that, although Zr and Y are both abundant in Precambrian wall rocks, neither is contributed to the SFCR melts by such a component. The consequences of these observations and resulting models of mixing are discussed in the following sections.

DISCUSSION

Three general petrogenetic models were mentioned as potential mechanisms for producing the observed isotopic and trace-element variations. That these correlations require some form of mixing of end members with significantly different values seems well established. *Magma mixing* would require partial melting of different, and probably physically separate, source regions and subsequent mixing of these fluid melts. *Contamination* is the result of en masse incorporation (assimilation) of tracts of country rock through which a magma passes as it rises within the crust and mantle. *Source mixing* envisions a previous "enriching' event within part of the subcontinental lithosphere (mantle metasomatism) or lower crust, which is then melted along with "normal" or "depleted" mantle to produce the correlated isotopic variations. All models require a thermal event to produce melting. A contamination model requires sufficient heat within the zone of assimilation so that small amounts of heat produced by the magma crystallizing can melt the incorporated tracts of country rock. Trace element data cast doubt on the viability of bulk assimilation of SFCR country rock. The Rb/Y and Nb/Y results suggest that Y values of average upper crust in the SFCR region are far too high and pluton values too low for simple wall-rock assimilation. Although Y contents of lower crustal rocks might well be lower than those of upper crustal Precambrian rocks sampled, the necessity of providing high Rb/Sr, high $\epsilon_{Sr}(t)$, and LREE-enriched "upper end-member" magmas from lower crust becomes more difficult.

Although evaluating models of enriched (metasomatized) mantle or lower crust is made difficult by the inherent flexibility of the model and inaccessibility of the deep-seated "study area," several parameters in the region of the SFCR cast doubt on its adequacy without additional upper crustal components. Mafic dikes within the Idaho batholith are abundant, and many show emplacement-level, synplutonic (magma mixing) relations with the granites (Hyndman and Foster, 1988). If all mixing were source mixing, synplutonic dikes and evidence of high-level mixing should be uncommon. Eocene volcanic and plutonic rocks of

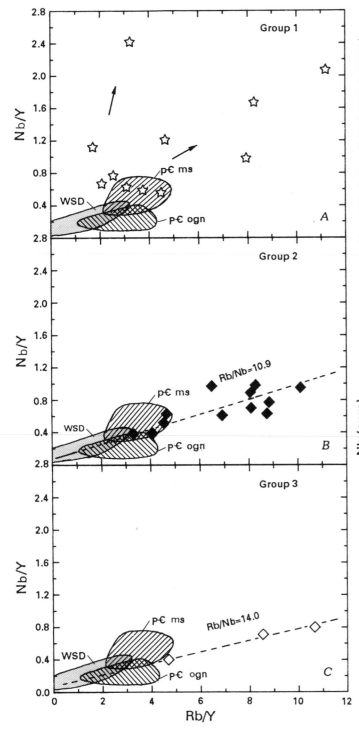

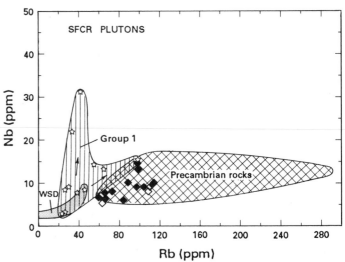

Figure 9. Covariation of Rb/Y and Nb/Y in SFCR plutons (symbols as in Fig. 5). Fields of WSD plutons and Precambrian orthogneisses and metasedimentary rocks (Fig. 8) are patterned as in Figure 5. Note that none of these fields provides an acceptable source for the high Rb/Y and high Nb/Y components of any of the SFCR pluton groups. A: Group 1 plutons show large scatter, with at least two trends required. Arrows define Rb/Nb trends at about 0.8 (steeper) and 6.0 as shown. B: Regression of Group 2 results (dashed line) indicates an average Rb/Nb of 10.9. This trend could be produced by mixing of any of the three sources shown with a high Rb/Y, Nb/Y component. Alternatively, a partial melt of any of the three under conditions increasing Rb/Y dramatically and Nb/Y to a lesser extent in the melt could achieve the same result. C: Group 3 samples are limited but define an array with Rb/Nb of about 14.0. The high Rb/Nb suggests crustal involvement and might be produced by either of the mechanisms discussed for Group 2.

Figure 10. Rb versus Nb diagram, showing coherent variations of Groups 2 and 3 (symbols as in Fig. 5) between the distributions of data for WSD plutons and Precambrian samples. Comparison with Figure 9 demonstrates that anomalous Rb/Y and Nb/Y variations are due largely to greatly reduced Y in SFCR magmas. Group 1 distributions, however, still reflect much higher Nb relative to Rb and support a minimum of 3 sources for these components, as appears indicated by Sm/Nd and Nd isotopic variations. The high Nb, low Rb/Nb component, apparent only in Group 1, is more typical of oceanic island basalt (OIB) sources than of continental-crustal or volcanic-arc sources, and helps explain the scatter in other trace-element variations in this group.

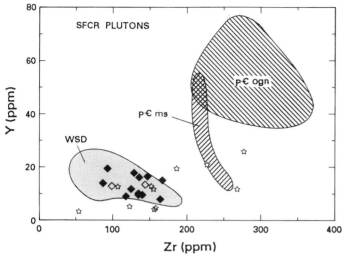

Figure 11. Covariation of Zr and Y documents the inadequacy of bulk wall-rock assimilation as a source of high ϵ_{Sr}, low ϵ_{Nd} components. The presence of these components in SFCR Groups 2 and 3, however, suggests partial melting of such upper crustal sources under conditions where Y and the heavy REE remain in the residue, possibly in garnet or hornblende. This is consistent with the light REE enrichment indicated in Table 1 and Figure 5. Zr and Y in Group 1 data are positively correlated (r = 0.70), demonstrating that the high Nb component of these magmas is not "anomalous" in Zr/Y relative to the other components. Symbols and patterns as in Figure 5.

TABLE 3. REGRESSION PARAMETERS FOR MIXING TRENDS IN SFCR

X-axis	Y-axis	Slope	Y-Intercept	r
GROUP #1 PLUTONS				
Nd/Sr	$\epsilon_{Sr}(t)$	1931.6	-38.13	0.82
Sr/Nd	$\epsilon_{Nd}(t)$	0.2456	-13.35	0.91
Sm/Nd	$\epsilon_{Nd}(t)$	238.6	-42.71	0.70
Sm/Sr	$\epsilon_{Sr}(t)$	11453	-34.07	0.85
1/Sr	$\epsilon_{Sr}(t)$	105566	-95.63	0.68
Rb	Nb	0.1386	3.732	0.83
Rb	Y	0.26585	0.0007	....
GROUP #2 PLUTONS				
Nd/Sr	$\epsilon_{Sr}(t)$	2247	-41.83	0.66
Sr/Nd	$\epsilon_{Nd}(t)$	0.02976	-11.75	0.57
Sm/Nd	$\epsilon_{Nd}(t)$	-11.85	-8.81	-0.38
1/Sr	$\epsilon_{Sr}(t)$	183162	-199.7	0.91
Rb/Y	Nb/Y	0.09198	0.06638	0.75
Nb	Nb	7.372	19.22	0.61
Sr	Zr	0.1912	22.93	0.77
GROUP #3 PLUTONS				
Rb/Y	Nb/Y	0.07149	0.0676	0.99

the Challis type (Armstrong, 1974; Fleck and Criss, 1985; Criss and Fleck, 1987) yield Sr$_i$ as low as 0.704, yet presumably encountered or were derived from the same lithosphere as the Late Cretaceous granites. Dikes associated with these epizonal plutons show no evidence of mixing with Idaho batholith or wall rocks. Hart (1985) provided valuable evidence of enriched mantle in Tertiary basalts in the tectonically extended region of the western Snake River Plain, but these rocks are far from granitic, have Sr$_i$ less than 0.708, and show no covariation of $\delta^{18}O$ with isotopic or trace-element parameters. The Idaho batholith contains true granites, including two-mica granites (Criss and Fleck, 1987; Hoover, 1987), with Si$_i$ > 0.730 and correlated $\delta^{18}O$, ϵ_{Sr}, ϵ_{Nd}, and trace-element variations. The volume of high-silica magma severely extends models requiring a largely subcrustal source. Finally, the strong geographic relation of the 0.712 Sr$_i$ contour in the Idaho batholith to exposures of Precambrian wall rocks (cf., Figs. 6.1 and 6.2 of Criss and Fleck, 1987) suggests a genetic link between exposed upper crust and high initial ratios.

Magma mixing is considered here the most probable model of petrogenesis of SFCR plutons. Synplutonic mafic dikes exhibit mixing relations with the granitic bodies (Hyndman and Foster, 1988). Partial melting of a siliceous Proterozoic crust at depths of 15 to 20 km provides the best source of the high–ϵ_{Sr}, low–ϵ_{Nd} components of SFCR magmas. By melting this heterogeneous source within the stability field of garnet and zircon, Y and the heavy REE can be reduced in the resulting melt. A less probable alternative might involve crystal fractionation of these minerals or

hornblende prior to mixing, but the amount of fractionation would be very large with hornblende. High-Sr tonalite (arc andesitic) melts with low Rb/Sr, Rb/Nb, and $\epsilon_{Sr}(t)$ are likely candidates for another end member of SFCR magmas, as discussed by Fleck and Criss (1985). Finally, magmas enriched in high-field-strength elements such as Nb and Zr, but with low to moderate REE and Sr may represent a suite of intermediate Sr$_i$ magmas. These could represent lower crust, enriched subcontinental lithosphere, or within-plate melts (Pearce and others, 1984; Leeman and Hawksworth, 1986). Sm/Nd results for Group 3 plutons suggest a possible high-level component derived from Middle Proterozoic metasedimentary rocks either as melts or by small amounts of contamination of other mixtures. This is supported to some degree by total REE results by Hoover (1987), but magma mixing is shown to be dominant by some of the trace-element results.

Linear regression (York, 1969) of isotopic and trace-element trends (Table 3) permits approximation of end-member concentrations for Groups 1 and 2 (Table 4). These end members, identified by their Sr isotopic ratios as the low or high value for each group, represent the melts prior to mixing, not the source compositions. Group 1 plutons require high Sr concentrations (about 1,250 ppm) for the lower end member (A). A plagioclase-rich source or Sr-enriched subcontinental lithosphere are possible candidates. Zr, Nb, and Rb are low in this melt, which is similar to volcanic arc magmas except for the enormous Sr concentration. The high end member of Group 1 plutons (B) is based on

TABLE 4. MIXING-MODEL END-MEMBERS AND SFCR WALL-ROCK AVERAGES

Element/ Ratio	Group #1 A	Group #1 B	Anom.	Group #2 C	Group #2 D	WSD Ave.	PE Sed.	PE ogn	CC1 Hart (1985)	CC2 Hart (1985)
$\varepsilon_{Sr}(t)$	-11.2	60	0	60	675	-14.7	824	1073	65	504
$\varepsilon_{Nd}(t)$	4.3	-10.3	0	-10.4	-11.3	5.66	-13.63	-10.65	-10	-10
Rb	23	85	30	65	135	19.07	121	150	20	95
Sr	1250	725	250	725	210	571	221	159	415	276
Zr	93	275	275	160	63	111	309	257		
Nb	5.8	15	40	7	13	3.8	18.02	11.5		
Y	6.6	23	15	13	17	18.5	38.8	51.1		
Sm	3.4	5.5	5.5	2.1	5.2	3.08	8.76	8.99	4.4	4.5
Nd	17.4	38	23	14	25	14.19	47.45	42.69	22	26
Rb/Sr	0.0184	0.1172	0.1200	0.0897	0.6429	0.0334	0.5475	0.9434	0.0482	0.3442
Sm/Nd	0.1954	0.1447	0.2391	0.1500	0.2080	0.2171	0.1846	0.2106	0.2000	0.1731
Sr/Nd	72	19	11	52	8	40	5	4	19	11
Sr/Sm	368	132	45	345	40	185	25	18	94	61
Sr/Zr	13.4	2.6	0.9	4.5	3.3	5.1	0.7	0.6		
Rb/Nb	4.0	5.7	0.8	9.3	10.4	5.0	6.7	13.0		
Rb/Y	3.5	3.7	2.0	5.0	7.9	1.0	3.1	2.9		
Nb/Y	0.88	0.65	2.67	0.54	0.76	0.21	0.46	0.23		

exclusion of a high-Nb, high-Zr component, which Rb, Nb, Zr, and Y results indicate must be present in Group 1 magmas (end member "Anom"). End member B is clearly from an old, LREE-enriched source, as $\varepsilon_{Nd}(t)$ must be about –10.3 and Sm/Nd is about 0.14 to 0.15 (Table 4). This represents a Proterozoic $\varepsilon_{Nd}(t)$ similar to orthogneisses of the SFCR, but $\varepsilon_{Sr}(t)$ values are retarded more like a lower crustal, perhaps granulitic source. Sr in this component remains high, but not unreasonable for lower crustal partial melts. Zr, Nb, and Nd are very high in end-member "Anom," reflecting both a LREE-enriched partial melt and the elevated high-field-strength elements of within-plate magmas. Sm/Nd ratios are very low, reflecting this. Rb/Nb in Group 1 rocks are low, but with large dispersion due to at least three components in the melts (A, B, and Anom).

Group 2 plutons show only the most modest variation in $\varepsilon_{Nd}(t)$, but most other parameters require significant differences in end members. Values of $\varepsilon_{Sr}(t)$, $\varepsilon_{Nd}(t)$, Sr, and Sm/Nd in the low end member (C) are the same or nearly the same as in end member B of Group 1 (Table 4). In fact, the constant trends in these parameters suggest that B and C are merely variations in a lower crustal source with identification complicated by the Anom component. The Anom component has the character of sublithospheric, high-Nb, high-Zr, within-plate melts. Small amounts of the Anom component may be present in some Group 2 plutons (Fig. 10), but whether this accounts for differences in components B and C cannot be determined. The high-$\varepsilon_{Sr}(t)$ end member of Group 2 melts (D) is clearly upper crustal in origin. Whereas $\varepsilon_{Sr}(t)$ is low in components B and C, measured values in Group 2 require a component with $\varepsilon_{Sr}(t) > 400$. A mantle or lower crustal source is highly improbable. Proterozoic upper crust is the preferred source of component D, which is similar to an average of

observed wall-rock metasedimentary rocks and orthogneisses (Table 4), except in Zr and Y. As mentioned for lower crustal components, partial melting with garnet and zircon in the residue could produce the required reduction in these elements. This fractionating event would have occurred as a part of Cretaceous anatexis, however, whereas the formation of Rb-depleted lower crust must have occurred during the Middle Proterozoic.

The components of Group 2 plutons, with the exception of any contribution from the Anom end member (Table 4), were derived from Proterozoic crust or a combination of crust and enriched subcontinental lithosphere. Partial melting of lower crust, such as that calculated by Hart (1985) and shown as CC1 (Table 4), can yield melts with elemental abundances very similar to components B and C (Table 4). Using bulk distribution coefficients of 0.2, 0.5, 1.5, and 1.1 for Rb, Sr, Sm, and Nd, respectively, a good match is obtained for batch melts of 10 to 15 percent. Isotopic ratios of CC1 were modified from those of Hart (1985) to reflect 1800-Ma Proterozoic lower crust. A granulite facies event is postulated at 1500 Ma, when abundant orthogneisses (once granodiorite to granite) were emplaced in the 1800-Ma crust. Assuming an original Rb/Sr of 0.344 (Hart's [1985] value for CC2 upper crust; see Table 4) was reduced to his CC1 value of 0.048 at 1500 Ma, at 80 Ma this granulitic crust would have had an average $^{87}Sr/^{86}Sr$ of 0.7091 ($\varepsilon_{Sr} = 65$). That value is similar to the lowest values of the "main phase" of the Bitterroot lobe of the Idaho batholith immediately northeast of the SFCR (Fleck and Criss, 1985). In that study this lower limit was considered to represent the average for lower crust for the region. Group 2 plutons of the SFCR can be modeled successfully as mixtures of upper-crust (CC2) and lower-crust (CC1) components derived by partial melting. Heat for this anatexis could have been supplied by the abundant synplutonic dikes (Hyndman and Foster, 1988).

Group 3 rocks have low $\epsilon_{Nd}(t)$ and intermediate $\epsilon_{Sr}(t)$ as well as some of the characteristics of melts contaminated by metasedimentary rocks. The low isotopic ratios are typical of Rb-depleted sources and may reflect a combination of lower crustal and metasedimentary upper crustal sources. The latter may be due primarily to simple wall-rock contamination caused by the proximity of samples to the margins of large sedimentary septa (Hoover, 1987; Myers, 1982). Like Group 2, Group 3 rocks have high Rb/Nb ratios and strong crustal signatures. Model ages calculated from Sm/Nd results suggest crustal residences of 1700 to 2000 Ma, but because the ultimate degree of mixing and partial-melt fractionation of Sm/Nd are not constrained, these estimates could be inaccurate.

ACKNOWLEDGMENTS

I am grateful to William P. Leeman, William K. Hart, Ronald Kistler, Marvin Lanphere, and an anonymous reviewer for thoughtful reviews that provided substantial improvements in the manuscript. I appreciate analytical work by Susan Gunn, John Hawk, and Mary Taylor. Robert Criss gets special thanks for advice and encouragement as well as for $\delta^{18}O$ data, which were discussed in our previous joint papers, but are compared to Nd variations here. Finally, I thank Lawford Anderson for convening the symposium and shepherding manuscripts for this volume.

REFERENCES CITED

Allegre, C. J., and Minster, J. F., 1978, Quantitative models of trace element behavior in magmatic processes: Earth and Planetary Science Letters, v. 38, p. 1–25.

Armstrong, R. L., 1974, Geochronometry of the Eocene volcanic-plutonic episode in Idaho: Northwest Geology, v. 3, p. 1–15.

—— , 1975, The geochronometry of Idaho: Isochron/West, no. 14, 50 p.

—— , 1976, The geochronometry of Idaho: Isochron/West, no. 15, p. 1–33.

Armstrong, R. L., Taubeneck, W. H., and Hales, P. O., 1977, Rb-Sr and K-Ar geochronometry of Mesozoic granitic rocks and their Sr isotopic composition, Oregon, Washington, and Idaho: Geological Society of American Bulletin, v. 88, p. 397–411.

Briqueu, L., and Lancelot, J. R., 1979, Rb-Sr systematics and crustal contamination models for calc-alkaline igneous rocks: Earth and Planetary Science Letters, v. 43, p. 385–396.

Brooks, H. C., and Vallier, T. L., 1978, Mesozoic rocks and tectonic evolution of eastern Oregon and western Idaho, in Howell, D. G., and McDougall, K. A., eds., Mesozoic paleogeography of the western United States: Pacific Section, Society of Economic Paleontologists and Mineralogists Pacific Coast Paleogeography Symposium 2, p. 133–145.

Criss, R. E., and Fleck, R. J., 1987, Petrogenesis, geochronology, and hydrothermal systems of the northern Idaho Batholith and adjacent areas based on $^{18}O/^{16}O$, D/H, $^{87}Sr/^{86}Sr$, K-Ar, and $^{40}Ar/^{39}Ar$ studies: U.S. Geological Survey Professional Paper 1436, p. 95–137.

DePaolo, D. J., 1981, Trace element and isotopic effects of combined wallrock assimilation and fractional crystallization: Earth and Planetary Science Letters, v. 53, p. 189–202.

DePaolo, D. J., and Wasserburg, G. J., 1976, Nd isotopic variations and petro-

genetic models: Geophysical Research Letters, v. 3, no. 5, p. 249–252.

—— , 1977, The sources of island arcs as indicated by Nd and Sr isotopic studies: Geophysical Research Letters, v. 4, no. 10, p. 465–468.

—— , 1979, Petrogenetic mixing models and Nd-Sr isotopic patterns: Geochimica et Cosmochimica Acta, v. 43, p. 615–627.

Fleck, R. J., and Criss, R. E., 1985, Strontium and oxygen isotopic variations in Mesozoic and Tertiary plutons of central Idaho: Contributions to Mineralogy and Petrology, v. 90, p. 291–308.

Fleck, R. J., Greenwood, W. R., Hadley, D. G., Anderson, R. E., and Schmidt, D. L., 1980, Rubidium-strontium geochronology and plate-tectonic evolution of the southern part of the Arabian Shield: U.S. Geological Survey Professional Paper 1131, 33 p.

Hart, W. K., 1985, Chemical and isotopic evidence for mixing between depleted and enriched mantle, northwestern U.S.A.: Geochimica et Cosmochimica Acta, v. 49, p. 131–144.

Hoover, A. L., 1987, Transect across the Salmon River suture, South Fork of the Clearwater River, western Idaho; Rare earth element geochemical, structural, and metamorphic study [M.S. thesis]: Corvallis, Oregon State University, 138 p.

Hyndman, D. W., and Foster, D. A., 1988, The role of tonalites and mafic dikes in the generation of the Idaho batholith: Journal of Geology, v. 96, p. 31–46.

Leeman, W. P., and Hawksworth, C. J., 1986, Open magma systems; Trace element and isotopic constraints: Journal of Geophysical Research, v. 91, p. 5901–5912.

Menzies, M. A., Leeman, W. P., and Hawksworth, C. J., 1983, Isotope geochemistry of Cenozoic volcanic rocks reveals mantle heterogeneity below western U.S.A.: Nature, v. 303, p. 205–209.

Myers, P. E., 1982, Geology of the Harpster area, Idaho County, Idaho: Idaho Bureau of Mines and Geology Bulletin 25, 46 p.

Norrish, K., and Chappell, B. W., 1967, X-ray fluorescence spectrography, in Zussman, J., ed., Physical methods in determinative mineralogy: London, Academic Press, p. 161–214.

Nye, C. J., and Reid, M. R., 1986, Geochemistry of primary and least fractionated lavas from Okmok volcano, central Aleutians; Implications of arc magma genesis: Journal of Geophysical Research, v. 91, p. 10271–10287.

O'Nions, R. K., Hamilton, P. J., and Evensen, N. M., 1977, Variations in $^{143}Nd/^{144}Nd$ and $^{87}Sr/^{86}Sr$ ratios in oceanic basalts: Earth and Planetary Science Letters, v. 34, p. 13–22.

Pearce, J. A., Harris, N.B.W., and Tindle, A. G., 1984, Trace element discrimination diagrams for the tectonic interpretation of granitic rocks: Journal of Petrology, v. 25, p. 956–983.

Taubeneck, W. H., 1971, Idaho batholith and its southern extension: Geological Society of America Bulletin, v. 82, p. 1899–1928.

Taylor, H. P., 1980, The effects of assimilation of country rocks by magmas on $^{18}O/^{16}O$ and $^{87}Sr/^{86}Sr$ systematics on igneous rocks: Earth and Planetary Science Letters, v. 47, p. 243–254.

Vallier, T. L., and Brooks, H. C., editors, 1987, The geology of the Blue Mountains: U.S. Geological Survey Professional Paper 1436, 196 p.

Vallier, T. L., Brooks, H. C., and Thayer, T. P., 1977, Paleozoic rocks of eastern Oregon and western Idaho, in Stewart, J. H., and others, eds., Paleozoic paleogeography of the western United States: Pacific Section, Society of Economic Paleontologists and Mineralogists Pacific Coast Paleogeography Symposium 1, p. 455–466.

York, D., 1969, Least-squares fitting of a straight line with correlated error: Earth and Planetary Science Letters, v. 5, p. 320–324.

Zindler, A., Hart, S. R., and Frey, F. A., 1979, Nd and Sr isotope ratios and rare earth element abundances in Reykjanes peninsula basalts; Evidence for mantle heterogeneity beneath Iceland: Earth and Planetary Science Letters, v. 45, p. 249–262.

MANUSCRIPT SUBMITTED AUGUST 18, 1987
REVISED MANUSCRIPT SUBMITTED SEPTEMBER 29, 1988
MANUSCRIPT ACCEPTED BY THE SOCIETY FEBRUARY 7, 1989

Geological Society of America
Memoir 174
1990

Chapter 22

The Colville Igneous Complex; Paleogene volcanism, plutonism, and extension in northeastern Washington

Diane H. Carlson
Geology Department, California State University, Sacramento, California 95819
Falma J. Moye
Department of Geology, Idaho State University, Pocatello, Idaho 83209

ABSTRACT

The name "Colville Igneous Complex" is proposed to include the Colville batholith and genetically related volcanic rocks. The Colville batholith, originally described as a Mesozoic composite granitic intrusion, has been redefined to include Paleocene orthogneisses and leucocratic granitic rocks and Eocene plutonic suites emplaced during early Tertiary extension in northeastern Washington. The volcanic component is coeval with the Eocene plutonic suite of the batholith. The batholith was emplaced into pre-Tertiary rocks of the Omineca crystalline belt, which includes Precambrian and Paleozoic gneisses and eugeoclinal rocks, considered part of the allochthonous Quesnel terrane which attached to the continent in Jurassic time.

The Colville Igneous Complex is divided into three components: (1) 65 ± 4 Ma orthogneisses of the Okanogan dome or complex and similar gneisses in the Kettle and Lincoln complexes; (2) 61 to 54 Ma leucocratic granitic rocks; and (3) 53 to 47 Ma intermediate to felsic volcanic-plutonic rocks. The leucocratic granites and younger volcanic-plutonic rocks are divided on the basis of age, geochemical discrimination, and emplacement mechanism. The older leucocratic granites are silica-rich, corundum-normative, and Sr and light rare earth element enriched, and they form several large, discrete, compositionally zoned plutons and intrusive suites. The younger volcanic-plutonic assemblage contains two suites: an older, compositionally restricted (68 to 72 wt% SiO_2), Sr-enriched medium-K suite, and a younger, intermediate to felsic, high-K, calc-alkalic suite.

The Colville batholith intruded during early Tertiary northwest-southeast crustal extension. The orthogneisses are characterized by a penetrative mylonitic fabric and kinematic indicators that indicate tectonic transport parallel to the extension direction. The leucocratic granites cut the gneisses but locally have a similar kinematic overprint. The younger plutonic assemblage was emplaced during maximum extension and includes northeast-trending dike swarms and elongate plutons that locally contain a weak mylonitic fabric. Coeval volcanic rocks were extruded from and confined to northeast-trending grabens.

Carlson, D. H., and Moye, F. J., 1990, The Colville Igneous Complex; Paleogene volcanism, plutonism, and extension in northeastern Washington, *in* Anderson, J. L., ed., The nature and origin of Cordilleran magmatism: Boulder, Colorado, Geological Society of America Memoir 174.

INTRODUCTION

The Colville batholith was described by Pardee (1918) as a composite granitic intrusion, probably Mesozoic in age. This definition was further expanded by Waters and Krauskopf (1941) to include gneissic rocks of the Okanogan dome that were interpreted as a protoclastic border. Staatz (1964) recognized a suite of Tertiary intrusive rocks that intrude the older granitic rocks and suggested that the name Colville batholith be reserved for the granitic rocks of probable Cretaceous age. Carlson (1984) defined the Colville batholith to include parts of the Okanogan, Kettle, and Lincoln domes or complexes, 61 to 54 Ma leucocratic granite plutons that locally contain a mylonitic fabric, and Eocene plutons and dike swarms. For this chapter, we use the definition proposed by Carlson (1984) for the batholith, and propose "Colville Igneous Complex" as an inclusive name for the batholithic components and cogenetic volcanic rocks.

Plutonic rocks of batholithic dimension and metamorphic complexes encompass a large part of the Omineca crystalline belt in northeastern Washington and southern British Columbia (Wheeler, 1970). Early workers suggested that the orogenic emplacement of the "gneiss domes" and "Cretaceous" granitic rocks was a single event followed by postorogenic Eocene volcanism and plutonism (Waters and Krauskopf, 1941; Fox and others, 1977). Recent radiometric-age studies, however, have shown that the Colville batholith contains no dated Cretaceous units and that all plutons range in age from Paleocene to Eocene (Atwater and Rinehart, 1984).

The purpose of this chapter is to present geological, geochemical, and radiometric age data to discriminate the components of the igneous complex and to discuss the emplacement history of each. The complex is divided into: (1) 65-Ma orthogneisses of the Okanogan, Kettle, and Lincoln complexes; (2) Paleocene-Eocene (61 to 54 Ma) leucocratic granitic rocks; and (3) Eocene (53 to 47 Ma) intermediate to felsic, intrusive, and volcanic rocks. The leucocratic granites and volcanic-plutonic assemblage are characterized by distinct geochemical signatures and emplacement mechanisms that possibly reflect different source regions.

REGIONAL GEOLOGIC SETTING

The Omineca crystalline belt (Fig. 1) is a complex geologic province that includes Paleozoic and Mesozoic metasedimentary rocks, Proterozoic to Jurassic medium- to high-grade orthogneiss and paragneiss, and Cretaceous and Tertiary batholiths. The Colville Igneous Complex lies in the southern part of the belt, which extends north into Canada and includes the Shuswap Metamorphic Complex as well as other Tertiary volcanic and intrusive rocks (Fig. 1). The southern part of the Shuswap Complex has been named the Okanagan Complex by Okulitch (1984) and contains remnants of a Mesozoic magmatic arc built on North American craton and transitional crust and tectonic slivers of the Quesnel terrane, which docked in the Jurassic and caused ex-

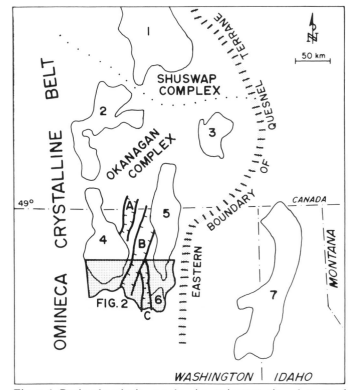

Figure 1. Regional geologic map showing major tectonic and structural features in southern part of Omineca crystalline belt. Gneiss domes or metamorphic core complexes are numbered as follows: 1, Frenchman's Cap—Monashee Complex; 2, Thor Odin and Pinnacles; 3, Valhalla; 4, Okanogan; 5, Kettle; 6, Lincoln; and 7, Selkirk. Grabens are lettered: A = Toroda Creek, B = Republic, C = Keller.

treme crustal shortening and high-grade metamorphism. In northeastern Washington, the Okanagan Complex contains the Okanogan, Kettle, and Lincoln core complexes, which are separated by three northeast-trending, en echelon grabens that formed in response to Paleogene extension.

Gneissic rocks associated with the Colville batholith include compositionally varied paragneiss and orthogneiss that are considered to be the oldest rocks in the Omineca belt. Fox and others' (1977) synthesis of regional studies in Canada suggests that the parent material of the gneiss is late Precambrian to late Paleozoic in age. Hansen and Goodge (1988) interpret the age of metamorphism and deformation of the Okanogan complex gneisses as Jurassic to Early Cretaceous, synchronous with extreme crustal shortening associated with accretion of the Quesnel terrane and representing a period of extreme crustal shortening. This coincided with movement on east-directed thrust sheets in the foreland thrust belt (Price and Mountjoy, 1970; Price, 1981) and deep crustal shear zones that moved high-grade metamorphic rocks from deep to shallow crustal levels (Brown and Read, 1983; Okulitch, 1984). Final uplift, mylonitization, and emplacement of core complexes was coeval with Paleocene and Eocene magmatic activity, as evidenced by widespread resetting of K-Ar radiometric ages during the Tertiary thermal event (Atwater, 1985; Hansen and Goodge, 1988; Mathews, 1981). It should be noted that structures formed during Mesozoic crustal shortening have been largely overprinted by Paleogene extensional features. A COCORP seismic reflection profile across the area (Potter and others, 1986) shows deeper west-dipping structures cut by east-dipping extensional features that root near the Moho. Graben faulting and detachment faulting on the margins of the Okanogan, Kettle, and Lincoln complexes during Paleogene extension were synchronous with, and probably permitted emplacement of, the Colville batholith and eruption of coeval volcanic rocks within the grabens.

COLVILLE IGNEOUS COMPLEX

The Colville Igneous Complex contains Paleocene orthogneisses associated with the Okanogan, Kettle, and Lincoln complexes and two chemically and temporally distinct igneous assemblages that include Paleocene-Eocene leucocratic granites and Eocene intrusive and coeval volcanic rocks. The leucocratic granites comprise a number of large, discrete plutons and intrusive suites (Fig. 2) that form the main mass of the Colville batholith (Carlson, 1984, 1989). The Eocene volcanic-plutonic assemblage includes epizonal plutons, dike swarms, and volcanic and volcaniclastic rocks that are structurally controlled by the northeast-trending grabens.

Gneissic rocks

The Kettle, Okanogan, and Lincoln complexes contain compositionally varied, medium- to high-grade gneisses that range in age from Permian-Triassic to Paleocene (Atwater and Rinehart, 1984). On the basis of Rb/Sr and fission-track ages (Fox and others, 1976) and crosscutting relations, the gneisses probably formed in response to shortening and high-grade metamorphism during accretion of the Quesnel terrane in the Jurassic and were later partially remobilized and uplifted during Paleogene extension. Higher structural levels in the complexes are characterized by a penetrative mylonitic fabric and other kinematic indicators in Paleocene-age orthogneisses that record top-to-the-east movement in the Kettle (Rhodes and Cheney, 1981) and Lincoln complexes (C. D. Rinehart, personal communication, 1984), and top-to-the-west sense of shear in the Okanogan complex (Hansen, 1983; Tempelman-Kluit and Parkinson, 1986; Volk, 1986). Fabrics produced during top-to-the-east shearing and compression associated with accretion of the Quesnel terrane have been largely overprinted at exposed structural levels by the Paleogene extensional features.

In general, the timing of metamorphism and age of protoliths are poorly established in the gneisses of the Okanogan, Kettle, and Lincoln complexes. Preliminary U/Pb work (D. Parkinson, personal communication, 1986) indicates that orthogneisses exposed along the southern margin of the Okanogan dome are 65 ± 4 Ma (Table 1). Because these gneisses are closely related in time and have a mylonitic fabric that parallels the fabric developed locally in the leucocratic granites, they are considered part of the Colville batholith. The granite of Daisy Trail along the southwest edge of the Kettle complex (Fig. 2) shows a progressive increase in penetrative mylonitic fabric northward and ultimately grades into the gneisses of the dome (Holder, 1986). It is probable that some of the Kettle gneisses are coeval with, or were at least remobilized during emplacement of the batholith. The Lincoln complex may be the southern continuation of the Kettle dome (C. D. Rinehart, personal communication, 1985) and contains lineated hornblende-biotite granitoids and migmatitic gneisses that yield 50-Ma K/Ar ages (Atwater and Rinehart, 1989).

Paleocene-Eocene leucocratic granitic rocks

The leucocratic granites range in age from 61 to 54 Ma (Table 1) and form the main mass of the Colville batholith. Plutons and intrusive suites (Fig. 2) include the Moses pluton (Singer, 1984), Coyote Creek pluton (Orazulike, 1982), granite of Daisy Trail (Holder, 1986), and the Coulee Dam Intrusive Suite (Carlson, 1989), which is equivalent to the Keller Butte pluton of Carlson (1984). These plutons range in composition from hornblende-free biotite granodiorite to granite (Fig. 3) and typically have a low color index (<5). The leucocratic granitic rocks contain varying proportions of quartz, oligoclase, and microcline (Fig. 3), with accretionary apatite, zircon, ±allanite, and 1 to 2 percent spessartine garnet in late-stage pegmatitic phases. There is a conspicuous lack of mafic to intermediate intrusive units in the main mass of the batholith. Contacts between individual plutons generally have equivocal age relations, indicating that intrusion of magmas was very closely spaced in time. The plutons are typically steep sided and were intruded to fairly shallow levels, as indicated by quench textures, intrusive breccia pipes, and a general lack of roof rocks. The Coulee Dam Intrusive Suite is associated with Mo-Cu porphyry mineralization at the Mount Tolman deposit (Utterback, 1984).

The Coyote Creek pluton and granite of Daisy Trail, which are adjacent to the Okanogan and Kettle complexes, respectively, cut the orthogneisses, yet locally contain a mylonitic foliation that grades into the penetrative mylonitic fabric of the core complexes (Singer, 1984; Atwater, 1985; Holder, 1986; Volk, 1986). In addition, the Coulee Dam Intrusive Suite is elongate parallel to the Republic and Keller grabens and is also cut by the graben-bounding faults, as evidenced by steeply dipping cataclastic zones as much as 1,000 m wide (Carlson, 1984). These relations indicate that the main mass of the batholith intruded during the very early stages of graben formation and emplacement of the Okanogan, Kettle, and Lincoln complexes during Paleogene extension.

Moses pluton. The Moses pluton is an immense body of leucocratic granite (>250 km^2) located along the southeastern margin of the Okanogan complex (Fig. 2) (Atwater and Rinehart, 1984). Singer (1984) named and divided the Moses pluton into three concentrically arranged coeval phases on the basis of textural and compositional variation. The interior phase or main

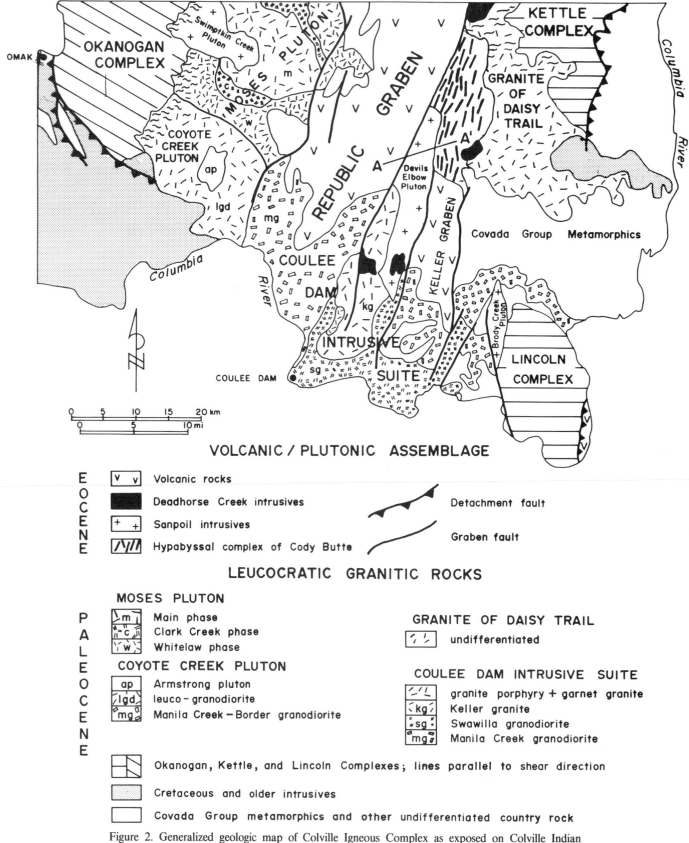

Figure 2. Generalized geologic map of Colville Igneous Complex as exposed on Colville Indian Reservation (after Atwater and Rinehart, 1984).

TABLE 1. RADIOMETRIC AGES FOR IGNEOUS ROCKS OF THE COLVILLE IGNEOUS COMPLEX

Unit	Mineral	Method	Mineral Age (Ma)	Source
KLONDIKE MOUNTAIN FORMATION				
quartz latite lava	hornblende	A/Ar	46.3 ± 1.7	1
quartz latite lava	biotite	K/Ar	47.4 ± 1.6	1
DEADHORSE SUITE				
Deadhorse granite	biotite	K/Ar	49.6 ± 0.3	2
Joe Moses stock	biotite	K/Ar	49.7 ± 0.4	2
SANPOIL SUITE				
Sanpoil Volcanics lava	biotite	K/Ar	48.5 ± 0.3	3
Sanpoil Volcanics lava	biotite	K/Ar	50.3 ± 0.4	3
Scatter Creek Rhyodacite	hornblende	K/Ar	49.4 ± 0.3	3
Scatter Creek Rhyodacite	biotite	K/Ar	50.3 ± 0.3	3
Devils Elbow Pluton	biotite	K/Ar	49.9 ± 0.3	3
Devils Elbow Pluton	biotite/hornblende	K/Ar	45.2 ± 1.1/47.7 ± 1.2	2
Devils Elbow Pluton	biotite	K/Ar	49.6 ± 1.2	3
Swimptkin Creek Pluton	biotite/hornblende	K/Ar	49.2 ± 1.5/49.4 ± 1.5	3
Swimptkin Creek Pluton	biotite	K/Ar	49.5 ± 1.2	3
Kettle Crest Pluton	biotite/hornblende	K/Ar	45.2 ± 1.1/47.7 ± 1.2	3
O'BRIEN CREEK SUITE				
quartz latite tuff	biotite	K/Ar	53.1 ± 1.5	
LEUCOCRATIC GRANITE SUITE				
Moses Pluton-				
Clark Creek Phase	biotite	K/Ar	49.4 ± 1.2	2
Armstrong pluton	biotite	K/Ar	52.5 ± 1.3	2
Coyote Creek pluton	biotite	K/Ar	51.1 ± 1.3	4
Coulee Dam Intrusive Suite				
Manila Creek granodiorite	K-feldspar	K/Ar	51.2 ± 1.8	5
Manila Creek granodiorite	sphene	U/Pb	54.0 ± 2.0	6
Swawilla granodiorite	biotite	K/Ar	58.8 ± 2.2	7
Keller granite	biotite	K/Ar	61.3 ± 2.3	7
Granite of Daisy Trail	biotite	K/Ar	49.9 ± 0.3	2
Granite of Daisy Trail	monazite	U/Pb	55.0 ± 3.0	6
OKANOGAN COMPLEX				
Mission Creek gneiss	biotite	K/Ar	47.2 ± 1.4	2
Mission Creek gneiss	zircon	U/Pb	65 ± 1.5	6
Mission Creek gneiss	zircon	U/Pb	65 ± 2.0	1

Sources: 1. Pearson and Obradovich (1977); 2. Atwater and Rinehart (1984); 3. Atwater and Rinehart (1989); 4. Fox and others (1976); 5. Armstrong and others (1982); 6. D. Parkinson (written communication, 1986); and 7. W. Utterback and R. Badley (*in* Atwater and Rinehart, 1984)

phase is a coarse-grained, equigranular granite that has a low color index (2 to 4) and contains equal proportions of quartz, microcline, and oligoclase. It is gradational more than a kilometer into the Clark Creek phase, which is a medium-grained granite to granodiorite that contains sparse microcline phenocrysts. The outermost phase, or Whitelaw, is characterized by an aplopeg-matite texture and is gradational with the Clark Creek phase over a short distance. Contacts between the phases give equivocal age relations, which suggests that the units are coeval. Near the Okanogan complex, the Clark Creek phase contains inclusions of the 65-Ma gneisses and contains a primary flow foliation and lineation that parallels the penetrative mylonitic fabric in the complex (Singer, 1984).

Coyote Creek pluton. The Coyote Creek pluton was named by Fox and others (1976) for granitic rocks exposed to the southeast of the Okanogan complex (Fig. 2). On the basis of limited crosscutting relations, the Coyote Creek pluton appears to be older than the Moses pluton (Singer, 1984). Orazulike (1982) studied the Coyote Creek pluton in detail and divided the pluton into three phases on the basis of textural and chemical criteria. These phases include a border granodiorite, leucocratic grano-diorite, and equigranular granite. The border granodiorite has a

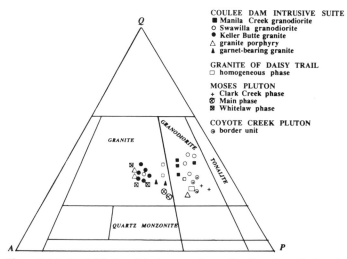

Figure 3. Modal QAP plot of the leucocratic granites (data from Carlson, 1984; Holder, 1986; Singer, 1984). Classification fields are from Streck-eisen (1976).

higher color index (<10) and contains subhedral pink microcline megacrysts and abundant disc-shaped inclusions (Broch, 1979). The most distinctive phase is the leucocratic granodiorite, which is coarse-grained, has a low color index (<5), and contains K-feldspar megacrysts as long as 15 cm and rounded "eyes" of smokey quartz. The equigranular granite of Orazulike (1982) (Armstrong pluton of Atwater and Rinehart, 1984) is a circular plug of equigranular granite that is contained entirely within the leucocratic granodiorite. The younger Armstrong pluton is in sharp contact with the leucocratic granodiorite, and dikes emanating from the Armstrong pluton contain inclusions of the leucocratic granodiorite.

The leucocratic granodiorite, along the northwestern border of the Coyote Creek pluton, contains a primary lineation that parallels the penetrative S-C mylonites of the 65-Ma Okanogan complex gneisses (Volk, 1986). This suggests that the Coyote Creek pluton intruded during top-to-the-west movement in the Okanogan complex during Paleogene extension.

Coulee Dam Intrusive Suite. Along the southern end of the Republic and Keller grabens, a suite of five coeval granitic units is well exposed at and to the northeast of Coulee Dam (Fig. 2). The Coulee Dam Intrusive Suite is 55 ± 3 m.y. old, based on K/Ar and U/Pb ages (Table 1). From oldest to youngest, the Coulee Dam Intrusive Suite contains the Manila Creek Grano-diorite, Swawilla Granodiorite, Keller Butte Granite, granite porphyry, and a garnet-bearing granite (Carlson, 1989). To the northwest, the Manila Creek Granodiorite is contiguous with the border granodiorite of the Coyote Creek pluton. The Swawilla Granodiorite is medium grained and typically equigranular, but locally contains subhedral K-feldspar megacrysts; it is most similar to the Clark Creek phase of the Moses pluton. The Keller Butte Granite forms one of the interior units in the Coulee Dam Intrusive Suite and is virtually indistinguishable from the leuco-

cratic granodiorite of the Coyote Creek pluton. The large K-feldspar megacrysts and the quartz eyes are distinctive. The granite porphyry is a textural variation of the Keller Butte Granite that has well-developed quartz eyes and quench textures that probably formed in response to venting and rapid pressure release of volatiles (Carlson, 1984, 1986). Northeast of Coulee Dam, the granite porphyry forms a small plug that is elongate north-northeast, parallel to the Republic graben. Elsewhere, it occurs as small plugs and diffuse zones in the megacrystic Keller Granite and leucocratic granodiorite of the Coyote Creek pluton. The garnet-bearing granite is the youngest unit in the suite and occurs as irregular-shaped masses of aplo-pegmatite and as dikes that cut all of the other units. Garnet is spessartitic and formed at the expense of biotite; muscovite and magnetite are present as magmatic reaction products of the breakdown of biotite.

Contacts between the units are sharp, unchilled, and dip steeply away from the interior of the suite. The outer Manila Creek Granodiorite is foliated locally along contacts with meta-sedimentary roof and wall rocks. Schistose country rocks are locally contorted into low-amplitude chevron folds that are cut by postkinematic andalusite (Carlson, 1984). Thus, the outermost units in the suite record a somewhat forcible intrusion. The suite as a whole was emplaced rapidly, because 53-Ma lavas of the O'Brien Creek Formation rest unconformably on the suite. Emplacement was probably accommodated by vertical uplift and doming of the roof, along with east-west extension associated with the opening of the grabens and detachment faulting above the Okanogan, Kettle, and Lincoln complexes. The upper part of the Keller Butte Granite, in the interior of the suite, contains a fabric that records a top-to-the-west sense of shear. It is very likely that the roof rocks were being detached as the suite was intruded.

Granite of Daisy Trail. A large body (>350 km²) of leucocratic granite located between the southwest margin of the Kettle complex and the eastern boundary fault of the Republic graben (Fig. 2) has been named the granite of Daisy Trail (At-water and Rinehart, 1984; Holder, 1986). The granite of Daisy Trail is coarse grained and locally megacrystic; it is similar in composition and texture to the Keller Butte Granite in the Coulee Dam Intrusive Suite and the leucocratic granodiorite of the Coyote Creek pluton. To the north, the granite of Daisy Trail cuts the Kettle complex gneisses but also contains a penetrative mylo-nitic fabric with prominent C and S surfaces that give a top-to-the-east sense of shear similar to that found in the Kettle complex (Holder, personal communication, 1983). On the basis of K/Ar and U/Pb age determinations (Table 1), the Daisy Trail dates from 55 Ma, and was intruded during the early stages of movement on the Kettle complex.

Eocene volcanic-plutonic assemblage

Eocene rocks in the Colville Igneous Complex comprise three regionally correlatable volcanic units and their subvolcanic equivalents that range in age from 53 to 47 Ma (Table 1). Muessig (1962) originally described the Tertiary volcanic section and suggested that associated hypabyssal dikes and plugs represented comagmatic intrusive rocks. Pearson and Obradovich (1977) suggested a regional correlation of lithologically and temporally similar rocks across northeastern Washington and southern British Columbia. In a study at the southern end of the Republic graben, Moye (1984) demonstrated that volcanic and intrusive equivalents could be correlated using major- and trace-element geochemistry along with temporal and spatial relations.

The Eocene assemblage includes formal volcanic stratigraphy and plutonic rock units defined by Muessig (1962), and informally named volcanic subunits and intrusive rocks defined by Atwater and Rinehart (1984), Moye (1984), and Carlson (1984). Volcanic rocks are largely confined to northeast-trending grabens; intrusive rocks form complex dike swarms, elongate intrusions parallel to the grabens, and irregular plug-like intrusions. From oldest to youngest, the Eocene volcanic/plutonic assemblage includes the following.

O'Brien Creek Suite. The O'Brien Creek Suite includes biotite rhyolite dikes and plugs that are localized along and within the Republic and Keller grabens and coeval volcanic rocks of the O'Brien Creek Formation. The O'Brien Creek Formation, the basal Tertiary unit, comprises volcaniclastic, epiclastic, and pyroclastic rocks (Muessig, 1962) and dates from 53.1 ± 1.5 Ma based on K-Ar age determinations (Table 1). In addition, Atwater and Rinehart (1984) and Moye (1984) included biotite rhyodacite lava flows in the Keller graben and in the southern end of the Republic graben in the O'Brien Creek Suite. These flows were deposited unconformably on an erosional surface on the older leucocratic granite and pre-Tertiary country rocks. The thickness and distribution of the O'Brien Creek Formation is highly varied because it was deposited on irregular topography in the early stages of graben subsidence. The O'Brien Creek Formation has been correlated with the Kettle River and Springbrook Formations in British Columbia (Pearson and Obradovich, 1977). The intrusive equivalent of the O'Brien Creek Formation has been informally named the Rhyolite Porphyry of Thirtymile Creek (Moye, 1984) and consists of biotite rhyolite dikes and plugs that are locally indistinguishable from the lava flows in hand specimen.

Both intrusive and extrusive phases of this suite are distinguished from younger intrusive and extrusive rocks by the presence of euhedral biotite books about 1 mm in size and small to large embayed quartz grains set in a light tan to greenish aphanitic groundmass. In addition, both the intrusive and extrusive phases characteristically contain xenoliths of pre-Tertiary argillite that range in size up to several centimeters, although most are smaller than 1 cm.

On the basis of volcanic facies relations, vent areas have been inferred near the southern end of the Republic graben (Moye, 1984) and in southern British Columbia, where the Shingle Creek Porphyry, a likely correlative, has been described as a volcanic neck (Bostock, 1966).

Sanpoil Suite. The Sanpoil Suite contains the Sanpoil Volcanics and several subvolcanic intrusions, including the Scatter Creek Rhyodacite (Muessig, 1962), the Devil's Elbow pluton (Moye, 1984; Atwater and Rinehart, 1984), and the Swimptkin Creek, Brody Creek, and Kettle Crest plutons (Atwater and Rinehart, 1984). The age of the suite is approximately 49 Ma based on K-Ar dating (Table 1). This suite comprises the largest volume and most widely distributed of the Eocene igneous rocks. Correlative volcanic rocks in southern British Columbia include the upper Marron Formation (Monger, 1968) as well as age-equivalent but geochemically dissimilar alkalic volcanic and intrusive rocks of the Coryell batholith.

The Sanpoil Volcanics is a widespread unit of dominantly dacite to rhyodacite lava flows and flow breccias with subordinate pyroclastic tuffs and tuff breccias. Thickness estimates range from 1,500 m at the southern Republic graben (Moye, 1984), to 1,200 m at the northern end of the Republic graben (Muessig, 1967), to 1,000 m in the Toroda Creek graben (Pearson, 1967). Thicknesses of individual flows are highly varied, ranging from less than 10 m to more than 300 m in the center of the Republic graben (Moye, 1982, 1984).

Lava flows of the Sanpoil Volcanics are characteristically porphyritic dacite to rhyodacite with varied proportions of phenocrystic plagioclase, hornblende, biotite, and augite. Less abundant, but commonly present, are phenocrysts of pigeonite, subcalcic augite, and hypersthene; phenocrysts of quartz are rare. The groundmass is generally microcrystalline to cryptocrystalline quartz and potassium feldspar.

The Scatter Creek Rhyodacite is a regionally widespread porphyritic hypabyssal unit that locally grades upward into the Sanpoil Volcanics lava flows within the Republic graben (Muessig, 1967; Moye, 1982, 1984). This unit is characterized by variable amounts of hornblende, biotite, plagioclase, and augite phenocrysts in a microcrystalline or glassy groundmass; quartz phenocrysts are also rare in this unit. Among the phenocrysts, hornblende and plagioclase are the dominant phases.

The Scatter Creek Rhyodacite, along with the older rhyolite porphyry of Thirtymile Creek, comprises the hypabyssal complex of Cody Butte in the horst blocks adjacent to the Republic graben (Fig. 2). The Cody Butte consists of varied proportions of rhyolite and rhyodacite in complexly interfingering swarms of sheeted dikes and irregular plugs with dimensions too small or exposure too inadequate to permit map delineation. Pre-Eocene rocks comprise up to 25 percent of the complex, including Covada Group metamorphic rocks and the Paleocene leucocratic granite of the Colville batholith; these country rocks form elongate, northeast-trending slivers that are engulfed by the hypabyssal intrusions.

Dikes in the hypabyssal complex of Cody Butte have a dominant N20°E trend and moderate to steep dips, indicating that northwest-southeast extension controlled dike emplacement and graben formation (Fig. 4). In addition, there is a marked

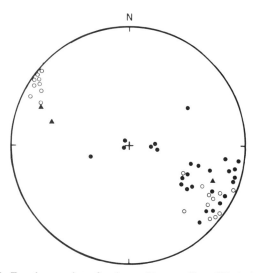

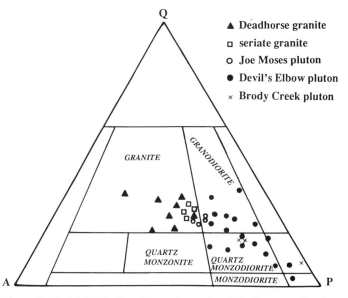

Figure 4. Equal-area plot of poles to Eocene dikes (filled circles) in hypabyssal complex of Cody Butte illustrating dominant northwest-southeast extension direction which controlled emplacement of Eocene intrusive rocks. Mineral lineations from adjacent Okanogan and Kettle orthogneisses (open circles) are from Hansen and Goodge (1988) and Rhodes and Cheney (1981), respectively. Poles to graben faults are shown with triangles.

Figure 5. Modal QAP plot of intrusive rocks of the Eocene volcanic-plutonic assemblage. Classification fields are from Streckeisen (1976).

decrease in the ratio of dikes to country rock away from the graben border faults, suggesting that intrusion of the dikes was strongly controlled by the extension associated with the formation of the Republic graben (Moye and others, 1982; Moye, 1984). The amount of extension estimated to accommodate the volume of dike material at the southern end of the Republic graben is about 10 km (Moye, 1984).

The Devil's Elbow pluton is one of several large zoned intrusions of intermediate composition exposed in the area; others include the Swimptkin Creek, Brody Creek, and Kettle Crest plutons (Atwater and Rinehart, 1984). The composition ranges from diorite to granodiorite, but averages quartz monzonite (Fig. 5). These intrusions locally grade into hypabyssal roof rocks, and in the case of the Devil's Elbow body, intrude their volcanic cover. These plutons range in age from 45.2 ± 1.1 to 49.6 ± 1.2 Ma (Table 1).

The Devil's Elbow pluton exemplifies the great compositional and textural zonation in these intrusions. The pluton grades upward from a medium-grained, equigranular hornblende quartz monzodiorite to a fine-grained, subporphyritic biotite-hornblende granodiorite at intermediate levels to porphyritic biotite-hornblende granodiorite at the uppermost exposures. The porphyritic roof rocks are virtually indistinguishable from the Scatter Creek Rhyodacite. Figure 6 illustrates the relation between the roof of the pluton and the hypabyssal complex of Cody Butte. The contact between the roof and the Scatter Creek Rhyodacite is shown as intrusive, based on Scatter Creek radiometric ages being older than the main equigranular quartz monzodiorite phase of the pluton. Contact relations in outcrop show that the units are mutually intrusive (Moye, 1984, 1987).

Deadhorse Suite. This suite includes the Deadhorse Creek granite and rhyolite domes east of West Fork (Moye, 1984), seriate granite and Joe Moses Creek stock (Carlson, 1984), and, at the northern end of the Republic graben, the Long Alec, Herron Creek, and other quartz monzonite intrusions (Muessig, 1967; Parker and Calkins, 1964). Modal composition of this suite ranges from granodiorite to granite (Fig. 5). Field relations unequivocally show that this unit intrudes rocks of the Sanpoil suite; therefore, it represents the youngest igneous activity in the southern end of the Republic graben (Moye and others, 1982; Moye, 1984). However, K-Ar age dates for the granites overlap ages determined for the Devils Elbow and Swimptkin Creek plutons and are older than ages for the Kettle Crest pluton; this inconsistency in radiometric age dates has not been resolved. To the north, clasts of quartz monzonite intrusions are found in volcaniclastic rocks of the Klondike Mountain Formation, the youngest of the Eocene volcanic sequence (Muessig, 1967). This suggests that the intrusions had been unroofed prior to the youngest volcanic event in the region.

At the southern end of the Republic graben, intrusive rocks of this unit occur as small plugs and dikes. Extrusive rocks occur as small domes and dikes that are localized in the center of the Republic graben and fed small flows (Moye, 1982, 1984). Volcanic rocks are aphyric biotite rhyolite; glassy groundmass is locally preserved. Intrusive and hypabyssal rocks include seriate granite; equigranular, medium-grained biotite granite; subporphyritic hornblende-biotite granodiorite; and fine-grained, subporphyritic biotite rhyolite dikes.

Klondike Mountain Formation. The Klondike Mountain Formation described by Muessig (1962) is the youngest and most

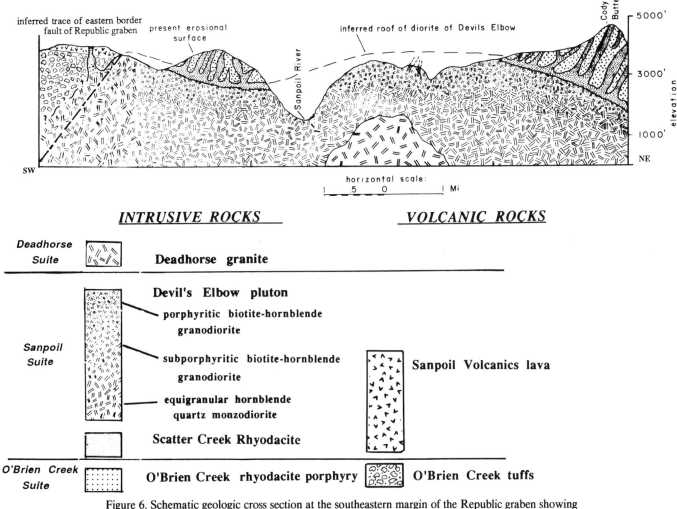

Figure 6. Schematic geologic cross section at the southeastern margin of the Republic graben showing textural and compositional variation of the Devil's Elbow pluton in relation to the overlying hypabyssal complex of Cody Butte. Line of section is shown in Figure 2. Modified from Moye (1987).

areally restricted of the Eocene volcanic units (Pearson and Obradovich, 1977). As described by Muessig, it includes volcanic and volcaniclastic deposits that unconformably overlie the Sanpoil Volcanics. The unit is confined to the northern half of the Republic graben, the Toroda Creek graben, and several other localities in northeastern Washington and southern British Columbia; none are in the area included in Figure 2. Few dikes or plugs have been recognized, and the present limited distribution is inferred to closely approximate the original areal extent.

Volcaniclastic deposits of the Klondike Mountain Formation locally consist of thick slide breccias containing Sanpoil-age intrusive rock clasts as well as pre-Tertiary metamorphic rocks (Pearson and Obradovich, 1977). Volcanic deposits are distinguished from the older Sanpoil lavas by the virtual absence of porphyritic lavas and the tendency to form volcanic domes.

ANALYTICAL METHODS

Representative samples from the Colville Igneous Complex were selected for analysis of major elements, trace elements, and rare earth elements (REE). Between 1.0 kg (volcanic rocks) and 5 kg (coarser granites) of each sample was crushed and ground using standard laboratory procedures; samples of coarse-grained granites were split, and duplicate samples were analyzed in order to insure sample homogeneity and analytical precision.

Major elements and trace elements Rb, Ba, Sr, Zr, V, Ni, Cr, and Y were analyzed by x-ray fluorescence (XRF) at Washington State University and at Franklin and Marshall College. Samples were prepared following the procedures outlined in Hooper and Atkins (1969), and analyzed using U.S. Geological Survey standards G-2, AGV-1, GSP-1, BCR-1, and PCC-1. Th and Ta were determined by instrumental neutron activation analysis at Washington State University.

Selected samples of the Coulee Dam Intrusive Suite and Eocene intrusive rocks were also analyzed for REE and additional trace elements by inductively coupled plasma (ICP) emission spectrometry at Kings College, London, England. The technique used for dissolution of samples is the same as that described in Walsh and others (1981).

GEOCHEMISTRY

The leucocratic granitic rocks and younger volcanic-plutonic assemblage are chemically distinct. This is best shown on an AFM diagram (Fig. 7), where the Eocene volcanic-plutonic rocks define a calc-alkalic trend that is richer in MgO than the more alkali-rich leucocratic granite. On the basis of the alkali-lime index of Peacock (1931), the Eocene assemblage is, in general, calc-alkalic. Although a definitive alkali-lime index is precluded by a limited range of composition in the leucocratic granites, the indication is that the granites differ from the Eocene assemblage and may have a more calcic index. In general, the leucocratic granites tend to be higher in silica and lower in potassium than the Eocene volcanic-plutonic rocks (Fig. 8). Although temporally and spatially related to the Eocene rocks, the O'Brien Creek Suite is chemically more similar to the leucocratic granites.

Paleocene-Eocene leucocratic granitic rocks

The leucocratic granites are distinct in that they are peraluminous and rich in silica. The peraluminous nature of the leucocratic granites is implied by molecular $Al_2O_3/(CaO + Na_2O + K_2O)$ ratios more than 1.15 and in excess of 2 percent corundum in the norm. Using the classification scheme proposed by Miller (1985), the leucocratic granites are weakly peraluminous; biotite is the only aluminous phase present and garnet is restricted to the late-stage differentiates.

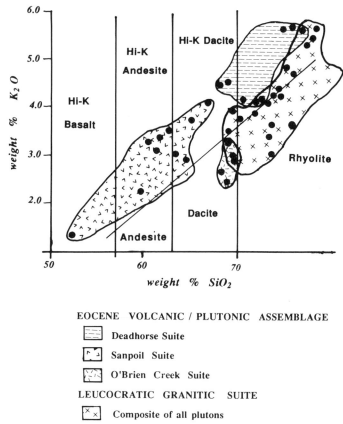

EOCENE VOLCANIC / PLUTONIC ASSEMBLAGE

    ⬚   Deadhorse Suite

    ⬚   Sanpoil Suite

    ⬚   O'Brien Creek Suite

LEUCOCRATIC GRANITIC SUITE

    ⬚   Composite of all plutons

Figure 8. Potash-silica variation diagram illustrating compositional variation between leucocratic granites and Eocene volcanic-plutonic assemblage. Data points shown are from Tables 2 and 3; outline of fields is based on additional data that are available from the authors on request. Classification is based on Peccarillo and Taylor (1976).

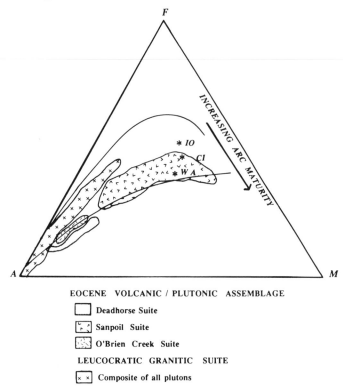

EOCENE VOLCANIC / PLUTONIC ASSEMBLAGE

    ⬚   Deadhorse Suite

    ⬚   Sanpoil Suite

    ⬚   O'Brien Creek Suite

LEUCOCRATIC GRANITIC SUITE

    ⬚   Composite of all plutons

Figure 7. AFM plot of leucocratic granites and Eocene volcanic-intrusive rocks compared to Brown's (1982) classification of volcanic arcs. WA = western America arc; CI = continental interior arc; IO = ocean island arc.

In general, individual units in the leucocratic granitic rocks tend to be chemically homogeneous. Variation between units in individual plutons or related intrusive suites show small but predictable major-element variation. The greatest variation is in the percentage of silica, which varies from 66 wt.% in the more mafic border units to 76 wt.% in the youngest, most evolved phases of the Coulee Dam Intrusive Suite (Fig. 9) and the Coyote Creek pluton (Table 2). Alumina, CaO, TiO_2, P_2O_5, MnO, FeO, and MgO decrease with increasing silica, whereas Na_2O and K_2O show the opposite relation (Fig. 9). The major-element chemistry reflects the variation in mineralogy; biotite and plagioclase decrease, whereas the percentages of quartz and microcline increase in the younger, more evolved units of the suite.

Available trace-element and REE chemistry data for the leucocratic granites indicate that Sr is enriched with respect to Rb (Table 2), which corresponds to the inferred calcic character, and lower K_2O than rocks of equal silica content in the Eocene volcanic-plutonic assemblage. The leucocratic granites are also lower in Ba than the Eocene volcanic-plutonic rocks (Tables 2 and 3). The lack of mafic mineral phases throughout the leuco-

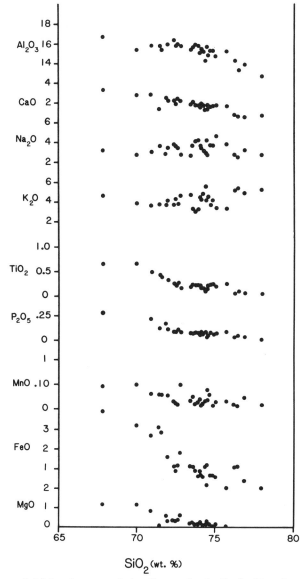

Figure 9. Major element variation diagram for the Coulee Dam Intrusive Suite (from Carlson, 1989).

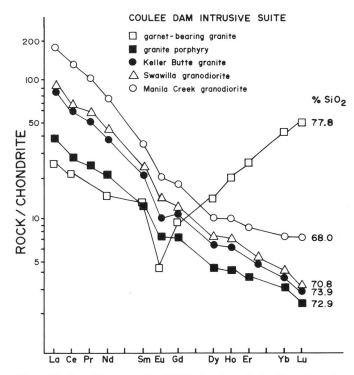

Figure 10. Chondrite normalized REE plot of the Coulee Dam Intrusive Suite.

cratic granites accounts for the low Zr values observed. REE data are available only for the Coyote Creek pluton (Orazulike, 1982) and the Coulee Dam Intrusive Suite (Carlson, 1984). Because these rocks are similar in composition to the other leucocratic granites, they are assumed to be representative of the entire suite. Except for the garnet-bearing granite, the Coulee Dam Intrusive Suite is enriched in LREE relative to HREE; La/Lu ranges from 260 in the least siliceous Manila Creek Granodiorite to 162 in the most siliceous granite porphyry (Table 4). In addition, the overall abundance of REE decreases systematically from the least siliceous to the more evolved units in both the Coulee Dam Intrusive Suite (Fig. 10) and the Coyote Creek pluton (Orazulike, 1982). However, the most evolved garnet-bearing granite is anomalous

in that it has a distinct negative Eu anomaly and is enriched in HREE with respect to LREE. The Eu anomaly reflects the lower percentage of modal plagioclase in this unit, whereas the HREE are contained in the garnet. The nearly parallel slopes and the progressive decrease in REE throughout the rest of the suite suggest that the individual units are petrogenetically related, probably by removal of REE–rich accessories such as monazite, apatite, allanite, and zircon from the magma (Carlson, 1984).

The chemistry of the leucocratic granites was normalized to hypothetical ocean ridge granites (ORG) and plotted on a Pearce diagram (Fig. 11) for comparison with granites of known tectonic setting. Compared to an ORG, the leucocratic granites are enriched in large ion lithophile elements (LIL) and depleted in high field strength elements (HFS). The leucocratic granites are most similar to oceanic volcanic-arc granites from Jamaica (Fig. 11). However, the Colville granites contain more Rb and Ta and less Yb than the Jamaican granites, which probably reflects the influence of continental crust in the Colville granites.

On the basis of preliminary isotope data, the leucocratic granites have moderate (0.707 to 0.708) initial strontium ratios (Carlson and others, 1988) and a 1,700-Ma inherited Pb component (D. Parkinson, personal communication, 1985). This, together with the high silica and La/Lu values and low Rb/Sr ratios, suggests that the leucocratic granites may have formed by small degrees of partial melting of a high-Sr, Middle Proterozoic, sialic lower crust. The restricted compositional range, in terms of silica and other major elements, further suggests that there was

TABLE 2. SELECTED BULK ROCK GEOCHEMICAL ANALYSES FOR THE PALEOCENE LEUCOCRATIC GRANITIC ROCKS

	Manila Creek Granodiorite*			Swawilla granodiorite				Keller Butte Granite			granite porphyry		garnet-bearing granite	
	81-182	DMO352	DMO202	81-30E	82M379	81-32	81-184	81-187	81-191	81-192	81-10A	81-10C	82-73A	81-52
major element, weight percent														
SiO_2	68.02	66.03	68.47	70.76	70.00	72.76	72.85	75.90	71.20	73.24	73.89	71.57	77.81	74.17
TiO_2	0.66	0.58	0.30	0.30	0.49	0.31	0.24	0.17	0.26	0.22	0.15	0.43	0.07	0.21
Al_2O_3	15.79	17.08	16.79	15.75	16.63	15.84	15.56	14.56	16.16	15.80	15.75	15.74	13.62	14.67
Fe_2O_3	1.49	2.14	1.15	n.d.	n.d.	n.d.	n.d.	n.d.	n.d.	n.d.	n.d.	n.d.	n.d.	n.d.
FeO	2.09	2.45	1.31	n.d.	n.d.	n.d.	n.d.	n.d.	n.d.	n.d.	n.d.	n.d.	n.d.	n.d.
FeOt	......	......	......	1.63	3.05	1.63	1.33	0.91	1.36	1.04	0.68	2.55	0.11	1.40
MnO	0.10	0.08	0.07	0.06	0.60	0.50	0.05	0.04	0.03	0.02	0.03	0.06	0.03	0.04
MgO	1.14	1.33	0.42	0.40	0.99	0.43	0.25	0.17	0.24	0.17	0.08	0.23	0.00	0.24
CaO	3.05	5.14	3.57	2.14	2.94	2.18	2.05	1.45	2.03	1.90	1.27	1.49	0.78	1.84
Na_2O	2.65	3.23	3.71	4.28	3.74	4.33	4.70	4.23	4.75	5.35	5.00	5.01	3.54	3.41
K_2O	3.55	1.65	4.08	4.09	3.59	3.98	3.30	3.64	3.80	2.96	4.09	3.80	5.22	4.37
P_2O_5	0.25	0.29	0.13	0.12	0.24	0.12	0.09	0.06	0.08	0.07	0.05	0.12	0.01	0.06
Total	98.67	100.00	100.00	99.53	102.27	101.63	100.42	101.13	99.91	100.77	100.99	101.00	101.19	100.41
trace elements, in ppm														
Rb	139	100	119	135	132	126	135	126	93	89	144	134	178	152
Sr	485	732	879	712	430	717	528	494	729	673	502	404	61	368
Ba	1157	679	1540	1548	862	1610	654	805	1576	847	866	200	66	1251
Zr	486	268	124	157	179	167	113	96	146	125	81	184	53	106
Y	21	21	n.d.	12	25	16	16	11	10	11	15	21	20	12
Th†	15	10	6	15	n.d.	n.d.	8	n.d.	n.d.	n.d.	6	n.d.	n.d.	n.d.
Ta†	2.7	3.7	5.9	4.2	n.d.	n.d.	4.9	n.d.	n.d.	n.d.	4.4	n.d.	n.d.	n.d.

TABLE 2. SELECTED BULK ROCK GEOCHEMICAL ANALYSES FOR THE PALEOCENE LEUCOCRATIC GRANITIC ROCKS (continued)

| | COYOTE CREEK PLUTON | | | | | | GRANITE OF DAISY TRAIL | | | | MOSES PLUTON | | | |
| | Leucocratic granodiorite | | | granite | | | | | | | Clark Creek Phase | | Main Phase | Whitelaw phase |
	DMO255	DMO275	DMO383	DMO210	DMO233	DMO237	WH1231	WH146	WH8	WHBRN	SS341	SS354		
major element, weight percent														
SiO_2	70.91	71.54	73.04	76.15	77.57	74.47	70.06	71.82	74.43	76.19	70.37	73.43	73.56	71.53
TiO_2	0.35	0.24	0.20	0.18	0.10	0.17	0.21	0.31	0.27	0.17	0.30	0.30	0.21	0.22
Al_2O_3	16.04	16.15	15.94	12.78	13.11	14.68	17.44	16.30	15.06	14.58	17.17	15.30	15.70	15.94
Fe_2O_3	1.10	0.46	0.28	0.37	0.00	0.29	0.61	0.53	0.48	0.25	0.69	0.61	0.31	0.54
FeO	1.27	0.52	0.32	0.42	0.00	0.33	0.69	0.60	0.55	0.29	0.79	0.70	0.35	0.62
MnO	0.06	0.03	0.02	0.04	0.02	0.04	0.05	0.02	0.02	0.03	0.02	0.02	0.01	0.03
MgO	0.71	0.11	0.09	0.13	0.00	0.05	0.34	0.50	0.18	0.43	0.19	0.13	0.05	0.00
CaO	3.16	2.00	2.06	0.70	0.53	1.21	2.89	2.02	1.39	1.14	2.66	2.06	1.80	1.27
Na_2O	3.31	5.29	4.95	3.79	3.99	4.12	4.63	4.33	3.35	3.26	4.38	3.76	3.75	3.37
K_2O	2.96	3.57	3.03	5.38	4.64	4.58	2.99	3.49	4.21	3.63	3.33	3.60	4.20	6.42
P_2O_5	0.14	0.08	0.07	0.07	0.05	0.06	0.08	0.09	0.06	0.04	0.09	0.09	0.06	0.07
Total	100.01	99.99	100.00	100.01	100.01	100.00	99.99	100.01	100.00	100.01	99.99	100.00	100.00	100.02
trace elements, in ppm														
Rb	79	108	79	140	170	147	n.d.	n.d.	n.d.	n.d.	n.d.	n.d.	n.d.	n.d.
Sr	491	780	743	210	108	477	n.d.	n.d.	n.d.	n.d.	n.d.	n.d.	n.d.	n.d.
Ba	684	1330	1050	818	215	809	n.d.	n.d.	n.d.	n.d.	n.d.	n.d.	n.d.	n.d.
Zr	152	133	132	152	63	114	n.d.	n.d.	n.d.	n.d.	n.d.	n.d.	n.d.	n.d.
Y	n.d.	n.d.	n.d.	n.d.	n.d.	n.d.	n.d.	n.d.	n.d.	n.d.	n.d.	n.d.	n.d.	n.d.
Th†	14	8	7	20	3	13	n.d.	n.d.	n.d.	n.d.	n.d.	n.d.	n.d.	n.d.
Ta†	3.7	4.3	5.0	5.9	6.7	5.5	n.d.	n.d.	n.d.	n.d.	n.d.	n.d.	n.d.	n.d.

*Border granodiorite is grouped with the Manila Creek granodiorite in the Coulee Dam Intrusive Suite.

†Trace element analyses by INAA.

Data sources: DMO specimens from Orazulike (1982); WH specimens from Holder (1986); SS specimens from Singer (1984).

TABLE 3. SELECTED BULK-ROCK GEOCHEMICAL ANALYSES FOR THE EOCENE VOLCANIC PLUTONIC ASSEMBLAGE

	O'Brien Creek Suite					Sanpoil Suite						
	1	2	3	4	5	6	7	8	9	10	11	12
major elements, weight percent												
SiO_2	68.41	67.63	69.14	67.51	67.89	64.40	62.71	56.13	71.37	59.95	52.52	62.70
TiO_2	0.34	0.40	0.27	0.33	0.37	0.63	0.73	1.09	0.24	0.83	0.92	0.69
Al_2O_3	15.86	15.28	16.01	17.33	15.58	15.12	15.70	15.93	11.24	15.28	17.40	15.02
Fe_2O_3	1.24	1.31	0.05	1.14	1.50	1.88	2.06	n.d.	n.d.	2.94	1.96	2.03
FeO	0.68	0.80	0.87	0.80	0.80	2.26	2.96	n.d.	n.d.	2.82	6.27	3.37
MnO	0.03	0.04	0.03	0.03	0.05	0.07	0.08	0.15	0.03	0.11	0.15	0.07
MgO	0.62	1.20	0.38	0.59	1.43	2.52	3.14	10.06	0.33	3.65	5.27	3.03
CaO	2.68	2.47	2.06	3.08	2.87	3.81	4.67	9.03	2.33	5.51	8.53	4.32
Na_2O	4.84	4.11	5.19	4.85	4.81	3.51	3.70	1.89	3.33	4.07	3.03	3.32
K_2O	2.97	3.17	2.81	2.34	2.59	3.84	3.04	1.54	3.57	2.17	1.03	3.54
P_2O_5	0.10	0.13	0.07	0.10	0.11	0.27	0.28	0.30	0.10	0.36	0.23	0.26
LOI	2.64	3.23	2.75	1.60	1.81	1.74	0.93	n.d.	n.d.	1.19	2.42	2.20
Total	100.41	99.99	100.13	99.70	100.11	100.05	100.00	99.52	98.91	99.53	99.73	99.55
FeO*	1.80	2.20	1.36	1.83	2.42	3.95	4.81	8.09	2.32	5.47	8.03	4.20
trace elements, in ppm												
Rb	62	79	72	55	55	106	76	30	101	46	31	84
Sr	1095	879	1063	1454	909	873	946	347	1019	1305	579	924
Ba	1269	1342	1235	1092	1059	1344	1347	833	1439	793	520	1341
Zr	87	97	69	75	58	190	146	136	168	66	117	212
Y	<2	<2	<2	<2	<2	6	9	22	14	12	20	6
V	32	51	29	41	62	83	109	n.d.	n.d.	144	205	98
Ni	4	11	3	4	19	25	28	n.d.	n.d.	22	18	37
Cr	10	34	9	38	16	83	114	n.d.	n.d.	53	98	97
Ta†	n.d.	n.d.	n.d.	n.d.	n.d.	n.d.	n.d.	15	n.d.	n.d.	n.d.	n.d.
Th†	n.d.	n.d.	n.d.	n.d.	n.d.	n.d.	n.d.	1.41	n.d.	n.d.	n.d.	n.d.
Rb/Sr	0.056	0.084	0.067	0.037	0.060	0.121	0.080	0.092	0.099	0.035	0.053	0.090

TABLE 3. SELECTED BULK-ROCK GEOCHEMICAL ANALYSES FOR THE EOCENE VOLCANIC PLUTONIC ASSEMBLAGE (continued)

	13	14	15	16	17	18	19	20	21	22	23
					SANPOIL SUITE					DEADHORSE SUITE	
major elements, weight percent											
SiO_2	61.70	66.35	60.69	64.87	63.46	67.36	67.79	65.53	72.51	7604	75.23
TiO_2	0.79	0.56	0.80	0.64	0.80	0.51	0.45	0.56	0.19	0.26	0.20
Al_2O_3	15.51	14.99	15.61	15.48	14.81	15.09	14.32	15.25	15.02	11.09	14.19
Fe_2O_3	2.68	3.06	3.00	3.79	3.19	2.32	1.66	1.32	0.64	0.48	n.d.
FeO	2.61	0.64	2.11	1.04	1.24	1.07	1.10	2.10	0.58	0.92	n.d.
MnO	0.09	0.05	0.08	0.06	0.10	0.06	0.04	0.07	0.04	0.04	0.02
MgO	3.42	2.33	3.49	1.64	2.72	1.77	1.81	2.18	0.24	0.74	0.40
CaO	4.79	3.19	5.13	3.83	5.12	2.73	1.86	3.92	1.63	1.10	1.65
Na_2O	3.64	3.46	3.31	3.86	3.16	3.88	3.28	3.87	4.35	0.22	3.19
K_2O	3.26	3.84	3.16	2.76	2.94	4.12	4.30	2.59	3.75	5.40	3.30
P_2O_5	0.33	0.21	0.33	0.24	0.37	0.19	0.14	0.15	0.04	0.07	0.07
LOI	1.53	1.90	2.15	1.93	2.54	1.27	2.95	2.20	0.52	3.42	n.d.
Total	100.35	100.58	99.86	100.14	100.45	100.37	99.70	99.74	99.51	99.78	98.80
FeO^*	5.02	3.39	4.81	4.45	4.11	3.16	2.59	3.29	1.16	1.35	0.55
trace elements, in ppm											
Rb	79	106	77	67	58	125	125	117	124	109	171
Sr	963	758	1014	771	984	678	668	410	740	133	483
Ba	1291	1323	1328	1184	1181	1313	1222	1000	1224	459	860
Zr	197	191	177	118	181	171	137	159	74	73	109
Y	5	10	5	6	18	2	10	20	2	2	19
V	117	73	119	104	115	64	57	88	18	30	n.d.
Ni	40	38	27	19	50	25	21	24	3	16	n.d.
Cr	125	74	94	62	132	68	54	76	20	46	n.d.
Ta[†]	n.d.	n.d.	n.d.	n.d.	n.d.	n.d.	n.d.	n.d.	n.d.	n.d.	7
Th[†]	n.d.	n.d.	n.d.	n.d.	n.d.	n.d.	n.d.	1.41	n.d.	n.d.	1.8
Rb/Sr	0.082	0.139	0.075	0.086	0.058	0.184	0.187	0.285	0.167	0.891	0.354

O'Brien Creek Suite: 1. N-1, rhyodacite porphyry; 2. N-2, rhyodacite lava; 3. 91680-5, rhyodacite lava; 4. 72981-1, rhyodacite lava flow; 5. 71180-7, rhyodacite porphyry.

Sanpoil Suite: 6. 91181-4, Devil's Elbow pluton, sub-porphyritic granodiorite; 7. N61G, Devil's Elbow quartz monzodiorite; 8. 81-17, Devil's Elbow diorite; 9. 82-150B, Joe Moses stock biotite granodiorite; 10. 71481-2, Devil's Elbow quartz monzodiorite; 11. N-5, Devil's Elbow quartz diorite; 12. 82980-10, Scatter Creek Rhyodacite; 13. 71170-2, Scatter Creek Rhyodacite; 14. 81280-6, Sanpoil bt-hb dacite lava; 15. 72281-7, Sanpoil bt-cpx andesite lava; 16. 9280-1, Sanpoil bt-cpx dacite lava; 17. R-12, Sanpoil bt-cpx dacite lava; 18. 81280-9, Sanpoil rhyodacite intrusion; 19. 8480-9, Sanpoil rhyodacite intrusion; 20. 92080-2, Klondike Mountain lava.

Deadhorse Suite: 21. 91780-2, Deadhorse pluton granite; 22. 9480-1, rhyolite dome; 23. 81-180B, seriate granite.

*FeO = total iron.

†trace elements analyses by INAA.

TABLE 4. RARE EARTH ELEMENT ANALYSES FOR SELECTED SPECIMENS FROM
THE PALEOCENE LEUCOCRATIC GRANITIC ROCKS*
AND THE EOCENE VOLCANIC/PLUTONIC ASSEMBLAGE†

| | PALEOCENE LEUCOCRATIC GRANITIC ROCKS | | | | | EOCENE VOLCANIC/PLUTONIC ASSEMBLAGE | | |
	81-182	81-30E	81-184	81-10A	82-73	81.17	81-180B	82-150B
rare earth elements, in ppm								
La	62.41	28.19	27.89	12.97	8.74	20.15	22.97	29.03
Ce	115.70	53.92	51.27	24.16	17.55	45.06	41.88	53.15
Pr	12.28	7.00	6.14	3.11	2.25	6.24	5.24	6.20
Nd	47.64	27.26	24.19	13.21	10.00	18.87	21.25	23.00
Sm	7.09	4.12	4.28	2.54	2.92	5.93	3.96	3.54
Eu	1.54	1.13	0.77	0.54	0.34	1.53	0.64	0.78
Gd	4.93	2.65	3.05	1.92	3.04	5.12	2.88	2.64
Dy	3.43	1.68	2.14	1.55	5.52	4.31	2.07	1.92
Ho	0.76	0.53	0.45	0.32	1.52	0.82	0.42	0.52
Er	1.96	0.97	1.07	0.87	6.37	2.36	10.10	1.14
Yb	1.61	0.73	0.80	0.76	10.17	1.99	0.80	0.98
Lu	0.24	0.09	0.08	0.08	1.80	0.29	0.09	0.14
Total	259.59	128.27	122.13	62.03	70.22	122.67	112.30	123.04

*See Table 2 for major and trace element data and unit descriptions.
†See Table 3 for major and trace element data and unit descriptions.

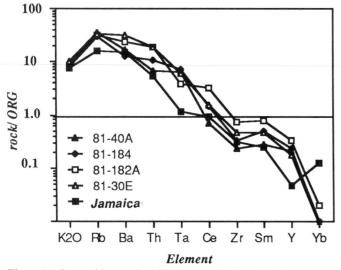

Figure 11. Ocean ridge granite (ORG) normalized geochemical patterns for oceanic island arc granite from Jamaica (Pearce and others, 1984) and the leucocratic granites.

minimal high-level fractional crystallization involved in the generation of individual units in the leucocratic granites.

Eocene volcanic-plutonic units

The Eocene volcanic-plutonic units are predominantly intermediate in composition; rocks of dacite to rhyodacite in the volcanic section and diorite to quartz monzodiorite dominate the intrusive rocks; volumetrically, silicic rocks are less abundant. Variation diagrams of major and trace elements discriminate the O'Brien Creek Suite as a geochemically distinct magmatic event (Fig. 12). Discrimination using Peacock's (1931) alkali-lime index indicates that the Sanpoil and Deadhorse suites are calc-alkalic. The limited compositional range of the O'Brien Creek Suite precludes classifying this unit by the alkali-lime index; however, it has a weakly defined trend, indicating a calcic index similar to the leucocratic granites.

Major-element discrimination between the O'Brien Creek Suite and the younger Sanpoil and Deadhorse suites and Klondike Mountain Formation is best illustrated by the potash versus silica plot (Fig. 8), which shows that the O'Brien Creek Suite is medium-K dacite and rhyolite, based on the classification by Peccarillo and Taylor (1976), and is compositionally restricted in terms of silica content with a range of 68 to 72 wt.% SiO_2. The younger volcanic and intrusive rocks are considered high-K acid andesite to rhyolite; within these suites, there is a distinct compositional gap between 67 and 70 wt.% SiO_2. Other major elements do not as clearly discriminate the O'Brien Creek Suite from the younger volcanic and intrusive units. In addition, the limited silica range of the O'Brien Creek Suite precludes defining enrichment or depletion trends for other major elements; rather, those elements are described as enriched or depleted at a given silica content relative to the younger rocks in the Eocene volcanic-plutonic asemblage. Alumina shows some enrichment in the O'Brien Creek Suite; however, because some of the analyses are

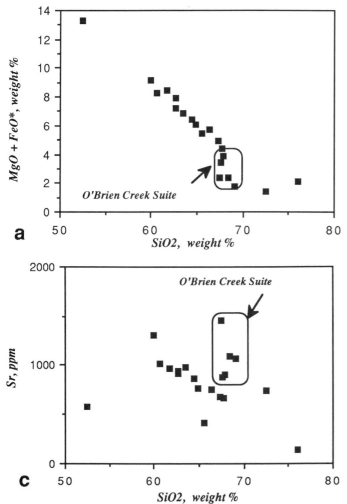

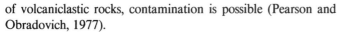

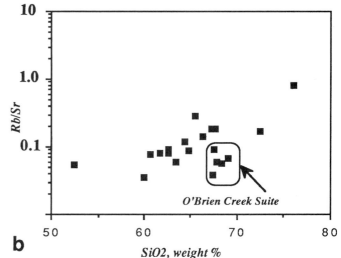

Figure 12. Variation diagrams for the Eocene volcanic-plutonic assemblage: a = FeO + MgO/SiO$_2$ plot; b = Rb/Sr versus SiO$_2$ plot; c = Sr/SiO$_2$ plot.

of volcaniclastic rocks, contamination is possible (Pearson and Obradovich, 1977).

The Sanpoil and Deadhorse suites show well-defined trends for major oxides plotted against silica. FeO and MgO decrease with increasing silica (Fig. 12a), probably due to the abundance of hornblende and pyroxene in the more mafic units; TiO$_2$ and P$_2$O$_5$ show similar trends; this reflects the decrease in apatite and sphene, which are abundant in the more mafic rocks of the suite but rare in the rhyolites and granites. CaO also decreases systematically with silica; however, alumina does not show a well-defined trend, possibly due to the range in the percentage of total feldspar throughout the suite.

Trace-element data also discriminate the O'Brien Creek Suite geochemically (Fig. 12b, c). It is relatively enriched in Sr, Ba, and Zr and depleted in Rb, Y, Ni, and Cr compared to Sanpoil and Deadhorse suite rocks of similar SiO$_2$ content. Sr enrichment may be tied to the high percentage of phenocrystic plagioclase (30 to 50 percent) in the O'Brien Creek Formation.

The Eocene volcanic-plutonic asemblage has a REE signature (Fig. 13) similar to the leucocratic granites in that the LREE are enriched with respect to HREE: La/Lu ranges from 69 in the more mafic (55.7 percent SiO$_2$) of the Sanpoil intrusives to 255

in a silica-rich (72.6 percent SiO$_2$) Deadhorse intrusive (Table 4). There is also a slight negative Eu anomaly in the Deadhorse intrusive and more felsic Sanpoil intrusive, which reflects a slightly lower percentage of modal plagioclase in each of the units.

Geochemical data were normalized to N-type mid-ocean ridge basalt (MORB) (Pearce, 1982) and hypothetical ocean ridge granite (ORG) (Pearce and others, 1984) to compare the behavior of LIL and HFS elements in the medium-K and high-K suites to the leucocratic granites and to possible mafic parental magmas. Compared to ORG, the LIL are moderately enriched (2 to 40× ORG) and the HFS are weakly depleted (0.8 to 80× ORG) (Fig. 14a). Monzodiorite of the Devil's Elbow pluton (N-5) shows the least enrichment of LIL and least depletion of HFS. Silicic rhyolite domes (9480-1) of the Deadhorse suite show the greatest enrichment and depletion of LIL and HFS, respectively. Rhyodacite intrusives from the O'Brien Creek suite show strong enrichment in Ba and strong depletion in Y, similar to that observed in the leucocratic granites. Compared to a N-type MORB (Fig. 14b), the Eocene volcanic-plutonic assemblage is enriched in Sr, K$_2$O, Rb, Ba, P$_2$O$_5$, and Zr but depleted in TiO$_2$ and Y. The most mafic unit in the suite (No. 11) shows the least enrichment and depletion compared to a N-type MORB. As might be expected, the more silicic units show the greatest degree of enrichment and depletion.

Limited isotope data indicate that the O'Brien Creek Suite has high initial Sr ratios (0.711), whereas the Sanpoil suite has lower values (0.706 to 0.708) (Carlson and others, 1988). These preliminary results suggest that the O'Brien Creek Suite may represent a melt with a significant upper-crustal component,

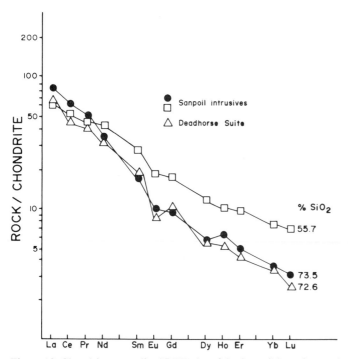

Figure 13. Chondrite normalized REE plot of the Sanpoil intrusives and Deadhorse suite granite.

whereas the Sanpoil suite may reflect an increased involvement of subcrustal components.

DISCUSSION

The Colville Igneous Complex was emplaced during the transition from earlier crustal thickening to Paleogene extension and records the opening of the Republic and Keller grabens and movement on the Okanogan, Kettle, and Lincoln complexes. Evidence for contemporaneity of graben formation and movement on the complexes is given by the Coyote Creek pluton (Atwater, 1985). According to Atwater (1985), emplacement of the Coyote was structurally controlled along the southeastern margin by the western bounding fault of the Republic graben (Fig. 2), whereas the northwestern contact with the Okanogan complex is intrusive and contains an incipient mylonitic fabric and mineral lineation that parallel the penetrative mylonitic fabric in the gneisses of the complex. Together, the Coulee Dam Intrusive Suite and granite of Daisy Trail show similar relations. The Keller granite and granite porphyry of the Coulee Dam Intrusive Suite are elongate parallel to the grabens, yet the Keller granite is cataclastically deformed by the eastern bounding fault of the Republic graben (Carlson, 1984). Where the granite of Daisy Trail intrudes the Kettle complex, it contains a kinematic overprint similar to that in the Kettle gneisses. This suggests that emplacement of the leucocratic granites was guided by the same northwest-southeast–directed extension that formed the grabens and that emplacement was temporally related to ductile movement on the Okanogan, Kettle, and Lincoln complexes.

The leucocratic granites were rapidly unroofed before volcanism and plutonism associated with the Eocene assemblage occurred. Rapid unroofing of the leucocratic granites is required by the O'Brien Creek Formation, which rests unconformably on weathered Keller Granite. The leucocratic granites intruded to epizonal levels before crystallization was complete, because

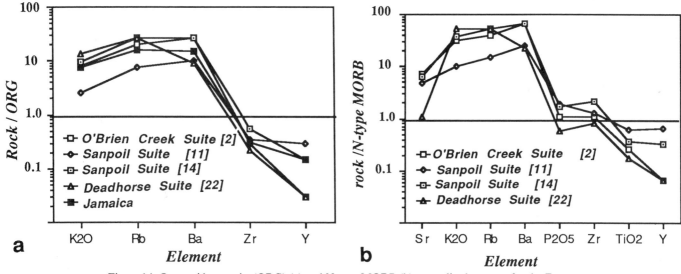

Figure 14. Ocean ridge granite (ORG) (a) and N-type MORB (b) normalized patterns for the Eocene volcanic-plutonic assemblage.

quench textures and intrusive breccias and other evidence of near-surface venting is common. The paucity of roof rocks may be explained by doming of the surface in association with the shallow level of emplacement and/or by detachment of the roof during the beginning stages of extension. Intrusion to an epizonal level was probably aided by extension.

The volcanic-plutonic assemblage records the period of maximum extension during the Eocene. Volcanic rocks vented along the graben faults and are preserved in the down-dropped blocks. The subvolcanic sheeted dikes in the hypabyssal complex of Cody Butte are strongly controlled by extension, which also produced the grabens, as are the subvolcanic, cauldron-like intrusives of the Sanpoil suite. The volume of dikes to country rock in the Cody Butte requires at least 10 km of extension of the crust (Moye and others, 1987). Movement on the Okanogan complex continued through the Eocene, as indicated by the 49-Ma Swimptkin Creek pluton (Fig. 2), which contains a mineral lineation that parallels the penetrative mylonitic lineation in the complex. The structural control of the Sanpoil intrusives further supports the interpretation that graben formation was contemporaneous with deformation in the complexes and that movement lasted at least until 49 Ma.

The chemistry and isotopic signature of the Colville Igneous Complex suggests that the leucocratic granites and volcanic-plutonic assemblage were derived from different source areas. That the leucocratic granites are not associated with more mafic border units and are silica rich, LREE enriched, compositionally restricted with respect to silica and other major elements, and have intermediate initial strontium ratios, suggest that the granites may have formed by small degrees of partial melting in the lower crust. The melting may have been initiated during the period of crustal thickening. However, intrusion of the magma was guided during the beginning stages of extension. The O'Brien

Creek Formation is chemically similar to the leucocratic granites, except for higher Sr values and much higher initial strontium ratios. This may be a function of contamination by a strontium-enriched upper crust. Melting of the upper crustal levels was probably aided by the ascent of leucocratic magmas, which resulted in an increased geothermal gradient. The lower initial strontium values in the more mafic Sanpoil suite may be attributed to involvement of subcrustal components during the period of maximum extension.

The Colville Igneous Complex was emplaced during the transition from compression and crustal thickening to extension and thinning of the crust that affected much of the Cordillera. The Colville rocks record this transition and also the timing of detachment on the Okanogan, Kettle, and Lincoln complexes and development of the intervening graben structures.

ACKNOWLEDGMENTS

Many geologists who were part of the U.S. Geological Survey Colville Indian Reservation Mapping Project contributed to the ideas presented in this chapter: B. F. Atwater, K. F. Fox, Jr., C. D. Rinehart, J. W. Goodge, V. L. Hansen, G. McCarley-Holder, R. W. Holder, F. Simms, and S. Singer. W. C. Utterback is recognized for his thought-provoking ideas on the origin of the Colville batholith and its relation to mineralization at Mt. Tolman. We thank W. R. Hackett, C. D. Rinehart, and B. P. Rhodes for thorough and very helpful reviews of the chapter. We are indebted to C. D. Rinehart, K. F. Fox, Jr., and B. F. Atwater and the U.S. Geological Survey for supporting this work and to the Colville Confederated Tribes for granting access on the reservation. D. Carlson also acknowledges support from a California State University–Sacramento Research Assigned Time Grant.

REFERENCES CITED

Armstrong, R. L., Harakal, J. E., and Hollister, V. F., 1982, Eocene mineralization at Mount Tolman (Keller), Washington, and Silver Dyke, Montana: Isochron/West, no. 33, p. 9.

Atwater, B. F., 1985, The contemporaneity of the Republic graben and Okanogan gneiss dome: Geological Society of America Abstracts with Programs, v. 6, p. 381.

Atwater, B. F., and Rinehart, C. D., 1984, Preliminary geologic map of the Colville Indian Reservation: U.S. Geological Survey Open-File Report 84-389, 117 p.

——— , 1989, Geologic map of the Colville Indian Reservation: U.S. Geological Survey Miscellaneous Field Studies Map (in press).

Bostock, H. H., 1966, Feldspar and quartz phenocrysts in the Shingle Creek porphyry, British Columbia: Geological Survey of Canada Bulletin 126, 70 p.

Broch, M. J., 1979, Igneous and metamorphic petrology, structure, and mineral deposits of the Mineral Ridge area, Colville Indian Reservation, Washington [M.S. thesis]: Pullman, Washington State University, 204 p.

Brown, R. L., and Read, P. B., 1983, Shuswap terrane of British Columbia; A Mesozoic "core complex": Geology, v. 11, p. 164–168.

Carlson, D. H., 1984, Geology and petrochemistry of the Keller Butte pluton and associated intrusive rocks in the south half of the Nespelem and the north half of the Grand Coulee Dam quadrangles, and the development of cataclasites and fault lenses along the Manila Pass fault, northeastern Washington [Ph.D. thesis]: Pullman, Washington State University, 184 p.

——— , 1986, REE chemistry and evolution of intrusive rocks associated with the Colville batholith near Grand Coulee Dam, Washington: Geological Society of America Abstracts with Programs, v. 18, p. 93.

——— , 1989, Geology and geochemistry of the Coulee Dam Intrusive Suite and associated younger intrusions, Colville batholith, Washington: U.S. Geological Survey Bulletin 1846 (in press).

Carlson, D. H., Fleck, R. J., and Moye, F. J., 1988, Geochemistry and isotopic character of the Paleogene Colville Igneous Complex, northeastern Washington: Geological Society of America Abstracts with Programs, v. 20, no. 6, p. 409.

Fox, K. F., Jr., Rinehart, C. D., Engles, J. C., and Stern, T. W., 1976, Age of emplacement of the Okanogan gneiss dome, north-central Washington: Geological Society of America Bulletin, v. 87, p. 1217–1224.

Fox, K. F., Jr., Rinehart, C. D., and Engles, J. C., 1977, Plutonism and orogeny in north-central Washington; Timing and regional context: U.S. Geological Survey Professional Paper 989, 27 p.

Hansen, V. L., 1983, Kinematic interpretation of mylonitic rocks in the Okanogan dome, north-central Washington, and implications for dome evolution [M.S. thesis]: Missoula, University of Montana, 47 p.

Hansen, V. L., and Goodge, J. W., 1988, Metamorphism, structural petrology, and regional evolution of the Okanogan complex, northeastern Washington, *in* Ernst, G., ed., Metamorphism and crustal evolution of the western United States; Rubey v. VII: Englewood Cliffs, New Jersey, Prentice-Hall, p. 223–270.

Holder, R. W., 1986, Emplacement and geochemical evolution of Eocene plutonic rocks in the Colville batholith [Ph.D. thesis]: Pullman, Washington State University, 189 p.

Hooper, P. R., and Atkins, A., 1969, The preparation of fused samples in X-ray fluorescence analysis: Mineral Magazine, v. 37, p. 409–413.

Mathews, W. M., 1981, Early Cenozoic resetting of potassium-argon dates and geothermal history of north Okanagan area, British Columbia: Canadian Journal of Earth Sciences, v. 18, p. 1310–1319.

Miller, C. F., 1985, Are strongly peraluminous magmas derived from pelitic sedimentary sources?: Journal of Geology, v. 93, p. 673–689.

Monger, J.W.H., 1968, Early Tertiary stratified rocks, Greenwood map area (82 E/2), British Columbia: Geological Survey of Canada Paper 67-42, 39 p.

Moye, F. J., 1982, Eocene Sanpoil Volcanics of northeast Washington: Geological Society of America Abstracts with Programs, v. 14, p. 343.

——, 1984, Geology and petrochemistry of Tertiary igneous rocks in the western half of the Seventeenmile Mountain Quadrangle, Ferry County, Washington [Ph.D. thesis]: Moscow, University of Idaho, 187 p.

——, 1987, Republic graben, *in* Hill, M. L., ed., Cordilleran section: Boulder, Colorado, Geological Society of America, Centennial Field Guide, v. 1, p. 399–402.

Moye, F. J., Carlson, D. C., and Utterback, B., 1982, Volcanism and plutonism in a portion of northeastern Washington: Geological Society of America Abstracts with Programs, v. 14, p. 218.

Moye, F. J., Carlson, D. H., and Hackett, W. R., 1987, Tectonic implicatons of Paleogene igneous activity in the northwestern United States: Geological Society of America Abstracts with Programs, v. 19, p. 435.

Muessig, S. F., 1962, Tertiary volcanic and related rocks of the Republic area, Ferry County, Washington: U.S. Geological Survey Professional Paper 450-D, p. D56–D58.

——, 1967, Geology of the Republic and part of the Aeneas Quadrangle, Ferry County, Washington: U.S. Geological Survey Bulletin 1216, 135 p.

Okulitch, A. V., 1984, The role of the Shuswap Metamorphic Complex in Cordilleran tectonism; A review: Canadian Journal of Earth Sciences, v. 21, p. 1171–1198.

Orazulike, D. M., 1982, Igneous petrology and petrochemical variation in the Coyote Creek pluton, Colville batholith, and its relation to mineralization in Squaw Mountain, Colville Indian Reservation, Washington [Ph.D. thesis]: Pullman, Washington State University, 275 p.

Pardee, J. T., 1918, Geology and mineral deposits of the Colville Indian Reservation, Washington: U.S. Geological Survey Bulletin 677, 186 p.

Parker, R. L., and Calkins, J. A., 1964, Geology of the Curlew Quadrangle, Ferry County, Washington: U.S. Geological Survey Bulletin 1169, 95 p.

Peacock, M. S., 1931, Classification for the recognition of igneous rock series: Journal of Geology, v. 39, p. 54–67.

Pearce, J. A., 1982, Trace element characteristics of lavas from destructive plate boundaries, *in* Thorpe, R. S., eds., Andesites: New York, John Wiley and Sons, p. 525–548.

Pearce, J. A., Harris, N.B.W., and Tindle, A. G., 1984, Trace element discrimination diagrams for tectonic interpretation of granitic rocks: Journal of Petrology, v. 25, part 4, p. 956–983.

Pearson, R. C., 1967, Geologic map of the Bodie Mountain Quadrangle, Ferry and Okanogan counties, Washington: U.S. Geological Survey Geological Quadrangle Map GQ-636, scale 1:62,500.

Pearson, R. C., and Obradovich, J. D., 1977, Eocene rocks in northeast Washington; Radiometric ages and correlation: U.S. Geological Survey Bulletin 1433, 41 p.

Peccarillo, A., and Taylor, S. R., 1976, Geochemistry of Eocene calc-alakline volcanic rocks from the Kastamonu area, northern Turkey: Contributions to Mineralogy and Petrology, v. 58, p. 63–87.

Potter, C. J., and 7 others, 1986, COCORP deep seismic reflection of the interior of the North American Cordillera, Washington and Idaho; Implications for orogenic evolution: Tectonics, v. 5, no. 7, p. 1007–1025.

Price, R. A., 1981, The Cordilleran foreland thrust and fold belt in the southern Canadian Rocky Mountains, *in* Price, N. J., and MacClay, K., eds., Thrust and nappe tectonics: Geological Society of London Special Paper 9, p. 427–448.

Price, R. A., and Mountjoy, E. W., 1970, Geologic structure of the Canadian Rocky Mountains between Bow and Athabaska rivers; A progress report, *in* Wheeler, J. O., ed., Structure of the southern Canadian Cordillera: Geological Association of Canada Special Paper 6, p. 7–26.

Rhodes, B. P., and Cheny, E. S., 1981, Low-angle faulting and the origin of the Kettle Dome, a metamorphic core complex in northeastern Washington: Geology, v. 9, p. 366–369.

Singer, S. H., 1984, Geology of the west half of the Disautel 15-minute Quadrangle, Okanogan County, Washington [M.S. thesis]: Moscow, University of Idaho, 101 p.

Staatz, M. H., 1964, Geology of the Bald Knob Quadrangle, Ferry and Okanogan counties, Washington: U.S. Geological Survey Bulletin 1161-F, p. F-1–F-79.

Streckeisen, A. L., 1976, To each plutonic rock its proper name: Earth Science Review, v. 12, p. 1–33.

Tempelman-Kluit, D., and Parkinson, D., 1986, Extension across the Eocene Okanagan crustal shear in southern British Columbia: Geology, v. 14, p. 318–321.

Utterback, W. E., editor, 1984, Revised geology and mineral potential of the Colville Indian Reservation: Department of Geology, Colville Confederated Tribe, 81 p.

Volk, J., 1986, Structural analysis and kinematic interpretation of rocks in the southern portion of the Okanogan gneiss dome, north-central Washington [M.S. thesis]: Pullman, Washington State University, 156 p.

Walsh, J. N., Buckely, F., and Barker, J., 1981, The simultaneous determination of the rare-earth elements in rocks using inductively coupled plasma source spectrometry: Chemical Geology, v. 33, p. 141–153.

Waters, A. C., and Krauskopf, K., 1941, Protoclastic border of the Colville batholith: Geological Society of America Bulletin, v. 52, p. 1355–1418.

Wheeler, J. D., 1970, Introduction, *in* Wheeler, J. O., ed., Structure of the southern Canadian Cordillera: Geological Association of Canada Special Paper 6, p. 1–5.

MANUSCRIPT SUBMITTED JULY 15, 1987
REVISED MANUSCRIPT SUBMITTED FEBRUARY 26, 1988
MANUSCRIPT ACCEPTED BY THE SOCIETY FEBRUARY 7, 1989

Geological Society of America
Memoir 174
1990

Chapter 23

Two traverses across the Coast batholith, southeastern Alaska

Fred Barker
U.S. Geological Survey, Box 25042, Denver Federal Center, Denver, Colorado 80225
Joseph G. Arth
U.S. Geological Survey, National Center, Reston, Virginia 22092

ABSTRACT

Two traverses across the Coast batholith from Haines, Alaska, to Bennett, British Columbia (Skagway traverse), and from Ketchikan, Alaska, to Hyder, British Columbia (Ketchikan traverse), indicate the following general features.

(1) The batholith sutures, or stitches, Taku, Alexander, and Stikine terranes, which consist largely of tectonically thickened Paleozoic to Jurassic oceanic, volcanic, flyschoid, and carbonate rocks; cratonic rocks are absent.

(2) The batholith consists of discrete units or suites, episodically emplaced: the Skagway traverse shows western tonalitic gneiss (57 to 70 percent SiO_2, 68[?] Ma), central massive tonalite (59 to 71 percent SiO_2, 54 Ma) and minor tonalitic gneiss, and eastern massive granite (74 to 77 percent SiO_2, 52 to 48 Ma); the Ketchikan traverse shows western foliated tonalite (55 to 58 percent SiO_2, 55 to 57 Ma), central migmatitic dioritic to tonalitic gneiss (50 to 64 percent SiO_2, ca. 127 Ma), and eastern massive granodiorite and granite (61 to 71 percent SiO_2, 54 to 52 Ma).

(3) Emplacement of the batholith was syn- to post-accretionary and coeval with subduction.

(4) Most rocks are calc-alkalic, have moderate contents of K, high Sr, low Rb, and mildly enriched light rare earth elements (REE), except that minor high-SiO_2 granite of the Skagway traverse shows low Sr and moderate Rb; on the Qz-Or-(Ab+An) normative plot, compositions lie between high-Al basalt and the trondhjemite-granodiorite-granite field; initial $^{87}Sr/^{86}Sr$ ratios (SIR) are 0.7049–0.7060 (Skagway) and 0.7046–0.7066 (Ketchikan); initial $^{143}Nd/^{144}Nd$ ratios (NIR) are 0.51229–0.51240 (Ketchikan). Polarity of SIR are only found in the Ketchikan traverse, where western foliated tonalites have higher values than eastern granodiorite and granite.

West of the batholith, 93- to 89-Ma tonalite and granodiorite intruded Taku terrane and is chemically similar (60 to 67 percent SiO_2) to that of the batholith, but is isotopically and mineralogically distinct.

Proposed origins for the various suites of plutons are consistent in both traverses with their position relative to the migmatitic gneisses. Most massive plutons to the east of the gneisses in both traverses probably formed by fractionation of subduction-related high-Al tholeiite coupled by mixing with melts from metamorphosed mafic to siliceous igneous rocks and flysch of Mesozoic to Paleozoic age. A few smaller high-SiO_2 granite bodies may be largely melt of flysch or siliceous igneous rocks. Foliated tonalitic plutons to the west of the mignatites (Ketchikan traverse) display less subduction component and may have formed by melting of the mafic parts of the Mesozoic migmatitic gneiss.

Barker, F., and Arth, J. G., 1990, Two traverses across the Coast batholith, southeastern Alaska, *in* Anderson, J. L., ed., The nature and origin of Cordilleran magmatism: Boulder, Colorado, Geological Society of America Memoir 174.

INTRODUCTION

Coast batholith (Coast Plutonic Complex of many Canadian workers) is the largest Cordilleran batholith of North America. It underlies much of the Coast Mountains of British Columbia and southeastern Alaska, extending more than 1,700 km from near lat 49°N at the British Columbia–Washington boundary to well north of lat 61°N in the Yukon Territory (Hutchison, 1970; Roddick and Hutchison, 1974; Roddick, 1983a). Its breadth ranges from about 50 to 200 km. Early studies in British Columbia by Dawson (1881, 1888) and Brooks (1906) noted the existence of a great batholith, perhaps of Mesozoic age. The general nature and extent of the batholith in southeastern Alaska and nearby British Columbia were delineated by Buddington (1927), Buddington and Chapin (1929), and Hutchison (1982). Berg and others (1988) presented the geology of the Coast batholith in the Ketchikan area.

The Coast batholith is of continental-marginal type, but it differs from those of the western United States and Mexico in that it formed entirely in accreted rocks of general oceanic origin, and its eastern margin is located more than 200 km west of the miogeoclinal and other rocks of the North American craton. The northern third of the batholith, from the Prince Rupert area to the Yukon Territory (Fig. 1), is bounded on the east by Paleozoic and Mesozoic rocks of Stikine terrane (Stikinia), and on the west by the late Paleozoic to early Mesozoic Taku terrane, the early Paleozoic to Jurassic rocks of the Alexander terrane and the overlying Gravina-Nutzotin belt (Berg and others, 1988).

The western margin of the Coast batholith in southeastern Alaska is generally delineated by a remarkably linear geomorphic and geologic feature termed the Coast Range megalineament by Brew and Ford (1978). Rocks along this western margin, at least in the Ketchikan–Prince Rupert area, show 10 to 30 km of uplift (Hollister, 1982; Crawford and Hollister, 1982; Kenah and Hollister, 1983).

The Coast batholith in southeastern Alaska consists of three general parts: foliated western tonalite (IUGS Subcommission terminology), central migmatitic gneisses (especially in the Ketchikan region) of quartz dioritic to tonalitic compositions, and eastern massive granodiorite and granite. Intrusion was episodic, as discussed below. In addition, tonalites found just west of the megalineament on Revillagigedo Island (Fig. 2, units ti and mb) are generally similar in chemistry to those of the batholith, but are part of a geographically separate and temporally distinct episode of plutonism (ca. 90 Ma; Arth and others, 1988) found in Taku terrane, and are not considered part of the Coast batholith.

This paper summarizes geochemical and geochronological results and genetic interpretations obtained from two traverses across the Coast batholith, one from Haines to Skagway, Alaska, and north to near Bennett, British Columbia (Skagway traverse); the other from near Ketchikan on Revillagigedo Island to Hyder, Alaska, and British Columbia (Ketchikan traverse). For the Skagway traverse, a new geological reconnaissance map, and petrologic, geochronologic, chemical, and isotopic data were given in Barker and others (1986). A preliminary report on migmatitic gneisses in the Ketchikan area was made by Barker and Arth (1984). Tonalitic through granitic plutons of the Ketchikan traverse were the subject of a petrologic, geochronlogic, chemical, and isotopic study by Arth and others (1988).

COMPONENTS OF THE BATHOLITH

Skagway and Ketchikan traverses

The geology of the Coast batholith along the Skagway traverse in northernmost southeastern Alaska, as reported by Barker and others (1986), is shown in Figure 1. Geology along the Ketchikan traverse in southernmost southeastern Alaska (Fig. 2) is from Berg and others (1988) and Arth and others (1988). The major plutonic rocks found in these two traverses are described briefly in this section, and were described more thoroughly in Barker and Arth (1984), Barker and others (1986), Arth and others (1988), and Berg and others (1988).

The Skagway traverse (Fig. 1) consists of (1) Cretaceous(?) quartz dioritic to tonalitic orthogneiss in both the southwestern and central parts of the batholith; (2) 54 Ma (the abbreviation Ma is used in accord with the North American Stratigraphic Code wherein qualifiers such as "age" or "before the present" are implied) massive tonalite and granodiorite (the "tonalite of Skagway" of Barker and others, 1986) in the central part; (3) 53 to 48 Ma granites of Summit Lake and Clifton in the central and eastern parts; and (4) 72 Ma granite of Log Cabin, along the northeastern margin of the batholith.

The Ketchikan traverse (Fig. 2) consists of (1) 57 to 55 Ma foliated western tonalite and quartz diorite (unit wt); (2) Early Cretaceous, central migmatitic gneisses to quartz dioritic to granodioritic compositions (unit gc); (3) 54 to 52 Ma massive eastern granodiorite and granite (unit eg); (4) quartz dioritie and tonalite plutons, ca. 90 Ma, just west of the Coast batholith in the Taku terrane (unit ti); and (5) minor, epizonal mid-Tertiary plutons found both in the batholith and to the west of the Taku terrane (unit mi).

Western tonalite and orthogneiss

The southwestern part of the Skagway traverse (Fig. 1) consists of heterogeneous quartz dioritic and tonalitic gneiss that is partly migmatitic, screens or pendants of metasedimentary biotite gneiss, and lenticular masses of relatively homogeneous tonalite gneiss. The orthogneisses are typically gray, medium- to coarse-grained, and contain both hornblende and biotite. The gneiss along the southwestern margin of the batholith, at Lutak Inlet, shows highly sheared mortar structure in thin section, and overgrowths of metamorphic green hornblende on magmatic brown cores. The mortar gneiss gave $^{206}Pb/^{238}U$ and $^{207}Pb/^{235}U$ ages on zircon of 68.2 Ma and 67.3 Ma, respectively. These ages may represent the time of magmatic crystallization or the influence of a later thermal or tectonic event. Homogeneous

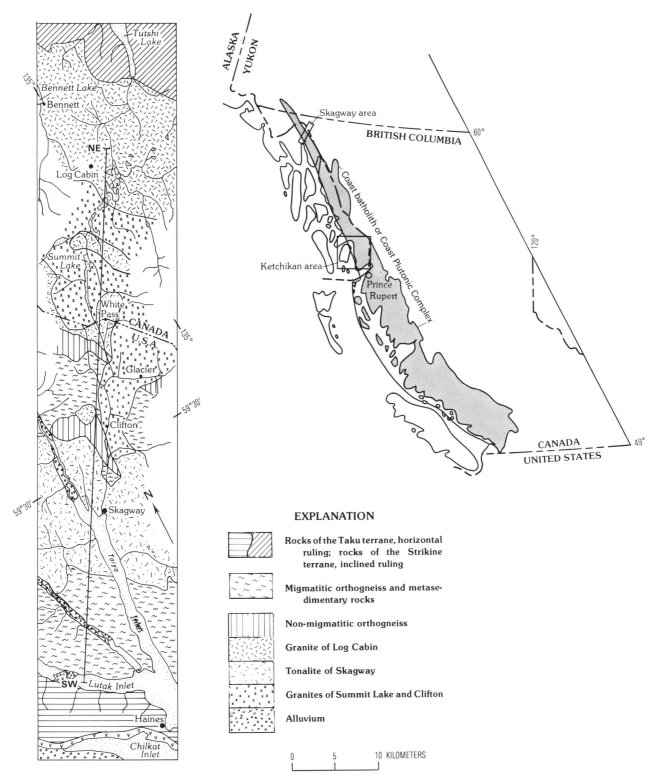

Figure 1. Index map of the Skagway and Ketchikan traverses and geologic map of Skagway traverse (Barker and others, 1986), showing line of northeast-southwest section of Figure 3a.

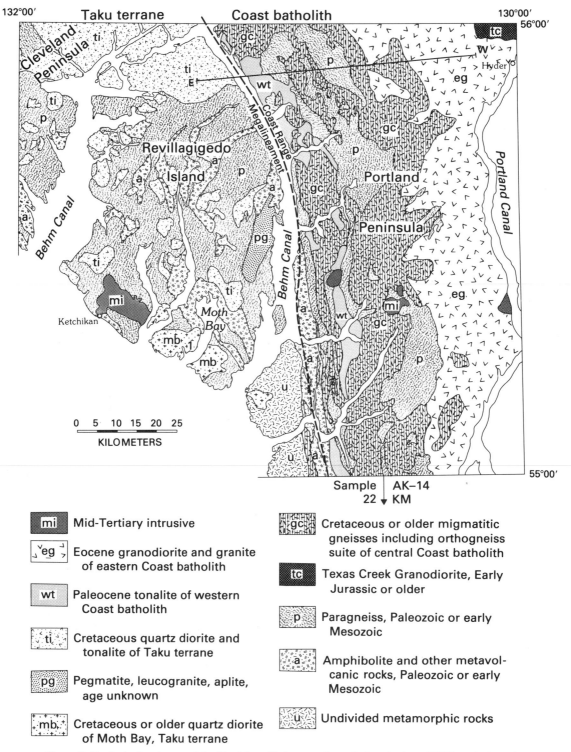

Figure 2. Geologic sketch map of the Ketchikan-Hyder area, from Arth and others (1988) and adapted from Berg and others (1988), showing line of east-west section of Figure 3b.

hornblende-biotite tonalitic gneiss several kilometers to the southwest gave a K-Ar age on hornblende of 59.9 Ma, which may represent the time of uplift or resetting by a post-emplacement thermal event. This rock is petrographically similar to the Tonalite Sill east of Juneau (Brew, 1981) dated at 67 Ma by the U-Pb method on zircon (Gehrels and others, 1983).

In the Ketchikan-Hyder area (Fig. 2), hornblende-biotite quartz dioritic and tonalitic gneiss (unit wt) is well exposed along the western margin of the batholith in the deep fiords that cut into Portland Peninsula. This gneiss is medium gray, coarse-grained, and well foliated. The foliation may have formed either by flow during emplacement or by regional stress. This gneiss occurs as lenticular to tabular masses parallel to subparallel to the schistosity of the enclosing gneisses and schists. This rock is probably part of the "Tonalite Sill" of Brew (1981), but has consistently younger ages of 55 to 57 Ma as determined by the U-Th-Pb method on zircons in the Ketchikan quadrangle and adjacent quadrangles to the north (Bradfield Canal quadrangle) and to the south Prince Rupert quadrangle).

Central gneisses

Orthogneisses are found in the central region of the Coast batholith in both Skagway and Ketchikan traverses. Such rocks form a very extensive mass in the Ketchikan traverse (Fig. 2, unit gc), whereas in the Skagway traverse, they consist of three fragments of 3 to 10 km maximum horizontal dimension (Fig. 1).

Typical orthogneiss of the Skagway traverse is hornblende-biotite tonalite in composition, well foliated, shows light and dark streaking of mafic minerals, is medium to coarse grained, and medium gray. This rock gives discordant U-Pb ages on zircon: $^{206}Pb/^{238}U = 61.7$ Ma, $^{207}Pb/^{235}U = 66.1$ Ma, and $^{208}Pb/^{232}Th$ = 71.0 Ma. K-Ar ages of 49.4 Ma on biotite and of 54.7 Ma on hornblende are also discordant. The time of magmatic crystallization probably is older than the $^{206}Pb/^{238}U$ age of 61.7 Ma. The K-Ar ages probably indicate resetting of older, metamorphic or magmatic ages by heat from the nearby granite of Clifton at 48 Ma.

The orthogneiss of Ketchikan traverse (Central Gneiss Complex of Hutchison, 1970; and Barker and Arth, 1984) is markedly heterogeneous, being migmatitic. It is medium to dark gray, medium to coarse grained, banded by quartzofeldspathic and hornblende-biotitic layers or streaks about 1 cm to 1 m thick, well foliated, and cut by various streaks and blebs of aplite and pegmatite. These aplite-pegmatite bodies constitute a few percent to more than 10 percent of the migmatite. They lie both parallel and at various angles to the foliation of the gneiss matrix. Their contacts with the matrix range from sharp to diffuse; some show a poor foliation, but most are massive. Their contents of hornblende and biotite typically are low, but these phases are concentrated locally. Slabs and irregular fragments of pelitic gneiss and metagraywacke that range from a few meters to several kilometers in maximum dimension are scattered in the migmatitic orthogneiss. Several samples of the migmatitic orthogneiss were dated

by the U-Pb method on zircon. The ages range from 117 to 140 Ma and are mostly discordant. One sample gives a concordant age of 127 Ma. These rocks are thus taken to be Early Cretaceous.

Eastern granodiorite and granite

The 54 to 48 Ma intrusives that form the eastern parts of the Coast batholith in our two traverses comprise tonalitic, granodioritic, and granitic rocks. In addition, the northeastern part of the batholith at the Skagway traverse consists of a large (10 to 13 km in breadth, Fig. 1) mass of biotite-hornblende granite, informally termed the granite of Log Cabin. It has SiO_2 contents of 67 to 73 percent and dates from 72 Ma by the U-Pb method on zircon. This mass, though physically a part of the Coast batholith at this latitude, is unique and not found elsewhere. Its age and chemical character are like those of plutons in the Surprise Lake batholith 50 to 80 km to the east and emplaced in rocks of the Stikine terrane (Ballantyne and Littlejohn, 1982). The granite of Log Cabin thus belongs to the extensive suite of intrusives of the Stikine terrane; it is only a part of the Coast batholith by coincidence, and will not be considered further here.

The eastern suite of the Skagway traverse consists of two general intrusive types: the tonalite of Skagway and the granites of Summit Lake and Clifton. The tonalite of Skagway actually forms the central part of the batholith at Skagway, and in that sense should not be grouped with the eastern suite. However, a smaller body of similar tonalite, found 20 km north of Skagway at White Pass (Fig. 1), has a U-Pb age of 54 Ma on zircon, has a massive post-tectonic fabric, and has a chemical character like that of the eastern suite at Hyder and along Portland Canal. Thus, we consider it to be an intrusive of the eastern suite. The tonalite of Skagway is light gray, medium to coarse grained, typically massive but locally flow-foliated, homogeneous except for ubiquitous centimeter-size dark inclusions, and ranges in composition from tonalite to granodiorite. It shows two petrographic varieties, one in which hornblende and biotite are euhedral, the other in which those minerals are anhedral. A K-Ar age on biotite near Skagway of 52.4 Ma indicates that the pluton cooled to 300°C within about 2 m.y. after its emplacement.

The major intrusives of the eastern suite of Skagway traverse also include the granites of Summit Lake and Clifton. Because these rocks are similar to each other and the contacts between them could not be located easily in the field, they are considered together. These biotite granites are pink to buff, massive, homogeneous, fine grained (Clifton) and medium grained (Summit Lake), and sparsely cut by aplite and pegmatite. Miarolitic cavities near Clifton indicate shallow emplacement. The U-Pb ages on zircon of Summit Lake are concordant at 52 Ma; those of Clifton are concordant at 48 Ma.

The eastern granodiorites and granites of the Ketchikan traverse (Fig. 2, unit eg) are buff to pink to gray, massive, typically homogeneous, and medium to coarse grained. Like the eastern rocks of Skagway traverse, these rocks sharply crosscut older

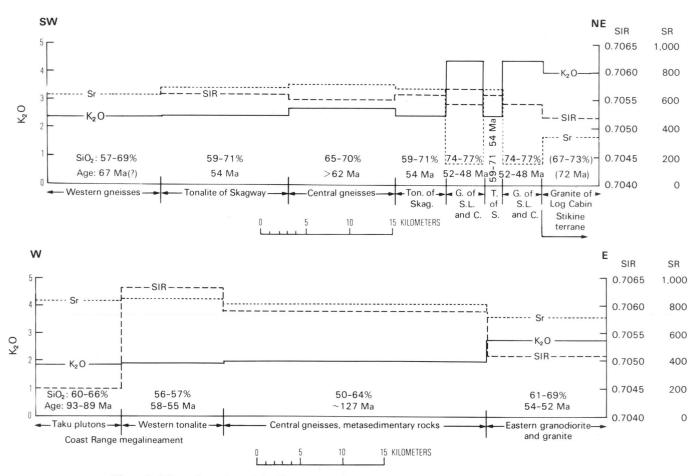

Figure 3. Schematic sections of the Skagway and Ketchikan traverses, showing K₂O (weight percent), Sr (ppm), SIR, range of SiO₂, and ages of suites.

rocks. Most samples have concordant or near-concordant U-Pb zircon ages of 54 to 52 Ma, which is taken as the age of emplacement. One sample, however, is 127 to 99 Ma by U-Pb and U-Th, and 51 Ma by the K-Ar technique on hornblende. This is interpreted as the result of inherited zircon in a rock of ca. 51 Ma.

Plutons of Taku terrane

Plutons of quartz diorite and tonalite that range in maximum horizontal dimension from a few to more than 60 km lie west of the western margin of the Coast batholith in the Taku terrane of Revillagigedo Island and Cleveland Peninsula (Fig. 2, unit ti). They extend from the Coast Range megalineament to as much as 45 km to the west. These rocks typically are medium gray, slightly to moderately foliated, and homogeneous. Magmatic garnet and epidote are common (Zen and Hammarstrom, 1984), and most varieties contain both hornblende and biotite. Clinopyroxene, which we have not found in Coast batholith intrusives, is a minor phase in some of this tonalite of the Taku terrane. These rocks give near-concordant U-Pb ages on zircon of 93 to 89 Ma and K-Ar ages on hornblende as old as about 90 Ma.

Mid-Tertiary plutons

Several small plutons of Oligocene to Miocene age intrude the Coast batholith and Taku terrane (Fig. 2, unit mi). One pluton, intruded into central gneisses of the batholith at Quartz Hill (Ketchikan quadrangle), contains a major molybdenum deposit (Hudson and others, 1981). These plutons are volumetrically very minor in the batholith, however, and will not be considered further.

SUMMARY OF CHRONOLOGIC, GEOGRAPHIC, CHEMICAL, AND ISOTOPIC FEATURES

Four distinguishing features of the Coast batholith along the Ketchikan and Skagway traverses are listed in Table 1 and shown graphically in Figure 3. These features include age, position in the batholith, major- and minor-element chemistry, and Sr and Nd isotopic initial ratios. These four will be discussed individually here, prior to our synthesis in the last section.

Ages of plutons within the Coast batholith, like other Cordilleran batholiths, reflect episodic emplacement. The major plutonic events were: (1) formation of the plutonic protoliths of the

TABLE 1. SUMMARY OF SOME CHEMICAL AND ISOTOPIC FEATURES OF THE MAJOR UNITS FOUND IN KETCHIKAN–HYDER (K-H) AND SKAGWAY (S) TRAVERSES*

	Traverse	Age	SiO_2	K_2O	Rb	Sr	La_N	Lu_N	SIR	NIR
Granites of Summit Lake and Clifton	S	52-48	74-77	4.18-4.65	125-201	87-210	67-140	6.9-12	0.7048-0.7060	n.d.
Eastern granodiorite and granite	K-H	54-52	61-69	1.83-3.69	47-110	543-904	43-113	3.2-9.7	0.7046-0.7056	0.51240
Tonalite of Skagway	S	54	59-71	1.81-3.05	48-75	531-830	27-95	4.0-7.4	0.7054-0.7058	n.d.
Western tonalite	K-H	58-55	56-57	1.83-2.01	47-75	784-904	43-64	4.9-8.3	0.7063-0.7064	0.51229-0.51238
Central orthogeneiss	S	>62?	65-70	2.24-3.19	52-83	712	149-186	2.9-3.7	0.7055	n.d.
Western orthogeneiss	S	67?	57-69	1.74-305	45.64	479-775	27-152	1.4-8.6	n.d.	n.d.
Taku plutons	K-H	93-89	60-66	1.18-2.49	32-66	600-1070	49-70	6.3-7.7	0.7041-0.7049	0.51246-0.51265
Central gneisses	K-H	ca. 127	50-64	1.44-3.57	26-107	727-899	46-213	4.6-19	0.7052-0.7066	n.d.

*Ages in millions of years, SiO_2 and K_2O in weight percent, Rb and Sr in parts per million, La normalized to chondritic values (0.328) and Lu ditto (0.0349), SIR = $^{87}Sr/^{86}Sr$ initial ratio and NIR = ^{144}Nd initial ratio. Data from Barker and Arth (1984), Barker and others (1986), and Arth and others (1988). n.d. = not determined.

central gneiss of K-H Traverse at about 120 to 140 Ma, (2) intrusion of deep-seated plutons at ca. 90 Ma west of the batholith in the Taku terrane, (3) injection of tabular to lenticular bodies of tonalite ("Tonalite Sill") in the westernmost part of the batholith, and (4) generation and emplacement of great volumes of siliceous plutons in the eastern part of the batholith from 54 to 48 Ma. Intrusion of the western tonalites may have started in the north and progressed southward. We suggest this on the basis of available U/Pb ages (mostly concordant) in southeast Alaska, from south to north, as follows:

Quadrangle	Age in m.y.	Reference
Prince Rupert	55	(Arth and others, 1988)
Ketchikan	56	(Arth and others, 1988)
Bradfield Canal	57	(Arth and others, 1988)
Petersburg	64	(Gehrels and others, 1983)
Juneau	67	(Gehrels and others, 1983)
Skagway	68?	(Barker and others, 1986)

Position of plutonic units from west to east, or southwest to northeast, is generally found to be quartz diorite and tonalite both west of, and in the western part of, the batholith; both mafic to tonalitic gneisses and massive tonalite and granodiorite in the central part; and massive granodiorite and granite in the eastern 30 to 40 percent of the batholith. Thus, there is a general progression of more siliceous and potassic intrusives from west to east, as Buddington (1927) pointed out, but this change is more step-wise than continuous, and some reversals are present (see Figs. 1, 2, and 3).

The distinguishing chemical features of the batholith, based on 70 analyses of major and trace elements from our two traverses (Barker and Arth, 1984; Barker and others, 1986; and Arth and others, 1988; and see our Table 1) may be summarized briefly as follows.

1. The Coast batholith is dominantly tonalite, but approximately 20 percent at Ketchikan and 30 to 35 percent at Skagway is granite, 10 to 15 percent at each traverse is granodiorite, and less than 5 percent is quartz diorite.

2. All intrusive units are calc-alkalic, as shown by plots of the Alk-F-M diagram of Irvine and Baragar (1971), the total alkali-SiO_2 diagram of Kuno (1969), and the $FeO*/MgO-SiO_2$ (where $FeO* = FeO + O.9Fe_2O_3$) plot of Miyashiro (1974).

3. Rocks of intermediate SiO_2 contents, in keeping with the tonalitic character of more than half of the batholith, are abundant (Table 1). Furthermore, all units of the batholith except the Paleocene western tonalite show wide ranges of SiO_2: the central orthogneisses of the Ketchikan traverse show a range of 14 percent, western gneisses of the Skagway traverse show a range of 12 percent, tonalite of Skagway also shows 12 percent, and the eastern granodiorite and granite show an overall range from 61 to 77 percent. The central orthogneisses of the Ketchikan traverse have major-element abundances like those of Gill's (1981) averages of high-K orogenic andesite.

4. K_2O contents show the common increase with SiO_2 of most Cordilleran batholiths: samples of the central gneisses of the

Ketchikan traverse show the greatest increase, and those of the western orthogneiss and tonalite the smallest increase (Table 1). However, none of these major units shows very low K_2O or very high K_2O; all, even the high-SiO_2 granites of the Skagway traverse at 4.2 to 4.6 percent K_2O, show moderate values.

5. Na_2O contents for most rocks of the batholith are 3 to 4 percent.

6. Although Al_2O_3 contents decrease steeply as SiO_2 increases, rocks of 50 to 65 percent SiO_2 contain 16 to 18 percent Al_2O_3. The mafic to intermediate rocks thus are of high Al_2O_3 type.

7. Sr abundances are high for all rocks except in the 52 to 48 Ma granites of the Skagway traverse: most rocks contain 500 to 900 ppm (Table 1), and show a decrease of Sr with increasing SiO_2.

8. Rb abundances are generally quite low, with a maximum of about 200 ppm. Changes of Rb reflect those of K_2O and show mild increase with increasing SiO_2.

9. REE patterns typically are slightly concave upward, have La_N values of 27 to 213 and Lu_N of 1.4 to 19 (Table 1), and exhibit either no or small Eu anomalies, except for the negative anomalies of the granites of Summit Lake and Clifton ($Eu/Eu* = 0.3-0.4$).

Initial ratios of $^{87}Sr/^{86}Sr$ (SIR) and of $^{143}Nd/^{144}Nd$ (NIR) do not show large ranges: SIR = 0.7041 to 0.7066 and NIR = 0.51229 to 0.51265. However, these ratios show significant differences from one unit of the batholith to another (Table 1). Note that SIR of Taku plutons are the lowest (0.7041 to 0.7050). SIR of the western tonalite, just east of the Taku terrane, are the highest (0.7063 to 0.7064), excepting the single value of 0.7066 of an aplite dike in the central gneisses of Ketchikan traverse. In addition, SIR of the 54 to 48 Ma eastern intrusives (0.7046 to 0.7061) tend to be generally lower than those of the older, more mafic gneisses. NIR of Taku plutons are higher than those of the Coast batholith. On a SIR-NIR plot (Arth and others, 1988), points of the Taku intrusives lie in or near the intersection of Zartman's (1984) fields for island-arc rocks and for young or mafic crustal rocks, whereas Coast batholithic rocks plot wholly in the field of crustal rocks.

Pillowform mafic inclusions are found in Coast batholith intrusives, and are believed to represent coeval, mantle-derived magmas. Analyses of two of these (Barker and others, 1986) indicate that they are high-Al, tholeiitic basalts. Comparison of many chemical abundances and SIR of these inclusions with the lowest SiO_2 members of suites of batholithic rocks shows many close similarities (Table 2).

CONCLUSIONS

The Coast batholith in southeastern Alaska formed in a complex tectonic regime in which the Alexander and Taku terranes were accreted to the Stikine terrane (Monger and others, 1982) and which overlay a long-lived subduction zone where Farallon and Kula plates plunged northeastward (e.g., see Byrne

**TABLE 2. COMPARISON OF SOME CHEMICAL ABUNDANCES AND SIR's OF
TWO BASALTIC INCLUSIONSAND OF LEAST-SILICEOUS MEMBERS OF BATHOLITHIC
SUITES THAT SHOW WIDE RANGES OF SiO$_2$***

	Inclusions		Batholithic Rocks			
	AK-203	AK-213l	Central Gneiss (K-H)	Western tonalite (K-H)	Western gneiss (S)	Tonalite of Skagway
SiO$_2$	48.2	53.4	50.7	55.8	57.3	58.6
Al$_2$O$_3$	20.2	18.6	19.5	18.5	18.6	17.8
FeO*	9.36	7.86	8.23	6.99	6.32	6.23
MgO	7.84	4.46	3.70	3.70	3.35	2.62
K$_2$O	1.94	1.81	1.92	1.89	1.74	1.93
TiO$_2$	1.41	1.37	1.04	0.85	1.04	0.94
Rb	48	48	55	75	45	55
Sr	749	830	n.d.	784	762	n.d.
Zr	160	115	220	150	216	140
Ta	0.70	0.73	0.40	0.55	0.58	0.74
Cr	24	15	12	26	11	12
SIR	n.d.	0.7056	0.7052-0.7066	0.7063-0.7064	n.d.	0.7054-0.7058

*Sources and abbreviations as in Table 1.

1979; Engebretson and Cox, 1984). The batholith is composed of older orthogneisses, foliated tonalites, and younger massive intrusives. The emplacement of some of the plutonic rocks within the Coast batholith or adjacent to its bounds is partly accidental. However, the longitudinal continuity of several major units of the batholith, considered in conjunction with the variability of the accreted rocks on either side of it, indicates major control by a uniform mechanism that must include the subjacent subduction of the downgoing oceanic slab.

Development of the batholith along our two traverses may be summarized in two modes. One involves tectonics, age, and relative positions of rocks; the other involves geochemistry and petrology.

Summary of the first mode innvolves the following.

1. Development of a continental-margin magmatic arc in Early Cretaceous time (ca. 127 Ma) either in Stikine terrane or in an oceanward terrane that is poorly preserved in the graywacke and pelites found near the central gneisses east of Ketchikan (Fig. 2), and extending south into British Columbia (Hutchison, 1982; Roddick, 1983b).

2. Westward-directed thrusting and high-temperature, moderate-pressure metamorphism (see, e.g., Godwin, 1975; Monger and others, 1982; Crawford and Hollister, 1982; Crawford and others, 1987) to emplace and metamorphose the central gneisses of Ketchikan traverse (Barker and Arth, 1984). The timing of this thrusting, as determined by Woodsworth and others (1983) and Saleeby (1987) by their dating of syntectonic intrusives in rocks immediately west of the Coast batholith, is about 100 Ma.

3. Intrusion of the moderately evolved (SiO$_2$ = 60 to 66

percent, Table 1) Taku plutons at 90 Ma. Crawford and others (1987) also reported folding, kyanite-grade metamorphism, and shearing at 90 Ma in the Prince Rupert area.

4. Possible emplacement and metamorphism of western and central orthogneisses of the Skagway traverse in Late Cretaceous time, if their ^{206}Pb/^{238}Pb ages on zircon are magmatic ones (detailed work on this problem is needed). Late Cretaceous zircon ages, uplift, and thrusting in the Coast batholith of the Prince Rupert–Terrace area were described by Woodsworth and others (1983) and Crawford and others (1987).

5. A prolonged latest Cretaceous to Paleocene "event" (or series of events), at ca. 67 to 55 Ma, depending on location, involved emplacement of the western tonalities and a thermal pulse from the Skagway-Juneau area to the Ketchikan and Prince Rupert areas, as well as extensive uplift, generation of upright isoclinal folds, and injection of the large dioritic Kasiks pluton in the central batholith between Prince Rupert and Terrace (see summary of Crawford and others, 1987). Crawford and others (1987) also proposed that all these tonalitic and dioritic plutons rose through the crust along steep ductile shear zones. Magnetic results (Griscom, 1977; Roddick, 1983b) indicate the existence of a large crustal mass of mafic rock under the western margin of the Coast batholith, which may be related to the western tonalites and which also may have caused the thermal pulse. The foliation of these western tonalites may have been induced by regional stress, rather than simply by flow of partly crystalline magma; relative movement between the Taku terrane and the central gneisses also may have occurred at this time.

6. Abrupt shifting of the locus of magmatism 20 to 50 km eastward or northeastward at 54 to 48 Ma, accompanied by a

change to more siliceous plutons. This was accompanied by change to a neutral-stress or tensional regime, and emplacement of an enormous amount of tonalitic to granitic magma, perhaps as the motion of oceanic plates relative to North America changed from a subductive mode to the present one of transverse motion.

Summary of the second mode, the geochemistry and petrology of our traverses, consists of several major features and their implications.

1. Tonalite is the predominant rock of the Coast batholith. Granite and granodiorite are of lesser abundance. Hornblende and/or biotite are the dominant mafic phases. Magmatic epidote, garnet, and muscovite are absent or rare (though the first two phases are characteristics of Taku plutons), and these intrusives (except Taku plutons) probably crystallized at less than 6 to 8 kbar pressure.

2. The several suites of gneisses and younger, massive intrusives that compose the batholith, with the exception of the young granites of the Skagway traverse, show a coherent calc-alkalic chemistry with SiO_2 of 50 to 71 percent, moderate K_2O of 1.4 to 3.7 percent, low Rb of 26 to 110 ppm, and abundant Sr of 479 to 1,070 ppm. Individual suites show ranges of SiO_2 as large as 14 percent (Table 1). Coeval pillowform inclusions found in both gneiss and tonalite are of high-Al, magmatic arc–type tholeiite, and are compositionally identical (except for K_2O, which infiltrated from wall rocks into these inclusions) to the least siliceous and most mafic batholitic rocks. This relation suggests a direct link between basaltic liquid, presumably generated from the underlying subduction-zone system, and rocks of the batholith.

3. Analyses of mineral phases of analyzed central migmatic gneisses (Ketchikan traverse) of 53 to 63 percent SiO_2 and least-squares modeling (F. Barker and R. Christian, 1986, unpublished results) indicate that closed-system fractionation of approximately equal proportions of hornblende and plagioclase from a mafic parent magma may account for the compositional variation of this suite. On the other hand, compositional trends of the younger plutons extend (e.g., as on the normative plot of Qz-Or-(Ab+An); see Barker and others, 1986) from basaltic end

members to siliceous end members including trondhjemitic, granodioritic, and granitic compositions. Thus, mixing models in which the siliceous end members would be generated by melting of accreted crustal rocks also are tenable. However, the nature of the lower to intermediate crustal rocks of this region is not known, and well-constrained mixing models cannot as yet be constructed.

4. The presence of only small positive or negative Eu anomalies in Coast batholitic rocks (excepting the granites of Summit Lake and Clifton of the Skagway traverse) is compatible with fractional crystallization or partial melting where both hornblende and plagioclase are residual, with hornblende selectively rejecting Eu and plagioclase selectively incorporating Eu from the liquid (Arth and Barker, 1976).

5. Sr and Nd isotopic ratios reflect an origin for the magmas in Paleozoic or younger accreted oceanic to continental-slope crustal rocks, or from isotopically similar basalts and andesites of continental-margin magmatic arcs. The small differences in these ratios from one suite of the batholith to another presumably reflect differences in their sources, but they cannot at present be related to specific crustal or mantle rocks. However, SIR of an analyzed basaltic inclusion from tonalite of Skagway is in the range of SIR of its host tonalite.

6. The high SiO_2 (74 to 77 percent), 52 to 48 Ma, high-level granites of the Skagway Traverse show several pronounced differences in major- and minor-element abundances from all other suites of the Coast batholith (Table 1). They probably formed largely by melting of crustal rocks. If so, their SIR of 0.7048 to 0.7060 indicate that their source rocks were isotopically like the remainder of the Coast batholith, of generally oceanic or younger crustal character.

ACKNOWLEDGMENTS

We thank M. L. Crawford, W. C. Day, and Z. E. Peterman for helpful reviews of the manuscript.

REFERENCES CITED

Arth, J. G., and Barker, F., 1976, Rare-earth partitioning between hornblende and dacitic liquid and implications for the genesis of trondhjemitic-tonalitic magmas: Geology, v. 4, p. 534–536.

Arth, J. G., Barker, F., and Stern, T. W., 1988, Coast batholith and Taku plutons near Ketchikan, Alaska; Petrography, geochronology, geochemistry, and isotopic character, in Sinha, A. K., ed., Frontiers in petrology: American Journal of Science, v. 288A, p. 461–489.

Ballantyne, S. B., and Littlejohn, A. L., 1982, Uranium mineralization and lithogeochemistry of the Surprise Lake batholith, Atlin, British Columbia, in Maurice, Y. T., ed., Uranium in granites: Geological Survey of Canada Paper 81–23, p. 145–155.

Barker, F., and Arth, J. G., 1984, Preliminary results, Central Gneiss Complex of the Coast Range batholith, southeastern Alaska; The roots of a high-K, calc-alkaline arc?: Physics of the Earth and Planetary Interiors, v. 35, p. 191–198.

Barker, F., Arth, J. G., and Stern, T. W., 1986, Evolution of the Coast Batholith along the Skagway Traverse, Alaska and British Columbia: American Mineralogist, v. 71, p. 632–643.

Berg, H. C., Elliott, R. L., and Koch, R. D., 1988, Geologic map of the Ketchikan and Prince Rupert quadrangles, Alaska: U.S. Geological Survey Miscellaneous Investigations Map I–1807, scale 1:250,000.

Brew, D. A., 1981, The Coast plutonic complex sill, southeastern Alaska: U.S. Geological Survey Circular 823–B, p. B96–B99.

Brew, D. A., and Ford, A. B., 1978, Megalineament in southeastern Alaska marks southwest edge of Coast Range batholithic complex: Canadian Journal of Earth Sciences, v. 15, p. 1763–1772.

Brooks, A. H., 1906, The geography and geology of Alaska: U.S. Geological Survey Professional Paper 45, 327 p.

Buddington, A. F., 1927, Coast Range intrusives of southeastern Alaska: Journal of Geology, v. 35, p. 224–246.

Buddington, A. F., and Chapin, T., 1929, Geology and mineral deposits of southeastern Alaska: U.S. Geological Survey Bulletin 800, 398 p.

Byrne, T., 1979, Late Paleocene demise of the Kula-Pacific spreading center: Geology, v. 7, p. 341–344.

Crawford, M. L., and Hollister, L. S., 1982, Contrast of metamorphic and structural histories across the Work Channel Lineament, Coast Plutonic Complex, British Columbia: Journal of Geophysical Research, v. 87, p. 3849–3860.

Crawford, M. L., Hollister, L. S., and Woodsworth, G. J., 1987, Crustal deformation and regional metamorphism across a terrane boundary, Coast Plutonic Complex, British Columbia: Tectonics, v. 6, no. 3, p. 343–361.

Dawson, G. M., 1881, Sketch of the geology of British Columbia: Geological Magazine, v. 8, p. 156–162, 214–227.

—— , 1888, Report on an exploration in the Yukon District, N.W.T., and adjacent northern portion of British Columbia: Geology and Natural History Survey of Canada Annual Report, v. 8, part 1, Report B, p. 31B–38B, 237B–238B.

Engebretson, D. C., and Cox, A., 1984, Relative motions between oceanic plates of the Pacific Basin: Journal of Geophysical Research, v. 89, p. 10291–10310.

Gehrels, G. E., Brew, D. A., and Saleeby, J. B., 1983, U-Pb zircon ages of major intrusive suites in the Coast plutonic-metamorphic complex near Juneau, southeastern Alaska: Geological Association of Canada Program with Abstracts, v. 8, p. A26.

Gill, J. B., 1981, Orogenic andesites and plate tectonics: Berlin, Springer-Verlag, 380 p.

Godwin, C. I., 1975, Imbricate subduction zones and their relationship with Upper Cretaceous to Tertiary porphyry deposits in the Canadian Cordillera: Canadian Journal Earth Sciences, v. 12, p. 1362–1378.

Griscom, A., 1977, Interpretation of aeromagnetic data, *in* Berg, H. C., and others, eds., Mineral resources of the Granite Fiords Wilderness Study Area, Alaska: U.S. Geological Survey Bulletin 1403, 151 p.

Hollister, L. S., 1982, Metamorphic evidence for rapid (2 mm/yr) uplift of a portion of the Central Gneiss Complex, Coast Mountains, British Columbia: Canadian Mineralogist, v. 20, p. 319–332.

Hudson, T., Arth, J. G., and Muth, K. G., 1981, Geochemistry of intrusive rocks associated with molybdenite deposits, Ketchikan Quadrangle, southeastern Alaska: Economic Geology, v. 76, p. 1125–1232.

Hutchison, W. W., 1970, Metamorphic framework and plutonic styles in the Prince Rupert region of the Central Coast Mountains, British Columbia: Canadian Journal of Earth Sciences, v. 7, p. 376–405.

—— , 1982, Geology of the Prince Rupert-Skeena Map Area, British Columbia: Geological Survey of Canada Memoir 394, 116 p.

Irvine, T. N., and Baragar, W.R.A., 1971, A guide to the chemical classification of the common volcanic rocks: Canadian Journal of Earth Sciences, v. 8, p. 523–548.

Kenah, C., and Hollister, L. S., 1983, Anatexis in the Central Gneiss Complex, British Columbia, *in* Atherton, M. P., and Gribble, C. D., eds., Migmatites, melting, and metamorphism; Proceedings of the Geochemical Group of the Mineralogical Society: Shiva Geology Series, p. 142–162.

Kuno, H., 1969, Andesite in time and space: Oregon Department of Geology and Mineral Industries Bulletin 65, p. 13–20.

Miyashiro, A., 1974, Volcanic rock series in island arcs and active continental margins: American Journal of Science, v. 275, p. 321–355.

Monger, J.W.H., Price, R. A., and Tempelman-Kluit, D. J., 1982, Tectonic accretion and the origin of the two major metamorphic and plutonic welts in the Canadian Cordillera: Geology, v. 10, p. 70–75.

Roddick, J. A., 1983a, Circum-Pacific plutonic terranes; An overview, *in* Roddick, J. A., ed., Circum-Pacific plutonic terranes: Geological Society of America Memoir 159, p. 1–3.

—— , 1983b, Geophysical review and composition of the Coast Plutonic Complex, south of latitude 55°N: *in* Roddick, J. A., ed., Circum-Pacific plutonic terranes: Geological Society of America Memoir 159, p. 195–211.

Roddick, J. A., and Hutchison, W. W., 1974, Setting of the Coast Plutonic Complex, British Columbia: Pacific Geology, v. 8, p. 91–108.

Saleeby, J. B., 1987, The inner boundary of the Alexander terrane in southern SE Alaska; Part 2, Southern Revillagigedo Island (RI) to Cape Fox (CF): Geological Society of America Abstracts with Programs, v. 19, p. 828.

Woodsworth, G. J., Loveridge, W. D., Parrish, R. R., and Sullivan, R. W., 1983, Uranium-lead dates from the Central Gneiss Complex and Ecstall pluton, Prince Rupert map area, British Columbia: Canadian Journal of Earth Sciences, v. 20, p. 1475–1483.

Zartman, R. E., 1984, Lead, strontium, and neodymium isotopic characterization of mineral deposits relative to their geologic environments: Proceedings of the 27th International Geological Congress, v. 12, p. 83–106.

Zen, E-an, and Hammarstrom, J. M., 1984, Magmatic epidote and its petrologic significance: Geology, v. 12, p. 515–518.

Manuscript Submitted December 15, 1987
Revised Manuscript Submitted April 15, 1988
Manuscript Accepted by the Society February 7, 1989

Printed in U.S.A.

Index

[Italic page numbers indicate major references]

Typeset by WESType Publishing Services, Inc., Boulder, Colorado
Printed in U.S.A. by Malloy Lithographing, Inc., Ann Arbor, Michigan